FEMINIST FRONTIERS

EIGHTH EDITION

Verta Taylor

Nancy Whittier

Leila J. Rupp

Higher Education

Boston   Burr Ridge, IL   Dubuque, IA   New York
San Francisco   St. Louis   Bangkok   Bogotá   Caracas   Kuala Lumpur
Lisbon   London   Madrid   Mexico City   Milan   Montreal   New Delhi
Santiago   Seoul   Singapore   Sydney   Taipei   Toronto

 **Higher Education**

Published by McGraw-Hill, an imprint of The McGraw-Hill Companies, Inc., 1221 Avenue of the Americas, New York, NY 10020. Copyright © 2009, 2007, 2004, 2001, 1997, 1993, 1989, 1983. All rights reserved. No part of this publication may be reproduced or distributed in any form or by any means, or stored in a database or retrieval system, without the prior written consent of The McGraw-Hill Companies, Inc., including, but not limited to, in any network or other electronic storage or transmission, or broadcast for distance learning.

This book is printed on acid-free paper.

1 2 3 4 5 6 7 8 9 0 DOC/DOC 0 9 8

ISBN: 978-0-07-340430-1
MHID: 0-07-340430-6

Editor in Chief: *Michael Ryan*
Publisher: *Frank Mortimer*
Sponsoring Editor: *Gina Boedeker*
Marketing Manager: *Leslie Oberhuber*
Editorial Assistant: *Jordan Killam*
Project Manager: *Amanda Peabody*
Manuscript Editor: *Tom Briggs*

Design Manager: *Allister Fein*
Text Designer: *Marianna Kinigakis*
Cover Designer: *Scott Ratinoff*
Production Supervisor: *Tandra Jorgensen*
Composition: *9/11 Palatino by ICC Macmillan Inc.*
Printing: *45# New Era Matte, R. R. Donnelley & Sons/Crawfordsville, IN*

Cover: Walking Women by Katherine Doughty. Media: Acrylic on canvas. Image © Katherine Doughty/www.katharinedoughty.com. About the artist: A long standing theme in her work, the walking figures connect to determination, survival, and the myriad of choices available to human beings. The walking figure is included in her ongoing "Alphabet Series," which depicts an archetypal journey following the sequence of the alphabet. Miss Doughty is a multimedia artist working in painting, sculpture, and jewelry.

Credits: The credits section for this book begins on page A-1 and is considered an extension of the copyright page.

Library of Congress Cataloging-in-Publication Data

Feminist frontiers / [edited by] Verta Taylor, Nancy Whittier, Leila J. Rupp. — 8th ed.
     p. cm.
  Includes bibliographical references.
  ISBN-13: 978-0-07-340430-1 (alk. paper)
  ISBN-10: 0-07-340430-6 (alk. paper)
    1. Feminism—United States. 2. Women—United States. 3. Sex role—United States. 4. Women—Cross-cultural studies. I. Taylor, Verta A. II. Whittier, Nancy, 1966-III. Rupp, Leila J., 1950-
HQ1426.F472 2009
305.420973—dc22   2008016460

The Internet addresses listed in the text were accurate at the time of publication. The inclusion of a Web site does not indicate an endorsement by the authors or McGraw-Hill, and McGraw-Hill does not guarantee the accuracy of the information presented at these sites.

www.mhhe.com

ABOUT THE EDITORS

VERTA TAYLOR is Professor and Chair of the Department of Sociology and an affiliated faculty member in Women's Studies at the University of California at Santa Barbara. She teaches courses on gender, feminism, women's studies, and social movements and has won numerous teaching awards, including an Ohio State University Distinguished Teaching Award, a Multicultural Teaching Award, an Outstanding Faculty Award from the Office of Gay, Lesbian, and Bisexual Student Services, and a University Distinguished Diversity Enhancement Award for her role as Chair of Undergraduate Studies in the Department of Sociology at Ohio State. She continues to be recognized for her teaching at the University of California. Professor Taylor also received the Sociologists for Women in Society's Mentoring Award, the John D. McCarthy Lifetime Achievement Award for her scholarship on social movements and collective action, the Simon and Gagnon Award for her career of scholarship in sexualities, and she has served as Feminist Lecturer for Sociologists for Women in Society. She has been member of more than a dozen editorial boards, served as Chair of the Sex and Gender, Collective Behavior and Social Movement, and Sexuality Sections of the American Sociological Association, and as Chair of the Committee on the Status of Gay, Lesbian, Bisexual, and Transgender Sociologists of the American Sociological Association.

Taylor is the author of *Rock-a-by Baby: Feminism, Self-Help, and Postpartum Depression*; and coauthor with Leila J. Rupp of *Survival in the Doldrums: The American Women's Rights Movement, 1945 to the 1960s* and *Drag Queens at the 801 Cabaret*, which won the 2005 book award from the Sex and Gender Section of the American Sociological Association. Her writings have also appeared in numerous scholarly collections and journals.

NANCY WHITTIER is Professor and former chair of the Department of Sociology and a member of the Women's Studies Program Committee at Smith College. She teaches courses on gender, social movements, queer politics, and research methods. She is the author of *Feminist Generations: The Persistence of the Radical Women's Movement* and *The Politics of Child Sexual Abuse* (forthcoming in 2009), and co-editor of *Social Movements: Identity, Culture, and the State*. Her work on the women's movement, social movement culture and collective identity, activist generations, and activism against child sexual abuse has appeared in numerous scholarly collections and journals.

LEILA J. RUPP is Professor of Women's Studies and Associate Dean of Social Sciences at the University of California, Santa Barbara, where she holds affiliated appointments in the Departments of History and Sociology. A historian by training, she teaches introductory women's studies and courses on sexuality and women's movements. She received an Academic Senate Distinguished Teaching Award in 2008, and while teaching at Ohio State University, won an Ohio State University Distinguished Teaching Award, a Multicultural Teaching Award, and an outstanding teaching award from the Ohio Academy of History. She also won awards at both Ohio State and the University of California for her contributions to gay, lesbian, bisexual, transgender, and queer students. She is the author of *Mobilizing Women for War: German and American Propaganda, 1939–1945*, *Worlds of Women: The Making of an International Women's Movement*, *A Desired Past: A Short History of Same-Sex Love in America*, and coauthor, with Verta Taylor, of *Survival in the Doldrums: The American Women's Rights Movement, 1945 to the 1960s* and *Drag Queens at the 801 Cabaret*, which won the 2005 book award from the Sex and Gender Section of the American Sociological Association. In addition, she has published numerous articles in journals and edited collections. She served as the editor of the *Journal of Women's History* from 1996 to 2004.

PREFACE

The first edition of *Feminist Frontiers* was conceived in the late 1970s at a time when many women inside and outside academia were beginning to recognize and challenge male domination. At the time of its publication, only a handful of books and anthologies written for classroom use presented a feminist perspective on women's lives.

The evolution of this book through eight editions reflects both the success of the women's movement and the incredible development of feminist scholarship over the past three decades. Women's studies courses have blossomed and spread to campuses in even the most conservative regions of the country. Feminist scholars have, in the meantime, refined and enlarged our understanding of how gender inequality operates and how it intersects with other systems of domination based on race, ethnicity, class, sexuality, nationality, and ability. There is no doubt that the situation of women has changed since the publication of the first edition of *Feminist Frontiers*. Gender inequality has not, however, disappeared.

We write this preface to the eighth edition of *Feminist Frontiers* with pride and excitement. We are proud to be part of the continuing women's movement; and we are excited about the burgeoning knowledge about how gender is connected to class, race, ethnicity, sexuality, and other differences and how forces of globalization in the contemporary world shape the experiences of women. We feel fortunate to be writing, teaching, and learning at a time when feminist thought and research are flourishing and deepening, despite the challenges we face both nationally and globally. It is, simultaneously, a time to enjoy the bounty of feminist scholarship and to sow new feminist seeds.

We developed *Feminist Frontiers* for use as the major—or supplementary—text in courses on women's studies, gender studies, or the sociology of women or gender. Because this book offers a general framework for analyzing women, society, and culture, it can also be used as a supplementary text in introductory sociology classes and in courses on social problems, comparative studies, and American studies.

Although we have retained some of the articles from previous editions of *Feminist Frontiers*—particularly writings that have become feminist classics—the book has been updated to include more recent scholarship. We have added fourteen new selections and nine new boxed inserts. We have continued to select readings that emphasize the diversity of women's experiences and the intersections of gender with race, ethnicity, class, sexuality, nationality, and ability. We have further strengthened the coverage of disability, transgender, and global issues. As in previous editions, the introductions to each section contain focused summaries of the readings and their relationship to each other, as well as discussion questions for each reading.

ORGANIZATION

Feminist Frontiers is organized into four major parts, each introduced by a sociological and feminist analysis. **Part One: Introduction** begins with a section representing the diversity of women's experiences and gender systems. That is followed by a section titled "Theoretical Perspectives," which presents social constructionist and intersectional theoretical approaches to gender. **Part Two: Gender, Culture, and Socialization** has two sections, "Representation, Language, and Culture" and "Socialization." **Part Three: Social Organization of Gender** has five sections, providing readings on work, families, sexualities, bodies, and violence against women. **Part Four: Social Change** includes articles on global politics and the state and on social protest and women's movements.

CRITERIA FOR SELECTION

As we set about selecting articles for this edition, we found an abundance of excellent pieces. We used the following criteria for choosing what to include:

- We wanted each selection to be engagingly written and accessible in style and language to readers from different disciplinary backgrounds.
- As a testament to the tremendous growth in the depth and complexity of feminist scholarship, we sought selections exploring a wide range of theoretical and substantive issues.
- We wanted this anthology to reflect a diversity of racial, ethnic, class, sexual, and cultural experiences.
- Given the increasingly powerful forces of globalization in our contemporary world, we looked for articles on different countries and on the impact of globalization on women.
- We sought to capture the cross-disciplinary nature of gender research.

CHANGES IN THE EIGHTH EDITION

The eighth edition contains fourteen new articles and nine new boxed inserts, representing the most current scholarship and public debates and expanding our coverage of issues important to feminist scholarship. We have deleted dated pieces while retaining readings that are classic in the field.

Central topics that continue to receive coverage in this edition include social constructionist theories of gender; feminist intersectionality theory; gendered and raced beauty standards; racialized gender socialization; gender, race, and ethnicity in the workplace; marriage and family issues; diverse sexualities; body issues; reproductive rights; violence against women; globalization; women and welfare; women's movements; and queer politics.

Additions to the text focus especially on expanding coverage of diverse women's experiences, both within the United States and around the globe, with new articles on such topics as teaching women's studies as a black woman, gender and disability, transgender feminism, fat activism, music videos, interracial families in Britain, drag queens, the politics of appearance in the workplace, medical constructions of heterosexuality in the United States in the 1950s, college women's sexuality, global histories of love between women, societal impacts on bodies, sex work, and the marriage promotion movement in the United States. In addition, new boxes illuminate such issues as feminism and disability, heteronormativity in reality television shows, rap as empowerment, gender in military recruitment, Hillary Clinton's gender presentation, global health, men and sexual harassment, gender and the Iraq War, and things you can do with a degree in women's studies.

Although the core focus remains on women and gender, this edition continues to offer consistent coverage of men and masculinity.

NEW READINGS IN THE EIGHTH EDITION

Every section has been updated with new selections. Section 1 begins with an article by **Kimberly Springer** on her experiences as a black women in the women's studies classroom and adds another by **Catherine Kudlick** on the gender implications of using a white cane as a blind woman. **Audre Lorde**'s classic piece "The Master's Tools Will Never Dismantle the Master's House" has been excerpted to keep the emphasis on her essential insights, which are central to women's studies. Section 2 strengthens consideration of transgender and disability issues by offering **Susan Stryker**'s thoughts on transgender feminism, along with **Rosemarie Garland-Thomson**'s thoughts on feminism and disability studies.

Section 3, "Representation, Language, and Culture," adds better coverage of contemporary media through an article by **Judy Taylor** on the Dove "Real Beauty" campaign, another by **T. Denean Sharpley-Whiting** on the representations of women of color in music videos, and boxed inserts on *The Bachelor* and rap. Two added articles in Section 4, on socialization, provide new perspectives: **France Winddance Twine** writes on "racial literacy" in British interracial families, and **Verta Taylor** and **Leila J. Rupp** reveal the messages imparted about gender and sexuality by drag queens. The boxed insert covers gender in military recruitment.

In Section 5, "Work," **Eileen Boris** contributes an article on the politics of appearance in the workplace, looking at women on the assembly line during the Second World War and women working as flight attendants in different historical periods. Section 6,

"Families," adds historical perspective through **Carolyn Herbst Lewis**'s piece on the ways that doctors in the United States used the pelvic exam to teach proper gender and sexual roles to women in the 1950s.

New pieces in Section 7, "Sexualities," deal with college women's heterosexual gender strategies (**Laura Hamilton**) and a global history of love between women (**Leila J. Rupp**). A new boxed insert explores the meaning of Hillary Clinton exposing a little cleavage early in her campaign. Section 8, "Bodies," offers **Anne Fausto-Sterling**'s recent consideration of how social factors, not just biology, affect such things as bones. Section 9, "Violence Against Women," adds a new box on sexual harassment.

Section 10, "Global Politics and the State," includes a new article on the feminist debate about sex work in global perspective (**Jo Doezema**) and another (**Melanie Heath**) on the movement in the United States to promote heterosexual marriage. A new box comes from a blog written by a young woman living in Baghdad during the U.S. invasion of Iraq.

Section 11 takes us back to the beginning by adding a new box on how a degree in women's studies can help you transform the world.

CONNECTIONS AMONG SECTIONS

Many of the articles in *Feminist Frontiers* make connections to topics covered in different sections, a sign of the multiple intersections of women's studies. For example, the concept of intersectionality, illustrated in the diverse and complex experiences covered in Section 1 and outlined in the theoretical articles in Section 2, can be traced through **Kimberlé Crenshaw**'s classic article on violence against women of color in Section 9 and **Andrea Smith**'s consideration of reproductive politics in the context of race, class, and ability. That we cannot talk about gender without acknowledging the ways that it is raced and classed is central to **T. Denean Sharpley-Whiting**'s article on music videos, **Yen Le Espiritu**'s article on Filipina girls, **France Winddance Twine**'s on interracial families, **Eileen Boris**'s on the politics of appearance, **Miliann Kang**'s on Korean manicurists, **Pierrette Hondagneu-Sotelo**'s on Latina domestics, **Denise Segura**'s on Chicana and Mexicana mothers, **Hung**

Cam Thai's on Vietnamese marriages, **Patricia Hill Collins**' on black sexual politics, **Becky Wangsgaard Thompson**'s on eating disorders, **Lila Abu-Lughod**'s on Muslim women, **Gwendolyn Mink**'s on welfare, and **Susan Muaddi Darraj**'s on Arab-American feminism.

Likewise, global forces appear throughout the volume, not just in the section on global politics: in **Chandra Talpade Mohanty**'s and **R. W. Connell**'s theoretical articles in Section 2, **Sharpley-Whiting**'s consideration of sex tourism, **Yen Le Espiritu**'s analysis of cross-national socialization practices and **Twine**'s article in Section 4, the pieces on Korean manicurists and Latina domestics in Section 5, the articles on Mexican and Mexican-American women and Vietnamese marriages in Section 6, the consideration of same-sex sexuality around the globe in Section 7, the consideration of African genital cutting in light of cosmetic labial surgery in the United States in Section 8, **Joane Nagel**'s piece on sexuality in wartime in Section 9, and **Grace Chang**'s article on Asian women workers fighting globalization, the overview of women's movements, and the Beijing documents in Section 11.

Other issues, too, cross sections. Transsexuality, transgenderism, and intersexuality appear in **Paula Gunn Allen**'s reflections on being Native American, **Suzanne Kessler**'s consideration of surgery on intersexed infants, **Susan Stryker**'s article, **Verta Taylor** and **Leila Rupp**'s article on "Learning from Drag Queens," **Nancy Naples**'s piece on queer parenting, the boxed insert "Stolen Bodies," the article on sexuality in wartime, and **Cathy Cohen**'s article on queer politics. Other connections across sections focus on work, bodies, disability, beauty, youth, motherhood, and migration.

SUPPLEMENTS

Companion Web site

The *Feminist Frontiers* Web site proves general information about the book and offers separate areas for students and instructors.

For the Student
The "Student side" of the site is organized to correspond to the eleven sections of the text. There are

practice test questions, an annotated list of Web links, and a link to Census 2000 updates.

For the Instructor
Instructor's Manual: The Instructor's Manual is organized to correspond to each section of the text. It offers learning objectives, discussion questions, summaries of the key points of the section introductions and readings, suggestions for assignments and exercises, and an annotated list of Web links.

Test Bank: The Test Bank offers multiple-choice, short answer, and essay questions on the section introductions and individual readings.

Visit the companion Web site at:
www.mhhe.com/taylorff8e

ACKNOWLEDGMENTS

We gratefully acknowledge the support, skill, and help of many people. We extend thanks to the authors of the articles, not only for writing the selected pieces but also for allowing us to reprint them here. At McGraw-Hill, we thank Gina Boedeker and Amanda Peabody for their encouragement and attention to detail in the production of the book and Tom Briggs for his expert copyediting. We also thank Fred Courtright for his services as permissions editor. Amber Ault was instrumental in shaping some section introductions for the third edition of the book, and we continue to appreciate her contributions for this and for developing some of the content for both the Instructor's Manual and the companion Web site. Nicole Raeburn provided invaluable research assistance and revisions of the Test Bank for earlier editions of the book, and Lisa Leitz put her charisma as a teacher to use in developing the Web site. We could not have completed this revision without the help of Kegan Allee, who brought her intellectual abilities, commitment to feminism, and incredible organizational skills to the project. From suggesting readings to assembling the manuscript, she was our mainstay. In addition, we are grateful to Eileen Boris and Juliet Williams for sharing with us their experiences teaching the previous edition and suggesting potential articles. Finally, we express our appreciation to students in our classes on the sociology of women, sex and gender, and women's studies at Smith College and the University of California, Santa Barbara. They have contributed to the development of this anthology by their thoughtful responses to potential articles.

The following scholars served as reviewers in the development of *Feminist Frontiers*:

Lori E. Amy, Georgia Southern University
Eileen Boris, University of California, Santa Barbara
Mariana Branda-Gheradi, College of the Canyons
Sharon Elise, California State University–San Marcos
Heather Hartley, Ph.D., Portland State University
Astrid Henry, Saint Mary's College
Kathryn M. Matthews, Saint Louis University
Rachel Raimist, University of Minnesota–Twin Cities

We continue to be grateful to Laurel Richardson, who, together with Verta Taylor, initiated the first edition of *Feminist Frontiers*. Special thanks go to Kate Weigand, who provided feedback and insight into the collection's organization and offered consistent encouragement and companionship. Jonah, Eva, and Isaac Weigand-Whittier are a constant source of inspiration as we seek to reconstruct gender. To them and to the students and colleagues who have touched our lives positively, we express our gratitude.

Verta Taylor
Nancy Whittier
Leila J. Rupp

CONTENTS

ABOUT THE EDITORS   *iv*
PREFACE   *v*

PART ONE: INTRODUCTION   1

Section One: Diversity and Difference   4

1   Being the Bridge: A Solitary Black Woman's Position in the Women's Studies Classroom as a Feminist Student and Professor, *Kimberly Springer*   7

2   White Privilege: Unpacking the Invisible Knapsack, *Peggy McIntosh*   12

   BOX: Haole Girl: Identity and White Privilege in Hawai'i, *Judy Rohrer*   19

3   Frontlines and Borders: Identity Thresholds for Latinas and Arab American Women, *Laura M. Lopez and Frances S. Hasso*   20

4   Where I Come from Is Like This, *Paula Gunn Allen*   34

   BOX: The Master's Tools Will Never Dismantle the Master's House, *Audre Lorde*   38

5   The Blind Man's Harley: White Canes and Gender Identity in America, *Catherine Kudlick*   39

Section Two: Theoretical Perspectives   49

6   "Night to His Day": The Social Construction of Gender, *Judith Lorber*   53

7   The Medical Construction of Gender, *Suzanne Kessler*   69

8   Transgender Feminism: Queering the Woman Question, *Susan Stryker*   83

9   Theorizing Difference from Multiracial Feminism, *Maxine Baca Zinn and Bonnie Thornton Dill*   89

   BOX: Feminism and Disability Studies, *Rosemarie Garland-Thomson*   95

10   Feminism Without Borders, *Chandra Talpade Mohanty*   97

11   Masculinities and Globalization, *R. W. Connell*   103

   BOX: Womanist, *Alice Walker*   114

PART TWO: GENDER, CULTURE, AND SOCIALIZATION   115

Section Three: Representation, Language, and Culture   117

12   Gender Stereotyping in the English Language, *Laurel Richardson*   120

   BOX: The Normalization of Heterogendered Relations in *The Bachelor*, *Gust Yep and Ariana Ochoa Camacho*   125

13   Feminist Consumerism and Fat Activists: Grassroots Activism and the Dove "Real Beauty" Campaign, *Judy Taylor*   127

14   Cosmetic Surgery: Paying for Your Beauty, *Debra L. Gimlin*   140

15   Hair Still Matters, *Ingrid Banks*   153

16   "I See the Same Ho": Video Vixens, Beauty Culture, and Diasporic Sex Tourism, *T. Denean Sharpley-Whiting*   162

   BOX: Rewriting Rap to Empower Teens, *Tara Parker-Pope*   173

Section Four: Socialization   174

17   Girls and Boys Together . . . but Mostly Apart: Gender Arrangements in Elementary Schools, *Barrie Thorne*   176

18   What Are Little Boys Made Of?, *Michael Kimmel*   187

BOX: The Making of a Soldier: Gender in Military Recruitment, *Kristen N. Nelson*   190

19   "We Don't Sleep Around Like White Girls Do": Family, Culture, and Gender in Filipina American Lives, *Yen Le Espiritu*   193

20   Bearing Blackness in Britain: The Meaning of Racial Difference for White Birth Mothers of African-Descent Children, *France Winddance Twine*   207

21   Learning from Drag Queens, *Verta Taylor and Leila J. Rupp*   223

PART THREE: SOCIAL ORGANIZATION OF GENDER   229

Section Five: Work   231

22   Sex Segregation in the U.S. Labor Force, *Christine E. Bose and Rachel Bridges Whaley*   233

BOX: Median Annual Earnings of Full-Time, Year-Round Workers by Education, Race, and Hispanic Origin, 2006, *Nancy Whittier*   242

23   Desirable Dress: Rosies, Sky Girls, and the Politics of Appearance, *Eileen Boris*   243

24   The Managed Hand: The Commercialization of Bodies and Emotions in Korean Immigrant–Owned Nail Salons, *Miliann Kang*   253

BOX: The Realities of Affirmative Action in Employment, *Barbara Reskin*   266

25   Maid in L.A., *Pierrette Hondagneu-Sotelo*   269

BOX: The Living Wage as a Women's Issue, *Eileen Boris*   287

Section Six: Families   288

26   Bridal Wave, *Melissa Morrison*   291

27   Waking Sleeping Beauty: The Premarital Pelvic Exam and Heterosexuality During the Cold War, *Carolyn Herbst Lewis*   294

28   Working at Motherhood: Chicana and Mexicana Immigrant Mothers and Employment, *Denise A. Segura*   308

29   Moral Dilemmas, Moral Strategies, and the Transformation of Gender: Lessons from Two Generations of Work and Family Change, *Kathleen Gerson*   322

30   For Better or Worse: Gender Allures in the Vietnamese Global Marriage Market, *Hung Cam Thai*   331

31   Queer Parenting in the New Millennium, *Nancy A. Naples*   342

Section Seven: Sexualities   346

32   Doing Desire: Adolescent Girls' Struggles for/with Sexuality, *Deborah L. Tolman*   348

33   Trading on Heterosexuality: College Women's Gender Strategies and Homophobia, *Laura Hamilton*   359

BOX: Hillary Clinton's Tentative Dip into New Neckline Territory, *Robin Givhan*   374

34   Black Sexual Politics, *Patricia Hill Collins*   375

35   Loving Women in the Modern World, *Leila J. Rupp*   389

36   Becoming 100% Straight, *Michael A. Messner*   400

Section Eight: Bodies   405

37   The Bare Bones of Sex: Part 1—Sex and Gender, *Anne Fausto-Sterling*   407

38 "A Way Outa No Way": Eating Problems Among African-American, Latina, and White Women, *Becky Wangsgaard Thompson* 421

39 Loose Lips Sink Ships, *Simone Weil Davis* 430

40 Beyond Pro-Choice Versus Pro-Life: Women of Color and Reproductive Justice, *Andrea Smith* 446

41 Welcome to Cancerland, *Barbara Ehrenreich* 458

BOX: Stolen Bodies, Reclaimed Bodies: Disability and Queerness, *Eli Clare* 467

Section Nine: Violence Against Women 469

42 Fraternities and Rape on Campus, *Patricia Yancey Martin and Robert A. Hummer* 471

43 Supremacy Crimes, *Gloria Steinem* 480

BOX: Understanding Sexual Harassment: A Primer for Dudes, *Silvana Naguib* 482

44 Mapping the Margins: Intersectionality, Identity Politics, and Violence Against Women of Color, *Kimberlé Crenshaw* 484

45 Sex and War: Fighting Men, Comfort Women, and the Military-Sexual Complex, *Joane Nagel* 494

PART FOUR: SOCIAL CHANGE 507

Section Ten: Global Politics and the State 510

46 The Globe Trotting Sneaker, *Cynthia Enloe* 512

47 Forced to Choose: Beyond the Voluntary v. Forced Prostitution Dichotomy, *Jo Doezema* 517

BOX: Femicide in Juárez, *Pheona Donohoe* 525

48 Do Muslim Women Really Need Saving? Anthropological Reflections on Cultural Relativism and Its Others, *Lila Abu-Lughod* 527

BOX: Baghdad Burning: Girl Blog from Iraq, *Riverbend* 536

49 The Lady and the Tramp (II): Feminist Welfare Politics, Poor Single Mothers, and the Challenge of Welfare Justice, *Gwendolyn Mink* 538

50 The Marriage Promotion Movement, *Melanie Heath* 543

Section Eleven: Social Protest and the Feminist Movement 554

51 The Women's Movement: Persistence Through Transformation, *Verta Taylor, Nancy Whittier, and Cynthia Fabrizio Pelak* 556

52 Feminists or "Postfeminists"? Young Women's Attitudes Toward Feminism and Gender Relations, *Pamela Aronson* 572

BOX: Transform the World: What You Can Do with a Degree in Women's Studies, *Nikki Ayanna Stewart* 583

53 From the Third World to the "Third World Within": Asian Women Workers Fighting Globalization, *Grace Chang* 585

54 Punks, Bulldaggers, and Welfare Queens: The Radical Potential of Queer Politics? *Cathy J. Cohen* 596

BOX: UN Commission Approves Declaration Reaffirming Goals of 1995 Women's Conference After U.S. Drops Antiabortion Amendment, *08 Mar 2005* 613

BOX: Fourth World Conference on Women Beijing Declaration 614

ACKNOWLEDGMENTS A-I

PART ONE

INTRODUCTION

What is gender? Our gender, and what it means to us and to others, affects the ways we interact with each other, the kinds of relationships we form, and our positions in our communities. As an element of social relationships, gender operates at multiple levels to categorize and distinguish people. But gender is also about social institutions that distribute power, resources, and status among various groups of women and men. As we shall see, gender also interacts with race, class, ethnicity, and sexuality. In other words, gender means different things, and has different consequences for status and power, depending on race, class, ethnicity, and sexuality.

What does it mean to be a woman? Thinking about women's experiences is a complicated task because women have as many differences from each other as commonalities. On the one hand, women everywhere suffer from restrictions, oppression, and discrimination because they are living in patriarchal societies. Yet gender is not the sole influence on any woman's life. Differences of race, ethnicity, class, sexuality, age, nation, region, and religion shape women's experiences. Moreover, these differences intersect with each other. For example, Asian-American women of various ages, sexual orientations, classes, and ethnic and national origins have different experiences.

The experience of being a woman may be quite different for distinct groups of women. For a white, upper-class, heterosexual, American woman, for example, femininity might entail being economically dependent on her husband, maintaining a delicate and refined physical appearance, and achieving social influence through child-raising and volunteer work. Womanhood for a middle-class African-American woman might mean providing financial support for her children, holding influential and respected positions within her church and community, yet being stereotyped by the dominant white culture as sexually promiscuous or unintelligent.

For a Mexican immigrant to the United States, femininity might mean being a good mother—which, as Denise Segura suggests in Section 6, may mean working long hours in order to support her children.

The experiences of men are similarly varied. Although men benefit from power and privilege over women, some groups of men also exercise power over other men, while other groups of men are excluded from economic or political influence due to their race, class, nationality, or sexual identity. To understand the position of a particular man, in other words, we must consider his gender, race, class, sexuality, age, and so forth, in order to understand the particular advantages and disadvantages he faces.

In short, gender is defined in various ways for different groups. Gender definitions bring with them a distinct set of restrictions and disadvantages for members in each group, as well as privileges and sources of power or resistance. The task for you as students, and for scholars of gender, is to recognize the patterns and persistence of male dominance while simultaneously recognizing these variations.

As if matters were not complex enough, feminist scholars also recognize that individuals have unique constellations of experiences. Each of us has our own story to tell. Each of us has multiple alliances and identifications with groups that shift through time and social context. The religious identity of childhood may be shunted aside during young adulthood, for example, only to be reclaimed in later years. Self-definitions as heterosexual may give way later in life to new identities as lesbian or bisexual. As biracial or bicultural or mixed-religion daughters, we might identify with the heritage of either parent or both. In addition, we have different degrees of allegiance to the gender standards of our particular groups. Some of us adopt prescriptions about masculinity or femininity wholeheartedly, others reject those prescriptions, and still others adopt some aspects of socially approved gender standards and reject others. Some of us identify strongly with the category—woman or man—to which we are assigned, while others identify as transgendered and seek either to identify with the other gender category or to construct an alternate gender identity. Although social forces such as sexism, racism, heterosexism, and class inequality shape our biographies, it is as individuals that we experience and make sense of our lives.

The task of feminist scholarship, and of this volume, is to illuminate the social and structural roots of our gendered experiences while simultaneously recognizing the complicated and unique factors that shape our lives. Feminist research builds upon and links two levels of analysis: structure and biography. The structural level looks at social institutions and cultural practices that create and sustain gender inequalities, and it links those inequalities to other systems of oppression, such as racism, ageism, and homophobia. The biographical level honors each individual's expression of her own experience. It pays attention to how individuals represent themselves and recognizes personal voice. As a result, we can learn how difference and commonality are structurally rooted and personally experienced. We can see how larger social forces affect our own and others' lives.

Feminist research is not just about analyzing the ways that social structures shape and restrict the lives of women. Of course, it is important to document the inequalities faced by various groups of women and to examine the ways that women have been oppressed and victimized based on gender. Experiences such as discrimination in hiring and pay, sexual violence, and legal subordination, for example, are undeniably central to gender. Yet feminist scholarship also emphasizes the sources of power that women find: how they define themselves, influence their social contexts, and resist the restrictions that they face. The articles in this volume view women not as passive victims of patriarchal social structures, but as actors who exercise control over their own lives find pleasure and fulfillment, and resist social constraints.

Further, feminist research is not just about documenting women's experiences. It is about recognizing the ways that gender shapes the lives of both women and men and analyzing a broad system of gender. The gender system affects not only the lives of individuals but the organization of other institutions in the larger society. By documenting

the influence of social structures on gender and highlighting individuals' complex mixture of domination, resistance, and complicity, feminist scholarship leads us to rethink the structural changes necessary to meet the needs of actual women and men.

Feminist theory and scholarship on gender, then, face a broad set of questions. Approaches to answering these questions vary enormously; we hope that you will recognize disagreement and debate, as well as cooperation, in the readings that follow. There are, however, some shared assumptions that run through the selections in this book.

First, feminist scholars view gender as pervasive, as part of every feature of social life and individual identity. It is impossible, therefore, to analyze any part of social life as if it were gender neutral. As a result, feminist scholars challenge the male bias hidden under claims of scientific objectivity in academic research. As you read these essays and those in other classes, ask yourself how the social conditions and practices of doing research reinforce or challenge gender inequities.

Second, feminist researchers understand systems of oppression as interlocking. Race, class, ethnicity, sexuality, and other systems of domination affect how one experiences gender. Therefore, although gender is a basic fact of social life, women and men in different positions in society experience their gender and the power or oppression that results from it differently. Just as feminist researchers challenge knowledge claims about "people" based on research on men, they question knowledge about "women" based on research on white, middle-class women.

Third, feminist scholars experiment with new ways of doing research, rethinking the relationship between the researcher and the researched. The scientific method of research assumes that there is a separation between the scholar and the subjects of research and that this separation is necessary to produce "objective" and "valid" research. Feminist researchers challenge this tenet. Treating women as "objects" of research contravenes feminist goals of equality by elevating the researcher's agenda and perspective above those of the researched. One of the major questions of feminist thought is how to do research that empowers both the researcher and the researched. How do we create social research practices in which researcher and researched collaborate in the process of interpreting the world? For some, the solution has been to write about their own lives; some acknowledge directly how their own biases affect their work; others study groups of which they are a part; still others do "participatory" or "action" research in which the researcher and the researched determine together the topics, methods, goals, and political action to follow from the project, so that the scholar is a participant in the project, but not its leader.

These are not only theoretical concerns; they are important ethical questions. What right does a scholar have to write about another person's life? How should scholars write about the lives of those who are different from themselves? How can feminist scholars use the skills and privileges of academic practice to diminish social inequality?

We invite you to engage in reading, thinking about, and doing feminist research. We hope that you will consider some of the central questions that run through this book. What are the commonalities and differences among women or among men? What, if anything, do women of different classes, races, or sexualities share in common? We hope that you will reflect on the complicated balance between oppression and resistance or between the pervasive influence of society and the ways that individuals and groups define themselves and carve out meaningful lives. We encourage you to discuss your ideas, to debate the issues this volume raises with your friends and classmates, to agree or disagree with the authors here, and to come to your own conclusions. We hope, too, that through this engagement you will consider how gender has shaped your life and how gender intersects with the other systems of inequality that affect you. We hope as well that you will share your understandings with others, becoming a researcher yourself and a theorist of your own and others' lives so that you might help empower us all and transform society.

Diversity and Difference

Conducting research about women has been the focus of feminist scholars since the 1960s. In recent years, researchers have looked especially closely at the differences and commonalities among women, and they have also examined how men's lives are shaped by cultural expectations of masculinity. Gender shapes women's and men's lives in complex ways, and scholars are interested in understanding these experiences in ways that can contribute to positive social change. Women everywhere face male dominance in various manifestations. Yet differences among women arise from factors such as race, ethnicity, class, sexual orientation, age, geographic region, and religion. Further, not all men possess the same advantages or social power. Men of subordinate racial or ethnic groups, social classes, or sexual orientations may have power relative to women in their own group but be subordinate in some ways to other men and to women in more powerful groups.

Recognizing that women are not a homogeneous group raises questions about the grounds for affiliation among women. Can we even speak of "woman" as a meaningful category, or is the diversity among women too great for any generalization? The readings in this section discuss points of similarity and difference among women and among men. Although these readings give only a sampling of the varied and rich experiences of women and men, they begin to illustrate the vast range of meanings that gender has for women and men in different groups. These readings also provide some key analytical frameworks and concepts for understanding the tension between the significance of gender as a category by which people are

grouped and the ways that gender is shaped by other forms of inequality and social distinctions.

The readings in this section examine the distinctions among women's experiences by showing how race, ethnicity, and age shape the lives of specific groups of women. The first reading in this section, Kimberly Springer's "Being the Bridge: A Solitary Black Woman's Position in the Women's Studies Classroom," tackles the similarities and differences among women directly. Recounting her experiences as a women's studies student and campus activist, Springer shows how being a black woman in a predominantly white feminist context pushed her to serve as a "bridge between cultures, races, and theories." For Springer, activism includes teaching and writing about black feminism and working to bring black feminists together outside of academia as well. What does Springer's experience suggest about how connections and coalitions among different groups of women might occur? Why are these connections important, and how are they limited? For Springer, activism and academic work are inextricably linked. Do you agree with her that scholarly study of gender must be linked to activism for social change? Why or why not?

Peggy McIntosh adds to Springer's analysis by focusing on the often-unrecognized ways that white women benefit from their racial category. In a classic piece, "White Privilege: Unpacking the Invisible Knapsack," McIntosh discusses the taken-for-granted systems and practices that privilege white women over women of color. She argues that much of what white women take for granted in daily life is in fact a result of their dominant social status. Documenting her own white privilege helps her understand how she benefits from this system and shows that racism cannot change through individual attitudes alone, but requires change in social institutions. How does her list of benefits from white privilege change your understanding of racism? How does it change your understanding of gender inequality, or of the degree to which women of different races share oppression in common? Can you think of other advantages to add to her list? If you are a member of another privileged group, can you construct a list of the benefits you receive by virtue of your gender, class, sexual orientation, religion, or nationality? If you are a member of a subordinated group, can you list some of the ways you are disadvantaged? Most readers will have some statuses that grant them privilege (such as white skin, male gender, heterosexuality, U.S. nationality, youth, or Christian religion) and some statuses that disadvantage them (such as nonwhite skin, female gender, lesbian or gay or bisexual sexual orientation, non-U.S. nationality, age, or non-Christian religion). In what ways do the forms of privilege and disadvantage that you possess interact? How does the boxed insert, "Haole Girl," suggest that even white skin may carry different degrees of privilege and disadvantage in different settings?

In "Frontlines and Borders: Identity Thresholds for Latinas and Arab American Women," Laura Lopez and Frances Hasso discuss how women experience their racial-ethnic identities differently at white-dominant universities and in their own ethnic communities. Latina and Arab-American students both experience the university as often hostile and culturally unfamiliar, but in different ways. Latinas faced stereotyping as unsuited for college education and found themselves left out of both Anglo and African-American social and political groups. Often coming from rich Latina cultural settings into a university with very few Latino/a students or faculty, they also felt culturally dislocated. Arab Americans, in contrast, were affected by tense political events in the Middle East, and often "came out" as Arab American in response to comments that stereotyped all Arabs as terrorists. Both groups responded to these pressures by reaffirming their ethnic identities, often heightening them by relearning native languages, finding other students who shared their identities, and strengthening ties to family and

community. As they strengthened community ties, however, they had to reckon with often-restrictive notions of gender and sexuality. In both home and university settings, the women negotiated borders between ethnic and Anglo culture and had concerns about ethnic "authenticity." Both groups faced contradictory pressures about their physical appearance (to appear more or less "ethnic") and worried about how to manage their ethnic communities' expectations of women's sexuality. Gaining a college education, however, had quite different effects on ethnic identity for the two groups: Latinas, who in this study were mostly first-generation college students, risked criticism from family and community for assimilating into Anglo culture; this was not an issue for the Arab-American women in this study because their families were highly educated. It is, however, a common concern for a variety of ethnic groups.

What ethnic, racial, and cultural groups are predominant on your campus? To what extent do other groups have access to their own cultural spaces and influence on the larger campus culture? How has your experience at college affected your own racial or ethnic identity, whether you are a member of a minority or majority group?

Paula Gunn Allen, similarly, suggests that assumptions about what it means to be a woman in Anglo-European culture do not hold in American Indian cultures. In "Where I Come from Is Like This," she draws on her bicultural experiences to explore the contradictions between the images of women embedded in Anglo and American Indian culture. The images of American Indian women she grew up with are ones of "practicality, strength, reasonableness, intelligence, wit, and competence," in contrast to Anglo-American ideas about women as "passive and weak." Again, we see the difficulty of generalizing about women's experiences. What are the assumptions about women that are part of your own culture?

The boxed insert by Audre Lorde, "The Master's Tools Will Never Dismantle the Master's House," also emphasizes the difficulties of accurately analyzing how systems of oppression affect peoples' lives. Lorde argues in this classic piece, excerpted here, that feminists must critically examine their own use of dominant concepts in their analysis of women's lives. She suggests that academic knowledge is based in an institution that historically has excluded women and people of color, and she asks whether academic knowledge can undermine the inequalities on which it is based. Do you think that the "regular" methods of scholarship and science are adequate to the task of understanding the diversity among women and the complexity of the gender system? Will new tools be necessary? What might they be? Lorde argues that encouraging women to relate to each other at the points of their differences promotes growth, creativity, and social change. Do these conversations across differences happen on your campus?

The final selection in this section focuses on how disability affects experiences of gender. In "The Blind Man's Harley: White Canes and Gender Identity in America," Catherine Kudlick explores the connections between gender and stereotypes of the helpless blind person. Blind people, Kudlick argues, experience condescension from the sighted world, and blind men experience this as emasculating. For Kudlick, entering a program to learn independent cane use challenged her sense of herself as helpless and also showed the ways that the training program equated independence with a macho attitude. Within the blind world, programs such as the one that Kudlick attended emphasize independence and self-determination for the blind and tend to equate greater assistance with femininity. As both men and women in the program "cast off [their] feminine selves" in order to be independent, Kudlick had to redefine her identity as a woman.

Can you think of examples of how other disabilities are equated with femininity and how the rehabilitation or independence of people with disabilities are conceptualized in macho terms? Can you think of counterexamples? How are the disabilities of veterans returning from the Iraq War understood in gender terms? In addition to disability, what other kinds of characteristics can be seen as feminizing for men? What does it mean for a woman to possess a "feminizing" characteristic?

Being the Bridge: A Solitary Black Woman's Position in the Women's Studies Classroom as a Feminist Student and Professor

Gloria Anzaldúa's autograph in my copy of *This Bridge Called My Back* reads, "*Para Kim, que te vaya bien con tus estudios. contigo, Gloria E. Anzaldúa 10.2.91.*" I doubt she knew the significant role her words and *This Bridge* would play in my development as an activist, a student of women's studies, and a professor. *Bridge* not only introduced me to the feminism of Asian-American, Latina, and Native American women, but on a basic level this text showed me the possibility of even *being* a Black feminist.[1] However, this particular bridge could only take me so far and from that point on I began to create, if you will, an expansion. The bridge I envision is like one in movies featuring rainforests and uncharted jungles: rickety ol' planks strung together with rope that looks like it's seen many hardships. But the bridge *exists;* someone took the time to build it and it awaits use, as well as reinforcement for those who will follow. Through awareness, activism, and scholarship, I hope to reinforce the bridge by replacing a few well-worn planks with constructive criticism of Black feminism's past, as well as self-critique of my own Black feminist praxis.

In this essay, I recall demands from white peers in the classroom that I *be* the bridge over which they cross from being racist to interrogating their own privilege and my refusal to do so. I also gingerly step onto the bridge I now provide as a scholar-activist in my academic work. Through these experiences I reflect upon *Bridge*'s impact on my life, my relationship to Black feminism, and my understanding of coalition-building. Feelings of wonderment, rage, isolation, and transformation within *Bridge* were guideposts for the socialization I underwent from an assimilated, working-class girl into a Black feminist woman. Call them stages of Black feminist development.

Feminism, as theorized in *Bridge,* was a guide mapping many potential directions for my analysis of the complexity of Black feminism. With this personal narrative I demonstrate the continuing existence of Black feminist activism from Black women active in the 1970s (Kate Rushin, Beverly Smith, Barbara Smith, Beverly Guy-Sheftall, Audre Lorde), many still active today. I oppose a media-generated image of a second-wave/third-wave fracture and speculate on the possibilities for an intergenerational Black feminist theory. Rather than competing with the Black feminists who came before me, as much predominately white third-wave feminist literature attests, I see myself as the bridge between my fore mothers and future Black feminists. Feminists must do coalition work on many levels simultaneously: connect with those outside the groups we choose to call home and examine our internal politics to determine what keeps us separated and reinventing the wheel.

BLACK GIRLHOOD AND INCIPIENT FEMINISM

There are perils to growing up Black and female in the United States, but there are also unimaginable joys and triumphs. Watching my young second-cousin, Skylar, grow up, I'm simultaneously filled with pride and trepidation. Her mother reminds me of my own mother: the best mother possible, trying to raise a healthy, whole African-American girl in a society that devalues her based on her race and gender. I try to assist, reminding Skylar how smart, beautiful, and truly bold she is through creative feminist gifts and encouraging words. However, there is only so much I can do to protect her from the racist, sexist, heterosexist attitudes that will eventually try to shape her into someone other than who she was meant to be. I often compose letters and practice conversations I'd like to have when she is old enough to comprehend my meaning.

> Dear Skylar Jade,
> What's up, Skydee-dy-dee? Are you keeping Mama busy with your activities and questions and just all-around brilliance? I remember the time we tried to go see a holiday light festival. You were in the backseat all strapped in, asking me why we couldn't, after all, go. I'd left my wallet at home and explained the situation. You asked for the 3rd or 4th time and I lost my patience and, with a heavy sigh, said, "BECAUSE, Sky, I don't have any money on me." From the backseat I heard this pre-teen (though you were only 5) sucking of teeth and an exasperated "I was just ASKING." That, my dear, was what Alice Walker and other women in our family would call acting "womanish," but I had to laugh because you were so SASSY. I hope you remain secure in who you are—a complex almost-young-woman who'll keep questioning until satisfied with the answers. Enclosed is a copy of Toni Morrison's *The Bluest Eye* Call me when you've read it. Kisses. Love, Cousin Kim

Part of the message I received growing up was "Each one, teach one." I try to apply this edict as I reach back to younger Black girls who have yet to figure out that feminism is not a "white girls' thing" or a "bad word"; to help young girls and women see that female empowerment is not a crotch-grabbing "video-ho" and that we can, in fact, say, "Sister, that is fucked-up behavior." As my dear friend, another Kimberly, says, we need to bring our whole selves to the table, not just the newly sexually-empowered parts. I want to offer my Black feminist experiences as just one of many options to get them through the times when the news media, popular culture, and even some of their peers try to tell them that they're not intelligent and beautiful because they don't fit the dominant norms of beauty or that they are not keeping it real unless they are singing about some man paying the bills.

Preparing to graduate in the spring of 1992, I sat trying to decide what protest message to write on my mortar board. Among the sea of Greek letters and accolades for years spent partying, I wanted my cap to reflect my growing Black feminist consciousness. Not that I hadn't gotten my apolitical groove on to Public Enemy a number of times, but my years at the University of Michigan were my own flashpoint. Onto the television came another round of bulletins about the

L.A. rebellion. A reporter asked a teenaged African-American girl a typically inane mainstream question: "What does the verdict in the Rodney King trial say to you?" I could feel my young sister's anguish as she choked out between tears, "It makes me feel like they think we don't matter at all." I knew then what to write on my mortarboard ("Burn, Hollywood, Burn"), but it was hard to see through my own tears as I felt similar feelings of worthlessness and defiance all at once. I think of that girl when I contemplate the shock of waking up from a deep assimilated sleep and into the cold reality of social injustice. How could I help her and others cross the icy waters of degradation threatening to overtake us all every time a bullet rips through the flesh of another sister or brother?

IDENTITY POLITICS/IDENTIFYING POLITICALLY

What does it mean that a white man, a gay white man, introduced me to feminism? Is my feminism any less legitimate than that of my classmate who came to feminism following years of sexual abuse at her father's hands? Is it any less legitimate than that of my friend whose lesbian mother raised her with feminist principles, as if *Free to Be You and Me* were the sugar on every child's morning cereal?

My resident advisor, Jim, taught me many things that year. He taught me what it meant to think critically about power and privilege. He taught me what it meant to have my first real bona fide crush on a gay man and opt instead for being a dear friend. He also suggested that I take Introduction to Women's Studies during my first year. He led this horse to water, but he didn't have to make me drink. I partook of every reading, required and suggested, that I could get my hands on. Finally, there was something, or rather many "someones," who could explain just what the hell it was I felt as I learned about Black women's history for the first time, who all the powerful Black figures were in Boogie Down Productions' song "You Must Learn," why someone would want to spell *woman* "womyn," and the import of my senior high/junior college paper on *Bowers v. Hardwick*.

For me this mixing of cultures and political allegiances meant that, early on, I had an abiding belief in building coalitions across identities. It sounds clichéd, but I really could not see how one could harbor prejudices toward entire groups of people if one had experienced discrimination and also entered into intimate relationships with people different from one's self. I'm sure the label "sell-out" was tossed at my back, but I was too busy, thrilled by the activism and camaraderie, to notice. As an activist in anti-racist work, defending suburban Detroit clinics with reproductive rights organizations, studying social movements, I encountered people with differing political priorities. While it was never easy to negotiate all the demands and a few friendships fell by the wayside, I never regret trying to bridge the externally-imposed divides between my political interests. In those interests for women's, lesbian/gay, and people of color's rights, I had my own hands-on practicum in how power and privilege circulate to positively and negatively impact movement outcomes.

Just when I was discovering what each aspect of my identity had to do with the others, postmodern theorists (mostly white, European men) tried to suck *all* the damn air out of the room and tell me there was no "I." I was also discovering how my powerlessness and privilege lived side-by-side, making for a very confused, angry, but oddly exhilarated young woman. In my Intro to Women's Studies course, one of the *Bridge* essays I elected to read was the dialogue between Beverly and Barbara Smith. Not having a sister myself, I could only read in awe: two Black feminists in the same family? They captured precisely the conflict I felt while taking advantage of my educational privilege for eight months of the year, then going "home" to my family and Black community during holidays:

> There are ways we act when Black people are together that white women will never see in a largely white context. Now, I don't think this is about acting white in a white context. It's about one, a lack of inspiration. Because the way you act with Black people is because they inspire the behavior. And I do mean inspire. And the other thing is that when you are in a white context, you think "Well, why bother? Why waste your time?" If what you're trying to do is get things across and communicate and what-have-you, *you talk in your second language.* (119, my emphasis)

Barely passing French my first year, I became bilingual in my Blackness and my feminist inclinations. What I had yet to learn was how to defend myself in this new language, this new land where different parts of me fought to lay claim to my time and energy. The Black Student Union protest or drive to a Clinic Defense in suburban Detroit? The United Coalition Against Racism meeting or the Take Back the Night March?

Like the 1970s Black feminists I would later study, I was torn between two lovers and, surely, feeling like a fool. I straddled the fence of my identity and burned out quickly trying to bring an anti-sexist analysis to my "race work" and an anti-racist sensibility to my "gender work." Not surprisingly, these two branches never met. It was like trying to keep two lovers from finding out about one another, but secretly wanting them to meet, fall in love, and forget all about me. Bringing an anti-heterosexist perspective to either aspect of my activism was, needless to say, an even rougher battle as I tried to be pro-lesbian/gay/bi rights and *still* get a date with one of the SNAGs (Sensitive New Age Guys) on campus. Was I being naive in thinking that, unlike Rushin in her "Bridge Poem," I would somehow be exempt from translating for everyone who selected which parts of me they wanted to encounter?

Inside the classroom a different battle was only just beginning. I tried to defend myself in my women's studies classes where I was "The Only One." The only Black woman, the only one who knew the importance of talking about hair and its racial and gender implications for Black women. The only one who thought, "You must be kidding" when professors at one of the most prestigious universities in the country spoke of being ghettoized. Tell it to the folks in Cabrini Green. The only one who cringed and slouched over self-consciously when a white professor declared, "Black women don't have body image issues. There's just a different aesthetic in the Black Community." Did you hear that, hips? You're just a different *aesthetic.* Yeah. Right. Donna Kate Rushin's poem rang in my ears: "Sick of being the sole Black friend to 34 individual white people." Sick of being the sole person in the room unimpressed when professors tokenized bell hooks on their otherwise all-white feminist theory syllabi.

The struggles with white feminists were not only with professors, but with teaching assistants of the next generation of feminist activism too. The TA for a required course interrogated me, "Well, 100-level students will want to know. *Are* you a feminist?" It made me angry that all the replies I could think of were not mine. Not the historically logical answer: "*Hell,* no, I'm not a feminist! Do I look like Sojourner Truth, waiting for some Northern suffragist to turn her back on me? I ain't no fool." That would be too "angry Black woman" and I might not pass the interview to facilitate the 100-level women's studies class, which I needed to fulfill my major. I opted for "Throw Her off the Scent Answer #2": "No, I'm not a feminist. I'm a *womanist.*" While appeasing my Birkenstock-wearing, cultural-feminist TA, it did nothing for me but give me a reprieve from committing myself to feminism or to non-Black status in the eyes of some of my friends and relatives. Still, I felt so good and authentic that I went out and bought my *own* pair of Birkenstocks— militantly **black** ones.

I kept those broke-down sandals as a memento of what I saw as a simpler time in my feminist trajectory. It was easier in undergraduate school for me to parrot the lines of my real and imagined mentors on the need for socialist revolution, Black liberation, and patriarchy's downfall. It wasn't that I didn't believe those things but just that I didn't think about them much. It was much easier to take these principles as my own, rather than wrestle with my inner-life contradictions: my middle-class aspirations, my vast amount of booklearning, a decreasing belief in god, the ability to get instantly weepy at a strong rendition of the gospel hymn "Goin' up' a Yonder," the desire for a throwdown revolution Che Guevara–style, and a penchant for a Black Panther in a black leather coat.

IN THE BELLY OF THE FEMINIST BEAST

In the face of all that confusion I went to graduate school. Thinking I'd find out who I was and what I wanted to be, or at least buy myself a little more time, I applied to and was accepted into a doctoral program in women's studies. It seemed like a logical next step, building on my undergraduate major in women's studies and sociology. I could continue finding ways to remain politically active because I would still be a student—or so I thought.

The program I chose was, at the time, one of two offering a Ph.D. in women's studies. I assumed that it was a feminist program—after all, what else would a women's studies program be? Not until I began studying social movements and organizations did I understand it in the context of the institutionalization and professionalization of an area founded by activists. I entered a women's studies program in which most faculty and students *studied* women, but not necessarily tried to investigate or apply feminism.[2] This was, in fact, a double-sided realization: slight dismay that I could no longer assume that women's studies equaled feminist studies, but a determination to focus on feminist theory in my own work.

After another Black woman left the program for one more suited to her interests and sanity, I was once again the only Black woman in the program.[3] In addition to my status as the only Black woman, I also encountered many students who hadn't majored in or taken women's studies courses as undergraduates. This lack of training had significant consequences on my intellectual and activist outlook. It baffled me that a few women's studies graduate students in my classes professed to do women's studies, but flushed at the thought of having to enter a classroom and talk about feminist perspectives on film, religion, science, politics, or any number of other topics. Soon I learned that many of the women opting for a certificate in women's studies, wasting valuable class time in my feminist theory course with asinine debates about standard vacuum cleaners versus Dustbusters, merely added the certificate to their resume in the hopes of landing a scarce teaching position in their respective fields. That's when I decided that there's meeting women where they are and there's leaving their asses by the side of the road (or at a very nice rest stop) if you've got places to go.

IT'S A LOVE/HATE THANG

Recently three constellations saved me from chewing through the rope I was holding. My academic research, a few students, and a posse of Black, Asian-American, Latina, and white feminist friends were, and still are, my bridge between women's studies and feminism, between academic professionalization and activism. That's what the hyphen in scholar-activist means to me: I can still think critically, write, and teach about ideas of social justice, democracy, and equality, while encouraging students and myself to participate in direct action that makes those ideas practical tools for living.

Part of my struggle as a scholar-activist is my research on 1970s Black feminist organizations. I read about several organizations, searched them out to join up, but found that they'd all disbanded around the time I was saving my allowance for candy and *Archie* comic books. So I decided to discover what happened to these organizations and, more important, how they did it in the first place. How did they get a group of Black women together in the same room for something besides planning Women's Day at church or getting their hair done, which for a long time was my limited experience of women's organizing activities? Over the course of twelve years, several hundred, if not thousands, of Black feminists laid the groundwork for Black feminist activism and the expansion of what we call feminist issues (including, but not limited to, the right to *have* children and informed consent about sterilization as valid reproductive rights). Black feminists in at least five organizations in Boston, New York, Chicago, and San Francisco participated in consciousness-raising groups with white women and in groups of only Black women where they started to believe that they were not crazy for being Black *and* feminist.

Though these groups ceased meeting by the early 1980s, they left a legacy inspiring me to document their existence. Kitchen Table Press pinned a button stating, "Black Feminism *LIVES!*" to every copy of the reprinted Combahee River Collective Statement! This feminism lives in me as I read and re-read feminist-of-color writings and as I try to relay to my students the excitement and danger of a time in women's movement history that I wasn't around for either.

As an instructor on social movements, I struggle to teach about identity politics. Some postmodernists view identity politics as essentialist, reinforcing ideas of how marginalized people "naturally" are. Well, in some ways essentialism is *essential.* As the Smith sisters and the Combahee River Collective note, there once was, and still is, value in *identifying politically* with people who look like you. Yet as Bernice Johnson Reagon points out, this does not mean we don't ever open the door to the place we call home. In fact, it often behooves us to collectively tear the roof off our ideas of home and invite others in to see what we can make of the future.

As much as I complain about students' lack of historical context or wish I could just uncritically enjoy my *Entertainment Weekly,* I wouldn't trade in my feminism for anything in the world. Every time I experience a student having that "click" of how to think critically about discrimination and social change, I have that same spark of recognition all over again. We are still working on a bridge to somewhere exciting, dangerous, and new.

Incredibly enough, I've seen a few frat boys experience that click while some young sisters try to get over on me, Sister/Teacher, because, after all, "You know what it's like to be the only Black woman in a classroom of white folks *and* not have done the classwork because of last night's Kappa step show." At that moment Black feminist organizations' lessons come back to haunt me: do not assume that because someone looks like you, they share your political and personal objectives; I return to the idea of identity politics and remind myself there is much intragroup coalition work to be done. Moreover, I must be aware of how my own internal identity politics can impede internal critique and connections with the Black woman I hope to be and with other Black women.

One way I sought to make the exchange between activism and scholarship was to help organize a Black Feminist Salon while living in Atlanta. Unfortunately for me, I was moving away soon after the group formed, but it filled me with hope and pride that we could get several sisters to sit in a room and share what it means to be Black and feminist, lesbian, straight, and bisexual. Living about a thousand miles away from the Salon is disappointing, but just getting it together lets me know I can build community wherever I go. Whether that community is with other Black women or with feminist women and men in my predominately white mountain town, the bridges I've learned to build are internal and transport well.

There is so much work to be done around gender that I will not be left to my leisure even if I live miles away from a critical mass of Black sisters and brothers. The work heterosexual Black feminists need to do in conjunction with our Black lesbian and gay counterparts around homophobia in Black communities is unending. The dialogues that Black women of all sexual orientations need to open up with one another about sexuality and competition and "diva-dissing" could fill hours of conversation and anthologies yet to be conceived. Continuing to push for a redefined Black masculinity that does not replicate patriarchy's worst tendencies is a project just beginning in academia and the street.

Feminism, specifically third-world feminism, has been a bridge, a lifeline, and even an extension of my being. Yet sometimes I wonder how much longer I can continue being a bridge between cultures, races, and theories. As a member of the Black Feminist Salon in Atlanta said, "I consider it my activism whenever I leave the house." This is a lifetime of work. Social change is a process. I will often be afraid inside and outside spaces I call home. Perhaps I can persuade myself to look forward to the challenges and growth that will come as I continue crossing the bridge built by *This Bridge Called My Back* twenty years ago.

What Donna Kate Rushin calls for is not throwing in the towel because we're sick of white folks and everyone else who looks to Black women to be political Mammys. Instead, she affirms the work we need to do internally as well as externally to continue waging battles that have yet to be fought. Rushin's determined words warrant repeating: "The bridge I must be/Is the bridge to my own power/I must translate/My own fears/Mediate/My own weaknesses/I must be the bridge to nowhere/But my true self/And then I will be useful." Amen, sistah Kate, amen!

NOTES

The author thanks AnaLouise Keating and Kimberly Wallace-Sanders for their extensive sisterly comments.

1. Equally critical in my personal-political Black feminist development was *Home Girls,* another Kitchen Table publication.

2. By the time I graduated from the program in 1999, I perceived students' greater dedication to critically engaging feminism.

3. The next year, sister Francis Wood came to the program, bringing heat and light.

R E A D I N G *2*   **Peggy McIntosh**

White Privilege: Unpacking the Invisible Knapsack

Through work to bring materials and perspectives from Women's Studies into the rest of the curriculum, I have often noticed men's unwillingness to grant that they are overprivileged in the curriculum, even though they may grant that women are disadvantaged. Denials that amount to taboos surround the subject of advantages that men gain from women's disadvantages. These denials protect male privilege from being fully recognized, acknowledged, lessened, or ended.

Thinking through unacknowledged male privilege as a phenomenon with a life of its own, I realized that since hierarchies in our society are interlocking, there was most likely a phenomenon of white privilege that was similarly denied and protected, but alive and real in its effects. As a white person, I realized I had been taught about racism as something that puts others at a disadvantage, but had been taught not to see one of its corollary aspects, white privilege, which puts me at an advantage.

I think whites are carefully taught not to recognize white privilege, as males are taught not to recognize male privilege. So I have begun in an untutored way to ask what it is like to have white privilege. This paper is a partial record of my personal observations and not a scholarly analysis. It is based on my daily experiences within my particular circumstances.

I have come to see white privilege as an invisible package of unearned assets that I can count on cashing in each day, but about which I was "meant" to remain oblivious. White privilege is like an invisible weightless knapsack of special provisions, assurances, tools, maps, guides, codebooks, passports, visas, clothes, compass, emergency gear, and blank checks.

Since I have had trouble facing white privilege, and describing its results in my life, I saw parallels here with men's reluctance to acknowledge male privilege. Only rarely will a man go beyond acknowledging that women are disadvantaged to acknowledging that men have unearned advantage, or that unearned privilege has not been good for men's development as human beings, or for society's development, or that privilege systems might ever be challenged and *changed.*

I will review here several types or layers of denial that I see at work protecting, and preventing awareness about, entrenched male privilege. Then I will draw parallels, from my own experience, with the denials that veil the facts of white privilege. Finally, I will list forty-six ordinary and daily ways in which I experience having white privilege, by contrast with my African-American colleagues in the same building. This list is not intended to be generalizable. Others can make their own lists from within their own life circumstances.

Writing this paper has been difficult, despite warm receptions for the talks on which it is based.[1] For describing white privilege makes one newly accountable. As we in Women's Studies work to reveal male privilege and ask men to give up some of their power so one who writes about having white privilege must ask, "Having described it, what will I do to lessen or end it."

The denial of men's overprivileged state takes many forms in discussions of curriculum change work. Some claim that men must be central in the curriculum because they have done most of what is important or distinctive in life or in civilization. Some recognize sexism in the curriculum but deny that it makes male students seem unduly important in life. Others agree that certain *individual* thinkers are male-oriented but deny that there is any *systemic* tendency in disciplinary frameworks or epistemology to over-empower men as a group. Those men who do grant that male privilege takes institutionalized and embedded forms are still likely to deny that male hegemony has opened doors for them personally. Virtually all men deny that male overreward alone can explain men's centrality in all the inner sanctums of our most powerful institutions. Moreover, those few who will acknowledge that male privilege systems have over-empowered them usually end up doubting that we could dismantle these privilege systems. They may say they will work to improve women's status, in the society or in the university, but they can't or won't support the idea of lessening men's. In curricular terms, this is the point at which they say that they regret they cannot use any of the interesting new scholarship on women because the syllabus is full. When the talk turns to giving men less cultural room, even the most thoughtful and fair-minded of the men I know will tend to reflect, or fall back on, conservative assumptions about the inevitability of present gender relations and distributions of power, calling on precedent or sociobiology and psychobiology to demonstrate that male domination is natural and follows inevitably from evolutionary pressures. Others resort to arguments from "experience" or religion or social responsibility or wishing and dreaming.

After I realized, through faculty development work in Women's Studies, the extent to which men work from a base of unacknowledged privilege, I understood that much of their oppressiveness was unconscious. Then I remembered the frequent charges from women of color that white women whom they encounter are oppressive. I began to understand why we are justly seen as oppressive, even when we don't see ourselves that way. At the very least, obliviousness of one's privileged state can make a person or group irritating to be with. I began to count the ways in which I enjoy unearned skin privilege and have been conditioned into oblivion about its existence, unable to see that it put me "ahead" in any way, or put my people ahead, overrewarding us and yet also paradoxically damaging us, or that it could or should be changed.

My schooling gave me no training in seeing myself as an oppressor, as an unfairly advantaged person, or as a participant in a damaged culture. I was taught to see myself as an individual whose moral state depended on her individual moral will. At school, we were not taught about slavery in any depth; we were not taught to see slaveholders as damaged people. Slaves were seen as the only group at risk of being dehumanized. My schooling followed the pattern which Elizabeth Minnich has pointed out: whites are taught to think of their lives as morally neutral, normative, and average, and also ideal, so that when we work to benefit others, this is seen as work that will allow "them" to be more like "us." I think many of us know how obnoxious this attitude can be in men.

After frustration with men who would not recognize male privilege, I decided to try to work on myself at least by identifying some of the daily effects of white privilege in my life. It is crude work, at this stage, but I will give here a list of special circumstances and conditions I experience that I did not earn but that I have been made to feel are mine by birth, by citizenship, and by virtue of being a conscientious law-abiding "normal" person of goodwill. I have chosen those conditions that I think in my case *attach somewhat more to skin-color privilege* than to class, religion, ethnic status, or geographical location, though these other privileging factors are intricately intertwined. As far as I can see, my African-American co-workers, friends, and acquaintances with whom I come into daily or frequent contact in this particular time, place, and line of work cannot count on most of these conditions.

1. I can, if I wish, arrange to be in the company of people of my race most of the time.
2. I can avoid spending time with people whom I was trained to mistrust and who have learned to mistrust my kind or me.
3. If I should need to move, I can be pretty sure of renting or purchasing housing in an area which I can afford and in which I would want to live.
4. I can be reasonably sure that my neighbors in such a location will be neutral or pleasant to me.
5. I can go shopping alone most of the time, fairly well assured that I will not be followed or harassed by store detectives.
6. I can turn on the television or open to the front page of the paper and see people of my race widely and positively represented.

7. When I am told about our national heritage or about "civilization," I am shown that people of my color made it what it is.

8. I can be sure that my children will be given curricular materials that testify to the existence of their race.

9. If I want to, I can be pretty sure of finding a publisher for this piece on white privilege.

10. I can be fairly sure of having my voice heard in a group in which I am the only member of my race.

11. I can be casual about whether or not to listen to another woman's voice in a group in which she is the only member of her race.

12. I can go into a bookshop and count on finding the writing of my race represented, into a supermarket and find the staple foods that fit with my cultural traditions, into a hairdresser's shop and find someone who can deal with my hair.

13. Whether I use checks, credit cards, or cash, I can count on my skin color not to work against the appearance that I am financially reliable.

14. I could arrange to protect our young children most of the time from people who might not like them.

15. I did not have to educate our children to be aware of systemic racism for their own daily physical protection.

16. I can be pretty sure that my children's teachers and employers will tolerate them if they fit school and workplace norms; my chief worries about them do not concern others' attitudes toward their race.

17. I can talk with my mouth full and not have people put this down to my color.

18. I can swear, or dress in secondhand clothes, or not answer letters, without having people attribute these choices to the bad morals, the poverty, or the illiteracy of my race.

19. I can speak in public to a powerful male group without putting my race on trial.

20. I can do well in a challenging situation without being called a credit to my race.

21. I am never asked to speak for all the people of my racial group.

22. I can remain oblivious to the language and customs of persons of color who constitute the world's majority without feeling in my culture any penalty for such oblivion.

23. I can criticize our government and talk about how much I fear its policies and behavior without being seen as a cultural outsider.

24. I can be reasonably sure that if I ask to talk to "the person in charge," I will be facing a person of my race.

25. If a traffic cop pulls me over or if the IRS audits my tax return, I can be sure I haven't been singled out because of my race.

26. I can easily buy posters, postcards, picture books, greeting cards, dolls, toys, and children's magazines featuring people of my race.

27. I can go home from most meetings of organizations I belong to feeling somewhat tied in, rather than isolated, out of place, outnumbered, unheard, held at a distance, or feared.

28. I can be pretty sure that an argument with a colleague of another race is more likely to jeopardize her chances for advancement than to jeopardize mine.

29. I can be fairly sure that if I argue for the promotion of a person of another race, or a program centering on race, this is not likely to cost me heavily within my present setting, even if my colleagues disagree with me.

30. If I declare there is a racial issue at hand, or there isn't a racial issue at hand, my race will lend me more credibility for either position than a person of color will have.

31. I can choose to ignore developments in minority writing and minority activist programs, or disparage them, or learn from them, but in any case, I can find ways to be more or less protected from negative consequences of any of these choices.

32. My culture gives me little fear about ignoring the perspectives and powers of people of other races.

33. I am not made acutely aware that my shape, bearing, or body odor will be taken as a reflection on my race.

34. I can worry about racism without being seen as self-interested or self-seeking.

35. I can take a job with an affirmative action employer without having my co-workers on the job suspect that I got it because of my race.

36. If my day, week, or year is going badly, I need not ask of each negative episode or situation whether it has racial overtones.

37. I can be pretty sure of finding people who would be willing to talk with me and advise me about my next steps, professionally.

38. I can think over many options, social, political, imaginative, or professional, without asking whether a person of my race would be accepted or allowed to do what I want to do.

39. I can be late to a meeting without having the lateness reflect on my race.

40. I can choose public accommodation without fearing that people of my race cannot get in or will be mistreated in the places I have chosen.

41. I can be sure that if I need legal or medical help, my race will not work against me.

42. I can arrange my activities so that I will never have to experience feelings of rejection owing to my race.

43. If I have low credibility as a leader, I can be sure that my race is not the problem.

44. I can easily find academic courses and institutions that give attention only to people of my race.

45. I can expect figurative language and imagery in all of the arts to testify to experiences of my race.

46. I can choose blemish cover or bandages in "flesh" color and have them more or less match my skin.

I repeatedly forgot each of the realizations on this list until I wrote it down. For me, white privilege has turned out to be an elusive and fugitive subject. The pressure to avoid it is great, for in facing it I must give up the myth of meritocracy. If these things are true, this is not such a free country; one's life is not what one makes it; many doors open for certain people through no virtues of their own. These perceptions mean also that my moral condition is not what I had been led to believe. The appearance of being a good citizen rather than a troublemaker comes in large part from having all sorts of doors open automatically because of my color.

A further paralysis of nerve comes from literary silence protecting privilege. My clearest memories of finding such analysis are in Lillian Smith's unparalleled *Killers of the Dream*, and Margaret Andersen's review of Karen and Mamie Fields' *Lemon Swamp*. Smith, for example, wrote about walking toward black children on the street and knowing they would step into the gutter; Andersen contrasted the pleasure that she, as a white child, took on summer driving trips to the south with Karen Fields' memories of driving in a closed car stocked with all necessities lest, in stopping, her black family should suffer "insult, or worse." Adrienne Rich also recognizes and writes about daily experiences of privilege, but in my observation, white women's writing in this area is far more often on systemic racism than on our daily lives as light-skinned women.[2]

In unpacking this invisible knapsack of white privilege, I have listed conditions of daily experience that I once took for granted, as neutral, normal, and universally available to everybody, just as I once thought of a male-focused curriculum as the neutral or accurate account that can speak for all. Nor did I think of any of these perquisites as bad for the holder. I now think that we need a more finely differentiated taxonomy of privilege, for some of these varieties are only what one would want for everyone in a just society, and others give license to be ignorant, oblivious, arrogant, and destructive. Before proposing some more finely tuned categorization, I will make some observations about the general effects of these conditions on my life and expectations.

In this potpourri of examples, some privileges make me feel at home in the world. Others allow me to escape penalties or dangers that others suffer. Through some, I escape fear, anxiety, insult, injury, or a sense of not being welcome, not being real. Some keep me from having to hide, to be in disguise, to feel sick or crazy, to negotiate each transaction from the position of being an outsider or, within my group, a person who is suspected of having too close links with a dominant culture. Most keep me from having to be angry.

I see a pattern running through the matrix of white privilege, a pattern of assumptions that were passed on to me as a white person. There was one main piece of cultural turf; it was my own turf, and I was among those who could control the turf. I could measure up to the cultural standards and take advantage of the many options I saw around me to make what the culture would call a success of my life. *My skin color was an asset for any move I was educated to want to make.* I could think of myself as "belonging" in major ways and of making social systems work for me. I could freely disparage, fear, neglect, or be oblivious to anything outside of the dominant cultural forms. Being of the main culture, I could also criticize it fairly freely. My life was reflected back to me frequently enough so that I felt, with regard to my race, if not to my sex, like one of the real people.

Whether through the curriculum or in the newspaper, the television, the economic system, or the general look of people in the streets, I received daily signals and indications that my people counted and that others *either didn't exist or must be trying, not very successfully, to be like people of my race.* I was given cultural permission not to hear voices of people of other races or a tepid cultural tolerance for hearing or acting on such voices. I was also raised not to suffer seriously from anything that darker-skinned people might say about my group, "protected," though perhaps I should more accurately say *prohibited,* through the habits of my economic class and social group, from living in racially mixed groups or being reflective about interactions between people of differing races.

In proportion as my racial group was being made confident, comfortable, and oblivious, other groups were likely being made unconfident, uncomfortable, and alienated. Whiteness protected me from many kinds of hostility, distress, and violence, which I was being subtly trained to visit in turn upon people of color.

For this reason, the word "privilege" now seems to me misleading. Its connotations are too positive to fit the conditions and behaviors which "privilege systems" produce. We usually think of privilege as being a favored state, whether earned or conferred by birth or luck. School graduates are reminded they are privileged and urged to use their (enviable) assets well. The word "privilege" carries the connotation of being something everyone must want. Yet some of the conditions I have described here work to systemically overempower certain groups. Such privilege simply *confers dominance,* gives permission to control, because of one's race or sex. The kind of privilege that gives license to some people to be, at best, thoughtless and, at worst, murderous should not continue to be referred to as a desirable attribute. Such "privilege" may be widely desired without being in any way beneficial to the whole society.

Moreover, though "privilege" may confer power, it does not confer moral strength. Those who do not depend on conferred dominance have traits and qualities that may never develop in those who do. Just as Women's Studies courses indicate that women survive their political circumstances to lead lives that hold the human race together, so "underprivileged" people of color who are the world's majority have survived their oppression and lived survivors' lives from which the white global minority can and must learn. In some groups, those dominated have actually become strong through *not* having all of these unearned advantages, and this gives them a great deal to teach the others. Members of so-called privileged groups can seem foolish, ridiculous, infantile, or dangerous by contrast.

I want, then, to distinguish between earned strength and unearned power conferred systemically. Power from unearned privilege can look like strength when it is, in fact, permission to escape or to dominate. But not all of the privileges on my list are inevitably damaging. Some, like the expectation that neighbors will be decent to you, or that your race will not count against you in court, should be the norm in a just society and should be considered as the entitlement of everyone. Others, like the privilege not to listen to less powerful people, distort the humanity of the holders as well as the ignored groups. Still others, like finding one's staple foods everywhere, may be a function of being a member of a numerical majority in the population. Others have to do with not having to labor under pervasive negative stereotyping and mythology.

We might at least start by distinguishing between positive advantages that we can work to spread, to the point where they are not advantages at all but simply part of the normal civic and social fabric, and negative types of advantage that unless rejected will always reinforce our present hierarchies. For example, the positive "privilege" of belonging, the feeling that one belongs within the human circle, as Native Americans say, fosters development and should not be seen as privilege for a few. It is, let us say, an entitlement that none of us should have to earn; ideally it is an *unearned entitlement.* At present, since only a few have it, it is an *unearned advantage* for them. The negative "privilege" that gave me cultural permission not to take darker-skinned others seriously can be seen as arbitrarily conferred dominance and should not be desirable for anyone. This paper results from a process of coming to see that some of the power that I originally saw as attendant on being a human being in the United States consisted in *unearned advantage* and *conferred dominance,* as well as other kinds of special circumstance not universally taken for granted.

In writing this paper I have also realized that white identity and status (as well as class identity and status) give me considerable power to choose whether to broach this subject and its trouble. I can pretty well decide whether to disappear and avoid and not listen and escape the dislike I may engender in other people through this essay, or interrupt, answer, interpret, preach, correct, criticize, and control to some extent what goes on in reaction to it. Being white, I am given considerable power to escape many kinds of danger or penalty as well as to choose which risks I want to take.

There is an analogy here, once again, with Women's Studies. Our male colleagues do not have a great deal to lose in supporting Women's Studies, but they do not have a great deal to lose if they oppose it either. They simply have the power to decide whether to commit themselves to more equitable distributions of power. They will probably feel few penalties whatever choice they make; they do not seem, in any obvious short-term sense, the ones at risk, though they and we are all at risk because of the behaviors that have been rewarded in them.

Through Women's Studies work I have met very few men who are truly distressed about systemic, unearned male advantage and conferred dominance. And so one question for me and others like me is whether we will be like them, or whether we will get truly distressed, even outraged, about unearned race advantage and conferred dominance and if so, what we will do to lessen them. In any case, we need to do more work in identifying how they actually affect our daily lives. We need more down-to-earth writing by people about these taboo subjects. We need more understanding of the ways in which white "privilege" damages white people, for these are not the same ways in which it damages the victimized. Skewed white psyches are an inseparable part of the picture, though I do not want to confuse the kinds of damage done to the holders of special assets and to those who suffer the deficits. Many, perhaps most, of our white students in the United States think that racism doesn't affect them because they are not people of color; they do not see "whiteness" as a racial identity. Many men likewise think that Women's Studies does not bear on their own existences because they are not female; they do not see themselves as having gendered identities. Insisting on the universal "effects" of "privilege" systems, then, becomes one of our chief tasks, and being more explicit about the *particular* effects in particular contexts is another. Men need to join us in this work.

In addition, since race and sex are not the only advantaging systems at work, we need to similarly examine the daily experience of having age advantage, or ethnic advantage, or physical ability, or advantage related to nationality, religion, or sexual orientation. Professor Marnie Evans suggested to me that in many ways the list I made also applies directly to heterosexual privilege. This is a still more taboo subject than race privilege: the daily ways in which heterosexual privilege makes some persons comfortable or powerful, providing supports, assets, approvals, and rewards to those who live or expect to live in heterosexual

pairs. Unpacking that content is still more difficult, owing to the deeper embeddedness of heterosexual advantage and dominance and stricter taboos surrounding these.

But to start such an analysis I would put this observation from my own experience: The fact that I live under the same roof with a man triggers all kinds of societal assumptions about my worth, politics, life, and values and triggers a host of unearned advantages and powers. After recasting many elements from the original list I would add further observations like these:

1. My children do not have to answer questions about why I live with my partner (my husband).
2. I have no difficulty finding neighborhoods where people approve of our household.
3. Our children are given texts and classes that implicitly support our kind of family unit and do not turn them against my choice of domestic partnership.
4. I can travel alone or with my husband without expecting embarrassment or hostility in those who deal with us.
5. Most people I meet will see my marital arrangements as an asset to my life or as a favorable comment on my likability, my competence, or my mental health.
6. I can talk about the social events of a weekend without fearing most listeners' reactions.
7. I will feel welcomed and "normal" in the usual walks of public life, institutional and social.
8. In many contexts, I am seen as "all right" in daily work on women because I do not live chiefly with women.

Difficulties and dangers surrounding the task of finding parallels are many. Since racism, sexism, and heterosexism are not the same, the advantages associated with them should not be seen as the same. In addition, it is hard to isolate aspects of unearned advantage that derive chiefly from social class, economic class, race, religion, region, sex, or ethnic identity. The oppressions are both distinct and interlocking, as the Combahee River Collective statement of 1977 continues to remind us eloquently.[3]

One factor seems clear about all of the interlocking oppressions. They take both active forms that we can see and embedded forms that members of the dominant group are taught not to see. In my class and place, I did not see myself as racist because I was taught to recognize racism only in individual acts of meanness by members of my group, never in invisible systems conferring racial dominance on my group from birth. Likewise, we are taught to think that sexism or heterosexism is carried on only through intentional, individual acts of discrimination, meanness, or cruelty, rather than in invisible systems conferring unsought dominance on certain groups. Disapproving of the systems won't be enough to change them. I was taught to think that racism could end if white individuals changed their attitudes; many men think sexism can be ended by individual changes in daily behavior toward women. But a man's sex provides advantage for him whether or not he approves of the way in which dominance has been conferred on his group. A "white" skin in the United States opens many doors for whites whether or not we approve of the way dominance has been conferred on us. Individual acts can palliate, but cannot end, these problems. To redesign social systems, we need first to acknowledge their colossal unseen dimensions. The silences and denials surrounding privilege are the key political tool here. They keep the thinking about equality or equity incomplete, protecting unearned

advantage and conferred dominance by making these taboo subjects. Most talk by whites about equal opportunity seems to me now to be about equal opportunity to try to get into a position of dominance while denying that *systems* of dominance exist.

Obliviousness about white advantage, like obliviousness about male advantage, is kept strongly inculturated in the United States so as to maintain the myth of meritocracy, the myth that democratic choice is equally available to all. Keeping most people unaware that freedom of confident action is there for just a small number of people props up those in power and serves to keep power in the hands of the same groups that have most of it already. Though systemic change takes many decades, there are pressing questions for me and I imagine for some others like me if we raise our daily consciousness on the perquisites of being light-skinned. What will we do with such knowledge? As we know from watching men, it is an open question whether we will choose to use unearned advantage to weaken invisible privilege systems and whether we will use any of our arbitrarily awarded power to try to reconstruct power systems on a broader base.

ACKNOWLEDGMENTS

I have appreciated commentary on this paper from the Working Papers Committee of the Wellesley College Center for Research on Women, from members of the Dodge seminar, and from many individuals, including Margaret Andersen, Sorel Berman, Joanne Braxton, Johnnella Butler, Sandra Dickerson, Marnie Evans, Beverly Guy-Sheftall, Sandra Harding, Eleanor Hinton Hoytt, Pauline Houston, Paul Lauter, Joyce Miller, Mary Norris, Gloria Oden, Beverly Smith, and John Walter.

NOTES

1. This paper was presented at the Virginia Women's Studies Association conference in Richmond in April 1986, and the American Educational Research Association conference in Boston in October 1986, and discussed with two groups of participants in the Dodge seminars for Secondary School Teachers in New York and Boston in the spring of 1987.
2. Andersen, Margaret, "Race and the Social Science Curriculum: A Teaching and Learning Discussion," *Radical Teacher*, November 1984, pp. 17–20. Smith, Lillian, *Killers of the Dream*, New York: W. W. Norton, 1949.
3. "A Black Feminist Statement," The Combahee River Collective, pp. 13–22 in G. Hull, P. Scott, B. Smith, Eds., *All the Women Are White, All the Blacks Are Men, but Some of Us Are Brave: Black Women's Studies*, Old Westbury, NY: The Feminist Press, 1982.

HAOLE GIRL: IDENTITY AND WHITE PRIVILEGE IN HAWAI'I

Judy Rohrer

This is a paper about what it means to be a white person in Hawai'i, what it means to be a haole. Hawaii's ethnically mixed population and history as an independent kingdom colonized by the United States makes being a white person here a completely different experience than anywhere else in the country. In Hawai'i, white does not blend in; it stands out. Having grown up in Hawai'i and now living here as an adult, I have struggled with my haole identity, mostly trying to figure out how to minimize, disguise, or get rid of it altogether. I have tried hard to be anything but a haole girl. Instead of continuing to try to escape, I decided to face it through research and writing. . . .

Who am I? It makes sense that I would have different answers at different times under different circumstances. Identity is relational, contested, contingent, negotiated, produced, manipulated, multiple, socially and historically constructed. In other words, it is never just one thing. "Our cultural identities are . . . always in a state of becoming, a journey in which we never arrive" (Hereniko 1994:407). Postmodern theorists encourage us to "play" with identities, putting them on and taking them off like hats or cloaks. Oppressed peoples are reclaiming and redefining their identities as sources of strength. Non-white feminist theorists have stressed the multiplicity, interconnectedness, and simultaneity of identities. I am not just a woman, but a white woman; not just a white woman, but a white lesbian; not just a white lesbian, but a white, educated, middle-class lesbian; not just a white, educated, middle-class lesbian, but a white, educated, middle-class, able-bodied lesbian. These identities are the ones about which I have spent the most time (re)constructing, thinking and educating myself. But what about haole? . . .

Use of the word haole can be found in precontact times in the *Kumulipo*, a creation chant and in written references to a type of pig, the pua'a haole. Most scholars agree that its earliest meanings were "foreigner, foreign, introduced, of foreign origin," as it is defined in the Pukui and Elbert *Hawaiian Dictionary*. Emily Hawkins, a Hawaiian language professor at the University of Hawai'i, states, "it was a word used for outsiders, or things that were not from here."[1] One of the first references describing a white person, in this case an English captain, is found in a biography published in 1838.[2]

I remember using knowledge of the epistemology of haole to try to counteract its sting.

When local (non-Hawaiian) kids would call me haole, I would say, "Haole means foreigner. You're a foreigner here too."

But it didn't matter.

Haole had taken on new meanings through years of colonialism and neo-colonialism.

The kids knew I was "da haole girl."

Years later I'm coming to understand that too.

. . . We cannot escape being haole; we have been too well-trained and the term carries too much meaning and history. Haole is not a positive identity for most white people in Hawai'i, not something we claim with pride, but something ascribed to us by a history, a culture and a language we may know little about. Our feelings about the term range from ambivalence to anger. In fact, some of us spend a good deal of energy ignoring or denying our haoleness. It is difficult for us to know how to choose to be/become haole. At this time, what I am searching for are ways to be not *so* haole, ways to reconstruct my haole identity. If identities are really manipulated, negotiable, and produced, then I want to become a different haole without denying the historical and contemporary context that shapes the term. I remind myself that while Hawai'i *is* very multicultural, the history behind that ethnic mix has built today's structures of unequal power and domination. . . .

What has helped me in figuring out where to go from here is feminist writing which attempts to question, unveil and deconstruct whiteness. On a certain level, haole can be thought of as a name for white privilege situated in Hawai'i. . . .

(continued)

I like the idea of being/becoming a "recovering haole." It is a subprocess of being a "recovering racist," a concept from anti-racism work. As a white person, I can never fully "recover" from being haole or racist, because these identities are so strongly constructed in our culture, in our beings. What I can do is work to acknowledge the privilege I have and act out of this self-awareness by becoming more accountable and responsible. This process of recovery is vital to my becoming a more whole person—vital, in fact, to my survival.

NOTES

1. As quoted in Vicki Viotti (1995:F8).
2. *Ibid.*

REFERENCES

Hereniko, Vilsoni. 1994. "Representations of Cultural Identities," pp. 406–434 in *Tides of History: The Pacific in the Twentieth Century,* edited by Kerry Howe, Robert Kiste and Brij Lal. Honolulu: University of Hawai'i Press.

Viotti, Vicki. 1995. "Haole: Is It a Dirty Word?" *Honolulu Advertiser* February 5:F8.

READING *3*　**Laura M. Lopez**
Frances S. Hasso

Frontlines and Borders: Identity Thresholds for Latinas and Arab American Women[1]

INTRODUCTION

I would like to say that I longed not to be defined by the gaze of the other, but to look out upon the world through eyes rooted in the boundaries of my own identity. But it is true that for much of my life I thought if I looked long enough I would find someone to tell me who I am. Turning to the world for some reflection of myself, however, I found only distortion. (Majaj 1994: 67)

This essay compares the ways in which Latina and Arab American women students experienced their racial-ethnic and gender identities at "home" and in a university environment.[2] These women's experiences have for the most part been excluded by a black/white dichotomy that is especially dominant in the sociological literatures on race and gender. Comparing the experiences of these two pan-national, racially diverse groups

enriches this literature by exploring how multiple sites of difference (race, class, national, cultural, and sexual) interact with systems of domination, and how these interactions, in turn, affect identity construction. Literally and figuratively, dominance and resistance are not black/white issues. Without undercutting the power of material and discursive anti–African American racism, this dichotomy limits analysis of racism against African Americans, excludes other racialized experiences, inhibits comparison across racialized groups, and, perhaps most importantly from our perspective, restricts the possibilities for alliances across racial-ethnic groups for the purpose of making social change.

While racial-ethnic identities in racist societies are defined and constructed by subordinate groups in a context of exclusion and misrepresentation, the process can also be empowering for minorities. In the educational system in particular, power relations are contradictory, producing not only oppression but its opposition—and opposition, in turn, avails itself of power's blind spots and loopholes. The educational system's greater or lesser discriminatory and dehumanizing constructions of the "third world"–origin minority "identity" elicit the minority subject's destabilization of dominant ideology's logic, while oppression and discrimination in turn create the oppressed's desire for empowerment, equality, and justice. (Pérez 1993: 269)

In response to racism and the configuration of racial-ethnic identities, both the Arab American women and Latinas interviewed found the university to be an identity threshold—a place where racial-ethnic identity was reconfigured. Both groups of women were excluded and misrepresented in a variety of ways. As underrepresented minorities, the Latinas contended with a myriad of messages that they were unqualified to be university students *because* of their racial-ethnic backgrounds. This was compounded by a dichotomized racial-ethnic discourse that often excluded their experiences as Latinas. The Arab American women grew up in a popular culture that almost uniformly denigrated their Arab and/or Muslim backgrounds, and live in a social environment in which political discourse about the Middle East is generally both uninformed and highly charged. For the Arab Americans, political conflicts related to the Middle East played out on campus in ways that created identity "frontlines."

Whereas racial-ethnic identities were emphasized in the university, both groups of women focused on issues of authenticity when discussing their "homes"—family, community, or nation. Language-knowledge, class mobility, and obedience to racial-ethnic gender and sexual norms affected whether the women felt and/or were treated as "authentic" community members. In addition, both groups discussed physical appearance (skin color, hair texture, and body size) as a focus of discipline and control within and outside their communities. Rather than being mutually exclusive categories, "home" and university experiences interactively defined racial-ethnic and gender identities; at the same time, different identity issues were stressed in the two settings.

METHOD AND REPRESENTATION

The findings in this report stem from a joint fieldwork project undertaken in the 1993–4 academic year during a graduate qualitative research methods course at the University of Michigan, Ann Arbor. Using the same interview guide, Frances Hasso conducted one- to two-hour semi-structured interviews with eight Arab American women students, and Laura Lopez did the same with eight Latinas; the groups were evenly split between undergraduate and graduate students.[3] Together we conducted two group interviews that included both Arab Americans and Latinas, one of which was designed to share information and get feedback on preliminary analysis.

The eight Arab American women interviewed had parents originally from Egypt, Palestine, Lebanon, Morocco, and combinations of these countries; three of the women had Euro-American mothers, and one (Mona) had a Euro-American father. Seven of the Arab Americans were born in the US and one (Suha) was naturalized as an infant. Three of the women identified as Muslim and five as Christian (although only one in each category was practicing). None of the Arab American women's parents were divorced, although one (Hana) had parents who were separated.

The call for interviews with Latinas drew only Chicanas and Puerto Rican women. Of the four women who identified as being of Puerto Rican descent, three were born and raised in New York and one grew up in Puerto Rico. The birth mother of one Puerto Rican woman (Linda) was of Euro-American descent (her stepmother, however, was Puerto Rican), and the birth father of another Puerto Rican woman (Margaret) was Asian (although she was raised solely by her single mother). The remaining four Latinas were Chicanas/Mexican Americans from Texas and California, one of whom was born in Mexico and naturalized in the US soon thereafter. One Latina gave no religious identification, and the remainder identified as Catholics (five practicing and two non-practicing). Five of the eight Latinas grew up with both birth parents (although not all fathers were consistently present or financially supportive); two had spent their childhoods partly with divorced mothers and partly in blended families; and one was raised by a single mother.

Five of the eight Latinas were from poor or working-class backgrounds. Additionally, one Puerto Rican said she was "low to middle class" (Linda), a Chicana said she was "middle-class" (Emma), and the Puerto Rican from the island said she was "high middle-class" (Lisa). Both parents of two Puerto Rican women (Linda and Lisa) had bachelor degrees (one had an MA); the single mother of another Puerto Rican woman (Margaret) had earned a BA as an adult; and the father of one Chicana

(Emma) had attended two years of college after earning a graduate equivalency diploma. The remaining four Latinas came from families in which neither parents nor siblings had ever attended college. Moreover, three of these women came from households in which neither parent had graduated from high school.

In contrast, all eight Arab American women had at least one college-educated parent (and usually both were college-educated). Seven out of the eight (Jamila is the exception) had at least one parent (and usually both) who had an advanced academic or professional degree. With the exception of one middle-class woman (Hana), all the remaining women came from upper middle-class backgrounds. While some of the women had spent parts of their childhoods living in the Arab world, when they lived in the US seven of the eight had grown up in mostly white, upper middle-class neighborhoods and went to schools (public and private) with similar characteristics. While they did not live in Arab neighborhoods, the parents of four women were involved in religious, professional, cultural, and/or political activities in Arab American communities.

It was not possible to compare the socio-economic indicators of the women interviewed with those of other Arab American and Latina/o students at the University of Michigan because of the absence of such data, including a complete lack of any information on Arab Americans as a group. According to university data, during the 1992–3 academic year, approximately 4.1 percent of the student body (undergraduate and graduate) were "Hispanic/Latino"; included in this category are persons of "Mexican, Puerto Rican, Cuban, Central or South American, or other Spanish culture or origin, regardless of race . . ." (University of Michigan, June 1993: 35).[4] During the 1992–3 academic year, approximately 76 percent of graduate and undergraduate students were categorized as "white," 8.4 percent as Asian American, 7.9 percent as African American, and 0.65 as Native American (University of Michigan, June 1993: 39, 41).

In this study, we are looking at "segments within segments" of communities intersected by a number of axes of difference, not least of which is that both "Arab American" and "Latina/o" are constructs that include different national, class, and religious backgrounds. In addition, while there are class differences among Arab Americans, US Census Bureau data indicate that they are significantly better off as a group than either Mexican Americans or Puerto Ricans, whose poor class standing has been connected to a long history of US colonization and exploitation of these two groups (Montejano 1987; Moore and Pachon 1993; Munóz, Jr 1989; Rodriguez 1989).[5] While there are many voices (e.g., men, working-class Arab American women, and upper middle-class Latinas) not represented in this study, those who are provide insights with respect to both racial-ethnic groups. Instead of emphasizing the representativeness of the women interviewed, we would prefer to stress the dynamic and context-specific nature of identity and identity formation, in keeping with the goal of "partial, locatable, critical knowledges sustaining the possibility of webs of connections" (Behdad 1993: 45, citing D. Haraway).

Renalo Rosaldo (1989) and others have argued that knowledge and theorizing occurs relationally and is always a subjective process involving the researcher and the researched. Our own subjectivities and experiences as an Arab American woman and a Chicana provided critical insights throughout this research project. We undertook the project as two women of color for whom racism has been a tangible part of growing up in the United States and our university experiences. As members of these respective communities, we also had expectations about the types of issues that would resonate with the women we interviewed. At the same time, we approached the project from an inductive perspective, being careful to remain open to differences of subjectivity and experience. Indeed, while our social and class locations and experiences were sometimes similar to those of the women interviewed, they were also different in many respects. Like Laura, three of the Latinas interviewed had been primarily raised by a single or divorced mother and a number of them had struggled economically growing up. Unlike Frances, none of the Arab American women came from working-class backgrounds.

OPPOSITIONALITY AND IDENTITY

According to Chela Sandoval, "oppositional consciousness" is an ideological strategy for subordinated persons confronting domination. It refers to

> the capacity to re-center depending upon the kinds of oppression to be confronted . . . [and it also] depends upon the ability to read the current situation of power and self-consciously choosing and adopting the ideological form best suited to push against its configurations, a survival skill well-known to oppressed peoples. (Sandoval 1991: 14–15)

This type of consciousness allows "weav[ing] 'between and among' oppositional ideologies," much like the clutch of an automobile allows a driver to "select, engage, and disengage gears in a system for the transmission of power" (Sandoval 1991: 14).

For the Latinas and Arab Americans interviewed, identity was redefined in opposition to the racialized narratives operative on campus. That is, while race, class, and gender identities were bound together, because racial-ethnic identities were emphasized by the dominant culture, they were usually the most salient in the university; gender was not irrelevant, but *less* relevant than racial-ethnic identity. Exclusion and misrepresentation in this setting contributed to a more definitive sense of "Arabness" or "Latinaness," and the women often relayed identity "coming out" stories. It is not that racial-ethnic identity did not exist as an affirming process, but that oppositionality *on campus* redefined it.

Oppositionality operated in different ways for the Arab American women and Latinas. The Latinas redefined their identities in opposition to the university's predominantly white environment, white racism, and a Eurocentric curriculum; they were told that they were "unqualified" and did not "belong" in a myriad of ways in this setting. On another level, however, their experiences were also shaped by tension and exclusion by students of color who had limited definitions of race. For the Arab American women, oppositionality was very much related to the way international events played out on college campuses. The Middle East's political-economic importance, its real frontlines of war and political crises, its ubiquity in the news, and the treatment of such issues in classrooms created "frontlines" in the university that compelled women to make identity decisions.

THE "FORCED ALIENATION" OF LATINAS

[P]eople talk about assimilation in one voice and alienation in another voice and I don't think that they're that separate—not in my life—they're not. If you could take anything from, you know, what I just splurted out, it would be that, that my life has been one of confused assimilation and forced alienation. (Linda)

Upon their entrance to the university, most of the Latinas interviewed found themselves relocated from racially diverse or predominantly Latino/a neighborhoods to a largely white educational institution and city. Latino/a students' relatively low representation at the university defined and exacerbated their sense of oppositionality. One Chicana (Emma) characterized this low representation by saying, "it was a long time before I found another Mexican." A Puerto Rican woman (Janie), who had described the university and surrounding community as "too white-bread," said it took her a long time to find other people of color on campus.

Further, most of the Latinas interviewed left communities where their cultural events, music, and food were more readily accessible and came to study at a university that lacked many of the cultural comforts of "home." As Emma put it, "there's nothing here of what I am used to . . . like food, music, you know all these. . . . I had to bring everything from back home to even have just a little bit."

Teresa, another Chicana observed:

It took me a while to figure out that they didn't have any Spanish radio stations . . . or TV stations [at that time] and it took me probably three months to figure out that the tortillas were in the frozen section . . . and the minute I opened the package I knew I wasn't going to like them. So that was really depressing.

Their sense of oppositionality to the dominant culture at the university was exacerbated by discriminatory encounters with white students and professors, and an academic discourse and environment that excluded their experiences. Margaret, a Puerto Rican/ Chinese American student, related the following:

I've almost always had white professors—white male professors . . . here at the university. . . . I don't know, I have always wondered about that because I go into the classroom and I never felt very comfortable talking to the professor . . . and I'm sure a lot of it is just me, but I wonder why it is that some of these other people feel so comfortable doing that, feel so comfortable being . . . loud or being whatever kind of way in class, which I wouldn't do because . . . maybe because it would attract too much attention, I don't know. . . . [I] can't really be myself or feel comfortable enough to ask questions in the middle of class. I know that the one time when I did have a Black professor here in one of my hard sciences courses. . . . I felt so comfortable—even though I rarely talked to the professor at all—but just walking in there, sitting down, I loved going to class because he was Black and I felt like "wow, somebody at least I feel like I can identify with," you know, who might at least be able to identify with me a little bit better.

Janie, also Puerto Rican, discussed feeling "out of place in school":

> I was probably the only Latina . . . in all of my classes, which was really sad. And I think being from out-of-state, and being Puerto Rican, and being lower-class, I think everything was just very difficult. So when I got here I felt really alienated. I had a tough time with the politics of being in graduate school. I did not get along with my advisor. . . . I just had a hard time.

A Chicana student encountered racist remarks on two different occasions at the beginning of her tenure in a PhD program. First, a white male literature professor criticized this US-born and educated woman (Anne) for her command of the English language, and she was within earshot on another occasion when another white male professor remarked that the students of color from her entering cohort "were just a joke." Linda, a Puerto Rican/Euro-American student, similarly noted:

> I was insulted, I was stepped on, I was criticized, I was questioned [by white students and professors] . . . to the point that, even if I thought that they were nice people or they had some particular personality characteristic that I might have wanted to hang out with, it was impossible for me to do that and maintain a sense of self-worth. . . . When people found out that I had minority fellowships, I was no longer a smart kid. You know, it wasn't the kind of research experience I had, it wasn't the college I went to, the classes I had, or the things that I said in class. It was that she's this minority, she has this fellowship. . . .

Feeling marginalized, the Latinas sought out other Latina/o students in social and political groups, and the few Latina/o professors on campus for mentorship. They attempted to build cultural spaces and small communities in opposition to an alienating academic community, which further contributed to a sense of "Latina-ness" or "woman of colorness," versus "them" or "whiteness." Some of the lighter-skinned Latinas even reacted negatively to being "mistaken for" or labeled as "white" by whites or other students of color in the university whose race thinking worked from only black/white scripts. Teresa, a light-skinned Chicana, relayed the following story about her first summer at the university:

> I guess, again, coming from California it was OK to mix different groups and nobody ever had any problems with it, you know, and people knew who you were or at least they had been exposed to more groups than just blacks and whites. And when I got here this summer I went to a party and one of the black guys that was there said "Who brought that white bitch?" and who they were talking about was me and I overheard that so it was sort of like "well, do I cuss this motherfucker out. . . ?"

Significantly, her angry response was not because she had been called "bitch" by another man (i.e., he was offending her as a woman), but because she had been called a "*white* bitch" by an African American.

Thus, as a result of racialized-cultural opposition from whites (and sometimes, African Americans), and the lack of the cultural comforts of home, "Latina" became a critical part of these women's identities in the university. Emma summarized this feeling when she said "I've become more conscientious about it [being Latina] . . . because who thinks about it when you're all the same? . . . Being up here makes me more aware and more proud of who I am." In addition to increasingly associating predominantly or even exclusively with other Latinas/os, these Latinas also learned or brushed up on Spanish language skills as necessary, and all but one (a student in the physical sciences) focused on Latino/a issues in their studies.

ARAB AMERICAN "FRONTLINES"

> [Misconceptions about the Middle East on campus] really stir feelings of rage and frustration [in me] and it's like an actual emotion rather than knowledge. And I think, how did it happen to me? What did my parents do to make me so wrapped up in it? . . . And my parents never—I almost wish they had—but they never sat me down and said: "This is the history of your [Palestinian] family. First they killed so and so." It just came out gradually, these things that happened, sad things and terrible things, but never explicitly. (Mona)

The racialized campus experiences of the Arab American women differed from those of the Latinas. They did not confront the dislocation experienced by the Latinas interviewed, largely because most of them came from upper middle-class backgrounds, lived in predominantly white neighborhoods, and attended schools with similar characteristics. Even as they remained "Arab" within their homes, as children, most of the Arab American women had assimilated in public contexts as much as they were allowed to until they became university students—avoiding "role conflict" by becoming "Americans by day and [Arabs] by night" (Swanson 1996: 244). When they reached the university, however, almost all were compelled to make identity decisions about their "Arab-ness"—whether or not to "come out," so to speak—largely in response to the way Middle East–related events played out on campuses.

These international events are highly politically charged and for the most part (mis)represented in both the media (Said 1981; Shaheen 1984; Shaheen 1993) and school and university classrooms. Recent examples include the 1990–1 Gulf War, the 1994 World Trade Center bombing, and the ongoing Arab-Israeli conflict. In university classroom situations, the Arab American women had to either disregard misrepresentations or racist characterizations of Arabs, Muslims, Islam, or Arab culture, or publicly confront their professors, teaching assistants, or fellow students. "Taking a stand" exposed their Arab American identities (if others did not already know), and often subjected them to being labelled a number of things that are assumed by the dominant culture to be inherently Arab or Muslim: "terroristic," anti-Semitic, violent, and unreasonably angry. As a result, confusion and silence were common responses to such misrepresentations.

(Mis)perceptions of the Arab-Israeli conflict in particular were often provocative for the Arab American women. One Palestinian/Euro-American graduate student remembered the following conversation with a white male housemate soon after arriving in Ann Arbor:

> He was seeing a Jewish girlfriend and he just found out I was Palestinian and he said, "well, that puts me in an awkward position. . . . I'm going out with a Jewish girlfriend, and you being Palestinian." I said, "Yeah, but I mean we're adults here. Why does that make a difference?" [she laughs slightly]. . . . And do you know what he said to me? He said, "If you ever did anything to hurt this girl, I will come after you and blow your head off." This is *a week* after I lived with this guy. And I was stuck with him for a whole four months. Can you believe that? (Katy)

This woman, whose hair is blondish and skin light-colored, told few others in her professional program that she is Palestinian American after this incident.

Another Palestinian/Euro-American graduate student discussed her ambivalent silence in classrooms at her "very Ivy League" undergraduate institution:

> I mean, I didn't feel comfortable saying my opinions [about the Middle East] in class or in really any setting, except with close friends, and even then it would be a little hard. I have a lot of Jewish friends and stuff who have an amazing blind spot when it comes to certain things. But definitely not in classes; I would not give my opinion; I always was restraining myself and saying I have to be diplomatic, I have to be understanding, I have to remember this, this, and the other thing, so I never actually brought it to a head by doing something. So, I just avoided it, but I knew I was consciously avoiding something, because I felt that it would cause trouble, but I can't prove that it would because I didn't. I had friends who told me about other incidents and it just scared me and I wasn't up to dealing with it. . . . (Mona)

Many women, including this Egyptian American undergraduate, remembered the 1990–1 Gulf War as making life particularly difficult for Arab Americans: "It was difficult because I have a lot of friends who are Jewish. . . . And so, you know, it was—it was difficult. . . . I was against the war and I didn't—I felt that most people were really just supporting the war out of blind patriotism and nothing else" (Amy). A Moroccan/Euro-American graduate student who had been politically active during the Gulf War described how she was accused at various points of being unpatriotic, un-American, and anti-Semitic: "I got obscene and pornographic hate mail, threatening me with rape. . . . My classmates spread a rumor . . . that I had given up my American citizenship" (Hana). Anti-Muslim sentiment was at such heights during the Gulf War, that for the first time she began identifying herself as a *Muslim* Arab American: "I wanted to set myself as much apart [as possible] from this culture and in line with that culture . . . and I thought that was one way to do it" (Hana).

While these incidents were frightening and alienating for the Arab American women, they also galvanized most of them to study the political debates into which they were inextricably pulled, and to be prepared for intellectual confrontations. All except one (Katy) of the Arab American women interviewed became politically active, took courses on the Arab-Israeli and other regional conflicts, studied the Arab countries from which they originated, and/or focused their studies on the Arab world during college. A Lebanese American woman discussed the effects of a course she took on the Arab-Israeli conflict:

> I became stronger with my identity as an Arab and a Lebanese. . . . Why I did, I'm not sure. . . . [When she was one of the few women and only Arab American to publicly disagree with the professor's and other students' analysis in a class of over 100 students] I don't know how to explain it, but I know I felt cornered [in class]. It's not because I'm anti-Jewish, but I am against what the Israeli government does. I'm against what the US does. Do you know what I'm saying? Um, so I identified more and more and that's where my Arab identity came into larger play. (Jamila)

Similar to the Latinas' responses to racism and exclusion on campus, all but one of the Arab American women learned or relearned Arabic, interrogated their families about their own histories, travelled to the Arab world, and/or socialized with other Arab Americans and Arabs. While many of the women became more comfortable with their "Arab-ness," most could not ignore the intertwining of oppositionality and identity. As one activist noted in relation to being attacked at the university for her political positions: "Isn't it funny how that [people attacking you] makes you feel more Arab, too? . . . [I]t's sort of like opposition defines you" (Michelle). While oppositionality generally strengthened racial-ethnic identity, for three of the Arab American women (two of whom were bi-racial), "coming out" was a personal, not public, process. As indicated by their narratives, some of these women remained afraid of the reputational and professional consequences of confronting racism and stressing their racial-ethnic identities in the university. In addition, as they became more aware of their histories and backgrounds, the cultural dilemmas became more stark for most of the women, who found themselves in situations where they felt neither "Arab" nor "American," in practice redefining both identities.

"BORDERED" RACIAL/GENDER IDENTITIES

In the remainder of the paper, we address racial/gender identities by looking at physical appearance, language knowledge, class mobility, and sexuality. These issues were most (but not exclusively) relevant in "home" spaces, and were often tied to whether women were treated as "authentic" community members. Physical appearance, language knowledge, class mobility, and obedience to cultural rules of behavior about gender and sexuality were important both to how others identified the Latinas and Arab American women and how they self-identified. These were interdependent processes: identity was socially constructed in relation to how others defined them.

The concept of "home" has been discussed by a number of feminist scholars (Martin and Mohanty 1986; Pratt 1984). Martin and Mohanty argue that some feminist scholars' "pursuit of safe places and ever-narrower conceptions of community relies on unexamined notions of home, family, and nation, and severely limits the scope of the feminist inquiry and struggle" (1986: 191–2). Even though most needed "home" for comfort, security, and sustenance, the women interviewed problematized these locations as sites of restrictive sexual norms and essentialized definitions of the "authentic" Latina or Arab woman.

The "borders" metaphor captures the conflicts and contradictions that arose for the Latinas and Arab American women as they negotiated within limiting definitions of identity. Over the past decade, the metaphor has characterized the experiences and geopolitical spaces of Latinas/os as a colonized people: they are products of interaction and exchange between different cultures, races, and nations with often diametrically opposed ideologies and cultural practices (Anzaldua 1987; Saldivar-Hull 1991). Borders, therefore, divide two or more different states of existence that may contradict each other, making conflicts common for those whose identities straddle such borders. The concept is also a metaphor for the histories, experiences, and social spaces of other "hybrid" peoples who are compelled to live in borders because conventional spaces do not accept their multiple identities (Anzaldua 1987). Thus, borders are also margins of safety, spaces in which "hybridity" is allowed.

APPEARANCE BORDERS

The relationship between physical appearance and "bordered" racial/gender identities was stressed in the individual and group interviews by Latinas and Arab American women. The women varied in terms of their physical features: they were light to dark-skinned; had "kinky," "nappy," "big," or straight hair, ranging from black to blonde; and had differently shaped facial features and body sizes. However they identified themselves, the Arab American women were frequently thought to be Greek, Latina, African American, African/Euro-American, or white, and the Latinas were sometimes assumed to be African American or white.

Women in both groups felt that hair and body size have been significant foci of discipline and control in different contexts. They discussed unsuccessful attempts at feathering, perming, or straightening their hair in order to look like white teenagers, and the gendered implications of some of their mothers' pressures to contain their "big" hair into tight braids, knots, or with hair clips. One Latina believed this pressure was actually about containing girls' sexuality, and an Arab American woman explained such control with a different feminist argument:

"[Y]our hair is too big, it's like uncontrollable." I think that's the thing about trying to keep women small, too, you know? . . . So why do we have to take up this much space [she curves both hands on the table facing each other about a foot apart], you know [everyone laughs]? (Michelle)

Both groups discussed body size standards within their communities as liberating in comparison to those dominant in US culture. Most US men, they believed, want "petite, they all want petite" (Amal). A Chicana joked about the US Southwest as a place "where men really appreciate women," and an Arab American woman joked about her father's Arab country of origin as "the only place in the world where I'm considered too thin." While variations in skin color occasionally came up as disciplinary issues *within* some homes and communities—with lighter skin considered more beautiful than darker skin for women—their discussions largely centered on how "external" groups perceived them based on their skin color.

The light-skinned Chicanas, as mentioned earlier, were often defined as white and ostracized by some students of color on campus. Carol said she "got literally ignored, brushed off by some people in the African American community because they thought I was white because I'm light skinned. . . . Some of them didn't accept me as a person of color, they had to be told."

Conversely, Janie felt that it was difficult to be both black and Puerto Rican within the African American community:

Last year I think I identified myself more with the racial aspect of it because I was getting so much—you know, it was like people were identifying me a lot by my race and it was frustrating for me. It was like "How can I explain to them?" . . . I don't identify myself by my race, but then I don't want to be excluded and that was important for me . . . but last year I started . . . saying that I was black Puerto Rican.

Another black Puerto Rican woman who had attended a predominantly black university as an undergraduate found herself in a similar situation when she began applying for graduate schools:

I put Puerto Rican on the box, or Hispanic, or whatever the box was at that time, my advisor told me "Why am I putting that?" and I said because that's what I am and he said "No, you're black" and I said, "You know, my grandfather is as African as your grandfather, but my experience isn't, my experience is a Puerto Rican experience." (Linda)

Thus, because discussions of race and ethnicity in the university were usually based on a black/white schema, the Latinas were often pigeon-holed into one or the other category, excluding their other identities and experiences.

All the darker-skinned Arab Americans said that as children they frequently wished they were lighter-skinned and lighter-haired, and less identifiably "Arab," especially during Middle East–related crises. Most had childhood memories of being called "niggers," "sand niggers," "Ayrabs," and "camel jockeys":

[B]ecause my hair's really curly and very tight curls, I got all kinds of—you know, some people would think I was Black so they would call me "nigger." Some people knew that my parents were from Egypt, so they . . . would say "sand nigger," I got that a lot. (Amy)

In response to constant harassment for her brown skin and kinky hair, Amy admitted: "I felt bad. I mean, when I was eight, I wanted to have blonde, straight hair, this was my ideal. And now I realize how hideous I would look if I had blonde straight hair."

While the less phenotypically "Arab" women were much less likely to have their physical appearances be sources of difference during their childhoods, this physical blending was problematic later in life when they wanted to affirm their "Arab-ness." The dissonance between their identification as Arab Americans and their physical appearance contributed to feeling "phoney" when using a self-identifier such as "Arab American" or "woman of color." Indeed, three of the four bi-racial Arab American women wished they looked darker. For example, when asked if she considered herself a woman of color, Hana said:

> It's really interesting that you should ask me this question because this for me is one of the most difficult issues . . . because I look white. I mean, it's very difficult because it's an identification that I feel very strongly about. And again, I think that very much came out of the Gulf War. . . . But I sometimes feel ridiculous saying it ["I am a woman of color"] because for people looking at me it's like: "What's this person talking about?" Which has always been something that is extremely complicated for me because I always wanted to look like my—like I was an Arab.

Six of the eight Latinas strongly identified as women of color, whereas only two of the eight Arab American women did so. The two Latinas and two of the six Arab Americans who did not identify as women of color identified instead as a Chicana, Puerto Rican, Lebanese, and Egyptian, respectively. The generally weaker "women of color" identification among the Arab Americans may be related to the fact that their school and neighborhood interactions have largely been with white people. At the same time, six of the eight Arab Americans strongly believed that they were not white and all eight were ambivalent about being legally categorized as such.

LANGUAGE BORDERS

Language knowledge existed as a marker of authenticity in both communities. Four of the eight Latinas interviewed spoke Spanish fluently; two of the four who did not grow up speaking Spanish fluently sought to learn the language as adults. Among the Arab American women, with the exception of one who was fluent in Arabic, five were learning or relearning the language, and two said they wanted to learn it. Latinas and Arab American women who did not speak Spanish or Arabic fluently often felt inadequate as a result in their respective communities. Indeed, some of the Latinas interviewed whose first language was Spanish resented other Latinas/os who did not speak Spanish. As Emma put it: "[I]t really

bugs me when some people are Mexican and they don't know Spanish."

Lack of language knowledge created a sense of distance from their racial-ethnic communities for both groups of women. As Margaret stated, "For me, not being fluent in Spanish has always been an insecurity . . . it has kind of been one of the things that has kept me apart from certain Latino communities . . . [because] there's some expectations on this campus that a Latino should speak Spanish." An Arab American similarly stated:

> I've had long conversations about the significance of feeling at home nowhere. When I'm here [in the US], I'm sure that I belong there [in the Arab world] and when I'm there, I'm sure I don't belong there. . . . Language has been a big issue simply because a lot of them [my relatives abroad] I can't speak with. (Hana)

Some of the women who were not fluent in Arabic or Spanish attributed "loss" of language to social obstacles. One Chicana (Anne) said that her parents were physically and psychologically sanctioned for speaking Spanish in school and she believed this resulted in her being discouraged from speaking the language as a child. Margaret believed that English was her first language because her Puerto Rican mother was educated in a US convent, where she was punished for speaking Spanish. Linda similarly said, "I minored in Spanish in college . . . but it wasn't something that was reinforced in our lives."

Loss of language was relevant for three of the four Arab American women, both of whose parents were of Arab descent; the fourth woman was almost fluent as a result of consistently traveling between the Arab world and the US. Like the Latinas, these Arab American women discussed how US racism and ethnocentrism compelled them to forget their Arabic when they were young and/or resulted in teachers discouraging their parents from using the language with them. An Arab American who was frequently harassed by white children because of her physical appearance also discussed her own resistance to maintaining her Arabic language knowledge when she was younger:

> I had a very bad attitude towards speaking Arabic. My mom would try to teach me periodically. You know, she'd get the books out and say, "Okay, this is *alef*, this is *bey*, this is *ley*" [the first three letters of the Arabic

alphabet]. And I really—I mean, I very much did not want any part of Arabic. Like I remember being seven and eight and her trying to teach me, and I remember thinking, "This is America, we have to speak English." . . . To speak the [Arabic] language would only make me more a part of something I didn't want to be a part of. (Amy)

Amy, who was relearning the language, regretted this loss of Arabic as an adult and saw a powerful relationship between language knowledge and racial-ethnic identity:

I really regret their [her parents] not having spoken [Arabic] at home and my not having learned the language when I was much younger, when it would have been easier. . . . And I really feel, too, since having been able to read and write a little bit, there is great power of the language to allow me to identify with that culture more. I just—it makes it so much easier when you get the window into that culture, do you know what I mean? (Amy)

CLASS BORDERS

Earlier, we discussed how many of the women interviewed were alienated in the academic setting and how in most cases this strengthened their racial-ethnic identities. A paradox arises for the Latinas, however, because many simultaneously feel alienated from their home communities as a result of their higher education and impending class mobility. Getting a university education created a distance—physically, economically and socially—between these Latinas and members of their families and communities, most of whom were poor to working-class and far less educated; they felt that their educations were privileging them in relation to their families and communities.

After being at the university for a year or so, a Chicana undergraduate from Texas (Emma) noted being disturbed and offended when she was told by a former teacher back home that she "sounded so different . . . so white." The interplay between class, race, and education was also apparent in her following statement:

[W]hen I go back home with my family—because I am the first one to go to college and I was the second one to graduate from high school . . . now they see me as like "Oh, well Miss College here." I don't know. My whole family is proud of me, but it's like in a sense

they're—some of them actually go "Oh, you think you're big shit because you're over there." (Emma)

Linda, a Puerto Rican graduate student, similarly stated:

Earlier on it was hard to justify being here and wanting the education and . . . having my father telling me that I was distancing myself from the community . . . but society expects education to be that method by which you go about change, so when you go back there you're not part of that community anymore. . . . [My family told me,] "College was OK, but what's this PhD business?" . . . I want to go back, but there is still that issue of, first, where do you put a PhD in the middle of East Harlem?

Anne, a Chicana graduate student, was concerned about trying to balance efforts to help her community "without alienating or intimidating them." Another Chicana graduate student remarked that while her parents were proud of what she was accomplishing, they did not really understand what she was doing. When she does go home she is careful not to let her "academic hat" place her above others:

I think my sister and my brother would be the first ones to slap me in the face—not literally, but you know—and say "You're at home now . . . don't impress us . . . we know you" . . . to them I'm still the same person [as when] I left. . . . But I think to my parents it's much more of a big deal that I'm getting [a PhD] than probably to anybody else. Even though I don't think they understand it themselves. . . . I guess in some sense I am my mother's dream come true, that she never went to school and at least I got that opportunity. (Teresa)

Education and upward mobility did not distance the Arab American women interviewed from their families and communities, for two related reasons: first, none of their families lived in Arab neighborhoods, where class differences are much more salient. And second, the women came from middle- to upper-middle-class backgrounds, in which at least one and usually both parents were highly educated. As one woman noted in response to this issue: "In fact, I feel like they've [her parents] obtained a certain level of education and there's actually great expectation on me to at least equal that or surpass it. . . . So if anybody is feeling intellectual inferiority, it's me not them" (Amy).

SEXUALITY BORDERS[6]

The women interviewed discussed the often repressive aspects of "home" with respect to gender, sexuality, and sexual practices. Both groups believed that being a woman in Latino/a and Arab cultures had its own limitations, especially with respect to controlling their sexuality as unmarried women. In asking women to discuss their formal and informal sexual educations, the major themes that arose were silence, denial, and control. The two groups diverged in a number of ways, however, most importantly in that the Latinas were particularly concerned about not becoming pregnant, whereas the Arab American women were most concerned with the implications of losing their virginity.

Latina scholars have argued that the sexual repression of Latinas begins early, and girls are taught to be "submissive, virtuous, respectful of elders and helpful of our mothers, long suffering, deferring to men, industrious, and devoted" (Ramos 1987: xxvi); the most common strategy has been to deny "young women's imminent sexuality" (Castillo 1991: 32). As one Chicana said, her mother "didn't know" and "didn't want to know" about her sexual development and practices. If sex was discussed in the Latinas' homes, it was often bluntly discouraged. This angered the Latinas interviewed, and most were taught to be ashamed of sexuality. When asked about her informal sex education, one Puerto Rican woman responded: "I didn't get anything from my mother, absolutely nothing. I think she did such a poor job with that; I'm sorry, but she did [she laughs]. She really dodged it." This silence and denial with respect to sexuality affected her later when she "couldn't look her mother in the face" after her first experience of sexual intercourse. Almost all the Latinas received their sexual educations from peers, in school, and/or from television. According to another Chicana: "[My mom] just once told me 'if you have anything you want to talk to me about, just ask me.' And the first time we talked about menstruation was when I already had it. . . . But as far as sex, never, never a conversation."

The sex education experiences of the Arab American women were more divided. Interestingly, all of the women whose parents are both Arab had very open discussions with one (not always the mother) or both parents about anatomy, sexuality, and even sexually transmitted diseases before the onset of their menstrual cycles. One woman said that she often tried on her older sister's and mother's sanitary napkins for fun before she got her first period, and another woman argued about female anatomy with her Arab father as an 11-year-old. Three of the four bi-racial Arab American women, in contrast, received little to no sexual education from their parents and were generally not encouraged to discuss sexuality issues. One of these women said that her first period was "traumatic—very traumatic. . . . I didn't know how to deal with the irregularity and cramps. . . . [I felt] isolated and abandoned [laughs], and I just survived." This woman, who was a virgin and engaged to be married, asked a number of questions about birth control during her individual interview.

While pre-marital sexual activity was discouraged by the Latinas' families, all the Arab American women received much stronger explicit and implicit messages that they should remain virgins until they married. "Nice Arab girls" were not supposed to lose their virginity before marriage. In order to control the sexuality of unmarried daughters, unchaperoned dating is generally strongly discouraged in Arab cultures, and Arab American girls are punished for violating these cultural norms (Aswad and Gray 1996). The virginity narrative was an especially strong source of internal conflict for the five Arab American women who had engaged in pre-marital sex. One respondent who eventually slept with a partner discussed this ambivalence:

> I went through a phase for a while, because I think a lot of Arabs—in-between women go through—which is that "If I lose my virginity, I can't marry an Arab.". . . It's awful, I mean it's awful. . . . I'm really glad that I didn't have sex earlier because my experiences with men have been on the whole extremely shitty and it seems to me like it would have just made everything worse.

A number of the Arab American women were sexually active with men but tried to abstain from intercourse. One of these women described her first experience of sexual intercourse with her Arab American boyfriend as a rape, which she believed he knew would force her to make a premature commitment to him: "Oh, yeah, I mean, I have slept with him, I wish we never did. I wish—because I know that I became more attached and closer to him. I think maybe, maybe . . . had I not slept with him, maybe I would not continue seeing him." Her primary concern after this was what would occur if she and her boyfriend did not marry: "What man is going to take me, a non-virgin, in our society?"

When asked if her parents had specifically warned her against having sex, an Arab American who had not engaged in sexual intercourse responded: "[T]hey never came out explicitly and said, you know, 'Don't sleep with anyone.' . . . [I]t was implicit in everything else that they said, do you know what I mean?" This Arab American demonstrated that ostracization from family and society was the most effective form of social control:

[I]t was always very clear in terms of sexual mores what was and wasn't permissible. . . . [I]f I ever got pregnant and I wasn't married, that they would have nothing to do with me. That would be the end of it. . . . And that, you know, instilled enough fear in me that I was never going to put myself in a situation, you know, where I would jeopardize my being related to them or them not having anything to do with me.[7]

The three Arab American women who had not engaged in pre-marital sex said that they were unwilling to do so until they married. One of these women stated that she remained a virgin

[n]ot because they'd [her parents] forbid me to, but just because I see—you know, sleeping with somebody is such an intimate thing and it binds you to them in ways that you're not bound to anybody else. And that's not something that . . . I just want to do with anyone.

Discussions about sex and the loss of virginity often brought up the fear of pregnancy or the consequences of unwanted early motherhood for the Latinas, a phenomenon highly informed by the fact that most of them came from poor to working-class backgrounds. These women had seen many friends and family members whose lives had been changed by early motherhood. One Puerto Rican woman said her "biggest fear was getting pregnant" at an early age as her mother had done when she was 19. She added, "[in] turning 19 and 20, for me to be able to make it that far and not to have a baby, that was like my goal in life." Fear of unplanned pregnancy also came up when women were asked their views of abortion, a right that all but one Latina strongly supported.

The Arab American women, in contrast, were much more ambivalent about abortion. While five of the eight stated they were pro-choice, most believed abortion was morally wrong, and all expressed discomfort with the idea.

Despite the fact that many of the women grew up in households where sex was not discussed and/or sexual expression was discouraged, a number of the Latinas and Arab Americans spoke about transgressing some of these cultural norms. Two of the Latinas interviewed disclosed that they had engaged in sexual relationships with women as well as men, and another had experimented with a female friend as a pre-adolescent. One Chicana said that she had to "change her thinking" about expressing her sexuality because she grew up in a very "restricted" household. She didn't want to be sexually repressed as she had seen her "father make [her] mother be." This theme is clearly articulated by a Puerto Rican, who said:

I've had to replace values. In the very beginning, that was part of my value system that "Oh, I can only be with one person" . . . but now that I've dated and that I've had—that I've been sexually intimate with people . . . it's not part of my value system anymore.

The Arab American women interviewed did not bring up sexual experiences with other women, possibly because they were uncomfortable discussing the issue. Five of the eight Arab American women interviewed had engaged in pre-marital sex despite strong messages to the contrary from their families and communities. Three of these women continued to feel ambivalent about their sexual activity, however, while two were more comfortable. According to one in the latter group:

[A]ll through high school, because my parents were so, like, "You can't date, you can't do this," that when I got to college, I was like, "Oh, let's check it out!" [We both laugh.] . . . I think that maybe when it all first started happening, I felt a little strange about it because I know that my parents were sort of like, "No pre-marital sex. No pre-marital sex.". . . But I don't feel like that about it anymore. . . I just do it because I think it's right and this is what I want to do and if you're not—. . . [I]f the person I want to marry does not accept that then that's not the kind of person I need to marry.

CONCLUSION

Whereas the Arab American women and Latinas interviewed differed along a variety of axes, all found the university to be a threshold for racial-ethnic identity. They discussed the university as a site where racial-ethnic identity was defined oppositionally, and "home" as culturally affirmative *and* a place with its own inflexible racial-ethnic/gender norms. Rather than being mutually exclusive categories, home and university sites emphasized different identity issues that were interactively defined. Although there is a common assumption, especially in non-academic circles, that racial-ethnic identities are natural and fixed, they are always being constructed and redefined in social interaction and through social practices. Anti-Arab and anti-Latina/o racisms were undergirded by different assumptions by the dominant culture, and, like identities, both were "performed" in daily interactions. While oppositional consciousness was governed by both "structural" location and context, subjective experiences ultimately meant that these Latinas and Arab American women practiced a range of identity strategies over time and tailored them for different sites. They responded in a variety of ways to rigid identity categories, providing evidence that racial-ethnic identity is a process of both external social construction and political self-definition.

NOTES

1. The authors share equal responsibility for this article. We thank Judith A. Howard, the anonymous reviewers of *Qualitative Sociology*, Tomás Almagner, Natalie Bennett, Mark Chesler, Jeff Dillman, Janet Hart, Moon-Kie Jung, Maria Teresa Koreck, Michael Sulieman, Steve Sumida, and Patricia Zavella for reading and commenting on the paper, which we presented at the August 1995 meeting of the American Sociological Association in Washington, DC.

2. We use the term "racial-ethnic" to capture both the racialization of people of color by the dominant culture *and* the idea that people of color can affirmatively define their histories, languages, and customs. We assume that racial-ethnic identities are not stable or unitary, but socially constructed, contingent and historical (Hall 1992; McCarthy and Crichlow 1993; Omi and Winant 1994). Similarly, oppression based on gender, race, class, and sexuality is interlocking and the intersections of these identities are multiple and dynamic (Alarcon 1991; Collins 1990; Crenshaw 1991; Zinn and Dill 1994; Harris 1991; Martin and Mohanty 1986; Mohanty 1991). For women of color, then, multiple hierarchies condition and define their material positions and subjective experiences.

3. The Arab world encompasses 21 Arab countries in North Africa and Southwest Asia and the Occupied Palestinian Territories. The term "Middle East" refers to these Arabic-speaking countries, as well as Turkey, Iran, Israel, and sometimes Pakistan and Afghanistan. "Latina/o" is an umbrella term used to describe peoples of Latin American or Spanish origin, including Chicanos and Puerto Ricans. The students interviewed were recruited through solicitations on the Arab American Student Association and the Latino/a electronic mail networks, personal contact, and word of mouth. Those who agreed to participate in the study were self-selected in that they identified as Arab Americans or Latinas and were willing to discuss identity issues. For convenience, we limited the sample to women who had US citizenship. We use pseudonyms to protect confidentiality.

4. The university does not track the specific racial-ethnic backgrounds of Latino/a students and does not keep records on their family income levels. In addition, it does not maintain separate records on Arab Americans, who are categorized as "white."

5. Based on 1990 census data, while the overall US official poverty rate was 13.1 percent, the rates were 26.3 percent for persons of Mexican origin, 31.7 percent for persons of Puerto Rican origin, and 14.5 percent for persons of Arab ancestry. Arab Americans 25 years or over were significantly more likely than the overall population to have received a high school diploma (82.4 compared to 75.2 percent), a bachelor's degree (36.3 to 20.3 percent), and a graduate degree (15.2 to 7.2 percent). Among Puerto Ricans, 53.4 percent received a high school diploma, 9.5 percent received a bachelor's degree, and 3.2 percent received a graduate degree. Among Mexican Americans the figures are 44.2 percent, 6.3 percent, and 2.0 percent, respectively (US Bureau of Census 1990).

6. The populations of Chicanas, Puerto Rican, and Arab American women students at the University of Michigan, Ann Arbor, are small. To safeguard confidentiality, which women were particularly concerned about when discussing sexuality, we do not attribute quotes in this section.

7. Aswad and Gray (1996) discuss the oppressive and affirmative functions of patrilineal family membership for Arabs and Arab Americans; Swanson (1996: 245) examines how these functions are used to "psychological[ly] coerce children [to ensure] compliance with parental expectations."

REFERENCES

Alarcon, N. 1991. "The theoretical subject(s) of this bridge called my back and Anglo American feminism," in *Criticism in the Borderlands: Studies in Chicano Literature, Culture and Ideology*, H. Calderon and J. D. Saldivar (eds). Durham, NC: Duke University Press.

Anzaldua, G. 1987. *Borderlands/La Frontera: The New Mestiza*. San Francisco, CA: Aunt Lute Books.

Aswad, B. C. and N. A. Gray. 1996. "Challenges to the Arab-American family and ACCESS," in *Family and Gender Among American Muslims: Issues Facing Middle Eastern Immigrants and Their Descendants*, B. C. Aswad and B. Bilgé (eds). Philadelphia, PA: Temple University Press.

Behdad, A. 1993. "Traveling to teach: Postcolonial critics in the American academy," in *Race, Identity, and Representation in Education*, C. McCarthy and W. Crichlow (eds). New York, NY: Routledge.

Castillo, A. 1991. "La macha: Toward a beautiful whole self," in *Chicana Lesbians: The Girls Our Mothers Warned Us About*, C. Trujillo (ed.). Berkeley, CA: Third Woman Press.

Collins, P. H. 1990. *Black Feminist Thought: Knowledge, Consciousness, and the Politics of Empowerment*. Boston: Unwin Hyman.

Crenshaw, K. 1991. "Demarginalizing the intersection of race and sex: A Black feminist critique of anti-discrimination doctrine," in *Feminist Legal Theory: Readings in Law and Gender*, K. Bartlett and R. Kennedy (eds). Boulder, CO: Westview Press.

Hall, S. 1992. "The question of cultural identity," in *Modernity and Its Futures*, S. Hall, D. Held, and T. McGrew (eds). Cambridge: Polity Press.

Harris, A. 1991. "Race and essentialism in feminist legal theory," in *Feminist Legal Theory: Readings in Law and Gender*, K. Bartlett and R. Kennedy (eds). Boulder, CO: Westview Press.

Majaj, L. S. 1994. "Boundaries: Arab/American," in *Food for Our Grandmothers: Writings by Arab-American and Arab-Canadian Feminists*, J. Kadi (ed.). Boston, MA: South End Press.

Martin, Biddy and Chandra Talpade Mohanty. 1986. "Feminist politics: What's home got to do with it?" in *Feminist Studies/Critical Studies*, Teresa de Lauretis (ed.). Bloomington, IN: Indiana University Press, 191–212.

Mohanty, C. 1991. "Under Western eyes: Feminist scholarship and colonial discourses," in *Third World Women and the Politics of Feminism*, C. Mohanty, A. Russo, and L. Torres (eds). Bloomington, IN: Indiana University Press.

Monlejano, D. 1987. *Anglos and Mexicans in the Making of Texas, 1836–1986*. Austin, TX: University of Texas Press.

Moore, J. and H. Pachon 1985. *Hispanics in the United States*. Englewood Cliffs, NJ: Prentice-Hall.

Munóz, C., Jr. 1989. *Youth, Identity, Power: The Chicano Movement*. London: Verso.

Omi, M. and H. Winant. 1994. *Racial Formation in the United States: From the 1960s to the 1990s*, 2nd ed. New York, NY: Routledge.

Pérez, L. E. 1993. "Opposition and the education of Chicana/os," in *Race, Identity and Representation in Education*, C. McCarthy and W. Crichlow (eds). New York, NY: Routledge.

Pratt, Minnie Bruce. 1984. "Identity: Skin blood heart," in *Yours in Struggle: Three Feminist Perspectives on Anti-Semitism and Racism*, Elly Bulkin, Minnie Bruce Pratt, and Barbara Smith. Brooklyn, NY: Long Haul Press.

Ramos, J. 1987. Introduction, in *Compañeras: Latina Lesbians (an Anthology)*, J. Ramos (ed.). New York, NY: Latina Lesbian Project.

Rodriguez, C. E. 1989. *Puerto Ricans: Born in the U.S.A.* Boston, MA: Unwin Hyman.

Rosaldo, R. 1989. *Culture and Truth: The Remaking of Social Analysis*. Boston, MA: Beacon Press.

Said, E. W. 1981. *Covering Islam: How the Media and the Experts Determine How We See the Rest of the World*. New York, NY: Pantheon Books.

Saldivar-Hull, S. 1991. "Feminism on the border: From gender politics to geopolitics," in *Criticism in the Borderlands: Studies in Chicano Literature, Culture and Ideology*, H. Calderon and J. D. Saldivar (eds). Durham, NC: Duke University Press.

Sandoval, C. 1991. "U.S. third world feminism: The theory and method of oppositional consciousness in the postmodern world," *Genders* 10: 1–24.

Shaheen, J. G. 1993. "Aladdin: Animated racism." *Cineaste* 20(1): 49.

Shaheen, J. G. 1984. *The TV Arab*. Bowling Green, OH: Bowling Green State University Popular Press.

Swanson, J. C. 1996. "Ethnicity, marriage, and role conflict: The dilemma of a second-generation Arab-American," in *Family and Gender Among American Muslims: Issues Facing Middle Eastern Immigrants and Their Descendants*, B. C. Aswad and B. Bilgé (eds). Philadelphia, PA: Temple University Press.

University of Michigan. 1993. *Faculty, Staff and Students of Color: A Statistical Profile for Academic Years 1982–83 through 1992–93*. Ann Arbor, MI: Office of Affirmative Action and Office of Minority Affairs (June).

US Bureau of the Census. 1990. "Persons of Hispanic origin in the U.S.," CP-3-3 (CPH-L-150), and "Ancestry of the population in the United States," CP-3-2 (CPH-L-149), in *1990 Census of Population and Housing*.

Zinn, M. B., and B. T. Dill (eds). 1994. *Women of Color in U.S. Society*. Philadelphia, PA: Temple University Press.

Where I Come from Is Like This

I

Modern American Indian women, like their non-Indian sisters, are deeply engaged in the struggle to redefine themselves. In their struggle they must reconcile traditional tribal definitions of women with industrial and postindustrial non-Indian definitions. Yet while these definitions seem to be more or less mutually exclusive, Indian women must somehow harmonize and integrate both in their own lives.

An American Indian woman is primarily defined by her tribal identity. In her eyes, her destiny is necessarily that of her people, and her sense of herself as a woman is first and foremost prescribed by her tribe. The definitions of woman's roles are as diverse as tribal cultures in the Americas. In some she is devalued, in others she wields considerable power. In some she is a familial/clan adjunct, in some she is as close to autonomous as her economic circumstances and psychological traits permit. But in no tribal definitions is she perceived in the same way as are women in western industrial and postindustrial cultures.

In the West, few images of women form part of the cultural mythos, and these are largely sexually charged. Among Christians, the madonna is the female prototype, and she is portrayed as essentially passive: her contribution is simply that of birthing. Little else is attributed to her and she certainly possesses few of the characteristics that are attributed to mythic figures among Indian tribes. This image is countered (rather than balanced) by the witch/goddess/whore characteristics designed to reinforce cultural beliefs about women, as well as western adversarial and dualistic perceptions of reality.

The tribes see women variously, but they do not question the power of femininity. Sometimes they see women as fearful, sometimes peaceful, sometimes omnipotent and omniscient, but they never portray women as mindless, helpless, simple, or oppressed. And while the women in a given tribe, clan, or band may be all these things, the individual woman is provided with a variety of images of women from the interconnected supernatural, natural, and social worlds she lives in.

As a half-breed American Indian woman, I cast about in my mind for negative images of Indian women, and I find none that are directed to Indian women alone. The negative images I do have are of Indians in general and in fact are more often of males than of females. All these images come to me from non-Indian sources, and they are always balanced by a positive image. My ideas of womanhood, passed on largely by my mother and grandmothers, Laguna Pueblo women, are about practicality, strength, reasonableness, intelligence, wit, and competence. I also remember vividly the women who came to my father's store, the women who held me and sang to me, the women at Feast Day, at Grab Days, the women in the kitchen of my Cubero home, the women I grew up with; none of them appeared weak or helpless, none of them presented herself tentatively. I remember a certain reserve on those lovely brown faces; I remember the direct gaze of eyes framed by bright-colored shawls draped over their heads and cascading down their backs. I remember the clean cotton dresses and carefully pressed hand-embroidered aprons they always wore; I remember laughter and good food, especially the sweet bread and the oven bread they gave us. Nowhere in my mind is there a foolish woman, a dumb woman, a vain woman, or a plastic woman, though the Indian women I have known have shown a wide range of personal style and demeanor.

My memory includes the Navajo woman who was badly beaten by her Sioux husband; but I also remember that my grandmother abandoned her Sioux husband long ago. I recall the stories about the Laguna woman beaten regularly by her husband in the presence of her children so that the children would not believe in the strength and power of femininity. And I remember the women who drank, who got into fights with other women and with the men, and who often won those battles. I have memories of tired women, partying women, stubborn women, sullen women, amicable women, selfish women, shy women, and aggressive women. Most of all I remember the women who laugh and scold and sit uncomplaining in the long sun on feast days and who cook wonderful food on wood stoves, in beehive mud ovens, and over open fires outdoors.

Among the images of women that come to me from various tribes as well as my own are White Buffalo Woman, who came to the Lakota long ago and brought them the religion of the Sacred Pipe, which they still practice; Tinotzin the goddess, who came to Juan Diego to remind him that she still walked the hills of her people and sent him with her message, her demand, and her proof to the Catholic bishop in the city nearby. And from Laguna I take the images of Yellow Woman, Coyote Woman, Grandmother Spider (Spider Old Woman), who brought the light, who gave us weaving and medicine, who gave us life. Among the Keres she is known as Thought Woman, who created us all and who keeps us in creation even now. I remember Iyatiku, Earth Woman, Corn Woman, who guides and counsels the people to peace and who welcomes us home when we cast off this coil of flesh as huskers cast off the leaves that wrap the corn. I remember Iyatiku's sister, Sun Woman, who held metals and cattle, pigs and sheep, highways and engines and so many things in her bundle, who went away to the east saying that one day she would return.

II

Since the coming of the Anglo-Europeans beginning in the fifteenth century, the fragile web of identity that long held tribal people secure has gradually been weakened and torn. But the oral tradition has prevented the complete destruction of the web, the ultimate disruption of tribal ways. The oral tradition is vital; it heals itself and the tribal web by adapting to the flow of the present while never relinquishing its connection to the past. Its adaptability has always been required, as many generations have experienced. Certainly the modern American Indian woman bears slight resemblance to her forebears—at least on superficial examination—but she is still a tribal woman in her deepest being. Her tribal sense of relationship to all that is continues to flourish. And though she is at times beset by her knowledge of the enormous gap between the life she lives and the life she was raised to live, and while she adapts her mind and being to the circumstances of her present life, she does so in tribal ways, mending the tears in the web of being from which she takes her existence as she goes.

My mother told me stories all the time, though I often did not recognize them as that. My mother told me stories about cooking and childbearing; she told me stories about menstruation and pregnancy; she told me stories about gods and heroes, about fairies and elves, about goddesses and spirits; she told me stories about the land and the sky, about cats and dogs, about snakes and spiders; she told me stories about climbing trees and exploring the mesas; she told me stories about going to dances and getting married; she told me stories about dressing and undressing, about sleeping and waking; she told me stories about herself, about her mother, about her grandmother. She told me stories about grieving and laughing, about thinking and doing; she told me stories about school and about people; about darning and mending; she told me stories about turquoise and about gold; she told me European stories and Laguna stories; she told me Catholic stories and Presbyterian stories; she told me city stories and country stories; she told me political stories and religious stories. She told me stories about living and stories about dying. And in all of those stories she told me who I was, who I was supposed to be, whom I came from, and who would follow me. In this way she taught me the meaning of the words she said, that all life is a circle and everything has a place within it. That's what she said and what she showed me in the things she did and the way she lived.

Of course, through my formal, white, Christian education, I discovered that other people had stories of their own—about women, about Indians, about fact, about reality—and I was amazed by a number of startling suppositions that others made about tribal customs and beliefs. According to the un-Indian, non-Indian view, for instance, Indians barred menstruating women from ceremonies and indeed segregated them from the rest of the people, consigning them to some space specially designed for them. This showed that Indians considered menstruating women unclean and not fit to enjoy the company of decent (nonmenstruating) people, that is, men. I was surprised and confused to hear this because my mother had taught me that white people had strange attitudes toward menstruation: they thought something was bad about it, that it meant you were sick, cursed, sinful, and weak and that you had to be very careful during that time. She taught me that menstruation was a normal occurrence, that I could go swimming or hiking or whatever else I wanted to do during my period. She actively scorned women who took to their beds, who were incapacitated by cramps, who "got the blues."

As I struggled to reconcile these very contradictory interpretations of American Indians' traditional beliefs concerning menstruation, I realized that the menstrual taboos were about power, not about sin or filth. My conclusion was later borne out by some tribes' own explanations, which, as you may well imagine, came as quite a relief to me.

The truth of the matter as many Indians see it is that women who are at the peak of their fecundity are believed to possess power that throws male power totally out of kilter. They emit such force that, in their presence, any male-owned or -dominated ritual or sacred object cannot do its usual task. For instance, the Lakota say that a menstruating woman anywhere near a yuwipi man, who is a special sort of psychic, spirit-empowered healer, for a day or so before he is to do his ceremony will effectively disempower him. Conversely, among many if not most tribes, important ceremonies cannot be held without the presence of women. Sometimes the ritual woman who empowers the ceremony must be unmarried and virginal so that the power she channels is unalloyed, unweakened by sexual arousal and penetration by a male. Other ceremonies require tumescent women, others the presence of mature women who have borne children, and still others depend for empowerment on postmenopausal women. Women may be segregated from the company of the whole band or village on certain occasions, but on certain occasions men are also segregated. In short, each ritual depends on a certain balance of power, and the positions of women within the phases of womanhood are used by tribal people to empower certain rites. This does not derive from a male-dominant view; it is not a ritual observance imposed on women by men. It derives from a tribal view of reality that distinguishes tribal people from feudal and industrial people.

Among the tribes, the occult power of women, inextricably bound to our hormonal life, is thought to be very great; many hold that we possess innately the blood-given power to kill—with a glance, with a step, or with a judicious mixing of menstrual blood into somebody's soup. Medicine women among the Pomo of California cannot practice until they are sufficiently mature; when they are immature, their power is diffuse and is likely to interfere with their practice until time and experience have it under control. So women of the tribes are not especially inclined to see themselves as poor helpless victims of male domination. Even in those tribes where something akin to male domination was present, women are perceived as powerful, socially, physically, and metaphysically. In times past, as in times present, women carried enormous burdens with aplomb. We were far indeed from the "weaker sex," the designation that white aristocratic sisters unhappily earned for us all.

I remember my mother moving furniture all over the house when she wanted it changed. She didn't wait for my father to come home and help—she just went ahead and moved the piano, a huge upright from the old days, the couch, the refrigerator. Nobody had told her she was too weak to do such things. In imitation of her, I would delight in loading trucks at my father's store with cases of pop or fifty-pound sacks of flour. Even when I was quite small I could do it, and it gave me a belief in my own physical strength that advancing middle age can't quite erase. My mother used to tell me about the Acoma Pueblo women she had seen as a child carrying huge ollas (water pots) on their heads as they wound their way up the tortuous stairwell carved into the face of the "Sky City" mesa, a feat I tried to imitate with books and tin buckets. ("Sky City" is the term used by the Chamber of Commerce for the mother village of Acoma, which is situated atop a high sandstone table mountain.) I was never very successful, but even the attempt reminded me that I was supposed to be strong and balanced to be a proper girl.

Of course, my mother's Laguna people are Keres Indian, reputed to be the last extreme mother-right people on earth. So it is no wonder that I got notably nonwhite notions about the natural strength and prowess of women. Indeed, it is only when I am trying to get non-Indian approval, recognition, or acknowledgment that my "weak sister" emotional and intellectual ploys get the better of my tribal woman's good sense. At such times I forget that I just moved the piano or just wrote a competent paper or just completed a financial transaction satisfactorily or have supported myself and my children for most of my adult life.

Nor is my contradictory behavior atypical. Most Indian women I know are in the same bicultural bind: we vacillate between being dependent and strong, self-reliant and powerless, strongly motivated and hopelessly insecure. We resolve the dilemma in various ways: some of us party all the time; some of us drink to excess; some of us travel and move around a lot; some of us land good jobs and then quit them; some of us engage in violent exchanges; some of us blow our brains out. We act in these destructive ways because we suffer from the societal conflicts caused by having to identify with two hopelessly opposed cultural definitions of women. Through this destructive dissonance we are unhappy prey to the self-disparagement common to, indeed demanded of, Indians living in the United States today. Our situation is caused by the exigencies of a history of invasion, conquest, and colonization whose searing marks are probably ineradicable. A popular bumper sticker on many Indian cars proclaims: "If You're Indian You're In," to which I always find myself adding under my breath, "Trouble."

III

No Indian can grow to any age without being informed that her people were "savages" who interfered with the march of progress pursued by respectable, loving, civilized white people. We are the villains of the scenario when we are mentioned at all. We are absent from much of white history except when we are calmly, rationally, succinctly, and systematically dehumanized. On the few occasions we are noticed in any way other than as howling, blood-thirsty beings, we are acclaimed for our noble quaintness. In this definition, we are exotic curios. Our ancient arts and customs are used to draw tourist money to state coffers, into the pocketbooks and bank accounts of scholars, and into support of the American-in-Disneyland promoters' dream.

As a Roman Catholic child I was treated to bloody tales of how the savage Indians martyred the hapless priests and missionaries who went among them in an attempt to lead them to the one true path. By the time I was through high school I had the idea that Indians were people who had benefited mightily from the advanced knowledge and superior morality of the Anglo-Europeans. At least I had, perforce, that idea to lay beside the other one that derived from my daily experience of Indian life, an idea less dehumanizing and more accurate because it came from my mother and the other Indian people who raised me. That idea was that Indians are a people who don't tell lies, who care for their children and their old people. You never see an Indian orphan, they said. You always know when you're old that someone will take care of you—one of your children will. Then they'd list the old folks who were being taken care of by this child or that. No child is ever considered illegitimate among the Indians, they said. If a girl gets pregnant, the baby is still part of the family, and the mother is too. That's what they said, and they showed me real people who lived according to those principles.

Of course the ravages of colonization have taken their toll; there are orphans in Indian country now, and abandoned, brutalized old folks; there are even illegitimate children, though the very concept still strikes me as absurd. There are battered children and neglected children, and there are battered wives and women who have been raped by Indian men. Proximity to the "civilizing" effects of white Christians has not improved the moral quality of life in Indian country, though each group, Indian and white, explains the situation differently. Nor is there much yet in the oral tradition that can enable us to adapt to these inhuman changes. But a force is growing in that direction, and it is helping Indian women reclaim their lives. Their power, their sense of direction and of self will soon be visible. It is the force of the women who speak and work and write, and it is formidable.

Through all the centuries of war and death and cultural and psychic destruction have endured the women who raise the children and tend the fires, who pass along the tales and the traditions, who weep and bury the dead, who are the dead, and who never forget. There are always the women, who make pots and weave baskets, who fashion clothes and cheer their children on at powwow, who make fry bread and piki bread, and corn soup and chili stew, who dance and sing and remember and hold within their hearts the dream of their ancient peoples—that one day the woman who thinks will speak to us again, and everywhere there will be peace. Meanwhile we tell the stories and write the books and trade tales of anger and woe and stories of fun and scandal and laugh over all manner of things that happen every day. We watch and we wait.

My great-grandmother told my mother: Never forget you are Indian. And my mother told me the same thing. This, then, is how I have gone about remembering, so that my children will remember too.

THE MASTER'S TOOLS WILL NEVER DISMANTLE THE MASTER'S HOUSE

Audre Lorde

... Advocating the mere tolerance of difference between women is the grossest reformism. It is a total denial of the creative function of difference in our lives. Difference must be not merely tolerated, but seen as a fund of necessary polarities between which our creativity can spark like a dialectic. Only then does the necessity for interdependency become unthreatening. Only within that interdependency of different strengths, acknowledged and equal, can the power to seek new ways of being in the world generate, as well as the courage and sustenance to act where there are no charters.

Within the interdependence of mutual (nondominant) differences lies that security which enables us to descend into the chaos of knowledge and return with true visions of our future, along with the concomitant power to effect those changes which can bring that future into being. Difference is that raw and powerful connection from which our personal power is forged.

As women, we have been taught either to ignore our differences or to view them as causes for separation and suspicion rather than as forces for change. Without community there is no liberation, only the most vulnerable and temporary armistice between an individual and her oppression. But community must not mean a shedding of our differences, nor the pathetic pretense that these differences do not exist.

Those of us who stand outside the circle of this society's definition of acceptable women; those of us who have been forged in the crucibles of difference—those of us who are poor, who are lesbians, who are Black, who are older—know that *survival is not an academic skill*. It is learning how to stand alone, unpopular and sometimes reviled, and how to make common cause with those others identified as outside the structures in order to define and seek a world in which we can all flourish. It is learning how to take our differences and make them strengths. *For the master's tools will never dismantle the master's house.* They may allow us temporarily to beat him at his own game, but they will never enable us to bring about genuine change. And this fact is threatening only to those women who still define the master's house as their only source of support.

Poor women and women of Color know there is a difference between the daily manifestations of marital slavery and prostitution because it is our daughters who line 42nd Street. If white american [*sic*] feminist theory need not deal with the differences between us, and the resulting difference in our oppressions, then how do you deal with the fact that the women who clean your houses and tend your children while you attend conferences on feminist theory are, for the most part, poor women and women of Color? What is the theory behind racist feminism?

In a world of possibility for us all, our personal visions help lay the groundwork for political action. The failure of academic feminists to recognize difference as a crucial strength is a failure to reach beyond the first patriarchal lesson. In our world, divide and conquer must become define and empower. . . .

Women of today are still being called upon to stretch across the gap of male ignorance and to educate men as to our existence and our needs. This is an old and primary tool of all oppressors to keep the oppressed occupied with the master's concerns. Now we hear that it is the task of women of Color to educate white women—in the face of tremendous resistance—as to our existence, our differences, our relative roles in our joint survival. This is a diversion of energies and a tragic repetition of racist patriarchal thought.

Simone de Beauvoir once said: "It is in the knowledge of the genuine conditions of our lives that we must draw our strength to live and our reasons for acting."

Racism and homophobia are real conditions of all our lives in this place and time. *I urge each one of us here to reach down into that deep place of knowledge inside herself and touch that terror and loathing of any difference that lives there. See whose face it wears.* Then the personal as the political can begin to illuminate all our choices.

READING *5*   **Catherine Kudlick**

The Blind Man's Harley: White Canes and Gender Identity in America

Several years ago, I completed a six-month residential rehabilitation program at the Colorado Center for the Blind (CCB), just south of Denver in Littleton. As someone who is legally blind but with much usable vision, I wanted to learn a set of skills that would help me function better with the vision I have; at the same time I hoped to change my attitudes about blindness. Thus, I picked—as far as I know—the most adventurous blindness rehabilitation program in the world, one that required me to be blindfolded all day in classes (wearing what we call "sleep-shades"), where I learned such things as cane travel, Braille, and living skills, all the while engaging in confidence builders such as going downhill skiing and participating in bizarre treasure hunts to the far reaches of Denver. The final graduation requirement consisted of being dropped alone somewhere unknown in the metropolitan area and having to make my way back to the CCB, being allowed to ask only one question.

Here I want to tell about one tiny aspect of my time at the Colorado Center: traveling through the streets of Denver using a long white cane. As a professor in the humanities, I am programmed to step back from my experiences and analyze them through the comfort of scholarly abstractions. For example, I might write of the program's particularly masculine reading of rugged individualism as part of mainstream American culture grafted awkwardly but firmly onto shifting gender identities transformed by blindness. Or I might cast everything in terms of "performativity" and "gender play," revealing how contested ideas of masculinity and femininity can be created even—and especially—for something as seemingly fixed as blindness. But first I would have to point out that terms such as *masculinity* and *femininity* are problematic, open as they are to interpretations contingent on social and cultural expectations that change over time. And who could resist describing the cane as a blind person's phallus? All of these observations have their place in this essay and may even be the abstract forces that ultimately shape it.

Still, my struggles in "blind boot camp" demanded that I come face to face with something much more visceral: my own deep-seated fears about blindness, and how these anxieties related to being a woman in a program that called upon me to "take it like a man." Such gender tensions constantly played themselves out in the choices I made between being safe and embracing the risks that make life worth living. These decisions shape how all human beings confront difference, as we read the actions—or inactions—of others through the internal lens of our dread. For a low-vision person like me, blindness represented the consummate defeat and blind people the embodiment of my failure. The blind of my imagination begged with tin cups in the street or groped in the dark, their heads raised and their arms stretched out in desperation. Above all, they stayed home, angry and bitter, passively accepting what fate had handed them. My blind were so emasculated that femininity did not have a safe dwelling place.

The six months at the Colorado Center blew away all my assumptions. The adventure put an end to my lifelong self-image as the pathetic little blind girl, at the same time destroying any illusions I might have had of one day discovering a conventional feminine self. Through their unbridled audaciousness, my fellow students and teachers—all of them blind—rescued blindness from the depths of pity and helped turn it into simply another way of being in the world. At the same time, I had to change how I thought about myself as a woman in order to triumph over adversity in this particular way. Yes, part of me wanted to kill off the helpless blind girl. But did this mean I would have to renounce femininity altogether? Would I have to come up with something completely new? And when all was said and done, who would take the little girl's place?

Public responses to the white cane as the ultimate symbol of helplessness and powerlessness only increased my dread of being associated with blind people. When I first started to use a cane, I was dumbfounded by the dramatic change in how most in the sighted world treated me just because I held a long thin piece of carbon fiber in my hand. It might be the flip side of what young powerless street kids must feel when they enter a room pointing a gun. One minute I stood there, an innocuous, competent, responsible adult, and the next my "stickmata" brought the wrath of human condescension raining down upon me, as people's voices grew artificially soft and solicitous. Most sighted people assumed I could do very little for myself and treated me like a dependent child or a delicate porcelain doll. Being female, I found these responses troubling enough. But the men around me at the Colorado Center—from my young biker buddies

who proclaimed themselves my "Guardian Hell's Angels" to my closest friend and confidant, a gay psychologist in his late fifties from the East Coast—all complained bitterly about how the sighted world's treatment of them as helpless dependents was robbing them of their masculinity.

To counter this image, the Colorado Center consciously sought to make the cane not just a symbol of independence but a means of achieving it. In operation for nearly a decade, the CCB was founded by members of the National Federation of the Blind (NFB), the world's largest organization run by and for blind people. The organization has a seductive philosophy that speaks to men and women alike at the same time that it sets the tone for a particular kind of masculine assertiveness. The real problem for blind people is not the lack of eyesight, the NFB philosophy claims, but rather social attitudes; given opportunity and proper training in alternative techniques, blindness can be reduced to a mere physical nuisance, and blind people can compete on terms of equality with their sighted peers doing just about anything.[1] People in the blindness field, as well as the blind man or woman on the street, tend to have strong feelings about the organization, either as enthusiastic defenders or as fierce critics decrying "federationists" as unthinking fanatics. The NFB constantly infuriates people because it takes unpopular and uncompromising stands, some of them seemingly at odds with the needs of the blind. In the early 1990s, for example, the organization generated huge controversy when it lobbied passionately against installing tactile warning strips along train platforms. Federationists saw such measures as "special treatment," more ammunition for the sighted world to see blind people as different; the more practical and less expensive solution, they argued, was good cane technique. But disagreement over who is qualified to teach this technique and how the requisite mobility skills should be taught has created another major rift within the blindness field.

Behind the dispute lurks a deep philosophical question that divides the world of rehabilitation training unmistakably along gender lines. On my first day at the center my travel instructor, Dirk, who had been totally blind for ten years after the sudden onset of diabetes, leaned back in his squeaky chair and bellowed: "Okay, Doc. Let me guess. If you learned to use a cane from someone at the state department of rehab, she was a very well-meaning middle-aged sighted lady who drove you to a quiet parking lot somewhere and made sure you didn't get lost." My jaw dropped because it seemed he had been following me before he even knew who I was. The majority opinion holds that sighted people are better equipped to teach someone mobility because they can see obstacles and have a better perspective on the big picture, which will help a blind traveler figure out certain complicated situations. For example, a blind instructor might not be able to know that one cannot enter a raised train platform without using a stairway located way down the block or might not be able to tell when a pedestrian crossing is only on one side of a busy intersection whizzing with cars. The bottom line of this argument rests on safety issues: a sighted instructor is in a better position to keep a new blind traveler out of danger. And as long as travel stays within the confines of predictable challenges, it's women's work.[2]

The NFB-inspired centers such as the one I attended have shaken up the rehab world because they exclusively employ low-vision or blind travel instructors. During my time at the CCB all of them happened to be men, though over the years several women have taught travel as well. Those who favor the blind-leading-the-blind approach argue that a blind person is in a better position to train and instill confidence in other blind people than a sighted person, however competent and enlightened that sighted person might be. If you do not have faith in a blind teacher, the reasoning goes, how can you possibly convince new travelers to believe in themselves? Anyone who has taken a gym class and watched the coach sip soda while students puffed their way around the track will appreciate how I thought about the well-meaning sighted professional who gave me my first cane. As for the argument that sighted people can offer help that a blind person cannot, the NFB points out that you will not always have a kind rehab lady to act as your guardian angel, so you had better learn how to puzzle out complex situations on your own. It is an appealing notion, one that too often seemed better in theory, such as the countless times we wandered around some godforsaken corner of Denver with a blind instructor, lost in the snow. On the other hand, we learned that it was okay to be lost, that people eventually find their way. Not just an extreme example of the masculine compulsion to avoid asking directions at any cost, this approach also underscored the search for self-sufficiency in a sighted world that often denies such independence to blind people, be they men or women.

Perhaps not surprisingly in our post-Freudian times, the NFB tries to reclaim masculinity for blindness

via cane length. This makes it possible to discern a person's blindness politics based on the type she or he might use. Most favor the red-bottomed cane offered by agencies that do not adhere to the NFB philosophy. These canes reach the middle of the chest and collapse by folding into sections, much like tent poles. At the top they have a black rubberized grip like that of a golf club, while for the bottom one can choose from a variety of nylon tip shapes and sizes described as marshmallows, cylinders, mushrooms, and balls, some of which roll and therefore require constant contact with the sidewalk while others remain stationary to facilitate tapping back and forth. For something that folds, they feel quite solid. Many travelers—both men and women—find these canes the best compromise between strength and portability. You can stuff them into your back pocket or lay them discreetly on a chair next to you in a restaurant. And if you don't feel like drawing attention to your blindness for every minute of your public life, these folding models offer an option. I have friends who passionately try to convince me that they are easier to use and transmit information more effectively, not to mention that they arc about 30 percent cheaper ($33 vs. $40) than the NFB canes. Alas, I found the folding canes heavy and tiring to use for any length of time. And, I should confess, they didn't seem as cool to me—I tended to think of them as akin to orthopedic shoes or thick glasses in the days before optometry became chic.

About thirty years ago, the NFB modified the style and use of the cane by coming up with a thin, rigid model made of carbon fiber. These sleek all-white canes with a metal tip at the bottom generally come to the bridge of one's nose. One CCB staff member, a woman from Nepal well under five feet tall, sported a cane that towered over her head. Users assert that the long canes enable you to walk more quickly because they give you more information sooner, like wearing a stronger pair of glasses that allows you to see farther away. As for the rigidity, the NFB philosophy seeks to make a point: you should not be ashamed of your blindness, and if a rigid cane is light and durable, why settle for anything less? These canes have major drawbacks, however. Their length makes it more likely that a user will get tangled up with fellow pedestrians, sometimes tripping them, causing the rigid cane to snap and splinter. Also, imagine going through life (restaurants, concerts, airplane trips, car rides, to name but a few situations) with the equivalent of a fishing pole that you constantly need to find places to store, particularly when you already feel obtrusive enough as a blind person. The NFB's arguments about strength and lightness shaped the cane industry so that folding ones have improved enormously on both counts, yet federationists still chide people for using them to hide their blindness. For the situations where rigid canes are impractical, the organization finally caved in to popular demand by making a very light-weight and compact telescoping cane, an elegant but (deliberately?) poorly designed object that collapses when you least expect it.

Students at the CCB were required to use the long, rigid canes, though several registered silent protests against the school and the NFB more generally by buying the shorter folding ones. The teachers, who could tell the difference between NFB and non-NFB canes by the sound of the metal tip, tried to tease people who used them in a friendly way ("What, you want to walk like an old lady?"), but usually the offenders ignored them. A few others, such as Jason, a tall guy whose sixty-nine-inch cane kept getting run over by buses, reverted to the folding models because they thought these canes held up better. Jason liked the length of the rigid NFB canes, though, so he had to mail-order extralong folding ones from a special place in Canada because the longest American ones were only sixty inches.

"I should think about getting me one of these folding canes," Dirk once admitted to me as we headed off to explore Littleton, causing me to stop dead in my tracks. A prospective student was visiting the center, and Dirk had traded canes in order to give him a sense of what the NFB ones were like. "The nylon tips are quiet so I could use them when I want to follow some slacker," he explained. But usually Dirk just turned his rigid NFB cane upside down, using the plastic top as the tip as he followed behind at a discreet distance. "Of course, the handle turns to crap pretty fast," he admitted, "but that's what duct tape is for." He rattled around in his snuff bag, spat, and added, "Never go anywhere without duct tape, one of the little-known miracles of the blind guy's tool kit. I've pasted up one or two canes with the silver stuff, enough to get me home and even add a couple hundred miles on 'em before they really give out."

The NFB's sense of rugged independence also translated into its philosophy and policies that discouraged using dog guides. Because numerous schools across the country specialize in working with dogs, a rehab center like the CCB could reasonably argue that it should

specialize in teaching cane travel. Besides, people should first have good cane mobility skills, lest they find themselves without their dog for some reason. But I think something else was also at work: the NFB seemed to be engaging with the sighted world's long-held belief that dogs served the more needy—and therefore less competent, more feminized—blind, that the dog leads the person rather than the person controlling the dog like any other tool. Rightly or wrongly, we internalized the message that using a dog was tantamount to copping out and creating unnecessary barriers with the sighted world because animals are intrusive.

Still, the center didn't rule out dogs altogether. Among the students, the ex–Hell's Angel Gavin had a dog, an unpleasant, high-strung German shepherd that wore a bandanna. Keyla had to spend most of her days curled up under one of the tables in the meeting room while her owner learned to travel with a long, rigid cane outside. I never understood why Gavin had Keyla in the first place, especially since he was clearly such a talented cane traveler; I could only figure that her surly growls helped maintain his tough-guy biker persona in a way a white cane never could. More often, our travel teachers gave certain students, including Harriet and Don, who had both experienced serious hearing loss, their blessing for getting dogs *after* they graduated. But the general message was clear: canes were about independence, confidence, assertiveness, and full social integration, while dogs were not.

Such a macho cane environment spawned an interesting culture that ran counter to everything most sighted Americans have thought about blind people and blindness. In public, the long, rigid canes clearly managed to surprise sighted people because the circumstances in which we used them confounded expectations of helpless blind people flailing alone in the world. Sometimes, for example, the whole center would go on chaotic outings that brought some twenty-five or thirty of us with our long canes fanning out through an unsuspecting Denver. Sighted culture never quite knows what to do when more than one blind person shows up, particularly if unaccompanied by sighted help. Sometimes I got the impression that we terrified people on the street, that they drew only the thinnest of lines between fearing for our safety and fearing for their lives. I would hear concerned mothers hurrying their intrigued children away or groups of African-American teenage guys shouting to us: "Go brothers and sisters!" More often, sighted people's anxiety manifested itself through bewildered and awkward questions about why the canes were so long. Unconsciously anyway, they seem to have picked up on the NFB cane's more potent macho dimensions.

In the hands of someone like my instructor Dirk, the cane became a Harley of sorts, with a whole vocabulary and series of rituals to match. For example, people who use the NFB canes must change the metal tip that meets the sidewalk every couple of weeks. Tough guys such as Dirk and my biker friends referred to the mundane fact of the tip wearing out as "blowing a tip" and had a whole classification system for describing what caused it. If one "blew out" on Dirk just a few days after he had put it on, it was "sissy" or "wimpy"; I think I once even heard one of the guys use the word "pussy" in this context. If someone like me went through one too quickly, however, it was my fault and not the tip's. Novices, particularly women, seemed to "burn through" tips at an alarming rate, because, the guys claimed, we scraped them too much along the sidewalk. But a tip's significance could also lie in the eye of the beholder: a few years ago I met a guy—no sissy—who saved every one he ever changed as a sign of all the miles he'd traveled with a cane. Then there was the whole issue of actually changing the tip. Novices heard that we should first lick the base where the old tip had been before attaching a new one, a disgusting thought if you imagine all the places a cane goes in a day. I must confess to wondering if this was really necessary, dismissing the advice as one of our rare boot-camp hazing moments. I later learned that some form of lubrication helped matters considerably, but, like most of my women friends at the center, I decided this was a man's work and cheerfully resorted to traditional flirtation rather than spit. Certain people—mostly men but also a few women—developed a reputation for being good tip changers, so the rest of us would go to them for help. Women had tested various makeups, skin creams, Vaseline, and even K-Y Jelly, whereas men simply spat and hoped for the best as they muscled the spent old tip off and a new one on.

The CCB offered a particularly macho environment in which to learn such basics. When I arrived for my training, the center had just relocated to a former YMCA, where the travel office had settled into the men's locker room, which still smelled distinctly of jock sweat. Moreover, the travel teachers and a few of the male students thought nothing of heading for the urinal well within earshot of our class. Several of us (both female and male) complained, but to little avail, since the guys didn't want to be bothered by having to troop upstairs only to wait in line. Within this bunkerlike setting, Dirk began with the essentials by giving informal lectures about urban planning, stoplights, traffic control, and—for anyone who cared to listen—about how cement was mixed and poured. He taught us about parking lots and traffic patterns by guiding our hands to a collection of matchbox cars he kept on his desk, which he'd arrange to create various complex scenarios.

"The best class a blind traveler could ever take would be driver's ed.," he stated matter-of-factly one day. "I've been thinking about assigning the State of Colorado's driver's handbook to all you students and making you pass that sucker of a test. In fact, if I had time, I'd introduce a bill before the state legislature to require all blind kids to take it."

I bristled. Driver's education class had been a huge emotional nemesis for me as a legally blind teenager in high school. "What's the point of making a bunch of blind people do *that*," I blurted out, for once not being the well-behaved student.

"Well, Doc," he said, leaning back in his squeaky chair as he always did when he knew he was about to win, "it's a jungle out there, a god-damned jungle. But there are rules of the jungle. In theory, anyway. You, little speck of a blind person, are out there surrounded by wild beasts, wild two-ton metal beasts whose lives just happen to be explained in a book like this very one provided for free by the marvelous state of Colorado. I don't know about you, but before I go out there, I'd want a fighting chance, and the only way to have it is to know what rules govern the jungle."

After such lectures, Dirk would take two or three of us out to an intersection to make us listen for the logic of traffic patterns. One frosty morning I found myself heading out with him and Jason, a pleasant young man who had started his training shortly after I had. Blind from birth and sheltered by his overprotective family until he had finished college, he was smart and articulate. But this poor kid from Oregon knew surprisingly little of the world, so, among other things, the CCB was teaching him to travel alone for the first time in his life.

As we walked north on the Prince Street overpass and heard a train pulling out of the light-rail station slightly ahead and to the right, Dirk stopped abruptly. The sun felt warm on my right ear, but even though I wore the thickest gloves imaginable, I already feared my frostbitten fingers were going to have to be amputated. "Okay, my friends," he ordered, "turn to your left, and tell me where we are. Hint: you have to listen."

I had been around Dirk long enough by that point to know that the obvious answer was seldom correct, but having racked my brain, I couldn't come up with anything better: "At the light-rail station?" I ventured.

"Perhaps. Mr. Krug?"

"I'd have to agree," Jason said, also sensing that this wasn't what Dirk wanted.

"Listen more carefully. The train is gone. What do you hear now?"

We stood fixed to the spot, concentrating.

A car somewhere to our left had stopped and was idling. "You can cross!" the person I assumed to be its driver shouted at us. "It's okay to go!"

I felt something long and thin brush my kneecaps. "No need to go anywhere just yet, Doc," Dirk said, gently pushing me back with his cane. "In fact, we won't cross anything today." I hadn't even realized that I had inched into the street. "Rule number one: don't listen to drivers. Like all our sighted friends, they mean well, but you need to understand your environment first. Rule number two: when you get to an intersection, stop and figure it out. What is your line of traffic, where are the cars headed? How fast are they going? When do they stop? Where? How long? Take as long as you need. Don't let anyone push you into going before you're absolutely sure where you are, where you want to go, and how you'll get there. Now what can you tell me about this intersection? First of all, what kind of intersection is it?"

"Busy," I joked, more out of fear than wit.

Jason chuckled in nervous agreement.

"That's right on the mark," Dirk said without sarcasm. "That's your first important piece of information. Now what kind of busy is it? Listen."

I thought hard about all the details of the environment, but truth be told, all I could hear were big roaring cars that sounded chaotic and dangerously close to where we stood. I figured just as long as I remained a little behind Dirk I would be okay. Things grew quiet, and I actually thought I heard the wind rustling in the trees across the street. Then one or two cars honked as they drove by, followed by a driver who shouted, "You folks need any help? I can pull up to that parking lot and walk you across."

"No thank you, sir," Dirk replied in his deadpan way. "We're just three blind people out for a nice walk in the country." Then turning to us, "Don't mind them.

Your job is to listen to the flow of cars. Are they going all the time or are they stopping?"

As I concentrated, the reality of the intersection began to take shape. When Dirk asked if I thought it had a traffic light, a stop sign, or nothing at all, I could tell instantly that it was a light because the cars clearly streamed through in batches. When the vehicles going perpendicular to where we stood came to a stop, those facing us would come toward us. I felt immensely pleased with myself for figuring this out.

"What if I told you that's only part of the story?" Dirk inquired. I sighed. "Good, it's a light," he allowed, perhaps sensing how defeated I felt; then, "But what kind of light? What kind of intersection is this? Is there anything special about it?"

The cars fell completely silent so that once again I noticed the strange mechanical clanging of the light-rail bell behind us and heard the hum of a train as it glided into the station. I stiffened with excitement as I collected the pieces of a puzzle and began snapping them into place: one set of cars passed back and forth in front of us, and when these stopped, another batch came straight toward us but turned either right or left rather than going through; *they couldn't go through because Church Street dead-ended into Prince Street at the light-rail station tracks!*

Ever the eager student, I blurted out my answer, half expecting it to be wrong.

"Excellent," Dirk said in the flat way he reserved for his highest praise. I felt I had been awarded a medal. "This is what is known as a 'T-intersection,'" he explained. "It's named after the print letter 'T.'" Then turning to Jason, he asked, "You ever seen the print letter 'T,' Mr. Krug?"

Jason seemed a little embarrassed. Blind from birth, he knew Braille better than most of the rest of us, but he had never written with pen and ink. Consequently, he had never had reason to learn the print alphabet. "No, I'm afraid not," he admitted.

"Here, my friend," Dirk said gently, "give me your back so I can draw it for you." I heard Jason step toward Dirk, who traced the letter first for Jason then for me on my own back. "Like this," he said to each of us as he ran his glove over the fabric, first down and then across at the top. "That's the print letter 'T.' Now imagine it being upside down like this." This time he drew the vertical line first, then put the horizontal one at the bottom, pushing harder where the two lines met to indicate where we stood. His touch was quick and direct, delicate and informative all at once.

"This is heady, important stuff," he growled, as we stood giddy with terror at the prospect of actually having to apply this knowledge. "But it's worthless crap if you don't put your cane out there to let them know you're intending to cross. As a blind guy, I could hold a line of twenty-five cars back all day long if I wanted just by putting my cane out there and showing with body posture that I want to cross. Your cane is your key to roam the road, to make the road yours. It's the simplest and most elegant tool, so you'd damn well better use it."

"But, Dirk," I protested, "it's easy for you to put your body on the line—guys are encouraged to do that beginning with when you're first starting to walk! We girls *never* learned to 'just put ourselves out there.' If anything, I'm hardwired to 'just keep my body in there,' thank you very much." I tried to make it light and funny, but I didn't like this kind of vulnerability one bit.

"Ah come on, Doc!" Dirk shouted over all the traffic. "For someone who's supposed to be so smart, you don't use that brain of yours very much—or maybe you use it too damn much! I'm not asking you to put your body on the line; I'm just saying use your goddamned cane!" At that moment, I smelled his habitual snuff, heard the distinct sound of expectoration, and cringed as I wondered where his spit had gone. "Blind people can't afford to be sissy-wimps if they want to be free in this world," he announced. "The way I see it, you can either put yourself out there or you can sit at home and wait for some well-meaning sighted person to come and rescue the damsel in distress. It's your choice, Doc."

A few days later Dirk wanted me to accompany him and a more advanced student to downtown Littleton so we could "visit the damn birds," Dirk's expression for audible pedestrian signals. Like Gavin, Finn was a tattoo-covered ex-biker, a large man in his early thirties who, like Dirk, had gone blind suddenly from diabetes. We had bonded on my first day at boot camp when Finn had given me a tour of the center. Even though he was a decade younger, he always called me "little sister," while still managing to treat me with genuine gallantry and respect.

"Rule number one," Dirk barked as we approached the chirping at the corner of Prince and Alamo, "ignore those things. They're put in by poor clueless sighted people and their lazy blind friends." The chirps and cuckoos have been a big bone of contention in the blindness community, making the NFB once again seem like it has taken a ridiculous stand against the better interests of blind people. After all, who in their right minds would attack a street signal that—at least in theory—allowed a blind person standing at an intersection to hear exactly when the light changed? Once you learn that cuckoo means cross north-south and chirp-chirp east-west (or is it that chirp-chirp means north-south and cuckoo means east-west?), all you have to do is arrive at the corner and wait patiently for the signal.

"My point exactly." I heard Dirk's voice ringing in my ear as he instinctively understood my confusion. "Plus, most audible signals are designed with vision in mind. They want you to know what drivers are seeing, when what you really need to know is what *you* should be *doing*. And no two of these suckers are ever alike. One might be way up top of a pole, and another practically on the frickin' ground or far away from the intersection. Some ping, some chirp, some do one thing one minute and another thing the next, and sometimes you have to push a button to activate them. And where's the button?" We laughed as Dirk noisily banged his cane into various poles and other nearby obstacles, including an innocent bystander who shouted "Hey!" when Dirk hit her. "Thank you for helping me make my point, ma'am," Dirk said by way of apology, turning back to us. "I suppose if cities really wanted to help, they'd raise crosswalks just slightly so your cane could lead you in the right direction, but it wouldn't matter that much once you learned how to use your cane." He claimed that the NFB metal tip's sensitivity allowed one to distinguish the paint of a crosswalk, a lesson I would master by the end of my training, though I wasn't completely confident. Dirk admitted that audible signals might be useful at irregular intersections or in the growing number of situations where traffic lights are geared toward maximizing traffic flow at the expense of pedestrians. "But if we have to have them, then they've got to be consistent and everybody plays by the same rules. And the bottom line is having good cane technique."

Dirk took me to the corner, spun me in a circle, told me an off-color joke, walked me to a store entrance, spun me around again, then plunked me at the corner. "Okay, Doc. Wait for the birdie, then tell me where you think you should go." By that point I was disoriented, not to mention that I remained preoccupied with simply finding the actual line that separated the sidewalk from the street. I felt around with my cane in a panic as the cuckoo started up, but I still couldn't get oriented.

"Here, Doc," Dirk said, taking me by the shoulders. "Now you're pointed in the right direction. Now what?" I stood through several cuckoo/chirp cycles, but even though I had a pretty good idea of what I thought must be north, the sun wasn't out that day, and the more I listened for the signal the less certain I was about my line of direction.

"Finn, my man, I'm going to step over here for a bit of snuff," Dirk announced and then headed off, fishing in his pocket. "Show our friend the doctor how it's done."

I could hear Finn's cane exploring to my right. "Here's the curb," he reported in his raspy voice, "give me your cane," whereupon he put his enormous hand on top of mine and ran the cane back and forth over a small indentation. "Here's the lip," he explained as my cane skipped over a small ridge and then down. "It's one of those blended curbs that my boys dig so much for skateboarding, so it's really hard to find, but here's the low point." I remembered one of Dirk's minilectures where he had described how city streets had been constructed to facilitate drainage. Just beyond the curb was a smooth area that gradually headed upward, then got rough. "Feel the difference between cement and asphalt?" Finn asked, guiding my cane first to one, then the other. The cement was definitely smoother, while the asphalt not only felt rough but grated more on my cane tip. I had the strange sensation of not knowing whether I was getting this information through sound or touch.

"Now here's the thing, little sister," Finn said as we stood there, "I know you're probably scared to death, but don't worry. I'll be right with you all the way, and I'll stand between you and the traffic." I felt much better, but my heart still pounded. When the cars started up after sitting at a light, they roared like a pack of lions that I knew was preparing to charge at me. We stood through several cycles, this time listening to the traffic patterns rather than the signals. We waved off the usual well-meaning drivers and occasional pedestrians. I was beginning to have a sense of the intersection now, realizing that Prince Street went two directions while Alamo went one way.

"Okay, sis, you say when we should go." My cane hand shook and my feet felt like blocks. The cars coming toward us started to roll, so I stepped into the street with all the enthusiasm of heading for my own execution. "You're doing great," Finn said. "Just keep those cars and me on your right and you'll be fine." Dirk had come up on my left, so that both men kept me in line with their canes when I strayed a little to the right or the left as we crossed. I felt this incredible sense of warmth and protection just from the occasional gentle tap of their canes against my shins. When we arrived at the other side, I heaved a huge sigh of relief.

About a month into my training, Dirk announced that the time had come for me to cross a busy intersection on my own. This put me into a panic far worse than anything I'd ever felt about setting foot in a formidable research library for the first time, walking into my Ph.D. qualifying exams, or going on my first job interview. This was, after all, literally about life and death. "Doc, you've got what it takes," Dirk reassured me. "But I'll let you off easy this time. You just cross that intersection at Prince and Alamo—the one you did already with Finn here—continue up one more block, and we'll meet you after you've reached the next corner. You leave now, we'll follow in ten." Somehow, knowing that my mauled body would be found reassured me enough that I set off.

I realize blind people travel busy intersections all the time without holding a press conference. But I freely admit that I burst into tears when I made it to the right spot, determined when to go, and walked a straight line to the other side, all this without being run over. I'm not talking figure of speech here: there was a lump in my throat, and soon the outer foam covering of my sleepshades was soggy. Few peacocks have walked with more pride than I did up to the next corner, where Dirk and Finn came up from behind to congratulate me, slapping my back and giving me high fives.

Then a terrifying thing happened. Just after Dirk asked me to analyze the traffic pattern of the new intersection, I felt something heavy collapse into my legs. Even before catching my balance and tearing off my sleepshades, I realized that it was a human body. Finn, my biker buddy and protector, a large man of considerable bulk and a serious diabetic, was having some kind of seizure. He had slid down onto the pavement, where he lay motionless at my feet. Dirk reached into his pocket for a handful of sugar candies that he always carried for his own emergencies and tried to feed them to Finn, who seemed barely able to chew, let alone swallow, and who was definitely not lucid. I pulled out my cell phone ready to call 911, but Dirk dictated a number, which I immediately dialed, assuming it was some diabetic hotline. But it turned out to be the number of the CCB. "Doc, just hold the line," Dirk commanded in a calm, authoritative voice. "When someone picks up, have them send one of the sighted employees with a car to the corner of Prince and Main. Our friend here just needs to get his blood sugar up, that's all."

Meanwhile, cars were driving up and asking if we needed help—we must have looked pretty needy at that point, three blind people at a street corner, one of them horizontal among the hardened chunks of dirty snow. Dirk waved them off, saying that we had the situation under control. I didn't feel so sure, but he was my teacher and seemed knowledgeable about diabetic crises.

I felt torn in many directions as I found myself in voice-mail hell waiting for a live human to answer. Sure, I had never experienced this kind of thing before, but here was a guy on the sidewalk, someone who I heard had just been in the hospital for a minor heart attack. Were we carrying this macho independence thing too far: *blind people can do anything, so why ask for help in the face of death?* To my relief, I heard a siren—apparently a passing motorist had called 911 anyway—and within seconds paramedics had pulled up. They loaded Finn into the van, sped off to the hospital, and that was the last I saw of him.

Until later that afternoon, when my big brother strolled into the center bitching about them cutting off his Harley shirt so they could give him injections. "Shit, man," he said in his gravelly voice, "that was my favorite shirt. But hey, I needed the shots. Oh well, gave up the bike and now the shirt. Fair trades for my life I guess."

Not surprisingly, the experience with Finn prompted some soul searching on my part: Would I have felt the same way if a sighted person had been there all along? Was I unable to trust someone's judgment merely because he was blind, and did this tap into my own lack of confidence, which I'd felt since childhood, the very thing that had brought me to the Colorado Center for the Blind in the first place? Or could my biker friend have been the victim of Dirk's NFB machismo, his need to prove that blind people could survive on their own? If this was so, then blindness could have killed Finn—not because it made him pathetic and powerless but rather because someone had selfishly sought to prove that blindness was *not* these things. Could I trust Dirk not to make me a martyr to the Cause by leaving me in a similar circumstance if I really needed help? Suppose the ambulance had not arrived when it did?

As much as I wanted to vilify him, I had tremendous respect for Dirk, who, it turned out, had been completely on target regarding Finn's situation. In fact, he had been on target about everything, just as he had been thorough, serious, and measured as a teacher. And ultimately I knew I had agreed to take certain risks by participating in the program to begin with; if I truly wanted to confront my worst fears about blindness, this was not the time to walk away.

With a strange combination of caution and renewed resolve, I threw myself back into my training. Once I could get a little distance, the experience taught me that the desire to be safe and the drive toward taking risks conflict with each other at the same time that they operate in tandem, not unlike our "masculine" and "feminine" sides. We humans must feel safe enough to take the risks that make life worth living. But at times we must also put ourselves in difficult, unfamiliar situations to find the safety we crave. Blindness—and perhaps other disabilities—puts this dynamic into a new perspective, forcing us to see how complex something like safety really is.

This is why, a few days later, when Dirk barked, "Okay, Doc, show us the way home!" I eagerly turned to lead him, Gavin, and Finn back to the center in time for lunch. I wanted to push past my fears of collapsing and struggling alone. I wanted to prove that I didn't have to be the helpless little blind girl who preferred to follow just to be sure I would be safe.

But simple resolve is never enough, as I learned all too quickly, for in my distraction and need to appear confident I missed some irregularity on the sidewalk and pitched forward, falling flat on my face. Thanks to the protection of the thick, foamy sleepshades, I had only a few minor cuts on my chin, lips, and hands, and a mouth full of gravel that I tried to remove with little delicate flicks of my tongue. "Just spit, Doc," Dirk said, almost tenderly. I hesitated. Good girls don't spit, especially not good little blind ones who have no way of knowing where it might go. "Well, Doc, what are you waiting for, the Red Sox to win the World Series?" Clearly now I had no choice but to gather up the full contents in my mouth and let it fly. "Hell, woman!" he exclaimed, "I believe you just spat on my cane!"

Later in our travels, Dirk's cane, which he said with pride had been held together with his infamous duct tape, finally split in two. "I've put hundreds of miles on this baby, all kinds of weather, all kinds of streets," he said with what could only have been nostalgia. "Now the old duct tape won't even hold her." He guided each of our hands to the damaged portion so we could see how well it had held up until the bitter end. When I asked Dirk if he would miss that particular cane, he said, "Nah, I'll just get a new one and call it 'Widow-Maker,' the same thing as the one before and the one before that."

Heading home to the center, Gavin announced, "Hey, you've got some pretty powerful spit there, Cathy K."

"Positively *toxic*," Finn chipped in. "Took Dirk's cane clean apart!"

Dirk spat what I imagined to be a wad of well-chewed snuff into the street. "Not bad for a girl," he laughed, patting my shoulder, "not bad at all."

It all *did* come down to spit. Dirk, a sensitive guy who had experienced firsthand the fall from mainstream society's masculine grace, showed both men and women how to cast off our feminine selves to counter the stereotypes of helplessness triggered by the sight of a white cane. Even though I suspect that my teacher's macho approach to travel covered over real fears, I gladly took up his invitation to march across the gender line. But of course I could never be a man. Instead, if I wanted to emerge from the nongendered hinterlands to which the double stigma of femininity and blindness had banished me, I would have to make my way to some new place where I could consider different ideas for my feminine self. Holding my cane, I wondered what a woman could possibly do with one in public to make it her own in a way analogous to Dirk's Harley. There was always fashion. But even if a long, elegant cane seemed more chic than a short, stubby one that folded into pieces, I still wanted to strut and spit and fix my fragility with duct tape.

Okay, so maybe it *is* about the phallus.

But it's also about acting in the world. Each time I trudged through Denver's ice and snow, faced packs of roaring cars, and picked myself up from a spectacular fall, I confronted the fact that I choreographed my gendered role to ensure my survival. So if Dirk had taught me to perform a new part as a blind woman, who was my audience? And would this be a onetime show or a lifelong run?

Years later, as I wait at a corner with my white cane, I realize that as much as my CCB show was for the entire world, a poor little blind girl still sits in the front row. Pathetic, but wanting to be bold, she is the ghost I could finally embrace after completing blind boot camp. And she is not about blindness; she is the little girl that every woman carries within, as all of us—blind or sighted—face the same choice: when and how do we take risks to strike that delicate balance between living safely and being a prisoner of an abstract place known as "home"? Dirk helped me understand that because blindness exaggerates so many expectations and fears, the blind-girl-turned-woman who wants to live a "normal" life has to push especially hard, perhaps even playing with gender now and then. So with my teacher's voice ringing in my ears, I step into the street. And with the grace of an elegant diva, I flaunt my long white cane, knowing I can spit like the best of the bikers.

ACKNOWLEDGMENTS

Special thanks to Emily Abel, Tony Candela, Sumi Colligan, Rosemarie Garland-Thomson, Sandra Harding, Georgina Kleege, Kim Neilsen, Kate Norberg, the participants of the Cross-Cultural Group in Women's History at the University of California, Davis, and the organizers of the session at the American Anthropological Association Meeting in 2001, where I first presented this work. Above all, I thank the students and staff of the CCB, especially "Dirk," to whom I dedicate this essay. All names and some identifying details in this essay have been changed.

NOTES

1. This is a compilation of statements from various NFB pamphlets available at http://www.nfb.org/. For the CCB's take, go to: http://www.cocenter.org/.
2. Statistical data from the organizations that represent those who teach blind people to travel support my firsthand impressions. The current directory of the Academy for Certification of Vision Rehabilitation and Education Professionals (available at http://www.acvrep.org/directory .aspx) lists 1,977 orientation and mobility instructors, approximately 1,504 of whom are women (418 are men, and 35 are of indeterminate gender based on first names), while the National Federation of the Blind's National Orientation and Mobility Certification (NOMC) lists 39 certificate holders, 11 women and 28 men (e-mail correspondence with Ronald Ferguson, Chair, NOMC Examination Committee, May 25, 2004).

Theoretical Perspectives

Theory is simply an effort to understand and explain the social world. Theories of gender are attempts to outline the major processes and social structures that give rise to the differences and inequalities between women and men and to analyze how these gender inequalities are connected to other major inequalities of race, class, sexuality, and nationality. You may notice as you read some of these selections that the language of theory is a bit different from some other forms of writing. Some of these readings may seem "harder" to you. In fact, the language in some of them *is* more complex as the authors attempt to make sense of abstract and complicated social processes. We hope that you will not be intimidated by this. Every student is smart enough to understand "theory," and the effort you put into reading these works will be rewarded in two ways: You will grasp the fascinating and provocative ideas the authors put forward, and you will gain a sense of your own competence. We are all theorists of gender, after all, whether we construct our theories in formal academic language or in everyday discussions with friends.

One important distinction in feminist theory is between *sex*, or the biological characteristics of men and women, and *gender*, or the social statuses and meanings assigned to women and men. Gender is one of the most important social distinctions. Societies define men and women as separate and distinct categories, and gender- or sex-based stratification is ubiquitous. Even our physical bodies (what might be considered an aspect of *sex*, or biology) are shaped and interpreted through societies' focus on differences between women and men. For example, men

are widely considered to be stronger than women, despite the fact that men's physical strength is also affected by social practices such as weight-training or manual labor. Women are considered to be biologically "softer" and more delicate than men, but these characteristics are produced in part by social practices such as clothing, hairstyle, and the shaving of body hair. Although there are undeniably physical or biological attributes that differ between women and men (including, but not limited to, reproductive organs), the distinction between biological sex and social gender is far from clear-cut.

Another central tenet of feminist theory about gender is *intersectionality*—the recognition that gender is inextricably entwined with race, class, sexuality, nationality, and other major distinctions. We cannot think about gender in the abstract, apart from other distinctions, because gender takes different forms for different groups. The ways that gender inequality manifests itself in the lives of women from different racial group are not just quantitatively distinct—that is, it's not just that some groups are more unequal than others. The manifestations of gender inequality are qualitatively distinct—the particular expectations and forms of subordination are different. While the selections in Section 1 demonstrated intersectionality, the selections in Section 2 seek to articulate what it is and to explain how it works.

Gender is also more than a feature of individuals. Behaviors are gendered (aggressive, nurturing), traits (strong, delicate), and even objects (pink or blue clothes, children's toys, power tools and household gadgets). As we saw in the previous section, gender distinctions overlap with race, class, sexuality, disability, nationality, and other inequalities. Feminist scholars seek to understand how societies construct the meaning of being a woman or a man and how gender affects individual identities, the ways people interact with each other, the ways social institutions are organized, and inequality.

Explanations of gender inequality fall into two basic schools of thought: the essentialist and the social constructionist. The *essentialist* position holds that the behaviors of men and women are rooted in biological and genetic factors, including differences in hormonal patterns, physical size, aggressiveness, the propensity to "bond" with members of the same sex, and the capacity to bear children. For the essentialist, the sexual division of labor in human societies is rooted in the sexual determination that is found in all species, from ants to deer to primates. Viewing such differences as a natural outgrowth of human evolution, essentialists contend that sex-based differences in responsibilities and the natural superiority of the male are inevitable, functional, and necessary for the survival of the species.

The second school of thought, the *social constructionist*, bases its position on a growing body of historical and anthropological research that points to wide variations in gender behavior and in the sexual division of labor among human societies throughout history. Social constructionists contend that the diversity of cultural understandings of gender is too great to be explained by biological factors. Instead, they argue, male dominance appears to be inevitable only because cultural ideas and beliefs have arisen to justify and perpetuate sex-based stratification systems that entitle men to greater power, prestige, and wealth than women. While such ideologies do not cause gender inequality, they certainly justify it as natural.

Gender is simultaneously socially constructed— "made up," artificial, created by people out of quite flimsy bases—and very real in its ramifications for individuals and for society as a whole. The task of theorists of gender is to explain this contradiction and the means by which gender becomes "real." The readings in this section present various approaches to understanding gender and its construction. In "'Night to His Day': The Social Construction of Gender," Judith

Lorber outlines a social constructionist approach. She defines gender as a social institution that rests on the "socially constructed statuses" of "man" and "woman." Even the apparently dimorphic physical characteristics of the two sexes, Lorber argues, are socially interpreted and emphasized. How does the social institution of gender create *sameness* among members of each gender and *difference* between women and men? How are the genders ranked in a hierarchy that privileges men over women?

In "The Medical Construction of Gender," Suzanne Kessler illustrates the powerful role medicine plays in the social construction of the categories of male and female. Kessler challenges the notion that the biological distinctions between women and men are natural rather than subject to social construction. Drawing on interviews with medical experts who have had extensive clinical experience managing babies born with genitals that are neither clearly male nor clearly female, Kessler discusses the standard practices used by the medical establishment to define the gender of intersexed infants. The primary consideration in physicians' gender assignments and corrective surgery is the ability to construct correctly formed genitals, not the other potential gender markers such as chromosomes, hormones, or psychological factors. Kessler argues that the view that gender consists of two mutually exclusive types—female and male—is created by these medical practices, despite biological evidence of greater natural variation in actual gender markers. Do you agree with the medical view that gender must be assigned immediately, decisively, and irreversibly when an intersexed child is born? What role, if any, do you think social factors should play in making decisions about gender identity? What does Kessler's article suggest about the relationship (if any) between biological differences and societal gender systems?

Susan Stryker examines the relationship between sex and gender further in "Transgender Feminism: Queering the Woman Question." Defining "transgender phenomena" as "anything that disrupts or denaturalizes normative gender" and exposes the processes that produce the illusion of gender as natural, Stryker asks how thinking about transgender changes the way we think about feminism. She suggests that transgender helps us think about how bodies are used to justify inequality, and she questions the distinction between "sex" and "gender." Stryker critiques the parts of feminist theory and activism that accept the category "woman" as straightforward and unproblematic and that therefore see transgender questions as, at best, irrelevant. In contrast, she recounts her own experiences with various forms of oppression to illustrate that transgender experiences can shed light on a range of other important social phenomena, from gender and sexual discrimination, to the controlling role of medicine, to state surveillance, to violence and hate crimes. Further, she suggests, transgender issues are a key connection between feminism and "queer politics" because they focus our attention on the relationships between gender, bodies, and sexuality. In her conclusion, Stryker argues that "how we live in our bodies is a vital source of knowledge for us all." How is your own embodied experience shaped by the demands of sex and gender? How is this experience affected by the degree to which your body and sense of yourself conform to what "women" or "men" are supposed to be like?

Stryker suggests that it is hard to imagine a future in which justice around any rising issue or form of social change has prevailed. What are the "claims of justice" that transgender issues make upon us? Can you imagine what a world in which those transformations had occurred would be like?

In "Theorizing Difference from Multiracial Feminism," Maxine Baca Zinn and Bonnie Thornton Dill develop a model of how race, class, and gender are related to one another. In this model, race and other "differences" among women are central to the task of understanding gender. Arguing that these different forms of inequality intersect with one another in a "matrix of domination" (Hill Collins), Baca Zinn and Dill discuss how experiences of gender vary according to race and class. Their multiracial feminist perspective is relevant to the experiences of women and men of all races, because, they contend, categories of dominance and power are constructed in relationship to subordinate categories. As race, class, and gender intersect, they create both oppression and opportunity for various groups of people. Multiracial feminism is not simply a theory of inequality and oppression,

however. Baca Zinn and Dill argue that individuals exercise their own agency, resisting the social structures that attempt to restrict them and finding ways to live satisfying lives.

Can you apply the multiracial feminist perspective to some of the readings from Section 1, "Diversity and Difference"? Which of the readings take a multiracial feminist perspective, and what would that perspective add to the readings that do not? Can you analyze a currently relevant topic on your own campus or in your own community using a multiracial feminist perspective? How is this perspective different from other points of view on that topic? As you read the remaining selections in this volume, consider the ways in which they are informed by a multiracial feminist perspective.

Chandra Talpade Mohanty expands on this perspective in her discussion of the shifting categories of "Third World women," "feminism," and "Third World feminism," in "Feminism Without Borders." She aims to define Third World women in a way that does not present them as a unified group, with any single culture or racial category. Instead, Third World women are an internally diverse group brought together by shared political allegiances and opposition to racism and imperialism. Similarly, the relationship between Third World women and feminism is varied. Mohanty argues that feminist politics have too often been linked to racism and imperialism, and yet Third World women's political actions address multiple oppressions simultaneously, including gender oppression. In this, Mohanty suggests that Third World women take what Baca Zinn and Dill would call a multiracial feminist perspective. But Mohanty, writing almost a decade after Baca Zinn and Dill, focuses more strongly on how Third World women's position is constructed within a *global* context. For Mohanty, analyzing Third World feminist politics is important for understanding industrial and postindustrial countries and politics as well, because of changing connections among nations, the rise of international corporations, and the migration of people from the Third World to industrialized countries. How would Mohanty understand recent developments in international trade agreements? Can you identify some current events that reflect the transnationalism that she discusses? What is the position of women in these events? As you read later selections in this volume, particularly those in Section 10, try to apply Mohanty's perspective.

R. W. Connell follows Mohanty's concern with how transnationalism and gender affect each other. Focusing specifically on the forms of masculinity that characterize global capitalism, Connell argues in "Masculinities and Globalization" that masculinity is defined in different ways in different contexts and time periods. In contrast to theorists who see masculinity as having one single definition, Connell emphasizes how different versions of masculinity exist in relation to each other. In this view, some kinds of masculinity, which she calls "hegemonic masculinity," characterize more powerful men, and other kinds of masculinity characterize subordinated men. Although masculinities are constructed in specific contexts, Connell emphasizes that they are linked to a global gender order. This global gender order specifies divisions of labor among nations and individuals (through production, work, and trade), creates power relations between women and men and among different nations, structures emotions, and represents gender through culture. What examples does she give of the effects of the global gender order on local masculinities? Can

you come up with some additional examples? How are the masculinities that prevail in your own community shaped by global forces?

Connell outlines the gender order and the prevailing masculinities during three major global time periods: conquest and settlement, empire, and postcolonial or neoliberal. What does she see as the major forms of masculinity during each period? In the selection's final section, Connell discusses local variations on "transnational business masculinity." Look at articles or pictures in a newspaper for examples of transnational business masculinity, and consider the extent to which they represent a Western model. What possibilities for social change in the gender order does Connell identify, and what does she see as barriers to those changes?

As you consider the various ways of thinking about gender presented in these articles, with which do you agree? As you read the selections in the rest of the book, consider the questions raised here about what gender is; how extensively women share commonalities of oppression or experience; how gender intersects with other forms of inequality such as race, class, or nationality; and how gender is part of our cultural systems of meaning and our institutions and social structures.

"Night to His Day": The Social Construction of Gender

Talking about gender for most people is the equivalent of fish talking about water. Gender is so much the routine ground of everyday activities that questioning its taken-for-granted assumptions and presuppositions is like thinking about whether the sun will come up.[1] Gender is so pervasive that in our society we assume it is bred into our genes. Most people find it hard to believe that gender is constantly created and recreated out of human interaction, out of social life, and is the texture and order of that social life. Yet gender, like culture, is a human production that depends on everyone constantly "doing gender" (West and Zimmerman 1987).

And everyone "does gender" without thinking about it. Today, on the subway, I saw a well-dressed man with a year-old child in a stroller. Yesterday, on a bus, I saw a man with a tiny baby in a carrier on his chest. Seeing men taking care of small children in public is increasingly common—at least in New York City. But both men were quite obviously stared at—and smiled at, approvingly. Everyone was doing gender—the men who were changing the role of fathers and the other passengers, who were applauding them silently. But there was more gendering going on that probably fewer people noticed. The baby was wearing a white crocheted cap and white clothes. You couldn't tell if it was a boy or a girl. The child in the stroller was wearing a dark blue T-shirt and dark print pants. As they started to leave the train, the father put a Yankee baseball cap on the child's head. Ah, a boy, I thought. Then I noticed the gleam of tiny earrings in the child's ears, and as they got off, I saw the little flowered sneakers and lace-trimmed socks. Not a boy after all. Gender done.

Gender is such a familiar part of daily life that it usually takes a deliberate disruption of our expectations of how women and men are supposed to act to pay attention to how it is produced. Gender signs and signals are so ubiquitous that we usually fail to note them—unless they are missing or ambiguous. Then we are uncomfortable until we have successfully placed the other person in a gender status; otherwise, we feel socially dislocated. In our society, in addition to man and woman, the status can be *transvestite* (a person who dresses in opposite-gender clothes) and *transsexual* (a person who has had sex-change surgery). Transvestites and transsexuals carefully construct their gender status by dressing, speaking, walking, gesturing in the ways prescribed for women or men—whichever they want to be taken for—and so does any "normal" person.

For the individual, gender construction starts with assignment to a sex category on the basis of what the genitalia look like at birth.[2] Then babies are dressed or adorned in a way that displays the category because parents don't want to be constantly asked whether their baby is a girl or a boy. A sex category becomes a gender status through naming, dress, and the use of other gender markers. Once a child's gender is evident, others treat those in one gender differently from those in the other, and the children respond to the different treatment by feeling different and behaving differently. As soon as they can talk, they start to refer to themselves as members of their gender. Sex doesn't come into play again until puberty, but by that time, sexual feelings and desires and practices have been shaped by gendered norms and expectations. Adolescent boys and girls approach and avoid each other in an elaborately scripted and gendered mating dance. Parenting is gendered, with different expectations for mothers and for fathers, and people of different genders work at different kinds of jobs. The work adults do, as mothers and fathers and as low-level workers and high-level bosses, shapes women's and men's life experiences, and these experiences produce different feelings, consciousness, relationships, skills—ways of being that we call feminine or masculine.[3] All of these processes constitute the social construction of gender.

Gendered roles change—today fathers are taking care of little children, girls and boys are wearing unisex clothing and getting the same education, women and men are working at the same jobs. Although many traditional social groups are quite strict about maintaining gender differences, in other social groups they seem to be blurring. Then why the one-year-old's earrings? Why is it still so important to mark a child as a girl or a boy, to make sure she is not taken for a boy or he for a girl? What would happen if they were? They would, quite literally, have changed places in their social world.

To explain why gendering is done from birth, constantly and by everyone, we have to look not only at the way individuals experience gender but at gender as a social institution. As a social institution, gender is one of the major ways that human beings organize their lives. Human society depends on a predictable division of labor, a designated allocation of scarce goods, assigned responsibility for children and others who cannot care for themselves, common values and their systematic transmission to new members, legitimate leadership, music, art, stories, games, and other symbolic productions. One way of choosing people for the different tasks of society is on the basis of their talents, motivations, and competence—their demonstrated achievements. The other way is on the basis of gender, race, ethnicity—ascribed membership in a category of people. Although societies vary in the extent to which they use one or the other of these ways of allocating people to work and to carry out other responsibilities, every society uses gender and age grades. Every society classifies people as "girl and boy children," "girls and boys ready to be married," and "fully adult women and men," constructs similarities among them and differences between them, and assigns them to different roles and responsibilities. Personality characteristics, feelings, motivations, and ambitions flow from these different life experiences so that the members of these different groups become different kinds of people. The process of gendering and its outcome are legitimated by religion, law, science, and the society's entire set of values.

In order to understand gender as a social institution, it is important to distinguish human action from animal behavior. Animals feed themselves and their young until their young can feed themselves. Humans have to produce not only food but shelter and clothing.

They also, if the group is going to continue as a social group, have to teach the children how their particular group does these tasks. In the process, humans reproduce gender, family, kinship, and a division of labor—social institutions that do not exist among animals. Primate social groups have been referred to as families, and their mating patterns as monogamy, adultery, and harems. Primate behavior has been used to prove the universality of sex differences—as built into our evolutionary inheritance (Haraway 1978). But animals' sex differences are not at all the same as humans' gender differences; animals' bonding is not kinship; animals' mating is not ordered by marriage; and animals' dominance hierarchies are not the equivalent of human stratification systems. Animals group on sex and age, relational categories that are physiologically, not socially, different. Humans create gender and age-group categories that are socially, and not necessarily physiologically, different.[4]

For animals, physiological maturity means being able to impregnate or conceive; its markers are coming into heat (estrus) and sexual attraction. For humans, puberty means being available for marriage; it is marked by rites that demonstrate this marital eligibility. Although the onset of physiological puberty is signaled by secondary sex characteristics (menstruation, breast development, sperm ejaculation, pubic and underarm hair), the onset of social adulthood is ritualized by the coming-out party or desert walkabout or bar mitzvah or graduation from college or first successful hunt or dreaming or inheritance of property. Humans have rituals that mark the passage from childhood into puberty and puberty into full adult status, as well as for marriage, childbirth, and death; animals do not (van Gennep 1960). To the extent that infants and the dead are differentiated by whether they are male or female, there are different birth rituals for girls and boys and different funeral rituals for men and women (Biersack 1984, 132–33). Rituals of puberty, marriage, and becoming a parent are gendered, creating a "woman," a "man," a "bride," a "groom," a "mother," a "father." Animals have no equivalents for these statuses.

Among animals, siblings mate and so do parents and children; humans have incest taboos and rules that encourage or forbid mating between members of different kin groups (Lévi-Strauss 1956, [1949] 1969). Any animal of the same species may feed another's young (or may not, depending on the species). Humans designate responsibility for particular children by kinship; humans frequently limit responsibility for children to the members of their kinship group or make them into members of their kinship group with adoption rituals.

Animals have dominance hierarchies based on size or on successful threat gestures and signals. These hierarchies are usually sexed, and in some species, moving to the top of the hierarchy physically changes the sex (Austad 1986). Humans have stratification patterns based on control of surplus food, ownership of property, legitimate demands on others' work and sexual services, enforced determinations of who marries whom, and approved use of violence. If a woman replaces a man at the top of a stratification hierarchy, her social status may be that of a man, but her sex does not change.

Mating, feeding, and nurturant behavior in animals is determined by instinct and imitative learning and ordered by physiological sex and age (Lancaster 1974). In humans, these behaviors are taught and symbolically reinforced and ordered by socially constructed gender and age grades. Social gender and age statuses sometimes ignore or override physiological sex and age completely. Male and female animals (unless they physiologically change) are not interchangeable; infant animals cannot take the place of adult animals. Human females can become husbands and fathers, and human males can become wives and mothers, without sex-change surgery (Blackwood 1984). Human infants can reign as kings or queens.

Western society's values legitimate gendering by claiming that it all comes from physiology—female and male procreative differences. But gender and sex are not equivalent, and gender as a social construction does not flow automatically from genitalia and reproductive organs, the main physiological differences of females and males. In the construction of ascribed social statuses, physiological differences such as sex, stage of development, color of skin, and size are crude markers. They are not the source of the social statuses of gender, age grade, and race. Social statuses are carefully constructed through prescribed processes of teaching, learning, emulation, and enforcement. Whatever genes, hormones, and biological evolution contribute to human social institutions is materially as well as qualitatively transformed by social practices. Every social institution has a material base, but culture and social practices transform that base into something with qualitatively different patterns and constraints. The economy is much more than producing food and goods and distributing them to eaters and users; family and kinship are not the equivalent of having sex and procreating; morals and religions cannot be equated with the fears and ecstasies of the brain; language goes far beyond the sounds produced by tongue and larynx. No one eats "money" or "credit"; the concepts of "god" and "angels" are the subjects of theological disquisitions; not only words but objects, such as their flag, "speak" to the citizens of a country.

Similarly, gender cannot be equated with biological and physiological differences between human females and males. The building blocks of gender are *socially constructed statuses*. Western societies have only two genders, "man" and "woman." Some societies have three genders—men, women, and *berdaches* or *hijras* or *xaniths*. Berdaches, hijras, and xaniths are biological males who behave, dress, work, and are treated in most respects as social women; they are therefore not men, nor are they female women; they are, in our language, "male women."[5] There are African and American Indian societies that have a gender status called *manly hearted women*—biological females who work, marry, and parent as men; their social status is "female men" (Amadiume 1987; Blackwood 1984). They do not have to behave or dress as men to have the social responsibilities and prerogatives of husbands and fathers; what makes them men is enough wealth to buy a wife.

Modern Western societies' *transsexuals* and *transvestites* are the nearest equivalent of these crossover genders, but they are not institutionalized as third genders (Bolin 1987). Transsexuals are biological males and females who have sex-change operations to alter their genitalia. They do so in order to bring their physical anatomy into congruence with the way they want to live and with their own sense of gender identity. They do not become a third gender; they change genders. Transvestites are males who live as women and females who live as men but do not intend to have sex-change surgery. Their dress, appearance, and mannerisms fall within the range of what is expected from members of the opposite gender, so that they "pass." They also change genders, sometimes temporarily, some for most of their lives. Transvestite women have fought in wars as men soldiers as recently as the nineteenth century; some married women, and others went back to being women and married men once the war was over.[6] Some were discovered when their wounds were treated; others not until they died. In order to work as a jazz musician, a man's occupation, Billy Tipton, a woman, lived most of her life as a man. She died recently at seventy-four, leaving a wife and three adopted sons for whom she was husband and father, and musicians with whom she had played and traveled, for whom she was "one of the boys" (*New York Times* 1989).[7] There have been many other such occurrences of women passing as men to do more prestigious or lucrative men's work (Matthaci 1982, 192–93).[8]

Genders, therefore, are not attached to a biological substratum. Gender boundaries are breachable, and individual and socially organized shifts from one gender to another call attention to "cultural, social, or aesthetic dissonances" (Garber 1992, 16). These odd or deviant or third genders show us what we ordinarily take for granted—that people have to learn to be women and men. Men who cross-dress for performances or for pleasure often learn from women's magazines how to "do femininity" convincingly (Garber 1992, 41–51). Because transvestism is direct evidence of how gender is constructed, Marjorie Garber claims it has "extraordinary power . . . to disrupt, expose, and challenge, putting in question the very notion of the 'original' and of stable identity" (1992, 16).

GENDER BENDING

It is difficult to see how gender is constructed because we take it for granted that it's all biology, or hormones, or human nature. The differences between women and men seem to be self-evident, and we think they would occur no matter what society did. But in actuality, human females and males are physiologically more similar in appearance than are the two sexes of many species of animals and are more alike than different in traits and behavior (Epstein 1988). Without the deliberate use of gendered clothing, hairstyles, jewelry, and cosmetics, women and men would look far more alike.[9] Even societies that do not cover women's breasts have gender-identifying clothing, scarification, jewelry, and hairstyles.

The ease with which many transvestite women pass as men and transvestite men as women is corroborated by the common gender misidentification in Westernized societies of people in jeans, T-shirts, and sneakers. Men with long hair may be addressed as "miss," and women with short hair are often taken for men unless they offset the potential ambiguity with deliberate gender markers (Devor 1987, 1989). Jan Morris, in *Conundrum,* an autobiographical account of events just before and just after a sex-change operation, described how easy it was to shift back and forth from being a man to being a woman when testing how it would feel

to change gender status. During this time, Morris still had a penis and wore more or less unisex clothing; the context alone made the man and the woman:

> Sometimes the arena of my ambivalence was uncomfortably small. At the Travellers' Club, for example, I was obviously known as a man of sorts—women were only allowed on the premises at all during a few hours of the day, and even then were hidden away as far as possible in lesser rooms or alcoves. But I had another club, only a few hundred yards away, where I was known only as a woman, and often I went directly from one to the other, imperceptibly changing roles on the way—"Cheerio, sir," the porter would say at one club, and "Hello, madam," the porter would greet me at the other. (1975, 132)

Gender shifts are actually a common phenomenon in public roles as well. Queen Elizabeth II of England bore children, but when she went to Saudi Arabia on a state visit, she was considered an honorary man so that she could confer and dine with the men who were heads of a state that forbids unrelated men and women to have face-to-unveiled-face contact. In contemporary Egypt, lower-class women who run restaurants or shops dress in men's clothing and engage in unfeminine aggressive behavior, and middle-class educated women of professional or managerial status can take positions of authority (Rugh 1986, 131). In these situations, there is an important status change: These women are treated by the others in the situation as if they are men. From their own point of view, they are still women. From the social perspective, however, they are men.[10]

In many cultures, gender bending is prevalent in theater or dance—the Japanese kabuki are men actors who play both women and men; in Shakespeare's theater company, there were no actresses—Juliet and Lady Macbeth were played by boys. Shakespeare's comedies are full of witty comments on gender shifts. Women characters frequently masquerade as young men, and other women characters fall in love with them; the boys playing these masquerading women meanwhile, are acting out pining for the love of men characters.[11] In *As You Like It*, when Rosalind justifies her protective cross-dressing, Shakespeare also comments on manliness:

> *Were it not better,*
> *Because that I am more than common tall,*
> *That I did suit me all points like a man:*
> *A gallant curtle-axe upon my thigh,*

A boar-spear in my hand, and in my heart
Lie there what hidden women's fear there will,
We'll have a swashing and martial outside,
As many other mannish cowards have
That do outface it with their semblances.

(I, i, 115–22)

Shakespeare's audience could appreciate the double subtext: Rosalind, a woman character, was a boy dressed in girl's clothing who then dressed as a boy; like bravery, masculinity and femininity can be put on and taken off with changes of costume and role (Howard 1988, 435).[12]

M Butterfly is a modern play of gender ambiguities, which David Hwang (1989) based on a real person. Shi Peipu, a male Chinese opera singer who sang women's roles, was a spy as a man and the lover as a woman of a Frenchman, Gallimard, a diplomat (Bernstein 1986). The relationship lasted twenty years, and Shi Peipu even pretended to be the mother of a child by Gallimard. "She" also pretended to be too shy to undress completely. As "Butterfly," Shi Peipu portrayed a fantasy Oriental woman who made the lover a "real man" (Kondo 1990b). In Gallimard's words, the fantasy was "of slender women in chong sams and kimonos who die for the love of unworthy foreign devils. Who are born and raised to be perfect women. Who take whatever punishment we give them, and bounce back, strengthened by love, unconditionally" (Hwang 1989, 91). When the fantasy woman betrayed him by turning out to be the more powerful "real man," Gallimard assumed the role of Butterfly and, dressed in a geisha's robes, killed himself: "because 'man' and 'woman' are oppositionally defined terms, reversals . . . are possible" (Kondo 1990b, 18).[13]

But despite the ease with which gender boundaries can be traversed in work, in social relationships, and in cultural productions, gender statuses remain. Transvestites and transsexuals do not challenge the social construction of gender. Their goal is to be feminine women and masculine men (Kando 1973). Those who do not want to change their anatomy but do want to change their gender behavior fare less well in establishing their social identity. The women Holly Devor called "gender blenders" wore their hair short, dressed in unisex pants, shirts, and comfortable shoes, and did not wear jewelry or makeup. They described their everyday dress as women's clothing: One said, "I wore jeans all the time, but I didn't wear men's clothes"

(Devor 1989, 100). Their gender identity was women, but because they refused to "do femininity," they were constantly taken for men (1987, 1989, 107–42). Devor said of them: "The most common area of complaint was with public washrooms. They repeatedly spoke of the humiliation of being challenged or ejected from women's washrooms. Similarly, they found public change rooms to be dangerous territory and the buying of undergarments to be a difficult feat to accomplish" (1987, 29). In an ultimate ironic twist, some of these women said "they would feel like transvestites if they were to wear dresses, and two women said that they had been called transvestites when they had done so" (1987, 31). They resolved the ambiguity of their gender status by identifying as women in private and passing as men in public to avoid harassment on the street, to get men's jobs, and, if they were lesbians, to make it easier to display affection publicly with their lovers (Devor 1989, 107–42). Sometimes they even used men's bathrooms. When they had gender-neutral names, like Leslie, they could avoid the bureaucratic hassles that arose when they had to present their passports or other proof of identity, but because most had names associated with women, their appearance and their cards of identity were not conventionally congruent, and their gender status was in constant jeopardy.[14] When they could, they found it easier to pass as men than to try to change the stereotyped notions of what women should look like.

Paradoxically, then, bending gender rules and passing between genders do not erode but rather preserve gender boundaries. In societies with only two genders, the gender dichotomy is not disturbed by transvestites, because others feel that a transvestite is only transitorily ambiguous—is "really a man or woman underneath." After sex-change surgery, transsexuals end up in a conventional gender status—a "man" or a "woman" with the appropriate genitals (Eichler 1989). When women dress as men for business reasons, they are indicating that in that situation, they want to be treated the way men are treated; when they dress as women, they want to be treated as women:

By their male dress, female entrepreneurs signal their desire to suspend the expectations of accepted feminine conduct without losing respect and reputation. By wearing what is "unattractive" they signify that they are not intending to display their physical charms while engaging in public activity. Their loud, aggressive banter contrasts with the modest demeanor that attracts men. . . . Overt signalling of a suspension of the rules preserves normal conduct from eroding expectations. (Rugh 1986, 131)

FOR INDIVIDUALS, GENDER MEANS SAMENESS

Although the possible combinations of genitalia, body shapes, clothing, mannerisms, sexuality, and roles could produce infinite varieties in human beings, the social institution of gender depends on the production and maintenance of a limited number of gender statuses and of making the members of these statuses similar to each other. Individuals are born sexed but not gendered, and they have to be taught to be masculine or feminine.[15] As Simone de Beauvoir said: "One is not born, but rather becomes, a woman . . . ; it is civilization as a whole that produces this creature . . . which is described as feminine" (1952, 267).

Children learn to walk, talk, and gesture the way their social group says girls and boys should. Ray Birdwhistell, in his analysis of body motion as human communication, calls these learned gender displays *tertiary sex characteristics* and argues that they are needed to distinguish genders because humans are a weakly dimorphic species—their only sex markers are genitalia (1970, 39–46). Clothing, paradoxically, often hides the sex but displays the gender.

In early childhood, humans develop gendered personality structures and sexual orientations through their interactions with parents of the same and opposite gender. As adolescents, they conduct their sexual behavior according to gendered scripts. Schools, parents, peers, and the mass media guide young people into gendered work and family roles. As adults, they take on a gendered social status in their society's stratification system. Gender is thus both ascribed and achieved (West and Zimmerman 1987). . . .

People go along with the imposition of gender norms because the weight of morality as well as immediate social pressure enforces them. Consider how many instructions for properly gendered behavior are packed into this mother's admonition to her daughter: "This is how to hem a dress when you see the hem coming down and so to prevent yourself from looking like the slut I know you are so bent on becoming" (Kincaid 1978).

Gender norms are inscribed in the way people move, gesture, and even eat. In one African society, men were supposed to eat with their "whole mouth, wholeheartedly, and not, like women, just with the lips, that is halfheartedly, with reservation and restraint" (Bourdieu [1980] 1990, 70). Men and women in this society learned to walk in ways that proclaimed their different positions in the society:

The manly man . . . stands up straight into the face of the person he approaches, or wishes to welcome. Ever on the alert, because ever threatened, he misses nothing of what happens around him. . . . Conversely, a well brought-up woman . . . is expected to walk with a slight stoop, avoiding every misplaced movement of her body, her head or her arms, looking down, keeping her eyes on the spot where she will next put her foot, especially if she happens to have to walk past the men's assembly. (70)

Many cultures go beyond clothing, gestures, and demeanor in gendering children. They inscribe gender directly into bodies. In traditional Chinese society, mothers bound their daughters' feet into three-inch stumps to enhance their sexual attractiveness. Jewish fathers circumcise their infant sons to show their covenant with God. Women in African societies remove the clitoris of prepubescent girls, scrape their labia, and make the lips grow together to preserve their chastity and ensure their marriageability. In Western societies, women augment their breast size with silicone and reconstruct their faces with cosmetic surgery to conform to cultural ideals of feminine beauty. Hanna Papanek (1979) notes that these practices reinforce the sense of superiority or inferiority in the adults who carry them out as well as in the children on whom they are done: The genitals of Jewish fathers and sons are physical and psychological evidence of their common dominant religious and familial status; the genitals of African mothers and daughters are physical and psychological evidence of their joint subordination.[16]

Sandra Bem (1981, 1983) argues that because gender is a powerful "schema" that orders the cognitive world, one must wage a constant, active battle for a child not to fall into typical gendered attitudes and behavior. In 1972, *Ms.* magazine published Lois Gould's fantasy of how to raise a child free of gender-typing. The experiment calls for hiding the child's anatomy from all eyes except the parents' and treating the child as neither a girl nor a boy. The child, called X, gets to do all the things boys *and* girls do. The experiment is so successful that all the children in X's class at school want to look and behave like X. At the end of the story, the creators of the experiment are asked what will happen when X grows up. The scientists' answer is that by then it will be quite clear what X is, implying that its hormones will kick in and it will be revealed as a female or male. That ambiguous, and somewhat contradictory, ending lets Gould off the hook; neither she nor we have any idea what someone brought up totally androgynously would be like sexually or socially as an adult. The hormonal input will not create gender or sexuality but will only establish secondary sex characteristics; breasts, beards, and menstruation alone do not produce social manhood or womanhood. Indeed, it is at puberty, when sex characteristics become evident, that most societies put pubescent children through their most important rites of passage, the rituals that officially mark them as fully gendered—that is, ready to marry and become adults.

Most parents create a gendered world for their newborn by naming, birth announcements, and dress. Children's relationships with same-gendered and different-gendered caretakers structure their self-identifications and personalities. Through cognitive development, children extract and apply to their own actions the appropriate behavior for those who belong in their own gender, as well as race, religion, ethnic group, and social class, rejecting what is not appropriate. If their social categories are highly valued, they value themselves highly; if their social categories are low status, they lose self-esteem (Chodorow 1974). Many feminist parents who want to raise androgynous children soon lose their children to the pull of gendered norms (Gordon 1990, 87–90). My son attended a carefully nonsexist elementary school, which didn't even have girls' and boys' bathrooms. When he was seven or eight years old, I attended a class play about "squares" and "circles" and their need for each other and noticed that all the girl squares and circles wore makeup, but none of the boy squares and circles did. I asked the teacher about it after the play, and she said, "Bobby said he was not going to wear makeup, and he is a powerful child, so none of the boys would either." In a long discussion about conformity, my son confronted me with the question of who the conformists were, the boys who followed their leader or the girls who listened to the woman teacher. In actuality, they both were, because they both followed same-gender leaders and acted in gender-appropriate ways. (Actors may wear makeup, but real boys don't.)

For human beings there is no essential femaleness or maleness, femininity or masculinity, womanhood or

manhood, but once gender is ascribed, the social order constructs and holds individuals to strongly gendered norms and expectations. Individuals may vary on many of the components of gender and may shift genders temporarily or permanently, but they must fit into the limited number of gender statuses their society recognizes. In the process, they recreate their society's version of women and men: "If we do gender appropriately, we simultaneously sustain, reproduce, and render legitimate the institutional arrangements. . . . If we fail to do gender appropriately, we as individuals—not the institutional arrangements—may be called to account (for our character, motives, and predispositions)" (West and Zimmerman 1987, 146).

> The gendered practices of everyday life reproduce a society's view of how women and men should act (Bourdieu [1980] 1990). Gendered social arrangements are justified by religion and cultural productions and backed by law, but the most powerful means of sustaining the moral hegemony of the dominant gender ideology is that the process is made invisible; any possible alternatives are virtually unthinkable. (Foucault 1972; Gramsci 1971)[17]

FOR SOCIETY, GENDER MEANS DIFFERENCE

The pervasiveness of gender as a way of structuring social life demands that gender statuses be clearly differentiated. Varied talents, sexual preferences, identities, personalities, interests, and ways of interacting fragment the individual's bodily and social experiences. Nonetheless, these are organized in Western cultures into two and only two socially and legally recognized gender statuses, "man" and "woman."[18] In the social construction of gender, it does not matter what men and women actually do; it does not even matter if they do exactly the same thing. The social institution of gender insists only that what they do is *perceived* as different.

If men and women are doing the same tasks, they are usually spatially segregated to maintain gender separation, and often the tasks are given different job titles as well, such as executive secretary and administrative assistant (Reskin 1988). If the differences between women and men begin to blur, society's "sameness taboo" goes into action (G. Rubin 1975, 178). At a rock-and-roll dance at West Point in 1976, the year women were admitted to the prestigious military academy for the first time, the school's administrators "were reportedly perturbed by the sight of mirror-image couples dancing in short hair and dress gray trousers," and a rule was established that women cadets could dance at these events only if they wore skirts (Barkalow and Raab 1990, 53).[19] Women recruits in the U.S. Marine Corps are required to wear makeup—at a minimum, lipstick and eye shadow—and they have to take classes in makeup, hair care, poise, and etiquette. This feminization is part of a deliberate policy of making them clearly distinguishable from men Marines. Christine Williams quotes a twenty-five-year-old woman drill instructor as saying: "A lot of the recruits who come here don't wear makeup; they're tomboyish or athletic. A lot of them have the preconceived idea that going into the military means they can still be a tomboy. They don't realize that you are a *Woman* Marine" (1989, 76–77).[20]

If gender differences were genetic, physiological, or hormonal, gender bending and gender ambiguity would occur only in hermaphrodites, who are born with chromosomes and genitalia that are not clearly female or male. Since gender differences are socially constructed, all men and all women can enact the behavior of the other, because they know the other's social script: "'Man' and 'woman' are at once empty and overflowing categories. Empty because they have no ultimate, transcendental meaning. Overflowing because even when they appear to be fixed, they still contain within them alternative, denied, or suppressed definitions" (Scott 1988, 49). Nonetheless, though individuals may be able to shift gender statuses, the gender boundaries have to hold, or the whole gendered social order will come crashing down.

Paradoxically, it is the social importance of gender statuses and their external markers—clothing, mannerisms, and spatial segregation—that makes gender bending or gender crossing possible—or even necessary. The social viability of differentiated gender statuses produces the need or desire to shift statuses. Without gender differentiation, transvestism and transsexuality would be meaningless. You couldn't dress in the opposite gender's clothing if all clothing were unisex. There would be no need to reconstruct genitalia to match identity if interests and lifestyles were not gendered. There would be no need for women to pass as men to do certain kinds of work if jobs were not typed as "women's work" and "men's work." Women would not have to dress as men in public life in order to give orders or aggressively bargain with customers.

Gender boundaries are preserved when transsexuals create congruous autobiographies of always having felt like what they are now. The transvestite's story also "recuperates social and sexual norms" (Garber 1992, 69). In the transvestite's normalized narrative, he or she "is 'compelled' by social and economic forces to disguise himself or herself in order to get a job, escape repression, or gain artistic or political 'freedom'" (Garber 1992, 70). The "true identity," when revealed, causes amazement over how easily and successfully the person passed as a member of the opposite gender, not a suspicion that gender itself is something of a put-on.

GENDER RANKING

Most societies rank genders according to prestige and power and construct them to be unequal, so that moving from one to another also means moving up or down the social scale. Among some North American Indian cultures, the hierarchy was male men, male women, female men, female women. Women produced significant durable goods (basketry, textiles, pottery, decorated leather goods), which could be traded. Women also controlled what they produced and any profit or wealth they earned. Since women's occupational realm could lead to prosperity and prestige, it was fair game for young men—but only if they became women in gender status. Similarly, women in other societies who amassed a great deal of wealth were allowed to become men—"manly hearts." According to Harriet Whitehead (1982):

> Both reactions reveal an unwillingness or inability to distinguish the sources of prestige—wealth, skill, personal efficacy (among other things)—from masculinity. Rather there is the innuendo that if a person performing female tasks can attain excellence, prosperity, or social power, it must be because that person is, at some level, a man. . . . A woman who could succeed at doing the things men did was honored as a man would be. . . . What seems to have been more disturbing to the culture—which means, for all intents and purposes, to the men—was the possibility that women, within their own department, might be onto a good thing. It was into this unsettling breach that the berdache institution was hurled. In their social aspect, women were complimented by the berdache's imitation. In their anatomic aspect, they were subtly insulted by his vaunted superiority. (108)

In American society, men-to-women transsexuals tend to earn less after surgery if they change occupations; women-to-men transsexuals tend to increase their income (Bolin 1988, 153–60; Brody 1979). Men who go into women's fields, like nursing, have less prestige than women who go into men's fields, like physics. Janice Raymond, a radical feminist, feels that transsexual men-to-women have advantages over female women because they were not socialized to be subordinate or oppressed throughout life. She says:

> We know that we are women who are born with female chromosomes and anatomy, and that whether or not we were socialized to be so-called normal women, patriarchy has treated and will treat us like women. Transsexuals have not had this same history. No man can have the history of being born and located in this culture as a woman. He can have the history of *wishing* to be a woman and of *acting* like a woman, but this gender experience is that of a transsexual, not of a woman. Surgery may confer the artifacts of outward and inward female organs but it cannot confer the history of being born a woman in this society. (1979, 114)

Because women who become men rise in the world and men who become women fall, Elaine Showalter (1987) was very critical of the movie *Tootsie,* in which Dustin Hoffman plays an actor who passes as a woman in order to be able to get work. "Dorothy" becomes a feminist "woman of the year" for standing up for women's rights not to be demeaned or sexually harassed. Showalter feels that the message of the movie is double-edged: "Dorothy's 'feminist' speeches . . . are less a response to the oppression of women than an instinctive situational male reaction to being treated like a woman. The implication is that women must be taught by men how to win their rights. . . . It says that feminist ideas are much less threatening when they come from a man" (123). Like Raymond, Showalter feels that being or having been a man gives a transsexual man-to-woman or a man cross-dressed as a woman a social advantage over those whose gender status was always "woman."[21] The implication here is that there is an experiential superiority that doesn't disappear with the gender shift.

For one transsexual man-to-woman, however, the experience of living as a woman changed his/her whole personality. As James, Morris had been a soldier,

foreign correspondent, and mountain climber; as Jan, Morris is a successful travel writer. But socially, James was far superior to Jan, and so Jan developed the "learned helplessness" that is supposed to characterize women in Western society:

> We are told that the social gap between the sexes is narrowing, but I can only report that having, in the second half of the twentieth century, experienced life in both roles, there seems to me no aspect of existence, no moment of the day, no contact, no arrangement, no response, which is not different for men and for women. The very tone of voice in which I was now addressed, the very posture of the person next in the queue, the very feel in the air when I entered a room or sat at a restaurant table, constantly emphasized my change of status.

> And if other's responses shifted, so did my own. The more I was treated as woman, the more woman I became. I adapted willy-nilly. If I was assumed to be incompetent at reversing cars, or opening bottles, oddly incompetent I found myself becoming. If a case was thought too heavy for me, inexplicably I found it so myself. . . . Women treated me with a frankness which, while it was one of the happiest discoveries of my metamorphosis, did imply membership of a camp, a faction, or at least a school of thought; so I found myself gravitating always towards the female, whether in sharing a railway compartment or supporting a political cause. Men treated me more and more as junior, . . . and so, addressed every day of my life as an inferior, involuntarily, month by month I accepted the condition. I discovered that even now men prefer women to be less informed, less able, less talkative, and certainly less self-centered than they are themselves; so I generally obliged them. (1975, 165–66)[22]

COMPONENTS OF GENDER

By now, it should be clear that gender is not a unitary essence but has many components as a social institution and as an individual status.[23]

As a social institution, gender is composed of:

Gender statuses, the socially recognized genders in a society and the norms and expectations for their enactment behaviorally, gesturally, linguistically, emotionally, and physically. How gender statuses are evaluated depends on historical development in any particular society.

Gendered division of labor, the assignment of productive and domestic work to members of different gender statuses. The work assigned to those of different gender statuses strengthens the society's evaluation of those statuses—the higher the status, the more prestigious and valued the work and the greater its rewards.

Gendered kinship, the family rights and responsibilities for each gender status. Kinship statuses reflect and reinforce the prestige and power differences of the different genders.

Gendered sexual scripts, the normative patterns of sexual desire and sexual behavior, as prescribed for the different gender statuses. Members of the dominant gender have more sexual prerogatives; members of a subordinate gender may be sexually exploited.

Gendered personalities, the combinations of traits patterned by gender norms of how members of different gender statuses are supposed to feel and behave. Social expectations of others in face-to-face interaction constantly bolster these norms.

Gendered social control, the formal and informal approval and reward of conforming behavior and the stigmatization, social isolation, punishment, and medical treatment of nonconforming behavior.

Gender ideology, the justification of gender statuses, particularly, their differential evaluation. The dominant ideology tends to suppress criticism by making these evaluations seem natural.

Gender imagery, the cultural representations of gender and embodiment of gender in symbolic language and artistic productions that reproduce and legitimate gender statuses. Culture is one of the main supports of the dominant gender ideology.

For an individual, gender is composed of:

Sex category, to which the infant is assigned at birth based on appearance of genitalia. With prenatal testing and sex-typing, categorization is prenatal. Sex category may be changed later through surgery or reinspection of ambiguous genitalia.

Gender identity, the individual's sense of gendered self as a worker and family member.

Gendered marital and procreative status, fulfillment or nonfulfillment of allowed or disallowed mating, impregnation, childbearing, kinship roles.

Gendered sexual orientation, socially and individually patterned sexual desires, feelings, practices, and identification.

Gendered personality, internalized patterns of socially normative emotions as organized by family structure and parenting.

Gendered processes, the social practices of learning, being taught, picking up cues, enacting behavior already learned to be gender appropriate (or inappropriate, if rebelling, testing), developing a gender identity, "doing gender" as a member of a gender status in relationships with gendered others, acting deferent or dominant.

Gender beliefs, incorporation of or resistance to gender ideology.

Gender display, presentation of self as a certain kind of gendered person through dress, cosmetics, adornments, and permanent and reversible body markers.

For an individual, all the social components are supposed to be consistent and congruent with perceived physiology. The actual combination of genes and genitalia, prenatal, adolescent, and adult hormonal input, and procreative capacity may or may not be congruous with each other and with sex-category assignment, gender identity, gendered sexual orientation and procreative status, gender display, personality, and work and family roles. At any one time, an individual's identity is a combination of the major ascribed statuses of gender, race, ethnicity, religion, and social class, and the individual's achieved statuses, such as education level, occupation or profession, marital status, parenthood, prestige, authority, and wealth. The ascribed statuses substantially limit or create opportunities for individual achievements and also diminish or enhance the luster of those achievements.

GENDER AS PROCESS, STRATIFICATION, AND STRUCTURE

As a social institution, gender is a process of creating distinguishable social statuses for the assignment of rights and responsibilities. As part of a stratification system that ranks these statuses unequally, gender is a major building block in the social structures built on these unequal statuses.

As a *process*, gender creates the social differences that define "woman" and "man." In social interaction throughout their lives, individuals learn what is expected, see what is expected, act and react in expected ways, and thus simultaneously construct and maintain the gender order: "The very injunction to be a given gender takes place through discursive routes: to be a good mother, to be a heterosexually desirable object, to be a fit worker, in sum, to signify a multiplicity of guarantees in response to a variety of different demands all at once" (Butler 1990, 145). Members of a social group neither make up gender as they go along nor exactly replicate in rote fashion what was done before. In almost every encounter, human beings produce gender, behaving in the ways they learned were appropriate for their gender status, or resisting or rebelling against these norms. Resistance and rebellion have altered gender norms, but so far they have rarely eroded the statuses.

Gendered patterns of interaction acquire additional layers of gendered sexuality, parenting, and work behaviors in childhood, adolescence, and adulthood. Gendered norms and expectations are enforced through informal sanctions of gender-inappropriate behavior by peers and by formal punishment or threat of punishment by those in authority should behavior deviate too far from socially imposed standards for women and men.

Everyday gendered interactions build gender into the family, the work process, and other organizations and institutions, which in turn reinforce gender expectations for individuals.[24] Because gender is a process, there is room not only for modification and variation by individuals and small groups but also for institutionalized change (Scott 1988, 7).

As part of a *stratification* system, gender ranks men above women of the same race and class. Women and men could be different but equal. In practice, the process of creating difference depends to a great extent on differential evaluation. As Nancy Jay (1981) says: "That which is defined, separated out, isolated from all else is A and pure. Not-A is necessarily impure, a random catchall, to which nothing is external except A and the principle of order that separates it from Not-A" (45). From the individual's point of view, whichever gender is A, the other is Not-A; gender boundaries tell the individual who is like him or her, and all the rest are unlike. From society's point of view, however, one

gender is usually the touchstone, the normal, the dominant, and the other is different, deviant, and subordinate. In Western society, "man" is A, "wo-man" is Not-A. (Consider what a society would be like where woman was A and man Not-A.)

The further dichotomization by race and class constructs the gradations of a heterogeneous society's stratification scheme. Thus, in the United States, white is A, African American is Not-A; middle class is A, working class is Not-A, and "African-American women occupy a position whereby the inferior half of a series of these dichotomies converge" (Collins 1990, 70). The dominant categories are the hegemonic ideals, taken so for granted as the way things should be that white is not ordinarily thought of as a race, middle class as a class, or men as a gender. The characteristics of these categories define the Other as that which lacks the valuable qualities the dominants exhibit.

In a gender-stratified society, what men do is usually valued more highly than what women do because men do it, even when their activities are very similar or the same. In different regions of southern India, for example, harvesting rice is men's work, shared work, or women's work: "Wherever a task is done by women it is considered easy, and where it is done by [men] it is considered difficult" (Mencher 1988, 104). A gathering and hunting society's survival usually depends on the nuts, grubs, and small animals brought in by the women's foraging trips, but when the men's hunt is successful, it is the occasion for a celebration. Conversely, because they are the superior group, white men do not have to do the "dirty work," such as housework; the most inferior group does it, usually poor women of color (Palmer 1989).

Freudian psychoanalytic theory claims that boys must reject their mothers and deny the feminine in themselves in order to become men: "For boys the major goal is the achievement of personal masculine identification with their father and sense of secure masculine self, achieved through superego formation and disparagement of women" (Chodorow 1978, 165). Masculinity may be the outcome of boys' intrapsychic struggles to separate their identity from that of their mothers, but the proofs of masculinity are culturally shaped and usually ritualistic and symbolic (Gilmore 1990).

The Marxist feminist explanation for gender inequality is that by demeaning women's abilities and keeping them from learning valuable technological skills, bosses preserve them as a cheap and exploitable reserve army of labor. Unionized men who could be easily replaced by women collude in this process because it allows them to monopolize the better paid, more interesting, and more autonomous jobs: "Two factors emerge as helping men maintain their separation from women and their control of technological occupations. One is the active gendering of jobs and people. The second is the continual creation of subdivisions in the work processes, and levels in work hierarchies, into which men can move in order to keep their distance from women" (Cockburn 1985, 13).

Societies vary in the extent of the inequality in social status of their women and men members, but where there is inequality, the status "woman" (and its attendant behavior and role allocations) is usually held in lesser esteem than the status "man." Since gender is also intertwined with a society's other constructed statuses of differential evaluation—race, religion, occupation, class, country of origin, and so on—men and women members of the favored groups command more power, more prestige, and more property than the members of the disfavored groups. Within many social groups, however, men are advantaged over women. The more economic resources, such as education and job opportunities, are available to a group, the more they tend to be monopolized by men. In poorer groups that have few resources (such as working-class African Americans in the United States), women and men are more nearly equal, and the women may even outstrip the men in education and occupational status (Almquist 1987).

As a *structure,* gender divides work in the home and in economic production, legitimates those in authority, and organizes sexuality and emotional life (Connell 1987, 91–142). As primary parents, women significantly influence children's psychological development and emotional attachments, in the process reproducing gender. Emergent sexuality is shaped by heterosexual, homosexual, bisexual, and sadomasochistic patterns that are gendered—different for girls and boys, and for women and men—so that sexual statuses reflect gender statuses.

When gender is a major component of structured inequality, the devalued genders have less power, prestige, and economic rewards than the valued genders. In countries that discourage gender discrimination, many major roles are still gendered; women still do most of the domestic labor and child-rearing, even while doing full-time paid work; women and men are segregated on the job and each does work considered "appropriate"; women's work is usually paid less than men's work. Men dominate the positions of authority and leadership in government, the military, and the law; cultural productions, religions, and sports reflect men's interests.

In societies that create the greatest gender difference, such as Saudi Arabia, women are kept out of sight behind walls or veils, have no civil rights, and often create a cultural and emotional world of their own (Bernard 1981). But even in societies with less rigid gender boundaries, women and men spend much of their time with people of their own gender because of the way work and family are organized. This spatial separation of women and men reinforces gendered differentness, identity, and ways of thinking and behaving (Coser 1986).

Gender inequality—the devaluation of "women" and the social domination of "men"—has social functions and a social history. It is not the result of sex, procreation, physiology, anatomy, hormones, or genetic predispositions. It is produced and maintained by identifiable social processes and built into the general social structure and individual identities deliberately and purposefully. The social order as we know it in Western societies is organized around racial, ethnic, class, and gender inequality. I contend, therefore, that the continuing purpose of gender as a modern social institution is to construct women as a group to be the subordinates of men as a group. The life of everyone placed in the status "woman" is "night to his day—that has forever been the fantasy. Black to his white. Shut out of his system's space, she is the repressed that ensures the system's functioning" (Cixous and Clément [1975] 1986, 67).

THE PARADOX OF HUMAN NATURE

To say that sex, sexuality, and gender are all socially constructed is not to minimize their social power. These categorical imperatives govern our lives in the most profound and pervasive ways, through the social experiences and social practices of what Dorothy Smith calls the "everyday/everynight world" (1990, 31–57). The paradox of human nature is that it is *always* a manifestation of cultural meanings, social relationships, and power politics; "not biology, but culture, becomes destiny" (Butler 1990, 8). Gendered people emerge not from physiology or sexual orientation but from the exigencies of the social order, mostly from the need for a reliable division of the work of food production and the social (not physical) reproduction of new members.

The moral imperatives of religion and cultural representations guard the boundary lines among genders and ensure that what is demanded, what is permitted, and what is tabooed for the people in each gender are well known and followed by most (Davies 1982). Political power, control of scarce resources, and, if necessary, violence uphold the gendered social order in the face of resistance and rebellion. Most people, however, voluntarily go along with their society's prescriptions for those of their gender status, because the norms and expectations get built into their sense of worth and identity as a certain kind of human being, and because they believe their society's way is the natural way. These beliefs emerge from the imagery that pervades the way we think, the way we see and hear and speak, the way we fantasize, and the way we feel.

There is no core or bedrock human nature below these endlessly looping processes of the social production of sex and gender, self and other, identity and psyche, each of which is a "complex cultural construction" (Butler 1990, 36). *For humans, the social is the natural.* Therefore, "in its feminist senses, gender cannot mean simply the cultural appropriation of biological sexual difference. Sexual difference is itself a fundamental—and scientifically contested—construction. Both 'sex' and 'gender' are woven of multiple, asymmetrical strands of difference, charged with multifaceted dramatic narratives of domination and struggle" (Haraway 1990, 140).

NOTES

1. Gender is, in Erving Goffman's words, an aspect of *Felicity's Condition:* "any arrangement which leads us to judge an individual's . . . acts not to be a manifestation of strangeness. Behind Felicity's Condition is our sense of what it is to be sane" (1983, 27). Also see Bem 1993; Frye 1983, 17–40; Goffman 1977.

2. In cases of ambiguity in countries with modern medicine, surgery is usually performed to make the genitalia more clearly male or female.

3. See J. Butler 1990 for an analysis of how doing gender *is* gender identity.

4. Douglas 1973; MacCormack 1980; Ortner 1974; Ortner and Whitehead 1981; Yanagisako and Collier 1987. On the social construction of childhood, see Ariès 1962; Zelizer 1985.

5. On the hijras of India, see Nanda 1990; on the xaniths of Oman, Wikan 1982, 168–86; on the American Indian berdaches, W. L. Williams 1986. Other societies that have similar institutionalized third-gender men are the Koniag of Alaska, the Tanala of Madagascar, the Mesakin of Nuba, and the Chukchee of Siberia (Wikan 1982, 170).

6. Durova 1989; Freeman and Bond 1992; Wheelwright 1989.

7. Gender segregation of work in popular music still has not changed very much, according to Groce and Cooper 1990, despite considerable androgyny in some very popular figures. See Garber 1992 on the androgyny. She discusses Tipton on pp. 67–70.

8. In the nineteenth century, not only did these women get men's wages, but they also "had male privileges and could do all manner of things other women could not: open a bank account, write checks, own property, go anywhere unaccompanied, vote in elections" (Faderman 1981, 44).

9. When unisex clothing and men wearing long hair came into vogue in the United States in the mid-1960s, beards and mustaches for men also came into style again as gender identifications.

10. For other accounts of women being treated as men in Islamic countries, as well as accounts of women and men cross-dressing in these countries, see Garber 1992, 304–52.

11. Dollimore 1986; Garber 1992, 32–40; Greenblatt 1987, 66–93; Howard 1988. For Renaissance accounts of sexual relations with women and men of ambiguous sex, see Laqueur 1990, 134–39. For modern accounts of women passing as men that other women find sexually attractive, see Devor 1989, 136–37; Wheelwright 1989, 53–59.

12. Females who passed as men soldiers had to "do masculinity," not just dress in a uniform (Wheelwright 1989, 50–78). On the triple entendres and gender resonances of Rosalind-type characters, see Garber 1992, 71–77.

13. Also see Garber 1992, 234–66.

14. Bolin describes how many documents have to be changed by transsexuals to provide a legitimizing "paper trail" (1988, 145–47). Note that only members of the same social group know which names are women's and which men's in their culture, but many documents list "sex."

15. For an account of how a potential man-to-woman transsexual learned to be feminine, see Garfinkel 1967, 116–85, 285–88. For a gloss on this account that points out how, throughout his encounters with Agnes, Garfinkel failed to see how he himself was constructing his own masculinity, see Rogers 1992.

16. Paige and Paige (1981, 147–49) argue that circumcision ceremonies indicate a father's loyalty to his lineage elders—"visible public evidence that the head of a

family unit of their lineage is willing to trust others with his and his family's most valuable political asset, his son's penis" (147). On female circumcision, see El Dareer 1982; Lightfoot-Klein 1989; van der Kwaak 1992; Walker 1992. There is a form of female circumcision that removes only the prepuce of the clitoris and is similar to male circumcision, but most forms of female circumcision are far more extensive, mutilating, and spiritually and psychologically shocking than the usual form of male circumcision. However, among the Australian aborigines, boys' penises are slit and kept open, so that they urinate and bleed the way women do (Bettelheim 1962, 165–206).

17. The concepts of moral hegemony, the effects of everyday activities (praxis) on thought and personality, and the necessity of consciousness of these processes before political change can occur are all based on Marx's analysis of class relations.

18. Other societies recognize more than two categories, but usually no more than three or four (Jacobs and Roberts 1989).

19. Carol Barkalow's book has a photograph of eleven first-year West Pointers in a math class, who are dressed in regulation pants, shirts, and sweaters, with short haircuts. The caption challenges the reader to locate the only woman in the room.

20. The taboo on males and females looking alike reflects the U.S. military's homophobia (Berube and D'Emilio 1984). If you can't tell those with a penis from those with a vagina, how are you going to determine whether their sexual interest is heterosexual or homosexual unless you watch them having sexual relations?

21. Garber feels that *Tootsie* is not about feminism but about transvestism and its possibilities for disturbing the gender order (1992, 5–9).

22. See Bolin 1988, 149–50, for transsexual men-to-women's discovery of the dangers of rape and sexual harassment. Devor's "gender blenders" went in the opposite direction. Because they found that it was an advantage to be taken for men, they did not deliberately cross-dress, but they did not feminize themselves either (1989, 126–40).

23. See West and Zimmerman 1987 for a similar set of gender components.

24. On the "logic of practice," or how the experience of gender is embedded in the norms of everyday interaction and the structure of formal organizations, see Acker 1990; Bourdieu [1980] 1990; Connell 1987; Smith 1987.

REFERENCES

Acker, Joan. 1990. Hierarchies, jobs, and bodies: A theory of gendered organizations. *Gender & Society* 4: 139–58.

Almquist, Elizabeth M. 1987. Labor market gendered inequality in minority groups. *Gender & Society* 1: 400–14.

Amadiume, Ifi. 1987. *Male daughters, female husbands: Gender and sex in an African society.* London: Zed Books.

Ariés, Philippe. 1962. *Centuries of childhood: A social history of family life,* translated by Robert Baldick. New York: Vintage.

Austad, Steven N. 1986. Changing sex nature's way. *International Wildlife,* May–June, 29.

Barkalow, Carol, with Andrea Raab. 1990. *In the men's house.* New York: Poseidon Press.

Bem, Sandra Lipsitz. 1981. Gender schema theory: A cognitive account of sex typing. *Psychological Review* 88: 354–64.

———. 1983. Gender schema theory and its implications for child development: Raising gender-aschematic children in a gender-schematic society. *Signs* 8: 598–616.

———. 1993. *The lense of gender: Transforming the debate on sexual inequality.* New Haven: Yale University Press.

Bernard, Jessie. 1981. *The female world.* New York: Free Press.

Bernstein, Richard. 1986. France jails 2 in odd case of espionage. *New York Times,* 11 May.

Berube, Allan, and John D'Emilio. 1984. The military and lesbians during the McCarthy years. *Signs* 9: 759–75.

Bettelheim, Bruno. 1962. *Symbolic wounds: Puberty rites and the envious male.* London: Thames and Hudson.

Biersack, Aletta. 1984. Paiela "women-men": The reflexive foundations of gender ideology. *American Ethnologist* 11: 118–38.

Birdwhistell, Ray L. 1970. *Kinesics and context: Essays on body motion communications.* Philadelphia: University of Pennsylvania Press.

Blackwood, Evelyn. 1984. Sexuality and gender in certain Native American tribes: The case of cross-gender females. *Signs* 10: 27–42.

Bolin, Anne. 1987. Transsexualism and the limits of traditional analysis. *American Behavioral Scientist* 31: 41–65.

———. 1988. *In search of Eve: Transsexual rites of passage.* South Hadley, Mass.: Bergin and Garvey.

Bourdieu, Pierre. [1980] 1990. *The logic of practice.* Stanford, Calif.: Stanford University Press.

Brody, Jane E. 1979. Benefits of transsexual surgery disputed as leading hospital halts the procedure. *New York Times,* 2 October.

Butler, Judith. 1990. *Gender trouble: Feminism and the subversion of identity.* New York and London: Routledge.

Chodorow, Nancy. 1974. Family structure and feminine personality. In Rosaldo and Lamphere.

———. 1978. *The reproduction of mothering.* Berkeley: University of California Press.

Cixous, Hélène, and Catherine Clément. [1975] 1986. *The newly born woman,* translated by Betsy Wing. Minneapolis: University of Minnesota Press.

Cockburn, Cynthia. 1985. *Machinery of dominance: Women, men and technical know-how.* London: Pluto Press.

Collins, Patricia Hill. 1990. *Black feminist thought: Knowledge, consciousness, and the politics of empowerment.* Boston: Unwin Hyman.

Connell, R. [Robert] W. 1987. *Gender and power: Society, the person, and sexual politics.* Stanford, Calif.: Stanford University Press.

Coser, Rose Laub. 1986. Cognitive structure and the use of social space. *Sociological Forum* 1: 1–26.

Davies, Christie. 1982. Sexual taboos and social boundaries. *American Journal of Sociology* 87: 1032–63.

de Beauvoir, Simone. 1953. *The second sex,* translated by H. M. Parshley. New York: Knopf.

Devor, Holly. 1987. Gender blending females: Women and sometimes men. *American Behavioral Scientist* 31: 12–40.

———. 1989. *Gender blending: Confronting the limits of duality.* Bloomington: Indiana University Press.

Dollimore, Jonathan. 1986. Subjectivity, sexuality, and transgression: The Jacobean connection. *Renaissance Drama,* n.s. 17: 53–81.

Douglas, Mary. 1973. *Natural symbols.* New York: Vintage.

Durova, Nadezhda. 1989. *The calvary maiden: Journals of a Russian officer in the Napoleonic wars,* translated by Mary Fleming Zirin. Bloomington: Indiana University Press.

Eichler, Margrit. 1989. Sex change operations: The last bulwark of the double standard. In *Feminist frontiers,* edited by Laurel Richardson and Verta Taylor. New York: Random House.

El Dareer, Asma. 1982. *Woman, why do you weep? Circumcision and its consequences.* London: Zed Books.

Epstein, Cynthia Fuchs, 1988. *Deceptive distinctions: Sex, gender and the social order.* New Haven: Yale University Press.

Faderman, Lillian. 1981. *Surpassing the love of men: Romantic friendship and love between women from the Renaissance to the present.* New York: William Morrow.

Foucault, Michel. 1972. *The archeology of knowledge and the discourse on language,* translated by A. M. Sheridan Smith. New York: Pantheon.

Freeman, Lucy, and Alma Halbert Bond. 1992. *America's first woman warrior: The courage of Deborah Sampson.* New York: Paragon.

Frye, Marilyn. 1983. *The politics of reality: Essays in feminist theory.* Trumansburg, N.Y.: Crossing Press.

Garber, Marjorie. 1992. *Vested interests: Cross-dressing and cultural anxiety.* New York and London: Routledge.

Garfinkel, Harold. 1967. *Studies in ethnomethodology.* Engelwood Cliffs, N.J.: Prentice-Hall.

Gilmore, David D. 1977. The arrangement between the sexes. *Theory and Society* 4: 301–33.

———. 1990. *Manhood in the making: Cultural concepts of masculinity.* New Haven: Yale University Press.

Goffman, Erving. 1977. The arrangement between the sexes. *Theory and Society* 4: 301–33.

———. Felicity's condition. *American Journal of Sociology* 89: 1–53.

Gordon, Tuula. 1990. *Feminist mothers.* New York: New York University Press.

Gramsci, Antonio. 1971. *Selections from the prison notebooks,* translated and edited by Quintin Hoare and Geoffrey Nowell Smith. New York: International Publishers.

Greenblatt, Stephen. 1987. *Shakespearean negotiations: The circulation of social energy in Renaissance England.* Berkeley: University of California Press.

Groce, Stephen B., and Margaret Cooper. 1990. Just me and the boys? Women in local-level rock and roll. *Gender & Society* 4: 220–29.

Haraway, Donna. 1978. Animal sociology and a natural economy of the body politic. Part I: A political physiology of dominance. *Signs* 4: 21–36.

———. 1990. Investment strategies for the evolving portfolio of primate females. In Jacobus, Keller, and Shuttleworth.

Howard, Jean E. 1988. Crossdressing, the theater, and gender struggle in early modern England. *Shakespeare Quarterly* 39: 418–41.

Hwang, David Henry. 1989. *M Butterfly.* New York: New American Library.

Jacobs, Sue-Ellen, and Christine Roberts. 1989. Sex, sexuality, gender, and gender variance. In *Gender and anthropology,* edited by Sandra Morgen. Washington, D.C.: American Anthropological Association.

Jay, Nancy. 1981. Gender and dichotomy. *Feminist Studies* 7: 38–56.

Kando, Thomas. 1973. *Sex change: The achievement of gender identity among feminized transsexuals.* Springfield, Ill.: Charles C Thomas.

Kincaid, Jamaica. 1978. Girl. *The New Yorker,* 26 June.

Kondo, Dorinne K. 1990a. *Crafting selves: Power, gender, and discourses of identity in a Japanese workplace.* Chicago: University of Chicago Press.

———. 1990b. *M. Butterfly:* Orientalism, gender, and a critique of essentialist identity. *Cultural Critique,* no. 16 (Fall): 5–29.

Lancaster, Jane Beckman. 1974. *Primate behavior and the emergence of human culture.* New York: Holt, Rinehart and Winston.

Laqueur, Thomas. 1990. *Making sex: Body and gender from the Greeks to Freud.* Cambridge, Mass.: Harvard University Press.

Lévi-Strauss, Claude. 1956. The family. In *Man, culture, and society,* edited by Harry L. Shapiro, New York: Oxford.

———. [1949] 1969. *The elementary structures of kinship,* translated by J. H. Bell and J. R. von Sturmer. Boston: Beacon Press.

Lightfoot-Klein, Hanny. 1989. *Prisoners of ritual: An odyssey into female circumcision in Africa.* New York: Harrington Park Press.

MacCormack, Carol P. 1980. Nature, culture and gender: A critique. In *Nature, culture and gender,* edited by Carol P. MacCormack and Marilyn Strathern. Cambridge, England: Cambridge University Press.

Matthaei, Julie A. 1982. *An economic history of women's work in America.* New York: Schocken.

Mencher, Joan. 1988. Women's work and poverty: Women's contribution to household maintenance in South India. In Dwyer and Bruce.

Morris, Jan. 1975. *Conundrum.* New York: Signet.

Nanda, Serena. 1990. *Neither man nor woman: The hijiras of India.* Belmont, Calif.: Wadsworth.

New York Times. 1989. Musician's death at 74 reveals he was a woman. 2 February.

Ortner, Sherry B. 1974. Is female to male as nature is to culture? In Rosaldo and Lamphere.

Ortner, Sherry B., and Harriet Whitehead. 1981. Introduction: Accounting for sexual meanings. In Ortner and Whitehead.

Paige, Karen Ericksen, and Jeffrey M. Paige. 1981. *The politics of reproductive ritual.* Berkeley: University of California Press.

Palmer, Phyllis. 1989. *Domesticity and dirt: Housewives and domestic servants in the United States, 1920–1945.* Philadelphia: Temple University Press.

Papanek, Hanna. 1979. *Family status production:* The "work" and "non-work" of women. *Signs* 4: 775–81.

Raymond, Janice G. 1979. *The transsexual empire: The making of the she-male.* Boston: Beacon Press.

Reskin, Barbara F. 1988. Bringing the men back in: Sex differentiation and the devaluation of women's work. *Gender & Society* 2: 58–81.

Rogers, Mary F. 1992. They were all passing: Agnes, Garfinkel, and company. *Gender & Society* 6: 169–91.

Rosaldo, Michelle Zimbalist, and Louise Lamphere (eds.). 1974. *Woman, culture, and society.* Stanford, Calif.: Stanford University Press.

Rubin, Gayle. 1975. The traffic in women: Notes on the political economy of sex. In *Toward an anthropology of women,* edited by Rayna R[app] Reiter. New York: Monthly Review Press.

Rugh, Andrea B. 1986. *Reveal and conceal: Dress in contemporary Egypt.* Syracuse, N.Y.: Syracuse University Press.

Scott, Joan Wallach. 1988. *Gender and the politics of history.* New York: Columbia University Press.

Showalter, Elaine. 1987. Critical cross-dressing: Male feminists and the woman of the year. In *Men in feminism,* edited by Alice Jardine and Paul Smith. New York: Methuen.

Smith, Dorothy E. 1987. *The everyday world as problematic: A feminist sociology.* Toronto: University of Toronto Press.

———. 1990. *The conceptual practices of power: A feminist sociology of knowledge.* Toronto: University of Toronto Press.

van der Kwaak, Anke. 1992. Female circumcision and gender identity: A questionable alliance? *Social Science and Medicine* 35: 777–87.

van Gennep, Arnold. 1960. *The rites of passage,* translated by Monika B. Vizedom and Gabrielle L. Caffee. Chicago: University of Chicago Press.

Walker, Molly K. 1992. Maternal reactions to fetal sex. *Health Care for Women International* 13: 293–302.

West, Candace, and Don Zimmerman. 1987. Doing gender. *Gender & Society* 1: 125–51.

Wheelright, Julie. 1989. *Amazons and military maids: Women who cross-dressed in pursuit of life, liberty and happiness.* London: Pandora Press.

Whitehead, Harriet. 1982. The bow and the burden strap: A new look at institutionalized homosexuality in Native North America. In *Sexual meanings: The cultural construction of gender and sexuality,* edited by Sherry B. Ornter and Harriet Whitehead. New York: Cambridge University Press.

Wikan, Unni. 1982. *Behind the veil in Arabia: Women in Oman.* Baltimore, Md.: Johns Hopkins University Press.

Williams, Christine L. 1989. *Gender differences at work: Women and men in nontraditional occupations.* Berkeley: University of California Press.

Williams, Walter L. 1986. *The spirit and the flesh: Sexual diversity in American Indian culture.* Boston: Beacon Press.

Yanagisako, Sylvia Junko, and Jane Fishburne Collier. 1987. Toward a unified analysis of gender and kinship. In *Gender and kinship: Essays toward a unified analysis,* edited by Jane Fishburne Collier and Sylvia Junko Yanagisako. Berkeley: University of California Press.

Zelizer, Viviana A. 1985. *Pricing the priceless child: The changing social value of children.* New York: Basic Books.

The Medical Construction of Gender

The birth of intersexed infants, babies born with genitals that are neither clearly male nor clearly female, has been documented throughout recorded time.[1] In the late twentieth century, medical technology has become sufficiently advanced to allow scientists to determine chromosomal and hormonal gender, which is typically taken to be the real, natural, biological gender, usually referred to as "sex."[2] Nevertheless, physicians who handle cases of intersexed infants consider several factors beside biological ones in determining, assigning, and announcing the gender of a particular infant. Indeed, biological factors are often preempted in physicians' deliberations by such cultural factors as the "correct" length of the penis and capacity of the vagina.

In the literature on intersexuality, issues such as announcing a baby's gender at the time of delivery, postdelivery discussions with the parents, and consultations with patients in adolescence are considered only peripherally to the central medical issues—etiology, diagnosis, and surgical procedures.[3] Yet members of medical teams have standard practices for managing intersexuality, which rely ultimately on cultural understandings of gender. The process and guidelines by which decisions about gender (re)construction are made reveal the model for the social construction of gender generally. Moreover, in the face of apparently incontrovertible evidence—infants born with some combination of "female" and "male" reproductive and sexual features—physicians hold an incorrigible belief that female and male are the only "natural" options. This paradox highlights and calls into question the idea that female and male are biological givens compelling a culture of two genders.

Ideally, to undertake an extensive study of intersexed infant case management, I would like to have had direct access to particular events, for example the deliveries of intersexed infants and the initial discussions among physicians, between physicians and parents, between parents, and among parents and family and friends of intersexed infants. The rarity with which intersexuality occurs, however, made this unfeasible.[4] Alternatively, physicians who have had considerable experience dealing with this condition were interviewed. I do not assume that their "talk" about how they manage such cases mirrors their "talk" in the situation, but their words do reveal that they have certain assumptions about gender and that they impose those assumptions via their medical decisions on the patients they treat.

Interviews were conducted with six medical experts (three women and three men) in the field of pediatric intersexuality: one clinical geneticist, three endocrinologists (two of them pediatric specialists), one psychoendocrinologist, and one urologist. All of them have had extensive clinical experience with various intersexed syndromes, and some are internationally known researchers in the field of intersexuality. They were selected on the basis of their prominence in the field and their representing four different medical centers in New York City. Although they know one another, they do not collaborate on research and are not part of the same management team. All were interviewed in the spring of 1985 in their offices. The interviews lasted between forty-five minutes and one hour. Unless further referenced, all quotations in this [reading] are from these interviews.[5]

THE THEORY OF INTERSEXUALITY MANAGEMENT

The sophistication of today's medical technology has led to an extensive compilation of various intersex categories based on the various causes of malformed genitals. The "true hermaphrodite" condition, where both ovarian and testicular tissue are present either in the same gonad or in opposite gonads, accounts for fewer than 5 percent of all cases of ambiguous genitals:[6] More commonly, the infant has either ovaries or testes, but the genitals are ambiguous. If the infant has two ovaries, the condition is referred to as female pseudohermaphroditism. If the infant has two testes, the condition is referred to as male pseudohermaphroditism. There are numerous causes of both forms of pseudohermaphroditism, and although there are life-threatening aspects to some of these conditions, having ambiguous genitals per se is not harmful to the infant's health.[7]Although most cases of ambiguous genitals do not represent true hermaphroditism, in keeping with the contemporary literature I will refer to all such cases as intersexed.

Current attitudes toward the intersex condition have been primarily influenced by three factors. First are the developments in surgery and endocrinology. Diagnoses of specific intersex conditions can be made with greater precision. Female genitals can be constructed that look much like "natural" ones, and some small penises can be enlarged with the exogenous application of hormones, although surgical skills are not sufficiently advanced to construct a "normal"-looking and -functioning penis out of other tissue.[8] Second, in the contemporary United States, the influence of the feminist movement has called into question the valuation of women according to strictly reproductive functions, and the presence or absence of functional gonads is no longer the only or the definitive criterion for gender assignment. Third, psychological theorists focus on "gender identity" (one's sense of oneself as belonging to the female or male category) as distinct from "gender role" (cultural expectations of one's behavior as "appropriate" for a female or male).[9] The relevance of this new gender identity theory for rethinking cases of ambiguous genitals is that gender must be assigned as early as possible if gender identity is to develop successfully. As a result of these three factors, intersexuality is considered a treatable condition of the genitals, one that needs to be resolved expeditiously.

According to all of the specialists interviewed, management of intersexed cases is based upon the theory of gender proposed first by John Money, J. G. Hampson, and J. L. Hempson in 1955 and developed in 1972 by Money and Anke A. Ehrhardt. The theory argues that gender identity is changeable until approximately eighteen months of age.[10] "To use the Pygmalion allegory, one may begin with the same clay and fashion a god or a goddess."[11] The theory rests on satisfying several conditions: The experts must ensure that the parents have no doubt about whether their child is male or female; the genitals must be made to match the assigned gender as soon as possible; gender-appropriate hormones must be administered at puberty; and intersexed children must be kept informed about their situation with age-appropriate explanations. If these conditions are met, the theory proposes, the intersexed child will develop a gender identity in accordance with the gender assignment (regardless of the chromosomal gender) and will not question her or his assignment and request reassignment at a later age.

Supportive evidence for Money and Ehrhardt's theory is based on only a handful of repeatedly cited cases, but it has been accepted because of the prestige of the theoreticians and its resonance with contemporary ideas about gender, children, psychology, and medicine. Gender and children are malleable; psychology and medicine are the tools used to transform them. This theory is so strongly endorsed that it has taken on the character of gospel. "I think we [physicians] have been raised in the Money theory," one endocrinologist said. Another claimed, "We always approach the problem in a similar way and it's been dictated, to a large extent, by the work of John Money and Anke Ehrhardt because they are the only people who have published, at least in medical literature, any data, any guidelines." It is provocative that this physician immediately followed this assertion with: "And I don't know how effective it really is." Contradictory data are rarely cited in reviews of the literature, were not mentioned by any of the physicians interviewed, and have not reduced these physicians' belief in the theory's validity.[12]

The doctors interviewed concur with the argument that gender must be assigned immediately, decisively, and irreversibly, and that professional opinions be presented in a clear and unambiguous way. The psychoendocrinologist said that when doctors make a statement about the infant, they should "stick to it." The urologist said, "If you make a statement that later has to be disclaimed or discredited, you've weakened your credibility." A gender assignment made decisively, unambiguously, and irrevocably contributes, I believe, to the general impression that the infant's true, natural "sex" has been discovered, and that something that was there all along has been found. It also serves to maintain the credibility of the medical profession, reassure the parents, and reflexively substantiate Money and Ehrhardt's theory.

Also according to this theory, if corrective surgery is necessary, it should take place as soon as possible. If the infant is assigned the male gender, the initial stage of penis repair is usually undertaken in the first year, and further surgery is completed before the child enters school. If the infant is assigned the female gender, vulva repair (including clitoral reduction) is usually begun by three months of age. Money suggests that if reduction of phallic tissue were delayed beyond the neonatal period, the infant would have traumatic memories of having been castrated.[13] Vaginoplasty, in those females having an adequate internal structure (e.g., the vaginal canal is near its expected location), is done between the ages of one and four years. Girls who require more complicated surgical procedures might not be surgically corrected until preadolescence.[14] The complete vaginal canal is typically constructed only when the body is fully grown, following pubertal feminization with estrogen, although some specialists have claimed surgical success with vaginal construction in the early childhood years.[15] Although physicians speculate about the possible trauma of an early-childhood "castration" memory, there is no corresponding concern that vaginal reconstructive surgery delayed beyond the neonatal period is traumatic.

Even though gender identity theory places the critical age limit for gender reassignment between eighteen months and two years, the physicians acknowledge that diagnosis, gender assignment, and genital reconstruction cannot be delayed for as long as two years, since a clear gender assignment and correctly formed genitals will determine the kind of interactions parents will have with their child.[16] The geneticist argued that when parents "change a diaper and see genitalia that don't mean much in terms of gender assignment, I think it prolongs the negative response to the baby. . . . If you have clitoral enlargement that is so extraordinary that the parents can't distinguish between male and female, it is sometimes helpful to reduce that somewhat so that the parent views the child as female." Another physician concurred: Parents "need to go home and do their job as child rearers with it very clear whether it's a boy or a girl."

DIAGNOSIS

A premature gender announcement by an obstetrician, prior to a close examination of an infant's genitals, can be problematic. Money and his colleagues claim that the primary complications in case management of intersexed infants can be traced to mishandling by medical personnel untrained in sexology.[17] According to one of the pediatric endocrinologists interviewed, obstetricians improperly educated about intersexed conditions "don't examine the babies closely enough

at birth and say things just by looking, before separating legs and looking at everything, and jump to conclusions, because 99 percent of the time it's correct. . . . People get upset, physicians I mean. And they say things that are inappropriate." For example, he said that an inexperienced obstetrician might blurt out, "I think you have a boy, or no, maybe you have a girl." Other inappropriate remarks a doctor might make in postdelivery consultation with the parents include, "You have a little boy, but he'll never function as a little boy, so you better raise him as a little girl." As a result, said the pediatric endocrinologist, "the family comes away with the idea that they have a little boy, and that's what they wanted, and that's what they're going to get." In such cases, parents sometimes insist that the child be raised male despite the physicians' instructions to the contrary. "People have in mind certain things they've heard, that this is a boy, and they're not likely to forget that, or they're not likely to let it go easily." The urologist agreed that the first gender attribution is critical: "Once it's been announced, you've got a big problem on your hands." "One of the worst things is to allow them [the parents] to go ahead and give a name and tell everyone, and it turns out the child has to be raised in the opposite sex."[18]

Physicians feel that the mismanagement of such cases requires careful remedying. The psychoendocrinologist asserted, "When I'm involved, I spend hours with the parents to explain to them what has happened and how a mistake like that could be made, *or not really a mistake but a different decision*" [my emphasis]. One pediatric endocrinologist said, "I try to dissuade them from previous misconceptions and say, 'Well, I know what they meant, but the way they said it confused you. This is, I think, a better way to think about it.'" These statements reveal physicians' efforts not only to protect parents from concluding that their child is neither male nor female or both, but also to protect other physicians' decision-making processes. Case management involves perpetuating the notion that good medical decisions are based on interpretations of the infant's real "sex" rather than on cultural understandings of gender.

"Mismanagements" are less likely to occur in communities with major medical centers where specialists are prepared to deal with intersexuality and a medical team (perhaps drawing physicians from more than one teaching hospital) can be quickly assembled. The team typically consists of the original referring doctor (obstetrician or pediatrician), a pediatric endocrinologist, a pediatric surgeon (urologist or gynecologist), and a geneticist. In addition, a psychologist, psychiatrist, or psychoendocrinologist might play a role. If an infant is born with ambiguous genitals in a small community hospital without the relevant specialists on staff, the baby is likely to be transferred to a hospital where diagnosis and treatment are available. Intersexed infants born in poor rural areas where there is less medical intervention might never be referred for genital reconstruction. Many of these children, like those born in earlier historical periods, will grow up and live through adulthood with the genital ambiguity—somehow managing.

The diagnosis of intersexed conditions includes assessing the chromosomal sex and the syndrome that produced the genital ambiguity and may include medical procedures such as cytologic screening; chromosomal analysis; assessing serum electrolytes; hormone, gonadotropin, and steroids evaluation; digital examination; and radiographic genitography.[19] In any intersexed condition, if the infant is determined to be a genetic female (having an XX chromosome makeup), then the treatment—genital surgery to reduce the phallus size—can proceed relatively quickly, satisfying what the doctors believe are psychological and cultural demands. For example, 21-hydroxylase deficiency, a form of female pseudohermaphroditism and one of the most common conditions, can be determined by a blood test within the first few days.

If, on the other hand, the infant is determined to have at least one Y chromosome, then surgery may be considerably delayed. A decision must be made whether to test the ability of the phallic tissue to respond to human chorionic gonadotropin (HCG), a treatment intended to enlarge the microphallus enough to be a penis. The endocrinologist explained, "You do HCG testing and you find out if the male can make testosterone. . . . You can get those results back probably within three weeks. . . . You're sure the male is making testosterone—but can he respond to it? It can take three months of waiting to see whether the phallus responds."

If the Y-chromosome infant cannot make testosterone or cannot respond to the testosterone it makes, the phallus will not develop, and the Y-chromosome infant will not be considered to be a male after all. Should the infant's phallus respond to the local application of testosterone or a brief course of intramuscular injections of low-potency androgen, the gender assignment problem is resolved, but possibly at some later cost, since the penis will not grow again at puberty when the rest of the body develops.[20] Money's case-management philosophy assumes that while it may be difficult for an

adult male to have a much smaller than average penis, it is very detrimental to the morale of the young boy to have a micropenis.[21] In the former case, the male's manliness might be at stake, but in the latter case, his essential maleness might be. Although the psychological consequences of these experiences have not been empirically documented, Money and his colleagues suggest that it is wise to avoid the problems of both the micropenis in childhood and the still-undersized penis postpuberty by reassigning many of these infants to the female gender.[22] This approach suggests that for Money and his colleagues, chromosomes are less relevant in determining gender than penis size, and, by implication, that "male" is defined not by the genetic condition of having one Y and one X chromosome or by the production of sperm but by the aesthetic condition of having an "appropriately" sized penis.

The tests and procedures required for diagnosis (and consequently for gender assignment) can take several months.[23] Although physicians are anxious not to make premature gender assignments, their language suggests that it is difficult for them to take a completely neutral position and to think and speak only of *phallic tissue* that belongs to an infant whose gender has not yet been determined or decided. Comments such as "seeing whether the male can respond to testosterone" imply at least a tentative male gender assignment of an XY infant. The psychoendocrinologist's explanations to parents of their infant's treatment program also illustrate this implicit male gender assignment. "Clearly this baby has an underdeveloped phallus. But if the phallus responds to this treatment, we are fairly confident that surgical techniques and hormonal techniques will help this child to look like a boy. But we want to make absolutely sure and use some hormone treatments and see whether the tissue reacts." The mere fact that this doctor refers to the genitals as an "underdeveloped" phallus rather than an overdeveloped clitoris suggests that the infant has been judged to be, at least provisionally, a male. In the case of the undersized phallus, what is ambiguous is not whether this is a penis but whether it is "good enough" to remain one. If, at the end of the treatment period, the phallic tissue has not responded, what had been a potential penis (referred to in the medical literature as a "clitoropenis") is now considered an enlarged clitoris (or "penoclitoris"), and reconstructive surgery is planned as for the genetic female.

The time-consuming nature of intersex diagnosis and the assumption, based on the gender identity theory, that gender be assigned as soon as possible thus present physicians with difficult dilemmas. Medical personnel are committed to discovering the etiology of the condition in order to determine the best course of treatment, which takes time. Yet they feel an urgent need to provide an immediate assignment and genitals that look and function appropriately. An immediate assignment that will need to be retracted is more problematic than a delayed assignment, since reassignment carries with it an additional set of social complications. The endocrinologist interviewed commented: "We've come very far in that we can diagnose, eventually, many of the conditions. But we haven't come far enough. . . . We can't do it early enough. . . . Very frequently a decision is made before all this information is available, simply because it takes so long to make the correct diagnosis. And you cannot let a child go indefinitely, not in this society you can't. . . . There's pressure on parents [for a decision], and the parents transmit that pressure onto physicians."

A pediatric endocrinologist agreed: "At times you may need to operate before a diagnosis can be made. . . . In one case parents were told to wait on the announcement while the infant was treated to see if the phallus would grow when treated with androgens. After the first month passed and there was some growth, the parents said they had given the child a boy's name. They could only wait a month."

Deliberating out loud on the judiciousness of making parents wait for assignment decisions, the endocrinologist asked rhetorically, "Why do we do all these tests if in the end we're going to make the decision simply on the basis of the appearance of the genitalia?" This question suggests that the principles underlying physicians' decisions are cultural rather than biological, based on parental reaction and the medical team's perception of the infant's societal adjustment prospects given the way the child's genitals look or could be made to look. Moreover, as long as the decision rests largely on the criterion of genital appearance, and male is defined as having a "good-sized" penis, more infants will be assigned to the female gender than the male.

THE WAITING PERIOD: DEALING WITH AMBIGUITY

During the period of ambiguity between birth and assignment, physicians not only must evaluate the infant's prospects of becoming a good male but also must manage the parents' uncertainty about a genderless child. Physicians advise that parents postpone announcing the gender of the infant until a gender has been explicitly assigned. They believe that parents should not feel compelled to disclose the baby's "sex" to other people. The clinical geneticist interviewed said that physicians "basically encourage them [parents] to treat it [the infant] as neuter." One of the pediatric endocrinologists reported that in France parents confronted with this dilemma sometimes give the infant a neuter name such as Claude. The psychoendocrinologist concurred: "If you have a truly borderline situation, and you want to make it dependent on the hormone treatment . . . then the parents are . . . told, 'Try not to make a decision. Refer to the baby as "baby." Don't think in terms of boy or girl.'" Yet, when asked whether this is a reasonable request to make of parents in our society, the physician answered: "I don't think so. I think parents can't do it."[24]

New York State requires that a birth certificate be filled out within forty-eight hours of delivery, but the certificate need not be filed with the state for thirty days. The geneticist tells parents to insert "child of" instead of a name. In one case, parents filled out two birth registration forms, one for each gender, and they refused to sign either until a final gender assignment had been made.[25] One of the pediatric endocrinologists claimed, "I heard a story, I don't know if it's true or not. There were parents of a hermaphroditic infant who told everyone they had twins, one of each gender. When the gender was determined, they said the other had died."

The geneticist explained that when directly asked by parents what to tell others about the gender of the infant, she says, "Why don't you just tell them that the baby is having problems and as soon as the problems are resolved we'll get back to you." A pediatric endocrinologist echoes this suggestion in advising parents to say, "Until the problem is solved, [we] would really prefer not to discuss any of the details." According to the urologist, "If [the gender] isn't announced, people may mutter about it and may grumble about it, but they haven't got anything to get their teeth into and make trouble over for the child, or the parents, or whatever." In short, parents are asked to sidestep the infant's gender rather than admit that the gender is unknown, thereby collaborating in a web of white lies, ellipses, and mystifications.[26]

Even as physicians teach parents how to deal with those who may not find the infant's condition comprehensible or acceptable, they also must make the condition comprehensible and acceptable to the parents, normalizing the intersexed condition for them. In doing so, they help the parents consider the infant's condition in the most positive way. There are four key aspects to this "normalizing" process.

First, physicians teach parents usual fetal development and explain that all fetuses have the potential to be male or female. One of the endocrinologists explains, "In the absence of maleness, you have femaleness. . . . It's really the basic design. The other [intersex] is really a variation on a theme." This explanation presents the intersex condition as a natural phase of fetal development. Another endocrinologist "like[s] to show picture[s] to them and explain that at a certain point in development males and females look alike and then diverge for such and such reason." The professional literature suggests that doctors use diagrams that illustrate "nature's principle of using the same anlagen to produce the external genital parts of the male and female."[27]

Second, physicians stress the normalcy of other aspects of the infant. For example, the geneticist tells parents, "The baby is healthy, but there was a problem in the way the baby was developing." The endocrinologist says the infant has "a mild defect, [which] just like anything could be considered a birth defect, a mole, or a hemangioma." This language not only eases the blow to the parents but also redirects their attention. Terms like "hermaphrodite" or "abnormal" are not used. The urologist said that he advised parents "about the generalization of sticking to the good things and not confusing people with something that is unnecessary."

Third, physicians (at least initially) imply that it is not the gender of the child that is ambiguous but the genitals. They talk about "undeveloped," "maldeveloped," or "unfinished" organs. From a number of the physicians interviewed came the following explanations:

At a point in time the development proceeded in a different way, and sometimes the development isn't complete and we may have some trouble . . . in determining what the *actual* sex is. And so we have to do a blood test to help us. [my emphasis]

The baby may be a female, which you would know after the buccal smear, but you can't prove it yet. If so, then it's a normal female with a different appearance. This can be surgically corrected.

The gender of your child isn't apparent to us at the moment.

While this looks like a small penis, it's actually a large clitoris. And what we're going to do is put it back in its proper position and reduce the size of the tip of it enough so it doesn't look funny, so it looks right.

Money and his colleagues report a case in which parents were advised to tell their friends that the reason their infant's gender was reannounced from male to female is that "the baby was . . . 'closed up down there.' [. . .] When the closed skin was divided, the female organs were revealed, and the baby discovered to be, *in fact*, a girl" [my emphasis]. It was mistakenly assumed to be a male at first because "there was an excess of skin on the clitoris."[28]

The message in these examples is that the trouble lies in the doctor's ability to determine the gender, not in the baby's gender per se. The real gender will presumably be determined/proven by testing, and the "bad" genitals (which are confusing the situation for everyone) will be "repaired." The emphasis is not on the doctors' creating gender but in their completing the genitals. Physicians say that they "reconstruct" the genitals rather than "construct" them. The surgeons reconstitute from remaining parts what should have been there all along. The fact that gender in an infant is "reannounced" rather than "reassigned" suggests that the first announcement was a mistake because the announcer was confused by the genitals. The gender always was what it is now seen to be.[29]

Finally, physicians tell parents that social factors are more important in gender development than biological ones, even though they are searching for biological causes. In essence, the physicians teach the parents Money and Ehrhardt's theory of gender development.[30] In doing so, they shift the emphasis from the discovery of biological factors that are a sign of the "real" gender to providing the appropriate social conditions to produce the "real" gender. What remains unsaid is the apparent contradiction in the assumption that a "real" or "natural" gender can be or needs to be produced artificially. The physician/parent discussions make it clear to family members that gender is not a biological given [even though, of course, the physicians' own procedures for diagnosis assume that it is] and that gender is fluid: The psychoendocrinologist paraphrased an explanation to parents thus: "It will depend, ultimately, on how everybody treats your child and how your child is looking as a person. . . . I can with confidence tell them that generally gender [identity] clearly agrees with the assignment." A pediatric endocrinologist explained: "I try to impress upon them that there's an enormous amount of clinical data to support the fact that if you sex-reverse an infant . . . the majority of the time the alternative gender identity is commensurate with the socialization, the way that they're raised, and how people view them, and that seems to be the most critical."

The implication of these comments is that gender identity (of all children, not just those born with ambiguous genitals) is determined primarily by social factors, that the parents and community always construct the child's gender. In the case of intersexed infants, the physicians merely provide the right genitals to go along with the socialization. Of course at so-called normal births, when the infant's genitals are unambiguous, the parents are not told that the child's gender is ultimately up to socialization. In those cases, doctors do treat gender as a biological given.

SOCIAL FACTORS IN DECISION MAKING

Most of the physicians interviewed claimed that personal convictions of doctors ought to play no role in the decision-making process. The psychoendocrinologist explained:

> I think the most critical factors [are] what is the possibility that this child will grow up with genitals which look like that of the assigned gender and which will ultimately function according to gender. . . . That's why it's so important that it's a well-established team, because [personal convictions] can't really enter into it. It has to be what is surgically and endocrinologically possible for that baby to be able to make it. . . . It's really much more within medical criteria. I don't think many social factors enter into it.

While this doctor eschews the importance of social factors in gender assignment, she argues forcefully that social factors are extremely important in the development of gender identity. Indeed, she implies that social factors primarily enter the picture once the infant leaves the hospital.

In fact, doctors make decisions about gender on the basis of shared cultural values that are unstated, perhaps even unconscious, and therefore considered objective rather than subjective. Money states the fundamental rule for gender assignment: "Never assign a baby to be reared, and to surgical and hormonal therapy, as a boy, unless the phallic structure, hypospadiac

or otherwise, is neonatally of at least the same caliber as that of same-aged males with small–average penises."[31] Elsewhere, he and his colleagues provide specific measurements for what qualifies as a micropenis: "A penis is, by convention, designated as a micropenis when at birth its dimensions are three or more standard deviations below the mean. . . . When it is correspondingly reduced in diameter with corpora that are vestigial, . . . it unquestionably qualifies as a micropenis."[32] A pediatric endocrinologist claimed that although "the [size of the] phallus is not the deciding factor, . . . if the phallus is less than two centimeters long at birth and won't respond to androgen treatments, then it's made into a female." There is no clearer statement of the formula for gender assignment than the one given by one well-published pediatric surgeon: "The decision to raise the child with male pseudohermaphroditism as a male or female is dictated entirely by the size of the phallus."[33]

These guidelines are clear, but they focus on only one physical feature, one that is distinctly imbued with cultural meaning. This becomes especially apparent in the case of an XX infant with normal female reproductive gonads and a "perfect" penis. Would the size and shape of the penis, in this case, be the deciding factor in assigning the infant as a "male," or would the "perfect" penis be surgically destroyed and female genitals created? Money notes that this dilemma would be complicated by the anticipated reaction of the parents to seeing "their apparent son lose his penis."[34] Other researchers concur that parents are likely to want to raise a child with a normal-shaped penis (regardless of size) as "male," particularly if the scrotal area looks normal and if the parents have had no experience with intersexuality.[35] Elsewhere, Money argues in favor of not neonatally amputating the penis of XX infants since fetal masculinization of brain structures would predispose them "almost invariably [to] develop behaviorally as tomboys, even when reared as girls."[36] This reasoning implies first that tomboyish behavior in girls is bad and should be avoided and second that it is preferable to remove the internal female organs, implant prosthetic testes, and regulate the "boy's hormones for his entire life than to overlook or disregard the perfection of the penis."[37]

The ultimate proof to the physicians that they intervened appropriately and gave the intersexed infant the correct gender assignment is that the reconstructed genitals look normal and function normally in adulthood. The vulva, labia, and clitoris should appear ordinary to the woman and her partner(s), and the vagina should be able to receive a normal-sized penis. Similarly, the man and his partner(s) should feel that his penis (even if somewhat smaller than the norm) looks and functions in an unremarkable way. Although there are no published data on how much emphasis the intersexed person, him- or herself, places upon genital appearance and functioning, physicians are absolutely clear about what they believe is important. The clinical geneticist said, "If you have . . . a seventeen-year-old young lady who has gotten hormone therapy and has breast development and pubic hair and no vaginal opening, I can't even entertain the notion that this young lady wouldn't want to have corrective surgery." The urologist summarized his criteria: "Happiness is the biggest factor. Anatomy is part of happiness." Money states, "The primary deficit [of not having sufficient penis]—and destroyer of morale—lies in being unable to satisfy the partner."[38] Another team of clinicians reveals its phallocentrism and argues that the most serious mistake in gender assignment is to create "an individual unable to engage in genital [heterosexual] sex."[39]

The equation of gender with genitals could have emerged only in an age when medical science can create genitals that appear to be normal and to function adequately, and an emphasis on the good phallus above all else could have emerged only in a culture that has rigid aesthetic and performance criteria for what constitutes maleness. The formulation "Good penis equals male; absence of good penis equals female" is treated in the literature and by the physicians interviewed as an objective criterion, operative in all cases. There is a striking lack of attention to the size and shape requirements of the female genitals, other than that the clitoris not be too big and that the vagina be able to receive a penis.[40]

In the late nineteenth century, when women's reproductive function was culturally designated as their essential characteristic, the presence or absence of ovaries (whether or not they were fertile) was held to be the ultimate criterion of gender assignment for hermaphrodites. As recently as 1955, there was some concern that if people with the same chromosomes or gonads paired off, even if they had different genitals, that "might bring the physician in conflict with the law for abetting the pursuit of (technically) illegal sex practices."[41] The urologist interviewed recalled a case from that period of a male child reassigned to "female" at the age of four or five because ovaries had been discovered.

Nevertheless, doctors today, schooled in the etiology and treatment of the various intersex syndromes, view decisions based primarily on chromosomes or gonads as wrong, although, they complain, the conviction that the presence of chromosomes or gonads is the ultimate criterion "still dictates the decisions of the uneducated and uninformed."[42] Presumably the educated and informed now know that decisions based primarily on phallic size, shape, and sexual capacity are right.

While the prospect of constructing good genitals is the primary consideration in physicians' gender assignments, another extramedical factor was repeatedly cited by the six physicians interviewed—the specialty of the attending physician. Although intersexed infants are generally treated by teams of specialists, only the person who coordinates the team is actually responsible for the case. This person, acknowledged by the other physicians as having chief responsibility, acts as spokesperson to the parents. Although all of the physicians claimed that these medical teams work smoothly, with few differences of opinion, several of them mentioned decision-making orientations that are grounded in particular medical specializations. One endocrinologist stated, "The easiest route to take, where there is ever any question, . . . is to raise the child as female. . . . In this country, that is usual if the infant falls into the hands of a pediatric endocrinologist. . . . If the decision is made by the urologists, who are mostly males, . . . they're always opting, because they do the surgery, they're always feeling they can correct anything." Another endocrinologist concurred: "[Most urologists] don't think in terms of dynamic processes. They're interested in fixing pipes and lengthening pipes, and not dealing with hormonal, and certainly not psychological issues. . . . 'What can I do with what I've got?'" Urologists were defended by the clinical geneticist: "Surgeons here, now I can't speak for elsewhere, they don't get into a situation where the child is a year old and they can't make anything."

Whether or not urologists "like to make boys," as one endocrinologist claimed, the following example from a urologist who was interviewed explicitly links a cultural interpretation of masculinity to the medical treatment plan. The case involved an adolescent who had been assigned the female gender at birth but was developing some male pubertal signs and wanted to be a boy. "He was ill-equipped," said the urologist, "yet we made a very respectable male out of him. He now owns a huge construction business—those big cranes that put stuff up on the building."

POSTINFANCY CASE MANAGEMENT

After the infant's gender has been assigned, parents generally latch onto the assignment as the solution to the problem—and it is. The physician as detective has collected the evidence, as lawyer has presented the case, and as judge has rendered a verdict. Although most of the interviewees claimed that parents are equal participants in the whole process, they gave no instances of parental participation prior to the gender assignment.[43] After the physicians assign the infant's gender, the parents are encouraged to establish the credibility of that gender publicly by, for example, giving a detailed medical explanation to a leader in their community, such as a physician or pastor, who will explain the situation to curious casual acquaintances. Money argues that "medical terminology has a special layman's magic in such a context, it is final and authoritative and closes the issue."[44] He also recommends that eventually the mother "settle [the] argument once and for all among her women friends by allowing some of them to see the baby's reconstructed genitalia." Apparently, the powerful influence of normal-looking genitals helps overcome a history of ambiguous gender.

Some of the same issues that arise in assigning gender recur some years later when, at adolescence, the child may be referred to a physician for counseling.[45] The physician then tells the adolescent many of the same things his or her parents had been told years before, with the same language. Terms like "abnormal," "disorder," "disease," and "hermaphroditism" are avoided; the condition is normalized and the child's gender is treated as unproblematic. One clinician explains to his patients that sex organs are different in appearance for each person, not just those who are intersexed. Furthermore, he tells the girls "that while most women menstruate, not all do . . . that conception is only one of a number of ways to become a parent; [and] that today some individuals are choosing not to become parents."[46] The clinical geneticist tells a typical female patient: "You are female. Female is not determined by your genes. Lots of other things determine being a woman. And you are a woman but you won't be able to have babies."

A case reported by one of the pediatric endocrinologists involving an adolescent female with androgen insensitivity provides an intriguing insight into the postinfancy gender-management process. She was told at the age of fourteen "that her ovaries weren't normal and had been removed. That's why she needed pills to look normal. . . . I wanted to convince her of her femininity. Then I told her she could marry and have normal sexual relations. . . . [Her] uterus won't develop but [she] could adopt children." The urologist interviewed was asked to comment on this handling of the counseling. "It sounds like a very good solution to it. He's stating the truth, and if you don't state the truth . . . then you're in trouble later." This is a strange version of "the truth," however, since the adolescent was chromosomally XY and was born with normal testes that produced normal quantities of androgen. There *were* no ovaries or uterus. Another pediatric endocrinologist, in commenting on the management of this case, hedged the issue by saying that he would have used a generic term like "the gonads." A third endocrinologist said she would say that the uterus had never formed.

Technically, these physicians are lying when, for example, they explain to an adolescent XY female with an intersexed history that her "ovaries . . . had to be removed because they were unhealthy or were producing 'the wrong balance of hormones.'"[47] We can presume that these lies are told in the service of what physicians consider a greater good—keeping individual/concrete genders as clear and uncontaminated as the notions of female and male are in the abstract. One clinician suggests that with some female patients it eventually may be possible to talk to them "about their gonads having some structures and features that are testicular-like."[48] This call for honesty may be based, at least partly, on the possibility of the child's discovering his or her chromosomal sex inadvertently from a buccal smear taken in a high school biology class. Today's litigious climate may be another encouragement.

In sum, the adolescent is typically told that certain internal organs did not form because of an endocrinological defect, not because those organs could never have developed in someone with her or his sex chromosomes. The topic of chromosomes is skirted.

There are no published studies on how these adolescents experience their condition and their treatment by doctors. An endocrinologist interviewed mentioned that her adolescent patients rarely ask specifically what is wrong with them, suggesting that they are accomplices in this evasion. In spite of the "truth" having been evaded, the clinician's impression is that "their gender identities and general senses of well-being and self-esteem appear not to have suffered."[49]

LESSONS FROM INTERSEX MANAGEMENT

Physicians conduct careful examinations of the intersexed infant's genitals and perform intricate laboratory procedures. They are interpreters of the body, trained and committed to uncovering the "actual" gender obscured by ambiguous genitals. Yet they also have considerable leeway in assigning gender, and their decisions are influenced by cultural as well as medical factors. What is the relationship between the physician as discoverer and the physician as determiner of gender? Where is the relative emphasis placed in discussions with parents and adolescents and in the consciousness of the physicians? It is misleading to characterize the doctors whose words are provided here as presenting themselves publicly to the parents as discoverers of the infant's real gender but privately acknowledging that the infant has no real gender other than the one being determined or constructed by the medical professionals. They are not hypocritical. It is also misleading to claim that the physicians' focus shifts from discovery to determination over the course of treatment: first the doctors regard the infant's gender as an unknown but discoverable reality; then the doctors relinquish their attempts to find the real gender and treat the infant's gender as something they must construct. They are not medically incompetent or deficient. Instead, I am arguing that the peculiar balance of discovery and determination throughout treatment permits physicians to handle very problematic cases of gender in the most unproblematic of ways.

This balance relies fundamentally on a particular conception of "natural."[50] Although the "deformity" of intersexed genitals would be immutable were it not for medical interference, physicians do not consider it natural. Instead, they think of, and speak of, the surgical/hormonal alteration of such "deformities" as natural because such intervention returns the body to what it ought to have been if events had taken their typical course. The nonnormative is converted into the normative, and the normative state is considered natural.[51] The genital ambiguity is remedied to conform to a "natural," that is, culturally indisputable gender dichotomy. Sherry Ortner's claim that the culture/nature distinction is itself a construction—a product of culture—is relevant here. Language and imagery help create and maintain a specific view of what is natural about the two genders and, I would argue, about the very idea of gender—that it consists of two exclusive types: female and male.[52] The belief that gender consists of two exclusive types is maintained and perpetuated by the medical community in the face of incontrovertible physical evidence that this is not mandated by biology.

The lay conception of human anatomy and physiology assumes a concordance among clearly dimorphic gender markers—chromosomes, genitals, gonads, hormones—but physicians understand that concordance and dimorphism do not always exist. Their understanding of biology's complexity, however, does not inform their understanding of gender's complexity. In order for intersexuality to be managed differently than it currently is, physicians would have to take seriously Money's assertion that it is a misrepresentation of epistemology to consider any cell in the body authentically male or female.[53] If authenticity for gender resides not in a discoverable nature but in someone's proclamation, then the power to proclaim something else is available. If physicians recognized that implicit in their management of gender is the notion that finally, and always, people construct gender, as well as the social systems that are grounded in gender-based concepts, the possibilities for real societal transformations would be unlimited. Unfortunately, neither in their representations to the families of the intersexed nor among themselves do the physicians interviewed for this study draw such far-reaching implications from their work. Their "understanding" that particular genders are medically (re)constructed in these cases does not lead them to see that gender *is always* constructed. Accepting genital ambiguity as a natural option would require that physicians also acknowledge that genital ambiguity is "corrected" not because it is threatening to the infant's life but because it is threatening to the infant's culture.

Rather than admit to their role in perpetuating gender, physicians "psychologize" the issue by talking about the parents' anxiety and humiliation in being confronted with an anomalous infant. They talk as though they have no choice but to respond to the parents' pressure for a resolution of psychological discomfort and as though they have no choice but to use medical technology in the service of a two-gender culture. Neither the psychology nor the technology is doubted, since both shield physicians from responsibility. Indeed, for the most part, neither physicians nor parents emerge from the experience of intersex case management with a greater understanding of the social construction of gender. Society's accountability, like their own, is masked by the assumption that gender is a given. Thus, the medical management of intersexuality, instead of illustrating nature's failure to ordain gender in these isolated, "unfortunate" instances, illustrates physicians' and Western society's failure of imagination—the failure to imagine that each of their management decisions is a moment when a specific instance of biological "sex" is transformed into a culturally constructed gender.

NOTES

1. For historical reviews of the intersexed person in ancient Greece and Rome, see Leslie Fiedler, *Freaks: Myths and Images of the Second Self* and Vern Bullough, *Sexual Variance in Society and History*. For the Middle Ages and Renaissance, see Michel Foucault, *History of Sexuality*. For the eighteenth and nineteenth centuries, see Michel Foucault, *Herculine Barbin* and Alice Domurat Dreger, *Hermaphrodites and the Medical Invention of Sex*. For the early twentieth century, see Havelock Ellis, *Studies in the Psychology of Sex*.

2. Traditionally, the term "gender" has designated psychological, social, and cultural aspects of maleness and femaleness, and the term "sex" has specified the biological and presumably more objective components. Twenty years ago, Wendy McKenna and I introduced the argument that "gender" should be used exclusively to refer to anything related to the categories "female" and "male," replacing the term "sex," which would be restricted to reproductive and "lovemaking" activities (Kessler and McKenna). Our reasoning was (and still is) that this would emphasize the socially constructed, overlapping nature of all category distinctions, even the biological ones. We wrote about gender chromosomes and gender hormones even though, at the time, doing so seemed awkward. I continue this practice here, but I follow the convention of referring to people with mixed biological gender cues as "intersexed" or "intersexuals" rather than as "intergendered" or "intergenderals." The latter is more consistent with my position, but I want to reflect both medical and vernacular usage without using quotation marks each time.

3. See, for example: M. Bolkenius, R. Daum, and E. Heinrich, "Paediatric Surgical Principles in the Management of Children with Intersex"; Kenneth I. Glassberg, "Gender Assignment in Newborn Male Pseudohermaphrodites"; and Peter A. Lee et al., "Micropenis. I. Criteria, Etiologies and Classification."

4. It is difficult to get accurate statistics on the frequency of intersexuality. Chromosomal abnormalities (like XOXX or XXXY) are registered, but those conditions do not always imply ambiguous genitals, and most cases of ambiguous genitals do not involve chromosomal abnormalities. None of the physicians interviewed would venture a guess on frequency rates, but all claimed that intersexuality is rare. One physician suggested that the average obstetrician may see only two cases in twenty years. Another estimated that a specialist may see only one a year or possibly as many as five a year. A reporter who interviewed physicians at Johns Hopkins Medical Center wrote that they treat, at most, ten new patients a year (Melissa Hendricks, "Is It a Boy or a Girl?"). The numbers are considerably greater if one adopts a broader definition of intersexuality to include all "sex chromosome" deviations and any genitals that do not look, according to the culturally informed view of the moment, "normal" enough. A urologist at a Mt. Sinai School of Medicine symposium on Pediatric Plastic and Reconstructive Surgery (New York City, 16 May 1996) claimed that one of every three hundred male births involves some kind of genital abnormality. A meticulous analysis of the medical literature from 1955 to 1997 led Anne Fausto-Sterling and her students to conclude that the frequency of intersexuality may be as high as 2 percent of live births, and that between 0.1 and 0.2 percent of newborns undergo some sort of genital surgery (Melanie Blackless et al., "How Sexually Dimorphic Are We?"). The Intersex Society of North America (ISNA) estimates that about five intersex surgeries are performed in the United States each day.

5. Although the interviews in this chapter were conducted more than ten years ago, interviews with physicians conducted in the mid-to late 1990s and interviews conducted with parents of intersexed children during that same time period . . . indicate that little has changed in the medical management of intersexuality. This lack of change is also evident in current medical management literature. See, for example, F. M. E. Slijper et al., "Neonates with Abnormal Genital Development Assigned the Female Sex: Parent Counseling," and M. Rohatgi, "Intersex Disorders: An Approach to Surgical Management."

6. Mariano Castro-Magana, Moris Angulo, and Platon J. Collipp, "Management of the Child with Ambiguous Genitalia."

7. For example, infants whose intersexuality is caused by congenital adrenal hyperplasia can develop severe electrolyte disturbances unless the condition is controlled by cortisone treatments. Intersexed infants whose condition is caused by androgen insensitivity are in danger of eventual malignant degeneration of the testes unless these are removed. For a complete catalog of clinical syndromes related to the intersexed condition, see Arye Lev-Ran, "Sex Reversal as Related to Clinical Syndromes in Human Beings."

8. Much of the surgical experimentation in this area has been accomplished by urologists who are trying to create penises for female-to-male transsexuals. Although there have been some advancements in recent years in the ability to create a "reasonable-looking" penis from tissue taken elsewhere on the body, the complicated requirements of the organ (requiring both urinary and sexual functioning) have posed surgical problems. It may be,

however, that the concerns of the urologists are not identical to the concerns of the patients. While data are not yet available from the intersexed, we know that female-to-male transsexuals place greater emphasis on the "public" requirements of the penis (for example, being able to look normal while standing at the urinal or wearing a bathing suit) than on its functional requirements (for example, being able to achieve an erection) (Kessler and McKenna, 128–132). As surgical techniques improve, female-to-male transsexuals (and intersexed males) might increase their demands for organs that look and function better.

9. Historically, psychology has tended to blur the distinction between the two by equating a person's acceptance of her or his genitals with gender role and ignoring gender identity. For example, Freudian theory posited that if one had a penis and accepted its reality, then masculine gender role behavior would naturally follow (Sigmund Freud, "Some Psychical Consequences of the Anatomical Distinctions Between the Sexes").

10. Almost all of the published literature on intersexed infant case management has been written or co-written by one researcher, John Money, professor of medical psychology and professor of pediatrics, emeritus, at Johns Hopkins University and Hospital, where he is director of the Psychohormonal Research Unit. Even the publications that are produced independently of Money reference him and reiterate his management philosophy. Although only one of the physicians interviewed has published with Money, they all essentially concur with his views and give the impression of a consensus that is rarely encountered in science. The one physician who raised some questions about Money's philosophy and the gender theory on which it is based has extensive experience with intersexuality in a nonindustrialized culture where the infant is matured differently with no apparent harm to gender development. Even though psychologists fiercely argue issues of gender identity and gender role development, doctors who treat intersexed infants seem untouched by these debates. There are still, in the late 1990s, few renegade voices from within the medical establishment. Why Money has been so single-handedly influential in promoting his ideas about gender is a question worthy of a separate substantial analysis. His management philosophy is conveyed in the following sources: John Money, J. G. Hampson, and J. L. Hampson, "Hermaphroditism: Recommendations Concerning Assignment of Sex, Change of Sex, and Psychologic Management"; John Money, *Sex Errors of the Body: Dilemmas, Education, Counseling;* John Money, Reynolds Potter, and Clarice S. Stoll, "Sex Reannouncement in Hereditary Sex Deformity: Psychology and Sociology of Habilitation"; Money and Ehrhardt; John Money, "Psychologic Consideration of Sex Assignment in Intersexuality"; John Money, "Psychological Counseling: Hermaphroditism"; John Money, Tom Mazur, Charles Abrams, and Bernard F. Norman, "Micropenis, Family Mental Health, and Neona-

tal Management: A Report on Fourteen Patients Reared as Girls"; and John Money, "Birth Defect of the Sex Organs: Telling the Parents and the Patient."

11. Money and Ehrhardt, 152.

12. One exception is the case followed by Milton Diamond in "Sexual Identity, Monozygotic Twins Reared in Discordant Sex Roles and a BBC Follow-up" and, with Keith Sigmundson, in "Sex Reassignment at Birth: Long-term Review and Clinical Applications."

13. Money, "Psychologic Consideration of Sex Assignment in Intersexuality."

14. Castro-Magana, Angulo, and Collipp.

15. Victor Braren et al., "True Hermaphroditism: A Rational Approach to Diagnosis and Treatment."

16. Studies of nonintersexed newborns have shown that, from the moment of birth, parents respond to their infant based on her or his gender. Jeffrey Rubin, F. J. Provenzano, and Z. Luria, "The Eye of the Beholder: Parents' Views on Sex of Newborns."

17. Money, Mazur, Abrams, and Norman.

18. There is evidence from other kinds of sources that once a gender attribution is made, all further information buttresses that attribution, and only the most contradictory new information will cause the original gender attribution to be questioned. Kessler and McKenna.

19. Castro-Magana, Angulo, and Collipp.

20. Money, "Psychologic Consideration of Sex Assignment in Intersexuality."

21. Technically, the term "micropenis" should be reserved for an exceptionally small but well-formed structure, a small, malformed "penis" should be referred to as a "microphallus" (Peter A. Lee et al.).

22. Money, Mazur, Abrams, and Norman, 26. A different view is argued by another leading gender-identity theorist: "When a little boy (with an imperfect penis) knows he is a male, he creates a penis that functions symbolically the same as those of boys with normal penises" (Robert J. Stoller, *Sex and Gender*).

23. W. Ch. Hecker, "Operative Correction of Intersexual Genitals in Children."

24. This way of presenting advice fails to understand that parents are part of a larger system. A pediatric endocrinologist told biologist Anne Fausto-Sterling that parents, especially young ones, are not independent actors. They rely on the advice of grandparents and older siblings, who, according to the physician, are more hysterical and push for an early gender assignment before all the medical data are analyzed (private communication, summer 1996).

25. Elizabeth Bing and Esselyn Rudikoff, "Divergent Ways of Parental Coping with Hermaphrodite Children."

26. These evasions must have many ramifications in everyday social interactions between parents, family, and friends. How people "fill in" the uncertainty such that interactions remain relatively normal is an interesting question that warrants further study. One of the pediatric

endocrinologists interviewed acknowledged that the published literature discusses intersex management only from the physicians' point of view. He asks, "How [do parents] experience what they're told, and what [do] they remember . . . and carry with them?" One published exception to this neglect of the parents' perspective is a case study comparing two different coping strategies. The first couple, although initially distressed, handled the traumatic event by regarding the abnormality as an act of God. The second couple, more educated and less religious, put their faith in medical science and expressed a need to fully understand the biochemistry of the defect. Bing and Rudikoff.

27. Tom Mazur, "Ambiguous Genitalia: Detection and Counseling," and Money "Psychologic Consideration of Sex Assignment in Intersexuality," 218.

28. Money, Potter, and Stoll, 211.

29. The term "reassignment" is more commonly used to describe the gender changes of those who are cognizant of their earlier gender, e.g., transsexuals—people whose gender itself was a mistake.

30. Although Money and Ehrhardt's socialization theory is uncontested by the physicians who treat intersexuality and is presented to parents as a matter of fact, there is actually much debate among psychologists about the effect of prenatal hormones on brain structure and ultimately on gender-role behavior and even on gender identity. The physicians interviewed agreed that the animal evidence for prenatal brain organization is compelling but that there is no evidence in humans that prenatal hormones have an inviolate or unilateral effect. If there is any effect of prenatal exposure to androgen, they believe it can easily be overcome and modified by psychosocial factors. It is this latter position, not the controversy in the field, that is communicated to the parents. For an argument favoring prenatally organized gender differences in the brain, see Milton Diamond, "Human Sexual Development: Biological Foundations for Social Development"; for a critique of that position, see Ruth Bleier, *Science and Gender. A Critique of Biology and Its Theories on Women.*

31. Money, "Psychological Counseling: Hermaphroditism," 610.

32. Money, Mazur, Abrams, and Norman, 18.

33. P. Donahoe, "Clinical Management of Intersex Abnormalities."

34. John Money, "Hermaphroditism and Pseudohermaphroditism."

35. Mojtaba Beheshti, Brian E. Hardy, Bernard M. Churchill, and Denis Daneman, "Gender Assignment in Male Pseudohermaphrodite Children." Of course, if the penis looked normal and the empty scrotum was overlooked, it might not be discovered until puberty that the male child was XX with a female internal structure.

36. Money, "Psychologic Consideration of Sex Assignment in Intersexuality," 216.

37. Weighing the probability of achieving a "perfect" penis against the probable trauma such procedures may entail is another social factor in decision making. According to an endocrinologist interviewed, if it seems that an XY infant with an inadequate penis would require as many as ten genital operations over a six-year period in order to have an adequate penis, the infant would be assigned the female gender. In this case, the endocrinologist's practical and compassionate concerns would override purely genital criteria.

38. Money, "Psychologic Consideration of Sex Assignment in Intersexuality," 217.

39. Castro-Magana, Angulo, and Collipp, 180.

40. It is unclear how much of this bias is the result of a general cultural devaluation of the female and how much is the result of physicians' belief in their ability to construct anatomically correct and functional female genitals.

41. John F. Oliven, *Sexual Hygiene and Pathology: A Manual for the Physician.*

42. Money, "Psychologic Consideration of Sex Assignment in Intersexuality," 215. Remnants of this anachronistic view can still be found, however, when doctors justify the removal of contradictory gonads on the grounds that they are typically sterile or at risk for malignancy (J. Dewhurst and D. B. Grant, "Intersex Problems"). Presumably, if the gonads were functional and healthy, their removal would provide an ethical dilemma for at least some medical professionals.

43. Although one set of authors argued that the views of the parents on the most appropriate gender for their child must be taken into account (Dewhurst and Grant, 1192), the physicians interviewed here denied direct knowledge of this kind of participation. They claimed that they personally had encountered few, if any, cases of parents who insisted on their child being assigned a particular gender. Yet each had heard about cases where a family's ethnicity or religious background biased them toward males. None of the physicians recalled whether this preference for male offspring meant the parents wanted a male regardless of the "inadequacy" of the penis, or whether it meant that the parents would have greater difficulty with a less-than-perfect male than with a "normal" female.

44. Money, "Psychological Counseling: Hermaphroditism," 613.

45. As with the literature on infancy, most of the published material on adolescents is on surgical and hormonal management rather than on social management. See, for example, Joel J. Roslyn, Eric W. Fonkalsrud, and Barbara Lippe, "Intersex Disorders in Adolescents and Adults."

46. Mazur, 421.

47. Dewhurst and Grant, 1193.

48. Mazur, 422.

49. Ibid.

50. For an extended discussion of different ways of conceptualizing what is natural, see Richard W. Smith, "What Kind of Sex Is Natural?"

51. This supports sociologist Harold Garfinkel's argument that we treat routine events as our *due* as social members and that we treat gender, like all normal forms, as a moral imperative. It is no wonder, then, that physicians conceptualize what they are doing as natural and unquestionably "right." Harold Garfinkel, *Studies in Ethnomethodology*.

52. Sherry B. Ortner, "Is Female to Male as Nature Is to Culture?"

53. Money, "Psychological Counseling: Hermaphroditism," 618.

REFERENCES

Beheshti, Mojtaba, Brian E. Hardy, Bernard M. Churchill, and Denis Daneman. "Gender Assignment in Male Pseudohermaphrodite Children." *Urology* 22, no. 6 (December 1983): 604–607.

Bing, Elizabeth, and Esselyn Rudikoff. "Divergent Ways of Parental Coping with Hermaphrodite Children." *Medical Aspects of Human Sexuality* (December 1970): 73–88.

Blackless, Melanie, Anthony Charuvastra, Amanda Derryck, Anne Fausto-Sterling, Karl Lauzanne, and Ellen Lee. "How Sexually Dimorphic Are We?" Unpublished manuscript, 1997.

Bleier, Ruth. *Science and Gender: A Critique of Biology and Its Theories on Women*. New York: Pergamon Press, 1984.

Bolkenius, M., R. Daum, and E. Heinrich. "Paediatric Surgical Principles in the Management of Children with Intersex." *Progress in Pediatric Surgery* 17 (1984): 33–38.

Braren, Victor, John J. Warner, Ian M. Burr, Alfred Slonim, James A. O'Neill Jr., and Robert K. Rhamy. "True Hermaphroditism: A Rational Approach to Diagnosis and Treatment." *Urology* 15 (June 1980): 569–574.

Bullough, Vern. *Sexual Variance in Society and History*. New York: John Wiley and Sons, 1976.

Castro-Magana, Mariano, Moris Angulo, and Platon J. Collipp. "Management of the Child with Ambiguous Genitalia." *Medical Aspects of Human Sexuality* 18, no. 4 (April 1984): 172–188.

Dewhurst, J., and D. B. Grant. "Intersex Problems." *Archives of Disease in Childhood* 59 (July–December 1984): 1191–1194.

Diamond, Milton. "Human Sexual Development: Biological Foundations for Social Development." In *Human Sexuality in Four Perspectives*, ed. Frank A. Beach, 22–61. Baltimore: The Johns Hopkins University Press, 1976.

———. "Sexual Identity, Monozygotic Twins Reared in Discordant Sex Roles and a BBC Follow-Up." *Archives of Sexual Behavior* 11, no. 2 (1982): 181–186.

———, and Keith Sigmundson. "Sex Reassignment of Birth: Long-term Review and Clinical Applications." *Archives of Pediatric and Adolescent Medicine* 151 (May 1997): 298–304.

Donahoe, P. "Clinical Management of Intersex Abnormalities." *Current Problems in Surgery* 28 (1991): 519–579.

Dreger, Alice Domurat. *Hermaphrodites and the Medical Invention of Sex*. Cambridge: Harvard University Press, 1998.

Ellis, Havelock. *Studies in the Psychology of Sex*. New York: Random House, 1942.

Fiedler, Leslie. *Freaks: Myths and Images of the Second Self*. New York: Simon and Schuster, 1978.

Foucault, Michael. *Herculine Barbin*. New York: Pantheon Books, 1978.

———. *History of Sexuality*. New York: Pantheon Books, 1980.

Freud, Sigmund. "Some Psychical Consequences of the Anatomical Distinctions Between the Sexes" (1925). In *The Complete Psychological Works*, trans. and ed. J. Strachy, vol. 18. New York: Norton, 1976.

Garfinkel, Harold. *Studies in Ethnomethodology*. Englewood Cliffs, N.J.: Prentice-Hall, 1967.

Glassberg, Kenneth I. "Gender Assignment in Newborn Male Pseudohermaphodites." *Urologic Clinics of North America* 7 (June 1980): 409–421.

Hecker, W. Ch. "Operative Correction of Intersexual Genitals in Children." *Progress in Pediatric Surgery* 17 (1984): 21–31.

Hendricks, Melissa. "Is It a Boy or a Girl?" *Johns Hopkins Magazine* 45, no. 5 (November 1993): 10–16.

Kessler, Suzanne J., and Wendy McKenna. *Gender: An Ethnomethodological Approach*. New York: Wiley-Interscience, 1978; Chicago: University of Chicago Press, 1985.

Lee, Peter A., Thomas Mazur, Robert Danish, James Amrhein, Robert M. Blizzard, John Money, and Claude J. Migeon. "Micropenis: I. Criteria, Etiologies and Classification." *The Johns Hopkins Medical Journal* 146 (1980): 156–163.

Lev-Ran, Arye. "Sex Reversal as Related to Clinical Syndromes in Human Beings." In *Handbook of Sexology II: Genetics, Hormones and Behavior*, ed. John Money and H. Musaph, 157–173. New York: Elsevier, 1978.

Mazur, Tom. "Ambiguous Genitalia: Detection and Counseling." *Pediatric Nursing* 9 (November/December 1983): 417–431.

Money, John. "Birth Defect of the Sex Organs: Telling the Parents and the Patient." *British Journal of Sexual Medicine* 10 (March 1983): 14.

———. "Hermaphroditism and Pseudohermaphroditism." In *Gynecologic Endocrinology*, ed. Jay J. Gold, 449–464. New York: Hoeber, 1968.

———. "Psychologic Consideration of Sex Assignment in Intersexuality." *Clinics in Plastic Surgery* 1 (April 1974): 215–222.

———. "Psychological Counseling: Hermaphroditism." In *Endocrine and Genetic Diseases of Childhood and Adolescence*, ed. L. I. Gardner, 609–618. Philadelphia: W. B. Saunders, 1975.

———. *Sex Errors of the Body: Dilemmas, Education, Counseling*. Baltimore: The Johns Hopkins University Press, 1968. Reprint, 1994.

————, and Anke A. Ehrhardt. *Man & Woman, Boy & Girl.* Baltimore: The Johns Hopkins University Press, 1972.

————, J. G. Hampson, and J. L. Hampson. "Hermaphroditism: Recommendations Concerning Assignment of Sex, Change of Sex, and Psychologic Management." *Bulletin of The Johns Hopkins Hospital* 97 (1955): 284–300.

————, Tom Mazur, Charles Abrams, and Bernard F. Norman. "Micropenis, Family Mental Health, and Neonatal Management: A Report on Fourteen Patients Reared as Girls." *Journal of Preventive Psychiatry* 1, no. 1 (1981): 17–27.

————, Reynolds Potter, and Clarice S. Stoll. "Sex Reannouncement in Hereditary Sex Deformity: Psychology and Sociology of Habilitation." *Social Science and Medicine* 3 (1969): 207–216.

Oliven, John F. *Sexual Hygiene and Pathology: A Manual for the Physician.* Philadelphia: J. B. Lippincott, 1955.

Ortner, Sherry B. "Is Female to Male as Nature Is to Culture?" In *Woman, Culture, and Society,* ed. Michelle Zimbalist Rosaldo and Louise Lamphere, 67–87. Stanford, Calif.: Stanford University Press, 1974.

Rohatgi, M. "Intersex Disorders: An Approach to Surgical Management." *Indian Journal of Pediatrics* 59 (1992): 523–530.

Roslyn, Joel J., Eric W. Fonkalsrud, and Barbara Lippe. "Intersex Disorders in Adolescents and Adults." *The American Journal of Surgery* 146 (July 1983): 138–144.

Rubin, Jeffrey, F. J. Provenzano, and Z. Luria. "The Eye of the Beholder: Parents' Views on Sex of Newborns." *American Journal of Orthopsychiatry* 44, no. 4 (1974): 512–519.

Slijper, F. M. E., S. L. S. Drop, J. C. Molenaar, and R. J. Scholtmeijer. "Neonates with Abnormal Genital Development Assigned the Female Sex: Parent Counseling." *Journal of Sex Education and Therapy* 20, no. 1 (1994): 9–17.

Smith, Richard W. "What Kind of Sex Is Natural?" In *The Frontiers of Sex Research,* ed. Vern Bullough, 103–111. Buffalo: Prometheus, 1979.

Stoller, Robert J. *Sex and Gender,* vol. 1. New York: J. Aronson, 1968.

READING *8* **Susan Stryker**

Transgender Feminism: Queering the Woman Question[1]

Many years ago, I paid a visit to my son's kindergarten room for parent-teacher night. Among the treats in store for us parents that evening was a chance to look at the *My Favorite Things* book that each child had prepared over the first few weeks of classes. Each page was blank except for a pre-printed line that said "My favorite color is (blank)," or "My favorite food is (blank)," or "My favorite story is (blank)"; students were supposed to fill in the blanks with their favorite things and draw an accompanying picture. My son had filled the blanks and empty spaces of his book with many such things as "green," "pizza" and "*Goodnight Moon,*" but I was unprepared for his response to "My favorite animal is (blank)." His favorite animal was "yeast." I looked up at the teacher, who had been watching me in anticipation of this moment. "Yeast?" I said, and she, barely suppressing her glee, said, "Yeah.

And when I asked why yeast was his favorite animal, he said, 'It just makes the category animal seem more interesting.'"

At the risk of suggesting that the category "woman" is somehow not interesting *enough* without a transgender supplement, which is certainly not my intent, I have to confess that there is a sense in which "woman," as a category of human personhood, is indeed, for me, *more* interesting when we include transgender phenomena within its rubric. The work required to encompass transgender within the bounds of womanhood takes women's studies, and queer feminist theorizing, in important and necessary directions. It takes us directly into the basic questions of the sex/gender distinction, and of the concept of a sex/gender system, that lie at the heart of Anglophone feminism, Once there, transgender phenomena ask us to follow basic feminist insights to their logical conclusion (biology is not destiny, and one is not born a woman, right?) And yet, transgender phenomena simultaneously threaten to refigure the basic conceptual and representational framework within which the category "woman" has been conventionally understood, deployed, embraced, and resisted.

Perhaps "gender," transgender tells us, is not related to "sex" in quite the same way that an apple is related to the reflection of a red fruit in the mirror; it is not a mimetic relationship. Perhaps "sex" is a category that, like citizenship, can be attained by the non-native residents of a particular location by following certain procedures. Perhaps gender has a more complex genealogy, at the level of individual psychobiography as well as collective sociohistorical process, than can be grasped or accounted for by the currently dominant binary sex/gender model of Eurocentric modernity. And perhaps what is to be learned by grappling with transgender concerns is relevant to a great many people, including nontransgendered women and men. Perhaps transgender discourses help us think in terms of embodied specificities, as *women's* studies has traditionally tried to do, while also giving us a way to think about gender as a system with multiple nodes and positions, as *gender* studies increasingly requires us to do. Perhaps transgender studies, which emerged in the academy at the intersection of feminism and queer theory over the course of the last decade or so, can be thought of as one productive way to "queer the woman question."[2]

If we define "transgender phenomena" broadly as anything that disrupts or denaturalizes normative gender, and which calls our attention to the processes through which normativity is produced and atypicality achieves visibility, "transgender" becomes an incredibly useful analytical concept. What might "transgender feminism"—a feminism that focuses on marginalized gender expressions as well as normative ones—look like?

As an historian of the United States, my training encourages me to approach currently salient questions by looking at the past through new eyes. Questions that matter now, historians are taught to think, are always framed by enabling conditions that precede them. Thus, when I want to know what transgender feminism might be, I try to learn what it has already been. When I learned, for example, that the first publication of the post-WWII transgender movement, a short-lived early-1950s magazine called *Transvestia*,[3] was produced by a group calling itself The Society for Equality in Dress,[3] I not only saw that a group of male

transvestites in Southern California had embraced the rhetoric of first-wave feminism and applied the concept of gender equality to the marginalized topic of cross-dressing; I also came to think differently about Amelia Bloomer and the antebellum clothing reform movement. To the extent that breaking out of the conventional constrictions of womanhood is both a feminist and a transgender practice, what we might conceivably call transgender feminism arguably has been around since the first half of the 19th century.

Looking back, it is increasingly obvious that transgender phenomena are not limited to individuals who have "transgendered" personal identities. Rather, they are signposts that point to many different kinds of bodies and subjects, and they can help us see how gender can function as part of a more extensive apparatus of social domination and control. Gender as a form of social control is not limited to the control of bodies defined as "women's bodies," or the control of female reproductive capacities. Because genders are categories through which we recognize the personhood of others (as well as ourselves), because they are categories without which we have great difficulty in recognizing personhood at all, gender also functions as a mechanism of control when some loss of gender status is threatened, or when claims of membership in a gender are denied. Why is it considered a heterosexist putdown to call some lesbians mannish? Why, if a working-class woman does certain kinds of physically demanding labor, or if a middle-class woman surpasses a certain level of professional accomplishment, is their feminine respectability called into question? Stripping away gender, and misattributing gender, are practices of social domination, regulation, and control that threaten social abjection; they operate by attaching transgender stigma to various unruly bodies and subject positions, not just to "transgendered" ones.[4]

There is also, however, a lost history of feminist activism by self-identified transgender people waiting to be recovered. My own historical research into 20th-century transgender communities and identities teaches me that activists on transgender issues were involved in multi-issue political movements in the 1960s and 1970s, including radical feminism. The ascendancy of cultural feminism and lesbian separatism by the mid-1970s—both of which cast transgender practices, particularly transsexuality, as reactionary patriarchal anachronisms—largely erased knowledge of this early transgender activism from feminist consciousness. Janice Raymond, in her outrageously transphobic book *The Transsexual Empire,* went so far as to suggest that "the problem of transsexualism would best be served by morally mandating it out of existence."[5] Even in this period, however, when identity politics effectively disconnected transgender feminism from the broader women's movement and before the queer cultural politics of the 1990s revitalized and expanded the transgender movement, it is possible to find startling historical episodes that compel us to reexamine what we think we know about the feminist history of the recent past. The Radical Queens drag collective in Philadelphia, for example, had a "sister house" relationship with a lesbian separatist commune during the early 1970s, and participated in mainstream feminist activism through involvement with the local chapter of N.O.W. In the later 1970s in Washington, D.C., secretive clubs for married heterosexual male cross-dressers began holding consciousness-raising sessions; they argued that to identify as feminine meant they were politically obligated to come out as feminists, speak out as transvestites, and work publicly for passage of the Equal Rights Amendment.[6]

In addition to offering a revisionist history of feminist activism, transgender issues also engage many of the foundational questions in the social sciences and life sciences as they pertain to feminist inquiry. The biological body, which is typically assumed to be a single organically unified natural object characterized by one and only one of two available sex statuses, is demonstrably no such thing. The so-called "sex of the body" is an interpretive fiction that narrates a complex amalgamation of gland secretions and reproductive organs, chromosomes and genes, morphological characteristics and physiognomic features. There are far more than two viable aggregations of sexed bodily being. At what cost, for what purposes, and through what means do we collapse this diversity of embodiment into the social categories "woman" and "man"? How does the psychical subject who forms in this material context become aware of itself, of its embodied situation, of its position in language, family, or society? How does it learn to answer to one or the other of the two personal pronouns "he" or "she," and to recognize "it" as a disavowed option that forecloses personhood? How do these processes vary from individual to individual, from place to place, and from time to time? These are questions of importance to feminism, usually relegated to the domains of biology and psychology, that transgender phenomena can help us think through. Transgender feminism gives us another axis,

along with critical race studies or disability studies, to learn more about the ways in which bodily difference becomes the basis for socially constructed hierarchies, and helps us see in new ways how we are all inextricably situated, through the inescapable necessity of our own bodies, in terms of race, sex, gender, or ability.

When we look cross-culturally and trans-historically at societies, as anthropologists and sociologists tend to do, we readily see patterns of variations in the social organization of biological reproduction, labor, economic exchange, and kinship; we see a variety of culturally specific configurations of embodiment, identity, desire, social status, and social role. Which of these patterns do we call "gender," and which do we call "transgender"? The question makes sense only in reference to an unstated norm that allows us to distinguish between the two. To examine "transgender" cross-culturally and trans-historically is to articulate the masked assumptions that produce gender normativity in any given (time-bound and geographically constrained) context. To examine "transgender" is thus to risk decentering the privileged standpoint of white Eurocentric modernity. It is to denaturize and dereify the terms through which we ground our own genders, in order to confront the possibility of radically different ways of being in the world. This, too, is a feminist project.[7]

A third set of concerns that make transgender feminism interesting for women's studies is the extent to which "transgender," for more than a decade now, has served as a laboratory and proving ground for the various postmodern and poststructuralist critical theories that have transformed humanities scholarship in general over the past half century, and which have played a role in structuring the generational debates about "second wave" and "third wave" feminism. This is a debate in which I take an explicitly partisan position, largely in response to the utterly inexcusable level of overt transphobia in second-wave feminisim.

An unfortunate consequence of the second-wave feminist turn to an untheorized female body as the ultimate ground for feminist practice (which has to be understood historically in the context of reactionary political pressures that fragmented all sorts of movements posing radical threats to the established order and required them to find new, often ontological, bases for political resistance) was that it steered feminist analysis in directions that ill equipped it to engage theoretically with the emerging material conditions of social life within advanced capitalism that collectively have come to be called, more or less usefully, "postmodernity." The overarching tendency of second-wave feminism to couch its political analyses within moral narratives that link "woman" with "natural," "natural" with "good," "good" with "true," and "true" with "right" has been predicated on an increasingly non-utilitarian modernist epistemology. Within the representational framework of Eurocentric modernity, which posits gender as the superstructural sign of the material referent of sex, transgender practices have been morally condemned as unnatural, bad, false, and wrong, in that they fundamentally misalign the proper relationship between sex and gender. The people who engage in such misrepresentations can be understood only as duped or duplicitous, fools or enemies to be pitied or scorned. The failure of second-wave feminism to do justice to transgender issues in the 1970s; 1980s, and afterward is rooted in its more fundamental theoretical failure to recognize the conceptual limits of modernist epistemology.[8]

Transgender theorizing in third-wave feminism begins from a different—postmodern—epistemological standpoint which imagines new ways for sexed bodies to signify gender. Within the feminist third wave, and within humanities scholarship in general, transgender phenomena have come to constitute important evidence in recent arguments about essentialism and social construction, performativity and citationality, hybridity and fluidity, anti-foundationalist ontologies and non-referential epistemologies, the proliferation of perversities, the collapse of difference, the triumph of technology, the advent of posthumanism, and the end of the world as we know it. While it is easy to parody the specialized and sometimes alienating jargon of these debates, the issues at stake are quite large, involving as they do the actual as well as theoretical dismantling of power relations that sustain various privileges associated with normativity and injustices directed at minorities. Because these debates are irreducibly political, because they constitute an ideological landscape upon which material struggles are waged within the academy for research funds and promotions, for tenure and teaching loads, transgender phenomena have come to occupy a curiously strategic location in the working lives of humanities professionals, whether they like it or not. This brings me at last to the crux of my remarks.

For all the reasons I have suggested, transgender phenomena are *interesting* for feminism, women's studies, gender studies, sexuality studies, and so forth. But *interesting,* by itself, is not enough, when hard decisions about budgets and staffing have to be made in academic departments, priorities and commitments actualized through classroom allocations and affirmative action hiring goals. *Interesting* also has to be *important,* and transgender is rarely considered important. All too often transgender is thought to name only a largely irrelevant class of phenomena that occupy the marginal fringe of the hegemonic gender categories man and woman, or else it is seen as one of the later, minor accretions to the gay and lesbian movement, along with bisexual and intersexed. At best, transgender is considered a portent of a future that seems to await us, for good or ill. But it remains a canary in the cultural coal mine, not an analytical workhorse for pulling down the patriarchy and other associated social ills. As long as transgender is conceived as the fraction of a fraction of a fraction of a movement, as long as it is thought to represent only some inconsequential outliers in a bigger and more important set of data, there is very little reason to support transgender concerns at the institutional level. Transgender will always lose by the numbers. The transgender community is tiny. In (so-called) liberal democracies that measures political strength by the number of votes or the number of dollars, transgender doesn't count for much, or add up to a lot. But there is another way to think about the importance of transgender concerns at this moment in our history.

One measure of an issue's potential is not how many people directly identify with it, but rather, how many other issues it can be linked with in a productive fashion. How, in other words, can an issue be *articulated,* in the double sense of "articulation," meaning both "to bring into language," and "the act of flexibly conjoining."[9] Articulating a transgender politics is part of the specialized work that I do as an activist transgender intellectual. How many issues can I link together through my experience of the category transgender?

To the extent I am perceived as a woman (which is most of the time), I experience the same misogyny as other women, and to the extent that I am perceived as a man (which happens every now and then), I experience the homophobia directed at gay men—both forms of oppression, in my experience, being rooted in a cultural devaluation of the feminine. My transgender status, to the extent that it is apparent to others, manifests itself through the appearance of my bodily surface and my shape, in much the same way that race is constructed, in part, through visuality and skin, and in much the same way that the beauty system operates by privileging certain modes of appearance. My transsexual body is different from most other bodies, and while this difference does not impair me, it has been medicalized, and I am sometimes disabled by the social oppression that takes aim at the specific form of my difference. Because I am formally classified as a person with a psychopathology known as Gender Identity Disorder, I am subject to the social stigma attached to mental illness, and I am more vulnerable to unwanted medical-psychiatric interventions. Because changing personal identification documents is an expensive and drawn-out affair, I have spent part of my life as an undocumented worker. Because identification documents such as drivers licenses and passports are coded with multiple levels of information, including previous names and "A.K.A.'s," my privacy, and perhaps my personal safety, are at risk every time I drive too fast or cross a border. When I travel I always have to ask myself—will some aspect of my appearance, some bit of data buried in the magnetic strip on some piece of plastic with my picture on it, create suspicion and result in my detention? In this era of terror and security, we are all surveiled, we are all profiled, but some of us have more to fear from the state than others. Staying home, however, does not make me safer. If I risk arrest by engaging in non-violent demonstrations, or violent political protest, the incarceration complex would not readily accommodate my needs; even though I am a post-operative male-to-female transsexual, I could wind up in a men's prison where I would be at extreme risk of rape and sexual assault. Because I am transgendered, I am more likely to experience discrimination in housing, employment, and access to health care, more likely to experience violence. These are not abstract issues: I have lost jobs, and not been offered jobs, because I am transgendered. I have had doctors walk out of exam rooms in disgust; I have had more trouble finding and retaining housing because I am transgendered; I have had my home burglarized and my property vandalized, and I have been assaulted, because I am transgendered.

Let me recapitulate what I can personally articulate through transgender: misogyny, homophobia, racism, looksism, disability, medical colonization, coercive psychiatrization, undocumented labor, border control, state surveillance, population profiling, the prison-industrial complex, employment discrimination, housing discrimination, lack of health care, denial of access to social services, and violent hate crimes. These issues are my issues, not because I think it's chic to be politically progressive. These issues are my issues, not because I feel guilty about being white, highly educated, or a citizen of the United States. These issues are my issues because my bodily being lives in the space where these issues intersect. I articulate these issues

when my mouth speaks the words that my mind puts together from what my body knows. It is by winning the struggles over these issues that my body as it is lived for me survives—or by losing them, that it will die. If these issues are your issues as well, then transgender needs to be part of your intellectual and political agenda. It is one of your issues.

I conclude now with some thoughts on yet another aspect of transgender articulation, the one mentioned in my title, which is how transgender issues articulate, or join together, feminist and queer projects. "Trans-" is troublesome for both LGBT communities and feminism, but the kind of knowledge that emerges from this linkage is precisely the kind of knowledge that we desperately need in the larger social arena.

Trans is not a "sexual identity," and therefore fits awkwardly in the LGBT rubric. That is, "transgender" does not describe a sexual orientation (like homosexual, bisexual, heterosexual, or asexual), nor are transgender people typically attracted to other transgender people in the same way that lesbians are attracted to other lesbians, or gay men to other gay men. Transgender status is more like race or class, in that it cuts across the categories of sexual identity.[10] Neither is transgender (at least currently, in Eurocentric modernity) an identity term like "woman" or "man" that names a gender category within a social system. It is a way of being a man or a woman, or a way of marking resistance to those terms. Transgender analyses of gender oppression and hierarchy, unlike more normative feminist analyses, are not primarily concerned with the differential operations of power upon particular identity categories that create inequalities within gender systems, but rather on how the system itself produces a multitude of possible positions that it then works to center or to marginalize.

Transgender practices and identities are a form of gender trouble, in that they call attention to contradictions in how we tend to think about gender, sex, and sexuality. But the transgender knowledges that emerge from these troubling contradictions, I want to argue, can yoke together queer and feminist projects in a way that helps break the impasse of identity politics that has so crippled progressive movements in the United States. Since the early 1970s, progressive politics have fragmented along identity lines practically to the point of absurdity. While it undoubtedly has been vital over the past few decades of movement history to enunciate the particularities of all our manifold forms of bodily being in the world, it is equally important that we now find new ways of articulating our commonalities without falling into the equally dead-end logic of total-izing philosophies and programs.

Transgender studies offers us one critical methodol-ogy for thinking through the diverse particularities of our embodied lives, as well for thinking through the commonalities we share through our mutual enmesh-ment in more global systems. Reactionary political move-ments have been very effective in telling stories about shared values—family, religion, tradition. We who work at the intersection of queer and feminist movements, we who have a different vision of our collective future, need to become equally adept in telling stories that link us in ways that advance the cause of justice, and that hold forth the promise of happy endings for all our strivings. Bringing transgender issues into women's studies, and into feminist movement building, is one concrete way to be engaged in that important work.

While it is politically necessary to include transgen-der issues in feminist theorizing and organizing, it is not intellectually responsible, nor ethically defensible, to teach transgender studies in academic women's studies without being engaged in peer-to-peer conver-sations with various sorts of trans- and genderqueer people. Something crucial is lost when academically-based feminists fail to support transgender inclusion in the academic workplace. Genderqueer youth who have come of age after the "queer '90s" are now pass-ing through the higher education system, and they increasingly fail to recognize the applicability of pre-vailing modes of feminist discourse for their own lives and experiences. How we each live our bodies in the world is a vital source of knowledge for us all, and to teach trans studies without being in dialog with trans people is akin to teaching race studies only from a position of whiteness, or gender studies only from a position of masculinity. Why is transgender not a cate-gory targeted for affirmative action in hiring, and val-ued the same way that racial diversity is valued? It is past time for feminists who have imagined that trans-gender issues have not been part of their own concerns to take a long, hard look in the mirror. What in their own constructions of self, their own experiences of gender, prevents their recognition of transgender peo-ple as being somehow like themselves—as people engaged in parallel, intersecting, and overlapping struggles, who are not fundamentally Other?

Transgender phenomena now present queer figures on the horizon of feminist visibility. Their calls for attention are too often received, however, as an uncomfortable solicitation from an alien and unthink-able monstrosity best left somewhere outside the vil-lage gates. But justice, when we first feel its claims upon us, typically points us toward a future we can scarcely imagine. At the historical moment when racial slavery in the United States at long last became mor-ally indefensible, and the nation plunged into civil war, what did the future of the nation look like? When greenhouse gas emissions finally become equally mor-ally indefensible, what shape will a post-oil world take? Transgender issues make similar claims of justice upon us all, and promise equally unthinkable transfor-mations.[11] Recognizing the legitimacy of these claims will change the world, and feminism along with it, in ways we can now hardly fathom. It's about time.

NOTES

1. This essay was first delivered as a keynote address at Third Wave Feminism, an international conference at the Institute for Feminist Theory and Research, University of Exeter, UK, July 25, 2002; and in revised form at the Presi-dential Session plenary on "Transgender Theory" at the National Women's Studies Association Annual Meeting, Oakland, California, June 17, 2006. Many of the ideas I present here have been worked out in greater detail in Stryker 1994,1998, 2004, and 2006; see also Zalewski. For another account of the relationship between recent femi-nist scholarship and transgender issues, see Heyes.

2. Meyerowitz 2002, p. 179.

3. My thoughts on the role of transgender phenomena for understanding United States history in general are signifi-cantly indebted to Joanne Meyerowitz; see Meyerowitz 2006.

4. Raymond, 178. See also Hausman, 9–14, for an overview of cultural feminist critiques of transsexuality, and Billings and Urban for a particularly cogent exposition and appli-cation of this approach.

5. Tommi Avicolli Mecca interview, November 19, 1998, in author's possession; see also Silverman and Stryker 2005, and Members of the Gay and Lesbian Historical Society 1998, for transgender involvement in progressive grass-roots political activism in the San Francisco Bay Area in the 1960s.

6. See Blackwood and Wieringa, and Morgan and Towle, on cross-cultural studies of transgender phenomena.

7. For a post-structuralist, anti-foundationalist critique of second-wave feminism, see Butler.

8. The concept of "articulation" is taken from Laclau and Mouffe 2001.

9. See Gamson on the trouble transgender presents to iden-tity movements.

10. On monstrosity and justice, see Sullivan 2006.

REFERENCES

Billings, Dwight B. and Thomas Urban. "The Sociomedical Construction of Transsexualism: An Interpretation and Critique." *Social Problems* 29 (1981), 266–282.

Blackwood, Evelyn and Saskia Wieringa, eds. *Female Desires: Same Sex Relations and Transgender Practices Across Cultures.* New York: Columbia University Press, 1999.

Butler, Judith. "Contingent Foundations: Feminism and the Question of 'Postmodernism.'" In Judith Butler and Joan Scott, eds., *Feminists Theorize the Political.* New York: Routledge, 1992. Pp. 3–21.

Gamson, Joshua. "Must Identity Movements Self-Destruct? A Queer Dilemma." *Social Problems* (1995) Vol. 42, no. 3, 390–406.

Heyes, Cressida. "Feminist Solidarity After Queer Theory: The Case of Transgender." *Signs* (2003) Vol. 28, no. 4, 1093–1120.

Laclau, Ernesto and Chantal Mouffe. *Hegemony and Socialist Strategy: Towards a Radical Democratic Politics.* London: Verso. 2001. Second Edition.

Mecca, Tommi Avicolli. Interview by Susan Stryker. November 19, 1998. Transcript in author's possession.

Members of the Gay and Lesbian Historical Society. "MTF Transgender Activism in San Francisco's Tenderloin: Commentary and Interview with Elliot Blackstone." *GLQ: A Journal of Lesbian and Gay Studies* 4:2 (1998), 349–372.

Meyerowitz, Joanne. *How Sex Changed: A History of Transsexuality in the United States.* Cambridge: Harvard University Press. 2002.

Meyerowitz, Joanne. "A New History of Gender." Paper delivered at Trans/Forming Knowledge: The Implications of Transgender Studies for Women's, Gender, and Sexuality Studies. University of Chicago, February 17, 2006. Podcast at http://humanities.uchicago.edu/orgs/cgs/Trans%20Conference%20Audio%20Files/Session%202_Intro_Meyerowitz.mp3. Accessed on June 27, 2006.

Morgan, Lynn M. and Evan B. Towle, "Romancing the Transgender Native: Rethinking the Use of the 'Third Gender' Concept." *GLQ: A Journal of Lesbian and Gay Studies* Vol. 8, no. 4, 469–497.

Raymond, Janice. *The Transsexual Empire: The Making of the She-Male.* New York: Teachers College Press. Reissued with new introduction, 1994; orig. pub. Boston: Beacon Press. 1979.

Silverman, Victor and Susan Stryker. *Screaming Queens: The Riot at Compton's Cafeteria.* Documentary film. (USA 2005).

Stryker, Susan. "(De)Subjugated Knowledges: An Introduction to Transgender Studies." In Susan Stryker and Stephen Whittle, eds., *The Transgender Studies Reader.* New York: Routledge. 2006. Pp. 1–18.

———. "My Words to Victor Frankenstein Above the Village of Chamounix: Performing Transgender Rage." *GLQ: A Journal of Lesbian and Gay Studies* 1:3 (1994), 237–254.

———. "Introduction: The Transgender Issue." *GLQ: A Journal of Lesbian and Gay Studies* 4:2 (1998), 145–158.

———. "Transgender Studies: Queer Theory's Evil Twin." *GLQ: A Journal of Lesbian and Gay Studies* 10:2 (Spring, 2004), 212–215.

Sullivan, Nikki. "Transmogrification: (Un)Becoming Others." In Susan Stryker and Stephen Whittle, eds., *The Transgender Studies Reader.* New York: Routledge. 2006. Pp. 552–564.

Zalewski, Marysia. "A Conversation with Susan Stryker." *International Feminist Journal of Politics* 5:1 (April 2003), 118–125.

READING *9*   **Maxine Baca Zinn**
Bonnie Thornton Dill

Theorizing Difference from Multiracial Feminism

Women of color have long challenged the hegemony of feminisms constructed primarily around the lives of white middle-class women. Since the late 1960s, U.S. women of color have taken issue with unitary theories of gender. Our critiques grew out of the widespread concern about the exclusion of women of color from feminist scholarship and the misinterpretation of our experiences,[1] and ultimately "out of the very discourses, denying, permitting, and producing difference."[2] Speaking simultaneously from "within and against" *both* women's liberation *and* antiracist movements, we have insisted on the need to challenge systems of domination,[3] not merely as gendered subjects but as women whose lives are affected by our location in multiple hierarchies.

Recently, and largely in response to these challenges, work that links gender to other forms of domination is increasing. In this article, we examine this connection further as well as the ways in which difference and diversity infuse contemporary feminist studies. Our analysis draws on a conceptual framework that we refer to as "multiracial feminism."[4] This perspective is an attempt to go beyond a mere recognition of diversity and difference among women to examine structures of domination, specifically the importance of race in understanding the social construction of gender. Despite the varied concerns and multiple intellectual stances which characterize the feminisms of women of color, they share an emphasis on race as a primary force situating genders differently. It is the centrality of race, of institutionalized racism, and of struggles against racial oppression that link the various feminist perspectives within this framework. Together, they demonstrate that racial meanings offer new theoretical directions for feminist thought.

TENSIONS IN CONTEMPORARY DIFFERENCE FEMINISM

Objections to the false universalism embedded in the concept "woman" emerged within other discourses as well as those of women of color.[5] Lesbian feminists and postmodern feminists put forth their own versions of what Susan Bordo has called "gender skepticism."[6]

Many thinkers within mainstream feminism have responded to these critiques with efforts to contextualize gender. The search for women's "universal" or "essential" characteristics is being abandoned. By examining gender in the context of other social divisions and perspectives, difference has gradually become important—even problematizing the universal categories of "women" and "men." Sandra Harding expresses the shift best in her claim that "there are no gender relations *per se*, but only gender relations as constructed by and between classes, races, and cultures."[7]

Many feminists now contend that difference occupies center stage as *the* project of women studies today.[8] According to one scholar, "difference has replaced equality as the central concern of feminist theory."[9] Many have welcomed the change, hailing it as a major revitalizing force in U.S. feminist theory.[10] But if *some* priorities within mainstream feminist thought have been refocused by

attention to difference, there remains an "uneasy alliance"[11] between women of color and other feminists.

If difference has helped revitalize academic feminisms, it has also "upset the apple cart" and introduced new conflicts into feminist studies.[12] For example, in a recent and widely discussed essay, Jane Rowland Martin argues that the current preoccupation with difference is leading feminism into dangerous traps. She fears that in giving privileged status to a predetermined set of analytic categories (race, ethnicity, and class), "we affirm the existence of nothing but difference." She asks, "How do we know that for us, difference does not turn on being fat, or religious, or in an abusive relationship?"[13]

We, too, see pitfalls in some strands of the difference project. However, our perspectives take their bearings from social relations. Race and class differences are crucial, we argue, not as individual characteristics (such as being fat) but insofar as they are primary organizing principles of a society which locates and positions groups within that society's opportunity structures.

Despite the much-heralded diversity trend within feminist studies, difference is often reduced to mere pluralism: a "live and let live" approach where principles of relativism generate a long list of diversities which begin with gender, class, and race and continue through a range of social structural as well as personal characteristics.[14] Another disturbing pattern, which bell hooks refers to as "the commodification of difference," is the representation of diversity as a form of exotica, "a spice, seasoning that livens up the dull dish that is mainstream white culture."[15] The major limitation of these approaches is the failure to attend to the power relations that accompany difference. Moreover, these approaches ignore the inequalities that cause some characteristics to be seen as "normal" while others are seen as "different" and thus, deviant.

Maria C. Lugones expresses irritation at those feminists who see only the *problem* of difference without recognizing *difference*.[16] Increasingly, we find that difference *is* recognized. But this in no way means that difference occupies a "privileged" theoretical status. Instead of using difference to rethink the category of women, difference is often a euphemism for women who differ from the traditional norm. Even in purporting to accept difference, feminist pluralism often creates a social reality that reverts to universalizing women:

> So much feminist scholarship assumes that when we
> cut through all of the diversity among women created
> by differences of racial classification, ethnicity, social

class, and sexual orientation, a "universal truth" concerning women and gender lies buried underneath. But if we can face the scary possibility that no such certainty exists and that persisting in such a search will always distort or omit someone's experiences, with what do we replace this old way of thinking? Gender differences and gender politics begin to look very different if there is no essential woman at the core.[17]

WHAT IS MULTIRACIAL FEMINISM?

A new set of feminist theories have emerged from the challenges put forth by women of color. Multiracial feminism is an evolving body of theory and practice informed by wide-ranging intellectual traditions. This framework does not offer a singular or unified feminism but a body of knowledge situating women and men in multiple systems of domination. U.S. multiracial feminism encompasses several emergent perspectives developed primarily by women of color: African Americans, Latinas, Asian Americans, and Native Americans, women whose analyses are shaped by their unique perspectives as "outsiders within"— marginal intellectuals whose social locations provide them with a particular perspective on self and society.[18] Although U.S. women of color represent many races and ethnic backgrounds—with different histories and cultures—our feminisms cohere in their treatment of race as a basic social division, a structure of power, a focus of political struggle, and hence a fundamental force in shaping women's and men's lives.

This evolving intellectual and political perspective uses several controversial terms. While we adopt the label "multiracial," other terms have been used to describe this broad framework. For example, Chela Sandoval refers to "U.S. Third World feminisms,"[19] while other scholars refer to "indigenous feminisms." In their theory text-reader, Alison M. Jagger and Paula M. Rothenberg adopt the label "multicultural feminism."[20]

We use "multiracial" rather than "multicultural" as a way of underscoring race as a power system that interacts with other structured inequalities to shape genders. Within the U.S. context, race, and the system of meanings and ideologies which accompany it, is a fundamental organizing principle of social relationships.[21] Race affects all women and men, although in different ways. Even cultural and group differences among women are produced through interaction within a racially stratified social order. Therefore, although we do not discount the importance of culture, we caution that cultural analytic frameworks that ignore race tend

to view women's differences as the product of group-specific values and practices that often result in the marginalization of cultural groups which are then perceived as exotic expressions of a normative center. Our focus on race stresses the social construction of differently situated social groups and their varying degrees of advantage and power. Additionally, this emphasis on race takes on increasing political importance in an era where discourse about race is governed by color-evasive language[22] and a preference for individual rather than group remedies for social inequalities. Our analyses insist upon the primary and pervasive nature of race in contemporary U.S. society while at the same time acknowledging how race both shapes and is shaped by a variety of other social relations.

In the social sciences, multiracial feminism grew out of socialist feminist thinking. Theories about how political economic forces shape women's lives were influential as we began to uncover the social causes of racial ethnic women's subordination. But socialist feminism's concept of capitalist patriarchy, with its focus on women's unpaid (reproductive) labor in the home failed to address racial differences in the organization of reproductive labor. As feminists of color have argued, "reproductive labor has divided along racial as well as gender lines, and the specific characteristics have varied regionally and changed over time as capitalism has reorganized."[23] Despite the limitations of socialist feminism, this body of literature has been especially useful in pursuing questions about the interconnections among systems of domination.[24]

Race and ethnic studies was the other major social scientific source of multiracial feminism. It provided a basis for comparative analyses of groups that are socially and legally subordinated and remain culturally distinct within U.S. society. This includes the systematic discrimination of socially constructed racial groups and their distinctive cultural arrangements. Historically, the categories of African American, Latino, Asian American, and Native American were constructed as both racially and culturally distinct. Each group has a distinctive culture, shares a common heritage, and has developed a common identity within a larger society that subordinates them.[25]

We recognize, of course, certain problems inherent in an uncritical use of the multiracial label. First, the perspective can be hampered by a biracial model in which only African Americans and whites are seen as racial categories and all other groups are viewed through the prism of cultural differences. Latinos and Asians have always occupied distinctive places within the racial hierarchy, and current shifts in the composition of the U.S. population are racializing these groups anew.[26]

A second problem lies in treating multiracial feminism as a single analytical framework, and its principle [sic] architects, women of color, as an undifferentiated category. The concepts "multiracial feminism," "racial ethnic women," and "women of color" "homogenize quite different experiences and can falsely universalize experiences across race, ethnicity, sexual orientation, and age."[27] The feminisms created by women of color exhibit a plurality of intellectual and political positions. We speak in many voices, with inconsistencies that are born of our different social locations. Multiracial feminism embodies this plurality and richness. Our intent is not to falsely universalize women of color. Nor do we wish to promote a new racial essentialism in place of the old gender essentialism. Instead, we use these concepts to examine the structures and experiences produced by intersecting forms of race and gender.

It is also essential to acknowledge that race is a shifting and contested category whose meanings construct definitions of all aspects of social life.[28] In the United States it helped define citizenship by excluding everyone who was not a white, male property owner. It defined labor as slave or free, coolie or contract, and family as available only to those men whose marriages were recognized or whose wives could immigrate with them. Additionally, racial meanings are contested both within groups and between them.[29]

Although definitions of race are at once historically and geographically specific, they are also transnational, encompassing diasporic groups and crossing traditional geographic boundaries. Thus, while U.S. multiracial feminism calls attention to the fundamental importance of race, it must also locate the meaning of race within specific national traditions.

THE DISTINGUISHING FEATURES OF MULTIRACIAL FEMINISM

By attending to these problems, multiracial feminism offers a set of analytic premises for thinking about and theorizing gender. The following themes distinguish this branch of feminist inquiry.

First, multiracial feminism asserts that gender is constructed by a range of interlocking inequalities, what Patricia Hill Collins calls a "matrix of domination."[30] The idea of a matrix is that several fundamental systems work with and through each other. People experience race, class, gender, and sexuality differently depending upon their social location in the structures of race, class, gender, and sexuality. For example, people of the same race will experience race differently depending upon their location in the class structure as working class, professional managerial class, or unemployed; in the gender structure as female or male; and in structures of sexuality as heterosexual, homosexual, or bisexual.

Multiracial feminism also examines the simultaneity of systems in shaping women's experience and identity. Race, class, gender, and sexuality are not reducible to individual attributes to be measured and assessed for their separate contribution in explaining given social outcomes, an approach that Elizabeth Spelman calls "popbead metaphysics," where a woman's identity consists of the sum of parts neatly divisible from one another.[31] The matrix of domination seeks to account for the multiple ways that women experience themselves as gendered, raced, classed, and sexualized.

Second, multiracial feminism emphasizes the intersectional nature of hierarchies at all levels of social life. Class, race, gender, and sexuality are components of both social structure and social interaction. Women and men are differently embedded in locations created by these cross-cutting hierarchies. As a result, women and men throughout the social order experience different forms of privilege and subordination, depending on their race, class, gender, and sexuality. In other words, intersecting forms of domination produce *both* oppression *and* opportunity. At the same time that structures of race, class, and gender create disadvantages for women of color, they provide unacknowledged benefits for those who are at the top of these hierarchies—whites, members of the upper classes, and males. Therefore, multiracial feminism applies not only to racial ethnic women but also to women and men of all races, classes, and genders.

Third, multiracial feminism highlights the relational nature of dominance and subordination. Power is the cornerstone of women's differences.[32] This means that women's differences are *connected* in systematic ways.[33] Race is a vital element in the pattern of relations among minority and white women. As Linda Gordon argues, the very meanings of being a white woman in the United States have been affected by the existence of subordinated women of color: "They intersect in conflict and in occasional cooperation, but always in mutual influence."[34]

Fourth, multiracial feminism explores the interplay of social structure and women's agency. Within the constraints of race, class, and gender oppression, women create viable lives for themselves, their families, and their communities. Women of color have resisted and often undermined the forces of power that control them. From acts of quiet dignity and steadfast determination to involvement in revolt and rebellion, women struggle to shape their own lives. Racial oppression has been a common focus of the "dynamic of oppositional agency" of women of color. As Chandra Talpade Mohanty points out, it is the nature and organization of women's opposition which mediates and differentiates the impact of structures of domination.[35]

Fifth, multiracial feminism encompasses wide-ranging methodological approaches, and like other branches of feminist thought, relies on varied theoretical tools as well. Ruth Frankenberg and Lata Mani identify three guiding principles of inclusive feminist inquiry: "building complex analyses, avoiding erasure, specifying location."[36] In the last decade, the opening up of academic feminism has focused attention on social location in the production of knowledge. Most basically, research by and about marginalized women has destabilized what used to be considered as universal categories of gender. Marginalized locations are well suited for grasping social relations that remained obscure from more privileged vantage points. Lived experience, in other words, creates alternative ways of understanding the social world and the experience of different groups of women within it. Racially informed standpoint epistemologies have provided new topics, fresh questions, and new understandings of women and men. Women of color have, as Norma Alarcón argues, asserted ourselves as subjects, using our voices to challenge dominant conceptions of truth.[37]

Sixth, multiracial feminism brings together understandings drawn from the lived experiences of diverse and continuously changing groups of women. Among Asian Americans, Native Americans, Latinas, and Blacks are many different national cultural and ethnic groups. Each one is engaged in the process of testing, refining, and reshaping these broader categories in its own image. Such internal differences heighten awareness of and sensitivity to both commonalities and differences, serving as a constant reminder of the importance of comparative study and maintaining a creative tension between diversity and universalization.

DIFFERENCE AND TRANSFORMATION

Efforts to make women's studies less partial and less distorted have produced important changes in academic feminism. Inclusive thinking has provided a way to build multiplicity and difference into our analyses. This has led to the discovery that race matters for everyone. White women, too, must be reconceptualized as a category that is multiply defined by race, class, and other differences. As Ruth Frankenberg demonstrates in a study of whiteness among contemporary women, all kinds of social relations, even those that appear neutral, are, in fact, racialized. Frankenberg further complicates the very notion of a unified white identity by introducing issues of Jewish identity.[38] Therefore, the lives of women of color cannot be seen as a *variation* on a more general model of white American womanhood. The model of womanhood that feminist social science once held as "universal" is also a product of race and class.

When we analyze the power relations constituting all social arrangements and shaping women's lives in distinctive ways, we can begin to grapple with core feminist issues about how genders are socially constructed and constructed differently. Women's difference is built into our study of gender. Yet this perspective is quite far removed from the atheoretical pluralism implied in much contemporary thinking about gender.

Multiracial feminism, in our view, focuses not just on differences but also on the way in which differences and domination intersect and are historically and socially constituted. It challenges feminist scholars to go beyond the mere recognition and inclusion of difference to reshape the basic concepts and theories of our disciplines. By attending to women's social location based on race, class, and gender, multiracial feminism seeks to clarify the structural sources of diversity. Ultimately, multiracial feminism forces us to see privilege and subordination as interrelated and to pose such questions as: How do the existences and experiences of all people—women and men, different racial-ethnic groups, and different classes—shape the experiences of each other? How are those relationships defined and enforced through social institutions that are the primary sites for negotiating power within society? How do these differences contribute to the construction of both individual and group identity? Once we acknowledge that all women are affected by the racial order of society, then it becomes clear that the insights of multiracial feminism provide an analytical framework, not solely for understanding the experiences of women of color but for understanding *all* women, and men, as well.

NOTES

1. Maxine Baca Zinn, Lynn Weber Cannon, Elizabeth Higginbotham, and Bonnie Thornton Dill, "The Costs of Exclusionary Practices in Women's Studies," *Signs* 11 (winter 1986): 290–303.

2. Chela Sandoval, "U.S. Third World Feminism: The Theory and Method of Oppositional Consciousness in the Postmodern World," *Genders* (spring 1991): 1–24.

3. Ruth Frankenberg and Lata Mani, "Cross Currents, Crosstalk: Race, 'Postcoloniality,' and the Politics of Location," *Cultural Studies* 7 (May 1993): 292–310.

4. We use the term "multiracial feminism" to convey the multiplicity of racial groups and feminist perspectives.

5. A growing body of work on difference in feminist thought now exists. Although we cannot cite all the current work, the following are representative: Michèle Barrett, "The Concept of Difference," *Feminist Review* 26 (July 1987): 29–42; Christina Crosby, "Dealing with Difference," in *Feminists Theorize the Political*, ed. Judith Butler and Joan W. Scott (New York: Routledge, 1992), 130–43; Elizabeth Fox-Genovese, "Difference, Diversity, and Divisions in an Agenda for the Women's Movement," in *Color, Class, and Country: Experiences of Gender*, ed. Gay Young and Bette J. Dickerson (London: Zed Books, 1994), 232–48; Nancy A. Hewitt, "Compounding Differences," *Feminist Studies* 18 (summer 1992): 313–26; Maria C. Lugones, "On the Logic of Feminist Pluralism," in *Feminist Ethics*, ed. Claudia Card (Lawrence: University of Kansas Press, 1991), 35–44; Rita S. Gallin and Anne Ferguson, "The Plurality of Feminism: Rethinking 'Difference,'" in *The Woman and International Development Annual* (Boulder: Westview Press, 1993), 3: 1–16; and Linda Gordon, "On Difference," *Genders* 10 (spring 1991): 91–111.

6. Susan Bordo, "Feminism, Postmodernism, and Gender Skepticism," in *Feminism/Postmodernism*, ed. Linda J. Nicholson (London: Routledge, 1990), 133–56.

7. Sandra G. Harding, *Whose Science? Whose Knowledge? Thinking from Women's Lives* (Ithaca: Cornell University Press, 1991), 179.

8. Crosby, 131.

9. Fox-Genovese, 232.

10. Faye Ginsberg and Anna Lowenhaupt Tsing, Introduction to *Uncertain Terms, Negotiating Gender in American Culture*, ed. Faye Ginsberg and Anna Lowenhaupt Tsing (Boston: Beacon Press, 1990), 3.

11. Sandoval, 2.

12. Sandra Morgan, "Making Connections: Socialist-Feminist Challenges to Marxist Scholarship," in *Women and a New Academy: Gender and Cultural Contexts*, ed. Jean F. O'Barr (Madison: University of Wisconsin Press, 1989), 149.

13. Jane Rowland Martin, "Methodological Essentialism, False Difference, and Other Dangerous Traps," *Signs* 19 (spring 1994): 647.

14. Barrett, 32.

15. bell hooks, *Black Looks: Race and Representation* (Boston: South End Press, 1992), 21.

16. Lugones, 35–44.

17. Patricia Hill Collins, Foreword to *Women of Color in U.S. Society*, ed. Maxine Baca Zinn and Bonnie Thornton Dill (Philadelphia: Temple University Press, 1994), xv.

18. Patricia Hill Collins, "Learning from the Outsider Within: The Sociological Significance of Black Feminist Thought," *Social Problems* 33 (December 1986): 514–32.

19. Sandoval, 1.

20. Alison M. Jagger and Paula S. Rothenberg, *Feminist Frameworks: Alternative Theoretical Accounts of the Relations Between Women and Men*, 3d ed. (New York: McGraw-Hill, 1993).

21. Michael Omi and Howard Winant, *Racial Formation in the United States: From the 1960s to the 1980s*, 2d ed. (New York: Routledge, 1994).

22. Ruth Frankenberg, *The Social Construction of Whiteness: White Women, Race Matters* (Minneapolis: University of Minnesota Press, 1993).

23. Evelyn Nakano Glenn, "From Servitude to Service Work: Historical Continuities in the Racial Division of Paid Reproductive Labor," *Signs* 18 (autumn 1992): 3. See also Bonnie Thornton Dill, "Our Mothers' Grief: Racial-Ethnic Women and the Maintenance of Families," *Journal of Family History* 13, no. 4 (1988): 415–31.

24. Morgan, 146.

25. Maxine Baca Zinn and Bonnie Thornton Dill, "Difference and Domination," in *Women of Color in U.S. Society*, 11–22.

26. See Omi and Winant, 53–76, for a discussion of racial formation.

27. Margaret L. Andersen and Patricia Hill Collins, *Race, Class, and Gender: An Anthology* (Belmont, Calif.: Wadsworth, 1992), xvi.

28. Omi and Winant.

29. Nazli Kibria, "Migration and Vietnamese American Women: Remaking Ethnicity," in *Women of Color in U.S. Society*, 247–61.

30. Patricia Hill Collins, *Black Feminist Thought: Knowledge, Consciousness, and the Politics of Empowerment* (Boston: Unwin Hyman, 1990).

31. Elizabeth Spelman, *Inessential Women: Problems of Exclusion in Feminist Thought* (Boston: Beacon Press, 1988), 136.

32. Several discussions of difference make this point. See Baca Zinn and Dill, 10; Gordon, 106; and Lynn Weber, in the "Symposium on West and Fenstermaker's 'Doing Difference,'" *Gender & Society* 9 (August 1995): 515–19.

33. Glenn, 10.

34. Gordon, 106.

35. Chandra Talpade Mohanty, "Cartographies of Struggle: Third World Women and the Politics of Feminism," in *Third World Women and the Politics of Feminism*, ed. Chandra Talpade Mohanty, Ann Russo, and Lourdes Torres (Bloomington: Indiana University Press, 1991), 13.

36. Frankenberg and Mani, 306.
37. Norma Alarçon, "The Theoretical Subject(s) of *This Bridge Called My Back* and Anglo-American Feminism," in *Making Face, Making Soul, Haciendo Caras: Creative and Critical Perspectives by Women of Color*, ed. Gloria Anzaldúa (San Francisco: Aunt Lute, 1990), 356.
38. Frankenberg. See also Evelyn Torton Beck, "The Politics of Jewish Invisibility," *NWSA Journal* (fall 1988): 93–102.

FEMINISM AND DISABILITY STUDIES

Rosemarie Garland-Thomson

The way we imagine disability in America is changing. Disability is becoming a diversity, inclusion and civil rights issue, rather than simply a medical problem, charity case or personal misfortune. The disability rights movement and civil rights legislation such as the Americans with Disabilities Act of 1990, which mandates full integration and prohibits discrimination, underwrite such changes.

People with disabilities are leaving the closet and the nursing home and entering workplaces, courtrooms and public debates.

A deaf Miss America reigned; Superman became quadriplegic; Barbie came out as a wheelchair user; Gallaudet University students demanded a deaf president; Casey Martin accessed golf tournaments with a cart.

The largest minority group in the United States, people with disabilities make up 30 percent of the U.S. population. Approximately one-third of entering college freshmen report having a disability. Disabled people are a vibrant and vocal constituency. Disability, we are learning, is a fundamental facet of human diversity.

Critical analysis of disability lags behind that of race, gender, ethnicity, sexual orientation and class both inside and outside the university. Still, there has emerged what I call the New Disability Studies, exploring disability as a historical system of thought and knowledge that represents some bodies as inferior—as in need of being somehow changed in order to conform to what the cultural imagination considers to be a standard body. To do this, it focuses on the myriad sites where culture elaborates disability.

Disability is everywhere in culture—Oedipus to the human genome—once scholars and teachers know how to look for it. The New Disability Studies ranges across such discourses as history, art, literature, religion, philosophy and rhetoric, engaging the critical conversations of aesthetics, epistemology, cultural studies, ethnic studies, feminism, the history of the body and issues of identity. It frames disability as a narrative about human differences we can chart over time, an interpretation of physiological and mental traits we can query, an exclusionary discourse we can excavate, and a fiction about bodily variation we can reveal.

Most important, these narratives shape the material world, determine the distribution of resources, inform human relations and mold our sense of who we are. In short, then, the New Disability Studies interrogates disability; it analyzes and challenges our collective stories about disability, redefining it as an integral part of all human experience and history.

Humanities scholarship in particular recognizes that disability is everywhere. For example, the blind, mad, lame, crippled and unusually embodied have particularly fired the imaginations and underwritten the metaphors of classic Western literature. From Sophocles to Toni Morrison, disability confers distinction on protagonists and drives narrative. Our first literary hero, Oedipus—whose name means "damaged foot"—begins a tradition that continues through Shakespeare's Richard the Third, Melville's monomaniacal amputee Ahab and Faulkner's modern monologist Benjy Compson.

The aim of much disability studies is to reimagine disability, to challenge our collective representations of disability as an exclusionary and oppressive system rather than as the natural and appropriate order of things. This accomplishes important cultural

(continued)

work. First, it shows disability as a significant human experience that occurs in every society, every family—and most every life. Second, it helps us *accept* that fact. Third, it helps *integrate* disability into our knowledge of human experience and history and to integrate disabled people into our culture.

The New Disability Studies points out that ability and disability are not so much a matter of the capacities and limitations of bodies, but more about what we expect from a body at a particular moment and place. Stairs disable people who need to use wheelchairs to get around, but ramps let them go places freely. Reading the print in a phone book or deciphering the patterns on a computer screen are abilities that our moment demands. So if our minds can't make sense of the patterns or our eyes can't register the print, we become disabled. In other words, we are expected to look, act, and move in certain ways, so we'll literally "fit" into the built environment. If we don't, we become disabled.

All bodies are shaped by their environments from the moment of conception; we transform constantly in response to our surroundings. The transformations that occur when body encounters world are what we call disability. The human body varies tremendously in its forms and functions. Our bodies need care; we all need assistance to live. Every life evolves into disability, making it perhaps the essential characteristic of being human. In spite of or perhaps because of this, the subject of disability both discomforts and compels many people.

Our society emphatically denies vulnerability, contingency and mortality. Modernity pressures us relentlessly toward standardizing bodies. This goal is largely now accomplishable in the developed world through technological and medical interventions that materially rationalize our bodies under the banner of progress and improvement.

Indeed, despite the popular call for "diversity," a deep and seldom challenged project of creating bodily uniformity marches forward in practices such as genetic engineering, selective abortion, reproductive technology, so-called physician-assisted suicide, surgical normalization, aesthetic standardization procedures and ideologies of health and fitness. A kind of new eugenics that aims to regularize our bodies supports all of these practices. Although we value biodiversity in our environment, we devalue physical and mental variety. We expect medicine to wipe away all disability. As a consequence, when disability does enter our lives, often our only available responses are silence, denial, shame or determined and desperate vows to "fight it." Seldom do we imagine disability as an aspect of all lives that our society, government and community should accommodate and include.

What would happen if our society fully recognized and validated human variation? What if we cultivated rather than reduced this rich distinctiveness? How would the public landscape change if the widest possible diversity of human forms, functions and behaviors were fully accommodated? How would such an understanding alter our collective sense of what is beautiful and proper? What would be the political significance of such inclusion? Applying the vibrant logic of biodiversity to humans reimagines a public sphere that values and makes a tenable space for the kinds of bodies variously considered old, retarded, crippled, blind, deaf, abnormal, ugly, deformed or excessive.

Disability is not a natural state of corporeal inferiority, inadequacy or excess—or a stroke of misfortune. Rather, it is a culturally fabricated narrative of the body, similar to the fictions of race and gender. The disability/ability system produces subjects by differentiating and marking bodies. Although this comparison of bodies is ideological rather than biological, it nevertheless penetrates into the formation of culture, legitimating an unequal distribution of resources, status and power within a biased social and architectural environment.

Disability is a broad term within which cluster ideological categories as varied as sick, deformed, abnormal, crazy, ugly, old, feebleminded, maimed, afflicted, mad or debilitated—all of which disadvantage people by devaluing bodies that do not conform to cultural standards. Thus the disability system functions to preserve and validate such privileged designations as beautiful, healthy, normal, fit, competent, intelligent—all of which provide cultural capital to those who can claim such status, who can reside within these subject positions. It is, then, the various interactions between bodies and world that materialize disability from the stuff of human variation and precariousness.

Feminism Without Borders

. . . The world we occupy now [is] a world that is definable only in relational terms, a world traversed with intersecting lines of power and resistance, a world that can be understood only in terms of its destructive divisions of gender, color, class, sexuality, and nation, a world that must be transformed through a necessary process of "pivoting the center" (to use Bettina Aptheker's words), for the assumed center (Europe and the United States) will no longer hold. But it is also a world with powerful histories of resistance and revolution in daily life and as organized liberation movements. And it is these contours that define the complex ground for the emergence and consolidation of Third World women's feminist politics. (I use the term "Third World" to designate geographical location and sociohistorical conjunctures. It thus incorporates so-called minority peoples or people of color in the United States.)

In fact, one of the distinctive features of contemporary societies is the internationalization of economies and labor forces. In industrial societies, the international division of economic production consisted in the geographical separation of raw material extraction (in primarily the Third World) from factory production (in the colonial capitals). With the rise of transnational corporations that dominate and organize the contemporary economic system, however, factories have migrated in search of cheap labor, and the nation-state is no longer an appropriate socioeconomic unit for analysis. In addition, the massive migration of excolonial populations to the industrial metropolises of Europe to fill the need for cheap labor has created new kinds of multiethnic and multiracial social formations similar to those in the United States. Contemporary postindustrial societies, thus, invite cross-national and cross-cultural analyses for explanation of their own internal features and socioeconomic constitution. Moreover, contemporary definitions of the Third World can no longer have the same geographical contours and boundaries they had for industrial societies. In the postindustrial world, systemic socioeconomic and ideological processes position the peoples of Africa, Asia, Latin America, and the Middle East, as well as "minority" populations (people of color) in the United States and Europe, in similar relationships to the state.

Thus, charting the ground for an analysis of Third World women and the politics of feminism is no easy task. First, there are the questions of definition: Who/what is the Third World? Do Third World women make up any kind of a constituency? On what basis? Can we assume that Third World women's political struggles are necessarily "feminist"? How do we/they define feminism? And second, there are the questions about context: Which/whose history do we draw on to chart this map of Third World women's engagement with feminism? How do questions of gender, race, and nation intersect in determining feminisms in the Third World? Who produces knowledge about colonized peoples and from what space/location? What are the politics of the production of this particular knowledge? What are the disciplinary parameters of this knowledge? What are the methods used to locate and chart Third World women's self and agency? Clearly, questions of definition and context overlap; in fact, as we develop more complex, nuanced modes of asking questions and as scholarship in a number of relevant fields begins to address histories of colonialism, capitalism, race, and gender as inextricably interrelated, our very conceptual maps are redrawn and transformed. How we conceive of definitions and contexts, on what basis we foreground certain contexts over others, and how we understand the ongoing shifts in our conceptual cartographies—these are all questions of great importance in this particular cartography of Third World feminisms.

I write this cartography from my own particular political, historical, and intellectual location, as a Third World feminist trained in the United States, interested in questions of culture, knowledge production, and activism in an international context. The maps I draw are necessarily anchored in my own discontinuous locations. In this [reading], then, I attempt to formulate an initial and necessarily noncomprehensive response to the above questions. Thus this [reading] offers a very partial conceptual map: it touches upon certain contexts and foregrounds particular definitions and strategies. I see this as a map that will of necessity have to be redrawn as our analytic and conceptual skills and knowledge develop and transform the way we understand questions of history, consciousness, and agency. This [reading] will also suggest significant questions and directions for feminist analysis—an analysis that is made possible by the precise challenges posed by "race" and postcolonial studies to the second wave of white Western feminisms, and by feminist anticapitalist critique to economic globalization and neoliberalism. I believe that these challenges suggest new questions for feminist historiography and epistemology, as well as point toward necessary reconceptualizations of ideas of resistance, community, and agency in daily life.

DEFINITIONS: THIRD WORLD WOMEN AND FEMINISM

Unlike the history of Western (white, middle-class) feminisms, which has been explored in great detail over the last few decades, histories of Third World women's engagement with feminism are in short supply. There is a large body of work on "women in developing countries," but this does not necessarily engage feminist questions. A substantial amount of scholarship has accumulated on women in liberation movements, or on the role and status of women in individual cultures. However, this scholarship also does not necessarily engage questions of feminist historiography. Constructing such histories often requires reading against the grain of a number of intersecting progressive discourses (e.g., white feminist, Third World nationalist, and socialist), as well as the politically regressive racist, imperialist, sexist discourses of slavery, colonialism, and contemporary capitalism. The very notion of addressing what are often internally conflictual histories of Third World women's feminisms under a single rubric, in one chapter, may seem ludicrous—especially since the very meaning of the term "feminism" is continually contested. For, it can be argued, there are no simple ways of representing these diverse struggles and histories. Just as it is difficult to speak of a singular entity called "Western feminism," it is difficult to

generalize about "Third World feminisms." But in much of my scholarship, I have chosen to foreground "Third World women" as an analytical and political category; thus I want to recognize and analytically explore the links among the histories and struggles of Third World women against racism, sexism, colonialism, imperialism, and monopoly capital. I am suggesting, then, an "imagined community" of Third World oppositional struggles—"imagined" not because it is not "real" but because it suggests potential alliances and collaborations across divisive boundaries, and "community" because in spite of internal hierarchies within Third World contexts, it nevertheless suggests a significant, deep commitment to what Benedict Anderson, in referring to the idea of the nation, calls "horizontal comradeship."[1]

The idea of imagined community is useful because it leads us away from essentialist notions of Third World feminist struggles, suggesting political rather than biological or cultural bases for alliance. It is not color or sex that constructs the ground for these struggles. Rather, it is the way we think about race, class, and gender—the political links we choose to make among and between struggles. Thus, potentially, women of all colors (including white women) can align themselves with and participate in these imagined communities. However, clearly our relation to and centrality in particular struggles depend on our different, often conflictual, locations and histories. This, then, is what indelibly marks this discussion of Third World women and the politics of feminism together: imagined communities of women with divergent histories and social locations, woven together by the political threads of opposition to forms of domination that are not only pervasive but also systemic. An example of a similar construct is the notion of "communities of resistance," which refers to the broad-based opposition of refugee, migrant, and black groups in Britain to the idea of a common nation: Europe 1992 (now the European Union). "Communities of resistance," like "imagined communities," is a political definition, not an essentialist one. It is not based on any ahistorical notion of the inherent resistance and resilience of Third World peoples. It is, however, based on a historical, material analysis of the concrete disenfranchising effects of Europe 1992 on Third World communities in Britain and the necessity of forming "resistant/oppositional" communities that fight this. However, while such imagined communities are historically and geographically concrete, their boundaries are necessarily fluid. They have to be, since the operation of power is always fluid and changing. Thus I do not posit any homogeneous configuration of Third World women who form communities because they share a "gender" or a "race" or a "nation." As history (and recent feminist scholarship) teaches us, "races" and "nations" haven't been defined on the basis of inherent, natural characteristics; nor can we define "gender" in any transhistorical, unitary way.[2] So where does this leave us?

Geographically, the nation-states of Latin America, the Caribbean, sub-Saharan Africa, South and Southeast Asia, China, South Africa, and Oceania constitute the parameters of the non-European Third World. In addition, black, Latino, Asian, and indigenous peoples in the United States, Europe, and Australia, some of whom have historic links with the geographically defined Third World, also refer to themselves as Third World peoples. With such a broad canvas, racial, sexual, national, economic, and cultural borders are difficult to demarcate, shaped politically as they are in individual and collective practice.

THIRD WORLD WOMEN AS SOCIAL CATEGORY

. . . Scholars often locate "Third World women" in terms of the underdevelopment, oppressive traditions, high illiteracy, rural and urban poverty, religious fanaticism, and "overpopulation" of particular Asian, African, Middle Eastern, and Latin American countries. Corresponding analyses of "matriarchal" black women on welfare, "illiterate" Chicana farmworkers, and "docile" Asian domestic workers also abound in the context of the United States. Besides being normed on a white, Western (read: progressive/modern) or non-Western (read: backward/traditional) hierarchy, these analyses freeze Third World women in time, space, and history. For example, in analyzing indicators of Third World women's status and roles, Momsen and Townsend (1987) designate the following categories of analysis: life expectancy, sex ratio, nutrition, fertility, income-generating activities, education, and the new international division of labor. Of these, fertility issues and Third World women's incorporation into multinational factory employment are identified as two of the most significant aspects of "women's worlds" in Third World countries.

While such descriptive information is useful and necessary, these presumably "objective" indicators by no means exhaust the meaning of women's day-to-day lives. The everyday, fluid, fundamentally historical and dynamic nature of the lives of Third World women is here collapsed into a few frozen "indicators" of their well-being. Momsen and Townsend (1987) state that in fact fertility is the most studied aspect of women's lives in the Third World (36). This particular fact speaks volumes about the predominant representations of Third World women in social-scientific knowledge production. And our representations of Third World women circumscribe our understanding and analysis of feminism as well as of the daily struggles women engage in these circumstances.

For instance, compare the analysis of fertility offered by Momsen and Townsend (as a social indicator of women's status) with the analysis of population policy and discussions on sexuality among poor Brazilian women offered by Barroso and Bruschini (1991). By analyzing the politics of family planning in the context of the Brazilian women's movement, and examining the way poor women build collective knowledge about sex education and sexuality, Barroso and Bruschini link state policy and social movements with the politics of everyday life, thus presenting us with a dynamic, historically specific view of the struggles of Brazilian women in the barrios. . . . Our definitions, descriptions, and interpretations of Third World women's engagement with feminism must necessarily be simultaneously historically specific and dynamic, not frozen in time in the form of a spectacle.

Thus if the above "social indicators" are inadequate descriptions/interpretations of women's lives, on what basis do Third World women form any constituency? First, just as Western women or white women cannot be defined as coherent interest groups, Third World women also do not constitute any automatic unitary group. Alliances and divisions of class, religion, sexuality, and history, for instance, are necessarily internal to each of the above groups. Second, ideological differences in understandings of the social mediate any assumption of a natural bond between women. After all, there is no logical and necessary connection between being female and becoming feminist. Finally, defining Third World women in terms of their "problems" or their "achievements" in relation to an imagined free white liberal democracy effectively removes them (and the liberal democracy) from history, freezing them in time and space.

A number of scholars in the United States have written about the inherently political definition of the term "women of color" (a term often used interchangeably with "Third World women," as I am doing here).[3] This term designates a political constituency, not a biological or even sociological one. It is a sociopolitical designation for people of African, Caribbean, Asian, and Latin American descent, and native peoples of the United States. It also refers to "new immigrants" to the United States in the last three decades: Arab, Korean, Thai, Laotian, and so on. What seems to constitute "women of color" or "Third World women" as a viable oppositional alliance is a common context of struggle rather than color or racial identifications. Similarly, it is Third World women's oppositional political relation to sexist, racist, and imperialist structures that constitutes our potential commonality. Thus it is the common context of struggles against specific exploitative structures and systems that determines our potential political alliances. It is this common context of struggle, both historical and contemporary, that the next section charts and defines.

WHY FEMINISM?

Before proceeding to consider the structural, historical parameters that lead to Third World women's particular politics, we should understand how women in different sociocultural and historical locations formulate their relation to feminism. The term "feminism" is itself questioned by many Third World women. Feminist movements have been challenged on the grounds of cultural imperialism and of shortsightedness in defining the meaning of gender in terms of middle-class, white experiences, internal racism, classism, and homophobia. All of these factors, as well as the falsely homogeneous representation of the movement by the media, have led to a very real suspicion of "feminism" as a productive ground for struggle. Nevertheless, Third World women have always engaged with feminism, even if the label has been rejected in a number of instances. In the introduction to a collection of writings by black and Third World women in Britain (Grewal et al. 1988), the editors are careful to focus on the contradictions, conflicts, and differences among black women, while emphasizing that the starting point for all contributors has been "the historical link between us of colonialism and imperialism" (Grewal et al. 1988, 6). The editors maintain that this book, the first publication of its kind, is about the "idea of Blackness" in contemporary Britain:

An idea as yet unmatured and inadequately defined, but proceeding along its path in both "real" social life and in the collective awareness of many of its subjects. Both as an idea and a process it is, inevitably, contradictory. Contradictory in its conceptualization because its linguistic expression is defined in terms of colour, yet it is an idea transcendent of colour. Contradictory in its material movements because the unity of action, conscious or otherwise, of Asians, Latin Americans and Arabs, Caribbeans and Africans, gives political expression to a common "colour," even as the State-created fissures of ethnicity threaten to engulf and overwhelm us in islands of cultural exclusivity. (I)

This definition of the idea of "Blackness" in Britain, and of "the unity of action" as the basis for black and Third World women's engagement with feminist politics, echoes the idea of a common context of struggle. British colonialism and the migration of colonized populations to the "home country" form the common historical context for British Third World women, as do, for instance, contemporary struggles against racist immigration and naturalization laws.[4]

The text that corresponds to *Charting the Journey* in the U.S. context was published a few years earlier, in 1981: *This Bridge Called My Back: Writings by Radical Women of Color*.[5] In the introduction to this groundbreaking book, Cherríe Moraga and Gloria Anzaldúa delineate the major areas of concern for a broad-based political movement of U.S. Third World women:

- how visibility/invisibility as women of color forms our radicalism;
- the ways in which Third World women derive a feminist political theory specifically from our racial/cultural background and experience;
- the destructive and demoralizing effects of racism in the women's movement;
- the cultural, class, and sexuality differences that divide women of color;
- Third World women's writing as a tool for self-preservation and revolution; and
- the ways and means of a Third World feminist future. (Moraga and Anzaldúa 1981, xxiv)

A number of ideas central to Third World feminisms emerge from these two passages. Aida Hurtado (1989) adds a further layer: in discussing the significance of the idea "the personal is political" to communities of white women and women of color in the United States, she distinguishes between the relevance of the public/ private distinction for American white middle- and upper-class women, and working-class women and women of color who have always been subject to state intervention in their domestic lives:

> Women of Color have not had the benefit of the economic conditions that underlie the public/private distinction. Instead the political consciousness of women of Color stems from an awareness that the public is *personally* political. Welfare programs and policies have discouraged family life, sterilization programs have restricted reproduction rights, government has drafted and armed disproportionate numbers of people of Color to fight its wars overseas, and locally, police forces and the criminal justice system arrest and incarcerate disproportionate numbers of people of Color. There is no such thing as a private sphere for people of Color except that which they manage to create and protect in an otherwise hostile environment. (Hurtado 1989, 849)

Hurtado introduces the contemporary liberal, capitalist state as a major actor and focus of activity for women of color in the United States. Her discussion suggests that in fact, the politics of "personal life" may be differently defined for middle-class whites and for people of color.[6] Finally, Kumari Jayawardena, writing about feminist movements in Asia in the late nineteenth and early twentieth centuries, defines feminism as "embracing movements for equality within the current system and significant struggles that have attempted to change the system" (Jayawardena 1986, 2). She goes on to assert that these movements arose in the context of the formulation and consolidation of national identities that mobilized anti-imperialist movements during independence struggles and the remaking of precapitalist religious and feudal structures in attempts to "modernize" Third World societies. Here again, the common link between political struggles of women in India, Indonesia, and Korea, for instance, is the fight against racist, colonialist states and for national independence.

To sum up, Third World women's writings on feminism have consistently focused on the idea of the simultaneity of oppressions as fundamental to the experience of social and political marginality and the grounding of feminist politics in the histories of racism and imperialism; the crucial role of a hegemonic state in circumscribing their/our daily lives and survival struggles; the significance of memory and writing in the creation of oppositional agency; and the differences, conflicts, and contradictions internal to Third World women's organizations and communities. In addition, they have insisted on the complex interrelationships between feminist, antiracist, and nationalist struggles. In fact, the challenge of Third World feminisms to white, Western feminisms has been precisely this inescapable link between feminist and political liberation movements. In fact, black, white, and other Third World women have very different histories with respect to the particular inheritance of post-fifteenth-century Euro-American hegemony: the inheritance of slavery, enforced migration, plantation and indentured labor, colonialism, imperial conquest, and genocide. Thus, Third World feminists have argued for the rewriting of history based on the specific locations and histories of struggle of people of color and postcolonial peoples, and on the day-to-day strategies of survival utilized by such peoples.

The urgency of rewriting and rethinking these histories and struggles is suggested by A. Sivanandan in his searing critique of the identity politics of the 1980s social movements in Britain, which, he argues, leads to a flight from class:

> For [the poor, the black, the unemployed] the distinction between the mailed fist and the velvet glove is a stylistic abstraction, the defining limit between consent and force a middle-class fabrication. Black youth in the inner cities know only the blunt force of the state, those on income support have it translated for them in a thousand not so subtle ways. If we are to extend the freedoms in civil society through a politics of hegemony, those who stand at the intersection of consent and coercion should surely be our first constituency and guide—a yardstick to measure our politics by. How do you extend a "politics of food" to the hungry, a "politics of the body" to the homeless, a "politics of the family" for those without an income? How do any of these politics connect up with the Third World? . . . Class cannot just be a matter of identity, it has to be the focus of commitment. (Sivanandan 1990, 18–19)

In foregrounding the need to build our politics around the struggles of the most exploited peoples of the world, and in drawing attention to the importance of a materialist definition of class in opposition to identity based social movements and discourses,

Sivanandan underscores both the significance and the difficulty of rewriting counterhegemonic histories. His analysis questions the contemporary identity-based philosophy of social movements that define "discourse" as an adequate terrain of struggle. While discursive categories are clearly central sites of political contestation, they must be grounded in and informed by the material politics of everyday life, especially the daily life struggles for survival of poor people—those written out of history.

NOTES

1. Anderson 1983, esp. 11–16.
2. See Scott 1986 and essays in *Signs* 1989.
3. See, for instance, Chela Sandoval's work on the construction of the category "Women of Color" in the United States and her theorization of oppositional consciousness (Sandoval 1983, 1991, and 2000). Norma Alarcón 1990 offers an important conceptualization of Third World women as subjects in her essay "The Theoretical Subject(s) of *This Bridge Called My Back* and Anglo-American Feminism." See also Moraga and Anzaldúa 1981, hooks 1984, and Anzaldúa 1987 for similar conceptualizations.

4. Grewal, Kay, Landor, Lewis, and Parmar 1988, 1; see also Bryan et al. 1985, Bhabha et al. 1985, and *Feminist Review* 1984.
5. Moraga and Anzaldúa 1981.
6. My use of Hurtado's analysis is not meant to suggest that the state does not intervene in the "private" sphere of the white middle and upper classes; merely that historically, people of color and white people have a differential (and hierarchical) relation to state rule.

REFERENCES

Alarçon, Norma. 1989. "The Theoretical Subject(s) of *This Bridge Called My Back* and Anglo-American Feminism." In *Chicana Criticism in a Social Context*, edited by H. Calderon and J.D. Saldivar. Durham, NC: Duke University Press.

Anderson, Benedict. 1983. *Imagined Communities: Reflections on the Origin and Spread of Nationalism*. New York: Verso Books.

Anzaldúa, Gloria. 1987. *Borderlands/La Frontera: The New Mestiza*. San Francisco: Spinsters/Aunt Lute.

Barroso, Carmen, and Christina Bruschini. 1991. "Building Politics from Personal Lives: Discussions on Sexuality Among Poor Women in Brazil." In *Third World Women and the Politics of Feminism*, edited by Chandra Talpade Mohanty, Ann Russo, and Lourdes Torres. Bloomington: Indiana University Press.

Bhaba, Jacqueline, et al. 1985. *Worlds Apart: Women Under Immigration and Nationality Law*. London: Pluto Press.

Bryan, Beverly, et al. 1985. *The Heart of the Race: Black Women's Lives in Britain*. London: Virago.

Feminist Review. 1984. Special Issue: *Many Voices, One Chant: Black Feminist Perspectives.* Vol. 17 (Autumn).

Grewal, S., Jackie Kay, Liliane Landor, Gail Lewis, and Pratibha Parmar, eds. 1988. *Charting the Journey: Writings by Black and Third World Women*. London: Sheba Feminist Publishers.

hooks, bell. 1984. *Feminist Theory: From Margin to Center*. Boston: South End Press.

Hurtado, Aida. 1989. "Relating to Privilege: Seduction and Rejection in the Subordination of White Women and Women of Color." *Signs* 14, no. 4 (summer): 833–55.

Jayawardena, Kumari. 1986. *Feminism and Nationalism in the Third World*. London: Zed Press.

Momsen, Janet Henshall, and Janet G. Townsend. 1987. *Geography of Gender in the Third World*. Albany: State University of New York Press.

Moraga, Cherrie, and Gloria Anzaldúa. 1981. *This Bridge Called My Back: Writings by Radical Women of Color*. Albany: Kitchen Table Press.

Sandoval, Chela. 2000. *Methodology of the Oppressed*. Minneapolis: University of Minnesota Press.

———. 1991. "U.S. Third World: The Theory and Method of Oppositional Consciousness in the Postmodern World." *Genders* 10 (spring): 1–24.

———. 1983. "Women Respond to Racism: A Report on the National Women's Studies Association Conference, Storrs, Connecticut." Occasional Paper Series. Oakland, Calif.: Center for Third World Organizing, 1995.

Scott, Joan. 1986. "Gender: A Useful Category of Historical Analysis." *American Historical Review* 91, no. 5: 1053–75.

Signs. 1989. Special Issue: *Common Grounds and Crossroads: Race, Ethnicity and Class in Women's Lives.* Vol. 14, no. 4 (summer).

Sivanandan, A. 1990. "All That Melts into Air Is Solid: The Hokum of the New Times." *Race and Class* 31, no. 3: 1–30.

Masculinities and Globalization

The current wave of research and debate on masculinity stems from the impact of the women's liberation movement on men, but it has taken time for this impact to produce a new intellectual agenda. Most discussions of men's gender in the 1970s and early 1980s centered on an established concept, the male sex role, and an established problem: how men and boys were socialized into this role. There was not much new empirical research. What there was tended to use the more abstracted methods of social psychology (e.g., paper-and-pencil masculinity/femininity scales) to measure generalized attitudes and expectations in ill-defined populations. The largest body of empirical research was the continuing stream of quantitative studies of sex differences—which continued to be disappointingly slight (Carrigan, Connell, and Lee 1985).

The concept of a unitary male sex role, however, came under increasing criticism for its multiple oversimplifications and its incapacity to handle issues about power (Kimmel 1987; Connell 1987). New conceptual frameworks were proposed that linked feminist work on institutionalized patriarchy, gay theoretical work on homophobia, and psychoanalytic ideas about the person (Carrigan, Connell, and Lee 1985; Hearn 1987). Increasing attention was given to certain studies that located issues about masculinity in a fully described local context, whether a British printing shop (Cockburn 1983) or a Papuan mountain community (Herdt 1981). By the late 1980s, a genre of empirical research based on these ideas was developing, most clearly in sociology but also in anthropology, history, organization studies, and cultural studies. This has borne fruit in the 1990s in what is now widely recognized as a new generation of social research on masculinity and men in gender relations (Connell 1995; *Widersprueche* 1995; Segal 1997).

Although the recent research has been diverse in subject matter and social location, its characteristic focus is the construction of masculinity in a particular milieu or moment—a clergyman's family (Tosh 1991), a professional sports career (Messner 1992), a small group of gay men (Connell 1992), a bodybuilding gym (Klein 1993), a group of colonial schools (Morrell 1994), an urban police force (McElhinny 1994), drinking groups in bars (Tomsen 1997), a corporate office on the verge of a decision (Messerschmidt 1997). Accordingly, we might think of this as the "ethnographic moment" in masculinity research, in which the specific and the local are in focus. (This is not to deny that this work *deploys* broader structural concepts simply to note the characteristic focus of the empirical work and its analysis.)

The ethnographic moment brought a much-needed gust of realism to debates on men and masculinity, a corrective to the simplifications of role theory. It also provided a corrective to the trend in popular culture where vague discussions of men's sex roles were giving way to the mystical generalities of the mythopoetic movement and the extreme simplifications of religious revivalism.

Although the rich detail of the historical and field studies defies easy summary, certain conclusions emerge from this body of research as a whole. In short form, they are the following.

Plural Masculinities A theme of theoretical work in the 1980s, the multiplicity of masculinities has now been very fully documented by descriptive research. Different cultures and different periods of history construct gender differently. Striking differences exist, for instance, in the relationship of homosexual practice to dominant forms of masculinity (Herdt 1984). In multicultural societies, there are varying definitions and enactments of masculinity, for instance, between Anglo and Latino communities in the United States (Hondagneu-Sotelo and Messner 1994). Equally important, more than one kind of masculinity can be found within a given cultural setting or institution. This is particularly well documented in school studies (Foley 1990) but can also be observed in workplaces (Messerschmidt 1997) and the military (Barrett 1996).

Hierarchy and Hegemony   These plural masculinities exist in definite social relations, often relations of hierarchy and exclusion. This was recognized early, in gay theorists' discussions of homophobia; it has become clear that the implications are far-reaching. There is generally a hegemonic form of masculinity, the most honored or desired in a particular context. For Western popular culture, this is extensively documented in research on media representations of masculinity (McKay and Huber 1992). The hegemonic form need not be the most common form of masculinity. Many men live in a state of some tension with, or distance from, hegemonic masculinity; others (such as sporting heroes) are taken as exemplars of hegemonic masculinity and are required to live up to it strenuously (Connell 1990a). The dominance of hegemonic masculinity over other forms may be quiet and implicit, but it may also be vehement and violent, as in the important case of homophobic violence.

Collective Masculinities   Masculinities, as patterns of gender practice, are sustained and enacted not only by individuals but also by groups and institutions. This fact was visible in Cockburn's (1983) pioneering research on informal workplace culture, and it has been confirmed over and over: in workplaces (Donaldson 1991), in organized sport (Whitson 1990; Messner 1992), in schools (Connell 1996), and so on. This point must be taken with the previous two: institutions may construct multiple masculinities and define relationships between them. Barrett's (1996) illuminating study of hegemonic masculinity in the U.S. Navy shows how this takes different forms in the different subbranches of the one military organization.

Bodies as Arenas   Men's bodies do not determine the patterns of masculinity, but they are still of great importance in masculinity. Men's bodies are addressed, defined and disciplined (as in sport; see Theberge 1991), and given outlets and pleasures by the gender order of society. But men's bodies are not blank slates. The enactment of masculinity reaches certain limits, for instance, in the destruction of the industrial worker's body (Donaldson 1991). Masculine conduct with a female body is felt to be anomalous or transgressive, like feminine conduct with a male body; research on gender crossing (Bolin 1988) shows the work that must be done to sustain an anomalous gender.

Active Construction   Masculinities do not exist prior to social interaction, but come into existence as people

act. They are actively produced, using the resources and strategies available in a given milieu. Thus the exemplary masculinities of sports professionals are not a product of passive disciplining, but as Messner (1992) shows, result from a sustained, active engagement with the demands of the institutional setting, even to the point of serious bodily damage from "playing hurt" and accumulated stress. With boys learning masculinities, much of what was previously taken as socialization appears, in close-focus studies of schools (Walker 1988; Thorne 1993), as the outcome of intricate and intense maneuvering in peer groups, classes, and adult-child relationships.

Contradiction   Masculinities are not homogeneous, simple states of being. Close-focus research on masculinities commonly identifies contradictory desires and conduct; for instance, in Klein's (1993) study of bodybuilders, the contradiction between the heterosexual definition of hegemonic masculinity and the homosexual practice by which some of the bodybuilders finance the making of an exemplary body. Psychoanalysis provides the classic evidence of conflicts within personality, and recent psychoanalytic writing (Chodorow 1994; Lewes 1988) has laid some emphasis on the conflicts and emotional compromises within both hegemonic and subordinated forms of masculinity. Life-history research influenced by existential psychoanalysis (Connell 1995) has similarly traced contradictory projects and commitments within particular forms of masculinity.

Dynamics   Masculinities created in specific historical circumstances are liable to reconstruction, and any pattern of hegemony is subject to contestation, in which a dominant masculinity may be displaced. Heward (1988) shows the changing gender regime of a boys' school responding to the changed strategies of the families in its clientele. Roper (1991) shows the displacement of a production-oriented masculinity among engineering managers by new financially oriented generic managers. Since the 1970s, the reconstruction of masculinities has been pursued as a conscious politics. Schwalbe's (1996) close examination of one mythopoetic group shows the complexity of the practice and the limits of the reconstruction.

If we compare this picture of masculinity with earlier understandings of the male sex role, it is clear that the ethnographic moment in research has already had important intellectual fruits.

Nevertheless, it has always been recognized that some issues go beyond the local. For instance, mythopoetic movements such as the highly visible Promise Keepers are part of a spectrum of masculinity politics; Messner (1997) shows for the United States that this spectrum involves at least eight conflicting agendas for the remaking of masculinity. Historical studies such as Phillips (1987) on New Zealand and Kimmel (1996) on the United States have traced the changing public constructions of masculinity for whole countries over long periods; ultimately, such historical reconstructions are essential for understanding the meaning of ethnographic details.

I consider that this logic must now be taken a step further, and in taking this step, we will move toward a new agenda for the whole field. What happens in localities is affected by the history of whole countries, but what happens in countries is affected by the history of the world. Locally situated lives are now (indeed, have long been) powerfully influenced by geopolitical struggles, global markets, multinational corporations, labor migration, transnational media. It is time for this fundamental fact to be built into our analysis of men and masculinities.

To understand local masculinities, we must think in global terms. But how? That is the problem pursued in this article. I will offer a framework for thinking about masculinities as a feature of world society and for thinking about men's gender practices in terms of the global structure and dynamics of gender. This is by no means to reject the ethnographic moment in masculinity research. It is, rather, to think how we can use its findings more adequately.

THE WORLD GENDER ORDER

Masculinities do not first exist and then come into contact with femininities; they are produced together, in the process that constitutes a gender order. Accordingly, to understand the masculinities on a world scale, we must first have a concept of the globalization of gender.

This is one of the most difficult points in current gender analysis because the very conception is counterintuitive. We are so accustomed to thinking of gender as the attribute of an individual, even as an unusually intimate attribute, that it requires a considerable wrench to think of gender on the vast scale of global society. Most relevant discussions, such as the literature on women and development, fudge the issue. They treat the entities that extend internationally (markets, corporations, intergovernmental programs,

etc.) as ungendered in principle—but affecting unequally gendered recipients of aid in practice, because of bad policies. Such conceptions reproduce the familiar liberal-feminist view of the state as in principle gender-neutral, though empirically dominated by men.

But if we recognize that very large scale institutions such as the state are themselves gendered, in quite precise and specifiable ways (Connell 1990b), and if we recognize that international relations, international trade, and global markets are inherently an arena of gender formation and gender politics (Enloe 1990), then we can recognize the existence of a world gender order. The term can be defined as the structure of relationships that interconnect the gender regimes of institutions, and the gender orders of local society, on a world scale. That is, however, only a definition. The substantive questions remain: what is the shape of that structure, how tightly are its elements linked, how has it arisen historically, what is its trajectory into the future?

Current business and media talk about globalization pictures a homogenizing process sweeping across the world, driven by new technologies, producing vast unfettered global markets in which all participate on equal terms. This is a misleading image. As Hirst and Thompson (1996) show, the global economy is highly unequal and the current degree of homogenization is often overestimated. Multinational corporations based in the three major economic powers (the United States, European Union, and Japan) are the major economic actors worldwide.

The structure bears the marks of its history. Modern global society was historically produced as Wallerstein (1974) argued, by the economic and political expansion of European states from the fifteenth century on and by the creation of colonial empires. It is in this process that we find the roots of the modern world gender order. Imperialism was, from the start, a gendered process. Its first phase, colonial conquest and settlement, was carried out by gender-segregated forces, and it resulted in massive disruption of indigenous gender orders. In its second phase, the stabilization of colonial societies, new gender divisions of labor were produced in plantation economies and colonial cities, while gender ideologies were linked with racial hierarchies and the cultural defense of empire. The third phase, marked by political decolonization, economic neocolonialism, and the current growth of world markets and structures of financial control, has seen gender divisions of labor remade on a massive scale in the "global factory" (Fuentes and

Ehrenreich 1983), as well as the spread of gendered violence alongside Western military technology.

The result of this history is a partially integrated, highly unequal and turbulent world society, in which gender relations are partly but unevenly linked on a global scale. The unevenness becomes clear when different substructures of gender (Connell 1987; Walby 1990) are examined separately.

The Division of Labor   A characteristic feature of colonial and neocolonial economies was the restructuring of local production systems to produce a male wage worker–female domestic worker couple (Mies 1986). This need not produce a "housewife" in the Western suburban sense, for instance, where the wage work involved migration to plantations or mines (Moodie 1994). But it has generally produced the identification of masculinity with the public realm and the money economy and of femininity with domesticity, which is a core feature of the modern European gender system (Holter 1997).

Power Relations   The colonial and postcolonial world has tended to break down purdah systems of patriarchy in the name of modernization, if not of women's emancipation (Kandiyoti 1994). At the same time, the creation of a westernized public realm has seen the growth of large-scale organizations in the form of the state and corporations, which in the great majority of cases are culturally masculinized and controlled by men. In *comprador* capitalism, however, the power of local elites depends on their relations with the metropolitan powers, so the hegemonic masculinities of neocolonial societies are uneasily poised between local and global cultures.

Emotional Relations   Both religious and cultural missionary activity has corroded indigenous homosexual and cross-gender practice, such as the native American *berdache* and the Chinese "passion of the cut sleeve" (Hinsch 1990). Recently developed Western models of romantic heterosexual love as the basis for marriage and of gay identity as the main alternative have now circulated globally—though as Altman (1996) observes, they do not simply displace indigenous models, but interact with them in extremely complex ways.

Symbolization   Mass media, especially electronic media, in most parts of the world follow North American and European models and relay a great deal of metropolitan content; gender imagery is an important part of

what is circulated. A striking example is the reproduction of a North American imagery of femininity by Xuxa, the blonde television superstar in Brazil (Simpson 1993). In counterpoint, exotic gender imagery has been used in the marketing strategies of newly industrializing countries (e.g., airline advertising from Southeast Asia)—a tactic based on the longstanding combination of the exotic and the erotic in the colonial imagination (Jolly 1997).

Clearly, the world gender order is not simply an extension of a traditional European-American gender order. That gender order was changed by colonialism, and elements from other cultures now circulate globally. Yet in no sense do they mix on equal terms, to produce a United Colours of Benetton gender order. The culture and institutions of the North Atlantic countries are hegemonic within the emergent world system. This is crucial for understanding the kinds of masculinities produced within it.

THE REPOSITIONING OF MEN AND THE RECONSTITUTION OF MASCULINITIES

The positioning of men and the constitution of masculinities may be analyzed at any of the levels at which gender practice is configured: in relation to the body, in personal life, and in collective social practice. At each level, we need to consider how the processes of globalization influence configurations of gender.

Men's bodies are positioned in the gender order, and enter the gender process, through body-reflexive practices in which bodies are both objects and agents (Connell 1995)—including sexuality, violence, and labor. The conditions of such practice include where one is and who is available for interaction. So it is a fact of considerable importance for gender relations that the global social order distributes and redistributes bodies, through migration, and through political controls over movement and interaction.

The creation of empire was the original "elite migration," though in certain cases mass migration followed. Through settler colonialism, something close to the gender order of Western Europe was reassembled in North America and in Australia. Labor migration within the colonial systems was a means by which gender practices were spread, but also a means by which they were reconstructed, since labor migration was itself a gendered process—as we have seen in relation to the gender division of labor. Migration from the colonized world to the metropole became (except for Japan) a mass process in the decades after World War II. There is also migration within the periphery, such as the creation of a very large immigrant labor force, mostly from other Muslim countries, in the oil-producing Gulf states.

These relocations of bodies create the possibility of hybridization in gender imagery, sexuality, and other forms of practice. The movement is not always toward synthesis, however, as the race/ethnic hierarchies of colonialism have been recreated in new contexts, including the politics of the metropole. Ethnic and racial conflict has been growing in importance in recent years, and as Klein (1997) and Tillner (1997) argue, this is a fruitful context for the production of masculinities oriented toward domination and violence. Even without the context of violence, there can be an intimate interweaving of the formation of masculinity with the formation of ethnic identity, as seen in the study by Poynting, Noble, and Tabar (1997) of Lebanese youths in the Anglo-dominant culture of Australia.

At the level of personal life as well as in relation to bodies, the making of masculinities is shaped by global forces. In some cases, the link is indirect, such as the working-class Australian men caught in a situation of structural unemployment (Connell 1995), which arises from Australia's changing position in the global economy. In other cases, the link is obvious, such as the executives of multinational corporations and the financial sector servicing international trade. The requirements of a career in international business set up strong pressures on domestic life: almost all multinational executives are men, and the assumption in business magazines and advertising directed toward them is that they will have dependent wives running their homes and bringing up their children.

At the level of collective practice, masculinities are reconstituted by the remaking of gender meanings and the reshaping of the institutional contexts of practice. Let us consider each in turn.

The growth of global mass media, especially electronic media, is an obvious "vector" for the globalization of gender. Popular entertainment circulates stereotyped gender images, deliberately made attractive for marketing purposes. The example of Xuxa in Brazil has already been mentioned. International news media are also controlled or strongly influenced from the metropole and circulate Western definitions of authoritative masculinity, criminality, desirable femininity, and so on. But there are limits to the power of global mass communications. Some local centers of mass entertainment differ from the Hollywood model, such as the Indian popular film industry centered in Bombay. Further, media research emphasizes that audiences are highly selective in their reception of media messages, and we must allow for popular recognition of the fantasy in mass entertainment. Just as economic globalization can be exaggerated, the creation of a global culture is a more turbulent and uneven process than is often assumed (Featherstone 1995).

More important, I would argue, is a process that began long before electronic media existed, the export of institutions. Gendered institutions not only circulate definitions of masculinity (and femininity), as sex role theory notes. The functioning of gendered institutions, creating specific conditions for social practice, calls into existence specific patterns of practice. Thus, certain patterns of collective violence are embedded in the organization and culture of a Western-style army, which are different from the patterns of precolonial violence. Certain patterns of calculative egocentrism are embedded in the working of a stock market; certain patterns of rule following and domination are embedded in a bureaucracy.

Now, the colonial and postcolonial world saw the installation in the periphery, on a very large scale, of a range of institutions on the North Atlantic model: armies, states, bureaucracies, corporations, capital markets, labor markets, schools, law courts, transport systems. These are gendered institutions and their functioning has directly reconstituted masculinities in the periphery. This has not necessarily meant photocopies of European masculinities. Rather, pressures for change are set up that are inherent in the institutional form.

To the extent that particular institutions become dominant in world society, the patterns of masculinity embedded in them may become global standards. Masculine dress is an interesting indicator: almost every political leader in the world now wears the uniform of the Western business executive. The more common pattern, however, is not the complete displacement of local patterns but the articulation of the local gender order with the gender regime of global model institutions. Case studies such as Hollway's (1994) account of bureaucracy in Tanzania illustrate the point; there, domestic patriarchy articulated with masculine authority in the state in ways that subverted the government's formal commitment to equal opportunity for women.

We should not expect the overall structure of gender relations on a world scale simply to mirror patterns known on the smaller scale. In the most vital of respects, there is continuity. The world gender order is unquestionably patriarchal, in the sense that it privileges men over women. There is a patriarchal dividend for men arising from unequal wages, unequal labor force participation, and a highly unequal structure of ownership, as well as cultural and sexual privileging. This has been extensively documented by feminist work on women's situation globally (e.g., Taylor 1985), though its implications for masculinity have mostly been ignored. The conditions thus exist for the production of a hegemonic masculinity on a world scale, that is to say, a dominant form of masculinity that embodies, organizes, and legitimates men's domination in the gender order as a whole.

The conditions of globalization, which involve the interaction of many local gender orders, certainly multiply the forms of masculinity in the global gender order. At the same time, the specific shape of globalization, concentrating economic and cultural power on an unprecedented scale, provides new resources for dominance by particular groups of men. This dominance may become institutionalized in a pattern of masculinity that becomes, to some degree, standardized across localities. I will call such patterns *globalizing masculinities*, and it is among them, rather than narrowly within the metropole, that we are likely to find candidates for hegemony in the world gender order.

GLOBALIZING MASCULINITIES

In this section, I will offer a sketch of major forms of globalizing masculinity in the three historical phases identified above in the discussion of globalization.

Masculinities of Conquest and Settlement

The creation of the imperial social order involved peculiar conditions for the gender practices of men. Colonial conquest itself was mainly carried out by segregated groups of men—soldiers, sailors, traders, administrators, and a good many who were all these by turn (such as the Rum Corps in early New South Wales, Australia). They were drawn from the more segregated occupations and milieu in the metropole, and it is likely that the men drawn into colonization tended to be the more rootless. Certainly the process of conquest could produce frontier masculinities that combined the occupational culture of these groups with an unusual level of violence and egocentric individualism. The vehement

contemporary debate about the genocidal violence of the Spanish conquistadors—who in fifty years completely exterminated the population of Hispaniola—points to this pattern (Bitterli 1989).

The political history of empire is full of evidence of the tenuous control over the frontier exercised by the state—the Spanish monarchs unable to rein in the conquistadors, the governors in Sydney unable to hold back the squatters and in Capetown unable to hold back the Boers, gold rushes breaking boundaries everywhere, even an independent republic set up by escaped slaves in Brazil. The point probably applies to other forms of social control too, such as customary controls on men's sexuality. Extensive sexual exploitation of indigenous women was a common feature of conquest. In certain circumstances, frontier masculinities might be reproduced as a local cultural tradition long after the frontier had passed, such as the gauchos of southern South America and the cowboys of the western United States.

In other circumstances, however, the frontier of conquest and exploitation was replaced by a frontier of settlement. Sex ratios in the colonizing population changed, as women arrived and locally born generations succeeded. A shift back toward the family patterns of the metropole was likely. As Cain and Hopkins (1993) have shown for the British empire, the ruling group in the colonial world as a whole was an extension of the dominant class in the metropole, the landed gentry, and tended to reproduce its social customs and ideology. The creation of a settler masculinity might be the goal of state policy, as it seems to have been in late-nineteenth-century New Zealand, as part of a general process of pacification and the creation of an agricultural social order (Phillips 1987). Or it might be undertaken through institutions created by settler groups, such as the elite schools in Natal studied by Morrell (1994).

The impact of colonialism on the construction of masculinity among the colonized is much less documented, but there is every reason to think it was severe. Conquest and settlement disrupted all the structures of indigenous society, whether or not this was intended by the colonizing powers (Bitterli 1989). Indigenous gender orders were no exception. Their disruption could result from the pulverization of indigenous communities (as in the seizure of land in eastern North America and southeastern Australia), through gendered labor migration (as in gold mining with Black labor in South Africa; see Moodie 1994), to ideological attacks on local gender arrangements (as in the missionary assault on the *berdache* tradition in North

America; see Williams 1986). The varied course of resistance to colonization is also likely to have affected the making of masculinities. This is clear in the region of Natal in South Africa, where sustained resistance to colonization by the Zulu kingdom was a key to the mobilization of ethnic-national masculine identities in the twentieth century (Morrell 1996).

Masculinities of Empire

The imperial social order created a hierarchy of masculinities, as it created a hierarchy of communities and races. The colonizers distinguished "more manly" from "less manly" groups among their subjects. In British India, for instance, Bengali men were supposed effeminate while Pathans and Sikhs were regarded as strong and warlike. Similar distinctions were made in South Africa between Hottentots and Zulus, in North America between Iroquois, Sioux, and Cheyenne on one side, and southern and southwestern tribes on the other.

At the same time, the emerging imagery of gender difference in European culture provided general symbols of superiority and inferiority. Within the imperial "poetics of war" (MacDonald 1994), the conqueror was virile, while the colonized were dirty, sexualized, and effeminate or childlike. In many colonial situations, indigenous men were called "boys" by the colonizers (e.g., in Zimbabwe; see Shire 1994). Sinha's (1995) interesting study of the language of political controversy in India in the 1880s and 1890s shows how the images of "manly Englishman" and "effeminate Bengali" were deployed to uphold colonial privilege and contain movements for change. In the late nineteenth century, racial barriers in colonial societies were hardening rather than weakening, and gender ideology tended to fuse with racism in forms that the twentieth century has never untangled.

The power relations of empire meant that indigenous gender orders were generally under pressure from the colonizers, rather than the other way around. But the colonizers too might change. The barriers of late colonial racism were not only to prevent pollution from below but also to forestall "going native," a well-recognized possibility—the starting point, for instance, of Kipling's famous novel *Kim* ([1901] 1987). The pressures, opportunities, and profits of empire might also work changes in gender arrangements among the colonizers, for instance, the division of labor in households with a large supply of indigenous workers as domestic servants (Bulbeck 1992). Empire might also affect the gender order of the metropole itself by changing gender ideologies, divisions of labor, and the nature of the metropolitan state. For instance, empire figured prominently as a source of masculine imagery in Britain, in the Boy Scouts, and in the cult of Lawrence of Arabia (Dawson 1991). Here we see examples of an important principle: the interplay of gender dynamics between different parts of the world order.

The world of empire created two very different settings for the modernization of masculinities. In the periphery, the forcible restructuring of economics and workforces tended to individualize, on one hand, and rationalize, on the other. A widespread result was masculinities in which the rational calculation of self-interest was the key to action, emphasizing the European gender contrast of rational man/irrational woman. The specific form might be local—for instance, the Japanese "salaryman," a type first recognized in the 1910s, was specific to the Japanese context of large, stable industrial conglomerates (Kinmonth 1981). But the result generally was masculinities defined around economic action, with both workers and entrepreneurs increasingly adapted to emerging market economies.

In the metropole, the accumulation of wealth made possible a specialization of leadership in the dominant classes, and struggles for hegemony in which masculinities organized around domination or violence were split from masculinities organized around expertise. The class compromises that allowed the development of the welfare state in Europe and North America were paralleled by gender compromises—gender reform movements (most notably the women's suffrage movement) contesting the legal privileges of men and forcing concessions from the state. In this context, agendas of reform in masculinity emerged: the temperance movement, compassionate marriage, homosexual rights movements, leading eventually to the pursuit of androgyny in "men's liberation" in the 1970s (Kimmel and Mosmiller 1992). Not all reconstructions of masculinity, however, emphasized tolerance or moved toward androgyny. The vehement masculinity politics of fascism, for instance, emphasized dominance and difference and glorified violence, a pattern still found in contemporary racist movements (Tillner 1997).

Masculinities of Postcolonialism and Neoliberalism

The process of decolonization disrupted the gender hierarchies of the colonial order and, where armed struggle was involved, might have involved a deliberate cultivation of masculine hardness and violence (as in South Africa; see Xaba 1997). Some activists and theorists of liberation struggles celebrated this, as a necessary response to colonial violence and emasculation; women in liberation struggles were perhaps less impressed. However one evaluates the process, one of the consequences of decolonization was another round of disruptions of community-based gender orders and another step in the reorientation of masculinities toward national and international contexts.

Nearly half a century after the main wave of decolonization, the old hierarchies persist in new shapes. With the collapse of Soviet communism, the decline of postcolonial socialism, and the ascendancy of the new right in Europe and North America, world politics is more and more organized around the needs of transnational capital and the creation of global markets.

The neoliberal agenda has little to say, explicitly, about gender: it speaks a gender-neutral language of "markets," "individuals," and "choice." But the world in which neoliberalism is ascendant is still a gendered world, and neoliberalism has an implicit gender politics. The "individual" of neoliberal theory has in general the attributes and interests of a male entrepreneur, the attack on the welfare state generally weakens the position of women, while the increasingly unregulated power of transnational corporations places strategic power in the hands of particular groups of men. It is not surprising, then, that the installation of capitalism in Eastern Europe and the former Soviet Union has been accompanied by a reassertion of dominating masculinities and, in some situations, a sharp worsening in the social position of women.

We might propose, then, that the hegemonic form of masculinity in the current world gender order is the masculinity associated with those who control its dominant institutions: the business executives who operate in global markets, and the political executives who interact (and in many contexts, merge) with them. I will call this *transnational business masculinity*. This is not readily available for ethnographic study, but we can get some clues to its character from its reflections in management literature, business journalism, and corporate self-promotion, and from studies of local business elites (e.g., Donaldson 1997).

As a first approximation, I would suggest this is a masculinity marked by increasing egocentrism, very conditional loyalties (even to the corporation), and a declining sense of responsibility for others (except for

purposes of image making). Gee, Hull and Lankshear (1996), studying recent management textbooks, note the peculiar construction of the executive in "fast capitalism" as a person with no permanent commitments, except (in effect) to the idea of accumulation itself. Transnational business masculinity is characterized by a limited technical rationality (management theory), which is increasingly separate from science.

Transnational business masculinity differs from traditional bourgeois masculinity by its increasingly libertarian sexuality, with a growing tendency to commodify relations with women. Hotels catering to businessmen in most parts of the world now routinely offer pornographic videos, and in some parts of the world, there is a well-developed prostitution industry catering for international businessmen. Transnational business masculinity does not require bodily force, since the patriarchal dividend on which it rests is accumulated by impersonal, institutional means. But corporations increasingly use the exemplary bodies of elite sportsmen as a marketing tool (note the phenomenal growth of corporate "sponsorship" of sport in the last generation) and indirectly as a means of legitimation for the whole gender order.

MASCULINITY POLITICS ON A WORLD SCALE

Recognizing global society as an arena of masculinity formation allows us to pose new questions about masculinity politics. What social dynamics in the global arena give rise to masculinity politics, and what shape does global masculinity politics take?

The gradual creation of a world gender order has meant many local instabilities of gender. Gender instability is a familiar theme of poststructuralist theory, but this school of thought takes as a universal condition a situation that is historically specific. Instabilities range from the disruption of men's local cultural dominance as women move into the public realm and higher education, through the disruption of sexual identities that produced "queer" politics in the metropole, to the shifts in the urban intelligentsia that produced "the new sensitive man" and other images of gender change.

One response to such instabilities, on the part of groups whose power is challenged but still dominant, is to reaffirm *local* gender orthodoxies and hierarchies. A masculine fundamentalism is, accordingly, a common response in gender politics at present. A soft version, searching for an essential masculinity among myths and symbols, is offered by the mythopoetic men's movement in the United States and by the religious revivalists of the Promise Keepers (Messner 1997). A much harder version is found, in that country, in the right-wing militia movement brought to world attention by the Oklahoma City bombing (Gibson 1994), and in contemporary Afghanistan, if we can trust Western media reports, in the militant misogyny of the Taliban. It is no coincidence that in the two latter cases, hardline masculine fundamentalism goes together with a marked anti-internationalism. The world system—rightly enough—is seen as the source of pollution and disruption.

Not that the emerging global order is a hotbed of gender progressivism. Indeed, the neoliberal agenda for the reform of national and international economics involves closing down historic possibilities for gender reform. I have noted how it subverts the gender compromise represented by the metropolitan welfare state. It has also undermined the progressive-liberal agendas of sex role reform represented by affirmative action programs, anti-discrimination provisions, child care services, and the like. Right-wing parties and governments have been persistently cutting such programs, in the name of either individual liberties or global competitiveness. Through these means, the patriarchal dividend to men is defended or restored, without an *explicit* masculinity politics in the form of a mobilization of men.

Within the arenas of international relations, the international state, multinational corporations, and global markets, there is nevertheless a deployment of masculinities and a reasonably clear hegemony. The transnational business masculinity described above has had only one major competitor for hegemony in recent decades, the rigid, control-oriented masculinity of the military, and the military-style bureaucratic dictatorships of Stalinism. With the collapse of Stalinism and the end of the cold war, Big Brother (Orwell's famous parody of this form of masculinity) is a fading threat, and the more flexible, calculative, egocentric masculinity of the fast capitalist entrepreneur holds the world stage.

We must, however, recall two important conclusions of the ethnographic moment in masculinity research: that different forms of masculinity exist together and that hegemony is constantly subject to challenge. These are possibilities in the global arena too. Transnational business masculinity is not completely homogeneous; variations of it are embedded in different parts of the world system, which may not be completely compatible. We may distinguish a Confucian variant, based in East Asia, with a stronger commitment to hierarchy and social consensus, from a secularized Christian variant, based in North America, with more hedonism and individualism and greater tolerance for social conflict. In certain arenas, there is already conflict between the business and political leaderships embodying these forms of masculinity: initially over human rights versus Asian values, and more recently over the extent of trade and investment liberalization.

If these are contenders for hegemony, there is also the possibility of opposition to hegemony. The global circulation of "gay" identity (Altman 1996) is an important indication that nonhegemonic masculinities may operate in global arenas, and may even find a certain political articulation, in this case around human rights and AIDS prevention.

REFERENCES

Altman, Dennis. 1996. Rupture or continuity? The internationalisation of gay identities. *Social Text* 48 (3): 77–94.

Barrett, Frank J. 1996. The organizational construction of hegemonic masculinity: The case of the U.S. Navy. *Gender Work and Organization* 3 (3): 129–42.

BauSteineMaenner, ed. 1996. *Kritische Maennerforschung* [Critical research on men]. Berlin: Argument.

Bitterli, Urs. 1989. *Cultures in conflict: Encounters between European and non-European cultures, 1492–1800.* Stanford, CA: Stanford University Press.

Bolin, Anne. 1988. *In search of Eve: Transsexual rites of passage.* Westport, CT: Bergin & Garvey.

Bulbeck, Chilla. 1992. *Australian women in Papua New Guinea: Colonial passages 1920–1960.* Cambridge, U.K.: Cambridge University Press.

Cain, P. J., and A. G. Hopkins. 1993. *British imperialism: Innovation and expansion, 1688–1914.* New York: Longman.

Carrigan, Tim, Bob Connell, and John Lee. 1985. Toward a new sociology of masculinity. *Theory and Society* 14 (5): 551–604.

Chodorow, Nancy. 1994. *Femininities, masculinities, sexualities: Freud and beyond.* Lexington: University Press of Kentucky.

Cockburn, Cynthia. 1983. *Brothers: Male dominance and technological change.* London: Pluto.

Cohen, Jon. 1991. NOMAS: Challenging male supremacy. *Changing Men* (Winter/Spring): 45–46.

Connell, R. W. 1987. *Gender and power.* Cambridge, MA: Polity.

———. 1990a. An iron man: The body and some contradictions of hegemonic masculinity. In *Sport, men and the gender order: Critical feminist perspectives,* edited by Michael A. Messner and Donald F. Sabo, 83–95. Champaign, IL: Human Kinetics Books.

———. 1990b. The state, gender and sexual politics: Theory and appraisal. *Theory and Society* 19: 507–44.

———. 1992. A very straight gay: Masculinity, homosexual experience and the dynamics of gender. *American Sociological Review* 57 (6): 735–5l.

———. 1995. *Masculinities.* Cambridge, MA: Polity.

———. 1996. Teaching the boys: New research on masculinity, and gender strategies for schools. *Teachers College Record* 98 (2): 206–35.

Cornwall, Andrea, and Nancy Lindisfarne, eds. 1994. *Dislocating masculinity: Comparative ethnographies.* London: Routledge.

Dawson, Graham. 1991. The blond Bedouin: Lawrence of Arabia, imperial adventure and the imagining of English-British masculinity. In *Manful assertions: Masculinities in Britain since 1800,* edited by Michael Roper and John Tosh, 113–44. London: Routledge.

Donaldson, Mike. 1991. *Time of our lives: Labour and love in the working class.* Sydney: Allen & Unwin.

———. 1997. Growing up very rich: The masculinity of the hegemonic. Paper presented at the conference Masculinities: Renegotiating Genders, June, University of Wollongong, Australia.

Enloe, Cynthia. 1990. *Bananas, beaches and bases: Making feminist sense of international politics.* Berkeley: University of California Press.

Featherstone, Mike. 1995. *Undoing culture: Globalization, postmodernism and identity.* London: Sage.

Foley, Douglas E. 1990. *Learning capitalist culture: Deep in the heart of Tejas.* Philadelphia: University of Pennsylvania Press.

Fuentes, Annette, and Barbara Ehrenreich. 1983. *Women in the global factory.* Boston: South End.

Gee, James Paul, Glynda Hall, and Colin Lankshear. 1996. *The new work order: Behind the language of the new capitalism.* Sydney: Allen & Unwin.

Gender Equality Ombudsman. 1997. *The father's quota.* Information sheet on parental leave entitlements, Oslo.

Gibson, J. William. 1994. *Warrior dreams: Paramilitary culture in post-Vietnam America.* New York: Hill & Wang.

Hagemann-White, Carol, and Maria S. Rerrich, eds. 1988. *FrauenMaennerBilder* [Women, imaging, men]. Bielefeld: AJZ-Verlag.

Hearn, Jeff. 1987. *The gender of oppression: Men, masculinity and the critique of Marxism.* Brighton, U.K.: Wheatsheaf.

Herdt, Gilbert H. 1981. *Guardians of the flutes: Idioms of masculinity.* New York: McGraw-Hill.

———, ed. 1984. *Ritualized homosexuality in Melanesia.* Berkeley: University of California Press.

Heward, Christine. 1988. *Making a man of him: Parents and their sons' education at an English public school 1929–1950.* London: Routledge.

Hinsch, Bret. 1990. *Passions of the cut sleeve: The male homosexual tradition in China.* Berkeley: University of California Press.

Hirst, Paul, and Grahame Thompson. 1996. *Globalization in question: The international economy and the possibilities of governance.* Cambridge, MA: Polity.

Hollstein, Walter. 1992. *Machen Sie Platz, mein Herr! Teilen statt Herrschen* [Sharing instead of dominating]. Hamburg: Rowohlt.

Hollway, Wendy. 1994. Separation, integration and difference: Contradictions in a gender regime. In *Power/gender: Social relations in theory and practice,* edited by H. Lorraine Radtke and Henderikus Stam, 247–69. London: Sage.

Holter, Oystein Gullvag. 1997. Gender, patriarchy and capitalism: A social forms analysis. Ph.D. diss., University of Oslo, Faculty of Social Science.

Hondagneu-Sotelo, Pierrette, and Michael A. Messner. 1994. Gender displays and men's power: The "new man" and the Mexican immigrant man. In *Theorizing masculinities,* edited by Harry Brod and Michael Kaufman, 200–218. Twin Oaks, CA: Sage.

Ito Kimio. 1993. *Otokorashisa-no-yukue* [Directions for masculinities]. Tokyo: Shinyo-sha.

Jolly, Margaret. 1997. From point Venus to Bali Ha'i: Eroticism and exoticism in representations of the Pacific. In *Sites of desire, economies of pleasure: Sexualities in Asia and the Pacific,* edited by Lenore Manderson and Margaret Jolly, 99–122. Chicago: University of Chicago Press.

Kandiyoti, Deniz. 1994. The paradoxes of masculinity: Some thoughts on segregated societies. In *Dislocating masculinity: Comparative ethnographies,* edited by Andrea Cornwall and Nancy Lindisfame, 197–213. London: Routledge.

Kaufman, Michael. 1997. Working with men and boys to challenge sexism and end men's violence. Paper presented at UNESCO expert group meeting on Male Roles and Masculinities in the Perspective of a Culture of Peace, September, Oslo.

Kimmel, Michael S. 1987. Rethinking "masculinity": New directions in research. In *Changing men: New directions in research on men and masculinity,* edited by Michael S. Kimmel, 9–24. Newbury Park, CA: Sage.

———. 1996. *Manhood in America: A cultural history.* New York: Free Press.

Kimmel, Michael S., and Thomas P. Mosmiller, eds. 1992. *Against the tide: Pro-feminist men in the United States, 1776–1990, a documentary history.* Boston: Beacon.

Kindler, Heinz. 1993. *Maske(r)ade: Jungen-und Maenner-arbeit fuer die Pratis* [Work with youth and men]. Neuling: Schwaebisch Gmuend und Tuebingen.

Kinmonth, Earl H. 1981. *The self-made man in Meiji Japanese thought: From Samurai to salary man.* Berkeley: University of California Press.

Kipling, Rudyard. [1901] 1987. *Kim*. London: Penguin.

Klein, Alan M. 1993. *Little big men: Bodybuilding subculture and gender construction*. Albany: State University of New York Press.

Klein, Uta. 1997. Our best boys: The making of masculinity in Israeli society. Paper presented at UNESCO expert group meeting on Male Roles and Masculinities in the Perspectives of a Culture of Peace, September, Oslo.

Lewes, Kenneth. 1988. *The psychoanalytic theory of male homosexuality*. New York: Simon & Schuster.

MacDonald, Robert H. 1994. *The language of empire: Myths and metaphors of popular imperialism, 1880–1918*. Manchester, U.K.: Manchester University Press.

McElhinny, Bonnie. 1994. An economy of affect: Objectivity, masculinity and the gendering of police work. In *Dislocating masculinity: Comparative ethnographies*, edited by Andrea Cornwall and Nancy Lindisfarne, 159–71. London: Routledge.

McKay, Jim, and Debbie Huber. 1992. Anchoring media images of technology and sport. *Women's Studies International Forum* 15 (2): 205–18.

Messerschmidt, James W. 1997. *Crime as structured action: Gender, race, class, and crime in the making*. Thousand Oaks, CA: Sage.

Messner, Michael A. 1992. *Power at play: Sports and the problem of masculinity*. Boston: Beacon.

———. 1997. *The politics of masculinities: Men in movements*. Thousand Oaks, CA: Sage.

Metz-Goeckel, Sigrid, and Ursula Mueller. 1986. *Der Mann: Die Brigitte-Studie* [The male]. Beltz: Weinheim & Basel.

Mies, Maria. 1986. *Patriarchy and accumulation on a world scale: Women in the international division of labour*. London: Zed.

Moodie, T. Dunbar. 1994. *Going for gold: Men, mines, and migration*. Johannesburg: Witwatersand University Press.

Morrell, Robert. 1994. Boys, gangs, and the making of masculinity in the White secondary schools of Natal, 1880–1930. *Masculinities* 2 (2): 56–82.

———, ed. 1996. *Political economy and identities in KwaZulu-Natal: Historical and social perspectives*. Durban, Natal: Indicator Press.

Nakamura, Akira. 1994. *Watashi-no Danseigaku* [My men's studies]. Tokyo: Kindaibugei-sha.

Oftung, Knut, ed. 1994. *Menns bilder og bilder av menn* [Images of men]. Oslo: Likestillingsradet.

Phillips, Jock. 1987. *A man's country? The image of the Pakeha male—a history*. Auckland: Penguin.

Poynting, S., G. Noble, and P. Tabar. 1997. "Intersections" of masculinity and ethnicity: A study of male Lebanese immigrant youth in Western Sydney. Paper presented at the conference Masculinities: Renegotiating Genders, June, University of Wollongong, Australia.

Roper, Michael. 1991. Yesterday's model: Product fetishism and the British company man, 1945–85. In *Manful assertions: Masculinities in Britain since 1800*, edited by Michael Roper and John Tosh, 190–211. London: Routledge.

Schwalbe, Michael. 1996. *Unlocking the iron cage: The men's movement, gender, politics, and the American culture*. New York: Oxford University Press.

Segal, Lynne. 1997. *Slow motion: Changing masculinities, changing men*. 2d ed. London: Virago.

Seidler, Victor J. 1991. *Achilles heel reader: Men, sexual politics and socialism*. London: Routledge.

Shire, Chenjerai. 1994. Men don't go to the moon: Language, space and masculinities in Zimbabwe. In *Dislocating masculinity: Comparative ethnographies*, edited by Andrea Cornwall and Nancy Lindisfarne, 147–58. London: Routledge.

Simpson, Amelia. 1993. *Xuxa: The mega-marketing of a gender, race and modernity*. Philadelphia: Temple University Press.

Sinha, Mrinalini. 1995. *Colonial masculinity: The manly Englishman and the effeminate Bengali in the late nineteenth century*. Manchester, U.K.: Manchester University Press.

Taylor, Debbie. 1985. Women: An analysis. In *Women: A world report*, 1–98. London: Methuen.

Theberge, Nancy. 1991. Reflections on the body in the sociology of sport. *Quest* 43:123–34.

Thorne, Barrie. 1993. *Gender play: Girls and boys in school*. New Brunswick, NJ: Rutgers University Press.

Tillner, Georg. 1997. Masculinity and xenophobia. Paper presented at UNESCO meeting on Male Roles and Masculinities in the Perspective of a Culture of Peace, September, Oslo.

Tomsen, Stephen. 1997. A top night: Social protest, masculinity and the culture of drinking violence. *British Journal of Criminology* 37 (1): 90–103.

Tosh, John. 1991. Domesticity and manliness in the Victorian middle class: The family of Edward White Benson. In *Manful assertions: Masculinities in Britain since 1800*, edited by Michael Roper and John Tosh, 44–73. London: Routledge.

United Nations Educational, Scientific and Cultural Organization (UNESCO). 1997. *Male roles and masculinities in the perspective of a culture of peace: Report of expert group meeting, Oslo, 24–28 September 1997*. Paris: Women and a Culture of Peace Programme, Culture of Peace Unit, UNESCO.

Walby, Sylvia. 1990. *Theorizing patriarchy*. Oxford, U.K.: Blackwell.

Walker, James C. 1988. *Louts and legends: Male youth culture in an inner-city school*. Sydney: Allen & Unwin.

Wallerstein, Immanuel. 1974. *The modern world-system: Capitalist agriculture and the origins of the European world-economy in the sixteenth century*. New York: Academic Press.

Whitson, David. 1990. Sport in the social construction of masculinity. In *Sport, men, and the gender order: Critical feminist perspectives*, edited by Michael A. Messner and Donald F. Sabo, 19–29. Champaign, IL: Human Kinetics Books.

Widersprueche. 1995. Special Issue: *Maennlichkeiten.* Vol. 56/57.

Williams, Walter L. 1986. *The spirit and the flesh: Sexual diversity in American Indian culture.* Boston: Beacon.

Xaba, Thokozani. 1997. Masculinity in a transitional society: The rise and fall of the "young lions." Paper presented at the conference Masculinities in Southern Africa, June, University of Natal-Durban, Durban.

WOMANIST

Alice Walker

Womanist

1. From *Womanish.* (Opp. of "girlish," i.e., frivolous, irresponsible, not serious.) A black feminist or feminist or color. From the black folk expression of mothers to female children, "You acting womanish," i.e., like a woman. Usually referring to outrageous audacious, courageous or *willful* behavior. Wanting to know more and in greater depth than is considered "good" for one. Interested in grown-up doings. Acting grown up. Being grown up. Interchangeable with another black folk expression: "You trying to be grown," Responsible. In charge. *Serious.*

   . . .

2. *Also:* A woman who loves other women, sexually and/or nonsexually. Appreciates and prefers women's culture, women's emotional flexibility (values tears as natural counterbalance of laughter), and women's strength. Sometimes loves individual men, sexually and/or nonsexually. Committed to survival and wholeness of entire people, male *and* female. Not a separatist, except periodically, for health. Traditionally universalist, as in: "Mama, why are we brown, pink, and yellow, and our cousins are white, beige, and black?" Ans.: "Well, you know the colored race is just like a flower garden, with every color flower represented." Traditionally capable, as in: "Mama, I'm walking to Canada and I'm taking you and a bunch of other slaves with me." Reply: "It wouldn't be the first time."

   . . .

3. Loves music. Loves dance. Loves the moon. *Loves the Spirit.* Loves love and food and roundness. Loves struggle. *Loves* the Folk. Loves herself. *Regardless.*

   . . .

4. Womanist is to feminist as purple to lavender.

PART TWO

GENDER, CULTURE, AND SOCIALIZATION

Everyone is born into a culture—a set of shared ideas about the nature of reality, standards of right and wrong, and concepts for making sense of social interactions. These ideas are put into practice in behaviors and material objects. As totally dependent infants, we are socialized—taught the rules, roles, and relationships of the social world we will inherit. In the process of growing up, we learn to think, act, and feel as we are "supposed to." As adults, we are embedded in our culture's assumptions and images of gender.

One of the earliest and most deeply seated ideas to which we are socialized is that of gender identity—the idea that "I am a boy" or "I am a girl." Because the culture promotes strong ideas about what boys and girls are like, most of us learn to think of ourselves in terms of our gender identity (our "boyness" or "girlness") and adopt behaviors that are sex-assigned in our culture. Thus, for example, a girl who plays quietly with dolls is viewed as behaving in a feminine or "ladylike" manner, and a boy who plays with trucks is seen as appropriately masculine, as "all boy." Children who do not display these gender-stereotypical behaviors may face disapproval or punishment from adults and teasing or shunning by other children. Children who do not feel that their gender is right—that their bodies do not match their sense of their own gender identity—have a very difficult time in our society. Consciously or unconsciously, adults and peers categorize children as boys or girls, respond to and regard them differently, and encourage them to adopt behaviors and attitudes on the basis of their sex. We raise, in effect, two different kinds of children: girls and boys.

Parents are strong socializing influences, and they provide the first and most deeply experienced socialization. Despite claims to the contrary, American parents treat girls and boys differently. Boys and girls have different toys, names, and room decor, and adults play with them in different ways. The stores in which parents shop for children's toys or clothing have separate aisles for boys' and girls' items, which can easily be identified by the dominant color (waves of pink packaging are a clue that the aisle contains girls' items). Even if parents monitor their actions in the hope of preventing sexism from affecting their child, other socializing influences—schools, mass media, and other children—bear down on children.

One of the primary socializing influences is language. When we learn to talk, we also learn the thought patterns and communication styles of our culture. Those patterns and styles reinforce differentiation by sex and perpetuate sex stereotyping, although the kind of stereotyping may vary from language to language. All languages teach their culture's ideas about men and women. They do it "naturally": As one learns a language, one learns the viewpoint of one's culture. In the English language, for example, the generic man is supposed to include males and females, as well as people of all races and ethnicities; but in linguistic practice, it does not, as Richardson shows in Section 3. People other than white and male are linguistically tagged in writing and in speech. For example, occupational categories are sex- or race-tagged if the person's sex or race does not fit cultural stereotypes about who will be in those occupations. Consider: doctor/woman doctor/black woman doctor or nurse/male nurse/Asian male nurse. Linguistic tags convey normative expectations about who should occupy particular positions in society and about the normality or legitimacy of white men's claim to powerful positions. When a child asks, "Were there any cave women?" for example, we realize the picture conveyed by the term "cavemen."

As societies have become more complex, the mass media increasingly have become centralized agents that transmit dominant cultural beliefs. Movements toward cultural heterogeneity are thwarted through the homogenizing effects of television, in particular. TV presents gender stereotypes in their purest and simplest forms. Whether the program is about African-American families, lawyers at work, white teenagers, talking animals, or bachelors searching for the perfect wife, the stereotyping messages about gender and race are endlessly repetitive. Children in the United States spend more time watching TV than they spend in school or interacting with parents or peers. Moreover, they believe that what they see on TV is an accurate representation of how the world is and should be organized. White middle-class male dominance and sexualized, passive femininity are the repetitive themes.

The socialization effected by the family, language, and the mass media is continued in the educational system. Schools are formally charged with teaching the young. While teaching reading, writing, and arithmetic, however, schools also teach conventional views of gender. They do so through patterns of staffing (male principals and custodians, female teachers and food servers), curriculum, the sex segregation of sports and activities (whether formal or informal), and different expectations for boys and girls. Children themselves reinforce these messages through sex-segregated play and the teasing of children who do not conform.

Socialization—whether through the home, the school, language, or the mass media—creates and sustains gender differences. Boys are taught that they will inherit the privileges and prestige of manhood and that they must be tough, aggressive, and interested in cars and sports. Girls, in contrast, learn that they are less socially valuable than boys and that they should be quiet, pretty, and interested in dolls, fashion, and boys. Subcultures that promote values and beliefs different from the mainstream do exist, and individuals do not necessarily internalize every message from the dominant culture. In fact, many children and adults challenge the culture of gender difference directly, and many others live their lives in ways that do not conform to the stereotypes and expectations for their gender. Nevertheless, traditional cultural views of gender are ubiquitous and powerful.

Through influential social institutions, then, children learn and consume a culture. Our culture is one that views men and masculinity as superior to women and femininity. It is a system that assigns different behaviors and attitudes to males and females and that further distinguishes between people of different racial and ethnic groups. As adults, we continue to be shaped by the books and magazines we read, the movies and TV shows we see, the music we enjoy, and the people with whom we spend time. The ways that gender is portrayed or represented in the culture—in mass media, schools, and public discussions—provide us with our only conceptual tools for thinking about men and women. It becomes nearly impossible to think about gender without being shaped by the images that surround us.

The readings in this part of Feminist Frontiers illustrate and explain different aspects of cultural constructions of gender and the socialization process. These systems of meaning shape how we understand ourselves and our social institutions. The readings document both the prevalence of conventional understandings in the culture and the presence of alternative messages. As you read, consider what kinds of influences conventional representations of gender have and what sources exist for challenging these images.

SECTION 3

Representation, Language, and Culture

Our gender culture includes the language we use and the images that surround us in advertising, mass media, and daily life. We are confronted by images of gender in all areas of our lives. In our language, mass media, and daily lives, we encounter particular definitions of what it means to be a woman or a man. Often we take these images for granted, and the ways that women and men are represented seem natural or inevitable. Yet language and media representations of gender shape the way we view ourselves and our relationships to each other and to the world around us. This section explores the images of women and men expressed in language and mass media, as well as their relationship to culture and daily life more broadly.

Laurel Richardson's "Gender Stereotyping in the English Language" demonstrates the major ways in which sexism pervades the structure and standard usage of modern American English. Her analysis reveals different expectations of women and men embedded in the language and shows how we internalize and reinforce gender differences, as we read, write, and speak English or hear it spoken. The reading raises questions about the relationships between language and social life, including connections between linguistic change and other forms of social change. What are some examples of sexist or nonsexist language? If you speak or have studied another language, compare its gender structure to that of English. Do you think using nonsexist language affects people's attitudes toward women? How? An interesting question for classroom debate is whether the word "guy" or the phrase "you guys" is gender neutral.

Judy Taylor's "Feminist Consumerism and Fat Activists" moves to the arena of advertising and daily life. Taylor contrasts how the Dove Campaign for Real Beauty talked about broader views of what kinds of bodies can be seen as beautiful with the much more radical redefinitions of feminine beauty advocated by a fat activist group. Although the Dove campaign challenged the view that only extremely thin women are beautiful, it nevertheless presented beauty as central to women's identities. In contrast, the fat activist group not only celebrated fat women's bodies but attempted to resist the idea that women are defined by their appearance. Yet while the Dove campaign reached a broad audience, the grassroots and radical nature of the fat activist group meant that it reached only a relatively small audience. What effect, if any, do you think the Dove campaign had on definitions of beauty and weight? Can you think of other advertising campaigns that challenged definitions of beauty or that presented alternative views of women or men more generally? How much power do you think advertising has to change gender? What limits its power? In contrast, what kinds of changes can grassroots campaigns like the one Taylor describes make?

Debra Gimlin describes one of the consequences of cultural messages of beauty on women: the high rates of cosmetic surgery. In "Cosmetic Surgery: Paying for Your Beauty," she discusses the phenomenal rise in the United States of elective cosmetic surgeries such as liposuction, breast augmentation (and reduction), blepharoplasty (eyelid surgery), facelift, and chemical peel. Ninety percent of patients undergoing such procedures are women. Criticism of such surgeries focus not only on the risks and costs but also on the increasing pressure for women to take advantage of medical advances to fight aging, imperfection, and ethnic deviations from an Anglo ideal of beauty.

Yet Gimlin, in interviewing women who had undergone plastic surgery at a Long Island clinic, challenges the notion that women are simply dupes of the culture. She finds that women set realistic and limited goals—not the attainment of perfect beauty—when they seek plastic surgery, and that the surgery often makes them feel better about their bodies and themselves. At the same time, they feel the need to construct elaborate defenses for having made this choice. Gimlin offers a complex view of cosmetic surgery. Do you think cosmetic surgery is a reasonable choice for women? How important are cultural ideals in making women dislike parts of their bodies? Can you imagine seeking cosmetic surgery for yourself?

Some of the women Gimlin interviewed disliked their Jewish or Italian noses or Asian eyes. Race, ethnicity, and class have a great deal to do with American ideals of beauty. Ingrid Banks, author of a book called *Hair Matters*, argues in "Hair Still Matters" that hair continues to carry complex meanings for African-American women. From Venus Williams and her controversial beaded braids to Yaya DaCosta Johnson, a contestant on "America's Next Top Model" who was considered "Afrocentric" because she did not straighten her hair, African-American women's hairstyles make statements about race, gender, sexuality, and culture. Banks listens to the voices of African-American women talking about how hair is perceived by others and how they feel about their own hair. She also connects the issue of hair to global issues of beauty and women's bodies. Given cultural images of white women with long, flowing hair, is it surprising that long hair signals femininity for many African-American women? What are the standards for beautiful hair for other racial or ethnic groups? Do other ethnic groups also attempt to

conform to white standards of beauty? Are there similar pressures for men? What do different hairstyles signal about the people who choose to wear them? Do you judge women's femininity and sexuality based on hairstyle?

T. Denean Sharpley-Whiting extends Banks's critique of standards of beauty for African-American women in "'I See the Same Ho': Video Vixens, Beauty Culture, and Diasporic Sex Tourism." Sharpley-Whiting focuses on the very narrow range of beauty depicted in hip-hop videos and the way these ideals affect African-American women and girls. The women who play the role of "video ho" or "eye candy" are universally light-skinned and long-haired and increasingly reflect an ideal of ethnically ambiguous or hybrid beauty. Even the most popular individual artists, such as Beyoncé Knowles or Faith Evans, conform to this standard of beauty, while hip-hop videos produced by African-American men present women as valuable primarily for their sexuality. Sharpley-Whiting argues that, most recently, the "fetishizing" of racial hybridity has led to an idealization of Brazilian women as a new ideal for black femininity in music videos such as Snoop Dogg's "Beauty." Along with this idealization of Brazilian women comes an increase in sex tourism and a marketing of Brazil as a hedonistic paradise to African-American men. In Sharpley-Whiting's view, black masculinity is also defined in conjunction with these definitions of black femininity. She sees this image of black masculinity as based on American privilege and—in its "color chauvinism"—white supremacy. Why is "ethnically ambiguous" beauty in demand? Why is this problematic?

Can you think of other examples of how black women are portrayed in hip-hop videos? How do these compare with music videos from other genres? Do you agree with Sharpley-Whiting about the narrowness of these images? What are the images of black men in hip-hop videos? What are the standards of masculine attractiveness? How does Sharpley-Whiting think narrow definitions of beauty and an emphasis on sexuality affect black women and girls? Do you agree with her? Do you think about the depictions of women when you consume hip-hop music or videos? How do they affect you?

We cannot emphasize too strongly the importance of language and mass media in the construction of our understanding of women's and men's positions in society. We are exposed to these images continually. Because the language we have acquired and the images we use are so deeply rooted and inseparable, it is very difficult for us to break free of them, to see and describe the world and our experiences in nonsexist ways. Yet women and other subordinate groups do attempt to construct alternative systems of meaning and to draw strength from cultures of resistance. The power to define has a major influence on our conceptions of others and ourselves.

Gender Stereotyping in the English Language

Everyone in our society, regardless of class, ethnicity, sex, age, or race, is exposed to the same language, the language of the dominant culture. Analysis of verbal language can tell us a great deal about a people's fears, prejudices, anxieties, and interests. A rich vocabulary on a particular subject indicates societal interests or obsessions (e.g., the extensive vocabulary about cars in America). And different words for the same subject (such as *freedom fighter* and *terrorist, passed away* and *croaked, make love* and *ball*) show that there is a range of attitudes and feelings in the society toward that subject.

It should not be surprising, then, to find differential attitudes and feelings about men and women rooted in the English language. Although English has not been completely analyzed, six general propositions concerning these attitudes and feelings about males and females can be made.

First, in terms of grammatical and semantic structure, women do not have a fully autonomous, independent existence; they are part of man. The language is not divided into male and female with distinct conjugations and declensions, as many other languages are. Rather, *women* are included under the generic *man*. Grammar books specify that the pronoun *he* can be used generically to mean *he or she*. Further, *man*, when used as an indefinite pronoun, grammatically refers to both men and women. So, for example, when we read *man* in the following phrases we are to interpret it as applying to both men and women: "man the oars," "one small step for man, one giant step for mankind," "man, that's tough," "man overboard," "man the toolmaker," "alienated man," "garbageman." Our rules of etiquette complete the grammatical presumption of inclusivity. When two persons are pronounced "man and wife," Miss Susan Jones changes her entire name to Mrs. Robert Gordon (Vanderbilt, 1972). In each of these correct usages, women are a part of man; they do not exist autonomously. The exclusion of women is well expressed in Mary Daly's ear-jarring slogan "the sisterhood of man" (1973:7–21).

However, there is some question as to whether the theory that *man* means everybody is carried out in practice (see Bendix, 1979; Martyna, 1980). For example, an eight-year-old interrupts her reading of "The Story of the Cavemen" to ask how we got here without cavewomen. A ten-year-old thinks it is dumb to have a woman post*man*. A beginning anthropology student believes (incorrectly) that all shamans ("witch doctors") are males because her textbook and professor use the referential pronoun *he*.

But beginning language learners are not the only ones who visualize males when they see the word *man*. Research has consistently demonstrated that when the generic *man* is used, people visualize men, not women (Schneider & Hacker, 1973; DeStefano, 1976; Martyna, 1978; Hamilton & Henley, 1982). DeStefano, for example, reports that college students choose silhouettes of males for sentences with the word *man* or *men* in them. Similarly, the presumably generic *he* elicits images of men rather than women. The finding is so persistent that linguists doubt whether there actually is a semantic generic in English (MacKay, 1983).

Man, then, suggests not humanity but rather male images. Moreover, over one's lifetime, an educated American will be exposed to the prescriptive *he* more than a million times (MacKay, 1983). One consequence is the exclusion of women in the visualization, imagination, and thought of males and females. Most likely this linguistic practice perpetuates in men their feelings of dominance over and responsibility for women, feelings that interfere with the development of equality in relationships.

Second, in actual practice, our pronoun usage perpetuates different personality attributes and career aspirations for men and women. Nurses, secretaries, and elementary school teachers are almost invariably referred to as *she*; doctors, engineers, electricians, and presidents as *he*. In one classroom, students referred to an unidentified child as *he* but shifted to *she* when discussing the child's parent. In a faculty discussion of the problems of acquiring new staff, all architects, engineers, security officers, faculty, and computer programmers were referred to as *he;* secretaries and file clerks were referred to as *she.* Martyna (1978) has noted that speakers consistently use *he* when the referent has a high-status occupation (e.g., doctor, lawyer, judge) but shift to *she* when the occupations have lower status (e.g., nurse, secretary).

Even our choice of sex ascription to nonhuman objects subtly reinforces different personalities for males and females. It seems as though the small (e.g., kittens), the graceful (e.g., poetry), the unpredictable (e.g., the fates), the nurturant (e.g., the church, the school), and that which is owned and/or controlled by men (e.g., boats, cars, governments, nations) represent the feminine, whereas that which is a controlling forceful power in and of itself (e.g., God, Satan, tiger) primarily represents the masculine. Even athletic teams are not immune. In one college, the men's teams are called the Bearcats and the women's teams the Bearkittens.

Some of you may wonder whether it matters that the female is linguistically included in the male. The inclusion of women under the pseudogeneric *man* and the prescriptive *he,* however, is not a trivial issue. Language has tremendous power to shape attitudes and influence behavior. Indeed, MacKay (1983) argues that the prescriptive *he* "has all the characteristics of a highly effective propaganda technique": frequent repetition, early age of acquisition (before age six), covertness (*he* is not thought of as propaganda), use by high-prestige sources (including university texts and professors), and indirectness (presented as though it were a matter of common knowledge). As a result, the prescriptive affects females' sense of life options and feelings of well-being. For example, Adamsky (1981) found that women's sense of power and importance was enhanced when the prescriptive *he* was replaced by *she.*

Awareness of the impact of the generic *man* and prescriptive *he* has generated considerable activity to change the language. One change, approved by the Modern Language Association, is to replace the prescriptive *he* with the plural *they*—as was accepted practice before the eighteenth century. Another is the use of *he or she.* Although it sounds awkward at first, the *he or she* designation is increasingly being used in the media and among people who have recognized the power of the pronoun to perpetuate sex stereotyping. When a professor, for example, talks about "the lawyer" as "he or she," a speech pattern that counteracts sex stereotyping is modeled. This drive to neutralize the impact of pronouns is evidenced further in the renaming of occupations: a policeman is now a police officer, a postman is a mail carrier, a stewardess is a flight attendant.

Third, linguistic practice defines females as immature, incompetent, and incapable and males as mature, complete, and competent. Because the words *man* and *woman* tend to connote sexual and human maturity, common speech, organizational titles, public addresses, and bathroom doors frequently designate the women in question as *ladies.* Simply contrast the different connotations of *lady* and *woman* in the following common phrases:

> Luck, be a lady (woman) tonight.
> Barbara's a little lady (woman).
> Ladies' (Women's) Air Corps.

In the first two examples, the use of *lady* desexualizes the contextual meaning of *woman.* So trivializing is the use of *lady* in the last phrase that the second is wholly anomalous. The male equivalent, *lord,* is never used, and its synonym, *gentleman,* is used infrequently. When *gentleman* is used, the assumption seems to be that certain culturally condoned aspects of masculinity (e.g., aggressivity, activity, and strength) should be set aside in the interests of maturity and order, as in the following phrases:

> A gentlemen's (men's) agreement.
> A duel between gentlemen (men).
> He's a real gentleman (man).

Rather than feeling constrained to set aside the stereotypes associated with *man,* males frequently find the opposite process occurring. The contextual connotation of *man* places a strain on males to be continuously sexually and socially potent, as the following examples reveal:

> I was not a man (gentleman) with her tonight.
> This is a man's (gentleman's) job.
> Be a man (gentleman).

Whether males, therefore, feel competent or anxious, valuable or worthless in particular contexts is influenced by the demands placed on them by the expectations of the language.

Not only are men infrequently labeled *gentlemen,* but they are infrequently labeled *boys.* The term *boy* is reserved for young males, bellhops, and car attendants, and as a putdown to those males judged inferior. *Boy* connotes immaturity and powerlessness. Only occasionally do males "have a night out with the boys." They do not talk "boy talk" at the office. Rarely does our language legitimize carefreeness in males. Rather, they are expected, linguistically, to adopt the responsibilities of manhood.

On the other hand, women of all ages may be called *girls*. Grown females "play bridge with the girls" and indulge in "girl talk." They are encouraged to remain childlike, and the implication is that they are basically immature and without power. Men can become men, linguistically, putting aside the immaturity of childhood; indeed, for them to retain the openness and playfulness of boyhood is linguistically difficult.

Further, the presumed incompetence and immaturity of women are evidenced by the linguistic company they keep. Women are categorized with children ("women and children first"), the infirm ("the blind, the lame, the women"), and the incompetent ("women, convicts, and idiots"). The use of these categorical designations is not accidental happenstance; "rather these selectional groupings are powerful forces behind the actual expressions of language and are based on distinctions which are not regarded as trivial by the speakers of the language" (Key, 1975:82). A total language analysis of categorical groupings is not available, yet it seems likely that women tend to be included in groupings that designate incompleteness, ineptitude, and immaturity. On the other hand, it is difficult for us to conceive of the word *man* in any categorical grouping other than one that extends beyond humanity, such as "Man, apes, and angels" or "Man and Superman." That is, men do exist as an independent category capable of autonomy; women are grouped with the stigmatized, the immature, and the foolish. Moreover, when men are in human groupings, they are invariably first on the list ("men and women," "he and she," "man and wife"). This order is not accidental but was prescribed in the sixteenth century to honor the worthier party.

Fourth, in practice women are defined in terms of their sexual desirability (to men); men are defined in terms of their sexual prowess (over women). Most slang words in reference to women refer to their sexual desirability to men (e.g., *dog, fox, broad, ass, chick*). Slang about men refers to their sexual prowess over women (e.g., *dude, stud, hunk*). The fewer examples given for men is not an oversight. An analysis of sexual slang,

for example, listed more than a thousand words and phrases that derogate women sexually but found "nowhere near this multitude for describing men" (Kramarae, 1975:72). Farmer and Henley (cited in Schulz, 1975) list five hundred synonyms for *prostitute*, for example, and only sixty-five for *whoremonger*. Stanley (1977) reports two hundred twenty terms for a sexually promiscuous woman and only twenty-two for a sexually promiscuous man. Shuster (1973) reports that the passive verb form is used in reference to women's sexual experiences (e.g., *to be laid, to be had, to be taken*), whereas the active tense is used in reference to the male's sexual experience (e.g., *lay, take, have*). Being sexually attractive to males is culturally condoned for women and being sexually powerful is approved for males. In this regard, the slang of the street is certainly not countercultural; rather, it perpetuates and reinforces different expectations in females and males as sexual objects and performers.

Further, we find sexual connotations associated with neutral words applied to women. A few examples should suffice. A male academician questioned the title of a new course, asserting it was "too suggestive." The title? "The Position of Women in the Social Order." A male tramp is simply a hobo, but a female tramp is a slut. And consider the difference in connotation of the following expressions:

> *It's easy.*
> *He's easy.*
> *She's easy.*

In the first, we assume something is "easy to do"; in the second, we might assume a professor is an "easy grader" or a man is "easygoing." But when we read "she's easy," the connotation is "she's an easy lay."

In the world of slang, men are defined by their sexual prowess. In the world of slang and proper speech, women are defined as sexual objects. The rule in practice seems to be: If in doubt, assume that *any* reference to a women has a sexual connotation. For both genders, the constant bombardment of prescribed sexuality is bound to have real consequences.

Fifth, women are defined in terms of their relations to men; men are defined in terms of their relations to the world at large. A good example is seen in the words *master* and *mistress*. Originally these words had the same meaning—"a person who holds power over servants." With the demise of the feudal system, however, these words took on different meanings. The masculine variant metaphorically refers to power over something, as in "He is the master of his trade"; the feminine variant metaphorically (although probably not in actuality) refers to power over a man sexually, as in "She is Tom's mistress." Men are defined in terms of their power in the occupational world, women in terms of their sexual power over men.

The existence of two contractions for Mistress (*Miss* and *Mrs.*) and but one for Mister (*Mr.*) underscores the cultural concern and linguistic practice: women are defined in relation to men. Even a divorced woman is defined in terms of her no-longer-existing relation to a man (she is still *Mrs. Man's Name*). But apparently the divorced state is not relevant enough to the man or to the society to require a label. A divorced woman is a *divorcée*, but what do you call a divorced man? The recent preference of many women to be called *Ms.* is an attempt to provide for women an equivalency title that is not dependent on marital status.

Sixth, a historical pattern can be seen in the meanings that come to be attached to words that originally were neutral: those that apply to women acquire obscene and/or debased connotations, but no such pattern of derogation holds for neutral words referring to men. The processes of *pejoration* (the acquiring of an obscene or debased connotation) and *amelioration* (the reacquiring of a neutral or positive connotation) in the English language in regard to terms for males and females have been studied extensively by Muriel Schulz (1975).

Leveling is the least derogative form of pejoration. Through leveling, titles that originally referred to an elite class of persons come to include a wider class of persons. Such democratic leveling is more common for female designates than for males. For example, contrast the following: *lord–lady; baronet–dame; governor–governess.*

Most frequently what happens to words designating women as they become pejorated, however, is that they come to denote or connote sexual wantonness. *Sir* and *mister,* for example, remain titles of courtesy, but at some time *madam, miss,* and *mistress* have come to designate, respectively, a brothelkeeper, a prostitute, and an unmarried sexual partner of a male (Schulz, 1975:66).

Names for domestic helpers, if they are females, are frequently derogated. *Hussy,* for example, originally meant "housewife." *Laundress, needlewoman, spinster* ("tender of the spinning wheel"), and *nurse* all referred to domestic occupations within the home, and all at some point became slang expressions for prostitute or mistress.

Even kinship terms referring to women become denigrated. During the seventeenth century, *mother* was used to mean "a bawd"; more recently *mother* (*mothuh f*—) has become a common derogatory epithet (Cameron, 1974). Probably at some point in history every kinship term for females has been derogated (Schulz, 1975:66).

Terms of endearment for women also seem to follow a downward path. Such pet names as Tart, Dolly, Kitty, Polly, Mopsy, Biddy, and Jill all eventually became sexually derogatory (Schulz, 1975:67). *Whore* comes from the same Latin root as *care* and once meant "a lover of either sex."

Indeed, even the most neutral categorical designations—*girl, female, woman, lady*—at some point in their history have been used to connote sexual immorality. *Girl* originally meant "a child of either sex"; through the process of semantic degeneration it eventually meant "a prostitute." Although *girl* has lost this meaning, *girlie* still retains sexual connotations. *Woman* connoted "a mistress" in the early nineteenth century; *female* was a degrading epithet in the latter part of the nineteenth century; and when *lady* was introduced as a euphemism, it too became deprecatory. "Even so neutral a term as *person,* when it was used as substitute for *woman,* suffered [vulgarization]" (Mencken, 1963:350, quoted in Schulz, 1975:71).

Whether one looks at elite titles, occupational roles, kinship relationships, endearments, or age-sex categorical designations, the pattern is clear. Terms referring to females are pejorated—"become negative in the middle instances and abusive in the extremes" (Schulz, 1975:69). Such semantic derogation, however, is not evidenced for male referents. *Lord, baronet, father, brother, nephew, footman, bowman, boy, lad, fellow, gentleman, man, male,* and so on "have failed to undergo the derogation found in the history of their corresponding feminine designations" (Schulz, 1975:67). Interestingly, the male word, rather than undergoing derogation, frequently is replaced by a female referent when the speaker wants to debase a male. A weak man, for example, is referred to as a *sissy* (diminutive of *sister*), and an army recruit during basic training is called a *pussy.* And when one is swearing at a male, he is referred to as a *bastard* or a *son of a bitch*—both appellations that impugn the dignity of a man's mother.

In summary, these verbal practices are consistent with the gender stereotypes that we encounter in everyday life. Women are thought to be a part of man, nonautonomous, dependent, relegated to roles that require few skills, characteristically incompetent and immature, sexual objects, best defined in terms of their relations to men. Males are visible, autonomous and independent, responsible for the protection and containment of women, expected to occupy positions on the basis of their high achievement or physical power, assumed to be sexually potent, and defined primarily by their relations to the world of work. The use of the language perpetuates the stereotypes for both genders and limits the options available for self-definition.

REFERENCES

Adamsky, C. 1981. "Changes in pronominal usage in a classroom situation." *Psychology of Women Quarterly* 5:773–79.

Bendix, J. 1979. "Linguistic models as political symbols: Gender and the generic 'he' in English." In J. Orasanu, M. Slater, and L. L. Adler, eds., *Language, Sex and Gender: Does la différence Make a Difference?* pp. 23–42. New York: New Academy of Science Annuals.

Cameron, P. 1974. "Frequency and kinds of words in various social settings, or What the hell's going on?" In M. Truzzi, ed., *Sociology for Pleasure*, pp. 31–37. Englewood Cliffs, N.J.: Prentice-Hall.

Daly, M. 1973. *Beyond God the Father.* Boston: Beacon Press.

DeStefano, J. S. 1976. Personal communication. Columbus: Ohio State University.

Hamilton, N., & Henley, N. 1982. "Detrimental consequences of the generic masculine usage." Paper presented to the Western Psychological Association meetings, Sacramento.

Key, M. R. 1975. *Male/Female Language.* Metuchen, N.J.: Scarecrow Press.

Kramarae, Cheris. 1975. "Woman's speech: Separate but unequal?" In Barrie Thorne and Nancy Henley, eds., *Language and Sex: Difference and Dominance*, pp. 43–56. Rowley, Mass.: Newbury House.

MacKay, D. G. 1983. "Prescriptive grammar and the pronoun problem." In B. Thorne, C. Kramarae, and N. Henley, eds., *Language, Gender, and Society*, pp. 38–53. Rowley, Mass.: Newbury House.

Martyna, W. 1978. "What does 'he' mean? Use of the generic masculine." *Journal of Communication* 28:131–38.

Martyna, W. 1980. "Beyond the 'he/man' approach: The case for nonsexist language." *Signs* 5:482–93.

Mencken, H. L. 1963. *The American Language.* 4th ed. with supplements. Abr. and ed. R. I. McDavis. New York: Knopf.

Schneider, J., & Hacker, S. 1973. "Sex role imagery in the use of the generic 'man' in introductory texts: A case in the sociology of sociology." *American Sociologist* 8:12–18.

Schulz, M. R. 1975. "The semantic derogation of women." In B. Thorne and N. Henley, eds., *Language and Sex: Difference and Dominance*, pp. 64–75. Rowley, Mass.: Newbury House.

Shuster, Janet. 1973. "Grammatical forms marked for male and female in English." Unpublished paper. Chicago: University of Chicago.

Stanley, J. P. 1977. "Paradigmatic woman: The prostitute." In D. L. Shores, ed., *Papers in Language Variation.* Birmingham: University of Alabama Press.

Vanderbilt, A. 1972. *Amy Vanderbilt's Etiquette.* Garden City, N.Y.: Doubleday.

THE NORMALIZATION OF HETEROGENDERED RELATIONS IN *THE BACHELOR*

Gust Yep and Ariana Ochoa Camacho

Offering the promise of heterosexual romance and a fairy tale ending, *The Bachelor* opened its fourth season on prime-time ABC with a male voice telling us "Once upon a time there was a charming young bachelor searching for a woman of his dreams." In this essay, we argue that *The Bachelor,* one of the top 25 shows in the Fall 2003 television lineup in the US (AllYourTV 2003), normalizes heterogendered relations in contemporary US society. Coined by Chrys Ingraham (1994), heterogender is a concept used to demystify the connection between gender and heterosexuality. In *The Bachelor,* heterogendered relations are upheld and reified while remaining strategically opaque. Through our reading of the show, we make such relations visible for critical analysis.

The Bachelor is a one-hour romance reality television series. The premise of the show revolves around a man, Bob Guiney in the Fall 2003 season, selecting from 25 women in his quest for a serious long-term relationship, and potentially marriage (ABC 2003). *The Bachelor* gives a behind-the-scenes look into the experience of the participants in a "unique" dating process (ABC 2003). The show focuses on rose ceremonies that reveal Guiney's process of elimination. At each ceremony, the bachelor is presented with a limited number of roses to give to the women. Through a carefully orchestrated demonstration, he hands each chosen woman a rose. Any woman he rejects simply does not receive a rose, and is forced to leave immediately. The finale involves Guiney rejecting one woman, and presenting a ring to the "one woman who captures his heart" (ABC 2003).

Heterogendered Relations in *The Bachelor*

The heterosexual imaginary constitutes an ideology that conceals the relationship between heterosexuality and gender, foreclosing any critical analysis of heterosexuality as an organizing institution in the modern West (Ingraham 1994). One powerful strategy for this closure is normalization. Normalization refers to the process of constructing, establishing, and (re)producing a taken-for-granted, unquestionable, and all-encompassing standard used to measure goodness, desirability, morality, rationality, and superiority (Gust Yep 2003).

Heterogender refers to the asymmetrical stratification of the sexes, privileging men and exploiting women, in the institution of patriarchal heterosexuality (Ingraham 1994). This is evident in the premise of the show with 25 women competing for the attention of one man. The bachelor has tremendous proactive power (e.g., he selects which women remain) while the women are given very limited reactive power (e.g., they can refuse the rose and immediately leave).

The Bachelor clearly reinforces current US standards of female beauty and objectification of the woman's body. In the first episode, Mike Fleiss, Executive Producer, tells the audience about how the women were selected: "Most importantly, they have to look good in the hot tub." The women undoubtedly submitted to the "tall, young, fit, and thin" beauty standard as one of the participants observed, "All the women are beautiful, gorgeous, and skinny." Although the bachelor typically described the women as "amazingly beautiful" and "extremely intelligent," the show focused on their physical appearance—body shape, clothing, makeup, and hairstyle. The women were mostly presented as objects of the male gaze. This was accomplished through two primary techniques. The first uses visual approaches that scan and scrutinize the women's bodies with the camera focusing on the women's breasts, buttocks, and legs as they dressed, entered and left the pool, or disrobed to catch the bachelor's attention. The second technique utilized plot devices that created situations for the women to expose their bodies such as pajama parties, water rides in an amusement park, and interactions in hot tubs and pools. In a number of these shots, the

(continued)

women's faces were absent or de-emphasized as they became interchangeable body parts for public consumption. On the other hand, reflecting the asymmetrical power relationships, the bachelor's body was hardly the object of scrutiny. The bachelor was presented as the subject of the gaze complete with agency and control of every situation in the show.

The verbal exchanges between the women tended to focus on the bachelor. As the episodes progressed, the women openly displayed their feelings of love and desire for the bachelor. The show simultaneously highlighted "cat fights" and open displays of rivalry among the women, and their sense of connection through intense competition for Guiney's affections. In the process, the ideal of a subservient, care-taking woman tending to the needs of her husband was continually reinforced as one participant in the show declared, "I will be the perfect wife because I like to mother. I like to actually take care of somebody like that, to cook for them." Another confessed, "I will make the best wife for Bob because I will be a servant to him." These archaic patriarchal gender roles are normalized throughout the show.

As the core premise of the show, the ideology of patriarchal heterosexuality was consistently invoked through connections with fairy tales. The narrative of the show was infused with statements such as "Once upon a time," "Cinderella," "fantasy date," and 'happily ever after" which signaled the heterosexual imaginary (Ingraham 1999). According to Ingraham, heterosexual imaginary is a

> belief system that relies on romantic and sacred notions of heterosexuality in order to create and maintain the illusion of well-being. At the same time this romantic view prevents us from seeing how institutionalized heterosexuality actually works to organize gender while preserving [current] racial, class, and sexual hierarchies. (1999, p. 16)

Throughout the episodes, many of the women discussed their dream weddings, marriage, and the details of being a good wife. These sound bites explicitly reinforced heteronormative standards for women. These homogenizing images exclude women who subscribe to different ideals in their relationships with men. Certainly these ideals exclude queer women altogether. However, in a house full of women, we saw allusions to queerness through homoeroticism. In episode three, in the pajama party scene, some women dance together moving their torsos and hips together seductively as Guiney watches. The editing accentuates the intention of these behaviors designed for the male gaze.

Audre Lorde's (1984, p. 116) notion of the "mythical norm" is reproduced in *The Bachelor*. By scrutinizing the heterogendered normative standards for women in this show, we expose the "white, thin, male, young, heterosexual, . . . and financially secure" figure referenced by Lorde (1984, p. 116). Lorde points out that "It is with this mythical norm that the trappings of power reside within [US] society" (1984, p. 116). Such power creates social relations that appear to be natural, normal, and beyond reproach. Through visibility and representation, it constructs what is attractive and desirable, what is loving, and who is lovable. Anyone who deviates from the mythical norm is pathologized, dismissed, silenced, or erased. Through invisibility and symbolic annihilation, love, desire, and human connection among individuals diverging from the mythical norm are rendered unintelligible. However, a closer examination of the mythical norm reveals that it is in a constant state of crisis. Although we recognize the material advantages and consequences associated with this norm, this mythical center is in perpetual need of those outside of it to define, maintain, and (re)affirm itself. Through critical analysis, these borders can be potentially shifted to change current social arrangements.

Conclusion

In this essay, we examined *The Bachelor* and argued that it reifies current heterogendered relations through the process of normalization. Although reality TV offers the promise of democratic access to the means of media production by making "ordinary people" into "stars," a closer examination suggests otherwise. Reality TV shows have become "the latest and most self-conscious in a string of transparently staged spectacles, complete with their own formulas" (Mark Andrejevic 2004, p. 3) which are controlled by global corporate giants that continue to reify social hierarchies to increase consumption and profit.

REFERENCES

ABC (2003) 'The Bachelor, about the show', [Online] Available at: http://abc.go.com/primetime/bachelor/show.html (13 Oct. 2003).

ALLYOURTV (2003). 'Ratings: the season so far'. [Online] Available at: http://www.allyourtv.com/ratingsseason.html (14 Nov. 2003).

Andrejevic, Mark (2004) Reality TV: The Work of Being Watched, Rowman & Littlefield, Lanham, MD.

The Bachelor (video recording) (2003) Episodes 1–6, ABC, 24 September, 1 October, 8 October, 22 October, 29 October, 5 November.

Ingraham, Chrys (1994) 'The heterosexual imaginary: feminist sociology and theories of gender', Sociological Theory, vol. 12, no. 2, pp. 203–219.

Lorde, Audre (1984) Sister Outsider: Essays and Speeches, The Crossing Press, Freedom, CA.

Yep, Gust (2003) 'The violence of heteronormativity in communication studies: notes on injury, healing, and queer-world making', Journal of Homosexuality, vol. 45, nos. 2–4, pp. 11–59.

READING *13* **Judy Taylor**

Feminist Consumerism and Fat Activists: Grassroots Activism and the Dove "Real Beauty" Campaign

I. INTRODUCTION

Some cultural critics suggest a limited transformative outcome when a corporation co-opts social movements' emancipatory ideals into marketing campaigns (Frank 1997; Potter and Weiland 2004). Virginia Slims, for instance, promoted an image of feminist independence in the "you've come a long way" marketing campaign, and yet sold women a highly addictive, cancer-causing product. While "feminist tobacco" contains obvious contradictions, today's transnational corporations employ a panoply of socially responsible wares ranging from fair-trade coffee to biodegradable yoga mats and organic frozen dinners (Johnston 2001). Because some such corporate strategies appear both well intentioned and well received, we move beyond cynical dismissal to empirically investigate and analyze corporate discourse to identify its transformative possibilities and contradictions. In this paper, we question whether transformative visions are exclusively linked with grassroots models for social change—models at the heart of feminist consciousness-raising.[1]

Our primary goal is to compare the discursive contributions of Dove's[2] "Campaign for Real Beauty"—a corporate project that claims to oppose restrictive feminine beauty standards and promote a more democratic vision of beauty—with those made by a grassroots, Toronto-based fat-activist organization that also targets feminine beauty ideals, Pretty, Porky, and Pissed Off (PPPO). We use a comparative approach to evaluate how each case challenges feminine beauty ideology, while taking into consideration the scale of its activism. Our analysis of the PPPO case relies on interviews with PPPO members, archival documentation of their events provided by activists, and media profiles and reviews of their shows. The Dove case draws primarily on their corporate website, multi-media advertisements, trade magazines and journals, and participant observation at Dove Real Beauty events. We also collected and analyzed mainstream news coverage. This research enabled us to understand and compare these parallel but very different campaigns, paying particular attention to questions of scale and their different cultural contexts, ideologies, tactics, intended audiences, and goals.

At the same political moment scholars bemoaned the constant assertion that feminism is dead (Hawkesworth 2004; Staggenborg and Taylor 2005), Dove launched its "Campaign for Real Beauty" in 2004 using feminist critiques and concerns about beauty ideals to re-vitalize the Dove brand. Billboard, television, and magazine ads depicted women who were wrinkled, freckled, pregnant, had stretch marks, or might be seen as fat (at least compared with the average media representation of women).[3] The campaign has generated commercial success (e.g., sales of firming lotion, the campaign's flagship product, far exceeded forecasts), media sensation (e.g., *People* 2005), and endorsements from celebrities (e.g., Oprah Winfrey), gender scholars (e.g., Susie Orbach), and professional associations (e.g., American Women in Radio and Television). The campaign, which started in the UK and quickly spread to North America, is now a major feature of Dove's global marketing.

While Dove uses a multi-million dollar, multi-media marketing campaign, PPPO employed radically different tactics to challenge hegemonic beauty standards. Frustrated with ill-fitting clothing options for plus-size women, a group of artists and activists from women's studies and queer activist communities formed PPPO in 1996. Their first event was a street protest in a trendy shopping district where members handed out candy and questioned passersby about their attitudes toward fat. PPPO went on to become one of Toronto's most popular queer cabaret acts, using song and dance to challenge misogynist attitudes about fat women and sexuality.

PPPO's grassroots activism and Dove's corporate campaign seem countervailing forces pulling beauty ideology in opposite directions—particularly since the beauty industry is thought to articulate and reproduce gendered beauty norms (Black 2004; Jeffreys 2005). The tendency is to summarily dismiss Dove's efforts to broaden beauty ideals, yet as feminist scholars, our hope is to better *understand* the nuances, possibilities, and contradictions of Dove's seemingly transformative aspirations, particularly when juxtaposed with the beauty critiques of grassroots activists. The Real Beauty Campaign promotes itself as a progressive force for women, aligns itself with certain feminist ideals and academics, engages in "grassroots" partnering to raise millions of dollars for eating disorder organizations and Girl Scouts programs to build self-esteem, has engaged with prominent gender scholars, and [has] been widely praised in the popular media. To make sense of its impact, our comparison of the Dove campaign with grassroots feminist activism has three objectives (1) document Dove's campaign discourse as an example of corporate appropriation of social movement ideals, thereby contributing to the important, but sparse, critical scholarship on this topic (Frank 1997; Heath and Potter 2004; Messner 2002)[4] (2) examine the transformative potential of the corporate versus the grassroots; and (3) speak to theoretical debates, suggesting the need for closer integration between political economic analysis and feminist scholarship of beauty ideology, cultural politics and grassroots activisms.[5] Thus, our comparative project combines political-economic scholarship with feminist understandings of social change, shedding light on prospects for counter-hegemonic action against oppressive feminine beauty standards.

First we outline the theoretical questions at stake—what is the ideology of feminine beauty, and how is this relevant to feminist social activism? Second, we provide brief case profiles, and third, we analyze the relationship between the cases and our twin concerns of feminine beauty ideology and feminist social action. We conclude by arguing that the Dove campaign is a manifestation of *feminist consumerism*, a phenomena with the potential to partially disrupt gender norms, but without provoking a substantive feminist transformation of beauty ideology. We use the term feminist consumerism to emphasize its evolution alongside a broader culture-ideology of consumerism, understood as a way of life dedicated to the possession and use of consumer goods (Kellner 1983:74), and rooted in the capitalist necessity of selling an ever-expanding roster of commodities in a globalized economy (Gottdiener 2000:281; Sklair 2001).[6] PPPO provides a counter-hegemonic critique of beauty and its relationship to capitalist consumerism, but we caution against a reification and romanticization of the scale of grassroots social activism, and suggest that the limitations of both actors help explain the continued salience of beauty ideology in women's lives.

II. IDEOLOGICAL CONTEXT: FEMININE BEAUTY AND FEMINIST PRAXIS

Ideology is a useful tool for feminists interested in understanding how ideas enable and preclude possibilities for transformative change. Recent theorizing sees ideology as organized around a set of ideas, normative claims, and value-structures that have an emotional component influencing their usage and appeal (see Thompson 2001; Fegan 1996; Ferree and Merrill 2000). Ideology may [conceal] domination, but cannot be juxtaposed to a singular, scientific truth. . . . Ideological processes naturalize and legitimize "ideas in pursuit of dominant interests," which are not imposed top-down, but involve a negotiation between individual subjects and dominant constructions (Fegan 1996, 184). Fegan employs the example of motherhood to demonstrate how ideology is internalized by women in their intimate lives—providing meaning and personal satisfaction—while it concomitantly reproduces and legitimates gender inequality through its discursive operations in the legal system (1996, 183). For our case studies, ideology is essential to appreciating how subjects internalize and resist feminine beauty ideals in the larger context of corporate consumer culture, and allows a substantive comparison of counter-hegemonic potential.

Feminist scholarship and activism since the 1970s has critiqued oppressive beauty standards that repress women's freedom, inhibit personal power and self-acceptance, and promote a destructive relationship with the body (Dworkin 1974; Banner 1983; Chernin 1981; Bover 1989; Brownmiller 1984; Bartky 1990). Drawing on these critiques, Naomi Wolf published *The Beauty Myth* in 1991—a feminist analysis of beauty standards that became one of the best-selling feminist books of all time—which suggested that women's gains from the second wave of the feminist movement were stymied by the existence of a "beauty myth" that disabled women from achieving full equality with men. While Wolf's work was a timely piece of public scholarship, exposing countless women to the idea of a hegemonic beauty regimen, more recent feminist scholarship on beauty draws from post-structuralism's emphasis on agency to problematize the idea of singularly oppressive beauty standards, and focus on the meaning embedded in beauty rituals. Scholars have observed women's collusion with, and participation in, the social construction of beauty, suggesting that women's "body work," whether through exercise, make-up, or plastic surgery, can function as a meaningful source of embodiment and even empowerment (Gimlin 2002; Davis 1995; Frost 1999).

The cultural turn has similarly influenced feminist scholars to problematize the aesthetic ideals surrounding thin and fat bodies. "Corpulence studies," for instance, draws on queer theory to question whether beauty standards surrounding body weight are straightforwardly oppressive, and deconstruct dualisms of thin/successful versus fat/oppressed. Corpulence studies has developed significant insights into food, gender, sexuality, and the body, specifically in relationship to fat bodies reviled as asexual, out of control, or morally repugnant (Braziel 2001; LeBesco 2001; Hartley 2001). Significantly, this scholarship has identified agency in fat bodies previously assumed to be monolithically oppressed, depressed, and psychologically traumatized. Braziel and LeBesco (2001) and Marilyn Wann (1999) suggest that not every fat girl wants to be thin, and that fatness is experienced in a variety of ways betwixt stereotypes of the asexual obese woman and the fat femme (Brazil 2001; Mazer 2001). Corpulence studies identifies agency, "everyday" forms of resistance, and the varied ways gender is constructed in bodies that defy idealized feminine beauty.

Problematizing the existence of a singular, oppressive beauty standard has been a useful corrective to monochromatic understandings of gender inequality and oppression. However, the emphasis on feminine beauty and the body as a site of individual meaning and empowering "play" is prone to a naive voluntarism that minimizes domination and the "normalizing power of cultural images" (Jeffreys 2005, 5; Bordo 1993, 21, 275). The cultural turn's insistence on individual agency risks complicity with a neo-liberal emphasis on individual (read: consumer) choice, and diverts attention from the political economy of corporate domination. Even scholars who emphasize the agency present in beauty practices have produced evidence suggesting that internalized hatred of fat bodies persists despite willful individual resistance, and is documented within the fat-acceptance movement (Gimlin 2002, 136). The persistence of domination in the realm of beauty ideals raises serious questions for our two cases of beauty rebellion, as well as for the cultural turn in beauty analysis. Can resistance to beauty ideals rely on therapeutic, individually-focused strategies, or must they also target the institutions and material structures that support hegemonic beauty standards?[7] How can individual transgression and resistance be re-incorporated into corporate structures—say in a jar of "woman-affirming" firming cream?[8]

[An analysis] of ideology can clarify how hegemonic beauty standards dominate and oppress, while simultaneously recognizing the agency present in beauty practices. [Emphasizing] ideology, [we] can move away from a voluntaristic and idealistic approach that either: (1) suggests that women can readily eschew internalized beauty ideals and embrace their non-conforming bodies; or (2) sanctions gender conformity through fashion, make-up, and plastic surgery. . . . Appreciating ideology allows us to recognize the beauty industry as a space where women construct "a bodily being in which they feel comfortable," while still identifying the symbolic violence it perpetuates, particularly since the "default position" for most women is idealized feminine beauty (Black 2004, 182–3, 189). While recognizing [that] individual manipulation of beauty ideals is important, the corporate beauty industry perpetuates and institutionalizes gender inequality by placing an inordinate emphasis on the personal appearance of women, (re)producing largely unattainable aesthetic standards (Hartley 2001, 64), and perpetuating misogynist and harmful cultural practices (e.g., labiaplasty and breast augmentation) (Jeffreys 2005). . . .

Feminist politics has been a central site for connecting personal and political battles; yet today, the popular consensus is that the women's movement is dead and that counter-hegemonic feminist ideologies have lost their critical edge (Staggenborg and Taylor 2005; Hawkesworth 2004).[9] Indeed, Dove's public campaign for a woman's "right" to feel beautiful might suggest that feminist ideals have become socially mainstream, rather than socially marginalized. This begs the question of how to differentiate between the gender ideals used by Dove to promote women's self-esteem through brand-building, and those promoted by grassroots fat activists like PPPO. Not all gender ideals are equally feminist, by which we mean committed to women's equality and empowerment in the face of institutionalized gender inequality, nor do they equally challenge the naturalization of women's subordinate status as it intersects with inequalities of class, race, and ethnicity. To explore the counter-hegemonic challenge to beauty ideologies and their relationship to feminist activism, we turn to our case studies.

III. THE CASES: FAT ACTIVISTS AND A CORPORATE CAMPAIGN FOR "REAL BEAUTY"

Pretty, Porky, and Pissed Off (PPPO)

Pretty, Porky, and Pissed Off emerged the way many "primary movement groups" (Rosenthal and Schwartz 1989) do—based on friendship and characterized by informality. The idea arose from a conversation in 1996 between Allyson Mitchell and Ruby Rowan, both artists

and women's studies students. While attending a conference on subcultures, they lamented the absence of attention to lesbian feminists active in the queer arts scene—women writing, playing in bands, making films and art that expressed feminist politics in varied and nuanced ways. The conversation turned to mundane matters—not being able to find cool pants that fit. Mitchell recalled of this conversation, "It was so familiar and so yuck, and so a known story for fat girls. Ruby was really pivotal in saying 'let's do something about it instead of bitching about it. We should start a fat girl group.'"

Mitchell, Rowan, and many of their friends who had already explored body issues in their artistic work, hoped the idea of a more formal group would resonate. However, friends needed to be "out" as fat, comfortable enough to perform the role of fat activist, able to confront strangers' phobias, and to endure curious or contemptuous stares. They planned an action for the following weekend in a trendy shopping district. Mitchell, Rowan, and ten friends dressed in campy polyester dresses and feather boas, danced to electronic music and passed out "fat facts," such as the average size of North American women. . . . As shoppers passed by, the activists gave them stickers or flyers, and asked, "Do you think I'm fat?"

PPPO participants found the event successful on multiple levels: they reached a large number of people, and the event received significant media attention. Besides feeling they had effectively communicated with the public, they gained an understanding of who they were and what they could do for and with one another. Characterizing participants as "a dyke network" of artists, performers, feminists, friends, and exes, Mitchell says the event solidified their identities as fat activists: "It was consciousness-raising among ourselves for us all to be there. It was borrowing from that feminist power in numbers, feeding off each other's affirmations and then trying to bleed that out to the crowd."

The group continued general interventions, like putting stickers and fliers in public spaces, but subsequent activism focused on performance pieces within the queer arts community. PPPO officially came together as a troupe of three (gradually expanding to eight) at a benefit show for "Pussy Palace," a women's bathhouse in Toronto facing legal challenges after a police raid. While two troupe members sang a rewritten version of the Reggae song "Wide Load," the third passed out peanut butter and jelly sandwiches to onlookers.

PPPO's group performances evolved with their political consciousness and everyday lived experiences. Planning meetings were as much concerned with processing feelings and experiences of "fat phobia," as with choreography. Some pieces evolved organically out of these discussions and reflected the group's growing camaraderie. For example, one PPPO member was rendered speechless when told, "Move it, fatty," by a man getting off the streetcar. This experience was catalyst for a piece called "Move It Fatty" in which the girl-gang comes to the rescue, throwing the significance of female friendship into sharp relief. In addition to building solidarity and community, PPPO experimented with importing a feminist politic and a therapeutic affect into spaces where queer camp predominated, and introduced increasingly complex political analyses of fat and consumerism. In a show titled "Big Judy," each member introduced her performance by talking about the personal politics and experiences that led her to become a fat activist, while "Chubway" attempted to reckon with the political economy of fat by critiquing the food industry and its promotion of unhealthy diets. Thus, PPPO brought a complex feminist analysis into a queer arts space in which neither hegemonic beauty standards, nor corporate capitalism were previously much critiqued.

In addition to cabaret-style shows, PPPO members held fundraisers for local and extra-local fat activism causes, such as Nomy Lamm's "fat camp" for kids (focusing on positive body image rather than weight loss). These included clothing swaps in working class neighborhoods where women paid five dollars for a bag of clothing that fit them. For PPPO activists, this kind of work exemplified their politics: it wasn't simply that they wanted corporations to produce larger sizes; they also wanted to create opportunities to resist consumerism, while recognizing the gender and class implications of fat bodies.

PPPO activists primarily performed in countercultural arts spaces, but they also performed in more mainstream venues and traveled outside Toronto, with mixed results. Some women did not understand the camp genre and complained that the show lampooned fat women. Arts-oriented audiences critiqued the group for not memorizing their lines or having simplistic choreography, missing the fact that performance for PPPO was a vehicle for political and cultural expression. Wearing tennis shoes with bottle caps nailed to the bottom enabled "tap" dancing, and black body suits were used to critique, rather than compete within

an ultra-thin and competitive women's dance world. Another site of contention was the media. Eager to communicate a message of health *and* bodily acceptance to large-bodied women and girls, PPPO activists regularly granted interviews, although members found it challenging to be cast dichotomously with public health officials as the voices (purportedly) denying the health risks of obesity.

At a meeting in 2003 to discuss a show that would require travel, arts grants, and significant time and resources, the group realized they did not want to take their activism to this new level, and PPPO disbanded. Expanding PPPO's reach would have required members to give up other activist, artistic, and employment commitments. Members celebrated the decision, however, proud of their accomplishments and committed to carrying on their fat activism. PPPO hoped another group would pick up where it left off, and in 2005, one did—the Fat Femme Mafia, a fat activist performance group that performs and organizes fat events in the Toronto area, and explicitly draws inspiration from PPPO's trailblazing work.[10] Thus far, Fat Femme Mafia is not the community PPPO once was, having only two members, but its intention to work within the public schools suggests a less insular approach to social change than taken by its predecessors.

The Dove Campaign: Real Women, Real Beauty, Real Feminism?

Just as PPPO's grassroots activism was winding down, Dove, a subsidiary of Unilever, and the largest skin care brand in the world, launched the "Real Women" Campaign in Britain. The campaign hinged on selecting "real" women rather than models for TV and print advertisements featuring their new line of "firming" products. The women appeared to be in their 20s and 30s, were multi-racial, and posed together smiling widely and frolicking, while wearing white cotton bras and underwear. Conventionally attractive, they radiated happiness and friendship. The success of this effort led to a significantly more complex and multitiered, multi-national "Campaign for Real Beauty" launched in September 2004. The campaign was orchestrated by some of the most powerful advertising, research, and public relations firms in the world, including Ogilvy and Mather, Mindshare, Edelman, and Lexis, Katz Media, The Downing Street Group, and others, in conjunction with creative teams within Unilever and Dove. While some marketing gurus advised against a refutation of conventional beauty, others found the cultural critique a good way to garner media attention and revitalize a 50-year-old brand.

Dove's fluid, multi-pronged approach made use of diverse organizational fields, ranging from billboards, television, interactive websites, and tie-ins with the mass media (e.g., *The Oprah Winfrey Show*). Dove's networking extended beyond media and corporate entities to include university researchers and non-profit agencies, and it commissioned a large-scale, multi-national survey of women's conceptions and practices, hiring scholars like Nancy Etcoff, Susie Orbach, and Naomi Wolf to contribute to the "The Dove Report: Challenging Beauty" (Etcoff et al., 2004). The Dove Campaign also forged alliances, using what it termed "grassroots partnering"; the Dove Self Esteem Fund was formed "to educate and inspire girls on a wider definition of beauty" in partnership with the American Girl Scouts. By 2005, Dove claimed to have already reached over 138,000 . . . girls [age 8–14] with programs like "Uniquely ME!" and "Body Talk." The campaign also expanded into the arts with an international photography exhibit, "Beyond Compare," featuring the work of 60 women photographers from 22 countries. The exhibit featured images of obesity, aging, dwarfs, eating disorders, lesbians, female body-builders, and women of various races and nationalities. Dove asked photographers to donate pictures they made depicting real beauty as they saw it, and in exchange, Dove made a contribution to the National Eating Disorders Information Centre (NEDIC), a Toronto-based non-profit agency whose website now features a prominent Dove hotlink.

Initially, the Dove campaign focused on provocative, conversational billboards where the public was asked to adjudicate women's attractiveness (e.g., fat or fabulous?). This format provided a space to debate feminine beauty ideals, and was a win-win situation for Dove: it could promote its products as beauty solutions, and at the same time, express concern with narrow beauty ideals. Dove soon moved toward a more explicitly normative position. The Dove Real Beauty Campaign website launched with the following text floating over the Dove insignia:

> For too long, beauty has been defined by narrow, stifling stereotypes. You've told us it's time to change all that. We agree. Because we believe real beauty comes in many shapes, sizes, and ages. It is why we started the Campaign for Real Beauty. And why we hope you'll take part. (Dove 2005a)

Thus, while responding to "real" women with cellulite and wrinkles (rather than unattainable air-brushed features), Dove diagnoses the problem as one caused by unrealistic media and advertising images, communicating their intention to make women feel more beautiful. On the website, women can post their picture, donate to one of Dove's campaigns, read Dove-commissioned research on beauty, or participate in web conversations in multiple nations and languages.

The website seamlessly connects its politics to its products. A section titled "Let's Dare to Love Our Hair" is followed by a list of Dove shampoos, conditioners, and styling aids. A list of Dove antiperspirants and lotions is prefaced by "Let's Make Peace with our Bodies." This pairing is explicit, and corporate spokespersons speak plainly and consistently about their dual goals: to "make women feel more beautiful" and to sell more Dove beauty products (e.g., *People* 2005). On the latter score, Dove attributes the success of its new product lines such as the Dove Firming Range (exceeding expectations by 120%) to the Campaign for Real Beauty.

IV. ANALYTIC COMPARISON: BEAUTY IDEOLOGIES, FEMINIST CONSUMERISM, AND GRASSROOTS ACTIVISM

In this section, we examine how each case relates to feminine beauty, and evaluate contributions to feminist praxis. Specifically our focus on hegemonic ideologies of beauty and the counter-hegemonic potential of feminism is designed to investigate whether PPPO and Dove achieve the same goal of de-legitimizing beauty ideologies, and identify contradictions involved in the framing process.

I. Beauty Ideology: Dove Makes Peace, While PPPO Wages War

Both the Dove Real Beauty Campaign and PPPO claim to challenge hegemonic beauty codes that articulate a virtually unachievable conception of physical beauty. Even defenders of beauty norms as socially and biologically inevitable, like evolutionary psychologist Nancy Etcoff, acknowledge that the top models exemplifying contemporary Western beauty are "genetic freaks" (1999, 12).

Dove's own multinational beauty survey found that only 2% of women describe themselves as beautiful (Etcoff et at., 2004, 11). Dove commits itself to changing this statistic through its provocative billboard campaign, which partially disrupts the ideology of feminine beauty by publicly portraying women not conventionally seen as beautiful, and hence not normally depicted on billboards advertising beauty products. By doing so, the campaign raised the ire of some male viewers. *Chicago Sun-Times* columnist Richard Roeper criticized the campaign for depicting average women, and suggested that if he wanted to see "plump gals bearing too much skin," he would have simply gone to Taste of Chicago (*People* 2005). Yet *Slate* advertising columnist Seth Stevenson said that the Dove models on giant billboards challenged his gendered beauty ideals in a positive way:

> When I first saw one of these smiley, husky gals on the side of a building, my brain hiccupped. . . . Here I was, staring at a "big-boned" woman in her underwear, but this wasn't an Adam Sandler movie, and I wasn't supposed to laugh at her. It felt almost revolutionary. (Stevenson 2005)

While the Dove campaign challenges one key element of beauty ideology (narrow beauty ideals), theorists remind us that ideology is a complex creature. Women are not simply "tricked" into seeking beauty. Beauty ideals . . . are internalized, rationalized, and socially legitimized. . . . The ideology of beauty suggests that every woman can, and should, feel beautiful, presenting beauty as a democratic gender "good," akin to life, liberty, and the pursuit of happiness. At the same time, beauty codes make clear that most women do not measure up aesthetically. Women are penalized for not being beautiful, and at the same time, are stigmatized, even pathologized, for not *feeling* beautiful, for having low self-esteem or behaviors like dieting, excessive exercising, or eating disorders.

The Dove campaign, while it contests narrow beauty codes, works within a hegemonic ideology of gendered beauty by refusing to challenge the idea that beauty is an essential part of a woman's identity, personhood, and social success, and legitimizing the notion that every woman should feel beautiful. For example, a television advertisement promoting Dove's "self-esteem" fund for young girls, features young girls along with their physical anxieties (e.g., they hate their freckles, feel fat, and want to be blonde); a voice-over then issues the following commands projected over their faces: "Let's tell her she's wrong. Let's tell her to be real. And brave. And true. And she'll be

beautiful. Beautiful. Beautiful. [Enter Dove logo] Let's make peace with beauty" (Dove 2005b). At the end of the commercial, and within the Dove campaign more generally, the social imperative for women to be and feel beautiful is not up for negotiation. Even though the social understanding of beauty is contested, the importance of beauty as a paramount value for women is reproduced and legitimized by the campaign's explicit and unceasing focus on beauty. Women's acceptance of their bodies as "beautiful" is demanded, rather than recognized as an inherently complex, fraught, and contradictory endeavor (particularly in the context of the mass media, beauty industry, weight-loss industry, and industrial food complex) or related to what women accomplish apart from looking pretty.[11] . . .

The Dove campaign recognizes that the pursuit of beauty is an important, internalized norm that cannot be easily abandoned or even de-prioritized, even though women may also actively critique its operation—an insight made clear from research emphasizing women's active involvement in beauty ideals and body work (Black 2004; Cahill 2003; Gimlin 2002). As an ideology, beauty is a complex process [related to] women's sense of self and the gender socialization process; many women are simultaneously critical of beauty ideals, the beauty industry, and their own physical attributes. The Dove campaign acknowledges the ways most women don't possess conventional beauty, and allows them to participate in a critique of narrow beauty norms, while encouraging women to "make peace with beauty" by channeling negative energy into self-acceptance, self-worth, and self-care via Dove products. In this sense, Dove's attempt to "democratize" beauty is deeply disingenuous. . . . Furthermore, the democratic ethos underlying the campaign (e.g., voting on whether a woman is fat or fabulous) suggests that challenging unhealthy, Eurocentric beauty norms is optional, a consumer *choice*—not an urgent necessity for social change in a world where beauty ideals and social respect are linked to inequalities based on sex, race, class, and body size.

Furthermore, while presenting non-standardized images of beauty, myriad cues of hegemonic beauty ideals are maintained in the Dove Campaign material. In one advertisement, hundreds of women converge at a city center in identical blonde wigs. They simultaneously tear off their wigs, thereby symbolically repudiating notions of attractive hair and embracing their locks. Reminiscent of Eve Ensler's *Vagina Monologues*, the accompanying web video features women talking about learning to love their hair. Three women are featured: one is blonde, white, attractive, with a slightly protruding stomach; the second is "super-model" beautiful, extremely thin, white, with lustrous long brown hair; and the third is an attractive, slight, light-skinned "ethnic" woman with blonde-frosted curly hair. These gendered beauty depictions are significant, since although the advertisement pans over non-conventionally beautiful women, the three women featured are young, attractive, relatively fair, and promote beautiful hair as an important personal attribute. This allows the campaign to associate youth, slenderness, and conventional beauty with the Dove brand, while opening the door to a handful of deviations (like the slightly protruding stomach) that construct brand loyalty. This is part of a gender-specific marketing strategy that cultivates brand loyalty using models and imagery that women can identify with, while conveying an appearance of corporate philanthropy (Corbett 2006). . . . Thus, Dove channels women's dissent to re-build its brand, while deflecting attention away from the conventional depictions of feminine beauty relied upon in Dove marketing.

One of the more insidious aspects of Dove's appropriation of feminist themes of empowerment and self-care is its reformulation of feminism as achieved principally through grooming and shopping. This association is ironic because many women have shied away from feminism precisely because they do not want to "burn their bras," or discontinue shaving and wearing make-up and deodorant. The radical feminism that might require them to be critical of gendered grooming and beauty ideology is absent in feminist consumerism, which is achieved precisely through purchasing and using beauty products. This reformulation enables women to wear an identity associated with self-respect, independence, personal strength, and collective identity and community, without doing any of the hard consciousness-raising work usually required to produce collective (rather than simply individual) transformation.[12]

Like the DOVE campaign, the PPPO critique did not reject the idea of physical feminine beauty. Yet a closer examination of its approach to "beauty" reveals important differences between the two campaigns, namely the PPPO's more complex and ambivalent relationship to the idealization of women's physical beauty, an interest in exploring the pain caused by beauty ideals, and a refusal to prioritize looking or

feeling beautiful as cornerstones of gendered identity. Rather than take on the lofty concept of "beauty," the activists in PPPO appropriate a more accessible moniker, "pretty," and immediately and alliteratively knock the gender ideal of "pretty" off its social pedestal by linking it to "porky" and "pissed off." In so doing, PPPO members embrace their non-conforming fat bodies and wage war with hegemonic beauty standards—actions far removed from Dove's reformist peace-making.

Unlike Dove's demand that women feel beautiful and love their "curves," PPPO activists did not straight-forwardly celebrate fat as fabulous.[13] Instead, PPPO activism involved open discussion of the terrors, contradictions, and pain involved with living in a fat body. One PPPO activist, speaking on a local radio program, commented, "I am a fat activist with an eating disorder." PPPO performances presented large bodies as sexually attractive and confident, but fat was not uncritically or automatically linked to beauty. Instead, the whole apparatus of judging women based on their physical appearance, and the kinds of gendered obsessions this creates, were themselves challenged through PPPO's activist performances. In "Fat Judy," for instance, PPPO activists explored how obsession with their non-conforming bodies caused physical discomfort, emotional suffering, and enduring pain.

. . . Like Dove, PPPO targeted women's feelings of inadequacy in relation to beauty, but unlike Dove's equation of *feeling* beautiful with *being* beautiful, PPPO recognized that not everyone would perceive their dancing, performing, non-conforming bodies as attractive. While the Dove campaign implicitly relied on images of attractive women, PPPO activist performances explicitly constructed dissonant images of beauty (e.g., dressing in body-hugging black leotards and dancing with iced cakes). These images engaged the obesophobia (e.g., the performance "Move It Fatty") underlying harmful body practices (Bordo 1993, 141). PPPO's radical disruption of hegemonic beauty ideology was at least partially derived from the de-stabilization of the heteronormative gaze. Strongly linked to a lesbian-arts community, PPPO activists did not prioritize the approval of men socially or performatively, and this may have allowed a more radical rejection of beauty as feminine aspiration. Whether a radical rejection of beauty ideology and the male gaze is a likely strategy for a corporate campaign is an important question for feminist praxis, and one to which we now turn.

2. Feminist Praxis: Consciousness, Community, and Consumerism

. . . Both the Dove Campaign and PPPO are crucial sites of contestation that may not be recognized as such. . . . Taylor's (1996, 175–177) study of post-partum depression self-help groups implicitly maps criteria—converting shame and fear into anger and pride, asserting the legitimacy of "deviant" behavior, embracing diversity as healthy and normal, and trying to change not just women's, but men's practices—for thinking about what can be considered feminist and transformational. These criteria help identify critical differences between Dove's and PPPO's contributions to feminist praxis—differences centering on the contrast between feminist consumerism and feminist community building and consciousness-raising.

The goal of facilitating women's emotional transformation and creating therapeutic spaces for women to process their feelings about hegemonic beauty standards is central to both campaigns; however, the "emotion cultures" and "emotion work" of each are constitutively distinct. In its performances and discourse, PPPO modeled therapeutic consciousness-raising. Members narrated painful stories, while song and dance segments were built around accessible stories of rejection, social exclusion, self-loathing, and reclaiming painful epithets (e.g., fatty, porky), with actors modeling an emotional trajectory of pain and isolation giving way to anger, and ending in a bold assertion of self-worth, or a collective assertion of burlesque sensuality.

Conversely, in the Dove Campaign, both pain and anger are avoided, suggesting a more limited model of consciousness raising, a greater focus on building positive associations that can be converted to brand loyalty, and an explicit connection between self-love and self-care through commodity consumption. Women featured on the Dove website and advertisements convey that they have been unhappy with different aspects of their bodies and appearances, but viewers are spared hearing about the details, and can instead click on Dove's "real" models to learn about their "favorite curves." Raised consciousness in the Dove campaign is presented as a happy awakening by casting off limited notions of attractiveness, and working with what one has to accentuate inner and outer beauty. For Dove, social acceptance and beauty should not be uncoupled. Rather, beauty should be reconceived and made accessible—a process that occurs through self-care via Dove beauty products. Because the central

importance of feminine beauty is not questioned by the Dove campaign, its architects need not include anger as an emotional stage. Anger would only be required if women were rejecting, rather than coming to terms with this basic social tenet. Dove's emotional register erases shame, fear, and anger, making personal pride and social change appear as painless, simple achievements—as simple as shopping itself.

Related to this, Dove and PPPO have very different ideas on deviance and challenging gendered beauty norms. On a basic level, PPPO does not prescribe changes in women's appearance, instead advocating female solidarity to alleviate the psychological toll of non-conformity. In stark contrast, Dove uses a smattering of deviant images to suggest a feeling of solidarity with "real" women, followed with product promotion framed as a way to express self-care. While both Dove and PPPO ask women to embrace their non-conforming bodies, Dove advocates feminist consumerism as a primary form of social critique. Most significantly, this critique obscures the contradictory desires underlying the Dove campaign: to condemn beauty standards, while promoting conformity to these same standards (e.g., by promoting firming and anti-aging creams). While Dove legitimizes conformity, PPPO asserts the "coolness" of feminine deviance in their performances, such as their mock West Side Story featuring a protagonist rejected from the gang for not being fat enough.[14] Perhaps because PPPO emerges from a queer, feminist friendship and activist network, deviance is already a central mode of operation and criterion for membership. Conversely, the Dove campaign enables more people to feel successful in achieving (heterosexual) mainstream social acceptance. Even the "uniform" of the two groups conveys this different approach to deviance: While the Dove campaign dresses models in white cotton bras and underwear, signifying cleanliness and purity, PPPO activists wore fat drag, donning black leotards and feather boas.

Dove's and PPPO's approach to diversity and inequality reflect the differing goals of feminist consumerism versus grassroots community building. Consumer culture allows for, and encourages, individual difference but does not emphasize structural [inequalities] or collective strategies for social change. In Dove's approach, multicultural diversity is embraced through visual images of women of different races, but the structural inequalities facing citizens (e.g., injustice, racism, inequality) and the disparate, racialized effects of beauty standards are not openly discussed. Interracial harmony is performed, but never part of the written text, or to state it another way, is seen but not heard. The Dove website similarly represents the problem of hegemonic beauty standards as global, and universally experienced. Dove's message, "Women of the World—Unite!" reflects a simplistic understanding of how women across different national contexts may share a common interest in beauty, while underplaying the significant barriers dividing women along lines of class, citizenship, race, ethnicity, religion, and language. In this way, feminist consumerism is a politically problematic strategy that resists labeling structural inequality, classism, or institutionalized racism and presents "an undifferentiated pastiche of differences, a grab bag in which no items are assigned any more importance or centrality than others" (Bordo 1993, 258).

In contrast to Dove's consumerist recognition of diversity without inequality, PPPO employed what it conceived of as a 3rd Wave feminist approach to fat activism and community building that explicitly recognized multiple axes of inequality. As a group, PPPO spent considerable time discussing intersectionality and providing community opportunities to impact social inequality, but were less concerned with *representing* racial difference through their performances. While PPPO was somewhat ethnically diverse, the group's commitment to anti-racism did not make its way into its activism. Class featured more prominently, in actions such as fundraisers for low-income kids to attend fat-positive camps and clothing swaps in low-income neighborhoods. . . .

In sum, while each case displayed a concern with feminine beauty ideology, they represented very different approaches to feminist praxis—a difference we would characterize as a disjuncture between feminist consumerism, and a grass-roots feminist focus on community building and consciousness raising. Feminist consumerism is . . . a corporate strategy that employs feminist themes of empowerment to market products to women, and shares consumerism's focus on individual consumption as a primary source of identity, affirmation, and social change. As with consumerism more generally (Sklair 2001, 5), feminist consumerism prioritizes commodity purchases above more ambitious goals such as de-centering the role of beauty in women's lives, processing negative emotions, or challenging men's relationship with feminine beauty. As such, feminist consumerism tends to obscure and minimize both structural and institutionalized gender inequalities that are difficult to resolve, and which

might cause negative emotional associations with brands. Thus, from a marketing perspective, feminist consumerism makes business sense, operating as it does within a larger pattern of consumer culture that markets dissent to build brand loyalty and increase sales.[15]

The extensive scale of Dove's corporate campaign cannot be denied, yet we question whether corporate channels enable counter-hegemonic critique, particularly given the campaign's complicity with beauty ideology outlined above. In contrast, PPPO's ability to incorporate negative emotions and build spaces for "deviant" behavior allowed it to construct a counter-hegemonic feminist project of community-building and consciousness-raising. PPPO's grassroots activism included a radical intersectional critique focused on women's personal relationships with food and fat, but also critiqued corporate capitalism and its role in promoting unhealthy eating habits and destructive body image. Although the scale on which these activities occurred was clearly limited when compared to Dove's multinational campaign, the group provided more room to process the negative emotions generated by gender inequality and beauty ideology, and raised awareness and solidarity among fat activists at the local scale.

V. CONCLUSION

Our objective has been to assess how the Dove Campaign for Real Beauty and the grassroots group Pretty, Porky, and Pissed Off (PPPO) did and did not challenge beauty ideology, and how this circumscribes or enables possibilities for feminist transformation. We conclude that the Dove Campaign for Real Beauty provides a critique that partially disrupts the narrowness of Western contemporary beauty codes, but systematically reproduces and legitimizes the hegemony of beauty ideology in women's personal lives in the service of expanding sales and corporate growth. Dove's approach, which we term feminist consumerism, encourages women to channel dissent and practice self-care by engaging with corporate marketing campaigns and purchasing beauty products. Though broadly accessible, Dove's critique of beauty ideology is diluted by its contradictory imperative to promote self-acceptance, while at the same time increasing sales by promoting women's consumption of products that encourage conformity to feminine beauty ideology. The Dove Campaign does not de-centre the role of beauty in women's lives, and suggests that beauty and self-acceptance can be accessed through the purchase of Dove beauty products. Dove's profit imperative helps explain the campaign's reproduction of hegemonic beauty ideologies, and its place within a larger hegemonic culture-ideology of consumerism. A more radical critique might negatively affect sales by alienating women who are emotionally invested in beauty ideology, and/or promote a kind of self-acceptance not contingent on beautification and commodification. Because the Dove campaign was framed in a market context that prioritizes profits and corporate growth, the critique of hegemonic beauty standards could not incorporate a critique of consumerism as an avenue to self-acceptance, or meaningfully address the class and racial inequalities linked with beauty ideals in late capitalist societies.

In the case of grassroots anti-fat activists, PPPO, we identified a more substantive counter-hegemonic attack on beauty standards that mocked these norms, and offered a radical, intersectional critique identifying the role of political-economic variables underlying women's unhealthy relationship to food, beauty, and the body. While offering a therapeutic venue for processing pain caused by the failure to conform to ideological beauty codes, the PPPO case suggests that counter-cultural activism is not necessarily solipsistic navel gazing; performances challenged the capitalist ideology of consumerism, offered a critique of hegemonic standards that attacked market institutions like corporations, and occurred within the more democratic context of civil society organizing, public sphere interventions, and the local spaces of queer theatre. These are significant achievements, but what should not be forgotten is the limits of the local: these grassroots actors were unable to connect with the scores of women and girls reached through the Dove campaign. While narrow in its reach, the impact of PPPO's counter-hegemonic critique of the beauty industry appears deep in terms of community building and identity construction for the women involved. Corporate entities were not transformed in such a grassroots project, but a critical consciousness was fostered and developed. . . .

The limitations of both the corporate and grassroots actors help explain the continued salience of beauty ideology in contemporary women's lives. While corporations and grassroots feminists both challenge hegemonic notions of feminine beauty, the scale and market location of the Dove case provide it [with] considerably greater influence through the mass market. Feminist consumerism offers a shallow critique that perpetuates beauty ideology, while counter-hegemonic grassroots praxis remains severely limited in scale; meanwhile, beauty ideology works to reproduce and legitimate gender inequality that generates billions of dollars in profit for the diet, cosmetic, and plastic surgery industries. This conclusion has implications for feminist praxis, and method. First, our case comparison speaks to the pressing need for collective action able to raise critical consciousness about beauty ideology amongst women and girls over a long time frame; our cases suggests that such a critique will not emerge from a corporate-market context, and is required at a scale that transcends grassroots resistance projects. Methodologically, our cases suggest the importance of feminist analyses that do not simply track micro-instances of cultural resistance, transgression, or fat bodies in revolt (LeBesco 2001, 77), but that also analyze the contemporary centralization of cultural power in key political-economic actors such as transnational corporations—actors that retain a tremendous potential to shape, normalize, and constrain the mind/body relationship in late capitalist culture.

NOTES

1. National organizations and feminist campaigns define feminism in the national public consciousness; yet collective identities are arguably forged at the local level (Reger 2002). Movement scholars have long understood the centrality of grassroots organizing to feminist (and other) social change initiatives, even though "the political" is often narrowly defined as a national-level occurrence targeting the state (Bookman and Morgan 1988; Naples 1998).

2. Dove is a beauty products company owned by Dutch multinational Unilever.

3. The Dove models range from size 6 to 12. While larger than the average fashion model (size 4), they are still smaller than the average American woman, who is a size 14.

4. This objective also responds to Gordon's decade-old assertion that corporate discourse is an important, yet neglected element of cultural studies scholarship (1995).

5. In part, this echoes Fraser's call for closer attention to how feminist struggles involve elements of symbolic recognition and material redistribution (Fraser and Naples 2004, 1113).

6. Analyses of Nike's campaigns surrounding women and sport have inspired concepts similar to ours, and are useful in explaining how corporations appropriate feminist ideas in marketing campaigns. Such analyses use terms such as "corporate feminism" (Messner 2002) and "celebrity feminism" (Cole and Hribar 1995). We are indebted to anonymous reviewers at *Signs* for flagging these parallel

analyses. We use the term "feminist consumerism" to emphasize its origins in consumerism's focus on commodity purchase and acquisition as a primary means to assert an identity, achieve the common good, express ethical (feminist) principles, and seek personal pleasure and social approval. Feminist consumerism is an effective marketing tool because it is part of a hegemonic "commonsense"of consumerism that allows Dove to credibly present itself as a vanguard of a consumer movement facilitating women's agitation and channeling resistance into commodity purchases. This involves a degree of agency, but as Messner notes, it is a "reproductive agency," which channels "women's actions and bodies within the power relations of the current gender order" (2002: 87).

7. While LeBesco uses queer theory to deconstruct the discourse of fatness as revolting, her suggestion that fat bodies are necessarily *in revolt*, is troubling, voluntaristic, and obscures the link between discursive constructions and material institutions. Using Judith Butler as her reference point, LeBesco suggests that "we just might be able to talk our way out of anything, even seemingly entrenched fat oppression, because speaking builds subjects" (2001, 77).

8. These questions are posed to the progressive left and feminists by critics who question the assumption that countercultural actions and non-conformist "play" necessarily subvert capitalist intuitions and material structures (Heath and Potter 2005, 21; Frank 1997; Jeffreys 2005).

9. Pronouncements on the "death of feminism" are themselves ideological, naturalizing the "end" of an era of feminist activism, and suggesting that women's concerns have been addressed and are not worth fighting for (Hawkesworth 2004).

10. According to an interview with Fat Femme Mafia activist Liz Brockest, "My dream is to be half as fundamental to fat folks as PPPO was and still is" (Foad 2006, 25).

11. This is part of a long-standing marketing strategy that superficially acknowledges women's problematic and conflicted relationship with food (e.g., emphasizing themes of obsession, danger, and loss of control), while denying, or minimizing the darker realities of these relationships. Bordo's deconstruction of advertisements suggests that even ads that de-stabilize gender expectations can work to reify inequitable gender norms (1993, 105–110, 131–34).

12. Cogent analyses of Nike's advertisements in the mid-1990s indicate a strikingly similar and successful precedent for selling feminism to women who need only wear Nike clothing to be "empowered," thereby channeling dissent into individual consumption, rather than collective organizing around the concept of "women" (Cole and Hribar 1995; Messner 2002, 88).

13. Celebrating fat as fabulous is a theme of many fat acceptance organizations and activists (e.g., Wann 1995).

14. Fat deviance is cool, yet unhealthy eating encouraged by the contemporary industrial-food system is also acknowledged. PPPO performances demonstrated a complex attraction/repulsion to food (e.g., sitting on cakes and then eating the mashed remnants off of their own bodies).

15. Dove is not the only corporation to use the marketing strategy of feminist consumerism. Nike also uses this strategy in various girl-power campaigns; the most recent features disaggregated women's body parts that re-appropriates derogatory labels (e.g., "thunder thighs") to sell athletic wear featured on well-toned (but not anorexic) body parts.

REFERENCES

Banner, Lois. 1983. *American Beauty,* Chicago: University of Chicago Press.

Bartky, Sandra. 1990. *Femininity and Domination. Studies in the Phenomenology of Oppression.* New York: Routledge.

Black, Paula. 2004. *The Beauty Industry: Gender, Culture, Pleasure.* New York: Routledge.

Bookman, Ann and Sandra Morgen, eds. 1988. *Women and the Politics of Empowerment.* Philadelphia: Temple University Press.

Bordo, Susan. 1993. *Unbearable Weight: Feminism, Western Culture, and the Body.* Los Angeles: University of California Press.

Bover, Shelley. 1989. *The Forbidden Body: Why Being Fat Is Not a Sin.* Northampton: Pandora.

Braziel, Jana Evans. 2002. "Sex and Fat Chics: Deterritorializing the Fat Female Body." In *Bodies Out of Bounds,* eds. J. Braziel and K. LeBesco, 231–256. Berkeley: University of California Press.

Braziel, Jana Evans and Kathleen LeBesco, eds. 2001. *Bodies Out of Bounds: Fatness and Transgression.* Berkeley: University of California Press.

Brownmiller, Susan. 1984. *Femininity.* New York: Linden Press.

Cahill, Ann. 2003. "Feminist Pleasure and Feminine Beautification." *Hypatia* 18(4):42–64.

Carroll, William. 1992. "Introduction: Social Movements and Counter-Hegemony in a Canadian Context." In *Organizing Dissent. Contemporary Social Movements in Theory and Practice,* ed. W. Carroll, 1–21. Canada: Garamond Press.

Chernin, Kim. 1981. *The Obsession: Reflections on the Tyranny of Slenderness.* New York: Harper and Row.

Cole, C. L. and Amy Hribar. 1995. "Celebrity Feminism: Nike Style, Post-Fordism, Transcendence and Consumer Power." *Sociology of Sport Journal* 12:347–369.

Corbett, Rachel. 2006. "Dove's Larger Models Spur Sales and Attention." *Women's ENews,* January 29, 2006. Accessed online at http://womensenews.org/article.cfm/dyn/aid/2617/context/cover/

Davis, Kathy. 1995. *Reshaping the Female Body; The Dilemma of Cosmetic Surgery.* New York: Routledge.

Dove Real Beauty Campaign. 2005a. Campaign Website. "Why the Campaign for Real Beauty?" Accessed online

January 4, 2006, at http://www.campaignforrealbeauty.ca/supports.asp?id=1560&length=short&section=campaign

Dove Real Beauty Campaign. 2005b. Campaign Website. "The NEW Dove Self-Esteem Fund TV Ad." Accessed online at http://www.campaignforrealbeauty.ca/flat2.asp?url=flat2.asp&id=1607

Dworkin, Andrea. 1974. *Women Hating.* New York: E. P. Dutton.

Etcoff, Nancy. 1999. *Survival of the Prettiest.* New York: Random House.

Etcoff, Nancy, Susie Orbach, Jennifer Scott and Heidi D'Ogstino. 2004. "The Real Truth About Beauty: A Global Report." Global report commissioned by Dove, a Unilever Beauty Brand. Accessed online at http://www.campaignforrealbeauty.ca/uploadedFiles/dove_white_paper_final.pdf

Fegan, Eileen. 1996. "'Ideology' After 'Discourse': A Reconceptualization for Feminist Analyses of Law." *Journal of Law and Society* 23(2):173–197.

Ferree, Myra Marx and David Merrill. 2000. "Hot Movements, Cold Cognition: Thinking About Social Movements in Gendered Frames." *Contemporary Sociology* 29(3):454–462.

Foad, Lisa. 2006. "A Big Fat Revolution," *XTRA!* February 16, 2006, 25.

Frank, Thomas. 1997. *The Conquest of Cool: Business Culture, Counter-Culture, and the Rise of Hip Consumerism.* Chicago: University of Chicago Press.

Frost, Liz. 2001. *Young Women and the Body. A Feminist Sociology.* Basingstoke, Hampshire: Palgrave.

Gimlin, Debra. 2002. *Body Work: Beauty and Self-Image in American Culture.* Berkeley: University of California Press.

Gottdiener, M., ed. 2000. *New Forms of Consumption. Consumers, Culture, and Commodification.* New York: Rowman and Littlefield.

Hartley, Cecilia. 2001. "Letting Ourselves Go: Making Room for the Fat Body in Feminist Scholarship." In *Bodies Out of Bounds: Fatness and Transgression,* eds. J. E. Braziel and K. LeBesco, 60–73. Berkeley: University of California Press.

Hawkesworth, Mary. 2004 "The Semiotics of Premature Burial: Feminism in a Postfeminist Age." *SIGNS* 29:961–985.

Heath, Joseph and Andrew Potter. 2004. *The Rebel Sell. Why the Culture Can't Be Jammed.* Toronto: HarperCollins.

Jeffreys, Sheila. 2005. *Beauty and Misogyny. Harmful Cultural Practices in the West.* New York: Routledge.

Johnston, Josée. 2001. "Consuming Global Justice: Fair Trade Shopping and the Search for Alternative Development Strategies." In *Protest and Globalization,* ed. J. Goodman, 38–56. Australia: Pluto Press.

Kellner, Douglas. 1983. "Critical Theory, Commodities and Consumer Society." *Theory, Culture and Society* 1(3):64–84.

LeBesco, Kathleen. 2001. "Queering Fat Bodies/Politics." In *Bodies Out of Bounds: Fatness and Transgression,* eds. J. Braziel and K. LeBesco, 74–90. Berkeley: University of California Press.

Mazer, Sharon. 2001. "She's So Fat . . . ; Facing the Fat Lady at Coney Island's Sideshows by the Seashore." In *Bodies Out of Bounds,* eds. J. Braziel J. and K. LeBesco, 257–276. Berkeley: University of California Press.

McLellan, David. 1995. *Ideology,* 2d ed. Great Britain: Open University Press.

Messner, Michael. 2002. *Taking the Field: Women, Men, and Sport.* Minneapolis: University of Minnesota Press.

Mitchell, Allyson, Lisa Bryn Rundle and Lara Karaian. 2001. *Turbo Chicks Talking Young Feminisms.* Toronto: Sumach Press.

Napes, Nancy and Nancy Fraser. 2004. "To Interpret the World and to Change It: An Interview with Nancy Fraser." *Signs* 29(4):1103–1124.

Naples, Nancy A., ed. 1998. *Community Activism and Feminist Politics. Organizing Across Race, Class and Gender.* New York: Routledge.

People Magazine. 2005, August 15. "Fat or Flab?" Pp. 116–117.

Prior, Molly. "Dove Ad Campaign Aims to Redefine Beauty." *The HBA Report. Women's Wear, Daily—The Retailer's Daily Newspaper.* October 8, 2004. Accessed online at www.wwd.com

Reger, Jo. 2002. Organizational Dynamics and Construction of Multiple Feminist Identities in the National Organization for Women. *Gender & Society* 16:710–727.

Rosenthal, Naomi and Michael Schwartz. 1989. Spontaneity and Democracy in Social Movements. *International Social Movement Research* 2:33–59.

Roth, Benita. 2004. *Separate Roads to Feminism: Black, Chicana, and White Feminist Movements in America's Second Wave.* Cambridge: Cambridge University Press.

Sklair, Leslie. 2001. *The Transnational Capitalist Class.* Malden: Blackwell Publishers.

Staggenborg, Suzanne and Verta Taylor. 2005. "Whatever Happened to the Women's Movement?" *Mobilization* 10:37–52.

Stevenson, Seth. 2005. "When Tush Comes to Dove. Real Women. Real Curves. Really Smart Ad Campaign." *Slate.* Posted August 1, 2005. Accessed online at http://www.slate.com/id/2123659/

Taylor, Verta. 1996. *Rock-a-by Baby: Feminism, Self-Help, and Post-Partum Depression.* New York: Routledge.

Thomson, Denise. 2001. *Radical Feminism Today.* London: Sage.

Wann, Marilyn. *Fat! So? Because You Don't Have to Apologize for Your Size!* Berkeley: Ten Speed Press.

Wolf, Naomi. 1991. *The Beauty Myth.* Toronto: Random House.

Cosmetic Surgery: Paying for Your Beauty

After several unsuccessful attempts to schedule an appointment, I finally managed to meet with Jennifer, a twenty-nine-year-old grade school teacher who volunteered to talk with me about her cosmetic surgery. On a typically cold November afternoon, I spoke with Jennifer in her apartment on the south shore of Long Island. Jennifer is 5 feet 6 inches tall and has long, straight blonde hair and expressive light blue eyes. That day she was dressed in an oversized gray pullover and black sweatpants. While we talked, she peeled and sliced the crudites that would be her contribution to the potluck engagement party that she was attending later that evening.

During our conversation, I noticed that by far the most prominent feature in her small studio apartment was the enormous black and chrome stair-climbing machine set slightly off from the center of the living room/bedroom. I learned that Jennifer spends forty minutes each day on this machine and works out with weights at a nearby gym three to four times a week. She eats no meat, very little oil or fat, and no sweets, and she drinks very little alcohol. Despite her rigorous body work routine, Jennifer's legs have remained a disappointment to her. Rather than lean and muscular, they look, by her account, thick and shapeless—particularly around her lower thighs and knees. Jennifer says that her decision to have liposuction was motivated primarily by her inability to reshape her legs through diet and exercise. During the procedure, the fatty deposits were removed from the insides of Jennifer's knees, making her legs appear slimmer and more toned.

Jennifer acknowledged her own significant ambivalence about taking surgical steps to alter her body. If possible, she would have preferred to shape her legs through aerobics, weight training, and dieting, rather than through liposuction, which Jennifer described as a final and desperate option. By her account, plastic surgery was the only way to alter physical attributes that she referred to as "genetic flaws," features that she could change through no other available means. Expressing some shame, as she says, "for taking the easy way out," Jennifer's guilt is not so great that she regrets having surgery. Indeed, she plans to have a second liposuction in the near future, this time to remove the fatty tissue from her upper and inner thighs.

Cosmetic surgery stands, for many theorists and social critics, as the ultimate invasion of the human body for the sake of physical beauty. It epitomizes the astounding lengths to which contemporary women will go to obtain bodies that meet current ideals of attractiveness. As such, plastic surgery is perceived by many to be qualitatively different from aerobics, hair styling, or even dieting. In this view, cosmetic surgery is not about controlling one's own body but is instead an activity so extreme, so invasive that it can only be interpreted as subjugation. Even more than women who may participate in other types of body-shaping activities, those who undergo cosmetic surgery appear to many observers—both casual and academic—to be so obsessed with physical appearance that they are willing to risk their very existence to become more attractive.

Not surprisingly, cosmetic surgery has been attacked by the scores of feminist writers who criticize body work generally.[1] While these attacks may be well deserved, the cosmetic surgery industry is expanding rapidly nevertheless. Board-certified plastic surgeons performed more than 2.2 million procedures in 1999, a 44 percent increase since 1996 and striking 153 percent increase since 1992. Liposuction, the most common cosmetic procedure in the United States, was performed 230,865 times (up 57 percent since 1996 and 264 percent since 1992), at a cost of approximately $2,000 per patient. Breast augmentation, with its price tag of nearly $3,000, was the second most common procedure, at 167,318 (a 51 percent increase since 1996). Blepharoplasty (eyelid surgery), the third most common, was performed on 142,033 patients at a cost of just under $3,000, followed by face-lift (72,793) at over $5,000, and chemical peel (51,519), at nearly $1,300.[2] Ninety percent of these operations are performed on women, as are virtually all breast augmentations and reductions, 87 percent of liposuctions, 91 percent of face-lifts, and 85 percent of blepharoplastics. In 1999, American women had 167,318 breast augmentations, 120,160 blepharoplasties, 201,083 liposuction procedures, and 66,096 face-lifts.[3]

Although strategies for surgically altering the body's appearance have been available for centuries, the practice has only recently become a mass phenomenon. Until recently, patients were most often men disabled by war or industrial accidents. Now the recipients are overwhelmingly women who are dissatisfied with their looks.[4] Today, aesthetic operations make up 45 percent of all plastic surgery.[5]

Cosmetic surgery is one of the fastest-growing specialities in American medicine.[6] Although the total number of physicians in the United States has little more than doubled in the last quarter of a century, the number of plastic surgeons has increased fourfold. At the end of World War II, there were only about 100 plastic surgeons in the country; in 1965, there were 1,133. By 1990, that number had tripled to 3,850. Moreover, these figures may underrepresent the total number of individuals performing aesthetic procedures today. Because it is not necessary to be a licensed plastic surgeon to perform cosmetic surgery, procedures such as face-lifts, eyelid corrections, and chemical peels may be performed by other specialists, such as dermatologists.[7]

Criticisms of surgical alternation of the female body multiply nearly as rapidly as the procedures themselves. One of the main critiques of cosmetic surgery derives from the dangers involved. Cosmetic surgery is undeniably painful and risky, and each operation involves specific potential complications. For instance, pain, numbness, bruising, discoloration, and depigmentation frequently follow a liposuction, often lingering up to six months after the operation. Face-lifts can damage nerves, leaving the patient's face permanently numb. More serious complications include fat embolisms, blood clots, fluid depletion, and even death. Health experts estimate that the chance of serious side effects from breast augmentation are between 30 percent and 50 percent. The least dramatic and most common of these include decreased sensitivity in the nipples, painful swelling or congestion of the breasts, and hardening of the breasts that makes it difficult to lie down comfortably or to raise the arms without shifting the implants.[8] More serious is the problem of encapsulation, in which the body reacts to foreign materials by forming a capsule of fibrous tissue around the implants. This covering can sometimes be broken down manually by the surgeon, but, even when successful, the procedure is extremely painful. When it is unsuccessful, the implants must be removed; in some cases, the surgeon must chisel the hardened substance from the patient's chest wall.

Clearly, the recipient of cosmetic surgery may emerge from the operation in worse shape than when she went in. Unsuccessful breast augmentations are often disfiguring, leaving the patient with unsightly scars and deformation. An overly tight face-lift produces a "zombie" look, in which the countenance seems devoid of expression. Following liposuction, the skin can develop a corrugated, uneven texture.

Finally, some criticisms of plastic surgery focus on the implications of such procedures for contemporary conceptualizations of the body and identity. Cosmetic surgery has expanded alongside specific technological developments, including advances in medical equipment like magnifying lenses, air drills for severing bone and leveling skin, and improved suturing materials, all of which enable surgical interventions to be performed with better results and less trauma for the patient.[9] According to some critics, these developments, and the increasing flexibility in body altering that they permit, are linked to cultural discourses likening the body to what Susan Bordo has called "cultural plastic." The body is now understood as having a potential for limitless change, "undetermined by history, social location or even individual biography."[10] Not only has the body come to stand as a primary symbol of identity, but it is a symbol with an unlimited capacity for alteration and modification. The body is not a dysfunctional object requiring medical intervention but a commodity, not unlike "a car, a refrigerator, a house, which can be continuously upgraded and modified in accordance with new interests and greater resources."[11] The body is a symbol of selfhood, but its relation to its inhabitant is shaped primarily by the individual's capacity for material consumption.

Of the various forms of body work, plastic surgery is surely the hardest to justify. The physical dangers are real. The symbolic damage done to all women by the apparent surrender of some to unattainable ideals of beauty is significant. Yet the criticisms also leave out a good deal. Most important, the criticisms operate either at the grand level of cultural discourse or the highly grounded level of physiological effect. As a result, they overlook the experience of the women who have plastic surgery. In this [reading], after first discussing the role of the doctor as a gatekeeper to plastic surgery, I focus on that experience.

First—and most important to those who undergo it—plastic surgery often works. This fact stands in contrast to a rhetoric that concentrates on the unattainable character of contemporary beauty ideals, portraying plastic surgery as a Sisyphean task. Critics of plastic surgery imply that those who undergo it will complete one operation only to discover some new flaw. Yet this is not the case. Somewhat to my surprise, many of the women I interviewed expressed enormous satisfaction with their procedures. While some did, indeed, intend to return for additional operations, others seemed content to have fixed a particular "flaw." I do not mean to argue that all contemporary ideals of beauty are, in fact, attainable. They are not. Neither do I mean to argue that women in contemporary America can escape the nagging self-doubts caused by those unattainable ideals. They cannot. But the ambitions of those women who undergo plastic surgery often stop far short of attaining ideal beauty. And given these limited ambitions—and within the cultural space marked out for the expression of female beauty—plastic surgery frequently achieves the exact goals intended by those who undergo it.

Second, criticisms of plastic surgery directed at gender issues often understate the extent to which this activity involves gender at an intersection with age, race, ethnicity, and even class. Many women surely undertake plastic surgery, most notably in the case of breast enlargement, to enhance distinctively female attributes. Others, however—Jewish and Italian women who have rhinoplasty, Chinese and Japanese women who have their eyes reshaped—do so in a distinctively ethnic context. And many others have plastic surgery in an attempt to reproduce the bodies of their youth. If plastic surgery speaks to the depredations of gender domination, we should recognize that it also speaks to the depredations of Anglo-Saxon ideals of beauty and the idealization of youth.

Third, the criticisms of plastic surgery ignore the complicated process by which the women who undergo surgical procedures integrate them into their identities. If not in feminist theory, then in popular culture, there lies an implicit notion that the benefits of plastic surgery are somehow inauthentic and, therefore, undeserved. Although the critics of plastic surgery insist that appearance should not be the measure of a woman's worth, the women who have plastic surgery are nonetheless participants in a culture in which appearance is taken as an expression of an inner state. To be able to purchase a new nose or wider eyes or thinner thighs seems, then, to sever the relationship between inner states and their outer expression. Where the women in aerobics classes are working hard to detach their identities from their bodies, the women who undergo plastic surgery must work even harder to reattach their identities to their new appearances. On the one hand, they are using plastic surgery to tell a story about themselves: I am the woman with svelte thighs or a button nose. On the other hand, they must also tell a story about plastic surgery in order to counter the charges of its inauthenticity. They must somehow show, to themselves even more than to others, that the new appearance is both deserved and a better indicator of the self than the old appearance—an appearance necessarily repositioned as "accidental." The result, then, is that the woman who has plastic surgery finds herself in a double bind. She is unhappy with her appearance, and so she takes the only steps she can to improve it. No matter how successful her efforts are—or how pleased she is with their outcome—the woman must ultimately defend her decision to purchase appearance and identity.

RESEARCH AND METHODS

The research for this [reading] involved fieldwork in a Long Island plastic surgery clinic and interviews with the surgeon and twenty of his female patients. Finding a location to study cosmetic surgery proved difficult because many women hesitate to admit that they have undergone such procedures and physicians are bound by doctor-patient confidentiality. Having organized my research around interviews and fieldwork in identifiable physical locations, I knew that I wanted to talk with a single surgeon's female patients, rather than a "snowball" sample of surgery clients, whom I could have located easily through advertisements in local newspapers, gyms, universities, or hairstyling salons. As a result, I needed to find a cosmetic surgeon who would permit me access to patients. My search for this doctor took nearly six months, during which time I contacted over twenty clinics and interviewed seven physicians.

I eventually chose to focus on the clinic of Dr. John Norris, a local surgeon specializing in aesthetic procedures. My discussions with the six other physicians proved to be a rich source of data about the cosmetic surgery industry and cosmetic surgeons themselves. I learned, for example, that cosmetic surgeons are frequently critical of their female clientele, seeing them as obsessed and impossible to please. Moreover, often believing that the physical imperfections that their clients observe are insignificant, surgeons sometimes suspect their patients of trying to solve emotional problems by altering their bodies.

I met John Norris at the gym where I studied aerobics. As a member of the gym, I spent a considerable amount of time there each week, both in research and on my own body work. John and his wife, Monica, were gym regulars who, like me, tended to exercise in the mornings, and I saw them several times each week. Even though I had met him previously, I contacted John formally, as I did the other cosmetic surgeons in the area. I explained my project to his receptionist and made an appointment to speak with him. After our second meeting, I asked John to allow me to interview twenty of his female clients. He agreed and asked his receptionist to contact women who might be willing to talk with me. After obtaining his patients' approval, John provided me with their names and telephone numbers. This procedure surely biased my sample in favor of successful cases. In addition to interviewing patients (one of whom I was able to interview both before and after she had surgery), I conducted several interviews with John. I also attended informational sessions at another local clinic to learn more about many of these procedures.

John conducts his enormously successful practice in two offices, one on Long Island and the other in Manhattan. I spoke with him at some length about his interest in aesthetic plastic surgery. He explained that although he had originally aspired to be a sculptor, he soon decided that a career in art would not provide an adequate income. As his interest in science developed, John opted instead for a medical career and for what he now refers to as the "excitement of sculpting human appearance." Believing that his work helps his patients to feel more satisfied with the way they look, more desirable, and more confident in their professional and private lives, John says that he derives enormous satisfaction from his career.

John is interested not only in "sculpting" the appearances of others; he is himself heavily involved in the culture of body work. In particular, John has participated in bodybuilding since he was fifteen years old and, at age fifty-one, still participates regularly in bodybuilding competitions. Moreover, John has personally undergone plastic surgery to remove the "love handles" that he says will develop at his waistline unless he maintains a body composition of no more than 3 percent body fat. As his medical career has progressed, John's training and competition have both fueled and been fueled by his interest in using surgery to rework the aesthetics of the body. While he began his career doing reconstructive and burn-correcting surgery in addition to cosmetic procedures, he now focuses almost exclusively on aesthetic plastic surgery, which he finds equally rewarding and more enjoyable.

Similar to the staff of Pamela's Hair Salon [discussed in another part of *Body Work: Beauty and Self-image in American Culture* (Berkeley: University of California Press, 2002), from which this reading is taken], John is a "true believer" in beauty ideology. Like the stylists, John not only dispenses the means of altering appearance but also is deeply involved in reworking his own appearance. Nevertheless, he is differentiated from them by his higher social status. Like Pamela's staff, John is able both to assess his clients' appearance "flaws" and to suggest particular techniques for correcting them. But, unlike Pamela's staff—and primarily because of his status as a medical professional—John's patients nearly always accept his advice. Simply put, John is different from Pamela's stylists because he not only dispenses "beauty" to his patients but also shapes the choices they make about their appearances.

Moreover, John regularly denies surgical candidates access to the body work he provides. He is selective in choosing his clientele, screening patients to ensure that they are suitable for the operations they request. Listening to the client's description of her physical imperfections, John determines whether or not her complaint is reasonable—whether or not her nose is really inappropriate for her face, her breasts are really too small, her ankles are really too thick, and so on. In making such judgments, John (like the beauticians at Pamela's) blurs the line between technique and aesthetics, effectively broadening his area of expertise. While understanding his activity as a process of determining the "appropriateness" of surgical candidates, he actually selects patients based in large part on his personal taste and sense of aesthetics. As a purveyor of body work, John positions himself not only as a surgeon but also as an expert in contemporary standards for female beauty.

In deciding whether patients are suitable candidates for the procedures they request, John judges not only the aesthetics of their appearance but also their psychological health. By his own account, John attempts to determine whether patients are trying to deal with personal crises (such as divorce) through plastic surgery. John says that when he talks with potential patients about their motivations for having cosmetic surgery, many express sadness or fear regarding a significant personal relationship, even to the point of breaking down in tears in his office. This reaction, he claims, suggests that patients should seek the services of "some other type" of professional presumably, a psychologist or marital counselor—rather than those of a cosmetic surgeon.

John has come to categorize patients in four conceptual types, distinguished primarily by their motivations for having surgery. The first of the groups includes individuals who are "self-motivated and realistic." These patients pursue surgery as a means of bringing their appearances in line with their inner self. Claiming that their bodies fail to represent them as the people they truly are, individuals in this group explain their desire for cosmetic surgery with statements such as "I don't feel like an old person. I don't want to look like one," or "I exercise and diet. I want to look like I do." These candidates, according to John, are adequately prepared for cosmetic surgery, with expectations that will likely be met by the procedures they undergo.

The second type of patient seeks out plastic surgery to please someone else. In John's description, this patient—usually a woman—is going through a painful breakup and, hoping that changing her appearance will reignite her partner's interest, turns to plastic surgery as a "last-ditch effort" to save her relationship. Breast augmentation—which, John notes with some amusement, is the surgical procedure most likely to precede divorce—is a common request among members of this category. John typically refuses to perform such procedures on patients who hope to use plastic surgery to solve some personal problem.

The third group in John's typology involves children, usually brought to the office by their parents. According to John, these patients' parents frequently say things such as "She has her father's nose," which the parents, rather than the children themselves, judge

as unattractive and requiring change. John makes it a practice to ask the adolescents what they think about the particular body part. According to him, they tend to be relatively satisfied with the "nose" or other problematic feature, finding it far less objectionable than the parents do. John advises parents not to "fix what isn't broken," to give the child a few years to "grow into" the feature and then broach the topic of surgery again if they feel it necessary.

The last group includes individuals John refers to as "flighty," who want surgery for any number of "bizarre" reasons. As an example, John described one woman who wanted to have rhinoplasty because a favorite movie star had undergone the procedure. In another case, a potential patient requested breast augmentation in order to look more like a celebrity her boyfriend admired. In such cases, John refuses to operate because he considers these individuals to be psychologically unstable and impossible to satisfy.

All told, John claims that he rejects two or three requests per week. His ability and willingness to deny service suggest another comparison between the plastic surgeon and the hairstylist: John is less dependent on his clientele than are the beauticians at Pamela's, who have little choice concerning whose hair they style or how they style it. At the same time, John's decisions to reject patients are linked to his medical and legal responsibility for the surgeries that he performs. Indeed, his motivations for denying surgical procedures suggest a wariness about trying to satisfy the desires of individuals whose expectations are unreasonable and who might hold him legally responsible for their inevitable dissatisfaction. In this sense, John is even more vulnerable to his clients than are the stylists at Pamela's. While a beautician might lose a client who dislikes her haircut, John could potentially lose much more to a patient who claims that he is responsible for some physical deformity, particularly if that patient decides to sue.

The patients I interviewed ranged in age from twenty-four to fifty. The procedures they underwent included breast augmentations, nose jobs, face-lifts, eye-reshaping procedures, tummy tucks, and liposuctions. All of the women were Asian-American or European American; three were of Semitic ancestry; and all but one (a full-time mother) held salaried jobs or were students at the time of the interviews. They were employed as opticians, medical technicians, receptionists, insurance agents, teachers, office administrators, hairstylists, and secretaries.

THE STORY OF A FACE-LIFT: ANN MARIE

Ann Marie, a slender, soft-spoken fifty-year-old medical technician with upswept blonde hair, was one of the first patients I interviewed. Married to her current and only husband for nearly thirty years, Ann Marie carries herself with a careful gentility. Dressed in snug-fitting woolen pants, low-heeled brown pumps and a fuzzy light mauve sweater, Ann Marie invites me into her small, tidy home and asks if I would like coffee. Anxious to begin my first interview, I refuse. Ann Marie brings her own drink back from the kitchen in a tiny, flower-painted china cup and saucer and begins telling me about her experiences with plastic surgery.

Ann Marie is not at all shy about discussing her face-lift. She actually seems eager to tell me the reasons for her decision. Her appearance began to change in her late thirties and forties when she developed "puffiness underneath the eyes" and "drooping upper eyelids." Most unattractive, by Ann Marie's account, "the skin of my throat started getting creepy." In her words, "You get to an age" when "you look in the mirror and see lines that were not there before." Because her physical appearance had begun to reflect the aging process, she explains, "All of a sudden, the need [for cosmetic surgery] was there."

While Ann Marie describes her need for a face-lift as "sudden," she had planned to have the procedure long before. She recalls that "about ten years ago," she spoke with several close friends about having a face-lift at some point in the future. She explains, "We talked about it a long time ago. I guess I have never accepted the axiom of growing old gracefully. I have always sworn I would never picture myself as a chubby old lady." Ann Marie and her friends "talked and decided that when the time was just right, we would definitely do it." Ann Marie is the only member of the group who actually went through with surgery.

Despite her resolve, Ann Marie did not enter into cosmetic surgery lightly. Instead, for several years she "thought about it from time to time. There was a lot to be considered." Among the issues she contemplated were the physical dangers involved in the operation, the risk of looking worse after the surgery than before, and the importance of choosing a well-qualified doctor with an excellent reputation. She explains, "You are putting your face in the hands of a surgeon; there is the possibility of absolute disaster, very possibly permanently. You have to choose the surgeon very carefully."

Ann Marie chose John Norris to perform the face-lift. Largely because he had performed an emergency procedure for her just over one year earlier, Ann Marie claims that she felt completely comfortable with him. "John was recommended to me by my dermatologist. I had an infection on my face; it was quite serious. The dermatologist told me I had to go to a plastic surgeon, and John was the only one he would recommend." Because of the dermatologist's recommendation and her satisfaction with John's earlier work, Ann Marie returned to him for the face-lift. She visited his office in Long Island for a consultation and, not long after her appointment, decided to go ahead with the procedure.

During their first meeting, Ann Marie had what she refers to as two "surprises": one was the price of the operation and the other the news that she would have to stop smoking. According to Ann Marie, John explained that "you will not heal as well if you continue to smoke. Because it impedes circulation, smoking decreases your ability to heal properly." She says, "The most difficult part was to stop smoking. I was puffing away a pack and a half a day for over twenty years." John told Ann Marie that she would not be able to smoke for three months before the surgery. She says, "I thought, What? I will never be able to do this. But I did, I stopped cold. That was the real sacrifice for me."

While giving up cigarettes may have been the greatest sacrifice for Ann Marie, there were clearly many others. For a full year, Ann Marie had to work "one day job, one night job, occasionally a third job" to afford the surgery. She had to "bank" four weeks of overtime at her primary job so she could take time off to recover from the procedure. She also postponed repairs on her home. She explains, "There were things my house needed, but my feeling was, I needed a face-lift more than my house did."

By providing me with a long and detailed account of her need for a face-lift and the sacrifices she was willing to make to have the procedure, Ann Marie hints at an awareness that her behavior is somehow subject to criticism, that it might be construed by others as superficial or shallow. With a hint of defensiveness, Ann Marie explains that she "needed" the face-lift—despite its financial costs and physical risks—not merely because she is concerned with her appearance, but because of pressures in "the workfield." She says, "Despite the fact that we have laws against age discrimination, employers do find ways of getting around it. I know women my age who do not get jobs or are relieved of jobs because of age. . . . [The face-lift] will ensure my work ability." Ann Marie, by her account, decided to have cosmetic surgery not due to narcissism but to concern for her professional well-being. Justifying her behavior as a career decision, she implies that she is sensitive to the social disapproval of plastic surgery, that she knows that the behavior requires some justification.

Even though Ann Marie believes that looking younger will help her professionally, she also admits that she has "not seen anything that has really changed in that area." Instead, the procedure has affected her primarily "on a personal basis, a social basis." Explaining these effects in more detail, she says, "I meet people I haven't seen for two or three years who will say, 'There is something different about you, but I don't know what it is.' I met a sister of a very good friend of mine in June, which is five months after my surgery. She looked at me and said, 'I don't know you.' I said, 'Of course you do. I've known you nearly all of my life.' She realized who I was and was astounded at my appearance."

This incident, along with several similar ones, has, by Ann Marie's account, improved her self-image. By attributing these experiences—and the resulting improvement in her self-perception—to her face-lift, Ann Marie justifies her decision to have cosmetic surgery. In contemporary Western culture, "feeling good" about oneself is understood to be worth considerable effort because it makes us better workers, spouses, and citizens. Among children, self-esteem is credited with the ability to improve grades and to discourage sex and illegal drug use. Ann Marie explains her choice to have plastic surgery as "a matter of personal esteem. If you feel you look better, you feel better about yourself." By granting cosmetic surgery the power to provide self-esteem, Ann Marie—like many of the other women I spoke with—effectively legitimizes an otherwise illegitimate activity.

At the same time, Ann Marie's defensiveness suggests that she is somewhat self-conscious about her choice. She describes her decision to have a face-lift as "not purely vanity," and then adds, "If it is vanity, so what? That does not make me a bad person. I don't want to look bad. I don't want to look my age. I want to look younger. I want smoother skin." By her account, Ann Marie is not "bad" or vain; in fact, she is actually a good person, as evidenced by the other forms of body work in which she participates. She explains, "My weight is only a variance of six pounds heavier from what it was thirty years ago. I keep in shape in addition

to the surgery. I jog, I exercise, I diet." Ann Marie has maintained her physical appearance of youth in every way possible—failing only to control the appearance of her facial skin, which she could not keep from "getting creepy." In her account, Ann Marie deserved the surgery—an act tinged with deception—because she has proved her moral character through other (physically demanding and highly symbolic) forms of work on her body. Ann Marie is entitled to an appearance that reflects those efforts, even if that appearance is obtainable only through cosmetic surgery.

"A DEEP, DARK SECRET": HAVING LIPOSUCTION

John arranged for me to speak with a twenty-seven-year-old woman named Bonnie who was planning to have cosmetic surgery. In sharp contrast to the other women I interviewed, Bonnie was hesitant to speak with me about the procedure, because, as she later said, she considered it to be "a deep, dark secret" that she had discussed with no one but her husband of five months. Bonnie worked out at the same gym that both John and I attended. Because she and I were previously acquainted, John suggested that Bonnie speak with me about the procedure she was considering, and she agreed. Over the next six months, Bonnie and I met several times to discuss cosmetic surgery; during that period, she decided to have liposuction, underwent the procedure, and recovered from it.

Having recently completed a master's degree at a New England university, Bonnie moved to the east end of Long Island to take a position as a chemist in a pharmaceutical firm. She explained to me that over the years she had spoken casually to various women about cosmetic surgery and had "fantasized about" having liposuction herself, though she had never considered it seriously. Prior to having the operation, Bonnie told me why she was reluctant to have cosmetic surgery:

It's always seemed to me to be one step too far. I have dieted and exercised my whole life, and sometimes I've gone over the edge and done some things that probably weren't very healthy, but I could always stop myself before I became totally obsessed. I guess I have always thought that I would never get so obsessed that I would allow my body to be cut into just so I could look better. At least that's what I had always hoped. I couldn't imagine myself as one of "them," as one of those weak women who would go that far.

Despite her stated objections to cosmetic surgery and her characterization of its patients as "weak," Bonnie underwent liposuction on the outside of her upper thighs. Bonnie described this area of her body as "flabby, no matter what I do. I exercise five or six times a week; I cycle with my husband. I do all the weight lifting that is supposed to tone up the muscles in those areas. Nothing works!" Nevertheless, Bonnie never seriously investigated the procedure until she finished graduate school and began full-time employment. She explained, "This is the first time I've ever made enough money to think about doing something like this. The liposuction will cost $2,000, which is less than it usually costs because I won't have to have general anesthesia, but it's still a lot of money."

Referring to her new job and home, Bonnie noted that she would never have considered having cosmetic surgery while she was living near her family and friends. "I wouldn't want any of my friends or my family to know about it, only my husband. My family would all be like, 'You don't need to have that done. You're crazy. You are thin enough already.' That doesn't keep me from thinking these lumps on my thighs are really ugly. They are the only thing I see when I look in the mirror."

Bonnie's hesitance to discuss liposuction with her friends stems from her perception of cosmetic surgery as part of a process of "giving in to pressure, giving in to these ideals about how women should look, when none of us real women are ever going to look like that." Bonnie believes that her friends would react to her interest in plastic surgery by making her "feel so ashamed, like I am not strong enough to accept myself like I am."

Unlike most of John's patients, Bonnie articulates her ambivalence about plastic surgery primarily in political rather than personal terms. Her description of her friends' imagined objections is one of many examples of her concern with the political meaning of her actions. In another, Bonnie explains that her own political view of cosmetic surgery is the main source of her conflict over having the procedure. She says, "I am not worried about problems with the operation itself. I know that Dr. Norris has a great reputation. I've talked to other people at the gym who have used him, and they were all really happy. He does so much of this stuff, I'm sure he's really good at it." Bonnie's concerns focus instead on the social and cultural significance of her action. "If I am proud to be a woman, then I should be proud to look like a woman, with a woman's butt and a woman's thighs." Reacting to her own accusations, she notes, "I am proud to be a woman, but I really hate it when I get a glimpse of my backside and I just look big. I feel terrible knowing that it is those areas of my body which are understood to be most 'female' that I dislike the most." Expressing her interest in cosmetic surgery as her only viable option for reducing her dissatisfaction with her appearance, she adds,

> I don't really know how to get around it, though, because I really do not like those parts of my figure. Plastic surgery seems like a pretty good way, and really, a pretty easy way, to deal with that dissatisfaction, to put those negative feelings behind me . . . to move on with the rest of my life. . . . I'd love to get dressed for work in the morning and have only the work in front of me, rather than, you know, what's literally behind me, be the thing that concerns me the most.

Bonnie is explicitly aware that the body and the self are linked. When she says that she dislikes the "female" parts of her figure, one can easily imagine replacing the term "figure" with the term "self." Indeed, it is Bonnie's ambivalence about her female identity that is most troubling to her; eradicating the physical signs of femininity—and the flaws inherent in those attributes—may enable her to construct a self that she believes to be less imperfect, more culturally acceptable, and that will allow her to focus more attention on other activities and concerns, including her career, the sports she enjoys, and her new marriage. At the same time, her decision to undergo liposuction comes at a considerable cost; Bonnie says explicitly that, if possible, she would prefer to change her perceptions rather than her body. The "pressure" she feels, however, limits her ability to rework her self-image, leaving her to choose between plastic surgery and a negative self-concept, two options that are unsatisfying. Bonnie's decision to undergo liposuction suggests that, in the end, the costs associated with plastic surgery are somehow less significant than those attached to her appearance flaws.

Obviously, Ann Marie and Bonnie present two quite disparate facets of the concerns women face as they consider having cosmetic surgery. While Ann Marie struggled to meet the financial and physical requirements of her face-lift, Bonnie agonized over the political dimension of her decision to have liposuction. So distinct are these preoccupations, in fact, that they can be conceptualized as opposite ends of a continuum, along which the perspectives of the other eighteen women I interviewed can be placed. For most of these women, the political implications of cosmetic surgery, though not entirely insignificant, were far less important than they were for Bonnie. The other women I interviewed were more often concerned with the health risks and financial costs of cosmetic surgery and with how they would look after their procedures.

While Ann Marie's and Bonnie's preoperative anxieties took different forms, both constructed elaborate justifications for plastic surgery. Like the other women I interviewed, Bonnie responds to the negative identity implications of plastic surgery by explaining that she has done all that is humanly possible to alter an imperfect body but that no act short of plastic surgery will allow her to live peacefully with herself. Invariably, the women's accounts involve bodies that were flawed in some way for which the individual claimed not to be responsible. Each woman's body was imperfect not because she had erred in her body work but because of aging, genetics, or some other physical condition that she could not control. Their flawed bodies are inaccurate indicators of character, and so they effectively lie about who the women really are. Accounts like these permit women to engage in cosmetic procedures with less guilt. Plastic surgery becomes for them not an act of deception but an attempt to align body with self.

"THE BODY I WAS MEANT TO HAVE": WHY WOMEN HAVE COSMETIC SURGERY

Whereas some writers have dealt with cosmetic surgery as if it were an attempt to attain idealized female beauty in order to gain the approval of men,[12] the women I interviewed claim that their goal in undergoing plastic surgery is neither to become beautiful nor to be beautiful specifically for husbands, boyfriends, or other significant individuals. Rather, they alter their bodies for their own satisfaction, in effect utilizing such procedures to create what they consider a normal appearance, one that reflects a normal self. While I do not accept their accounts without some skepticism, I believe that women who have plastic surgery are not necessarily doing so in order to become beautiful or to please particular individuals. Instead they are responding to highly restrictive notions of normality and the "normal" self, notions that neither apply to the population at large (in fact, quite the reverse) nor leave space for ethnic variation. Plastic surgery "works" for women

who have these procedures, but it works only within the context of a culture of appearance that is less about beauty than it is about control based on the physical representations of gender, age, and ethnicity.

My respondents claim that prior to having surgery, some particular physical feature stood in the way of their looking "normal." This feature distinguished them from others and prohibited them from experiencing "a happy, regular life," as Marcy, a twenty-five-year-old student, put it. Marcy decided at twenty-one to have the bony arch in the middle of her nose removed and its tip shortened. Before the procedure, Marcy had never been involved in a romantic relationship, a fact that she attributed to her "hook" nose and unattractive appearance. Marcy says, "I have always felt terrible about how pronounced it was. No matter how I wore my hair, it was in the middle of my face, and everybody noticed it. It's not like I could just wear my bangs long."

Marcy decided to have rhinoplasty near a date that was particularly symbolic for her. "I was having my nose done just before Valentine's Day. I thought to myself, maybe if I have my nose done for Valentine's Day, by next Valentine's Day, I'll have a Valentine!" Although she did not find a Valentine for the following year—she explained that dating "didn't happen until a few years later"—Marcy claimed that over time, the surgery allowed her to experience pleasure that she would otherwise have missed.

Because Marcy uses cosmetic surgery to make herself more appealing to others, her experience seemingly supports the criticisms of authors like Naomi Wolf. However, Marcy stresses that she does not expect plastic surgery to make her beautiful. Neither does she believe that winning male affection requires her to be beautiful. Quite the contrary, Marcy clearly imagines that a merely normal appearance is sufficient to garner the male attention she desires.

The women describe several ways in which their physical features have kept them from living ordinary lives. For example, Barbara, a twenty-nine-year-old bookkeeper, says that her breasts—which were, by her account, too small to fill out attractive clothing—made her appear "dumpy" and ill-proportioned. Her "flaw" contributed to a negative self-image, which in turn served to limit the education and career goals Barbara set for herself, the friendships she fostered, and the romantic and sexual relationships she pursued. Barbara decided to have her breasts augmented (from a 36A to a 36D) to become, in her words, "more attractive to myself and others." While her larger breasts have in fact made Barbara feel more attractive, she, like other patients I interviewed, nevertheless laments women's inability to be self-confident despite their physical shortcomings. She says, "For women, the appearance is the important thing. That's too bad that we can't worry about not being judged. [Small breasts] made a big difference in how I felt myself being perceived and how I felt about myself as a person."

Because physical attractiveness shapes the way women are "judged," appearance must be protected as women age. Like Ann Marie, several of the patients I interviewed underwent cosmetic procedures aimed at reducing the natural signs of aging. These women claim that aging had changed an acceptable appearance into an unacceptable one that reflected negatively on their identity. For instance, Sue, a forty-four-year-old optician, decided to have the loose skin around her eyes tightened. She discusses her motivations for having the operation: "My eyes had always been all right, nice eyes. I guess I had always liked my face pretty well, but with age, the skin around them started getting puffy. They just didn't look nice anymore. I looked tired, tired and old. That's why I had them fixed." While Sue had, according to her own account, once been satisfied with her appearance, she grew to dislike her face as the signs of aging became apparent. She used cosmetic surgery to regain the face she liked "pretty well."

Several women told me that they chose to have cosmetic surgery not to make themselves beautiful or outstanding in any particular way but simply to regain normal physical characteristics they had lost through aging.[13] Like Sue and Ann Marie, Tina, a forty-eight-year-old receptionist, used cosmetic surgery to combat the physical changes associated with growing older. Tina underwent liposuction to reduce what she referred to as "secretarial spread," the widening of her hips and buttocks that she believed had come with her twenty-five-year career in office management. She explains, "When I was younger, I had nice hips, curvy but narrow enough, and my rear was well-shaped. After a lifetime of sitting, growing older and flabbier, it had gotten really huge." Tina hoped to restore her appearance to its more youthful form. Believing that her only means of doing so was cosmetic surgery, Tina opted to have liposuction rather than surrender to the aging process that had so drastically altered her body.

Youth—or at least a youthful appearance—is not the only characteristic women attempt to construct or

regain through aesthetic procedures. Indeed, three of the patients I interviewed—all under the age of thirty—had cosmetic surgery to reduce the physical markers of ethnicity. These women underwent procedures intended to make their physical features more Anglo-Saxon. Marcy, a Jewish woman, notes that her rhinoplasty removed physical features "more frequently associated with Jewish people." Jodie, a twenty-eight-year-old student who also had her nose reshaped, says, "I had this Italian bump on my nose. It required a little shaving. Now, it looks better." By a "better" nose, Jodie implies a more Anglo-Saxon, less Italian, and therefore less ethnic nose. And Kim, a twenty-two-year-old Taiwanese American student, underwent a procedure to make her eyes appear more oval in shape. She said, "[Taiwanese people] regard girls with wide, bright eyes as beautiful. My eyes used to look a little bit as if I was staring at somebody. The look is not soft; it is a very stiff look." While none of these women consciously attempted to detach themselves from ethnicity, they nevertheless chose to ignore the fact that their efforts to appear "normal" explicitly diminished the physical markers of that ethnicity. Seemingly indifferent to this loss, they accept the notion that normalized (i.e., Anglo-Saxon) features are more attractive than ethnic ones.

All the women claimed that plastic surgery was, for them, a logical, carefully thought-out response to distressing circumstances that could not be otherwise remedied. They now perceive themselves to be more socially acceptable, more normal, and, in several cases, more outgoing. As Bonnie explains, "I got exactly what I wanted from this. My body isn't extraordinarily different, but now, I feel like, well, I have a cute bottom. I have a cuter figure. I don't feel like the one with the big butt anymore. And for me, that lets me put my body issues away pretty much."

At the same time, displaying some remnants of her original ambivalence about cosmetic surgery, Bonnie notes, "I wish that I could have said, 'To hell with it, I am going to love my body the way it is' . . . but I had tried to do that for fifteen years, and it didn't work." She adds, "Now, I know I'll never look like Cindy Crawford, but I can walk around and feel like everything is good enough."

Women who undergo plastic surgery report various other benefits. For instance, some say that they can now wear clothes that they could not have worn prior to their operations; others attest to having greater self-confidence or to being more extroverted. Jennifer explains, "When I walk out that door in the morning, my head might be a little bit higher when I'm wearing a certain outfit. Like, before I had [liposuction] done, it used to be, I feel good, but I hope no one will notice that my legs aren't too nice."

These women now wear bathing suits, dresses with low-cut necklines, and feminine and revealing lingerie. Wearing these clothes, and believing themselves to be attractive in them, shapes the women's perceptions of themselves and increases their self-confidence. Tara, a twenty-seven-year-old student, told me that before she had breast augmentation surgery, she avoided wearing bathing suits in public and rarely shopped for bras. She says, "[Breast augmentation] has given me more self-confidence than I ever had. I fit in when I'm with my girlfriends now. Before, I never went to the beach with anybody around. After I had [plastic surgery], I couldn't wait to buy a bra. I could never buy one before because I was so pathetically small." Having plastic surgery made Tara appear more "normal." She is now able to participate in activities from which she previously felt excluded.

Barbara, who also had breast augmentation surgery, recounted a similar experience. She says, "I used to wear super-padded bras when I dressed up, but they just never did it for me. I didn't look like the other women. But now, like tonight, I am going to a party, and I know I'll be able to fill out the dress." She added, "[Breast augmentation] has made me feel very confident. I think that's the difference."

Sandra, a forty-three-year-old office manager who had liposuction to reduce her "thick thighs" and "saddlebag" hips, explains that she underwent the procedure not only to appear youthful and wear feminine clothing, but also to approximate a cultural ideal involving social class. "I used to put on nice clothes and still look like a bag lady, you know, unsophisticated. Now I feel like I can wear good clothes and look like they are appropriate for me. Now, my body fits the clothes." Sandra likens appearance to a tableau of social class, both in the context of the clothing one chooses and the extent to which one's body appears to be "appropriate" for that clothing (and the social standing that it implies). Simply put, before Sandra's surgery, her "flabby" body had less class than her clothing. Her body undermined her efforts to use appearance to stake out a particular social location. In effect, it not only made her clothing an ineffective class identifier but also invalidated her claims to a particular status. Plastic surgery, however, has allowed Sandra to dis-

play social class through clothing. Cosmetic surgery legitimizes Sandra's claims to social status.

Other women I interviewed also claimed that cosmetic surgery helped them feel more self-confident. For example, Kim says, "I guess I feel better when I am out with friends, like maybe people will think I am attractive. I feel attractive and I guess, I act more attractive." Thus, the women imagine that they are now perceived more favorably and so behave in a manner that they believe is appropriate for "attractive" women. At the same time, the women recognize that they may simply be imagining others' perceptions of them and that their behaviors may have changed independently of any alteration in the way they are viewed. Kim says, "Maybe nobody even notices, but I feel like I look better. I guess just thinking I look better changes the way I act a little."

Nearly all of the women told me that their romantic partners believed the cosmetic procedures were unnecessary. Before her breast augmentation procedure, Tara's boyfriend voiced significant apprehension. "He was very, very frightened about it. He kept on telling me, 'I love you just the way you are,' that type of thing." And Barbara's fiance blamed himself for her dissatisfaction with her breasts. She recalls, "My fiance thought he was doing something wrong that would make me feel like this about myself." In many cases, the women's partners attempted to convince them not to undergo the surgery. Jennifer says her boyfriend "tried to talk me out of it, but finally he decided, 'If it's going to make you happy, go ahead and do it.'" Some of John's patients report that their partners have had mixed reactions to the results of the procedures. Barbara says that even though she has always considered her husband a "breast man, because his eyes would pop out if he saw a big-breasted woman," he nevertheless told her that she was "perfect" with small breasts. She adds, laughing, "He still says he liked me better before, but I'll tell you, I can't keep him off of me. I keep saying I'm taking them back for a refund."

The frequency with which I heard such assertions points to the considerable importance women attach to having "freely" chosen to have cosmetic surgery, independent of coercion by their lovers or the desire to please someone other than themselves. These assertions make sense in light of the women's accounts of their surgery. Plastic surgery cannot be both something women "deserve" and something that they are forced or manipulated into doing. In their accounts, plastic surgery is positioned as a final option for correcting a tormenting problem. This conception of plastic surgery is clearly inconsistent with an image of acts forced on them by others—particularly others who might actually benefit more from the procedures than do the women themselves.

PLASTIC SURGERY AND INAUTHENTICITY: THE HIGH PRICE OF BODY WORK

In turning "abnormal" bodies into "normal" ones, plastic surgery succeeds: the woman who participates in plastic surgery comes to possess the foundation (i.e., a normal body) of a normative self. However, plastic surgery fails as a method for constructing a positive self-concept because of the negative social and political meanings attached to it. Women participate in cosmetic surgery in a world that limits their choices and in which the flawed body is taken as a sign of a flawed character. Despite the negative connotations of plastic surgery, women opt to engage in such procedures because the alternative is more detrimental to self-image. However, most of the women I interviewed carry with them the burden of their decisions; the process of dealing with that burden exacts from them a considerable price.

Some of the costs of cosmetic surgery—including the danger of physical damage and the high financial price—are obvious to those who have undergone these procedures and perhaps even to those who have not. Most of these women had plastic surgery only after serious consideration (often accompanied by research into the medical technology involved in the operations). Likewise, few could easily afford the surgery they underwent; nearly all of them had to sacrifice some other large purchase or to weather financial hardship. Some have accrued considerable debt, while others had to request financial help from relatives. Only a very few of the women had health insurance that covered part of the cost.

Other costs associated with cosmetic surgery, while less concrete, are no less substantial. Specifically, after surgery, women must attempt to deal with the taint of inauthenticity these procedures imply. Although the body appears more normal, the character becomes suspect, with the self, by implication, becoming deviant. The unacceptable act of cosmetic surgery displaces the normative body as an indicator of character. Although the women I interviewed do not formulate the complexities and contradictions involved in their activities

in the way I have here, their accounts show that they struggle with a self-concept that continues to be deviant despite their now-normal appearance. Indeed, the accounts themselves—which attempt to deny inauthenticity by positioning cosmetic surgery as somehow owed to the women who partake of it—show that plastic surgery fails to align body and self.

These accounts suggest a singular conclusion with regard to the success of plastic surgery for establishing the normative identity. Women like Ann Marie and Bonnie—like participants in the aerobics classes [discussed in another part of *Body Work*]—invoke their rigorous body work regimens as evidence of moral rectitude and as the basis for their entitlement to cosmetic surgery. But although cosmetic surgery patients and aerobics participants seem to rely on the same symbols of identity, for women who undergo cosmetic surgery, those symbols fail to mitigate the body's negative implications for self. Had these women accepted their body work as an adequate indicator of identity, they would not have needed to turn to plastic surgery to correct their bodies' failings. Moreover, still needing to establish the "deceptive" act of plastic surgery as irrelevant to self (and to position the surgically altered, normative body as the true indicator of selfhood), these women revert to accounts that have already proved unsuccessful. Indeed, the negative implications for self inherent in cosmetic surgery require women to resort to accounts that they know—consciously or not—fail to support the normative identity. In so doing, these women attest to the failure of cosmetic surgery to position the transformed body as symbolic of self. Simply put, if plastic surgery were a successful method for constructing identity, these women would argue that the surgically altered body—rather than body work that has proved unsuccessful at shaping the body or establishing the self—serves to symbolize identity.

CONCLUSION

My research points to three general conclusions. The first bears on the reasons women have plastic surgery and suggests a modification of the criticisms of such procedures. The second bears on the ways in which women create accounts of plastic surgery, which are ignored by the criticisms of plastic surgery to date. The third returns more sympathetically to those criticisms.

None of the women I spoke to embarked casually on plastic surgery. The costs associated with these procedures—measured in dollars and the risk of physical damage—are well known. Although physicians may serve as gatekeepers by preventing some women from undergoing surgery, they rarely recruit patients directly. When surgeons actively market their practices—as did John Norris—they tend to do so indirectly, through advertisements in local magazines and shopping malls. And the women I interviewed did not report that they underwent surgery at the urging of a husband, parent, lover, or friend. Rather, the decision to seek surgery seems to have been theirs alone, at least in the immediate circumstances. To be sure, these decisions were shaped by broader cultural considerations—by notions of what constitutes beauty, by distinctively ethnic notions of beauty, and, most important, by the assumption that a woman's worth is measured by her appearance. Yet to portray the women I talked to as cultural dupes, as passively submitting to the demands of beauty, is to misrepresent them badly. A more appropriate image, I would suggest, is to present them as savvy cultural negotiators, attempting to make out as best they can within a culture that limits their options. Those who undergo plastic surgery may (ultimately) be misguided, but they are not foolish. They know what they are doing. Their goals are realistic, and they in fact achieve most of what they set out to accomplish with plastic surgery. Although their actions surely do, in the long run, contribute to the reproduction of a beauty culture that carries heavy costs for them and for all women, in the short run they have succeeded in their own limited purposes.

Second, plastic surgery requires a defense. Much like the women I studied in the aerobics classes, those who underwent plastic surgery are working hard to justify themselves. But the accounts of the women who have plastic surgery are very different from those of the women who attend the aerobics classes. The aerobics women use hard physical work as an indicator of character that allows them to sever their conception of the self from the body. In contrast, the women who have had plastic surgery work hard to reattach the self to the body. First, they must convince themselves that they deserve the surgery, whether by the hard work they put in at the gym or the effort they invest in saving the money for the procedure. In so doing, they make the surgery psychologically and ideologically their own. Second, they must convince themselves that their revised appearance is authentically connected to the self.[14] To do this, they invoke

essentialist notions of the self and corresponding notions of the body as accidental, somehow inessential or a degeneration from a younger body that better represented who they truly are.

I do not mean these observations as a defense of plastic surgery so much as an effort to understand that surgery and its implications. Indeed, if we are to distinguish plastic surgery from other forms of body work, we can do so on precisely the grounds I have just suggested. I am not convinced that reducing facial wrinkles is somehow less "real" than dyeing hair from gray to brown or even that eye surgery or rhinoplasty is somehow less authentic than a decision to have straight rather than curly hair. However, what characterizes the efforts of women in aerobics, hair salons, and, . . . in NAAFA [National Association to Advance Fat Acceptance], is that they attempt, in somewhat different ways and with varying degrees of success, to neutralize appearance as a measure of character. Far more than the other women I studied, the women who undergo plastic surgery help to reproduce some of the worst aspects of the beauty culture, not so much through the act of the surgery itself as through their ideological efforts to restore appearance as an indicator of character.

My own criticisms of plastic surgery are tempered by observations of [other] women described in [my book] *Body Work*. Although I have characterized plastic surgery as a research "site," parallel to an aerobics class or a group of women in a hair salon or the members of NAAFA, this parallel is in certain respects misleading. In the hair salon, in the aerobics class, and especially in NAAFA, I found women working together to find common solutions to a shared problem. But women who underwent plastic surgery were not a group in the same sense. For the most part, they did not know each other. They did not speak to each other. And although they may have had common problems with a common solution, they did not develop this solution cooperatively. In the other settings I studied, the local production of an alternative culture was very much in evidence. In the plastic surgery group, however, there were the aesthetic judgments of the plastic surgeon, the ignored opposition of friends and family, but no culture of its own. The women in the aerobics class, in the hair salon, and especially in NAAFA, all challenged a beauty culture, however haltingly, however partially. In contrast, the women who undergo plastic surgery are simply making do within a culture that they believe judges and rewards them for their looks.

NOTES

1. Ann Dally, *Women Under the Knife: A History of Surgery* (London: Hutchinson Radius, 1991); Eugenia Kaw, "Opening Faces: The Politics of Cosmetic Surgery and Asian-American Women," in *Many Mirrors: Body Image and Social Relations*, ed. N. Sank (New Brunswick, N.J.: Rutgers University Press, 1994), 241–65.

2. American Society of Plastic and Reconstructive Surgeons, *1999 Plastic Surgery Procedural Statistics* (Arlington Heights, Ill.: American Society of Plastic and Reconstructive Surgeons, www.plasticsurgery.org, March 2000); American Society of Plastic and Reconstructive Surgeons, *1999 Average Surgeon's Fees* (Arlington Heights, Ill.: American Society of Plastic and Reconstructive Surgeons, www.plasticsurgery.org, March 2000). Generally, surgeons' fees do not include anesthesia, operating-room facilities, or other related expenses.

3. American Society of Plastic and Reconstructive Surgeons, *1999 Gender Distribution. Cosmetic Procedures* (Arlington Heights, Ill.: American Society of Plastic and Reconstructive Surgeons, www.plasticsurgery.org, March 2000).

4. American Society of Plastic and Reconstructive Surgeons, *1999 Plastic Surgery Procedural Statistics* (Arlington Heights, Ill.: www.plasticsurgery.org, March 2000).

5. Joachim Gabka and Ekkehard Vaubel, *Plastic Surgery Past and Present: Origin and History of Modern Lines of Incision* (Basel: Karger, 1983), 29.

6. Susan Faludi, *Backlash: The Undeclared War on Women* (New York: Crown, 1991), 217.

7. Kathy Davis, *Reshaping the Female Body: The Dilemma of Cosmetic Surgery* (New York: Routledge, 1995), 21.

8. Robert M. Goldwyn, ed., *Long-Term Results in Plastic and Reconstructive Surgery*, 2d ed. (Boston: Little, Brown, 1980).

9. Barbara Meredith, *A Change for the Better* (London: Grafton Books, 1988).

10. Susan Bordo, "'Material Girl': The Effacements of Postmodern Culture," *Michigan Quarterly Review* 29 (1990): 657.

11. Joan Finkelstein, *The Fashioned Self* (Philadelphia: Temple University Press, 1991), 87.

12. Naomi Wolf; *The Beauty Myth: How Images of Beauty Are Used Against Women* (New York: William Morrow, 1991).

13. See Davis, *Reshaping the Female Body,* for similar findings.

14. Concern about authenticity may well be class-specific; however, because my sample is based on references from a plastic surgeon, it is likely to include those patients who are least troubled by what they have done.

R E A D I N G *15*   **Ingrid Banks**

Hair Still Matters

Williams' beaded braids, though popular with her fans and part of her identity the past few years, have long been a matter of annoyance to some opponents even when they don't come undone. . . . To bead or not to bead, that is the question now facing Williams. For the moment, she plans only to braid them a little tighter. "I shouldn't have to change," she said. "I like my hair."

—Associated Press, 1999

INTRODUCTION

I've always liked tennis, as both a player and fan. But who knew back in 1999 when Venus Williams was beginning to light a fire to the women's professional circuit that my interest in tennis and my scholarly research on black women and hair would collide? Though troubled by the racial, gendered, and cultural meanings of Williams being penalized for wearing beads in her hair during the Australian Open, I knew that once again I had some phat fodder for continuing to argue that hair STILL matters for black women.[1] The expectation to conform to white standards is nothing new in a society that privileges whiteness, and the expectation is becoming magnified for blacks in predominantly white spaces like professional tennis. In fact, in the late 1990s, descriptions of Venus Williams and basketball sensation Allen Iverson often included allusions to their hairstyles, braided and in rows, respectively. The coded racial language of sportscasters' coverage of Williams's tennis matches or Iverson's basketball games is indicative of the fascination and discomfort that white mainstream U.S. society continues to feel regarding African Americans in general, and particular black hairstyles and what they signify, whether real or imagined. Like the Afro, Williams's beaded braids and Iverson's corn-rows are exotic to some and threatening to others because they display a black aesthetic that is linked to an authentic or radical blackness in the imagination of many whites. Still, the gendered component of Williams's sanctioning during her 1999 match is equally as important as the racial one. For example, Williams's choice of hairstyle was rooted outside of mainstream constructions of femininity. By wearing beaded braids, Williams's expression of racialized gender sent the message to a predominantly white professional wom-en's tennis circuit that mainstream constructions of womanhood are insufficient in understanding black women's relationship to beauty culture. In fact, Williams's hairstyle sent a bold statement that the very notion of what constitutes femininity must not only be contested, but our understanding of womanhood must be expanded. Feminist scholars have done well in unmasking the gender politics of femininity and sexu-ality that are embedded in how the female body has been, for example, treated in popular media and sci-ence (Jaggar and Bord 1989; Bordo 1993). The female body in general, as a site where both empowerment and repression are played out, must be central to femi-nist projects in the 21st century. From a woman's right to choose what happens to her body with regard to abortion to female circumcision to the covering of women's bodies among Muslims, feminists, locally and globally, must continue to illuminate the contexts under which women's bodies are politicized, as well as depoliticized.

SITUATING HAIR IN ACADEMIA AND POPULAR CULTURE

To be sure, this is not fetish or trendy scholarship. Hair has been of interest to social theorists spanning the 20th century from Freud to Robin D. G. Kelley. Psycho-analysts were waxing theoretical poetic about the sex-ual symbolism of hair during the earlier period (Freud 1922). In reaction to psychoanalytic readings of hair symbolism, social meanings of hair emerged. More specifically in the latter part of the century, scholars focusing on blacks and hair emphasize the importance of hair among blacks in relationship to Africa (Morrow 1973), enslavement (Patterson 1982), constructions of

race (Mercer 1990), skin color, self-esteem, ritual, aes-thetics, and adornment (Mercer 1990), appropriate grooming practices (Tyler 1990), images of beauty, pol-itics, and identity (Grier and Cobbs 1968; Mercer 1990), and the intersection of race and gender (Craig 1997; Kelley 1997).

The scholarship on blacks and hair highlighting the difference that gender makes in understanding hair-styling practices among African Americans provides a similar gender intervention to that within general hair theorizing scholarship (Eilberg-Schwartz and Doniger 1995).

Several works have been written that engage beauty culture and black women (Giddings 1984; Hill Collins 1990; Caraway 1991; Rooks 1996; Craig 2002). In par-ticular, discussions by black women moved the debate about hair among people of African descent to one that also focuses on experience (Okazawa-Rey et al. 1986; Benton Rushing 1988; hooks 1988; Walker 1988; Hill Collins 1990; Caldwell 1991; Norsworthy 1991; Cleage 1993; Wade Gayles 1993; Davis 1994; Jones 1994; Gibson 1995; DuCille 1996; Rooks 1996). In these works the authors discuss personal experiences involving hair that intersect with race, gender, motherhood, free-dom, law, appropriation, and identity. In one of the most important texts focusing on black women and hair, *Hair Raising: Beauty, Culture, and African American Women,* Noliwe Rooks (1996) examines black hair care advertisements at the turn of the century in her inves-tigation of how dominant or mainstream ideologies of race and beauty forced African American women to produce and sell beauty products for an African Amer-ican female market. Rooks makes a strong case for understanding why gendered investigations of hair meanings in black communities are central for under-standing how black women negotiate mainstream beauty culture. More recently, provocative texts that examine the history of black hair in the U.S. (Byrd and Tharps, 2001) and personal reflections on hair (Harris and Johnson, 2001) have contributed greatly to schol-arship on black women and hair.

Similar to early anthropological writings that do not take into consideration the difference culture and gender make in understandings about hair, early feminist discussions about the relationship between femininity and hair focus on hair as an indelible marker of femininity. For example, Susan Brownmiller (1984) conflates the meanings of hair by reducing the inter-pretation of "good" hair and "bad" hair to mean the same thing for black women as it does for white women. Brownmiller collapses these terms despite racial and cultural difference. Her analysis demonstrates why these types of comparisons are problematic and how they disclaim the cultural significance of hair for black women by treating the issue as if it were *merely* a women's issue, and not an issue that traverses lines of race and culture.

Black hair is certainly not simply an academic matter. In fact, the debates that scholars engage [in] are clearly indicative of real-world tensions, as the literature on blacks and hair demonstrates. Within the context of black popular culture, hair has always been "pop." Spike Lee films such as *School Daze* and *Jungle Fever*, as well as the prime-time TV shows *Any Day Now, Girlfriends, Moesha, The Parkers*, and *The Practice*, have engaged the politically charged issue of black women's hair. For example, in Spike Lee's *School Daze*, a scene unfolds in the film that illustrates the intraracial tensions embedded in constructions of "good" hair and "bad" hair. In one episode of Lifetime Television Network's drama *Any Day Now*, a story line involving the different cultural meanings that black and white women ascribe to hair grooming practices illustrates difference race makes in understanding how women relate to beauty culture.

Rap artists such as Lauryn Hill and her former Fugees crew, The Lost Boyz, and The Roots have laced particular songs with explicit references to nappy hair.[2] Preceding the attention given to black hair on prime time and in popular music in the late 20th century and early 21st century was the emergence of the Afro almost three decades ago. Though today the Afro has less political meaning, in the late 1960s it was associated with a movement and a black woman. The movement was black power and the black woman was (and still is, even without her late 1960s, early 1970s Afro) Angela Davis. During an interview for *Hair Matters*, Taylor, a 48-year-old accountant, reminisced about her desire to wear an "Angela Davis Afro" during the early 1970s. Similar [to] yet different from Davis's recognition that law enforcement officers used her image (i.e., Afro) as a reason to detain and harass black women, Taylor explained that it was her Afro and *assumed* gender that led to her being detained during the early 1970s:

> When Afros came out, I wanted to wear an Afro. So I did everything and I finally got me a great big huge Angela Davis Afro. Whenever I would wear my Afro I'd get pulled over by the police because I drove a very sleek car and they always thought from the back of the head that I had to be male a lot of times because we [Black women and Black men] all wore the same hairstyle.

Taylor's understanding of why she was detained by police officers was based on both her Afro and mistaken gender-identity. Whereas Taylor presented an image of the Afro-wearing militant as male, which was supported by the general perception of the black militant at the time, Davis describes how race and gender merged to stigmatize and repress black women, a point that would surface almost twenty years later when black women's hair was at the center of legal battles.

In the late 1980s black female employees went to court to challenge a policy by Hyatt Hotels and American Airlines against the wearing of braids.[3] These companies couched their policy in terms that related to "appropriate" grooming practices, which they argued braids violated. In November 1996, another hair controversy hit a sururban middle school in Chicago. *The Atlanta Journal/Atlanta Constitution* ran a story that highlighted a ban on hairstyles, along with certain clothes and jewelry that school officials defined as "gang related paraphernalia." Hairstyles such as cornrows, dreadlocks, braids, and ponytails for boys would lead to suspension; hairstyles with zigzag parts for girls were disallowed. With a similar argument as the one used against Hyatt Hotels and American Airlines, critics argued that the school's policy appeared to restrict African Americans. To add, the weekly ABC news show *20/20* aired a segment that examined the tensions that many black professional women face when hair is at issue. Oprah Winfrey dedicated an entire show to the "black hair question." As the *Los Angeles Times* reported in an article that examined the rise in natural hairstyles among black women (and men), the *20/20* episode illustrated how "one woman was terminated because management saw her hairstyle as 'extreme,' and another woman was written up because her braids were deemed 'too ethnic'" (George 1998, E4).

MY RESEARCH ON BLACK WOMEN AND HAIR

My research is a departure from previous research and discussions as it serves as the first empirical study that examines why hair matters to black women and girls. Prior to my research, an empirically based book that centers on black women's views was absent in the literature and to this end, the study fills a void in the literature. Given that I identified a gap in research on this topic, how did I go about collecting data? By the fall of 1998, I completed forty-three individual interviews and five focus group interviews with African-American women and girls. The interviewees consisted of girls and women ranging from ages 12 to 76, from various walks of life. Individuals were recruited and interviewed in the San Francisco Bay Area, Los Angeles, Santa Barbara, and Atlanta. During a focus group interviewee, Wixie, a 45-year-old physician explained to me, "There's always a question of race, money, and sex. But I think for black women, it's race, money, sex, and hair. It transcends a cosmetic [or esthetic] issue because it is at the base historically, culturally, and socially." Indeed, the argument here presents hair as a cultural tool that shapes black women's ideas about race, gender, class, sexuality and images of beauty and power. In addition, my research illustrates that hair matters for black women are never merely arrested within esthetics. Indeed, it serves cultural theorists well in paying close to attention to why hair matters to black women. In stating that hair matters, I argue that identity matters.

HAIR AND FEMININITY

On January 3, 1999, hair, in relationship to black women, made prime time again on the ABC weekly one-hour drama *The Practice*. The show focuses on a group of attorneys in a Boston law firm. In this particular episode, Lucy, the white female receptionist in her early twenties, asks the black female attorney, Rebecca, if she's a lesbian. Rebecca, somewhat puzzled, replies no, but wonders why anyone would assume she is a lesbian. Lucy replies, "With that rump and no guy in your life, and that crop-cut butchy-do hair [I just assumed you were a lesbian]." Rebecca commences to wonder if the reason she doesn't get asked out is because she "looks butch." Though Rebecca's femininity is marked through her shapely posterior, which is loaded with racialized images of Black women's bodies, her hair becomes the ultimate marker of both her womanhood and sexuality. Ideas about the relationship between hair, femininity, and sexuality, as well as images of beauty and male perceptions of femininity,

surfaced as the women and girls addressed the question of whether hair is associated with femininity in any way.

Several of the women explained how long hair is associated with femininity and how their beliefs have been nurtured through the mainstream media or other external forces. For example, Pearl, a 45-year-old college counselor, explained that she felt most sexy with long hair:

PEARL: Oh I have [associated hair with femininity]. I think the sexiest hairstyle was for me, and this could come from advertisements, television, anywhere, was when my hair was longer and it was piled on top of my head and I would always have little ringlets on the side. And that could also be from my southern background and that's how southern women wore their hair a long time ago. It could stem from my mom. I'm not exactly sure where those images come from but I would look in the mirror and I would see how I look and say, "God, that is sexy, that looks gorgeous."

Pearl also associated her perception of long hair with her southern roots and mother, but still questioned how she learned what is feminine or sexy. Aria, a 30-year-old undergraduate student, also explained the relationship between long hair, femininity, and constructions of beauty but unlike Pearl, Aria perceived this relationship through gender and racial readings of hair:

ARIA: Oh please, yes. If I said no I'd be lying because for years we have been inundated with magazine pictures of white women and their beautiful bodies and their long flowing locks. We have seen commercials, they're [white women] in the magazine ads. You see them in school flippin' their hair all through the classroom. I mean I sit in class and I see these women changing their hairstyles in a fifty-minute class at least four different times, you know. It's like come on. We have romance novels that accentuate the long, silken tresses so there's so many different mediums that portray [long] hair as beautiful, as feminine, as silky. And then if you have a lack of hair, then your femininity sometimes is questioned.

Aria pointed to the white women on TV, in magazines, and in romance novels with long, flowing hair as representative of femininity in U.S. society. Therefore, femininity is not merely associated with long hair as described by Pearl but with white women. Aria made a connection to the historical construction of womanhood, also known as the "cult of the lady" or the "cult of true womanhood" that represented 19th century U.S. Victorian society (Giddings 1984). Similar to Aria's construction of femininity that does not include black women, this was also the case with the cult of true womanhood. Given that the cult was based on a socioeconomic class hierarchy,[4] as well as racist and sexist ideologies, there was no place for black women regardless of class status in the definition of "true" womanhood.

Aria ends by stating that if a woman lacks hair, her femininity is questioned. This idea was common among the women. They associated their understanding of what short hair means in relationship to sexuality and masculinity. Dianne, a 50-year-old retired material handler, explained that an understanding of what it means to be male and female is embedded in readings of hair length. She also presented a different way of approaching the image of long flowing hair among black women:

DIANNE: Oh yeah. Right or wrong, you'll say stuff like that's a feminine cut, that's not a feminine cut, or whatever. I think to the extent that you have this long flowing hair that's perceived as very feminine. And the shorter you go, the less feminine it seems to be. So I definitely think that there's some association with that. And the whole interesting thing with the long hair [is] that [it] has some tie back to mainstream culture because not a lot of people in our community have this flowing long hair, but that's defined as being feminine. So when [women] go really short, [people say] that looks too mannish or something. My sister got her hair cut really short one time and she was like, "oh now people are going to think that I look like a boy or something."

In Dianne's explanation of the relationship between femininity and hair, she presented a scale in which long hair (feminine) and short hair (masculine) exists at the extremes. "Mannish" is associated with "looking like a boy" and long, flowing hair becomes a powerful feminine trait. However, Dianne questioned placing

the image of long flowing hair among black people outside of black communities when she stated that based on her observations, there is not a critical mass of black folk who have long flowing hair. The more telling issue is how black people in general, and black women in particular, understand these meanings and how ideas that link long hair to femininity are actually acted out. In fact Indigo, a 28-year-old independent filmmaker and teacher, explained how her decision to grow dreadlocks has allowed her to fulfill the dream of having long hair.

INDIGO: I think certainly. I've just begun to take a look at the issue of dreadlocks because I look at myself and all my life I wanted to have long hair and now I get to have it with dreadlocks. The longer I let it grow I can have this long, flowing hair. Of course it won't look like Cheryl Tiegs's hair or, you know, Farah Fawcett's, but it will be my own hair.

Although similar to Aria's observation that white women's hair is the standard of long, flowing hair, Indigo sees length as outweighing texture. She demonstrated her perception of femininity through hair, and although she recognizes the problem in reinforcing the belief that long hair characterizes femininity, she challenged mainstream standards of beauty through the length of her dreadlocks. Although she doesn't have the stuff, in terms of texture and color, as do Tiegs and Fawcett, she does possess the feminine trait, long hair. Thus, Indigo's reading of hair permits black women to sit at the table of femininity, despite historical constructions of what constitutes womanhood and, therefore, beauty. But the desire to have long hair relates to perceptions of what is considered feminine and it is associated with white women. That is, even with long dreadlocks, the model of long hair, and therefore femininity, is white women like Cheryl Tiegs and Farah Fawcett.

Indigo also explained how shaving her head and having short hair shaped her understanding about hair and femininity. Like other women, she discussed the relationship between sexuality or perceived sexuality with hair, particularly in relationship to lesbianism.

INDIGO: For women, you know, it is a very important part of your appearance. Your face, your hair. I mean you can still be feminine and have no hair on your head. But you know, we have these judgments that only certain women can pull that off. I mean actually be bald, and still be considered feminine. I know when I shaved off [my hair or the] many times I've had my hair short, I was trying to compensate with earrings and all this kind of stuff. Trying not to wear as many pants because I felt like I was going to be, you know, categorized as a dyke, or you know, just deemed unattractive.

Cheryl, Jean, Kaliph, and Barbara[5] made similar comments in linking hair to sexuality, as well as being masculine:

CHERYL: Yeah, I think it is, unfortunately. I cut my hair [short] [and] the day I did it I went out to a club with my girl [in the nonromantic sense]. It wasn't that crowded, so we were kinda hangin' out together and I think we went on the dance floor. We weren't even really dancing together but we were, you know, dancing without partners and somebody came up to me and asked me if like we were together as like a lesbian couple. And she [my friend] wears dreads. And I was like, it's the hair, isn't it?

JEAN: Oh yeah, definitely. So you know, especially in this town [San Francisco Bay Area, California] people see a haircut and they say, oh, dyke.

KALIPH: Yes, definitely yes because, and now I'm thinking in terms of length and lack of length. I hear one of the concerns among my friends who wear their hair short and natural, that there is sometimes a misperception around sexuality like, oh you must be a lesbian if you wear your hair like that. And by definition if you're a lesbian that somehow there's a lack of femininity, you know, you're trying to be a man. You're trying to be male, masculine. So I think there is something about hair, particularly length of hair, that speaks to being feminine and being a woman.

BARBARA: In my view, no. But some men will see a woman with short hair, real short hair, and will think negatively. [Like] a butch cut. I've heard that.

Words such as "butch" and "dyke" describe how ideas about sexuality can be read through hair. Sexual identities are often placed on individuals based on

hair, which is why Cheryl concluded that it was her short haircut and her friend's dreadlocks that made others think they were a lesbian couple on the dance floor. Kaliph even shared that she has black female friends with close-cropped and natural hair that are concerned with being perceived as lesbian. Kaliph explained that hair length is related not only to sexuality but also to female attractiveness. For example, when Indigo compensated for the lack of hair on her head, she did so by accentuating what she understood as feminine. It was Indigo's concern with being labeled a lesbian and therefore unfeminine that guided her practice of wearing big earrings and more skirts and dresses. In fact, as if in a dialogue with Indigo, Mrs. Franklin, a 70-year-old retired instructor's assistant, supported this reading of hair and femininity:

MRS. FRANKLIN: Yes, I do [think hair is associated with femininity]. Because I like to see women with hair. Most women when they have their hair short, [they] got to get up in the morning [and start] puttin' on make-up, puttin' on earrings and all this kind of stuff so people won't take a second look and say, "Is that a man or a lady?"

Even though Mrs. Franklin appeared to be making a presumption that women with short hair have to highlight their femininity, her thoughts resonate in Indigo's personal account of her insecurities about how her womanhood, in relationship to sexuality, would be read. What Mrs. Franklin and Indigo demonstrate is that black women understand that femininity cannot be reduced to one thing. Although hair is important in black women's understanding of what constitutes femininity, it is not the only marker. However, their comments also contradict their understanding of a more complicated reading of femininity because if a black woman has long hair, it is not necessary for her to "play up" her femininity by adorning her body in ways that are defined as "feminine." Even if hair is only one of many markers of femininity, or lack thereof, it is definitely one of the most powerful.

Habiba is a 50-year-old writer and teacher. In her reading of the relationship between hair and femininity, she also discussed long hair but used the example of (black) men wearing dreads as indicative of femininity. Femininity is still read through long hair, but

Habiba challenged the belief that only women possess feminine characteristics when they have long hair. She also *explicitly* stated that hair is associated with femininity *and* sexuality:

HABIBA: [Hair is associated with femininity] and sexuality. People often times have their hands in each others hair, pubic [for example]. So [hair] is very, very sensual. Very, very feminine. And I think men growing the long hair, men with dreads, are also activating that. What is it? They're activating the feminine side. Yes, yes, yes. For men to have the long hair and the dreads. Oh, that's incredible.

Habiba also provided a different view of the sexual nature of hair. Her reading of the relationship between hair and sexuality involves sensuality. Although her discussion supports how long hair is associated with femininity, Habiba's perception of what it means to be masculine is not questioned when she sees black men with long hair. Unlike the explanations of what it means for a woman to wear particular short hairdos[6] that are perceived as male "do's" Habiba questioned static notions of gender identities for women and men even as she supported the idea that long hair is associated with femininity. However it is Semple's critique of gender readings of hair (she is a 22-year-old undergraduate student), like that posed by Habiba's, that view long hair as feminine, that present a challenge to how gender is socially constructed. Unlike other women, Semple discussed this matter within the context of black males and how their hairstyling practices relate to how they are perceived:

SEMPLE: Is hair associated with femininity? I mean, I can see where we've maybe been socialized to think certain hairstyles [are feminine]. [The artist formally known as] Prince is always thought of as being out the box because he wants to wear a perm and a short cut. Michael Jackson got a little bob cut and people wanted to feminize that whole image. But at the same time, a brother can grow locks down his back and still be seen as extremely masculine. I mean brothers are wearing braids now and people are still [associating certain hairstyles with femininity]. I mean there's an element of "gang society" who walks around with permed hair and curls in their hair.

Unlike Habiba, Semple sees long dreadlocks worn by black men as indicative of masculinity, not femininity. Styles or lengths that are perceived as feminine do not necessarily question the masculinity or sexuality of black men. Semple's discussion of femininity as being read through the hairstyling practices of black men provided a different lens from which to view how black women understand gender through their ideas about hair. Although Semple discussed the hairstyling practices of Michael Jackson and The Artist as influencing their feminization, it is in her discussion of gang culture and the hairstyling practices among younger black males, particularly those in urban areas, that undoubtedly influence and have been influenced by hip-hop culture and rap music, that she contested feminine constructions of hair. Although I am in no way suggesting that rap artist Snoop Dog is a gangster, his hairstyling practices sheds light on Semple's critique. When Snoop appeared on the MTV Music Awards show in New York City a few years ago his hair was freshly straightened with lots of "Shirley Temple" curls. A year or two later, he was on the same awards show with straightened hair that touched his shoulders. Despite Snoop's hairstyling practices that imitate popular hairstyling practices by (Black) women, his "manhood" is not called into question. Like other younger black males who are straightening their hair, wearing braids and cornrows, as well as barrettes and rubber bands [in] their hair, Snoop is still seen as masculine. In a recent DJ Quik music video "Youz a Gangsta," Snoop appears with individual braids with beads dangling elegantly at the end of each braid. DJ Quik's hairstyle changes from cornrows to a straightened style by the end of the video. In another recent video, "Thug Mentality," rap artist Krayzie Bone appears with beautiful cornrows, and one of his posse members stands by his side with the same type of braided and beaded style as Snoop in DJ Quik's video. The video represents the life of a thug, with car chases and gambling rounding out the message of the video. Despite their hairdos, in both of these videos, the masculinity and sexuality of the main characters are never questioned because they are gangstas and thugs. This was true in the 1970s as well within the urban pimp culture scene. No one challenged Ron O'Neal's masculinity in the blaxploitation film *Super Fly*. If anything, he was hyper-masculinized and seen as the perfect example of a "brother's brother." That is, a man's man. He had women, money, sharp clothes, a nice apartment, and a fancy car. And he had straightened ("fly") hair.

What Semple's observation suggests is that gender identity is not static, but given the comments by other women who addressed the relationship between hair and femininity, a nonstatic or even a cross-reading of gender does not occur when women's hairstyling practices resemble those that are considered masculine. Whereas all black men are not labeled as feminine or gay when they sport hairdos that are perceived as feminine, when black women wear their hair close-cropped, for example, they are constructed as being unfeminine, unattractive, masculine, and lesbian. As Indigo and Mrs. Franklin's comments demonstrate above, women have to play up their femininity in other ways.

CONCLUSION: FEMININITY, HAIR, AND GLOBALIZATION

Hair still matters, and though differences arise in different cultural and political contexts, for women, hair is never *simply* arrested within the aesthetic. Though global-studies scholars are raising important questions concerning globalization and its relationship to not merely Western societies, but the entire planet, hair went global a while back. "Through the seventies, stock imported from Europe was the only hair product sold to what the industry calls the 'Caucasian Trade.' Now that the European market is drying up, Asian hair goes to all races, in most cases, unless specially ordered. When you buy human hair in lengths for weaving and braiding, in wigs, and as male-replacement product, what you buy nine times out often is Asian hair" (Jones, 1994, p. 282). The average woman from Asia growing her hair for profit lives in poverty. It is an eerie feeling to realize that though these women will most likely remain living in a cycle of poverty, their hair exists within a global context.

Hair has gone global culturally as well. During the post–September 11 era, hair matters continue to make news, though within a different global and cultural context than what went down with Venus Williams in Australia in 1999. Consider the eyes of the Western/Christian world not merely on the Taliban restrictions placed on Afghani women, but also on the wider Islamic faith's teachings concerning the presentation of the female body. The hijab (veil) that covers the hair continues to be a source of great debate within and outside feminist circles. With the downfall of the Taliban government, some Afghani women proudly shed the all-encompassing burka (full body veil). However, many women continue to follow Afghan culture by continuing to wear the burka. As feminists, we would be remiss if we discounted the views of Islamic women outside and inside of Afghanistan who continue to don the hijab. Certainly, the issue of covering women's bodies among Muslims cannot be disengaged from patriarchy and the state, but as my research on U.S. black women conveys, women must be given a platform to speak, to theorize, about *their* existence from *their* various standpoints. As 22-year-old Mahbobo Sidiqi stated as she and the other women shed their burkas after entering a classroom at the University of Kabul to sit for college entrance exams along with men in February 2000, "My head is free. . . . No more headaches" (*Miami Herald*, February 7, 2002). Indeed, hair still matters, and it matters for women of color in profound ways as exemplified by what we can learn by recent events in the global culture.

ACKNOWLEDGMENT

I am indebted to Hung Cam Thai for his insightful comments and unwavering support. He is one of the finest *feminists* that I know.

NOTES

1. Ingrid Banks, *Hair Matters: Beauty, Power, and Black Women's Consciousness* (New York: New York University Press, 2000).
2. See Lauryn Hill's "Doo Wop (That Thing)," the Fugees' "Nappy Hair," and The Lost Boyz album "Love, Peace, and Nappiness."
3. See Paulette Caldwell's (1991) discussion of these cases.
4. For example, poor and working-class women, regardless of race, were not viewed as "true women." Those women who had to work outside of the home for economic necessity were excluded from the definition of a lady.
5. Cheryl is a 22-year-old graduate student, Jean is a 37-year-old architect, Kaliph is a 28-year-old graduate student, and Barbara is a 49-year-old Administrative Assistant II.
6. Not all short hairdos worn by women are viewed as unfeminine; what is meant here is particularly those hairdos that resemble traditional men's hairdos (e.g., short, cropped, buzz cuts).

REFERENCES

Banks, Ingrid. 2000. *Hair Matters: Beauty, Power and Black Women's Consciousness*. New York: University Press.

Benton Rushing, Andrea. 1988. "Hair-Raising." *Feminist Studies* 14(2) (Summer): 325–335.

Bordo, Susan. 1993. *Unbearable Weight: Feminism, Western Culture, and the Body*. Berkeley: University of California Press.

Brownmiller, Susan. 1984. *Femininity*. New York: London Press/Simon & Schuster.

Byrd, Ayana D., and Lori L. Tharps. 2001. *Hair Story: Untangling the Roots of Black Hair in America*. New York: St. Martin's Press.

Caldwell, Paulette M. 1991. "A Hair Piece: Perspectives on the Intersection of Race and Gender." *Duke Law Review*: 365–397.

Caraway, Nancie. 1991. *Segregated Sisterhood: Racism and the Politics of American Feminism*. Knoxville: University of Tennessee Press.

Cleage, Pearl. 1993. "Hairpeace: Requirement for Afro-American Women Writers to Discuss Hair." *African-American Review* 27(1) (Spring): 37.

Craig, Maxine. 2002. *Ain't I a Beauty Queen? Black Women, Beauty, and the Politics of Race*. New York: Oxford University Press.

———. 1997. "The Decline and the Fall of the Conk; or, How to Read a Process." *Fashion Theory: The Journal of Dress, Body and Culture* 1(4) (December): 399–419.

Davis, Angela Y. 1994. "Afro Images: Politics, Fashion, and Nostalgia." *Critical Inquiry* 21(1) (Autumn): 37.

DuCille, Ann. 1996 *Skin Trade*. Cambridge: Harvard University Press.

Eilberg-Schwartz, Howard, and Wendy Doniger, eds. 1995. *Off with Her Head! The Denial of Woman's Identity in Myth, Religion, and Culture*. Berkeley: University of California Press.

Freud, Sigmund. 1922. "Medusa's Hair." In *Collected Papers*, 105–106. London: Hogarth Press and the Institute of Psychoanalysis.

George, Lynell. 1998. "The Natural Look." *The Los Angeles Times*, August 6, E1.

Gibson, Aliona. 1995. *Nappy: Growing Up Black and Female in America*. New York: Harlem River Press.

Giddings, Paula. 1984. *When and Where I Enter: The Impact of Black Women on Race and Sex in America*. New York: Bantam Books.

Grier, William H., and Price M. Cobbs. 1968. *Black Rage*. New York: Basic Books.

Harris, Juliette, and Pamela Johnson. 2001. *Tenderheaded: A Comb-Bending Collection of Hair Stories*. New York: Pocket Books.

Hill Collins, Patricia. 1990. *Black Feminist Thought: Knowledge, Consciousness, and the Politics of Empowerment*. London: HarperCollins.

hooks, bell. 1988. "Straightening Our Hair." *Z Magazine* (Summer): 14–18.

Jagger, Alison, and Susan Bordo. 1989. *Gender/Body/Knowledge: Feminist Reconstructions of Knowing*. Newark, NJ: Rutgers University Press.

Jones, Lisa. 1994. *Bulletproof Diva: Tales of Race, Sex, and Hair*. New York: Doubleday.

Kelley, Robin D. G. 1997. "Nap Time: Historicizing the Afro." *Fashion Theory: The Journal of Dress, Body and Culture* 1(4) (December): 339–351.

Mercer, Kobena. 1990. "Black Hair/Style Politics." In *Out There: Marginalization and Contemporary Cultures*, Russell Ferguson et al., eds., 247–264. New York: The New Museum of Contemporary Art and MIT Press.

Morrow, Willie. 1973. *400 Years Without a Comb*. San Diego: Black Publishers of San Diego.

Norsworthy, Kym. 1991. "Hair Discovery." *Real News*, 2(1): 3, 8.

Okazawa-Rey, Margo, et al. 1986. "Black Women and the Politics of Skin Color and Hair." *Women's Studies Quarterly* 14 (1 and 2) (Spring/Summer): 13–14.

Patterson, Orlando. 1982. *Slavery and Social Death: A Comparative Study*. Cambridge: Harvard University Press.

Rooks, Noliwe. 1996. *Hair Raising: Beauty, Culture, and African American Women*. New Brunswick, NJ: Rutgers University Press.

Shipp, E. R. 1988. "Are Cornrows Right for Work?" *Essence*, February, 109–110.

Tyler, Bruce M. 1990. "Black Hairstyles: Cultural and Socio-political Implications." *The Western Journal of Black Studies* 14(4): 235–250.

Wade-Gayles, Gloria. 1993. "The Making of a Permanent Afro." In *Pushed Back to Strength: A Black Woman's Journey Home*, 133–158. Boston: Beacon Press.

Walker, Alice. 1988. "Oppressed Hair Puts a Ceiling on the Brain." In *Living by the Word*, 69–74. Orlando: Harcourt Brace Jovanovich.

"I See the Same Ho": Video Vixens, Beauty Culture, and Diasporic Sex Tourism

Every other video . . .
I see the same ho

> —*Tupac (featuring Nate Dogg,*
> *YGD Tha Top Dawg), "All About U"*

Watching the videos, you see the long curly hair
[and] think, "Man that would be nice to have some
long, curly hair."

> —*Sela, eighteen-year-old undergraduate*

Brazilian women are usually desirable, as often
women of mixed ethnicities are. . . . Our leaders
should make a law demanding intercultural
breeding to fill our planet . . . thus ending all the
world's problems.

> —*askmen.com, Top 99 Most Desirable*
> *Women 2005*

When Michelle "Micki" Burks decided to take on the role of eye candy in the now-defunct rap-reggae group Ruff Neck Sound System's music videos "Stick by Me" and "Luv Bump," little did she know that her decision would land her years later in the category of "video ho." Her performances in the music videos did not involve provocative backside acrobatics, but her video persona in "Luv Bump" is interestingly transmogrified into a "hoochie" by the video's end due to fast-living and hustling men. Shot in New York, the video aired in 1995 on the Rachel-hosted Black Entertainment Television format *Caribbean Rhythms*. At 5'8" with long brown highlighted hair and honey-toned skin, Micki attended the prestigious Berklee School of Music in Boston from 1986 to 1990. A soprano with a superb vocal range, she toured Europe and Japan, releasing an album called *Inca,* and then took up modeling with Models, Inc. in

Boston as a side gig until her music career took off. She met the Ruff Neck crew in the Boston music scene. Her then-boyfriend, Chris, was a well-known producer who had teamed with such venerable acts as the late Donnie Hathaway's daughter Lahla.

When asked about the moniker "video ho," she emphatically rejects any description of her experiences as degrading. She does nonetheless lament the portrayals of women in hip hop videos of late, stating that, "It is unnecessary. They don't have to treat the women like that." When asked if she would work in the emerging lucrative music video industry today if the opportunity presented itself again, the still-lithe thirty-six-year-old says with a laugh, "Yeah, if I were thinner [and] as a model not a 'video ho.'"

While sales in the music industry continue a downward spiral that even the gestalt of rapper 50 Cent's *The Massacre* (which moved over one million units in just under four days) cannot break, the music video DVD has emerged as a boon to the recording industry. In an April 7, 2004, press release, Jay Berman, Chairman of IFPI (International Federation of the Phonographic Industry), an affiliate of the Recording Industry Association of America (RIAA), the organization responsible for the world's largest music market, noted that music video sales are rapidly becoming an important revenue stream for the industry. The music video, popularized by the launch of cable television stations such as Black Entertainment Television (BET), Music Television (MTV), and Video Hits 1 (VH1), represents the lion's share of formatting for these stations. Launched in 1980, 1981, and 1985 respectively, the first popular music video to debut on MTV was The Buggles's "Video Killed the Radio Star," a video that predicted rather prematurely that the music video genre would supplant the radio. Music videos have exploded, with budgets as large as some indie film projects, more developed narratives and sets, and digital technology, which has also allowed for a clearer picture and a larger than life celluloid image.[1] The hip hop music video in particular also provides brand product placement with a bumping beat. Like a four- to six-minute advertisement, the music video DVD sells music and the fabulous lifestyle signified by whatever material acquisitions are worn (or not), driven, or drank within its frames—all at a general sticker price between thirteen and eighteen dollars. Borrowing from cultural critic Greg Tate's observations on hip hop culture in "Nigs R Us, or How Blackfolk Became Fetish Objects," the hip hop video has "collapsed art, commerce, and interactive technology into one mutant animal."[2] Similar to the film industry, which ties its potential box office take to A-list stars as well as well-known directors, the directors of music videos have become a highly sought after group, particularly veterans such as Hype Williams, Paul Hunter, Little X, and Chris Robinson.[3] Recording artists recognize that the music video can make or break a career, and heavy rotation on MTV, BET, and VH1 all but guarantees break-out success. Indeed, 70 percent of BET's programming, the go-to station for urban hip hop generationers, is music videos and infomercials. And the cable station reaches some eighty million homes.[4]

In "All About U," a Tupac Shakur, Nate Dogg, and YDG Tha Top Dawg collaboration, the rap artists bond over their disdain for "video ho's" and "groupies" who they encounter in every city they tour and video they see. Like Micki, many of these women are singers, professional models, dancers, and aspiring actresses, earning their rent, tuition monies, or commercial exposure for a day's work on a shoot. And some dance and shake for free for their five minutes of fame, jumping in front of the camera when Young Buck or any one of the St. Lunatics roll up on a North Nashville or North St. Louis block with a film crew in tow. As Atlanta hip hop industry insider and videographer Tiona McClodden suggests, "Many of the background video models use their bodies as demos because they know that much of what is shot will be left on the floor of the editing room. They have one opportunity. If they do something provocative enough to stand out, they anticipate that the shot just may remain in the final video."[5] That the impact of these sexually suggestive videos is undeniably regressive in terms of gender politics and young girls and women's self-identity is revealed in a 2003 year-long study conducted by the Center for AIDS Research (CFAR) at Emory University.

Tracking 522 Alabama girls' hip hop video consumption and behaviors, the study revealed that a higher consumption of hip hop videos corresponded negatively with higher frequency of sexually transmitted diseases, alcohol and drug abuse (60 percent), and multiple sex partners (twice as likely).

* * *

But just as important as the complex motivations behind young women's suggestive performances in hop-hop videos—rumps moving with the alacrity of a jackhammer, hips gyrating like a belly dancer on amphetamines, limbs akimbo, mouths agape in a perpetual state of the orgasmic "oh"—is the repetition of particular ideals of femininity. Hip hop is now as much about images as it is skills and beats. That the vast majority of the young women in these videos are either fairer-skinned, ethnically mixed, or of indeterminate ethnic/racial origins, with long, straight, or curly hair would suggest that along with the stereotype of hypersexuality and sexual accessibility, a particular type of beauty is offered up as ideal. In some respects, the majority of these women represent what historian Tiffany Patterson calls "ascriptive mulattas," that is, those whose physical beauty transcends chart, acteristics such as darker hues, full lips, and the like, historically prefigured as less than ideal (non-European). The "mulatta" figure, a pejorative term if ever there was one, is typically depicted as tragic because of her "in-between" racial status. Yet the "mulatta" has also been deemed in literary and film annals as the most ideal in the arena of feminine beauty, and the secretly longed for in the heterosexual marketplace of desire. This status comes about precisely because of her mixed-race heritage involving some configuration of "black" and "white," which in the European and American male imagination signals the perfect blending of skillfulness in matters of sex (read: black) and physical beauty (read: white).

The physical appeal to both white and black men of Gabrielle Union, Ciara, Beyoncé, and Tyra Banks falls into ascriptive mulatta territory, as did that of Lena Horne and Dorothy Dandridge—just ask the men at askmen.com where Union, Ciara, Banks, and Beyoncé are ranked among the 2006 edition of the top ninety-nine most desirable women. On any given segment of MTV's *Top Twenty*, or BET's *Rap City* and *106 & Park*, roughly 70 percent of the videos feature superbly toned, nubile, hybrid flesh. One could certainly argue that practically all seemingly black flesh in the

"New World" is a hybrid given the history of transracial contact. But it is precisely because of the enormous *range* of blackness (as a result of consensual and nonconsensual) sex that the incredibly narrow prototype of beauty is even more troubling.

As writer Kevin Powell argues in *Who's Gonna Take the Weight,* hip hop generationers still do not fully appreciate the range of black women's beauty. Even the fallout in the hip hop community from the 2002 Grammy Awards ceremony over Alicia Key's multiple Grammy wins over India Arie hinged unfortunately (and mistakenly I would add) for some on the issue of color. Another example is the ruckus over the fall 2004 season of *America's Next Top Model (ANTM),* a reality show that attempts to demystify high-fashion modeling by demonstrating that models, while born with certain assets like height, are primarily talent-development projects and that "can-do" attitudes go the distance. The show is undeniably in the service of beauty culture, which in general has been less accepting, if not hostile, to black women. However, in the 2004 season *ANTM* was UPN's highest-rated program among women ages eighteen to forty-nine as well as teens. As the network's newest cash cow, it was also one of the top ten programs among African American adults, and the highest-rated reality show among African Americans. Its host, übermodel Tyra Banks, consistently emphasizes personality over a particular "look." Nonetheless, the conclusion of the fall 2004 season caused viewer squabbles regarding the hair and skin color of the final two contestants, Yaya DaCosta Johnson and Eva Pigford. In an interview with *TV Guide*'s Daniel Coleridge, the runner-up, Yaya, a Brown University graduate, responded to the interviewer's perception of her "look" as "Afrocentric," a perception that may have contributed to her loss:

> I'm not Afrocentric, I'm just natural. But in this country, black women who don't straighten their hair with chemical processing are stereotyped and labeled. Not *all* black women with straight hair need chemical processing, but I would have to to achieve that look. Just because we don't straighten our hair doesn't mean we're trying to be anything else—we're being ourselves. If anything hurts me about that, it's that I wasn't allowed the luxury of being myself like the other girls were. Nobody asks Cassie, Ann or Amanda to be "less white." I'm used to having to defend my very being. That makes me a little sensitive.[6]

DaCosta Johnson's browner skin and unprocessed hair moved her into an Afrocentric space when compared to Eva Pigford's African American girl-next-door look with chemically straightened hair, light eyes, and lighter hue.

DaCosta Johnson's predicament on *Top Model* raises old questions in this new era on assimilation, identity, and beauty. And yet, the mixing bowl with a wee bit of nutmeg and cinnamon standard of beauty endorsed ostensibly by American culture (more specifically on Madison Avenue) parallels the shifting ideas of beauty in hip hop videos that are, some would argue, necessarily still derivative of a white ideal.

In "Generation E.A.: Ethnically Ambiguous," a feature in the Fashion & Style section of *The New York Times,* advertising executives and fashion magazine editors offered running commentaries that ranged from disquieting to just plain dim on marketing trends to "tweens," teens, and hip hop generationers in both the mainstream and high-end marketplace: "Today what's ethnically neutral, diverse, or ambiguous has tremendous appeal"; "What is perceived as good, desirable, successful is often a face whose heritage is hard to pin down"; "We're seeing more of a desire for the exotic, left-of-center beauty. . . . [It] represents the new reality of America, which includes considerable mixing. . . . It's the changing face of American beauty."[7] That racial categories are social constructs rather than biological realities—though this does not alter the lived experiences of those who occupy those categories—that "considerable" "race" mixing is not "a new reality" but has been historically widespread in the United States, and that America is not as "white" as it believes itself to be has been duly noted since at least the nineteenth century by writers and activists such as Frances Ellen Harper Watkins in her novel *Iola Leroy.* Even in *The Birth of a Nation,* a racist film posing as an American cinematic masterpiece, racial amalgamation is a core preoccupation because of its prevalence. The contemporary scholarly writing of philosophers of race Kwame Anthony Appiah and Naomi Zack are only a few examples of our awareness of the power of social constructs. Both Appiah and Zack have argued that "race" and therefore categories of race are biologically non-existent, dishonest, and in bad faith. That we as a culture cling to them relates more to our desires to enact and maintain social, political, and economic powers and privileges.

In effect, racial categories are themselves racist. In her 1993 book *Race and Mixed Race,* Zack argues presciently for the category of *gray*, an almost uncanny predecessor to "ethnically ambiguous." Therefore, the excited tone of discovery evoked in the "Generation E. A." article seems more than a bit out of touch. The rhetoric that still situates whiteness at the center of American beauty culture and darker hues on this schematic shifting to the left (one wonders what right of center beauty looks like) quite simply reinforces a hierarchy of beauty, as well as the notion of fixed racial categories. Indeed, ethnic ambiguity does not guarantee racial ambiguity, particularly in relationship to those possessing "African" ethnicities and origins. One may be ethnically mixed (ambiguous) but racially marked as black.

Despite the hubbub about Generation E.A., editors and ad executives admit that whiteness continues to dominate the beauty and fashion industries. Where does, pray tell, such a hierarchy leave Generation Non-E.A. (non–ethnically ambiguous) black women? In her widely read book *Beauty Myth*, Naomi Wolf relates how the beauty industry essentially creates angst in women regarding their choices—Yaya DeCosta Johnson, for example. While not a treatise against the beauty industry and practices of adornment (though some critics have reductively read the book as Wolf's feminist cri de coeur against lipstick wearing), *The Beauty Myth* in fact argues for something very basic: a women's right to choose. Wolf makes the radical assertion that women should choose how they want to look, without fear of employment discrimination, or of being castigated as unfeminine, or of being subjected to the litany of other charges leveled at those whose beauty practices (or lack thereof) run counter to dominant ideas about what it means to be a woman.

Women who choose not to indulge in beauty practices are often disadvantaged and made to feel guilty for their lack of conformity in a culture that overemphasizes physical appearance. Simultaneously women who embrace beauty products and their images still "second guess" themselves and are subject to descriptions such as "high maintenance" and "not natural." And those women who embrace beauty culture and also fall outside the current rage over Generation E.A. or Ascriptive Mulattas are left to endlessly negotiate a maze of images and ideas that are not especially affirming and seem, at each turn, to lead to a dead end.

* * *

As with the behavioral implications for hip hop video consumption, the collision between hip hop culture and beauty culture, the marketing and packaging of the "same" video girl who resembles the high-fashion model who resembles the latest Hollywood "It" girl, also has a clear and deleterious impact on what young black female consumers come to identify as desirable. And the desire to be desirable seems especially costly and laborious for young black women, as the product-hawking, image-projecting hip hop video pumps cash into the mainstream and hip hop's multibillion-dollar fashion and beauty industries. In effect, what young black women cannot be, they now buy.

Who can forget the purchased artifices of Lil' Kim? Her "so unpretty" motivations for doffing and donning colored contact lens, purported skin-lightening procedures, nose contourings, platinum hair, breast augmentation, and liposuction. The visceral pain she articulated watching her Svengali-lover-father figure and public and very private abuser, the Notorious B.I.G., marry the lighter-skinned, fairer-maned hip hop/R&B singer Faith Evans nine days after meeting her.[8] Or the cracks of insecurity seeping from her admission: "Halle Berry, Sally Richardson, Stacy Dash, Jada Pinkett? I used to wish I looked like them motherfuckers!"?[9] On the question of breast augmentation, she says, "I laughed at first. But then I went home and really thought about it. I went to the best, most expensive doctor available, but that was the most pain I ever felt in my life."[10]

As with Lil' Kim, the overwhelming majority of us black and Latina women offer our labor in a marketplace—one that still does not pay us equally—in order to purchase some happiness through beauty.[11] (The median weekly earnings of black women who worked full time in 2001 was $451 compared with $521 for white women, $518 for black men, and $694 for white men; these figures are for non-college-educated black women; in 2004, college-educated black women, roughly two million, outearned both the white women and Latinas.) Using data from over three thousand households surveyed by the Department of Commerce, marketers and corporations have determined that black women, with their increasing income, have the most influence on the growth in African American spending. Between 2001 and 2002, our spending on personal care products increased (by 18 percent), as did our expenditures on women's apparel and footwear (2 percent and 13 percent, respectively). Our generosity with ourselves was rivaled only by our generosity with others, as gift spending spiked by 155 percent.[12]

The July 2004 report released by *The U.S. Multicultural Women Market* suggests that the buying power of multicultural women (defined as African American, Asian American, and Hispanic American) will exceed $1 trillion by 2008 and African American women over eighteen years of age will keep the dominant share of the market. African American women's educational attainment is high; we are more confident and secure with ourselves, and one in four of us occupy professional or managerial positions. Yet, we are simultaneously least likely to be married (as our race loyalties tend to constrain our options) or even in fulfilling relationships with a female partner; dieting and exercise appear less of a concern while health risks are high. We are also very brand conscious, loyal, and receptive—or vulnerable, depending on your interpretation of the data—to media, and particularly to television.

Savvy marketers will continue to pitch products that seem to tap into our greatest strengths and deepest insecurities about beauty and desirability. Hair-care products accounted for $174 million of our disposable income in 2002.[13] Plastic surgery, once the strict domain of white women and a taboo subject, is now democratized and featured prominently in the same headline as the words "black or African American" in magazines and online portals such as *Essence, Newsweek,* and *AOL Black Voices* (though most African American women seek surgeries for breast reduction and tummy tucks). These spending trends on beauty and fashion have been chalked up to "African-American women hav[ing] finally just decided that it's time to love ourselves" by *Essence* beauty editor Miki Taylor.[14] While Asian American women also spend a great deal, more even, on fashion and beauty products and are just as brand conscious, they are also the leading consumers among women of financial services.[15] One wonders if our "loving ourselves" reflects our "security and confidence," or, given our marked receptivity to *all* media, our insecurity and self-doubt bred by the confluence of media, beauty, and hip hop culture? Shouldn't the slicing away, camouflage, and enhancement offered by plastic surgery and beauty products considered part of this new phenomenon of "loving ourselves" include a concomitant uptick in financial investments as well as diet- and exercise-related spending given our health risks? Purchased beauty is undeniably a depreciating asset, while health and financial solvency guarantees some degree of longevity. And yet, I am clearly aware that there are those hip hop generation women who would argue that if beauty enhancement lands you a "baller," it was money well spent.

In the end, despite all the hype about diversity and Generation E.A., hegemony prevails. Blondes, the stand-in for unadulterated whiteness, still have more fun. Generation E.A. comes in at quite a distant second, and Generation A.M. (Ascriptive Mulattas)—those left-of-center beauties—clinch third. Those of us who remain—the *un*aesthetically pleasing, racially marked plebeians, or Generation B (read: black)—anchor the bottom or the far left of the beauty schema, particularly with respect to mainstream culture.

Hip hop culture as represented through the "video vixens" and Madison Avenue collide on the beauty hierarchy in the ambiguous space between generations E.A. and A.M. And who determines the contours of this space? More often than not, it is black men. Besides sports—which has generated a cottage industry of books on the black male athlete—hip hop culture represents another cultural terrain dominated and shaped by black men. Certainly Erica Kennedy's hilarious debut novel *Bling!,* a tale of the hip hop industry, offers interesting commentary on black men as cultural brokers of desire who resemble modern-day Svengalis as they develop, control, and project what is desirable and equally cultivate the public's desire for E.A. and A.M. artists who nonetheless read "black."[16] In Kennedy's make-believe world that seamlessly channels the contradictions of hip hop culture, darker skin among women is a handicap to be overcome; dreaded, braided, or "happy to be nappy" hair are "no-no's"; and "big," as in body type, is definitely not beautiful.

Lest one get the impression that those women who self-identify as black and fall into the E.A. and A.M. categories of desirability do not also contend with demons not of their own making, they do. Idealization is often accompanied by alienation, "trophied" status, and petty jealousies. Anita Lewis, former Communications/Public Relations Liaison for Pennsylvania State Senator Vincent Hughes and one of *Philadelphia Business Journal's* "40 Under 40," admits that being a lighter-skinned black woman has its own challenges:

> The fighting began in middle school with other girls pulling my hair, trying to put glue in it, and taking swipes, with their fingernails, at my face. As a professional, there are those who think I have landed certain positions because of my looks. Undoubtedly, there are

those who may perceive me as less threatening, more acceptable. I cut my hair extremely short at one point in my career so that people, especially men, would take me seriously, stop fixating on my hair and listen to what I was saying. My looks may have allowed my foot in the door, but my talents and skills keep me there.[17]

Singer Beyoncé Knowles, part of a roundtable discussion with other professional black women featured in *Newsweek,* also spoke to these very issues of color and beauty and her experiences as a lighter-skinned black woman. Knowles, who is incidentally identified as part of "Generation E.A." in *The New York Times* article, ranked number eight on 2005's askmen.com's top ninety-nine, and somersaulted Jennifer Lopez off the "booty pedestal" with her "Bootylicious" anthem and appearance on *Q* magazine's cover with the headline, "The Ass that Shook the World," offered: "Well, I could complain about being light-skinned. But that's life. People judge you by the way you look, unfortunately. . . ."[18]

So while black men may have questionable standards of beauty for black women, they are not, unlike Madison Avenue, necessarily worshipping at the altar of white beauty. They linger rather, as I have suggested, somewhere between Generation E.A. and Generation A.M. That heterosexual black youth culture leans toward "left-of-center beauty" is a direct result of the political landscape, ideology, and social gains offered by both the civil rights and black power movements. While integration offered by the civil rights movement presented access to corridors, classrooms, and bedrooms heretofore inaccessible, the 1970s' slogan "Black Is Beautiful" carried over into the 1980s and helped shape the worldview of the hip hop generation. It is not so much that black is no longer beautiful but too familiar. The forbidden-fruit aura once enveloping white women has also been thoroughly demystified as they too avail themselves of the most hedonistic offerings of hip hop culture, ergo the pornographic videos *Girls Gone Wild* with Snoop Dogg and *Groupie Love* with G-Unit. Moreover, beauty culture's stoking of white women's obsession with thinness, the aim for 103 lbs. whether one is 5'1" or 5'10", disinvites the development of "junk in the trunk," those protuberant charms essentialized in hip hop culture. Most white women are left "assed out."

Besides breeding misogyny and sexism, a surprising ancillary effect of such black male privilege and

familiarity has been the desire for the unknown, the "exotic" feminine ideal. The ideal woman is indeed black-derived, curvy, and "thick," but she is "paprika'd" and salted with difference, as with the October 2004 Black-Irish-Cherokee-Asian "Eye Candy" centerfold in the hip hop magazine *XXL*, or December 2004's African-American-Egyptian-Brazilian "Eye Candy" spread. Beginning at opposite ends of the great chain of beauty's color spectrum, hip hop culture and mainstream beauty culture meet somewhere in the middle in their fetishization of ethnic brewing.

The desire for the unknown, the exotic and highly ethnically seasoned black woman of late has been satiated beyond U.S. borders—namely among the black diaspora in countries like Brazil. The mirror of Brazil is being reflected back on U.S. women. This latest "desire for the exotic," as the Generation E.A. article put it, then transcends not only "rigid social categories of race, class," but U.S. borders as well. Raquel Rivera has skillfully argued in *New York Ricans in the Hip-Hop Zone* that Latinas as the *buttapecans,* the *mamis,* have often served as the exotic detour in the predominantly black male world of hip hop. The interesting reality is that they too have now become part of "The Known World" (borrowing Edward P. Jones's Pulitzer Prize–winning novel's title). The search for the beautiful is now in the *favelas* (the ghettos) of Brazil. Hence it is no small surprise to see advertisements by Game, Inc., a company based out of Las Vegas, Nevada, for the porn collection *Hip-Hop Honeys: Brazil Boom Boom,* "with the bootylicious bodies that make Brazil a fantasy favorite for the hip hop generation" in "hip hop on a higher level" magazines like *XXL*.[19]

In some respects, hip hop generation African American men's latest fetish parallels Brazil's own fetishizing of racial admixture as embodied by the mulatta figure. In a country where a cliché on the order of "white woman to wed, mulatta to bed, black woman to work" is befitting, Alma Guillermoprieto, author of *Samba,* notes:

Mulatas are glorified sex fetishes, sanitized representations of what whites view as the savage African sex urge, but they are also, of course, tribute and proof of the white male's power: his sexual power, and his economic power, which allowed him to wrest the *mulata's* black mother away from her black partner. At the same time the *mulata* serves to perpetuate one of the myths that Brazilians hold most dear, that there is no racism in Brazil, that miscegenation has been natural and pleasant for both parties, that white people really, sincerely, do like black people. In fact, the aesthetic superiority accorded to light-skinned black women—*mulatas*—underlines the perceived ugliness of blacks before they have been "improved" with white blood. The white skin also serves to lighten a sexual force that in undiluted state is not only threatening but vaguely repulsive, and at the same time, the myth goes, irresistible.[20]

The fleshy hips, thighs, ample posterior, and thrust-forward breasts of the mulatta figure is offered as a sign of all things Brazilian, specifically Rio de Janeiro, as is Sugar Loaf, Corcovado (the Jesus Christ statue reigning majestically high above the city of Rio de Janeiro), the historic district of Lapa, Capoeira, and the *favelas*. As if taking cues from its northerly American neighborhoods, racial and ethnic brewing is celebrated but whiteness dominates the high-end billboards of Ipanema and the beauty industry. In interviewing a model talent scout for a May 2005 article on Brazil entitled "Beauty and the Beach," *Condé Nast Traveler* writer Julia Chapin uncovered that "right now what's hot are girls who have a European face but the body movements and attitude of a Latin." The talent scout admits that "dark-skinned girls from northern Brazil have a harder time getting work."[21]

The summer of 2003 brought the upbeat, radio-ready "Beautiful" collaboration between Snoop Dogg, Pharrell, and Uncle Charlie Wilson, formerly of the Gap Band. We all sang along in Pharrell's Marvin Gaye–esque falsetto, ignoring the first refrain offered by Snoop about "Long hair, wit'cha big fat booty." By the time Snoop arrived at, "Black and beautiful, you the one I'm choosin' / Hair long and black and curly like you're Cuban," some black women were singing, "No, No, No, No!" instead of "Yeah, Yeah, Yeah, Yeah!"—mocking the Pharrell and Charlie Wilson refrain. The heavily rotated Chris Robinson–directed video was shot on location in Brazil. Stunning because of the locale and the women, "Beautiful" the video provides a visual representation of the new black feminine ideal in hip hop culture with the charge to "Look far Southward!" to find it. Surrounded by a bevy of Brazilian beauties, Snoop and Pharrell move through this postcard-like sonata, showcasing the history of New World race mixing of imported African captives, indigenous Indians, and conquering Europeans. While some have argued that the video vixens were not

Brasilieras, the fact of the matter is that the video provides the illusion of an authentic Brazilian experience. The video has become perhaps the best advertisement the Brazilian travel and tourism industry could hope for in its recent attempts to tap into a specifically African American market.

Snoop is not the first hip hop artist to use Brazil and its women as backdrops, nor will he be the last. Indeed, southern rapper T.I. finds himself in Rio among frolicking women on Copacabana Beach in his 2006 "Why You Wanna" video. The Neptunes, the Pharrell Williams–Chad Hugo hit-making duo, acted in *Dude: We're Going to Rio*, the 2003 hip hop musical comedy directed by C. B. Harding. In this campy tale of love at first sight, Pharrell sees a travel poster for Brazil featuring a Brazilian woman with whom he falls in love, and he travels to Rio de Janeiro to find her. Ja Rule's video "Holla, Holla," directed by Hype Williams and from the 1999 CD *Venni Vetti Vicci*, broke ranks at the time of its release by featuring Brazilian women and shooting on location in Brazil. In an interview with AllHipHop .com, Ja Rule relates that

> At that point in Hip-Hop, it was still about your n*ggas in the videos with you. We flew out to Brazil, and it was magic instantly. We set up cameras, scouting ladies. There were mad beautiful chicks coming to the camera, and on the beach topless. All types of shit, man! I was extra amped! We turned the cameras on, and girls started flocking. We only brought one professional girl (Gloria Velez), and the rest were just girls from Brazil that wanted to get down.[22]

While "Holla, Holla" is an anthem to the rough-and-tumble life of thugdom, playin' bitches and poppin' snitches, "Beautiful" is purposely G-rated commercial fare, untarnished by bleeps; it is an ode to beauty by one of hip hop culture's legendary gangsta pimps, Snoop Dogg, a purveyor of style, a barometer for "what" and "who" is the "in" thing to do and screw.

When revolutionary writer Frantz Fanon wrote in his 1963 "handbook of the Black Revolution," *The Wretched of the Earth*, of "the pitfalls of national consciousness" and globalization with respect to developing nations and tourism, who would have imagined how prophetic his pronouncements were? And who would have thought that hip hop generation black men would join the Western bourgeois tourist "avid for the exotic . . . the beaches of Rio, the little Brazilian . . . girls . . ., [t]he banking magnates, the technocrats, and the big businessmen of the United States [who] have only to step onto a plane and they are wafted into subtropical climes, there for a space of a week or ten days to luxuriate in . . . delicious depravities"?[23] Despite, harrowing statistics about poverty, unemployment, incarceration, HIV/AIDS, and drug use, hip hop generation black men have been able to access, generate, and benefit from the unprecedented wealth that has made the United States the most powerful capitalist nation in the world.

The Selig Center for Economic Growth's survey *The Multicultural Economy 2004* reports that African Americans have enjoyed a steady rise in income, resulting in $723 billion in buying power as of September 2004, an increase of 3.9 percent over the $631 billion earned in 2002 as reported in the 2003 Target Market News' analysis *The Buying Power of Black America.* This extraordinary wealth generation has allowed them the means and opportunity to act in many respects with the same arrogance and license as their white American and European male contemporaries and the imperialist tourists of Fanon's era.

Latin America, Fanon wrote, is "Europe's brothel," and Brazil, in particular, has become to the heterosexual black American male what Tahiti was to the nineteenth-century painter Paul Gauguin—an idyllic place where one could "fuck, tan, and eat," or *"baiser, bronzer et bouffer,"* as the French Club Med experience was once described. According to a BBC report on sex tourism and prostitution in Brazil, sex work in Brazil is on the upswing, as Brazilian women and girls look for a way out of dire poverty. Brazil has been pressed into the role of purveyor of sex tourism as a result of the void left by Asia—specifically Thailand—and the tsunami crisis. A casualty of its savvy and relentless marketing, particularly with respect to women and sex, Brazil is identified as the land of samba, sensuality, the bikini wax, and the Brazilian *bunda,* a string/thong bikini.[24] Such are the obsessions with Brazilian sexuality that plastic surgeons offer a procedure called the Brazilian butt lift.[25] For a few Brazilian *reais,* which amount to nominal amounts in American dollars (and sometimes the promise of a better life for Brazilians in the United States), one can experience the fantasy that is Brazil—and generally from women from the *favelas.*

In Brazil, the reputedly large parties thrown by moguls such as Damon Dash and Sean "Puffy" Combs during Carnivale and the Brazilian fascination with all things Americana, especially mass-produced and globally exported black commodities such as music and music videos, provide cultural currency for hip hop generation black men that gives them a Brazilian ghetto tour pass that includes discounts on women. For those poor and working-class black men unable to procure the fantasy on the ground, their imaginations, like those writers of beguiling eighteenth- and nineteenth century travel narratives of exotic places and eager-to-be-had women, will travel for them. For a mere $72 including shipping and handling—a far cry from a $1,000 plane ticket to Rio—they can be transported to Brazil via pornographic visual aids like *Hip Hop Honeys: Brazil Boom Boom*'s three-volume set and a poster.

In 2004, African Americans spent $4.6 billion on travel, lodging, and transportation.[26] While the Caribbean and Africa have long been heavily marketed to African Americans by the travel and tourism industry, partnerships between the Brazilian government and African American media moguls like *Essence* magazine founder Clarence Smith have resulted in deal-brokering between Varig Airlines and Avocet Travel and Entertainment that now includes direct flights from New York to Salvador, Bahia. Brazil represents an untapped market for African American businesses, and vice versa. As *Brazil Online Magazine* suggests,

> This place (Brazil) has so much to offer African-Americans. Much more than any place on the continent of Africa. The environment here is stable; there is no civil war here. There are no famines on the scale of what a visitor would encounter in Africa. Brazil offers access to state of the art telecommunications, reliable banking systems, good roads and health facilities.[27]

Furthermore, the emergence of interest groups on the Web such as "African American Men & Brazilian Women" signals the global inclinations and democratization of wander lust and leisure afforded by the U.S. economic boom. Replete with visuals, The African American Men & Brazilian Women message board also provides insight into some of the kinds of leisure activities sought. There is a "do's and don'ts" list offered by one aficionado of Brazilian women. A sort of "Mr. Manners" for African American men traveling to Brazil, *ChgoBachelor31_4u* took his counsels from postings at Rioexposed.com and Brazilmensclub.com, sites that promote sex tourism. Among other things,

ChgoBachelor31_4u advises African American men not to "flirt with females unless your [*sic*] serious" or "go in the *favelas* unless your [*sic*] with someone you know & trust," but do "wear a condom," and "if your [*sic*] there (1) week you should average 10 females, if your [*sic*] there (2) weeks you should average 20 females," and finally, "Even if you dont [*sic*] need it fellas, 'blue devils' aka viagra. dont [*sic*] be ashamed to use it."[28]

For those interested in making "honest women" out [of] the *Brasilieras, bgcaliber1* offers some handy tips as well:

1. Though it may be tough . . . try to see her a few times in Brazil b4 bringing her back. Learn some Portuguese (or bring someone who knows the language) and try to ask around her neighborhood what type of girl she is from the local guys (last thing you want to do is bring back a full fledged hoe). See how her family is (full of nice spiritual people or a group of thieves). Remember, the apple doesn't fall far from the tree.

2. If you do eventually get her here, do not trust her to visit other girlfriends living here by herself. KEEP HER AWAY FROM OTHER BRAZILIAN GIRLS HERE IN THE STATES (unless you're absolutely sure the girl is living a clean simple life). If she has to visit, go with her. Unless you're independently wealthy and can afford to give her money to send back to Brazil, she'll want to start working. With limited English and no papers yet, where is the 1st place she'll think about going. You got it . . . THE STRIP CLUB! Once some of these girls find out how much other girls make in the sex trade . . . you're screwed!

3. Many of these girls really do just want the papers. Once they get them, many times it's . . . ADIOS! Unless you . . . (refer to #4 & #6).

4. If your libido isn't up to par, you better get those blue pills. The majority of Brasileras I know love sex and if you're not doing the job. . . .

5. Keep tabs and don't give too much freedom (at least in the beginning) to go off by herself (or not calling in to check up on her). Once again, refer to #2 & #4.

6. LEARN THE LANGUAGE! You will meet SO MANY MORE Brazilian women if you can even basically communicate [*sic*] with them and you will tend to keep them longer (never mind the fact that you will be able to understand what she's talking about on the phone). . . .

Good luck in finding your ideal woman brothers![29]

While many of my colleagues in second language acquisition studies cringe at such utilitarian approaches to language learning, as a professor of French studies, I can in principle appreciate *bgcaliber1*'s emphatic suggestion to learn the Portuguese language, despite the suggestion's questionable context. But that context necessarily feeds into the myth that these ethereal beauties, these "ideal wom[e]n," are sex goddesses to boot. They require constant monitoring for fear of cuckolding, are predisposed to work in the sex entertainment industry, and require flaccid-penised paramours to come with a prescription of Viagra. In the Brazilian woman, the African American male has met his sexual match—at least in these scripts of sexual insatiability penned by African American men. Better still, with all this talk of Viagra, the African American male, that quintessential cocksman, "the keeper of the impalpable gate," in Fanon speak, "that opens into the realm of orgies, of bacchanals, of delirious sexual sensations,"[30] has been bested by *Brasilieras.*

That the mania over Brazil has reached an interesting pitch is bizarrely revealed by a certain John Nicholson who claims to be an associate of pioneering filmmaker Warrington Hudlin, whose box office draws *Boomerang* and *House Party* helped to establish hip hop film as a subgenre of American cinema. Nicholson wants African American men on the African American Men & Brazilian Women message board to provide him and Hudlin insight into their Brazil connections as they are purportedly making a documentary on Brazil, much to the chagrin of many of the men who frequent the site:

This is John Nicholson, and i [*sic*] would like to address what appears to be some growing concerns expressed by some of the men about the motives and results of the documentary Warrington Hudlin and I are working on about african american [*sic*] men who love/enjoy the women in brasil. First, my 100% goal is to present a very fair and unbiased look at the entire situation on Rio. I have zero interest in making a T&A (tits and ass) documentary, this will be a serious and fair look at Rio.

Now some have expressed concerns that i [*sic*] am interested in doing this documentary at all. I and Warrington feel that its [*sic*] a compelling and interesting story to be told. Some have said that they prefer if we did not complete the documentary at [all], for fear that too many people will find out and ruin a "good thing." I think its [sic] fair to say that after Snoops [sic] music video, if it was a secret before, it certainly is not one now.

Men need to keep in mind, that the talk about Brasil is spreading in the african american [sic] community, and while my goal is to do a fair look at this issue, there may be others who might simply want to make a one sided and sensational type piece, that would not be fair and balanced. Maybe some show like Oprah will eventually send down a production team with hidden camera's [sic] and mics and blow brothers out [of] the water with the video.

Which is why its important to me that i [sic] complete this project and get it out there as soon as i [sic] can. I will gladly answers any concerns, issues or questions any of you may have, please feel free to email me at JNicholson30339@yahoo.com.[31]

What is most telling about Nicholson's posting is the exclusive reference to Rio de Janeiro, his use of "or," signaled by the slash between "love/enjoy," rather than "and" in reference to loving "or" enjoying Brazilian women, and the "good thing" his documentary will ruin—sexual paradise spoiled by a sea of competing African American males. African American men have choices. They can "love" Brazilian women, as many of them genuinely do, but *Brasilieras* can also be merely enjoyed, sampled like exotic victuals as *ChgoBachelor31_4u* suggests, depending on "if your [sic] there (1) week . . . (10 females) . . . (2) (20 females)." Indeed, the sheer number of Brazilian female dishes available depending on one's travel schedule rather resembles a colonial Indonesian rice table in which the wealthy colonists selected the finest and most succulent dishes from the isles of Asia.

The exclusive mention of Rio tells yet another story. The Avocet T&E-Varig deal to Bahia is targeted to African American females between the ages of twenty-five and fifty-five, seeking a more spiritual vacation. The first imported enslaved Africans arrived in Salvador, Bahia in the sixteenth century. Bahia and northern Brazil represent the stronghold of African culture with the ever-present martial-art school teaching the Angolan-inspired Capoeira and Yoruban-derived spiritual practices such as Candomblé Though sex tourism is a persistent problem in Salvador da Bahia and the North, and the Bahian Carnival is also ballyhooed on sex tourist sites like Brazilmensclub.com as such a celebration that "every man owes it to himself to go once in his life," Rio becomes the exclusive playground for

African American male sexual pre-rogatives. And the arrest of twenty-nine African American men on charges of sexual tourism with forty Brazilian sex workers (*garota de programa*, also known as GDP) on the schooner *Shangrilá* leaving the Marina da Glòria in Rio on June 11, 2005, demonstrate the exercising of those prerogatives. It is then not particularly surprising that Rio, the *favelas*, and the women are varyingly put to use in hip hop culture.

With "Beautiful," "Why You Wanna," *Dude: We're Going to Rio*, and "Holla, Holla" videos, Snoop, T.I., Pharrell, and Ja Rule not only represented the mobility, influence, and access to affluence available to African American hip hop generation men as part of our new global condition, but also offered up the latest fetishized commodity of beauty in the heterosexual African American male realm of desire. That the "Eye Candy" section of hip hop magazines like *XXL* and the Dirty South's *Ozone* feature video vixens remarkably similar to the women in "Beautiful" is no coincidence. That we seem to see the "same ho[s]," using Tupac's rancid poetic maneuver, in Brazil, in *XXL*, and in hip hop videos in general is unfortunately a conundrum of the new black gender politics that uses art, technological innovation, and globalization in the service of color chauvinism, sexist exploitation, and hair neurosis. It is a new black gender politics completely in the service of a jack-legged black masculinity. And that black masculinity has been cobbled together from the stultifying remains of white supremacy, media, and the undeserved privileges accrued globally by American manhood.

That young black women continue to negotiate these impossible ideals that literally gyrate around them in videos, assail them from above in Madison Avenue billboards, and stare back at them in mainstream and hip hop magazines in myriad ways is nothing new. We have always attempted to carve spaces for ourselves in an American culture that has resolutely tried to deny our very humanity and womanhood. But the spaces that have emerged in commercial hip hop are categorically one-dimensional. Beauty is nothing short of the helpmate to sex; and we have become reducible to our sexuality as the predominate arbiter of our reality. Into this rotten stew of hypersexuality and insatiability, one can add the distressing outcome of sexual abuse—of which young black women and girls are 10 percent more likely to be survivors.

NOTES

1. See Serge R. Denisoff, *Inside MTV* (New Brunswick, NJ: Rutgers University Press, 1988); and E. Ann Kaplan, *Rocking Around the Clock: Music Television, Postmodernism, and Consumer Culture* (New York: Methuen, 1987).

2. Greg Tate, "Nigs R Us, or How Blackfolk Became Fetish Objects," in *Everything but the Burden: What White People Are Taking from Black Culture* (New York: Broadway Books, 2003), 7.

3. It is no coincidence that I deliberately selected movies, directors, and films that seem to resonate with the thug/gangsta creed of top-shelf hip hop artists.

4. Johnnie L. Roberts, "Fine Tuning a New Act," *Newsweek*, February 7, 2005, 40.

5. All citations from author's interview with the filmmaker in 2005.

6. Daniel R. Coleridge, "Top Model's Yaya Stays Strong," *TV Guide Insider Online*, December 23, 2004.

7. Ruth La Ferla, "Generation E.A.: Ethnically Ambiguous" in Fashion & Style Section, *The New York Times*, December 28, 2003, 1.

8. Rob Marriott, *Vibe Hip-Hop Divas* (New York: Three Rivers Press, 2001), 134.

9. Ibid., 136.

10. Ibid., 136.

11. Charisse Jones, "Black Women Make 'Shifts' to Succeed," *USA Today*, January 2, 2004, A13. A recent study of wage earnings among college-educated women found however that black and Asian women outearn their similarly educated white female counterparts ($41,100, $43,700, and $37,800, respectively). Latino women with undergraduate degrees earned $37,600. College-educated black men ($45,000) earned less than white, Latino ($49,000), and Asian ($52,000) men. All minority men earned significantly less than white men, who took in $66,000. See *The Chronicle of Higher Education*, Section: Government & Politics, Volume 51: 31, 2004, A22.

12. Target Market News, "The Buying Power of Black America," 2003.

13. Veronica MacDonald, "Ethnic Hair Care: Acquisitions Are Changing the Market, but When It Comes to Product Development, Moisturization Remains the Mantra," *Happi-Household & Personal Products Industry*, 39(4): 60(9), April 2002.

14. Allison Samuels with Mary Carmichael, "Smooth Operations," *Newsweek*, July 5, 2004, 48.

15. *The U.S. Multicultural Women Market*, July 2004.

16. Erica Kennedy, *Bling!* (New York: Miramax Books, 2004).

17. Telephone interview with Lewis in 2005.

18. Allison Samuels, "Time to Tell It Like It Is: Sisters Talk Frankly About Black Men and White Colleagues, Money, Beauty—and the Prospect of Having to Choose Between Racial Disloyalty and Being Alone," *Newsweek*, March 3, 2003, 52.

19. Advertisement, *XXL*, June 2005, 121.

20. In Marshall Eakin's *Brazil: The Once and Future Country* (New York: St. Martin's, 1997), 136–37.

21. Julia Chapin, "Beauty and the Beach," *Condé Nast Traveler*, May 2005, http://www.concierge.com/cntraveler/articles/detail?articleId=6057.

22. Matt Barone, "Ja Rule: Rates the Hits," AllHipHop.com, October 2004.

23. Frantz Fanon, *The Wretched of the Earth* (New York: Grove, 1963), 153–54.

24. "Brazil Struggles to Curb Sex Tourism," BBC News World Edition, December 2, 2004.

25. Norman Boucher, "Is There a Doctor on the Set?" *Brown Alumni Magazine*, September–October 2004, 55.

26. Department of Commerce's Consumer Expenditure Survey, 2003 and 2004.

27. Peter Wagner, "Opening Doors to Bahia," *Brazil Online Magazine*, in Enterprise and Culture Section, April 2004.

28. *ChgoBachelor31_4u*, "Dos & Don'ts," AfricanAmericanMenBrazilianWomen@groups.msn.com, April 10, 2005, 8:45 A.M.

29. *bgcaliber1*, "Marrying a Brazilian Woman and Bringing Her Back to the States," AfricanAmericanMenBrazilianWomen@groups.msn.com, March 14, 2005, 5:00 A.M.

30. Frantz Fanon, *Black Skin, White Masks* (New York: Grove, 1967), 177.

31. *frihazeleyes30067*, "I'd Like to Address Some Concerns," March 20, 2005, 9:24 P.M.

REWRITING RAP TO EMPOWER TEENS

Tara Parker-Pope

A group of high school girls in Atlanta got tired of taunts and catcalls from men in the street. So they decided to rap about it:

> Imma give you yo number back
> Cause I don't like you and yo game is whack
> You see these boys just don't know how to act
> I try to walk away but they talk smack
> Take it to the streets

Creating rhymes about bad behavior may not seem like a meaningful way to battle harassment. But rewriting rap lyrics is one way educators are trying to harness the power of popular music to help build kids' self esteem and counter negative images of women in the media. The power of hip-hop to reach teens hasn't gone unnoticed by health researchers, who are now spending time on the dance floor and dissecting rap lyrics in hopes of finding ways to better communicate with young people.

The Atlanta teens are part of a group called HOTGIRLS (Helping Our Teen Girls In Real Life Situations). Although rap is often blamed for promoting degrading images of women, HOTGIRLS uses rap music to start conversations with girls about the challenges they face growing up.

Rewriting song lyrics helps girls "critically analyze the messages they encounter in the media and in their daily lives," said HOTGIRLS founder Carla E. Stokes. "Girls are using hip hop as a vehicle to reach their peers and raise awareness about issues that affect their lives."

The group has started the FIREGRL club, which takes teens into a recording studio to create their own versions of popular songs, such as "Let Me Tell You How You Talk to Me," a reworked version of Justin Timberlake's song "Sexy Back." Although everyone doesn't have access to a recording studio, Dr. Stokes notes that parents can discuss song lyrics with kids, and even encourage them to rewrite lyrics and perform their own more positive versions of popular songs.

"For a lot of parents, the response is to turn off the TV or the radio," said Dr. Stokes. "I don't think they can realistically shield their children from all the messages that are out there. I think the important thing to do is just talk to children about what they're hearing."

SECTION 4

Socialization

We are born into cultures that have definite ideas about men and women and their appropriate attitudes, values, and behaviors, although those ideas may differ dramatically across time and place. The dominant U.S. culture defines certain traits as masculine or feminine and values behaviors, occupations, and attitudes deemed the characteristics of men more highly than those associated with women. It assumes that what men do is right and normal. Women are judged in accordance with how well they conform to the male standard. This way of thinking is known as *androcentrism*. As children, we learn to see ourselves and others as girls or boys and to judge our own and others' behaviors according to standards of gender-appropriate behavior, which is why a boy wearing a skirt can be so disconcerting. If we don't know a person's gender, we barely know how to interact, which is why people whose gender cannot be easily discerned or is easily mistaken have such a hard time.

The articles in this section analyze the complex process of gender socialization from various perspectives. Learning about our culture begins in the family. We learn about gender not only from what our parents say but from what they do. When mothers have primary responsibility for raising children, both girls and boys learn that nurturing is more a responsibility of women than of men. Gender socialization continues in schools, peer groups, and religious institutions, and can be ongoing throughout life, as we learn the expectations of our college contexts, our workplaces, and the families we form as adults.

As we have all experienced, schools play an important role in gender socialization. By the time children

are in school, they not only have been socialized into their gender but also are able to negotiate how and in which situations gender will be socially salient. Barrie Thorne, in her classic article "Girls and Boys Together . . . but Mostly Apart: Gender Arrangements in Elementary Schools," argues for a more complex idea of gender as socially constructed and context specific. In her observations of social relations among children in elementary school, she finds that boys and girls are segregated and seen as different in the classroom and on the playground due both to teachers' actions and to the ways children socialize each other. Did your own experiences in elementary school conform to the patterns Thorne describes? Do you think anything has changed since Thorne first published this research in 1986?

A new concern with boys has emerged in recent decades. In "What Are Little Boys Made Of?" Michael Kimmel discusses the different ways that popular discourse defines the problems that confront boys, from violence, to attention deficit disorder, to the pressure to appear emotionally invulnerable. Kimmel argues that there are clear problems facing boys but that these problems stem from cultural expectations and peer pressure to conform to a narrow definition of masculinity. He critiques authors who argue that testosterone or other biological features make boys more violent, or more active, or less adapted to educational settings than girls. Instead, he suggests, boys' lives can be improved not only by addressing the emotional straightjacket forced upon them by gender norms but also by taking a feminist approach to eliminating gender inequality. Do you agree with Kimmel's argument? How are his observations about boys' experiences similar to those that Thorne describes? Can you think of examples from your own experiences of the pressures placed on boys to conform to notions of masculinity?

Because gender intersects with race, ethnicity, and class, our socialization experiences differ in complex ways. What a woman of color, for example, needs to teach her sons and daughters to enable them to survive in a white-male-dominated society is different from what a white mother needs to teach her children. These kinds of ethnic and racial differences, in turn, are compounded by differences in class status. Yen Le Espiritu, in "We Don't Sleep Around Like White Girls Do," explores the ways that gendered sex norms in Filipina-American families serve as a strategy of resistance to oppression for the community as a whole and at the same time limit the autonomy of Filipina women. By emphasizing the sexual looseness of white girls, Filipina girls and their parents assert their moral superiority and counter the stereotypes of Filipinas as either prostitutes or submissive mail-order brides. Rather than consider dominant white conceptions of racial and ethnic "others," Espiritu looks at Filipina constructions of whiteness. What generational differences are there between the Filipina girls Espiritu studies and their parents? What is the Filipina-American notion of white society? Do you think it is accurate?

France Winndance Twine, in "Bearing Blackness in Britain," also considers whiteness in her study of white birth mothers of African-descent children. She explores the ways that race and gender shape the experiences of members of interracial families and the strategies of what she calls "racial consciousness" and "racial literacy" that white birth mothers use to prepare their children for the racism they encounter. Once again, we see the ways that class, race, ethnicity, and gender intersect in shaping people's experiences and identities. How do black family members view white and black mothers differently? How important do you think racial literacy is, not just for these white mothers, but for people in general?

The final article, "Learning from Drag Queens," an excerpt from Verta Taylor and Leila Rupp's award-winning book *Drag Queens at the 801 Cabaret*, illustrates the complexity of gender and sexuality. Some of the drag queens at the 801 Cabaret in Key West, Florida, resisted socialization into masculinity, instead embracing femininity. And in their shows, they "trouble" gender and sexual identity, in the process challenging the way audience members think about what it means to be a woman or a man, what it means to be gay or straight. What can drag queens teach us about gender socialization? Do you agree that drag shows have the potential to bring about change?

Socialization, as you can see, is not a simple process; rather, it is shaped in profound ways by class, race, ethnicity, and sexuality. Why is gender socialization such a powerful force? How much agency do you think people have in accepting or resisting the forces of socialization?

17 **Barrie Thorne**

Girls and Boys Together . . . but Mostly Apart: Gender Arrangements in Elementary Schools

Throughout the years of elementary school, children's friendships and casual encounters are strongly separated by sex. Sex segregation among children, which starts in preschool and is well established by middle childhood, has been amply documented in studies of children's groups and friendships (e.g., Eder & Hallinan, 1978; Schofield, 1981) and is immediately visible in elementary school settings. When children choose seats in classrooms or the cafeteria, or get into line, they frequently arrange themselves in same-sex clusters. At lunchtime, they talk matter-of-factly about "girls' tables" and "boys' tables." Playgrounds have gendered turfs, with some areas and activities, such as large playing fields and basketball courts, controlled mainly by boys, and others—smaller enclaves like jungle-gym areas and concrete spaces for hopscotch or jump rope—more often controlled by girls. Sex segregation is so common in elementary schools that it is meaningful to speak of separate girls' and boys' worlds.

Studies of gender and children's social relations have mostly followed this "two worlds" model, separately describing and comparing the subcultures of girls and boys (e.g., Lever, 1976; Maltz & Borker, 1983). In brief summary: Boys tend to interact in larger, more age-heterogeneous groups (Lever, 1976; Waldrop & Halverson, 1975; Eder & Hallinan, 1978). They engage in more rough and tumble play and physical fighting (Maccoby & Jacklin, 1974). Organized sports are both a central activity and a major metaphor in boys' subcultures; they use the language of "teams" even when not engaged in sports, and they often construct interaction in the form of contests. The shifting hierarchies of boys' groups (Savin-Williams, 1976) are evident in their more frequent use of direct commands, insults, and challenges (Goodwin, 1980).

Fewer studies have been done of girls' groups (Foot, Chapman, & Smith, 1980; McRobbie & Garber, 1975),

and—perhaps because categories for description and analysis have come more from male than female experience—researchers have had difficulty seeing and analyzing girls' social relations. Recent work has begun to correct this skew. In middle childhood, girls' worlds are less public than those of boys; girls more often interact in private places and in smaller groups or friendship pairs (Eder & Hallinan, 1978; Waldrop & Halverson, 1975). Their play is more cooperative and turn-taking (Lever, 1976). Girls have more intense and exclusive friendships, which take shape around keeping and telling secrets, shifting alliances, and indirect ways of expressing disagreement (Goodwin, 1980; Lever, 1976; Maltz & Borker, 1983). Instead of direct commands, girls more often use directives which merge speaker and hearer, e.g., "let's" or "we gotta" (Goodwin, 1980).

Although much can be learned by comparing the social organization and subcultures of boys' and of girls' groups, the separate-worlds approach has eclipsed full, contextual understanding of gender and social relations among children. The separate-worlds model essentially involves a search for group sex differences and shares the limitations of individual sex difference research. Differences tend to be exaggerated and similarities ignored, with little theoretical attention to the integration of similarity and difference (Unger, 1979). Statistical findings of difference are often portrayed as dichotomous, neglecting the considerable individual variation that exists; for example, not all boys fight, and some have intense and exclusive friendships. The sex difference approach tends to abstract gender from its social context, to assume that males and females are qualitatively and permanently different (with differences perhaps unfolding through separate developmental lines). These assumptions mask the possibility that gender arrangements and patterns of similarity and difference may vary by situation, race, social class, region, or subculture.

Sex segregation is far from total, and is a more complex and dynamic process than the portrayal of separate worlds reveals. Erving Goffman (1977) has observed that sex segregation has a "with–then apart" structure; the sexes segregate periodically, with separate spaces, rituals, [and] groups, but they also come together and are, in crucial ways, part of the same world. This is certainly true in the social environment of elementary schools. Although girls and boys do interact as boundaried collectivities—an image suggested by the separate-worlds approach—there are other occasions when they work or play in relaxed and integrated ways. Gender is less central to the organization and meaning of some situations than others. In short, sex segregation is not static, but is a variable and complicated process.

To gain an understanding of gender which can encompass both the "with" and the "apart" of sex segregation, analysis should start not with the individual, nor with a search for sex differences, but with social relationships. Gender should be conceptualized as a system of relationships rather than as an immutable and dichotomous given. Taking this approach, I have organized my research on gender and children's social relations around questions like the following: How and when does gender enter into group formation? In a given situation, how is gender made more or less salient or infused with particular meanings? By what rituals, processes, and forms of social organization and conflict do "with–then apart" rhythms get enacted? How are these processes affected by the organization of institutions (e.g., different types of schools, neighborhoods, or summer camps), varied settings (e.g., the constraints and possibilities governing interaction on playgrounds vs. classrooms), and particular encounters?

METHODS AND SOURCES OF DATA

This study is based on two periods of participant observation. In 1976–1977 I observed for eight months in a largely working-class elementary school in California, a school with 8 percent Black and 12 percent Chicana/o students. In 1980 I did fieldwork for three months in a Michigan elementary school of similar size (around 400 students), social class, and racial composition. I observed in several classrooms—a kindergarten, a second grade, and a combined fourth-fifth grade—and in

school hallways, cafeterias, and playgrounds. I set out to follow the round of the school day as children experience it, recording their interactions with one another, and with adults, in varied settings.

Participant observation involves gaining access to everyday, "naturalistic" settings and taking systematic notes over an extended period of time. Rather than starting with preset categories for recording, or with fixed hypotheses for testing, participant observers record detail in ways which maximize opportunities for discovery. Through continuous interaction between observation and analysis, "grounded theory" is developed (Glaser & Strauss, 1967).

The distinctive logic and discipline of this mode of inquiry emerges from: (1) theoretical sampling—being relatively systematic in the choice of where and whom to observe in order to maximize knowledge relevant to categories and analysis which are being developed; and (2) comparing all relevant data on a given point in order to modify emerging propositions to take account of discrepant cases (Katz, 1983). Participant observation is a flexible, open-ended and inductive method, designed to understand behavior within, rather than stripped from, social context. It provides richly detailed information anchored in everyday meanings and experience.

DAILY PROCESSES OF SEX SEGREGATION

Sex segregation should be understood not as a given, but as the result of deliberate activity. The outcome is dramatically visible when there are separate girls' and boys' tables in school lunchrooms or sex-separated groups on playgrounds. But in the same lunchroom one can also find tables where girls and boys eat and talk together, and in some playground activities the sexes mix. By what processes do girls and boys separate into gender-defined and relatively boundaried collectivities? And in what contexts, and through what processes, do boys and girls interact in less gender-divided ways?

In the school settings I observed, much segregation happened with no mention of gender. Gender was implicit in the contours of friendship, shared interest, and perceived risk which came into play when children chose companions—in their prior planning, invitations, seeking of access, saving of places, denials of entry, and allowing or protesting of "cuts" by those who violated the rules for lining up. Sometimes children formed mixed-sex groups for play, eating, talking, working on a classroom project, or moving through space. When adults or children explicitly invoked gender—and this was nearly always in ways which separated girls and boys—boundaries were heightened and mixed-sex interaction became an explicit arena of risk.

In the schools I studied, the physical space and curricula were not formally divided by sex, as they have been in the history of elementary schooling (a history evident in separate entrances to old school buildings, where the words "Boys" and "Girls" are permanently etched in concrete). Nevertheless, gender was a visible marker in the adult-organized school day. In both schools, when the public address system sounded, the principal inevitably opened with: "Boys and girls . . . ," and in addressing clusters of children, teachers and aides regularly used gender terms ("Heads down, girls"; "The girls are ready and the boys aren't"). These forms of address made gender visible and salient, conveying an assumption that the sexes are separate social groups.

Teachers and aides sometimes drew upon gender as a basis for sorting children and organizing activities. Gender is an embodied and visual social category which roughly divides the population in half, and the separation of girls and boys permeates the history and lore of schools and playgrounds. In both schools—although through awareness of Title IX, many teachers had changed this practice—one could see separate girls' and boys' lines moving, like caterpillars, through the school halls. In the fourth–fifth-grade classroom the teacher frequently pitted girls against boys for spelling and math contests. On the playground in the Michigan school, aides regarded the space close to the building as girls' territory, and the playing fields "out there" as boys' territory. They sometimes shooed children of the other sex away from those spaces, especially boys who ventured near the girls' area and seemed to have teasing in mind.

In organizing their activities, both within and apart from the surveillance of adults, children also explicitly invoked gender. During my fieldwork in the Michigan school, I kept daily records of who sat where in the lunchroom. The amount of sex segregation varied: it was least at the first-grade tables and almost total among sixth-graders. There was also variation from classroom to classroom within a given age and from day to day. Actions like the following heightened the gender divide: In the lunchroom, when the two second-grade tables were filling, a high-status boy walked by the inside table, which had a scattering of both boys and girls, and said loudly, "Oooo, too many girls," as he headed for a seat at the far table. The boys at the inside table picked up their trays and moved, and no other boys sat at the inside table, which the pronouncement had effectively made taboo. In the end, that day (which was not the case every day), girls and boys ate at separate tables.

Eating and walking are not sex-typed activities, yet in forming groups in lunchrooms and hallways children often separated by sex. Sex segregation assumed added dimensions on the playground, where spaces, equipment, and activities were infused with gender meanings. My inventories of activities and groupings on the playground showed similar patterns in both schools: boys controlled the large fixed spaces designated for team sports (baseball diamonds, grassy fields used for football or soccer); girls more often played closer to the building, doing tricks on the monkey bars (which, for sixth-graders, became an area for sitting and talking) and using cement areas for jump rope, hopscotch, and group games like four-square. (Lever, 1976, provides a good analysis of sex-divided play.) Girls and boys most often played together in kickball, and in group (rather than team) games like four-square, dodgeball, and handball. When children used gender to exclude others from play, they often drew upon beliefs connecting boys to some activities and girls to others: A first-grade boy avidly watched an all-female game of jump rope. When the girls began to shift positions, he recognized a means of access to the play and he offered, "I'll swing it." A girl responded, "No way, you don't know how to do it, to swing it. You gotta be a girl." He left without protest. Although children sometimes ignored pronouncements about what each sex could or could not do, I never heard them directly challenge such claims.

When children had explicitly defined an activity or a group as gendered, those who crossed the boundary—especially boys who moved into female-marked space—risked being teased. ("Look! Mike's in the girls' line!"; "That's a girl over there," a girl said loudly, pointing to a boy sitting at an otherwise all-female table in the lunchroom.) Children, and occasionally adults, used teasing—especially the tease of "liking" someone of the other sex, or of "being" that sex by virtue of being in their midst—to police gender boundaries. Much of the teasing drew upon heterosexual romantic definitions, making cross-sex interaction risky and increasing social distance between boys and girls.

RELATIONSHIPS BETWEEN THE SEXES

Because I have emphasized the "apart" and ignored the occasions of "with," this analysis of sex segregation falsely implies that there is little contact between girls and boys in daily school life. In fact, relationships between girls and boys—which should be studied as fully as, and in connection with, same-sex relationships—are of several kinds:

1. "Borderwork," or forms of cross-sex interaction which are based upon and reaffirm boundaries and asymmetries between girls' and boys' groups.
2. Interactions which are infused with heterosexual meanings.
3. Occasions where individuals cross gender boundaries to participate in the world of the other sex.
4. Situations where gender is muted in salience, with girls and boys interacting in more relaxed ways.

Borderwork

In elementary school settings, boys' and girls' groups are sometimes spatially set apart. Same-sex groups sometimes claim fixed territories such as the basketball court, the bars, or specific lunchroom tables. However, in the crowded, multifocused, and adult-controlled environment of the school, groups form and disperse at a rapid rate and can never stay totally apart. Contact between girls and boys sometimes lessens sex segregation, but gender-defined groups also come together in ways which emphasize their boundaries.

"Borderwork" refers to interaction across, yet based upon and even strengthening, gender boundaries. I have drawn this notion from Fredrik Barth's (1969) analysis of social relations which are maintained across ethnic boundaries without diminishing dichotomized ethnic status.[1] His focus is on more macro, ecological arrangements; mine is on face-to-face behavior. But the insight is similar: groups may interact in ways which strengthen their borders, and the maintenance of ethnic (or gender) groups can best be understood by examining the boundary that defines the groups, "not the cultural stuff that it encloses" (Barth, 1969:15). In elementary schools there are several types of borderwork: contests or games where gender-defined teams compete; cross-sex rituals of chasing and pollution; and group invasions. These interactions are asymmetrical, challenging the separate-but-parallel model of "two worlds."

Contests Boys and girls are sometimes pitted against each other in classroom competitions and playground games. The fourth–fifth-grade classroom had a boys' side and a girls' side, an arrangement that reemerged each time the teacher asked children to choose their own desks. Although there was some within-sex shuffling, the result was always a spatial moiety system—boys on the left, girls on the right—with the exception of one girl (the "tomboy" whom I'll describe later), who twice chose a desk with the boys and once with the girls. Drawing upon and reinforcing the children's self-segregation, the teacher often pitted the boys against the girls in spelling and math competitions, events marked by cross-sex antagonism and within-sex solidarity. The teacher introduced a math game; she would write addition and subtraction problems on the board, and a member of each team would race to be the first to write the correct answer. She wrote two scorekeeping columns on the board: "Beastly Boys" . . . "Gossipy Girls." The boys yelled out, as several girls laughed, "Noisy girls! Gruesome girls!" The girls sat in a row on top of their desks; sometimes they moved collectively, pushing their hips or whispering "Pass it on." The boys stood along the wall, some reclining against desks. When members of either group came back victorious from the front of the room, they would do the "giving five" hand-slapping ritual with their team members.

On the playground a team of girls occasionally played a team of boys, usually in kickball or team two-square. Sometimes these games proceeded matter-of-factly, but if gender became the explicit basis of team solidarity, the interaction changed, becoming more antagonistic and unstable. Two fifth-grade girls played against two fifth-grade boys in a team game of two-square. The game proceeded at an even pace until an argument ensued about whether the ball was out or on the line. Karen, who had hit the ball, became annoyed, flashed her middle finger at the other team, and called to a passing girl to join their side. The boys then called out to other boys, and cheered as several arrived to play. "We got five and you got three!" Jack yelled. The game continued, with the girls yelling, "Bratty boys! Sissy boys!" and the boys making noises—"Weee haw," "Ha-ha-ha"—as they played.

Chasing Cross-sex chasing dramatically affirms boundaries between girls and boys. The basic elements of chase and elude, capture and rescue (Sutton-Smith, 1971) are found in various kinds of tag with formal rules and in informal episodes of chasing which punctuate life on playgrounds. These episodes begin with a provocation (taunts like "You can't get me!" or "Slobber monster!"; bodily pokes or the grabbing of possessions). A provocation may be ignored or responded to by chasing. Chaser and chased may then alternate roles. In an ethnographic study of chase sequences on a school playground, Christine Finnan (1982) observes that chases vary in number of chasers to chased (e.g., one chasing one or five chasing two); form of provocation (a taunt or a poke); outcome (an episode may end when the chased outdistances the chaser, or with a brief touch, being wrestled to the ground, or the recapturing of a hat or a ball); and use of space (there may or may not be safety zones).

Like Finnan (1982) and Sluckin (1981), who studied a playground in England, I found that chasing has a gendered structure. Boys frequently chase one another, an activity which often ends in wrestling and mock fights. When girls chase girls, they are usually less physically aggressive; they less often, for example, wrestle one another to the ground.

Cross-sex chasing is set apart by special names— "girls chase the boys"; "boys chase the girls"; "the chase"; "chasers"; "chase and kiss"; "kiss chase"; "kissers and chasers"; "kiss or kill"—and by children's animated talk about the activity. The names vary by region and school, but contain both gender and sexual meanings (this form of play is mentioned, but only briefly analyzed, in Finnan, 1982; Sluckin, 1981; Parrott, 1972; and Borman, 1979).

In "boys chase the girls" and "girls chase the boys" (the names most frequently used in both the California and Michigan schools) boys and girls become, by definition, separate teams. Gender terms override individual identities, especially for the other team ("Help, a girl's chasin' me!"; "C'mon, Sarah, let's get that boy"; "Tony, help save me from the girls"). Individuals may also grab someone of their sex and turn them over to the opposing team: Ryan grabbed Billy from behind, wrestling him to the ground. "Hey, girls, get 'im," Ryan called.

Boys more often mix episodes of cross-sex with same-sex chasing. Girls more often have safety zones, places like the girls' restroom or an area by the school wall, where they retreat to rest and talk (sometimes in animated postmortems) before new episodes of cross-sex chasing begin.

Early in the fall in the Michigan school, where chasing was especially prevalent, I watched a second-grade

boy teach a kindergarten girl how to chase. He slowly ran backwards, beckoning her to pursue him, as he called, "Help, a girl's after me." In the early grades chasing mixes with fantasy play, e.g., a first-grade boy who played "sea monster," his arms out-flung and his voice growling, as he chased a group of girls. By third grade, stylized gestures—exaggerated stalking motions, screams (which only girls do), and karate kicks—accompany scenes of chasing.

Names like "chase and kiss" mark the sexual meanings of cross-sex chasing, a theme I return to later. The threat of kissing—most often girls threatening to kiss boys—is a ritualized form of provocation. Cross-sex chasing among sixth-graders involves elaborate patterns of touch and touch avoidance, which adults see as sexual. The principal told the sixth-graders in the Michigan school that they were not to play "pom-pom," a complicated chasing game, because it entailed "inappropriate touch."

Rituals of Pollution   Cross-sex chasing is sometimes entwined with rituals of pollution, as in "cooties," where specific individuals or groups are treated as contaminating or carrying "germs." Children have rituals for transferring cooties (usually touching someone else and shouting, "You've got cooties!"), for immunization (e.g., writing "CV" for "cootie vaccination" on their arms), and for eliminating cooties (e.g., saying "no gives" or using "cootie catchers" made of folded paper) (described in Knapp & Knapp, 1976). While girls may give cooties to girls, boys do not generally give cooties to one another (Samuelson, 1980).

In cross-sex play, either girls or boys may be defined as having cooties, which they transfer through chasing and touching. Girls give cooties to boys more often than vice versa. In Michigan, one version of cooties is called "girl stain"; the fourth-graders whom Karkau (1973) describes used the phrase "girl touch." "Cootie queens" or "cootie girls" (there are no "kings" or "boys") are female pariahs, the ultimate school untouchables, seen as contaminating not only by virtue of gender, but also through some added stigma such as being overweight or poor.[2] That girls are seen as more polluting than boys is a significant asymmetry, which echoes cross-cultural patterns, although in other cultures female pollution is generally connected to menstruation and not applied to prepubertal girls.

Invasions   Playground invasions are another asymmetric form of borderwork. On a few occasions I saw girls invade and disrupt an all-male game, most memorably a group of tall sixth-grade girls who ran onto the playing field and grabbed a football which was in play. The boys were surprised and frustrated, and, unusual for boys this old, finally tattled to the aide. But in the majority of cases, boys disrupt girls' activities rather than vice versa. Boys grab the ball from girls playing four-square, stick feet into a jump-rope and stop an ongoing game, and dash through the area of the bars where girls are taking turns performing, sending the rings flying. Sometimes boys ask to join a girls' game and then, after a short period of seemingly earnest play, disrupt the game. Two second-grade boys begged to "twirl" the jump rope for a group of second-grade girls who had been jumping for some time. The girls agreed, and the boys began to twirl. Soon, without announcement, the boys changed from "seashells, cockle bells" to "hot peppers" (spinning the rope very fast), and tangled the jumper in the rope. The boys ran away laughing.

Boys disrupt girls' play so often that girls have developed almost ritualized responses: they guard their ongoing play, chase boys away, and tattle to the aides. In a playground cycle which enhances sex segregation, aides who try to spot potential trouble before it occurs sometimes shoo boys away from areas where girls are playing. Aides do not anticipate trouble from girls who seek to join groups of boys, with the exception of girls intent on provoking a chase sequence. And indeed, if they seek access to a boys' game, girls usually play with boys in earnest rather than breaking up the game.

A close look at the organization of borderwork—or boundaried interactions between the sexes—shows that the worlds of boys and girls may be separate, but they are not parallel, nor are they equal. The worlds of girls and boys articulate in several asymmetric ways:

1. On the playground, boys control as much as ten times more space than girls, when one adds up the area of large playing fields and compares it with the much smaller areas where girls predominate. Girls, who play closer to the building, are more often watched over and protected by the adult aides.
2. Boys invade all-female games and scenes of play much more than girls invade boys'. This, and boys' greater control of space, correspond with other findings about the organization of gender, and inequality, in our society: compared with men and boys, women and girls take up less space, and their space

and talk are more often violated and interrupted (Greif, 1982; Henley, 1977; West & Zimmerman, 1983).
3. Although individual boys are occasionally treated as contaminating (e.g., a third-grade boy who both boys and girls said was "stinky" and "smelled like pee"), girls are more often defined as polluting. This pattern ties to themes that I discuss later: it is more taboo for a boy to play with (as opposed to invade) girls, and girls are more sexually defined than boys.

A look at the boundaries between the separated worlds of girls and boys illuminates within-sex hierarchies of status and control. For example, in the sex-divided seating in the fourth–fifth-grade classroom, several boys recurrently sat near "female space": their desks were at the gender divide in the classroom, and they were more likely than other boys to sit at a predominantly female table in the lunchroom. These boys—two nonbilingual Chicanos and an overweight "loner" boy who was afraid of sports—were at the bottom of the male hierarchy. Gender is sometimes used as a metaphor for male hierarchies; the inferior status of boys at the bottom is conveyed by calling them "girls." Seven boys and one girl were playing basketball. Two younger boys came over and asked to play. While the girl silently stood, fully accepted in the company of players, one of the older boys disparagingly said to the younger boys, "You girls can't play."[3]

In contrast, the girls who more often travel in the boys' world, sitting with groups of boys in the lunchroom or playing basketball, soccer, and baseball with them, are not stigmatized. Some have fairly high status with other girls. The worlds of girls and boys are asymmetrically arranged, and spatial patterns map out interacting forms of inequality.

Heterosexual Meanings

The organization and meanings of gender (the social categories "woman/man," "girl/boy") and of sexuality vary cross-culturally (Ortner & Whitehead, 1981)—and, in our society, across the life course. Harriet Whitehead (1981) observed that in our (Western) gender system, and that of many traditional North American Indian cultures, one's choice of a sexual object, occupation, and dress and demeanor are closely associated with gender. However, the "center of gravity" differs in the two gender systems. For Indians, occupational pursuits provide the primary imagery of gender; dress and demeanor are secondary, and sexuality is least important. In our system, at least for adults, the order is reversed: heterosexuality is central to our definitions of "man" and "woman" ("masculinity/ femininity") and the relationships that obtain between them, whereas occupation and dress/demeanor are secondary.

Whereas erotic orientation and gender are closely linked in our definitions of adults, we define children as relatively asexual. Activities and dress/demeanor are more important than sexuality in the cultural meanings of "girl" and "boy." Children are less heterosexually defined than adults, and we have nonsexual imagery for relations between girls and boys. However, both children and adults sometimes use heterosexual language—"crushes," "like," "goin' with," "girlfriends," and "boyfriends"—to define cross-sex relationships. This language increases through the years of elementary school; the shift to adolescence consolidates a gender system organized around the institution of heterosexuality.

In everyday life in the schools, heterosexual and romantic meanings infuse some ritualized forms of interaction between groups of boys and girls (e.g., "chase and kiss") and help maintain sex segregation. "Jimmy likes Beth" or "Beth likes Jimmy" is a major form of teasing, which a child risks in choosing to sit by or walk with someone of the other sex. The structure of teasing and children's sparse vocabulary for relationships between girls and boys are evident in the following conversation, which I had with a group of third-grade girls in the lunchroom. Susan asked me what I was doing, and I said I was observing the things children do and play. Nicole volunteered, "I like running, boys chase all the girls. See Tim over there? Judy chases him all around the school. She likes him." Judy, sitting across the table, quickly responded, "I hate him. I like him for a friend." "Tim loves Judy," Nicole said in a loud, singsong voice.

In the younger grades, the culture and lore of girls contain more heterosexual romantic themes than those of boys. In Michigan, the first-grade girls often jumped rope to a rhyme which began: "Down in the valley where the green grass grows, there sat Cindy [name of jumper], as sweet as a rose. She sat, she sat, she sat so sweet. Along came Jason and kissed her on the cheek. First comes love, then comes marriage, then along comes Cindy with a baby carriage." Before a girl took her turn at jumping, the chanters asked her, "Who do you want to be your boyfriend?" The jumper always

proffered a name, which was accepted matter-of-factly. In chasing, a girl's kiss carried greater threat than a boy's kiss; "girl touch," when defined as contaminating, had sexual connotations. In short, starting at an early age, girls are more sexually defined than boys.

Through the years of elementary school, and increasing with age, the idiom of heterosexuality helps maintain the gender divide. Cross-sex interactions, especially when children initiate them, are fraught with the risk of being teased about "liking" someone of the other sex. I learned of several close cross-sex friendships, formed and maintained in neighborhoods and church, which went underground during the school day.

By the fifth grade a few children began to affirm, rather than avoid, the charge of having a girlfriend or a boyfriend; they introduced the heterosexual courtship rituals of adolescence. In the lunchroom in the Michigan school, as the tables were forming, a high-status fifth-grade boy called out from his seat at the table: "I want Trish to sit by me." Trish came over, and almost like a king and queen, they sat at the gender divide—a row of girls down the table on her side, a row of boys on his. In this situation, which inverted earlier forms, it was not a loss but a gain in status to publicly choose a companion of the other sex. By affirming his choice, the boy became unteasable (note the familiar asymmetry of heterosexual courtship rituals: the male initiates). This incident signals a temporal shift in arrangements of sex and gender.

Traveling in the World of the Other Sex

Contests, invasions, chasing, and heterosexually defined encounters are based upon and reaffirm boundaries between girls and boys. In another type of cross-sex interaction, individuals (or sometimes pairs) cross gender boundaries, seeking acceptance in a group of the other sex. Nearly all the cases I saw of this were tomboys—girls who played organized sports and frequently sat with boys in the cafeteria or classroom. If these girls were skilled at activities central in the boys' world, especially games like soccer, baseball, and basketball, they were pretty much accepted as participants.

Being a tomboy is a matter of degree. Some girls seek access to boys' groups but are excluded; other girls limit their "crossing" to specific sports. Only a few—such as the tomboy I mentioned earlier, who chose a seat with the boys in the sex-divided fourth-fifth grade—participate fully in the boys' world. That particular girl was skilled at the various organized sports which boys played in different seasons of the year. She was also adept at physical fighting and at using the forms of arguing, insult, teasing, naming, and sports-talk of the boys' subculture. She was the only Black child in her classroom, in a school with only 8 percent Black students; overall that token status, along with unusual athletic and verbal skills, may have contributed to her ability to move back and forth across the gender divide. Her unique position in the children's world was widely recognized in the school. Several times, the teacher said to me, "She thinks she's a boy."

I observed only one boy in the upper grades (a fourth-grader) who regularly played with all-female groups, as opposed to "playing at" girls' games and seeking to disrupt them. He frequently played jump rope and took turns with girls doing tricks on the bars, using the small gestures—for example, a helpful push on the heel of a girl who needed momentum to turn her body around the bar—which mark skillful and earnest participation. Although I never saw him play in other than an earnest spirit, the girls often chased him away from their games, and both girls and boys teased him. The fact that girls seek and have more access to boys' worlds than vice versa, and the fact that girls who travel with the other sex are less stigmatized for it, are obvious asymmetries, tied to the asymmetries previously discussed.

Relaxed Cross-Sex Interactions

Relationships between boys and girls are not always marked by strong boundaries, heterosexual definitions, or interacting on the terms and turfs of the other sex. On some occasions girls and boys interact in relatively comfortable ways. Gender is not strongly salient nor explicitly invoked, and girls and boys are not organized into boundaried collectivities. These "with" occasions have been neglected by those studying gender and children's relationships, who have emphasized either the model of separate worlds (with little attention to their articulation) or heterosexual forms of contact.

Occasions when boys and girls interact without strain, when gender wanes rather than waxes in importance, frequently have one or more of the following characteristics:

1. The situations are organized around an absorbing task, such as a group art project or creating a radio show, which encourages cooperation and lessens attention to gender. This pattern accords with other studies finding that cooperative activities reduce group antagonism (e.g., Sherif & Sherif, 1953, who studied divisions between boys in a summer camp; and Aronson et al., 1978, who used cooperative activities to lessen racial divisions in a classroom).

2. Gender is less prominent when children are not responsible for the formation of the group. Mixed-sex play is less frequent in games like football, which require the choosing of teams, and more frequent in games like handball or dodgeball, which individuals can join simply by getting into a line or a circle. When adults organize mixed-sex encounters—which they frequently do in the classroom and in physical education periods on the playground—they legitimize cross-sex contact. This removes the risk of being teased for choosing to be with the other sex.

3. There is more extensive and relaxed cross-sex interaction when principles of grouping other than gender are explicitly invoked—for example, counting off to form teams for spelling or kickball, dividing lines by hot lunch or cold lunch, or organizing a work group on the basis of interests or reading ability.

4. Girls and boys may interact more readily in less public and crowded settings. Neighborhood play, depending on demography, is more often sex- and age-integrated than play at school, partly because with fewer numbers, one may have to resort to an array of social categories to find play partners or to constitute a game. And in less crowded environments there are fewer potential witnesses to "make something of it" if girls and boys play together.

Relaxed interactions between girls and boys often depend on adults to set up and legitimize the contact.[4] Perhaps because of this contingency—and the other, distancing patterns which permeate relations between girls and boys—the easeful moments of interaction rarely build to close friendship. Schofield (1981) makes a similar observation about gender and racial barriers to friendship in a junior high school.

IMPLICATIONS FOR DEVELOPMENT

I have located social relations within an essentially spatial framework, emphasizing the organization of children's play, work, and other activities within specific settings and in one type of institution, the school. In contrast, frameworks of child development rely upon temporal metaphors, using images of growth and transformation over time. Taken alone, both spatial and temporal frameworks have shortcomings; fitted together, they may be mutually correcting.

Those interested in gender and development have relied upon conceptualizations of "sex-role socialization" and "sex differences." Sexuality and gender, I have argued, are more situated and fluid than these individualist and intrinsic models imply. Sex and gender are differently organized and defined across situations, even within the same institution. This situational variation (e.g., in the extent to which an encounter heightens or lessens gender boundaries, or is infused with sexual meanings) shapes and constrains individual behavior. Features which a developmental perspective might attribute to individuals and understand as relatively internal attributes unfolding over time may, in fact, be highly dependent on context. For example, children's avoidance of cross-sex friendship may be attributed to individual gender development in middle childhood. But attention to varied situations may show that this avoidance is contingent on group size, activity, adult behavior, collective meanings, and the risk of being teased.

A focus on social organization and situation draws attention to children's experiences in the present. This helps correct a model like "sex-role socialization," which casts the present under the shadow of the future, or presumed "endpoints" (Speier, 1976). A situated analysis of arrangements of sex and gender among those of different ages may point to crucial disjunctions in the life course. In the fourth and fifth grades, culturally defined heterosexual rituals ("goin' with") begin to suppress the presence and visibility of other types of interaction between girls and boys, such as nonsexualized and comfortable interaction and traveling in the world of the other sex. As "boyfriend/ girlfriend" definitions spread, the fifth-grade tomboy I described had to work to sustain "buddy" relationships with boys. Adult women who were tomboys often speak of early adolescence as a painful time when they were pushed away from participation in boys' activities. Other adult women speak of the loss of intense, even erotic ties with other girls when they entered puberty and the rituals of dating, that is, when they became absorbed into the situation of heterosexuality (Rich, 1980). When Lever (1976) describes

best-friend relationships among fifth-grade girls as preparation for dating, she imposes heterosexual ideologies onto a present which should be understood on its own terms.

As heterosexual encounters assume more importance, they may alter relations in same-sex groups. For example, Schofield (1981) reports that for sixth- and seventh-grade children in a middle school, the popularity of girls with other girls was affected by their popularity with boys, while boys' status with other boys did not depend on their relations with girls. This is an asymmetry familiar from the adult world; men's relationships with one another are defined through varied activities (occupations, sports), while relationships among women—and their public status—are more influenced by their connections to individual men.

A full understanding of gender and social relations should encompass cross-sex as well as within-sex interactions. "Borderwork" helps maintain separate, gender-linked subcultures, which, as those interested in development have begun to suggest, may result in different milieux for learning. Daniel Maltz and Ruth Borker (1983), for example, argue that because of different interactions within girls' and boys' groups, the sexes learn different rules for creating and interpreting friendly conversation, rules which carry into adulthood and help account for miscommunication between men and women. Carol Gilligan (1982) fits research on the different worlds of girls and boys into a theory of sex differences in moral development. Girls develop a style of reasoning, she argues, which is more personal and relational; boys develop a style which is more positional, based on separateness. Eleanor Maccoby (1982), also following the insight that because of sex segregation, girls and boys grow up in different environments, suggests implications for gender-differentiated prosocial and antisocial behavior.

This separate-worlds approach, as I have illustrated, also has limitations. The occasions when the sexes are together should also be studied, and understood as contexts for experience and learning. For example, asymmetries in cross-sex relationships convey a series of messages: that boys are more entitled to space and to the nonreciprocal right of interrupting or invading the activities of the other sex; that girls are more in need of adult protection, lower in status, more defined by sexuality, and may even be polluting. Different types of cross-sex interaction—relaxed, boundaried, sexualized, or taking place on the terms of the other sex—provide different contexts for development.

By mapping the array of relationships between and within the sexes, one adds complexity to the overly static and dichotomous imagery of separate worlds. Individual experiences vary, with implications for development. Some children prefer same-sex groupings; some are more likely to cross the gender boundary and participate in the world of the other sex; some children (e.g., girls and boys who frequently play "chase and kiss") invoke heterosexual meanings, while others avoid them.

Finally, after charting the terrain of relationships, one can trace their development over time. For example, age variation in the content and form of borderwork, or of cross- and same-sex touch, may be related to differing cognitive, social, emotional, or physical capacities, as well as to age-associated cultural forms. I earlier mentioned temporal shifts in the organization of cross-sex chasing, from mixing with fantasy play in the early grades to more elaborately ritualized and sexualized forms by the sixth grade. There also appear to be temporal changes in same- and cross-sex touch.

In kindergarten, girls and boys touch one another more freely than in fourth grade, when children avoid relaxed cross-sex touch and instead use pokes, pushes, and other forms of mock violence, even when the touch clearly expresses affection. This touch taboo is obviously related to the risk of seeming to *like* someone of the other sex. In fourth grade, same-sex touch begins to signal sexual meanings among boys as well as between boys and girls. Younger boys touch one another freely in cuddling (arm around shoulder) as well as mock-violence ways. By fourth grade, when homophobic taunts like "fag" become more common among boys, cuddling touch begins to disappear for boys, but less for girls.

Overall, I am calling for more complexity in our conceptualizations of gender and of children's social relationships. Our challenge is to retain the temporal sweep, looking at individual and group lives as they unfold over time, while also attending to social structure and context and to the full variety of experiences in the present.

ACKNOWLEDGMENTS

I would like to thank Jane Atkinson, Nancy Chodorow, Arlene Daniels, Peter Lyman, Zick Rubin, Malcolm Spector, Avril Thorne, and Margery Wolf for comments on an earlier version of this paper. Conversations with Zella Luria enriched this work.

NOTES

1. I am grateful to Frederick Erickson for suggesting the relevance of Barth's analysis.
2. Sue Samuelson (1980) reports that in a racially mixed playground in Fresno, California, Mexican-American but not Anglo children gave cooties. Racial as well as sexual inequality may be expressed through these forms.
3. This incident was recorded by Margaret Blume, who, for an undergraduate research project in 1982, observed in the California school where I earlier did fieldwork. Her observations and insights enhanced my own, and I would like to thank her for letting me cite this excerpt.
4. Note that in daily school life depending on the individual and the situation, teachers and aides sometimes lessened and at other times heightened sex segregation.

REFERENCES

Aronson, E., et al. 1978. *The Jigsaw Classroom.* Beverly Hills, Calif.: Sage.

Barth, F., ed. 1969. *Ethnic Groups and Boundaries.* Boston: Little, Brown.

Borman, K. M. 1979. "Children's interactions in playgrounds." *Theory into Practice* 18: 251–57.

Eder, D., & Hallinan, M. T. 1978. "Sex differences in children's friendships." *American Sociological Review* 43: 237–50.

Finnan, C. R. 1982. "The ethnography of children's spontaneous play." In G. Spindler, ed., *Doing the Ethnography of Schooling*, pp. 358–80. New York: Holt, Rinehart & Winston.

Foot, H. C., Chapman, A. J., & Smith, J. R. 1980. "Introduction." *Friendship and Social Relations in Children*, pp. 1–14. New York: Wiley.

Gilligan, C. 1982. *In a Different Voice: Psychological Theory and Women's Development.* Cambridge: Harvard University Press.

Glaser, B. G., & Strauss, A. L. 1967. *The Discovery of Grounded Theory.* Chicago: Aldine.

Goffman, E. 1977. "The arrangement between the sexes." *Theory and Society* 4: 301–36.

Goodwin, M. H. 1980. "Directive-response speech sequences in girls' and boys' task activities." In S. McConnell-Ginet,

R. Borker, & N. Furman, eds., *Women and Language in Literature and Society*, pp. 157–73. New York: Praeger.

Greif, E. B. 1982. "Sex differences in parent–child conversations." *Women's Studies International Quarterly* 3: 253–58.

Henley, N. 1977. *Body Politics: Power, Sex, and Nonverbal Communication*. Englewood Cliffs, N.J.: Prentice-Hall.

Karkau, K. 1973. *Sexism in the Fourth Grade*. Pittsburgh: KNOW, Inc. (pamphlet).

Katz, J. 1983. "A theory of qualitative methodology: The social system of analytic fieldwork." In R. M. Emerson, ed., *Contemporary Field Research*, pp. 127–48. Boston: Little, Brown.

Knapp, M., & Knapp, H. 1976. *One Potato, Two Potato: The Secret Education of American Children*. New York: W. W. Norton.

Lever, J. 1976. "Sex differences in the games children play." *Social Problems* 23: 478–87.

Maccoby, E. 1982. "Social groupings in childhood: Their relationship to prosocial and antisocial behavior in boys and girls." Paper presented at conference on The Development of Prosocial and Antisocial Behavior, Voss, Norway.

Maccoby, E., & Jacklin, C. 1974. *The Psychology of Sex Differences*. Stanford, Calif.: Stanford University Press.

Maltz, D. N., & Borker, R. A. 1983. "A cultural approach to male–female miscommunication." In J. J. Gumperz, ed., *Language and Social Identity*, pp. 195–216. New York: Cambridge University Press.

McRobbie, A., & Garber, J. 1975. "Girls and subcultures." In S. Hall & T. Jefferson, eds., *Resistance Through Rituals*, pp. 209–23. London: Hutchinson.

Ortner, S. B., & Whitehead, H. 1981. *Sexual Meanings*. New York: Cambridge University Press.

Parrott, S. 1972. "Games children play: Ethnography of a second-grade recess." In J. P. Spradley & D. W. McCurdy, eds., *The Cultural Experience*, pp. 206–19. Chicago: Science Research Associates.

Rich, A. 1980. "Compulsory heterosexuality and lesbian existence." *Signs* 5: 631–60.

Samuelson, S. 1980. "The cooties complex." *Western Folklore* 39: 198–210.

Savin-Williams, R. C. 1976. "An ethological study of dominance formation and maintenance in a group of human adolescents." *Child Development* 47: 972–79.

Schofield, J. W. 1981. "Complementary and conflicting identities: Images and interaction in an interracial school." In S. R. Asher & J. M. Gottman, eds., *The Development of Children's Friendships*, pp. 53–90. New York: Cambridge University Press.

Sherif, M., & Sherif, C. 1953. *Groups in Harmony and Tension*. New York: Harper.

Sluckin, A. 1981. *Growing Up in the Playground*. London: Routledge & Kegan Paul.

Speier, M. 1976. "The adult ideological viewpoint in studies of childhood." In A. Skolnick, ed., *Rethinking Childhood*, pp. 168–86. Boston: Little, Brown.

Sutton-Smith, B. 1971. "A syntax for play and games." In R. E. Herron and B. Sutton-Smith, eds., *Child's Play*, pp. 298–307. New York: Wiley.

Unger, R. K. 1979. "Toward a redefinition of sex and gender." *American Psychologist* 34: 1085–94.

Waldrop, M. F., & Halverson, C. F. 1975. "Intensive and extensive peer behavior: Longitudinal and cross-sectional analysis." *Child Development* 46: 19–26.

West, C., & Zimmerman, D. H. 1983. "Small insults: A study of interruptions in cross-sex conversations between unacquainted persons." In B. Thorne, C. Kramarae, & N. Henley, eds., *Language, Gender, and Society*. Rowley, Mass.: Newbury House.

Whitehead, H. 1981. "The bow and the burden strap: A new look at institutionalized homosexuality in Native America." In S. B. Ortner & H. Whitehead, eds., *Sexual Meanings*, pp. 80–115. New York: Cambridge University Press.

What Are Little Boys Made Of?

To hear some tell it, there's a virtual war against boys in America. Best-sellers' subtitles counsel us to "protect" boys, to "rescue" them. Inside, we hear how boys are failing at school, where their behavior is increasingly seen as a problem. Therapists advise anguished parents about boys' fragility, their hidden despair and despondence. Boys, we read, are depressed, suicidal, emotionally shut down.

And why? It depends on whom you ask. The backlash chorus—the cultural right as well as the authors of some of these books—chant "feminism." Because of feminism, they say, America has been so focused on girls that we've forgotten about the boys. Other writers blame patterns of male development, while still others find in feminism not the problem but its solution.

There's no question that there's a boy crisis. Virtually all the books cite the same statistics: boys are four to five times more likely to kill themselves than girls, four times more likely to be diagnosed as emotionally disturbed, three times more likely to be diagnosed with attention deficit disorder, and 15 times more likely to be victims of violent crime. The debate concerns the nature of the crisis, its causes, and, of course, its remedies. The startling number of advice manuals that have appeared in the past couple of years—almost all by male therapists—alternate between psychological diagnoses and practical advice about how to raise boys.

One group, epitomized by therapist Michael Gurian (*A Fine Young Man, The Wonder of Boys*), suggests that boys are both doing worse than ever and doing worse than girls thanks to feminists' efforts. Gurian argues that as feminists have changed the rules, they've made boys the problem. By minimizing the importance of basic biological differences, and establishing girls' standards as the ones all children must follow, feminists have wrecked boyhood. Along with Australian men's movement guru Steve Biddulph (*Raising Boys*), Gurian argues that our educational system forces naturally rambunctious boys to conform to a regime of obedience. With testosterone surging through their little limbs, boys are commanded to sit still, raise their hands, and take naps.

To hear these critics tell it, we're no longer allowing boys to be boys. We've misunderstood boy biology, and cultural meddling—especially by misinformed women—won't change a thing. It's nature, not nurture, that propels boys toward obnoxious behavior, violence, and sadistic experiments on insects. What makes boys boys is, in a word, testosterone, that magical, catch-all hormone that drives them toward aggression and risk-taking, and challenging this fact gives them the message, Gurian says, that "boyhood is defective."

This facile biological determinism mars otherwise insightful observations. Gurian adroitly points out the nearly unbearable pressure on young boys to conform, to resort to violence to solve problems, to disrupt classroom decorum. But he thinks it's entirely due to biology—not peer culture, media violence, or parental influence. And Biddulph agrees: "Testosterone equals vitality," he writes. All we have to do is "honor it and steer it into healthy directions." This over-reliance on biology leads both writers to overstate the differences between the sexes and ignore the differences among boys and among girls. To argue that boys have a harder time in school ignores all reliable evidence from sources such as Myra and David Sadker's *Failing at Fairness: How America's Schools Cheat Girls.*

These misdiagnoses lead to some rather bizarre excuses for boys' behavior, and to the celebration of all things masculine as the simple product of that pubertal chemical elixir. In *The Wonder of Boys*, Gurian cities bewilderingly incongruous rites of passage, such as "military boot camp, fraternity hazings, graduation day, and bar mitzvah," as essential parts of every boy's life. Hazing and bar mitzvahs? Have you read any reports of boys dying at the hands of other boys at bar mitzvahs? Biddulph explains boys' refusal to listen to adult authority by reference to the "fact" that their ear canals develop in irregular spurts, "leading to a period of hearing loss." And did you know that baritone singers in Welsh choruses have more testosterone than tenors— and have more sex! Where do they get this stuff?

More chilling, though, are their strategies for intervention. Gurian suggests reviving corporal punishment both at home and at school—but only when administered privately with cool indifference and never in the heat of adult anger. (He calls it "spanking responsibly.") Biddulph, somewhat more moderately, proposes that boys start school a year later than girls, so they'll be on a par intellectually.

The problem is, there's plenty of evidence that boys are not "just boys" everywhere and in the same ways. If it's all biological, why is the slightest deviation from expected manly behavior so cruelly punished? Why aren't Norwegian or French or Swiss boys as violent, homophobic, and misogynist as many are in the U.S.? Boys are not doomed to be victims of what Alan Alda once facetiously called "testosterone poisoning." On the contrary, they can become men who express their emotions and treat their partners respectfully, who listen as well as act, and who love and nurture their children.

But how do we get there? Another group of therapists, including Dan Kindlon and Michael Thompson, and William Pollack, eschew testosterone-tinged testimonials and treat masculinity as an ideology to be challenged. For them, we need to understand the patterns of boys' development to more effectively intervene and set boys on the path to a manhood of integrity.

To do that, Kindlon and Thompson write in *Raising Cain,* we must contend with the "culture of cruelty" that forces a boy to deny emotional neediness, "routinely disguise his feelings," and end up emotionally isolated. In *Real Boys,* Pollack calls it the "Boy Code" and the "mask of masculinity"—a kind of swaggering attitude that boys embrace to hide their fears, suppress dependency and vulnerability, and present a stoic front.

These two books are the biggest sellers and their authors the most visible experts on boyhood. Pollack's book is far better. The most influenced by feminism, his observations provide an important parallel to psychologist Carol Gilligan's work on how assertive, confident, and proud girls "lose their voices" when they hit adolescence. At the same moment, Pollack says, boys find the inauthentic voice of bravado, of constant posturing, of foolish risk-taking and gratuitous violence. The Boy

Code teaches them that they are supposed to be in power and thus to act like it. They "ruffle in a manly pose," as Yeats once put it, "for all their timid heart."

Unfortunately, these therapists' explanations don't always track. For one thing they all use examples drawn from their clinical practices but then generalize casually from their clients to all boys. And, alas, "all" is limited almost entirely to middle-class, suburban white boys. Cute blond boys stare at us from the books' covers, while inside the authors ignore large numbers of boys whose pain and low self-esteem may have to do with insecurities and anxieties that are more economically and politically rooted. Gurian's books disingenuously show one boy of color on each cover, but there's nary a mention of them inside. Kindlon and Thompson generalize from their work at an elite prep school.

If all the boys are white and middle class, at least they're not all straight. Most therapists treat homosexuality casually, dropping in a brief reference, "explaining" it as biological, and urging compassion and understanding before returning to the more "important" stuff. Only Pollack devotes a sensitive and carefully thought-out chapter to homosexuality and he actually uses the term "homophobia."

The cause of all this posturing and posing is not testosterone, of course, but privilege. In adolescence, both boys and girls get their first real dose of gender inequality, and that is what explains their different paths. The interventions recommended by Kindlon and Thompson—allowing boys to have their emotions; accepting a high level of activity; speaking their language; treating them with respect; using discipline to guide and build; modeling manhood as emotionally attached (all of which are good suggestions and applicable to girls, also)—don't address male entitlement. Indeed, of the male therapists, only Pollack and James Gilligan (*Violence*) even seem to notice it. For the others, boys' troubles are all about fears suppressed, pain swallowed. Kindlon and Thompson write that the "culture of cruelty imposes a code of silence on boys, requiring them to suffer without speaking of it and to be silent witnesses to acts of cruelty to others."

The books that are written with an understanding of male privilege—and the need to challenge it—are the ones that offer the most useful tools to improve boys' lives. Books by Myriam Miedzian and by Olga Silverstein and Beth Rashbaum, published several years ago, offer critiques of traditional boyhood and well-conceived plans for support and change. Eschewing biological determinism, these books see in feminism a blueprint for transforming both boyhood and manhood. Feminism encourages men—and their sons—to be more emotionally open and expressive, to develop empathic skills, and to channel emotional outbursts away from violence. And feminism demands the kinds of societal changes that make this growth possible.

That's all the more necessary, because there really is a boy crisis in America—not the crisis of inverted proportions that claims boys are the new victims of a feminist-inspired agenda run amok. The real boy crisis usually goes by another name. We call it "teen violence," "youth violence," "gang violence," "violence in the schools." Let's face facts: men and boys are responsible for 85 percent of all violent crimes in this country, and their victims are overwhelmingly male as well. From an early age, boys learn that violence is not only an acceptable form of conflict resolution, but one that is admired. Four times more teenage boys than teenage girls think fighting is appropriate when someone cuts into the front of a line. Half of all teenage boys get into a physical fight each year.

"Rescuing" or "protecting" isn't the answer, say British high school teachers Jonathan Salisbury and David Jackson. As their title, *Challenging Macho Values*, shouts, they want to take issue with traditional masculinity, to disrupt the facile "boys will be boys" model, and to erode boys' sense of entitlement. And for Paul Kivel (*Boys Will Be Men*), raising boys to manhood means confronting racism, sexism, and homophobia—both in our communities and in ourselves. These books are loaded with hands-on practical advice to help adolescents raise issues, confront fears, and overcome anxieties, and to help teachers dispel myths, encourage cooperation, and discourage violent solutions to perceived problems. Salisbury and Jackson's book will be most valuable to teachers seeking to transform disruptive behavior; Kivel's is geared more to parents, to initiate and continue those sensitive and difficult conversations. The most valuable material helps parents and teachers deconstruct sexuality myths and challenge sexual harassment and violence. "We believe that masculine violence is intentional, deliberate, and purposeful," write Salisbury and Jackson. "It comes from an attempt by men and boys to create and sustain a system of masculine power and control that benefits them every minute of the day." Forget testosterone; it's sexism! Even if these two books are less gracefully written and more relentlessly critical of traditional

boyhood, they are the only ones to recognize that not all boys are the same, and that one key to enabling boys to express a wider range of emotions is to challenge the power and privilege that is part of their cultural heritage.

Gilligan and Miedzian, along with James Garbarino (*Lost Boys*), understand that the real boy crisis is a crisis of violence—specifically the cultural prescriptions that equate masculinity with the capacity for violence. Garbarino's fortuitously timed study of youthful offenders locates the origins of men's violence in the way boys swallow anger and hurt. Among the boys he studied, "deadly petulance usually hides some deep emotional wounds, a way of compensating through an exaggerated sense of grandeur for an inner sense of violation, victimization, and injustice." In other words, as one prison inmate put it, "I'd rather be wanted for murder than not wanted at all."

Gilligan is even more specific. In his insightful study of violence, he places its origins in "the fear of shame and ridicule, and the overbearing need to prevent others from laughing at oneself by making them weep instead." The belief that violence is manly is not carried on any chromosome, not soldered into the wiring of the right or left hemisphere, not juiced by testosterone. (Half of all boys don't fight, most don't carry weapons, and almost all don't kill: are they not boys?) Boys learn it. Violence, Gilligan writes, "has far more to do with the cultural construction of manhood than it does with the hormonal substrates of biology."

That's where feminism comes in. Who, after all, has offered the most trenchant critique of that cultural construction but feminists? That's why the books written by women and men that use a feminist perspective (Gilligan, Kivel, Miedzian, Pollack, Salisbury and Jackson, and Silverstein and Rashbaum) are far more convincing than those that either repudiate it (Gurian, Biddulph) or ignore it (Kindlon and Thompson).

Frankly, I think the antifeminists such as Gurian and Biddulph (and the right wing in general) are the real male bashers. When they say boys will be boys, they mean boys will be uncivilized animals. In their view, males are biologically propelled to be savage, predatory, sexually omnivorous creatures, hard-wired for violence. As a man, I find this view insulting.

Feminists imagine, and demand, that men (and boys) can do better. Feminism offers the possibility of a new boyhood and a new masculinity based on a passion for justice, a love of equality, and the expression of a full range of feelings.

THE MAKING OF A SOLDIER: GENDER IN MILITARY RECRUITMENT

Kristen N. Nelson

The slogan "An Army of One" summons potential recruits to join a solid, unified team. Implied in the concept of joining an Army of One is a stripping of individuality and an adoption of the mentality and lifestyle of the "One." In reality, the U.S. military is made up of a diverse group of individuals, all of whom have been affected in different ways by intersections of gender, race, class, and nationality. The military uses print ad campaigns that encourage a heterogeneous pool of potential recruits to aspire to the ideal of the Mythic American Warrior. This fictional combatant is usually a U.S. citizen, *either* male *or* female, and heterosexual. Most individuals of any race or class meeting these guidelines can aspire to some version of the ideal.

Through the construction of the Mythic American Warrior, the U.S. military fosters conformity to mainstream standards of gender and heterosexuality. Representations of the ideal combatant reinforce the hegemony of White American masculinity. Because not all potential recruits can adopt the traits of hegemonic masculinity, the idealization of the Mythic Warrior fosters inequality. Yet, in significant ways, this fictional fighter subverts dominant standards of femininity and challenges often-racist hierarchies of masculinities.

The characteristics of the ideal American Soldier are clearly portrayed in the intersectional representations of race, gender, and nationality in military recruitment literature. Constructions of the ideal fighter vary based on individuals' social identities. An analysis of ten brochures that were on display at a Boston Army recruiting station in the Spring of 2005 clarifies the dually hegemonic and subversive nature of these representations.

All ten brochures highlight the intersectionality of race and gender; however, the longest, a 20-page booklet titled *The Making of a Soldier*, is especially revealing. While this pamphlet shows Black and White men in authoritative poses, no Asian-identifiable men are shown in combat or climbing walls. One man who looks East Asian is wearing surgeon's scrubs. Another, the only East Asian soldier pictured in camouflage in the collection, is seated and looking pensively toward an artificial source of light. He is dressed in camouflage, but he is not depicted in training or battle. This pamphlet reflects the multiplicity of masculinities available to potential recruits and suggests that the norm for masculinity shifts across lines of race.

Of course, East Asian soldiers hold combat positions in the military. Yet, this brochure propagates the controlling image of Asian American men as "effeminate, in the image of the 'model minority'" (Espiritu, 1997). The conflation of pensive, inactive poses with femininity and overt violence with masculinity only reinforces constricting gender norms. Nonetheless, the construction of the Asian American soldier as intelligent enough to serve as an Army doctor, yet not physically violent enforces the damaging conception that Asian men are less "truly masculine" than men of other races.

Images in *The Making of a Soldier* and other recruitment brochures also invoke colonialism, an institution that shaped the racialized construction of hegemonic and inferior masculinities (Connell, 2001). Three pamphlet pictures exemplify the centrality of colonialism to representations of the Mythic American Warrior. *The Making of a Soldier* features a picture of a White male soldier in camouflage kneeling to talk to a small African or Afro Latina girl. The sandy background of the picture suggests it was taken somewhere outside the United States (this picture also appears in *Army Linguist*, another brochure in the collection). A one-page foldout brochure, *Army Special Forces*, shows a Black combatant holding a gun in a woodsy area and pointing the way for a line of distraught-looking young brown-skinned women. The silhouette of another male soldier with a gun is blurred in the background, and the Black soldier in the foreground appears focused, authoritative, and tense. In a third pamphlet, *A World of Possibilities Awaits You: U.S. Air Force, Cross into the Blue*, a White male Air Force member dressed in camouflage is pictured holding a small, scared-looking East Asian girl with dirt on her shirt and a bandage on her elbow. He holds a protective hand on her wounded arm.

The colonialism and "White Man's Burden" ideology depicted in these brochures evoke R. W. Connell's discussion of how masculinities affect both colonizers and the colonized. Connell asserts in "The Men and the Boys" that "the formation of masculinities and the meaning of men's bodies is persistently connected with the racialization of global society. 'Race' . . . is understood as a hierarchy of bodies, and this has become inextricably mixed with the hierarchy of masculinities" (61). The use of an authoritative Black soldier in *Army Special Forces* disrupts the archetype of White westerners overtaking foreign lands and asserting their masculinity over effeminate native men and helpless, brown-skinned women. Yet the concept of superior American masculinity and the objectification, disempowerment, and exoticization of Third World women persist in these images.

The fictional American Warrior in military recruitment literature both perpetuates and subverts dominant constructions of racialized masculinity. This ideal soldier also reproduces and rejects hegemonic standards of femininity. One pamphlet, *Where Is That Girl That Lived in Your Mind*, addresses women who are considering becoming Marines. This brochure reproduces oppressive ideas about the femininity of mothering, but also offers empowering images of women that counter mainstream ideals of feminine beauty. Like the others in the collection, the photographs in this brochure reflect the intersections of race and gender.

The cover of *Where Is That Girl That Lived in Your Mind* features the softly-lit face of a young White woman, and asks the potential recruit in a (femininely) cursive font to remember "that girl in your mind" who, among other things, "threw harder" when she only "threw like a girl." This message could be viewed as stifling or empowering. On one hand, the pamphlet reinforces the essentialist belief that to throw like a girl is not to throw hard enough. On the other, the brochure encourages women who have been raised according to dominant gender ideology to exceed the low physical expectations placed on them because of their sex.

Where Is That Girl That Lived in Your Mind both promotes and rejects dominant ideas about women's work. One panel carries the message that being a female Marine in a predominantly male corps means "Equal opportunity. Equal training. And equal expectations. Advancement based on performance. Not gender." Implicit here is an acknowledgment of the "high rates of sex segregation [in the workplace] that foster inequities" (Bose and Whaley, this volume). Thus, *Where Is That Girl* addresses the fact that American women in many occupations experience gender discrimination.

The brochure assures the reader that when a woman joins the Marines, she will not be forced to give up her womanhood: "We don't expect or want you to compromise your femininity. You are a woman. Be a woman. Live the life you want to live. Raise a family if you choose." While the earlier acknowledgment of gender inequality is admirable, the pamphlet reassures women by reference to the exact characteristics often used to justify their oppression. To suggest that the life women want to live is a family life is to perpetuate the "ideological position that women's biological abilities to bear . . . children are 'natural' and therefore fundamental to women's 'fulfillment'" (Segura, this volume), even the fulfillment of women who challenge widespread gender norms by joining the Marines.

Interestingly, the military's visual representation of women as a group does not conform to dominant standards of beauty. There are no starved-looking women in these brochures. In the pictures of military personnel (and thus excluding the female "natives" discussed above), the Black body is not sexualized (as discussed by Collins, this volume). The only Black woman photographed with her hair visible appears in *Where Is That Girl That Lived in Your Mind*. This Black Marine's hair is straightened and styled in a short bob, marking her as heterosexual, but not overly feminine (see Banks, this volume).

Together, the ten pamphlets reveal much about the construction of the Mythic American Warrior under intersecting matrices of oppression. Men are more likely to be represented than women: 66% of those pictured are men; 33% are women. Men are also almost twice as likely as women to be depicted in camouflage (45% of the time, vs. 23% of the time

(continued)

for women) or carrying guns (15% of the time, vs. 8% of the time for women). Although women are depicted as soldiers and Marines, they continue to be represented as fragile and gentle, photographed in violent roles at a substantially lower rate than men. The male Mythic American Warrior is tough and combative (depending on his race); his female counterpart demonstrates her patriotism by joining the military, but also preserves femininity and only sometimes takes on physically aggressive roles.

By idealizing the qualities of the Mythic Warrior (in all her incarnations), the military encourages a diverse pool of potential recruits to recruit a limited set of racialized masculinities and femininities. It is perhaps not surprising that military cultural representations invoke colonialism, a racialized hierarchy of masculinities, and hint at "women's place" as caregivers. Yet, together, these brochures do not offer a monolithic expression of oppressive norms. Rather, they portray a shifting and complex ideal. Representations of the Mythic American Warrior constrict potential recruits according to dominant standards. However, these pamphlets also offer expressions of gender and race that defy norms of self-representation and behavior based on social identity. Through various constructions of gender, race, and nationality, U.S. military recruitment literature invites recruits into a world governed by hegemonic norms, while simultaneously promising opportunities for unconventional empowerment.

REFERENCES

Banks, I. (2008). Hair still matters. In L. Richardson, V. Taylor, & N. Whittier (Eds.), *Feminist Frontiers* in this volume. New York: McGraw-Hill.

Bose, C. E. & Whaley, R. B. (2008). Sex segregation in the U.S. labor force. In L. Richardson, V. Taylor, & N. Whittier (Eds.), *Feminist Frontiers* in this volume. New York: McGraw-Hill.

Connell, R. W. (2001). *The Men and the Boys.* Berkeley: University of California Press.

Espiritu, Y. L. (1997). *Asian American Women and Men.* Thousand Oaks, CA: Sage.

Hooks, B. (2008). Selling hot pussy: Representations of Black female sexuality in the cultural marketplace. In L. Richardson, V. Taylor, & N. Whittier (Eds.), *Feminist Frontiers* in this volume. New York: McGraw-Hill.

Segura, D. A. (2008). Working at motherhood: Chicana and Mexicana immigrant mothers and employment.

In L. Richardson, V. Taylor, & N. Whittier (Eds.), *Feminist Frontiers* in this volume. New York: McGraw-Hill.

U.S. Air Force (n.d.). *A world of possibilities awaits you: U.S. Air Force, cross into the blue* [Brochure].

U.S. Air Force. (n.d.). *Air Force combat control* [Brochure].

U.S. Army. (2003). *Army linguist* [Brochure].

U.S. Army. (2003). *Army Special Forces* [Brochure].

U.S. Army. (2003). *Army warrant officer flight training* [Brochure].

U.S. Army (2002). *The making of a soldier* [Brochure].

U.S. Marines. (n.d.). *A message for family members* [Brochure].

U.S. Marines. (n.d.). *A standard of excellence: Marine Corps guaranteed enlistment options* [Brochure].

U.S. Marines. (n.d.). *Toma el camino que pocos tienen el valor de tomar* [Brochure].

U.S. Marines. (n.d.). *Where is that girl that lived in your mind* [Brochure].

"We Don't Sleep Around Like White Girls Do": Family, Culture, and Gender in Filipina American Lives

I want my daughters to be Filipino especially on sex. I always emphasize to them that they should not participate in sex if they are not married. We are also Catholic. We are raised so that we don't engage in going out with men while we are not married. And I don't like it to happen to my daughters as if they have no values. I don't like them to grow up that way, like the American girls.

—Filipina Immigrant Mother

I found that a lot of the Asian American friends of mine, we don't date like white girls date. We don't sleep around like white girls do. Everyone is really mellow at dating because your parents were constraining and restrictive.

—Second-Generation Filipina daughter

Focusing on the relationship between Filipino immigrant parents and their daughters, this article argues that gender is a key to immigrant identity and a vehicle for racialized immigrants to assert cultural superiority over the dominant group. In immigrant communities, culture takes on a special significance: not only does it form a lifeline to the home country and a basis for group identity in a new country, it is also a base from which immigrants stake their political and sociocultural claims on their new country (Eastmond 1993, 40). For Filipino immigrants, who come from a homeland that was once a U.S. colony, cultural reconstruction has been especially critical in the assertion of their presence in the United States—a way to counter the cultural Americanization of the Philippines, to resist the assimilative and alienating demands of U.S. society, and to reaffirm to themselves their self-worth in the face of colonial, racial, class,

and gendered subordination. Before World War II, Filipinos were barred from becoming U.S. citizens, owning property, and marrying whites. They also encountered discriminatory housing policies, unfair labor practices, violent physical encounters, and racist as well as anti-immigrant discourse.[1] While blatant legal discrimination against Filipino Americans is largely a matter of the past, Filipinos continue to encounter many barriers that prevent full participation in the economic, social, and political institutions of the United States (Azores-Gunter 1986–87; Cabezas, Shinagawa, and Kawaguchi 1986–87; Okamura and Agbayani 1997). Moreover, the economic mobility and cultural assimilation that enables white ethnics to become "unhyphenated whites" is seldom extended to Filipino Americans (Espiritu 1994). Like other Asians, the Filipino is "always seen as an immigrant, as the 'foreigner-within,' even when born in the United States" (Lowe 1996, 5). Finally, although Filipinos have been in the United States since the middle of the 1700s and Americans have been in the Philippines since at least the late 1800s, U.S. Filipinos—as racialized nationals, immigrants, and citizens—are "still practically an invisible and silent minority" (San Juan 1991, 117). Drawing from my research on Filipino American families in San Diego, California, I explore in this article the ways racialized immigrants claim through gender the power denied them by racism.

My epigraphs, quotations of a Filipina immigrant mother and a second-generation Filipina daughter, suggest that the virtuous Filipina daughter is partially constructed on the conceptualization of white women as sexually immoral. This juxtaposition underscores the fact that femininity is a relational category, one that is co-constructed with other racial and cultural categories. These narratives also reveal that women's sexuality and their enforced "morality" are fundamental to the structuring of social inequalities. Historically, the sexuality of racialized women has been systematically demonized and disparaged by dominant or oppressor groups to justify and bolster nationalist movements, colonialism, and/or racism. But as these narratives indicate, racialized groups also criticize the morality of white women as a strategy of resistance—a means of asserting a morally superior public face to the dominant society.

By exploring how Filipino immigrants characterize white families and white women, I hope to contribute to a neglected area of research: how the "margins" imagine and construct the "mainstream" in order to assert superiority over it. But this strategy is not without costs. The elevation of Filipina chastity (particularly that of young women) has the effect of reinforcing masculinist and patriarchal power in the name of a greater ideal of national/ethnic self-respect. Because the control of women is one of the principal means of asserting moral superiority, young women in immigrant families face numerous restrictions on their autonomy, mobility, and personal decision making. Although this article addresses the experiences and attitudes of both parents and children, here I am more concerned with understanding the actions of immigrant parents than with the reactions of their second-generation daughters.

STUDYING FILIPINOS IN SAN DIEGO

San Diego, California has long been a favored area of settlement for Filipinos and is today the third-largest U.S. destination for Filipino immigrants (Rumbaut 1991, 220).[2] As the site of the largest U.S. naval base and the Navy's primary West Coast training facility, San Diego has been a primary area of settlement for Filipino navy personnel and their families since the early 1900s. As in other Filipino communities along the Pacific Coast, the San Diego community grew dramatically in the twenty-five years following passage of the 1965 Immigration Act. New immigration contributed greatly to the tripling of San Diego county's Filipino American population from 1970 to 1980 and its doubling from 1980 to 1990. In 1990, nearly 96,000 Filipinos resided in the county. Although they made up only 4 percent of the county's general population, they constituted close to 50 percent of the Asian American population (Espiritu 1995). Many post-1965 Filipino immigrants have come to San Diego as professionals—most conspicuously as health care workers. A 1992

analysis of the socioeconomic characteristics of recent Filipino immigrants in San Diego indicated that they were predominantly middle-class, college-educated, and English-speaking professionals who were more likely to own than rent their homes (Rumbaut 1994). At the same time, about two-thirds of the Filipinos surveyed indicated that they had experienced racial and ethnic discrimination (Espiritu and Wolf, forthcoming).

The information on which this article is based comes mostly from in-depth interviews that I conducted with almost one hundred Filipinos in San Diego.[3] Using the "snowball" sampling technique, I started by interviewing Filipino Americans whom I knew and then asking them to refer me to others who might be willing to be interviewed. In other words, I chose participants not randomly but rather through a network of Filipino American contacts whom the first group of respondents trusted. To capture the diversity within the Filipino American community, I sought and selected respondents of different backgrounds and with diverse viewpoints. The sample is about equally divided between first-generation immigrants (those who came to the United States as adults) and Filipinas/os who were born and/or raised in the United States. It is more difficult to pinpoint the class status of the people I interviewed. To be sure, they included poor working-class immigrants who barely eked out a living, as well as educated professionals who thrived in middle- and upper-class suburban neighborhoods. However, the class status of most was much more ambiguous. I met Filipinos/as who toiled as assembly workers but who, through the pooling of income and finances, owned homes in middle-class communities. I also discovered that class status was transnational, determined as much by one's economic position in the Philippines as by that in the United States. For example, I encountered individuals who struggled economically in the United States but owned sizable properties in the Philippines. And I interviewed immigrants who continued to view themselves as "upper class" even while living in dire conditions in the United States. These examples suggest that the upper/middle/working-class typology, while useful, does not capture the complexity of immigrant lives. Reflecting the prominence of the U.S. Navy in San Diego, more than half of my respondents were affiliated with or had relatives affiliated with the U.S. Navy.

My tape-recorded interviews, conducted in English, ranged from three to ten hours each and took place in offices, coffee shops, and homes. My questions were open-ended and covered three general areas: family and immigration history, ethnic identity and practices, and community development among San Diego's Filipinos. The interviewing process varied widely: some respondents needed to be prompted with specific questions, while others spoke at great length on their own. Some chose to cover the span of their lives; others focused on specific events that were particularly important to them. The initial impetus for this article on the relationship between immigrant parents and their daughters came from my observation that the dynamics of gender emerged more clearly in the interviews with women than in those with men. Because gender has been a marked category for women, the mothers and daughters I interviewed rarely told their life stories without reference to the dynamics of gender (see Personal Narratives Group 1989, 4–5). Even without prompting, young Filipinas almost always recounted stories of restrictive gender roles and gender expectations, particularly of parental control over their whereabouts and sexuality.

I believe that my own personal and social characteristics influenced the actual process of data collection, the quality of the materials that I gathered, and my analysis of them. As a Vietnam-born woman who immigrated to the United States at the age of twelve, I came to the research project not as an "objective" outsider but as a fellow Asian immigrant who shared some of the life experiences of my respondents. During the fieldwork process, I did not remain detached but actively shared with my informants my own experiences of being an Asian immigrant woman: of being perceived as an outsider in U.S. society, of speaking English as a second language, of being a woman of color in a racialized patriarchal society, and of negotiating intergenerational tensions within my own family. I do not claim that these shared struggles grant me "insider status" into the Filipino American community; the differences in our histories, cultures, languages, and, at times, class backgrounds, remain important. But I do claim that these shared experiences enable me to bring to the work a comparative perspective that is implicit, intuitive, and informed by my own identities and positionalities—and with it a commitment to approach these subjects with both sensitivity and rigor. In a cogent call for scholars of color to expand on the premise of studying "our own" by studying other "others," Ruby Tapia argues that such implicitly comparative projects are important because they permit us to "highlight the different and *differentiating* functional

forces of racialization" (1997, 2). It is with this deep interest in discovering—and forging—commonalities out of our specific and disparate experiences that I began this study on Filipino Americans in San Diego.

"AMERICAN" AND WHITENESS: "TO ME, AMERICAN MEANS WHITE"

In U.S. racial discourse and practices, unless otherwise specified, "Americans" means "whites" (Lipsitz 1998, 1). In the case of Asian Americans, U.S. exclusion acts, naturalization laws, and national culture have simultaneously marked Asians as the inassimilable aliens and whites as the quintessential Americans (Lowe 1996). Excluded from the collective memory of who constitutes a "real" American, Asians in the United States, even as citizens, remain "foreigners-within"—"non-Americans." In a study of third- and later-generation Chinese and Japanese Americans, Mia Tuan (1998) concludes that, despite being longtime Americans, Asians—as racialized ethnics—are often assumed to be foreign unless proven otherwise. In the case of Filipinos who emigrated from a former U.S. colony, their formation as racialized minorities does not begin in the United States but rather in a "homeland" already affected by U.S. economic, social, and cultural influences (Lowe 1996, 8).

Cognizant of this racialized history, my Filipino respondents seldom identify themselves as American. As will be evident in the discussion below, they equate "American" with "white" and often use these two terms interchangeably. For example, a Filipina who is married to a white American refers to her husband as "American" but to her African American and Filipino American brothers-in-law as "black" and "Filipino," respectively. Others speak about "American ways," "American culture," or "American lifestyle" when they really mean *white* American ways, culture, and lifestyle. A Filipino man who has lived in the United States for thirty years explains why he still does not identify himself as American: "I don't see myself just as an American because I cannot hide the fact that my skin is brown. To me, American means white." A second-generation Filipina recounted the following story when asked whether she defined herself as American:

> I went to an all-white school. I knew I was different. I wasn't American. See, you are not taught that you're American because you are not white. When I was in the tenth grade, our English teacher asked us what our

nationality was, and she goes how many of you are Mexican, how many of you are Filipino, and how many of you are Samoan and things like that. And when she asked how many of you are American, just the white people raised their hands.

Other Asian Americans also conflate *American* and *white*. In an ethnographic study of Asian American high school students, Stacey Lee reports that Korean immigrant parents often instructed their children to socialize only with Koreans and "Americans." When asked to define the term *American*, the Korean students responded in unison with "White! Korean parents like white" (Lee 1996, 24). Tuan (1998) found the same practice among later-generation Chinese and Japanese Americans: the majority use the term *American* to refer to whites.

CONSTRUCTING THE DOMINANT GROUP: THE MORAL FLAWS OF WHITE AMERICANS

Given the centrality of moral themes in popular discussions on racial differences, Michele Lamont (1997) has suggested that morality is a crucial site to study the cultural mechanisms of reproduction of racial inequality. While much has been written on how whites have represented the (im)morality of people of color (Collins 1991; Marchetti 1993; Hamamoto 1994), there has been less critical attention to how people of color have represented whites.[4] Shifting attention from the otherness of the subordinate group (as dictated by the "mainstream") to the otherness of the dominant group (as constructed by the "margins"), this section focuses on the alternative frames of meaning that racially subordinate groups mobilize to (re)define their status in relation to the dominant group. I argue that female morality—defined as women's dedication to their families and sexual restraint—is one of the few sites where economically and politically dominated groups can construct the dominant group as other and themselves as superior. Because womanhood is idealized as the repository of tradition, the norms that regulate women's behaviors become a means of determining and defining group status and boundaries. As a consequence, the burdens and complexities of cultural representation fall most heavily on immigrant women and their daughters. Below, I show that Filipino immigrants claim moral distinctiveness for their community by representing "Americans" as morally flawed, themselves

as family-oriented model minorities, and their wives and daughters as paragons of morality.

FAMILY-ORIENTED MODEL MINORITIES: "WHITE WOMEN WILL LEAVE YOU"

In his work on Italian immigrant parents and children in the 1930s, Robert Anthony Orsi (1985) reports that the parents invented a virtuous Italy (based on memories of their childhood) that they then used to castigate the morality of the United States and their U.S.-born or -raised children. In a similar way, many of my respondents constructed their "ethnic" culture as principled and "American" culture as deviant. Most often, this morality narrative revolves around family life and family relations. When asked what set Filipinos apart from other Americans, my respondents—of all ages and class backgrounds—repeatedly contrasted close-knit Filipino families to what they perceived to be the more impersonal quality of U.S. family relations.[5] In the following narratives, "Americans" are characterized as lacking in strong family ties and collective identity, less willing to do the work of family and cultural maintenance, and less willing to abide by patriarchal norms in husband/wife relations:

> American society lacks caring. The American way of life is more individual rather than collective. The American way is to say I want to have my own way. (Filipina immigrant, fifty-four years old)
>
> Our [Filipino] culture is different. We are more close-knit. We tend to help one another. Americans, ya know, they are all right, but they don't help each other that much. As a matter of fact, if the parents are old, they take them to a convalescent home and let them rot there. We would never do that in our culture. We would nurse them; we would help them until the very end. (Filipino immigrant, sixty years old)
>
> Our [Filipino] culture is very communal. You know that your family will always be there, that you don't have to work when you turn eighteen, you don't have to pay rent when you are eighteen, which is the American way of thinking. You also know that if things don't work out in the outside world, you can always come home and mommy and daddy will always take you and your children in. (Second-generation Filipina, thirty-three years old)
>
> Asian parents take care of their children. Americans have a different attitude. They leave their children to their own resources. They get baby sitters to take care

of their children or leave them in day care. That's why when they get old, their children don't even care about them. (Filipina immigrant, forty-six years old)

Implicit in negative depictions of U.S. families as uncaring, selfish, and distant is the allegation that white women are not as dedicated to their families as Filipina women are to theirs. Several Filipino men who married white women recalled being warned by their parents and relatives that "white women will leave you." As one man related, "My mother said to me, 'Well, you know, don't marry a white person because they would take everything that you own and leave you.'" For some Filipino men, perceived differences in attitudes about women's roles between Filipina and non-Filipina women influenced their marital choice. A Filipino American navy man explained why he went back to the Philippines to look for a wife:

> My goal was to marry a Filipina. I requested to be stationed in the Philippines to get married to a Filipina. I'd seen the women here and basically they are spoiled. They have a tendency of not going along together with their husband. They behave differently. They chase the male, instead of the male, the normal way of the traditional way is for the male to go after the female. They have sex without marrying. They want to do their own things. So my idea was to go back home and marry somebody who has never been here. I tell my son the same thing: if he does what I did and finds himself a good lady there, he will be in good hands.

Another man who had dated mostly white women in high school recounted that when it came time for him to marry, he "looked for the kind of women" he met while stationed in the Philippines: "I hate to sound chauvinistic about marriages, but Filipinas have a way of making you feel like you are a king. They also have that tenderness, that elegance. And we share the same values about family, education, religion, and raising children."

The claims of family closeness are not unique to Filipino immigrants. For example, when asked what makes their group distinctive, Italian Americans (di Leonardo 1984), Vietnamese Americans (Kibria 1993), South Asian Americans (Hickey 1996), and African Americans (Lamont 1997) all point proudly to the close-knit character of their family life. Although it is difficult to know whether these claims are actual perceptions or favored self-legitimating answers, it is nevertheless important to note the gender implications

of these claims. That is, while both men and women identify the family system as a tremendous source of cultural pride, it is women—through their unpaid housework and kin work—who shoulder the primary responsibility for maintaining family closeness. As the organizers of family rituals, transmitters of homeland folklores, and socializers of young children, women have been crucial for the maintenance of family ties and cultural traditions. In a study of kinship, class, and gender among California Italian Americans, di Leonardo argues that women's kin work, "the work of knitting households together into 'close, extended families,'" maintains the family networks that give ethnicity meaning (1984, 229).

Because the moral status of the community rests on women's labor, women, as wives and daughters, are expected to dedicate themselves to the family. Writing on the constructed image of ethnic family and gender, di Leonardo argues that "a large part of stressing ethnic identity amounts to burdening women with increased responsibilities for preparing special foods, planning rituals, and enforcing 'ethnic' socialization of children" (1984, 222). A twenty-three-year-old Filipina spoke about the reproductive work that her mother performed and expected her to learn:

> In my family, I was the only girl, so my mom expected a lot from me. She wanted me to help her to take care of the household. I felt like there was a lot of pressure on me. It's very important to my mom to have the house in order: to wash the dishes, to keep the kitchen in order, vacuuming, and dusting and things like that. She wants me to be a perfect housewife. It's difficult. I have been married now for about four months and my mother asks me every now and then what have I cooked for my husband. My mom is also very strict about families getting together on holidays, and I would always help her to organize that. Each holiday, I would try to decorate the house for her, to make it more special.

The burden of unpaid reproductive and kin work is particularly stressful for women who work outside the home. In the following narrative, a Filipina wife and mother described the pulls of family and work that she experienced when she went back to school to pursue a doctoral degree in nursing:

> The Filipinos, we are very collective, very connected. Going through the doctoral program, sometimes I think it is better just to forget about my relatives and

just concentrate on school. All that connectedness, it steals parts of myself because all of my energies are devoted to my family. And that is the reason why I think Americans are successful. The majority of the American people they can do what they want. They don't feel guilty because they only have a few people to relate to. For us Filipinos, it's like roots under the tree, you have all these connections. The Americans are more like the trunk. I am still trying to go up to the trunk of the tree but it is too hard. I want to be more independent, more like the Americans. I want to be good to my family but what about me? And all the things that I am doing. It's hard. It's always a struggle.

It is important to note that this Filipina interprets her exclusion and added responsibilities as only racial when they are also gendered. For example, when she says, "the American people they can do what they want," she ignores the differences in the lives of white men and white women—the fact that most white women experience similar competing pulls of family, education, and work.

RACIALIZED SEXUALITY AND (IM)MORALITY: "IN AMERICA, . . . SEX IS NOTHING"

Sexuality, as a core aspect of social identity, is fundamental to the structuring of gender inequality (Millett 1970). Sexuality is also a salient marker of otherness and has figured prominently in racist and imperialist ideologies (Gilman 1985; Stoler 1991). Historically, the sexuality of subordinate groups—particularly that of racialized women—has been systematically stereotyped by the dominant groups.[6] At stake in these stereotypes is the construction of women of color as morally lacking in the areas of sexual restraint and traditional morality. Asian women—both in Asia and in the United States—have been racialized as sexually immoral, and the "Orient"—and its women—has long served as a site of European male-power fantasies, replete with lurid images of sexual license, gynecological aberrations, and general perversion (Gilman 1985, 89). In colonial Asia in the nineteenth and early twentieth centuries, for example, female sexuality was a site for colonial rulers to assert their moral superiority and thus their supposed natural and legitimate right to rule. The colonial rhetoric of moral superiority was based on the construction of colonized Asian women as subjects of sexual desire and fulfillment and European colonial

women as the paragons of virtue and the bearers of a redefined colonial morality (Stoler 1991). The discourse of morality has also been used to mark the "unassimilability" of Asians in the United States. At the turn of the twentieth century, the public perception of Chinese women as disease-ridden, drug-addicted prostitutes served to underline the depravity of "Orientals" and played a decisive role in the eventual passage of exclusion laws against all Asians (Mazumdar 1989, 3–4). The stereotypical view that all Asian women were prostitutes, first formed in the 1850s, persisted. Contemporary American popular culture continues to endow Asian women with an excess of "womanhood," sexualizing them but also impugning their sexuality (Espiritu 1997, 93).

Filipinas—both in the Philippines and in the United States—have been marked as desirable but dangerous "prostitutes" and/or submissive "mail-order brides" (Halualani 1995; Egan 1996). These stereotypes emerged out of the colonial process, especially the extensive U.S. military presence in the Philippines. Until the early 1990s, the Philippines, at times unwillingly, housed some of the United States's largest overseas airforce and naval bases (Espiritu 1995, 14). Many Filipino nationalists have charged that "the prostitution problem" in the Philippines stemmed from U.S. and Philippine government policies that promoted a sex industry—brothels, bars, and massage parlors—for servicemen stationed or on leave in the Philippines. During the Vietnam War, the Philippines was known as the "rest and recreation" center of Asia, hosting approximately ten thousand U.S. servicemen daily (Coronel and Rosca 1993; Warren 1993). In this context, all Filipinas were racialized as sexual commodities, usable and expendable. A U.S.-born Filipina recounted the sexual harassment she faced while visiting Subic Bay Naval Station in Olongapo City:

> One day, I went to the base dispensary. . . . I was dressed nicely, and as I walked by the fire station, I heard catcalls and snide remarks being made by some of the firemen. . . . I was fuming inside. The next thing I heard was, "How much do you charge?" I kept on walking. "Hey, are you deaf or something? How much do you charge? You have a good body." That was an incident that I will never forget. (Quoted in Espiritu 1995, 77)

The sexualized racialization of Filipina women is also captured in Marianne Vilanueva's short story "Opportunity" (1991). As the protagonist, a "mail-order bride" from the Philippines, enters a hotel lobby to meet her American fiancé, the bellboys snicker and whisper *puta* (whore): a reminder that U.S. economic and cultural colonization in the Philippines always forms a backdrop to any relations between Filipinos and Americans (Wong 1993, 53).

Cognizant of the pervasive hypersexualization of Filipina women, my respondents, especially women who grew up near military bases, were quick to denounce prostitution, to condemn sex laborers, and to declare (unasked) that they themselves did not frequent "that part of town." As one Filipina immigrant said,

Growing up [in the Philippines], I could never date an American because my dad's concept of a friendship with an American is with a G.I. The only reason why my dad wouldn't let us date an American is that people will think that the only way you met was because of the base. I have never seen the inside of any of the bases because we were just forbidden to go there.

Many of my respondents also distanced themselves culturally from the Filipinas who serviced U.S. soldiers by branding them "more Americanized" and "more Westernized." In other words, these women were sexually promiscuous because they had assumed the sexual mores of white women. This characterization allows my respondents to symbolically disown the Filipina "bad girl" and, in so doing, to uphold the narrative of Filipina sexual virtuosity and white female sexual promiscuity. In the following narrative, a mother who came to the United States in her thirties contrasted the controlled sexuality of women in the Philippines with the perceived promiscuity of white women in the United States:

In the Philippines, we always have chaperons when we go out. When we go to dances, we have our uncle, our grandfather, and auntie all behind us to make sure that we behave in the dance hall. Nobody goes necking outside. You don't even let a man put his hand on your shoulders. When you were brought up in a conservative country, it is hard to come here and see that it is all freedom of speech and freedom of action. Sex was never mentioned in our generation. I was thirty already when I learned about sex. But to the young generation in America, sex is nothing.

Similarly, another immigrant woman criticized the way young American women are raised: "Americans are so liberated. They allow their children, their girls,

to go out even when they are still so young." In contrast, she stated that, in "the Filipino way, it is very important, the value of the woman, that she is a virgin when she gets married."

The ideal "Filipina," then, is partially constructed on the community's conceptualization of white women. She is everything that they are not: she is sexually modest and dedicated to her family; they are sexually promiscuous and uncaring. Within the context of the dominant culture's pervasive hypersexualization of Filipinas, the construction of the "ideal" Filipina—as family-oriented and chaste—can be read as an effort to reclaim the morality of the community. This effort erases the Filipina "bad girl," ignores competing sexual practices in the Filipino communities, and uncritically embraces the myth of "Oriental femininity." Cast as the embodiment of perfect womanhood and exotic femininity, Filipinas (and other Asian women) in recent years have been idealized in U.S. popular culture as more truly "feminine" (i.e., devoted, dependent, domestic) and therefore more desirable than their more modern, emancipated sisters (Espiritu 1997, 113). Capitalizing on this image of the "superfemme," mail-order bride agencies market Filipina women as "'exotic, subservient wife imports' for sale and as alternatives for men sick of independent 'liberal' Western women" (Halualani 1995, 49; see also Ordonez 1997, 122).

Embodying the moral integrity of the idealized ethnic community, immigrant women, particularly young daughters, are expected to comply with male-defined criteria of what constitute "ideal" feminine virtues. While the sexual behavior of adult women is confined to a monogamous, heterosexual context, that of young women is denied completely (see Dasgupta and DasGupta 1996, 229–31). In the next section, I detail the ways Filipino immigrant parents, under the rubric of "cultural preservation," police their daughters' behaviors in order to safeguard their sexual innocence and virginity. These attempts at policing generate hierarchies and tensions within immigrant families—between parents and children and between brothers and sisters.

THE CONSTRUCTION(S) OF THE "IDEAL" FILIPINA: "BOYS ARE BOYS AND GIRLS ARE DIFFERENT"

As the designated "keepers of the culture" (Billson 1995), immigrant women and their behavior come under intensive scrutiny both from men and women of their own groups and from U.S.-born Americans

(Gabbacia 1994, xi). In a study of the Italian Harlem community from 1880 to 1950, Orsi reports that "all the community's fears for the reputation and integrity of the domus came to focus on the behavior of young women" (1985, 135). Because women's moral and sexual loyalties were deemed central to the maintenance of group status, changes in female behavior, especially that of growing daughters, were interpreted as signs of moral decay and ethnic suicide and were carefully monitored and sanctioned (Gabbacia 1994, 113).

Although details vary, young women of various groups and across space and time—for example, second-generation Chinese women in San Francisco in the 1920s (Yung 1995), U.S.-born Italian women in East Harlem in the 1930s (Orsi 1985), young Mexican women in the Southwest during the interwar years (Ruiz 1992), and daughters of Caribbean and Asian Indian immigrants on the East Coast in the 1990s (Dasgupta and DasGupta 1996; Waters 1996)—have identified strict parental control on their activities and movements as the primary source of intergenerational conflict. Recent studies of immigrant families also identify gender as a significant determinant of parent-child conflict, with daughters more likely than sons to be involved in such conflicts and instances of parental derogation (Rumbaut and Ima 1988; Woldemikael 1989; Matute-Bianchi 1991; Gibson 1995).

Although immigrant families have always been preoccupied with passing on their native culture, language, and traditions to both male and female children, it is daughters who have the primary burden of protecting and preserving the family. Because sons do not have to conform to the image of an "ideal" ethnic subject as daughters do, they often receive special day-to-day privileges denied to daughters (Haddad and Smith 1996, 22–24; Waters 1996, 75–76). This is not to say that immigrant parents do not place undue expectations on their sons; rather, these expectations do not pivot around the sons' sexuality or dating choices.[7] In contrast, parental control over the movement and action of daughters begins the moment they are perceived as young adults and sexually vulnerable. It regularly consists of monitoring their whereabouts and forbidding dating (Wolf 1997). For example, the immigrant parents I interviewed seldom allowed their daughters to date, to stay out late, to spend the night at a friend's house, or to take an out-of-town trip.

Many of the second-generation women I spoke to complained bitterly about these parental restrictions. They particularly resented what they saw as gender inequity in their families: the fact that their parents placed far more restrictions on their activities and movements than on their brothers'. Some decried the fact that even their younger brothers had more freedom than they did. "It was really hard growing up because my parents would let my younger brothers do what they wanted but I didn't get to do what I wanted even though I was the oldest. I had a curfew and my brothers didn't. I had to ask if I could go places and they didn't. My parents never even asked my brothers when they were coming home." As indicated in the following excerpt, many Filipino males are cognizant of this double standard in their families:

> My sister would always say to me, "It's not fair, just because you are a guy, you can go wherever you want." I think my parents do treat me and my sister differently. Like in high school, maybe 10:30 at night, which is pretty late on a school night, and I say I have to go pick up some notes at my friend's house, my parents wouldn't say anything. But if my sister were to do that, there would be no way. Even now when my sister is in college already, if she wants to leave at midnight to go to a friend's house, they would tell her that she shouldn't do it.

When questioned about this double standard, parents generally responded by explaining that "girls are different":

> I have that Filipino mentality that boys are boys and girls are different. Girls are supposed to be protected, to be clean. In the early years, my daughters have to have chaperons and curfews. And they know that they have to be virgins until they get married. The girls always say that is not fair. What is the difference between their brothers and them? And my answer always is, "In the Philippines, you know, we don't do that. The girls stay home. The boys go out." It was the way that I was raised. I still want to have part of that culture instilled in my children. And I want them to have that to pass on to their children.

Even among self-described Western-educated and "tolerant" parents, many continue to ascribe to "the Filipino way" when it comes to raising daughters. As one college-educated father explains,

> Because of my Western education, I don't raise my children the way my parents raised me. I tended to be a little more tolerant. But at times, especially in

certain issues like dating, I find myself more towards the Filipino way in the sense that I have only one daughter so I tended to be a little bit stricter. So the double standard kind of operates: it's alright for the boys to explore the field but I tended to be overly protective of my daughter. My wife feels the same way because the boys will not lose anything, but the daughter will lose something, her virginity, and it can be also a question of losing face, that kind of thing.

Although many parents discourage or forbid dating for daughters, they still fully expect these young women to fulfill their traditional roles as women: to marry and have children. A young Filipina recounted the mixed messages she received from her parents:

This is the way it is supposed to work: Okay, you go to school. You go to college. You graduate. You find a job. *Then* you find your husband, and you have children. That's the whole time line. *But* my question is, if you are not allowed to date, how are you supposed to find your husband? They say "no" to the whole dating scene because that is secondary to your education, secondary to your family. They do push marriage, but at a later date. So basically my parents are telling me that I should get married and I should have children but that I should not date.

In a study of second-generation Filipino Americans in northern California, Diane Wolf (1997) reports the same pattern of parental pressures: Parents expect daughters to remain virgins until marriage, to have a career, *and* to combine their work lives with marriage and children.

The restrictions on girls' movement sometimes spill over to the realm of academics. Dasgupta and Das-Gupta (1996, 230) recount that in the Indian American community, while young men were expected to attend faraway competitive colleges, many of their female peers were encouraged by their parents to go to the local colleges so that they could live at or close to home. Similarly, Wolf (1997, 467) reports that some Filipino parents pursued contradictory tactics with their children, particularly their daughters, by pushing them to achieve academic excellence in high school but then "pulling the emergency brake" when they contemplated college by expecting them to stay at home, even if it meant going to a less competitive college, or not going at all. In the following account, a young Filipina relates that her parents' desire to

"protect" her surpassed their concerns for her academic preparation:

My brother [was] given a lot more opportunity educationally. He was given the opportunity to go to Miller High School that has a renowned college preparatory program but [for] which you have to be bussed out of our area.[8] I've come from a college prep program in junior high and I was asked to apply for the program at Miller. But my parents said "No, absolutely not." This was even during the time, too, when Southside [the neighborhood high school] had one of the lowest test scores in the state of California. So it was like, "You know, mom, I'll get a better chance at Miller." "No, no, you're going to Southside. There is no ifs, ands, or buts. Miller is too far. What if something happens to you?" But two years later, when my brother got ready to go on to high school, he was allowed to go to Miller. My sister and I were like, "Obviously, whose education do you value more? If you're telling us that education is important, why do we see a double standard?"

The above narratives suggest that the process of parenting is gendered in that immigrant parents tend to restrict the autonomy, mobility, and personal decision making of their daughters more than that of their sons. I argue that these parental restrictions are attempts to construct a model of Filipina womanhood that is chaste, modest, nurturing, and family-oriented. Women are seen as responsible for holding the cultural line, maintaining racial boundaries, and marking cultural difference. This is not to say that parent-daughter conflicts exist in all Filipino immigrant families. Certainly, Filipino parents do not respond in a uniform way to the challenges of being racial-ethnic minorities, and I met parents who have had to change some of their ideas and practices in response to their inability to control their children's movements and choices:

I have three girls and one boy. I used to think that I wouldn't allow my daughters to go dating and things like that, but there is no way I could do that. I can't stop it. It's the way of life here in America. Sometimes you kind of question yourself, if you are doing what is right. It is hard to accept but you got to accept it. That's the way they are here. (Professional Filipino immigrant father)

My children are born and raised here, so they do pretty much what they want. They think they know everything. I can only do so much as a parent. . . . When I try to teach my kids things, they tell me that I sound like an old record. They even talk back to me sometimes. . . . The first time my daughter brought her boyfriend to the house, she was eighteen years old. I almost passed away, knocked out. Lord, tell me what to do? (Working-class Filipino immigrant mother)

These narratives call attention to the shifts in the generational power caused by the migration process and to the possible gap between what parents say they want for their children and their ability to control the young. However, the interview data do suggest that intergenerational conflicts are socially recognized occurrences in Filipino communities. Even when respondents themselves had not experienced intergenerational tensions, they could always recall a cousin, a girlfriend, or a friend's daughter who had.

SANCTIONS AND REACTIONS: "THAT IS NOT WHAT A DECENT FILIPINO GIRL SHOULD DO"

I do not wish to suggest that immigrant communities are the only ones in which parents regulate their daughters' mobility and sexuality. Feminist scholars have long documented the construction, containment, and exploitation of women's sexuality in various societies (Maglin and Perry 1996). We also know that the cultural anxiety over unbounded female sexuality is most apparent with regard to adolescent girls (Tolman and Higgins 1996, 206). The difference is in the ways immigrant and nonimmigrant families sanction girls' sexuality. To control sexually assertive girls nonimmigrant parents rely on the gender-based good girl/bad girl dichotomy in which "good girls" are passive, threatened sexual objects while "bad girls" are active, desiring sexual agents (Tolman and Higgins 1996). As Dasgupta and DasGupta write, "the two most pervasive images of women across cultures are the goddess and whore, the good and bad women" (1996, 236). This good girl/bad girl cultural story conflates femininity with sexuality, increases women's vulnerability to sexual coercion, and justifies women's containment in the domestic sphere.

Immigrant families, though, have an additional strategy: they can discipline their daughters as racial/national subjects as well as gendered ones. That is, as self-appointed guardians of "authentic" cultural memory, immigrant parents can attempt to regulate their daughters' independent choices by linking them to cultural ignorance or betrayal. As both parents and children recounted, young women who disobeyed parental strictures were often branded "non-ethnic," "untraditional," "radical," "selfish," and "not caring about the family." Female sexual choices were also linked to moral degeneracy, defined in relation to a narrative of a hegemonic white norm. Parents were quick to warn their daughters about "bad" Filipinas who had become pregnant outside marriage.[9] As in the case of "bar girls" in the Philippines, Filipina Americans who veered from acceptable behaviors were deemed "Americanized"—as women who have adopted the sexual mores and practices of white women. As one Filipino immigrant father described "Americanized" Filipinas: "They are spoiled because they have seen the American way. They go out at night. Late at night. They go out on dates. Smoking. They have sex without marrying."

From the perspective of the second-generation daughters, these charges are stinging. The young women I interviewed were visibly pained—with many breaking down and crying—when they recounted their parents' charges. This deep pain, stemming in part from their desire to be validated as Filipina, existed even among the more "rebellious" daughters. One twenty-four-year-old daughter explained:

My mom is very traditional. She wants to follow the Filipino customs, just really adhere to them, like what is proper for a girl, what she can and can't do, and what other people are going to think of her if she doesn't follow that way. When I pushed these restrictions, when I rebelled and stayed out later than allowed, my mom would always say, "That is not what a decent Filipino girl should do. You should come home at a decent hour. What are people going to think of you?" And that would get me really upset, you know, because I think that my character is very much the way it should be for a Filipina. I wear my hair long, I wear decent makeup. I dress properly, conservative. I am family oriented. It hurts me that she doesn't see that I am decent, that I am proper and that I am not going to bring shame to the family or anything like that.

This narrative suggests that even when parents are unable to control the behaviors of their children, their (dis)approval remains powerful in shaping the emotional lives of their daughters (see Wolf 1997). Although better-off parents can and do exert greater controls over their children's behaviors than do poorer parents

(Wolf 1992; Kibria 1993), I would argue that all immigrant parents—regardless of class background—possess this emotional hold on their children. Therein lies the source of their power: As immigrant parents, they have the authority to determine if their daughters are "authentic" members of their racial-ethnic community. Largely unacquainted with the "home" country, U.S.-born children depend on their parents' tutelage to craft and affirm their ethnic self and thus are particularly vulnerable to charges of cultural ignorance and/or betrayal (Espiritu 1994).

Despite these emotional pains, many young Filipinas I interviewed contest and negotiate parental restrictions in their daily lives. Faced with parental restrictions on their mobility, young Filipinas struggle to gain some control over their own social lives, particularly over dating. In many cases, daughters simply misinform their parents of their whereabouts or date without their parents' knowledge. They also rebel by vowing to create more egalitarian relationships with their own husbands and children. A thirty-year-old Filipina who is married to a white American explained why she chose to marry outside her culture:

> In high school, I dated mostly Mexican and Filipino. It never occurred to me to date a white or black guy. I was not attracted to them. But as I kept growing up and my father and I were having all these conflicts, I knew that if I married a Mexican or a Filipino, [he] would be exactly like my father. And so I tried to date anyone that would not remind me of my dad. A lot of my Filipina friends that I grew up with had similar experiences. So I knew that it wasn't only me. I was determined to marry a white person because he would treat me as an individual.[10]

Another Filipina who was labeled "radical" by her parents indicated that she would be more open-minded in raising her own children: "I see myself as very traditional in upbringing but I don't see myself as constricting on my children one day and I wouldn't put the gender roles on them. I wouldn't lock them into any particular way of behaving." It is important to note that even as these Filipinas desired new gender norms and practices for their own families, the majority hoped that their children would remain connected to Filipino culture.

My respondents also reported more serious reactions to parental restrictions, recalling incidents of someone they knew who had run away, joined a gang, or attempted suicide. A Filipina high-school counselor relates that most of the Filipinas she worked with "are really scared because a lot of them know friends that are pregnant and they all pretty much know girls who have attempted suicide." A 1995 random survey of San Diego public high schools conducted by the federal Centers for Disease Control and Prevention (CDC) found that, in comparison with other ethnic groups, female Filipino students had the highest rates of seriously considering suicide (45.6 percent) as well as the highest rates of actually attempting suicide (23 percent) in the year preceding the survey. In comparison, 33.4 percent of Latinas, 26.2 percent of white women, and 25.3 percent of black women surveyed said they had suicidal thoughts (Lau 1995).

CONCLUSION

Mainstream American society defines white middle-class culture as the norm and whiteness as the unmarked marker of others' difference (Frankenberg 1993). In this article, I have shown that many Filipino immigrants use the largely gendered discourse of morality as one strategy to decenter whiteness and to locate themselves above the dominant group, demonizing it in the process. Like other immigrant groups, Filipinos praise the United States as a land of significant economic opportunity but simultaneously denounce it as a country inhabited by corrupted and individualistic people of questionable morals. In particular, they criticize American family life, American individualism, and American women (see Gabbacia 1994, 113). Enforced by distorting powers of memory and nostalgia, this rhetoric of moral superiority often leads to patriarchal calls for a cultural "authenticity" that locates family honor and national integrity in the group's female members. Because the policing of women's bodies is one of the main means of asserting moral superiority, young women face numerous restrictions on their autonomy, mobility, and personal decision making. This practice of cultural (re)construction reveals how deeply the conduct of private life can be tied to larger social structures.

The construction of white Americans as the "other" and American culture as deviant serves a dual purpose: It allows immigrant communities both to reinforce patriarchy through the sanctioning of women's (mis)behavior and to present an unblemished, if not morally superior, public face to the dominant society. Strong in family values, heterosexual morality, and a hierarchical family structure, this public face erases the Filipina "bad girl" and ignores competing (im)moral practices in the Filipino communities. Through the oppression of Filipina women and the denunciation of white women's morality, the immigrant community attempts to exert its moral superiority over the dominant Western culture and to reaffirm to itself its

self-worth in the face of economic, social, political, and legal subordination. In other words, the immigrant community uses restrictions on women's lives as one form of resistance to racism. This form of cultural resistance, however, severely restricts the lives of women, particularly those of the second generation, and it casts the family as a potential site of intense conflict and oppressive demands in immigrant lives.

ACKNOWLEDGMENTS

I gratefully acknowledge the many useful suggestions and comments of George Lipsitz, Vince Rafael, Lisa Lowe, Joane Nagel, Diane Wolf, Karen Pyke, and two anonymous reviewers for *Signs.* I also would like to thank all those Filipinos/as who participated in this study for their time, help, and insights into immigrant lives.

NOTES

1. Cordova 1983; Sharma 1984; Scharlin and Villanueva 1992; Jung 1999.
2. Filipino settlement in San Diego dates back to 1903, when a group of young Filipino *pensionados* enrolled at the State Normal School (now San Diego State University).
3. My understanding of Filipino American lives is also based on the many conversations I have had with my Filipino American students at the University of California, San Diego, and with Filipino American friends in the San Diego area and elsewhere.
4. A few studies have documented the ways racialized communities have represented white Americans. For example, in his anthropological work on Chicano joking, José Limón (1982) reports that young Mexican Americans elevate themselves over whites through the telling of "Stupid-American" jokes in which an Anglo American is consistently duped by a Mexican character. In her interviews with African American working-class men, Michele Lamont (1997) finds that these men tend to perceive Euro Americans as immoral, sneaky, and not to be trusted. Although these studies provide an interesting and compelling window into racialized communities' views of white Americans, they do not analyze how the rhetoric of moral superiority often depends on gender categories.
5. Indeed people around the world often believe that Americans have no real family ties. For example, on a visit to my family in Vietnam, my cousin asked me earnestly if it was true that American children put their elderly parents in nursing homes instead of caring for them at home. She was horrified at this practice and proclaimed that, because they care for their elders, Vietnamese families are morally superior to American families.
6. Writing on the objectification of black women, Patricia Hill Collins (1991) argues that popular representations of

black females—mammy, welfare queen, and Jezebel—all pivot around their sexuality, either desexualizing or hypersexualizing them. Along the same line, Native American women have been portrayed as sexually excessive (Green 1975), Chicana women as "exotic and erotic" (Mirande 1980), and Puerto Rican and Cuban women as "tropical bombshells, . . . sexy, sexed and interested" (Tafolla 1985, 39).
7. The relationship between immigrant parents and their sons deserves an article of its own. According to Gabbacia, "Immigrant parents fought with sons, too, but over different issues: parents' complaints about rebellious sons focused more on criminal activity than on male sexuality or independent courtship" (1994, 70). Moreover, because of their mobility, young men have more means to escape—at least temporarily—the pressures of the family than young women. In his study of Italian American families, Orsi reports that young men rebelled by sleeping in cars or joining the army, but young women did not have such opportunities (1985, 143).
8. The names of the two high schools in this excerpt are fictitious.
9. According to a 1992 health assessment report of Filipinos in San Francisco, Filipino teens have the highest pregnancy rates among all Asian groups and, in 1991, the highest rate of increase in the number of births as compared with all other racial or ethnic groups (Tiongson 1997, 257).
10. The few available studies on Filipino American intermarriage indicate a high rate relative to other Asian groups. In 1980, Filipino men in California recorded the highest intermarriage rate among all Asian groups, and Filipina women had the second-highest rate, after Japanese American women (Agbayani-Siewert and Revilla 1995, 156).

REFERENCES

Agbayani-Siewert, Pauline, and Linda Revilla. 1995. "Filipino Americans." In *Asian Americans: Contemporary Trends and Issues*, ed. Pyong Gap Min, 134–68. Thousand Oaks, Calif.: Sage.

Azores-Gunter, Tania Fortunata M. 1986–87. "Educational Attainment and Upward Mobility: Prospects for Filipino Americans." *Amerasia Journal* 13(1):39–52.

Billson, Janet Mancini. 1995. *Keepers of the Culture: The Power of Tradition in Women's Lives*. New York: Lexington.

Cabezas, Amado, Larry H. Shinagawa, and Gary Kawaguchi. 1986–87. "New Inquiries into the Socioeconomic Status of Pilipino Americans in California." *Amerasia Journal* 13(1):1–21.

Collins, Patricia Hill. 1991. *Black Feminist Thought: Knowledge, Consciousness, and the Politics of Empowerment*. New York: Routledge.

Cordova, Fred. 1983. *Filipinos: Forgotten Asian Americans, a Pictorial Essay, 1763–1963*. Dubuque, Iowa: Kendall/Hunt.

Coronel, Sheila, and Ninotchka Rosca. 1993. "For the Boys: Filipinas Expose Years of Sexual Slavery by the U.S. and Japan." *Ms.*, November/December, 10–15.

Dasgupta, Shamita Das, and Sayantani DasGupta. 1996. "Public Face, Private Space: Asian Indian Women and Sexuality." In *"Bad Girls/Good Girls": Women, Sex, and Power in the Nineties*, ed. Nan Bauer Maglin and Donna Perry, 226–43. New Brunswick, N.J.: Rutgers University Press.

di Leonardo, Micaela. 1984. *The Varieties of Ethnic Experience: Kinship, Class, and Gender Among California Italian-Americans*. Ithaca, N.Y.: Cornell University Press.

Eastmond, Marita. 1993. "Reconstructing Life: Chilean Refugee Women and the Dilemmas of Exile." In *Migrant Women: Crossing Boundaries and Changing Identities*, ed. Gina Buijs, 35–53. Oxford: Berg.

Egan, Timothy. 1996. "Mail-Order Marriage, Immigrant Dreams and Death." *New York Times*, May 26, 12.

Espiritu, Yen Le. 1994. "The Intersection of Race, Ethnicity, and Class: The Multiple Identities of Second Generation Filipinos." *Identities* 1(2–3):249–73.

———. 1995. *Filipino American Lives*. Philadelphia: Temple University Press.

———. 1997. *Asian American Women and Men: Labor, Laws, and Love*. Thousand Oaks, Calif.: Sage.

Espiritu, Yen Le, and Diane L. Wolf. Forthcoming. "The Paradox of Assimilation: Children of Filipino Immigrants in San Diego." In *Ethnicities: Children of Immigrants in America*, ed. Ruben Rumbaut and Alejandro Portes. Berkeley: University of California Press; New York: Russell Sage Foundation.

Frankenberg, Ruth. 1993. *White Women, Race Matters: The Social Construction of Whiteness*. Minneapolis: University of Minnesota Press.

Gabbacia, Donna. 1994. *From the Other Side: Women, Gender, and Immigrant Life in the U.S., 1820–1990*. Bloomington: Indiana University Press.

Gibson, Margaret A. 1995. "Additive Acculturation as a Strategy for School Improvement." In *California's Immigrant Children: Theory, Research, and Implications for Educational Policy*, ed. Ruben Rumbaut and Wayne A. Cornelius, 77–105. La Jolla: Center for U.S.-Mexican Studies, University of California, San Diego.

Gilman, Sander L. 1985. *Difference and Pathology: Stereotypes of Sexuality, Race, and Madness*. Ithaca, N.Y.: Cornell University Press.

Green, Rayna. 1975. "The Pocahontas Perplex: The Image of Indian Women in American Culture." *Massachusetts Review* 16(4):698–714.

Haddad, Yvonne Y., and Jane I. Smith. 1996. "Islamic Values Among American Muslims." In *Family and Gender Among American Muslims: Issues Facing Middle Eastern Immigrants and Their Descendants*, ed. Barbara C. Aswad and Barbara Bilge, 19–40. Philadelphia: Temple University Press.

Halualani, Rona Tamiko. 1995. "The Intersecting Hegemonic Discourses of an Asian Mail-Order Bride Catalog: Pilipina 'Oriental Butterfly' Dolls for Sale." *Women's Studies in Communication* 18(1):45–64.

Hamamoto, Darrell Y. 1994. *Monitored Peril: Asian Americans and the Politics of Representation*. Minneapolis: University of Minnesota Press.

Hickey, M. Gail. 1996. "'Go to College, Get a Job, and Don't Leave the House Without Your Brother': Oral Histories with Immigrant Women and Their Daughters." *Oral History Review* 23(2):63–92.

Jung, Moon-Kie. 1999. "No Whites: No Asians: Race, Marxism and Hawaii's Pre-emergent Working Class." *Social Science History* 23(3):357–93.

Kibria, Nazli. 1993. *Family Tightrope: The Changing Lives of Vietnamese Immigrant Community*. Princeton, N.J.: Princeton University Press.

Lamont, Michele. 1997. "Colliding Moralities Between Black and White Workers." In *From Sociology to Cultural Studies: New Perspectives*, ed. Elisabeth Long, 263–85. New York: Blackwell.

Lau, Angela. 1995. "Filipino Girls Think Suicide at Number One Rate." *San Diego Union-Tribune*, February 11, A-1.

Lee, Stacey J. 1996. *Unraveling the "Model Minority" Stereotype: Listening to Asian American Youth*. New York: Teachers College Press.

Limón, José E. 1982. "History, Chicano Joking, and the Varieties of Higher Education: Tradition and Performance as Critical Symbolic Action." *Journal of the Folklore Institute* 19(2/3):141–66.

Lipsitz, George. 1998. *The Possessive Investment in Whiteness: How White People Profit from Identity Politics*. Philadelphia: Temple University Press.

Lowe, Lisa. 1996. *Immigrant Acts: On Asian American Cultural Politics.* Durham, N.C.: Duke University Press.

Maglin, Nan Bauer, and Donna Perry. 1996. "Introduction." In *"Bad Girls/Good Girls": Women, Sex, and Power in the Nineties,* ed. Nan Bauer Maglin and Donna Perry, xiii–xxvi. New Brunswick, N.J.: Rutgers University Press.

Marchetti, Gina. 1993. *Romance and the "Yellow Peril": Race, Sex, and Discursive Strategies in Hollywood Fiction.* Berkeley: University of California Press.

Matute-Bianchi, Maria Eugenia. 1991. "Situational Ethnicity and Patterns of School Performance among Immigrant and Nonimmigrant Mexican-Descent Students." In *Minority Status and Schooling: A Comparative Study of Immigrant and Involuntary Minorities,* ed. Margaret A. Gibson and John U. Ogbu, 205–47. New York: Garland.

Mazumdar, Suchetta. 1989. "General Introduction: A Woman-Centered Perspective on Asian American History." In *Making Waves: An Anthology by and About Asian American Women,* ed. Asian Women United of California, 1–22. Boston: Beacon.

Millett, Kate. 1970. *Sexual Politics.* Garden City, N.Y.: Doubleday.

Mirande, Alfredo. 1980. "The Chinano Family: A Reanalysis of Conflicting Views." In *Rethinking Marriage, Child Rearing, and Family Organization,* ed. Arlene S. Skolnick and Jerome H. Skolnick, 479–93. Berkeley: University of California Press.

Okamura, Jonathan, and Amefil Agbayani. 1997. "*Pamantasan:* Filipino American Higher Education." In *Filipino Americans: Transformation and Identity,* ed. Maria P. Root, 183–97. Thousand Oaks, Calif.: Sage.

Ordonez, Raquel Z. 1997. "Mail-Order Brides: An Emerging Community." In *Filipino Americans: Transformation and Identity,* ed. Maria P. Root, 121–42. Thousand Oaks, Calif.: Sage.

Orsi, Robert Anthony. 1985. *The Madonna of 115th Street: Faith and Community in Italian Harlem, 1880–1950.* New Haven, Conn.: Yale University Press.

Personal Narratives Group. 1989. "Origins." In *Interpreting Women's Lives: Feminist Theory and Personal Narratives,* ed. Personal Narratives Group, 3–15. Bloomington: Indiana University Press.

Ruiz, Vicki L. 1992. "The Flapper and the Chaperone: Historical Memory among Mexican-American Women." In *Seeking Common Ground: Multidisciplinary Studies,* ed. Donna Gabbacia. Westport, Conn.: Greenwood.

Rumbaut, Ruben. 1991. "Passages to America: Perspectives on the New Immigration." In *America at Century's End,* ed. Alan Wolfe, 208–44. Berkeley: University of California Press.

———. 1994. "The Crucible Within: Ethnic Identity, Self-Esteem, and Segmented Assimilation Among Children of Immigrants." *International Migration Review* 28(4):748–94.

Rumbaut, Ruben, and Kenji Ima. 1988. *The Adaptation of Southeast Asian Refugee Youth: A Comparative Study.* Washington, D.C.: U.S. Office of Refugee Resettlement.

San Juan, E., Jr. 1991. "Mapping the Boundaries: The Filipino Writer in the U.S." *Journal of Ethnic Studies* 19(1):117–31.

Scharlin, Craig, and Lilia V. Villanueva. 1992. *Philip Vera Cruz: A Personal History of Filipino Immigrants and the Farmworkers Movement.* Los Angeles: University of California, Los Angeles Labor Center, Institute of Labor Relations, and Asian American Studies Center.

Sharma, Miriam. 1984. "Labor Migration and Class Formation among the Filipinos in Hawaii, 1906–46." In *Labor Immigration Under Capitalism: Asian Workers in the United States Before World War II;* ed. Lucie Cheng and Edna Bonacich, 579–611. Berkeley: University of California Press.

Stoler, Ann Laura. 1991. "Carnal Knowledge and Imperial Power: Gender, Race, and Morality in Colonial Asia." In *Gender at the Crossroads of Knowledge: Feminist Anthropology in the Postmodern Era,* ed. Micaela di Leonardo, 51–104. Berkeley: University of California Press.

Tafolla, Carmen. 1985. *To Split a Human: Mitos, Machos y la Mujer Chicana.* San Antonio, Tex.: Mexican American Cultural Center.

Tapia, Ruby. 1997. "Studying Other 'Others.'" Paper presented at the Association of Pacific Americans in Higher Education, San Diego, Calif., May 24.

Tiongson, Antonio T., Jr. 1997. "Throwing the Baby out with the Bath Water." In *Filipino Americans: Transformation and Identity,* ed. Maria P. Root, 257–71. Thousand Oaks, Calif.: Sage.

Tolman, Deborah L., and Tracy E. Higgins. 1996. "How Being a Good Girl Can Be Bad for Girls." In *"Bad Girls/Good Girls": Women, Sex, and Power in the Nineties,* ed. Nan Bauer Maglin and Donna Perry, 205–25. New Brunswick, N.J.: Rutgers University Press.

Tuan, Mia. 1998. *Forever Foreigners or Honorary Whites? The Asian Ethnic Experience Today.* New Brunswick, N.J.: Rutgers University Press.

Villanueva, M. 1991. *Ginseng and Other Tales from Manila.* Corvallis, Oreg.: Calyx.

Warren, Jenifer. 1993. "Suit Asks Navy to Aid Children Left in Philippines." *Los Angeles Times,* March 5, A3.

Waters, Mary C. 1996. "The Intersection of Gender, Race, and Ethnicity in Identity Development of Caribbean American Teens." In *Urban Girls: Resisting Stereotypes, Creating. Identities,* ed. Bonnie J. Ross Leadbeater and Niobe Way, 65–81. New York: New York University Press.

Woldemikael, T. M. 1989. *Becoming. Black American: Haitians and American Institutions in Evanston, Illinois.* New York: AMS Press.

Wolf, Diane L. 1992. *Factory Daughters: Gender; Household Dynamics, and Rural Industrialization in Java.* Berkeley: University of California Press.

———. 1997. "Family Secrets: Transnational Struggles Among Children of Filipino Immigrants." *Sociological Perspectives* 40(3):457–82.

Wong, Sau-ling. 1993. *Reading Asian American Literature: From Necessity to Extravagance.* Princeton, N.J.: Princeton University Press.

Yung, Judy. 1995. *Unbound Feet: A Social History of Chinese Women in San Francisco.* Berkeley: University of California Press.

Bearing Blackness in Britain: The Meaning of Racial Difference for White Birth Mothers of African-Descent Children

Is there not something unseemly, in our society, about the spectacle of a white woman mothering a black child? A white woman giving totally to a black child; a black child totally and demandingly dependent for everything, sustenance itself from a white woman. The image of a white woman suckling a black child . . . such a picture says there is no difference. (Williams, 1991, pp. 226–27)

Thus, although there are limits to the experience of many "white" people when compared to "black" people, there is no single truth about racism which only "blacks" can know. To assert that the latter is so is, in fact, to condemn "white" people to a universal condition which implies possession of a permanent essence which inevitably sets them apart. (Miles, 1989)

On 30 August 1998, the British Broadcasting Corporation (BBC) aired a documentary entitled *Love in Black and White* as part of the "Windrush" series acknowledging the achievements and experiences of British blacks and celebrating the anniversary of the landing of the *S.S. Empire Windrush*. Fifty years earlier the *S.S. Windrush* had landed at the Tilbury Dock in London on 22 June 1948 filled with 492 would-be-settlers from Jamaica, many of them ex-servicemen who had served in the war in Britain and had then returned to the West Indies to receive their discharges and war benefits (Scobie, 1972, p. 194).

Love in Black and White represents a significant departure from mainstream representations of the black British experience in that it privileges the experiences of five white women (and their adult children) who had married and established families with black Caribbean men. The inclusion of white mothers of African-descent children in a documentary series celebrating black

Caribbeans and how they have transformed British culture signals a growing public recognition of the part that white mothers play in the "reproduction" of the black British community. However, despite their presence in this documentary, they have typically been invisible in media and government reports concerned with racism and anti-racism in contemporary Britain.[1] White mothers of African-descent children appear to occupy a paradoxical and pivotal role in the reproduction of black Britishness. Thus, if we are to understand contested meanings of transatlantic blackness, Britishness, racism and antiracism, then an analysis of the experiences of white mothers in British multiethnic families is of critical importance.

Until now the degree to which white mothers of multiracial families experience forms of racial abuse and racial exclusions has received little attention. According to the 1997 Annual Report of the Commission for Racial Equality, however, 64 white women and 15 Irish women filed applications for assistance in racial discrimination cases in the United Kingdom.[2,3] There is now a growing body of feminist scholarship on racism and anti-racism among white women in organised racist and anti-racist movements (Ware, 1992; Blee, 1991; 1997). With a few notable exceptions, nevertheless, there has been little sustained theoretical or empirical analysis of the ways in which racism and anti-racism structure the maternal experiences of white mothers of African-descent children (Frankenberg, 1993; Luke, 1994; Twine, 1998).

Foundational analyses of gender inequality and motherhood (de Beauvoir, 1952; Rich, 1976; Chodorow, 1978; Ruddick, 1985) among white middle-class women in the US and Western Europe have not explored the degree to which *transracial* mothers, that is, white mothers who are socially defined as belonging to a racial group presumed to be racially distinct from that of their *birth* children, conceptualise and experience racism. White women who give birth to children whose physical bodies (and relationships with black men) may disqualify them from membership in the "white" community provide a lens through which to examine the multiple meanings of racial difference. Their experiences also illuminate the limits of racial privilege for those whose families of reproduction transgress the prescribed ideals of their local communities. An analysis of the racialised experiences of white mothers of African-descent children provide a necessary corrective to earlier literature that conflated various forms of discrimination and assumed *racially unified* and mono-ethnic family formations. Elizabeth Spelman critiques feminist scholars who have failed theoretically to account for the intersections of race, class, and gender hierarchies:

> Women mother in societies that may be racist and classist as well as sexist and heterosexist. Are we to believe that a woman's mothering is informed only by her relationship to a husband or a male lover and her experience of living in a male-dominated society, but not by her relation to people of other classes and races and her experience of living in a society in which there are race and class hierarchies? (Spelman, 1988, p. 85)

How then, in view of these more nuanced analyses of intersecting forms of discrimination, do we evaluate the impact of racism on white women parenting children who are socially classified as "black" or "mixed-race"? Several recently published memoirs by US white feminist mothers (Reddy, 1994; Lazarre, 1996) have begun to illuminate some of the ways that racial hierarchies structure the emotional experience of mothering for white women who are parenting in the context of long-term domestic partnerships with black men. However, with the notable exception of these memoirs by US feminist scholars, few ethnographic analyses of racism have not yet offered empirical explorations of white parents' experience of negotiating racism and acquiring an anti-racist consciousness as they parent African-descent children (Twine, 1998; in press).

In 1995, when I initially began to explore the impact of racism upon white birth mothers parenting their children of African descent in England, I sought to understand how white mothers (and their black partners) mediate, interpret and respond to white suprem-

acist ideologies.[4] As a black feminist theorist and ethnographer concerned with the contingent nature of white racial privilege for women whose relationships with black men constitute a transgression of orthodox ideologies of social respectability, I found that critical race theorists or feminist theorists had focused little attention on a growing population of white mothers of African-descent children in Britain. If we are to develop a sophisticated understanding of transformations in the meaning of Britishness, blackness, and contemporary racisms, then an analysis of the consciousness and practices of white women who are members of black British families is invaluable.

In this essay, drawing upon both public discussions and private focused life history interviews with white women and their black Caribbean family members in the East Midlands of Britain, I will examine one of the paradoxes that emerged when I asked black women and men to consider the impact of racism upon the white birth mothers of African-descent children in their families. By exploring the perceptions and expectations that black family members have of white mothers of African-descent children, my aim is to illuminate the dilemmas for some white women who must contend with their own "racialisation" by black family members.[5]

When I began to pursue these questions with black family members of white women, I found that black Caribbean women and men typically perceived their white relatives as unable to "equip" their children to cope with racism because, as *whites*, they could not "empathise" with them not having experienced racism. White mothers, in particular, were described as racially disadvantaged because they are perceived as being incapable of feeling racism. In other words, the black family members interviewed distinguished between racial "empathy" and "sympathy," arguing that while white mothers could sympathise with their children they did not typically possess racial *empathy*, the ability to experience the pain of racism, and thus could not really understand the impact of racism upon their children.

In addition to this paradoxical discourse, I found that, because white mothers must often manage the presumed "racial" divide between themselves and their children, they may sometimes work harder (than black mothers of children of Anglo-European and African descent) to acquire an understanding of how racial difference (and thus racism) impacts their children. In other words, if they are conscious of the assumptions made about their maternal competence (and if their children report racism to them) they may be more likely than their black peers to develop *proactive* anti-racist parental strategies.[6] In other words, the presumed racial differences between themselves and their African-descent children may advantage them by calling into attention the cultural work that must be done in order to prepare their children to negotiate racist ideologies and racist structures.

RESEARCH METHODS

Between 1995 and 1998 I conducted eight months of field research in London and the East Midlands of Britain.[7] I also interviewed white and black parents who were members of interracial families. This chapter draws upon data from this research and focuses upon the life histories of 95 parents of African-descent children in Britain. I interviewed a snowball sample of 95 black and white parents that included 65 white birth mothers and their black family members between the ages of 28 and 70 years. The white women interviewed were the birth mothers of children whose fathers were either African-Caribbean, African-American or black British men in relationships that ranged from a period of several months to more than 30 years.[8] In order to evaluate how gender structures the dynamics of transracial motherhood, I also interviewed a comparable group of 14 white English fathers of African-descent children who resided in the same communities as the white mothers interviewed.

During my field research I lived in the home of an African-Caribbean education officer employed by the Leicestershire City Council, who was also actively involved with the African-Caribbean Education Working Group and was thus linked to virtually all of the recognised local African-Caribbean community members and leaders. I also attended and participated in private family events and African-Caribbean cultural events, interviewing residents who self-identified as either West Indian, black, African Caribbean, or mixed race with origins in Antigua, Barbados, Dominica, Guyana, Jamaica, Montserrat, St. Kitts-Nevis, Trinidad and Tobago, and the United States. The families interviewed reported that their parents had immigrated to England between 1955 and 1965.

THE LOCAL CONTEXT: THE EAST MIDLANDS

Leicester, which is known as a "hosiery" manufacturing city, is located 90 miles north of London in the East Midlands of England. Leicester's textiles continue to consti-

tute a major segment of its economic base and it continues to be a principal supplier of the British knitwear industry. Approximately 30 per cent of the local adult population works in the industry, and according to a recently published City Council report, Leicestershire "has the largest number of people employed in the manufacture of hosiery, knitwear and fabrics in the United Kingdom" (1993, p. 42).

During the 1970s Leicester served as the national headquarters of the National Front,[9] a right-wing political party that represented the unification of the League of Empire Loyalists, the British National Party, and the Racial Preservation Society. John Solomos (1993) has described the political aims of the National Front thus: "to provide a new arena for the far right activism, outside the Conservative Party and as an independent organisation."[10] As the site of an organised racist political party, Leicester also became a logical political organising base for anti-racist organisers. As Solomos notes,

> Between 1977 and 1979 the activities of the National Front also became the focus for anti-racist political mobilisation orchestrated by the Anti-Nazi League and Rock Against Racism. (Solomos, 1993, p. 190)

Leicester became a national testing ground for racist and anti-racist political organising. For example, a 1990 Report notes that:

> The Leicester Racial Attacks Monitoring Project, better known as RAMP, was set up at the end of 1986. This was a direct response to the high level of racist incidents being reported to the Highfields and Belgrave Law Centre.[11]

Some of the local white anti-racist activists became the parents of African-descent children and members of black Caribbean extended families.

Another distinctive aspect of Leicester is the size of its ethnic minority population. Outside of London it is the local authority with the highest percentage of all ethnic minorities and has one of the largest Asian Indian populations with origins in East Africa (Kenya, Malawi, Tanzania, and Uganda) (see Leicester City Council, 1996). In 1994, the total population of Leicester was 293, 400 with whites constituting 71.5 per cent.[12] South Asians constitute 23.7 per cent of the local population, making it one of the largest Asian communities in the United Kingdom.[13] Leicester ranks second in terms of absolute numbers of Asians and *first* for its population of Indian origin, according to the 1991 census. The Indian population of 60,297 constitutes 22.3 per cent of Leicester's residents, making it the largest in absolute numbers in any city in the United Kingdom (Leicester City Council, 1996). In striking contrast, the local black population, which is sub-divided on the census into black Caribbean, black African and black Other, constitutes just 2.4 per cent of the local population (it is ranked 35th in size for the UK). The African-Caribbean population, a segment of the larger black population, comprises only 1.5 per cent of the total local population.

The size of the Leicester's Asian Indian population is relevant to this study because Indians constitute 78 per cent of the ethnic population and thus ethnics of Asian origin outnumber those of African-Caribbean origin by nearly 10 to 1.[14] In a context in which the African-Caribbean population views itself as the older and more established ethnic community, the African Caribbeans argued that the newer Asian Indian population has managed to secure control over much of the local community resources targeted for ethnic minorities. Religious, linguistic and other cultural differences between the black Caribbean and Asian (Indian, Pakistani, Bangladeshi, and East African Asian) communities appear to have generated tensions between the African-Caribbean and Asian ethnic communities. Consequently, there appears to be some shared resentment by both the indigenous white population and the black Caribbean community towards the Asian community which is perceived to be experiencing rapid upward mobility.[15] This phenomenon poses particular problems for the white *working-class* mothers of African-descent children—who tend to reside in communities where the dominant ethnic minority population is Asian (typically Bangladeshi or Indian) because their children are sometimes mistaken for Asian and consequently discriminated against.

RACIAL LOGIC AND RACIAL EMPATHY

In my conversations with the black relatives (including sisters-in-law, domestic partners/spouses and adult children) of white mothers parenting birth children of African-descent, I uncovered a racial logic that can best be understood as characterised by doubts concerning a white mother's ability to parent a child (or children) of African descent properly. It was assumed that white mothers were in fact both "racist"

towards their own children and racially "disadvantaged" because of their social experience as "white" persons with familial ties to a white community.[16] Recall, for example, that I was informed that white mothers of "black" children were unable to empathise with the racism that their children experience because they cannot personally experience racism. Black women whose brothers had established domestic partnerships with white women argued that white women were not adequately prepared to raise black children because they could not understand, or "feel," racism the way a black mother could.

The scepticism regarding white mothers' ability to empathise with their children is illustrated by the comments of Camille, a recognised black leader in the local African-Caribbean community. Like many of the UK-born black women I interviewed, Camille opposed interracial relationships but because two of her brothers had established domestic partnerships with local white women she had reluctantly become part of a multiracial extended family.[17] When I asked her to share her views on white women parenting African-descent children, she argued that white mothers are typically ill-prepared to deal with racism.

> I don't think white mothers have that understanding of what it means to be black . . . sometimes they haven't dealt with their own racism. They meet a system that's racist and they don't know how to deal with it. I don't think they're always ready . . . in terms of being prepared for racism—they haven't dealt with their own racism. I think a lot of time [white mothers] aren't prepared mentally, aren't emotionally prepared —just don't know what they're dealing with. They haven't had the sociological discussions around racism. What it is, how it affects people, that kind of thing . . . somehow the forums aren't there to discuss it.

Camille's comments must be understood in the context of her ongoing personal and professional experiences with anti-black racism. As a social worker she has acquired extensive experience providing supervision and treatment for African-Caribbean children who have been placed in foster care, often in response to neglect, abuse or family disintegration. She reported to me that the majority of her cases involve children of dual heritage who have one white parent and one black Caribbean or black British parent. Her experiences have led her to conclude that due to anti-black racism in British society black children are at risk and this risk is heightened when there is a white mother parenting.

However, when I asked Camille to elaborate on how her own parents (Jamaican blacks) had helped her to cope with racism as a child, she began to contradict herself. She had suggested, for example, that only *black* parents know how to prepare their children, but it soon became clear that her parents had not provided her with the very preparation she described. For example, because her parents had grown up in Jamaica they did not appear to have had an understanding of the particular kind of racism that their children encountered in England. Alluding perhaps to her own parents, she said:

> Some black parents feel they need to fit into society and that they're guests within this society and therefore have to behave that way. I think that, in some respects, we were protected [from racism] because we had black parents. I don't think they were always aware of the level of racism. I don't know that we even got into any discussions about it. I don't know that they had particularly good strategies for dealing with it either, because I can remember when I was at school I had tremendous problems [with racism]—it really affected my education—in terms of levels of racism . . . it wasn't something that I discussed openly [with my parents] at the time. I just felt—you needed to get on with it.

Fiona, the 36-year-old mother of a four-year-old daughter, also described coping with racism alone with no effective guidance from her parents. Her parents immigrated from Antigua in the 1960s, and were described as lacking a vocabulary for discussing race or racism in Britain. When asked how her Antiguan parents helped her to cope with the racism she encountered as a child, she describes her mother's failure to understand the racism that she encountered routinely at school.

> We very rarely discussed [racism], you know. From my parents—nothing. For example, I came home one day from school and said to my mother that a teacher told me that I had rubber lips, and all she said is, "Don't take any notice." She appeared not to recognise my pain, appeared not to want to talk about it in any further detail, and the sad fact is that I think my parents were internalised racists. I'll give you an example of why. My mother once said to me when I was 17 that if

I ever brought an African home that I could walk out the back door straight away because she didn't want a blue-black African in her home. [When I asked whether her parents had actively discussed racism with her or tried to prepare her for racism, she said:] No, they didn't. No. A lot of what I've learned and what I've been able to articulate and what I've been able to discuss came once I left home. . . . Even when I married a white man, there was never any discussion about how we would cope or what problems we might face or how they felt about it.

Fiona's experience is not unrepresentative of the childhood experiences described to me by other black Caribbean women I interviewed. Although black women tended to argue that black parents could better understand their children because they had personally encountered racism, their descriptions often contradicted this theory. While Fiona did not argue that white women were not prepared to parent, she did express scepticism about her daughter's white father's ability to comprehend the impact of racism on his daughter. Fiona and Camille's attitudes illustrate a pattern that I found in interviews with black women, in which black women applied a different maternal standard to white mothers of black children than they did to their own mothers.

How are we to understand this differential? In my conversations with black women, they often expressed their frustration and anger towards their black siblings and other local men who established families with white women. They interpreted this as a rejection of local black women, whom they felt were disadvantaged because they tended to come from more religious families than white women. I was repeatedly told that black teenage girls, unlike white girls, are not allowed to date or go out at night. However, their brothers are given these liberties. Consequently, they argued that their white female peers are not supervised or restricted by their parents so they are able at a young age to frequent the same nightclubs and leisure places that the young black men in their age cohort frequent. The black men pair up with white girls as teenagers before their black female peers acquire the same liberties as their black male peers. This has generated some tensions between black and white mothers in some multiracial extended families. In cases in which black women view white women as a threat to the reproduction of black families that consist of two black parents, they may be highly critical of their own white sisters-in-law parenting their nieces and nephews. In response to the growing numbers of interracial families, some black women invoke a maternal hierarchy in which they called into question the emotional and cultural competence of white mothers of African-descent children.

Carmen, another black woman of Jamaican origin, whose white sister-in-law was parenting her nieces and nephews, provides an analysis that paralleled that of Camille. A 33-year-old university student, Carmen has two siblings (a brother and a sister) who have established families with white English partners. When asked to compare her own situation as a black mother (whose youngest daughter has a white father) to that of a white mother of "black" children, she replied:

> Who you are, your culture, your identity . . . comes through the mother. And so therefore your cultural awareness, your ability to deal with racism (as we've been discussing) and a lot of other things will be defined by your mother. And that doesn't matter whether you're African Caribbean, European, Asian, whatever. It's the mother who brings the children up. And so I think that where the mother is black and the father is white . . . the children will stand a better chance of being more culturally rooted than when the mother is white because the [white] mother will pass on her own traditions, sometimes will stifle the tradition of her kids, will actively tell them that they're not black.

Like several other mothers interviewed, Carmen places the primary responsibility for parenting upon the mothers and does not appear to hold fathers accountable or responsible to the same degree as mothers. While few black mothers presented critiques of patriarchal arrangements that required women to bear the primary burden for childcare, occasionally a black mother would challenge this assumption and offer a more critical analysis of traditional gender roles. For example, Jamilha, the 39-year-old mother of two sons, who self-identifies as a feminist, identified "patriarchy" and traditional gender roles as a serious problem for both married and single white mothers of African-descent children. She agreed with other black mothers that

> It's not that their white parents don't love them, but they don't know what it's like and so children in that position do need black input. And a lot of them don't get that much [black cultural knowledge] if they happen to be with a white mother.

However, in contrast to other mothers, Jamilha identified "patriarchy" and traditional gender roles as a serious handicap for both married and single white mothers. She argued that the African-descent children of white mothers who lived with their black fathers did not necessarily have more access to support in preparing the children to cope with racism.

> Even if the black father has been around, they still treat the child as if, well, the child is the child of the mother. The child is seen [by the father] as within the sphere of the mother for the nurturing and all of that, you know, patriarchy. You know what women's roles and what men's roles are. So I'm not quite sure whether there is a black influence even when black men are around. [Black fathers] will still very much feel that they need to be letting the mother bring up the children.

With few exceptions, the view that white mothers are expected to take the primary role in socialising and caring for children seemed to be shared by black Caribbean men and women in the extended family. Carmen, who has nieces and nephews who are being parented by a white mother, described her brother's parenting responsibilities in this way:

> A lot of the black men tend to take a back seat rather than actually doing anything about their partners' understanding of being black, about black culture, about community.[18]

As I became more familiar with Leicestershire and spent more time living in this community, I became interested in exploring further the patterns of contradictory racial logic operating here. I also wanted to compare black and white mothers parenting children of dual African-Caribbean and Anglo-English heritage in the same extended families. Although the black women interviewed had typically been parented by two black Caribbean parents whom, they reported, rarely addressed the topic of discrimination, they continued to insist that white mothers were less adequately prepared than black Caribbean women to parent African-descent children. Such beliefs persisted in spite of their acknowledgement that they themselves had rarely received explicit support when they shared stories of racist incidents with their parents. Moreover, according to their reports, many of their parents, like some white parents interviewed, seemed unaware of the kind and extent of the institutionalised racism their children were encountering in Britain. In fact, what I found striking about the narratives of the black professional mothers interviewed is how similar they are to those of the white mothers interviewed. None of the black women reported having received any explicit education or guidance about racism at home (with two black parents} whereas several of the white parents of African-descent children described having formulated and implemented strategies to teach their children to recognise and counter multiple forms of racism.

BLACK FATHERS

David, a black[19] father, had been in a committed relationship with his white wife, Simone, for more than 16 years. Childhood sweethearts, they had had two sons who were four and eight. Asked to describe his relationship with his wife, David expressed admiration and respect for her "character" and remarked upon her "strength." However, when asked to compare his wife's experiences as a white mother with those of black mothers of African-descent children, he too employed the ideology of "racial empathy," invoked by the black women I interviewed. He advanced the belief that as a white woman, since his wife had not experienced racism, she was unable to *feel* the pain that her children would inevitably feel.

> My wife is always going to see things differently to a black mother anyway. Black mothers traditionally are very strong and very protective of their children, but when the ugly head of racism starts rearing its head, black mothers deal with it a lot. For example, they know—they can *feel* [racism]. They're doing it from an *empathetic* position. They [experience] the racism themselves, so they know how to challenge the racism. [My italics]

Like many other black parents interviewed, David also assumed that if one has experienced racism first-hand, then one automatically knows how to challenge it. He did not consider the social ostracism and racial exclusion that his wife had experienced (from her natal family and from other whites) to be a form of racial abuse. Although he acknowledged how much privilege she had "lost," for example, he did not consider that experience a parallel one that she could draw upon to empathise with their children's experience of racism. In other words, he did not appear to consider her racial

privilege contingent upon her willingness to form familial relationships exclusively with white men, even as he appeared to recognise that his wife had been subjected to certain forms of racial abuse. For example, he noted that:

> She's classed as a second-class citizen. It's a deal [black men] can never pay back [to their white partners]. And the majority of them don't realise it. They don't realise how much their partners have lost—none of them. But I see what she's lost . . . when I go to the family get-togethers and I look around the room and I'm the only black face and my children are the only black kids in that environment.

As another example of what she had lost, David revealed that Simone's brother "[whom] she looked up to" had not spoken to her since her marriage to him. They no longer had contact and Simone had experienced considerable overt hostility from several other members of her family as well. Other white mothers I interviewed had also been expelled from their families for refusing to abort or to give their children up for adoption, yet this experience was rarely recognised or conceptualised by them or their black family as an experience with racial discrimination.

This view that white mothers are unable to "feel" racism or "equip" their children to address it was also extended to white fathers who were described by their black partners as unprepared to cope with the racism their children were likely to encounter. For example, one black mother expressed the fear, not uncommon among the black mothers interviewed, that she might die before her children reached adulthood. She was especially concerned that her white husband would be unable to respond properly to racism on an emotional level.

> I don't think [their white father] could deal with [racism]. And I don't think he could very well *equip* them because, again, he doesn't have the understanding. I think he would deal with them in *sympathy,* but he couldn't deal with them as I would, in *empathy.* In some ways that's perhaps not a bad thing. The first time [my daughter] came home from school and said that she'd been subjected to racism I just sat on the bottom of the step and cried because I just felt it so personally. [My italics]

However, because fathers are not expected to parent to the same degree as mothers, most of the focus was placed upon the mothers. Black women thus tended to interpret *whiteness,* in and of itself, as an undifferentiated marker of inexperience with racism, rarely acknowledging that gender, class inequality and marital status mitigate the way that *white* women experience racial privileges. White mothers were typically described to me in terms that placed emphasis upon their "whiteness" without recognition of the ways in which their marital status, class, age and tenure in the local community might hyperwhiten and unwhiten them. Their maternal and familial ties to blacks were deemphasised in these discourses.[20] A similar phenomenon has been explored by John Hartigan, Jr (1997) in his analysis of US whites living in working-class and "underclass" communities. He emphasises the "uneven reproduction and experience of whiteness" and provides an example of a white woman whose grandchildren are of African descent. Describing how ideologies of racial difference and racism impact upon her as a member of a multiracial family, he notes:

> Relating to her grandchildren racialised her because it brought her into zones where only her racialness would be read; attending to her "black" grandchildren made her whiter even though she promoted no notion of racial superiority. It is notable that in such heterogeneous family sites, race retained an indelible content, no more diluted than if these members were in homogenous family groups. . . . For Esther, the complexity of their racialness (hers, her daughters', their children's) had expanded exponentially. Whereas as an individual she could efface the significance of race with her friends ("we don't get into that stuff"), as a family member she had become racialised in a manner outside her control of will, both by her nurturing role and by the positions in which it placed her. (1997, p. 202)

Like Hartigan, I found that white parents, particularly mothers, were racialised in this community in ways that they could not anticipate nor control by their family members. This had particular consequences for white mothers parenting black children who lacked an education and had not been involved in organised anti-racist politics. Since they do not typically constitute an organised political constituency, their concerns as white parents of African-descent children do not register in public debates. Moreover, they were not recognised as having struggles that parallel those of the black parents of African-descent children.

Thus far, I have explored the assumptions made by the black family members of white mothers in order to highlight the *discursive* field that white mothers negotiate without the benefit of formal channels and with few, if any, sources of anti-racist support. In contrast to black mothers (who are assumed to possess a sophisticated understanding of racism naturally) white mothers are sometimes expected to acquire a sophisticated understanding of racism even before having children. I have also analysed how black family members tend to conceptualise white mothers' ability to cope with racism. Among the seventy families interviewed, both working-class and middle-class blacks exhibited a pattern of perceiving white women as less capable of relating to their children because as white women they are incapable of understanding racism. It was assumed that white mothers were not the targets of racism and thus would not always respond appropriately, but such understandings are in direct contrast to those of many white mothers. I now turn to a discussion of the racial consciousness and racial literacy of five white mothers who are representative of a subset of the white women interviewed from working-class and middle-class origins.

RACIAL CONSCIOUSNESS, RACIAL LITERACY: WHITE MOTHERS' ANALYSES

An analysis of white mothers' own perceptions of how racism shapes their experiences as parents of children, who may be classified as "black" or Asian in public spaces, is useful when analysing how racism impacts upon them. Among the 65 white birth mothers interviewed, virtually all reported that they had been subjected to some form of racial harassment or racial abuse when their pregnancy was revealed and they decided not to sever their ties to their children through abortion or adoption. While not all mothers articulated an understanding of the forms of racism their children could encounter, mothers who had sustained relationships with black Caribbean women and men tended to give similar responses as black women to questions about the areas of discrimination that their children would face. They identified the same areas as black women: education, employment, police harassment and surveillance and routine racial abuse. And they developed various strategies for securing the networks of support that they anticipated their children would need (Twine, 1998; in press). In the following section I will draw on taped interviews with five white mothers who are representative of the working-class and middle-class mothers interviewed to explore their understanding of race and racism as mothers. They include: (1) two lone mothers raising their children without any assistance from their children's father, (2) two mothers who have sustained long-term marriages and (3) one divorced mother.

Diana, the 49-year-old mother, who described herself as a "white women defending a black family," was representative of white parents who had previously been actively involved in anti-racist and anti-fascist political work in London. Her involvement in anti-racist work mediated her encounters with racism as a white member of a black family. As Diana says,

> I knew about institutional racism. I knew about racial harassment, so I knew that when I stepped out on the street with my black child, the chances were that I would get harassed in some way or another. And I was ready for that. I was ready for someone to call me a name. I was ready for somebody to throw something at me ... I had that in my head, that that could happen. I wasn't ready for somebody to doubt that he was mine. It just hadn't occurred to me at all. So it was a real shock the first time. After that I was ready for it [whenever I was questioned about my son's origins by a stranger] ... my answer would just be straight "No, he's mine." I bore him. He was in my womb. I carried him for nine months, just like any other child.

Diana's statement illustrates how the perceived racial difference between herself and her son undermines her experience of her maternal status in public spaces. In this case, she must negotiate doubts about her biological relatedness to her own child.[21] This aspect of discrimination was never reported or commented upon by black mothers whose children resembled their white fathers in skin colour and phenotype.

Beverly, a 45-year-old mother of two young adults, argued that her husband does not recognise the forms of racialised exclusion that she experiences on a regular basis. She argues that racism has marginalised her from her children and husband. Her analysis of her situation provides another example of how she believes that racism affects here as a white mother when she is in public spaces. As she says:

> Well, I suffer from second-hand racism. [My husband] said, "You can't understand racism in the sense that a black person can understand racism because when you're out on your own in the street, you're the white person on your own." But I'll always say [to my family] ... when my kids were small, say I was standing in front of them [and the store clerk] would serve me—then they'd try to serve the kids because they didn't think we were a family ... and that even happens to me and [my husband] today when we're out shopping—people don't always associate that you're together.

In the above quote we can see that Beverly interprets the absence of recognition that she receives as a mother related to her children as a form of racism. While it may be problematic to expand racism to include this type of experience, it is important to recognise the language that she employs to describe the challenge posed to her "relatedness" to her birth children. Her relation to her children is not visible and she experiences this symbolic assault as a form of racism. Middle-class and working-class women identified this as a routine occurrence. However, black family members did not mention this kind of treatment when I asked them to evaluate the impact of racism on their white family members. Consequently, the white mothers interviewed reported that they seldom, if ever, received racial empathy from their children or other black family members when they encountered racial abuse because they were considered members of a racially privileged group. Their racialised experiences remained invisible to some family members.

RACIAL LITERACY AND ACTIVIST MOTHERS

Some of the university-educated mothers interviewed were conscious of and informed about multiple forms of racism. Educated in this arena or *racially literate,* they related examples of working very hard to provide their children with social experiences and other resources that would counter the racism they might face in their lives (see Twine, 1998). Several of the mothers interviewed were white women of working-class origin who met the fathers of their children while they were university students or white collar workers in multiethnic community organisations. The following remarks made by Jennifer, a 46-year-old welfare rights activist who is raising her seven-year-old daughter alone, are typical of how these activist mothers tended to conceptualise racism. Jennifer, who grew up in an exclusively white rural village, did not have any contact with people of colour before she attended the University of Kent at Canterbury, but her awareness of racism has become acute as her remarks illustrate:

> I think racism in this country is very insidious . . . compared with some European countries where it's very overt. You know, you'll go somewhere and you'll see black people literally quite separate from white people. . . . They're not included by the white people as part of society . . . racist arguments are presented quite openly. I think here there is a traditional English hypocrisy that you don't actually say things openly. It's always . . . behind the scenes, and I realised how closely it's woven into the English psyche, both gender phobia and racism, I think particularly. . . . Where I work [in the Welfare Department] . . . has helped me to at least think about some of those things as well as having [my daughter]. . . . I've learned about racism, that it's an insidious thing, that it's so much a part of all our traditions and our ways of thinking that it's something that you have to be aware of all the time. It's almost made me much more critical, I think of white liberal thinking because . . . that can be in a sense a more dangerous racism. You know the so-called colour-blind approach to things.

In contrast to both working-class white women with less education and to university-educated black women, Jennifer sought to employ her racial and class privilege (as a professional) taking an active role in the state school her daughter attended. As the white mother of an African-descent child, she actively sought to mediate and minimise the effects of racism on her daughter. And here, too, she was fully conscious of how her racial privilege as a white woman operated to her advantage in her struggles to protect her daughter. As she described the position she found herself in:

> I've become involved in the school because I'm interested in supporting it anyway, but I realise that also I want to pave the way for her. I'm also very conscious of the fact that if there is an issue that I take up, they will deal with me as a white person. And that's what I mean about the sort of ambiguity, that I may have access into . . . institutional society as a white person that a black person wouldn't have. . . . And, obviously, I will use that to her advantage. A black mother of a black

child or mixed-race child would have a very different experience in that respect because if there was an issue at school . . . she wasn't happy with, then she will immediately encounter some sort of racial stereotyping . . . a list of cultural expectations.

In contrast to Jennifer, who has black friends and who lives in a predominantly black and Asian residential community, Claire's case illustrated the isolation that many such mothers feel, caught as they often are between racialised communities. Although Claire, the 37-year-old mother of a teenage son, was also a university-educated professional, she described the many difficulties that she has had in locating discursive spaces in which to discuss the struggles that she was experiencing as a transracial mother.

> I don't have somebody at work that I feel that close to, that I can share those very specific issues with. I know there's lots of nice people around, but I don't know anyone else who is struggling to raise a black child and would be prepared to talk to me about it. Because even within the black community . . . they're seeing my son as white.

She expressed the fear that some black people would suspect her of trying to use her black son to secure quick entry into and intimacy with the black community. So she avoided discussions of her African-descent son with black co-workers even though most of them appeared to know that her son was of African descent because they referred me to her when I asked to meet white parents of African-descent children.

Somewhat ironically, Claire's reluctance to identify herself as the mother of an African-descent child placed her at risk of being perceived by some blacks as ashamed and thus keeping her son's existence in the "closet." Her silence, born of her fear of offending black colleagues, was thus misinterpreted by them as shame or racism, as I discovered when one of her black colleagues confided that "she doesn't tell anyone that her son is black." This example illustrates how difficult it is for some middle-class white mothers to locate a forum in which they feel comfortable sharing their concerns and receiving support or advice from other parents of African-descent children. This issue seemed to be more problematic for women who were not natives of Leicestershire and thus had no organic networks of childhood or school friends in whom they could confide.

When asked how she thought black mothers perceived her, Claire offered the following analysis,

They make assumptions about your experiences and about what you know. I find it difficult to be articulate about my specific experiences because there is no one to talk to about it.

As a white teacher in a school serving a predominantly Asian and African Caribbean population, Claire had acquired a sophisticated analysis of how institutional racism operates to target black students for exclusion or expulsion from school at much higher rates than white students. She speculated that her son, for example, had been accused of being a drug dealer at school simply because he was black. While she acknowledged having been a bit "naïve" in her twenties when she first became a parent, Claire contended that she had since developed a more complex understanding of how racism operated in her son's life.

For example, Claire, like Jennifer, made a concerted effort to deploy her racial privileges and university education to challenge the racist practices of school officials and police, as illustrated by the following remarks:

They were threatening to throw him out, so we had to go to the governors and defend him. . . . The other situations have been . . . more about trouble that his friends have got into. And because they're all white, somebody watching can't distinguish between the white kids so they'll go, "Oh, there was a black one with them." And in the end, he gets into trouble when he might only have been sort of a bystander. . . . Because he's 6'3" and he's the only black one in that particular group, he gets sort of fingered out for various things that he hasn't actually done. He has spent a night in a [prison] cell. He has been stopped on numerous occasions for, you know, standing on the street corner with a sports bag.

Like several other university mothers interviewed, Claire was very conscious that the police respond to her differently than they would, for example, a university educated black woman or a working-class white mother who did not exhibit a similar understanding of her legal lights. Comparing herself to a black mother she had witnessed in a similar situation, she said.

There was no politeness. There was no extra . . . leeway for her, and I felt I was given leeway in comparison to her . . . [the police] don't deal with me like that.

Fighting back tears as she spoke of her most recent encounter with the police, Claire described constant fear for her son's well-being, acknowledging that her experience was nothing when compared with what black mothers must endure daily. Once, when her son failed to return home after ten hours, she decided to phone the local police. As she described it:

I've been really paranoid given what's been happening lately with him being stopped in the streets . . . I thought the police had got him. So I rang the police station and said "This is Claire Cunningham. Have you got my son in custody?" They tapped through [the computer] and said, "No there's no Cunningham being held in Leicestershire." The police asked "Why are you ringing at this point? He's not been missing that long." So I said, "My son is 6'3", black and male. Your officers have been giving him a lot of hassle recently. They've stopped him on numerous occasions as he's got his key in this door coming into our home. Squad cars have stopped him and asked 'What are you doing?' because this is not in a black area. What's a 6'3" black male doing entering a house in a white, middle-class area?" So I said to this chap on the phone, "I'm really sorry and I know that I'm going to offend you personally but your officers have been spending far too much attention on my son. I have to eliminate this as a possibility."

Claire's experiences are the type of racism that members of the black community routinely manage. Nevertheless, they have become associated almost exclusively with blacks (and the Irish). It is precisely these "limits" on the intergenerational transfer of their white racial privilege that white mothers engaged in transracial caretaking alliances encounter. The fact that white privilege has "limits" is not always recognised by black family members when they calculate the impact of racism on their white family members, a perspective undercutting the amount of racial "empathy" that white women can expect to receive from their families and friends. Although the white mothers interviewed held a broad range of understandings about how racial privilege intersects with gender, age and class hierarchies, most argued that their social "suffering" and "abuse" as members of black families are not recognised and had consequences for them as mothers.

Another white mother, Britney, who is less educated than Claire, has arrived at the same analysis. While Britney is now divorced, she had been married for

more than ten years and raised her children with epi-
sodic support from her former Jamaican black husband. She described her daughters as "an extension of
me" and did not differ from the university-educated
mothers in her analysis of her children's hypervisibility
(and thus vulnerability) to school administrators and
the police because of their skin colour.

> When my children were in school, there were very few
> what we called in the old days "half-castes." Now
> today they would be called "black." . . . But I always
> did say to them that if ever they were out in a group, if
> there was anybody was doing anything wrong, they
> would be the ones to be singled out [by the police]
> because they were different. They stuck out . . . [from
> whites] but because they got colour in them, which
> they understood [was a problem].

While parents expressed concern for their daughters'
self-esteem because they were sometimes subjected to
racial abuse, they argued that racism was gendered and
that teenage girls were less likely to be racially harassed
by the police on a regular basis. And because parents
assumed that their sons would experience more frequent and vulgar forms of racial abuse in public spaces,
they seemed to develop a more heightened and proactive perspective about sons' needs [rather than reactive
anti-racist consciousness]. Proactive strategies included
things like teaching their sons how to respond to the
police politely and to *document* instances of racial harassment or police abuse, asking their *white* peers to report
incidents and act collectively as witnesses.

CONCLUSION: MINDING THE RACIAL GAPS IN MULTIRACIAL FAMILIES

I have traced racial logics and ideologies circulating
within interracial families that "naturalise" and
"racialise" a mother's ability to empathise with her
children. In my field research and focused interviews I
identified a discourse of maternal incompetence in
which black family members assumed white birth
mothers' inability to mother properly. Thus maternal
incompetence is racialised. White mothers may find
themselves parenting children in a familial context in
which their black family members suspect them of not
possessing racial "empathy." They are assumed to be
less prepared to parent their children because of their
"whiteness" and have to manage the presumed "racial
gap" between themselves and their children.

This raises the question, "Why do black women
typically invoke the trope of maternal incompetence as
a code for white women's vulnerability?" In a context
in which two-parent black families are idealised but are
increasingly less common as a family form, this may be
a code for other types of vulnerabilities that black
women experience in their efforts to establish and sustain two-parent black families. My attendance at black
community events called to my attention the central
role that white women occupy as the domestic partners, mothers, and aunts of some of the most successful
and visible black leaders in Leicester. Some black
women pointed out to me that their children would be
competing with the "black" children of white women
and would have less access to resources. They feared
that perhaps "biracial" children had access to resources
and privileges that their children lacked.

One consequence of these assumptions of maternal
incompetence is that the black family members (particularly their mothers and sisters of their partners) may
challenge their right to parent. They may also be
excluded from the very familial social networks that
black women argue that they need in order to develop
appropriate maternal skills. For some mothers this
leads to their feeling isolated within their family and as
not occupying the same moral sphere as the black
mothers in the family.

When compared with the black mothers (who had
children of multiracial ancestry), white mothers of
children of African ancestry expressed the same fears
that their children might be distinguished from black
children with two black parents. However, black mothers reasoned that since they shared the same "racial"
identity as their children, they were prepared to
empathise with their pain and respond appropriately.
As members of the black community, black mothers
felt equipped to compensate for the "horizontal hostility" their children might experience within that community. Both middle-class black and white mothers
who lived in professional enclaves feared that their
children might be excluded from certain black "social"
circles because of their more privileged lifestyles. They
feared that their children's greater access to material
resources and social experiences could generate
tensions and class-based cultural differences between
them and the children of working-class or low-income
blacks depriving them of the emotional and social support of that segment of the community.

The differences in racial logics that I detected in the
families I interviewed appear to be further exacerbated

by traditional gender ideologies that dictated that children be given what Sharon Hays has described as "intensive mothering" and that place primary responsibility for the transference to children of a black identity and African-Caribbean culture on mothers alone. My research suggests that white women, who are the birth mothers of African-descent children, may be parenting in a familial context in which racial empathy is assumed to follow naturally from racial resemblance. In other words, black family members often perceive white mothers as lacking racial empathy because they do not share their children's racial location. Thus, it is assumed that they do not typically have a proper understanding of racism and thus cannot feel (or respond appropriately) to their children's pain as a black mothers would. In spite of this widely held view, I found little validity to these claims; white mothers are not a homogeneous group.

The white mothers who were attempting to transfer a black identity to their children perceived access to black Caribbean social networks as desirable because they believed that they were a reliable source of emotional and social support for their children if they experienced racism. However, these same mothers expressed apprehension that their children would be rejected by the black community if they did not display specific cultural behaviours or traits defined as "black" traits by some segments of the black community. In some families these cultural traits were explicitly class-linked and reflective of immigration and educational histories. They included an ability to display certain forms of culinary preferences, musical tastes, hair care, hygiene, clothing styles, humour and Patois-speaking skills. The black women interviewed confirmed that the black community evaluates the children of white women on the basis of these learned cultural behaviours. For example, Camille, the black social worker mentioned earlier, perceived differences in the way such children were viewed by the black community:

> I don't think they [black children with one white parent] are necessarily accepted by the black community. They are treated differently from black children (with two black parents),

This issue of acceptable "black" cultural behaviour is complicated by the absence of a unitary and fixed conception of what constitutes "black" British or Caribbean cultural traits among the various African-Caribbean diasporic communities in Leicester.

While some white mothers expressed concerns that racial difference and racism were strong enough to disrupt their maternal bond with their children, others expressed the belief that the mother/child bond transcends race so that their children's experience of being labelled racially other would not threaten that primary intimacy. Others expressed both the fear of losing that bond and the fear that they wouldn't know how to comfort their children. Several white mothers, for example, expressed concerns about being eventually rejected by their children because they had not said the "right things" or known how to respond when issues of racial difference and racism emerged. But in spite of the numerous examples given of black parental failure (e.g., to empathise, to teach about racism) none of the black parents interviewed expressed fears of being rejected by their children. Thus, regardless of how they responded to racism and assumed racial difference, white mothers were assumed to lack the social experiences (including racial discrimination) black family members considered necessary to insure maternal competence, whereas all black mothers were believed to possess maternal competence by virtue of belonging to the same race as their children.

Black mothers of very light or white-skinned children argued that their children did not need physically to resemble them because no matter how closely they resembled their white fathers they still shared their mother's racial status. In this way, they de-emphasised physical resemblance while arguing that racial sameness and thus racial resemblance is a consequence of the way that the *white* Anglo-British population responds to anyone who possesses traces of visible African ancestry. An assumed absence of racial differences between black mothers and their children reaffirmed black mothers' belief that they possessed the adequate racial empathy and maternal competence. The inability of white mothers, however, to claim membership in the same racial category as their children combined with cultural beliefs about racial difference appeared to undermine their maternal competence (and authority) even when they had acquired sophisticated analyses of racism.

As we have seen, black mothers were not required by the black community (or their families) to *prove* that they possessed the skills necessary to mediate racism while white mothers experienced considerable scepticism (and occasionally even intense criticism) about their maternal abilities if they failed to demonstrate a sufficiently sophisticated understanding of everyday racism. White mothers, who had children who were not perceived as white, had to strive continually to diminish the perceived "racial" gap that prevailed between themselves and their children. It might be argued that since white mothers of Anglo-British and African-descent children perceive them as belonging to their own racial category (whatever the degree of physical resemblance), they may have more motivation to develop and/or articulate some forms of pro-active anti-racist strategies. In contrast, due to a belief in a *shared* racial position, black mothers presumed their own maternal competence whereas white mothers were perceived, by others as well as themselves, as needing to earn competence in this area. White mothers who had children who were not perceived to be white continually had to work to diminish the perceived "racial" gap between themselves and their children, efforts that often led to more sophisticated and proactive strategies to counter racism.

ACKNOWLEDGMENTS

I am very grateful to David Theo Goldberg, Abebe Zegeye and the anonymous reviewer of *Social Identities* for their insightful comments on an earlier version of this paper. I would like to thank Nelista Cuffy, an African-Caribbean anti-racist education officer, and Rachel Hunte for their enthusiasm and support of this research. Ms Cuffy facilitated this research by providing me with numerous referrals to white mothers of African-descent children and to members of the African-Caribbean community in Leicestershire. I also thank Tani Barlow, Kathleen Blee, Jacqueline Nassy Brown, Avery Gordon and Jonathan Warren for their insightful comments on this project.

I also benefited from the comments of the following audiences: the Stanford Humanities Center, the Sociology Department's Colloquium on Race and Ethnicity at the University of Wisconsin at Madison, and the Gendered Politics of Reproduction session, organised by Carole Browner and Caroline Bledsoe for the Annual Meetings of the American Anthropological Association held 2–4 December 1996, in Philadelphia, Pennsylvania. Special thanks go to Gail Hanlon, whose critical editorial comments on this paper were invaluable. This paper is based upon research that was funded by the University of Washington at Seattle and the University of California at Santa Barbara.

NOTES

1. For example, several reports published by the Commission for Racial Equality document the racial violence in housing and education. However, while these reports identify black and Asian families, they do not generally acknowledge multiracial families that include white parents or white women who are the lone parents of African-descent children. See *Living in Terror: A Report on Racial Violence and Harassment in Housing* (1986), *Racial Harassment on Local Authority Housing Estates* (1981), and *Racial Violence and Harassment* (1986).
2. The report did not state whether these applications involved white women who were members of multiracial families.
3. The largest number of applications were filed by Caribbean women, who submitted 232 applications for assistance in racial discrimination cases to the Commission for Racial Equality in 1997.
4. This line of inquiry represented an extension of my earlier research in the United States and Brazil (Twine *et al.*, 1991; 1996; in press), and was also inspired by the work of feminist anti-racist scholars such as Kathleen Blee (1991), Vron Ware (1992) and Ruth Frankenberg (1993).
5. Previous British research on interraciality and transracial familial relations which has typically focused upon: (1) interracial families in London (Benson, 1981); (2) the racial identity of children (Wilson, 1987); or (3) the racism that children encounter (Tizard and Phoenix, 1993). By contrast, my research is concerned with how white *birth* mothers mediate, interpret and respond to anti-black racism as parents. Second, this study belongs to the nascent body of ethnographic research being conducted by US-based "whiteness studies" scholars rather than to what are known as the racial identity research studies.
6. See Twine (1998) for a brief discussion of several of the specific strategies employed by white mothers to minimise the racism that their children will encounter.
7. My original research design involved a comparative study of three different cities in England which included London, Leicester and Liverpool. After conducting pilot research in London and Leicester, I decided to conduct a focused community study of an African-descent community that, in contrast to London and Liverpool, has been neglected by researchers concerned with multiracial families. This enabled me to reside in one community for an extended period of time rather than dividing my time between three cities with very different histories of immigration and ethnic populations. It is my hope that this will generate a more richly textured ethnography that is sensitive to the uniqueness of this locale. I also selected Leicester because it has been an important site for organised racism.
8. While marital status was not a criterion of inclusion, I did attempt to over-interview in the category of mothers who had sustained a domestic partnership or marriage for a

minimum of ten years. Long-term relationships enabled me to explore in depth changes in their racial consciousness and parenting practices. I also interviewed a comparable sample of white fathers with black female partners in order to evaluate how gender affected the experience of racism. This also enabled me to consider how black women raising children with white male partners raising children in the same residential communities converge and diverge.

9. For a discussion of the basis of support for the National Front, see Ann Phizacklea and Robert Miles (1980) *Labour and Racism* and Cashmore (1987) *The Logic of Racism.*

10. The National Front reaped electoral rewards in local elections of 1976 and 1977 prior to the period when Margaret Thatcher served as Prime Minister (1979–1991).

11. Leicester Racial Attacks Monitoring Project, "Report 1990," RAMP Publications, 1991.

12. The 1991 Census was the first in the United Kingdom to include a question on ethnic origin.

13. I am following the British use of the term "Asian" which typically includes South Asians with origins in Bangladesh, India, Pakistan and East Africa while excluding the Chinese and other East Asians. The Chinese were counted as a separate category on the 1991 UK census. The Chinese constitute 0.3 per cent of the local population.

14. Pakistanis and Bangladeshis constitute 1.0 per cent and 0.4 per cent, respectively, of the population.

15. Tariq Modood and his research associates at the London Policy Institute have documented significant differences among Asian ethnic groups along axes of class, immigrant status, tenure in Britain and religion. For example, there appear to be profound economic differences between Bangladeshis as a whole and Indians in some communities. The diversity of the Asian population and economic differences are not always accounted for in the evaluations by non-Asians of Asian upward mobility.

16. Black scholars examining the African diaspora in Britain have described the anger that some black women feel towards local black men for dating and desiring white women (Brown, 1998). I encountered this same phenomenon in Leicester. In private and public discussions local

black women described their unsuccessful attempts to establish long-term relationships with black men. Their frustration with the increasing population of black men with white partners was sometimes articulated in their evaluations of the maternal competence and racial empathy of white women in their families.

17. Black women described their unsuccessful struggles to establish long-term monogamous relationships with local black men. Several women were considering immigrating to the United States because they considered this their only alternative if they hoped to establish a family with a black man. In a context in which black men routinely establish domestic partnerships and marriages with white women, relationships between black women and white men remain very stigmatised in Leicester among the black women I interviewed. This is not unique to the black community in Leicester. This same pattern has been found by US scholars working in port cities in England. For example, see Jacqueline Nassy Brown (1998).

18. She also interpreted the multiple and varied racial labels that white mothers employed to acknowledge that their children are of European/British ancestry as well as African as evidence that they are racist and don't understand racism. For example, *some* white mothers, like black Caribbean parents, employed terms such as "mixed race" or "half caste" or "African English" to distinguish black children with *one* black parent from black children with two black parents.

19. Although he was born in Leicester, England he self-identifies as Bajan. His parents immigrated from Barbados in the 1960s. His parents refer to the grandchildren who have one white parent as half-caste.

20. In his analysis of whites living in Detroit, John Hartigan Jr provides a much needed analysis of the ways that working class and poor whites, who are located in residential, friendship and familial networks that include US blacks, must manage their own racialisation (Hartigan, 1997).

21. My work is indebted to and inspired by that of Ruth Frankenberg, who has argued that racism "rebounds" onto white women.

REFERENCES

Benson, S. (1981) *Ambiguous Ethnicity: Interracial Families in London,* Cambridge and London: Cambridge University Press.

Blee, K. (1991) *Women of the Klan: Gender and Racism in the 1920s,* Berkeley and Los Angeles: University of California Press.

——— (1997) "Mothers in Race-Hate Movements," *The Politics of Motherhood: Activist Voices from Left to Right,* Hanover and London: University Press of New England.

Brown, J. (1998) "Black Liverpool, Black America, and the Gendering of Diasporic Space," *Cultural Anthropology,* 13 (3): 291–325.

Calhoun, C. (1995) *Critical Social Theory,* Cambridge and Oxford: Basil Blackwell.

Chodorow, N. (1978) *The Reproduction of Mothering: Psychoanalysis and the Sociology of Gender,* Berkeley and Los Angeles: University of California Press.

Collins, P. H. (1994) "Shifting the Center: Race, Class and Feminist Theorizing About Motherhood," in E. N. Glenn, G. Chang and L. R. Forcey (eds), *Mothering: Ideology, Experience and Agency,* New York/London: Routledge.

——— (1990) *Black Feminist Thought: Knowledge, Consciousness and the Politics of Empowerment,* Unwin Hyman.

Commission for Racial Equality (1981) *Racial Harassment on Local Authority Housing Estates,* London: CRE.

—— (1987) *Living in Terror: A Report on Racial Violence and Harassment in Housing,* London: CRE.

—— (1997) *Annual Report,* London: CRE.

—— (1996) *Annual Report,* London: CRE.

de Beauvoir, S. (1953) *The Second Sex,* translated by H. M. Parshley, New York: Alfred Knopf.

Essed, P. (1990) *Understanding Everyday Racism: Towards an Interdisciplinary Theory,* Newbury Park, CA and London: Sage Publications.

Frankenberg, R. (1993) *White Women, Race Matters: The Social Construction of Whiteness,* Minneapolis: University of Minnesota Press.

Gilroy, P. (1987) *There Ain't No Black in the Union Jack: The Cultural Politics of Race and Nation,* Chicago: University of Chicago Press.

Glenn, E. N., G. Chang and L. R. Forcey (eds) (1994) *Mothering: Ideology, Experience and Agency,* New York/London: Routledge.

Hartigan, J. Jr (1998) "Locating White Detroit," in R. Frankenberg (ed), *Displacing Whiteness: Social and Cultural Criticism,* Durham, NC and London: Duke University Press.

Hays, S. (1996) *The Cultural Contradictions of Motherhood,* New Haven, CT: Yale University Press.

Ladd-Taylor, M. and L. Umanksy (1998) *"Bad" Mothers: The Politics of Blame in Twentieth-Century America,* New York: New York University Press.

Lazarre, J. (1996) *Beyond the Whiteness of Whiteness: Memoir of a White Mother of Black Sons,* Durham and London: Duke University Press.

Leicester City Council (1996) *Leicester Key Facts: Ethnic Population.*

Luke, C. (1994) "White Women in Interracial Families: Reflections on Hybridization, Feminine Identities and Racialized Othering," *Feminist Issues,* 14 (2): 49–72.

Miles, R. (1989) *Racism,* London: Routledge.

Modood, T. and R. Berthoud (1997) *The Fourth National Survey of Ethnic Minorities: Diversity and Disadvantage,* London: Policy Studies Institute.

Phillips, M. and T. Phillips (1998) *Windrush: The Irresistible Rise of Multi-Racial Britain,* a companion to the BBC series, London: HarperCollins.

Phizacklea, A. and R. Miles (1980) *Labour and Racism,* London: Routledge.

Ragoné, H. (1998) "Incontestable Motivations," in S. Franklin and H. Ragoné (eds), *Reproducing Reproduction: Kinship, Power and Technological Innovation,* Philadelphia: University of Pennsylvania Press.

Reddy, M. (1994) *Crossing the Color Line: Race, Parenting and Culture,* New Brunswick, NJ: Rutgers University Press.

Rich, A. (1976) *Of Woman Born: Motherhood as an Institution,* New York: W. W. Norton.

Ruddick, S. (1989) *Maternal Thinking: Toward a Politics of Peace,* Boston: Beacon Press.

Scobie, E. (1972) *Black Britannia: a History of Blacks in Britain,* Chicago: Johnson Publishing Company.

Solomos, J. (1993) *Race and Racism in Britain,* 2nd ed, New York: St Martin's Press.

Spelman, E. (1988) *Inessential Woman: Problems of Exclusion in Feminist Thought,* Boston, MA: Beacon Press.

Tizard, B. and A. Phoenix (1993) *Black, White or Mixed Race? Race and Racism in the Lives of Young People of Mixed Parentage,* New York and London: Routledge.

Troyna, B. and R. Hatcher (1992) *Racism in Children's Lives: A Study of Mainly White Primary Schools,* London and New York: Routledge.

Twine, F. W. (in press) "Transracial Mothering and Anti-Racism: The Case of White Mothers of African-Descent Children in Britain," *Feminist Studies,* 25 (3, Fall).

—— (1998) *Racism in a Racial Democracy: The Maintenance of White Supremacy in Brazil,* New Brunswick NJ: Rutgers University Press.

—— (1998) "Managing Everyday Racisms: White Mothers of African-Descent Children in Britain," in J. O'Brien and J. Howard (eds), *Everyday Inequalities: Critical Inquiries,* London: Blackwell Publishers.

—— (1996) "Brown Skinned White Girls: Class, Culture and the Construction of White Identity in Suburban Communities," *Gender, Place and Culture: A Journal of Feminist Geography,* 3 (2, July): 205–24.

Twine, F. W., J. W. Warren and F. Ferrandiz (1991) *Just Black? Multiracial Identity,* New York: Filmmakers Library.

Ware, V. (1992) *Beyond the Pale: White Women, Racism and History,* London and New York: Verso Press.

—— (1996) "Island Racism: Gender, Place and White Power," *Feminist Review,* 54: 65–86.

Williams, P. (1991) *The Alchemy of Race and Rights: Diary of a Law Professor,* Cambridge and London: Harvard University Press.

Wilson, A. (1981) "In Between: The Mother in the Interracial Family," *New Community: Journal of the Commission for Racial Equality,* 9 (2): 208–15.

—— (1987) *Mixed Race Children: A Study of Identity,* London: Allen and Unwin.

Verta Taylor and Leila J. Rupp

Learning from Drag Queens

Drag queens can teach us a lot about sexual desire —especially our own.

In American society, people tend to think of males and females and heterosexuals and homosexuals as distinct and opposite categories. Drag performances challenge the biological basis of gender and the fixed nature of sexual identity. As a place where for an hour or two gay is normal and straight is other, drag shows use entertainment to educate straight people about gay, lesbian, bisexual, and transgendered lives.

Milla, one of the drag queens who performed at the 801 Cabaret, the Key West club we studied for our book *Drag Queens at the 801 Cabaret,* once proclaimed, with both exuberance and self-mockery, "We're going to be in classrooms all around the world! . . . No more George Washington, no more Albert Einstein, you'll be learning from us!" All the drag queens in the troupe laughed, but in fact, as we came to realize, they do teach their audience members complex lessons about the porous boundaries of gender and sexuality. Drag shows may be entertaining, and diverse people may flock to them to have a good time, but that does not belie the impact that a night of fun can have. The drag queens are, we think, more than entertainers. As Sushi, the house queen, insisted in a newspaper interview, "We're not just lip-synching up here, we're changing lives by showing people what we're all about." In the process of showing people what they are all about, they bring together diverse individuals, illustrating the official Key West philosophy that we are "One Human Family." How exactly do they do that? And do people take away the lessons they teach?

These were some of the questions we explored by studying the 801 Girls, a troupe of gay men who perform as drag queens every night of the year for mixed crowds of tourists and local residents, women and men, heterosexual, gay, lesbian, bisexual, and transgender people. The performers are economically marginal men who make barely enough to support themselves in a town where property is expensive and affordable housing is in short supply, as Barbara Ehrenreich conveyed so vividly in her depiction of Key West in *Nickel and Dimed: On (Not) Getting By in America.* We interviewed in all sorts of contexts and spent time with eight drag queens to find out why they do what they do and what their performances and interactions with audience members mean to them. We spent night after night at the shows, taping their banter and the songs they lip-synch and talking to audience members. And we recruited diverse people to come back the next day and talk to us about the shows in a focus-group setting. That is how we learned that there is more to drag shows than meets the eye.

DRAG SHOWS

Drag shows have a long history as central institutions in gay communities and as places where, at least in tourist towns, straight people come in contact with gay life. From the drag balls in cities such as New York and Chicago in the 1920s to the famous Finocchio's in San Francisco in the 1940s and the popularity of RuPaul and Lady Chablis in the 1990s, men dressed in women's clothing have served as a visible segment of the gay community and have also enthralled straight audiences. The 801 Girls are no exception. On a one-by-four-mile island closer to Cuba than to Miami, populated by diverse communities—Cuban, Bahamian, gay and lesbian, hippie, and increasingly Central American and Eastern European—drag queens are central to the mix. They are everywhere: on stage, on the streets, at benefits. As the local paper put it, "You know you're from Key West when . . . your Mary Kay rep is a guy in drag."

The shows at the 801 Cabaret are an institution in Key West, described by visitors as "the best show in town." Every night at quarter after ten, four or five of the girls take to the sidewalk outside the bar, hand out flyers for the show, and banter with passersby. That is how they recruit an audience. Some tourists avert their eyes or cross the street, but most are intrigued, stop to chat, and many decide to come to the show. Upstairs over a gay bar, the cabaret has small tables up front where unsuspecting tourists serve as props for the girls, a bar in the center, and mostly standing-room-only space around the bar. Gay men congregate and cruise at the back, behind the bar.

A typical show consists of 15 to 20 numbers, some performed individually and some in groups. There is a lot of interaction with the audience, which sets the show apart from similar ones performed at gay bars across the country. But in terms of the repertoire of songs, the comedy, and the dialogue, what happens at the 801 is typical of a style of drag that emerged in conjunction with the gay and lesbian movement, a style of drag that goes beyond female impersonation.

For these drag queens, although they dress in women's clothing and can be as beautiful as biological women, there is no pretending. They announce from the start that they are gay men, they talk in men's voices, they make jokes about their large clitorises and "manginas" and complain that they are having "testical difficulties" when the music does not work. Some do not even shave their legs or underarms or tuck their genitals. Inga, a statuesque blond from Sweden, would be introduced as "Inga with a pinga," and Milla, often mistaken for African American, sometimes appeared with a dildo gripped in her crotch, calling attention to the real item hidden away. Sushi occasionally pulls down her dress and bra to reveal her male chest, provoking the same kind of wild audience response a real female stripper might, even though the sight of male nipples is nothing new in a tropical town where men do not need to wear shirts walking down the street. Sushi also performs "Crazy World" from *Victor/Victoria*, a song about a world "full of crazy contradictions." Behind a sheer white curtain, she strips down to nothing but keeps her genitals tucked between her legs as she backs off stage, revealing what transgender activists would call a "gender-queer" body.

For the final number of the weekend shows, R.V. Beaumont, who perfected drag while working at Disney World and learned to do Bette Midler numbers from watching Bette Midler impersonators, used to change out of drag on stage to the Charles Aznevour ballad, "What Makes a Man a Man?," transforming

himself from woman to man. And a regular feature of the Saturday night "Girlie Show" is Kylie, Sushi's best friend from high school, who does a mean California valley girl, stripping entirely to "Queen of the Night," leaving the audience with the contrast between her blond wig, makeup, high heels, and well-hung body. These are the ways they educate their audiences about the performativity of gender and the slipperiness of sexual desire.

"TROUBLING" GENDER

The drag queens at the 801, at least some of them, have slipped back and forth between genders. Milla, who grew up in a working-class family in St. Petersburg, Florida, with an alcoholic and abusive father, "decided that I wanted to be a woman." She (the drag queens tend to use their drag names and female pronouns, although they also switch back and forth with some ease) got hormones from a counselor she was seeing for her adolescent drug problems by telling him that she would get them anyway from the drag queens on the street. She grew breasts and went out dressed as a woman and had "the men fall over, all over me, and with no clue, no clue." She loved it and seriously considered sex-reassignment surgery. But then "I started to love myself. I pulled away from that whole effeminate side . . . and I became a man." Milla continues to attract men and women of all sexual desires and pronounces herself "omnisexual."

Gugi, born to a Puerto Rican family in Chicago, also passed for a woman for a time. "What I've always wanted was to be a woman," Gugi said, although she added, "I don't know if it is because I wanted to be a woman or because I was attracted to men that I preferred to be a woman." She also took hormones for a time and grew breasts, but she stopped because "it wasn't the right time. . . . I did it to get away from my dad's death" and a painful breakup with a lover.

The one who is in charge of the shows and makes everything happen is Sushi, who never looks like a man even out of drag. Sushi, whose Japanese mother married an American G.I., describes herself as "some place in between" a woman and a man. She began to dress in drag in high school and for a time was a street prostitute in Los Angeles. At first, she thought that wanting to wear women's clothing meant that she wanted to be a woman, but then she came to realize that it just meant that she was a drag queen. "I know I'm a drag queen; I finally realized that I'm a gay man who puts on women's clothing and looks good." Yet she still worries that she is really a closeted transgendered person. One night we asked her the difference between being a drag queen and being transgendered and she replied, "A drag queen is someone like Kylie who has never ever thought about cutting her dick off."

What it means about the social basis of gender that men can look like beautiful women is not lost on audience members. A local straight woman described thinking of them as women during the show. A straight male tourist agreed, saying of Milla, "She was a woman." His wife agreed: "Uh-huh, she was a woman. It never even entered my mind. She was a beautiful woman." A young straight woman, at her first drag show, explained that she thought of them as both. "Back and forth, I think. Yeah, I was confused and went back about twelve times." A gay man, as if echoing what at least some of the girls might say about themselves, said, "I don't think of them as really any of it. I feel like they're their own thing. I feel like a drag queen is something completely different. . . . It's way more than being a woman and it's definitely not being a man."

As that last comment suggests, there is more going on here than just mimicking traditional female beauty. Even the girls who are the most beautiful in drag—Sushi, Milla, Inga, and Gugi—do not really look like women, because they are too tall or have muscled arms or men's waists and buttocks. They are beautiful as drag queens. And they perform alongside other girls who are old or overweight or do not shave their chests and who perform numbers that criticize traditional feminine ideals of beauty. Scabola Feces, whose very name belies any hint of impersonating beautiful women, performs "Wedding Bell Blues" in a ripped-up wedding dress, Coke-bottle glasses, and a mouthful of fake rotten buck teeth, and R.V. appears in hair curlers as a hooker or madam in such songs as "The Oldest Profession" and "When You're Good to Mama."

Their performances force audience members to think differently about what it means to be a man, what it means to be a woman. A local gay man described "older married couples" watching R.V. perform "What Makes a Man a Man?" "with their jaws hitting the floor. Especially when the eyelashes come off and the wig and the makeup disappears like that. . . . And they're like, I think they're still shocked when they leave that way like, 'Oh my god, I don't believe it.' They want to believe that they're women and it's hard for them to

accept that they're not." This is what feminist scholars mean when they talk of "troubling" gender, causing people to think outside the binary of male/female. The 801 girls are very good teachers.

AROUSING NEW SEXUAL DESIRES

The drag queens also have an impact by arousing sexual desires in audience members not congruent with their sexual identities. A central part of the show involves bringing audience members on stage to represent different sexual identity categories. The drag queens call for a straight man, a gay man, a straight woman, and a lesbian, sometimes a bisexual or transsexual. While this seems to affirm the boundaries of sexual desire, the intent of the drag queens is quite the opposite. First of all, they allow a great deal of latitude in who represents what categories, and audience members are creative, so that gay men might call out that they are lesbians and straight women might play lesbian for a night. And then, once on stage, during the time that we studied the shows, the girls arranged the couples in positions simulating sex acts, the two women as the drag queens say "bumping pussy" and the gay man on his back with the straight man crouched over his pelvis. Each participant got a shot of liquor poured into his or her mouth with a lot of teasing about fellatio.

Usually the people on stage really get into the act. One night the straight woman seemed eager to have the lesbian touch her and said she was "willing to try pussy-licking." Another time one of our research assistants volunteered as the lesbian, and a woman there with her husband came up to her and said, "I'm totally straight, but that just turned me on" and kissed her on the mouth. A young straight woman described feeling sorry for a young straight man brought up on stage. "I thought for him it had to be confusing because the drag queen that was coming on to him was, to me, the prettiest, and I kept thinking, 'God, that's a guy, that's a guy.' . . . And he's probably thinking, 'God, she's hot.' Forgetting that she's a he. And I think that when she got on top of him, he was probably embarrassed because he was turned on." Sometimes audience members take the initiative. One night a very thin young woman in skimpy clothes came onstage to dance with Desiray, a new member of the troupe who became a drag queen because he fell in love with the show as a tourist. The woman stripped down to a thong and eventually grabbed Desiray to mime having anal sex with her.

For the drag queens, a central part of the show is the arousal of straight men. They love to move through the crowd and touch and fondle them. One night a straight couple got in a fight because the man got an erection when Sushi grabbed his penis. A straight woman tourist, on the other hand, loved when the girls fondled her husband. "It's like here's this man touching my husband, it's like really cool. And he's standing there letting him." She found this the "sexiest" part of the show, "there was something crackling the most. . . . The line was crossed the most at that moment. . . . And I liked it." Her husband described his own response: "I'm sitting there and there's a little bit of me saying, 'This is sexually exciting' and there's another part of me saying, 'Wait a minute, don't do this. You're not supposed to be sexually excited, this is a man." At one show, a very macho young man there with his girlfriend took one look at Sushi and confided in us, "I could do her."

And it is not just straight men who experience sexual desires outside their identities. A lesbian described feeling very attracted to Milla: "She was so sexy," and a straight woman agreed, commenting that "I was very drawn to her sexually. I felt like kissing her. And I'm not gay at all." Yet she described being attracted because Milla "was a woman. She was a beautiful woman." Another straight woman "started falling in love with" Milla and announced, "I want to make love with her." When Sushi and Milla, or Sushi and Gugi, perform the lesbian duet "Take Me or Leave Me" from *Rent*, it has a powerful erotic impart on all sorts of audience members. More than once, during the shows, straight women started kissing their women friends. One night two Mormon women on vacation without their husbands started talking with us. By the end of the show, one confided that, if she were going to be with a woman, she would choose her friend.

As a result of these kinds of interactions and responses, many people at the shows conclude that the labels of "gay" and "straight," like "man" and "woman," just do not fit. For one gay man, "You leave them at the door." Said another, the drag queens are "challenging the whole idea of gender and so forth and they're breaking that down." A straight male tourist put it this way: "I think that one of the beauties of attending a show like this is that you do realize that you . . . shouldn't walk out and say, 'I only like men,' and you shouldn't say 'I only like women,' and it all kind of blends together a lot more so than maybe what

we want to live in our normal daily lives." Because the drag shows have the potential to arouse powerful desires that people perceive as contrary to their sexual identities, they have a real impact on people's thinking about the boundaries of heterosexuality.

DRAG QUEENS CREATING CHANGE

And this is just what the drag queens intend, as Milla's and Sushi's opening comments suggest. Kylie announces, "I intend to challenge people." Sushi explains that "I'm not just doing a number. . . . I'm trying to make more of an experience, a learning thing. . . . And I have a platform now to teach the world. . . . Even less than five minutes of talking to somebody, just that little moment I share with somebody from New Zealand or Africa or your college professor or whoever, they go back to their hometown. They remember that five-minute conversation, they realize, 'I'm not gonna call this person a fag,' you know what I mean?" Says Milla, "We are attractive to everybody. We have taken gender and thrown it out of the way, and we've crossed a bridge here. And when we are all up there, there is no gay/straight or anything."

One of the remarkable things about the drag shows is the way they bring people together across all kinds of boundaries, not just differences in gender and sexual identities. Inga described the audiences as ranging "from the worst faggot to the butchiest lesbian to the happily married couple with the kids, the honeymoon people, the people who hate gays but maybe thought it was something interesting." A gay male tourist thought the shows had a "really big mass appeal to a cross section of everyone," and in fact we have met Mormons, brides out on the town the night before their weddings, transsexuals, grandmothers and grandfathers, female strippers, bikers, and everyone in between. Although the shows express and affirm pride in gay or lesbian or bisexual or transgender identities, they also emphasize what we all have in common.

Milla, putting a negative spin on it, confessed once, "What I love the most is that all these people come to our shows—professors, doctors, lawyers, rich people—and they're as fucked up as we are." Margo, a sixty-something New Yorker who also wrote a column for the local gay newspaper, introduced the classic gay anthem "I Am What I Am" in a more positive way: "The next song I'm going to do for you will explain to everyone who, what, and why we are. We are not taxi drivers or hotel clerks or refrigerator repair people. We are drag queens and we are proud of what we do. Whether you are gay or straight, lesbian, bisexual, trisexual, transgender, asexual, or whatever in between, be proud of who you are." Sushi, too, preaches a message of pride and love. One night she raised her glass to toast to gay love and then corrected herself, "Oh no, here's to love. To love, baby, all across the world." Another time, more vulgarly, she introduced her best friend Kylie and announced, "This is the person that . . . told me that I was special and that every single one of you is special no matter if you suck a cock or lick a pussy." Using words that typically describe same-sex sex acts to divide people into new categories, the drag queens bring together gay men and straight women, lesbians and straight men.

The audience takes in the lessons. A gay New Yorker put it this way, "The message really comes across that it doesn't matter who you are." Another gay man commented that, at the 801, "Everybody is equally fabulous." A local straight woman realtor who had seen the shows many times commented to us, "They bring a gay guy up, then a straight woman, and a straight man, and a lesbian. By the end, you just think, 'What's the difference?'" Summing up the hopes and dreams of the drag queens, a young gay man with theatrical ambitions explained that the show "signifies for me . . . that we have these differences but here we are all together within this small space. Communing, interacting, being entertained, having a good time and everything is going well . . . and I think the idea being to make some sort of, like, utopia or this is the way it could be. Once we all leave this bar, if we can all see four different people that are different and commune together, or at least respect each other, then when we leave this bar, wouldn't the world be a little bit better place?"

The drag queens do indeed work to make the world a better place. As one of the few ways that straight people encounter gay culture—where, in fact, straight people live for an hour or two in an environment where gay people are the majority—drag shows, especially in a tourist town like Key West, have the potential to bring people together and to create new gender and sexual possibilities. Precisely because drag shows are entertaining, they attract people who might never otherwise be exposed to gay politics. As one female audience member put it, they "take something difficult and make it light." Because the shows arouse visceral emotions, even sexual desires that fall outside people's usual sexual identities, they have the potential to make a real impact. Through a complex process of separating people into gender and sexual identity categories, then blurring and playing with those boundaries, and then bringing people all together again, the drag queens at the 801 succeed, as the comments of audience members attest, in "freeing people's minds," "removing their blinders," "opening their minds," sometimes even "changing their lives." The diverse individuals who flock to the 801 come away with an experience that makes it a little less possible to think in a simple way about gender and sexuality or to ignore the experiences of gay, lesbian, bisexual, and transgendered people in American society.

RECOMMENDED RESOURCES

Patricia Gagné and Richard Tewskbury, eds. *Gendered Sexualities: Advances in Gender Research,* Volume 6 (JAI, 2002). A collection of articles that explore the intersection of gender and sexuality.

Esther Newton. *Mother Camp: Female Impersonators in America* (University of Chicago Press, 1972). The classic account of drag queens in the late 1960s, just before the emergence of the gay liberation movement.

Leila J. Rupp and Verta Taylor. *Drag Queens at the 801 Cabaret* (University of Chicago Press, 2003). A full analysis of the drag queens, their shows, and their impact on audiences.

Steven P. Schacht with Lisa Underwood, eds. *The Drag Queen Anthology* (Harrington Park Press, 2004). An interdisciplinary collection of articles about drag queens in different parts of the world.

PART THREE

SOCIAL ORGANIZATION OF GENDER

The processes of gender socialization that begin in early childhood prepare us for participation in society as adult women and men. Socialization alone, however, cannot account for the differences in power and prestige between men and women in almost all societies. Gender encompasses more than the socialized differences between individual women and men. As Judith Lorber points out in Section 2, gender also affects the way that social institutions—from family to medicine to politics—are structured. Key to feminist analyses is an understanding of the role of a society's institutions in perpetuating gender inequality.

Like other forms of social inequality, gender inequality includes the unequal distribution of three different kinds of valued commodities. First, inequality entails differential access to power, defined as the ability to carry out one's will despite opposition. Second, inequality includes differential access to the sources of prestige, defined as the ability to command respect, honor, and deference. Third, differential access to wealth, or economic and material resources, is important to inequality. Those who have access to any one of these resources—power, prestige, or wealth—occupy a position from which they are likely to gain access to the others and thereby reinforce their status over those who have less. In the case of gender-stratified social systems, men's greater access to power, prestige, and wealth enhances their opportunities to exploit women and decreases women's ability to resist.

Of course, not all men have equal access to power, prestige, or wealth. Men of subordinated racial or ethnic groups, working-class and poor men, disabled men, transsexual and transgendered men, and many gay or old men are also excluded from socially sanctioned sources of power, prestige, and wealth. Women, too, vary in their degree of access to power, prestige, and wealth; white or upper-class women receive benefits from their class and race even while they are penalized for their gender. As we have seen, gender is one system of domination that interacts with other systems based on race, class, ethnicity, sexuality, nationality, and ability. The task of feminist scholars is to trace the intersections of gender and other systems of domination, examining the varied ways that gender inequality is expressed and reinforced in social institutions.

Institutions construct systems of inequality in a variety of ways. Economic and legal systems; political, educational, medical, religious, and familial institutions; mass media; and the institutions of science and technology—all reinforce the ideology of women's inferiority and preserve men's greater access to power, prestige, and wealth. How? The structures of institutions are gendered in that they privilege men and those traits labeled masculine, and penalize women and the traits labeled feminine. Such institutions engage in practices that discriminate against women, exclude or devalue women's perspectives, and perpetuate the idea that differences between women and men and the dominance of men are natural. In addition, the control of these institutions usually rests in the hands of men, and as social scientists understand, dominant groups tend to behave in ways that enhance their own power.

Institutions establish various kinds of rewards and punishments that encourage women to behave in submissive ways, and such submissive behavior in turn perpetuates the idea that women are naturally submissive. For example, a complex social system in the United States exerts strong pressures on women to enter into heterosexual marriages. Families train daughters to be wives and mothers; high school events require opposite-sex dates; college fraternities and sororities promote heterosexual coupling; widespread violence against women encourages them, ironically, to seek male protection; and men's higher incomes mean that heterosexual marriage tends to improve a woman's standard of living.

A woman's failure to marry constitutes a violation of social prescriptions and often leaves her economically disadvantaged and socially suspect. On the other hand, despite women's increasing participation in the paid labor force, in heterosexual marriage the burden of care work—raising children and attending to the home—still usually falls disproportionately on women, a dynamic that helps maintain the inequality between men and women in the work world.

It is important to reiterate that gender stratification is not the only form of inequality affecting women's and men's lives and the structure of social institutions. Institutions that disadvantage racial or ethnic groups, sexual minorities, older people, people with disabilities, the poor, or particular religious or class-based groups also discriminate against both women and men who belong to those groups. Understanding women's oppression as a function of the social organization of gender necessitates understanding the intersectionality of systems of domination.

The following articles examine how particular institutions express, construct, and maintain gender inequality. They analyze the ways that women's subordination is maintained in work, families, sexuality, treatment of and attitudes about bodies, and violence against women. The articles do not simply document women's submission, however. They also describe the ways that women and men in various groups resist oppression and attempt to exercise control over their choices and their lives. To what extent are women or men able to resist the structures of gender, and to what extent are they controlled by gendered institutions?

SECTION 5

Work

Work for pay influences many aspects of our lives: our economic prosperity, our social status, our residence, our relationships with family members and friends, our health, and our access to health care. Our work experiences influence how we come to view others, ourselves, and the social world around us. Reciprocally, how we are situated in society often influences the kind of work we do and our compensation for that work.

In traditional societies, division of labor based on sex and age did not necessarily correspond to differences in the importance assigned to different tasks: "women's work" might be considered just as socially valuable as "men's work." In societies like the United States, however, social divisions of labor based on gender, race, ethnicity, age, and other factors reflect and perpetuate power differences among groups. As we have already seen in Section 1, "Diversity and Difference," and Section 2, "Theoretical Perspectives," gender is profoundly shaped by class, race, and ethnicity in ways that are especially critical in the realm of work.

This section begins with Christine Bose and Rachel Whaley's exploration of the continued concentration of women in predominantly female and men in predominantly male occupations. The most common occupations for women include secretary, cashier, and nurse, while truck drivers and carpenters are almost always men. In "Sex Segregation in the U.S. Labor Force," Bose and Whaley discuss the different ways of measuring sex segregation; the nature of sex segregation in white-collar, pink-collar, clerical, and blue-collar jobs; and the various explanations for the persistence of sex segregation into the twenty-first century. They

also argue that sex segregation matters: It is a cause of inequities in earnings (see the table on earnings) and leads to tokenism and lack of occupational mobility. Thinking about the people you know, how many are in non-sex-segregated jobs? What factors hinder people from finding work outside the traditional gender-appropriate occupations? How important is outright discrimination compared to people's socialization? Has affirmative action made a difference (see the boxed insert by Nancy Whittier on the realities of affirmative action)? What do you think can be done to end sex segregation in the labor force?

The next article in this section looks back in time to explore two cases in which the clothing women wore to work reveals a great deal about the complicated dynamics of women's employment. In "Desirable Dress: Rosies, Sky Girls, and the Politics of Appearance," Eileen Boris looks at World War II, when women factory workers donned masculine attire, and the airline industry in the 1960s, when "sky girls" wore sexy uniforms as a marketing strategy, to show the ways that employers, the state, unions, and women themselves struggled over what women would wear and for what purpose. We see the way that women's sexuality, either constrained or mobilized in the interests of employers, is far more than a private matter in the workplace. How did class, race, ethnicity, and age shape the struggles over women's clothing and appearance in these two very different cases? How would you describe the interests of male workers, employers, the state, and different groups of women workers in these cases? Can you think of contemporary examples of the politics of appearance at work?

231

Miliann Kang, in her article on Korean women's work in nail salons, looks at another form of gendered and embodied labor. Class, race, and ethnicity are central to Kang's story, not just in terms of the characteristics of the labor force but also with regard to the style of "body labor" expected by clients. In her rich ethnographic study, Kang differentiates white upper- and middle-class women's interest in pampering from black working-class women's preference for technical skill from the expectation of efficiency at a reasonable price on the part of the clients of a mixed-race, mid-level salon. What do the different interests of manicurists' clients tell us about racialized gender? What other jobs involve "body labor"? What does Kang see as positive about the interactions among women that she documents?

Sex segregation and racial-ethnic patterns of employment are also at the heart of Pierrette Hondagneu-Sotelo's "Maid in L.A.," a study of Latina domestic workers in Los Angeles. Talking with immigrant women, mostly from Latin America, who work as live-in and live-out nannies and housekeepers and as housecleaners, Hondagneu-Sotelo learns why they choose particular kinds of jobs at different times. New immigrants without the support of family and friends must often take jobs as live-ins, the least desirable position because of the lack of privacy, social isolation, long hours, incessant demands, and low pay. We hear how these Latina women feel about the houses they must clean, the children they care for, and the food (or lack thereof) their employers provide. We understand why, as soon as they can, women choose to work on a live-out basis, in their own homes and communities, and why some choose housecleaning as the most autonomous job.

Hondagneu-Sotelo puts these women's experiences into the context of immigration, transnational motherhood, and racial stereotyping. Like Kang's manicurists, Hondagneu-Sotelo's domestic workers are part of a global economy that is shaped by gender, class, and race/ethnicity. In what ways are the domestics similar to manicurists in New York? In what ways are they different? What determines whether domestic workers see their jobs as good jobs? Think about the relationship between their lives and the lives of the women who employ them. What do the experiences of Latina domestics tell us about why a living wage is a women's issue (see the boxed insert by Eileen Boris)?

As these articles demonstrate, women's race, ethnicity, nationality, age, and social class affect both the structural opportunities available to them in the labor force and their interpretations of these experiences. What experiences, if any, do you think women in the labor force share by virtue of their gender?

R E A D I N G *22* **Christine E. Bose**
Rachel Bridges Whaley[1]

Sex Segregation in the U.S. Labor Force

Sex segregation in the workplace is manifested in many ways—in the extent to which women and men are concentrated in different industries, establishments, occupations, and jobs, and in the extent to which any particular job is dominated by workers of one sex. An occupation is usually considered female or male dominated if it is at least 75 percent female or male. For example, 7 of the 10 most common occupations for women are dominated by female workers including secretary (98 percent), cashier (78 percent), and registered nurse (93 percent) (Women's Bureau 1999) (see Table 1). Similarly, the majority of the most common occupations for men are male dominated, such as truck driver (94 percent) and carpenter (98 percent) (U.S. Census Bureau 1998a) (see Table 2). The only occupation

among the top 10 (largest numbers) for both men and women is miscellaneous salaried manager, which is 70 percent male (Women's Bureau 1999). Such occupational "integration" is rare and its positive effects are frequently diluted because the particular jobs offered by employers or firms are sex segregated.

Occupational segregation may entail the physical separation of workers of different social groups (sex and racial or ethnic groups). For example, between 1920 and 1940 in North Carolina's tobacco industry, workers were physically separated and segregated into sex-typed and race-typed tasks. Black women tobacco workers were located in one building or on one floor, designed for "dirty" prefabrication work such as stripping the leaves, and white women were in

TABLE 1 TEN MOST COMMON OCCUPATIONS FOR WOMEN, 1998

Women's Common Occupations[1]	Percent Women
Secretaries	98
Cashiers	78
Managers and administrators, n.e.c.[1]	30
Sales supervisors and proprietors	40
Registered nurses	93
Nursing aides, orderlies, and attendants	89
Elementary school teachers	84
Bookkeepers, accounting clerks	93
Waiters and waitresses	78
Sales workers, other commodities[2]	68
Average labor-force occupation	46

[1]Not elsewhere classified or miscellaneous.
[2]Includes foods, drugs, health, and other commodities.

TABLE 2 TEN MOST COMMON OCCUPATIONS FOR MEN, 1998

Men's Common Occupations	Percent Women
Managers and administrators, n.e.c.	30
Truck drivers	5
Sales supervisors and proprietors	40
Construction laborers	16
Freight, stock, and material handlers	24
Janitors and cleaners	35
Fabricators and assemblers	33
Carpenters	1
Cooks	41
Sales representatives, commodities, wholesale	26

Source: U.S. Census, Statistical Abstract accessed on 4/10/00 at http://www.census.gov/prod/99pubs/99statab/sec13.pdf
Note: Occupational categories drawn from this source are slightly less detailed than those for women's occupations.

another building or on another floor, inspecting and packing the product. Meanwhile black men hauled materials between locales and white men acted as supervisors and inspectors (Jones 1984). A more recent example can be found in the baking industry. Female bakers are located in retail establishments (e.g., supermarkets) while men make up the majority of wholesale bakers (Steiger and Reskin 1990).

The sex segregation of any occupation can change over time, even while the segregation of the entire labor force remains fairly stable. Occupations are more likely to shift from male to female domination than the reverse. Public-school teaching made this transition in the late nineteenth century; clerical workers, telephone operators, waiters and waitresses, and bank tellers were resegregated by the middle of the twentieth century from male to female jobs. More recently, residential real estate sales and pharmacy work have become female dominated. Women have made significant inroads into other male-dominated jobs such as bartending and insurance adjustment, which now appear to be sex integrated but may be merely in transit to becoming female dominated. According to Barbara Reskin and Patricia Roos (1990), the fundamental reason that a job is resegregated from male to female domination is a shortage of male workers. That shortage occasionally happens when an occupation is rapidly expanding, using up the supply of suitable men. In most cases, however, men are leaving a job that has become less attractive because the work process has been downgraded in terms of skills or the job rewards are less. Consequently, the decrease in prestige and pay of an occupation occurs before women enter it. As a result, women's integration into apparently prestigious male-dominated jobs can be a hollow victory.

MEASURING SEX SEGREGATION

One way to understand the extent to which men and women do different work is to examine the proportion of workers of the same sex in each occupation, as was done above. To this end, it is seen that most men and women work in occupations where workers of the same sex predominate. Indeed, only a fraction of women work in occupations that are dominated by men (Kraut and Luna 1992).

Another method is to examine the extent to which male and female workers are clustered in a small number of occupations. Reskin and Irene Padavic (1994) report that 33 percent of women workers are employed in the top 10 occupations sex-typed female compared to about 25 percent of men being clustered in the top 10 occupations sex-typed male.

The most common way to measure sex segregation is to calculate an index of sex segregation, also called an *index of dissimilarity*, which ranges from 0 to 100. Its value is interpreted as the percentage of workers of one sex that would have to change occupations so that men and women have the same distribution in each occupation. An index of 0 implies perfect integration while an index of 100 suggests that the sexes are completely segregated from each other. In 1990 the index was 53, which means 53 percent of women workers (or approximately 28 million individuals) would need to be redistributed into other occupations if all occupations were to have the same percentage of women and men that are in the entire labor force (Reskin and Padavic 1994).

Researchers have calculated the occupational sex segregation index, using the preferred detailed Census job categories, for different historical periods. It is generally agreed that the index stayed fairly high and steady, between 65 and 69, from 1900 through 1960 (Gross 1968) and perhaps as late as 1970 (Jacobs 1989). If one focuses on nonagricultural jobs, there was only a six-point decline in sex segregation in the 60 years between 1910 and 1970, dropping from 74 to 68. Through the 1970s, however, it dropped another 8 points to 60 in 1980 (Jacobs 1989b). In the 1980s, the segregation index continued to drop but at a much slower rate (Reskin and Roos 1990).

In 1940 a comparable index of occupational *race* segregation, calculated separately for blacks and whites of each sex, was rather high at 65 among women and 44 among men. These rates actually increased through 1960 but declined thereafter with the advent of affirmative-action legislation. By 1980, the greater racial segregation among working women had declined to match that of men, reaching 26 to men's 30 by 1990 (King 1992; Reskin 1994). During this same 50-year time span, occupational sex segregation rates among both blacks and whites remained almost twice as high as race segregation among men (Reskin and Padavic 1994). Indeed, Joyce Jacobsen (1994) has concluded that the slowed decline in occupational sex segregation, combined with high rates of firm-level segregation, make it unlikely that sex segregation rates will become as low as race segregation rates by the 2000 census.

SEX SEGREGATION IN SPECIFIC CATEGORIES OF OCCUPATIONS

White-Collar Occupations

As a group, white-collar occupations typically command high salaries, prestige, and autonomy. Yet further inspection reveals considerable variation in their earnings as well as considerable sex segregation. There is a hierarchy of occupations within the classification white-collar. Imagine a pyramid. Executives, physicians, lawyers, and college professors are at the top of the pyramid, while nurses, librarians, and elementary school and secondary-school teachers form part of the middle third. The bottom third includes clerical workers, sales workers, and some service workers. More women are in white-collar occupations today than ever before but where?

In 1900 only 9 percent of women workers were employed in professional occupations and only 1 percent in managerial occupations. Ninety years later 17 percent of working women are in a professional specialty and 11 percent are in executive, administrative, and managerial occupations (U.S. Census Bureau 1990). In fact, women are 49 percent of all workers in executive, administrative, and managerial occupations and 53 percent in professional specialties, respectively (U.S. Census Bureau 1998a). Does this mean occupational sex segregation is no longer a problem? Unfortunately the answer is no.

Industry, firm, and job segregation channels women into the lower-paid, less autonomous, and less prestigious positions that often lack opportunities for upward advancement. For example, although women are about 50 percent of financial managers, they tend to be segregated in small bank branches rather than in loan and investment departments at headquarters (Silver 1981, cited in Reskin and Phipps 1988). Women are 63 percent of personnel and labor relations managers, a service-focused occupation with median annual earnings of $50,080, but only 35 percent of managers in marketing, advertising, and public relations who earn an average $57,100 a year (U.S. Census Bureau 1998a; U.S. Bureau of Labor Statistics 1997).

Women are currently about 27 percent of all lawyers, a remarkable increase from the 1900 figure of .8 percent. Yet, in a recent study of 200 male and female lawyers, Patricia MacCorquodale and Gary Jensen found that "Not a single respondent, male or female, would choose an equally qualified female attorney over a male attorney when considering who would command more respect in court" (1993, 590). Stereotypes and prejudices influence which firms hire women lawyers, the cases they are given, and whether they make partner. Research suggests that the path to partnership is considerably more demanding for women, who must present themselves as "super lawyers" to dissuade the sexist doubts of current partners (Kay and Hagan 1998, 741).

The barriers that women face when they attempt to move into higher-status positions, with greater responsibility, decision-making power, and authority, are widespread in male-dominated occupations. The phenomenon is so common that it has been termed the *glass-ceiling effect*, a phrase that helps people visualize the very real barrier to upward mobility on the job for women workers. The glass ceiling is created by a variety of organizational barriers and discrimination. . . .

Although the gender balance in the broad categories of executive, administrative, and managerial occupations and professional specialties appears to be about 50–50 and thousands of women are managers, doctors, and college professors, occupational segregation continues to limit women's options. In fact, 70 percent of women professionals, but only 27 percent of men professionals, are employed as teachers, librarians, and counselors or in health assessment and treating occupations such as nurse or dietitian (U.S. Census Bureau 1990).

Pink-Collar Occupations

There is a cluster of white-collar occupations that are more commonly labeled pink-collar occupations because they are female dominated. For example, women are approximately 93 percent of registered nurses, 98 percent of preschool and kindergarten teachers, 84 percent of elementary-school teachers, and 81 percent of librarians (U.S. Census Bureau 1998a; Women's Bureau 1999). These professional jobs are occasionally labeled semiprofessions because they lack some of the characteristics that identify an occupation as professional. Semiprofessions tend to be less prestigious, have less autonomy, and command lower salaries than full professions. Nursing and teaching at the elementary-school level are among the top 10 occupations for women, but women earn an average of only $38,168 as registered nurses and $35,204 as elementary-school teachers. Semiprofessionals are usually located in a bureaucratic setting where persons other than fellow professional workers set most administrative rules and professional norms.

In contrast to the relatively large proportion of women who have attempted to enter traditionally male-dominated occupations (e.g., manager, doctor, or lawyer), men are much less likely to enter the traditionally female-dominated domain of pink-collar occupations. Currently, 8 percent of registered nurses, 16 percent of elementary-school teachers, and 20 percent of librarians are men (U.S. Census Bureau 1998a; Women's Bureau 1999). Contrary to the lower wages that women command when they enter male-dominated occupations, men who enter female-dominated occupations often receive higher wages than women in similar positions. Yet the wage gap is almost negligible in nursing and elementary-school teaching, where women earn 95 percent and 90 percent of what men earn. It is important that both women and men who work in female-dominated occupations earn relatively less than women and men who work in male-dominated occupations; "women's work" is generally devalued and underpaid (England and Herbert 1993). Men in female-dominated occupations often find themselves on the fast track or on a "glass escalator"; upward mobility is encouraged and supported for them, for example, in occupations such as bank teller or airline flight attendant.

Clerical Occupations

The history of clerical work represents an example of the feminization of an occupation. At the beginning of the twentieth century, women were only 4 percent of clerical workers. Clerical work was a small, male-dominated occupation with relatively high prestige; it incorporated a diversity of tasks ranging from correspondence to bookkeeping. As the economy grew to be dominated by business and as paperwork proliferated, the need for clerical workers increased drastically. Employers drew on the ready supply of educated, working-class women who were eager to leave domestic service and factory work and enter these "cleaner" jobs. Companies intentionally divided up and restructured clerical work, creating female-dominated typists, whose jobs were mechanized by the previously invented typewriter, and filers, both having less autonomy than the accounting, bookkeeping, and cashier work initially reserved for men (Davies 1982).

Today women are 99 percent of secretaries, 94 percent of typists, and 97 percent of receptionists (U.S. Census Bureau 1998a), while being only 31 percent of shipping clerks, 41 percent of purchasing managers, and 57 percent of accountants and auditors. Secretarial work now employs more women than any other occupation. Compared to other prevalent women's occupations, the median weekly salary for secretaries ($430) is ranked fifth, well behind the higher earnings of the top-ranked registered nurses ($734) (Women's Bureau 1999). Secretarial work and other clerical positions tend to have short promotion ladders and typically do not lead to professional or managerial positions (Nakano Glenn and Feldberg 1989). Over the last century, clerical work has become tedious, requires lower skills, and is highly supervised. Clerical workers are often overeducated and find the work does not allow them to utilize all their skills (Nakano Glenn and Feldberg 1989).

Blue-Collar Occupations

Approximately 39 percent of men and 11 percent of women work in blue-collar occupations, which are counted by the Census under the headings of precision production, craft, and repair occupations and as machine operators, fabricators, and laborers (U.S. Census Bureau 1990). Like most occupational categories, blue-collar work includes a diverse array of occupations ranging from skilled through semiskilled to unskilled. Four blue-collar jobs—truck driver, carpenter, construction laborer, and automobile mechanic—were among the 10 leading occupations for men in 1990. All four are almost completely male dominated ranging from 99 percent (automobile mechanic) to 89 percent male (truck driver). Except for skilled occupations (e.g., electrician, carpenter, and plumber) and supervisory positions, blue-collar work offers little room for autonomy or creativity, requires hard physical labor, and is often dangerous.

Blue-collar work appeals to women although they find it hard to gain access to such positions. Historically, work in the manufacturing sector, particularly in unionized mills and plants, offered several advantages over the service jobs traditionally open to women. A study of women in the steel industry in the 1970s found that they preferred the higher wages, job security, health-care benefits, opportunity for shift work, and slower pace of blue-collar work over the harsh reality of working in sales or waitressing (Fonow 1993). In fact these tangible benefits outweighed the negative experiences in blue-collar work.

EXPLANATIONS OF SEX SEGREGATION

The history of work in the United States and elsewhere reveals a pattern of sex typing, defining some jobs as appropriate for men and others as women's work. But the origins of sex segregation in work are usually attributed to emerging industrialization. Sex segregation was created, in part, by gendered social expectations for women and men. For example, the ideas surrounding men as breadwinners and the "family wage" functioned to keep married women out of the labor force; and when single, divorced, or widowed women worked, these notions kept their wages lower than men's. The assumption was that all women had fathers and then husbands to care for them. Since men were considered the typical employees, part-time work, which women needed to be compatible with children's school hours, was virtually nonexistent except in the form of factory outwork or taking in laundry. Legal barriers constrained women's opportunities as well. Protective legislation limited women's options by defining how many hours, when (day versus night), and in which occupations they could work. In a reciprocal fashion, such segregation reinforced gendered power relations by limiting women's access to good jobs and by increasing their dependency on men. Through these processes, jobs became gendered. In other words, certain job titles as well as work tasks and skills became defined as male as distinct from female. This process is almost unnoticeable except when a job is newly created (and fought over by men and women) or its stereotype changes. A clear example of the latter case is the redefinition of clerical work as women's work by 1940 when, previously, it had been dominated by men.

Present-day researchers explain sex segregation in a variety of ways ranging from theories about individuals' behaviors to those emphasizing labor-market processes and social structure. The earliest sociological explanation focused on individual socialization, suggesting that the gender-stereotypical lessons people learn in childhood about masculine men and feminine women determine the academic fields they study and the occupations they choose. This view, however, is only partially supported. The jobs available to members of different social groups, such as women, blacks, or Hispanics, play a much greater role in determining our occupational status than any gender (or race) lessons we were taught as children. Workers are constrained by the opportunities available to them, by structural forces external to individuals.

One of the most important economic perspectives that, like socialization theory, focuses on individuals is human capital theory. Human capital is considered to be those characteristics or skills that make a worker more productive and attractive to an employer. To explain why women are predominantly employed in female-dominated occupations, human-capital theorists make many assumptions. First, they assume that all workers choose educational fields and occupations primarily with an eye toward maximizing lifetime earnings. They further assume that women consider work to be secondary to family and are only employed for short periods of time. Following from these assumptions, human-capital theorists expect women to select educational fields that require little investment in training and occupations that require skills that will not depreciate during occasional absences from the labor force. The assumption is that the resulting female-dominated occupations will be low skilled, have short career ladders, be amenable to intermittent employment, and pay more at entry than male-dominated jobs, where pay increases depend on on-the-job training. These assumptions are based on a 1950s understanding of women's roles.

Thus it is not surprising that researchers have shown that the human-capital perspective does not explain occupational sex segregation. It cannot explain why women enter low-skilled, female-dominated jobs when there are low-skilled, male-dominated jobs available. Worse still, most female-dominated occupations do not make it any easier to combine work and family than male-dominated occupations.

Counter to human-capital or socialization theorists, structural theorists argue that features of work can create behaviors, rather than individual behavior shaping occupational characteristics. For example, working in female-dominated occupations that are monotonous, have poor benefits and low wages, and lack autonomy can lead to high turnover rates. Researchers found that the same negative occupational characteristics lead to turnover among male workers, too (Reskin and Hartmann 1986). In other words, jobs can influence the attitudes, ambitions, and job preferences of workers, who are malleable and responsive to changing job situations.

The notion that institutional forces largely determine people's life chances is central to the various social-structural perspectives on occupational sex segregation. Social-control theory points to the social pressures that women and men encounter before and during employment. Both men and women are often discouraged from seeking employment in sex-atypical positions. Steel mill jobs were offered to women only after a federal court ordered steel companies to end discrimination against them. Even then the mills and male workers did not embrace the idea of women workers with open arms. In fact, women applicants reported feeling strongly discouraged by management, who questioned their interest and ability to deal with the negative aspects of the work (Fonow 1993). Men who attempt to enter traditionally female occupations are similarly discouraged by questions concerning their sexual orientation, manhood, and reasons for wanting to work with children or patients (Williams 1992).

In spite of such stereotyping, working people are not merely at the mercy of social institutions. They are also active participants in shaping sex segregation. Both sex typing and race typing of jobs can develop out of workers' struggles over new or existing occupations (Baron 1991; Milkman 1987). When the occupations of typist (originally called typewriter) or computer programmer were created, workers contended over which sex should fill them. When the existing occupation of typesetter changed from using hot-metal type to electronic composition in the 1970s, women actively entered jobs that men chose to leave (Roos 1990). Such resegregation in jobs from male to female is partially, but not entirely, responsible for the gradual decline in sex segregation during the 1980s (Jacobs 1989b).

Other processes, such as hiring procedures, help explain why women find employment in female-dominated occupations. When employers depend upon referrals from current employees for new employees, they tend to receive applications from workers of the same sex and race as those currently employed. The reason is that workers' informal networks of friends and family tend to include people of their own sex or racial group. Thus if an employer asks white men for referrals, names of other white men are proposed. Informal networks have been found to be very helpful for applicants; the sharing of information about job openings and promotion opportunities is critical to gaining access to higher-status and better-paying positions. This benefit, however, appears to be an advantage only for men. When women rely upon informal networks to learn about job openings, more often than not they end up in female-dominated occupations (Drentea 1998). When employers use open-recruitment methods, which they have to do if they are subject to affirmative-action laws, they are more likely to receive applications from workers who differ in sex, race, and ethnicity.

Open recruitment does not guarantee women access to sex-atypical jobs, however. Other organizational barriers make it difficult for women to break away from female-dominated occupations. For example, apprenticeship programs for various blue-collar jobs may have age limits, so that women who try to enter programs after having children are deemed too old, or they may require unnecessary previous experience including high school shop class. Seniority systems that are not plantwide and thus not transferable across departments may discourage women in clerical positions from taking more traditionally male jobs. The use of secretarial and typing pools in large offices hurts women's opportunities to be noticed and considered for promotion. Recent evidence suggests that sex segregation has a feedback effect. That is, employers tend to promote or hire women into management-level positions only if other women currently hold positions at the same level (Cohen, Broschak, and Haveman 1998). In other words, promotion or advancement in management for women occurs more often in female-dominated ladders. Until employers take the "risk" and hire women for positions not currently held by women, current practices will perpetuate sex segregation.

While many organizational or geographic barriers to sex-atypical occupations are grounded in administrative policies that have little to do with an employer's prejudices, discriminatory actions by employers and other male workers play an important role in the perpetuation of segregation. Recall the situation of women lawyers discussed above. Current law firm partners, who make decisions about granting new partnerships, have prejudices that can make it difficult for women to obtain partner status (Kay and Hagan 1998). Although discrimination against workers on the basis of sex and race is illegal, it persists nonetheless, as evidenced by the number of legitimate complaints of discrimination heard by the Equal Employment Opportunity Commission and other institutions.

CONSEQUENCES OF SEX SEGREGATION

Why does it matter that men and women are physically separated at work? What are the implications of sex-typed occupations? Sex segregation in the workplace matters for the same reason that the U.S. Supreme Court outlawed school segregation in 1964; among socially unequal groups, separate is not equal. The separation of men and women, as well as members of different racial or ethnic groups, into different jobs makes it easier to treat them differently and helps maintain stereotypes about men's and women's work-related characteristics (skills, aspirations, experience). It makes possible the devaluation of women's skills and abilities.

The remainder of this [reading] briefly highlights some of the major consequences of occupational sex segregation, including the wage gap, tokenism, and hindered mobility. Other consequences include women's lower Social Security and retirement benefits as a result of earning less during employment and having worked in less profitable industries that may not provide pensions (Hogan, Perrucci, and Wilmoth 2000). Sexual harassment appears to be a major consequence of sex segregation. When women are a numerical minority in an office or section of a plant, they are very likely to experience various forms of sexual harassment ranging from hostile environment to sexual coercion. . . .

The wage gap is a major consequence of occupational sex segregation. Among full-time, year-round workers age 25 years and over, women earn an average of 74 cents for every men's dollar (U.S. Bureau of Labor Statistics, 1999). The current wage gap represents a historical narrowing of earnings inequality; between 1930 and 1980 it fluctuated between 55 and 64 percent (Reskin and Padavic 1994, 103). However, only two-fifths of women's wage improvement in the last 20 years is due to an increase in their real wages; the remaining three-fifths is due to the fall in men's real wages.

Occupational sex segregation helps explain the wage gap in several ways. First, women and men work in different occupations. The occupations in which men predominate pay higher wages. Second, even when one compares women and men in the same occupational grouping, one finds that sex segregation in industries, establishments, departments, and jobs results in lower wages for women workers. Women engineers earn $800 less per week than men engineers (Andersen 1997, 105). The median weekly income for female machine operators is $228, yet for male machine operators it is $415 (Andersen 1997, 105). Although the occupations of engineer and machine operator are male dominated, sales occupations appear well integrated; 50 percent of sales workers are women (U.S. Census Bureau 1998a); however, retail or wholesale, men and women sell different items. In large department stores, for example, men sell large appliances on commission, while women work in noncommission departments such as sportswear. Consequently, the median weekly earning for men in this "integrated" occupational category is $603 while women earn $352 (U.S. Census Bureau 1998b).

The broad categorization of sales occupations only appears integrated. Upon closer examination, the segregation of women into the retail industry and into positions such as cashier reveal the extent to which sales occupations are really not integrated. Third, female-dominated jobs often have a shorter career ladder and fewer possibilities for upward job mobility. As a result, women's jobs not only have a glass ceiling but also a "sticky floor" (Berheide 1992).

Researchers have debated the extent to which sex segregation actually explains the wage gap. Other explanations point to human-capital characteristics, job characteristics, and organizational and regional differences. Donald Tomaskovic-Devey (1995) compared the ability of sex composition to explain the wage gap in both jobs and occupations. He found that the number of women employees in jobs explains 46 percent of the earnings differential for women and men while sex composition in occupations explains 33 percent. Similarly, the segregation of men and women into different occupations and industries when they begin their careers explains 42 percent of the earnings gap while gender differences in human capital and occupational aspirations account for only 14 and 10 percent of the gap, respectively (Marini and Fan 1997). . . .

Women and men who enter nontraditional occupations may encounter varieties of "boundary heightening" by majority-group members; this situation also occurs when people of color enter predominantly white organizations (Kanter 1977). When one class of worker makes up only 15 percent of a work group or organization, majority-group members are likely to act in ways that strengthen or make more visible the differences between their own group and the minority group. Much of this activity involves discriminatory treatment that may have direct impact on a token person's work environment, physical and mental well-being, and opportunity for advancement. In the case of female tokens, employee events may take on a decidedly masculine theme involving football or cars to which female co-workers may not even be invited. Thus women may be effectively excluded from the informal networks that prove so important in obtaining better jobs. Dress codes also set women apart in a very visible manner. In addition to boundary-heightening actions, majority-group workers may attempt to discourage women workers altogether. When women first entered steel work, male workers attempted to sabotage their work. Women fire fighters report concerns as to whether co-workers will back them up in dangerous situations. Finally, when women are members of a token group in the workplace they are often "oversupervised" and scrutinized.

The discriminatory treatment of women in male-dominated occupations does not mirror the experience of men in female-dominated occupations. Although female nurses and librarians often interact with male nurses and librarians in stereotypical ways (e.g., asking a male nurse to help change a tire), male tokens receive more rewards as a result of their numerical minority than disadvantages (Williams 1992). For example, rather than being labeled a "bitch" or an "Iron Maiden" for working hard and overachieving, a man in a sex-atypical position will be encouraged to move ahead and will often be placed on the fast track. The glass escalator experienced by many token male employees reveals the extent to which the token's experience is dependent upon gender. Female and male tokens are not treated similarly by co-workers, potential mentors, and bosses.

In sum, the consequences of occupational segregation are substantial. Occupations can provide income, autonomy, security, social status, and upward mobility. Occupational segregation, however, serves as a major institutional factor shaping and limiting women's (and men's) employment options, ultimately, reinforcing a gendered distribution of power and social status.

CONCLUSION

Throughout much of the twentieth century, rates of occupational sex segregation were consistent and high, only declining since 1970 from 68 to 53. In white-collar, pink-collar, clerical, and blue-collar occupations, the jobs at the top of the hierarchy tend to be male dominated; when women are allowed into those specialties, it is usually because the jobs have changed in some way to be less attractive to men. Although occupational segregation per se is not illegal, discriminatory hiring and promotion practices are prohibited in firms covered by affirmative-action legislation. Unfortunately, many states are overturning affirmative-action laws and policies. This trend is likely to slow any progress made toward the inclusion of more women and minorities in highly skewed male occupations. The best-supported explanations for the persistence of occupational sex segregation are those that focus on institutional and socially constructed antecedents rather than individual characteristics or gender differences. Perhaps surprisingly, the rapid, large increase in women's recorded employment over the last few decades has done proportionately little to reduce occupational sex stereotyping and the overall sex segregation of workers. Attitudes about the desirability of women's work may have changed, but the social organization of the specific jobs women hold has not always done so. Some occupations have become more sex integrated or have switched from male to female dominated. Yet other factors have counterbalanced this trend, including the decline of sex-integrated occupations in agriculture or the growth of new and existing sex-segregated occupations in the service sector. The consequence is continuing high rates of sex segregation that foster gender inequities.

NOTE

1. The co-authors have equally contributed to this chapter and their order is alphabetical.

REFERENCES

Andersen, Margaret L. (1997). *Thinking About Women: Sociological Perspectives on Sex and Gender*. Boston: Allyn and Bacon.

Baron, Ava. (1991). *Work Engendered: Toward a New History of American Labor*. Ithaca, NY: Cornell University Press.

Berheide, Catherine White. (1992). "Women still 'stuck' in low level jobs." *Women in Public Services: A Bulletin for the Center for Women in Government* 3 (Fall). Albany: Center for Women in Government, State University of New York.

Cohen, Lisa E., Joseph P. Broschak, and Heather A. Haveman. (1998). "And then there were more? The effect of organizational sex composition on the hiring and promotion of managers." *American Sociological Review*, 63:711–727.

Davies, Margery W. (1982). *Women's Place Is at the Typewriter: Office Work and Office Workers 1870–1930*. Philadelphia: Temple University Press.

Drentea, Patricia. (1998). "Consequences of women's formal and informal job search methods for employment in female-dominated jobs." *Gender & Society*, 12:321–338.

England, Paula and Melissa S. Herbert. (1993). "The pay of men in 'female' occupations: Is comparable worth only for women?" Pp. 28–48 in *Doing "Women's Work": Men in Nontraditional Occupations*. Christine L. Williams (ed.). Newbury Park, CA: Sage.

Fonow, Mary Margaret. (1993). "Occupation/ steelworker: Sex/ female." Pp. 217–222 in *Feminist Frontiers III*. Laurel Richardson and Verta Taylor (eds.). New York: McGraw-Hill.

Gross, Edward. (1968). "*Plus ça change:* The sexual segregation of occupations over time." *Social Problems,* 16:198–208.

Hogan, Richard, Carolyn C. Perrucci, and Janet M. Wilmoth. (2000). "Gender inequality in employment and retirement income effects of marriage, industrial sector, and self-employment." Pp. 27–54 in *Advances in Gender Research, Vol. 4, Social Change for Women and Children.* Vasilikie Demos and Marcia Texler Segal (eds.). Stamford, CT: JAI.

Jacobs, Jerry. (1989). "Long-term trends in occupational segregation by sex." *American Journal of Sociology,* 95:160–173.

Jacobsen, Joyce P. (1994). "Trends in work force sex segregation: 1960–1990." *Social Science Quarterly,* 75(1):204–211.

Jones, Beverly W. (1984). "Race, sex, and class; black female tobacco workers in Durham, North Carolina, 1920–1940, and the development of female consciousness." Pp. 228–233 in *Feminist Frontiers IV.* Laurel Richardson, Verta Taylor, and Nancy Whittier (eds.). New York: McGraw-Hill.

Kanter, Rosabeth Moss. (1977). *Men and Women of the Corporation.* New York: Basic.

Kay, Fiona M. and John Hagan. (1998). "Raising the bar: The gender stratification of law-firm capital." *American Sociological Review,* 63:728–743.

King, Mary C. (1992). "Occupational segregation by race and sex, 1940–88." *Monthly Labor Review,* 115:30–36.

Kraut, Karen and Molly Luna. (1992). *Work and Wages: Facts on Women and People of Color in the Workforce.* Washington, DC: National Committee on Pay Equity.

MacCorquodale, Patricia and Gary Jensen. (1993). "Women in the law: Partners or tokens?" *Gender & Society,* 7:582–593.

Marini, Margaret Mooney and Pi-Ling Fan. (1997). "The gender gap in earnings at career entry." *American Sociological Review,* 62:588–604.

Milkman, Ruth. (1987). *Gender at Work: The Dynamics of Job Segregation by Sex During World War II.* Urbana: University of Illinois Press.

Nakano Glenn, Evelyn and Roslyn L. Feldberg. (1989). "Clerical work: The female occupation." Pp. 287–311 in *Women: A Feminist Perspective.* Jo Freeman (ed.). Mountain View, CA: Mayfield.

Reskin, Barbara F. (1994). "Segregating workers: Occupational differences by sex, race, and ethnicity." Paper presented at the annual meeting of the Population Association of America in San Francisco.

Reskin, Barbara F. and Heidi I. Hartmann. (1986). *Women's Work, Men's Work: Sex Segregation on the Job.* Washington, DC: National Academy Press.

Reskin, Barbara F. and Irene Padavic. (1994). *Women and Men at Work.* Thousand Oaks, CA: Pine Forge.

Reskin, Barbara F. and Patricia A. Roos (eds.). (1990). *Job Queues, Gender Queues: Explaining Women's Inroads into Male Occupations.* Philadelphia: Temple University Press.

Reskin, Barbara F. and Polly A. Phipps. (1988). "Women in male-dominated professional and managerial occupations."

Pp. 190–205 in *Women Working: Theories and Facts in Perspective,* Second Edition. Ann Helton Stromberg and Shirley Harkess (eds.). Mountain View, CA: Mayfield.

Roos, Patricia A. (1990). "Hot-metal to electronic composition: Gender, technology, and social change." Pp. 275–298 in *Job Queues, Gender Queues: Explaining Women's Inroads into Male Occupations.* Barbara F. Reskin and Patricia A. Roos (eds.). Philadelphia: Temple University Press.

Silver, Catherine Bodare. (1981). "Public bureaucracy and private enterprise in the U.S.A. and France: Contexts for the attainment of executive positions by women." In *Access to Power: Cross-National Studies of Women and Elites.* Cynthia Fuchs Epstein and Rose Laub Coser (eds.). London: George Allen and Unwin.

Steiger, Thomas and Barbara F. Reskin. (1990). "Baking and baking off: Deskilling and the changing sex makeup of bakers." Pp. 257–274 in *Job Queues, Gender Queues: Explaining Women's Inroads into Male Occupations.* Barbara F. Reskin and Patricia A. Roos (eds.). Philadelphia: Temple University Press.

Tomaskovic-Devey, Donald. (1995). "Sex composition and gendered earnings inequality: A comparison of job and occupational models." Pp. 23–56 in *Gender Inequality at Work.* Jerry A. Jacobs (ed.). Thousand Oaks, CA: Sage.

U.S. Bureau of Labor Statistics. (1997). "Table 1. Table A-1. National employment and wage data from the occupational employment statistics survey by occupation, 1997." [Web Page]. Accessed 3 August 1999. Available at http://stats.bls.gov;80/news.release/ocwage.t01.htm.

———. (1999). "D-20 median weekly earnings of full-time wage and salary workers by selected characteristics." [Web Page]. Accessed 13 August 1999. Available at http://www.bls.gov/cpseeq.htm.

U.S. Census Bureau. (1990). "Table 20. Occupation of employed persons: 1990." P. 20 in *Census of the Population. Social and Economic Characteristics. United States.* Washington, DC: Bureau of the Census.

———. (1998a). *The Official Statistics™.* "No. 672. Employed civilians, by occupations, sex, race, and Hispanic origin: 1983 and 1997." *Statistical Abstract of the United States.* [Web Page]. Accessed 7 August 1999. Available at http://www.census.gov/prod/3/98pubs/98statab/cc98stab.htm.

———. (1998b). *The Official Statistics™.* "No. 696. Full-time wage and salary workers—number and earnings: 1985 to 1997." *Statistical Abstract of the United States.* [Web Page]. Accessed 7 August 1999. Available at http://www.census.gov/prod/3/98pubs/98statab/cc98stab.htm.

Williams, Christine L. (1992). "The glass escalator: Hidden advantages for men in the 'female' professions." Pp. 193–207 in *Men's Lives,* Third Edition. Michael S. Kimmel and Michael A. Messner (eds.). Boston: Allyn and Bacon.

Women's Bureau, Department of Labor. (1999) "20 leading occupations of employed women: 1998 annual averages." [Web Page]. Accessed 7 August 1999. Available at http://www.dol.gov/dol/wb/public/wb_pubs/201ead98.htm.

MEDIAN ANNUAL EARNINGS OF FULL-TIME, YEAR-ROUND WORKERS BY EDUCATION, RACE, AND HISPANIC ORIGIN, 2006

Nancy Whittier

Education	WOMEN				
	All Races	White	Black	Hispanic	Asian
Overall	41,518	42,036	36,590	30,874	50,177
Less than high school**	22,416	23,050	20,050	20,097	21,634
High school graduate	29,410	29,791	27,890	25,878	28,863
Some college	35,916	36,284	33,326	30,849	46,905
Associate's degree	40,463	40,450	41,381	38,922	37,038
Bachelor's degree	53,201	53,590	50,077	46,032	55,160
Master's degree	63,216	63,343	57,206	57,630	70,159
Professional degree	100,734	99,958	*	*	*
Doctoral degree	91,733	94,791	*	*	80,277

Education	MEN				
	All Races	White	Black	Hispanic	Asian
Overall	57,791	59,064	42,703	36,795	70,832
Less than high school	29,746	30,197	26,846	26,206	27,764
High school graduate	42,466	43,795	35,727	35,656	37,661
Some college	48,431	49,458	42,389	40,592	44,856
Associate's degree	51,485	52,578	41,714	43,591	53,816
Bachelor's degree	76,749	78,879	55,063	56,178	76,532
Master's degree	97,038	98,655	69,790	87,102	101,149
Professional degree	143,615	143,893	*	*	139,078
Doctoral degree	125,393	128,690	*	*	122,971

Note: The categories of white and black include both Hispanics and non-Hispanics; the category Hispanic includes Hispanics of any race. All racial categories refer to people who reported only that category.
*No data were available for these categories due to small sample size.
**No data were available for Black women with less than 9th grade education; figure represents only those with 9th–12th grade but no degree. Figures for other races, less than high school, include those with less than 9th grade education and those with 9th–12th grade but no degree.
Source: U.S. Census Bureau, Current Population Survey, 2007 Annual Social and Economic Supplement. Table PINC-04. "Educational Attainment—People 18 Years Old and Over, by Total Money Earnings in 2006, Work Experience in 2006, Age, Race, Hispanic Origin and Sex."
http://pubdb3.census.gov/macro/032007/perinc/new04_000.htm

Desirable Dress: Rosies, Sky Girls, and the Politics of Appearance

In oral interviews some thirty-five years after the Second World War, former Rosie the Riveters recalled their experiences of wearing slacks for the first time. "I felt kind of funny because I didn't really have the figure for slacks. I was pretty buxom," one white welder confessed. "Of course, we got quite used to it, and later I wore them all the time; even on my day off." Another white woman explained, "Pants were just becoming fashion for women and I felt like, gee whiz, it made me look like I was different. I was working someplace and nobody else was and people would look at me." A Mexican American also admitted, "I felt kind of funny wearing pants. Then at the same time, I said, 'Oh, what the heck.'" Though donning overalls and jeans, clothes associated with rough masculinity, initially seemed "very odd," even embarrassing, some war workers only reluctantly returned to dresses after leaving the factory for office, retail, or other spaces of women's labor.[1] For slacks—along with having "your hair tied up" and wearing "a welder's helmet"—brought, as a white worker at the Boston Navy Yard admitted, "liberation." Pants, associated with hegemonic masculinity, could signify power and freedom.[2]

During the 1930s, pants on women were unacceptable in industrial workplaces "because of a possible production hazard in distracting male employees," arbitration relations experts Frank Elkouri and Edna Asper Elkouri found, but "in the 1940s many plants *required* women to wear slacks to avoid danger involved in working around industrial machinery."[3] Whether or not dress requirements disciplined employee bodies, served to guarantee efficiency or check against accidents and the expense of worker compensation, or opened new possibilities for sexual or gendered identities was hardly predetermined. Employers could demand slacks, women could wear them, but what dress was desirable varied with the beholder. A "strug-gle over the breeches," to recall Anna Clark's characterization for linking "the personal with the political in working class history,"[4] pitted management, federal agencies, male workers, male-dominated trade unions, and women workers of various persuasions.

Work clothes and street clothes, the height of heels, the length of skirts, or the curl of hair, has generated an interdisciplinary literature that addresses the significance of appearance for self and group worth. The new fashion and dress history has emphasized how clothing "articulates the body, making it sociable and identifiable," as theorist Joanne Entwistle has argued: "Understanding dress in everyday life requires understanding not just how the body is represented within the fashion system and its discourses on dress, but also how the body is experienced and lived and the role dress plays in the presentation of the body/self."[5] Whether looking at nineteenth-century male "citizen workers," young Italian and Jewish immigrant women in early twentieth-century New York, African-American washerwomen in 1880s Atlanta, or live-out domestics in 1920s Washington, DC, historians have contrasted the coverings of the workplace, often considered erasers of independence and worth, with the raiments of the streets, indicative of citizenship and autonomy.[6]

Dress and appearance may provide clues to class, racialized gender, and/or cultural identities. Stephen Norwood and Nan Enstad have highlighted the ways that both white US born and European immigrant working-class women a century ago questioned the authority of their betters on the picket line through forging their own fashion. According to Vicki Ruiz, Mexican American flappers, cannery workers by day, also created style in relation to new popular cultural forms, particularly the cinema, thus challenging standards of propriety or "respectability."[7] Beauty contests, as Dorothy Sue Cobble and others have shown, constructed a workplace culture that both reinforced employer representations of their product and fulfilled the desires of wage-earning women to be more than laboring bodies, that is, to be sexually desirable ones.[8] Some scholars, however, have emphasized danger in the workplace rather than women's pleasure or agency. Daniel E. Bender and Steve Meyer, for example, have historicized sexual harassment in the garment trade and the automobile industry, suggesting how "predatory patterns" served to maintain gender definitions of skill and the sexual division of labor, in which women remained associated with low pay and lesser status.[9]

This essay rethinks two cases where issues of self-fashioning, appearance, sexuality, employer strictures, and state policy intertwined: the shop floors of the Second World War and the flight cabins of postwar airlines. I locate my discussion in gendered workplaces: the first, male-dominated manufacturing in which women labored "for the duration"; the second, a prototypical female service industry in which fierce competition led to selling sexual allure along with comfort and safety. Wartime factories existed to produce defense materials as rapidly as possible, so that any distraction—whether bathroom breaks, socializing, or sexual expressiveness—that interfered with output, managers sought to curb or suppress, just as they had in the manufacturing sector, especially where women workers clustered. In contrast, female sexuality could be integral to the production of services and thus enhance profit. So airline management sought to harness the appearance as well as the carework of their "hostesses," who offered attentiveness and sexual fantasy along with meals and pillows.

Before the late 1960s, sky girls, later called stewardesses and then, with the new feminism, the gender neutral flight attendant, operated under a cloak of respectability. Clothed in uniform dress suits that were tailored to the body, they emanated the attractiveness of the girl next door whose beauty and charm marked her marriageability. To the extent that air safety was more precarious in the first decades of commercial flight, personal characteristics that led to being hired put these women in harm's way. But because looking good was integral to the job, flight attendants could display sexual attractiveness to obtain better conditions as workers in a way not available to women in manufacturing. The performance of femininity courted dangers for Rosies both in the form of industrial hazards and male responses to the presence of "sweater girls" and women in pants. Indeed, overalls and other cover-ups served to differentiate the Rosies from male counterparts by hailing them as women in drag, even while individuals, including butch lesbians, found new freedoms through such attire.[10]

The state had oversight over both war manufacturing and postwar aviation, and thus historical access to these wage-earners often comes through official sources. These include government reports, such as inspections of Second World War factories, letters to state agencies, such as the wartime Fair Employment Practice Committee (FEPC), and Congressional hearings, such as on the airline industry. Formal complaints to government agencies and the courts further contain cultural and economic assumptions, as do articles in popular magazines and newspapers, that link appearance to job performance. However mediated by these sources, voices of wage-earning women in both the 1940s and 1960s announced new expectations of womanhood, beauty, and sexual expressiveness. But while management attempted to suppress women's bodies in the shipyards and other wartime workplaces, twenty years later airlines promoted the body of the flight attendant. In both examples, state mediation—through sources available as well as actual public policies—complicates our attempt to unravel pleasure and constraint in dressing, grooming, and sexual presence on the job.

SAFETY, SLACKS, OR SWEATERS

Like paintings and daguerreotypes of mill girls and male craftsmen in the mid-nineteenth century, photographs and movie footage of women riveters and welders during the Second World War reveal proud workers posing with the accoutrements of their trade.[11] Work clothes, like toots, marked their status as contributors to the war effort. The factories and shipyards of the Second World War were not the first time that appearance on the job generated public concern and reform efforts,[12] but the surge of unionization offered a space for individual workers to contest appearance regulations—despite discrimination by some unions and locals.[13] Such women rejected the disciplining of their bodies by management, male coworkers, or government agencies, including those charged with aiding them, like the US Women's Bureau or, for African Americans, the FEPC. But not all women wage-earners responded alike to employer dress codes, government safety rules, or persistent protective labor laws for women. Contesting notions of ladyhood, respectability, and sexuality marked the early 1940s as one of those moments when distinctions within the working-class and between workers and middle-class reformers, black as well as white, characterized the politics of appearance.

The "Case of the Woman in the Red Pants" highlights that there was more to slacks than the mere wearing of them. Pants could express employer control and female subjectivity, but also political resistance to the power and authority of supervisors. "Redhead" Carolyn Miller, a UAW activist, came to the Ford Motor Company line in 1944 wearing bright red slacks. The supervisor issued a reprimand, "saying that such a display of curves on the human body would certainly upset the whole male work force," and "docked" her pay by a half-hour. Form hugging garments certainly evoked such speculation; "tight sweaters, snug slacks, and feminine artifices of color and style were distracting influences," "hazards" to the workmen, *Business Week* had lamented in 1942, especially when "a very shapely sweater girl wanders in to take her place in the swing shift."[14] In this case, coworkers responded by establishing a picket line.[15] The union also took her grievance to the industrial "umpire" Harry Shulman, who ruled on the question of "whether a lady's red slacks constituted a production hazard because of a tendency to distract male employees." In revoking the disciplinary action against Miller, Shulman mocked the foreman's singling out red as the color of sexual desire even as he reinforced the trope of prowling men and distracting women: "Apparently bright green slacks were tolerated. And there was no effort at specification of other articles of clothing, or the fit thereof, which might be equally seductive of employees [sic] attention. Yet it is common knowledge that wolves, unlike bulls, may be attracted by colors other than red and by various other enticements in the art and fit of female attire."[16] Union stewards undoubtedly grieved on an appearance issue and coworkers walked out because the case involved lost of pay, Still this incident suggests how workplace appearance could not merely signify individual preference but also reflect struggles between workers and employers that were gendered as well as racialized and classed.[17]

Wartime propaganda portrayed overalls as glamorous, hoping to attract a factory labor force by feeding into a work culture that emphasized appearance, make-up, and beauty. Some suggested that a happy workforce would be an efficient one, that women's looks could compensate for wartime drab.[18] One management journal advised in 1943, "any uniform which adds bulges in the wrong places is not conducive to employee contentment."[19] Some women found personal power through appearance in the previously

masculinized shop floors of automobile and aircraft.[20] Yet sometimes a sweater was just a sweater. The Office of War Information might reinforce the "rumor that a tightly sweatered working companion takes a man's eyes off his machine." But women might put a sweater over their coveralls or uniforms because the factory "didn't have a lot of heat."[21]

Uniforms—issued by some wartime plants—and standardized dress regulations—in place at others—certainly represented "a form of social control," effacing rather than enhancing the body and, by implication, the self.[22] "The management issued strict rules to govern the dress of shipyard women," participant observer Katherine Anthony reported on Moore Dry Dock in Richmond, California. However, these "rules [were] based fully as much on the principles of concealment and sexless propriety as on the purported aims of safety."[23] Journalist and clothing designer Elizabeth Hawes, who worked at a New Jersey factory, claimed "the girls leaped to the conclusion that it [clothing regulation] was all a plot to make them unattractive and spoil their sex appeal."[24] Councilors for women employees in company social welfare departments may have lobbied for "dressing rooms and lunch rooms," but their job was "to get the girls to wear caps" and other protective gear.[25] The presence of these "women guards," who "stalked vigilantly through the warehouses, the workshops, and the rest rooms, looking for the coy curl unconfined by a bandanna, the bejeweled hand, and the revealing sweater," Anthony recounted, suggested the need to police the defiance of women wage-earners from strictures to conceal their femininity issued by management and protective agencies, like the Women's Bureau.[26]

Government agencies stressed safety and output, but in keeping with a quest for self-definition, women workers also interpreted these warnings on the dangers of undesirable dress as attacks on their sex-appeal. The Bureau of Home Economics advised, "Know your job and dress for it," stressing "action room," "'safety-first' features," and "time-saving styles."[27] The Women's Bureau insisted on "more attention to proper work clothing" in dangerous workplaces like ordnance plants. Nonetheless, the new women factory workers "have most of the foremen buffaloed and cowed," reported a Women's Bureau investigator about the Minneapolis Federal Cartridge Corporation in 1942. Women wore "high heels, no caps, dangling jewelry, rings, etc., but the foremen seemed afraid to do any thing about it,"[28] she harshly judged. Other women workers complained about "the girls themselves, who seem to consider it [working in a plant] a lark rather than a job. They come in bandbox attire, hair dressed every week, and don't dare touch anything without gloves," one union activist wrote to the Bureau.[29] Instructions on safe clothes for women war workers had included short hair, to be concealed in a net, headdress, or cap.[30] In defying the regulations of management and warnings of government agencies, women recruits risked reinforcing the stereotype of the factory girl, self-conscious rather than class or union conscious, in the pursuit of good looks.

Women subtly fought against attempts to police their dress and undermine their sexual expressiveness. According to Anthony, "giddy charmers skirted the bare fringe of the management's dress regulations, and by a variety of cunning devices succeeded in revealing as much as possible of the delights beneath. (One such was wont to say with titillating gusto that underneath her well-fitting and well-filled overalls she wore 'nothing . . .')"[31] An African-American woman remembered the need to distinguish gender identity: "We had to wear bandannas and hard hats and keep them on all the time, but most all the women in the shipyards would tie their hair up and then leave a piece of hair out in the front—bangs—so you could look ladylike. So you could know the men from the women."[32] Mocking the reasoning of women in the rubber plants, fictionalized "Thelma McClung" asked, "How is anybody going to know that a girl is a glamour girl if she's garbed in mechanized attire?"[33]

Such depictions ironically reduced welders and riveters to their sex, constituting a discourse that reminded onlookers of what bulky clothes hid to emphasize the woman underneath. The femaleness of office workers, who painted legs to imitate unavailable nylons and wore tight sweaters, was expected;[34] their labor was no threat to men's jobs and breadwinner status. But those who did men's work were another matter. Thus, a riveter heard from her boss: "you're a woman, you'll always be a woman, and if you don't put that hair in you'll have the damnedest permanent you've ever had because that weld is hot."[35] This supervisory response to women with bangs was double-edged, combining a warning about safety with words that named women as women, that is, as not men, in part for frivolous obsession with looks. If always a woman, then could a woman be a real worker, worthy of a man's wage?[36]

Race influenced responses to appearance. African-American women pointed to advantages that white women gained from their racialized bodies. As a black woman lifting hundred-ton iron ducts, that is, doing men's work, charged, the foreman "stopped one of the white girls from doing anything because he could go around with her."[37] Another lamented how they "were timed in going to the rest rooms. While the white girls sat and read papers and powdered from quarter to half and an hr." The wearing of overalls made it impossible for women to climb down from a welding station and get to a toilet and back in fifteen minutes.[38]

Reactions to African American women searching for wartime employment illuminate contrasting class-based notions of appearance within the black community. In October 1943, twenty-year-old Rosie Gray, a former laundress, sought better-paying bench work at Briggs, only one of a number of factories where a white man accepted her application and "told her to wait until she was sent for."[39] The Ward Employment Club, a neighborhood race advancement group, referred Gray to the Detroit field office of the FEPC—the agency created to end discrimination in government contracts and employment related to the war effort.[40] Gray told her story to FEPC examiner Lethia W. Clore—a college-educated African American, who, like an earlier generation of club women, promoted a concept of respectable, modest womanhood forged in reaction to demeaning images of Sapphire and Jezebel. In Clore's mind, for the betterment of the race, black women had to adhere to employer expectations of proper appearance. The reason for Gray's lack of success, Clore recorded, "was probably more than the fact that she is a member of the Negro race." The complaint file read: "personal appearance is definitely one reason why she had not been employed. She was anything but well groomed." Clore informed Gray: "personal appearance is prerequisite number one in the search for employment and particularly so in the plants where the hiring of Negro women is a new experiment," and then advised, "much needed attention to the hair. Dark tailored clothing and a less conspicuous hat." Gray also "displayed a rather belligerent attitude."[41]

About another black woman denied a job in 1943, Clore wrote: "Fact #1 to prohibit the upgrading of this complainant is her personal appearance. On the day she visited the office, this was not enhanced by her wearing slacks that were too tight and too short, a vivid coat, dark nail polish and no hat. In some departments her size would definitely prohibit her employment."[42] Like the shipyard supervisor who "went about among the girls of his jurisdiction with a bottle of acetone and a handkerchief and forced them to remove their nail polish and lipstick" in response to his wife's complaints about "the temptations,"[43] Clore judged the presentation of working-class women as dangerous. But danger for her came from attacks on the reputation of black womanhood, not the threat of sexually available war workers on men's morals and output.

Sexiness and respectability accounted for two contrasting representations of womanhood. A photograph staged by Los Angeles community activists to counter images of women as "pachucas" or "female zoot suiters"—that is, as disrupters of the war effort—displayed a group of Mexican American defense workers garbed in modest dresses and neat hair styles, though one posed in pants as if to announce her factory status.[44] This photograph exhibited a presentation of womanhood closely related to respectability—that of ladyhood, redefined as adherence to proper feminine dress. Distinctions appeared class-based within the white community as well. Some women may have donned a "uniform" at work, but at the day's end, "dressed as a lady." A machinist at the Watertown Arsenal explained that after work, "I stayed long enough to get my face on and high heels and hose so that even the guard at the gate said, 'Miss Kenney, you sure don't look like a factory worker.'"[45] Others drew a distinct line between work clothes and chosen clothes. They recoiled from using "shoe stamps for work boots" with steel-toes, "which meant we didn't have ration stamps left for dress shoes." With discretionary income, they purchased "expensive clothes" and luxury accessories.[46] A woman from "a classy family" donned "designer" overalls to distinguish herself from coworkers,[47] most of whom understood real glamour to [lie] in an enhanced realm of consumption marked by shopping and nightlife, not behind plant gates.[48] While many women took pride in their accomplishments as workers, they also stressed going "to the dances," having "my hair curled" and wearing lipstick, that is, they remembered being in the plants as coterminous [with], but not the same as, their initiation into a fashionable beauty culture. In this sense, they resembled earlier generations of laborers who distinguished their real identity from workplace representations of themselves. With war's end, one white woman claimed, "I think seventy percent of the women were delighted to get out of slacks and bandannas,"[49] that is, to return to desirable, feminine dress. This recollection varied from laments over having to give up pants.

UNIFORMS, DESIGNER SUITS, AND HOT PANTS

Unlike the entrance of women into Second World War factories where their very presence contested masculine prerogative, threatened the male rate for the job, and challenged efficient running of the assembly line, postwar airlines welcomed women to the lower-paid and temporary job of sky hostess. The glamour associated with the stewardess attracted white women to the occupation, and they in turn lured customers even before their popular metamorphosis as "sex objects in the sky."[50] These "girls" were to be "the epitome of fine womanhood," full of "charm, poise, grace, loveliness," with training that in later life would create the ideal wife, mother, and citizen. By the late 1960s flight attendants were to offer "coffee, tea, or fly me," not merely seat passengers and evacuate them in an emergency.[51] But, influenced by the new feminism, increased numbers sought a long term career and fought for better working conditions. Unionized flight attendants urged the newly established Equal Employment Opportunities [sic] Commission (EEOC) and the courts to overturn employer regulations and prehire contracts that forced them out because of perceived deviations in appearance due to age, pregnancy, weight, and marriage. Flight attendants wielded their sex as a weapon even as they questioned the cultural association of youth with beauty and sexual availability. Sexuality as both power and discipline pervaded their attempts to promote workplace justice.[52]

Stewardesses became the face of flight; their service, the reason to board a particular carrier. American Airlines' requirements for the job in 1957 were typical: "'a wholesome all-American girl type' between twenty and twenty-six years of age; between five feet, two inches and five feet, eight inches tall; of 'proportionate weight' not exceeding 130 pounds; single; in good health; attractive; and . . . [possessive of] 'considerable personable charm as well as a high degree of intelligence and enthusiasm.'"[53] The three to five, all white, selected out of every hundred applicants attended special schools for about a month, where management began to discipline their bodies. A more militant attendant explained forty years later, "You've got to be willing to go anywhere—and to cut your hair."[54] In 1958, shortness meant hair above the collar. Airlines established additional grooming and deportment rules, teaching how to make up ("sparingly") and how to "walk erect, sit like a lady," and generally carry oneself.[55] "You could only wear one shade of lipstick," another recalled. Applications asked about "distracting scars, moles, large pores, noticeable blemishes, and excessive facial hair" as well as body measurements. Interviewers graded prospective stewardesses "on the basis of 'first impression, figure, hips, legs, hands, hair, eyes, teeth, and complexion.'"[56] As one "blond, thirty-two-year-old veteran of ten years" told *Newsweek* in 1963, the companies always emphasized youth, but desired looks changed: "it was strictly pug-nosed, freckled, all-American types. Then it was bosoms, and now they want girls who can hardly fit between the seats when they walk down the aisle."[57]

Dress marked cultural shifts; as the hemline went up, the girl next door image morphed into a hipper, more stylish, and explicitly sexier representation of womanhood.[58] The first stewardesses in 1930 were nurses, all "petite" in size, trained as caregivers of a different sort than later bringers of food with a smile. They wore "flowing capes and shower-cap-type hats" and draped grey smocks over nurses' uniforms. Soon they donned green twill. Even after the color switched to blue, fashion designers in the 1960s found stewardesses resembling "World War II WAC corporals."[59] The uniforms of commercial airlines evoked the military, both to signify a chain of command from pilot to stewardess but also to quell fears of flying by associating the practice with an image of strength. By the 1950s, individually fitted uniforms followed the contours of their wearers, emphasizing the very bodies that they contained.[60] Sexuality, however, was submerged in promotions of classiness. In "pillbox hats and white gloves," stewardesses served elegant meals to well-dressed passengers; they epitomized "American women"—"neat hair, trim suits, nice shoes, white gloves"—judged as "the best dressed in the world."[61]

In the 1960s, airlines sought "High Style in Bid for Business," though explicit sexuality soon would trump revamped glamour. Oleg Cassini, Emilio Pucci, Pierre Balmain, and other haute couturiers upgraded the stewardess uniform. Some airlines branded their image in bizarre ways that relied on feminine bodies. Alaska Airlines turned to a "Gay Nineties-Gold Rush theme," with floor-length "skirts . . . of red velour," evocative of the prostitute's salon, removed after takeoff to reveal a "street-length version," while Braniff introduced the "air strip," in which attendants shed "four layers of outer garments during each trip." About this "dazzling ensemble of colorful raiment,

topped by a plastic space helmet," one stewardess stated: "it makes you feel like a real female and not a busboy"—perhaps in keeping with the false eyelashes the airline also urged her to wear.[62] This reaction contrasted with the growing perception that the jet-age stewardess was a glorified cocktail waitress, catering to ever greater numbers of passengers.[63] American Airlines dressed attendants in miniskirts and fishnet stockings, succumbing to rising hemlines that the carriers previously had insisted had to fall "at least one inch below the lowest part of the knee." Of this new look, one male passenger admitted: "Very distracting . . . but then, what else is there to look at?" Stewardesses rejected fishnets for hurting their feet. The stockings went, but shorter dresses remained, since the women viewed "longer lengths as 'frumpy and unfeminine.'"[64] In 1970, Eastern Airlines announced that its uniform "doesn't look like one. It's a pants suit designed by David Crystal"—but the company reassured that wearers "still look like a girl."[65]

By then, airlines were bolder in their use of sex. Southwest Airlines based its image on the appeal of women flight attendants and ticket agents, "dressed in high boots and hot-pants," who promised "love" to male commuters. But, as a TWA (Trans World Airlines) stewardess protested, "I don't think of myself as a sex symbol or a servant. I think of myself as somebody who knows how to open the door of a 747 in the dark, upside down, and under water."[66] The Civil Aeronautics Board, which required attendants on planes and specified their training, concurred. Nothing in the regulations specified their serving meals or flirting with customers.[67] But the Aeronautics Board never grounded a carrier for sex discrimination; it refused involvement when feminist unionists in 1974 threatened a slowdown unless airlines withdrew objectifying advertisements. Indeed, attendants' "animosity" over National Airlines' "sexist 'Fly Me'" promotion fueled their militancy during a lengthy 1975 strike.[68]

Proudly chosen for their looks and molded to fit a corporate image, stewardesses nonetheless wielded appearance as a weapon for group advancement. Photographs accompanying accounts of labor disputes pictured coffered and trim women holding protest signs rather than cocktail trays. Striking World Airways attendants traded miniskirts for bikinis when walking a 1970 picket line.[69] The strategic use of beauty comes through most powerfully in the prolonged battle over employer mandated age ceilings. This practice instituted in the 1950s led to dumping attendants just as they had gained enough seniority to command better wages and, along with dismissal upon marriage, kept turnover rates high, impeding unionization and job attachment. Women fought these bars to occupational longevity by insisting that age had nothing to do with the ability to perform the job, but did so by capturing public attention through their attractiveness.

Thus, in 1963 stewardesses working for American challenged reporters to "'Look Us Over.'" Newspapers described them as "posed prettily in their form-fitting blue uniforms for the benefit of admiring photographers." Asked by the women, "'what's the matter with us when we hit 32?' 'Not a thing!' was the overwhelming response from the press corps."[70] Another paper sexualized flight attendant Dusty Roads as it portrayed "fire flashing from her big baby blues, and the rest of her poured elegantly into a form-fitting blue uniform (measurements, 36–24–36)." It recounted her declaration, "'A Lolita I'm not! So at thirty-five, do I look like an old bag?'" To which the reporter explained, "Dusty stands a long-legged five ft. eight and weighs one-hundred-twenty-five pounds and has natural blonde hair, if you get the picture, fellows."[71] As *Newsweek* commented, "Who is American Airlines to tell a thirty-two-year-old doll something her mirror does not confirm?"[72]

The looks of aging stewardesses generated commentary during congressional hearings that led to passage of the Age Discrimination in Employment Act (ADEA) of 1967. Congressmen struggled with the apparent anomaly of still youthful workers condemned as too old. They reflected cultural constructions of womanhood in gallantly defending the beauty of the women, though at the end the stewardesses failed to gain legislative redress. At one point Representative James H. Scheuer (D-New York) "asked one of the over-thirty stewardesses to 'stand up so we can see the dimensions of the problem.'" He then proclaimed opposition "with my dying breath the notion that a woman is less beautiful, less appealing, less sensitive after thirty, and I'm sure my colleagues would agree."[73] Photographed outside the Capitol, as perfect embodiments of American womanhood, the stewardesses objected to both being defined as over the hill and to the airline's selling of sex through dress.[74] Their spokesperson Colleen Boland, President of the Air Line Stewards and Stewardesses, Local 500, Transport Workers Union of America, responded to proposals for miniskirt uniforms, with

accompanying quips like "then we could really fly the friendly thighs of United," by noting, "If this is to be the portent of the future, then this competitive-minded industry will soon be pleading to throw out or be exempt from such prudish laws as might prevent topless or bottomless outfits for their stewardesses . . . The purpose of the airline industry is supposed to be Interstate Commerce—not sex."[75]

Courts agreed. Airlines argued for a Bona Fide Occupational Qualification (BFOQ) exemption under Title VII, that only women who possessed certain characteristics could perform the labor. But, as the US District Court for the Northern District of Texas ruled in 1981, "Southwest is not a business where vicarious sex entertainment is the primary service provided. Accordingly, the ability of the airline to perform its primary business function, the transportation of passengers, would not be jeopardized by hiring males."[76] Neither did BFOQ apply when it came to marriage bars, a proxy for appearance that also expressed concern about pregnancy and motherhood being unfit conditions for flight. Courts initially upheld weight requirements insofar as men also came under such discipline and no fundamental right attached to sex or race was involved—even though the law was supposed to dislodge sexual stereotypes from personnel matters.[77] By the 1970s, collective bargaining victories and strike threats eliminated age and marriage bars and modified pregnancy rules.[78]

Protestors were sticking with the occupation, unlike the majority of attendants who left for marriage after less than three years. They rejected "the old image of being fly girls. We're professional career women and mothers." They had been "getting sick and tired of being looked at over the negotiating table as sweet young things who will take anything that the men on the other side want to give you," confessed a United worker in 1972. "Appearances are important," they admitted, "But, we think the policy is administered unfairly and in a degrading and humiliating way."[79] Such women formed the short-lived Stewardesses for Women's Rights. In rejecting sexual stigmatization, they gendered labor struggles for dignity and personal worth, while aligning more with the women's movement than the male dominated unions in their trade. By the late 1970s, uniforms had regained a look of respectability and the flight attendant workforce began to diversify in age, gender, and even race.[80]

Earlier discussions rarely stepped outside of an assumed whiteness. Only in the mid-1950s—under prodding from civil rights organizations, the New York State Commission Against Discrimination, and the President's Committee on Government Contract Compliance—did major airlines begin to hire African Americans for anything but the most menial labor.[81] Still they were slow to have black women as stewardesses and, when they did, such women conformed to regulations crafted with white women as the norm. They had to be respectable and appear middle-class. TWA's first one, UCLA undergraduate Mary Tiller, was light skinned, with features close to the Caucasian ideal.[82] A decade later, the EEOC found probable cause for race discrimination when an airline rejected a black woman "on basis of distinctive racial feature of appearance."[83] Even after African-American women regularly interacted with airline customers in the 1980s, management insisted they conform to hegemonic white femininity; American, for example, prohibited "an all-braided hairstyle."[84]

SUBJECT TO APPEARANCE

Wartime factory workers, moved into shop floors previously occupied by men, and postwar flight attendants, placed on planes to appeal to men, labored in vastly different settings. Rosies toiled in ship's holes or factory nooks, where without observation sexual banter could spin into violence. Harassment of flight attendants was in public view, usually by customers rather than coworkers. State policies and actions helped to create both workplaces, but sexuality and appearance had contrasting implications for the processes of manufacturing and service labor. Moreover, the Second World War constituted an arena for sexual politics that, while opening up new possibilities, only could prefigure later sexual revolutions. In these cases neither sexuality nor larger gendered subjectivities were predetermined or constant; they were continually being created and defined not only by management but by working people themselves.

Wartime generated the need for "Rosie the Riveters," even as workplace regulations sought to restrain their aura as sexual beings in the name of efficiency and output. Though overalls and helmets denied dominant gendered constructions of femininity, covering up called attention to what was underneath; rather than suppressed, female sexuality pervaded wartime production, but not necessarily to the benefit of women who remained marked by their sex when real workers were male. Women sought to bring back what was denied through beautification either on the job or through consumption made possible by earnings from the job.

Stewardesses also maintained a double-edged stance toward their status as a desirable figure. Defined by beauty and glamour by employers and the public, they protested such criteria as a job requirement even as they deployed their appearance to fight dismissal on the grounds of age. Many individuals came to the occupation precisely because they wished to look like a stewardess. Rather than buying into managerial construction of their bodies through their own appearance labors, their deployment of sexual appeal moved toward a different consciousness of bodily rights, even as they may have reinforced hegemonic ideals.[85] Where most wartime examples underscore individual expressions of self, the attendants' response to managerial definitions of appearance suggests the power inherent in unionization, especially where women are in the leadership, for grievances associated with womanhood itself. Where antidiscrimination machinery hardly existed in the 1940s, by the late 1960s, multiple avenues of redress had developed, including arbitration and bargaining, courts, legislation, and regulatory commissions. Moreover, cultural expectations of respectable and appropriate workplace dress had shifted with an apparent "sexual revolution."

Desirable dress, whether pants, sweaters, or miniskirted uniforms, contains symbolic meaning, but whose sexual subjectivity is expressed is not always clear. Even if imposed by employers or curtailed by regulatory rules, dress may generate new notions of self, as for women who found liberation through the wearing of pants and those who measured up as a sky girl. Appearance may be a proxy for other forms of contestation. But looks might also be a conveyer of pleasure that makes work just a little more humane.

ACKNOWLEDGMENTS

I would like to thank research assistants Danielle Swiontek, Jill Jensen and Carolyn Herbst Lewis, grants from the UCSB Academic Senate and ISBER, and readings by Dorothy Sue Cobble, Victoria Hattam, and Ava Baron. I also would like to acknowledge Kathleen Barry, Steve Meyer, and Elizabeth Escobedo, who generously shared their outstanding work-in-progress.

NOTES

1. "Marye Stumph," "Betty Jeanne Boggs," "Beatrice Morales Clifton," in Sherna Berger Gluck, *Rosie the Riveter Revisited: Women, The War, and Social Change* (Boston, 1987), 62, 111, 210.

2. Interview in Nancy Baker Wise and Christy Wise, *A Mouthful of Rivets: Women at Work in World War II* (San Francisco, 1994), 105.

3. Frank Elkouri and Edna Asper Elkouri, *How Arbitration Works*, 4th edition (Washington, 1985), 768.

4. Anna Clark, *The Struggle for the Breeches: Gender and the Making of the British Working Class* (Berkeley, 1995), 1.

5. Quoted in Barbara Burman and Carole Turbin, "Introduction: Material Strategies Engendered," *Gender and History* 14 (November 2002), 378; Joanne Entwistle, "The Dressed Body," in *Body Dressing*, Joanne Entwistle and Elizabeth Wilson, eds. (Oxford, 2001), 55.

6. David Montgomery, *Citizen Worker: The Experience of Workers in the United States with Democracy and the Free Market During the Nineteenth Century* (New York, 1993); Kathy Peiss, *Cheap Amusements: Working Women and Leisure at Turn of the Century New York* (Philadelphia, 1986); Elizabeth Ewen, *Immigrant Women and the Land of Dollars: Life and Culture on the Lower East Side, 1890–1925* (New York, 1985); Tera Hunter, *To "Joy My Freedom": Southern Black Women's Lives and Labors After the Civil War* (Cambridge, 1997); Elizabeth Clark-Lewis, *Living In, Living Out: African American Domestics in Washington, D.C., 1910–1940* (Washington, 1994).

7. Stephen Norwood, *Labor's Flaming Youth: Telephone Operators and Worker Militancy, 1878–1923* (Urbana, 1990); Nan Enstad, *Ladies of Labor, Girls of Adventure: Working Women, Popular Culture, and Labor Politics at the Turn of the Twentieth Century* (New York, 1999); Vicki Ruiz, "'Star Struck': Acculturation, Adolescence, and the Mexican American Woman, 1920–1940," in *Small Worlds: Children and Adolescents in America, 1850–1950*, eds. Elliott West and Paula Petrik (Lawrence, 1992), 61–80.

8. Dorothy Sue Cobble, *Dishing It Out: Waitresses and Their Unions in the Twentieth Century* (Urbana, 1991), 127; Vicki Howard, "'At the Curve of Exchange': Postwar Beauty Culture and Working Women at Maidenform," in *Beauty and Business: Commerce, Gender, and Culture in Modern America*, ed. Philip Scranton (New York, 2001), 195–216.

9. Daniel E. Bender, "'Too Much of Distasteful Masculinity': Historicizing Sexual Harassment in the Garment Sweatshop and Factory," *Journal of Women's History* 15 (Winter 2004), 91–116; Steve Meyer, "Workplace Predators: Sexuality and Harassment on the U.S. Automotive Shop Floor, 1930–1970," *Labor: Studies in Working-Class History of the Americas* 1 (Spring 2004), 77–93.

10. In her novel of he-she identity before Stonewall, Leslie Feinberg portrays the dress of such butches in the factory, where they were hired to replace drafted men, as well as their outfits in the bars. See *Stone Butch Blues* (Ithaca, NY, 1993).

11. Kathleen L. Endres, *Rosie the Rubber Worker: Women Workers in Akron's Rubber Factories During World War II* (Kent, Ohio, 2000).

12. Marc Linder, "Smart Women, Stupid Shoes, and Cynical Employers: The Unlawfulness and Adverse Health Consequences of Sexually Discriminatory Workplace Footwear Requirements for Female Employees," *Iowa Journal of Corporation Law* 22 (Winter 1997), 306–9.

13. Ruth Milkman, *Gender at Work: The Dynamics of Job Segregation by Sex During WWII* (Urbana, 1987); Nancy F. Gabin, *Feminism in the Labor Movement: Women and the United Auto Workers, 1935–1975* (Ithaca, 1990).

14. "A New Headache," *Business Week*, October 17, 1942, 48.

15. Quoted in Steve Meyer, "'The Woman in the Red Slacks': Men and Women on the Automotive and Aircraft Shop Floor During World War II," 54, unpublished paper presented at the 1999 North American Labor History Conference, Wayne State, in author's possession.

16. Elkouri and Elkouri, *How Arbitration Works*, 109; Meyer, "'The Woman in the Red Slacks,'" 1, 54–56; Karl E. Klare, "Power/Dressing: Regulation of Employee Appearance," *New England Law Review* 25 (Summer 1992), 1429–1430.

17. Eileen Boris, "'You Wouldn't Want One of 'Em Dancing with Your Wife'; Racialized Bodies on the Job in WWII," *American Quarterly* 50 (March 1998), 77–108.

18. Page Dougherty Delano, "Making Up for War: Sexuality and Citizenship in Wartime Culture,'" *Feminist Studies* 26 (Spring 2000), 33–68; Leila J. Rupp, *Mobilizing Women for War: German and American Propaganda, 1939–1945* (Princeton, 1978), 93–99, 146–66.

19. "Fashion Invades the Factory," *Personnel* 19 (January 1943), 593–94, quoted in Meyer, "'The Woman in the Red Slacks,'" 45–46.

20. Meyer, "Workplace Predators."

21. Quoted in Endres, *Rosie the Rubber Worker*, 102.

22. Diana Crane, *Fashion and Its Social Agendas: Class, Gender, and Identity in Clothes* (Chicago, 2000), 89–90.

23. Katherine Anthony, *Wartime Shipyard: A Study in Social Disunity* (Berkeley, 1947), 21.

24. Elizabeth Hawes, *Why Women Cry or Wenches with Wrenches* (Cornwall, NY, 1943), 89.

25. "Ford Motor Company, Detroit—April 20th: Employment of Women," Report, Box 19, file: "Michigan 1941," Papers of the Women's Bureau (RG86), Field Service Division, Field Office Files, Region V, National Archives (NA).

26. Anthony, *Wartime Shipyard*, 21.

27. Clarice L. Scott, *Work Clothes for Women*, Textiles and Clothing Division, Bureau of Home Economics, US Department of Agriculture, Farmers' Bulletin No. 1905 (Washington, DC, June 1942), 3.

28. Letter to Miss Anderson and Miss Nienburg from Ethel Erickson, October 24, 1942, Box 194, file: "Twin Cities Ordnance Plant, 1942/44," RG86, Division of Research,

Women Workers in WWII, 1940–1945, National Archives (NA).

29. Laura S. Parsons to Mary Anderson, August 1, 1943, RG86, Box 385, file: "Equal Pay-1943," NA.

30. Office of War Information, "Safe clothes for women war workers," photo by Ann Rosener, March 1943, Bendix Aviation Plant, Brooklyn, NY, American Memory Project, Library of Congress, LC-USE6-D-009751.

31. Anthony, *Wartime Shipyard*, 21, 32.

32. Interview in Wise and Wise, *A Mouthful of Rivets*, 13.

33. Endres, *Rosie the Rubber Worker*, 101.

34. Interview in Wise and Wise, *A Mouthful of Rivets*, 21.

35. Interview in Wise and Wise, *A Mouthful of Rivets*, 13.

36. Alice Kessler-Harris, *A Women's Wage: Historical Meanings and Social Consequences* (Lexington, 1990).

37. Letter to President from Mrs. Jackie Miller, San Mateo, Cal., 1943, Reel 112F, folder: "Boilermakers' Auxiliary Union Issue, Aug. 29, 1943, Exhibit C," in file: "Moore Drydock," RG228, FEPC Papers, San Bruno Branch, NA.

38. Letter to Mr. Routledge from Mrs. Doris Mae Williams, Vancouver, Washington, May 4,1944, No. 12-BR-339, reel 110F, folder "Kaiser Company," RG228, FEPC Papers, microfilm edition.

39. Memo to Mr. William T. McKnight from Lethia W. Clore, October 12, 1943, Roll 58F, file, "Briggs #2," in FEPC Papers. For the politics of respectability, Evelyn Brooks Higginbotham, *Righteous Discontent: The Women's Movement in the Black Baptist Church, 1880–1920* (Cambridge, MA, 1993), 185–229.

40. Merl E. Reed, *Seedtime for the Modern Civil Rights Movement: The President's Committee on Fair Employment Practice, 1941–1946* (Baton Rouge, 1991); Eileen Boris, "The Gender of Discrimination: Race, Sex, and Fair Employment," in *Women and the United States Constitution: History, Interpretation, and Practice*, Sibyl A. Schwarzenbach and Patricia Smith, eds. (New York, 2003), 273–91.

41. Memo to McKnight, October 12, 1943.

42. Memo to McKnight from Clore, Oct. 21,1943, Case No. 5-BR-1233, Reel 60F, folder "Hudson Motor Car Company," RG228, FEPC Papers, microfilm edition.

43. Anthony, *Wartime Shipyard*, 21.

44. "Mexican-American Girls Meet in Protest," *Eastside Journal*, June 16, 1943, cited by Elizabeth Escobedo, "Rosita the Riveter: Mexican American Women at Work for the War, and Their Community," unpublished paper, 2003 WAWH Conference, in possession of the author.

45. Interview in Wise and Wise, *A Mouthful of Rivets*, 100.

46. Interview in Wise and Wise, *A Mouthful of Rivets*, 54, 112, 49.

47. Interview in Wise and Wise, *A Mouthful of Rivets,*195.

48. Lizabeth Cohen, *A Consumer's Republic: The Politics of Mass Consumption in Postwar America* (New York, 2003).

49. Interviews in Wise and Wise, *A Mouthful of Rivets*, 163, 190.

50. Paula Kane, *Sex Objects in the Sky: A Personal Account* (Chicago, 1974).

51. Lindsay Van Gelder, "Coffee, Tea or Fly Me," *Ms.* (1973), 87–91, 105; Cathleen M. Dooley, "Battle in the Sky: A

Cultural and Legal History of Sex Discrimination in the United States Airline Industry, 1930–1980," unpublished Ph.D. Dissertation, University of Arizona, 2001, 83, 108.

52. Kathleen M. Barry, *Femininity in Flight: Flight Attendants, Glamour, and Pink-Collar Activism in the 20th Century United States* (forthcoming, Duke University Press) offers the most comprehensive analysis. See also her "Lifting the Weight: Flight Attendants' Challenges to Enforced Thinness," *Iris: A Journal About Women.* (Winter/Spring 1999), 50–54; Dorothy Sue Cobble, "'A Spontaneous Loss of Enthusiasm': Workplace Feminism and the Transformation of Women's Service Jobs in the 1970s," *International Labor and Working Class History* 56 (Fall 1999), 27–30, and *The Other Women's Movement: Workplace Justice and Social Rights in Modern America* (Princeton, 2004), 74–77, 207–11.

53. "50 Start Training as Stewardesses," *New York Times*, November 25, 1957, 39; Fredric C. Appel, "Airlines Vie with Cupid for Stewardesses," *New York Times*, April 26, 1965, 33; "Why Airlines Run a 'Bride School,'" *Business Week*, December 11, 1965, 164.

54. Dirk Johnson, "Behind a Glamorous Image, Flying Working Class," *New York Times*, November 24, 1993, A22.

55. "Glamor [sic] Girls of the Air," *Life*, August 25, 1958, 68, 73.

56. Quoted in Van Gelder, "Coffee, Tea or Fly Me," 87, 90.

57. "32 Skidoo," *Newsweek*, April 8, 1963, 56–57.

58. Dooley, "Battle in the Sky," 112–18.

59. Joseph Carter, "First Hostesses Hired in Thirties," *New York Times*, April 28, 1963, 90; "A 3-Month Airline Experiment Turns 50 Years Old," *New York Times*, May 13, 1980, B16; William Barry Furlong, "Fustest with the Hostess," *New York Times*, May 15, 1960, SM74; "Airlines: Up from Betty Grable," *Newsweek*, September 4, 1967, 58.

60. Jeanne Molli, "Uniforms Get a Personal Touch, Too," *New York Times*, March 21, 1962, 44.

61. Adam Bryant, "Air Chortle Is Now Boarding," *New York Times*, October 2, 1994, E5; Phyllis Lee Levin, "British Designers Arrive," *New York Times*, April 20, 1960, 35. For example, "Now more service 'In a class by itself'!" advertisement, *New York Times*, June 4, 1957, 18.

62. Tania Long, "Airways Turn to High Style in Bid for Business," *New York Times*, April 2, 1967, 199; "The Wild Hue Yonder," *Life*, December 3, 1965, 76; Peter Bart, "Advertising: New Airline Image," *New York Times*, April 3, 1963, 72; "Pan Am Stewardess Gets a New Uniform," *New York Times*, February 18, 1965, 37; "Couturiers Design for Stewardesses," *New York Times*, May 5, 1965, 40.

63. "Stewardess' Job Different Cup of Tea," *Los Angeles Times*, December 7, 1969, O12.

64. Long, "Airways Turn to Hight Style"; Julie Byrne, "Men Eye New Air Hostess Uniforms," *New York Times*, October 25, 1970, N21; Molli, "Uniforms Get a Personal Touch, Too"; "Up from Betty Grable."

65. "Our non-stops to Atlanta," advertisement, *New York Times*, March 16, 1970, 16.

66. *Wilson v. Southwest Airlines*, 517 F. Supp. 292 (1981), 295; Southern Airways, Inc. and Air Line Stewards and

Stewardesses Associatioin (TWU), Decision of System Board of Adjustment, Grievance: Termination of C. Poag and G. Duckworth, September 14, 1966, 7, TWU Collection, Box 32, "Local 550, ATD—1966," Tamiment Library.

67. "Appendix A," Statement at Hearing, Equal Employment Commission, *Stewardess Employment by the United States Air Transport Industry,* September 12, 1967, O'Donnell & Schwartz, Attorneys for Transport Workers Union of America, 9–10, TWU Collection, Box 32, "Local 550, ATD—1967."

68. "Stewardesses Protest Suggestive Airline Ads," *New York Times,* June 30, 1974, 33; Steven Rattner, "National Airlines Shutdown Is Nearing Four Months, *New York Times,* December 29, 1975, 44.

69. Don Smith, "Airline Employes [sic] Revolt Against Merger," *Los Angeles Times,* December 20, 1969, B9; Marsha Chambers, Stewardesses Exchange Trays for Picket Signs," *New York Times,* November 6, 1973, 73; "Women Wear Bikinis for Strike Duty," *Los Angeles Times,* June 23, 1970, A8.

70. Christina Kirk, "Skidoo at 32? No! Say 'Mature' Hostesses to Airline That Wants to Clip Their Wings," *Sunday News,* May 19, 1963, np, TWU Collection, Box 32, "Local 550, ATD—1963"; Flora Davis, *Moving the Mountain: The Women's Movement in America Since 1960* (New York, 1991), 16–25.

71. Theo Wilson, "She's 36–24–36, Alas 32-Plus: Air Hostesses Fighting Retirement Age," *Daily News,* April 18, 1963, 3.

72. "32 Skidoo," 57.

73. Quoted in Van Gelder, "Coffee, Tea or Fly Me," 89.

74. "House Panel Hears Complaint of Stewardesses," *New York Times,* September 3, 1965, 12.

75. Boland in US Congress, Senate. *Age Discrimination in Employment,* Hearings Before the Subcommittee on Labor of the Committee on Labor and Public Welfare, 90th Congress, First Session (Washington, 1967), 202.

76. *Wilson v. Southwest Airlines* at 14; *Diaz v. Pan American World Airways, Inc.,* 311 F. Supp. 559 (S.D. Fla. 1970), at 442.

77. Barry, "Lifting the Weight," 50–54; Dooley, "Battle in the Sky," 313–64.

78. Georgia Panter Nielsen, *From Sky Girl to Flight Attendant: Women and the Making of a Union* (Ithaca, 1982), 100–10.

79. Betty Liddick, "Tail Slogan Hits Bottom, Say Stewardesses," *Los Angeles Times,* January 25, 1974, E1; Robert Lindsey, "Air Stewardesses Fight Weight Rules," *New York Times,* March 4, 1972, 29, 54.

80. Cobble, *The Other Women's Movement,* 207–11.

81. Mohawk, a New York regional carrier, was the first in 1957. See Cobble, *The Other Women's Movement,* 83.

82. Memo to Wilkins, Marshall, Carter, Wright from Herbert Hill, "Re: Employment Discrimination in Airlines Industry—New York State," April 1, 1957; "Draft Press Release—May 16, 1958"; Bob Greene, "First Negro TWA Hostess Takes to The Air," *The Call* (Kansas City, MO), March 20, 1959, all in RG9–002, Box 1/folder 7, Records of the Division of Civil Rights, AFL-CIO Papers, George Meany Memorial Archives.

83. Decision No. 7090, August 19, 1969, 2 FEPC 236 (1971).

84. *Rogers v. American Airlines,* 527 F. Supp. 229 (1981), 231–33.

85. Melissa Tyler and Pamela Abbott, "Chocs Away: Weight Watching in the Contemporary Airline Industry," *Sociology* 32 (August 1998), 433–50, highlights body labor but in light of Foucauldian disciplining. More persuasive is Barry, *Femininity in Flight,* who offers discourses of skill as an alternative to sexual banter.

READING *24* **Miliann Kang**

The Managed Hand: The Commercialization of Bodies and Emotions in Korean Immigrant–Owned Nail Salons

The title of [Arlie] Hochschild's (1983) groundbreaking study of emotional labor, *The Managed Heart,* provides a rich metaphor for the control and commercialization of human feeling in service interactions. The title of this article, "The Managed Hand," plays on Hochschild's to capture the commercialization of both human feelings and bodies and to introduce the concept of body labor, the provision of body-related services and the management of feelings that accompanies it. By focusing on the case study of Korean immigrant manicurists and their relations with racially and socioeconomically diverse female customers in New York City nail salons, I broaden the study of emotional labor to illuminate its neglected embodied dimensions and to examine the intersections of gender, race, and class in its performance.

The past decade has witnessed a turn toward "Bringing Bodies Back In" (Frank 1990) to theory and research in sociology and feminist scholarship. What can be gained by "bringing the body back in" to the study of emotional labor and, more broadly, of gendered work? What are the dimensions of body labor, and what factors explain the variation in the quality and quantity of its performance? An embodied perspective on gendered work highlights the feminization of the body-related service sector and the proliferation of intricate practices of enhancing the appearance of the female body. A race, gender, and class perspective highlights the increasing role of working-class immigrant women in filling body-related service jobs and the racialized meanings that shape the processes of emotional management among service workers.

This study compares nail salons in three racially and socioeconomically diverse settings, employing participant observation and in-depth interviews ($N = 62$) in the tradition of feminist ethnography and the extended case method. After providing a brief overview of the case study of Korean-owned nail salons in New York City, the data presentation maps out the physical and emotional dimensions of body labor in three different nail salons and explains patterns of variation according to the race and class of the clientele and neighborhood.

In addition to contributing original empirical research on Korean immigrant women's work in the new and expanding niches of body service work, this article broadens the scholarship on emotional labor by addressing its performance by racial-ethnic and immigrant women in the global service economy. It demonstrates how the gendered processes of physical and emotional labor in nail salon work are steeped with race and class meanings that reinforce broader structures of inequality and ideologies of difference between women.

THEORETICAL FRAMEWORK

Emotional Labor in Body Service Work: Race, Gender, and Class Intersections

Work on the body requires not only physical labor but extensive emotional management, or what Hochschild's (1983) seminal work describes as emotional labor. The concept of body labor makes two important

contributions to the study of emotional labor: (1) It explores the embodied dimensions of emotional labor and (2) it investigates the intersections of race, gender, and class in shaping its performance. By bringing together an embodied analysis of emotional labor with an integrative race, gender, and class perspective, I show how this case study of nail salon work retheorizes emotional labor to have greater applicability to gendered occupations dominated by racialized immigrant women.

Building on Hochschild's (1983) work, studies of emotional labor have illuminated the increasing prevalence of emotional management in specific occupations and industries, the gendered composition of the emotional labor force, wage discrimination, burnout, and other occupational health issues (Hall 1993; Leidner 1999; Lively 2000; Wharton 1999). Steinberg and Figart (1999) provide a comprehensive overview of the field that examines both qualitative case studies of the contours of emotional labor in specific work sites and quantitative investigations of its prevalence and its impact on job satisfaction and compensation. Despite the many dimensions of emotional labor that have been addressed by feminist scholars, the body-related contours of emotional labor as it is manifested in low-wage service work dominated by racial-ethnic women, particularly in the beauty industry, have yet to be examined in depth.

While the study of beauty and the beauty industry presents a rich opportunity to explore the emotional work involved in servicing female bodies, this literature has focused attention almost exclusively on the experiences of middle-class white women consumers and their physical and psychological exploitation by the male-dominated beauty industry (Banner 1983; Bordo 1993; Chapkis 1986; Wolf 1991), neglecting the substandard working conditions, unequal power relations, and complex emotional lives of the women who provide these services. Several excellent ethnographies of beauty salons (Gimlan 1996; Kerner Furman 1997) have explored the dimensions of class and age in beauty shop culture, but they have not addressed the experiences of women of color as either customers or body service workers. Studies of the bodies of women of color, while illuminating cultural representations of racialized bodies as inferior and exotic (hooks 1990) and studying the politics of body alteration, particularly regarding hair (Banks 2000; Rooks 1996), have also neglected the actual interactions between consumers and providers of body-related services and the hierarchies that govern these exchanges.

In addition to neglecting emotional work in body service jobs, the literature on emotional labor has framed the processes of interactive service work primarily through a gender lens and paid less attention to the crosscutting influences of gender, race and class. Russell Hochschild's original case study of flight attendants and subsequent applications to other female-dominated occupations have emphasized the gendered employment experiences of native-born white women as paralegals (Pierce 1995), nannies and au pairs (Macdonald 1996), fast food and insurance sales workers (Leidner 1993), and police officers (Schmitt and Yancey Martin 1999). My research expands this work not only in its empirical focus on immigrant women of color doing gendered, emotional labor but through the theoretical framework of race, gender, and class as "interactive systems" and "interlocking categories of experience" (Anderson and Hill Collins 2001, xii). This framework critiques additive models that append race and class to the experiences of white middle-class women and instead highlights the simultaneity and reciprocity of race, gender, and class in patterns of social relations and in the lives of individuals (Baca Zinn 1989; Hill Collins 1991; hooks 1981; Hurtado 1989; Nakano Glenn 1992; Ngan-Ling Chow 1994). Thus, I demonstrate that different expectations or "feeling rules" (Hochschild 1983, x) shape the performance of emotional labor by women according to the racial and class context.

Drawing from Hochschild's (1983) definition of emotional labor, I incorporate this intersectional analysis to define important parallels and distinctions between the concepts of body labor and emotional labor. First, Hochschild's definition of emotional labor focuses on a particular form that "requires one to induce or suppress feeling in order to sustain the outward countenance that produces the proper state of mind in others—in this case, the sense of being cared for in a convivial and safe place" (1983, 7). While Hochschild develops this definition in reference to the specific case of flight attendants and the feeling rules that govern their work, this kind of caring, attentive service has become a widely generalized definition, rather than being regarded as one particular form of emotional labor performed by mostly white, middle-class women largely for the benefit of white, middle- and upper-class men. Korean-owned nail salons thus serve as a contrasting site to explore other forms of emotional labor that emerge in work sites that are differently gendered, differently racialized, and differently classed. The patterns of emotional labor described in this study can illuminate similar sites in which emotional labor involves women serving women (as opposed to mainly women serving men), and is not necessarily governed by the social feeling rules of white, middle-class America.

Furthermore, while Hochschild and other scholars of emotional labor have examined certain embodied aspects of emotional labor concerned with gendered bodily display, ranging from control of weight to smiles, this study highlights emotional management regarding bodily contact in service interactions. The dynamics of extended physical contact between women of different racial and class positions complicate and intensify the gendered performance of emotional labor. Body labor not only demands that the service worker present and comport her body in an appropriate fashion but also that she induces customers' positive feelings about their own bodies. This is a highly complicated enterprise in a culture that sets unattainable standards for female beauty and pathologizes intimate, nurturing physical contact between women, while it normalizes unequal relations in the exchange of body services.

By investigating the understudied area of body-related service occupations through an intersectional race, gender, and class analysis, this study of body labor reformulates the concept of emotional labor to dramatize how the feeling rules governing its exchange are shaped by interlocking oppressions that operate at the macro level (Hill Collins 1991) and then emerge as different styles of emotional service at the micro level.

BACKGROUND FOR THE STUDY

In this section, I provide context for my study by describing nail salons as a niche for Korean immigrant women's work and discussing the dynamics of race and ethnicity in its development. As one of the few arenas in which immigrant and native-born women encounter each other in regular, sustained, physical contact, Korean immigrant women–owned nail salons in New York City illuminate the complex performance and production of race, gender, and class as they are constructed in feminized work sites in the global service economy. Since the early 1980s, Korean women in New York City have pioneered this new ethnic niche with more than 2,000 Korean-owned nail salons throughout the metropolitan area, or approximately 70 percent of the total, as estimated by the Korean American Nail Association of New York. Each salon employs an average of five workers, suggesting an occupational niche of roughly 10,000 women. While the New York State licensing bureau does not keep track of nail salon licenses by ethnic group, their figures reveal an overall 41-percent growth in the nail industry (from 7,562 licensed nail technicians in 1996 to 10,684 in 2000) in New York City, Westchester County, and Nassau County. These numbers undercount a sizable number of women who do not possess licenses or legal working status.

While concentrating on Korean immigrant women, this study examines both race and ethnicity as salient categories of analysis. I designate the salon owners and workers according to ethnicity, but I recognize shared racial positions that push not only Korean but also other Asian immigrant women into this niche. For example, in New York, there is a significant presence of Chinese- and Vietnamese- as well as Korean-owned nail salons, and on the West Coast, the niche is almost solely dominated by Vietnamese women (www.nailsmag.com). Common factors such as limited English-language ability, unrecognized professional credentials from their countries of origin, undocumented immigration status, and coethnic resources in the form of labor, start-up capital, and social networks explain why Asian immigrant women of various ethnic groups cluster in the nail salon industry. Similarities across Asian ethnic groups include not only the human capital of the women themselves but also the conditions of the labor market and the U.S. racial hierarchy that they encounter. Through their shared race, gender, and class locations, Asian women have been coveted as productive and docile workers, whose "nimble fingers" (Ong 1987) make them desirable and exploitable in an increasingly feminized, impoverished, and unprotected labor force (Cheng and Bonacich 1984; Hu-DeHart 1999). Racialized perceptions of Asian women as skilled in detailed handiwork and massage further contribute to customers' preference for their manicuring services, as evidenced by the fact that many customers racially identify the salons as owned by Asians or "Orientals," as opposed to by specific ethnic group.

In sum, because it would be methodologically unsound to generalize findings based on a limited sample of Korean women to include all Asian immigrant women in the nail industry, this study maintains ethnicity as the significant category for describing the workers and owners but frames differences between the customers and variation in service interactions according to race. Thus, I discuss the different dimensions of Korean-immigrant women's performance of body labor through the integrative lens of race, gender, and class rather than a more specific focus on Korean ethnicity.

RESEARCH DESIGN AND METHOD

This study situates itself within feminist methodology and epistemology by beginning from the standpoint of women to investigate the "relations of ruling" in contemporary capitalist society (Smith 1987). At the same time, it does not privilege gender as the only or the most important framework for defining and investigating differences and aims instead for an understanding of race, gender, and class as crosscutting forces. By examining contrasting patterns of body labor between women of different racial and class backgrounds, this study reconstructs theories of emotional labor by addressing its embodied dimensions and the simultaneous influence of gender, race, and class on its performance. In doing so, it follows the extended case method of making critical interventions in existing theory by explaining anomalies between similar phenomena, rather than seeking generalizations toward the discovery of new theory, as in the contrasting approach of grounded theory. According to Burawoy (1991, 281), the primary architect of the extended case method, "The importance of the single case lies in what it tells us about society as a whole rather than about the population of similar cases." Thus, my study examines cases of specific nail salons, not to formulate generalizations about all similar nail salons but instead to explain how social forces influence variation in the service interactions at these sites.

The data collection for this project involved 14 months of fieldwork in New York City nail salons. The research design included in-depth interviews ($N = 62$) and participant observation at three sites: (1) "Uptown Nails," located in a predominantly white, middle- and upper-class commercial area; (2) "Downtown Nails," located in a predominantly Black (African American and Caribbean) working- and lower-middle-class commercial neighborhood; and (3) "Crosstown Nails," located in a racially mixed lower-middle and middle-class residential and commercial area. I spent at least 50 hours at each salon over the course of several months. In the case of Crosstown Nails, which was located near my home, visits were shorter (2 to 3 hours) and more frequent (several times a week). The other two salons required long commutes, so I usually visited once a week for 6 to 7 hours.

In addition to hundreds of unstructured conversational interviews conducted as a participant-observer, the research included in-depth structured interviews with 10 Korean nail salon owners, 10 Korean nail salon workers, 15 Black customers, and 15 white customers. The customers interviewed at each salon are as follows. Uptown Nails included a lawyer, professor, pharmacist, flight attendant, secretary, personal trainer, accessories importer, homemaker (formerly a computer programmer), fashion designer, and real estate broker. Customers interviewed at Downtown Nails included a package clerk, student/waitress, student/mother, grocery cashier, ambulatory service driver, county government administrative assistant, laboratory technician, nanny, therapist, and elementary school principal. At Crosstown Nails, I interviewed 10 customers (five white, five Black). The white customers included a bartender, high school teacher, hairdresser, homemaker, and retired insurance bookkeeper. The Black customers included a clinical researcher, theater technician/musician, management consultant, homemaker, and student.

In-depth interviews averaged 45 minutes for customers and two hours for owners and workers. Customers were interviewed in English at the salon while they were having their manicures, and when necessary, a follow-up meeting or telephone interview was arranged. Owners and workers were interviewed in both Korean and English, depending on their preference and level of fluency. Bilingual research assistants helped with translation, transcription, and follow-up interviews. I tape-recorded interviews in which consent was given, but in cases in which respondents refused, I took extensive handwritten notes that I typed immediately afterward. Both customers and service providers are referred to by pseudonyms that approximate the names they use in the salons. This convention captures the naturalistic setting where even coworkers commonly refer to each other by the "American name" that they employ at work. I have added a surname to citations and descriptions of owners and workers to differentiate customers from service providers.

Finally, I conducted key respondent interviews with two officials of the Korean Nail Salon Association of New York, two Korean ethnic press journalists, one New York State licensing official, and a representative of a Korean-operated nail school. I interviewed two Vietnamese nail salon owners and one Chinese and one Russian manicurist to provide preliminary comparisons to other ethnically owned nail salons. To provide comparisons to other Korean-owned small businesses, I engaged in limited participant observation in a Korean-owned grocery store and interviewed the owner and manager.

FINDINGS

The Contours of Body Labor

Body labor involves the exchange of body-related services for a wage and the performance of physical and emotional labor in this exchange. My study's findings illustrate three dimensions of body labor: (1) the physical labor of attending to the bodily appearance and pleasure of customers, (2) the emotional labor of managing feelings to display certain feeling states and to create and respond to customers' feelings regarding the servicing of their bodies, and (3) variation in the performance of body labor as explained through the intersection of gender with race and class. These dimensions vary across the different research sites and emerge as three distinct patterns of body labor provision: (1) high-service body labor involving physical pampering and emotional attentiveness serving mostly middle- and upper-class white female customers, (2) expressive body labor involving artistry in technical skills and communication of respect and fairness when serving mostly working- and lower-middle-class African American and Caribbean female customers, and (3) routinized body labor involving efficient, competent physical labor and courteous but minimal emotional labor when serving mostly lower-middle and middle-class racially mixed female customers. The data presentation admittedly flattens some of the variation within each site to clarify distinctions between them, but this typology highlights the dominant physical and emotional style of service at each salon.

Uptown Nails: High-Service Body Labor

A seasoned Korean manicurist who has worked at Uptown Nails for nearly 10 years, Esther Lee is in high demand for her relaxing and invigorating hand massages. She energetically kneads, strokes, and pushes pressure points, finishing off the massage by holding each of the customer's hands between her own and alternately rubbing, slapping, and gently pounding them with the flare that has wooed many a customer into a regular nail salon habit. Margie, a white single woman in her mid-30s who works for an accounting firm, smiles appreciatively and squeezes Esther's hand: "I swear, I couldn't stay in my job without this!" Esther reciprocates a warm, somewhat shy smile.

Uptown Nails boasts leafy green plants, glossy framed pictures of white fashion models showing off well-manicured hands, recent fashion magazine subscriptions stacked neatly on a coffee table, and classical CDs on the stereo system. The salon has been in operation for 13 years, and three of the six employees have worked there for more than 10 years. The customers sit quietly sipping their cappuccinos, updating their appointment books, or at times politely conversing with each other about the weather or the color of the nail polish they are wearing. Located in a prosperous business district of Manhattan, an Uptown Nails manicuring experience involves not only the filing and polishing of nails but attention to the customer's physical and emotional comfort. From the gentle removal of undernail dirt, to the careful trimming of cuticles and buffing of calluses, to the massaging of hands and feet, Korean manicurists literally rub up against their customers, who are mostly white middle- and upper-class women. The owner, one of the earliest pioneers in the nail salon industry, currently operates six very profitable salons in prime Manhattan locations and visits this salon only once a week to take care of paperwork. The owner, manager, and employees are all middle-aged Korean women with fluent English-language ability, reflecting the greater expectations for communications with customers. The physical dimensions of body labor in Uptown Nails, including hot cotton towels, bowls of warm soaking solution, sanitized utensils, and calming background music, all indicate considerable attention to creating a pleasurable sensory experience for the customer. Particular attention is given to avoiding nicks and cuts and sterilizing and apologizing profusely when they occur.

In addition to this extensive physical pampering, Uptown Nails prioritizes the emotional needs of customers regarding the servicing of their bodies. The mostly white middle-class customers at this salon place great importance on emotional attentiveness as a crucial component of the service interaction. Kathy, a personal trainer, elaborated,

> Having them done is a pleasure, a luxury. Doing them myself is tedious, having them done is a treat. It's the whole idea of going and having something nice done for myself. If I do them myself, it's just routine upkeep of my body—like washing your hair or keeping your

clothes clean. . . . Of course it makes it more enjoyable if they are friendly and can talk to you. If they can't remember my name that's okay, but I think they should recognize me.

The proper performance of body labor thus transforms a hygienic process, otherwise equated with washing hair or clothes, into a richly rewarding physical and emotional experience. The satisfaction Kathy experiences from the manicure derives not only from the appearance of the nails but the feeling of being special that accompanies attentive body servicing. To generate this feeling, customers expect the manicurist to display a caring demeanor and engage in pleasant one-on-one conversation with them.

Service providers recognize customers' high expectations with regard to both the physical and emotional dimensions of body labor, and they respond accordingly. Judy Cha, a 34-year-old who immigrated in 1993, describes the emotional and physical stressors that accompany high-service body labor, particularly giving massages to earn tips and engaging in conversation.

> Three years ago we didn't give a lot of massages but now customers ask more and more. It makes me weak and really tired. . . . I guess because I don't have the right training to do it in a way that doesn't tire my body. Some manicurists give massage all the time to get tips, but sometimes I don't even ask them if I'm tired. Owners keep asking you to ask them, but on days I'm not feeling well, I don't ask. . . . One of my biggest fears working in the salon is, what if I don't understand what the customer is saying? They don't really talk in detail, just say, "how is the weather." But in order to have a deeper relationship, I need to get past that and to improve my English. It makes it very stressful.

Thus, manicurists work hard to conform to the high service expectations of middle-class white women, but while the performance of caring, attentive emotional labor is noticeably higher than that afforded in the other research sites, it often does not meet customers' expectations. In particular, many Uptown Nails customers disapprove of the use of Korean language by the manicurists as a violation of proper attentiveness in beauty service transactions and suspect that they are being talked about (Kang 1997).

Cathy Hong, a 32-year-old manicurist who immigrated in 1999, sums up the assumptions many of the

Uptown Nails customers have regarding access to a regular manicure delivered with high-service body labor: "These women get their nails done regularly because it has become a habit to them, they take it for granted. Just as we wash our face daily, American women get their nails done."

Downtown Nails: Expressive Body Labor

Entering another borough, the scene inside Downtown Nails differs as radically as the neighborhoods in which these two salons are located. Squeezed between a Caribbean bakery and a discount clothing store, a worn-out signboard displays the single word "NAILS" and a painting of a graceful, well-manicured hand holding a long-stemmed rose and pointing to a staircase leading to the second-story entrance. Upon being buzzed in through the locked door, the customer is greeted with a display of hundreds of brightly colored airbrushed nail tips lining an entire wall. The noise level in the salon is high, as various electronic nail-sculpting tools create a constant buzz to match the flow of the lively conversations among the mostly Black customers. On a weekend afternoon, Downtown Nails is filled to capacity, and the wait for a preferred "nail artist" can be more than an hour. Mostly Caribbean and African American women, the customers engage in animated conversations while sharing coco buns and currant rolls from the downstairs bakery. The banter ranges from vivid accounts of a recent mugging near the salon to news about the pay freeze in the nearby hospital where many of the women work as nurses or technicians.

A far cry from the spa-like pampering experience of Uptown Nails, a nail job at Downtown Nails is closer to a stint on a factory assembly line: highly mechanized and potentially toxic. Absent are the elaborate sanitizing machines and solutions, let alone the soft pampering touches. Despite these appearances, body labor at Downtown Nails involves a complex mix of physical and emotional labor that accommodates customers' desires to express a unique sense of self through their nail designs and their expectations that service providers demonstrate both individual respect and appreciation to the community.

The manicurists, or nail artists, provide less of the traditional, attentive style of emotional labor but focus their emotional management on communicating a sense of respect and fairness. These women tend to be

more recent immigrants from more working-class backgrounds with less English-language fluency and are more likely to be working without legal immigration status or licenses. The owners, Mr. and Mrs. Lee, are a married couple, both formerly school teachers, who immigrated in 1981 to pursue better educational opportunities for their children. Two years after their arrival, they opened a salon in this location because the rent was affordable, the customer base was strong, and they reside in a nearby neighborhood. The customers at Downtown Nails span a broad range in socioeconomic status but most are working to lower-middle class.

The importance of the physical appearance of the nails themselves as opposed to the pampering experience of receiving these services is dramatized by customers' concern with the design of the nails versus the massage and other services that customers at Uptown Nails regard as integral and Downtown Nails customers view as extraneous. Jamilla, a 26-year-old African American part-time student and waitress, proudly displays her inch-and-a-half-long nails, each one adorned with the skyline of New York City in bold black, framed by an orange and yellow sunset. A regular patron of Downtown Nails for six years, she explains why she is willing to spend "$50–$60 every two weeks" for elaborate hand-painted designs:

> Because I don't like looking like anyone else. My nails say "me." They're the first thing people notice about me. I have big hands for a female. I never had those long, thin ladylike fingers. My father used to say my hands were bigger than his. I want long nails because they make my hands look more feminine.

Indicating a preference for nails that reflect very different norms of femininity than the demure, pastel tones prevalent at Uptown Nails, Jamilla elaborates further on her nail aesthetics. "It all depends on my mood. Like this design makes me feel like I'm on top of the city, like it can't bring me down [laughing]. . . . No one's gonna mess with you when you got nails like these." Jamilla's pride in having originally designed nails that no one else can reproduce suggests the importance of her nails as an expression of her individuality that also communicate a sense of self-efficacy and protection, as indicated in her comments that no one would "mess" with a woman with nails like hers. To meet the expectations of customers such as Jamilla, body labor at Downtown Nails calls for development of expertise in sculpting and painting original nail designs rather than in the soothing, pampering services offered at Uptown Nails. Thus, the physical demands of body labor are not less but simply of a different type.

Similarly, the emotional dimensions of body labor at Downtown Nails are not different in degree so much as kind. The customer's race and class location intersect to produce much lower expectations among working-class Black customers for emotional attentiveness than the white middle-class women at Uptown Nails. While it is clearly less attentive, Serena, an African American grocery store cashier, assesses the emotional labor at Downtown Nails positively.

> It's very good, I'm satisfied with it. They really just do the nails, no massages. That's fine with me. I just go in with my Walkman and listen to some good music and maybe just have a little basic conversation.

Customers at Downtown Nails rarely are on a first-name basis with the service providers, and their preference for a particular manicurist is based much more on her technical skills than her emotional attentiveness. Serena elaborated,

> There are a few people I like and I go to whoever's open, but I'll stay away from certain people. I know they're not good cause I hear other people complain—I see someone come back and say that their nail cracked the next day, or I see someone get nicked with a filer. . . . No, it's not because they're rude or anything, it's because I know they don't do a good job. . . . Just like some people just can't do hair, some people just can't do nails.
>
> [Regarding relations with her current manicurist] I feel comfortable with her, but it's more that she does an excellent job. If a wrap cracks or looks funny or I lose a nail, I'm not going back to her no matter how nice she is.

While many working-class Black customers like Serena give little importance to a caring, attentive emotional display, they demand another style of emotional labor.

Emotional labor at Downtown Nails calls less for sensitivity to pampering of individual customers and more for demonstration of values of respect and fairness that recognize the complex dynamics of Korean businesses operating in Black neighborhoods. This includes efforts such as sponsoring a Christmas party to thank customers for their patronage, participating in community events, displaying Afro-centric designs, and playing R&B and rap music. Mrs. Lee, the co-owner of the salon, allows regulars to run an informal tab when they are short of money and keeps a change jar that customers dip into for bus fare, telephone calls, or other incidentals. It is not uncommon for customers to drop by even when they are not getting their nails done to use the bathroom or leave shopping bags behind the front desk while they complete errands. These efforts at "giving back to the community" entail a distinct form of emotional labor that conforms not to white middle-class women's feeling rules of privilege and pampering but to Black working-class women's concerns about being treated with respect and fairness.

Jamilla described the importance of a sense of fairness and respect to Black customers and how this demands a particular form of emotional labor from Korean manicurists.

> It's kind of a Catch-22. Some customers feel like they're getting disrespected if you don't refer back to them or if you're having a side conversation. Then the Koreans get upset and think African Americans have an attitude, which then makes them talk more about us. You see, in the African American community, you can't outright say anything you want to say because we always have our guard up. We get it all the time, from the cops or whoever. I've seen it in the Hispanic community too—this thing about honor and respect. "Don't disrespect me just because I'm Black or Hispanic. What I say does count."

Thus, while the caring, pampering style of service is virtually absent at Downtown Nails, another form of emotional labor is necessary to negotiate and avoid conflicts with customers that can quickly become racialized into heated confrontations (Lee 2002). Serena described a scene at another salon that illustrates how the failure to perform appropriately respectful emotional labor can quickly erupt into shouting matches that take on racialized and anti-immigrant overtones: "I've seen some customers really go off on them, 'You're not in your country, speak English.'" Her comments underscore how the race and class of the neighborhood complicate the processes of emotional management inside the salons.

Although disagreements between Downtown Nails' customers and workers do arise, at times resulting in heated exchanges, the relations in the salon are congenial overall, as the expressive style of emotional labor enables customers and service providers to voice and, for the most part, "work out" their differences. Mrs. Lee explained that she prefers serving Black customers for this reason and actually moved back to working in a low-income Black neighborhood after working for a period in Long Island.

> Working in the white neighborhood didn't match my personality. I don't deal well with picky customers. . . . In the Black neighborhood, it's more relaxed. They don't leave tips but they don't expect so much service either. . . . [In Long Island] they want you to go slow and spend time with them. Here I just concentrate on doing a good job and working quickly.

Service providers invest less energy in displaying and creating convivial feeling states, which in some cases allows for a genuine affinity with Black customers and less of a sense of burnout from the effort involved in the manufacture of falsely convivial feelings.

Expressive body labor thus prioritizes both the meanings of the nails as a form of self-expression to working-class Black customers and the expression of symbolic but tangible efforts to respond to the feeling rules of respect and fairness governing Korean immigrant service providers in predominantly Black working-class neighborhoods.

Crosstown Nails: Routinized Body Labor

Located on the second floor above a fashionable boutique, Crosstown Nails is clean but sparse and utilitarian. In many ways, this salon is representative of the most prevalent style of service offered in Korean-owned nail salons: fast, cheap, basic manicures and pedicures with no frills. The McDonald's of the nail salon industry, Crosstown Nails offers a manicure that is standardized and predictable in both its physical and emotional aspects.

This salon often has customers waiting, but even when it is busy, the line moves quickly as each customer is whisked in and out of the manicuring seat with crisp efficiency. The customer chooses her nail color, presents it to the manicurist who asks her to specify the desired shape of the nail, and then soaks her nails briefly in a softening solution. Depending on her preference, her nails are either trimmed or pushed back. The manicurist offers to give a massage, but it is perfunctory and lasts usually not more than a minute. After carefully layering on two coats of polish and a quick-drying topcoat, the customer moves to a heated hand dryer where she converses with other customers or more often "zones out."

Many customers come from the neighboring hospital during lunch hour or after work. Situated on the edge of a fashionable, high-rent, racially diverse residential district and a lower-income but also racially mixed neighborhood, Crosstown Nails captures the broad range of customer interactions that many Korean service providers negotiate in a given day. In large, high-immigrant-receiving cities such as New York, service interactions often involve multiracial rather than binary interactions between Korean and Blacks or Koreans and whites.

Susan Lee, age 39, founded Crosstown Nails in 1989 and is the sole owner. Divorced with one son, age 10, she emigrated in 1982 from Seoul with her husband, a graduate student. She graduated college with a degree in tourism and worked as a travel agent in Korea. In New York City, she first worked in a retail store in Manhattan, then began to work in a nail salon in Brooklyn to support her husband while he studied. After their marriage ended, she brought her mother from Korea in 1988 and with her help opened a convenience store, which failed shortly thereafter. She then opened Crosstown Nails a year later, and the business has thrived.

The secret of Crosstown Nail's success is its ability to appeal to customers who lack excess disposable income and normally would not indulge in a professional manicure but are attracted by the convenience and price. Julia, a white bartender, commented,

> I'm kind of a ragamuffin, so it kind of surprises me that I get them done as often as I do, which is still much less than most people in the city. It's just so easy to do here, and cheap.

Julia's description of herself as a "ragamuffin" suggests that she does not adhere to strict codes of femininity in her dress or other beauty routines, as indicated by her casual peasant skirt and no makeup. Nonetheless, easy and cheap access draws her into purchasing regular manicures.

Many customers at Crosstown Nails seek manicures not as a pampering experience or as creative expression but as a utilitarian measure to enhance their self-presentation at work. Merna, an Afro-Caribbean clinical researcher, explained,

> I only get them done about every two months. I don't want to get attached to it. For some women it's such a ritual, it becomes a job—maintaining the tips and stuff. I'm presenting my hands all day long so it's worth it to me to spend some time and money to make sure they look good.

Merna regards manicured nails as a professional asset more than a core aspect of a gendered self. Thus, the style of her nails and the meaning she gives to them is more similar to the white middle-class customers at Crosstown Nails than to the Black working-class customers at Downtown Nails.

In general, middle-class Black customers like Merna mostly exhibited similar nail aesthetics to those of middle-class white women, suggesting the greater importance of class over race in influencing nail styles and expectations of body labor, particularly in routinized settings such as Crosstown Nails.

DISCUSSION

The concept of emotional labor addresses how service providers present and manipulate their feelings to communicate a sense of caring and attentiveness to customers, or in Hochschild's (1983, 6) words, where "the emotional style of offering service is part of the service itself." This study of interactions in Korean-owned nail salons enriches the literature on emotional labor by expanding it to include embodied dimensions, or body labor. The embodied aspects of emotional labor not only heighten the intensity of commercialized feeling exchanges but they also point out variation in these exchanges beyond the white middle-class settings explored by most researchers. Nail salon services, and body labor more generally, are gendered work processes, but they are enacted in different forms according to the influences of race and class.

In what ways is nail salon work gendered? In what ways are these gendered work processes remolded by race and class? Understanding the influence of race and class on the gendered performance of body labor in Korean-owned nail salons illuminates how gendered work processes reflect and reproduce racial and class inequalities at the level of social structures. Nail salon work is gendered in four major dimensions: (1) It involves mostly female actors, as both service providers and customers; (2) it focuses on the construction of beauty according to feminine norms; (3) it is situated in feminized, semiprivate spaces; and (4) it involves the gendered performance of emotional labor.

In describing each of these dimensions, I do not emphasize how socialized gender roles are acted out in these establishments, but rather how gender operates as a social institution that lays the groundwork for the very existence of these businesses and frames the interactions that occur within them. Thus, I conceptualize these small businesses according to the model of gendered institutions (Marx Ferree and Hall 1996) and examine how they are constructed from the ground up through gendered ideologies, relations, and practices that sustain systematic gender inequality at the micro level of sex differences, at the meso level of group conflict, and [at] the macro levels of power, social control, and the division of labor. At the same time, I argue that as gendered institutions, they cannot be separated from forces of racial and class inequality.

If, as Paul Gilroy (1993, 85) asserted, "gender is the modality in which race is lived," then race, and I argue class as well, are lived in these nail salons and other body-service sites as differences in gendered styles of body labor. Interactions in Korean female immigrant–owned nail salons illustrate how the gendered practices of body labor become the locus of expressing and negotiating race and class hierarchies between white, Black, and Asian women. High-service body labor, as performed at Uptown Nails, is similar to the style of caring, attentive emotional labor practiced by Hochschild's flight attendants and conforms to the feeling rules of white middle-class women. Expressive body labor focuses on the physical appearance and artistry of the nails and the communication of respect and fairness in serving mostly working- and lower-middle-class African American and Caribbean women customers at Downtown Nails. Routinized body labor stresses efficiency, predictability, affordability, and competency in physical labor and a courteous but no-frills style of emotional labor geared toward mostly lower-middle- and middle-class racially mixed female customers at Crosstown Nails.

These patterns of body labor conform to the racial and class positions of the customers and the associated feeling rules that define their service expectations. At Uptown Nails, race, gender, and class intersect to produce an emotionally and physically pampering form of body labor that conforms to the expectations of white, professional women for caring and attentive service. These women have high expectations regarding massages, cleanliness, sensitive touch, and friendly conversation while Black, working-class women at Downtown Nails expect minimal pampering and focus on the appearance, originality, and durability of the nails themselves. At Crosstown Nails, class prevails over race as both Black and white women of middling socioeconomic status view the nails instrumentally as a no-nonsense professional asset rather than conforming to traditional notions of pampered femininity. Thus, they trade off the physical pleasure and emotional attentiveness of high-service treatment for the convenience and price of routinized body labor.

Black middle-class women at Crosstown Nails share this instrumental view of nails and a preference for a routinized, hassle-free manicure. The style of nails and the meaning given to them by Black middle-class women radically differ from the working-class Black women at Downtown Nails, who value nail art as a form of self-expression and demand emotional labor that communicates respect and fairness. This contrast between the Black middle-class and working-class women customers at Crosstown and Downtown Nails again suggests the greater salience of class over race in determining the type of body labor.

What structural factors explain the differences in the provision of body labor in these three sites? These body labor types, while enacted at the micro level, reflect the social conditions of the neighborhoods in which the salons are located and the clientele they serve. Because of the reliance on tips in white middle-class neighborhoods, service providers have greater incentive to cater to the emotional needs of customers such as those at Uptown Nails to increase their earnings. In the Black working-class neighborhoods where tipping is not a widespread practice, nail salon workers guarantee their economic livelihood by establishing a base of regular customers who seek them out for their technical and artistic abilities more than their emotional or physical attentiveness. In routinized body labor settings serving lower-middle-class women of mixed races, service providers maximize their earnings by generating a high turnover of customers who receive satisfactory but not special emotional and physical treatment.

These patterns of body labor service reflect and reproduce racial and class inequalities between women. Korean service providers learn to respond to white middle- and upper-class customers' emotional pampering and physical pleasure, thereby reinforcing the invisible sense of privilege claimed by these customers. The expressive practices of creating artful nails and troubleshooting potential problems with Black working-class customers, while helping to smooth relations, can also serve to emphasize racial meanings in these interactions and enforce a sense of difference. The routinized style of body labor reflects the generic social position of women whose bodies are neither privileged nor pathologized but simply treated with routine efficiency.

CONCLUSIONS

Exchanges of manicuring services set up complex emotional and embodied interactions between diverse women. In introducing and exploring the dimensions of body labor, this article challenges the scholarship on emotional labor to take more seriously the growth in body-related service jobs and to address the differences in these service interactions not simply in terms of gendered processes but through the lens of race, gender, and class intersections. Thus, not only does the concept of body labor add embodied dimensions to emotional labor, but it also makes it more applicable to low-wage service work performed by immigrant women of color.

This study situates the practice of body labor in Korean-owned nail salons within the restructuring of the global economy and the transplantation of the practices of enhancing bodily appearance from private households into new forms of public urban space. A manicure is no longer something a woman gives herself, her daughter, or a girlfriend in the quiet of her own bathroom, but it is something that she increasingly purchases in a nail salon. In purchasing these services, she not only expands the boundaries of the service economy to include formerly private regimens of personal hygiene, but she also encounters the "other," often an immigrant woman of different racial and class background through physical contact that can generate highly charged feelings on both sides. These feelings manifest and are worked out differently in distinct styles of body labor that emerge through the intersection of gendered work processes with customers' racial and class positions and their associated service expectations.

Although so far I have drawn parallels between this process of exchanging body services for a wage with the commercialization of feelings in emotional labor, another parallel can be drawn to the encroachment of the capitalist system into the area of social reproduction. Nakano Glenn (1992) and others have illuminated how the performance of household work such as cleaning, cooking, and caring for children and the elderly has become increasingly part of the capitalist market, and these low-paying, unprotected jobs (nanny, elderly caregiver, nurses, aide) are most often filled by immigrant women of color. This study has illustrated how similar to these dynamics of commodifying reproductive labor and farming it out at low wages to less privileged women, body services and the emotional labor accompanying it (what I have conceptualized as body labor) have become increasingly commercialized and designated as racialized immigrant women's work.

While this article has concentrated on my case study of nail salons, the concept of body labor can be applied to many other occupations, especially female-dominated service professions in which service providers and customers are of different race and class origins, including hairdressers, masseuses, nannies, nurses, doctors, personal trainers, and prostitutes.

Finally, in mapping out the racial, gendered, and classed complexity of body labor, this article highlights a kernel of social change that lies in negotiating service interactions between women of different classes, racial

and ethnic backgrounds, and immigrant statuses. While these interactions often mimic structures of power and privilege, they also create opportunities to contest these structures. The Korean salon owner of Downtown Nails learns to respect and show appreciation for Black working-class patrons. Korean manicurists at Uptown Nails assert their knowledge and expertise over their white middle-class customers. Routinized service at Crosstown Nails equalizes treatment of women across race and class.

From the customer's side, a weekly trip to the local nail salon can become a lesson in relating to a woman of a radically different social position, whom she would rarely encounter in her own milieu. As these emotional and embodied interactions reflect larger systems of status and power, by rewriting the unspoken feeling rules of these interactions, women can take small but important steps in the creation of more equal relations with other women. Nakano Glenn (2002, 16–17) wrote that "contesting race and gender hierarchies may involve challenging everyday assumptions and practices, take forms that do not involve direct confrontation, and occur in locations not considered political." Exchanges involving body labor in Korean-owned nail salons are one such location where these everyday assumptions and practices can be recognized and possibly renegotiated.

ACKNOWLEDGMENTS

I would like to thank Catherine Berheide, C. N. Le, Jennifer Lee, Sara Lee, Susan Walzer and Chris Bose, Minjeong Kim, and the *Gender & Society* anonymous reviewers for valuable comments and suggestions. My dissertation committee at New York University, Craig Calhoun, Jeff Goodwin, and Ruth Horowitz, and readers, Troy Duster and Kathleen Gerson, guided the theory and research design. Thanks to Liann Kang, Wi Jo Kang, Nora Choi-Lee, Jung-hwa Hwang, Eunja Lee, and especially Jiwon Lee for research assistance. Research was supported in part by New York University, the Social Science Research Council's Committee on International Migration, Skidmore College, and Grinnell College. By recognizing this study with the Cheryl Allyn Miller award, Sociologists for Women in Society provided encouragement and intellectual community. I am grateful to Myra Marx Ferree, Mitchell Duneier, and members of the Feminist Seminar and Race and Ethnicity Seminar for inviting me to present and for responding to an earlier version of this article at the University of Wisconsin–Madison, 2001.

REFERENCES

Anderson, Margaret, and Patricia Hill Collins. 2001. *Race, class, and gender: An anthology.* Belmont, CA: Wadsworth.

Baca Zinn, Maxine. 1989. Family, race, and poverty in the eighties. *Signs: Journal of Women in Culture and Society* 14:856–74.

Banks, Ingrid. 2000. *Hair matters: Beauty, power, and Black women's consciousness.* New York: New York University Press.

Banner, Lois. 1983. *American beauty.* New York: Alfred A. Knopf.

Bordo, Susan. 1993. *Unbearable weight: Feminism, Western culture and the body.* Berkeley: University of California Press.

Burawoy, Michael. 1991. *Ethnography unbound.* Berkeley: University of California Press.

Chapkis, Wendy. 1986. *Beauty secrets.* Boston: South End.

Cheng, Lucie, and Edna Bonacich. 1984. *Labor immigration under capitalism: Asian workers in the United States before World War 2.* Berkeley: University of California Press.

Frank, Arthur W. 1990. Bringing bodies back in: A decade review. *Theory, Culture, and Society* 7:131–62.

Gilroy, Paul. 1993. *The Black Atlantic: Modernity and double consciousness.* Cambridge, MA: Harvard University Press.

Gimlan, Debra. 1996. Pamela's place: Power and negotiation in the hair salon. *Gender & Society* 10:505–26.

Hall, Elaine J. 1993. Waitering/waitressing: Engendering the work of table servers. *Gender & Society* 7:329–46.

Hill Collins, Patricia. 1991. *Black feminist thought: Knowledge, consciousness, and the politics of empowerment.* New York: Routledge.

Hochschild, Arlie. 1983. *The managed heart: The commercialization of human feeling.* Berkeley: University of California Press.

hooks, bell. 1981. *Ain't I a woman: Black women and feminism.* Boston: South End.

———. 1990. *Black looks: Race and representation.* Boston: South End.

Hu-DeHart, Evelyn. 1999. *Across the Pacific: Asian Americans and globalization.* Philadelphia: Temple University Press.

Hurtado, Aida. 1989. Relating to privilege: Seduction and rejection in the subordination of white women and women of color. *Signs: Journal of Women in Culture and Society* 14:833–55.

Kang, Miliann. 1997. Manicuring race, gender, and class: Service interactions in New York City Korean nail salons. *Race, Gender, and Class* 4:143–64.

Kerner Furman, Frida. 1997. *Facing the mirror: Older women and the beauty shop culture.* New York: Routledge.

Lee, Jee-Young Jennifer. 2002. *Civility in the city: Blacks, Jews, and Koreans in urban America.* Cambridge, MA: Harvard University Press.

Leidner, Robin. 1993. *Fast food, fast talk: Service work and the routinization of everyday life.* Berkeley: University of California Press.

———. 1999. Emotional labor in service work. *Annals of the American Academy of Political and Social Science* 561:81–95.

Lively, Kathryn. 2000. Reciprocal emotion management: Working together to maintain stratification in private law firms. *Work and Occupations* 27:32–63.

Macdonald, Cameron. 1996. Shadow mothers: Nannies, au pairs, and invisible work. In *Working in the service society*, edited by Cameron Lynne Macdonald and Carmen Sirianni. Philadelphia: Temple University Press.

Marx Ferree, Myra, and Elaine J. Hall. 1996. Rethinking stratification from a feminist perspective: Gender, race, and class in mainstream textbooks. *American Sociological Review* 61:929–50.

Nakano Glenn, Evelyn. 1992. From servitude to service work: Historical continuities in the racial division of paid reproductive labor. *Signs: Journal of Women in Culture and Society* 18:1–43.

———. 2002. *Unequal freedom: How race and gender shaped American citizenship and labor.* Cambridge, MA: Harvard University Press.

Ngan-Ling Chow, Esther. 1994. Asian American women at work. In *Women of color in U.S. society*, edited by Maxine Baca Zinn and Bonnie Dill Thornton. Philadelphia: Temple University Press.

Ong, Aihwa. 1987. *Spirits of resistance and capitalist discipline: Factory women in Malaysia.* Albany: State University of New York Press.

Pierce, Jennifer L. 1995. *Gender trials: Emotional lives in contemporary law firms.* Berkeley: University of California Press.

Rooks, Noliwe. 1996. *Hair rising: Beauty, culture, and African American women.* New Brunswick. NJ: Rutgers University Press.

Schmitt, Frederika E., and Patricia Yancey Martin. 1999. Unobtrusive mobilization by an institutionalized rape crisis center: "All we do comes from victims." *Gender & Society* 13:364–84.

Smith, Dorothy. 1987. *The everyday world as problematic: A feminist sociology.* Boston: Northeastern University Press.

Steinberg, Ronnie, and Deborah Figart. 1999. Emotional labor since *The Managed Heart. Annals of the American Academy of Political and Social Science* 561:8–26.

Wharton, Amy. 1999. The psychological consequences of emotional labor. *Annals of the American Academy of Political and Social Science* 561:158–77.

Wolf, Naomi. 1991. *The beauty myth: How images of beauty are used against women.* New York: William Morrow.

THE REALITIES OF AFFIRMATIVE ACTION IN EMPLOYMENT

Barbara Reskin

Affirmative action policies and practices reduce job discrimination against minorities and white women, although their effects have not been large. Some critics charge that affirmative action's positive effects have been offset by its negative effects on white men, on productivity, and on the merit system.

For many people, the most troubling aspect of affirmative action is that it may discriminate against majority-group members (Lynch 1997). According to 1994 surveys, 70 to 80 percent of whites believed that affirmative action sometimes discriminates against whites (Steeh and Krysan 1996, p. 139). Men are more likely to believe that a woman will get a job or promotion over an equally or more qualified man than they are to believe that a man will get a promotion over an equally or more qualified woman (Davis and Smith 1996).

Several kinds of evidence indicate that whites' fears of reverse discrimination are exaggerated. Reverse discrimination is rare both in absolute terms and relative to conventional discrimination.[1] On every measured outcome, African-American men were much more likely than white men to experience discrimination, and Latinos were more likely than non-Hispanic men to experience discrimination (Heckman and Siegelman 1993, p. 218). Statistics on the numbers and outcomes of complaints of employment discrimination also suggest that reverse discrimination is rare.

According to national surveys, relatively few whites have experienced reverse discrimination. Only 5 to 12 percent of whites believe that their race has cost them a job or a promotion, compared to 36 percent of African Americans (Steeh and Krysan 1996, pp. 139–40). Of 4,025 Los Angeles workers, 45 percent of African Americans and 16 percent of Latinos said that they had been refused a job because of their race, and 16 percent of African Americans and 8 percent of Latinos reported that they had been discriminated against in terms of pay or a promotion (Bobo and Suh 1996, Table 1). In contrast, of the 863 whites surveyed, less than 3 percent had ever experienced discrimination in pay or promotion,

and only one mentioned reverse discrimination. Nonetheless, two-thirds to four-fifths of whites (but just one-quarter of African Americans) surveyed in the 1990s thought it likely that less qualified African Americans won jobs or promotions over more qualified whites (Taylor 1994a; Davis and Smith 1994; Steeh and Krysan 1996, p. 139).[2]

Alfred Blumrosen's (1996, pp. 5–6) exhaustive review of discrimination complaints filed with the Equal Employment Opportunity Commission offers additional evidence that reverse discrimination is rare. Of the 451,442 discrimination complaints filed with the EEOC between 1987 and 1994, only 4 percent charged reverse discrimination (see also Norton 1996, pp. 44–5).[3] Of the 2,189 discrimination cases that federal appellate courts decided between 1965 and 1985, *less* than 5 percent charged employers with reverse discrimination (Burstein 1991, p. 518).

Allegations of reverse discrimination are less likely than conventional discrimination cases to be supported by evidence. Of the approximately 7,000 reverse-discrimination complaints filed with the EEOC in 1994, the EEOC found only 28 credible (Crosby and Herzberger 1996, p. 55). Indeed, U.S. district and appellate courts dismissed almost all the reverse-discrimination cases they heard between 1990 and 1994 as lacking merit.

How can we reconcile the enormous gulf between whites' perceptions that they are likely to lose jobs or promotions because of affirmative action and the small risk of this happening? The white men who brought reverse-discrimination suits presumably concluded that their employers' choices of women or minorities could not have been based on merit, because men are accustomed to being selected for customarily male jobs (*New York Times*, March 31, 1995).[4] Most majority-group members who have not had a first-hand experience of competing unsuccessfully with a minority man or woman or a white woman cite media reports as the source of their impression that affirmative action prompts employers to favor minorities and women (Hochschild 1995, pp. 144, 308).[5] It seems likely that politicians' and the media's emphasis on "quotas" has distorted the public's understanding of what is required and permitted in the name of affirmative action (Entman 1997).

There is no evidence that affirmative action reduces productivity or that workers hired under affirmative action are less qualified than other workers. In the first place, affirmative action plans that compromise valid educational and job requirements are illegal. Hiring unqualified workers or choosing a less qualified person over a more qualified one because of their race or sex is illegal and is not condoned in the name of affirmative action (U.S. Department of Labor, Employment Standards Administration n.d. (b), p. 2). Second, to the extent that affirmative action gives women and minority men access to jobs that more fully exploit their productive capacity, their productivity and that of their employers should increase.

Although many Americans believe that affirmative action means that less qualified persons are hired and promoted (Verhovek 1997, p. 32), the evidence does not bear this out. According to a study of more than 3,000 workers hired in entry-level jobs in a cross-section of firms in Atlanta, Boston, Detroit, and Los Angeles, the performance evaluations of women and minorities hired under affirmative action did not differ from those of white men or female or minority workers for whom affirmative action played no role in hiring (Holzer and Neumark 1998). In addition, Columbus, Ohio, female and minority police officers hired under an affirmative action consent decree performed as well as white men (Kern 1996). Of nearly 300 corporate executives surveyed in 1979, 72 percent believed that minority hiring did not impair productivity (*Wall Street Journal* 1979); 41 percent of CEOs surveyed in 1995 said affirmative action improved corporate productivity (Crosby and Herzberger 1996, p. 86).[6]

The consequences of affirmative action reach beyond workers and employers by increasing the pools of skilled minority and female workers. When affirmative action prompts employers to hire minorities or women for positions that serve the public, it can bring services to communities that would otherwise be underserved. For example, African-American and Hispanic physicians are more likely than whites and Anglos to practice in minority communities (Komaromy et al. 1996). Graduates of the Medical School at the University of California at San Diego who were admitted under a special admissions program were more likely to serve inner-city and rural communities and saw more poor patients than those admitted under the regular procedures (Perm, Russell, and Simon 1986).

Women's and minorities' employment in non-traditional jobs also raises the aspirations of other members of excluded groups by providing role models and by signaling that jobs are open to them. Some minorities and women do not pursue jobs or promotions because they expect to encounter discrimination (Mayhew 1968, p. 313). By reducing the perception that discriminatory barriers block access to certain lines of work, affirmative action curtails this self-selection (Reskin and Roos 1990, p. 305). In addition, the economic gains provided by better jobs permit beneficiaries to invest in the education of the next generation.

The tension between affirmative action and merit is the inevitable result of the conflict between our national values and what actually occurs in the nation's workplaces. As long as discrimination is more pervasive than affirmative action, it is the real threat to meritocracy. But because no one will join the debate on behalf of discrimination, we end up with the illusion of a struggle between affirmative action and merit.

NOTES

1. Lynch's (1989, p. 53) search for white male Southern Californians who saw themselves as victims of reverse discrimination turned up only 32 men.
2. Younger whites, those from more privileged backgrounds, and those from areas with larger black populations—especially black populations who were relatively well off—were the most likely to believe that blacks benefited from preferential treatment (Taylor 1994b).
3. Two percent were by white men charging sex, race, or national-origin discrimination (three-quarters of these charged sex discrimination), and 1.8 percent were by white women charging race discrimination (Blumrosen 1996, p. 5).
4. Occupational segregation by sex, race, and ethnicity no doubt contributes to this perception by reinforcing the notion that one's sex, color, or ethnicity is naturally related to the ability to perform a particular job.

(continued)

5. The disproportionate number of court-ordered interventions to curtail race and sex discrimination in cities'
   police and fire departments (Martin 1991) and the large
   number of court challenges by white men (Bureau of
   National Affairs 1995, pp. 5–12) probably contributed
   to the public's impression that hiring quotas are
   common.
6. No data were provided on the proportion who believed
   that affirmative action hampered productivity.

REFERENCES

Blumrosen, Alfred W. 1996. *Declaration*. Statement submitted to the Supreme Court of California in response
   to Proposition 209, September 26.

Bobo, Larry, and Susan A. Suh. 1996. "Surveying Racial
   Discrimination: Analyses from a Multi-Ethnic Labor
   Market." Working Paper No. 75, Russell Sage Founda-
   tion, New York.

Bureau of National Affairs. 1995. *Affirmative Action After
   Adarand: A Legal, Regulatory, Legislative Outlook.*
   Washington, DC: The Bureau of National Affairs.

Burstein, Paul. 1991. " 'Reverse Discrimination' Cases in
   the Federal Courts: Mobilization by a Countermovement." *Sociological Quarterly* 32:511–28.

Crosby, Faye J., and Sharon D. Herzberger. 1996. "For
   Affirmative Action." Pp. 3–109 in *Affirmative Action:
   Pros and Cons of Policy and Practice*, ed. R. J. Simon.
   Washington, DC: American University Press.

Davis, James A., and Tom W. Smith. 1994. *General Social
   Survey* [MRDF]. Chicago, IL: National Opinion
   Research Center [producer, distributor].

———. 1996. *General Social Survey* [MRDF]. Chicago,
   IL: National Opinion Research Center [producer,
   distributor].

Entman, Robert M. 1997. "Manufacturing Discord: Media in
   the Affirmative Action Debate." *Press/Politics* 2:32–51.

Heckman, James J., and Peter Siegelman. 1993. "The Urban
   Institute Audit Studies: Their Methods and Findings."
   Pp. 187–229 in *Clear and Convincing Evidence. Measurement
   of Discrimination in America*, ed. M. Fix and R. J. Struyk.
   Washington, DC: The Urban Institute.

Hochschild, Jennifer. 1995. *Facing Up to the American
   Dream*. Princeton, NJ: Princeton University Press.

Holzer, Harry J., and David Neumark. Forthcoming 1998.
   "Are Affirmative Action Hires Less Qualified?
   Evidence from Employer–Employee Data on New
   Hires." *Journal of Labor Economics*.

Kern, Leesa. 1996. "Hiring and Seniority: Issues in Policing
   in the Post-Judicial Intervention Period." Department
   of Sociology, Ohio State University, Columbus, OH:
   Unpublished manuscript.

Komaromy, Miriam, Kevin Grumbach, Michael Drake,
   Karen Vranizan, Nicole Lurie, Dennis Keane, and
   Andrew Bindman. 1996. "The Role of Black and
   Hispanic Physicians in Providing Health Care for
   Underserved Populations." *New England Journal of
   Medicine* 334:1305–10.

Lynch, Frederick R. 1989. *Invisible Victims: White Males and
   the Crisis of Affirmative Action*. New York: Greenwood.

———. 1997. *The Diversity Machine: The Drive to Change the
   White Male Workplace*. New York: Free Press.

Martin, Susan E. 1991. "The Effectiveness of Affirmative
   Action: The Case of Women in Policing." *Justice
   Quarterly* 8:489–504.

Mayhew, Leon. 1968. *Law and Equal Opportunity: A Study
   of Massachusetts Commission Against Discrimination.*
   Cambridge, MA: Harvard University Press.

New York Times. 1995. "Reverse Discrimination Complaints
   Rare. Labor Study Reports." *New York Times*, March 31,
   p. A23.

Norton, Eleanor Holmes. 1996. "Affirmative Action in the
   Workplace." Pp. 39–48 in *The Affirmative Action Debate*,
   ed. G. Curry. Reading, MA: Addison-Wesley.

Penn, Nolan E., Percy J. Russell, and Harold J. Simon.
   1986. "Affirmative Action at Work: A Survey of
   Graduates of the University of California at San Diego
   Medical School." *American Journal of Public Health*
   76:1144–46.

Reskin, Barbara F., and Patricia Roos. 1990. *Job Queues, Gender
   Queues*. Philadelphia, PA: Temple University Press.

Steeh, Charlotte, and Maria Krysan. 1996. "The Polls—
   Trends. Affirmative Action and the Public, 1970–1995."
   Public Opinion Quarterly 60:128–58.

Taylor, Marylee C. 1994a. "Beliefs About the Preferential
   Hiring of Black Applicants: Sure It Happens, But
   I've Never Seen It." Pennsylvania State University,
   University Park, PA. Unpublished manuscript.

———. 1994b. "Impact of Affirmative Action on Beneficiary
   Groups: Evidence from the 1990 General Social
   Survey." *Basic and Applied Social Psychology* 15: 143–78.

U.S. Department of Labor, Employment Standards
   Administration, Office of Federal Contract Compliance
   Programs [cited as OFCCP]. The Rhetoric and the
   Reality About Federal Affirmative Action at the
   OFCCP." Washington, DC: U.S. Department of Labor.

Verhovek, Sam Howe. 1997. "In Poll, Americans Reject
   Means but Not Ends of Racial Diversity." *New York
   Times*, December 14, 1, 32.

Wall Street Journal. 1979. "Labor Letter: A Special News
   Report on People and Their Jobs in Offices, Fields and
   Factories: Affirmative Action Is Accepted by Most
   Corporate Chiefs." *Wall Street Journal*, April 3, p. 1.

Maid in L.A.

The title of this [reading] was inspired by Mary Romero's 1992 book, *Maid in the U.S.A.*, but I am also taking the pun to heart: most Latina immigrant women who do paid domestic work in Los Angeles had no prior experience working as domestics in their countries of origin. Of the 153 Latina domestic workers that I surveyed at bus stops, in ESL classes, and in parks, fewer than 10 percent reported having worked in other people's homes, or taking in laundry for pay, in their countries of origin. This finding is perhaps not surprising, as we know from immigration research that the poorest of the poor rarely migrate to the United States; they simply cannot afford to do so.

Some of the Latina immigrant women who come to Los Angeles grew up in impoverished squatter settlements, others in comfortable homes with servants. In their countries of origin, these women were housewives raising their own children, or college students, factory workers, store clerks, and secretaries; still others came from rural families of very modest means. Regardless of their diverse backgrounds, their transformation into housecleaners and nanny/housekeepers occurs in Los Angeles. I emphasize this point because images in popular culture and the media more or less identify Latinas with domestic workers—or, more precisely, as "cleaning gals" and "baby-sitters," euphemisms that mask American discomfort with these arrangements. Yet they take on these roles only in the United States, at various points in their own migration and settlement trajectories, in the context of private households, informal social networks, and the larger culture's racialized nativism.

Who are these women who come to the United States in search of jobs, and what are those jobs like? Domestic work is organized in different ways, and in this [reading] I describe live-in, live-out, and house-cleaning jobs and profile some of the Latina immigrants who do them and how they feel about their work. The [reading] concludes with a discussion of why it is that Latina immigrants are the primary recruits to domestic work, and I examine what they and their employers have to say about race relations and domestic work.

LIVE-IN NANNY/HOUSEKEEPER JOBS

For Maribel Centeno, newly arrived from Guatemala City in 1989 at age twenty-two and without supportive family and friends with whom to stay, taking a live-in job made a lot of sense. She knew that she wouldn't have to spend money on room and board, and that she could soon begin saving to pay off her debts. Getting a live-in job through an agency was easy. The *señora*, in her rudimentary Spanish, only asked where she was from, and if she had a husband and children. Chuckling, Maribel recalled her initial misunderstanding when the *señora*, using her index finger, had drawn an imaginary "2" and "3" in the palm of her hand. "I thought to myself, well, she must have two or three bedrooms, so I said, fine. 'No,' she said. 'Really, really big.' She started counting, 'One, two, three, four . . . two-three rooms.' It was twenty-three rooms! I thought, huy! On a piece of paper, she wrote '$80 a week,' and she said, 'You, child, and entire house.' So I thought, well, I have to do what I have to do, and I happily said, 'Yes.'"

"I arrived on Monday at dawn," she recalled, "and I went to the job on Wednesday evening." When the *señora* and the child spoke to her, Maribel remembered "just laughing and feeling useless. I couldn't understand anything." On that first evening, the *señora* put on classical music, which Maribel quickly identified. "I said, 'Beethoven.' She said, 'Yeah,' and began asking me in English, 'You like it?' I said 'Yes,' or perhaps I said, 'Si,' and she began playing other cassettes, CDs. They had Richard Clayderman and I recognized it, and when I said that, she stopped in her tracks, her jaw fell open, and she just stared at me. She must have been thinking, 'No schooling, no preparation, no English, how does she know this music?'" But the *señora*, perhaps because of the language difficulty, or perhaps because she felt upstaged by her live-in's knowledge of classical music, never did ask. Maribel desperately wanted the *señora* to respect her, to recognize that she was smart, educated, and cultivated in the arts. In spite of her best status-signaling efforts, "They treated me," she said, "the same as any other girl from the countryside." She never got the verbal recognition that she desired from the *señora*.

Maribel summed up her experiences with her first live-in job this way: "The pay was bad. The treatment was, how shall I say? It was cordial, a little, uh, not racist, but with very little consideration, very little respect." She liked caring for the little seven-year-old boy, but keeping after the cleaning of the twenty-three-room house, filled with marble floors and glass tables, proved physically impossible. She eventually quit not because of the polishing and scrubbing, but because being ignored devastated her socially.

Compared to many other Latina immigrants' first live-in jobs, Maribel Centeno's was relatively good. She was not on call during all her waking hours and throughout the night, the parents were engaged with the child, and she was not required to sleep in a child's bedroom or on a cot tucked away in the laundry room. But having a private room filled with amenities did not mean she had privacy or the ability to do simple things one might take for granted. "I had my own room, with my own television, VCR, my private bath, and closet, and a kind of sitting room—but everything in minia-ture, Thumbelina style," she said. "I had privacy in that respect. But I couldn't do many things. If I wanted to walk around in a T-shirt, or just feel like I was home, I couldn't do that. If I was hungry in the evening, I wouldn't come out to grab a banana because I'd have to walk through the family room, and then everybody's watching and having to smell the banana. I could never feel at home, never. Never, never, never! There's always something invisible that tells you this is not your house, you just work here."

It is the rare California home that offers separate maid's quarters, but that doesn't stop families from hiring live-ins; nor does it stop newly arrived Latina migrant workers from taking jobs they urgently need. When live-ins cannot even retreat to their own rooms, work seeps into their sleep and their dreams. There is no time off from the job, and they say they feel con-fined, trapped, imprisoned.

"I lose a lot of sleep," said Margarita Gutiérrez, a twenty-four-year-old Mexicana who worked as a live-in nanny/housekeeper. At her job in a modest-sized condominium in Pasadena, she slept in a corner of a three-year-old child's bedroom. Consequently, she found herself on call day and night with the child, who sometimes went several days without seeing her mother because of the latter's schedule at an insurance company. Margarita was obliged to be on her job twenty-four hours a day; and like other live-in nanny/housekeepers I interviewed, she claimed that she could scarcely find time to shower or brush her teeth. "I go to bed fine," she reported, "and then I wake up at two or three in the morning with the girl asking for water, or food." After the child went back to sleep, Margarita would lie awake, thinking about how to leave her job but finding it hard to even walk out into the kitchen. Live-in employees like Margarita literally have no space and no time they can claim as their own.

Working in a larger home or staying in plush, pri-vate quarters is no guarantee of privacy or refuge from the job. Forty-four-year-old Elvia Lucero worked as a live-in at a sprawling, canyon-side residence, where she was in charge of looking after twins, two five-year-old girls. On numerous occasions when I visited her there, I saw that she occupied her own bedroom, a beautifully decorated one outfitted with delicate antiques, plush white carpet, and a stenciled border of pink roses painstakingly painted on the wall by the employer. It looked serene and inviting, but it was only three steps away from the twins' room. Every night one of the twins crawled into bed with Elvia. Elvia dis-liked this, but said she couldn't break the girl of the habit. And the parents' room lay tucked away at the opposite end of the large (more than 3,000 square feet), L-shaped house.

Regardless of the size of the home and the splendor of the accommodations, the boundaries that we might normally take for granted disappear in live-in jobs. They have, as Evelyn Nakano Glenn has noted, "no clear line between work and non-work time," and the line between job space and private space is similarly blurred.[1] Live-in nanny/housekeepers are at once socially isolated and surrounded by other people's ter-ritory; during the hours they remain on the employers' premises, their space, like their time, belongs to another. The sensation of being among others while remaining invisible, unknown and apart, of never being able to leave the margins, makes many live-in employees sad, lonely, and depressed. Melancholy sets in and doesn't necessarily lift on the weekends.

Rules and regulations may extend around the clock. Some employers restrict the ability of their live-in employees to receive telephone calls, entertain friends, attend evening ESL classes, or see boyfriends during the workweek. Other employers do not impose these sorts of restrictions, but because their homes are located on remote hillsides, in suburban enclaves, or in gated communities, their live-in nanny/housekeepers are effectively kept away from anything resembling social life or public culture. A Spanish-language radio station, or maybe a *telenovela*, may serve as their only link to the outside world.

Food—the way some employers hoard it, waste it, deny it, or just simply do not even have any of it in their kitchens—is a frequent topic of discussion among Latina live-in nanny/housekeepers. These women are talking not about counting calories but about the social meaning of food on the job. Almost no one works with a written contract, but anyone taking a live-in job that includes "room and board" would assume that adequate meals will be included. But what constitutes an adequate meal? Everyone has a different idea, and using the subject like a secret handshake, Latina domestic workers often greet one another by talking about the problems of managing food and meals on the job. Inevitably, food enters their conversations.

No one feels the indignities of food more deeply than do live-in employees, who may not leave the job for up to six days at a time. For them, the workplace necessarily becomes the place of daily sustenance. In some of the homes where they work, the employers are out all day. When these adults return home, they may only snack, keeping on hand little besides hot dogs, packets of macaroni and cheese, cereal, and peanut butter for the children. Such foods are considered neither nutritious nor appetizing by Latina immigrants, many of whom are accustomed to sitting down to meals prepared with fresh vegetables, rice, beans, and meat. In some employers' homes, the cupboards are literally bare. Gladys Villedas recalled that at one of her live-in jobs, the *señora* had graciously said, " 'Go ahead, help yourself to anything in the kitchen.' But at times," she recalled, "there was nothing, nothing in the refrigerator! There was nothing to eat!" Even in lavish kitchens outfitted with Subzero refrigerators and imported cabinetry, food may be scarce. A celebrity photographer of luxury homes that appear in posh magazines described to a reporter what he sees when he opens the doors of some of Beverly Hills' refrigerators: "Rows of cans of Diet Coke, and maybe a few remains of pizza."[2]

Further down the class ladder, some employers go to great lengths to economize on food bills. Margarita

Gutiérrez claimed that at her live-in job, the husband did the weekly grocery shopping, but he bought things in small quantities—say, two potatoes that would be served in half portions, or a quarter of a watermelon to last a household of five all week. He rationed out the bottled water and warned her that milk would make her fat. Lately, she said, he was taking both her and the children to an upscale grocery market where they gave free samples of gourmet cheeses, breads, and dips, urging them all to fill up on the freebies. "I never thought," exclaimed Margarita, formerly a secretary in Mexico City, "that I would come to this country to experience hunger!"

Many women who work as live-ins are keenly aware of how food and meals underline the boundaries between them and the families for whom they work. "I never ate with them," recalled Maribel Centeno of her first live-in job. "First of all, she never said, 'Come and join us,' and secondly, I just avoided being around when they were about to eat." Why did she avoid mealtime? "I didn't feel I was part of that family. I knew they liked me, but only because of the good work I did, and because of the affection I showered on the boy; but apart from that, I was just like the gardener, like the pool man, just one more of their staff." Sitting down to share a meal symbolizes membership in a family, and Latina employees, for the most part, know they are not just like one of the family.

Food scarcity is not endemic to all of the households where these women work. In some homes, ample quantities of fresh fruits, cheeses, and chicken stock the kitchens. Some employer families readily share all of their food, but in other households, certain higher-quality, expensive food items may remain off-limits to the live-in employees, who are instructed to eat hot dogs with the children. One Latina live-in nanny/housekeeper told me that in her employers' substantial pantry, little "DO NOT TOUCH" signs signaled which food items were not available to her; and another said that her employer was always defrosting freezer-burned leftovers for her to eat, some of it dating back nearly a decade.

Other women felt subtle pressure to remain unobtrusive, humble, and self-effacing, so they held back from eating even when they were hungry. They talked a lot about how these unspoken rules apply to fruit. "Look, if they [the employers] buy fruit, they buy three bananas, two apples, two pears. So if I eat one, who took it? It's me," one woman said, "they'll know it's me." Another nanny/housekeeper recalled: "They would bring home fruit, but without them having to say it, you just knew these were not intended for you. You understand this right away, you get it." Or as another put it, "Las Americanos have their apples counted out, one for each day of the week." Even fruits growing in the garden are sometimes contested. In Southern California's agriculture-friendly climate, many a residential home boasts fruit trees that hang heavy with oranges, plums, and peaches, and when the Latina women who work in these homes pick the fruit, they sometimes get in trouble.[3] Eventually, many of the women solve the food problem by buying and bringing in their own food; early on Monday mornings, you see them walking with their plastic grocery bags, carting, say, a sack of apples, some chicken, and maybe some prepared food in plastic containers.

The issue of food captures the essence of how Latina live-in domestic workers feel about their jobs. It symbolizes the extent to which the families they work for draw the boundaries of exclusion or inclusion, and it marks the degree to which those families recognize the live-in nanny/housekeepers as human beings who have basic human needs. When they first take their jobs, most live-in nanny/housekeepers do not anticipate spending any of their meager wages on food to eat while on the job, but in the end, most do—and sometimes the food they buy is eaten by members of the family for whom they work.

Although there is a wide range of pay, many Latina domestic workers in live-in jobs earn less than minimum wage for marathon hours: 93 percent of the live-in workers I surveyed in the mid-1990s were earning less than $5 an hour (79 percent of them below minimum wage, which was then $4.25), and they reported working an average of sixty-four hours a week.[4] Some of the most astoundingly low rates were paid for live-in jobs in the households of other working-class Latino immigrants, which provide some women their first job when they arrive in Los Angeles. Carmen Vasquez, for example, had spent several years working as a live-in for two Mexican families, earning only $50 a week. By comparison, her current salary of $170 a week, which she was earning as a live-in nanny/housekeeper in the hillside home of an attorney and a teacher, seemed a princely sum.

Many people assume that the rich pay more than do families of modest means, but working as a live-in in an exclusive, wealthy neighborhood, or in a twenty-three-room house, provides no guarantee of a high salary. Early one Monday morning in the fall of 1995, I was standing with a group of live-in nanny/housekeepers on a corner across the street from the Beverly Hills Hotel. As they were waiting to be picked up by their employers, a large Mercedes sedan with two women (a daughter and mother or mother-in-law?) approached, rolled down the windows, and asked if anyone was interested in a $150-a-week live-in job. A few women jotted down the phone number, and no one was shocked by the offer. Gore Vidal once commented that no one is allowed to fail within a two-mile radius of the Beverly Hills Hotel, but it turns out that plenty of women in that vicinity are failing in the salary department. In some of the most affluent Westside areas of Los Angeles—in Malibu, Pacific Palisades, and Bel Air—there are live-in nanny/housekeepers earning $150 a week. And in 1999, the *Los Angeles Times* Sunday classified ads still listed live-in nanny/housekeeper jobs with pay as low as $100 and $125.[5] Salaries for live-in jobs, however, do go considerably higher. The best-paid live-in employee whom I interviewed was Patricia Paredes, a Mexicana who spoke impeccable English and who had legal status, substantial experience, and references. She told me that she currently earned $450 a week at her live-in job. She had been promised a raise to $550, after a room remodel was finished, when she would assume weekend housecleaning in that same home. With such a relatively high weekly salary she felt compelled to stay in a live-in job during the week, away from her husband and three young daughters who remained on the east side of Los Angeles. The salary level required that sacrifice.

But once they experience it, most women are repelled by live-in jobs. The lack of privacy, the mandated separation from family and friends, the round-the-clock hours, the food issues, the low pay, and especially the constant loneliness prompt most Latina immigrants to seek other job arrangements. Some young, single women who learn to speak English fluently try to move up the ranks into higher-paying live-in jobs. As soon as they can, however, the majority attempt to leave live-in work altogether. Most live-in nanny/housekeepers have been in the United States for five years or less; among the live-in nanny/housekeepers I interviewed, only two (Carmen Vasquez and the relatively high-earning Patricia Paredes) had been in the United States for longer than that. Like African American women earlier in the century, who tired of what the historian Elizabeth Clark-Lewis has called "the soul-destroying hollowness of live-in domestic work,"[6] most Latina immigrants try to find other options.

Until the early 1900s, live-in jobs were the most common form of paid domestic work in the United States, but through the first half of the twentieth century they were gradually supplanted by domestic "day work."[7] Live-in work never completely disappeared, however, and in the last decades of the twentieth century, it revived with vigor, given new life by the needs of American families with working parents and young children—and, as we have seen, by the needs of newly arrived Latina immigrants, many of them unmarried and unattached to families. When these women try to move up from live-in domestic work, they see few job alternatives. Often, the best they can do is switch to another form of paid domestic work, either as a live-out nanny/housekeeper or as a weekly housecleaner. When they do such day work, they are better able to circumscribe their work hours, and they earn more money in less time.[8]

LIVE-OUT NANNY/HOUSEKEEPERS

When I first met twenty-four-year-old Ronalda Saavedra, she was peeling a hard-boiled egg for a dog in the kitchen of a very large home where I was interviewing the employer. At this particular domestic job, the fifth she had held since migrating from El Salvador in 1991, she arrived daily around one in the afternoon and left after the children went to bed. On a typical day, she assisted the housekeeper, a middle-aged woman, with cleaning, laundry, and errands, and at three o'clock she drove off in her own car to pick up the children—a nine-year-old boy, whom she claimed was always angry, and his hyperactive six-year-old brother.

Once the children were put to bed, Ronalda Saavedra drove home to a cozy apartment that she shared with her brother in the San Fernando Valley. When I visited her, I saw that it was a tiny place, about half the size of the kitchen where we had first met; but it was pleasantly outfitted with new bleached oak furniture, and the morning sunshine that streamed in through a large window gave it a cheerful, almost spacious feel. Ronalda kept a well-stocked refrigerator, and during our interview she served me *pan dulce*, coffee, and honeydew melon.

Like many other women, Ronalda had begun her work stint in the United States with a live-in job, but she vastly preferred living out. She slept through the night in peace, attended ESL classes in the morning, ate what she wanted when she wanted it, and talked daily on the phone with her fiancé. All this was possible because live-out jobs are firmly circumscribed. Even when women find it difficult to say no to their employers when they are asked, at the last minute, to stay and work another hour or two, they know they will eventually retreat to their own places. So while the workday tasks and rhythms are similar to those of live-ins, the job demands on live-outs stop when they exit the houses where they work and return to their own homes, usually small and sometimes crowded apartments located in one of Los Angeles' many Latino neighborhoods. For such women with husbands or with children of their own, live-out jobs allow them to actually live with their family members and see them daily.

Live-out nanny/housekeepers also earn more money than live-ins. Most of them work eight or nine hours a day, and of those I surveyed, 60 percent worked five days a week or fewer. Their mean hourly wages were $5.90—not an exorbitant wage by any means, but above the legal minimum, unlike the wages of their peers in live-in jobs. Ronalda earned $350 for her forty-hour workweek, making her hourly wage $8.75. On top of this, her employer gave her an additional $50 to cover gasoline expenses, as Ronalda spent a portion of each afternoon driving on errands, such as going to the dry cleaners, and ferrying the children home from school and then to and from soccer practices, music lessons, and so on. In the suburban landscape of Los Angeles, employers pay an extra premium for nanny/housekeepers who can provide this shuttling service. Only Latina nanny/housekeepers with experience, strong references, English skills, and an impressive array of certificates and licenses enjoy earnings that reach Ronalda's level.

Today, most Americans who hire a domestic worker to come into their homes on a daily basis do so in order to meet their needs for *both* housecleaning and child care. Most Latina nanny/housekeepers work in households where they are solely responsible for these tasks, and they work hard to fit in the cleaning and laundry (most of them don't cook) while the children are napping or at school. Some of them feel, as one woman said, that they need to be "octopuses," with busy arms extended simultaneously in all directions. A big part of their job requires taking care of the children; and various issues with the children present nanny/housekeepers with their greatest frustrations. Paradoxically, they also experience some of their deepest job satisfaction with these children with whom they spend so much time.

After what may be years of watching, feeding, playing with, and reprimanding the same child from birth to elementary school, day in and day out, some nanny/housekeepers grow very fond of their charges and look back nostalgically, remembering, say, when a child took her first steps or first learned nursery rhymes in Spanish. Ronalda, an articulate, highly animated woman who told stories using a lot of gestures and facial expressions, talked a great deal about the children she had cared for in her various jobs. She imitated the voices of children she had taken care of, describing longingly little girls who were, she said, "*muy* nice" or "*tan* sweet," and recalled the imaginary games they would play. Like many other nanny/housekeepers, she wept freely when she remembered some of the intimate and amusing moments she had spent with children she no longer saw. She also described other children who, she said, were dour, disrespectful, and disobedient.

Many live-out nanny/housekeepers made care work—the work of keeping the children clean, happy, well nourished, and above all safe—a priority over housecleaning duties. This sometimes created conflicts with their employers, who despite saying that their children should come first still expected a spotless house. "The truth is," explained Teresa Portillo, who looked after a child only on the weekends, "when you are taking care of children, you can't neglect anything, absolutely nothing! Because the moment you do, they do whatever little *travesura*, and they scrape their knees, cut themselves or whatever." Nanny/housekeepers fear they will be sent to jail if anything happens to the children.

Feeding the children is a big part of the job. Unlike their live-in peers, when live-out nanny/housekeepers talk about food, they're usually concerned with what the children eat or don't eat. Some of them derive tremendous pleasure and satisfaction from bringing the children special treats prepared at their own homes— maybe homemade flan or *pan con crema*, or simply a mango. Some nanny/housekeepers are also in charge, to their dismay, of feeding and cleaning the children's menagerie of pets. Many feel disgusted when they have to bathe and give eyedrops to old, sick dogs, or clean the cages of iguanas, snakes, lizards, and various rodents. But these tasks are trivial in comparison to the difficulties they encounter with hard-to-manage children. Mostly, though, they complain about permissive, neglectful parents.

Not all nanny/housekeepers bond tightly with their employers' children, but most are critical of what they perceive as their employers' careless parenting—or, more accurately, mothering, for their female employers typically receive the blame. They see mothers who may spend, they say, only a few minutes a day with their babies and toddlers, or who return home from work after the children are asleep. Soraya Sanchez said she could understand mothers who work "out of necessity," but all other mothers, she believed, hired nanny/housekeepers because they just didn't like being with their own kids. "*La Americana* is very selfish, she only thinks about herself," she said. "They prefer not to be with their children, as they find it's much easier to pay someone to do that." Her critique was shared by many nanny/housekeepers; and those with children of their own, even if they didn't live with them, saw their own mothering as far superior. "I love my kids, they don't. It's just like, excuse the word, 'shitting kids'" said Patricia Paredes. "What they prefer is to go to the salon, get their nails done, you know, go shopping, things like that. Even if they're home all day, they don't want to spend time with the kids because they're paying somebody to do that for them." For many Latina nanny/housekeepers, seething class resentments find expression in the rhetoric of comparative mothering.

When Latina immigrant women enter the homes of middle-class and upper-middle-class Americans, they encounter ways of raising children very different from those with which they are familiar. As Julia Wrigley's research has shown, the child-rearing values of many Latina and Caribbean nannies differ from those of their employers, but most are eager to do what middle-class parents want—to adopt "time out" discipline measures instead of swatting, or to impose limits on television viewing and Nintendo.[9] Some of them not only adapt but come to genuinely admire and appreciate such methods of child rearing. Yet they, too, criticize the parenting styles they witness close up in the homes where they work.

Some nanny/housekeepers encounter belligerent young children, who yell at them, call them names, and throw violent temper tantrums; and when they do, they blame the parents. They are aghast when parents, after witnessing a child scratch or bite or spit at them, simply shrug their shoulders and ignore such behavior. Parents' reactions to these incidents were a litmus test of sorts. Gladys Villedas, for example, told me that at her job, a five-year-old "grabbed my hair and pulled it really hard. Ay! It hurt so much I started crying! It really hurt my feelings because never in my own country, when I was raising my children, had this happened to me. Why should this happen to me here?" When she complained to her employer, she said the employer had simply consulted a child-rearing manual and explained that it was "a stage." Not all nanny/housekeepers encounter physically abusive children, but when they do, they prefer parents who allow them the authority to impose discipline, or who back them up by firmly instructing their children that it is not okay to kick or slap the nanny. Nanny/housekeepers spoke glowingly about these sorts of employers.

When nanny/housekeepers see parent-child interactions in the homes where they work, they are often put off and puzzled by what they observe. In these moments, the huge cultural gulf between Latina nanny/housekeepers and their employers seems even wider than they had initially imagined. In the home where Maribel Centeno was working as a live-out nanny/housekeeper, she spent the first few hours of her shift doing laundry and housecleaning, but when a thirteen-year-old boy, of whom she was actually very fond, arrived home from school, her real work began. It was his pranks, which were neither malicious nor directed at her, and parental tolerance of these, that drove her crazy. These adolescent pranks usually involved items like water balloons, firecrackers, and baking soda made to look like cocaine. Recently the boy had tacked up on his parents' bedroom door a condom filled with a small amount of milk and a little sign that read, "Mom and Dad, this could have been my life." Maribel thought this was inappropriate behavior; but more bewildering and disturbing than the boy's prank was his mother's reaction—laughter. Another nanny/housekeeper had reacted with similar astonishment when, after a toddler tore apart a loaf of French bread and threw the pieces, balled like cotton, onto the floor, the father came forward not to reprimand but to record the incident with a camcorder. The regularity with which their employers waste food astounds them, and drug use also raises their eyebrows. Some nanny/housekeepers are instructed to give Ritalin and Prozac to children as young as five or six, and others tell of parents and teens locked in their separate bedrooms, each smoking marijuana.

Nanny/housekeepers blame permissive and neglectful parents, who they feel don't spend enough time with their own children, for the children's unruly behavior and for teen drug use. "The parents, they say 'yes' to everything the child asks," complained one woman. "Naturally," she added, "the children are going to act

spoiled." Another nanny/housekeeper analyzed the situation this way: "They [the parents] feel guilty because they don't spend that much time with the kids, and they want to replace that missed time, that love, with toys."

Other nanny/housekeepers prided themselves on taming and teaching the children to act properly. "I really had to battle with these children just to get them to pay attention to me! When I started with them, they had no limits, they didn't pick up their toys, and they couldn't control their tempers. The eldest—oof! He used to kick and hit me, and in public! I was mortified," recalled Ronalda Saavedra. Another woman remarked of children she had looked after, "These kids listened to me. After all, they spent most of the time with me, and not with them [the parents]. They would arrive at night, maybe spend a few moments with the kids, or maybe the kids were already asleep." Elvia Areola highlighted the injustice of rearing children whom one will never see again. Discussing her previous job, she said, "I was the one who taught that boy to talk, to walk, to read, to sit! Everything! She [the child's mother] almost never picked him up! She only picked him up when he was happy." Another nanny/housekeeper concluded, "These parents don't really know their own children. Just playing with them, or taking them to the park, well, that's not raising children. I'm the one who is with them every day."

Nanny/housekeepers must also maneuver around jealous parents, who may come to feel that their children's affections have been displaced. "The kids fall in love with you and they [the parents] wonder why. Some parents are jealous of what the kids feel toward you," said Ronalda Saavedra, "I'm not going to be lying, 'I'm your mommy,' but in a way, children go to the person who takes care of them, you know? That's just the way it is." For many nanny/housekeepers, it is these ties of affection that make it possible for them to do their job by making it rewarding. Some of them say they can't properly care for the children without feeling a special fondness for them; others say it just happens naturally. "I fall in love with all of these children. How can I not? That's just the way I am," one nanny/housekeeper told me. "I'm with them all day, and when I go home, my husband complains that that's all I talk about, what they did, the funny things they said." The nanny/housekeepers, as much as they felt burdened by disobedient children, sometimes felt that these children were also a gift of sorts, one that parents—again, the mothers—did not fully appreciate. "The babies are so beautiful!" gushed Soraya Sanchez. "How is it that a mother can lose those best years, when their kids are babies. I mean, I remember going down for a nap with these little babies, how we'd cuddle. How is it that a person who has the option of enjoying that would prefer to give that experience to a stranger?" Precisely because of such feelings, many Latina immigrants who have children try to find a job that is compatible with their own family lives. Housecleaning is one of those jobs.

HOUSECLEANERS

Like many working mothers, every weekday morning Marisela Ramírez awoke to dress and feed her preschooler, Tomás, and drive him to school (actually, a Head Start program) before she herself ventured out to work, navigating the dizzying array of Los Angeles freeways. Each day she set off in a different direction headed for a different workplace. On Mondays she maneuvered her way to Pasadena, where she cleaned the stately home of an elderly couple; on Tuesdays she alternated between cleaning a home in the Hollywood Hills and a more modest-sized duplex in Glendale; and Wednesdays took her to a split-level condominium in Burbank. You had to keep alert, she said, to remember where to go on which days and how to get there!

By nine o'clock she was usually on the job, and because she zoomed through her work she was able to finish, unless the house was extremely dirty, by one or two in the afternoon. After work, there were still plenty of daylight hours left for Marisela to take Tomás to the park, or at least to take him outside and let him ride down the sidewalk on his kid-sized motorized vehicle before she started dinner. Working as a housecleaner allowed Marisela to be the kind of wife and mother she wanted to be. Her job was something she did, she said, "because I have to"; but unlike her peers who work in live-in jobs, she enjoyed a fairly regular family life of her own, one that included cooking and eating family meals, playing with her son, bathing him, putting him to bed, and then watching *telenovelas* in the evenings with her husband and her sister. On the weekends, family socializing took center stage, with *carne asadas* in the park; informal gatherings with her large Mexican family, which extended throughout Los Angeles; and music from her husband, who worked as a gardener but played guitar in a weekend *ranchera* band.

Some might see Marisela Ramírez as just another low-wage worker doing dirty work, but by her own account—and gauging by her progress from her starting point—she had made remarkable occupational strides. Marisela had begun working as a live-in nanny/housekeeper in Los Angeles when she was only fifteen years old. Ten years later, the move from live-in work to housecleaning had brought her higher hourly wages, a shorter workweek, control over the pace of work, and flexibility in arranging when she worked. Cleaning different houses was also, she said, less boring than working as a nanny/housekeeper, which entailed passing every single day "in just one house, all week long with the same routine, over and over."

For a while she had tried factory work, packaging costume jewelry in a factory warehouse located in the San Fernando Valley, but Marisela saw housecleaning as preferable on just about every count. "In the factory, one has to work very, very fast!" she exclaimed. "And you can't talk to anybody, you can't stop, and you can't rest until it's break time. When you're working in a house, you can take a break at the moment you wish, finish the house when you want, and leave at the hour you decide. And it's better pay. It's harder work, yes," she conceded, "but it's better pay."

"How much were you earning at the factory?" I asked.

"Five dollars an hour; and working in houses now, I make about $11, or even more. Look, in a typical house, I enter at about 9 A.M., and I leave at 1 P.M., and they pay me $60. It's much better [than factory work]." Her income varied, but she could usually count on weekly earnings of about $300. By pooling these together with her husband's and sister's earnings, she was able to rent a one-bedroom bungalow roofed in red tile, with a lawn and a backyard for Tomás's sandbox and plastic swimming pool. In Mexico, Marisela had only studied as far as fifth grade, but she wanted the best for Tomás. Everyone doted on him, and by age four he was already reading simple words.

Of the housecleaners I surveyed, the majority earned, like Marisela, between $50 and $60 per housecleaning, which usually took about six hours. This suggests an average hourly wage of about $9.50, but I suspect the actual figure is higher.[10] Women like Marisela, who drive their own cars and speak some English, are likely to earn more than the women I surveyed, many of whom ride the buses to work. Marisela was typical of the housecleaners whom I surveyed in having been in the United States for a number of years. Unlike nanny/housekeepers, most of the housecleaners who were mothers themselves had all their children with them in the United States. Housecleaning, as Mary Romero has noted, is a job that is quite compatible with having a family life of one's own.

Breaking into housecleaning is tough, often requiring informal tutelage from friends and relatives. Contrary to the image that all women "naturally" know how to do domestic work, many Latina domestic workers discover that their own housekeeping experiences do not automatically transfer to the homes where they work. As she looked back on her early days in the job, Marisela said, "I didn't know how to clean or anything. My sister taught me." Erlinda Castro, a middle-aged women who had already run her own household and raised five children in Guatemala, had also initially worked in live-in jobs when she first came to Los Angeles. Yet despite this substantial domestic experience, she recalled how mystified she was when she began housecleaning. "Learning how to use the chemicals and the liquids" in the different households was confusing, and, as friends and employers instructed her on what to do, she began writing down in a little notebook the names of the products and what they cleaned. Some women learn the job by informally apprenticing with one another, accompanying a friend or perhaps an aunt on her housecleaning jobs.

Establishing a thriving route of *casas* requires more than learning which cleaning products to use or how to clean quickly and efficiently. It also involves acquiring multiple jobs, which housecleaners typically gain by asking their employers if they have friends, neighbors, or acquaintances who need someone to clean their houses; and because some attrition is inevitable, they must constantly be on the lookout for more *casas*. Not everyone who wants to can fill up her entire week.

To make ends meet when they don't have enough houses to clean, Latina housecleaners in Los Angeles find other ways to earn income. They might prepare food—say, tamales and *crema*—which they sell door-to-door or on the street; or they might sell small amounts of clothing that they buy wholesale in the garment district, or products from Avon, Mary Kay cosmetics, and Princess House kitchenware. They take odd jobs, such as handing out flyers advertising dental clinics or working at a swap meet; or perhaps they find something more stable, such as evening janitorial work in office buildings. Some housecleaners work swing shift in garment factories, while others work three days a week as a nanny/housekeeper and try to fill the remaining days with housecleaning jobs. Some women supplement

their husband's income by cleaning only one or two houses a week, but more often they patch together a number of jobs in addition to housecleaning.

Housecleaning represents, as Romero has written, the "modernization" of paid domestic work. Women who clean different houses on different days sell their labor services, she argues, in much the same way that a vendor sells a product to various customers.[11] The housecleaners themselves see their job as far preferable to that of a live-in or live-out nanny/housekeeper. They typically work alone, during times when their employers are out of the home; and because they are paid "by the job" instead of by the hour, they don't have to remain on the job until 6 or 7 P.M., an advantage much appreciated by women who have families of their own. Moreover, because they work for different employers on different days, they are not solely dependent for their livelihood on one boss whom they see every single day. Consequently, their relationships with their employers are less likely to become highly charged and conflictual; and if problems do arise, they can leave one job without jeopardizing their entire weekly earnings. Since child care is not one of their tasks, their responsibilities are more straightforward and there are fewer points of contention with employers. Housecleaning is altogether less risky.

Housecleaners also see working independently and informally as more desirable than working for a commercial cleaning company. "The companies pay $5 an hour," said Erlinda Castro, whose neighbor worked for one, "and the women have to work their eight hours, doing up to ten, twenty houses a day! One does the vacuuming, the other does the bathroom and the kitchen, and like that. It's tremendously hard work, and at $5 an hour? Thank God, I don't have to do that." Two of the women I interviewed, one now a live-out nanny/housekeeper and the other a private housecleaner, had previously worked for cleaning services, and both of them complained bitterly about their speeded-up work pace, low pay, and tyrannical bosses.

Private housecleaners take enormous pride in their work. When they finish their job, they can see the shiny results, and they are proud of their job autonomy, their hours, their pay, and, most important, what they are able to do with their pay for themselves and for their families. Yet housecleaning brings its own special problems. Intensive cleaning eventually brings physical pain, and sometimes injury. "Even my bones are tired," said fifty-three-year-old Lupe Vélez; and even a relatively young woman like Celestina Vigil at age thirty-three was already reporting back problems that she attributed to her work. While most of them have only fleeting contact with their employers, and many said they work for "good people," just about everyone has suffered, they said, "inconsiderate persons" who exhort them to work faster, humiliate them, fail to give raises, add extra cleaning tasks without paying extra, or unjustly accuse them of stealing or of ruining a rug or upholstery. And the plain old hard work and stigma of cleaning always remain, as suggested by the answer I got when I asked a housecleaner what she liked least about her job. "The least?" she said, with a wry smile. "Well, that you have to clean."

DOMESTIC JOB TRAJECTORIES AND TRANSNATIONAL MOTHERHOOD

As we have seen, private paid domestic work is organized into suboccupations, each with different pay scales, tasks, and hours.[12] Although they share many similarities, each job arrangement has its own different problems and rewards. In this section I discuss the movement between the three suboccupations and some of the family characteristics of the women who fill these jobs.

Some researchers have called live-in domestic work "the bridging occupation," because in various periods and places, it allowed rural migrant women to acculturate to the city and learn new ways of living.[13] Unlike Irish immigrant women or the black women who went from the South to the North to work as domestics in the early twentieth century, and unlike many private domestics in Europe and Latin America in the past, most Latina immigrants doing paid domestic work in the United States are *not* new to the city. Yet for many of them in Los Angeles today, especially those who are single and have very limited options for places to work and live, live-in jobs do serve as an initial occupational step. As Table 1 shows, new arrivals and women who have lived in the United States five years or less concentrate in live-in jobs (60 percent). In contrast, the majority of housecleaners (83 percent) and live-out nanny/housekeepers (69 percent) have lived in the United States for more than five years. Some begin their live-in jobs literally within forty-eight hours after arriving in Los Angeles, while some housecleaners have lived in the United States for twenty years or more. For newly arrived immigrant women without papers, a live-in job in a private home may feel safer, as private homes in middle- and upper-middle-class

TABLE 1   TYPE OF DOMESTIC WORK, LENGTH OF RESIDENCE IN THE UNITED STATES, AND MEAN HOURLY WAGES

	Live-ins (percent) (n = 30)	Live-outs (percent) (n = 64)	Housecleaners (percent) (n = 59)
Five years or less in United States	60	31	17
More than five years in United States	40	69	83
Mean hourly wage	$3.80	$5.90	$9.50

neighborhoods are rarely, if ever, threatened by Immigration and Naturalization Service raids.[14]

As the years pass, the women who took live-in jobs learn some English, gain knowledge of other job possibilities, and learn to use their social networks to their occupational advantage. Most of them eventually move out of live-in work. Some return to their countries of origin, and others look to sales, factory work, or janitorial work. But given the low pay of those jobs—in 1999, garment workers in Los Angeles were earning $5.00 an hour, and nonunion janitors with six years of experience were earning $6.30 an hour—many of them transition into some form of domestic day work.[15] As they abandon their live-in positions for live-out nanny/housekeeper and housecleaner jobs, their wages increase. For these women, the initial misery suffered in their live-in jobs makes other domestic work look if not good then at least tolerable—and certainly better than where they started.

For Latina immigrants in Los Angeles today, live-in domestic work does serve as an occupational bridge of sorts, but it often leads only to other types of domestic jobs. These individual trajectories match historical transformations in the occupation. Much as live-in jobs were once the dominant form of paid domestic work, and then gave way to arrangements in which domestics continued to work daily for one employer but lived with their own families, and finally to modernized "job work" or periodic housecleaning, so many Latina immigrants today traverse these three different types of jobs. Some roughly follow the historical order, moving from live-in to live-out nanny/housekeeper jobs, and then to housecleaning, but their modest occupational mobility does not always follow such a linear course.

As Mexican and Central American immigrant women move into live-out and housecleaning jobs, their family lives change. With better pay and fewer hours of work, they become able to live with their own family members. Among those I surveyed, about 45 percent of the women doing day work were married, but only 13 percent of the live-ins were married. Most women who have husbands and children with them in Los Angeles do not wish to take live-in jobs; moreover, their application for a live-in job is likely to be rejected if they reveal that they have a husband, a boyfriend, or children living in Los Angeles. As one job seeker in an employment agency waiting room put it, "You can't have a family, you can't have anyone [if you want a live-in job]." Live-out nanny/housekeepers often face this family restriction too, as employers are wary of hiring someone who may not report for work when her own children come down with the flu.

Their subminimum wages and long hours make it impossible for many live-in workers to bring their children to Los Angeles; other live-ins are young women who do not have children of their own. Once they do have children who are either born in or have immigrated to Los Angeles, most women try to leave live-in work to be with them. Not all the women can do so, and sometimes their finances or jobs force them to send the children "back home" to be reared by grandmothers. Clearly, performing domestic work for pay, especially in a live-in job, is often incompatible with caring for one's own family and home.[16]

The substantial proportion of Latina domestic workers in Los Angeles whose children stay in their countries of origin are in the same position as many Caribbean women working in domestic jobs on the East Coast, and as the Filipinas who predominate in domestic jobs in many cities around the globe. This is what I label "transnational motherhood" . . . ; in a 1997 article Ernestine Avila and I coined this term as we examined how Latina immigrant domestic workers are transforming their own meanings of motherhood to accommodate these spatial and temporal separations.[17] As Table 2 suggests, these arrangements are most common among women with live-in jobs, but live-in domestic workers and single mothers are not the only ones who rely on them.[18]

These transnational arrangements are not altogether new. The United States has a long history of incorpo-

TABLE 2   TYPE OF DOMESTIC WORK, MARITAL STATUS, AND LOCATION OF CHILDREN

	Live-ins (percent) (n = 30)	Live-outs (percent) (n = 64)	Housecleaners (percent) (n = 59)
Single (included the widowed, divorced, or separated)	87	55	54
Married	13	45	46
	DOMESTIC WORKERS WITH CHILDREN		
	(n = 16)	(n = 53)	(n = 45)
All children in United States	18	58	76
At least one child "back home"	82	42	24

rating people of color through coercive systems of labor that do not recognize family rights, including the right to care for one's own family members. As others have pointed out, slavery and contract labor systems were organized to maximize economic productivity, and offered few supports to sustain family life.[19] Today, international labor migration and the job characteristics of paid domestic work, especially live-in work, virtually impose transnational motherhood on many Mexican and Central American women who have children of their own.

At the other end of the spectrum are the housecleaners, who earn higher wages than live-ins (averaging $9.50 an hour vs. $3.80) and who work fewer hours per week than live-ins (twenty-three vs. sixty-four). The majority of them (76 percent) have all their children in the United States, and they are the least likely to experience transnational spatial and temporal separations from their children. Greater financial resources and more favorable job terms enhance housecleaners' abilities to bring their children to the United States. As we have seen, weekly housecleaning is dominated by relatively well-established women with more years of experience in the United States, who speak some English, who have a car, and who have job references. Because their own position is more secure, they are also more likely to have their children here.

And because they tend to work fewer hours per week, have greater flexibility in scheduling, and earn higher wages than the live-ins, they can live with and care for their children.

With respect to their ability to care for their own children, live-out nanny/housekeepers fall between live-ins and weekly cleaners—predictably, since they are also in an intermediate position in their earnings, rigidity of schedule, and working hours. Live-out domestic workers, according to the survey, earn $5.90 an hour and work an average workweek of thirty-five hours, and 42 percent of those who are mothers reported having at least one of their children in their country of origin.

THE DOMINANCE OF CENTRAL AMERICAN AND MEXICAN IMMIGRANT WOMEN

Paid domestic work has long been a racialized and gendered occupation, but why today are Central American women hugely over-represented in these jobs in Los Angeles in comparison with Mexicans (whose immigrant population is of course many times larger)? In the survey I conducted of 153 Westside Latina domestic workers, 75 percent of the respondents were from Central America; of those, most were from El Salvador and Guatemala. And in census counts, Salvadoran and Guatemalan women are, respectively, twelve times and thirteen times more likely than the general population to be engaged in private domestic work in Los Angeles.[20] Numerous studies paint a similar picture in other major U.S. cities, such as Washington, D.C., Houston, and San Francisco; one naturally wonders why this should be so.[21]

In Los Angeles, the heavy concentration of Central American women in paid domestic work is partially explained by the location of L.A.'s primary Central American immigrant neighborhood, the Pico-Union/Westlake area, just west of the small, high-rise downtown. As UCLA sociologist David Lopez and his colleagues explain, "A large proportion of Central Americans tend to reside closer to the middle-class neighborhoods of the Westside and the San Fernando Valley . . . while Mexicans are concentrated in the more isolated areas east and south of Downtown Los Angeles.[22] It is certainly quicker to drive or take a bus to the Westside from the Pico Union area than it is from East L.A. But there is more to this story than spatial location and L.A. transportation systems: distinct migration patterns have also influenced these occupational concentrations.

Mexican migration to the United States goes back over a hundred years, initially driven by labor recruitment programs designed to bring in men to work in agriculture. Since the late 1960s, it has shifted from a primarily male population of temporary or sojourner workers to one that includes women and entire families; these newcomers have settled in rural areas, cities, and suburbs throughout the United States, but disproportionately in California. Many Mexican women who migrated in the 1970s and 1980s were accompanied by their families and were aided by rich social networks; the latter helped prevent the urgency that leads new immigrants to take live-in jobs. Even those unmarried Mexican women who did migrate on their own, despite being opposed and sometimes stigmatized by their family and community, were often assisted by friends and more sympathetic family members. By the 1990s, more unmarried Mexican women were going north, encouraged in part by help from female friends and kin. When Mexican women arrive in the United States, many of them enjoy access to well-developed, established communities whose members have long been employed in various industries, particularly agriculture, construction, hotels, food-processing plants, and garment factories. Compared to their Central American peers, Mexican women are more likely to have financial support from a husband; because fewer Mexican immigrant women must work outside their home, they have lower rates of overall participation in the labor force than do Central American women.[23] Their social networks also give Mexican women greater variety in their employment options; paid domestic work is only one of their alternatives.

Salvadoran and Guatemalan women migrating to the United States have done so under different circumstances than Mexican women. For Central Americans coming to *el norte*, there was no long-standing labor program recruiting men who could then bring, or encourage the migration of, their wives and daughters. In fact, as Terry Repak's study shows, some of the early pioneers of Salvadoran migration to Washington, D.C., were women, themselves informally recruited by individual members of the diplomatic corps precisely because they were desired as private domestics.[24] More significantly, Salvadoran and Guatemalan women and men left their countries in haste, often leaving their children behind, as they fled the civil wars, political violence, and economic upheaval of the 1980s. Theirs are immigrant communities that subsisted without legal status for nearly two decades, grew rapidly, and remain very poor. Even Guatemalan and Salvadoran women who arrived in the United States in the late 1980s and early 1990s could not count on finding communities of well-established compatriots who could quickly and efficiently situate them in jobs in restaurants, hotels, factories, or other industries. In fact, as some of the most compelling ethnographies of Salvadorans in San Francisco and on Long Island have shown, Central Americans' relatively shallow U.S. roots have left their social networks extremely impoverished and sometimes fractured.[25] For Central American women arriving on their own, without husbands and children in tow, desperate and lacking information about jobs—and at a crucial historical moment when American families were seeking to resolve their own child care and housekeeping problems—live-in jobs were both attractive and available.

Family structures and marriage patterns may have also contributed to the preponderance of Central American women in paid domestic work. El Salvador has traditionally had one of the lowest marriage rates in the hemisphere, especially among the urban poor, where common-law marriages and legacies of internal and intra–Central America labor migration—mostly for work on coffee plantations—have encouraged the formation of female-headed households.[26] Thus Salvadoran women have been more likely to migrate on their own and accept live-in jobs.[27] Their large numbers in this lowest rung of domestic work would then explain their eventual disproportionate concentration in all types of private paid domestic work, following the pattern discussed above.

The experience of Central American women might also be compared to that of Asian immigrant women, who have been entering the United States at increasing rates. The latter are an extremely heterogeneous group, but on average—and this is particularly true of Chinese, Indian, and Filipina women—they arrive with much higher levels of education, better English language skills, and more professional credentials than do their Latina peers. They are also more likely to have legal status; and members of some groups, especially Korean immigrant women, enjoy access to jobs in family businesses and ethnic enclaves.[28] At the same time, the generally poorer and less-educated women from Vietnam, Laos, and Cambodia have been able to withstand periods of underemployment and unemployment because they are officially sanctioned political refugees and therefore enjoy access to welfare and resettlement assistance from the federal government. While some individual Asian immigrant women are working in paid domestic work, they have not developed social networks that channel them into this niche.

It is particularly striking that Filipina immigrants predominate in this occupation elsewhere around the globe, but not in the United States. Worldwide, about two-thirds of Filipina migrants in countries as different as Italy, Canada, Hong Kong, Taiwan, Singapore, Saudi Arabia, and Jordan, do paid domestic work; but in the United States, their high levels of education and fluent English enable most of them to enter higher status occupations that require more skills than does domestic work. In 1990, 71 percent of the Filipinas in the United States were working in managerial, professional, technical/sales, and administrative support jobs, and only 17 percent were employed in service jobs.[29] They are disproportionately concentrated in the health professions, the result of formal recruitment programs designed to fill U.S. nursing shortages.[30] Experience in the health professions leads many Filipinas to take jobs in elder care; and though some work as nanny/housekeepers in Los Angeles, many of them as live-ins, in my numerous discussions with employers, Latina employees, attorneys, and owners and employees of domestic employment agencies, no one ever mentioned Filipina housecleaners.

Nevertheless, Filipina immigrants are doing paid domestic work in the United States. Interviews conducted by Rhacel Parreñas with twenty-six Filipina domestic workers in Los Angeles reveal that many of these women have college diplomas and are working in homes because they are older and face age discrimination; they tend to earn more as care providers for the elderly ($425 per week) and more as nanny/housekeepers ($350 per week) than do Latina immigrants in these same jobs.[31] When it comes to caring for their children, some employers prefer Filipina nanny/housekeepers because they speak English well (English is the official language of schools and universities in the Philippines), and because they tend to be highly educated. Paradoxically, these qualities may predispose some employers to *not* choose Filipinas as domestic employees. At three domestic employment agencies, the owners told me that they rarely placed Filipina job applicants, because they were deemed "uppity," demanding, and likely to lie about their references. Racial preferences, as the next section suggests, shape the formation of Latina domestic workers and their employment in Los Angeles.

NARRATIVES OF RACIAL PREFERENCES

In a race-conscious society, everyone has racial preferences and prejudices, and Latina domestic workers
and the women who employ them are no exception.
When choosing someone to work in their homes, many
employers prefer Latinas, because as "others" in language, race-ethnicity, and social class, they are outside
white, English-speaking, middle-class social circles
and are thus seen as unlikely to reveal family secrets
and intimacies. If they do tell someone about the
family fight they witnessed, that someone is likely to
be another Latina nanny or a member of their own
family—in either case, no one who matters to the
employers. This fear of exposure sometimes prevents
employers from choosing white, English-speaking job
candidates. "She was non-Hispanic, and I wasn't sure
if I could trust her," said one woman of a prospective
employee. Another employer had been advised not to
hire a white woman as a nanny/housekeeper because
an immigrant would be less likely to recognize her
philanthropic family's name and to engage in bribery
or kidnapping. Other women told me that they did not
want a European au pair or midwestern (white) teenager taking care of their children because they would
probably be young, irresponsible teens, more interested in cavorting with boyfriends, cruising the beach,
and stargazing in Hollywood than in doing their job.
Employers may also prefer to hire Latina nannies, as
research conducted by Julia Wrigley suggests, because
they view them as more submissive than whites.[32]

While some of the older employers I interviewed
had hired African American housecleaners and domestics in the past, none were now doing so. Of the relatively few black women working in paid domestic
work in contemporary Los Angeles, most are immigrants from Belize and Brazil, and some employers
remain adamantly opposed to hiring black women to
work in their homes. One domestic employment
agency owner told me that some clients had requested
that he never send black women to interview for a job.
And at an informal luncheon, arranged by one of the
employer interviewees, one of them cleared her throat
and then offered, with some awkward hesitation,
"Uhm, ah, I would never hire a black woman. I'd be
too scared to, and I'd be especially scared if her boyfriend came around." The women, all of them relatively upper-class white matrons, had nodded in silent
agreement. The old stereotype of the bossy black maid
is apparently alive and well, now joined by newer terrifying images associated with young black men; but

since African-American women are not pursuing
domestic work jobs in Los Angeles, most employers
need never confront their own racial fears directly. It is,
after all, Latina immigrant women who are queuing
up for domestic jobs in private homes.

When I talked with them, most employers expressed
genuine appreciation for the effort, dedication, and
work that these women put into their homes and children. They viewed Latina domestic workers as responsible, trustworthy, and reliable employees who have "a
really strong work ethic." And while plenty of employers spoke at length about Latina women as ideally
suited to caring for children, relying on images of
Latinas as exceptionally warm, patient, and loving
mothers, there was no similar racialized image of
cleanliness. No one said, for instance, "She cleans like
a Mexican." Such a phrase may sound offensive, but
the absence of any such generalization is striking when
nearly everyone hired to do cleaning in Los Angeles is
Mexican or Central American.

Indeed, some of the employers I interviewed did
make this kind of statement—to associate their own
northern European heritage with superior cleaning and
hygiene. A few of them offered remarks such as "People associate very clean homes with Dutch people," or
"My mother's German and she cleans, you know, like
Germans clean." These women did not necessarily
claim that they were excellent cleaners, only that they
belonged to racial-ethnic groups associated with cleanliness. None of them described their domestic employees
as "dirty," but the adjective has been commonly featured
in racial epithets directed at Mexicans in the Southwest
and at domestic workers just about everywhere. The historian Phyllis Palmer, who has written compellingly
about dirt, domesticity, and racialized divisions among
women, notes that while dirt and housework connote
inferior morality, white middle-class women transcend
these connotations by employing women different from
themselves to do the work. "Dirtiness," Palmer notes,
"appears always in a constellation of the suspect qualities that, along with sexuality, immorality, laziness, and
ignorance, justify social rankings of race, class and gender. The 'slut,' initially a shorthand for 'slattern' or
kitchen maid, captures all of these personifications in a
way unimaginable in a male persona."[33]

Employers are not the only ones who hold strong
racial-ethnic preferences and prejudices. Latina domestic workers at the bus stops, at the agencies, and in the
public parks readily agreed on who were their worst
employers: Armenians, Iranians, Asians, Latinos,
blacks, and Jews, especially Israeli Jews. "I'll never

work again for *un chino*!" or *"Los armenios* [Armenians] are the worst," they tell each other. These statements were echoed in the individual interviews, as well as by the preferences job candidates register at employment agencies, and they seem to mirror what Latino men who work as day laborers think about their similarly racialized employers in Los Angeles.[34] Anyone marked as "nonwhite," it seems, is at risk of being denounced as a cheap, abusive, and oppressive employer, one to be avoided at all costs.

There are a number of factors at work here. Many of the employers in these racial-ethnic groups are immigrants themselves, albeit entrepreneurial and professional immigrants with substantially more resources than the Latinas they hire to care for their homes and children. Many had belonged to elites in their countries of origin, accustomed to having servants in their homes who would be expected to perform all sorts of jobs on demand. Some of them bring these expectations with them when they come to the United States. When Latina domestic workers are expected to massage the *señora*'s feet with oil, or scrub the kitchen floor on their hands and knees, they take offence. Others are wholly unprepared to iron Hindu saris, or to follow kosher food preparation and serving practices in the homes of Orthodox Jews. At the same time, the immigrant and ethnic employers may have been accustomed in their countries of origin to paying slave wages, and the tenuous financial situations of some makes them unable to pay minimum wage. Some newly arrived women who find their first job working as a live-in for other working-class Latino immigrant families may receive as little as $25 or $50 a week in exchange for their round-the-clock services.

Latina immigrants also operate under racist assumptions, many of which they learn in the United States. They quickly pick up the country's racial hierarchies and racist stereotypes. "Jews are cheap," "Mexican Americans and blacks are lazy," or *"Los chinos* are too bossy," they say. The regional racial hierarchy also fixes Jews, Armenians, and Iranians in low positions. *"Los Americanos,"* the term they typically use to refer to employers marked only "white," are almost never singled out by ethnicity and are rarely criticized or negatively labeled as a group.

Conversely, Latina domestic workers single out the race of particular employers who happen to be both "bad employers" and "racialized" as nonwhite. One Mexican housecleaner who maintained that Latino employers were among the most exploitative was Lupe Vélez. When I probed why she felt this way, she cited as evidence her experiences with one employer, a man from Monterrey, Mexico. A large, verbally abusive man, he had called her a pig, he went out of his way to deny her food when he sat down to eat with his family, and he had unfairly accused her of scratching and ruining a stove top. These deeply felt, painful experiences were recounted tearfully.

Yet as we talked longer, I discovered that in Los Angeles, Lupe had worked in three different Latino homes; she spoke of a Mexican American teacher who had treated her well and paid her fairly. Mutual fondness, respect, and closeness had grown between the two, who had unsuccessfully conspired at matchmaking between their young adult children. How could she maintain that Latinos were the "worst" employers when in fact a Mexican American had been among her best employers? In recalling her bad experience with the Mexican man, Lupe Vélez singled out his racial-ethnic identity. As she recalled that painful experience, his being Mexican and consistently acting abusively toward her became the most salient features about him. She applied "Latino," a racial marker, to this man, labeled an abusive, bad employer, but not to the teacher whom she had favored.

I suspect that when Latina domestic workers denounce Jewish employers, a similar process is at work. In those cases, they may only identify as Jewish those employers who are abusive and who are, as Orthodox Jews or recently emigrated Israeli Jews, unambiguously marked as Jewish. They might not recognize the other Jews for whom they work. Or perhaps Latina domestic workers' disdain for Jewish employers is testimony to the force of contemporary anti-Semitism. It is no small irony that a major provider of legal services for Latina domestic workers in Los Angeles is a Jewish nonprofit organization.[35]

Some Latina domestic workers related counternarratives, criticizing their peers for relying on racial stereotypes and hasty racial judgments. One Salvadoran housecleaner cited her Moroccan employer as one of the most gracious because she always served her a hot lunch, sitting down to chat with her; another related her appreciation of an African American bachelor, an ex-basketball player, who kept a messy house but paid her very generously; still another felt warmly toward her Korean employer who did not pay well, but who passed many choice housecleaning jobs on to her. Yet the voices of these women were drowned out by the louder, frequently blanket condemnations that other Latina domestic workers offered about their racially marked minority and immigrant employers. Amid the public clamor of racialized nativism that propelled California ballot initiatives against health and education services for undocumented immigrants and their children, against affirmative action, and against bilingual education (Propositions 187, 209, and 227 respectively), Latina immigrant domestic workers learn their own version of regional racism.

In this [reading], I conveyed briefly some of the life textures and the daily trials and triumphs experienced by Latina immigrants who work as housecleaners, live-out nanny/housekeepers, and live-in nanny/housekeepers. The Mexican, Salvadoran, and Guatemalan women who occupy these jobs come from diverse class, regional, and cultural locations, and they bring different expectations to their jobs. Once in the United States, however, they share a set of similar experiences part because of the way that their domestic work is structured.

NOTES

1. Glenn 1986: 141.
2. Lacher 1997: 1.
3. One nanny/housekeeper told me that a *señora* had admonished her for picking a bag of fruit, and wanted to charge her for it; another claimed that her employer had said she would rather watch the fruit fall off the branches and rot than see her eat it.
4. Many Latina domestic workers do not know the amount of their hourly wages; and because the lines between their work and nonwork tend to blur, live-in nanny/housekeepers have particular difficulty calculating them. In the survey questionnaire I asked live-in nanny/housekeepers how many days a week they worked, what time they began their job, and what time they ended, and I asked them to estimate how many hours off they had during an average workday (39 percent said they had no time off, but 32 percent said they had a break of between one and three hours). Forty-seven percent of the women said they began their workday at 7 A.M. or earlier, with 62 percent ending their workday at 7 P.M. or later. With the majority of them (71 percent) working five days a week, their average workweek was sixty-four hours. This estimate may at first glance appear inflated; but consider a prototypical live-in nanny/housekeeper who works, say, five days a week, from 7 A.M. until 9 P.M., with one and a half hours off during the children's nap time (when she might take a break to lie down or watch television). Her on-duty work hours would total sixty-four and a half hours per week. The weekly pay of live-in nanny/housekeepers surveyed ranged from $130 to $400, averaging $242. Dividing this figure by sixty-four yields an hourly wage of $3.80. None of the live-in nanny/housekeepers were charged for room and board—and . . . this practice is regulated by law—but 86 percent said they brought food with them to their jobs. The majority reported being paid in cash.
5. See, e.g., Employment Classified Section 2, *Los Angeles Times*, June 6, 1999, G9.
6. Clark-Lewis 1994: 123. "After an average of seven years," she notes in her analysis of African American women who had migrated from the South to Washington, D.C., in the early twentieth century, "all of the migrant women grew to dread their live-in situation. They saw their occupation as harming all aspects of their life" (124). Nearly all of these women transitioned into day work in private homes. This pattern is being repeated by Latina immigrants in Los Angeles today, and it reflects local labor market opportunities and constraints. In Houston, Texas, where many Mayan Guatemalan immigrant women today work as live-ins, research by Jacqueline Maria Hagan (1998) points to the tremendous obstacles they face in leaving live-in work. In Houston, housecleaning is dominated by better-established immigrant women, by Chicanas and, more recently, by the commercial cleaning companies—so it is hard for the Maya to secure those jobs. Moreover, Hagan finds that over time, the Mayan women who take live-in jobs see their own social networks contract, further reducing their internal job mobility.
7. Several factors explain the shift to day work, including urbanization, interurban transportation systems, and smaller private residences. Historians have also credited the job preferences of African American domestic workers, who rejected the constraints of live-in work and chose to live with their own families and communities, with helping to promote this shift in the urban North after 1900 (Katzman 1981; Clark-Lewis 1994: 129–35). In many urban regions of the United States, the shift to day work accelerated during World War I, so that live-out arrangements eventually became more prevalent (Katzman 1981; Palmer 1989). Elsewhere, and for different groups of domestic workers, these transitions happened later in the twentieth century. Evelyn Nakano Glenn (1986: 143) notes that Japanese immigrant and Japanese American women employed in domestic work in the San Francisco Bay Area moved out of live-in jobs and into modernized day work in the years after World War II.
8. Katzman 1981; Glenn 1986.
9. Wrigley 1995.
10. Keep in mind that the survey questionnaire was administered at three different types of sites: bus stops, ESL evening classes, and parks where nannies congregate with the children in their charge. Housecleaners who drive and have their own cars, and who speak some English, typically earn more money and are able to clean more houses per week. Because my survey is biased toward Latina domestic workers who ride the buses and attend

ESL classes, those housecleaners earning higher wages are not taken into account.

11. Romero 1992.

12. In addition to the jobs of live-in nanny/housekeepers, live-out nanny/housekeepers, and weekly or biweekly housecleaners, an increasingly important and growing segment of the domestic workforce is engaged in elder care. That, too, is organized in different ways; and though the occupation lies beyond the parameters of this study (much of it is formally organized and contracted for by the state or medical organizations), some Latina immigrants are privately contracted for jobs as elders' companions and caretakers, as *damas de compañía.*

13. Smith 1973; McBride 1976.

14. The only news report of INS raids involving nannies working in private homes in Los Angeles that came to my attention as I did this research involved a nanny working for a top-ranking Latino INS agent, Jorge Guzman. In 1996 armed plainclothes INS agents illegally raided Guzman's home, and allegedly fondled and made sexual advances toward the domestic worker. Guzman claimed that the raid was part of a ten-year program of internal anti-Latino harassment directed at him. After he filed suit, the U.S. Justice Department agreed to pay him $400,000 to settle (McDonnell 1999).

15. Personal communication, Cynthia Cranford, March 1999; Cleeland 1999.

16. Rollins 1985; Glenn 1986; Romero 1992. See Romero 1997 for a study focusing on the perspective of domestic workers' children. Although the majority of respondents in that study were children of day workers, and none appear to have been children of transnational mothers, they still recall that their mothers' occupation had significant costs for them.

17. Hondagneu-Sotelo and Avila 1997.

18. Central American women seem more likely than Mexican women to leave their children in their country of origin, even if their husbands are living with them in the United States, perhaps because of the multiple dangers and costs associated with undocumented travel from Central America to the United States. The civil wars of the 1980s, continuing violence and economic uncertainty, greater difficulties and costs associated with crossing multiple national borders, and stronger cultural legacies of socially sanctioned consensual unions may also contribute to this pattern for Central Americans.

19. Glenn 1986; Dill 1988.

20. The figures on Salvadoran and Guatemalan women are taken from an analysis of the 1990 census data by the sociologists David E. Lopez, Eric Popkin, and Edward Telles (1996); they also found that Mexican immigrants were only 2.3 times as likely as those in the general population to be engaged in paid domestic work.

21. See Salzinger 1991; Hagan 1994, 1998; Repak 1995.

22. Lopez, Popkin, and Telles 1996: 298.

23. According to 1990 PUMS Census data, about 70 percent of Central American women between the ages of 24 and 60 in Los Angeles County are in the labor force, while only 56 percent of their Mexican peers are. Among this same group, 71 percent of Mexican immigrant women but only 56 percent of their Central American peers are married and living with a spouse. To put it even more starkly, 28 percent of Mexican immigrant women and 43 percent of Central American women report living with family members or adults other than their spouses.

24. Repak 1995.

25. Mahler 1995; Menjívar 2000.

26. Some studies estimate that as many as 50 percent of poor households in San Salvador were formed by "free unions" rather than marriage by law. This pattern is related not just to internal and intra-Central American labor migration but also to urban poverty, as there is no need to secure inheritance rights when there is no property to share (Nieves 1979; Repak 1995).

27. Countries with traditions of consensual marriages afford women more migration opportunities (Donato 1992).

28. A survey conducted in Los Angeles and Orange County in 1986 revealed that 45 percent of Korean immigrants were self-employed; many were business owners in the Korean ethnic economy (Min 1996: 48).

29. Mar and Kim 1994.

30. Between 1966 and 1985 nearly 25,000 Filipina nurses came to work in the United States, and another 10,000 came between 1989 and 1991. Filipinas who were formally recruited through government programs then informally recruited their friends and former nursing school classmates (Ong and Azores 1994).

31. Parreñas 2001.

32. Wrigley 1995.

33. Palmer 1989: 140.

34. Personal communication with UCLA professor Abel Valenzuela, fall 1998.

35. Bet Tzedek Legal Services.

REFERENCES

Clark-Lewis, Elizabeth. 1994. *Living In, Living Out: African American Domestics in Washington, D.C. 1910–1940.* Washington, D.C.: Smithsonian Institution Press.

Cleeland, Nancy. 1999. "Garment Jobs: Hard, Bleak, and Vanishing." *Los Angeles Times*, March 11, A1, A14–16.

Dill, Bonnie Thornton. 1988. "'Making Your Job Good Yourself': Domestic Service and the Construction of Personal Dignity." In *Women and the Politics of Empowerment*, edited by Ann Bookman and Sandra Morgen, 33–52. Philadelphia: Temple University Press.

Donato, Katharine. 1992. "Understanding U.S. Immigration: Why Some Countries Send Women and Others Send Men." In *Seeking Common Ground: Multidisciplinary Studies of Immigrant Women in the United States*, edited by Donna Gabaccia, 159–84. Westport, Conn.: Praeger.

Glenn, Evelyn Nakano. 1986. *Issei, Nisei, Warbride*. Philadelphia: Temple University Press.

Hagan, Jacqueline Maria. 1994. *Deciding to Be Legal: A Maya Community in Houston*. Philadelphia: Temple University Press.

———. 1998. "Social Networks, Gender, and Immigrant Incorporation." *American Sociological Review* 63: 55–67.

Hondagneu-Sotelo, Pierrette, and Ernestine Avila. 1997. "'I'm Here, But I'm There': The Meanings of Latina Transnational Motherhood." *Gender and Society* 11: 548–71.

Katzman, David M. 1981. *Seven Days a Week: Women and Domestic Service in Industrializing America*. Urbana: University of Illinois Press.

Lacher, Irene. 1997. "An Interior Mind." *Los Angeles Times*, March 16, E1, E3.

Lopez, David E., Eric Popkin, and Edward Telles. 1996. "Central Americans: At the Bottom, Struggling to Get Ahead." In *Ethnic Los Angeles*, edited by Roger Waldinger and Mehdi Bozorgmehr, 279–304. New York: Russell Sage Foundation.

Mahler, Sarah J. 1995. *American Dreaming: Immigrant Life on the Margins*. Princeton: Princeton University Press.

Mar, D., and M. Kim. 1994. "Historical Trends." In *The State of Asian Pacific America: Economic Diversity, Issues, and Policies*, edited by Paul Ong, 13–30. Los Angeles: LEAP Asian Pacific American Public Policy Institute and UCLA Asian American Studies Center.

McBride, Theresa. 1976. *The Domestic Revolution: The Modernization of Household Service in England and France, 1820–1920*. New York: Holmes and Meier.

McDonnell, Patrick J. 1999. "U.S. to Pay $400,000 to INS Agent in Bias Suit." *Los Angeles Times*, January 21, B1, B5.

Menjívar, Cecilia. 2000. *Fragmented Ties: Salvadoran Immigrant Networks in America*. Berkeley: University of California Press.

Min, Pyong Gap. 1996. *Caught in the Middle: Korean Communities in New York and Los Angeles*. Berkeley: University of California Press.

Nieves, Isabel, 1979. "Household Arrangements and Multiple Jobs in San Salvador." *Signs* 5:139–50.

Ong, Paul, and Tania Azores. 1994. "Health Professionals on the Front Line." In *The State of Asian Pacific America: Economic Diversity, Issues, and Policies*, edited by Paul Ong, 139–63. Los Angeles: LEAP Asian Pacific American Public Policy Institute and UCLA Asian American Studies Center.

Palmer, Phyllis. 1989. *Domesticity and Dirt: Housewives and Domestic Servants in the United States, 1920–1945*. Philadelphia: Temple University Press.

Parrenas, Rhacel Salazar. 2001. *Servants of Globalization: Women, Migration, and Domestic Work*. Stanford, Calif.: Stanford University Press.

Repak, Terry A. 1995. *Waiting on Washington: Central American Workers in the Nation's Capital*. Philadelphia: Temple University Press.

Rollins, Judith. 1985. *Between Women: Domestics and Their Employers*. Philadelphia: Temple University Press.

Romero, Mary. 1992. *Maid in the U.S.A.* New York: Routledge.

Romero, Mary. 1997. "Who Takes Care of the Maid's Children? Exploring the Costs of Domestic Service." In *Feminism and Families*, edited by Hilde L. Nelson, 63–91. New York: Routledge.

Salzinger, Leslie. 1991. "A Maid by Any Other Name: The Transformation of 'Dirty Work' by Central American Immigrants." In *Ethnography Unbound: Power and Resistance in the Modern Metropolis*, by Michael Burawoy et al., 139–60. Berkeley: University of California Press.

Smith, Margo L. 1973. "Domestic Service as a Channel of Upward Mobility for the Lower-Class Woman: The Lima Case." In *Female and Male in Latin America: Essays*, edited by Ann Pescatello, 192–207. Pittsburgh: University of Pittsburgh Press.

Wrigley, Julia. 1995. *Other People's Children*. New York: Basic Books.

THE LIVING WAGE AS A WOMEN'S ISSUE

Eileen Boris

Why is the living wage a women's issue? First, women will benefit the most from the introduction of living wages. Women are the largest group of low-income workers; among women, single mothers and women of color are the lowest paid. Women compose 60% of minimum wage workers when, even with California's recent increase to nearly $7 an hour, the minimum wage is dollars below a living wage. In an era when over half of women are in the labor force and the majority of mothers with small children are employed, women need a salary that allows them to make ends meet as much as men do. We can't count on men to support us, even if we wanted to. Those with partners understand that during periods of recession and spiraling costs of living, even two jobs may not be enough if none pay a living wage.

Second, living wages can counter welfare reform's race to the bottom. Marriage often isn't forever and sometimes parents never marry. For women who become household heads, welfare reform has shredded the safety net of public assistance. "Work-first" requirements flood the service sector with former recipients whose abundance serves to maintain low wages and counter the organizing efforts of immigrant, especially Latino, workers in hotels and nursing homes. Living wages help to stabilize all wages.

Third, a living wages ordinance might just keep the city from contracting out work, bypassing unionization. Women in public employee unions not only receive higher wages and greater benefits but also are more likely to have social supports to aid the juggling of family and wage labor.

Finally, the living wage promises to re-value the work of care. In a locale like Santa Barbara, those making less than a living wage cluster in service occupations funded by the state and often administrated and performed by non-profits: such as elder care, child care, and home health care. These are the jobs dismissed as unskilled because the work consists of tasks performed often by women for family members. Rather than again basing pay on the identity of the worker, we need to reward the identity of the work. A decent standard of living for all within our community benefits us all.

SECTION 6

Families

Families are a fundamental social unit. In families we develop a sense of ourselves as individuals and as members of a primary group. We internalize messages about our position in the community, the nation, and the world. We are taught systems of belief, usually consistent with the society in which we live, about appropriate roles for particular kinds of people. For example, we learn to think differently about men and women, elders and children, and people of various races, classes, and social statuses. We also learn how we are expected to treat the people we encounter in the world around us.

It is within families that members of a society first develop ideas and feelings about themselves as gendered individuals. When we are children, the socialization we receive contains strong messages about the appropriate attitudes and behaviors for males and females. When we are adults, families are where we spend much of our time, divide up the work of meeting our physical and emotional needs, and care for others, such as children or aging family members. Families usually organize these interpersonal roles according to what they consider appropriate for men or women. Yet families come in many forms, even within one society. The normative family structure of a married mother and father, in which the man is employed outside the home while the woman cares for their children, no longer represents the majority of families. Instead, a family may be a single parent with children, a couple with no children, lesbian or gay parents and their children, or a group of people who share a household. As a result, individuals' experiences with families vary widely.

Feminist scholars examine the family as a major source of the reproduction of inequality in a society.

Researchers investigate how the organization of family life supports women's oppression in society through its ideologies, economics, distribution of domestic tasks, and intimate relations. Reciprocally, researchers examine the impact of demographic, technological, economic, and political structures on women's and men's power and positions in their families.

At the same time, feminist scholars examine families as a source of women's strength and resistance. Alternative family forms are one way to restructure family lives; in addition, families may provide a source of resistance to other forms of oppression, such as racism or poverty. Feminist family studies emphasize the ways that race, ethnicity, sexuality, and class influence our family experiences.

In the first selection, "Bridal Wave," Melissa Morrison discusses Americans' cultural obsession with weddings. From rampant weddings on television, to a plethora of wedding books and magazines, to a whole industry dedicated to planning and producing the "perfect wedding," weddings occupy a central position in American life. Mass media representations of weddings, Morrison contends, promote a very expensive model of the perfect wedding and encourage consumers to desire weddings that imitate those of celebrities and the wealthy. Morrison argues that the event of the wedding, in fact, is emphasized in popular culture far more than the actual marriage relationship that it formalizes. Reality TV shows are only one reflection of this pattern. Despite the media wedding frenzy, actual couples often choose to live together rather than marrying and to marry, on average, at later ages. And while the presidential administration of George W. Bush invested in attempts to promote marriage for low-income people (see Melanie Heath's article in Section 10), opposition to same-sex marriage remains entrenched. Yet, ironically, legalization of same-sex marriage would produce large increases in earnings for the wedding industry.

What are the components of the "perfect wedding," as depicted in mainstream culture? How does this compare to weddings that you have attended? How do mass media depictions of weddings influence what people expect of their own weddings? Do you agree with Morrison that weddings are emphasized to the detriment of actual marriages?

The next selection, Carolyn Herbst Lewis's "Waking Sleeping Beauty: The Premarital Pelvic Exam and Heterosexuality During the Cold War," looks back in time to the 1950s, showing how the family is more than an intimate institution. Doctors in the 1950s saw families as the building block of a strong nation, one able to resist the Communist threat, and offered their expertise in teaching brides-to-be how to have appropriate sex on their wedding nights as the key to marital harmony, happy families, and national security. Through the premarital pelvic exam, they sought to ensure that what they assumed would be a woman's first experience with sexual intercourse would be pleasurable and appropriately gendered. What assumptions did doctors make about how couples should have sex? How did they connect sexual intercourse to the fight against Communism? In what ways are families politicized today?

After the fairy-tale wedding and the honeymoon, heterosexual women confront the challenge of balancing work and family, and their strategies vary according to class, ethnicity, culture, and nationality. Denise Segura analyzes how Chicana and Mexicana immigrant mothers view their lives as employed mothers in "Working at Motherhood: Chicana and Mexicana Immigrant Mothers and Employment." She finds that many Mexicana immigrants in the study viewed working for pay as an important part of motherhood because the income helped support their families. Many Chicana mothers, in contrast, who had grown up in the United States, had been socialized to the American notion of a separation between spheres of work and family and therefore expressed more ambivalence about combining employment and mothering. The article illustrates how the meaning and practice of motherhood are socially constructed and thus vary among different groups of women. How is the relationship between working outside the home and raising children defined in the culture in which you grew up?

In the next selection, "Moral Dilemmas, Moral Strategies, and the Transformation of Gender: Lessons from Two Generations of Work and Family Change," Kathleen Gerson addresses the same issue from a generational perspective. For young heterosexual women and men, dividing up the responsibilities of earning income and caring for children and home is a major challenge. Gerson argues that the idea that women and men have different moral responsibilities—with women responsible for caring for others and men responsible for supporting others through their work—is at the core of this dilemma. While women are seen as achieving fulfillment through connections to others, men's fulfillment is seen as coming from their independent efforts in the work world. Although this ideology remains powerful, Gerson shows that contemporary reality is far different. Large numbers of women work for pay, and men's incomes have declined to the point that many of them could no longer play the breadwinner role in any case. Yet change in the work of caring for others has been slower, with women still expected to do the bulk of child care while employers are reluctant to accommodate the caring work of either women or men employees.

When Gerson interviewed women and men coming of age around the turn of the millennium, she found that they sought to achieve relationships in which they could be both autonomous and connected, and in which they would share work and child care. Reflecting on their own parents, the first generation to raise children after the changes wrought by feminism, they viewed mothers' employment and fathers' involvement with children very positively. And overall, neither young men nor young women expected to find fulfillment solely through either work or family. Young women, however, were less likely than young men to prefer traditional gender relationships, and both women and men had fallback positions in case their ideals did not occur: women felt strongly that they wanted to be economically self-supporting, and men expected to be the primary breadwinners despite desiring connections with wives and children.

The conflicts are large between economic needs to work and the desire for personal autonomy, on the one hand, and caring demands and the desire for intimacy and connection, on the other. Yet Gerson suggests that these dilemmas also create the possibility for change, as women and men wrestle with their own hopes and confront the social institutions that make those hopes difficult to realize. What are your own expectations about work and family? What kinds of jobs and family support systems would you need in order to fulfill these expectations? To what extent have you been able to fulfill these expectations, if you have already formed your own independent household? As you reflect on the choices and situations faced by your own parents, how do your experiences compare to theirs, and to those of the people Gerson interviewed? What changes have occurred in family and paid labor over the past generation, and what has remained unchanged? What do you see as the main obstacles to further change in work and family lives?

In "For Better or Worse: Gender Allures in the Vietnamese Global Marriage Market," Hung Cam Thai shows how ideas of gender shape marriage strategies in quite different ways for Vietnamese male migrants to the United States and for women living in Vietnam. Women in Vietnam, he argues, are expected to "marry up" to men who are more highly educated, better employed, and older. But women who pursue higher education may lose their opportunity to marry up–in effect, "pricing themselves out" of the marriage market because by the time they finish their education they are not only too highly educated but too old to marry up. Reluctant to marry down in Vietnam and sacrifice their status and independence, they look for spouses who have immigrated to the United States, hoping to find a more egalitarian gender system there. Vietnamese male migrants to the United States, in contrast, often find themselves in low-status and low-paying jobs, despite their education or higher class status in Vietnam. For them, a wife from Vietnam provides the hope of a traditional marriage in which they can gain the respect that they have lost in the workplace. As Thai shows, these women and men bring very different hopes to their marriages, both shaped by complicated intersections of gender, nationality, class, and culture. What do you think will happen to couples like these?

How do their expectations compare to those of other cultures and communities with which you are familiar?

In the last selection, "Queer Parenting in the New Millennium," Nancy Naples argues that lesbian and gay parents produce social change simply by living their daily lives openly. The *heteronormative* family that she discusses is one in which a man and woman, married to each other, bear and raise children, and gain social approval and legal benefits. Both queer parenthood and queer marriage, Naples suggests, have the potential to challenge the dominance of this form of family. Yet that model remains highly influential, as Naples shows. She juxtaposes her own legally and socially marginal experience as an expectant nonbiological mother, in which she must come out as a lesbian in order to claim her status as parent, with her partner's experience of being welcomed into the sisterhood of women by sharing pregnancy stories with heterosexual women. The widespread political opposition to the legalization of same-sex marriage is another indication of the marginalization of queer families. As Naples discusses, there has been considerable debate within gay and lesbian activist organizations about whether same-sex marriage is an important political goal or whether it would simply promote assimilation by queer people into a heterosexual model. What is Naples' conclusion about this debate? What is your opinion? To what extent do you think that visible lesbian and gay parents contribute to social change? What media representations of lesbian or gay parenting or marriage can you think of, and how do these compare to the hostile political climate that Naples describes?

For most women, these articles suggest, family relationships are a complicated mixture of accommodation and resistance to gender oppression. Nevertheless, expectations and experiences within families differ for women and men of different races, ethnicities, classes, and sexual identities. In what ways do women, in these readings and in your own observation, accept or challenge traditional definitions of their family roles? How do they make choices about the relationship of paid employment to mothering? How do they gain power and fulfillment through family relationships, and how do these relationships constrict them? How are the answers to these questions different for men?

Bridal Wave

It's wedding season. Actually, it's wedding year. You might even say it's wedding millennium.

Seems like every time I turn on the TV these days, I'm blinded by the white of yet another Vera Wang gown: *For Better or for Worse, A Wedding Story, 'Til Death Do Us Part: Carmen & Dave, In Style's* annual celebrity wedding TV special, the dowry exchange known as *Trista & Ryan's Wedding*—it's all nuptials, all the time. When the one-off Fox special *Who Wants to Marry a Multi-Millionaire?* first aired a mere four years ago, viewers were shocked—shocked!—that something as superficial as a TV game show could unite a man and woman in the eyes of god and country. Today, the culminating prize of second-generation reality shows like *The Bachelor* and *The Bachelorette* is a ring, and no one even shrugs. Not since Charles and Diana's televised 1981 nuptials has marriage been such a ratings-grabber. The difference is that while the Prince and Princess of Wales had a TV marriage because they were well known, these days people are well known because they get married on TV.

It's the same story at the magazine rack: There are no fewer than 10 wedding-themed titles at my nearest Borders, each as thick as an encyclopedia and as chock-full of information. They inform brides-to-be (and bride wannabes) about everything they could possibly need to know for the ceremony: the best lipstick for wedding photos, how to style an updo, which bouquet suits an allergy-prone bride, where to buy a gold-leaf fondant cake, where to seat divorced parents.

The ostentatious, overly labored displays of emotion; the formulaic plots; the urgency to skip over relationship-building and get directly to the act—it all looks a lot like porn. The same way porn shows the act of lovemaking without reference to love, wedding porn fetishistically focuses on the ceremony without reference to the profound sentiments—and contemporary problems—that it represents. And so, from *The Bachelorette* to *Modern Bride*, the wedding itself has become the point of marriage. Any reference to what comes afterwards, i.e., the stuff women's magazines refer to as the "work" of marriage, well . . . hey, did we mention that Trista's shoes are the most expensive ever made for a wedding?

Offscreen, marriage is actually in something of a slump. Fewer Americans are marrying and more are choosing to live together instead (11 million in 2000, compared to 6.4 million a decade earlier). If they do marry, they're waiting longer to do it (the average age is 25 for women, up from 20 in 1960). With the average wedding costing more than $22,000 (up 50 percent from 1990), the "wedding-industrial complex," as sociologist Chrys Ingraham identified it in her 1999 book *White Weddings: Romancing Heterosexuality in Popular Culture*, has a huge stake in making the wedding, if not marriage itself, look like the latest must-have.

The bridal industry and ratings-hungry TV networks aren't the only ones waving the wedding flag these days. In fact, wedding porn has found some strange bedfellows, as a pop culture that was already wedding-saturated has been enlisted in a PR offensive by the Bush administration to bring heteros back onto the matrimonial ark. Bush's $1.5 billion effort aims to encourage low-income couples to tie the knot, yet the fact that marriage is no longer a social and financial necessity for a woman's survival and a man's reputation means the campaign must avoid pointing out that, like sex, the part that follows the big climax is far messier and more complicated than the ecstatic moment would lead us to believe.

However, President Bush was quick to clarify that he was talking about brides and grooms, not brides and brides. Though the Bush administration would presumably gnaw off its collective legs before declaring itself in step with Hollywood, on the subject of queer nuptials, the two entities seem to be in tacit agreement. Because on television, the story's much the same: The far right can say what they will about Hollywood's liberal agenda, but while a flurry of real-life same-sex weddings have occurred in San Francisco and Massachusetts, on TV the only gay people featured in weddings are wedding planners and stylists. The *Queer Eye* guys may be busy readying some slob for his upcoming nuptials, but the Fab Five won't be putting on Armani tuxes for their own walks down the aisle anytime soon. *Will & Grace*, groundbreaking for its portrayal of gays, only allows its straight female stars—first Grace, now Karen—to marry in its season-finale weddings.

Even celebrities who used to scandalize with their bed-hopping are now troth-pledging. Death-obsessed Jane's Addiction guitarist Dave Navarro and professional babe Carmen Electra may have gone about it unconventionally—their wedding invitation, photographed by David LaChappelle, showed them as corpses on his-and-hers morgue slabs—but their MTV reality series, *'Til Death Do Us Part,* revealed a couple consumed by the minutiae of event planning, and followed them through cake tastings, dress fittings, first-dance-song-choosing (they selected Sade's "By Your Side"), and prewedding yoga and colonics sessions. The Bush administration, despite seeming unaware of any pop culture since Steve & Eydie, was surely rubbing its beringed hands together in glee throughout: If these two heathens can find it in their hearts to merge their tax status, surely they'll set an example for America's pierced and tattooed youth.

Back in the day, Dan Quayle knew just how powerful a televised example could be when he condemned the fictional Murphy Brown for bearing a child out of wedlock. These days Marriage Savers, a promarriage advocacy group founded by former newsman Mike McManus, attributes the fact that a majority of Americans believe it's a good idea for couples to live together before marriage to the influence of movies and TV shows that depict wanton cohabitation. More to the point, Celia Duncan, the editor of British *CosmoGIRL!,* credited a recent 1.6 percent bump in British marriages to celebrity nuptials like those of the former Posh Spice to soccer star David Beckham. "The fact that so many celebrities are getting married does make a difference," she's quoted as saying in the U.K. business journal *Total Business Online* in November 2002. "They have a huge sway on society."

Stateside, nothing says traditional American values like weddings—they're big, they're expensive, and they involve a lot of shopping. In *White Weddings*, Ingraham points out that TV, movie, and celebrity weddings reaffirm outdated stereotypes: that women are concerned primarily with romantic love and shopping; that they're willing to give up their own careers or ideals for the status and perceived security of being a wife; and that a relationship is "true" only if it's codified by marriage—which, by default, restricts it to heterosexuals. And the events are invariably celebrations of well-off white people with the occasional bridesmaid of color thrown in as a nod to multiculturalism.

What's onscreen clearly reflects the wedding industry's targeted consumer: upper-income whites. Ingraham quotes the statistic that today's newlyweds earn twice the country's average household income and that whites (the race featured almost exclusively in bridal-magazine photos) marry at a higher rate than blacks or Hispanics. More tellingly, she points out the ways in which media consolidation has made the wedding-as-spectacle culturally ubiquitous. Media monolith Disney, for example, is the parent company of a dozen film production and distribution companies, including Touchstone Pictures, which made the *Father of the Bride* movies. It also owns ABC, home of *The Bachelor* and *The Bachelorette.* And among its 25-plus cable networks is Lifetime, which broadcasts wedding specials like *The "I Do" Diaries* and *Royal Weddings.* Of course, Disney's classic animated fairy tales like *Cinderella, Snow White and the Seven Dwarfs, Beauty and the Beast,* and *The Little Mermaid* typically end in weddings, and that's no doubt the inspiration for Disney's wedding business at its theme parks. (The "Ultimate Fairy Tale Wedding," available for a hundred grand, features a glass carriage that parades the bride down Main Street to meet her prince, who rides a white stallion.)

Women's magazines and the likes of *People* have always chronicled the weddings of Hollywood's brightest stars, but celebrity weddings have more recently become a genre of their own. *In Style* has taken the nuptial stargazing to new levels of obsession. It's not enough to feature "57 Pages of Dream Weddings," as promised in the February 2004 issue; now *In Style* publishes a separate celebrity wedding issue as thick as *Modern Bride* and its doorstop ilk, and broadcasts ABC specials on some of the weddings featured in the magazine.

In Style Weddings functions under the assumption that if you're going to get married, you might as well get married like a celebrity—and, in its parlance, that includes everyone from *Sabrina, the Teenage Witch* star Melissa Joan Hart to former Jerry Seinfeld squeeze Shoshanna Lonstein. The spring 2004 issue featured nearly 500 pages of information and instruction: Readers learned that Debbie Matenopoulos's fivetier cake was made by the Cake Divas, that Lonstein served sea bass at her reception, and that Geraldo Rivera bought his rings at Harry Winston. (No mention was made of the fact that it was Rivera's fifth time down the aisle.)

Journalists have written of the *In Style* "curse"—weddings or engagements that are no sooner celebrated in the magazine than they disappear faster than the latest Bennifer flick; victims have included J. Lo and Ojani Noa, J. Lo and Puff Daddy (as he was known at the time), Tara Reid and Carson Daly, and Drew Barrymore and Tom Green. The banner example is *In Style*'s March 2001 issue, which featured actor Courtney Thorne-Smith in her wedding dress on its cover, with a lengthy account of her Hawaii wedding within. By the time the issue came out, Thorne-Smith was already in the process of divorcing.

But as long as the caterers got paid, who cares? The stars of hit Fox series and actor-singer hyphenates can write off such expensive debacles as lessons in personal growth (and subjects for discussion in future magazine interviews). It's not so easy for the 401(k) class and those below. In that light, it's worth wondering how President Bush figures that marriage is the solution to poverty: If the couples have the kind of wedding pop culture encourages them to have, they'll be even poorer than when they started out. *In Style*'s spring wedding issue was chockablock with reasons why weddings are so pricey—some obvious (Reem Acra veil, $3,000; rose and snowberry bouquet, $350; vineyard rental for ceremony, $5,000) and some not so obvious (bride's handbag, $690; yo-yo favors for the kids, $2.50 a pop; wine carrier gift for out-of-town guests, $78 each).

It's wedding as shopping spree, and the implication seems to be, the more expensive the wedding, the more successful the marriage. Trista and Ryan's December 2003 nuptials, detailed exhaustively in a three-episode ABC reality miniseries, took the wedding-as-shopping metaphor to its most ostentatious level. Apart from the bride's aforementioned diamond-studded shoes, which the show's publicity repeatedly mentioned, the broadcast ran a tally of the items that added up to a $3.77 million ceremony: $750,000 location; $500,000 in pink roses; $155,000 for reception food and drink; $75,000 wedding dress; $15,000 wedding cake. Given that money is always cited as one of the most contentious issues for married couples, it would seem that the industry is sabotaging its own aim. Then again, maybe that's the point: Multiple marriages mean multiple expenditures.

Along those lines, it also seems that the wedding industry couldn't disagree more with the Bush administration's stringent anti–gay marriage stance. How could they, when snatching a piece of the gay wedding cake translates into such huge revenues? Forbes.com recently calculated a $16.8 billion annual "gay-marriage windfall" if laws were changed to legalize same-sex marriages. Specifically, the April 4, 2004, article noted, companies like Tiffany, Williams-Sonoma, and Marriott International would nicely benefit (it went on to helpfully provide their New York Stock Exchange abbreviations for any early investors). Forbes.com based its calculations on the assumption that gay couples would marry at the same rates as heterosexual couples, and spend the same amount of money, figuring, for example, $1.66 billion on collective engagement rings and $1.7 billion on honeymoons.

I'm not pretending to be such a savvy feminist that I'm impervious to wedding porn's siren song; I've fallen victim myself. Spending time with *In Style Weddings* had the same effect on me as an afternoon with *Vogue:* I was overtaken by the Fever. By the time I had reached the account of *Dawson's Creek* star Kerr Smith's Palm Springs nuptials, I had my own wedding planned: the Monique Lhuillier gown, the Audrey Hepburn upsweep, my mother's wedding ring. I wanted the party. I wanted all my family and friends to fly in and look at me at my most princesslike. (I'd gift them each with a wine basket for their effort.) Despite my own carefully deliberated belief that marriage is not for me, I still wanted a fondant cake decorated with my and my partner's initials.

I don't blame every entry in the current glut of wedding-themed shows for craven commercialism and fairy-tale portrayals. A recent episode of TLC's *A Wedding Story* (oddly enough, the least commercial of the current wedding media) revealed what it is, beyond the consumer booty and vicarious celebrity, that attracts us to wedding coverage. The episode was about a Liberian couple who had been separated by civil war, lost touch, then found each other again after each had escaped to the United States. At their best, partnerships can be seen as the symbolic opposite of war. They're about building lives, not destroying them. And weddings—when separated from the rampant heterosexual consumerism that too often attends them—are the threshold of creation: of a new family, new alliances, and new generations.

But this episode was exceptional, like a porno with a plot. And most of the audience was likely sitting there with the remote, poised for the buttercream-frosted money shot.

Waking Sleeping Beauty: The Premarital Pelvic Exam and Heterosexuality During the Cold War

In 1966 physician William F. Sheeley wrote an editorial for the *Journal of the American Medical Association* urging his colleagues to take a more active interest in the sex lives of their patients. "That basic unit without which few societies can survive—the family—depends upon discipline and control of sexual behavior," he cautioned. "Without such control, the family soon breaks down, and soon thereafter the whole society comes crashing down—like the mighty Roman Empire, which is no more."[1]

Although it would be easy to dismiss Sheeley's editorial as overly dramatic, in fact, his statements echo the fears and anxieties expressed by numerous physicians writing in American medical journals throughout the 1950s and 1960s. In essence, these physicians engaged in a three-part dialogue over female heterosexual health, marital stability, and community security. At the intersection of these three conversations was the premarital consultation and physicians' efforts at sexual instruction as a means of ensuring both the psychosexual adjustment of their patients and the stability of their patients' marriages. The healthy female orgasm was the key to it all.

In the 1950s and 1960s, physicians devoted a great deal of attention to marking the accepted parameters of "normal" female heterosexual behavior, particularly the distinction between vaginal and clitoral orgasms. Their efforts were, in part, a response to the 1953 publication of Alfred Kinsey's *Sexual Behavior in the Human Female*. While Kinsey dismissed the vaginal orgasm and instead pointed to the clitoris as the site of female sexual pleasure, physicians, with little dissent, maintained their commitment to the vaginal orgasm well into the mid-1960s, when the conversation on female heterosexual health began to wane in medical journals.[2]

At the same time that physicians honed their definition of female heterosexual health, they also stressed the importance of a healthy sex life to the marital relationship. Physicians asserted that just as a vaginal orgasm was integral to a woman's psychosexual health, the performance of healthy heterosexual gender and sexual roles—as evidenced by a satisfying sexual relationship—was crucial to the establishment and maintenance of a stable marriage.[3] Physicians ultimately extended their concern for marital stability out into the larger community, arguing that marriages and the families they created were the foundations of a morally secure citizenry. Moral security translated into political stability and military strength. Writing during the turbulence and uncertainty of the Cold War, physicians worried that "unhealthy," "maladjusted," and even extramarital sexual behavior was just as threatening to American society as were the Soviets and their nuclear bombs. Some physicians even went so far as to assert that changing trends in American sexual behavior were "part and parcel of the Communist program to change American sexual mores, [resulting] in a breakdown of the family and collapse of society as a whole, clearing the way for an easy Communist takeover."[4]

Citing rising rates of venereal disease and divorce, as well as the increasing sexual permissiveness of the nation's youth, physicians throughout these decades likened what they saw as "sexual chaos" to a contagion threatening the very health and safety of the nation—a contagion that could only be checked by containing sexual behavior within heterosexual marriage.[5] Physicians did not stop there; containment was only the first step. As Sheeley illustrated, physicians believed that the family units created by heterosexual marriages formed the building blocks of the national community. Physicians therefore sought to reinforce American society against moral and political subversion by strengthening individual marriages.[6] They insisted that the most effective means of doing so was to ensure that couples were practicing the "right kind" of sex.

In articles, letters, and editorials in the professional medical journals, as well as in conference presentations and books, physicians promoted a model of heterosexuality that underscored the era's prescribed gender roles, including their race- and class-based assumptions.[7] Using a specific definition of sexual health, physicians did not assume that heterosexual performance indicated a patient was sexually "normal." In fact, sexual "deviancy" was not their only concern. Instead, physicians maintained distinctions between "good" and "bad" heterosexual identity and performance. In their estimation, sexual preference and conduct were inseparable from gender identification and performance. Consequently, physicians claimed a passive and receptive vaginal orgasm as the hallmark of a well-adjusted and normal femininity. A woman's ability to achieve vaginal orgasm during intercourse with her husband was both symptom and cure, as it verified her appropriate gender and sexual role performance—a passive and feminine wife yielding to her active and masculine husband.[8] Vaginal intercourse that culminated in a vaginal orgasm was, therefore, the definition of the "right kind" of sex.

Yet despite the assumption that this was the normal and healthy exercise of heterosexuality, it was not presumed to be instinctive. For example, physicians and psychiatrists cited the rising divorce rate as a sign of widespread sexual maladjustment caused by ignorance and fear, particularly on the part of women. Young brides approached their wedding nights ill-prepared for initiation into marital heterosexuality; consequently, as physician Nadina Kavinoky maintained, the trauma of even a small amount of bleeding and pain often led to unhappy marriages and divorce.[9]

Proper instruction and preparation before the marriage promised a quick antidote to the nation's sexual difficulties. This article considers how physicians proposed to communicate their definition of healthy marital heterosexuality to their patients through the use of a premarital pelvic examination. The pelvic exam, as part of a state-mandated premarital consultation intended to monitor the spread of venereal disease, enabled physicians to monitor a woman's response to penetration and thereby estimate her ability to experience vaginal orgasm. Physicians asserted that, by ensuring that young women knew what to expect on their wedding nights, and, even more importantly, how to have the right kind of orgasm, they had a special role to play in contributing to marital stability. These stable marriages,

in turn, would serve as the foundation for a morally secure nation.[10] In short, physicians believed that the fully functioning American family—including healthy sexual performance—was part of the national arsenal used to combat the chaos and immorality encouraged by the looming Soviet threat. Thus, the premarital pelvic exam stood at the intersection of physicians' assertions regarding heterosexual health, marital stability, and community security. In the ideological battle against communism, the premarital pelvic exam afforded the ideal opportunity for them to practice a unique form of preventive medicine.

THE FATHERLY PHYSICIAN AS SEXUAL INSTRUCTOR

While American medicine was already a prestigious profession in the mid-twentieth century, the standardization of various specialties, including obstetrics and gynecology as distinct from general family practice, was still underway.[11] This drive towards specialization and standardization encouraged the emergence of medical journals such as *General Practice, Fertility and Sterility*, and *Obstetrics and Gynecology* in the early 1950s. Like the *Journal of the American Medical Association (JAMA)*, they quickly became more than a forum for informing physicians of advances in medical science. They also served as a means of reinforcing hegemony among physicians both as a larger group and within various specialties. This growth of professional identity was aided by the heightened prestige attached to Cold War science and the role of modern medicine in preventing the spread of infectious disease and improving the quality of life for the nation's citizens.[12]

In this context, physicians came to believe that they—even more than ministers or parents—were the best guides for a young couple seeking a mutually satisfying marital relationship. Their medical and anatomical expertise as well as their role as "father-confessor" to their patients made them knowledgeable and authoritative advisors.[13] As physician Jed Pearson explained, "The physician wishing to do premarital counseling is admirably equipped because of his broad medical and cultural education. In addition he needs only the attributes of personal warmth, sympathetic understanding, and an objectivity in approach to each patient's problems in order to succeed."[14] Although general practitioners and obstetrician-gynecologists emphasized how particularly well-suited their fields were to addressing matters related to female heterosexual health, they also claimed responsibility for ensuring the sexual well-being of the entire family unit on a long-term basis.

This emphasis on treating the family as well as the individual reflected physicians' concern with the family as the site of psychosexual development. Psychoanalytic theories of sexuality had become increasingly influential in the United States throughout the 1930s and 1940s. European psychiatrists seeking refuge in the United States brought with them a commitment to Freudian methods and theories. At the same time, the nature of psychiatric treatment shifted from rural state institutions for the "disturbed" to urban psychoanalysts treating a middle-class clientele with the time and money to attend to their mental and emotional well-being. Thus, psychiatrists became increasingly concerned not simply with curing the insane, but tending to the maladjusted as well. In this context, sexual behavior became an indicator of psychological health.[15] The rejection of more than one million men from military service due to mental and neurological disorders, coupled with those dismissed for being homosexuals, suggested to many in positions of power that the mental and sexual health problems of individuals were adversely affecting the nation. This was well demonstrated in 1950 Congressional hearings on the "homosexual problem," which linked medical discourse on homosexuality with issues of national security.[16] Because homosexuality was classified as a psychiatric disorder, the medical profession was the logical place to look for a solution to the problem.

General practitioners and psychiatrists agreed that prevention was just as important as treatment. Because the family played a pivotal role in Freudian theories of psychosexual development, the medical profession turned to the home as the main bastion against homosexuality and other psychosexual disturbances, such as frigidity. With the focus on the family, general practitioners became the primary source of medical intervention. Obstetrician-gynecologists were a close second. If they were successful, then the healthy families they produced would nurture healthy individuals. These families would serve as the building blocks of a healthy community and, by extension, a healthy nation.

THE RIGHT KIND OF SEX

The key to understanding how and why physicians constructed their role as sexual counselor lies in their belief that psychosexual development, while a natural and predetermined process, was not innate. Various factors could disrupt an individual's advancement to normal, mature, adult heterosexuality—a mother who was too doting, a father who was too distant, and, for women, a wedding night that was less than tender. An individual's psychosexual maladjustment held the potential for long-term impact on society, for psychosexually maladjusted parents—especially mothers—could not help but raise psychosexually maladjusted children.[17] Consequently, physicians placed great importance on a woman's transition into marital heterosexuality. In some sense, the wedding night was considered the last chance to overcome any previously induced sexual trauma and to set women on the path to psychosexual wellness. Surely, this was all much too important to be left to chance.

Greatly influenced by Freudian theories of psychosexual development, physicians characterized healthy female heterosexuality by such factors as passive acceptance of male sexual direction, a soft and submissive femininity, and a self-sacrificial drive to motherhood. The vagina formed the epicenter of this heterosexuality, as it served both as the site of the successful performance of heterosexual intercourse and as the only healthy outlet for female orgasm. Unlike male orgasm, which was considered necessary for male sexual health as well as for reproduction, female orgasm was a *goal*, but certainly not a *necessity*. As obstetrician Eugene Hamilton reminded readers of *Missouri Medicine*, "The male orgasm is a biologic necessity for the preservation of the species. For the female it is a luxury."[18] As evidence that the female orgasm was superfluous, physicians offered the explanation that "the normal woman is not so easily aroused [as the male] and may only on occasion achieve a climax."[19] Female sexual responsiveness, they asserted, was a latent energy that must be awakened by the more active energy of their partners, presumably their husbands. As psychoanalyst Helen Deutsch concluded, "The awakening of the vagina to full sexual functioning is entirely dependent upon the man's activity; and [the] absence of spontaneous vaginal activity constitutes the physiologic background of feminine passivity."[20] An active, or sexually aggressive, woman might arouse male anxieties of castration and thereby interfere with male heterosexual performance and psychosexual adjustment. Thus, female sexual passivity, as demonstrated through a woman's vaginal orgasm, was important not only to experiencing a satisfying and healthy sex life, but also to ensuring that a woman as well as her husband would be able to maintain the roles and identities "normal" for their sex.

The emphasis placed on vaginal orgasm reflected the discourse surrounding the nature of female sexuality that engaged the medical profession in the mid-twentieth century, particularly the debate over the valid definition of frigidity and the superiority of the vagina over the clitoris as the locus of female heterosexual pleasure. Neither physicians nor psychiatrists denied the existence of or possibility for clitoral orgasm; rather, they insisted that the clitoris was the primary organ of sexual pleasure during childhood, but in puberty, and particularly with the approach of marriage, a healthy, mature woman transferred her focus to the vagina.[21] This transfer was not so much physical as it was psychological; thus, the woman who failed to transfer suffered from a psychological neurosis that manifested itself in the inability to have a vaginal orgasm. In other words, she was frigid. Although a clitoral orgasm would still be physically possible, the mature woman would willingly and consciously defer to the vagina, maintaining a role of passive reception of the penis and restricting her sexual pleasure to that induced by penetration. The definition of frigidity used by physicians and psychiatrists in the mid-twentieth century did not simply correlate to the absence of sexual desire or sensation. Certainly, that was one form of frigidity, but physicians and psychiatrists primarily stressed the importance and pervasiveness of frigidity as *inappropriate*, not absent, sexual outlet. This frigidity would manifest itself in the failure to achieve a vaginal orgasm—or, worse yet, a consistent reliance on the clitoris for pleasure.[22]

Linked to this inappropriate sexual outlet was inappropriate gender role behavior. In addition to her improper sexual performance, a frigid woman would display improper gender identifications as well. If these women married in an attempt to create a normal life for themselves or to mask their psychosexual immaturity, "the marital union may be characterized by refusal to assume any serious obligation of wifehood or motherhood." Two of the era's most widely cited medical theorists of female sexuality, Edmund Bergler and William Kroger, warned that symptoms included interest in such activities as playing cards, participating in sports, traveling alone, and "perhaps even [the] aggressive pursuit of a career." At the same time, wives who became so obsessively involved in their homemaker duties that they stifled or neglected their husbands might also be frigid.[23]

Conversely, the psychosexually well-adjusted woman would recognize her husband's role as the head of the household and eagerly embrace her duties in the home. This included submitting to his sexual direction. Her ability to experience exclusively vaginal orgasm served as evidence of the extent to which a woman had adjusted to her role as wife and mother. Likewise, a truly healthy heterosexuality was indicated by appropriate psychosexual gender identity and corresponding heterosexual and social role performance. In the 1950s and 1960s, physicians writing in medical journals often cited a subconscious rejection of femininity and the maternal role as the main factor in female sexual disorder.[24] Women who failed to conform to expected standards of femininity were considered to be cases of latent frigidity or undiagnosed sexual dysfunction.

The definition of "healthy" sexuality and its accompanying gender ideology were further marked by assumptions of race and class. Throughout the medical journals, patients, like their physicians, were presumed to be white, heterosexual, and middle class. In fact, from 1950 to 1969 homosexuals, the working class, and women of color appeared in *JAMA* and the *New England Journal of Medicine* only in discussions of abnormal cases, pathologic behaviors, and especially in regard to lesbians, as the causes of neurosis in men. Chastity and modesty were often linked to the patient's (white) race, as physicians believed that "[e]mbarrassment at having the vulva exposed, looked at, or touched is a normal reaction, more deeply instilled in some racial groups than others."[25] As a result, physicians expected that their white patients would be in greater need of sensitivity and reassurance during the pelvic exam than their patients of color would be. Physicians also asserted that class and cultural backgrounds would determine a couple's "ability to fulfill their masculine or feminine destiny as parents" as well as "the pattern of the couple's relationship."[26] Intermarriage between different socioeconomic backgrounds produced further complications because, as one physician explained in 1966, "It is difficult for the middle class people to understand the behavior of the lower class male, and even more difficult for the female to understand comparable behavior." Although "lower class" men generally had more sexual experience, according to the physicians, middle-class men were more sophisticated and more sensitive to the needs of their partners. While the lower-class man was "unconcerned" with his partner's pleasure, the middle-class man "considers himself a failure if his wife doesn't have an orgasm."[27]

These assumptions are extremely important when we consider that physicians repeatedly stressed the need for a well-adjusted heterosexuality as the basis for a healthy femininity and maternal role. The implication of the race and class biases of the physicians was that only white and middle-class women could fully adjust to their own "psychosexual destinies" and, by extension, ensure that they would be able to guide the next generation to healthy adulthood. Perhaps fortunately, physicians did not attempt to "cure" the sexual problems of those who were neither white nor middle-class. Instead, they focused their attention on the psychosexual development of their patients—white, middle-class, and heterosexual women. For these women, unhealthy sexual behavior, such as frigidity, homosexuality, or nymphomania, indicated a maladjusted psychosexual identity or a rejection of femininity that needed remedying before a woman damaged herself, her children, and her community.[28]

Because the vaginal orgasm was the epicenter of healthy heterosexuality, the bride became the focus of the physician's premarital consultation, and the pelvic exam became the most important part of the office visit. Physicians worried that if a woman was too anxious, she might resist penetration and thereby undermine the successful performance of heterosexuality in her marriage. They imagined that the patient who was fearful of the pelvic exam would most likely be fearful of penetration in general.[29] Rather than approaching the exam as a means of observing how well patients had adjusted to intercourse after marriage, physicians in the 1950s and 1960s proposed using the pelvic exam as a means of instructing unmarried women in how to prepare for marital intercourse. In particular, physicians hoped to pre-empt any emotional or physical trauma that might be inflicted by a less-than-tender wedding night, which, of course, was presumed to be the patient's initial sexual intercourse. Consequently, physicians repeatedly advised their colleagues to perform a thorough, yet gentle, premarital pelvic exam that would quell any unspoken fears their patient might have of penetration.[30]

In their concern for the psychosexual development of their female patients, physicians expected women to lack both sexual knowledge and experience. While physicians recognized that information about marriage and sexuality was readily available to the public, they dismissed many of the sources as inadequate or misleading. Much of this information, they insisted, left young women confused, anxious, and ill-prepared.

They asserted that physicians should employ their medical knowledge and moral authority to set the record straight about healthy and normal heterosexual performance. For example, at the same time that editor Helen Gurley Brown was advising women to explore the joys of premarital sexuality, one *JAMA* editor reminded her colleagues that, "As every nice girl in Western culture knows, it is the male who is the [sexual] aggressor, while the passive female submits with either good or bad grace."[31] In particular, physicians sought to combat any anxieties regarding painful penetration or sexual incompatibility induced by misinformed gossip with girlfriends by educating women in just "how adequately [their] own sex organs are prepared to receive the erect penis."[32] The premarital pelvic exam offered the perfect opportunity for them to do so.

THE PREMARITAL PELVIC EXAM

By the end of the Second World War, widespread state premarital exam legislation had been in effect for only a decade at best. Although Oregon, Texas, and Wisconsin had laws as early as 1913 requiring a signed certificate verifying that a physical examination had confirmed that a man was free of venereal disease before a marriage ceremony could be performed, no state presumed to require a comparable declaration from a woman. Indeed, Wisconsin legislators had repeatedly killed bills proposing physical inspections for VD for brides because they "objected to having their young daughters 'pawed over'" by physicians.[33] But in the 1930s this sentiment had begun to change. The increasing professionalization of American medicine brought new respect and authority to physicians, interfering with legislators' ability to object to their examinations on grounds of decency and morality. At the same time, physicians began to organize as a force lobbying for public health policy.[34] While some physicians, legislators, and public health officials continued to protest that mandatory exams were a gross invasion of their patients' privacy, lawmakers' desire to eradicate VD and preserve the health of the population proved more persuasive.[35] In 1935, the Connecticut legislature passed the first state law mandating premarital physical examinations for both men and women prior to the issuance of a marriage license. Within four years, seventeen additional states enacted similar legislation.[36]

Generally speaking, state laws simply required blood tests and venereal disease screenings for brides and grooms. However, within fifteen years of the initial Connecticut legislation, physicians also advocated the use of the premarital consultation to discuss matters of sexual adjustment with their patients.[37] Although control of VD remained the original intent of the laws, physicians acknowledged that "the clear objective [of the premarital consultation was] to foster and preserve a sound family unit, a happy marriage, and healthy children." By 1964, the number of states with such laws had doubled to thirty-seven. "Thus," wrote the editors of *JAMA*, "the legal machinery is set up to bring young people to the physician before marriage, at a time when ignorance and fear about sex can be evaluated most easily and, hopefully, overcome."[38]

Recognizing that restrictions on time and expenses meant that premarital counseling was usually limited to a single visit with the bride alone, physicians focused their attention on the pelvic exam. The model premarital pelvic exam was outlined in a 1954 article in *JAMA* by obstetrician-gynecologist Nadina Kavinoky. Following inspection of the female genitalia, Kavinoky suggested that the physician should approach the topic of sexual adjustment. Because "a fearful virgin must first be taught to cooperate and relax," the physician should instruct the patient in relaxing and contracting the vaginal sphincter and pubococcygeus muscles. This exercise, Kavinoky promised, would enable "even the fearful virgin" to learn "how to cooperate and develop a more spontaneous rhythm." Once the patient was comfortable with these exercises, then the physician should proceed with the second step in the premarital pelvic examination: the insertion of a well-lubricated instrument into the patient's vagina so that "the virgin [could] realize that there is a normal opening in the hymen that leads into a deep vaginal canal." After the initial penetration, the physician should instruct the patient to "bear down" and insert the tube further into the vaginal canal. "The rate at which [the patient] introduces the tube and her facial expression reveal her anxiety," Kavinoky explained matter-of-factly, but "the return of color to her face and her relief, as she discovers no bleeding and no pain, convinces the physician of the therapeutic value of this simple procedure."[39]

Kavinoky's method of introducing the young woman to penetration became the accepted method for the premarital exam for the next two decades.[40] The exercises she implemented reflected the influence of psychoanalytic theories of psychosexual development, particularly the emphasis on penetration and the vagina's welcoming reception of the penis. In addition, Kavinoky was clearly relying on the work of gynecologist Arnold Kegel, who developed the series of vaginal and pubococcygeal contractions that became known as "Kegel exercises."

Like most physicians and psychiatrists of the time, Kegel pointed to involuntary muscular contractions during orgasm as the true indicator of mature female sexuality. While Kegel recognized that many women who experienced solely clitoral orgasms considered their sex lives to be satisfactory, he dismissed the clitoral orgasm as a crutch. Once women were able to transfer their focus to the vagina, Kegel reported in a 1953 letter to the editors of the *JAMA*, they appeared to "forget the clitoris" entirely.[41] But Kegel warned that even a woman who was otherwise sexually well-adjusted could be traumatized by a "rough first experience."[42] Like the other physicians writing in American medical journals at this time, Kegel failed to see the premarital consultation as an opportunity to advise grooms on how best to approach the act of initial penetration. Instead, physicians seemed to suggest that warning the bride to be patient and not resistant would be enough to get the couple through their first attempts at intercourse. Kegel's letter reflects a common suggestion that so long as the vagina was not resistant to penetration, marital heterosexuality would work itself out. After all, a woman's orgasm was more emotional than it was physical, and motherhood, not orgasm, was the ultimate fulfillment of her psychosexual destiny.

Perhaps this insistence on a compliant vagina and an emotional orgasm explains why virtually none of the material on the premarital consultation, including Kegel's letter to the editor and Kavinoky's article, made any mention of female arousal. Even Kavinoky's educational exercise in heterosexual performance remained just as clinical as the standard pelvic exam. Although the exercise was intended to prepare women for intercourse, it was not meant to replicate the sex act exactly. Consequently, physicians who used or advocated the use of Kavinoky's model premarital pelvic exam created a tricky situation. On the one hand, they wanted to demonstrate to their patients that penetration was nothing to fear and to convey the message that penetration should lead to orgasm. On the other hand, they did not want to arouse their patients. This fine line that physicians walked was illustrated by physician Janet Towne, whose article on premarital counseling offered a perplexing scenario.[43]

Towne described a patient having difficulty performing Kegel exercises. Her proposed solution was to induce muscular contraction by penetrating the vagina—in effect attempting to trick the vagina into an instinctive contraction. But, Towne warned, if the patient displayed an "erotic" response to the doctor's penetration, then the exam must end immediately. In short, while doctors wanted to tell their female patients how to respond sexually, they did not actually want to make them do it in their offices. This is certainly understandable. After all, it had been several decades since physicians had last advocated stimulating their patients to orgasm as a course of treatment for various nervous disorders. But, whereas the physicians administering "therapeutic massage" were able to argue that their activities were not sexual because penetration had not occurred, physicians administering exams such as Towne's or Kavinoky's could not claim the same.[44] Penetration had, in fact, taken place. Instead, physicians identified their procedure as non-sexual on the basis of their definitions of what heterosexual intercourse looked like, specifically penetration by a penis.

For example, Towne made a telling assumption: she only warned that attempting to induce a "vaginal response" was dangerous if the physician was male. Towne did not imagine a situation in which a woman might respond erotically to penetration by another woman. This reflects the physicians' assumption that lesbians, as psychosexually maladjusted women, would rely on clitoral stimulation rather than vaginal penetration in their lovemaking.[45] At the same time, Towne's assumption reinforced the assertion that the medical instrument should not be viewed as a mere substitute for the penis. Without a penis, it could not really be sex.

But there is something else at work here. In Towne's illustration, sexual response and sexual arousal are two separate and independent things. Most importantly, sexual arousal was not necessary to evoke "erotic" response. This helps to explain why Towne, like Kegel and Kavinoky, believed it was possible for physicians to train their patients in vaginal response without arousing them. In essence, the woman's sexual needs or desires were peripheral to her passive reception of the penis, as demonstrated by her embrace of the medical instrument without any need for sexual stimulation. Therefore, despite their purported concern for ensuring that women had satisfying sexual experiences in marriage, physicians actually endorsed a vision of "normal" heterosexual performance that perpetuated the emphasis on male sexual needs—a compliant vagina—rather than encouraging women to pursue physical sexual pleasure.

In fact, the physicians' goal was to create sexual partners who were compliant rather than eager. Physicians advised their female patients that pleasure would come later, once they had "gotten used to" penetration; women should be neither too fearful nor too eager. In the midst of all this discussion of fearful virgins, the idea that a woman might be too eager to begin heterosexual intercourse might seem a bit counterintuitive. Yet physicians repeatedly insisted that couples must not bring unrealistic expectations to the marriage bed. Wilfred Hulse warned that "[o]wing to the increased emphasis on female orgasm, the young bride and her spouse may occasionally become depressed and discouraged if she does not experience orgasm from the very beginning of married life."[46] In order to reassure the husband that it was no masculine failing on his part and the wife that it was no reflection on her femininity, physicians were urged to advise couples that it often took time and patience before a young bride could experience a fully satisfying sexual life. Like Kegel, these physicians believed that vaginal orgasm, while the only natural expression of female sexuality, was not necessarily instinctive. In some sense, they imagined themselves as coaches—not only overseeing their athletes' performance training, but also counseling them in reasonable goals and expectations. Gynecologist Patricia Lawrence cautioned that marital sexuality "is a learned technique requiring experience and practice," and "for the bride, responsiveness must often be cultivated."[47] Another gynecologist, Charles Flowers, advised that a woman should not expect to orgasm on her wedding night. Instead, "the bride should understand that coitus is a beautiful and tender expression of affection in which she achieves the giving of herself and body." Flowers continued, "She may be reminded of the first party or dance that she attended. The newness of the occasion, her excitement in wearing her first evening dress and high heeled shoes compensated for the lack of agility in herself and her dancing partner."[48] But why, after all their talk about the importance of the wedding night for setting the stage for healthy sexual and marital adjustment, would physicians counsel brides not to expect to orgasm on their wedding nights?

WAKING SLEEPING BEAUTY

Physicians stressed the need to coax women into orgasm because their vision of normal heterosexuality relied upon a confluence of gender performance, heterosexual development, and psychological health. This vision was best depicted in psychoanalyst Marie Bonaparte's 1953 volume *Female Sexuality*. The volume's cover professed that while "The Kinsey Report Gives the Facts—This Book Explains the *WHY* and *WHEREFORE*" of female sexuality. Bonaparte likened healthy female heterosexual development to the fairytale Sleeping Beauty. She asserted that "the little girl who is destined to be truly feminine must generally have abandoned clitoridal [*sic*] masturbation before she succeeds in obtaining end-pleasure [vaginal orgasm]." Bonaparte continued, "[L]ike the Sleeping Beauty, pierced in the hand—the hand of guilty masturbation . . . the preformed libidinal organization of the little girl will sink into slumber until such time as the husband's advent through the briars of the hymeneal forest awakes her from sleep. Such would be the ideal development of our little girls."[49]

In the traditional story of Sleeping Beauty, an evil witch puts a curse on a beautiful young princess. Despite all the efforts of her parents and their subjects to circumvent the conditions of the curse, on her sixteenth birthday the princess pricks her hand on a spinning wheel and she and the kingdom fall into a deep slumber. One hundred years later, a brave prince penetrates the forest that has grown around the castle. Finding Sleeping Beauty, he takes the liberty of kissing her motionless lips. Much to his joy, his kiss breaks the spell and she awakens and gratefully marries him.

In the fairytale maintained by Bonaparte and the physicians, Sleeping Beauty—personifying the ideal sexuality of all women—is asleep and will only be roused by the passions of the bridegroom. Unlike the woman in the fairytale who woke after just one kiss, the real-life Sleeping Beauty will awaken slowly, by the gentle persistence of her prince. But this version of the story has a second hero, as only the efforts of the physician will ensure that the prince succeeds, particularly in his navigation of the "hymeneal forest" that stands between him and his bride. Indeed, while the prince in the fairytale simply had to hack his way through a century's worth of briar growth, the real-life groom faced the physical and psychological barrier of the hymen.

Physicians agreed that the hymen was "the most misunderstood structure of feminine anatomy."[50] They cautioned that women coming in for their first pelvic exam might fear that inspection of the hymen would expose "past indiscretions or evidence of masturbation" or, conversely, that the exam would rupture the hymen, removing all evidence of virginity.[51] A ruptured or softened hymen, they assumed, indicated that counseling was not needed. Gynecologist Eleanor Easley explained, "If the hymen is well dilated already . . . I don't want to waste time on unnecessary or inappropriate advice."[52]

But physicians expected that most women would approach their first pelvic exam as well as their wedding night with their hymens intact. They also expected these women to be afraid that rupturing the hymen would be painful. Physician Martin Goldberg warned that "there is often considerable fear that sex will be terribly painful, that the hymen will be resistant, or that somehow the vagina is not 'big enough'." He continued, "Conversely, some young husbands may fear hurting their wives and may be concerned about rupturing the hymen or making first entry. Or they, too, may fear that their genitals are not large enough to perform the sex act successfully."[53] Physicians noted that this anxiety on the part of the bridegroom as well as the bride could easily be overcome by premarital dilation of the hymen. As Easley noted, "men are happy for the doctor to take over part of the job of preparing the hymen for intercourse." But, she explained, "some gynecologists . . . believe that unless the difficulties are insurmountable, dilation is the husband's job, and that it teaches him fundamental lessons in consideration for his wife."[54]

Easley's suggestion that the hymen should be left intact so that the husband can learn "fundamental lessons" in how to approach his wife on their wedding night was not one that was lauded by other physicians. Indeed, most physicians believed that hymeneal dilation was too sensitive of a job for a "bungling" bridegroom.[55] Physician Irving J. Sands cautioned readers of the *New York State Journal of Medicine* that "The act of defloration in the female may set up a chain of reactions either for a happy and satisfying sexual marital life or for a frustrating and disappointing one."[56] Guiding a fearful bride into a healthy sexuality rooted in her openness to penetration was more important than a husband's right to conquest. Thus, physicians' focus was entirely on the bride's fear of penetration and removing any physical or psychological obstacles that might exist.[57]

In addition to verbally reassuring the patient about the elasticity of her vagina, physicians also advocated performing exercises to dilate the hymen prior to marriage. The patient could be instructed in digitally stretching her vaginal opening in a warm bath. Other women were given a dilator to use, for, as one physician explains, "This will accomplish not only dilation of the hymen but also get the patient used to something being inserted into the vagina."[58] In the case of the patient who objected to self-dilation on the grounds that it too closely resembled masturbation, one physician advised that "The remark that she is now a grown woman about to enter marriage and that she should take an adult attitude about such things suffices to reassure her."[59] Most physicians, however, accepted the idea that many women found manipulating their own genitals to be "distasteful" and instead expected patients to prefer that the physician use a set of dilators to gradually increase vaginal elasticity for them.[60] Many authors noted that consent (often written) was required from the patient's fiancé, and, in some cases, her parents, in order to perform this dilation.[61] They repeatedly emphasized that the decision to pursue this course of treatment was one that must be considered carefully *by the couple*. Even though physicians preferred dilation to take place within a situation they controlled so as to best avoid physical or emotional trauma, they assumed that a woman's body belonged not merely to their patient, but also to her future husband and even her family. Their authority as physicians only extended so far as the husband-to-be was willing to grant it. If a groom refused to agree to medical dilation, the physician could not perform it, no matter how despicable he found the groom's attitude to be.[62]

Like Kavinoky's exercise, the methods of dilation of the hymen recommended by physicians clearly served several functions. At the most basic level, premarital dilation ensured that the vagina was able to be penetrated and that no physical impediments to intercourse remained. This included rupturing or stretching the hymen so that penetration would not be painful or traumatic. There was also a psychological or emotional dimension to dilation. If the woman was frightened, then the various exercises would allow her to experience "first hand" the elasticity of her vagina without any pressure to perform sexually. There was also a psychological or emotional effect for the absent groom, as premarital dilation removed any fears he might have had about injuring his bride. The result of this premarital preparation via both hymeneal dilation and Kavinoky's exercises was a woman who came to her marriage bed with an open mind and a compliant vagina. If all went as physicians hoped, marital consummation would be painless. The groom had no reason to fear causing pain or bleeding, and yet he could still feel secure in the fact that he was the first

man to have intercourse with his wife. Likewise, the bride had no reason to fear penetration, but she could still offer herself to her husband with a clear conscience. Even if she did not orgasm, the couple would surely be on the path to a healthy sexual relationship. Although the physician might never hear a word of thanks from either of them, he could feel confident that he had played a key role in effecting this fairytale ending.

CONCLUSION

"The family," physician Verna Stevens-Young explained, "is in essence the unit around which our communities are built."[63] Psychosexually well-adjusted individuals engaging in normal heterosexual intercourse promised to create stable marriages and secure families. And, according to the logic driving physicians in the decades of the Cold War, these strong families would produce strong communities, which would come together to form a strong nation capable of leading the free world. Marriages thus became imbued with great social and political, as well as personal, significance in the 1950s and 1960s. Conforming to the accepted model of heterosexual performance—both within the bedroom and outside of it—indicated not only a couple's sexual health, but also their adherence to the "American" way of life. Those who did not (because they could not or would not) were suspect.

In the premarital consultation, physicians intended to guide their patients into these satisfying and healthy marital relationships. Although their focus was on the heterosexual behavior of newly married couples, their motives clearly extended further, into the moral security of the community. With most states mandating premarital medical examinations as a prerequisite to obtaining a marriage license, physicians believed that they had both the opportunity and the expertise to discuss matters of sexual adjustment with their female patients, and thereby strengthen the moral fiber of American society.[64] If, as physician H. T. McGuire claimed in 1952, "the family unit is the keystone of the arch of our democracy," then satisfying marital sexuality was the foundation of the family unit. Making sure that women were not fearful of penetration was the physician's role in ensuring its success.[65]

In the decades before the resurgent feminist movement insisted that the personal is political, American physicians made the same point by linking healthy heterosexual vaginal orgasm, which they considered the prerequisite for marital stability, to the shoring up of the national security state. Sexuality therefore became part of the domestic policies of the Cold War not only in the exclusion and persecution of those individuals labeled as deviants, but also in the disciplining and control of the sexual behavior of those individuals considered to be normal. The line between the personal and the political did, in fact, blur as sexuality was used as a weapon of both national defense and political subterfuge. In matters of the state, as well as in matters of the heart, sex and politics make frequent, if somewhat strange, bedfellows.

ACKNOWLEDGMENTS

I would like to thank Leila Rupp, Jane Sherron De Hart, Katherine Jellison, Sandra Dawson, April Haynes, Elizabeth Stordeur Pryor, David Schuster, Matt Sutton, Warren Wood, A. J. Lewis, and the anonymous readers for the *Journal of Women's History* for their helpful comments.

NOTES

1. William F. Sheeley, M.D., "Sex and the Practicing Physician," *Journal of the American Medical Association*, hereafter *JAMA*, 195 (January 1966): 133.

2. Alfred C. Kinsey, Wardell B. Pomeroy, Clyde E. Martin, and Paul H. Gebhard, *Sexual Behavior in the Human Female* (Philadelphia: W. B. Saunders Company, 1953). Although Jane Gerhard has situated Kinsey as a link between the conservative definitions of heterosexual health that appeared in the early twentieth century and the sexually liberating ideology of second-wave feminism, Kinsey's research had little impact on the discussion of heterosexual health in the professional journals during the 1950s and early 1960s. Most mention of Kinsey was to dismiss his research and reaffirm the profession's commitment to the vaginal orgasm. Jane Gerhard, *Desiring Revolution: Second-Wave Feminism and the Rewriting of American Sexual Thought 1920–1982* (New York: Columbia University Press, 2001), chap. 2.

3. Sex as a cornerstone of stable marriage became well accepted among psychologists and marriage experts in the early twentieth century. Perhaps the best known proponent is Th. H. Van de Velde, M.D., *Ideal Marriage: Its Physiological and Technique* (New York: Random House, 1930).

4. Collin E. Cooper, M.D., Letter to the Editor, *JAMA* 209 (August 1969): 941. Cooper's letter was one of nine written to the editors of *JAMA* condemning their recent advocacy of secular sex education programs in the nation's schools. Other authors suggested that sex education was Communist inspired, based on a Swedish model of immorality, and anti-Christian. Editorial, "Sex Education in the Schools," *JAMA* 2008 (May 1969): 1016. Physicians were not the only authorities linking sexual behavior and citizenship. During the height of the Cold War, sexual "deviance" was suspect at best and treasonous at worst. See John D'Emilio, "The Homosexual Menace: The Politics of Sexuality in Cold War America," in *Passion and Powers: Sexuality in History*, eds. Kathy Peiss and Christina Simmons

(Philadelphia: Temple University Press, 1989), 226–40; David Caute, *The Great Fear: The Anti-Communist Purge Under Truman and Eisenhower* (New York: Simon & Schuster, 1978); Margot Canaday, "Building a Straight State: Sexuality and Social Citizenship Under the 1944 G.I. Bill," *Journal of American History* 90 (December 2003): 935–57; Robert J. Corber, *In the Name of National Security: Hitchcock, Homophobia, and the Political Construction of Gender in Postwar America* (Durham, NC: Duke University Press, 1993); David Campbell, *Writing Security: United States Foreign Policy and the Politics of Identity* (Minneapolis: University of Minnesota Press, 1992), 150–60; and Robert D. Dean, *Imperial Brotherhood: Gender and the Making of Cold War Foreign Policy* (Amherst: University of Massachusetts Press, 2001.

5. In 1958, the editors of the *New England Journal of Medicine*, hereafter *NEJM*, attributed the decline in the nation's morals (as evidenced by increasing pre- and extra-marital sexual activity among women) to three factors: the culture of leisure and self-indulgence that characterized American society at mid-century, the sexual emancipation of women, and Cold War uncertainty about the future. Editorial, "Syphilis on the March," *NEJM* 259 (September 1958): 496. See also Nicholas J. Fiumara, M.D., M.Ph., Bernard Appel, M.D., William Hill, M.D., and Herbert Mescon, M.D., "Venereal Disease Today," *NEJM* 260 (September 1959): 863–68.

6. Sheeley, "Sex and the Practicing Physician," 133; Editorial, "Stock of the Puritans," *NEJM* 270 (January 1964): 104–5; Irving J. Sands, M.D., "Marriage Counseling as a Medical Responsibility," *New York State Journal of Medicine* 54 (July 1954): 2050–56; Jed W. Pearson, Jr., M.D., "The Physician's Role in Premarriage Counseling," *American Journal of Obstetrics and Gynecology*, hereafter *AJOG*, 71 (February 1956): 363–67; Raymond W. Waggoner, M.D., Sc.D., "Marriage Counseling as a Responsibility of the Physician," *Journal of the Arkansas Medical Society*, hereafter *JAMS*, 64 (November 1967): 211–14; O. Sturgeon English, M.D., "The Role of the General Practitioner in Counselling [*sic*] Before

and After Marriage," *Delaware State Medical Journal* 24 (November 1952): 312–19; Robert H. Fagan, M.D., "The Role of the Obstetrician-Gynecologist in Marital Maladjustment," *AJOG* 89 (June 1964): 328–34; and Herman I. Kantor, M.D., "The Premarital Consultation," *The Mississippi Doctor* 64 (February 1968): 79–81.

7. Elaine Tyler May, *Homeward Bound: American Families in the Cold War Era* (New York: Basic Books, 1988); Stephanie Coontz, *The Way We Never Were: American Families and the Nostalgia Trap* (New York: Basic Books, 1992); Joanne Meyerowitz, ed., *Not June Cleaver: Women and Gender in Postwar America 1945–1960* (Philadelphia: Temple University Press, 1994); and Jessica Weiss, *To Have and to Hold: Marriage, the Baby Boom, and Social Change* (Chicago: University of Chicago Press, 2000).

8. Sheeley, "Sex and the Practicing Physician," 133; "Medical News: Submissive Women Arise and Marriages Fall," *JAMA* 184 (April 1963): 47; Charles E. Flowers, Jr., M.D., "Premarital Examination and Counseling," *Obstetrics & Gynecology,* hereafter *OG,* 20 (July 1962): 143–47; Sands, "Marriage Counseling as a Medical Responsibility," 2050–56; Janet E. Towne, M.D., "Premarital Counseling," *The Medical Clinics of North America* 45 (January 1961): 53–62; Pearson, "The Physician's Role," 363–67; Waggoner, "Marriage Counseling as a Responsibility of the Physician," 211–14; English, "The Role of the General Practitioner," 312–19; and Eugene G. Hamilton, M.D., "Frigidity in the Female," *Missouri Medicine* 58 (October 1961): 1040–51.

9. Nadina R. Kavinoky, M.D., "Premarital Medical Examination," *JAMA* 156 (October 1954): 692. See also Congress on Medical Education, "Obstacles to Population Control," *JAMA* 197 (April 1966): 643–54; Max Levin, M.D., "The Physician and the Sexual Revolution," *NEJM* 273 (December 1965): 1366–69; Wilfred C. Hulse, M.D., "The Management of Sexual Conflict in General Practice," *JAMA* 150 (November 1952): 846–49; Seymour L. Halleck, M.D., "Sex and Mental Health on Campus," *JAMA* 200 (May 1967): 684–90; Robert L. Tolle, M.D., "Sex and Marriage," *Southern Medical Journal* 60 (June 1967): 615–18; Lena Levine, M.D., "The Young Man and Woman Marry: Diagnosis and Treatment of Pre-Marital and Marital Ills," *Journal of the American Medical Woman's Association, hereafter JAMWA,* 18 (March 1963): 227–31; Martin Goldberg, M.D., "Counseling Sexually Incompatible Marriage Partners," *Postgraduate Medicine,* hereafter *PM,* 42 (July 1967): 62–68; Eleanor B. Easley, "The Premarital Examination." *North Carolina Medical Journal* 15 (March 1954): 105–10; John Parks, "Premarital Gynecologic Examination," *PM* 30 (November 1961): 476–78; and Patricia Ann Lawrence, M.D., "The Responsibility of the Gynecologist in Premarital Counseling," *AJOG* 96 (September 1966): 80–86.

10. Ibid. See also Sheeley, "Sex and the Practicing Physician," 133; Flowers, "Premarital Examination and Counseling," 143–47; Sands, "Marriage Counseling as a Medical Responsibility," 2050–56; Towne, "Premarital Counseling," 53–62; Pearson, "The Physician's Role," 363–67; Waggoner, "Marriage Counseling as a Responsibility of the Physician," 211–44; Editorial, "Sex and Medicine," *JAMA* 197 (July 1966): 643–54; J. P. Greenhill, M.D., Letter to the Editor, *JAMA* 159 (September 1955): 398; S. Leon Israel, M.D., "Teaching the Art of Caring for Women," *JAMA* 191 (February 1965): 393–96; S. Leon Israel, M.D., "The Role of the Physician in Family Life Education," *Michigan Medicine* 66 (May 1967): 567–71; Mary S. Calderone, "Sexual Problems in Medical Practice," *JAMWA* 23 (February 1968): 140–46; Lena Levine, M.D., "Preventive Measures for Marital Adjustment," *JAMA* 61 (August 1964): 72–74; John H. Holzaepfel, M.D., "Premarital Examinations and Conception Control," *Western Journal of Surgery Obstetrics & Gynecology* (November–December 1957): 379–81; English, "The Role of the General Practitioner," 312–19; J. Allan Offen, M.D., "The Role of the Gynecologist in Family and Marriage Counseling," *OG* 13 (March 1959): 302–10; Jed W. Pearson, Jr., M.D., "Premarital Counseling," *Medical Annals of the District of Columbia* 36 (January 1967): 1–2, 76; Sylvester W. Trythall, M.D., "The Premarital Law: History and a Survey of Its Effectiveness in Michigan," *JAMA* 187 (March 1964): 900–903; James R. Rappaport, M.D., "Sex in Marriage Counseling," *Maryland State Medical Journal* (September 1966): 35–40; Robert H. Fagan, M.D., "Premarital and Marital Counseling and the Family Doctor," *Medical Times,* hereafter *MT,* 93 (June 1965): 671–74; C. A. Johnson, M.D., "The Pre-Marital Lecture," *South Dakota Journal of Medicine and Pharmacy* (February 1959): 91–92, 106; Frederick J. Hofmeister and Robert P. Reik, "The Complete Office Examination," *PM* (February 1960): 235–40; Robert Chez, M.D., "Obtaining the Sexual History in the Female Patient," *General Practice,* hereafter *GP,* 30 (October 1964): 120–24; and Paul Popenoe, Sc.D., "Marriage Counseling," *GP* 6 (October 1952): 53–60.

11. Paul Starr, *The Social Transformation of American Medicine: The Rise of a Sovereign Profession and the Making of a Vast Industry* (New York: Basic Books, 1982); John Duffy, *From Humors to Medical Science: A History of American Medicine* (Chicago: University of Illinois Press. 1993); Stuart W. Leslie, *The Cold War and American Science: The Military-Industrial-Academic Complex at MIT and Stanford* (New York: Columbia University Press, 1993); and Rosemary Stevens, *American Medicine and the Public Interest: A History of Specialization* (Berkeley: University of California Press, 1971, 1998). Although obstetrician-gynecologists and general practitioners were struggling to distinguish their practices from one another, the material I am discussing in this article reveals a striking agreement on methods and ideology. Therefore, when I use the term "physicians" in this article, I am referring to both unless otherwise stated.

12. Starr, *The Social Transformation of American Medicine,* 333–51.

13. Luigi Mastroianni, M.D., discussion of Fagan, "The Role of the Obstetrician-Gynecologist," 334. See also Kavinoky, "Premarital Medical Examination," 692; Congress on Medical Education, "Obstacles to Population Control," 643–54; Sheeley, "Sex and the Practicing Physician," 133; Levin, "Preventive Measures," 1366–69; Hulse, "The Management of Sexual Conflict in General Practice," 846–49; Tolle, "Sex and Marriage," 615–18; Levine, "The Young Man and Woman Marry," 227–31; Flowers, "Premarital Examination and Counseling," 143–47; Sands, "Marriage Counseling as a Medical Responsibility," 2050–56; Towne, "Premarital Counseling," 53–62; Pearson, "The Physician's Role," 363–67; Waggoner, "Marriage Counseling as a Responsibility of the Physician," 211–14; Goldberg, "Counseling Sexually Incompatible Marriage Partners," 62–68; Easley, "The Premarital Examination," 105–10; Parks, "Premarital Gynecologic Examination," 476–78; Lawrence, "The Responsibility of the Gynecologist in Premarital Counseling," 80–86; "Sex and Medicine," 643–54; Greenhill, Letter to the Editor, 398; Israel, "Teaching the Art of Caring for Women," 393–96; Israel, "The Role of the Physician," 567–71; Calderone, "Sexual Problems in Medical Practice," 140–46; Levine, "Preventive Measures," 72–74; Holzaepfel, "Premarital Examinations and Conception Control," 379–81; English, "The Role of the General Practitioner," 312–19; Offen, "The Role of the Gynecologist in Family and Marriage Counseling," 302–10; Pearson, "Premarital Counseling," 1–2, 76; Trythall, "The Premarital Law," 900–903; Rappaport, "Sex in Marriage Counseling," 35–40; Fagan, "The Role of the Obstetrician-Gynecologist," 328–34; Fagan, "Premarital and Marital Counseling," 671–74; Johnson, "The PreMarital Lecture," 91–92, 106; Hofmeister and Reik, "The Complete Office Examination," 235–40; Chez, "Obtaining the Sexual History in the Female Patient," 120–24; and Popenoe, "Marriage Counseling," 53–60.

14. Pearson, "The Physician's Role," 693.

15. On shifts in psychiatric practices, see Starr, *The Social Transformation of American Medicine*; Juliet Mitchell, *Psychoanalysis and Feminism: A Radical Reassessment of Freudian Psychoanalysis* (1974; reprint; New York: Basic Books, 1974, 2000); and Joseph Schwartz, *Cassandra's Daughter: A History of Psychoanalysis* (New York: Penguin Books, 1999). The correlation between sexual behavior and mental health became increasingly racialized in the postwar period—especially for unwed mothers. See Rickie Solinger, *Wake Up Little Susie: Single Pregnancy and Race Before Roe v. Wade* (New York: Routledge, 2000); and Regina G. Kunzel, "White Neurosis, Black Pathology: Constructing Out-of-Wedlock Pregnancy in the Wartime and Postwar United States," in Meyerowitz, *Not June Cleaver*, 304–31. On the medicalization of sexual behavior and identity, see Jennifer Terry, *An American Obsession: Science, Medicine, and Homosexuality in Modern Society* (Chicago: University of Chicago Press, 1999); Joanne Meyerowitz, *How Sex Changed: A History of Transsexuality in the United States* (Cambridge, MA: Harvard University Press, 2002); and Carol Groneman, *Nymphomania: A History* (New York: W.W. Norton & Company, 2000).

16. See Terry, *An American Obsession*, chap. 11; and Allen Bérubé, *Coming Out Under Fire: The History of Gay Men and Women in World War Two* (New York: The Free Press, 1990).

17. Philip Wylie, *Generation of Vipers* (New York: Rinehart & Co., 1942); Edward A. Strecker, M.D., *Their Mothers' Sons: The Psychiatrist Examines an American Problem* (New York: J.B. Lippincott and Co., 1946); Strecker and Vincent T. Lathbury, M.D., *Their Mothers' Daughters* (New York: J.B. Lippincott and Co., 1956); and Ferdinand Lundberg and Marynia F. Farnham, M.D., *Modern Woman: The Lost Sex* (New York: Harper & Brothers, Publishers, 1947).

18. Hamilton, "Frigidity in the Female," 1043. See also Flowers, "Premarital Examination and Counseling," 146.

19. Towne, "Premarital Counseling," 58.

20. Helene Deutsch, *The Psychology of Women, Volume II—Motherhood* (New York: Grune & Stratton, 1945).

21. G. Lombard Kelly, M.D., "Query: Vaginal Orgasm," *JAMA* 146 (July 1951): 978–79; Hamilton, "Frigidity in the Female," 1040; William S. Kroger, M.D., and S. Charles Freed, M.D., "Psychosomatic Aspects of Frigidity," *JAMA* 143 (June 1950): 526–32; Edmund Bergler, M.D., "The Problem of Frigidity," *Psychiatric Quarterly* 18 (July 1944): 374–90; and William S. Kroger, M.D., and S. Charles Freed, M.D., Letter to the Editor, *JAMA* 144 (October 1950): 570–71.

22. According to Edmund Bergler and William Kroger, Freud called this transfer a "push of passivity" that occurred around the onset of puberty. Failure to transfer resulted in the "penalty" of frigidity. Edmund Bergler and William S. Kroger, *Kinsey's Myth of Female Sexuality* (New York: Grune & Stratton, 1954), 69–70.

23. Kroger and Freed, "Psychosomatic Aspects," 526–32.

24. Beverley T. Mead, M.D., "Sexual Problems," *MT* 90 (October 1962): 1033–37; Kroger and Freed, "Psychosomatic Aspects"; Goldberg, "Counseling Sexually Incompatible Marriage Partners," 62–68; and Hamilton, "Frigidity in the Female," 1040–51.

25. Kavinoky, "Premarital Medical Examination," 692. As if to prove this point, the only photographic representations of female genitalia that I have found in my research were of African American women. See Hofmeister and Reik, "The Complete Office Examination," 235–40. Emily Martin provides an excellent discussion of the racialization of women's healthcare in *The Woman in the Body: A Cultural Analysis of Reproduction* (Boston: Beacon Press, 1992).

26. Kavinoky, "Premarital Medical Examination," 694.

27. Rappaport, "Sex in Marriage Counseling," 36.

28. See, for example, Lawrence, "The Responsibility of the Gynecologist in Premarital Counseling," 84; and Hamilton, "Frigidity in the Female," 1040–51.

29. Lena Levine suggested that observing a patient's reaction to penetration during the pelvic exam would "serve as a guide to the physician as to the kind of information and explanations required" of sexual behavior. Levine, "The Young Man and Woman Marry," 228. Similar opinions are implied by Blanche Lockard, M.D., "A Program for Pre-Marital Counseling," *Mississippi Doctor* 37 (June 1959): 9–11; Kavinoky, "Premarital Medical Examination," 692–93; Paul Scholten, M.D., "The Premarital Examination," *JAMA* 168 (November 1958): 1173; and Towne, "Premarital Counseling," 56. Health educator Terri Kapsalis has argued that "the pelvic exam is in effect the staging of sex and gender, particularly the staging of femininity and female sexuality" in *Public Privates: Performing Gynecology from Both Ends of the Speculum* (Durham, NC: Duke University Press, 1997), 14. Barbara Ehrenreich and Deirdre English have discussed physicians' belief that the pelvic exam simulated heterosexual intercourse and therefore could be used to evaluate a woman's sexual adjustment in *For Her Own Good: 150 Years of the Experts' Advice to Women* (New York: Anchor Books, 1978), 274–80.

30. The importance of a gentle pelvic exam was best described by Louis G. Fournier, M.D., in "Practical Considerations for the General Practitioner in His Role as a Gynecologist," *New York State Journal of Medicine* (November 1952): 2765–70: "You cannot roughly barge into a vagina, causing 'embarrassment, discomfort, and pain, and expect to outline adequately the contents of that particular pelvis." Unlike today, physicians writing in these journals expected this to be a woman's first visit to the gynecologist, unless she had some sort of medical condition that would have necessitated an earlier visit. So in addition to assuaging fears about sexual intercourse, physicians also had to keep in mind that this was probably the patient's first experience with the speculum.

31. Ethel M. Albert, PhD, "Modern Women—Freedom or Bondage," *JAMA* 183 (March 1963), 38.

32. Kavinoky, "Premarital Medical Examination," 693.

33. Carl N. Neupert, M.D., to Lee D. Cady, M.D., 28 October 1937, Lee D. Cady Papers, Western Historical Manuscript Collection, University of Missouri, Columbia MO, hereafter Cady Papers.

34. For further reading on physicians as public health advocates, see Allan M. Brandt, *No Magic Bullet: A Social History of Venereal Disease in the United States Since 1880* (New York: Oxford University Press, 1985); Leslie J. Reagan, *When Abortion Was a Crime: Women, Medicine and Law in the United States, 1867–1973* (Berkeley: University of California Press, 1997); Starr, *Social Transformation;* and Stevens, *American Medicine and the Public Interest.*

35. Physician Lee D. Cady, who led the medical profession's campaign for premarital syphilis testing in Missouri, repeatedly emphasized the privacy violation inherent in a mandated physical exam. See, for example, Cady's 1939 radio address, "Missouri's Pre-marital Examination Laws," f. 22, Cady Papers.

36. Trythall, "The Premarital Law," 900; and Phillip K. Condit, M.D., M.P.H., and A. Frank Brewer, M.D., "Premarital Examination Laws—Are They Worthwhile?" *American Journal of Public Health* 43 (July 1953): 880–87.

37. Robert Latou Dickinson advocated the use of the premarital consultation to discuss matters of sexual adjustment with their patients as early as 1928; however, widespread support of this idea did not appear in the medical journals for nearly twenty-five years. Wendy Kline has discussed Dickinson's position in *Building a Better Race: Gender, Sexuality, and Eugenics from the Turn of the Century to the Baby Boom* (Berkeley: University of California Press, 2001), chap. 5. See also Ethel M. Nash, M.A., Lucie Jessner, M.D., and D. Wilfred Abse, M.D., *Marriage Counseling in Medical Practice* (Chapel Hill: University of North Carolina Press, 1964), 223; and R. L. Dickinson, "Premarital Consultation," *JAMA* 117 (November 1941): 1687–92.

38. Editorial, "Premarital Laws," *JAMA* 187 (March 1964): 948. Physicians repeatedly described the laws necessitating a premarital physical or venereal exam as an "opportunity" to provide premarital counseling about sex. See, for example, Condit and Brewer, "Premarital Examination Laws," 880–87; Levine, "The Young Man and Woman Marry," 227–31; English, "The Role of the General Practitioner," 312–19; and Waggoner, "Marriage Counseling as a Responsibility of the Physician," 211–14.

39. Kavinoky, "Premarital Medical Examination," 692–95.

40. Articles that specifically cited Kavinoky as a model include Towne, "Premarital Counseling," 53–62; Pearson, "The Physician's Role," 363–67; Scholten, "The Premarital Examination," 117–77; and Ethel M. Nash, M.A., and Lois M. Louden, M.A., "The Premarital Medical Examination and the Carolina Population Center: What Patients Desire," *JAMA* 210 (December 1969): 2365–69. See also Clark E. Vincent, *Human Sexuality in Medical Education and, Practice* (Springfield, IL: Charles C Thomas Publisher, 1968), 21. The editors of the 1964 volume *Marriage Counseling in Medical Practice,* listed Kavinoky's article as an important step "in the evolution of the premarital examination." Nash, Jessner, and Abse, *Marriage Counseling in Medical Practice,* 223. Although they do not cite Kavinoky, Abraham Stone, M.D., and Lena Levine, M.D., emphasize the importance of the initial pelvic exam in establishing the pattern for women's response to penetration in general. See Stone and Levine, *The Premarital Consultation: A Manual for Physicians* (New York: Grune & Stratton, 1956).

41. Arnold H. Kegel, M.D., Letter to the Editor, *JAMA* 153 (December 1953): 1303–4.

42. Ibid.

43. Towne, "Premarital Counseling," 57.

44. Rachel Maines, *The Technology of Orgasm* (Baltimore: Johns Hopkins University Press, 1999).

45. The medical community's discussion of frigidity makes clear that physicians and psychiatrists associated clitoral

stimulation with latent or active lesbianism and vaginal orgasm with "normal" heterosexual response. Kroger and Freed, "Psychosomatic Aspects," 526–32; Bergler, "The Problem of Frigidity," 374–90; Deutsch, *The Psychology of Women* and Marie Bonaparte, *Female Sexuality* (New York: International "Universities Press, Inc., 1953).

46. Hulse, "The Management of Sexual Conflict in General Practice," 848.

47. Lawrence, "The Responsibility of the Gynecologist in Premarital Counseling," 83.

48. Flowers, "Premarital Examination and Counseling," 146.

49. Bonaparte, *Female Sexuality,* 56. One physician not only cited Bonaparte in his bibliography, but also used the language of "sleeping beauty" to describe the normal sexual awakening for women. See Hamilton, "Frigidity in the Female," 1044.

50. Parks, "Premarital Gynecologic Examination," 477. One article described the pelvic exam as a planned invasion: "The hymen can be easily and almost painlessly infiltrated with 2% Xylocaine, beginning at 6 o'clock and proceeding around the entire periphery of the hymeneal ring." Flowers, "Premarital Examination and Counseling," 144. Flowers's article was reprinted in Nash, Jessner, and Abse, *Marriage Counseling in Medical Practice.*

51. Kavinoky, "Premarital Medical Examination," 692–95.

52. Easley, "The Premarital Examination," 107. The only physician who suggested that premarital sexual activity did not indicate sexual satisfaction was Lawrence, "The Responsibility of the Gynecologist in Premarital Counseling," 81. Likewise, because the pregnant bride was already on the path to fulfilling her psychosexual destiny, most physicians assumed that she had fully adjusted to heterosexuality, even if she had done so beyond the parameters of a legal and moral marriage.

53. Goldberg, "Counseling Sexually Incompatible Marriage Partners," 64.

54. Easley, "The Premarital Examination," 108.

55. Questions and Answers: Frigidity," *JAMA* 173 (June 1960): 971.

56. Sands, "Marriage Counseling as a Medical Responsibility," 2052.

57. Several physicians used the term "snug," including Fagan, "Premarital and Marital Counseling," 671, and "The Role of the Obstetrician-Gynecologist," 330; and Lawrence, "The Responsibility of the Gynecologist," 81.

58. Lockard, "A Program for Pre-Marital Counseling," 10.

59. Holzaepfel, "Premarital Examinations and Conception Control," 380.

60. Kavinoky, "Premarital Medical Examination," 693. The term "super-virgin" was used by Kavinoky to indicate a woman with a malformed hymen or vaginal canal that made the vaginal opening less than 1 cm. She emphasized that the physician should use this term when consulting with the couple regarding the appropriate course of treatment, because "The word 'small' has too many inaccurate implications." Similarly, John Parks advised that "Great care must be taken to avoid giving the patient a feeling that she is small, infantile, or genitally inferior." Parks, "Premarital Gynecologic Examination," 478.

61. Flowers, "Premarital Examination and Counseling," 144; Fagan, "Premarital and Marital Counseling," 672; Easley, "The Premarital Examination," 108; Lockard, "A Program for Pre-Marital Counseling," 10; and Pearson, "Premarital Counseling," 2. Parks suggested that the decision to dilate would be made solely by the fiancé, "Premarital Gynecologic Examination," 477; Towne indicates that the permission of the patient's family may also be necessary even before the pelvic exam can be administered ("Premarital Counseling," 55).

62. There is no indication of how many fiancés actually refused to grant permission for dilation. As physician Charles E. Flowers, Jr., noted, "It is indeed a rare and poorly adjusted groom who must reassure himself at the expense of his wife's dyspareunia." "Premarital Examination and Counseling," 144.

63. Verna Stevens-Young, M.D., discussion of English, "The Role of the General Practitioner," 317.

64. The ideological struggles of the Cold War were often cloaked in the language of sexual morality and gender performance. Consider, for example, the infamous Kitchen Debate between Soviet Premier Nikita Khrushchev and American Vice President Richard Nixon, or the gendered language of George Kennan's Long Telegram. See May, *Homeward Bound*, chap. 1; and Frank Costigliola, Unceasing Pressure for Penetration': Gender, Pathology, and Emotion in George Kennan's Formation of the Cold War," in *Journal of American History* (March 1997): 1309–39.

65. H. T. McGuire, M.D., discussion of English, "The Role of the General Practitioner," 317.

Working at Motherhood: Chicana and Mexicana Immigrant Mothers and Employment[1]

In North American society, women are expected to bear and assume primary responsibility for raising their children. This socially constructed form of motherhood encourages women to stay at home during their children's early or formative years, and asserts activities that take married mothers out of the home (for instance, paid employment) are less important or "secondary" to their domestic duties.[2] Motherhood as a social construction rests on the ideological position that women's biological abilities to bear and suckle children are "natural," and therefore fundamental to women's "fulfillment." This position, however, fails to appreciate that motherhood is a culturally formed structure whose meanings can vary and are subject to change.

Despite the ideological impetus to mother at home, over half of all women with children work for wages.[3] The growing incongruence between social ideology and individual behaviors has prompted some researchers to suggest that traditional gender role expectations are changing (for example, greater acceptance of women working outside the home).[4] The profuse literature on the "ambivalence" and "guilt" employed mothers often feel when they work outside the home, however, reminds us that changes in expectations are neither absolute nor uncontested.

Some analysts argue that the ambivalence felt by many employed mothers stems from their discomfort in deviating from a socially constructed "idealized mother," who stays home to care for her family.[5] This image of motherhood, popularized in the media, schoolbooks, and public policy, implies that the family and the economy constitute two separate spheres, private and public. Hood argues, however, that the notion of a private–public dichotomy largely rests on the experiences of white, leisured women and lacks immediate relevance to less privileged women (for instance,

immigrant women, women of color), who have historically been important economic actors both inside and outside the home.[6] The view that the relationship between motherhood and employment varies by class, race, and/or culture raises several important questions. Do the ideology of motherhood and the "ambivalence" of employed mothers depicted within American sociology and feminist scholarship pertain to women of Mexican descent in the United States? Among these women, what is the relation between the ideological constructions of motherhood and employment? Is motherhood mutually exclusive from employment among Mexican-heritage women from different social locations?

In this [reading] I explore these questions using qualitative data gathered from thirty women of Mexican descent in the United States—both native-born Chicanas (including two Mexico-born women raised since preschool years in the US) and resident immigrant Mexicanas.[7] I illustrate that notions of motherhood for Chicanas and Mexicanas are embedded in different ideological constructs operating within two systems of patriarchy. Contrary to the expectations of acculturation models, I find that Mexicanas frame motherhood in ways that foster a more consistent labor market presence than do Chicanas. I argue that this distinction—typically bypassed in the sociological literature on motherhood, women and work, or Chicano Studies—is rooted in their dissimilar social locations—that is, the "social spaces" they engage within the social structure created by the intersection of class, race, gender, and culture.[8]

I propose that Mexicanas, raised in a world where economic and household work often merged, do not dichotomize social life into public and private spheres, but appear to view employment as one workable domain of motherhood. Hence, the more recent the time of emigration, the less ambivalence Mexicanas express regarding employment. Chicanas, on the other hand, raised in a society that celebrates the expressive functions of the family and obscures its productive economic functions, express higher adherence to the ideology of stay-at-home motherhood and correspondingly more ambivalence toward full-time employment—even when they work.

These differences between Mexicanas and Chicanas challenge current research on Mexican-origin women that treats them as a single analytic category (for instance, "Hispanic") as well as research on contemporary views of motherhood that fails to appreciate diversity among women. My examination of the intersection of motherhood and employment among Mexican immigrant women also reinforces emerging research focusing on women's own economic and social motivations to emigrate to the United States (rather than the behest of husbands and/or fathers).[9]

My analysis begins with a brief review of relevant research on the relationship between motherhood and employment. Then I explore this relationship in greater detail, using in-depth interview data. I conclude by discussing the need to recast current conceptualizations of the dilemma between motherhood and employment to reflect women's different social locations.

THEORETICAL CONCERNS

The theoretical concerns that inform this research on Chicana/Mexicana employment integrate feminist analyses of the hegemonic power of patriarchy over work and motherhood with a critique of rational choice models and other models that overemphasize modernity and acculturation. In much of the literature on women and work, familial roles tend to be portrayed as important constraints on both women's labor market entry and mobility. Differences among women related to immigrant status, however, challenge this view.

Within rational choice models, motherhood represents a prominent social force behind women's job decisions. Becker and Polachek, for example, argue that women's "preference" to mother is maximized in jobs that exact fewer penalties for interrupted employment, such as part-time, seasonal, or clerical work.[10] According to this view, women's pursuit of their rational self-interest reinforces their occupational segregation within low-paying jobs (for example, clerical work) and underrepresentation in

higher-paying, male-dominated jobs that typically require significant employer investments (for example, specialized training). Employers may be reluctant to "invest" in or train women workers who, they perceive, may leave a job at any time for familial reasons.[11] This perspective views motherhood as a major impediment to employment and mobility. But it fails to consider that the organization of production has developed in ways that make motherhood an impediment. Many feminist scholars view this particular development as consistent with the hegemonic power of patriarchy.

Distinct from rational choice models, feminist scholarship directs attention away from individual preferences to consider how patriarchy (male domination/female subordination) shapes the organization of production, resulting in the economic, political, and social subordination of women to men.[12] While many economists fail to consider the power of ideological constructs such as "family" and "motherhood" in shaping behavior among women, employers, and the organization of production itself, many feminist scholars focus on these power dynamics.

Within feminist analyses, motherhood as an ideology obscures and legitimizes women's social subordination because it conceals particular interests within the rubric of a universal prerogative (reproduction). The social construction of motherhood serves the interest of capital by providing essential childbearing, child care, and housework at a minimal cost to the state, and sustains women as a potential reservoir of labor power, or a "reserve army of labor."[13] The strength of the ideology of motherhood is such that women continue to try to reconcile the "competing urgencies"[14] of motherhood and employment despite the lack of supportive structures at work or within the family.

Because employers view women as mothers (or future mothers), they encounter discrimination in job entry and advancement.[15] Because women are viewed as mothers, they also work a "second shift" at home.[16] The conflict between market work and family work has caused considerable ambivalence within women. Berg, for example, notes that one of the dominant themes in analyzing women and work is the "guilt" of employed mothers based on "espousing something different" from their own mothers.[17]

The notion Berg describes of "conflict" or "guilt" rests on several suppositions. The first assumption is that motherhood is a unilaterally oppressive state; the second, that employed mothers feel guilt; and the third, that today's employed mothers do not have working mothers (which partially explains their "guilt feelings"). Inasmuch as large numbers of working-class, immigrant, and racial ethnic women have long traditions of working in the formal and informal economic sectors, such assumptions are suspect.

Research on women of Mexican descent and employment indicates their labor force participation is lower than that of other women when they have young children.[18] Moreover, Chicanas and Mexicanas are occupationally segregated in the lowest-paying of female-dominated jobs.[19] Explanations for their unique employment situation range from analyses of labor market structures and employer discrimination[20] to deficient individual characteristics (for instance, education, job skills)[21] and cultural differences.[22]

Analyses of Chicana/Mexicana employment that utilize a cultural framework typically explain the women's lower labor force participation, higher fertility, lower levels of education, and higher levels of unemployment as part of an ethnic or cultural tradition.[23] That is, as this line of argument goes, Chicano/Mexican culture emphasizes a strong allegiance to an idealized form of motherhood and a patriarchal ideology that frowns upon working wives and mothers and does not encourage girls to pursue higher education or employment options. These attitudes are supposed to vary by generation, with immigrant women (from Mexico) holding the most conservative attitudes.[24]

There are two major flaws in the research on Chicana/Mexicana employment, however. First, inconsistency in distinguishing between native-born and resident immigrant women characterizes much of this literature. Second, overreliance on linear acculturation persists. Both procedures imply either that Chicanas and Mexicanas are very similar, or that they lie on a sort of "cultural continuum," with Mexican immigrants at one end holding more conservative behaviors and attitudes grounded in traditional (often rural) Mexican culture, and U.S.-born Chicanos holding an amalgamation of cultural traditions from Mexico and the United States.[25] In terms of motherhood and employment, therefore, Mexicanas should have more "traditional" ideas about motherhood than U.S.-born Chicanas. Since the traditional ideology of motherhood typically refers to women staying home to "mother" children rather than going outside the home to work, Mexicanas theoretically should not be as willing to work as Chicanas or North American women in general—unless there is severe economic need. This

formulation, while logical, reflects an underlying emphasis on modernity—or the view that "traditional" Mexican culture lags behind North American culture in developing behaviors and attitudes conducive to participating fully in modern society.[26] Inasmuch as conventional North American views of motherhood typically idealize labor market exit to care for children, embracing this prototype may be more conducive to maintaining patriarchal privilege (female economic subordination to men) than facilitating economic progress generally. In this sense, conceptualizations of motherhood that affirm its economic character may be better accommodating to women's market participation in the United States.

The following section discusses the distinct views of motherhood articulated by Chicanas and Mexicanas and their impact on employment attitudes and behaviors. In contrast to the notion that exposure to North American values enhances women's incentives to work, proportionately more Chicanas than Mexicanas express ambivalence toward paid employment when they have children at home. I analyze these differences among a selected sample of clerical, service, and operative workers.

METHOD AND SAMPLE

This paper is based on in-depth interviews with thirty Mexican-origin women—thirteen Chicanas and seventeen Mexicanas—who had participated in the 1978 to 79 or 1980 to 81 cohorts of an adult education and employment training program in the greater San Francisco Bay Area.[27] All thirty respondents had been involved in a conjugal relationship (either legal marriage or informal cohabitation with a male partner) at some point in their lives before I interviewed them in 1985, and had at least one child under eighteen years of age. At the time of their interviews, six Chicanas and fourteen Mexicanas were married; seven Chicanas and three Mexicanas were single parents.

On the average, the married Chicanas have 1.2 children at home; the Mexicanas report 3.5 children. Both Chicana and Mexicana single mothers average 1.6 children. The children of the Chicanas tend to be preschool age or in elementary school. The children of the Mexicanas exhibit a greater age range (from infant to late adolescence), reflecting their earlier marriages and slightly older average age.

With respect to other relevant characteristics, all but two Mexicanas and five Chicanas had either a high school diploma or its equivalent (GED). The average age was 27.4 years for the Chicanas and thirty-three years for the Mexicanas.[28] Upon leaving the employment training program, all the women secured employment. At the time of their interviews, about half of the Chicanas ($n = 7$) and three-fourths of the Mexicanas ($n = 12$) were employed. Only two out of the seven (28 percent) employed Chicanas worked full-time (thirty-five or more hours per week) whereas nine out of the twelve (75 percent) employed Mexicanas worked full-time. Most of the Chicanas found clerical or service jobs (for example, teacher assistants); most of the Mexicanas labored in operative jobs or in the service sector (for example, hotel maids), with a small minority employed as clerical workers.

I gathered in-depth life and work histories from the women to ascertain:

1. what factors motivated them to enter, exit, and stay employed in their specific occupations;
2. whether familial roles or ideology influenced their employment consistency; and
3. whether other barriers limited their job attachment and mobility.

My examination of the relationship between motherhood and employment forms part of a larger study of labor market stratification and occupational mobility among Chicana and Mexican immigrant women.[29]

MOTHERHOOD AND EMPLOYMENT

Nearly all of the respondents, both Chicana and Mexicana, employed and nonemployed, speak of motherhood as their most important social role. They differ sharply in their employment behaviors and views regarding the relationship between motherhood and market work. Women fall into four major groups. The first group consists of five *Involuntary Nonemployed Mothers*, who are not employed but care full-time for their children. All of these women want to be employed at least part-time. They either cannot secure the job they want and/or feel pressured to be at home mothering full-time.

The second group consists of six *Voluntary Nonemployed Mothers* who are not employed but remain out of the labor force by *choice*. They feel committed to staying at home to care for preschool and/or elementary school age children.

The third category, *Ambivalent Employed Mothers*, includes eleven employed women. They have either preschool or elementary school age children. Women in this group believe that employment interferes with motherhood and feel "guilty" when they work outside the home. Despite these feelings, they are employed at least part-time.

The fourth group, *Nonambivalent Employed Mothers*, includes eight employed women. What distinguishes these women from the previous group is their view that employment and motherhood seem compatible social dynamics irrespective of the age of their children. All eight women are Mexicanas. Some of these women believe employment could be problematic, however, *if* a family member could not care for their children or be at home for the children when they arrived from school.

Chicanas tend to fall in the second and third categories, whereas Mexicanas predominate in the first and fourth groups. Three reasons emerged as critical in explaining this difference:

1. the economic situations of their families;
2. labor market structure (four-fifths of the nonemployed Mexicanas were involuntarily unemployed); and
3. women's conceptualizations of motherhood, in particular, their expressed *need* to mother.

Age of the women and number of children did not fall into any discernible pattern; therefore, I did not engage them in depth within my analysis.

First, I consider the situation of the Voluntary Nonemployed Mothers, including three married Chicanas, one single-parent Mexicana, and one single-parent Chicana. All but one woman exited the labor market involuntarily (for reasons such as layoffs or disability). All five women remain out of the labor force by choice. Among them, the expressed need to mother appears strong—overriding all other concerns. They view motherhood as mutually exclusive from employment. Lydia, a married Chicana with a small toddler, articulates this perspective:

Right now, since we've had the baby, I feel, well he [her husband] feels the same way, that I want to spend this time with her and watch her grow up. See, because when I was small my grandmother raised me so I felt this *loss* [her emphasis] when my grandmother died. And I've never gotten that *real love*, that mother love from my mother. We have a friendship, but we don't have that "motherly love." I want my daughter to know that I'm here, especially at her age, it's very important for them to know that when they cry that mama's there. Even if it's not a painful cry, it's still important for them to know that mommy's there. She's my number one—she's all my attention . . . so working-wise, it's up to [her husband] right now.

Susana, a Chicana single parent with a five-year-old child, said:

I'm the type of person that has always wanted to have a family. I think it was more like I didn't have a family-type home when I was growing up. I didn't have a mother and a father and the kids all together in the same household all happy. I didn't have that. And that's what I want more than anything! I want to be different from my mother, who has worked hard and is successful in her job. I don't want to be successful in the same way.

Lydia, Susana, and the other voluntarily unemployed Chicanas adamantly assert that motherhood requires staying home with their children. Susana said: "A good mother is there for her children all the time when they are little and when they come home from school." All the Chicanas in this category believe that motherhood means staying home with children—even if it means going on welfare (AFDC). This finding is similar to other accounts of working-class women.[30]

The sense shared among this group of women that motherhood and employment are irreconcilable, especially when children are of preschool age, is related to their social locations. A small minority of the Chicanas had been raised by nonemployed mothers ($n = 3$). They feel they should stay at home with their children as long as it's economically feasible. Most of the Chicanas, however, resemble Lydia and Susana, who had been raised by employed mothers. Although these women recognize that their mothers had worked out of economic need, they believe they did not receive sufficient love and care from their mothers. Throughout their interviews, this group of Chicanas expressed hostility and resentment against their employed mothers for leaving them with other caretakers. These feelings contribute to their decisions to stay at home with their children, and/or their sense of "guilt" when they are employed. Their hostility and guilt defy psychoanalytic theories that speculate that the cycle of gender

construction locking women into "exclusive mothering" roles can be broken if the primary caretaker (the mother) undertakes more diverse roles.[31] Rather, Chicanas appear to value current conceptionalizations of motherhood that prioritize the expressive work of the mother, as distinct from her economic activities.

This group of Chicanas seems to be pursuing the social construction of motherhood that is idealized within their ethnic community, their churches, and society at large.[32] Among Chicanos and Mexicanos the image of *la madre* as self-sacrificing and holy is a powerful standard against which women often compare themselves.[33] The Chicana informants also seem to accept the notion that women's primary duty is to provide for the emotional welfare of the children, and that economic activities which take them outside the home are secondary. Women's desire to enact the socially constructed motherhood ideal was further strengthened by their conviction that many of their current problems (for instance, low levels of education, feelings of inadequacy, single parenthood) are related to growing up in families that did not conform to the stay-at-home-mother/father-as-provider configuration. Their evaluation of the close relationship between motherhood and economic or emotional well-being of offspring parallels popular emphasis on the primacy of individual efforts and the family environment to emotional vigor and achievement.[34]

Informants in this group speak to a complex dimension of mothering and gender construction in the Chicano/Mexicano communities. These women reject their employed mothers' organization of family life. As children, most had been cared for by other family members, and now feel closer to their grandmothers or other female relatives than to their own biological mothers. This causes them considerable pain—pain they want to spare their own children. Many, like Susana, do not want to be "successful" in the tradition of their own employed mothers. Insofar as "success" means leaving their children with other caretakers, it contradicts their conceptualization of motherhood. Rather, they frame "success" in more affective terms: having children who are happy and doing well in school. This does not suggest that Chicanas disagree with the notion that having a good job or a lucrative career denotes "success." They simply feel that successful careers could and should be deferred until their children are older (for instance, in the upper grades of elementary school) and doing well academically and emotionally.

Only one married Mexicana, Belen, articulated views similar to those of the Chicanas. Belen left the labor market in 1979 to give birth and care for her newborn child. It is important to note that she has a gainfully employed husband who does not believe mothers should work outside the home. Belen, who has two children and was expecting a third when I interviewed her, said:

> I wanted to work or go back to school after having my first son, but my husband didn't want me to. He said, "No one can take care of your child the way you can." He did not want me to work. And I did not feel right having someone else care for my son. So I decided to wait until my children were older.

Belen's words underscore an important dynamic that impacted on both Mexicana and Chicana conceptualizations of motherhood: spousal employment and private patriarchy. Specifically, husbands working in full-time, year-round jobs with earnings greater than those of their wives tended to pressure women to mother full-time. Women who succumb to this pressure become economically dependent on their husbands and reaffirm male authority in the organization of the family. These particular women tend to consider motherhood and employment in similar ways. This suggests that the form the social construction of motherhood takes involves women's economic relationship to men as well as length of time in the United States.

Four Mexicanas and one Chicana were involuntarily nonemployed. They had been laid off from their jobs or were on temporary disability leave. Three women (two Mexicanas/one Chicana) were seeking employment; the other two were in the last stages of pregnancy but intended to look for a job as soon as possible after their child's birth. All five women reported feeling "good" about being home with their children but wanted to rejoin the labor force as soon as possible. Ideologically these women view motherhood and employment as reconcilable social dynamics. As Isabel, an unemployed production worker, married with eight children, said:

> I believe that women always work more. We who are mothers work to maintain the family by working outside, but also inside the house caring for the children.

Isabel voiced a sentiment held by all of the informants—that women work hard at motherhood.

Since emigrating to the U.S. about a decade ago, Isabel had been employed nearly continuously, with only short leaves for childbearing. Isabel and nearly all of the Mexicanas described growing up in environments where women, men, and children were important economic actors. In this regard they are similar to the Nonambivalent Employed Mothers—all of whom are also Mexicanas. They tended not to dichotomize social life in the same way as the Voluntary Nonemployed Chicanas and Ambivalent Employed informants.

Although all of the Chicanas believe that staying home best fulfills their mother roles, slightly fewer than half actually stay out of the labor market to care for their young children. The rest of the Chicanas are employed and struggling to reconcile motherhood with employment. I refer to these women as Ambivalent Employed Mothers. They express guilt about working and assert they *would not work* if they did not have to for economic reasons. Seven of these women are Chicanas; four are Mexicanas.

To try and alleviate their guilt and help meet their families' economic goals, most of the Chicanas work in part-time jobs. This option permits them to be home when their children arrive from school. Despite this, they feel guilty and unhappy about working. As Jenny, a married Chicana with two children, ages two and four, who is employed part-time, said:

> Sure, I feel guilty. I *should* [her emphasis] be with them [her children] while they're little. He [her husband] really feels that I should be with my kids all the time. And it's true.

Despite their guilt, most of the women in this group remain employed because their jobs offer them the means to provide for family economic betterment—a goal that transcends staying home with their children. However, women's utilization of economic rationales for working sometimes served as a smokescreen for individualistic desires to "do something outside the home" and to establish a degree of autonomy. Several women, for example, stated that they enjoyed having their "own money." When I asked these women to elaborate, they typically retreated to a familistic stance. That is, much of *her* money is used *for the family* (for example, child care, family presents, clothing). When money is used *for the woman* (makeup, going out with the girls) it is often justified as necessary for her emotional well-being, which in turn helps her to be a good wife and mother.

The Mexicana mothers who are employed express their ambivalence somewhat differently from the Chicanas. One Mexicana works full-time; the other three are employed part-time. Angela, a Mexicana married with one child and employed full-time as a seamstress, told me with glistening eyes:

> Always I have had to work. I had to leave my son with the baby-sitter since he was six months old. It was difficult. Each baby-sitter has their own way of caring for children, which isn't like yours. I know the baby-sitter wouldn't give him the food I left. He always had on dirty diapers and was starving when I would pick him up. But there wasn't any other recourse. I had to work. I would just clean him and feed him when I got home.

Angela's "guilt" stemmed from her inability to find good, affordable child care. Unlike most of the Mexicanas, who had extensive family networks, Angela and her husband had few relatives to rely on in the U.S. Unlike the Chicana informants, Angela did not want to exit the labor market to care for her child. Her desire is reinforced by economic need; her husband is irregularly employed.[35] For the other three Mexicanas in this group, guilt as an employed mother appears to have developed with stable spousal employment. That is, the idea of feeling guilty about full-time employment emerged *after* husbands became employed in secure, well-paying jobs and "reminded" them of the importance of stay-at-home, full-time motherhood. Lourdes, who was married with eight children and working as a part-time hotel maid said:

> I was offered a job at a—factory, working from eleven at night to seven in the morning. But I had a baby and so I wasn't able to work. I would have liked to take the job because it paid $8.25 an hour. I couldn't though, because of my baby. And my husband didn't want me to work at night. He said, "If we both work at night, who will take care of the children?" So I didn't take the job.

To thwart potential guilt over full-time employment and to ease marital tension (if she had taken this job she would have earned more money than her husband), Lourdes declined this high-paying job. When her child turned two, she opted to work part-time as a hotel maid. Lourdes, and the other Mexicanas employed part-time, told me that they *would* work full-time *if* their husbands supported their preferences. Mexicanas' ambivalence, then, is related to unease

about their children's child care situations, as well as to anger at being held accountable to a narrow construction of motherhood enforced by their husbands.

All Ambivalent Employed Mothers report worrying about their children while at work. While this does not necessarily impair their job performance, it adds another psychological or emotional burden on their shoulders. This burden affects their ability to work full-time (overtime is especially problematic) or seek the means (especially schooling) to advance in their jobs.

Women seem particularly troubled when they have to work on weekends. This robs them of precious family time. As Elena, a Chicana single parent with two children, ages nine and three, who works part-time as a hotel maid, said:

> Yes, I work on weekends. And my kids, you know how kids are—they don't like it. And it's hard. But I hope to find a job soon where the schedule is fixed and I won't have to work on weekends—because that time should be for my kids.

There is a clear sense among the women I interviewed that a boundary between *time for the family* and *market time* should exist. During times when this boundary folds, women experience both internal conflict (within the woman herself) and external conflict (among family members). They regard jobs that overlap on family time with disfavor and unhappiness. When economic reasons compel women to work during what they view as family time, they usually try to find as quickly as possible a different job that allows them to better meet their mother roles.

Interestingly, the Chicanas appear less flexible in reconciling the boundaries of family time and market time than the Mexicanas. That is, Chicanas overwhelmingly "choose" part-time employment to limit the amount of spillover time from employment on motherhood and family activities. Mexicanas, on the other hand, overwhelmingly work full-time ($n = 9$) and attempt to do both familial caretaking and market work as completely as possible.

This leads us to consider the fourth category I call Nonambivalent Employed Mothers. This category consists of Mexicana immigrants, both married and single-parent (six and two women, respectively). Mexicanas in this group do not describe motherhood as a *need* requiring a separate sphere for optimal realization. Rather, they refer to motherhood as one function of womanhood compatible with employment insofar as employment allows them to provide for their family's economic subsistence or betterment. As Pilar, a married Mexicana with four children, employed full-time as a line supervisor in a factory, said: "I work to help my children. That's what a mother should do." This group of Mexicanas does not express *guilt* over leaving their children in the care of others so much as *regret* over the limited amount of time they could spend with them. As Norma, a Mexicana full-time clerical worker who is married with two children ages three and five, said:

> I don't feel guilty for leaving my children because if I didn't work they might not have the things they have now. . . . Perhaps if I had to stay at home I would feel guilty and frustrated. I'm not the type that can stay home twenty-four hours a day. I don't think that would help my children any because I would feel pressured at being cooped up [*encerrada*] at home. And that way I wouldn't have the same desire to play with my daughters. But now, with the time we have together, we do things that we want to, like run in the park, because there's so little time.

All of the Mexicanas in this group articulate views similar to Norma's. Their greater comfort with the demands of market and family work emanates from their social locations. All of the Mexicanas come from poor or working-class families, where motherhood embraced both economic and affective features. Their activities were not viewed as equal to those of men, however, and ideologically [the] women saw themselves as *helping* the family rather than *providing* for it.

Few Mexicanas reported that their mothers were wage-laborers (*n* = 3); rather, they described a range of economic activities they remembered women doing "for the family."[36] Mexicanas from rural villages (*n* = 7) recounted how their mothers had worked on the land and made assorted products or food to sell in local marketplaces. Mexicanas from urban areas (*n* = 5) also discussed how their mothers had been economically active. Whether rural or urban, Mexicanas averred that their mothers had taught them to "help" the family as soon as possible. As Norma said:

> My mother said: "It's one thing for a woman to lie around the house but it's a different thing for the work that needs to be done. As the saying goes, Work is never done; the work does you in [*El trabajo acaba con uno; uno nunca acaba con el trabajo*]."

Lourdes and two other Mexicanas cleaned houses with their mothers after school. Other mothers sold clothes to neighbors, cooked and sold food, or did assorted services for pay (for example, giving penicillin shots to neighbors). The Mexicanas do not view these activities as "separate" or less important than the emotional nurturing of children and family. Rather, they appreciate both the economic and the expressive as important facets of motherhood.

Although the Mexicanas had been raised in worlds where women were important economic actors, this did not signify gender equality. On the contrary, male privilege, or patriarchy, characterizes the organization of the family, the economy, and the polity in both rural and urban Mexican society.[37] In the present study, Mexicanas indicated that men wielded greater authority in the family, the community, and the state than women. Mexicanas also tended to uphold male privilege in the family by viewing both domestic work and women's employment as "less important" than the work done by men. As Adela, a married Mexicana with four children, said: "Men are much stronger and do much more difficult work than women." Mexicanas also tended to defer to husbands as the "head" of the family—a position they told me was both "natural" and "holy."[38]

WORKING AT MOTHERHOOD

The differences presented here between the Chicanas and Mexicanas regarding motherhood and employment stem from their distinct social locations. Raised in rural or working-class families in Mexico, the Mexicanas described childhoods where they and their mothers actively contributed to the economic subsistence of their families by planting crops, harvesting, selling homemade goods, and cleaning houses. Their situations resonate with what some researchers term a family economy, where all family members work at productive tasks differentiated mainly by age and sex.[39] In this type of structure, there is less distinction between economic life and domestic life. Motherhood in this context is both economic and expressive, embracing employment as well as child-rearing.

The family economy the Mexicanas experienced differs from the family organization that characterizes most of the Chicanas' childhoods. The Chicanas come from a world that idealizes a male wage earner as the main economic "provider," with women primarily as consumers and only secondarily as economic actors.[40] Women in this context are mothers first, wage earners second. Families that challenge this structure are often discredited, or perceived as dysfunctional and the source of many social problems.[41] The ambivalence Chicanas recurrently voice stems from their belief in what Kanter calls "the myth of separate worlds."[42] They seek to realize the popular notion or stereotype that family is a separate structure—a haven in a heartless world. Their attachment to this ideal is underscored by a harsh critique of their own employed mothers and themselves *when* they work full-time. Motherhood framed within this context appears irreconcilable with employment.

There are other facets to the differences between Chicanas and Mexicanas. The Mexicanas, as immigrant women, came to the United States with a vision of improving the life chances of their families and themselves. This finding intersects with research on "selective immigration." That is, Mexican immigrants tend to possess higher levels of education than the national average in Mexico, and a wide range of behavioral characteristics (for instance, high achievement orientation) conducive to success in the United States.[43]

The Mexicanas emigrated hoping to work—hence their high attachment to employment, even in physically demanding, often demeaning jobs. Mexican and Chicano husbands support their wives' desires to work *so long as* this employment does not challenge the patriarchal structure of the family. In other words, so long as the Mexicanas: (1) articulate high attachment to motherhood *and* family caretaker roles, (2) frame their employment in terms of family economic goals, and (3) do not ask men to do equal amounts of housework or child care, they encounter little resistance from husbands or other male family members.

When Mexican and Chicano husbands secure good jobs, however, they begin pressuring wives to quit working or to work only part-time. In this way, Mexican and Chicano men actively pursue continuity of their superordinate position within the family. This suggests that the way motherhood is conceptualized in both the Mexican and Chicano communities, particularly with respect to employment, is wedded to male privilege, or patriarchy. Ironically, then, Mexicanas' sense of employment's continuity with motherhood enhances their job attachment but does not challenge a patriarchal family structure or ethos.

Similarly, Chicanas' preference for an idealized form of motherhood does not challenge male privilege in their community. Their desire to stay at home to mother exercised a particularly strong influence on the employment behavior of single-parent Chicanas and women with husbands employed in relatively good jobs. This preference reflects an adherence to an idealized, middle-class lifestyle that glorifies women's domestic roles, as well as to maintenance of a patriarchal family order. Chicanas feel they should stay at home to try and provide their children with the mothering they believe children should have—mothering that many of them had not experienced. Chicanas also feel compelled by husbands and the larger community to maintain the status of men as "good providers." Men earning wages adequate to provide for their families' needs usually urged their wives to leave the labor market. While the concept of the good provider continues to be highly valued in our society, it also serves as a rationale that upholds male privilege ideologically and materially, and reinforces the myth of separate spheres that emanates from the organization of the family and the economy.

CONCLUSION

By illustrating how Chicanas and Mexicanas differ in their conceptualizations and organization of the motherhood and employment nexus, this study demonstrates how motherhood is a culturally formed structure with various meanings and subtexts. The vitality of these differences among a group whose members share a common historical origin and many cultural attributes underscores the need for frameworks that analyze diversity among all groups of women. Most essential to such an undertaking is a critique of the privileging of the "separate spheres" concept in analyses of women and work.

The present study provides additional coherence to recent contentions that the private–public dichotomy lacks immediate relevance to less privileged women (for instance, Chicana and Mexican immigrant women). In the process of illustrating how Chicanas and Mexicanas organized the interplay between motherhood and employment, it became clear that a more useful way of understanding this intersection might be to problematize motherhood itself. Considering motherhood from the vantage point of women's diverse social locations revealed considerable heterogeneity in how one might speak of it. For example, motherhood has an economic component for both groups of women, but it is most strongly expressed by Mexicana immigrants. The flavor of the expressive, however, flows easily across both groups of women, and for the Mexicanas embraces the economic. What this suggests is that the dichotomy of the separate spheres lacks relevance to Chicanas and Mexicanas and other women whose social origins make economic work necessary for survival.

This leads us to consider the relative place and function of the ideology of motherhood prevalent in our society. Motherhood constructed to privilege the woman who stays at home serves a myriad of functions. It pushes women to dichotomize their lives rather than develop a sense of fluidity across roles, responsibilities, and preferences. Idealized, stay-at-home motherhood eludes most American women with children. As an ideology, however, it tells them what "should be," rendering them failures *as women* when they enter the labor market. Hence the feelings of ambivalence that characterized employed mothers' lives for the most part—except those who had not yet internalized these standards. The present research provided examples of such women, along with the understanding that other women from different social locations may demonstrate distinct ways of organizing the motherhood–employment nexus as well.

Feminist analyses of women and work emphasize the role of patriarchy to maintain male privilege and domination economically and ideologically. It is important to recognize that male privilege is not experienced equally by all men, and that patriarchy itself can be expressed in different ways. The present study found that notions of motherhood among Mexicanas and Chicanas are embedded in different ideological constructs operating within two systems of patriarchy. For Mexicanas, patriarchy takes the form of a corporate family model, with all members contributing to the common good. For Chicanas, the patriarchal structure centers more closely around a public–private dichotomy that idealizes men as economic providers and women primarily as caretakers-consumers.

The finding that women from more "traditional" backgrounds (such as rural Mexico) are likely to approach full-time employment with less ambivalence than more "American" women (such as the Chicanas) rebuts linear acculturation models that assume a negative relationship between ideologies (such as motherhood) constructed within "traditional" Mexican society and employment. It also complements findings on the negative relationship between greater length of time in the United States and high aspirations among Mexicans.[44] This suggests that employment problems (for example, underemployment, unemployment) are related less to "traditional" cultural configurations than to labor market structure and employment policies. Understanding the intersections between employment policy, social ideology, and private need is a necessary step toward expanding possibilities for women in our society.

NOTES

1. This article is a revised version of "Ambivalence or Continuity? Motherhood and Employment Among Chicanas and Mexican Immigrant Women," *AZTLAN, International Journal of Chicano Studies Research* (1992). I would like to thank Maxine Baca Zinn, Evelyn Nakano Glenn, Arlie Hochschild, Beatriz Pesquera, and Vicki Ruiz for their constructive feedback and criticism of earlier drafts of this paper. A special thanks goes to Jon Cruz for his assistance in titling this paper. Any remaining errors or inconsistencies are my own responsibility. This research was supported in part by a 1986–87 University of California President's Postdoctoral Fellowship.

2. Betsy Wearing, *The Ideology of Motherhood, A Study of Sydney Suburban Mothers* (Sydney: George Allen and Unwin, 1984); Barbara J. Berg, *The Crisis of the Working Mother, Resolving the Conflict Between Family and Work* (New York: Summit Books, 1986); Nancy Folbre "The Pauperization of Motherhood: Patriarchy and Public Policy in the United States," *Review of Radical Political Economics* 16 (1984). The view that mothers should not work outside the home typically pertains to married women. Current state welfare policies (e.g., Aid to Families with Dependent Children [AFDC], workfare) indicate that single, unmarried mothers belong in the labor force, not at home caring for their children full-time. See Naomi Gerstel and Harriet Engel Gross, "Introduction," in N. Gerstel and H. E. Gross, eds., *Families and Work* (Philadelphia: Temple University Press, 1987), pp. 1–12; Deborah K. Zinn and Rosemary C. Sarri, "Turning Back the Clock on Public Welfare," in *Signs: Journal of Women in Culture and Society* 10 (1984), pp. 355–370; Nancy Folbre "The Pauperization of Motherhood"; Nancy A. Naples, "A Socialist Feminist Analysis of the Family Support Act of 1988," *AFFILIA* 6 (1991), pp. 23–38.

3. Allyson Sherman Grossman, "More than Half of All Children Have Working Mothers," Special Labor Force Reports—Summaries, *Monthly Labor Review* (February 1982), pp. 41–43; Howard Hayghe, "Working Mothers Reach Record Number in 1984," *Monthly Labor Review* 107 (December 1984), pp. 31–34; U.S. Bureau of the Census "Fertility of American Women: June 1990," *Current Population Report,* Series P-20, No. 454 (Washington, D.C.: United States Government Printing Office, 1991). In June 1990,

over half (53.1 percent) of women between the ages of 18 and 44 who had had a child in the last year were in the labor force. This proportion varied by race: 54.9 percent of white women, 46.9 percent of Black women, and 44.4 percent of Latinas were in the labor force. See U.S. Bureau of the Census (1991), p. 5.

4. Simon and Landis report that a 1986 Gallup Poll indicates that support for married women to work outside the home is considerably greater than 1938 levels: 76 percent of women and 78 percent of men approve (1989: 270). Comparable 1938 levels are 25 percent and 19 percent, respectively, of women and men. The 1985 Roper Poll finds the American public adhering to the view that a husband's career supersedes that of his wife: 72 percent of women and 62 percent of men agree that a wife should quit her job and relocate if her husband is offered a good job in another city (1989: 272). In the reverse situation, 20 percent of women and 22 percent of men believe a husband should quit his job and relocate with his wife (1989: 272). Simon and Landis conclude: "The Women's Movement has not radicalized the American woman: she is still prepared to put marriage and children ahead of her career and to allow her husband's status to determine the family's position in society" (1989: 269). Rita J. Simon and Jean M. Landis, "Women's and Men's Attitudes About a Woman's Place and Role," *Public Opinion Quarterly* 53 (1989), pp. 265–276.

5. Arlie Hochschild with Anne Machung, *The Second Shift, Working Parents and the Revolution at Home* (New York: Viking Penguin Books, 1989); Kathleen Gerson, *Hard Choices* (Berkeley: University of California Press, 1985); Barbara J. Berg, *The Crisis of the Working Mother, Resolving the Conflict Between Family and Work* (New York: Summit Books, 1986). The concept of "separate spheres" is approached in a variety of ways and often critiqued. See Michele Barrett, *Women's Oppression Today, Problems in Marxist Feminist Analysis* (London: Verso Press, 1980); Nona Glazer "Servants to Capital: Unpaid Domestic Labor and Paid Work," *Review of Radical Economics* 16 (1984), pp. 61–87. Zaretsky contends that distinct family and market spheres arose with the development of industrial capitalism: "Men and women came to see the family as separate from the economy, and personal life as a separate sphere of life divorced from the larger economy." See Eli Zaretsky, *Capitalism, the Family and Personal Life* (New York: Harper Colophon Books, 1976), p. 78. This stance is substantially different from that of early radical feminist approaches, including Firestone, who argued that the separation antedates history. See Shulamith Firestone, *The Dialectic of Sex* (New York: Bantam Books, 1970). Other scholars assert that the relations of production and reproduction are intertwined and virtually inseparable. See Heidi Hartmann, "Capitalism, Patriarchy and Job Segregation by Sex," in Martha Blaxall and Barbara Reagan, eds., *Women and the Work Place* (Chicago: University of Chicago Press, 1976), pp. 137–169.

6. Hood argues that the "ideal" of stay-at-home motherhood and male provider has historically been an unrealistic standard for families outside the middle and upper classes. She points out that early surveys of urban workers indicate between 40 and 50 percent of all families supplemented their income with the earnings of wives and children. See Jane C. Hood, "The Provider Role: Its Meaning and Measurement," *Journal of Marriage and the Family* 48 (May 1986), pp. 349–359.

7. It should be noted that native-born status is not an essential requirement for the ethnic label "Chicana/o." There are numerous identifiers used by people of Mexican descent, including: Chicana/o, Mexican, Mexican-American, Mexicana/o, Latina/o, and Hispanic. Often people of Mexican descent use two or three of the above labels, depending on the social situation (e.g., "Mexican-American" in the family or "Chicana/o" at school). See John A. Garcia, "Yo Soy Mexicano . . . Self-Identity and Sociodemographic Correlates," *Social Science Quarterly* 62 (March, 1981), pp. 88–98; Susan E. Keefe and Amado M. Padilla, *Chicano Ethnicity* (Albuquerque, NM: University of New Mexico Press, 1987). My designation of study informants as either "Chicana" or "Mexicana" represents an analytic separation that facilitates demonstrating the heterogeneity among this group.

8. Patricia Zavella, "Reflections on Diversity Among Chicanos," *Frontiers* 2 (1991), p. 75.

9. See Rosalia Solorzano-Torres, "Female Mexican Immigrants in San Diego County," in V. L. Ruiz and S. Tiano, eds., *Women on the U.S.-Mexico Border: Responses to Change* (Boston: Allen and Unwin, 1987), pp. 41–59; Reynaldo Baca and Bryan Dexter, "Mexican Women, Migration and Sex Roles," *Migration Today* 13 (1985), pp. 14–18; Sylvia Guendelman and Auristela Perez-Itriago, "Double Lives: The Changing Role of Women in Seasonal Migration," *Women's Studies* 13 (1987), pp. 249–271.

10. Gary S. Becker, "Human Capital, Effort, and the Sexual Division of Labor," *Journal of Labor Economics* 3 (1985 Supplement), pp. S33–S58; Gary S. Becker, *A Treatise on the Family* (Cambridge, MA: Harvard University Press, 1981); Solomon W. Polachek, "Occupational Self-Selection: A Human Capital Approach to Sex Differences in Occupational Structure," *Review of Economics and Statistics* 63 (1981), pp. 60–69; S. Polachek, "Occupational Segregation Among Women: Theory, Evidence, and a Prognosis" in C. B. Lloyd, E. S. Andrews, and C. L. Gilroy, eds., *Women in the Labor Market* (New York: Columbia University Press, 1981), pp. 137–157; S. Polachek, "Discontinuous Labor Force Participation and Its Effect on Women's Market Earnings," in C. Lloyd, ed., *Sex Discrimination and the Division of Labor* (New York: Columbia University Press, 1975), pp. 90–122. Becker's classic treatise, *Human Capital*, uses the following example borrowed from G. Stigler, "The Economics of Information," *Journal of Political Economy* (June 1961): "Women spend less time in the labor force than men and, therefore, have less incentive than residents

of the area to invest in knowledge of specific consumption activities." See Gary S. Becker, *Human Capital* (Chicago: University of Chicago Press, 1975), p. 74.

11. Some institutional economists argue that "statistical discrimination" is one critical labor market dynamic that often impedes women and minorities. See Kenneth Arrow, "Economic Dimensions of Occupational Segregation: Comment I," *Signs: Journal of Women in Culture and Society* 1 (1987), pp. 233–237; Edmund Phelps, "The Statistical Theory of Racism and Sexism," in A. H. Amsden, ed., *The Economics of Women and Work* (New York: St. Martin's Press, 1980), pp. 206–210. This perspective suggests that prospective employers often lack detailed information about individual applicants and therefore utilize statistical averages and normative views of the relevant group(s) to which the applicant belongs in their hiring decisions (e.g., college-educated men tend to be successful and committed employees; all women are potential mothers; or women tend to exit the labor force for childbearing).

Bielby and Baron pose an important critique to the underlying rationale of statistical discrimination. They argue that utilizing perceptions of group differences between the sexes is "neither as rational nor as efficient as the economists believe." That is, utilizing stereotypical notions of "men's work" and "women's work" is often costly to employers and therefore irrational. This suggests that sex segregation is embedded in organizational policies which reflect and reinforce "belief systems that are also rather inert." See William T. Bielby and James N. Baron, "Undoing Discrimination: Job Integration and Comparable Worth," in C. Bose and G. Spitze, eds., *Ingredients for Women's Employment Policy* (New York: State University of New York Press, 1987), pp. 216, 221–222.

12. Annette Kuhn, "Structure of Patriarchy and Capital in the Family," in A. Kuhn and Annemarie Wolfe, eds., *Feminism and Materialism: Women and Modes of Production* (London: Routledge and Kegan Paul, 1978); Heidi Hartmann, "Capitalism, Patriarchy, and Job Segregation by Sex," in Martha Blaxall and Barbara Reagan, eds., *Women and the Work Place* (Chicago: University of Chicago Press, 1976), pp. 137–169; H. Hartmann, "The Family as the Locus of Gender, Class, and Political Struggle: The Example of Housework," *Signs: Journal of Women in Culture and Society* 6 (1981), pp. 366–394; Michele Barrett, *Women's Oppression Today, Problems in Marxist Feminist Analysis* (London: Verso Press, 1980).

13. Lourdes Beneria and Martha Roldan, *The Crossroads of Class and Gender, Industrial Homework, Subcontracting, and Household Dynamics in Mexico City* (Chicago: University of Chicago Press, 1987); L. Beneria and Gita Sen, "Accumulation, Reproduction, and Women's Role in Economic Development: Boserup Revisited," in E. Leacock and H. I. Safa, eds., *Women's Work: Development and Division of Labor by Gender* (Massachusetts: Bergin and Garvey Publishers, 1986), pp. 141–157; Dorothy Smith, "Women's Inequality

and the Family," in N. Gerstel and H. E. Gross, eds., *Families and Work* (Philadelphia: Temple University Press, 1987), pp. 23–54.

14. This phrase was coined by Arlie R. Hochschild and quoted in Lillian B. Rubin, *Intimate Strangers, Men and Women Together* (New York: Harper and Row, 1983).

15. Rosabeth Moss Kanter, *Men and Women in the Corporation* (New York: Basic Books, 1977). Bielby and Baron note: "Employers expect certain behaviors from women (e.g., high turnover) and therefore assign them to routine tasks and dead-end jobs. Women respond by exhibiting the very behavior employers expect, thereby reinforcing the stereotype." Bielby and Baron, "Undoing Discrimination: Job Integration and Comparable Worth," p. 221.

16. Arlie Hochschild with Anne Machung, *The Second Shift, Working Parents and the Revolution of Home* (New York: Viking Penguin Books, 1989).

17. Barbara J. Berg, *The Crisis of the Working Mother, Resolving the Conflict Between Family and Work* (New York: Summit Books, 1986), p. 42.

18. Howard Hayghe, "Working Mothers Reach Record Number in 1984," *Monthly Labor Review* 107 (December 1984), pp. 31–34; U.S. Bureau of the Census, "Fertility of American Women: June 1990" in Current Population Report, Series P-20, No. 454 (Washington D.C.: United States Government Printing Office, 1991); U.S. Bureau of Census Report, "Fertility of American Women: June 1986," in Current Population Report, Series P-20. No. 421 (Washington, D.C.: United States Government Printing Office). In June 1986 (the year closest to the year I interviewed the respondents where I found relevant data), 49.8 percent of all women with newborn children were in the labor force. Women demonstrated differences in this behavior: 49.7 percent of white women, 51.1 percent of Black women, and 40.6 percent of Latinas with newborn children were in the labor force. See U.S. Bureau of the Census, "Fertility of American Women: June 1986" (1987), p. 5.

19. Bonnie Thornton Dill, Lynn Weber Cannon, and Reeve Vanneman, "Pay Equity: An Issue of Race, Ethnicity, and Sex" (Washington D.C.: National Commission on Pay Equity, February, 1987); Julianne Malveaux and Phyllis Wallace, "Minority Women in the Workplace," in K. S. Koziara, M. Moskow, and L. Dewey Tanner, eds., *Women and Work: Industrial Relations Research Association Research Volume* (Washington D.C.: Bureau of National Affairs, 1987), pp. 265–298; Vicki L. Ruiz, "'And Miles to go . . .': Mexican Women and Work, 1930–1985" in L. Schlissel, V. L. Ruiz, and J. Monk, eds., *Western Women, Their Land, Their Lives* (Albuquerque: University of New Mexico Press, 1988), pp. 117–136.

20. Mario Barrera, *Race and Class in the Southwest: A Theory of Racial Inequality* (Notre Dame, IN: University of Notre Dame Press, 1979); Tomas Almaguer, "Class, Race, and Chicano Oppression," *Socialist Revolution* 5 (1975), pp. 71–99; Denise Segura, "Labor Market Stratification:

The Chicana Experience," *Berkeley Journal of Sociology* 29 (1984), pp. 57–91.

21. Marta Tienda and P. Guhleman, "The Occupational Position of Employed Hispanic Women," in G. J. Borjas and M. Tienda, eds., *Hispanics in the U.S. Economy* (New York: Academic Press, 1985), pp. 243–273.

22. Edgar J. Kranau, Vicki Green, and Gloria Valencia-Weber, "Acculturation and the Hispanic Woman: Attitudes Towards Women, Sex-Role Attribution, Sex-Role Behavior, and Demographics," *Hispanic Journal of Behavioral Sciences* 4 (1982), pp. 21–40; Alfredo Mirande and Evangelina Enriquez, *La Chicana, The Mexican American Woman* (Chicago: University of Chicago Press, 1979).

23. Kranau, Green, and Valencia-Weber, "Acculturation and the Hispanic Woman," pp. 21–40; Alfredo Mirande, *The Chicano Experience: An Alternative Perspective* (Notre Dame, IN: University of Notre Dame Press, 1985).

24. Vilma Ortiz and Rosemary Santana Cooney, "Sex-Role Attitudes and Labor Force Participation Among Young Hispanic Females and Non-Hispanic White Females," *Social Science Quarterly* 65 (June 1984), pp. 392–400.

25. Susan E. Keefe and Amado M. Padilla, *Chicano Ethnicity* (Albuquerque: University of New Mexico Press, 1987); Richard H. Mendoza, "Acculturation and Sociocultural Variability," in J. L. Martinez Jr. and R. H. Mendoza, eds., *Chicano Psychology*, 2nd ed. (New York: Academic Press, 1984), pp. 61–75.

26. Maxine Baca Zinn, "Mexican-American Women in the Social Sciences," *Signs: Journal of Women in Culture and Society* 8 (1982), pp. 259–272; M. Baca Zinn, "Employment and Education of Mexican-American Women: The Interplay of Modernity and Ethnicity in Eight Families," *Harvard Educational Review* 50 (February 1980), pp. 47–62; M. Baca Zinn, "Chicano Family Research: Conceptual Distortions and Alternative Directions," *Journal of Ethnic Studies* 7 (1979), pp. 59–71.

27. For additional information on the methods and sample selection, I refer the reader to Denise A. Segura, "Chicanas and Mexican Immigrant Women in the Labor Market: A Study of Occupational Mobility and Stratification," unpublished Ph.D. dissertation, Department of Sociology, University of California, Berkeley (1986).

28. The ages of the Chicanas range from 23 to 42 years. The Mexicanas reported ages from 24 to 45. The age profile indicates that most of the women were in peak childbearing years.

29. Denise A. Segura, "Chicanas and Mexican Immigrant Women in the Labor Market."

30. For an example, see Betsy Wearing, *The Ideology of Motherhood, A Study of Sydney Suburban Mothers* (Sydney: George Allen and Unwin, 1984).

31. For an example, see Nancy Chodorow, *The Reproduction of Mothering* (Berkeley: University of California Press, 1979).

32. Manuel Ramirez III and Alfredo Castaneda, *Cultural Democracy, Bicognitive Development, and Education* (New York: Academic Press, 1974); Robert F. Peck and Rogelio Diaz-Guerrero, "Two Core-Culture Patterns and the Diffusion of Values Across Their Borders," *International Journal of Psychology* 2 (1967), pp. 272–282; Javier I. Escobat and E. T. Randolph, "The Hispanic and Social Networks," in R. M. Becerra, M. Karno, and J. I. Escobar, eds., *Mental Health and Hispanic Americans: Clinical Perspectives* (New York: Grune and Stratton, 1982).

33. Alfredo Mirande and Evangelina Enriquez, *La Chicana, The Mexican American Woman* (Chicago: University of Chicago Press, 1979); Margarita Melville, "Introduction" and "Matrascence" in M. B. Melville, ed., *Twice a Minority: Mexican American Women* (St. Louis: C. V. Mosby., 1980), pp. 1–16; Gloria Anzaldúa, *Borderlands, La Frontera: The New Mestiza* (San Francisco: Spinsters/Aunt Lute Book Co., 1987); Linda C. Fox, "Obedience and Rebellion: Re-Vision of Chicana Myths of Motherhood," *Women's Studies Quarterly* (Winter, 1983), pp. 20–22.

34. Talcott Parsons and Robert Bales, *Family, Socialization, and Interaction Processes* (New York: Free Press, 1955); Robert H. Bradley and Bettye M. Caldwell, "The Relation of Infants' Home Environments to Achievement Test Performance in First Grade: A Follow-up Study," *Child Development* 55 (1984), pp. 803–809; Toby L. Parcel and Elizabeth G. Menaghan, "Maternal Working Conditions and Child Verbal Facility: Studying the Intergenerational Transmission of Inequality from Mothers to Young Children," *Social Psychology Quarterly* 53 (1990), pp. 132–147; Avshalom Caspi and Glen H. Elder, "Emergent Family Patterns: The Intergenerational Construction of Problem Behavior and Relationships," in R. Hinde and J. Stevenson Hinde, eds., *Understanding Family Dynamics* (New York: Oxford University Press, 1988).

35. For a full discussion of the interplay between economic goals and economic status of the respondents and their employment decisions, I refer the reader to Denise Segura, "The Interplay of Familism and Patriarchy on Employment among Chicana and Mexican Immigrant Women," in the *Renato Rosaldo Lecture Series Monograph* 5 (Tucson, AZ: The University of Arizona, Center for Mexican American Studies, 1989), pp. 35–53.

36. Two of the Mexicanas reported that their mothers had died while they were toddlers and therefore they were unable to discuss their economic roles.

37. Patricia M. Fernandez-Kelly, "Mexican Border Industrialization, Female Labor-Force Participation and Migration," in J. Nash and M. P. Fernandez-Kelly, eds., *Women, Men, and the International Division of Labor* (Albany: State University of New York Press, 1983), pp. 205–223; Sylvia Guendelman and Auristela Perez-Itriago, "Double Lives: The Changing Role of Women in Seasonal Migration," *Women's Studies* 13 (1987), pp. 249–271; Reynaldo Baca and Dexter Bryan, "Mexican Women, Migration and Sex Roles," *Migration Today* 13 (1985), pp. 14–18.

38. Research indicates religious involvement plays an important role in gender beliefs. See Ross K. Baker, Laurily K. Epstein,

and Rodney O. Forth, "Matters of Life and Death: Social, Political, Religious Correlates of Attitudes on Abortion," *American Politics Quarterly* 9 (1981), pp. 89–102; Charles E. Peek and Sharon Brown, "Sex Prejudice Among White Protestants: Like or Unlike Ethnic Prejudice?" *Social Forces* 59 (1980), pp. 169–185. Of particular interest for the present study is that involvement in fundamentalist Christian churches is positively related to adherence to traditional gender role ideology. See Clyde Wilcox and Elizabeth Adell Cook, "Evangelical Women and Feminism: Some Additional Evidence," *Women and Politics* 9 (1989), pp. 27–49; Clyde Wilcox, "Religious Attitudes and Anti-Feminism: An Analysis of the Ohio Moral Majority," *Women and Politics* 48 (1987), pp. 1041–1051. Half of the Mexicanas (and all but two Chicanas) adhered to the Roman Catholic religion; half belonged to various fundamentalist Christian churches (e.g., Assembly of God). Two Chicanas belonged to other Protestant denominations. I noticed that the women who belonged to the Assembly of God tended to both work full-time in the labor market and voice the strongest convictions of male authority in the family. During their interviews many of the women brought out the Bible and showed me the biblical passages that authorized husbands to "rule" the family. Catholic women also voiced traditional beliefs regarding family structure but did not invoke God.

39. Frances Rothstein, "Women and Men in the Family Economy: An Analysis of the Relations Between the Sexes in Three Peasant Communities," *Anthropological Quarterly* 56 (1983), pp. 10–23; Ruth Schwartz Cowan, "Women's Work, Housework, and History: The Historical Roots of Inequality in Work-Force Participation," in N. Gerstel and H. E. Gross, eds., *Families and Work* (Philadelphia: Temple University Press, 1987), pp. 164–177; Louise A. Tilly and Joan W. Scott, *Women, Work, and Family* (New York: Holt, Rinehart and Winston, 1978).

40. Jessie Bernard, "The Rise and Fall of the Good Provider Role," *American Psychologist* 36 (1981), pp. 1–12; J. Bernard, *The Future of Motherhood* (New York: Penguin Books, 1974); Jane C. Hood, "The Provider Role: Its Meaning and Measurement," *Journal of Marriage and the Family* 48 (May, 1986), pp. 349–359.

41. Lorraine O. Walker and Mary Ann Best, "Well-Being of Mothers with Infant Children: A Preliminary Comparison of Employed Women and Homemakers," *Women and Health* 17 (1991), pp. 71–88; William J. Doherty and Richard H. Needle, "Psychological Adjustment and Substance Use Among Adolescents Before and After a Parental Divorce," *Child Development* 62 (1991), pp. 328–337; Eugene E. Clark and William Ramsey, "The Importance of Family and Network of Other Relationships in Children's Success

in School," *International Journal of Sociology of the Family* 20 (1990), pp. 237–254.

42. Rosabeth Moss Kanter, *Men and Women of the Corporation* (New York: Basic Books, 1977).

43. John M. Chavez and Raymond Buriel, "Reinforcing Children's Effort: A Comparison of Immigrant, Native-Born Mexican American and Euro-American Mothers," *Hispanic Journal of Behavioral Sciences* 8 (1986), pp. 127–142; Raymond Buriel, "Integration with Traditional Mexican-American Culture and Sociocultural Adjustment" in J. L. Martinez, Jr. and R. H. Mendoza, eds., *Chicano Psychology*, 2nd ed. (New York: Academic Press, 1984), pp. 95–130; Leo R. Chavez, "Households, Migration and Labor Market Participation: The Adaptation of Mexicans to Life in the United States," *Urban Anthropology* 14 (1985), pp. 301–346.

44. Raymond Buriel, "Integration with Traditional Mexican-American Culture and Sociocultural Adjustment," in J. L. Martinez, Jr. and R. H. Mendoza, eds., *Chicano Psychology*, 2nd ed. (New York: Academic Press, 1984), pp. 95–130. In their analysis of differences in educational goals among Mexican-Americans, Buriel and his associates found that "third-generation Mexican Americans felt less capable of fulfilling their educational objectives." See Raymond Buriel, Silverio Caldaza, and Richard Vasquez, "The Relationship of Traditional Mexican American Culture to Adjustment and Delinquency Among Three Generations of Mexican American Adolescents," *Hispanic Journal of Behavioral Sciences* 4 (1982), p. 50. Similar findings were reported by Nielsen and Fernandez: "We find that students whose families have been in the U.S. longer have *lower* [their emphasis] aspirations than recent immigrants." See Francois Nielsen and Roberto M. Fernandez, *Hispanic Students in American High Schools: Background Characteristics and Achievement* (Washington D.C.: United States Government Printing Office, 1981), p. 76.

In their analysis of Hispanic employment, Bean and his associates reported an unexpected finding—that English-proficient Mexican women exhibit a greater "constraining influence of fertility" on their employment vis-à-vis Spanish-speaking women. They speculate that more acculturated Mexican women may have "a greater desire for children of higher quality," and therefore "be more likely to devote time to the informal socialization and education of young children." They wonder "why this should hold true for English-speaking but not Spanish-speaking women." See Frank D. Bean, C. Gray Swicegood, and Allan G. King, "Role Incompatibility and the Relationship Between Fertility and Labor Supply Among Hispanic Women" in G. J. Borjas and M. Tienda, eds., *Hispanics in the U.S. Economy* (New York: Academic Press, 1985), p. 241.

Moral Dilemmas, Moral Strategies, and the Transformation of Gender: Lessons from Two Generations of Work and Family Change[1]

Choosing between self-interest and caring for others is one of the most fundamental dilemmas facing all of us. To reconcile this dilemma, modern societies in general—and American society in particular—have tried to divide women and men into different moral categories. Since the rise of industrialism, the social organization of moral responsibility has expected women to seek personal development by caring for others and men to care for others by sharing the rewards of independent achievement.

Although labeled "traditional," this gendered division of moral labor represents a social form and cultural mandate that rose to prominence in the mid-twentieth century but reached an impasse as the postindustrial era opened new avenues for work and family life. (Among the voluminous works on this subject, see Kimmel 1996; Ryan 1981; Welter 1966.) At the outset of the twenty-first century, women and men face rising conflicts over how to resolve the basic tensions between family and work, public and private, autonomy and commitment. They are searching for new strategies for reconciling an "independent self" with commitment to others.

While the long-term trajectory of change remains unclear, new social conditions have severely undermined the link between gender and moral obligation. The young women and men who have come of age amid this changing social landscape face risks and dangers, but they also inherit an unprecedented opportunity to forge new, more egalitarian ways to balance self-development with commitment to others. To enable them to do so, however, we must reshape work and family institutions in ways that overcome beliefs and practices that presume gender differences in moral responsibility.

Drawing on insights from my research on how contemporary young women and men negotiate the conflicts between family and work, I explore how new social conditions are compelling them to reconsider traditional strategies for reconciling self-development with caring for others. Social change has undermined earlier resolutions to these dilemmas but does not offer clear avenues for creating new ones. My research on the "children of the gender revolution" suggests that young women and men cannot rely on inflexible gender categories to resolve the conflict between autonomy and care, but they are encountering social and cultural obstacles to creating gender-neutral strategies for apportioning moral labor. . . .

STUDYING GENDER CHANGE: FINDINGS FROM A NEW GENERATION

During the last several decades, I have studied two pivotal generations. My earlier research examined how the women and men who came of age in the 1970s and 1980s helped forge changes in gender, work, and family life as they reacted to new structural and cultural conditions (Gerson 1985, 1993). My current research focuses on how the generation who grew up in these changing households and are now entering adulthood are responding to a world where nontraditional family forms predominate and gender inequality has been seriously questioned. In significant ways, the older group can be viewed as the "parents of the gender revolution" and the generation now coming of age as the "children of the revolution" (Gerson 2001). They have watched their parents cope with the erosion of the breadwinner-homemaker ethos, and they must now devise their own strategies in the face of continuing work and family change.

To discover how new generations are experiencing and responding to these vast social changes, I conducted in-depth, life history interviews with 120 young women and men between the ages of 18 and 32. They were randomly selected from a range of economic and social contexts, including inner-city, outer-city, and suburban neighborhoods throughout the New York metropolitan area. They are evenly divided between women and men, with an average age of 24, and are economically and racially diverse, with 54 percent non-Hispanic whites, 21 percent African Americans, 18 percent Hispanics, and 8 percent Asians.

Most lived in families that underwent changes that cannot be captured in the static categories of household types. That said, a large majority lived in some form of nontraditional arrangement before reaching 18. About 40 percent lived in a single-parent home at some point in their childhood, and 7 percent saw their parents break up after they left home.[2] About one-third grew up in homes where both parents held full-time jobs of relatively equal importance, at least at some point during their childhood.[3] The remaining 27 percent described growing up in homes that were generally traditional in the sense that mothers worked intermittently, secondarily, or not at all, although most of these households underwent some form of change as mothers went to work or marriages faced crises. As a whole, the group experienced the full range of changes now emerging in family, work, and gender arrangements.

The interviews reveal how growing up amid a shifting gender and family order has prompted a new generation to rethink the age-old conflict between self-interest and responsibility to others. Taking lessons from their parents and their parents' generation, but facing new quandaries of their own, these young women and men are crafting moral strategies that challenge traditional views of gender. Their emerging views on how to balance autonomy and commitment, to define care, and to develop a personal identity amid ambiguous social shifts are presented below. While these views suggest a blurring of gender boundaries, they also underscore how persisting obstacles are creating a gap between young women's and men's emerging egalitarian aspirations and their far more limited opportunities for achieving them. The next section thus considers how pervasive barriers to both gender equality and work-family integration are creating a new gender divide between women who seek personal independence and men who worry about losing traditional privileges.

NEW DILEMMAS, AMBIGUOUS STRATEGIES

How does this generation view its moral choices? As adult partnerships have become more fluid and voluntary, they are grappling with how to form relationships that balance commitment with autonomy and self-sufficiency. As their mothers have become essential and often sole breadwinners for their households, they are searching for new ways to define care that do not force them to choose between spending time with their children and earning an income. And in the face of rising work-family conflicts, they are looking for definitions of personal identity that do not pit their own development against creating committed ties to others. As young women and men wrestle with these dilemmas, they are questioning a division of moral responsibility that poses a conflict between personal development and caring for others.

Seeking Autonomy, Establishing Commitment

The decline of permanent marriage has raised new and perplexing questions about how to weigh the need and desire for self-sufficiency against the hope of creating an enduring partnership. In wrestling with this quandary, young women and men draw on lessons learned in their families and personal relationships. Yet, they also recognize that past experiences and encounters can provide, at best, a partial and uncertain blueprint for the future.

Few of the women and men who were interviewed reacted in a rigidly moralistic way to their parents' choices. Among those whose parents chose to divorce (or never marry), about 45 percent viewed the breakup as a prelude to growing difficulty, but the other 55 percent supported the separation and felt relief in its aftermath. Danisha, a 21-year-old African American, concluded that conflict would have emerged had her parents stayed together:

> I have personally met a lot of miserable children whose parents stayed together. For me, it would have been worse—because eventually, a lot of the civility they had toward each other would have broken down into hostility. They got out while it was good.

And at 26, Erica, who grew up in a white middle-class suburb, supported her parents' decision to separate and received more support from each of them in its aftermath:

I knew my parents were going to get divorced, because I could tell they weren't getting along. They were acting out roles rather than being involved. They were really drifting apart, so it was something perfectly natural to me. In the new situation, I spent more valuable time with my parents as individuals. So time with my father and mother was more meaningful to me and more productive.

Among those whose parents stayed together, almost 60 percent were pleased with and, indeed, inspired by, their parents' lifelong commitment, but about 40 percent concluded that a breakup would have been better than the persistently unhappy, conflict-ridden relationship they watched unfold. Amy, a 24-year-old Asian American, explains:

I always felt my parents would have divorced if they didn't have kids and didn't feel it was so morally wrong. They didn't really stick together because they were in love. I know all couples go through fights and stuff, but growing up, it seemed like they fought a lot, and each of them has made passing comments—like "Oh, I would have divorced your mom by now" or "I would have left your dad a thousand times." [So] I wouldn't have broken down or been emotionally stressed if my parents divorced. I didn't want to hear the shouting, and I didn't want to see my mom cry anymore. And I was also afraid of my dad, because he would never lay a hand on my mom, but he's scary. He could be violent.

Whether their parents stayed together or parted, most concluded that neither steadfast commitment nor choosing to leave has moral meaning in the abstract. The value of enduring commitment depends on the quality of the relationship it embodies.

When considering their own aspirations, almost everyone hopes to establish a committed, lasting relationship with one partner. Yet, they also hold high standards for what a relationship should provide and anticipate risks in sustaining such a commitment. Across the divides of gender, race, and class, most agree that a satisfying and worthwhile relationship should offer a balance between autonomy and sharing, sacrifice and support. At 26, Michael, an African American who was raised by his mother in a working-class suburb, is convinced that only economic independence can provide a proper base for commitment with his girlfriend:

I don't want the fifties type of marriage, where I come home with a briefcase and she's cooking. She doesn't

have to cook. I just want her to have a career of her own. I want things to be comfortable. And somewhere down the line, if I lose my job or things start going crazy in the marriage, I want to be able to set my goals, and she can do what she wants, because we both have this economic base and the attitude to do it. That's what marriage is about.

Amy imagines a partnership that is equal and fluid, capable of adapting to circumstances without relinquishing equity:

I want a fifty-fifty relationship, where we both have the potential of doing everything. Both of us working, and in dealing with kids, it would be a matter of who has more flexibility with regard to their career. And if neither does, then one of us will have to sacrifice for one period, and the other for another.

Most acknowledge, however, that finding a lasting and satisfying relationship represents an ideal that is hard to reach. If it proves unattainable, they agree that being alone is better than remaining in an unhappy or destructive union. Building a full life thus means developing the self in multiple ways. At 29, Maria, who grew up in a close-knit Hispanic household where both parents worked, is careful to build her life in many directions:

I want to be with somebody, to have this person to share your life with—that you're there for as much as they're there for you. But I can't settle. If I don't find it, then I cannot live in sorrow. It's not the only thing that's ultimately important. If I didn't have my family, if I didn't have a career, if I didn't have friends, or if I didn't have the things that I enjoy doing, I would be equally unhappy. This is just one thing. Maybe it takes a little bit more of the pie than some other things—but it's still just a slice of the pie.

Across the range of personal family experiences, most also agree that children suffer more from an unhappy home than from separated parents.[4] Miranda, whose parents parted when her father returned to Mexico in her teens, looks back from the vantage point of 27 and concludes,

For people to stay together in spite of themselves, just for the child, they're damaging the child. It's almost like a false assumption that you can do something for the sake of the child while you're being drained. Because the life is getting sucked out of you. How can you give life when it's sucked out of you?

Women and men both wonder if it is possible to establish relationships that strike a good balance between self-affirmation and commitment, providing and receiving support. Having observed their parents and others struggle with varying degrees of success against the strictures of traditional gender categories, they are hopeful but guarded about the possibilities for resolving the tension between autonomy and commitment in their own lives.[5] At 20, Chris, a Native American whose parents shared work and caretaking, is thus beginning to wonder:

> I thought you could just have a relationship, that love and being happy was always needed in life, and I've learned that you've got to be able to draw that line. It's a difficult thing, and you've got to know how to do it. And that would be my fear. Where am I cutting into my job too much? Where am I cutting into the relationship too much? And how do I divide it, and can it actually be done at all? Can you blend these two parts of your world?

Care as Time, Care as Money

If the rise of fluid adult partnerships has heightened the strains between commitment and autonomy, then the rise of employed mothers and the decline of sole male breadwinners have made the meaning of care ambiguous. Now that most children—whether living in single-parent or two-parent households—depend on the earnings of their mothers, parents face conflicts in balancing the need to provide economic support with the need to devote time and attention.

Rigid notions of gendered caring do not fit well with most family experiences, and the majority express support for parents who transgressed traditional gender categories. Among those who grew up in two-earner households, four out of five support such an arrangement, most with enthusiasm. Across race, class, and gender groups, they believe that two incomes provided the family with increased economic resources, more flexibility against the buffeting of economic winds, and greater financial security. For Serena, a 26-year-old African American, her parents' two jobs allowed her to avoid the privations of her friends and peers:

> Both my parents worked and a lot of parents in this neighborhood, one stayed home or some were on welfare. So a lot of my peers thought we were, like, upper class because both parents had cars and we went to private schools. When I was in my late teens and actually realized where I fit into the picture, it made me really appreciate my parents.

And Jason, also 26 and white, finds inspiration in his upwardly mobile parents' example as hard workers who made things better for their children in the process:

> I would say [both parents' working] made things better for the family because their being so dedicated to providing, to working, they helped that ethic of having to work and not wasting time. So it's instilled in me and my sister the ethic to work.

Of course, this means they see a mother's employment as largely beneficial. Whether in a two-parent or single-parent home, women and men agree that an independent base enhanced a mother's sense of self, contributed to greater parental equality, and provided an uplifting model. Rachel, 24 and from a white, working-class background, explains,

> I don't think that I missed out on anything. I think it served as a more realistic model. I've heard all that stuff about how children need a parent at home, but I don't think that having her stay home with me, particularly considering her temper, would have been anything other than counterproductive. The reality is that I'm going to have to work, and a lot of women in her generation chose not to work and did or didn't have the option. She had a choice, and she did what she wanted, and I think that's really great.

Kevin, 25 and from a middle-class, white family, agrees:

> For quite a while, my mom was the main breadwinner. She was the one who was the driving force in earning money. My mother's persona was really hard working, and that's something I've strived to be with and to emulate. I didn't think it was wrong in any way. I actually feel it's a very positive thing. Whatever my relationships, I always want and appreciate people who work, and I'm talking about female involvement. It's part of who I am, and it makes me very optimistic knowing that hard work can get you somewhere.

They also deemed highly involved fathers, whether in two-earner or single-parent households, as worthy examples. Daniel, now 23, describes his Irish father's atypical working hours and parental involvement:

My father was always around. He's a fire fighter, so he had a lot of free time. When he was home, he was usually coaching me and my brother or cooking dinner or taking us wherever we wanted to go. He was the only cook up until me and my brother started doing it. So I want to make sure that, if I get married and have kids, I'm there for my kids.

In contrast, those who grew up in a largely traditional household expressed more ambivalence. Although half felt fortunate to have had a mother devoted primarily to their care, the other half would have preferred for their mothers to pursue a more independent life. At 21, Justin, who grew up in a white, largely middle-class suburb, looks back on his mother's domestic focus with a strong conviction that it took its toll on the whole household:

She was very involved [and] always around. And I appreciated it, but I felt guilty that maybe I was taking too much. It's just that she wasn't happy. And she didn't give us any responsibilities at all. I guess that made her feel good to have someone rely on her. She felt needed more. And in the long run, obviously that's not something good.

And at 30, Sarah, also white and middle-class, agreed, pointing out that a mother's "sacrifice" may evoke mixed feelings:

I wish my mom had worked so that she would have been happier. Her identity was very much as a mother, and that was a sort of a void and pain. Because that's all she was, and that was not enough. She would say that it was, but that's not what I saw. She just seemed really unhappy a lot of time. She was just overinvolved with us, and if we did something separate from her, that was a major problem. I wouldn't mind her being supermom if that was really okay with her. But I got the message that she was giving up all of this other stuff to do it, and we should feel bad about it.

Breadwinning fathers may also elicit mixed reactions. Their economic contributions are appreciated but not necessarily deemed sufficient. A good father,

most concluded, takes time and offers emotional support as well. At 29, Nick, who grew up in a white working-class neighborhood and remembers feeling frustrated by his own father's distance, is seeking joint custody of his own young daughter:

I have seen a lot of guys who have kids and have never changed a diaper, have never done anything for this child. Don't call yourself daddy. Even when she was saying, "Oh, she might not be yours," it didn't matter to me. This child is counting on me.

In this context, care becomes a slippery concept. Across family circumstances, these young adults judge an ideal parent—whether mother or father—to be one who supports her or his children both economically and emotionally. At 21, Antonio, who grew up in a three-generational Hispanic household and whose father died of alcoholism, has concluded that fathers should give their children the time and emotional support typically expected of a mother:

[An ideal father] is a strong, balanced man. He's a daddy but he has the understanding of a mommy. He can care for you and protect you and guide you. . . . That's what I want to do with my kids. I want to make sure that I have time. I don't want to leave them in front of a TV set all day, because what they're learning is not coming from me. So I want to be there or, if not, I want to be in a position where I can take you with me.

If fathers should resemble traditional conceptions of mothers, then mothers should resemble fathers when it comes to work outside the home. Gabriel, a white 25-year-old who was raised by his father after his parents divorced when he was in grade school, explains,

In terms of splitting parental stuff, it should be even. Kids need a mother and a father. And I'm really not high on the woman giving up her job. I have never wanted to have a wife who didn't make a salary. But not for the sake of leeching off of her, but so that she was independent.

And Miranda agrees that mothering means providing money as well as care:

My mother has completely and entirely dedicated herself to me in the true sense; she has always been very selfless and very involved and fully responsible for me financially. I wouldn't feel comfortable if I didn't think I could make that kind of commitment.

If such an ideal proves beyond reach, as many expect it will be, women and men agree that families should apportion moral labor however best fits their circumstances—whether or not this means conforming to classic notions of gender difference. Mothers can and often do demonstrate care through paid work and fathers through involvement. Now 26 and raising a child on her own, Crystal, an African American, rejects a natural basis for mothering:

> I don't really believe in the mother instinct. I don't believe that's natural. Some people really connect with their children, and some people just don't. I think it should be whoever is really going to be able to be there for that child.

In the end, the material and emotional support a child receives matters more than the type of household arrangement in which it is provided. Michelle, a 24-year-old of Asian descent who watched her parents struggle in an unhappy marriage and then separate after she and her brother left home, focuses on emotional support rather than family composition:

> As long as the child feels supported and loved, that's the most important thing. Whether it's a two-parent home, a single-parent home, the mother is working, or anything, it's just really important for the child to have a good, strong foundation.

Identity Through Love, Identity Through Work

In a world where partnerships are fragile and domesticity is devalued, young women and men are confronting basic questions about identity and self-interest. Do they base their personal well-being and sense of self on public pursuits or private attachments? What balance can or should be struck between them?

In pondering their parents' lives, most could find no simple way to define or measure self-interest. While a minority uphold traditional gendered identities, most do not find such resolutions viable. Women are especially likely to conclude that it is perilous to look to the home as the sole source of satisfaction or survival. Reflecting on the many examples of mothers and other women who languished at home, who were bereft when marriages broke up, or who found esteem

in the world of paid work, 9 out of 10 express the hope that their lives will include strong ties to the workplace and public pursuits. Sarah, now a psychologist with a long-term lesbian partner who works "constantly," has high hopes but also nagging worries:

> I have a lot of conflicts now—work versus home and all of that stuff. But I would feel successful if I had a life with a lot of balance and that I'd made time for people who were important to me and made a real commitment to the people that I care about. And also, to work—I would be dedicated to work. And work and home would be connected. It would all be integrated, and it would be an outgrowth of my general way of being.

On the other side of the gender divide, many men have also become skeptical of work-centered definitions of masculine identity. As traditional jobs have given way to unpredictable shifts in work prospects, they are generally guarded about the prospect of achieving stable work careers. Having observed fathers and friends who found work either dissatisfying or too demanding, two-thirds of the men concluded that, while important, work alone could not provide their lives with meaning. These young men hope to balance paid work and personal attachments without having to sacrifice the self for a job or paycheck. Traditional views persist, but they increasingly compete with perspectives that define identity in more fluid ways. Widely shared by those who grew up in different types of families, these outlooks also transcend class and race differences. They cast doubt on some postfeminist assertions that a "new traditionalism" predominates among young women and men (Crittenden 1999). When asked how he would like to divide care-taking and breadwinning, Kevin considers the possibilities:

> Whoever can do it and whoever's capable of doing it, but it should be divided evenly. If there's something I can't do, just that I don't have the talent to do it, I would hope the other person would be able to. And the same goes the other way. My parents were like that. It was a matter of who was able to do what. There were hundreds of times when my dad made our lunches. And my sister claims that his were better than my mom's.

Yet, beyond the apparent similarities, a gender divide emerges. With one-third of men—but far fewer women—preferring traditional arrangements over all others, women are more likely to uphold flexible views of gender for themselves and their partners. More important, women and men both distinguish between their ideals and their chances of achieving them. If most hope to integrate family and work—and to find partners with whom to share the rewards and burdens of both—far fewer believe they can achieve this lofty aspiration. It is difficult to imagine integrating private with public obligations when most workplaces continue to make it difficult to balance family and job. And it is risky to build a life dependent on another adult when relationships are unpredictable. In this context, both women and men acknowledge that their actual options may fall substantially short of their ideals. For women, finding the right job and the right partner may seem too much to expect. Maria laments,

> Sometimes I ask myself if it's unrealistic to want everything. I think a lot of people would settle for something that is not what they wished, and, to me, that feels worse. It's a Catch 22, because you could wait so long, you never get anything, or you could settle for something and then be cut off from something else.

And men agree, although they are more likely to focus on the constraints of the workplace, as Peter, 27 and white, implies: "I want as even a split as possible. But with my hours, I don't think it could be very even."

AN EMERGING GENDER DIVIDE: AUTONOMY AND NEOTRADITIONALISM AS FALLBACK POSITIONS

The ideal of a balanced self continues to collide with an intransigent social world. New generations must thus develop contingent strategies for less than ideal circumstances. If egalitarian aspirations cannot be reached, what options remain? Here, women and men tend to diverge. Indeed, even as they are developing similar ideals, they are preparing for different outcomes. If an egalitarian commitment proves unworkable, most men would prefer a form of "modified traditionalism" in which they remain the primary if not sole family breadwinner and look to a partner to provide the lion's share of domestic care. Women, in contrast, tend to look toward autonomy as preferable to any form of traditionalism that would leave them and their children economically dependent on someone else.

As young women and men consider the difficulties of building balanced, integrated lives, they move from ideals to consider the fallback positions that would help them avert worst-case scenarios. Here, as we see below, the gender gap widens. Women, in hoping to avoid economic and social dependence, look toward autonomy, while men, in hoping to retain some traditional privileges, look toward modified forms of traditional arrangements. Yet, both groups hope to resolve these conflicts as they construct their lives over time.

Women and Autonomy

Among the women, 9 out of 10 hope to share family and work in a committed, mutually supportive, and egalitarian way. Yet, most are skeptical that they can find a partner or a work situation that will allow them to achieve this ideal. Integrating caretaking with committed work remains an uphill struggle, and it seems risky to count on a partner to sustain a shared vision in the long run. Even a modified version of traditionalism appears fraught with danger, for it creates economic vulnerability and constricted options in the event that a relationship sours or a partner decides to leave. Four out of five women thus prefer autonomy to a traditional marriage, concluding that going it alone is better than being trapped in an unhappy relationship or being abandoned by an unreliable partner. Danisha explains,

> Let's say that my marriage doesn't work. I won't ever go into marriage believing that, but just in case, I want to establish myself, because I don't ever want to end up, like, "What am I gonna do?" I want to be able to do what I have to do and still be okay. You can't take a cavalier attitude that things will just work out. Things will work out if you put some effort into making it work out.

Autonomy for women means, at its core, economic self-sufficiency. A life that is firmly rooted in the world of paid work provides the best safeguard against being stuck in a destructive relationship or being left without the means to support a family. Healthy relationships, they reason, are based on a form of economic individualism in which they do not place their economic fate in the hands of another. Rachel declares,

> I'm not afraid of being alone, but I am afraid of being with somebody who's a jerk. I can spend the rest of my life alone, and as long as I have my sisters and my friends, I'm okay. I want to get married and have children, but I'm not willing to just do it. It has to be under the right circumstances with the right person.

Men and Neotraditionalism

Young men express more ambivalence about the choice between autonomy and traditionalism. If a committed, egalitarian ideal proves out of reach, about 40 percent would opt for independence, preferring to stress the autonomous self so long associated with manhood and now increasingly affirmed by women as well. But 6 out of 10 men would prefer a modified traditionalism in which two earners need not mean complete equality. This split among men reflects the mix of options they confront. Work remains central to constructing a masculine identity, but it is difficult to find work that offers either economic security or good opportunities for family involvement. Without these supports, men are torn between avoiding family commitments and trying to retain some core advantages provided by traditional arrangements.

From men's perspective, opting for the autonomy conferred by remaining unmarried, unattached, or childless relieves them of the economic burden of earning a family wage in an uncertain economy, but it also risks cutting them off from close, committed, and lasting intimate connections. A neotraditional arrangement, in contrast, offers the chance to create a family built around shared breadwinning but less than equal caretaking. In this scenario, men may envision a dualearner arrangement but still expect their partner to place family first and weave work around it. Josh, a white 27-year-old who was raised by his father after his mother was diagnosed with severe mental illness, asserts,

> All things being equal, it should be shared. It may sound sexist, but if somebody's gonna be the breadwinner, it's going to be me. First of all, I make a better salary. If she made a much better salary, then I would stay home, but I always feel the need to work, even if it's in the evenings or something. And I just think the child really needs the mother more than the father at a young age.

Modified traditionalism provides a way for men to cope with economic uncertainties and women's shifting status without surrendering some valued privileges. It collides, however, with women's growing desire for equality and rising need for economic self-sufficiency.

Resolving Moral Dilemmas over Time

In the absence of institutional supports, postponing ultimate decisions becomes a key strategy for resolving the conflicts between commitment and self-development. For women as much as men, the general refrain is, "You can't take care of others if you don't take care of yourself." Michael wants to be certain his girlfriend has created a base for herself at the workplace before they marry, hoping to increase the chances the marriage will succeed and to create a safety net if it fails:

> There are a lot of problems when two people are not compatible socially, economically. When Kim gets these goals under her belt, and I have my goals established, it'll be a great marriage. You have to nurture the kind of marriage you want. You have to draw it out before you can go into it.

For Jennifer, 19 and white, autonomy also comes first. Commitment may follow, but only when she knows there is an escape route if the relationship deteriorates:

> I will have to have a job and some kind of stability before considering marriage. Too many of my mother's friends went for that—let him provide everything— and they're stuck in a relationship they're not happy with because they can't provide for themselves or the children they now have. The man is not providing for them the way they need, or he's just not a good person. Most of them have husbands who make a lot more money, or they don't even work at all, and they're very unhappy, but they can't leave. So it's either welfare or putting up with somebody else's crap.

Establishing an independent base becomes an essential step on the road to other goals, and autonomy becomes a prerequisite for commitment. This developmental view rejects the idea that individualism and commitment are in conflict by defining the search for independence as a necessary part of the process of becoming able to care for others. To do that, women as well as men tend to look to work, and its promise of autonomy, to complete the self. For those with children as well as those who are childless, lifelong commitments can be established when "you feel good enough about yourself to create a good relationship." Shauna, a 30-year-old African American who was raised by her mother and stepfather, explains,

> If you're not happy with yourself, then you can't be happy with someone else. I'm not looking for someone to fill a void. I think that's what a lot of people do when

they look for relationships, and that's not what it's about. It's about sharing yourself with the other person, and when you're content and happy with who you are, then you can give more of yourself to someone else, and that's the type of person that I want to be with.

These strategies are deeply felt and intensely private responses to social and personal conflicts that seem intractable. More fundamental solutions await the creation of systematic supports for balancing work and family and for providing women and men with equal opportunities at the workplace and in the home. Without these supports, new generations must cope as best they can, remaining both flexible and guarded. Andrew, a white 27-year-old, has concluded that rigid positions are not helpful in an unpredictable world:

I would like to have an equal relationship, but I don't have a set definition for what that would be like. I would be fine if both of us were working and we were doing the same thing, but it would depend on what she wants, too. If she thought, "Well, at this point in my life, I don't want to work," or if I felt that way, then it would be fine for one person to do more work in some respects. But I would like it to be equal—just from what I was exposed to and what attracts me.

Anita, a 26-year-old Hispanic, agrees:

I don't want to be on my own for the rest of my life, but right now it's fine, so I can figure out who I am. I don't want to look back later and say I totally ignored my needs. I'm realizing that things are so impermanent, and my expectations can only get me so far.

CONCLUSION: TOWARD A NEW MORAL ORDER?

Deeply rooted social and cultural changes have created new moral dilemmas while undermining a traditional gendered division of moral labor. The widespread and interconnected nature of these changes suggests that a fundamental, irreversible realignment is under way. Less clear is whether it will produce a more gender-equal moral order or will, instead, create new forms of inequality. The long-term implications are necessarily cloudy, but this ambiguity has created some new opportunities along with new risks.

While large-scale social forces are propelling change in a general direction, the specific forms it takes will depend on how women and men respond, individually and collectively, to the dilemmas they face. Those who have come of age during this period are adopting a growing diversity of moral orientations that defies dichotomous gender categories. Their experiences point to a growing desire for a social order in which women and men alike are afforded the opportunity to integrate the essential life tasks of achieving autonomy and caring for others.

Yet, persistent inequalities continue to pose dilemmas, especially for those who aspire to integrate home and work in a balanced, egalitarian way. To understand these processes, we need to focus on the social conditions that create such dilemmas and can transform, and potentially dissolve, the link between gender and moral responsibility. Of course, eradicating this link might only mean that women are allowed to adopt the moral strategies once reserved for men. We also need to discover how to enable everyone, regardless of gender, class, or family situation, to balance care of others with care of self.

The possibilities have never been greater for creating humanistic, rather than gendered, conceptions of moral obligation. New moral dilemmas have prompted women and men to develop innovative strategies, but the long-term resolution of these dilemmas depends on reorganizing our social institutions to foster gender equality and a better balance between family and work. Freud once commented that a healthy person is able "to love and to work." Achieving this vision depends on creating a healthy society, where all citizens are able to combine love and work in the ways they deem best.

NOTES

1. My deep thanks go to Sociologists for Women in Society for honoring me with the 1998 Feminist Lectureship and to the sociology departments and Women's Studies Programs at the University of Georgia and the University of North Texas for their generous support and warm hospitality.

2. Of this group, more than 27 percent lived largely with a single parent, including 7 percent whose parents shared joint custody and 5 percent who lived with single, custodial fathers. The rest saw one or both of their parents remarry and form a new, two-parent household.

3. A larger proportion of households were dual-earning, but they varied in the degree of equality between parents' jobs and did not necessarily include both biological parents.
4. Amato and Booth (1997) confirmed this viewpoint. Respondents also argue that both parents should sustain

strong ties to their children whether or not they remain together.
5. Cancian (1987) provided an in-depth analysis of innovative attempts among couples to create interdependent relationships, in which both women and men are responsible for love.

REFERENCES

Amato, Paul, and Alan Booth. 1997. *A generation at risk: Growing up in an era of family upheaval.* Cambridge, MA: Harvard University Press.

Cancian, Francesca M. 1987. *Love in America: Gender and self-development.* Cambridge, UK, and New York: Cambridge University Press.

Crittenden, Danielle. 1999. *What our mothers didn't tell us: Why happiness eludes the modern woman.* New York: Simon & Schuster.

Gerson, Kathleen. 1985. *Hard choices: How women decide about work, career, and motherhood.* Berkeley and Los Angeles: University of California Press.

———. 1993. *No man's land: Men's changing commitments to family and work.* New York: Basic Books.

———. 2001. Children of the gender revolution: Some theoretical questions and findings from the field. In *Restructuring work and the life course,* edited by Victor W. Marshall, Walter R. Heinz, Helga Krueger, and Anil Verma. Toronto, Canada: University of Toronto Press.

Kimmel, Michael. 1996. *Manhood in America: A cultural history.* New York: Free Press.

———. 2000. *The gendered society.* New York: Oxford University Press.

Ryan, Mary. 1981. *Cradle of the middle class.* New York and Cambridge, UK: Cambridge University Press.

R E A D I N G *30*   **Hung Cam Thai**

For Better or Worse: Gender Allures in the Vietnamese Global Marriage Market

Men and women like Minh and Thanh have dreams, but their dreams clash. He wants the best of tradition and she wants the best of modernity. He believes the respect he has been searching for did not arrive with him when he migrated to the United States almost 20 years ago, but instead was left back safely in Vietnam. She feels that the marital respect she needs is waiting for her in the United States and that she will get it when she joins him through marriage migration. Minh, 37, represents one of the more than two million *Viet Kieus*, or Vietnamese people living overseas, who make up an aging diaspora that largely began in the mid-1970s, after the postwar years. He is also one of over a million *Viet Kieus* who returned to visit family

and friends during the year 2000, a dramatic increase from the 160,000 who did so in 1993 (Nhat 1999). Thanh, 32, will soon join Minh as one of over 200,000 women *and* men worldwide who come to the United States each year through marriage migration, the number one mechanism for contemporary *legal* migration to the United States. In general, females have dominated in U.S.-bound migration since the 1930s (Houstoun, Kramer, and Barrett 1984) and, historically, women more often than men have migrated as spouses (Thornton 1992). Women currently make up more than 65 percent of all marriage migrants. While male marriage migrants make up about a quarter of all men who enter the United States each year, female marriage migrants make up over 40 percent of all women who enter (USINS 1999a; USINS 1999b).

During 14 months of fieldwork done in phases in Vietnam and in the United States from 1997 to 2001, I got to know couples like Minh and Thanh. In addition to understanding their distinct national and local cultures, I paid particular attention to some of their most private matrimonial thoughts—thoughts that they have not yet disclosed to each other. For they are in a migration waiting period, a period in which the women are waiting to be united with their husbands through migration. In this distinct and emergent global marriage market, the immigrant Vietnamese men typically go to Vietnam to marry through arrangement and subsequently return to their places of residence in the Vietnamese diaspora (most are from the United States, Canada, France, and Australia) to initiate paperwork to sponsor their wives. During this waiting period, I came to know them by first entering the lives of the brides in Vietnam and later the U.S.-based grooms.

The marriage of Minh and Thanh characterizes a distinct and growing global stream over the past 40 years of immigrant or immigrant-origin men returning to their home countries for marriage partners through processes of family-forming migration (Lievans 1999), thus significantly transforming gender and race relations in the communities of both origin and destination. Same-ethnic individuals constitute an estimated two-thirds of all marriage migration couples, and among international marriage migrants of U.S. non-citizen permanent residents, who are presumably immigrants, almost 90 percent of them are women (Thornton 1992; USINS 1999a; USINS 1999b). Like many international marriages between same-ethnic individuals, especially in Asia, the marriage of Minh and Thanh was arranged. While there are varying flexible meanings of marriage arrangements and class compositions, I focus on marriages of the two "unmarriageables"—highly educated women in Vietnam and overseas Vietnamese men who do low-wage work. These couples make up roughly 55 percent ($n = 38$) of the 69 marriages I studied.

GLOBALIZATION AND MARRIAGE SQUEEZES ACROSS THE VIETNAMESE DIASPORA

Before I began this study, I was fully aware that Vietnamese people worldwide are pressed unusually, if not uniquely, by what demographer Daniel Goodkind (1997) calls the "double marriage squeeze," which has resulted from a high male mortality rate during the Vietnam War and the larger number of men than women who emigrated during the last quarter of the 20th century. A shortage of one sex or the other in the age group in which marriage generally occurs is often termed a marriage squeeze (Guttentag and Secord 1983). The Vietnamese double marriage squeeze specifically refers to the low ratio of males to females in Vietnam and the unusually high ratio of males to females in the Vietnamese diaspora, especially in Australia and in the United States. For example, by 1999, among people between the ages of 30 to 34 years in Vietnam, statistically speaking, there were approximately 92 men for every 100 women. At the other end of the diaspora in 2000, among Vietnamese Americans between 25 to 29 years, there were 129 men for every 100 women; for the age group of 30 to 34, there were about 135 men for every 100 women. While these numbers are important, they tell only part of the story about the recent dramatic rise in Vietnamese transpacific marriages. The link between demographic numbers, intensified transnational and global processes in Vietnam and worldwide, new contours of kinship, and the intersection of gender and class in marriage markets throughout the Vietnamese diaspora provides a much more in-depth look at social processes involved in the emergence of a Vietnamese transpacific marriage market.

The most striking aspect about marriages of the two unmarriageables like Minh and Thanh is that they have globalized and reversed the marriage gradient, an old and almost universal pattern that women "marry up" and men "marry down," which is to say women marry older men who earn more money and have more education and, conversely, men marry younger women who earn less money and have less education (Fitzgerald 1999). But depending on the measure one uses in the marriages I studied, it is difficult to tell who is "from below." In demographic marriage market language (Guttentag and Secord 1983), women worldwide often find that the pool of marriageable men declines as they move up the educational ladder. Thanh is part of this emerging group of highly educated women in Vietnam who have delayed or avoided marriage with local men. These women have found the pool of marriageable men in Vietnam, who are employed and successful relative to them, to be too small. More importantly, Thanh's status as a highly educated woman made her unmarriageable to many men still influenced by the Asian and Confucian ideologies of hierarchical relations in terms of gender, age, and class. Like highly educated African-American women, women like Thanh in Vietnam are a "surplus" relative to their educated male counterparts. Minh, on the other hand, belongs to a group of surplus men, accumulated in part by the scattering of post-war Vietnamese migration, who are unable to find marriage partners partly because of their current low-wage work status. Some of these men, though certainly not all, experienced tremendous downward mobility as they migrated overseas.

Men like Minh who work in the low-wage labor market made up 80 percent of the men in my study. These men generally work for hourly wages, though some work in ethnic enterprises where salaries are negotiated "under the table." For the most part, they work long hours for low pay. In contrast, women like Thanh represent almost 70 percent of the brides. These women come from college-educated backgrounds, with about 40 percent having advanced degrees and working as doctors, lawyers, computer programmers, and the like. The remaining 60 percent are teachers, service sector workers in foreign companies, etc. To be sure, not all college-educated women in my study married low-wage working men, and not all low-wage working men married college-educated women. Men like Minh and women like Thanh are unmarriageable along both gender and class lines. Statistically, because of the double marriage squeeze, there is simply a surplus of women relative to men in Vietnam and a surplus of *Viet Kieu* men relative to *Viet Kieu* women overseas. But their unmarriageability does not end there. If the demography of the double marriage squeeze is a structural condition propelling these transpacific marriages, the cultural belief in the marriage gradient is perhaps a more powerful force driving these marriages. Vietnamese women and men worldwide have not dared to break the marriage-gradient norm in their local marriage market. They believe, as other unmarriageables do, that by globalizing the gradient, they have somehow solved the potential problem of breaking the marriage-gradient norm. That is, if a man is from a first-world country, he has the "up," while a woman from third-world Vietnam has the "down." And though it is no surprise that the economic divide between the "first-world" and "third-world" would inherently penetrate deeply into the private lives of Vietnamese transpacific couples, it is not always clear *who* has the third-world life in marriages of the two unmarriageables.

Globalization seems like a perfect solution to the dual problem facing the Vietnamese diaspora of "too few women here" and "too few men there," yet there is an untold story about the unanticipated collision of gender ideologies and strategies many of these couples will face.

Couples like Minh and Thanh—the unmarriageables—will bump into a clash of dreams as the women join their husbands overseas. Looking far across the Pacific, both were enamored, not necessarily by the economic, but powerfully by the gender allures of the other side: on one end of the Vietnamese diaspora, for educated women like Thanh, a man living overseas in a modern country will respect women more than men still held back by ancient traditions in Vietnam; on the other end of the diaspora, for low-wage working men like Minh, it is precisely these ancient traditions that he desired and perceived [that] are still maintained by women in Vietnam, the sort of traditions that he believes have been eroded by America's modernity.

Both have turned to the old and new, relying foremost on the tradition of marriage arrangements vis-à-vis family members to introduce them to each other. Yet, it is the new globalizing culture of Vietnam that offered them that opportunity. In 1986, after having no contact with the outside world for over a decade, the Vietnamese government adopted a new economic policy known as *doi moi*. It did not end state ownership, but encouraged private enterprise, free markets, and global engagement. Particularly in the 1990s, Saigon was reemerging as a major international city, first within the Asian landscape and soon to the rest of the world. At the time, Vietnam was in the news and was projected to be one of Asia's next "tigers" (Pierre 2000). Recognizing an enticing labor and consumer market of 80 million people, foreign companies were eager to move their factories there and make their products known. Globalization rapidly opened impersonal markets of capital, goods, and labor, and in conjunction with these markets, it also opened a rather personal market of emotions and marriages. Like global corporations and factories that recently moved to Vietnam because of its large supply of labor, one of the reasons *Viet Kieu* men go there for brides is because they have a much larger selection of marriage partners. However, unlike locals who eagerly work at foreign factories mainly for the monetary rewards, Vietnamese transpacific brides don't always share the same reasons for choosing to marry *Viet Kieu* men.

THE HIGHLY EDUCATED BRIDE'S STORY

Twenty years ago, Thanh's father was a math teacher at Le Buon Phong, a prestigious high school in Saigon. After the war, Thanh's uncle, her mother's younger brother, and his family were among the few thousands of Vietnamese who were airlifted out of Vietnam on April 30, 1975, when Saigon surrendered to North Vietnamese military troops. They eventually settled in Houston, one of the larger Vietnamese enclaves in the United States, and started a successful restaurant business specializing in *pho*, the popular Vietnamese beef noodle soup. Remittances—money sent back—from Thanh's uncle helped her parents open a small candy factory in the late 1980s which now has over 40 employees. Like the "new class of everywhere" in the global economy, her parents are now members of a class that represents a small but very visible percentage of families in Vietnam who enjoy access to overseas resources, such as Thanh's uncle and the remittances he sends home. They are part of a *Viet Kieu economy*, of which remittance plays an important role, that has grown from roughly $35 million in 1993 to an estimated $2 billion in 2000 (Pierre 2000). The remittance upward mobility is of course associated with Thanh's educational and social mobility. It has helped Thanh, her parents' only child, earn not only a good high school education, but also continue to study law and take lessons at international English schools in Saigon.

After graduating from Le Buon Phong High School, Thanh and a small group of her female friends did not choose early marriage, a path that most of their peers took soon after high school. Although Thanh and her friends did want to marry one day, they all wanted to further their schooling. Of her seven close female friends from high school, only one did not go to college. That friend opted for early marriage. The rest, including Thanh, quietly took various professional routes. Most went into fields traditionally reserved for women, including education and nursing. Two went on for higher education. Thanh obtained a law degree, and the other friend went on to become a prestigious physician at Vinh Bien, a private hospital catering to Saigon's middle class. Four of the seven, now in their early 30s, remain single. The pathways of Thanh and her four friends who chose singlehood illustrate a quiet gender revolution among highly educated women in Vietnam. These women have opted for singlehood in a culture where marriage is not only presumed, but often coerced. And if marriage is not achieved by a certain age, women and men are often dismissively referred to as simply "*e*," a derogatory term referring to commodities that are unmarketable. In contrast, women (often young and beautiful) and men (often educated and financially secure) who fare well on the marriage market are considered "*dat*," or scarce goods. As Thanh explained to me:

> I am already "e" in Vietnam. You know, at 32 here, it's hard to find a decent husband. I knew that when I decided to get a good education here that many men would be intimidated by me. But it was important to me to get an education, and I know that for women, marriage is more important. In Asian cultures, but maybe in Vietnam especially, the men do not want their wives to be better than them. I think for me it's harder, too, because my parents are successful here so on the outside [to the outsider] we are very successful.

In truth, Thanh is not completely "e" for there have been several men who, sometimes with their families, have come to propose marriage to her. In contemporary Vietnam, arranging marriage remains common practice, though more so in villages than in urban areas. For women in Vietnam, especially those who have passed the social marriageability age, individual and family success often come with being unmarriageable. Thanh had several proposals for marriage arrangements when she was in her mid-20s before she got her law degree, all from men who wanted to marry down socially and economically. Now, at age 32 and highly educated, she believes that marrying up is no longer an option as there are few available men in that category. Marrying down is not an appealing choice either, although she has many suitors in that category. Speaking in the marriage gradient mode, Thanh explains:

> When I look up, there are few men "up there" who I could see as suitable husbands. But those men, the few men I know who have more education and who are more successful than I am, usually want to marry young, beautiful women. To them, I am now too old. The backward thing about life is that the men below are very unappealing. And of course there are many of them! There are many, many non-quality men I could choose from, but that's what they are—non-quality.

Thanh's marriage procrastination was partially anchored in her confused class and gender status, for her educational and remittance upward mobility puts her one up locally, but one down globally. On the one hand, if by tradition, a man is to be above her, he must be the one to provide economically, but given that she married a low-wage worker, she may end up being the one to seek economic security through her own means. On the other hand, by traditional Vietnamese culture, Thanh knows her high educational status would not necessarily help her escape the gender subordination in marital life in Vietnam for few men she knows respect women in the every-day contours of marriage. On our third and final interview, Thanh and I walked along the Saigon River early one evening. As the city's buildings rose arrogantly in the background through the din of countless motorcycles, cycles, and taxis, she explained to me, with a sense of disconsolation:

> In Vietnam, it is hard being single, female, and old. People will criticize and laugh at you. People always ask me, "Where are your husband and children? And when I think about that, I realize that I have two choices. I can marry a man in Vietnam who is much less educated and less successful than me who I will have to support and who will likely abuse me emotionally or physically or dominate me in every possible way. Or I can marry a *Viet Kieu* man. *At least Viet Kieu men live in modern countries where they respect women.*

Ultimately, Thanh's priority, as an educated woman, in the selection of a marriage partner is for someone to respect her and for a marriage in which a man does not control her like most men in Vietnam she observes do. As Thanh explained to me:

> When I find a nice man "below" me who I could marry, he wouldn't want to marry me because he's afraid that I'll take control of the house or that if anything goes wrong in the marriage, I could turn to my family for help. Most men in Vietnam want to control their wives, they want their wives to be subordinate even when she is more successful and educated. That leaves me with very few choices in Vietnam, you see, because I for sure don't want a man to take control of me.

THE LOW-WAGE WORKING GROOM'S STORY

Through complicated logics of transnationality, Thanh found a suitable spouse across the Pacific. But if Thanh's desire for respect was prompted by her educational and remittance upward mobility, her husband's need for respect was prompted by his migratory downward mobility. Minh, whose hands, facial expressions, and graying hair make him seem older than his 37 years, was the only member of his family to leave Vietnam during "wave II" of the boat refugee exodus that took place after the war (Zhou and Bankston 1998). As the eldest son, he holds a position of distinction and responsibility of six siblings in a family of educators. Both of his parents were teachers of philosophy at Le Buon Phong, where they have known Thanh's parents for many years. Today, three of Minh's sisters are teachers and his two brothers are successful merchants in Saigon.

In 1985, at the age of 21, Minh, then a man of intellectual ambition and curiosity, had just completed his third year of engineering school when his parents asked him if he wanted to go to America. They didn't know anyone overseas at the time, but they knew of several people, among the many hundreds of thousands of refugees, who had fled and safely reached a Western country. Of those who successfully made the trip, over 90 percent eventually settled in France, Australia, Canada, or the United States (Merli 1997). Minh's parents also knew that as many as half of the refugees on any particular boat trip did not succeed. They died along the way due to starvation, pirate attacks, and often, in the case of women and children, rape and murder en route to a refugee camp. Many were also caught by the Vietnamese government and severely punished with long prison sentences. Nevertheless, his parents were confident that he would make it and have a better life abroad. After all, they spent their entire life savings to put him on one of the safest and most reputable boats run by private individuals, to leave the Mekong Delta for Western lands of opportunity via refugee camps in Southeast Asia. Like the Underground Railroad established for slave escapes during the American civil war, details about these refugee boats were kept secret. But unlike the railroads, the boats were made accessible only to wealthy or well-connected families. Many who were not wealthy, such as Minh's family, managed to pool their resources so that one person could go, usually a son. They saw this as an investment made with a hope of high returns, as in the case of Minh's family.

Today, Minh considers himself one of the lucky ones. After surviving two years—a lifetime to Minh—in a refugee camp in Malaysia, he was selected in 1987 for entry to the United States. Many people he met at the camp ended up in less desirable places, like Finland, Belgium, or Hungary. As with current migration from Vietnam, the United States was then considered the top destination choice, followed by Canada, France, and Australia. Minh arrived in rural Wyoming under the sponsorship of a local Catholic church. Like many of the churches scattered across the United States who sponsored Indochinese refugees from the late 1970s to the mid-1990s (Zhou and Bankston 1998), his church sponsored only one individual. He spent the first five years of his life in America as the only person of color in a rural town in Wyoming, the name of which he doesn't even want to remember. Like many Vietnamese refugees of the past three decades, Minh decided to migrate a second time. He wanted to go to Little Saigon, the most highly concentrated Vietnamese enclave outside of Vietnam, located in a seemingly quiet Los Angeles suburb, though today plagued by urban problems reported regularly by the media (Leonard and Tran 2000a; 2000b; *Los Angeles Times* 1995; Marosi and Tran 2000; Pad-dock and Dizon 1991; Terry 1999). But he had little money and no connections in or around Los Angeles. Then one day, in one of the Vietnamese-produced newspapers in the United States that flourished following the influx of refugees, Minh read about a Chinese restaurant called the Panda Garden that needed dishwashers. Unfortunately, it was not in Los Angeles but in a small town called Quincy, ninety miles from Seattle. Minh heard that Seattle also had many Vietnamese people and he thought a move there would bring him closer to other refugees.

Eleven years later, at age 37, Minh still lives in Quincy and works at the Panda Garden. He is now a deep fryer and an assistant cook, which is several steps up from the dishwashing position he was first given. Although to him, an assistant cook carries less stigma than a dishwasher, it is far from the engineering career he envisaged in his pre-migration years. Though known as one of the best and most authentic ethnic restaurants in town, the Panda mainly serves a "white American" clientele who, according to the owners, probably wouldn't know the differences between authentic Chinese food and Sara Lee frozen dinners. Quincy is similar to many suburban towns in Middle America—not quite rural, but far from urban. People who live here drive to Seattle to shop and eat if they have money, but stay in town if they want to see a movie. Minh knows five other Vietnamese people in the town, all men, and three of them work with him at the restaurant. He shares a modest three-bedroom apartment with the barest of furnishings with these co-workers.

Similar to many *Viet Kieu* people, Minh is a good example of a giver caught in the irony of a remittanceship.

Receivers of remittances enjoy first-world consumption, while their givers often only enjoy it when they go to Vietnam: on returning to a first-world setting, some givers, like Minh, regress to a third-world consumption pattern. Like Thanh's family, Minh's family enjoys remittances, albeit much smaller ones than Thanh's family enjoys from her uncle. He earns approximately $1,400 a month in Quincy and sends $500 of that back to his family. That amount is much higher than the average of $160 the grooms in my study send to their wives and/or families on a monthly basis. At $900, his remaining budget would be considered way below the poverty level anywhere in the United States. But his family has more than enough constant capital from his remittances to keep connected in the small, though conspicuous, circles of families who have overseas kin networks.

And while Minh's family enjoy their new consumption patterns, Minh finds himself lacking the luxury they afford—most importantly the luxury of having the kind of respect he was used to before migration, particularly the kind of respect he once had in intimate markets. Minh remembered vividly that in his early 20s, he had been considered a good catch among his peers. He was heading for an engineering career and was from a well-respected family. Recounting stories of masculinity from his early adulthood, Minh told me that young men he knew had not one, but several, girlfriends at a time, and that it was accepted and celebrated. After all, life after the war was particularly difficult for many families he knew. But he was relatively fortunate, for his parents were well-respected teachers with a small, but steady, income and, therefore, could afford to spend small amounts of money on leisure activities and materials that bought them some status in their pre-remittance circles. As he told me in one conversation when we were talking, with beers and cigarettes in our hands, rather loudly in the hot and sizzling kitchen where he worked:

> Life here now is not like life in Vietnam back then. My younger brothers and sisters used to respect me a lot because I was going to college and I was about to get my degree. Many young women I met at the time liked me, too, because I came from a good family and I had status [*dia di*]. But now, because I don't have a good job here, people don't pay attention to me. That's the way my life has been since I came to the United States. And I don't know if I'm lucky or unlucky, but I think it's hard for a [Vietnamese] man to find a wife here if he doesn't make good money. If you have money,

everyone will pay attention [to you], but if you don't, you have to live by yourself.

For the most part, that's what Minh has done in the 16 years since he arrived in the United States. In his social world, Minh believes money can, and often does, buy love, and that if you don't have much of it, you live "by yourself." His yearly income puts him just above the poverty level for a single man, but when I did a budget analysis of his expenditures, I discovered that after remittances, his available funds place him well below the poverty level. The long hours that often accompany low-wage work have also made it particularly difficult for him to meet and court marriage partners. If Minh worked long hours for a law firm or a large business corporation, he would not only get financial rewards, but also the status and prestige which men often use as a trade-off in marriage markets. If he were a blue collar white man in Quincy, he could go to church functions, bowling alleys, or bars to meet and court women in the local marriage market. For Minh—a single immigrant man—who does low-wage work in a low-status job with long hours in Middle America, the prospect of marriage has been, and remains, low. Like highly educated women such as Thanh, men like Minh are on the market for more than just intimacy. They are on it for respect, a sense of respect for marital life which they perceive they cannot find in their local marriage market. For men in general, but especially for working-class men, as sociologist Lillian Rubin (1994) argues in a compelling study, a sense of self is deeply connected to the ability to provide economically for the family. For low-wage workers like Minh, the ability to provide, or lack thereof, is sharply linked to earning respect in marital life. As Minh movingly explained to me:

> I don't know if other men told you this, but I think the main reason why a lot of *Viet Kieu* men go back to Vietnam for a wife is because the women here [*Viet Kieu*] do not respect their husbands if the husbands can not make a lot of money. I think that's why there are a lot of *Viet Kieu* women who marry white men, because the white men have better jobs than us. Many *Viet Kieu* women, even though they are not attractive and would not be worth much if there were a lot of them, would not even look at men like me because we can't buy them the fancy house or the nice cars. *I need my wife to respect me as her husband. If your wife doesn't respect you, who will?*

AND SO THEY MEET

Although Minh was headed for upward mobility in 1985 before he migrated to the United States, and would have become an engineer one day if he had remained in Vietnam, he is now an assistant cook and has spent the bulk of his adult working life in the confines of a small Chinese restaurant in Middle America. He hasn't read a book in recent memory. In fact, he didn't have much to share about what he does, except work, or what he owns, except a used Toyota Tercel he recently bought. Meanwhile, Thanh is a relatively successful lawyer in urban Saigon, where Chanel perfume from Paris and American designer Ann Taylor's shirts are essential components of her daily life. Thanh speaks very good English, the language we used when she and I met in Vietnam; Minh and I spoke Vietnamese when I interviewed him in Quincy, Washington. Thanh is currently attending an international adult English school to obtain her English proficiency degree and her current reading list includes Fitzgerald's *The Great Gatsby*. She often prides herself on the fact that she is not as thin as the average woman in Vietnam, nor does she conform to the stereotypical image of Vietnamese women with long, straight black hair. Instead, Thanh has a perm with red highlights and she spends a large part of her leisure time taking aerobics classes at the Saigonese Women's Union, an emerging activity among Saigon's middle class. Pointing to her access to and practice of modernity, she often joked, "Some people in Vietnam think that I'm a *Viet Kieu* woman."

Minh and Thanh, thus, live in noticeably different social worlds. They were united by a network of kin and acquaintanceship that was spatially separated, yet held together by the histories, memories, and connections of the prewar years. This network of kin helped arrange the marriage of the two and started when Minh's siblings expressed concerns that their eldest brother appeared lonely and "needed" a wife, though they never asked him. After all, he was the eldest brother and the only sibling not yet married and still childless. The average age of marriage for his three younger sisters was 21 and for his two brothers, 24. His next brother's eldest child is now attending her first year at Le Buon Phong High School, a sign to Minh that he's getting old. Minh was often embarrassed when asked, "Why didn't you bring your lady friend back to visit us, too?" What his family did not understand on his first few visits back was that long hours of work, as well as the scarcity of Vietnamese women (relative to men) in the United States in general and Quincy in particular, were reasons why the "lady friend generally was too busy to make the trip home *this time*."

If Minh's choice to return to Vietnam to find a wife was propelled by siblings and then followed by his individual discretion, Thanh's entrance into the transpacific marriage market was the complete opposite. Both faced structural and demographic limitations in their local marriage markets, but in different and reversed ways. On the one hand, Minh knew very *few* Vietnamese-American women, and those he knew usually earned the same amount of, or more, money than he did, which made him a *less* attractive marriage candidate in the United States. Research has shown that in the low-wage labor market among Asian Americans, especially in California, women tend to get jobs more easily, work longer hours, and earn more money than men (Espiritu 1999). In contrast, Thanh knew *many* single men in Saigon, but those she knew were far below her in educational status and made much *less* money than she did working as a part-time lawyer and for her father's factory, all of which made her a *less* attractive marriage candidate in Vietnam. By Vietnamese standards—and for some, by any global standard— women like Thanh come from solidly middle-class backgrounds, through acquired or inherited wealth, educational mobility, or remittances. Thanh's education, combined with the income she and her family generate, have been real trade-offs on the transpacific marriage market. As Thanh explained to me:

Any *Viet Kieu* man can come here to find a wife. And he can surely find a beautiful woman if he wants because there are many beautiful young women willing to marry anyone to go overseas. I think there is something different when you talk about *Viet Kieu* men coming back here to marry. They look for a real marriage. And a marriage that will last forever. And so it's important to them to check everything about the woman they will marry and her background. These men [*Viet Kieu* men] want a woman who is educated and who comes from an educated family, because that means she comes from a good family. And if her family has money, he knows she just doesn't want to marry him to go overseas because she already has a comfortable life in Vietnam.

Fearful that they may be seen as sex-workers, local women in Vietnam who want a transpacific spouse rarely allow themselves to be courted by foreign men in public spaces as is the case for women in Taiwan,

Thailand, Singapore, Malaysia, Hong Kong, and other Asian countries I've visited and learned about. According to most women and men I talked to in Vietnam, *Viet Kieu* men often come back and visit local bars and dance clubs in search of "one-night stands" either with prostitutes or non-prostitutes, but they would never marry women they meet in those public spaces. If women are fearful of the possibility of being sexually exploited, *Viet Kieu* men are wary of being used as a "bridge" to cross the Pacific (Ong 1999). These reasons, as well as the availability of transnational networks, have propelled women in Vietnam and Vietnamese men who live overseas to rely on the old practice of marriage arrangements by family and kin members, rather than engaging in individual courtship, what we call "free love" practices of choosing a marriage partner. As in the case of arranged marriages among other ethnic groups, marriage candidates in the Vietnamese diaspora believe that family members make the best judgements in their interests when looking for a spouse. Here, Thanh explained the logics of marriage arrangements that may seem illogical to a foreigner:

It's very easy to trick people now. Both men and women can trick each other. Women will pretend to love so they can go abroad and men will pretend to love so they can get a one-night relationship. And so that is why people will choose a family member who could investigate both sides for them. Most of the cases I know are similar to mine. Usually a *Viet Kieu* man says he wants a wife, and then he will call a family here who will search for him. His family member will try to contact friends, neighbors, whoever he can in search of a suitable wife who happens to also be waiting for an overseas man to court her. There's always a lot of women willing to marry a *Viet Kieu* man, even though she may never have thought about it until someone asks them. If you have a family member to choose for you, as my uncle helped me get to know my husband, you will end up with a real marriage. Otherwise, it can be risky for both people if they meet each other on their own.

The marriage arrangement between Minh and Thanh was initiated by Minh's parents, who have known Thanh's family for over two decades. Even though Thanh's father taught at Le Buon Phong two decades ago, and was a friend and colleague of Minh's parents, the current consumption gap between the two families has created a social distance over the years. When Minh's siblings convinced him to search for a wife in Vietnam, he was hesitant at first, but later followed their advice when his parents promised that they would invest time and care in finding the most suitable spouse. According to Minh, however, they were surprised to discover that arranging a marriage for a *Viet Kieu* was more complicated than they had anticipated:

> I thought that it would be easy for them to find someone. I thought all they had to do was mention a few things to their friends, and within days, they could describe a few possible people to me. But my parents told me that they were afraid that women just wanted to use our family to go abroad. We had many people get involved, many people wanted to be matchmakers for the family and added so much anxiety and fear about people's intentions. But the first choice for them was to find a woman from a wealthy family so that they were sure she wasn't just interested in money because if she has money, she would already be comfortable in Vietnam. And it would have been best if she had family in the United States already, because we would know that they already have overseas people who help them out so they would not expect to become dependent on us. In Vietnamese, you know, there is this saying, "When you choose a spouse, you are choosing his/her whole family."

Thanh's family was finally contacted by Minh's parents, a traditional way of arranging marriages in which a groom's parents represent him to propose, often with rituals and a ceremonial language that date back for centuries. Like most brides in my study, Thanh relied on an overseas relative—in this case, Thanh's uncle, Tuan—for advice on Minh's economic and social situation in the United States. The family discovered that Minh was a low-wage worker, but a full-time worker nonetheless. Virtually all of the locals I met in Vietnam viewed overseas men as a two-tiered group: the "successful" who succeeded in owning ethnic enterprises or through obtaining an education, and the "indolent" without full-time jobs who were perceived as being welfare-dependent or as participants in underground economies, such as gambling. Some saw the latter group as men who took up valuable "spots" that others from Vietnam could have filled. "If I had gotten a chance to go," I heard many men say, "I would be so rich by now." Most people, however, did not have an explanation for a man like Minh, who is neither lazy nor extremely successful. Thanh's uncle, Tuan, seemed to know more men in Houston who were not only

unemployed, but also alcoholics and gamblers. Her parents were worried that their daughter was unmarriageable as there was certainly no shortage of young and younger women in Vietnam for local men *her* age to marry. In addition, Thanh was already convinced that she was "e." All three were concerned that Thanh was facing a life of permanent singlehood for she was getting old by Vietnamese standards. In the back and front of these pre-arrangement thoughts, all three parties—Thanh's uncle, her parents, and herself—saw the option of marrying Minh, a *Viet kieu* man, [as] more desirable than marrying a local man in Vietnam. For Thanh's parents, Minh's status as a full-time worker *and* someone who sent remittances back home to his family translated into a potentially suitable husband. For her uncle, most *Viet Kieu* single men he knew were part of an underclass of which Minh was not a part. For Thanh, Minh's geographical advantage translated into something socially priceless: a man living in a modern country will respect women.

CLASH OF DREAMS

Women like Thanh want a respectful marriage based on principles of gender equality. By these principles, women expect to work for a wage, share in making social and economic decisions for their future households, and have their husbands share in the household division of labor. Above all, they did *not* want to live in multi-generational households serving as the dutiful daughter-in-law and housewife, the two often inseparable and presumed roles historically delegated to women in Vietnam. Many express that reluctance, for they know numerous *Viet Kieu* men who live with their parents or plan to do so in the future when their parents are old. The women's concern about having to live in multi-generational households is anchored in the fact that in Vietnamese culture, and more generally in Asia, elderly parents prefer to, and often do, live with their sons, usually the eldest one. Much less is known about the fact that it is their daughters-in-law, the wives of their sons, who do the fundamental daily caring work.

For Thanh, living with one's in-laws is the most symbolic act of feminine submission. For Minh, a wife's insistence on a nuclear household represents a desire for an equal marriage—and is one of the gendered anxieties of modernity:

> Vietnamese women, they care for their husbands and they are more traditional. I think non-VN women and

Viet Kieu women, are too modern. just want to be equal with their husbands and I don't think that it is the way husband and wife should be. [What do you mean?] I mean that husband and wife should not be equal. The wife should listen to husband most of the time. That is how they will have a happy life together. If the woman try to be equal they will have problems. . . . I know many Vietnamese men here who abandon their parents because their wives refuse to live with their parents. If my parents were in America, I would definitely plan for them to live with me when they are old. But because they are in Vietnam, they are living with one of my brothers.

Instead of seeking peasant village women or uneducated ones like white Europeans and Americans who search for wives through commercialized systems of mail-order brides, men like Minh seek marriage arrangement with educated women as part of a careful gender strategy for a perceived future marital stability. Minh outlines his strategy:

For me, I want to marry an educated woman because she comes from a good, educated family. It's very hard to find a poor woman or an uneducated woman who comes from an uneducated family, because if they are uneducated [the family] they don't know how to teach their daughters about morals and values. I know many men, *Viet Kieu* and foreign men, who go to Vietnam to marry beautiful young women, but they don't ask why do those women marry them? Those women only want to use their beauty to go overseas and they will leave their husbands when they get the chance. They can use their beauty to find other men. I would never marry a beautiful girl from a poor, uneducated family. You see, the educated women, they know it's important marry and stay married forever. As they say in Vietnam, "tram nam han phuc," [a hundred years of happiness]. Educated women must protect their family's reputation in Vietnam by having a happy marriage, not end in divorce.

UNIMAGINABLE FUTURES

At first glance, Minh and Thanh seem as if they are from different social worlds, two worlds accidentally assembled by a complex Vietnamese history. But once closely acquainted with them, we learn that they are very much alike. First is the class of their past—both sets of their parents were educated and middle class. Second, they are both lonely human faces of globalization who lack the emotional and intimate details that

adults of their social worlds enjoy. Most importantly, it seems, because of the gendered meanings embedded in their opposite trails of class mobility, they both long for marital respect, the kind of respect they perceive is scarce in their local marriage market. From Minh's side of the gender scene, he experienced downward mobility quickly and immensely as a result of migration and is eager to get back the respect he has lost. Thanh, a woman who has, in part, priced herself out of the local marriage market by acquiring a higher education, paid for by a remittance upward mobility, wants a man who respects her as an equal and as a woman who embraces modernity. He wants to regain what he sees as something men like him have lost, while she has, in part, challenged the local marriage norm and, in effect, the "control-norm" in the gender world of Vietnam.

The global forces and global histories that have mobilized their marriage—and their clashed dreams—will assuredly usher in marital conflicts. These conflicts will lead to several possibilities as women quietly migrate to join their husbands overseas. In a happy global story, Minh will join in the feminist revolution and leave behind the tradition he never had as he moves forward with his new marriage. I believe some, but few, men will join women in this revolution. In a tragic global story, these couples may end in divorce or worse, women like Thanh will be abused by their husbands. Many women like Thanh have thought about this possibility and have told me that their connection to transnational networks will ensure that they avoid abusive marriages. The most likely possibility for married couples like Minh and Thanh is that men will get what they want in the market of respect and women will consent to subordination in the name of family and kinship. Thanh will enjoy some aspects of modernity she cannot acquire in Vietnam, but she will be burdened by tradition she doesn't expect to see in the United States. For she will be going from a patriarchal frying pan to a patriarchal fire, but with one big difference. In the United States she has more support for her desire for gender equity where more women dare to quit a marriage if they don't get it. But she has the powerful burden of tradition in Vietnam to hold her back from choosing this option.

In Vietnam, marriage is an important matter not only because it unites two people, but also because it has significant implications for extended networks of kin (Tran 1991). In a culture where divorce is stigmatized and where saving face is a sacred activity especially among the educated and middle class, if Thanh daringly divorces her husband, she will cause her family and kin a loss of reputation in Vietnam and overseas, a risk she told me she is unlikely to take. If she stays in the marriage, she will give up her need for the respect and equality she thinks are waiting for her

in the United States. And she will likely serve as the traditional wife Minh needs in order for him to gain back the respect he left back in Vietnam almost 20 years ago. Simply put, Vietnamese politics of kinship promise that couples like Minh and Thanh will remain married—for better or worse.

ACKNOWLEDGMENTS

This is a revised version of another paper previously published under the title "Clashing Dreams: Highly-Educated Vietnamese Brides and Their Low-Wage Overseas Husbands," in *Global Woman* (New York: Metropolitan Books, 2003), edited by Arlie Russell Hochschild and Barbara Ehrenreich. Versions of this paper were also presented at the 2002 annual meetings of American Sociological Association in Chicago, and at the 2003 annual meetings of the West and the Pacific Regional Association for Asian American Studies in Pomona, California. I would like to very much thank Arlie Russell Hochschild, Barbara Ehrenreich, Verta Taylor, and Leila Rupp for comments on previous drafts. Thanks to Ingrid Banks for conversations and feedback. And to Barrie Thorne for guidance at every step of the way.

REFERENCES

Espiritu, Yen Le. 1999. "Gender and Labor in Asian Immigrant Families." *American Behavioral Scientist* 42: 628–647.

Fitzgerald, Tina Katherine. 1999. *Who Marries Whom? Attitudes in Marital Partner Selection.* Ph.D. Dissertation: University of Colorado.

Goodkind, Daniel. 1997. "The Vietnamese Double Marriage Squeeze." *The Center for Migration Studies of New York* 31: 108–128.

Guttentag, Marcia, and Paul F. Secord. 1983. *Too Many Women? The Sex Ratio Question.* Beverly Hills: Sage Publications.

Houstoun, Marion F., Roger G. Kramer, and Joan Mackin Barrett. 1984. "Female Predominance in Immigration to the United States since 1930s: A First Look." *International Migration Review* 18: 908–963.

Leonard, Jack, and Mai Tran. 2000a. "Agents Target Little Saigon Crime Groups." *Los Angeles Times*, October 7, p. A1.

Leonard, Jack, and Mai Tran. 2000b. "Probes Take Aim at Organized Crime in Little Saigon; Crackdown: Numerous Agencies Target Gambling, Drug Sales, Counterfeit Labels and Credit Card Scams." *Los Angeles Times*, October 7, p. B7.

Lievans, John. 1999. "Family Forming Migration from Turkey and Morocco to Belgium." *International Migration Review* 33: 717–744.

Los Angeles Times. 1995. "Cooler Days in Little Saigon." *Los Angeles Times*, August 8, p. B8.

Marosi, Richard, and Mai Tran. 2000. "Little Saigon Raids Dismantle Crime Ring, Authorities Say; Probe: Asian Syndicate Supplied Most Illegal Gambling Machines in Orange County, Police Say. Fifteen Are Arrested." *Los Angeles Times*, September 29, p. B3

Merli, Giovanna M. 1997. "Estimation of International Migration for Vietnam, 1979–1989." Unpublished paper, Department of Sociology and Center for Studies in Demography and Ecology. Seattle: University of Washington.

Nhat, Hong. 1999. "Hankering for '*Viet Kieu*' Money." *Vietnam Economic News* 9, no. 50 (December), p. 12.

Ong, Aihwa. 1999. *Flexible Citizenship: The Cultural Logics of Transnationality.* Durham, N.C.: Duke University Press.

Paddock, Richard C., and Lily Dizon. 1991. "3 Vietnamese Brothers in Shoot-out Led Troubled Lives." *Los Angeles Times*, p. A3.

Pierre, Andrew J. 2000. "Vietnam's Contradictions." *Foreign Affairs* 79.

Rubin, Lillian. 1994. *Families on the Fault Line: America's Working Class Speaks About the Family, the Economy, Race and Ethnicity.* New York: HarperCollins.

Terry, Don. 1999. "Passions of Vietnam War Are Revived in Little Saigon; Shop's Ho Chi Minh Poster Sets off Violence." *New York Times*, February 11, p. A20.

Thornton, Michael C. 1992. "The Quiet Immigration: Foreign Spouses of U.S. Citizens, 1945–1985." Pp. 64–76 in *Racially Mixed People in America*, edited by Maria P. Root. Newbury Park, CA: Sage Publications.

Tran, Dinh Huou. 1991. "Traditional Families in Vietnam and the Influence of Confucianism." Pp. 27–53 in *Sociological Studies on the Vietnamese Family*, edited by Rita Lijestrom and Tuong Lai. Hanoi: Social Sciences Publishing House.

USINS. 1999a. "International Matchmaking Organizations: A Report to Congress by the Immigration & Naturalization Service." *A Report to Congress*.

USINS. 1999b. *Statistical Yearbook of the Immigration and Naturalization Service, 1997.* Washington, D.C.: U.S. Government Printing Office.

Zhou, Min, and Carl L. Bankston. 1998. *Growing Up American: How Vietnamese Children Adapt to Life in the United States.* New York: Russell Sage Foundation.

Nancy A. Naples

Queer Parenting in the New Millennium

Earlier this year, the SWS Executive Council passed a resolution opposing a U.S. constitutional amendment prohibiting same-sex marriage. On 13 July, the Federal Marriage Amendment, which is designed as a constitutional amendment that would define marriage as the union of a man and a woman, reached the Senate floor.[1] Many senators expressed dismay that the legislation was brought to the floor for debate given the obvious lack of votes needed for passage (a constitutional amendment must be approved by two-thirds majority of both the Senate and the House of Representatives). However, sponsors of the legislation argued that their haste in bringing the vote to the Senate floor was prompted by the judicial decision in Massachusetts to permit same-sex marriage, which "could spread throughout the nation and undermine traditional marriage" (Hulse 2004).

Many conservative politicians believe that the Defense of Marriage Act, which was signed into law by President Bill Clinton in 1996,[2] does not go far enough in protecting "traditional marriage." President George W. Bush, who called for the constitutional amendment early in 2004, argues that same-sex marriage would undermine "the welfare of children and the stability of society."[3] Of course, feminist sociologists have long pointed out that it is poverty, not failure to marry, that contributes most to the instability of families and undermines children's welfare. Yet the Bush administration has earmarked approximately one million dollars to promote traditional marriage for women receiving public assistance in the legislation to reauthorize the welfare program Temporary Assistance to Needy Families. The contradictory expressions of support for marriage as a cure for many of the ills in society for different-sex couples and the opposition to marriage for same-sex couples has led even those of us who were critics of gay and lesbian movement organizations' focus on obtaining marriage rights to rethink our positions (Walters 2004).

I recall a campus visit to the University of California–Irvine, by Torie Osborn, former executive director of the National Gay and Lesbian Task Force organization, who was invited by the gay and lesbian faculty and staff group to discuss her book *Coming Home to America* (1996). When she began to talk about the campaign for same-sex marriage, several faculty members and graduate students in the audience became quite impatient, stressing that this normalizing goal would lead inevitably to assimilation into a heterosexist regime, undermine radical queer organizing, and further marginalize those who did not fit into a monogamous dyad. Furthermore, they passionately argued, same-sex marriage serves to co-opt efforts to decouple legal rights from the institution of marriage (Fineman 1995; O'Brien 2004). As more people lay claim to the institution, political struggles for universal health care, tax benefits, and other benefits that now accrue primarily through marriage will lose constituents. Osborn forcefully explained that she had just concluded a multicity tour to promote her book and, much to her surprise, was greeted with a tremendous level of passion and mobilizing efforts around same-sex marriage, civil unions, and partnership legislation. She believed that this energy could be tapped for other progressive issues. Accordingly, she argued, organizers need to meet people where they are and help facilitate their political goals, not criticize them for a lack of consciousness around the constraints of marriage as a patriarchal and heterosexist institution.

Some members of the gay, lesbian, bisexual, and transgendered community who argue against organizing on behalf of same-sex marriage assert that this issue is of little interest to communities of color and that it is primarily white, middle-class lesbians and gay men who will reap the benefits of marriage. In contrast, in a survey of attendees at Black Gay Pride events in 2000, 30 percent ranked marriage/domestic partnership as one of "the three most important issues facing the Black GLBT [gay, lesbian, bisexual, transgendered] community" (Battle et al. 2002, 26–27). In addition, the researchers found that women surveyed were "more likely than men and transgender people to view marriage and domestic partnership as a key issue for Black GLBT people" (Battle et al. 2002, 27). Since more than one thousand benefits accrue to couples through marriage, the economic benefits are sizable. Same-sex marriage would diminish the cost of legal paperwork that lesbians and gay men must complete to protect themselves and their children (Chambers 2001).

Protection of children is often used as the primary justification for the defense of traditional marriage legislation.[4] But of course, gays and lesbians already have children and will continue to do so despite the challenges they often face in the process (Dalton 2001). In fact, in the United States, in states such as Connecticut (where I live), gays and lesbians can apply to be coparents to the children they have with their partners despite the fact that they cannot marry.[5] Queer parenting can destabilize gender essentialism and other taken-for-granted assumptions about gender, sexuality, and family as well as pose challenges to regimes of normalization that shape contemporary institutions (Sullivan 2001). Of course, gay and lesbian parents are not a new phenomenon. In fact, it has been 15 years since the publication of *Heather Has Two Mommies* (Newman and Souza 1989), a children's book that has been banned from public school libraries in a number of U.S. cities. With the establishment of sperm banks and advances in reproductive technologies, gays and lesbians as well as infertile heterosexual couples, single women, and professional women who desire more control over the timing of births have been able to expand their reproductive options, at least if they have the funds to pay for these services. However, in some states, lesbians and single women can be denied infertility treatment (Murphy 2001).

In the context of the heated debate over same-sex marriage, my partner and I are expecting twin girls. As lesbians, our decision to have children poses a direct challenge to the heteronormativity that pervades everyday life. After a series of interviews with obstetricians in the area and a few hospital tours of labor and delivery facilities, my partner and I decided to work with a lesbian nurse midwife who is located in a Catholic hospital. Surprisingly, this is the only hospital in our area with nurse-midwives who work autonomously. Although they operate under the supervision of an obstetrician, they can manage prenatal care and deliver without the presence of physicians in routine deliveries. The fact that one of the two nurse-midwives is also a lesbian (we located her through our lesbian network) is ironic given the persistence and vehemence with which the Catholic Church has opposed same-sex marriage and civil union legislation in Connecticut and elsewhere. Regardless, the hospital is close to our home, is smaller, offers more flexibility than the public hospital in our city, and has accessible parking.

We are the only lesbian couple in our racially diverse childbirth class. My presence as the only woman coach in the class serves as a direct challenge to the gender essentialism associated with pregnancy, childbirth, and parenting. In contrast, as a pregnant woman, my partner finds herself easily drawn into conversations with the heterosexual women about the biological and emotional experiences of pregnancy and childbirth, highlighting how little of this world she shared before the pregnancy. Stein (1997) noted that a lesbian who becomes a biological mother can enjoy a new societal acceptance that renders lesbian identity less salient. In contrast, the comother must assert and explain her relationship to the child in every interaction, outing herself and her family form in multiple settings throughout each day.

The process of adopting her own children further reinscribes the nonbiological comother's otherness in a variety of frustrating ways. The adoption procedure includes a thorough assessment of personal background, including a criminal background check, and a home study by the Department of Children and Family Services to assess how suitable the home is for "the proper rearing of children." Some courts require the appointment of a guardian *ad litem* to represent the child in the court proceedings and may require an announcement in the newspaper to notify any potential interested parties about the adoption. In adoptions by step-fathers or step-mothers who are married to the biological parent, the process is streamlined, another privilege that accrues through marriage. According to Dalton (2001), second-parent adoptions can take up to 10 months, leaving lesbian and gay coparents at risk of losing their children if something happens to the birth mother before the adoption process is complete. In the case of assisted reproduction, the names of nonbiological fathers who are married to the biological mothers can be placed on the birth certificate automatically. As a result of the court ruling permitting same-sex marriage in Massachusetts, a lesbian coparent who was married to her partner could put her name on her child's birth certificate (Ross 2004). This marks a new chapter in state regulation of lesbian and gay sexuality and an official decoupling of reproduction and heterosexual privilege (Polikoff 2002).

However, when couples who live in other states decide to marry in Massachusetts, it is unclear whether their marriages will be recognized by home states. Several cases are now pending that will test the portability of marriage rights for same-sex couples.

Another alternative is for couples to enter into civil unions, which became legal in Vermont on 1 July 2000.[6] Maureen Murphy, a civil rights and family law attorney who founded the Connecticut Gay and Lesbian Law Association, cautions lesbians and gay men in Connecticut who wish to apply for coparent adoption against obtaining a civil union in Vermont. She explained that "entering into a civil union before completing adoption matters could complicate the adoption process—or even make you ineligible to adopt (especially if you are considering international adoptions)" (True Colors 2004).

The salience of the heteronormative family form is evident everywhere we turn. As a child-free lesbian couple, my partner and I could pass seemingly unnoticed in our everyday lives. Exceptions occur when we ask a hotel clerk for a queen size bed rather than two double beds and are met with a look of horror, as happened on one trip to Norway. Having children as a lesbian couple foregrounds our relationship in ways that we could not have anticipated, even though our fields of study are gender and sexuality. With few exceptions, my partner and I must define our relationship with the children-to-be to doctors, nurses, baby store employees, and in some new ways, to family and friends (Sullivan 2001).

We are changing the field of vision for those we interact with as we come out about our decision and "have children" together (Naples 2001). Our own field of vision and understanding of how heteronormativity shapes our worldview is also being altered as we become publicly visible as pregnant lesbian and partner. On one recent occasion, as we were waiting to order food at a roadside stand, a woman and her two children joined us in line. She turned to my partner who, at the time, was about six months pregnant, and asked, "Do you know what you're having?" My partner replied, "Fish and chips." After an awkward pause, she realized that she answered the wrong question. Similarly, too much time has been spent answering the wrong question: "Is the call for same-sex marriage an assimilationist or transformative strategy?" Rather, I believe the question we need to ask and answer is, "How can we harness the political energy that has been unleashed by the debates over same-sex marriage and queer parenting to destabilize the taken-for-granted notions of what counts as a family and what can be in the best interests of children in a resilient and inclusive society?" As Bernstein (2001, 440) argues, "Legal change may reduce the costs of coming out and transform public consciousness in the long run, but it is unlikely that by itself legal change will create acceptance or transform dominant cultural values." Queering family and parenting, and destabilizing the powerful hegemony of heteronormativity, involves daily negotiations, strategic choices, and a commitment to challenging heterosexual privilege in everyday life. At the same time, efforts to control and limit marriage have raised awareness among the members of the lesbian, gay, bisexual, and transgendered people about the costs as well as the benefits of campaigns for same-sex marriage.

ACKNOWLEDGMENTS

My thanks to Mary Bernstein for sharing her research and insights and for reviewing earlier drafts of this article and to Valerie Jenness and Jodi O'Brien for their helpful comments.

NOTES

1. On 22 July, the U.S. House of Representatives approved The Marriage Protection Act, which bars all federal courts, including the U.S. Supreme Court, from hearing cases concerning the constitutionality of the Defense of Marriage Act. It also prohibits states, U.S. territories, and American Indian tribes from recognizing same-sex marriage licenses issued in other jurisdictions. Only state courts could hear cases concerning same-sex marriage. However, the vote (233 to 194) indicates that there are insufficient votes needed to pass the Federal Marriage Amendment in the House.

2. The Defense of Marriage Act permits each state to recognize or deny any marriage-like relationship between persons of the same sex that has been recognized in another state. It also explicitly defines marriage as "a legal union of one man and one woman as husband and wife" and states that a spouse "refers only to a person of the opposite sex who is a husband

or a wife." To date, 38 states have enacted laws denying the recognition of same-sex unions, which is the same number of states needed to amend the United States Constitution.

3. Many conservatives who argue against same-sex marriage draw on social science literature to make their case (Stacey and Biblarz 2001). For an insightful analysis of the challenges of participating as a public intellectual in the debates around same-sex marriage and gay and lesbian parenting, see Stacey (2004).

4. Adam (2003) noted that almost 40 states have either passed legislation or are trying to pass legislation that would prohibit same-sex marriage. In stark contrast, laws recognizing same sex relationships have been passed in many industrial countries including South Africa, Germany, France, and New Zealand (Adam 2003, 259).

5. In addition to Connecticut, seven states plus Washington, D.C., recognize second-parent adoption. Judges have ruled in favor of second-parent adoptions in at least 20 other states.

6. In 2003, a lesbian couple who reside in Vermont and who took advantage of Vermont's civil union law won the right to have their names on their adoptive child's birth certificate after a Mississippi judge ruled in their favor (their adoptive child was born in that state) (Lambda Legal Defense and Education Fund 2003).

REFERENCES

Adam, Barry D. 2003. The Defense of Marriage Act and American exceptionalism: The "gay marriage" panic in the United States. *Journal of the History of Sexuality* 12 (2): 259–76.

Battle, Juan, Cathy J. Cohen, Dorian Warren, Gerard Fergerson, and Suzette Audam. 2002. *Say it loud: I'm Black and I'm proud.* New York: Policy Institute of the National Gay and Lesbian Task Force.

Bernstein, Mary. 2001. Gender transgressions and queer family law: Gender, queer family policies, and the limits of law. In *Queer families, queer politics: Challenging culture and the state.* New York: Columbia University Press.

Chambers, David. 2001. "What if?" The legal consequences of marriage and the legal needs of lesbian and gay male couples. In *Queer families, queer politics: Challenging culture and the state.* New York: Columbia University Press.

Dalton, Susan E. 2001. Protecting our parent-child relationships: Understanding the strengths and weaknesses of second-parent adoption. In *Queer families, queer politics: Challenging culture and the state,* edited by Mary Bernstein and Renate Reimann. New York: Columbia University Press.

Fineman, Martha. 1995. *The neutered mother, the sexual family and other twentieth century tragedies.* New York: Routledge.

Hulse, Carl. 2004. Gay-marriage ban faces loss in early vote. *New York Times,* 14 July.

Lambda Legal Defense and Education Fund. 2003. Mississippi judge orders state to list lesbian mothers on child's birth certificate. News release, 19 March.

Murphy, Julien S. 2001. Should lesbians count as infertile couples? Antilesbian discrimination in assisted reproduction. In *Queer families, queer politics: Challenging culture and the state,* edited by Mary Bernstein and Renate Reimann. New York: Columbia University Press.

Naples, Nancy A. 2001. A member of the funeral: An introspective ethnography. In *Queer families, queer politics:* *Challenging culture and the state,* edited by Mary Bernstein and Renate Reimann. New York: Columbia University Press.

Newman, Leslea, and Diana Souza. 1989. *Heather has two mommies.* New York: Alyson.

O'Brien, Jodi. 2004. Seeking normal? Considering same-sex marriage. *Seattle Journal of Social Justice* 2. Retrieved from http://www.law.seattleu.edu/sjsj/current.htm.

Osborn, Torie. 1996. *Coming home to America.* New York: St. Martin's.

Polikoff, Nancy D. 2002. Raising children: Lesbian and gay parents face the public and the courts. In *Creating change: Sexuality, public policy and civil rights,* edited by J. D'Emilio, W. B. Turner, and U. Vaid. New York: St. Martin's.

Ross, Casey. 2004. Moms the word—Lesbian couple first on birth certificate. *Boston Herald,* 16 July.

Stacey, Judith. 2004. Marital suitors court social science spinsters: The unwittingly conservative effects of public sociology. *Social Problems* 51 (1): 131–45.

Stacey, Judith, and Timothy Biblarz. 2001. (How) does the sexual orientation of parents matter? *American Sociological Review* 66 (2): 159–83.

Stein, Arlene. 1997. *Sex and sensibility: Stories of a lesbian generation.* Berkeley: University of California Press.

Sullivan, Maureen. 2001. Alma mater: Family "outings" and the making of the modern other mother (MOM). In *Queer families, queer politics: Challenging culture and the state,* edited by Mary Bernstein and Renate Reimann. New York: Columbia University Press.

True Colors, Inc. Sexual Minority Youth and Family Services of Connecticut. 2004. *Co-parent adoption tips and tidbits.* Retrieved from http://www.ourtruecolors.org/kinnections/co_parent.htm.

Walters, Suzanna. 2004. Gay marriage in America. *Political Sociology: States, Power, and Societies* 10 (2): 1, 4.

SECTION 7

Sexualities

The processes of socialization encourage women and men to develop different views of and approaches to sexuality and intimate relationships. Women learn strong interpersonal and emotional skills in preparation for roles as wives and mothers and for employment in professions associated with care work, such as teaching and nursing. At the same time, women's and men's different positions in social institutions mean that we enter our intimate and sexual relationships with different amounts and kinds of resources, power, networks, and expectations. In addition, we are surrounded by a culture that portrays women and men as having intrinsically different sexual needs, desires, and obligations. And as we have already seen, such differences between women and men are shaped as well by class, race, ethnicity, sexuality, nationality, ability, and age. The readings in this section discuss how even such a seemingly personal matter as sexuality is *socially constructed* in various ways in different contexts.

We begin with Deborah Tolman's "Doing Desire: Adolescent Girls' Struggles for/with Sexuality," an examination of how adolescent girls understand their sexuality. Adolescents have been the subject of considerable recent public debate over sexuality, with many politicians suggesting that teenage sexual activity should be discouraged. Yet adolescence is the life stage during which we begin to develop our sexual selves and form a sense of our intimate connections to others. Tolman examines how diverse adolescent girls construct desire, tracing the complex mix of pleasure and desire with danger and fear, highlighting differences of sexual identity. As a result

of the cultural repression of women's sexuality, Tolman argues, adolescent girls are "denied full access to the power of their own desire." How do the girls Tolman discusses come to understand their sexual selves in this context? What are the "possibilities of empowerment"?

In the next selection, Laura Hamilton's "Trading on Heterosexuality: College Women's Gender Strategies and Homophobia," we see the ways that the Greek party scene on a public university campus shapes the gender strategies of young heterosexual white women. Desirability in the eyes of men is achieved by adhering to traditional white feminine standards—being blond, tanned, slim, and sexy—and by maintaining social distance from women marked as lesbian through their appearance and/or lack of interest in men. At the same time, women at the top of the Greek party system hierarchy feel free to kiss and caress other women as a way of arousing men. Hamilton argues that this research illustrates the ways that women's homophobia operates differently than men's. Does this analysis of a midwestern university resonate with your own experience? How does Hamilton see these heterosexual college women's behavior as reinforcing gender inequality? How might this situation be changed?

From a very different perspective, Patricia Hill Collins takes up the relationship among race, gender, and sexuality in an excerpt from her award-winning book *Black Sexual Politics: African Americans, Gender, and the New Racism.* Making connections between historical and contemporary cultural phenomena, Collins analyzes the role of sexuality in what she calls "the new racism" of the twenty-first century. The dominant culture has long portrayed black bodies as hypersexualized, with different consequences for women and men. How does hypersexualization affect black women and men? How does sexuality enter into the new racism Collins discusses?

The concept of the social construction of sexuality—so central to Collins' analysis—has been most extensively developed in considering the history of same-sex sexuality. In "Loving Women in the Modern World," Leila Rupp explores the history, since the nineteenth century, of female-bodied individuals who have desired, loved, married, or engaged in sexual activity with women in various places around the world. She argues that we need to understand the different ways that women conceptualized their desires before and after creation of the category "lesbian." Looking at women who married other women, women who desired other women, and women who claimed different kinds of identities based on their desires, she suggests that we need to disabuse ourselves of the notion of "progress" from hostility in the "bad old days" to enlightenment in the present. The story is more complicated. What are some of the ways that women have formed relationships with other women in different times and places? What does the history of female same-sex sexuality tell us about the social construction of sexuality? What different conceptions are there of women who love women?

In the final article in this section, "Becoming 100% Straight," Michael Messner raises similar questions about adolescent male sexuality. Using his own experience as a student-athlete, he rethinks his conviction that he had always been entirely heterosexual by analyzing a crush he developed on another boy and his subsequent hostile reaction to him. Contrasting his own story to that of Tom Waddell, a closeted gay male athlete, he raises questions about the connections among heterosexuality, masculinity, and sport. He argues that men perform masculinity and heterosexuality through sport, and he asks why and what kind of consequences follow from that performance. How do you read Messner's story of his turn against Timmy? How important do you think sport is for young men today? Do you think sport has similar or different consequences for women as they perform femininity and heterosexuality? How do Messner's stories compare to Tolman's analysis of adolescent girls' sexual desires?

Like family life, sexuality and intimate relationships are both a source of support and strength for women and a location of oppression. What do these readings suggest about how diverse women find sexuality to be a means of fulfillment and an expression of self-definition? In contrast, how do the readings show sexuality to be a means of social control? How is sexuality shaped differently for people in different social groups?

Doing Desire: Adolescent Girls' Struggles for/with Sexuality

In order to perpetuate itself, every oppression must corrupt or distort those various sources of power within the culture of the oppressed that can provide energy for change. For women, this has meant suppression of the erotic as a considered source of power and information within our lives. (Lorde 1984, 53)

Recent research suggests that adolescence is the crucial moment in the development of psychological disempowerment for many women (e.g., Brown and Gilligan 1992; Gilligan 1990). As they enter adolescence, many girls may lose an ability to speak about what they know, see, feel, and experience evident in childhood as they come under cultural pressure to be "nice girls" and ultimately "good women" in adolescence. When their bodies take on women's contours, girls begin to be seen as sexual, and sexuality becomes an aspect of adolescent girls' lives; yet "nice" girls and "good" women are not supposed to be sexual outside of heterosexual, monogamous marriage (Tolman 1991). Many girls experience a "crisis of connection," a relational dilemma of how to be oneself and stay in relationships with others who may not want to know the truth of girls' experiences (Gilligan 1989). In studies of adolescent girls' development, many girls have demonstrated the ironic tendency to silence their own thoughts and feelings for the sake of relationships, when what they think and feel threatens to be disruptive (Brown and Gilligan 1992). At adolescence, the energy needed for resistance to crushing conventions of femininity often begins to get siphoned off for the purpose of maintaining cultural standards that stand between women and their empowerment. Focusing explicitly on embodied desire, Tolman and Debold (1993) observed similar patterns in the process of girls learning to look at,

rather than experience, themselves, to know themselves from the perspective of men, thereby losing touch with their own bodily feelings and desires. It is at this moment in their development that many women will start to experience and develop ways of responding to their own sexual feelings. Given these realities, what are adolescent girls' experiences of sexual desire? How do girls enter their sexual lives and learn to negotiate or respond to their sexuality?

Despite the real gains that feminism and the sexual revolution achieved in securing women's reproductive rights and increasing women's sexual liberation (Rubin 1990), the tactics of silencing and denigrating women's sexual desire are deeply entrenched in this patriarchal society (Brown 1991). The Madonna/whore dichotomy is alternately virulent and subtle in the cultures of adolescents (Lees 1986; Tolman 1992). Sex education curricula name male adolescent sexual desire; girls are taught to recognize and to keep a lid on the sexual desire of boys but not taught to acknowledge or even to recognize their own sexual feelings (Fine 1988; Tolman 1991). The few feminist empirical studies of girls' sexuality suggest that sexual desire is a complicated, important experience for adolescent girls about which little is known. In an ethnographic study, Fine noticed that adolescent girls' sexuality was acknowledged by adults in school, but in terms that denied the sexual subjectivity of girls; this "missing discourse of desire" was, however, not always absent from the ways girls themselves spoke about their sexual experiences (Fine 1988). Rather than being "educated," girls' bodies are suppressed under surveillance and silenced in the schools (see also Lesko 1988). Although Fine ably conveys the existence of girls' discourse of desire, she does not articulate that discourse. Thompson collected 400 girls' narratives about sexuality, romance, contraception, and pregnancy (Thompson 1984, 1990) in which girls' desire seems frequently absent or not relevant to the terms of their sexual relationships. The minority of girls who spoke of sexual pleasure voiced more sexual agency than girls whose experiences were devoid of pleasure. Within the context of girls' psychological development, Fine's and Thompson's work underscores the need to understand what girls' experiences of their sexual desire are like.

A psychological analysis of this experience for girls can contribute an understanding of both the possibilities and limits for sexual freedom for women in the current social climate. By identifying how the culture has become anchored in the interior of women's lives—an interior that is birthed through living in the exterior of material conditions and relationships—this approach can keep distinct women's psychological responses to sexual oppression and also the sources of that oppression. This distinction is necessary for avoiding the trap of blaming women for the ways our minds and bodies have become constrained.

METHODOLOGICAL DISCUSSION

Sample and Data Collection

To examine this subject, I interviewed thirty girls who were juniors in an urban and a suburban public high school ($n = 28$) or members of a gay and lesbian youth group ($n = 2$). They were 16.5 years old on average and randomly selected. The girls in the larger study are a heterogeneous group, representing different races and ethnic backgrounds (Black, including Haitian and African American; Latina, including Puerto Rican and Colombian; Euro-American, including Eastern and Western European), religions (Catholic, Jewish, and Protestant), and sexual experiences. With the exception of one Puerto Rican girl, all of the girls from the suburban school were Euro-American; the racial/ethnic diversity in the sample is represented by the urban school. Interviews with school personnel confirmed that the student population of the urban school was almost exclusively poor or working class and the students in the suburban school were middle and upper-middle class. This information is important in that my focus is on how girls' social environments shape their understanding of their sexuality. The fact that girls who live in the urban area experience the visibility of and discourse about violence, danger and the consequences of unprotected sex, and that the suburban girls live in a community that offers a veneer of safety and stability,

informs their experiences of sexuality. Awareness of these features of the social contexts in which these girls are developing is essential for listening to and understanding their narratives about sexual experiences.

The data were collected in one-on-one, semistructured clinical interviews (Brown and Gilligan 1992). This method of interviewing consists of following a structured interview protocol that does not direct specific probes but elicits narratives. The interviewer listens carefully to a girl, taking in her voice, and responding with questions that will enable the girl to clarify her story and know she is being heard. In these interviews, I asked girls direct questions about desire to elicit descriptions and narratives. Most of the young women wove their concerns about danger into the narratives they told.

Analytic Strategy

To analyze these narratives, I used the Listening Guide—an interpretive methodology that joins hermeneutics and feminist standpoint epistemology (Brown et al. 1991). It is a voice-centered, relational method by which a researcher becomes a listener, taking in the voice of a girl, developing an interpretation of her experience. Through multiple readings of the same text, this method makes audible the "polyphonic and complex" nature of voice and experience (Brown and Gilligan 1992, 15). Both speaker and listener are recognized as individuals who bring thoughts and feelings to the text, acknowledging the necessary subjectivity of both participants. Self-consciously embedded in a standpoint acknowledging that patriarchal culture silences and obscures women's experiences, the method is explicitly psychological and feminist in providing the listener with an organized way to respond to the coded or indirect language of girls and women, especially regarding topics such as sexuality that girls and women are not supposed to speak of. This method leaves a trail of evidence for the listener's interpretation, and thus leaves room for other interpretations by other listeners consistent with the epistemological stance that there is multiple meaning in such stories. I present *a* way to understand the stories these young women chose to tell me, our story as I have heard and understood it. Therefore, in the interpretations that follow I include my responses, those of an adult woman, to these girls' words, providing information about girls' experiences of sexual desire much like countertransference informs psychotherapy.

Adolescent Girls' Experiences of Sexual Desire

The first layer of the complexity of girls' experiences of their sexual desire was revealed initially in determining whether or not they felt sexual feelings. A majority of these girls (two-thirds) said unequivocally that they experienced sexual desire; in them I heard a clear and powerful way of speaking about the experience of feeling desire that was explicitly relational and also embodied. Only three of the girls said they did not experience sexual feelings, describing silent bodies and an absence of or intense confusion about romantic or sexual relationships. The remaining girls evidenced confusion or spoke in confusing ways about their own sexual feelings. Such confusion can be understood as a psychic solution to sexual feelings that arise in a culture that denigrates, suppresses, and heightens the dangers of girls' sexuality and in which contradictory messages about women's sexuality abound.

For the girls who said they experienced sexual desire, I turned my attention to how they said they responded to their sexual feelings. What characterized their responses was a sense of struggle; the question of "doing desire"—that is, what to do when they felt sexual desire—was not straightforward for any of them. While speaking of the power of their embodied feelings, the girls in this sample described the difficulties that their sexual feelings posed, being aware of both the potential for pleasure and the threat of danger that their desire holds for them. The struggle took different shapes for different girls, with some notable patterns emerging. Among the urban girls, the focus was on how to stay safe from bodily harm, in and out of the context of relational or social consequences, whereas among the suburban girls the most pronounced issue was how to maintain a sense of themselves as "good" and "normal" girls (Tolman 1992). In this article, I will offer portraits of three girls. By focusing on three girls in depth, I can balance an approach to "variance" with the kind of case study presentation that enables me to illustrate both similarities and differences in how girls in the larger sample spoke about their sexual feelings. These three girls represent different sexual preferences—one heterosexual, one bisexual, and one lesbian.[1] I have chosen to forefront the difference of sexual preference because it has been for some women a source of empowerment and a route to community; it has also been a source of divisiveness among feminists. Through this approach, I can illustrate *both* the similarities and differences in their experiences of sexual desire, which are nested in their individual experiences as well as their social contexts. Although there are many other demarcations that differentiate these girls—social class, race, religion, sexual experience—and this is not the most pervasive difference in this sample,[2] sexual preference calls attention to the kinds of relationships in which girls are experiencing or exploring their sexual desire and which take meaning from gender arrangements and from both the presence and absence of institutionalization (Fine 1988; Friend 1993). Because any woman whose sexuality is not directly circumscribed by heterosexual, monogamous marriage is rendered deviant in our society, all adolescent girls bear suspicion regarding their sexuality, which sexual preference highlights. In addition, questions of identity are heightened at adolescence.

Rochelle Doing Desire   Rochelle is a tall, larger, African-American girl who is heterosexual. Her small, sweet voice and shy smile are a startling contrast to her large body, clothed in white spandex the day of our interview. She lives in an urban area where violence is embedded in the fabric of everyday life. She speaks about her sexual experience with a detailed knowledge of how her sexuality is shaped, silenced, denigrated, and possible in relationships with young men. As a sophomore, she thought she "had to get a boyfriend" and became "eager" for a sexual relationship. As she describes her first experience of sexual intercourse, she describes a traditional framing of male–female relationships:

> I felt as though I had to conform to everything he said that, you know, things that a girl and a guy were supposed to do, so like, when the sex came, like, I did it without thinking, like, I wish I would have waited . . . we started kissing and all that stuff and it just happened. And when I got, went home, I was like, I was shocked, I was like, why did I do that? I wish I wouldn't a did it.
>
> *Did you want to do it?*
>
> Not really. Not really. I just did it because, maybe because he wanted it, and I was always like tryin' to please him and like, he was real mean, mean to me, now that I think about it. I was like kind of stupid, cause like I did everything for him and he just treated me like I was nothing and I just thought I had just to stay with him because I needed a boyfriend so bad to make my life complete but like now it's different.

Rochelle's own sexual desire is absent in her story of defloration—in fact, she seems to be missing altogether. In a virtual caricature of dominant cultural conventions of femininity, Rochelle connects her disappearance at the moment of sex—"it just happened"—to her attempts to fulfill the cultural guidelines for how to "make [her] life complete." She has sex because "he wanted it," a response that holds no place for whether or not she feels desire. In reflecting on this arrangement, Rochelle now feels she was "stupid . . . to do everything for him" and in her current relationship, things are "different." As she explains: "I don't take as much as I did with the first guy, cause like, if he's doin' stuff that I don't like, I tell him, I'll go, I don't like this and I think you shouldn't do it and we compromise, you know. I don't think I can just let him treat me bad and stuff."

During the interview, I begin to notice that desire is not a main plot line in Rochelle's stories about her sexual experiences, especially in her intimate relationships. When I ask her about her experiences of sexual pleasure and sexual desire, she voices contradictions. On one hand, as the interview unfolds, she is more and more clear that she does not enjoy sex: "I don't like sex" quickly becomes "I hate sex . . . I don't really have pleasure." On the other hand, she explains that

> there are certain times when I really really really enjoy it, but then, that's like, not a majority of the times, it's only sometimes, once in a while . . . if I was to have sex once a month, then I would enjoy it . . . if I like go a long period of time without havin' it then, it's really good to me, cause it's like, I haven't had something for a long time and I miss it. It's like, say I don't eat cake a lot, but say, like every two months, I had some cake, then it would be real good to me, so that's like the same thing.

Rochelle conveys a careful knowledge of her body's hunger, her need for tension as an aspect of her sexual pleasure, but her voiced dislike of sex suggests that she does not feel she has much say over when and how she engages in sexual activity.

In describing her experiences with sexuality, I am overwhelmed at how frequently Rochelle says that she "was scared." She is keenly aware of the many consequences that feeling and responding to her sexual desire could have. She is scared of being talked about and getting an undeserved reputation: "I was always scared that if I did that (had sexual intercourse) I would be portrayed as, you know, something bad." Even having sex within the confines of a relationship, which has been described by some girls as a safe haven for their sexuality (Rubin 1990; Tolman 1992), makes her vulnerable; she "could've had a bad reputation, but luckily he wasn't like that"; he did not choose to tell other boys (who then tell girls) about their sexual activity. Thinking she had a sexually transmitted disease was scary. Because she had been faithful to her boyfriend, having such a disease would mean having to know that her boyfriend cheated on her and would also make her vulnerable to false accusations of promiscuity from him. Her concern about the kind of woman she may be taken for is embedded in her fear of using contraception: "When you get birth control pills, people automatically think you're having sex every night and that's not true." Being thought of as sexually insatiable or out of control is a fear that many girls voice (Tolman 1992); this may be intensified for African-American girls, who are creating a sexual identity in a dominant cultural context that stereotypes Black women as alternately asexual and hypersexual (Spillers 1984).

Rochelle's history provides other sources of fear. After her boyfriend "flattened [her] face," when she realized she no longer wanted to be with him and broke off the relationship, she learned that her own desire may lead to male violence. Rochelle confided to me that she has had an abortion, suffering such intense sadness, guilt, and anxiety in the wake of it that, were she to become pregnant again, she would have the baby. For Rochelle, the risk of getting pregnant puts her education at risk, because she will have to sacrifice going to college. This goal is tied to security for her; she wants to "have something of my own before I get a husband, you know, so if he ever tries leavin' me, I have my own money." Given this wall of fears, I am not surprised when Rochelle describes a time when simply feeling desire made her "so scared that I started to cry." Feeling her constant and pervasive fear, I began to find it hard to imagine how she can feel any other feelings, including sexual ones.

I was thus caught off guard when I asked Rochelle directly if she has felt desire and she told me that she does experience sexual desire; however, she explained "most of the time, I'm by myself when I do." She launched, in breathless tones, into a story about an experience of her own sexual desire just the previous night:

> Last night, I had this crank call. . . . At first I thought it was my boyfriend, cause he likes to play around, you

know. But I was sitting there talking, you know, and thinking of him and then I found out it's not him, it was so crazy weird, so I hang the phone up and he called back, he called back and called back. And then I couldn't sleep, I just had this feeling that, I wanted to have sex so so bad. It was like three o'clock in the morning. And I didn't sleep the rest of the night. And like, I called my boyfriend and I was tellin' him, and he was like, what do you want me to do, Rochelle, I'm sleeping! [Laughs.] I was like, okay, okay, well I'll talk to you later, bye. And then, like, I don't know, I just wanted to, and like, I kept tossin' and turnin'. And I'm trying to think who it was, who was callin' me, cause like, it's always the same guy who always crank calls me, he says he knows me. It's kinda scary. . . . I can't sleep, I'm like, I just think about it, like, oh I wanna have sex so bad, you know, it's like a fever, drugs, something like that. Like last night, I don't know, I think if I woulda had the car and stuff, I probably woulda left the house. And went over to his house, you know. But I couldn't, cause I was baby-sitting.

When I told her that it sounds a little frightening but it sounds like there's something exciting about it, she smiled and leaned forward, exclaiming, "Yeah! It's like sorta arousing." I was struck by the intensity of her sexual feelings and also by the fact that she is alone and essentially assured of remaining alone due to the late hour and her responsibilities. By being alone, not subject to observation or physical, social, emotional, or material vulnerability, Rochelle experienced the turbulent feelings that are awakened by this call in her body. Rochelle's desire has not been obliterated by her fear; desire and fear both reverberate through her psyche. But she is not completely alone in this experience of desire, for her feelings occur in response to another person, whom she at first suspects is her boyfriend speaking from a safe distance, conveying the relational contours of her sexual desire. Her wish to bring her desire into her relationship, voiced in her response of calling her boyfriend, is in conflict with her fear of what might happen if she did pursue her wish—getting pregnant and having a baby, a consequence that Rochelle is desperate to avoid.

I am struck by her awareness of both the pleasure and danger in this experience and how she works the contradiction without dissociating from her own strong feelings. There is a brilliance and also a sadness in the logic her body and psyche have played out in the face of her experiences with sexuality and relationships. The psychological solution to the dilemma that desire means for her, of feeling sexual desire only when she cannot respond as she says she would like to, arises from her focus on these conflicts as personal experiences, which she suffers and solves privately. By identifying and solving the dilemma in this way, Rochelle is diminished, as is the possibility of her developing a critique of these conflicts as not just personal problems but as social inequities that emerge in her personal relationships and on her body. Without this perspective, Rochelle is less likely to become empowered through her own desire to identify that the ways in which she must curtail herself and be curtailed by others are socially constructed, suspect, and in need of change.

Megan Doing Desire   Megan, a small, freckled, perky Euro-American, is dressed in baggy sweats, comfortable, unassuming, and counterpointed by her lively engagement in our interview.[3] She identifies herself as "being bisexual" and belongs to a gay youth group; she lives in a city in which wealth and housing projects coexist. Megan speaks of knowing she is feeling sexual desire for boys because she has "kind of just this feeling, you know? Just this feeling inside my body." She explains: "My vagina starts to kinda like act up and it kinda like quivers and stuff, and like I'll get like tingles and and, you can just feel your hormones (laughing) doing something weird, and you just, you get happy and you just get, you know, restimulated kind of and it's just, and Oh! Oh!" and "Your nerves feel good." Megan speaks about her sexual desire in two distinct ways, one for boys and one for girls. In our interview, she speaks most frequently about her sexual feelings in relation to boys. The power of her own desire and her doubt about her ability to control herself frighten her: "It scares me when I'm involved in a sexual situation and I just wanna go further and further and cause it just, and it scares me that, well, I have control, but if I even just let myself not have control, you know? . . . I'd have sex and I can't do that." Megan knows that girls who lose control over their desire like that can be called "sluts" and ostracized.

When asked to speak about an experience of sexual desire, Megan chooses to describe the safety of a heterosexual, monogamous relationship. She tells me how she feels when a boyfriend was "feeling me up"; not only is she aware of and articulate about his bodily reactions and her own, she narrates the relational synergy between her own desire and his:

> I just wanted to go on, you know? Like I could feel his penis, you know, 'cause we'd kinda lied down you know, and, you just really get so into it and intense and, you just wanna, well you just kinda keep wanting to go on or something, but it just feels good. . . . His penis being on my leg made, you know, it hit a nerve or something, it did something because it just made me start to get more horny or whatever, you know, it just made me want to do more things and stuff. I don't know how, I can't, it's hard for me to describe exactly how I felt, you know like, (intake of breath) . . . when he gets more excited then he starts to do more things and you can kind of feel his pleasure and then you start to get more excited.

With this young man, Megan knows her feelings of sexual desire to be "intense," to have a momentum of their own, and to be pleasurable. Using the concrete information of his erection, she describes the relational contours of her own embodied sexual desire, a desire that she is clear is her own and located in her body but that also arises in response to his excitement.

Although able to speak clearly in describing a specific experience she has had with her desire, I hear confusion seep into her voice when she notices that her feelings contradict or challenge societal messages about girls and sexuality:

> It's so confusing, 'cause you have to like say no, you have to be the one to say no, but why should you be the one to, cause I mean maybe you're enjoying it and you shouldn't have to say no or anything. But if you don't, maybe the guy'll just keep going and going, and you can't do that, because then you would be a slut. There's so [much] like, you know, stuff that you have to deal with and I don't know, just I keep losing my thought.

Although she knows the logic offered by society—that she must "say no" to keep him from "going and going," which will make her "a slut"—Megan identifies what is missing from that logic, that "maybe you're"—she, the girl—"the one who is enjoying it." The fact that she may be experiencing sexual desire makes the scripted response—to silence his body—dizzying. Because she does feel her own desire and can identify the potential of her own pleasure, Megan asks the next logical question, the question that can lead to outrage, critique, and

empowerment: "Why should you have to be the one to [say no]?" But Megan also gives voice to why sustaining the question is difficult; she knows that if she does not conform, if she does not "say no"—both to him and to herself—then she may be called a slut, which could lead to denigration and isolation. Megan is caught in the contradiction between the reality of her sexual feelings in her body and the absence of her sexual feelings in the cultural script for adolescent girls' sexuality. Her confusion is an understandable response to this untenable and unfair choice: a connection with herself, her body, and sexual pleasure or a connection with the social world.

Megan is an avid reader of the dominant culture. Not only has she observed the ways that messages about girls' sexuality leave out or condemn her embodied feelings for boys, she is also keenly aware of the pervasiveness of cultural norms and images that demand heterosexuality:

> Every teen magazine you look at is like, guy this, how to get a date, guys, guys, guys, guys, guys. So you're constantly faced with I have to have a boyfriend, I have to have a boyfriend, you know, even if you don't have a boyfriend, just [have] a fling, you know, you just want to kiss a guy or something. I've had that mentality for so long.

In this description of compulsory heterosexuality (Rich 1983), Megan captures the pressure she feels to have a boyfriend and how she experiences the insistence of this demand, which is ironically in conflict with the mandate to say no when with a boy. She is aware of how her psyche has been shaped into a "mentality" requiring any sexual or relational interests to be heterosexual, which does not corroborate how she feels. Compulsory heterosexuality comes between Megan and her feelings, making her vulnerable to a dissociation of her "feelings" under this pressure.

Although she calls herself bisexual, Megan does not describe her sexual feelings for girls very much in this interview. In fact, she becomes so confused that at one point she says she is not sure if her feelings for girls are sexual:

> I mean, I'll see a girl I really really like, you know, because I think she's so beautiful, and I might, I don't know. I'm so confused. . . . But there's, you know, that same mentality as me liking a guy if he's really cute, I'm like, oh my God, you know, he's so cute. If I see a

woman that I like, a girl, it's just like wow, she's so pretty, you know. See I can picture like hugging a girl; I just can't picture the sex, or anything, so, there's something being blocked.

Megan links her confusion with her awareness of the absence of images of lesbian sexuality in the spoken or imagistic lexicon of the culture, counterpointing the pervasiveness of heterosexual imagery all around her. Megan suggests that another reason that she might feel "confused" about her feelings for girls is a lack of sexual experience. Megan knows she is feeling sexual desire when she can identify feelings in her own body—when her "vagina acts up"—and these feelings occur for her in the context of a sexual relationship, when she can feel the other person's desire. Because she has never been in a situation with a girl that would allow this embodied sexual response, she posits a connection between her lack of sexual experience with girls and her confusion.

Yet she has been in a situation where she was "close to" a girl and narrates how she does not let her body speak:

> There was this one girl that I had kinda liked from school, and it was like really weird 'cause she's really popular and everything. And we were sitting next to each other during the movie and, kind of her leg was on my leg and I was like, wow, you know, and that was, I think that's like the first time that I've ever felt like sexual pleasure for a girl. But it's so impossible, I think I just like block it out, I mean, it could never happen. . . . I just can't know what I'm feeling. . . . I probably first mentally just say no, don't feel it, you know, maybe. But I never start to feel, I don't know. It's so confusing. 'Cause finally it's all right for me to like a girl, you know? Before it was like, you know, the two times that I really, that it was just really obvious that I liked them a lot, I had to keep saying no no no no, you know, I just would not let myself. I just hated myself for it, and this year now that I'm talking about it, now I can start to think about it.

Megan both narrates and interprets her dissociation from her embodied sexual feelings and describes the disciplinary stance of her mind over her body in how she "mentally" silences her body by saying "no," preempting her embodied response. Without her body's feelings, her embodied knowledge, Megan feels confused. If she runs interference with her own sexual feelings by silencing her body, making it impossible for her to feel her desire for girls, then she can avoid the problems she knows will inevitably arise if she feels sexual feelings she "can't know"—compulsory heterosexuality and homophobia combine to render this knowledge problematic for her. Fearing rejection, Megan keeps herself from feelings that could lead to disappointment, embarrassment, or frustration, leaving her safe in some ways, yet also psychologically vulnerable.

Echoing dominant cultural constructions of sexual desire, Megan links her desire for girls with feelings of fear: "I've had crushes on some girls . . . you can picture yourself kissing a guy but then if you like a girl a lot and then you picture yourself kissing her, it's just like, I can't, you know, oh my God, no (laughs), you know it's like scary . . . it's society . . . you never would think of, you know, it's natural to kiss a girl." Megan's fear about her desire for girls is different from the fears associated with her desire for boys; whereas being too sexual with boys brings the stigma of being called a "slut," Megan fears "society" and being thought of as "unnatural" when it comes to her feelings for girls. Given what she knows about the heterosexual culture in which she is immersed—the pressure she feels to be interested in "guys" and also given what she knows about homophobia—there is an inherent logic in Megan's confused response to her feelings for girls.

Melissa Doing Desire   Melissa, dressed in a flowing gypsy skirt, white skin pale against the lively colors she wears, is clear about her sexual desire for girls, referring to herself as "lesbian"; she is also a member of a gay/lesbian youth group. In speaking of her desire, Melissa names not only powerful feelings of "being excited" and "wanting," but also more contained feelings; she has "like little crushes on like millions of people and I mean, it's enough for me." Living in a world defined as heterosexual, Melissa finds that "little crushes" have to suffice, given a lack of opportunity for sexual exploration or relationship: "I don't know very many people my age that are even bisexual or lesbians . . . so I pretty much stick to that, like, being hugely infatuated with straight people. Which can get a little touchy at times . . . realistically, I can't like get too ambitious, because that would just not be realistic."

At the forefront of how Melissa describes her desire is her awareness that her sexual feelings make her vulnerable to harm. Whereas the heterosexual girls in this study link their vulnerability to the outcomes of responding to their desire—pregnancy, disease, or getting a bad reputation—Melissa is aware that even the existence of her sexual desire for girls can lead to anger or violence if others know of it: "Well I'm really lucky that like nothing bad has happened or no one's gotten mad at me so far, that, by telling people about them, hasn't gotten me into more trouble than it has, I mean, little things but not like, anything really awful. I think about that and I think it, sometimes, I mean, it could be more dangerous." In response to this threat of violence, Melissa attempts to restrain her own desire: "Whenever I start, I feel like I can't help looking at someone for more than a few seconds, and I keep, and I feel like I have to make myself not stare at them or something." Another strategy is to express her desire covertly by being physically affectionate with other girls, a behavior that is common and acceptable; by keeping her sexuality secret, she can "hang all over [girls] and stuff and they wouldn't even think that I meant anything by it." I am not surprised that Melissa associates feeling sexual desire with frustration; she explains that she "find(s) it safer to just think about the person than what I wanna do, because if I think about that too much and I can't do it, then that'll just frustrate me," leading her to try to intervene in her feelings by "just think[ing] about the person" rather than about the more sexual things she "want(s) to do." In this way, Melissa may jeopardize her ability to know her sexual desire and, in focusing on containing what society has named improper feelings, minimize or exorcise her empowerment to expose that construction as problematic and unjust.

My questions about girls' sexual desire connect deeply with Melissa's own questions about herself; she is in her first intimate relationship, and this interview proves an opportunity to explore and clarify painful twinges of doubt that she had begun to have about it. This relationship began on the initiative of the other girl, with whom she had been very close, rather than out of any sexual feelings on Melissa's part. In fact, Melissa was surprised when her friend had expressed a sexual interest, because she had not "been thinking that" about this close friend. After a history of having to hold back her sexual desire, of feeling "frustrated" and being "hugely infatuated with straight people," rather than having the chance to explore her sexuality, Melissa's response to this potential relationship was that she "should take advantage of this situation." As the interview progresses, Melissa begins to question

whether she is sexually attracted to this girl or "it's just sort of like I just wanted something like this for so long that I'm just taking advantage of the situation."

When I ask Melissa questions about the role of her body in her experience of sexual desire, her confusion at first intensifies:

Is that [your body] part of what feels like it might be missing?

(eight-second pause) It's not, well, sometimes, I mean I don't know how, what I feel all the time. It's hard like, because I mean I'm so confused about this. And it's hard like when it's actually happening to be like, OK, now how do I feel right now? How do I feel right now? How am I gonna feel about this? . . . I don't know, 'cause I don't know what to expect, and I haven't been with anyone else so I don't know what's supposed to happen. So, I mean I'm pretty confused.

The way she speaks about monitoring her body suggests that she is searching for bodily feelings, making me wonder what, if anything, she felt. I discern what she does not say directly: that her body was silent in these sexual experiences. Her hunger for a relationship is palpable: "I really wanted someone really badly, I think, I was getting really sick of being by myself. . . . I would be like God, I really need someone." The desperation in her voice, and the sexual frustration she describes, suggest that her "want" and "need" are distinctly sexual as well as relational.

One reason that Melissa seems to be confused is that she felt a strong desire to be "mothered," her own mother having died last year. In trying to distinguish her different desires in this interview, Melissa began to distinguish erotic feelings from another kind of wanting she also experienced: she said that "it's more of like but I kind of feel like it's really more of like a maternal thing, that I really want her to take care of me and I just wanna touch someone and I just really like the feeling of just how I mean I like, when I'm with her and touching her and stuff. A lot, but it's not necessarily a sexual thing at this point." In contrast to her feelings for her girlfriend, Melissa describes feeling sexually attracted to another girl. In so doing, Melissa clarifies what is missing in these first sexual adventures, enabling her to know what had bothered her about her relationship with her girlfriend:

I don't really think I'm getting that much pleasure, from her, it's just, I mean it's almost like I'm getting experience, and I'm sort of having fun, it's not even that exciting, and that's why I think I don't really like her . . . because my friend asked me this the other day, well, I mean does it get, I mean when you're with her does it get really, I don't remember the word she used, but just really, like what was the word she used? But I guess she meant just like, exciting [laughing]. But it doesn't, to me. It's weird, because I can't really say that, I mean I can't think of like a time when I was really excited and it was like really, sexual pleasure, for me, because I don't think it's really like that. I mean not that I think that this isn't good because, I don't know, I mean, I like it, but I mean I think I have to, sort of realize that I'm not that much attracted to her, personally.

Wanting both a relationship and sexual pleasure, a chance to explore closeness and her sexual curiosity, and discovering that this relationship leaves out her sexual desire, Melissa laments her silent body: "I sort of expect or hope or whatever that there would be some kind of more excited feeling just from feeling sexually stimulated or whatever. I would hope that there would be more of a feeling than I've gotten so far." Knowing consciously what she "knows" about the absence of her sexual feelings in this relationship has left her with a relational conflict of large proportions for her: "I'm not that attracted to her and I don't know if I should tell her that. Or if I should just kind of pretend I am and try to . . . anyway." I ask her how she would go about doing that—pretending that she is. She replies, "I don't think I could pretend it for too long." Not being able to "pretend" to have feelings that she knows she wants as part of an intimate relationship, Melissa faces a dilemma of desire that may leave her feeling isolated and lonely or even fraudulent.

ADOLESCENT GIRLS' SEXUAL DESIRE AND THE POSSIBILITIES OF EMPOWERMENT

All of the girls in this study who said they felt sexual desire expressed conflict when describing their responses to their sexual feelings—conflict between their embodied sexual feelings and their perceptions of how those feelings are, in one way or another, anathema or problematic within the social and relational contexts of their lives. Their experiences of sexual desire are strong and pleasurable, yet they speak very often not of the power of desire but of how their desire may get them into trouble. These girls are beginning to voice the internalized oppression of their women's bodies; they knew and spoke about, in explicit or more indirect ways, the pressure they felt to silence their desire, to dissociate from those bodies in which they inescapably live. Larger societal forces of social control in the form of compulsory heterosexuality (Rich 1983), the policing of girls' bodies through school codes (Lesko 1988), and media images play a clear part in forcing this silence and dissociation. Specific relational dynamics, such as concern about a reputation that can easily be besmirched by other girls and by boys, fear of male violence in intimate relationships, and fear of violent repercussion of violating norms of heterosexuality are also audible in these girls' voices.

To be able to know their sexual feelings, to listen when their bodies speak about themselves and about their relationships, might enable these and other girls to identify and know more clearly the sources of oppression that press on their full personhood and their capacity for knowledge, joy, and connection. Living in the margins of a heterosexual society, the bisexual and lesbian girls voice an awareness of these forces as formative of the experiences of their bodies and relationships; the heterosexual girls are less clear and less critical about the ways that dominant constructions of their sexuality impinge on their embodied and relational worlds. Even when they are aware that societal ambivalence and fears are being played out on their minds and bodies, they do not speak of a need for collective action, or even the possibility of engaging in such activities. More often, they speak of the danger of speaking about desire at all. By dousing desire with fear and confusion, or simple, "uncomplicated" denial, silence, and dissociation, the girls in this study make individual psychological moves whereby they distance or disconnect themselves from discomfort and danger. Although disciplining their bodies and curbing their desire are a very logical and understandable way to stay physically, socially, and emotionally safe, they also heighten the chance that girls and women may lose track of the fact that an inequitable social system, and not a necessary situation, renders women's sexual desire a source of danger rather than one of pleasure and power in their lives. In "not knowing" desire, girls and women are at risk for not knowing that there is nothing wrong with having sexual feelings and responding to them in ways that bring joy and agency.

Virtually every girl in the larger study told me that no woman had ever talked to her about sexual desire and pleasure "like this"—in depth, listening to her speak about her own experiences, responding when she asked questions about how to masturbate, how to have cunnilingus, what sex is like after marriage. In the words of Rubin: "The ethos of privacy and silence about our personal sexual experience makes it easy to rationalize the refusal to speak [to adolescents]" (1990, 83; Segal 1993). Thompson (1990) found that daughters of women who had talked with them about pleasure and desire told narratives about first intercourse that were informed by pleasure and agency. The recurrent strategy the girls in my study describe of keeping their desire under wraps as a way to protect themselves also keeps girls out of authentic relationships with other girls and women. It is within these relationships that the empowerment of women can develop and be nurtured through shared experiences of both oppression and power, in which collectively articulated critiques are carved out and voiced. Such knowledge of how a patriarchal society systematically keeps girls and women from their own desire can instigate demand and agency for social change. By not talking about sexual desire with each other or with women, a source for empowerment is lost. There is a symbiotic interplay between desire and empowerment: to be empowered to desire one needs a critical perspective, and that critical perspective will be extended and sustained through knowing and experiencing the possibilities of desire and healthy embodied living. Each of these girls illustrates the phenomenon observed in the larger study—the difficulty for girls in having or sustaining a critical perspective on the culture's silencing of their sexual desire. They are denied full access to the power of their own desire and to structural supports for that access.

Common threads of fear and joy, pleasure and danger, weave through the narratives about sexual desire in this study, exemplified by the three portraits. Girls have the right to be informed that gaining pleasure and a strong sense of self and power through their bodies does not make them bad or unworthy. The experiences of these and other adolescent girls illustrate why girls deserve to be educated about their sexual desire. Thompson concludes that "to take possession of sexuality in the wake of the anti-erotic sexist socialization that remains the majority experience, most teenage girls need an erotic education" (1990, 406). Girls need to be educated about the duality of their sexuality, to have safe contexts in which they can explore both danger and desire (Fine 1988), and to consider why their desire is so dangerous and how

they can become active participants in their own redemption. Girls can be empowered to know and act on their own desire, a different educational direction than the simplistic strategies for avoiding boys' desire that they are offered. The "just say no" curriculum obscures the larger social inequities being played out on girls' bodies in heterosexual relationships and is not relevant for girls who feel sexual feelings for girls. Even adults who are willing or able to acknowledge that girls experience sexual feelings worry that knowing about their own sexual desire will place girls in danger (Segal 1993). But keeping girls in the dark about their power to choose based on their own feelings fails to keep them any safer from these dangers. Girls who trust their minds and bodies may experience a stronger sense of self, entitlement, and empowerment that could enhance their ability to make safe decisions. One approach to educating girls is for women to speak to them about the vicissitudes of sexual desire—which means that women must let themselves speak and know their own sexual feelings, as well as the pleasures and dangers associated with women's sexuality and the solutions that we have wrought to the dilemma of desire: how to balance the realities of pleasure and danger in women's sexuality.

Asking these girls to speak about sexual desire, and listening and responding to their answers and also to their questions, proved to be an effective way to interrupt the standard "dire consequences" discourse adults usually employ when speaking at all to girls about their sexuality. Knowing and speaking about the ways in which their sexuality continues to be unfairly constrained may interrupt the appearance of social equity that many adolescent girls (especially white, middle-class young women) naively and trustingly believe, thus leading them to reject feminism as unnecessary and mean-spirited and not relevant to their lives. As we know from the consciousness-raising activities that characterized the initial years of second-wave feminism, listening to the words of other girls and women can make it possible for girls to know and voice their experiences, their justified confusion and fears, their curiosities. Through such relationships, we help ourselves and each other to live in our different female bodies with an awareness of danger, but also with a desire to feel the power of the erotic, to fine-tune our bodies and our psyches to what Audre Lorde has called the "yes within ourselves" (Lorde 1984, 54).

NOTES

1. The bisexual girl and the lesbian girl were members of a gay/lesbian youth group and identify themselves using these categories. As is typical for members of privileged groups for whom membership is a given, the girls who feel sexual desire for boys and not for girls (about which they were asked explicitly) do not use the term "heterosexual" to describe themselves. Although I am aware of the debate surrounding the use of these categories and labels to delimit women's (and men's) experience, because my interpretive practice is informed by the ways society makes meaning of girls' sexuality, the categories that float in the culture as ways of describing the girls are relevant to my analysis. In addition, the bisexual and lesbian girls in this study are deeply aware of compulsory heterosexuality and its impact on their lives.

2. Of the thirty girls in this sample, twenty-seven speak of a desire for boys and not for girls. This pattern was ascertained by who appeared in their desire narratives and also by their response to direct questions about sexual feelings for girls, designed explicitly to interrupt the hegemony of heterosexuality. Two of the thirty girls described sexual desire for both boys and girls and one girl described sexual desire for girls and not for boys.

3. Parts of this analysis appear in Tolman (1994).

REFERENCES

Brown, L. 1991. Telling a girl's life: Self authorization as a form of resistance. In *Women, Girls and Psychotherapy: Reframing Resistance,* ed. C. Gilligan, A. Rogers, and D. Tolman. New York: Haworth.

Brown, L., E. Debold, M. Tappan, and C. Gilligan. 1991. Reading narratives of conflict for self and moral voice: A relational method. In *Handbook of Moral Behavior and Development: Theory, Research, and Application,* ed. W. Kurtines and J. Gewirtz. Hillsdale, NJ: Lawrence Erlbaum.

Brown, L., and C. Gilligan. 1992. *Meeting at the Crossroads: Women's Psychology and Girls' Development.* Cambridge, MA: Harvard University Press.

Fine, Michelle. 1988. Sexuality, schooling and adolescent females: The missing discourse of desire. *Harvard Educational Review* 58:29–53.

Friend, Richard. 1993. Choices, not closets. In *Beyond Silenced Voices,* ed. M. Fine and L. Weis. New York: State University of New York Press.

Gilligan, Carol. 1989. Teaching Shakespeare's sister. In *Making Connections: The Relational World of Adolescent Girls at Emma Willard School,* ed. C. Gilligan, N. Lyons, and T. Hamner. Cambridge, MA: Harvard University Press.

———. 1990. Joining the resistance: Psychology, politics, girls and women. *Michigan Quarterly Review* 29:501–36.

Lees, Susan. 1986. *Losing Out: Sexuality and Adolescent Girls.* London: Hutchinson.

Lesko, Nancy. 1988. The curriculum of the body: Lessons from a Catholic high school. In *Becoming Feminine: The Politics of Popular Culture,* ed. L. Roman. Philadelphia: Falmer.

Lorde, Audre. 1984. The uses of the erotic as power. In *Sister Outsider: Essays and Speeches.* Freedom, CA: Crossing Press.

Rich, Adrienne. 1983. Compulsory heterosexuality and lesbian existence. In *Powers of Desire: The Politics of Sexuality,* ed. A. Snitow, C. Stansell, and S. Thompson. New York: Monthly Review Press.

Rubin, Lillian. 1990. *Erotic Wars: What Happened to the Sexual Revolution?* New York: HarperCollins.

Segal, Lynne. 1993. Introduction. In *Sex Exposed: Sexuality and the Pornography Debate,* ed. L. Segal and M. McIntosh. New Brunswick, NJ: Rutgers University Press.

Spillers, Hortense. 1984. Interstices: A small drama of words. In *Pleasure and Danger: Exploring Female Sexuality,* ed. C. Vance. Boston: Routledge and Kegan Paul.

Thompson, Sharon. 1984. Search for tomorrow: On feminism and the reconstruction of teen romance. In *Pleasure and Danger: Exploring Female Sexuality,* ed. C. Vance. Boston: Routledge and Kegan Paul.

———. 1990. Putting a big thing in a little hole: Teenage girls' accounts of sexual initiation. *Journal of Sex Research* 27:341–61.

Tolman, Deborah L. 1991. Adolescent girls, women and sexuality: Discerning dilemmas of desire. *Women, Girls, and Psychotherapy: Reframing Resistance,* ed. C. Gilligan, A. Rogers, and D. Tolman. New York: Haworth.

———. 1992. Voicing the body: A psychological study of adolescent girls' sexual desire. Unpublished dissertation, Harvard University.

———. 1994. Daring to desire: Culture and the bodies of adolescent girls. In *Sexual Cultures: Adolescents, Communities and the Construction of Identity,* ed. J. Irvine. Philadelphia: Temple University Press.

Tolman, Deborah, and Elizabeth Debold. 1993. Conflicts of body and image: Female adolescents, desire, and the no-body. In *Feminist Treatment and Therapy of Eating Disorders,* ed. M. Katzman, P. Failon, and S. Wooley. New York: Guilford.

Trading on Heterosexuality: College Women's Gender Strategies and Homophobia

Scholars note that homophobia plays a central role in the construction of masculinities (Connell 1987; Corbett 2001; Kimmel 2001; Pascoe 2005). Indeed, as Corbett (2001) notes, the term *faggot* stands in for more than sexual insult: It connotes a failure to be fully masculine. "Real" men repudiate the feminine or that which they perceive to be weak, powerless, and inconsequential (Kimmel 2001). The hegemonic form of masculinity thus supports men's dominance over women and other men in subordinated positions because of race, class, or sexuality (Connell 1995). The literature on masculinities suggests that homophobia occurs when men try to perform hegemonic masculinity. By verbally or physically attacking men whom they perceive as not masculine, men may reassert their own manhood (Corbett 2001; Kimmel 2001; Pascoe 2005). When relying solely on this conceptualization, homophobia takes on gendered characteristics, underscoring a particular masculine manifestation of antihomosexual behaviors as quintessentially homophobic.

Past research seems to support the association of homophobia with men: For instance, studies often find that women have more positive attitudes toward homosexuality (Loftus 2001). Giddens (1992, 28) has even predicted that women will be the vanguard in creating a space for "the flourishing of homosexuality." Yet, it is possible that women's homophobia remains obscured when conceptualizing homophobia as a singular phenomenon. As Stein (2005) suggests, homophobia can take many forms and operate through multiple mechanisms. Homophobia may also be central to the development of certain feminine selves but not in the same way as for masculine selves. Because women and men are in different positions with regard to power, women's homophobia may support gendered identities that are most successful in garnering men's approval (Rich 1980). Some women may distance themselves from others who

do not perform the erotic selves that they perceive as valued by men. These women may exhibit homophobia to maintain the believability of their traditionally feminine identities.

In this article, I draw on ethnographic and interview data from a women's floor of a residence hall on a public university campus to suggest that heterosexual women may display homophobia against lesbians as they negotiate status in a gender-inegalitarian erotic market. First, I describe the Greek party scene on this campus, the erotic hierarchy linked to it, and lesbians' low ranking within this hierarchy. I then explain that women who were active partiers excluded lesbians from social interactions and spaces while critical partiers and nonpartiers were more inclusive. Finally, I describe how heterosexual women conceptualized the same-sex eroticism that they used to garner men's attention and the consequences that this had for lesbians. I conclude by discussing how gender inequality and heteronormitivity combine to create homophobia among women.

GENDER STRATEGIES: "TRADING ON" HETEROSEXUALITY

Scholars have used Swidler's (1986) concept of "strategies of action" to show how women create "gender strategies" that help them navigate inegalitarian gender conditions. A gender strategy is a course of action that attempts to solve a problem using the cultural conceptions of gender available to the individual (Handler 1995; Hochschild 1989). Gender strategies are thus both cognitive and behavioral. They are not, however, always reflexive. In interaction, decisions and actions often occur quickly and nonreflexively. Women may fall into well-established patterns of behavior that pull from available cultural definitions of femininity and masculinity. Consequently, they can engage in gender strategies without awareness of the gendered aspects of their actions (P. Y. Martin 2003).

Gender strategies involve the use of particular gender presentations over others. These presentations do not reflect preexisting internal qualities but become engrained in people's bodies through the constant repetition of particular movements, acts, and thoughts (Butler 1990; K. A. Martin 1998). Premised on gender difference, heterosexuality is one of the key mechanisms through which women and men learn to embody gender. Given women's subordinate position, much of what makes a woman traditionally feminine is her ability and desire to attract a man (Bartky 1990). Women learn to produce feminine bodies and to have desires for men that conform to heterosexual imperatives. Many of the roles from which they gain their identities—such as girlfriend, wife, and mother—further emphasize the centrality of heterosexuality to gender identity (Jackson 1996).

Depending on the rules governing a particular social field, some gender presentations will garner more rewards than others will (McCall 1992). As Connell (1995) notes, while political, cultural, and economic practices benefit hegemonic masculinity, they but subordinate masculinities that eschew heteronormativity. Many of these same practices similarly disadvantage women. However, femininities that conform to heteronormative ideals of feminine charm and beauty can operate as a form of embodied cultural capital (McCall 1992).[1] One strategy that women may use to deal with gender inequalities is to "trade on" their embodied capital (Chen 1999). That is, they may rely on their ability to signal heterosexuality to acquire better treatment and more status than other women (Butler 1990; McCall 1992; Rich 1980; Schwalbe et al. 2000). Homophobia can result when women who have embodied capital disassociate themselves from those who do not. Any benefits that women may accrue through homophobia come at a cost: They ultimately reinforce the gendered inequalities that made such a gender strategy necessary (Schwalbe et al. 2000).

Gendered-embodied capital is not equally available to all individuals: Instead, material resources, the physicality of bodies, and prior gender performances all restrict the femininities/masculinities that individuals can enact. Audiences hold people accountable for the types of gender performances that they expect from particular bodies in particular social positions (Bettie 2005). Gender identities thus reference locations within

social hierarchies. Hegemonic masculinity, for example, relies not only on heterosexuality but also on race and class statuses (Chen 1999). Similarly, women's embodied capital privileges whiteness and requires classed knowledge and resources (Bettie 2005; Collins 1990). Therefore, heterosexual women in socially dominant race and class positions may have greater access to the dividends of hegemonic masculinity as they are most likely to embody cultural notions of an "ideal" femininity.

EROTIC MARKETS AND HETEROSEXUAL PRIVILEGE

A ubiquitous element of youth cultures, erotic markets are expanding to include larger segments of the population for longer periods of their lives. Erotic markets are public sexualized scenes in which individuals present erotic selves that are subject to the judgments and reactions of others (Collins 2004). These markets require a mass of individuals who share similar assumptions about the kinds of sexual activity that are open for negotiation and how to interpret the sexual activity that does occur.

Many erotic markets operate using heteronormative cultural logics. This does not mean that all people within these scenes are heterosexual or that all erotic behaviors in this scene occur between women and men; rather, the available cultural understandings in heterosexual erotic markets reflect heteronormative ideas about sexuality, what "sex" is, and for whom it is performed. Because heterosexuality presumes gender difference, these meanings also code "real" sex as that which is penetrative or initiated by men and position women as desired objects rather than desiring subjects (Armstrong 1995; Jackson 1996). As a result, same-sex eroticism between conventionally feminine women becomes a performance for men, one that inevitably ends in heterosexual sex (Jenefsky and Miller 1998).

Within erotic markets, hierarchical rankings sort individuals by both successful participation *and* perceived desirability to potential partners. These rankings often transfer into other social relationships, marking status even when individuals are outside of erotic markets. Rankings are determined, in part, through social activities that are "organized by flirtation and sexual carousing" (Collins 2004, 253). Individuals who are not skilled, interested, or successful at engaging in these activities face exclusion from this avenue to status and the social networks of those who are high status. They must also perform gender in ways that others recognize as legitimate and desirable. For women within heterosexual erotic markets, this means performing a conventionally feminine identity.

Heterosexual relations are often organized in ways that benefit men (Jackson 1996). Past research has documented the gender imbalance in power, resources, and status that operates in erotic markets on college campuses—particularly those in which Greek organizations are present (Armstrong, Hamilton, and Sweeney 2006; Boswell and Spade 1996; Handler 1995; Holland and Eisenhart 1990; Martin and Hummer 1989; Stombler and Martin 1995). In these situations, women can use heterosexual performances to access benefits through their relations with men (Schwalbe et al. 2000). Many women who identify as heterosexual are privileged in heterosexual erotic markets in ways that lesbians are not and invest in maintaining their privilege (Rich 1980). These investments may not be fully conscious—women's participation in the heterosexual erotic system can preclude the kind of social contact with lesbians that fosters acceptance.

SOCIAL DISTANCE: ASSESSING HOMOPHOBIA AMONG WOMEN

Social distance is the degree of closeness that people are willing to tolerate in their interactions with a stigmatized group (Gentry 1987). Goffman's (1963) work on stigma suggests that people often avoid encounters with stigmatized individuals because of interactional ambiguities and a fear of contamination by association. Inserting social distance is one way to mitigate these perceived costs of engaging in social interaction with "different" individuals (Milner 2004).

Particularly among women, homophobia often appears as a form of social distance.[2] Socialized into "niceness," women may not always participate in the direct, aggressive, and publicly visible behaviors that many equate with homophobia among men (Gilligan 1982; K. A. Martin 2003). Research on adolescents suggests that women often use exclusionary projects—such as the maintenance of social distance—to mark the difference between themselves and "others" (Eder 1985; Merten 1997). In college, lesbians pose unique interactional threats to heterosexual women if they fail to engage in the appropriate erotic activities or present traditionally gendered selves in heterosexual erotic markets. Heterosexual women may also feel that lesbians are sexualizing the previously "safe" (i.e., hetero-

sexual) backstage area of the residence hall floor. By maintaining social distance from lesbians, many heterosexual women assuage their fears of status contamination and quell anxieties about their own sexuality.

METHOD AND DATA

Data for this study are from ethnographic observation, individual, and group interviews conducted at a large midwestern research university as part of a project on collegiate life.[3] One goal of the project is to understand how dominant groups on campus maintain and reproduce environments in which they are privileged. For example, all 43 of the women in this study were white. In addition, most came from middle- to upper-class families, identified as heterosexual, and had traditionally feminine gender presentations. Only two identified as lesbian, six were from working-class families, one was born outside of the United States, and another was isolated for her noncompliance with norms of appearance. Therefore, most embodied a femininity that the prevailing erotic market of the campus rewarded—if they chose to participate.

Most of the data were collected as part of an ethnography conducted throughout the 2004–2005 academic year on a women's floor in a mixed-gender residence hall that was identified by students and staff as a "party dorm." The title does not refer to partying within the residence hall itself; instead, students are attracted to this residence hall because it offers the most direct route into the dominant party scene on campus. Students from all residence halls gather outside of this and other party dorms en route to parties, making a party dorm a good site to study the dominant party culture on campus. Roughly one-third of incoming students are housed in party dorms; these residence halls feed the greatest number of students into the Greek system (which includes about 20 percent of students). While students cannot choose to live in party dorms, they can request certain areas of the campus. Some selectivity does occur, as many students pick particular areas because of the party dorms within them. Yet, even party dorms include students who are at least initially less party oriented.

A research team including one faculty member, five graduate students, and three undergraduates conducted the ethnography; five team members identified as heterosexual women and one as a gay man. Our team occupied a room on the floor we were observing. During the first semester, at least one member of the research team was there three to four weekday afternoons and evenings and one to two weekend afternoons and evenings per week. In the second semester, I was there two weekday evenings and one weekend evening weekly. Members of the team took notes about each interaction after the observation periods were completed. Interviews with floor residents occurred throughout the academic year and lasted between 1.5 to 2.5 hours. After each interview, we took notes. I conducted the majority of interviews but also relied on data collected by others. I used Atlas Ti to analyze interview transcripts and all notes.

Researchers formed different types of relationships with women based on their age, position in the university, and shared interests and/or tastes. As I identify as white, upper-middle-class, and heterosexual and have a fairly traditional gender presentation, I was able to connect with most women on the floor. Yet, this did not hinder me in forming close relationships with the out lesbians on the floor or several of the working-class women. As women on the floor generally associated with those of similar status, they often did not realize that individual researchers also knew others on the floor. This allowed me to move among different social groups with ease. Researchers only brought up sensitive topics in interview settings. However, discussions about issues such as sexuality did occur spontaneously. Our relationships with respondents did not change perceptibly after completing interviews or observing these sensitive discussions, perhaps because we did not reveal our own political and social attitudes.

Of the 53 women in the hall, we interviewed 43. This article focuses on the 43 residents with whom we completed interviews. All of these women were first-or second-year students. As older students—particularly seniors—may age out of the party culture, this study is most representative of processes occurring in the early years of college. Although all women on the floor were part of the ethnography, interview data allowed me to confirm social distance to lesbians. During interviews, women referred to their actual contact with lesbians on campus, what—if anything—they did to maintain social distance, and their preferred level of contact. In no case did women present attitudes that did not match observed behaviors toward out lesbians on the hall. Based on observations, the 11 women who are not included in the article are representative of other women in the hall in terms of their orientation to partying and fall into levels of social distance in proportions similar to the rest of the hall.[4]

I accepted the sexual orientation that women claimed across multiple data points—in interviews, surveys that we administered, and interactions with friends or the research team. The women who identified as heterosexual did not indicate otherwise across any of these settings in the course of an entire academic year. Recognizing that sexual identity may be concealed, is fluid, and may vary across multiple dimensions (i.e., political, social, sexual, etc.), it is entirely plausible that some of the heterosexual women in this study may privately see themselves as bisexual or lesbian or acknowledge this in different social contexts or during later periods of their lives. I am limited to the reported self-understandings of sexual identity that were in play during the ethnography. Regardless of their self-understandings in other aspects of their lives, the women who claimed public heterosexual identities could profit in keeping social distance from out lesbians. As I discuss later, many of them did simultaneously imitate same-sex erotic practices, but they generally did so *only with an audience of men*.

I also include data from a group interview with lesbian and bisexual women on campus conducted in spring 2004 to examine the impact of heterosexual women's same-sex eroticism on other women's experiences of social space on campus. This group interview was obtained through student organizations on campus and covered a variety of topics including sexuality, relationships, partying, and the Greek scene. Although they are marginalized, gay, lesbian, bisexual, and transgendered students do have resources geared toward recognizing their needs; for instance, they have access to alternative housing, support groups, discussion forums, rights-oriented organizations, and a few social venues. Yet, these resources and institutional policies against discrimination by sexual orientation do little to challenge the heterosexual social world on campus, and, for first-year students who are placed in "party dorms," knowledge of them may be limited.

THE EROTIC HIERARCHY OF THE GREEK PARTY SYSTEM

Although only one of the many social "games" on campus, the Greek party scene is the largest and most well known among students. Many arrive on campus anticipating participation in the drunken social world portrayed by MTV and other youth media as "college"; in fact, students often head off to party before they attend their first college class or unpack their possessions. Erotic interactions between men and women play a central part in this world.

The Greek Party Scene

The Greek party scene is a sexualized social arena that is temporally and spatially specific. It occurs in the evenings in fraternities and in popular bars known for their laxness in enforcing laws against underage drinking. All of these fraternities are effectively white organizations; the few Black and multicultural Greek organizations do not have on-campus houses that can accommodate large parties. Although fraternity houses host parties with varying themes, they all revolve around a predictable "party routine" in which women are expected to drink, flirt, and socialize (Armstrong et al. 2006). Bars often serve as secondary sites for those who party at fraternities. Thus, the party scene achieves a level of cohesiveness. As one respondent put it, regardless of where you are, "it's the same party, exactly the same frat, the same people." Fraternities have a monopoly on this scene because they provide "free" alcohol to underaged women who otherwise might not be able to obtain it. This resource, combined with little university policing and private ownership of communal spaces, allows them to dictate almost every aspect of the parties they hold (Armstrong et al. 2006).

For example, many fraternities operated a one-way transport system in front of the "party dorm" that we observed. Starting the week before school began, fraternity men waited in the latest sport utility vehicles to drive women to their parties. First-year women clustered in this area and had little control over their destinations. Fraternity men also dictated party themes, most pressuring women to arrive scantily clad. Women described attending parties such as "Golf Pro/Tennis Ho," "Trophy Wife and James Bond Husband," "Playboy Mansion," and "CEO/Secretary Ho." In addition, fraternities screened admission into their parties. One evening I observed a fraternity member selecting what appeared to be the most attractive and scantily clad women to receive the first ride; sometimes he even split up friendship groups. Women also reported that fraternity men rejected non-Greek men to create a favorable gender ratio. Finally, fraternity men determined the flow of guests and alcohol in their houses. Several women described men luring them into private spaces to receive alcohol. One noted that "Every guy [asks] you wanna drink, you wanna, oh, come see

this . . . oh, let's close this, and closes the door, and I just get so annoyed."[5]

For women, participation in this scene was not contingent on Greek status. Greek women did frequent the scene more heavily—often partying a few weeknights along with the weekend evenings; however, nearly all (49 out of 53) of the residents on the hall attended at least one fraternity party before they had the chance to join sororities. Although only 20 women on the floor became "Greek," most women who started by participating in this scene continued to do so. Many participated because they perceived few other options; on several occasions, women explained that they had "nothing else to do but drink." As one resident complained, the social scene is "so concentrated on the fraternities and fraternity-type partying."

Choosing not to participate also came at a cost. Several nonpartying women lived near each other in an area of the hall that the most social women labeled "the Dark Side." This phrase operated as a code word for "losers" and "antisocial" people. Although the women who coined the phrase hid its meaning, women on "the Dark Side" eventually found out why others called them by this name. These women and others who did not invest heavily in the party scene reported feeling lonely and left out. As one explained, "I thought people would be more open, and college was going to be a great place where I have all these friends, and I'm just really making some acquaintances and no friendships yet." Because of the dominant party culture of the hall, nonpartying women typically remained unaware of others like them.

Women's Erotic Status

The party scene privileged individuals who actively participated in the erotic market. Because fraternity men controlled important party resources, one had to attract their attention to be included in the party. A woman explained, "Well, I flirt with guys. . . . I just pretty much do that so we can go play flippy cup (a drinking game) or get free beer." The lesbians on the hall found this exchange to be intolerable. One described a party she attended as follows:

> I was uncomfortable . . . in the sense that all of the girls kind of have to compete with each other to get the alcohol, and it just screams so much like prostitution to me. You know, even if they're not literally having sex with the guys, it's just like they're . . . selling their flirtiness for beer or something, and that's just so not me.

She felt that fraternity men treated women who were unwilling to "trade on" their erotic interest as lower status and less deserving of alcohol. For this reason, she no longer attended Greek parties. The other lesbian on the hall never attempted to attend, stating, "I will never go. I don't want to go. It's not my scene at all."

Most heterosexual women who partied found men's erotic attention both important and rewarding. One woman noted that the best thing about "kissing guys" at parties was not physical pleasure but "know[ing] that a guy's attracted to you and is willing to kiss you. It's kinda . . . like a game to play just to see." Women even felt that not receiving this attention could be damaging to one's self-esteem. A woman with a long-term boyfriend described the costs of not seeking men's approval: "I was like the little conservative, country bumpkin in my outfit. I was like, no, I'm not going to get any of the attention. They're not going to waste their time with me. . . . You need to flirt; that's good for your confidence." Failing to signal interest in obtaining men's approval could also result in embarrassment. Another woman said that she was mortified when she unknowingly showed up at the "CEO/ Secretary Ho" party dressed as an actual secretary wearing a long-sleeved blouse and a knee-length skirt. When she walked in the door, a fraternity member flashed her a sarcastic thumbs-up, telling her, "Nice outfit."

The importance that most women placed on men's erotic interest translated into a clear hierarchy among them. At the top of this hierarchy stood "the blonde." By definition, all "blonde" women were white, having tan skin and light-colored hair. They were also thin, trendy, and sociable. Women felt that men found all of these traits to be desirable. One woman explained that being "blonde" was when "all the guys are like, 'Oh my god they are so hot.'" The seemingly organic nature of the "blonde" appearance belayed the extensive bodily work that went into managing a "blonde" body. For example, navigating the line between "good" and "bad" tan (looking "orange," as the women put it) involved knowing how to tan and when to stop. Many women struggled to maintain slender physiques while engaged in a party lifestyle that involved drinking a lot of beer and eating late-night pizza. Money was also essential; women often used colored contacts, hair straighteners, and salon hair coloring to appear more "blonde."

"Blondeness" also implied erotic interest in and appeal to heterosexual men. Part of indicating their interest in men involved actively working to avoid signaling homosexuality. For example, a woman told me about having a rainbow-colored arm cast in junior high, noting that she would never get one now as people might think that she was a lesbian. These women often assumed that others who did not exhibit a high-status gender presentation were lesbians. During a discussion in a dorm room one evening, several of them recoiled with disgust at a picture of tennis star Serena Williams, noting that her extremely defined muscles made her look "mannish" and like a lesbian. Because sexual orientation is not necessarily visually apparent, they equated gender conformity with sexual conformity. Most heterosexual women believed that this method could detect lesbians, whom they assumed to be "boyish." Both out lesbians on the floor dressed "sportier" than other women (often in sweatpants or T-shirts and rarely in makeup—even at night). After the women came out as lesbians, others insisted that they already had guessed based on their appearance. As one noted, "Definitely you can tell . . . there are people that have the stereotype. . . . They've got a way about them that they're probably gay."

Although heterosexual women generally did not believe that lesbians could be "hot," several did reevaluate their ranking of lesbians based on this possibility. When I asked one woman how she would feel about having a "hot" lesbian roommate, she explained,

> If my roommate was a lesbian and she was more feminine, I think I would be more comfortable. . . . [If she was] like me—she looked girly—it wouldn't matter if she liked guys or girls. But if it was someone that was really boyish, I think it would be hard for me to feel comfortable.

As Gamson (1998) noted of talk show audiences, heterosexual women on the hall often found the idea of lesbians who conformed to gender norms less problematic than those who did not. Regardless of her actual availability to men, the "hot lesbian" would at least look available.

However, if she were unwilling to enter the party scene and "sell her flirtiness for beer," a hot lesbian—like any other woman—would find her access to erotic status severely limited. The lesbians on the floor were thus doubly disadvantaged; first, by their refusal to participate in the erotic market and then by their choice not to perform "blondeness."

MAPPING SOCIAL DISTANCE FROM LESBIANS

Women on the floor had varied relationships to the Greek party scene. Most were highly invested in this scene, but a number were critical or opted out of the party scene altogether. As illustrated by Figure 1, women also differed in their willingness to interact, establish relationships, and share personal space with lesbians. All of the women who were most involved in the party scene fell into the two outer rings of social distance, while those who invested less required less social distance from lesbians.

Active Partiers

I defined active partiers as those women who (a) reported attending a fraternity party at least once a week for the majority of the academic year and (b) gen-

erally expressed satisfaction with this scene. Thirty women met these criteria; 19 of them joined sororities. I spent hours talking to women in this group as they prepared hair, makeup, and outfits for "going out." For most of them, partying was one of the major activities of college life. One avid partier explained, "I guess the only things I feel like I do here are study and party. My life is split between those things." Many emphasized the thrill of dressing "all sexy" for these parties. As a woman noted of a Playboy mansion party, "It's an excuse for everyone to just like dress in the sluttiest little thing that they can pull off without looking like complete trash. It was just so fun because you have an excuse to just like let loose, and there were so many people there." Along with the erotic energy of this scene, they also took pleasure in drinking. One woman exclaimed, "I almost feel getting drunk is like—I'm so happy! I guess that's what we mostly do." These women also felt that partying was a ubiquitous part of campus

FIGURE I   LEVELS OF SOCIAL DISTANCE FROM HOMOSEXUALITY

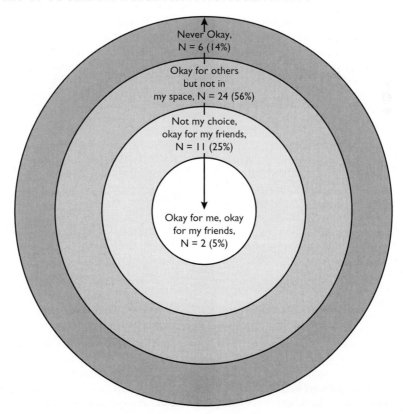

Never Okay, N = 6 (14%)

Okay for others but not in my space, N = 24 (56%)

Not my choice, okay for my friends, N = 11 (25%)

Okay for me, okay for my friends, N = 2 (5%)

life ("There's always a party going on here, you know?") in which almost every student was perceived to participate ("That's what practically everybody is doing on the weekends").

Among active partiers, there was a distinction between women who felt that homosexuality was "never okay" and those who felt that homosexuality was "okay for others but not in my space." For the six heterosexual women in the "never okay" category, religious beliefs were the guiding principle shaping their desired level of social distance from gays and lesbians. All of these women grew up in religious communities or rural towns. They saw homosexuality as a clear-cut moral issue; it was always wrong for both men and women. As two roommates explained:

R1: We've been sheltered around diversity.... Everybody's a farmer, everybody's the same.

R2: Hardly [any] gays or anything, so we're not used to all this gay pride stuff, and it's like, What are they doing? Read the Bible.

None, however, were part of Christian groups on campus; in fact, these groups did not approve of participation in the sexualized and wild party scene. Instead, women in the "never okay" category used religious objections that reflected the cultural logics of their homogeneous hometown communities rather than intense personal involvement with organized religion.

These women were frank in interviews and with peers about their beliefs, often saying homosexuality physically disgusted them. They struggled with what they felt to be an offensive new environment in which different values prevailed. For example, one night a frustrated woman told me and several others how tired she was of looking at "that" (the GLBT—Gay, Lesbian, Bisexual, and Transgendered—Rainbow week bulletin board just outside her door). She said vehemently, "I just want to take a big black marker and write "straighten up . . . straighten up your future.""

Others generally tolerated these women's verbal denouncements of homosexuality, labeling them as ignorant or provincial only during interviews. However, one of these women faced exclusion on the floor because she rejected her assigned lesbian roommate in such a negative fashion. This woman slandered her lesbian roommate as a "dyke" to others on the floor, engaged in loud verbal assaults on her, and made a show of changing her clothing elsewhere. Eventually the lesbian roommate chose to move out, and a friend with a similar conservative religious background moved in. Many floor residents ostracized this woman and her new roommate. She reported, "A lot of people don't say hi, don't smile, don't acknowledge us because they think I am this bad person."

Gamson (1998) notes that in talk shows, a similar process often occurs; audiences will isolate individuals with the most prejudiced views so as to define themselves as comparatively tolerant. Floor residents identified these women as "bigots" because they directly mistreated a lesbian, explicitly made it about her sexuality, cited religious morality, and made it political by hanging a "Vote for Bush" poster on their door. As Eliasoph and Lichterman (2003) note, Americans generally avoid political discussion because they see it as too divisive. A resident elaborated, "It could maybe make her uncomfortable if her roommate was a lesbian . . . [but] she shouldn't go around blabbering it." Although this woman understood the desire not to share a room with a lesbian, she found the public and unsophisticated way in which the other woman handled it to be objectionable.

The 24 women in the homosexuality as "okay for others but not in my space" category displayed this sort of sophistication, walking the line between the competing values of openness to diversity and dissociation from low-status lesbians. They were aware of the need to respect the discourse of diversity acceptance promoted by university staff and officials through numerous and visible "Celebrate Diversity" decorations and activities. The increasing visibility of gay characters in television shows that many of them watched (including The O.C. and MTV's The Real World) also signaled that appearing gay friendly was hip and fashionable. These women responded in interviews as to "prove" their tolerance, often in comparison to others with less socially acceptable views. As one noted, "It just doesn't faze me. I think you can do whatever you want to do, and I never was brought up that gay is wrong—like shaking the Bible." Another woman explained, "I mean, if they want to be gay, that's great. I don't have anything against it. I would rather someone come out?... than being scared, but I dunno because I'm not."

Awareness of cultural values for diversity, however, does not always translate into acceptance of marginalized groups. Researchers suggest that most whites now engage in "symbolic racism," framing their negative views toward other racial groups in ways that do not seem outwardly racist while continuing to engage in more indirect forms of discrimination (Schuman, Steeth, and Bobo 1988). Women in this category similarly avoided openly prejudiced statements about homosexuality or gays and lesbians as a group but still kept lesbians out of their social spheres. As one woman carefully noted of lesbians, "There's always going to be people that are different, but here I'm not friends with those people." Their lack of lesbian friends was not a consequence of the circumstances. The women in this group were generally aware of the two lesbians on the hall, mentioning their presence in interviews and interactions. One of the lesbians even noted that she was friendly with some of these women until she came out; then it was as if they were strangers.

Women in this group managed to avoid lesbians on the hall without appearing to contradict their "openness" to diversity by using the language of taste. Rather than highlighting lesbians' sexual preference as problematic, these women cited differences in interests, personal styles, or social chemistry. For example, one woman in this category also moved away from her lesbian roommate but maintained that it was mismatched personalities that led to her switch. As she explained during the interview, "I just don't like living with her because it's hard. We don't talk, and so I don't like that atmosphere." Even when talking with each other about lesbians on the hall, women in this group rarely said they disliked lesbians because of their sexual orientation. One woman told me about a conversation she had with another heterosexual woman who said that she would not want to move in with the lesbian (despite tension with her current roommate) because "she's bigger and she's weird." When I looked confused about this, the woman I was interviewing leaned in and whispered, "[She's] a lesbian."

The preference for social distance from lesbians was most apparent when I asked women to consider lesbians in their personal space. Almost invariably, they were concerned about being "checked out" by lesbian room- or floormates: "I'd be freaked out changing. I know I sound so close-minded, but truthfully I would be like scared. Like, is she watching me change or will she hit on me?" In a residence hall where private space is public space, lesbians introduce interactional ambiguity. Women were familiar with men eroticizing them—even on their floor and in their rooms—but lesbians added the possibility of an unfamiliar sexual gaze. One woman noted, "Having a lesbian on the floor has scared me. When I'm in the shower and I know she's next to me . . . I get nervous. 'Cause I never thought about a girl looking at me that way." In her opinion, even shared floor spaces were more comfortable when assumed to be heterosexual.

Critical Partiers and Nonpartiers

These 13 women shared an orientation to the party system that was different than for women in the outer two levels of social distance. They afforded the party scene less importance, choosing to define themselves through other avenues. I identified five of these women as critical partiers because, although they participated in the party scene, they consistently critiqued it. When I asked one critical partier where she partied the most, she said, "Whichever [place] I hate the least that week." The only critical partier or nonpartier to join the Greek system, she did so as an attempt to make friends but refused to be "fake and try to please people." She disliked the elitism of the party scene, where "people base stuff on money," judging others through their ownership of designer goods. Another woman maintained that she did not always have to party in the Greek scene, stating, "Tell me what I'm missing out on that I can't find with other people. . . . It's not worth it to me." She and her roommate, another critical partier, chose not to go through the process of visiting and eventually joining sororities, often referred to as "rush." They even posted what they called an "anti-rush" message on their door: "Yes, that's right. We quit. The two females who live in this room have been officially disqualified [by choice] from the rush process." This was a bold move in a context where the Greek system was highly valued.

I defined 11 women as nonpartiers because they chose to opt out of the Greek party system. Many of these women noted that they did not enjoy partying. One explained, "I'm not a big party person. . . . I'm not a big person on drinking, and I don't like being around people that are totally drunk, acting like idiots." Several of them reported being made fun of by other floor members. One woman, for instance, told me that a floormate chided, "You haven't drank and you're at college? Come on." For several who opted out, financial or personal issues led them to value school differently.

Some of these girls don't even go to class. It's like they just live here. They stay up until 4:00 in the morning. [I want to ask,] "Do you guys go to class? Like what's your deal? . . . You're paying a lot of money for this. . . . If you want to be here, then why aren't you trying harder?"

Her contempt reflects the fact that partying is also a classed activity—one that not everyone can afford.

Critical partiers and nonpartiers fell into two groups: those who were willing to have lesbian friends and those who were willing to consider public lesbian identities for themselves. The 11 women in the homosexuality as "not my choice, but okay for my friends" category believed in the benefits of diversity in college. Many were curious about meeting new people and learning about their experiences. One woman, a friend of a lesbian on the floor, enthusiastically detailed the positives of having a lesbian roommate, exclaiming, "I don't care, I'd be inquisitive! I'd want to know about . . . what they've dealt with and what their views are on gay pride like 'I wear the rainbow.'" Another woman talked about her interest in the gay and lesbian community in the town, sparked by her contact with a bisexual woman. She explained, "I'm really into everything different. Anything to have an experience is just so cool." For these women, contact with gays and lesbians was seen as a form of personal enrichment—"an experience" that could be consumed.

A few women in this group, however, felt that one's sexual orientation was not what made someone a desirable friend. They typically noted that a lesbian roommate would be the same as any other roommate—only a problem if they did not get along with each other. As one woman noted, she "loved" her lesbian friend because she was "real" and "down-to-earth." Another described her close lesbian friend, saying,

> She says what's on her mind and I love that. I just I get a kick out of half of the things she says, and the other half I just really appreciate that she's honest. . . . That's a good quality in anyone.

These two women did not think their friend's "gayness" made her fun and unique; they each enjoyed their lesbian friend for other aspects of her personality such as candor, wit, and sincerity.

While perhaps they were positive influences in the lives of individual lesbians, these women did not challenge the overall marginalization of lesbians. When they protested the exclusion of their lesbian friends, they did so in private or anonymously. For example, several of them privately expressed fierce hatred for the "bigots" on the floor. But, rather than speaking to the resident assistant or bringing up tolerance as a floor issue, they admitted to secretly writing things on the door of these two women. They realized that other people on the floor were not as accepting of lesbians as they were but did nothing to change this. As one noted, "It just sucks that not everyone can be open-minded."

The two women who felt that homosexuality was "okay for me, okay for my friends" had the smallest social distance from homosexuality. Both identified as lesbians and felt shunned because of their sexuality. One explained of her roommate, "She was really nice the day I met her, and then after I told her I was gay, she changed." Based on this reaction, the woman felt she needed to be careful about who she told. When I asked her if many people knew at first that she was a lesbian, she said, "No, take a look at the floor I was on, the building I was in. Of course not. I didn't want people to gang up on me." When she moved into a new residence hall, she decided that it was best to signal her sexuality only subtly by hanging her gay pride flag. She noted, "I learned my lesson from directly telling a roommate. . . . Honestly, I would have kept it a secret until I found out how she felt about it. If she was against it, I would have kept it secret." This woman was willing to hide her sexuality rather than face a negative reaction.

The other woman had a similar experience with her roommate. She and her roommate never actually talked about her sexuality, nor did the roommate directly confront her about it. Instead, the roommate indirectly signaled her disgust for lesbianism. The woman who identified as a lesbian explained,

> I was watching this show on VH1. It showed a clip from Melissa Etheridge's wedding, and I remember she made this disgusted noise and commented on it, but it stuck out to me obviously—like I see how you feel about this.

A week later this roommate had "a full out conversation about how disgusting [lesbianism] was" with a woman who lived next door. This conversation occurred in the lesbian's room, but the women who were talking never acknowledged her presence. Even in her own private space, she felt dismissed and ignored.

Both lesbians also reported that they felt unwelcome on campus. When I asked one woman if she thought that students were accepting of homosexuality, she made a clear distinction between how she felt in Adams (a relatively small alternative residence hall she moved to midyear) versus other places on campus. She noted that in most places, "I just feel uncomfortable. Like here (Adams), I'm totally comfortable with everybody. . . . If they're Adams kids I know that they're accepting." Outside this pocket, however, the two lesbians often felt isolated. As the other woman explained, "I assumed that everyone was straight, just like the rest of the world, where everyone assumes that everyone is straight." In classes, she reported sensing intolerance that kept her from being more open.

> There have been a couple times that I've kind of come close to saying something about [my sexuality], and I hold myself back because I know. For example . . . my English teacher is actually out and he's alluded to it a couple of times, talking about his partner. And the reactions that I've seen [my classmates] have to it, have kept me from [disclosing it].

For both women, college life involved constantly monitoring their surroundings, determining when they could be open, when they could not, and what spaces allowed them to be "lesbians."

APPROPRIATING LESBIAN EROTICISM

Although lesbians received clear messages that their sexuality was not welcome, same-sex eroticism of a certain kind thrived. Active partiers frequently engaged in same-sex sexual behaviors in the party scene. Their ability to do so without social stigma depended on maintaining social distance from those who identified as lesbians. Heterosexual women's appropriation of lesbian eroticism for their own use put lesbians in a difficult position. Woman-to-woman eroticism had its place on campus among those who identified as heterosexual, but out lesbians often encountered disgust or hostility.

Same-Sex Eroticism Among "Straight Girls"

Only active partiers, those in the two outer rings of social distance from lesbians, participated in same-sex eroticism (4 out of 6 women in the "never okay" group; 17 out of 24 women in the "okay for others but not in my space" group). Same-sex eroticism included kissing (on the mouth, often involving tongues) and fondling (of breasts and buttocks), particularly while dancing; no heterosexual women reported oral or digital stimulation of the genitals. These women openly

discussed such behaviors with researchers, talked about them with their friends, and posted pictures of themselves kissing women in their rooms and on the Internet.[6] Heterosexual women who were more open about homosexuality did not either engage in the same behavior or advertise it in the same way.

As Jenefsky and Miller (1998) note, the performance of lesbianism for men may signal heterocentric eroticism. Women on the floor who engaged in this behavior claimed that they intended their same-sex kissing for an audience of heterosexual men. Several noted that they liked to get reactions from men. One described, "You get guys that you just like to see their expressions. It's just so funny to see them be like, 'Oh my god, I can't believe you just did that, that was awesome.'" Another woman explained, "Guys said, 'Do it, do it!' just screwing around. . . . [They] were like, 'These girls are going to kiss!' So you think you're cooler and guys think you're cooler." The value in the same-sex kiss, therefore, was in the attention that it could garner from men. Like a sexy outfit or new stilettos, heterosexual women could deploy same-sex eroticism as a statement of style to get attention amid a sea of scantily dressed young women. One resident even noted that unlike doing drugs, this way of getting attention did not cause bodily harm.

Heterosexual women were careful to claim that their kisses had little meaning behind them, noting that they were not involved and not "serious." They often contextualized their behaviors so that others (and perhaps themselves) would interpret them as heterosexual. As two roommates told me when I asked if they had ever seen two girls kissing,

R1: Well, sometimes we're drunk. (Both laughing)
R2: Like trashed.
R1: We have a wall of shame of pictures.
R2: Sometimes we get a little out of control and trashed, but it's not like we're going crazy on each other. Like, it's just to be funny. It's random kisses. It's not serious.
R1: Right (laughs). It's not like I want you or anything. Eww.

Women often attributed these kisses to alcohol. Among this crowd, however, intoxication was rarely an embarrassing state. Drunken pictures were most likely to make it into public view as they provided proof that one could party hard. Same-sex sexuality was just another way to mark oneself as edgy and spontaneous—"stepping outside of your box," as one woman called it.

Floor residents who employed woman-to-woman eroticism were careful to distinguish their behaviors from those whom they considered to be "real lesbians." As many felt that lesbians were identifiable through their unfeminine appearance, they seemed sure that those in their social networks were heterosexual even if sexual orientation was never a topic of conversation. As one respondent noted,

R: It's totally different if you're into it. Like lesbians or something. It's just your friend.
I: How can you tell like if somebody is really into it or not?
R: I don't know. I always just assumed everyone wasn't. Just 'cause it's people I knew. I've never seen real lesbians kiss.

All of these women agreed that you only kissed close friends whom you trusted to be heterosexual. One even described it as a "bonding" activity between her and another woman on the floor. When they saw other women kissing at parties, they usually applied the same assumptions.

These women felt that encountering lesbians making out in the heterosexual space of the party scene was unlikely. They understood that women achieved status and even basic inclusion in the party scene through their ability to attract men. In their eyes, most lesbians were incapable of doing so; lesbians were "boyish" and "weird" and therefore unlikely to be "hot" or "blonde." They assumed that lesbians simply could not succeed in passing as heterosexual women. This assumption allowed them to construct seeming boundaries between their same-sex erotic practices and those of who they deemed to be "real" or "actual" lesbians. The maintenance of these boundaries played a central role in their ability to maintain heterosexual identities and define their behaviors as hetero-, rather than homo-, erotic.

Reducing Lesbian Spaces

Heterosexual women's enactment of same-sex eroticism worked to further marginalize lesbians. Displays of eroticism between women perceived as undesirable to heterosexual men invited ridicule or worse. Because the heterosexual party scene encompassed all Greek houses, many off-campus houses, and all but a few bars in town, lesbians were effectively excluded (both by choice and by design) from most public erotic spaces in town. A lesbian in a focus group suggested that het-

erosexual women even encroached on the few lesbian- and gay-friendly party spots. Della's, the bar to which she referred, is a widely known gay bar.

> One night I was at Della's and waiting for my friends to meet me there. I'm sitting alone at this table, and a group of approximately 50 girls in matching T-shirts with sorority lettering across the front, came in, took over the dance floor, and were makin' out and givin' lap dances to each other. . . . I called [my friend] and I was talkin' to her about how just disgusted I was by it because it's making a mockery of us. These two girls overheard me cause I was being loud (laughter). . . . And I tried to explain to them that if I went to the straight bar with my girlfriend and stood next to her, let alone kissed her, that would not be okay. But that these little girls kissing and giggling is A-okay because it's implied that there's no pleasure there or that it's to please men rather than to please themselves.

This woman experienced the sorority women's presence in her space as invasive and their behavior as insulting. Acting as heterosexual "tourists," these sorority women consumed the experience of the "exotic other" but could safely leave it behind (Casey 2004). As most erotic spaces privileged their sexuality, they felt entitled enough to invade one of the few lesbian-identified spaces in pursuit of a thrill.

None of the women in the focus group felt that heterosexual women's use of same-sex eroticism would lead to claiming a lesbian identity. One explained, "There doesn't seem to be any . . . authentic lesbian in between there." However, heterosexual women's enactment of same-sex eroticism in a gay bar suggests that their appropriation may not be only about garnering men's attention. It is possible that claiming a heterosexual identity allows them to enjoy experimentation with other women. On the floor, two roommates told me and another woman about a night when they danced together naked. They did this alone and were not recounting the story to get men's attention. Yet neither described this experience as a "lesbian" encounter, instead jokingly dismissing it as something to do when they were bored. They may have privately experienced this as a moment of questioning their sexuality; however, their ability to tell others without facing challenges to their heterosexual identity was dependent on the existence of out lesbians from whom they could differentiate themselves.

As Casey (2004) notes, heterosexual women's intrusion into gay and lesbian identified spaces can reduce lesbians' comfort, safety, and sense of inclusion. Women who claimed heterosexual identities may have experienced freedom from men's gaze and possibly played with same-sex desire while in the bar; however, as a result of their intrusion, lesbians lost the right to define the meaning of same-sex eroticism in their own space. By claiming same-sex eroticism as a heterosexual practice, heterosexual women made lesbian desire invisible and reconfigured it as a performance for men. Ironically, in the lesbian bar take-over, heterosexual women took up space with their bodies and their sexuality—something that scholars find to be particularly difficult for women (K. A. Martin 1998; Tolman 2002). Yet they did so only at the cost of women who were more disenfranchised on campus than they were.

DISCUSSION

The literature on masculinities suggests that men's dominance over women encourages adherence to heteronormative ideals of manhood that support aggression against gays (Connell 1987; Corbett 2001; Pascoe 2005). These analyses present the flip side of that story; women's efforts to navigate inegalitarian gender contexts may fortify their efforts to meet heteronormative standards of femininity. Although disadvantaged relative to men, heterosexual women may raise their status among other women by distancing themselves from those who do not perform traditionally feminine identities. Lesbians, who often avoid signaling availability to men through behavior or appearance, thus encounter systematic social exclusion.

Past scholarship may have minimized homophobia among women because it does not look the same as among men. Men's homophobia often takes the form of physical or verbal violence against gay men. My analyses suggest that homophobia among women instead renders lesbians socially invisible. For example, when someone covertly dismantled the Rainbow Week bulletin board in the hall, no one, save the resident assistant, said anything. The unceremonious removal of the board and its subsequent replacement with healthy eating suggestions fittingly represented the situation of the lesbians on the floor. Most of the floor was so busy avoiding them, they were almost socially nonexistent.

The problem of lesbian visibility is deeply rooted in heteronormative cultural meanings that are fundamentally gendered. They reflect the idea that women's sexuality is a direct consequence of men's desire, socially

transforming sex acts between women into erotic fodder for heterosexual men (Jenefsky and Miller 1998). When heterosexual women engage in same-sex eroticism for an audience of men or in lesbian-identified spaces, they make it difficult for lesbians to mark their erotic activities as nonheterosexual. In contrast, heterosexual men may feel that homosexuality is a persistent threat (Armstrong 1995). As a result of the fundamentally gendered nature of sexuality, heterosexual men often ward off accusations of homosexuality while lesbians have to struggle to make their sexuality visible.

Because of the invisibility of lesbian sexuality, lesbians often have to deliberately signal their unavailability to men through dress, group affiliation, and choice of social space (Armstrong 1995). This may mean both choosing not to participate in heterosexual erotic markets and creating a less feminine gender appearance. As my data suggest, however, these are two key mechanisms through which women can gain status in gender inegalitarian conditions. Many lesbians face a dilemma: They can make their lesbian identity visible and face social invisibility or struggle with the invisibility of their sexual identity but benefit from social inclusion. Women's homophobia thus relies on heteronormative understandings of sexuality to keep lesbians marginalized.

My analyses suggest that homophobia among women (heterosexism) is tightly linked to gender inequality (sexism). When disempowered, women may rely on gender strategies that access compensatory benefits through their relationships with men (Schwalbe et al. 2000). These gender strategies require traditionally feminine gender presentations that become the primary form of embodied capital available to women in specific social contexts. First, women have to be in disadvantaged positions vis-à-vis men to need their "patronage" for achieving status. Social and structural inequalities that divide men and women into two different groups also naturalize the gender differences that they produce. Second, heteronormative cultural logics that assume the "otherness" of appropriate sexual partners must be in play. These logics privilege women who work to attract and please men, often through their gender performances. Although ultimately supporting their own subordination, women who benefit from these conditions can rely on homophobia to maintain the status quo.

My work also indicates that women's embodied capital is race and class specific. "Blonde" gender presentations are only possible for those who can produce long, straight blonde hair and "tan" skin. In addition, this appearance requires knowledge about styles and trends and the money necessary to buy and embody them. Not everyone is, therefore, capable of producing the kind of femininity that can bring benefits in the erotic market of the Greek party scene. Although my analyses do not detail how race or class statuses impact women's gender strategies, it is possible that women with reduced access to the rewards of heterosexual performance have more room for gender flexibility. However, some Black feminists such as Collins (1991) and Smith (1982) indicate that when heterosexuality is among the few privileges available to women, they may invest heavily in "maintaining 'straightness'" (Smith 1982, 171). For this reason, women marginalized because of their race, ethnicity, and/or class background may exercise strategies of social distancing from lesbians with more vehemence. This remains a topic for further examination.

ACKNOWLEDGEMENTS

This article is part of a larger project about collegiate life that the author conducted in collaboration with Elizabeth A. Armstrong, director of the study. The author wishes to thank her for her insights and support. Thanks is also given to Sibyl Bedford, Katie Bradley, Teresa Cummings, Aimee Lipkis, Evelyn Perry, Brian Sweeney, and Amanda Tanner for research assistance. The author also appreciates Elizabeth A. Armstrong, Nancy Davis, Donna Eder, Timothy Hallett, and Brian Powell for comments on the article and is grateful to Dana Britton, Christine Williams, and anonymous reviewers for their helpful suggestions.

NOTES

1. Connell's (1987) concept of emphasized femininity suggests that women may benefit by complying with men's domination. However, he argues that women have little institutional leverage or reason for marginalizing other women and fails to account for women's active use of their heterosexuality to gain status or power.
2. Many have recognized the problems with the term *homophobia* (see Adam 1998). Unfortunately, there are few other terms that are as widely recognized and understood.
3. I assigned pseudonyms to the names of locations and buildings to protect the anonymity of respondents.
4. Two of these women left the school midyear before we could interview them. Five women were too uncomfortable talking about themselves to do an interview. Four said they were too busy for an interview.
5. Not all fraternities or fraternity men engage in these behaviors. However, women reported similar experiences at all of the most popular fraternities on campus.
6. Recent survey results from the National Center for Health Statistics indicate an unexpected increase in reports of same-sex experiences among 18- to 29-year-old women, most of whom do not identify as lesbian or bisexual (Mosher, Chandra, and Jones 2005).

REFERENCES

Adam, Barry D. 1998. Theorizing homophobia. *Sexualities* 1:387–404.

Armstrong, Elizabeth A. 1995. Traitors to the cause? Understanding the lesbian/gay "bisexuality debates." In *Bisexual politics: Theories, queries, & visions,* edited by N. Tucker. Binghamton, NY: Haworth.

Armstrong, Elizabeth A., Laura Hamilton, and Brian Sweeney. 2006. Sexual assault on campus: A multilevel, integrative approach to party rape. *Social Problems* 53: 483–99.

Bartky, Sandra. 1990. *Femininity and domination.* New York: Routledge.

Bettie, Julie. 2005. *Women without class: Gender, race, and identity,* Berkeley: University of California Press.

Boswell, A. Ayres, and Joan Z. Spade. 1996. Fraternities and collegiate rape culture: Why are some fraternities more dangerous places for women? *Gender & Society* 10:133–47.

Butler, Judith. 1990. *Gender trouble: Feminism and the subversion of identity.* New York: Routledge.

Casey, Mark. 2004. De-dyking queer space(s): Heterosexual female visibility in gay and lesbian spaces. *Sexualities* 7:446–61.

Chen, Anthony. 1999. Lives at the center of the periphery, lives at the periphery of the center: Chinese American masculinities and bargaining with hegemony. *Gender & Society* 13:584–607.

Collins, Patricia Hill. 1991. *Black feminist thought: Knowledge, consciousness, and the politics of empowerment.* New York: Routledge.

Collins, Randall. 2004. *Interaction ritual chains.* Princeton, NJ: Princeton University Press.

Connell, R. W. 1987. *Gender and power: Society, the person, and sexual politics.* Palo Alto, CA: Stanford University Press.

———. 1995. *Masculinities.* Berkeley: University of California Press.

Corbett, Ken. 2001. Faggot = Loser. *Studies in Gender and Sexuality* 2:3–28.

Eder, Donna. 1985. The cycle of popularity: Interpersonal relations among female adolescents. *Sociology of Education* 58:154–65.

Eliasoph, Nina, and Paul Lichterman. 2003. Culture in interaction. *American Journal of Sociology* 108:735–94.

Gamson, Josh. 1998. *Freaks talk back: Tabloid talk shows and sexual nonconformity.* Chicago: University of Chicago Press.

Gentry, Cynthia S. 1987. Social distance regarding male and female homosexuals. *Journal of Social Psychology* 127:199–208.

Giddens, Anthony. 1992. *The transformation of intimacy: Sexuality, love, and eroticism in modern societies* Cambridge, UK: Polity.

Gilligan, Carol. 1982. *In a different voice: Psychological theory and women's development.* Cambridge, MA: Harvard University Press.

Goffman, Erving. 1963. *Stigma: Notes on the management of spoiled identity.* Englewood Cliffs, NJ: Prentice-Hall.

Handler, Lisa. 1995. In the fraternal sisterhood: Sororities as gender strategy. *Gender & Society* 9:236–55.

Hochschild, Arlie Russell. 1989. *The second shift.* New York: Avon Books.

Holland, Dorothy C., and Margaret C. Eisenhart. 1990. *Educated in romance: Women, achievement, and college culture.* Chicago: University of Chicago Press.

Jackson, Stevi. 1996. Heterosexuality and feminist theory. In *Theorising heterosexuality,* edited by D. Richardson. Buckingham, UK: Open University Press.

Jenefsky, Cindy, and Diane H. Miller. 1998. Phallic intrusion: Girl-girl sex in Penthouse. *Women's Studies International Forum* 21:375–85.

Kimmel, Michael S. 2001. Masculinity as homophobia: Fear, shame, and silence in the construction of gender identity. In *The masculinities reader,* edited by S. Whitehead and F. Barrett. Cambridge, UK: Polity.

Loftus, Jeni. 2001. America's liberalization in attitudes toward homosexuality, 1973 to 1998. *American Sociological Review* 66:762–82.

Martin, Karin A. 1998. Becoming a gendered body: Practices of preschools. *American Sociological Review* 63:494–511.

———. 2003. Giving birth like a girl. *Gender & Society* 17:54–72.

Martin, Patricia Y. 2003. "Said and done" versus "saying and doing": Gendering practices, practicing gender at work. *Gender & Society* 17:342–66.

Martin, Patricia Y., and Robert A. Hummer. 1989. Fraternities and rape on campus. *Gender & Society* 3:457–73.

McCall, Leslie. 1992. Does gender fit? Bourdieu, feminism, and conceptions of social order. *Theory and Society* 21:837–67.

Merten, Don E. 1997. The meaning of meanness: Popularity, competition, and conflict among junior high school girls. *Sociology of Education* 70:175–91.

Milner, Murray Jr. 2004. *Freaks, geeks, and cool kids: American teenagers, schools, and the culture of consumption.* New York: Routledge.

Mosher, William D., Anjani Chandra, and Jo Jones. 2005. *Sexual behavior and selected health measures: Men and women 15–44 years of age.* Hyattsville, MD: National Center for Health Statistics.

Pascoe, C. J. 2005. "Dude, you're a fag": Adolescent masculinity and the fag discourse. *Sexualities* 8:329–46.

Rich, Adrienne. 1980. Compulsory heterosexuality and lesbian existence. *Signs* 5:631–60.

Schuman, Howard, Charlotte Steeth, and Lawrence Bobo. 1988. *Racial attitudes in America: Trends and interpretations.* Cambridge, MA: Harvard University Press.

Schwalbe, Michael, Sandra Godwin, Daphne Holden, Douglas Schrock, Shealy Thompson, and Michele Wolkomir. 2000. Generic processes in the reproduction of inequality: An interactionist analysis. *Social Forces* 79:419–52.

Smith, Barbara. 1982. Toward a Black feminist criticism. In *But some of us are brave,* edited by G. T. Hull, P. B. Scott, and B. Smith. Old Westbury, NY: Feminist Press.

Stein, Arlene. 2005. Make room for Daddy: Anxious masculinity and emergent homophobias in neopatriarchical politics. *Gender & Society* 19:601–20.

Stombler, Mindy, and Patricia Y. Martin. 1995. Bringing women in, keeping women down: Fraternity "little sister" organizations. *Journal of Contemporary Ethnography* 23: 150–84.

Swidler, Anne. 1986. Culture in action: Symbols and strategies. *American Sociological Review* 51:273–86.

Tolman, Deborah. 2002. *Dilemmas of desire: Teenage girls talk about sexuality.* Cambridge, MA: Harvard University Press.

HILLARY CLINTON'S TENTATIVE DIP INTO NEW NECKLINE TERRITORY

Robin Givhan

There was cleavage on display Wednesday afternoon on C-SPAN2. It belonged to Sen. Hillary Clinton.

She was talking on the Senate floor about the burdensome cost of higher education. She was wearing a rose-colored blazer over a black top. The neckline sat low on her chest and had a subtle V-shape. The cleavage registered after only a quick glance. No scrunch-faced scrutiny was necessary. There wasn't an unseemly amount of cleavage showing, but there it was. Undeniable.

It was startling to see that small acknowledgment of sexuality and femininity peeking out of the conservative—aesthetically speaking—environment of Congress. After all, it wasn't until the early '90s that women were even allowed to wear pants on the Senate floor. It was even more surprising to note that it was coming from Clinton, someone who has been so publicly ambivalent about style, image and the burdens of both.

The last time Clinton wore anything that was remotely sexy in a public setting surely must have been more than a decade ago, during Bill Clinton's first term in office when she was photographed wearing a black Donna Karan gown that revealed her shoulders. It was one of Karan's "cold-shoulder" dresses, inspired, Karan once noted, because a woman's shoulders remain sensuous and appealing regardless of her age.

Throughout Clinton's time as first lady, she wore clothes that were feminine and stately. But sexiness was not part of the image. Her second inaugural gown was by Oscar de la Renta. The original version or the gold lace dress had cap sleeves and a wide, jewel neckline. Clinton altered it so that it had long sleeves and a high, almost Victorian collar.

When she appeared on the cover of the December 1998 issue of *Vogue,* just after the Monica Lewinsky scandal had peaked, she wore another de la Renta gown, this one with a boat neck and long sleeves. She looked glamorous, regal and defiant. But one was not even tempted to mention the s-word.

By the time Clinton launched her first campaign for the Senate, she had found a desexualized uniform: a black pantsuit. Not a fitted, provocative suit, but merely an understated, flattering one. Clothes were off the table. End of discussion.

But as she has embarked on her campaign for president, she has given up the uniform. In its place has been a wide array of suits and jackets, in everything from dull khaki to canary yellow and sofa florals. Once again, she is playing the fashion field.

The cleavage, however, is an exceptional kind of flourish. After all, it's not a matter of what she's wearing but rather what's being revealed. It's tempting to say that the cleavage stirs the same kind of discomfort that might be churned up after spotting Rudy Giuliani with his shirt unbuttoned just a smidge too far. No one wants to see that. But really, it was more like catching a man with his fly unzipped. Just look away!

Not so long ago, Jacqui Smith, the new British home secretary, spoke before the House of Commons showing far more cleavage than Clinton. If Clinton's was a teasing display, then Smith's was a full-fledged come-on. But somehow it wasn't as unnerving. Perhaps that's because Smith's cleavage seemed to be presented so forthrightly. Smith's fitted jacket and her dramatic necklace combined to draw the eye directly to her bosom. There they were . . . all part of a bold, confident style package.

With Clinton, there was the sense that you were catching a surreptitious glimpse at something private. You were intruding—being a voyeur. Showing cleavage is a request to be engaged in a particular way. It doesn't necessarily mean that a woman is asking to be objectified, but it does suggest a certain confidence and physical ease. It means that a woman is content being perceived as a sexual person in addition to being seen as someone who is intelligent, authoritative, witty and whatever else might define her personality. It also means that she feels that all those other characteristics are so apparent and undeniable, that they will not be overshadowed.

To display cleavage in a setting that does not involve cocktails and hors d'oeuvres is a provocation. It requires that a woman be utterly at ease in her skin, coolly confident about her appearance, unflinching about her sense of style. Any hint of ambivalence makes everyone uncomfortable. And in matters of style, Clinton is as noncommittal as ever.

READING *34* *Patricia Hill Collins*

Black Sexual Politics

2001: The career of Jennifer Lopez skyrockets. A Puerto Rican woman, Lopez's rise to fame came after her feature film appearance as Selena, the first Chicana superstar. News of J-Lo is everywhere; especially her much discussed love relationship and subsequent break-up with hip-hop artist Puff Daddy (aka P Diddy). One special feature of Lopez's routinely makes the news—her seemingly large bottom. From late night American talk shows to South African radio programs to Internet websites, J-Lo's butt is all the rage. Recognizing its value, it is rumored that Lopez insures her buttocks for 1 billion dollars, as one website mischievously described it, 500 million dollars per cheek.

2000: The photo insert for *Survivor,* Destiny's Child third CD, shows the three African American women standing legs akimbo, holding hands, and dressed in animal skin bikinis. Selling over 15 million albums and singles worldwide, *Survivor's* success reflects a savvy marketing strategy that promoted the song "Independent Woman" as part of the soundtrack for the hit movie *Charlie's Angels* and foreshadowed the success of group member Beyoncé Knowles. *Survivor's* message of female power also fuels its popularity. Counseling women to be resilient and financially independent, Destiny's Child proclaim, "I'm a survivor, I'm gonna make it." *Survivor* suggests sexual independence as well. In their highly popular song "Bootylicious," written by Beyoncé, they refer to their butts as "jelly" and ask, "Can you handle it?" The term *bootylicious* proves to be so popular that, along with *hottie* and *roadrage,* it is added to the 2002 edition of *Merriam-Webster's Collegiate Dictionary.*

1925: Born in a poor community in East St. Louis, Missouri, African American entertainer Josephine Baker moves to Paris. She becomes a sensation in the American production of *La Revue Nègre.* Performing barebreasted in a jungle setting and clad only in a short skirt of banana leaves, Ms. Baker's rump-shaking banana dance becomes an instant hit with Parisian audiences. When asked whether she will return to the United States, Ms. Baker replies, "they would make me sing mammy songs and I cannot feel mammy songs, so I cannot sing them." Instead, in 1937 Ms. Baker becomes a French citizen and garners lifelong accolades as the "Black Venus" of France. Upon her death in 1975, she receives a twenty-one-gun salute, the only such honor given by France to an American-born woman.[1]

1816: After several years of being exhibited in Paris and London as the "Hottentot Venus," Sarah Baartman, a Khoi woman from what is now South Africa, dies. In the London exhibit, she is displayed caged, rocking back and forth to emphasize her supposedly wild and dangerous nature. She wears a tight-fitting dress whose brown color matches her skin tones. When ordered to do so, she leaves her cage and parades before the audience who seems fascinated with what they see as her most intriguing feature—her buttocks. Some in the audience are not content to merely look. One eyewitness recounts with horror how Baartman endures poking and prodding, as people try to ascertain for themselves whether her buttocks are real. In the context of popular London shows that display as forms of entertainment talking pigs, animal monsters and human oddities such as the Fattest Man on Earth, midgets, giants, and similar "freaks of nature," these reactions to Baartman's exhibition are not unusual. Upon Sarah Baartman's death, George Cuvier, one of the fathers of modern biology, claims her body in the interests of science. Her subsequent dissection becomes one of at least seven others completed on the bodies of women of color from 1814 to 1870. Their goal—to advance the field of classical comparative anatomy.[2]

Contemporary sexual politics in the United States present African American women and men with a complicated problem. From the display of Sarah Baartman as a sexual "freak" of nature in the early nineteenth century to Josephine Baker dancing bare-breasted for Parisian society to the animal-skin bikinis worn by "bootylicious" Destiny's Child to the fascination with Jennifer Lopez's buttocks, women of African descent have been associated with an animalistic, "wild" sexuality. Expressed via an ever-changing yet distinctive constellation of sexual stereotypes in which Sarah Baartman's past frames J-Lo's present, this association of sexuality with Black women helps create ideas about racial difference. Black men have their own variety of racial difference, also constructed from ideas about violence and dangerous sexuality. African American heavyweight boxer Jack Johnson certainly sparked controversy when, in 1910, he fought the formerly unbeaten White champion Jim Jeffries. During the fight itself, over 30,000 men stood outside the *New York Times'* offices, waiting to hear the outcome. Johnson's bloody victory sparked race riots in every Southern state. Johnson's predilection for White women only fueled the fires of White reaction. When authorities discovered that Johnson was having an affair with an eighteen-year-old blonde from Minnesota, they charged him under the Mann Act with engaging in white slavery. Johnson's ability to wield violence and his seeming attractiveness to White women made him threatening to White middle-class men.[3] For both women and men, Western social thought associates Blackness with an imagined uncivilized, wild sexuality

and uses this association as one lynchpin of racial difference. Whether depicted as "freaks" of nature or as being the essence of nature itself, savage, untamed sexuality characterizes Western representations of women and men of African descent.[4]

For their respective audiences, the distinctive sexualized spectacles performed by Baartman, Baker, Destiny's Child, and Lopez invoke sexual meanings that give shape to racism, sexism, class exploitation, and heterosexism. Each spectacle marks the contradictions of Western perceptions of African bodies and of Black women's agency concerning the use of their bodies. Together they frame an invented discourse of *Black sexuality*.[5] For French and British audiences, Sarah Baartman served as a sign of racial difference used to justify the growing belief in the superiority of White civilization and the inferiority of so-called primitive peoples necessary for colonialism. Her treatment helped create modern Black sexual stereotypes of the jezebel, the mammy, and the welfare queen that, in the United States, helped uphold slavery, Jim Crow segregation, and racial ghettoization.[6] Illustrating through stark historical example how common sense understandings of race and gender flow smoothly into those of biology, medicine, and Western science itself, her body marked the intersection of entertainment, science, and commerce. Sarah Baartman could be enjoyed while alive and, upon her death, studied under the microscope for the burgeoning field of comparative anatomy. As South African writer Yvette Abrahams and filmmaker Zola Maseko's video recording on the life of Baartman point out, we know little about Baartman's agency in this arrangement.[7] What Baartman lost by being displayed as a "freak" is far clearer to us through our modern sensibilities than what she might have gained for herself and her family.

Baartman may not have been aware of the power of the sexual stereotypes that were created in her image, but women of African descent who followed most certainly were.[8] Black women struggled to exercise agency and self-definition concerning these images and the social practices that they defended. Evidently aware of the sexual stereotypes applied to women of African descent, Josephine Baker played the part of the "primitive," but for her own reasons.[9] Baker entertained the French with her openness about her body, an important example of how an imagined, uncivilized, wild sexuality remained associated with Blackness within Western social thought and continued as a sign of racial difference. But was Baker really sexually liberated, or was her performance a carefully planned illusion that, in the African American trickster tradition, was designed to titillate and manipulate the tastes of her European audiences? Baker's biography suggests a level of sophistication that enabled her to move far beyond her initial depiction as a bare-breasted "primitive." Baker may have initially done banana dances, but from her point of view, she escaped performing the ubiquitous "mammy songs" assigned to Hattie McDaniel, Ethel Waters, and other talented African American women then performing in the United States. In France, Baker ensured that she was well compensated for her performances.

The work of contemporary artists such as Destiny's Child also invokes the contradictions of sexualized spectacle and Black women's agency or self-determination. Transported from the immediacy of live stage performances, Destiny's Child perform in the intimate yet anonymous terrain of CDs, music videos, movies, Internet websites, and other forms of contemporary mass media. Here each consumer of "Independent Woman" or "Bootylicious" can imagine a one-on-one relationship with one, two, or all three members of Destiny's Child, whose images and artistry are purchased, rented, or downloaded under the control of the consumer. Under conditions of racial segregation, mass media provides a way that racial difference can safely enter racially segregated private spaces of living rooms and bedrooms. Destiny's Child may not be like the girls next door, but they can be seen on home theater and heard via headphones within the privacy of individual consciousness. In this new mass media context, Black sexual stereotypes are rendered virtually invisible by their ubiquity; yet, they persist through a disconnected mélange of animal skins, sexually explicit lyrics, breast worship, and focus on the booty. Destiny's Child may entertain and titillate; yet, their self-definitions as "survivors" and "independent women" express female power and celebration of the body and booty. The women in Destiny's Child are also wealthy. Just who is being "controlled" in these new arenas? For what purpose? Their message contains a defiance denied to Bartmann and Baker—"It's my body, it's my booty, and I'll do what I want with it—can you handle it?"

What are we to make of Jennifer Lopez? As a Latina,[10] where does she fit in this story of Western constructions of "wild" Black sexuality, the social construction of racial difference, and Black people's reactions to them? Like Josephine Baker before her, Jennifer Lopez is celebrated and makes a considerable amount of money. Elevating Jennifer Lopez's buttocks to icon status invokes historical meanings of Black female sexuality and takes the politics of race and sexuality to an entirely new plane. In this case, a Latina brushed with the hint of Blackness and not clearly of African descent carries the visible sign of Black sexuality. In order to be marketed, Black sexuality need not be associated solely with bodies that have been racially classified as "Negro," "mulatto," or "Black." Western imaginations have long filled in the color, moving women from Black to White and back again depending on the needs of the situation. In antebellum Charleston, South Carolina, and New Orleans, Louisiana, White men desired quadroons and octoroons as prostitutes because such women looked like White women, but they were actually Black women, with all that that implied about women's sexuality.[11] J-Lo's fluid ethnicity in her films, from the Chicana in *Selena* to the racial/ethnic ambiguity in subsequent roles, illustrates the shifting contours of racial/ethnic classification. When it comes to "hot-blooded" Latinas, one might ask which part of their "blood" carries the spice of sexual looseness?[12] This all seems to be a far cry from the commodification of Sarah Baartman's—buttocks—or is it?

The fact that these examples involve women of actual or imputed African descent is no accident because the racial difference assigned to Black people has often come in gender specific forms. In the nineteenth century, women stood as symbols of race and women from different races became associated with differentially valued expressions of sexuality. During this period marked by the rise of European nationalism, England, France, Spain, Portugal, Germany, the Netherlands, and Italy all jockeyed with varying degrees of success to define themselves as nation-states. Each followed its own distinctive path in constructing its own national identity and that of its colonies. Yet they shared one overriding feature—the treatment of women within each respective nation-state as well as within the colonies were important to national identity.[13] Ideas of pure White womanhood that were created to defend women of the homeland required a corresponding set of ideas about hot-blooded Latinas, exotic Suzy Wongs, wanton jezebels, and stoic native squaws. Civilized nation-states required uncivilized and backward colonies for their national identity to have meaning, and the status of women in both places was central to this entire endeavor. In this context, Black women became icons of hypersexuality.[14]

Men of African descent were also seen as hyper-sexual beings that have generated similar icons.[15] During the era of live entertainment, and until the onset of the technologies that made mass media possible, men were objectified differently from women. The West African slave trade and Southern auction blocks treated both Black women's and men's bodies as objects for sale, yet women participated in sexual spectacles to a greater degree than did men, because Western ideas about women and femininity itself have long been more tightly wedded to ideas about women's physical beauty and sexual attractiveness. Even today, men are far more likely to stare at and comment upon women's breasts, buttocks, legs, face, and other body parts than are women to subject men's bodies to this type of scrutiny. Like all women, Black women were objects to be seen, enjoyed, purchased, and used, primarily by White men with money. African women's sexuality may have piqued the prurient interest of Western audiences, but African men's sexuality was seen as dangerous and in need of control. Live expressions of Black male sexuality needed to be hidden from White spectators, especially audiences that might contain White women. Until recently, the very tenets of female respectability made it impossible for a female audience to cheer on a live male sex show, especially a White female audience viewing Black men as sexual beings. Assumptions of heterosexuality also inhibit males viewing other males as sexual objects. A situation in which White men view Black male bodies as sexual objects potentially creates a homoerotic space that is incompatible with ideas of straight White masculinity.

Mass media technologies profoundly altered this reliance on face-to-face spectatorship and live entertainment. Television, video, DVD, and the Internet enabled images of Black women and men to enter living rooms, bedrooms, family rooms, and other private domestic spaces. Black male images could now enter private White spaces, one step safely removed because these were no longer live performances and Black men no longer appeared in the flesh. These technological advances enabled the reworking of Black male sexuality that became much more visible, yet was safely contained. Take, for example, the stylized music video performances of hip-hop artists. Camera angles routinely are shot from a lower position than the rapper in question, giving the impression that he is looming over the viewer. In real life, being this close to young African American men who were singing about sex and violence and whose body language included fists, angry gestures, and occasional crotch-grabbing might be anxiety provoking for the typical rap and hip-hop consumer (most are suburban White adolescents). Yet viewing these behaviors safely packaged within a music video protects consumers from any possible contact with Black men who are actually in the videos. Just who are these videos for? What are the imagined race, gender, and sexual orientations of the viewers? Black men have long given performances that placed sexuality center stage—Elvis Presley, Mick Jagger, and rapper Eminem all recognized and profited from this reality—but the sexual implications of viewing Black men in the flesh rarely made it out of African American settings where such performances had a different meaning. It is one thing to visit a Black nightclub to hear singer Millie Jackson's live performance of raunchy blues or gather in a neighbor's living room to listen to Redd Foxx records. It is entirely another to sit in an interracial audience and listen to comedian Eddie Murphy's uncensored boasting concerning Black male sexual prowess; or to count the times within a music video that the camera hones in on rapper Ja Rule's crotch.

Western perceptions of the sexuality of men of African descent also became central to the national identities of European nation-states engaged in colonial projects. England, France, and other colonial powers constructed their national identities by manipulating ideas about men in the home country and in their colonies. The United States followed a similar path, with ideas about race and masculinity intertwined with ideas about American citizenship.[16] Like their female counterparts, men of African descent were also perceived to have excess sexual appetite, yet with a disturbing additional feature, a predilection for violence. In this context, the "White heroes" of Western Europe and the United States became constructed in relation to the "Black beasts" of Africa.[17] Moreover, both were used to signal the hierarchical relationship between colonizers and colonies. Overall, colonialism, slavery, and racial segregation relied upon this discourse of Black sexuality to create tightly bundled ideas about Black femininity and Black masculinity that in turn influenced racial ideologies and racial practices.

As these systems of racial rule recede in the post–civil rights era, what if anything is taking their place? Over one hundred years ago, African American intellectual William E. B. DuBois predicted that the problem of the twentieth century would be the presence of the color line. By that, DuBois meant that the policies of colonialism and racial segregation were designed to create, separate, and rank the various "races" of man. Until legally outlawed in the 1950s and 1960s, the color line policies of Jim Crow racial segregation kept the vast majority of African Americans from quality educations, good jobs, adequate health care, and the best neighborhoods. In contrast, the problem of the twenty-first century seems to be the seeming *absence* of a color line. Formal legal discrimination has been outlawed, yet contemporary social practices produce virtually identical racial hierarchies as those observed by DuBois. By whatever measures used in the United States or on a global scale, people of African descent remain disproportionately clustered at the bottom of the social hierarchy. The effects of these historical exclusions persist today under a new racism.[18]

It is important to note that the new racism of the early twenty-first century has not replaced prior forms of racial rule, but instead incorporates elements of past racial formations. As a result, ideas about race, gender, sexuality, and Black people as well as the social practices that these ideas shape and reflect remain intricately part of the new racism, but in changed ways. The new racism thus reflects a situation of permanence and change. Just as people of African descent were disadvantaged within prior forms of economic organization, a similar outcome exists today. On a global scale, wealth and poverty continue to be racialized. This is permanence. At the same time, racial hierarchy is produced in a context of massive economic, political, and social change that organizes racial hierarchy differently. The processes used to maintain the same outcome are also different. In a similar fashion, ideas about sexuality and gender that were very much a part of prior forms of racial rule remain as important today. They too are differently organized to produce remarkably similar results.

First, new forms of global capitalism frame the new racism. Globalization itself is certainly not new—it was a core characteristic of former patterns of racism. The African slave trade had a global reach and its legacy created the contemporary African Diaspora. The colonial wealth of Europe was based on a global system of racial subordination of people of color. Yet the increasing concentration of capital in the hands of fewer and fewer corporations distinguishes the contemporary global capitalism from its nineteenth-century counterpart. Today, relatively few transnational corporations are driving the world economy and their decisions affect the global distribution of wealth and poverty. These new forms of global organization have polarized world populations. On one end are elites who are wealthy beyond the imagination, and who have the freedom to come and go as they please, wherever and whenever they want. The locals, the people who are stuck in one place, without jobs, and for whom time seems to creep by, populate the other end.[19]

People of African descent are routinely disadvantaged in this global economy in which corporations make the decisions and in which "the company is free to move; but the consequences of the move are bound to stay."[20] Within a global context, Black people and other people of color are those more likely to lose jobs in local labor markets. They are the ones who lack control over oil, mineral wealth, or other natural resources on their land; who lose their land to global agribusiness; and who are denied basic services of electricity and clean water, let alone the luxury goods of the new information age. The benefits of telecommunications and other new technologies have had a far greater impact on Whites than on people of African descent and other people of color. For example, though Europe and North America constitute 20 percent of the world's population, two-thirds of all televisions and radios are owned and controlled in these two regions.[21]

The new racism is also characterized by a changing political structure that disenfranchises people, even if they appear to be included. In the United States, for example, people may vote, but corporations and other propertied entities wield tremendous influence in deciding the outcome of elections because they fund campaigns. All levels of government have been affected by a growing concentration of economic power that has fostered corporate influence over public policy. This same process operates in a transnational context. Global corporations increasingly dominate national, regional, and local governance. This concentrated economic power erodes the authority of national governments and has created unprecedented migrations of people and jobs both within and between nation-states. The ineffectiveness of transnational governance and domestic policies of racial desegregation in reducing Black poverty suggests an important link joining the experiences of people of African descent with postcolonial governance and the experiences of African Americans in the United States with racial desegregation. The outcome is reconfigured social hierarchies of race, class, gender, and sexuality, with people of African descent clumped at the bottom. Patterns of desegregation and subsequent resegregation of African Americans in the United States resemble the decolonization and recolonization that characterizes the global context.[22]

The new racism also relies more heavily on mass media to reproduce and disseminate the ideologies needed to justify racism. There are two themes here—the substance of racial ideologies under the new racism and the forms in which ideologies are created, circulated, and resisted. Ideas about Black sexuality certainly appear in contemporary racial ideologies. But the growing significance of Black popular culture and mass media as sites for creating and resisting racial ideologies is also striking. The films, music, magazines, music videos, and television shows of global entertainment, advertising, and news industries that produce superstars like Jennifer Lopez help manufacture the consent that makes the new racism appear to be natural, normal, and inevitable.[23]

The challenges of the new racism have been especially pronounced for African American women and men, the subjects of this [article]. The issues associated with the politics of the new racism and with the manipulation of ideologies within them, in the case of African Americans, the discourse on Black sexuality, affect everyone. But the specific form that race and gender politics take for African Americans can serve as an important site for examining these larger issues. Moreover, the African American community contains a crucial subpopulation in these debates. A generation of young African American men and women who were born after the struggles for civil rights, Black power, and African nation-state independence has come of age under this new racism. Referred to as the hip-hop generation, this group has encountered, reproduced, and resisted new forms of racism that continue to rely on ideas about Black sexuality. Expecting a democratic, fair society with equal economic opportunities, instead, this group faced disappearing jobs, crumbling schools, drugs, crime, and the weakening of African American community institutions. The contradictions of the post–civil rights era affect all African Americans, yet they have been especially pronounced for Black youth.[24]

AMERICA—A SEXUALLY REPRESSIVE SOCIETY?

Sexualized Black bodies seem to be everywhere in contemporary mass media, yet within African American communities, a comprehensive understanding of sexual politics remains elusive. In a social context that routinely depicts men and women of African descent as the embodiment of deviant sexuality, African American politics has remained curiously silent on issues of gender and sexuality. As a result, African Americans lack a vibrant, public discussion of the complex issues that the prevailing discourse on Black sexuality has raised for African American men and women. In more candid moments, however, some African American thinkers stress how damaging the absence of a self-defined Black sexual politics can be. As African American cultural critic Cheryl Clarke pointed out over twenty years ago:

> Like all Americans, black Americans live in a sexually repressive culture. And we have made all manner of compromise regarding our sexuality in order to live here. We have expended much energy trying to debunk the racist mythology which says our sexuality is depraved. Unfortunately, many of us have overcompensated and assimilated the Puritan value that sex is for procreation, occurs only between men and women, and is only valid within the confines of heterosexual marriage. . . . Like everyone else in America who is ambivalent in these respects, black folk have to live with the contradictions of this limited sexual system by repressing or closeting any other sexual/erotic urges, feelings, or desires.[25]

Given the saturation of American mass media with sexual themes, and the visibility of sexualized spectacles that include men and women of African descent within movies, music videos, and popular music in particular, Clarke's comments may seem to be odd. How can American culture be "sexually repressive" when sexuality seems to be everywhere? White actresses routinely play roles that include graphic sex scenes. Moreover, Black women are not downtrodden rape victims, but instead, also seem to be in control of their own sexuality. Director Spike Lee's African American leading lady Nola Darling seemed to be calling the shots in *She's Gotta Have It,* Lee's groundbreaking film about Black female sexuality. Destiny's Child and J-Lo certainly do not seem "repressed." How can African Americans be sexually "closeted" when Black sexuality itself serves as an icon for sexual freedom?

For African Americans, these questions are crucial, especially in the context of the post–civil rights era in which Black popular culture and mass media are increasingly important for racial rule. Sexual regulation occurs through repression, both by eliminating sexual alternatives and by shaping the public debates that do exist. In order to prosper, systems of oppression must regulate sexuality, and they often do so by manufacturing ideologies that render some ideas commonsensical while obscuring others. The expanding scope of mass media makes this process more visible and, more important, in the United States, does seem to have produced a "sexually repressive culture."

The treatment of human sexuality in American society reflects a curious combination of censorship and excessive visibility (e.g., hypervisibility), of embarrassed silences and talk-show babble. On the one hand, since colonial times, selected groups within U.S. society have striven to suppress a wide range of sexual ideas and practices.[26] American colonists paid close attention to the sexual behavior of individuals, not to eliminate sexual expression but to channel it into what they thought was its proper setting and purpose, namely, as a "duty and a joy within marriage, and for purposes of procreation."[27] More recently, the election of conservative Republican Ronald Reagan in 1980 emboldened the Christian Right to advance a fundamentalist family values discourse. Resembling the colonial discourse from the 1600s, the contemporary family values position argues (1) all sexual practices should occur only within the confines of heterosexual marriage; (2) the fundamental purpose of sexuality is procreation; and (3) children should be protected from all sexual information with the exception of abstinence as the preferred form of birth control before marriage.

This historical and contemporary agenda that has suppressed and often censored a range of ideas concerning human sexuality has made it difficult to have open, candid, and fact-based public debates. This censorship not only affects public dialogues but it also influences research on human sexuality.[28] Heterosexism, with its ideas about what constitutes normal and deviant sexuality holds sway to the point where significant gaps exist in the social science literature on human sexuality. Despite the conservative thrust since 1980, the suppression of a range of ideas about human sexuality is not new. Research done in the 1950s by Alfred Kinsey and his colleagues at Indiana University provides a textbook case of sexual censorship. Kinsey's work treated all sexual practices, including homosexuality and bisexuality, as inherently "normal" and defined the array of sexual practices reported by study participants as benign indicators of human difference. But Kinsey's work virtually ground to a halt when funding for this line of scientific research dried up.

It has taken the field some time to recover from this censorship. In essence, heterosexism and its accompanying assumptions of heterosexuality operate as a hegemonic or taken-for-granted ideology that has influenced research on human sexuality. Societal norms that install heterosexuality as the only way to be normal still hold sway.[29] For example, the term *sexuality* itself is used so synonymously with *hetero*sexuality that schools, churches, and other social institutions treat heterosexuality as natural, normal, and inevitable. Studying sexual practices that stray too far from prevailing norms, for example, sex outside of marriage, adolescent sexuality, homosexuality, and formerly taboo sexual practices such as anal and oral sex, become situated within a social problems framework. This approach not only stigmatizes individuals and groups who engage in alternative sexual practices but it also reinforces views of human sexuality itself as being a problem that should not be discussed in public. Alternately, research on human sexuality is often annexed to bona fide social problems, for example, adolescent pregnancy and people living with HIV/AIDS. Sexuality seems to be everywhere, but research that investigates variations in human sexuality outside of a social problems framework has only recently come to the forefront.

The treatment of sex education in American public schools illustrates how a sexually repressive culture strives to render human sexuality invisible. Sex education remains a hot topic, with students receiving spotty information at best. Topics that are important to adolescents have been difficult to include within sex education programs. Despite high student interest and a growing recognition that comprehensive sex education might save lives, programs tend to shy away from discussing sexuality before marriage, the use of contraception, homosexuality, and other controversial topics. Ironically, the checkered pattern of research on human sexuality offers a good case for how heterosexism operates as a system of power that negatively affects straight and lesbian, gay, bisexual, and transgendered (LGBT) students alike. Because adolescents of all sexual orientations are in the process of forming sexual identities, they are especially affected by heterosexism. For example, despite a high adolescent pregnancy rate, worrisome increases in the rate of HIV infection among American adolescents, and emerging research demonstrating that high school students grappling with LGBT identities are more prone to depression and suicide, the reluctance to talk openly about human sexuality within U.S. schools places students at risk. Similarly, a special report on adolescent sexuality points to the difficulties of collecting data on adolescent conceptions of abstinence.[30] Anecdotal reports suggest that many adolescents who engage in oral sex think that they are practicing abstinence because they are refraining from genital sexual intercourse. These practices may protect them from pregnancy, but they also expose adolescents to risks of sexually transmitted diseases, including HIV.[31]

Despite these repressive practices, on the other hand, sexual ideas and images within contemporary U.S. society enjoy a visibility that would have been unheard of in Kinsey's 1950s America. Recognizing that sex sells, corporations increasingly use it to sell cars, toothpaste, beer, and other consumer goods. This media saturation has made sexual spectacles highly visible within American popular culture. Soap operas, prime time television, billboards, music videos, movies, and the Internet all contain explicit sexual material. Making sex highly visible in marketplace commodity relations becomes important to maintaining profitability within the U.S. capitalist political economy. The goal is neither to stimulate debate nor to educate, but to sell products.

In the absence of other forums, talk shows on network television provide one important public medium for gaining sexual information. Unfortunately, such shows foster the commodification of sexuality. Stressing sexually explicit conversations that titillate rather than instruct, talk shows illustrate how marketplace relations profit from sexual spectacles. By the early 2000s, this market had segmented into a variety of shows, each carving out its specific identity, often based on distinctive norms regarding race, class, gender, and sexuality.[32] For example, *The Montel Williams Show* routinely trumpets the benefits of the heterosexual family, primarily by extolling the role of fathers in their children's lives. By itself, this message is fairly innocuous. However, the show's format creates sexual spectacles that function as modern-day morality plays about race, gender, and sexuality. Mr. Williams, an African American, routinely conducts paternity tests for women who are not "sure" who fathered their babies. The potential fathers are invited to hear the results of the paternity test on the air, with a stern talk by Mr. Williams concerning their "responsibility" to those branded as fathers by DNA evidence. This family drama is played out repeatedly, with Mr. Williams readying himself to deliver the message to wayward young men—if you take it out of your pants, you need to take care of your babies. Moreover, as an African American man married to a White woman, on his show Mr. Williams repeatedly brings on working-class, interracial couples in which young White mothers try to get their sexually irresponsible Black boyfriends to claim paternity. If this weren't enough, Mr. Williams also devotes shows to the pain experienced by biracial children in search of their wayward parents.

The Maury Povich Show also trades in this racial family drama, but with more emphasis on race and sexuality. Not only does Mr. Povich, a White American, present shows in which White women seek paternity tests for their Black male partners, Mr. Povich presents Black women and Black men in an especially stark light. One show, for example, featured a Black woman who brought on nine Black men as candidates for her six-month-old daughter's "baby daddy."[33] All nine failed the paternity test. After the revelation, with cameras rolling in search of the all-important "money shot,"[34] Mr. Povich followed the distraught young mother backstage, and volunteered to keep working with her until she had tracked down the Black deadbeat dad. Like Mr. Williams, Mr. Povich delivers a message about responsibility to the DNA-branded fathers. Via the choice of topic, and showing the African American woman whose sexuality was so out of control that she had no idea who had fathered her child, Mr. Povich panders to longstanding societal beliefs about Black sexuality.

The crying and raw emotion solicited on Mr. Williams's and Mr. Povich's shows pales in comparison to the staged sexual spectacles of *The Jerry Springer Show*. Reminiscent of the London freak shows of Sarah Bartmann's time, Mr. Springer's shows routinely combine sexuality and violence, two sure-fire audience builders. Here participants are invited to come on the air and reveal "secrets" to seemingly unsuspecting spouses, lovers, and friends. The "secrets" routinely involve cheating, lying, and false paternity. By his choice of guests, Mr. Springer's show also takes sexual spectacles to an entirely new level. Morbidly obese women parade across the stage in bikinis, verbally taunting the audience to comment on their appearance. In a context in which women's bodies are routinely sexualized, displaying seemingly hideous female bodies is designed to shock and solicit ridicule. These confessional talk shows also routinely conduct paternity tests, show pictures of babies who lack legal fathers, discuss sexual infidelity, and display audience members in sexually explicit clothing (or lack thereof). For many Americans, these shows substitute for public discussions of sexuality because few other outlets are available.

African Americans are well represented in the public spectacles provided by Mr. Williams's, Mr. Povich's, and Mr. Springer's talk shows. Guests on all three programs are clearly working-class, with many of them Black and Latino. These shows are not just about sexuality; they also signal clear messages about race and class. They depict the challenges of explaining a new, interracial class structure that can no longer rely on biological notions of race to differentiate poor people (assumed to be Black) from middle-class people (assumed to be White). In the new multicultural America, Blacks can be middle class (the hugely popular *Cosby Show* broke that barrier in the 1980s) and, in fact, a certain degree of Black middle-class visibility is needed to buttress arguments of equal opportunity (Oprah Winfrey and Montel Williams both exemplify this need for visible, accomplished Blacks). But how does one explain the persistence of poverty among *White* Americans if poverty has long been attributed to Black biological inferiority? They are not biologically Black, but their poverty and downward mobility can be explained if they are seen as being culturally or socially Black. Whites who embrace Black culture become positioned closer to Blacks and become stigmatized. In the context of the new racism, cultural explanations for economic success and poverty substitute for biological arguments concerning intelligence or genetic dispositions for immorality or violence.

Viewing stories about historically taboo interracial sexuality between White women and Black men becomes the new sexual spectacle, where working-class White women become "darkened" by their sexual relationships with irresponsible working-class Black men.[35] When accused of paternity by these "trashy" White women, Black men are depicted as proud of their irresponsible sexual behavior. Certainly White men are given paternity tests on these shows, but typically these are working-class or poor White men who are hauled in by working-class White mothers of their alleged children. In contrast to the White women who point the finger of paternity at both Black and White men, Black women rarely identify White men as the potential fathers of their babies. Given the history of interracial, institutionalized rape of Black women by White men, White fathers of Black children would hardly be newsworthy. Instead, Black women are presented as being so reckless that they do not know who fathered their children or, sharing a common fate with their White sisters, they point the finger at irresponsible Black men. Despite similarities that link all three shows, they do offer different scripts for solving the problems of these sexual spectacles. Part of the appeal of *The Montel Williams Show* lies in his role in this family drama—Williams

plays the part of the caring yet stern Black patriarch who provides the fatherly discipline that so many of his guests seemingly lack. In contrast, Mr. Povich presents himself as a kindly White father, showing concern for his emotional albeit abnormal guests. Mr. Springer is merely a ringmaster—he doesn't get near his guests, preferring instead to watch the cursing and chair throwing from a safe distance. Discipline them, listen to them, or dismiss them—all three solutions apply to working-class and poor guests. Apparently, middle-class Americans (even Black ones) have little difficulty identifying which sexual partner conceived their children. Affluent, thirty-something White women awaiting the results of paternity tests for their biracial babies just do not appear on any of these shows.

Much more is at stake here than the accuracy of the depictions of African American women and men within talk shows and other forms of mass media. African Americans and Black culture are highly visible within the American movies, music, sports, dance, and fashion that help shape contemporary ideologies of race, gender, sexuality, and class in a global context. Sexual spectacles travel, and they matter. Historical context disappears, leaving seemingly free-floating images in its wake that become the new vocabulary that joins quite disparate entities. Terms such as "primitive," "backward," "jungle," "wild," and "freak" uncritically cycle through contemporary global culture, leaving undisturbed the pejorative historical meanings associated with this vocabulary. But history hides in the shadows of these terms, because these concepts are incomprehensible without a social context to give them meaning. For example, the pervasive use of animal imagery persists within some expressions of contemporary Black popular culture, as suggested by the decision to clothe Destiny's Child in animal-skin bikinis on their album cover. These depictions eerily resemble past practices of associating Africans with animals, particularly apes, monkeys, and chimpanzees. The choice of animal may change—no longer apes, Black men have taken on new identities as "dogs" energetically engaged in chasing the (kitty) "cat"—but associating Black men and women with lusty, animal sexual practices apparently has not. Although different meanings may be associated with animal imagery, Snoop Doggy Dog, Little Bow Wow, and the classic phrase "you my main dog" all invoke this same universe of animal imagery. Moreover, representations of Black men as "dogs" who have replaced the cool "cats" of prior eras of African American jazzmen, as well as the video "hos" who populate rap music videos suggest the emergence of an increasingly sophisticated gender-specific expression of ideas about Blackness sold in the global marketplace. Josephine Baker's banana dance and Destiny's Child's "Bootylicious" would be meaningless without this history, even if those enjoying the images do not consciously see the connections.

African American theorist Cornel West identifies the paradox of a sexually repressive culture that, on the one hand, seems saturated with sexuality, but that, on the other hand, suppresses education and open dialogue concerning human sexuality. To West, race matters: "the paradox of the sexual politics of race in America is that, behind closed doors, the dirty, disgusting, and funky sex associated with Black people is often perceived to be more intriguing and interesting, while in public spaces talk about Black sexuality is virtually taboo."[36] Black sexuality is routinely invoked within American society, namely, the alleged sexual prowess of the Black men accused of fathering babies with White women, but analyzing it is discouraged. The result is a society fraught with contradictions. For example, well-off White teenagers can drive expensive cars to racially segregated high schools and college campuses that admit only a few handpicked African Americans, all the while booming the latest sexually explicit lyrics of their favorite Black hip-hop artist. American viewers can sit in their living rooms viewing talk shows that censure the African American man accused of fathering three out-of-wedlock children with two different White women, yet still be intrigued by his sexual prowess. Legions of young American men can wonder what it would be like to get Beyoncé Knowles from Destiny's Child or Jennifer Lopez in bed.

Like other Americans, African Americans must make sense of this curious sexual climate that accompanies the new racism. This task is made even more difficult by the fact that African Americans are included in these debates, often serving as examples of what *not* to be or, alternately, as icons of sexual freedom served up as the antidote to American sexual repression. As part of the color-blind racism that has accompanied the erasure of the color line, the ubiquitous *inclusion* of images of Black sexuality that permeate contemporary movies, television shows, and music videos can replicate the power relations of racism today just as effectively as the *exclusion* of Black images did prior to the 1960s. Thus, Cheryl Clarke's observation that African Americans live in a sexually repressive culture speaks less to the prominence of representations of Black sexuality within an increasingly powerful mass media than to the *function* of these images in helping to construct a "limited sexual system."

NOTES

1. Asante 1993.
2. The details of this version come from Fausto-Sterling 1995. Depending on the intent of the author, Sarah Baartman's story takes on different meanings. For example, Anne Fausto-Sterling's account focuses on the nineteenth-century scientists who relentlessly probed her body and used Baartman as a vehicle for redefining Western concepts of race, gender, and sexuality. Fausto-Sterling's version points out how we learn much more about European scientists themselves via their treatment of Sarah Baartman than we gain any accurate information about her. In contrast, in his groundbreaking essay "The Hottentot and the Prostitute: Toward an Iconography of Female Sexuality," Sander Gilman's account traces how ideas about the Hottentot Venus as an icon of Black sexuality were crucial to nineteenth-century European perceptions of women's sexuality (Gilman 1985, 76–108). Advancing a materialist analysis, Zine Magubane takes issue with Gilman's claim that, by the eighteenth century, the sexuality of African men and women became the icon for deviant sexuality in general. Rather, Magubane contends that the Baartman exhibition encapsulated the debates that were occurring concerning colonial labor needs (Magubane 2001). Grounded in a cultural studies framework, Susie Prestney explores how the image of the Hotten-

tot Venus was central to conceptions of difference, especially those of freak shows and similar spectacles (Prestney 1997). Taking a different approach, Yvette Abrahams challenges the flawed historiography on the Khoi people and indigenous people in general that places Baartman outside history (Abrahams 1998). Finally, my own rendering of this narrative in *Black Feminist Thought* (Collins 2000a, 136–137, 141–145), and in this volume aim to place Sarah Baartman in an intersectional analysis of how race, class, gender, and sexuality affect women of African descent.
3. Bederman 1995, 1–5.
4. I use the terms *representations, stereotypes,* and *controlling images* to refer to the depiction of people of African descent within Western scholarship and popular culture. Each term has a different history. Representations need not be stereotypical and stereotypes need not function as controlling images. Of the three, controlling images are most closely tied to power relations of race, class, gender, and sexuality. For a discussion of controlling images, see Collins 2000a, 69–96.
5. As used here, the term *invented* resembles Benedict Anderson's notion of an *imagined* community (Anderson 1983). In his important study of nationalism, Anderson contends that members of nations can never know one another.

They "imagine" or "invent" a community. Racial categories such as White, Black, and native are all, in this sense, invented. Also, the term *discourse* has a particular meaning of a set of ideas and practices that, when taken together, organize both the way a society defines certain truths about itself and the way it deploys social power. An invented discourse is in some sense an oxymoron in that all discourses are social constructions that simultaneously shape and reflect actual social relations. For a good use of the term *invented* as the frame of an argument, see Oyèrónké Oyĕwùmí's book *The Invention of Women: Making an African Sense of Western Gender Discourses* (Oyĕwùmí 1997). All invented discourses typically contain contradictions and are often hotly contested, certainly the case with invented discourses on Black sexuality. For historical treatments of the invention of discourses of Black sexuality, see Jordan 1968, 136–178, especially 150–151; and D'Emilio and Freedman 1997, 34–37.

6. Collins 2000a, 69–96.

7. Abrahams 1998; Maseko 1998.

8. Morton 1991; Jewell 1993; Davis 1994; Asante 1994; Turner 1994.

9. The theme of primitivism of non-Western peoples was used to justify colonialism and slavery. For an analysis of how this idea was constructed and used, see Young 1995; Torgovnick 1990; McClintock 1995.

10. The term *Latina* addresses some of the multifaceted debates within contemporary racial theory that demonstrate the fluidity of racial classification. Research on how the different histories of people of African descent within Latin American countries coupled with a philosophy of "racial democracy" shows how Latin American populations approach race and ethnicity differently (Winant 2001, 219–248). In this context, Lopez's history as a Puerto Rican is significant, especially regarding the changing meaning of race in the United States as evidenced in the 2000 census (Rodriguez 2000). The category *Latina* refers to a wide range of national histories and migration streams into a new American ethnicity of *Hispanic*. Historically, Puerto Ricans have been viewed as reflecting a mulatto mixture resulting from European and African backgrounds as compared to a mestizo mixture of European and Indian of Chicana or Mexican-American populations. But the very categories of mulatto and mestizo may mask more than they reveal about the fluidity of racial and ethnic classification throughout the Americas. Both Puerto Rico and Mexico have varying combinations of racial mixtures, a situation that generates different approaches to skin color, hair texture, and the racial order itself. These ideas become layered upon North American ideas concerning race.

11. D'Emilio and Freedman 1997, 102–103.

12. Ironically, the theme of racial mixture of African, Indians, and Whites falters when Spain and Portugal are in the mix. Latinas have Spanish blood, but the Whiteness of this lineage can be questioned. Moors brought dark skin and Islam to Spain and intermingled with its peoples. Ferdinand and Isabella were celebrated for unifying Spain, "civilizing" it, and insisting on Catholicism as the way to prove membership and belonging in the emerging Spanish nation. Thus, Moors with their heathen Muslim beliefs and their dark skin became coded as savages.

13. The relationship among colonialism, European nationalism, and women has been explored by a variety of authors. For a representative work, see Yuval-Davis 1997.

14. People of African descent were not the only ones whose sexuality was pathologized in this process. Whereas the black/white binary is the anchor that frames all others, different race/gender groups found their sexuality differentially stereotyped and pathologized in this process. Enslaving people of African descent not only required enforcing the master/slave relationship, it also required erasing the presence of indigenous peoples (who faced genocidal policies) as well as claiming land that had been historically governed by Mexico (Takaki 1993). Racial ideologies constructed the sexualities of multiple groups in relation to one another (D'Emilio and Freedman 1997). Justifying slavery also required establishing a social class hierarchy among Whites while hiding the effects of this hierarchy under the assumed privileges attached to Whiteness.

15. For an early discussion of Black male sexuality, see Jordan 1968, 151–152. For more recent works that build on historical work, see Ferber 1998; Riggs 1999; Jones 1993.

16. For an analysis of how this process operated in the late nineteenth and early twentieth centuries, see Somerville 2000; Bederman 1995.

17. For a classic work on this process, see Hoch 1979.

18. The changes generated by postcoloniality, global capitalism, and new technologies have sparked a lively debate about the contours and meaning of the new racism in the United States. Some scrutinize the transformation of contemporary U.S. society as a racialized social system composed of structural and ideological dimensions (Bonilla-Silva 1996). When it comes to African Americans, structurally, American society has not made the gains in desegregating its housing, schools, and employment promised by the civil rights movement (Massey and Denton 1993). One study of Atlanta, Georgia, revealed that neighborhood-level racial resegregation is emerging as a new spatial pattern within major American cities, even those with a politically enfranchised and highly visible Black middle class (Orfield and Ashkinaze 1991). Other research points to the growth of a prison-industrial complex as an important new site for institutionalized racism confronting working-class and poor African Americans and Latinos (Miller 1996). Ideologically, a belief in upholding "color blindness" masks the continued inequalities of contemporary racism. By proclaiming that equal treatment of *individuals* under the law is sufficient for addressing racism, this ideology redefines *group*-based, antiracist remedies such as affirmative action as being "racist" (Crenshaw 1997). For a critique of color blindness and an

analysis of how this racial ideology merits rethinking in the United States, see Guinier and Torres 2002.

19. For a thorough analysis of how globalization shapes contemporary racial formations, see Winant's analysis of the United States, South Africa, Brazil, and Europe in the post–World War II era (Winant 2001). Feminist analysis has also produced a broad literature on globalization and women's economic status, some of it focused on racism, sexism, and issues of globalization. For representative theoretical work in this tradition, see Alexander 1997; Mohanty 1997. African American scholars have also focused more attention on the global political economy. For representative works in this tradition, see Wilson 1996; Brewer 1994; Squires 1994.

20. Bauman 1998, 9.

21. Lusane 1997, 114.

22. M. Jacqui Alexander's discussion of the tourist industry in the Bahamas provides an especially insightful analysis of the effects of globalization on nation-state autonomy and on social problems within the Bahamas (Alexander 1997).

23. Cultural studies and studies of mass media underwent massive growth after 1980. For general work on the media, see Gitlin 2001. For race and media, see Entman 2000. The field of Black cultural studies has generated a range of literature. For representative works, consult Bobo 1995; Kelley 1994; Kelley 1997; Rose 1994; Wallace 1990; Gilroy 2000; Ransby and Matthews 1993; Gates 1992; Neal 2002; Watkins 1998; Cashmore 1997; Caponi 1999; Dent 1992b; Hall 1992; and Dyson 1996.

24. Kitwana 2002.

25. Clarke 1983, 199.

26. D'Emilio and Freedman suggest that the suppression of a range of sexual practices was part of colonization. Comparing the sexual practices of Native Americans, which varied widely, with European colonialist perceptions of such practices, in every region where Europeans and indigenous peoples came into contact, Europeans judged the sexual life of natives as "savage" and their own practices as "civilized." For example, most indigenous peoples did not associate either nudity or sexuality with sin. They accepted premarital intercourse, polygamy, or institutionalized homosexuality, all practices that were condemned by European church and state (D'Emilio and Freedman 1997, 6–7). They point out, "perhaps the most striking contrast between English and Indian sexual systems was the relative absence of sexual conflict among native Americans, due in part to their different cultural attitudes toward both property and sexuality. . . . In cultures in which one could not 'own' another person's sexuality, prostitution—the sale of sex—did not exist prior to the arrival to European settlers. Rape—the theft of sex—only rarely occurred, and it was one of the few sexual acts forbidden by Indian cultures" (D'Emilio and Freedman 1997, 8).

27. D'Emilio and Freedman 1997, 16.

28. A 1995 report published by the Social Science Research Council charts the political difficulties that have plagued scientific studies of sexuality within American social science (di Mauro 1995).

29. Hegemony is also a mode of social organization wherein the dissent of oppressed groups is absorbed and thereby rendered politically useless. Moreover, in hegemonic situations, power is diffused throughout a social system such that multiple groups police one another and suppress each other's dissent. For example, if African Americans come to believe the dominant ideology and accept ideas about Black masculinities and Black femininities constructed within the dominant framework, then Black political dissent about gender and about all things tied to gender becomes weakened. Because they are used to justify existing social hierarchies, hegemonic ideologies may seem invincible. But ideologies of all sorts are never static. Instead, they are always internally inconsistent and are always subject to contestation (Magubane 2001).

30. Remez 2000.

31. This history of suppression of sex education and the limits on discussions that do exist have an especially negative impact on African American adolescents. HIV/AIDS has had a significant impact on African American youth. For statistics, see http://www.cdc.gov/hiv/pubs/Facts/afam.pdf.

32. For an analysis of talk shows, especially the production of "trashy" talk shows, see Grindstaff 2002. Grindstaff does not emphasize race, but her study of how talk shows replicate and reproduce ideas about social class and gender provides insight into the general process of ideology construction and contestation. She notes that talk shows are typically geared to women, feature working-class guests, and aim to display ordinary people engaged in extraordinary behavior.

33. Mark Anthony Neal and Hortense Spillers offer two different interpretations of the emergence of the term "baby daddy" to describe unmarried fatherhood among African American men. Neal's chapter "Baby Mama (Drama) and Baby Daddy (Trauma): Post-Soul Gender Politics" uses Black popular culture (Neal 2002, 57–97). In contrast, Spillers's essay "Mama's Baby, Papa's Maybe: An American Grammar Book," also examines unmarried fatherhood in the context of American race relations and the exploitation of Black bodies under slavery (Spillers 2000).

34. Grindstaff borrows the phrase the "money shot" from pornography to describe the efforts of producers to get ordinary people to deliver strong emotions such as joy, sorrow, rage, or remorse that can be seen in visible, bodily terms. Crying, shaking, running, and other evidence of emotion besides just talk are solicited. As Grindstaff points out, "Like pornography, daytime talk is a narrative of explicit revelation in which people 'get down and dirty' and 'bare it all' for the pleasure, fascination, or repulsion of viewers. Like the orgasmic cum shot of pornographic films, the money shot of talk shows makes visible the precise moment of letting go, of losing control, of

surrendering to the body and its 'animal' emotions" (Grindstaff 2002, 19). This is why Mr. Povich followed the woman backstage—he was in search of an authentic money shot.

35. Sociologist Abby Ferber describes how White supremacist literature remains obsessed with this theme of inter-racial

sexuality generally and of protecting the body of the White woman (and thus the White race) from Black penetration. White women who willingly partner with Black men become redefined as "darkened," trashy women (Ferber 1998).

36. West 1993, 83.

REFERENCES

Abrahams, Yvette. 1998. "Images of Sara Bartman: Sexuality, Race, and Gender in Early-Nineteenth-Century Britain." *Nation, Empire, Colony: Historicizing Gender and Race.* Ed. Ruth Roach Pierson and Nupur Chadhuri, 220–236. Bloomington: Indiana University Press.

Alexander, M. Jacqui. 1997. "Erotic Autonomy as a Politics of Decolonization: An Anatomy of Feminist and State Practice in the Bahamas Tourist Industry." *Feminist Genealogies, Colonial Legacies, Democratic Futures.* Ed. M. Jacqui Alexander and Chandra Talpade Mohanty, 63–100. New York: Routledge.

Anderson, Benedict. 1983. *Imagined Communities: Reflections on the Origin and Spread of Nationalism.* London: Verso.

Asante, Kariamu Welsh. 1993. "Josephine Baker." *Black Women in America: An Historical Encyclopedia.* Ed. Darlene Clark Hine, 75–78. Vol. 1. New York: Carlson Publishing.

———. 1994. "Images of Women in African Dance: Sexuality and Sensuality as Dual Unity." *Sage* 8, no. 2 (fall): 16–19.

Bauman, Zygmunt. 1998. *Globalization: The Human Consequences.* New York: Columbia University Press.

Bederman, Gail. 1995. *Manliness and Civilization: A Cultural History of Gender and Race in the United States, 1890–1917.* Chicago: University of Chicago Press.

Bobo, Jacqueline. 1995. *Black Women as Cultural Readers.* New York: Columbia University Press.

Bonilla-Silva, Eduardo. 1996. "Rethinking Racism: Toward a Structural Interpretation." *Americam Sociological Review* 62 (June): 465–480.

Brewer, Rose. 1994. "Race, Class, Gender and U.S. State Welfare Policy: The Nexus of Inequality for African American Families." *Color, Class and Country: Experiences of Gender.* Ed. Gay Young and Bette J. Dickerson, 115–127. London: Zed.

Caponi, Gena Dagel, ed. 1999. *Signifyin(g), Sanctifyin', & Slam Dunking: A Reader in African American Expressive Culture.* Amherst: University of Massachusetts Press.

Cashmore, Ellis. 1997. *The Black Culture Industry.* New York: Routledge.

Clarke, Cheryl. 1983. "The Failure to Transform: Homophobia in the Black Community." *Home Girls: A Black Feminist Anthology.* Ed. Barbara Smith, 197–208. New York: Kitchen Table Press.

Collins, Patricia Hill. 2000a. *Black Feminist Thought: Knowledge, Consciousness, and the Politics of Empowerment.* New York: Routledge.

Crenshaw, Kimberlé Williams. 1997. "Color Blindness, History, and the Law." *The House That Race Built.* Ed. Wahneema Lubiano, 280–288. New York: Pantheon.

D'Emilio, John, and Estelle B. Freedman. 1997. *Intimate Matters: A History of Sexuality in America.* Chicago: University of Chicago Press.

Dent, Gina, ed. 1992b. *Black Popular Culture.* Seattle: Bay Press.

di Mauro, Diane. 1995. *Sexuality Research in the United States: An Assessment of the Social and Behavioral Sciences.* New York: Social Science Research Council, Sexuality Research Assessment Project.

Dyson, Michael Eric. 1996. *Between God and Gangsta Rap: Bearing Witness to Black Culture.* New York: Oxford University Press.

Entman, Robert M., and Rojecki Andrew. 2000. *The Black Image in the White Mind: Media and Race in America.* Chicago: University of Chicago Press.

Fausto-Sterling, Anne. 1995. "Gender, Race, and Nation: The Comparative Anatomy of 'Hottentot' Women in Europe, 1815–1817." *Deviant Bodies: Critical Perspectives on Difference in Science and Popular Culture.* Ed. Jennifer Terry and Jacqueline Urla, 19–48. Bloomington: Indiana University Press.

Ferber, Abby L. 1998. *White Man Falling: Race, Gender, and White Supremacy.* Lanham, Md.: Rowman & Littlefield.

Gates, Henry Louis. 1992. *Loose Canons: Notes on the Culture Wars.* New York: Oxford University Press.

Gilman, Sander L. 1985. *Difference and Pathology: Stereotypes of Sexuality, Race, and Madness.* Ithaca, N.Y.: Cornell University Press.

Gilroy, Paul. 2000. *Against Race: Imagining Political Culture Beyond the Color Line.* Cambridge, Mass.: Belknap Press of Harvard University Press.

Gitlin, Todd. 2001. *Media Unlimited: How the Torrent of Images and Sounds Overwhelms Our Lives.* New York: Henry Holt.

Grindstaff, Laura. 2002. *The Money Shot: Trash, Class, and the Making of TV Talk Shows.* Chicago: University of Chicago Press.

Guinier, Lani, and Gerald Torres. 2002. *The Miner's Canary: Enlisting Race, Resisting Power, Transforming Democracy.* Cambridge, Mass.: Harvard University Press.

Hall, Stuart. 1992. "What Is This 'Black' in Black Popular Culture?" *Black Popular Culture.* Ed. Gina Dent, 21–33. Seattle: Bay Press.

Hoch, Paul. 1979. *White Hero, Black Beast: Racism, Sexism, and the Mask of Masculinity.* London: Pluto Press.

Jewell, K. Sue. 1993. *From Mammy to Miss America and Beyond: Cultural Images and the Shaping of U.S. Social Policy.* New York: Routledge.

Jones, Jacquie. 1993. "The Construction of Black Sexuality: Towards Normalizing the Black Cinematic Experience." *Black American Cinema.* Ed. Manthia Diawara, 247–256. New York: Routledge.

Jordan, Winthrop D. 1968. *White over Black: American Attitudes Toward the Negro, 1550–1812.* New York: W. W. Norton.

Kelley, Robin D. G. 1994. *Race Rebels: Culture, Politics, and the Black Working Class.* New York: Free Press.

———. 1997. *Yo' Mama's DisFUNKtional!: Fighting the Culture Wars in Urban America.* Boston: Beacon Press.

Kitwana, Bakari. 2002. *The Hip Hop Generation: Young Blacks and the Crisis in African-American Culture.* New York: Basic Books.

Lusane, Clarence. 1997. *Race in the Global Era: African Americans at the Millennium.* Boston: South End Press.

Magubane, Zine. 2001. "Which Bodies Matter? Feminism, Poststructuralism, Race, and the Curious Theoretical Odyssey of the 'Hottentot Venus.'" *Gender & Society* 15, no. 6: 816–834.

Maseko, Zola. 1998. *The Life and Times of Sara Baartman: "The Hottentot Venus."* New York: First Run/Icarus Films.

Massey, Douglas S., and Nancy A. Denton. 1993. *American Apartheid: Segregation and the Making of the Underclass.* Cambridge, Mass.: Harvard University Press.

McClintock, Anne. 1995. *Imperial Leather: Race, Gender, and Sexuality in the Colonial Contest.* New York: Routledge.

Miller, Jerome G. 1996. *Search and Destroy: African-American Males in the Criminal Justice System.* New York: Cambridge University Press.

Mohanty, Chandra Talpade. 1997. "Women Workers and Capitalist Scripts: Ideologies of Domination, Common Interests, and the Politics of Solidarity." *Feminist Genealogies, Colonial Legacies, Democratic Futures.* Ed. M. Jacqui Mohanty Chandra and Talpade Alexander, 3–29. New York: Routledge.

Morton, Patricia. 1991. *Disfigured Images: The Historical Assault on Afro-American Women.* New York: Greenwood Press.

Neal, Mark Anthony. 2002. *Soul Babies: Black Popular Culture and the Post-Soul Aesthetic.* New York: Routledge.

Orfield, Gary, and Carole Ashkinaze. 1991. *The Closing Door: Conservative Policy and Black Opportunity.* Chicago: University of Chicago Press.

Oyĕwùmí, Oyèrónké. 1997. *The Invention of Women: Making an African Sense of Western Gender Discourses.* Minneapolis: University of Minnesota Press.

Prestney, Susie. 1997. "Inscribing the Hottentot Venus: Generating Data for Difference." *At the Edge of International Relations: Postcolonialism, Gender & Dependency.* Ed. Phillip Darby, 86–105. New York: Pinter.

Ransby, Barbara, and Tracye Matthews. 1993. "Black Popular Culture and the Transcendence of Patriarchal Illusions." *Race and Class* 35, no. 1: 57–68.

Remez, Lisa. 2000. "Oral Sex Among Adolescents: Is It Sex or Abstinence?" *Family Planning Perspectives* 32, no. 6: 298–304.

Riggs, Marlon T. 1999. "Black Macho Revisited: Reflections of a SNAP! Queen." *Black Men on Race, Gender, and Sexuality.* Ed. Devon W. Carbado, 306–311. New York: New York University Press.

Rodriguez, Clara E. 2000. *Changing Race: Latinos, the Census, and the History of Ethnicity in the United States.* New York: New York University Press.

Rose, Tricia. 1994. *Black Noise: Rap Music and Black Culture in Contemporary American.* Hanover, N.H.: Wesleyan University Press.

Somerville, Siobhan B. 2000. *Queering the Color Line: Race and the Invention of Homosexuality in American Culture.* Durham, N.C.: Duke University Press.

Spillers, Hortense J. 2000. "Mama's Baby, Papa's Maybe: An American Grammar Book." *The Black Feminist Reader.* Ed. Joy James and T. Denean Sharpley-Whiting, 57–87. Malden Mass.: Blackwell.

Squires, Gregory D. 1994. *Capital and Communities in Black and White: The Intersections of Race, Class, and Uneven Development.* Albany: State University of New York Press.

Takaki, Ronald T. 1993. *A Different Mirror: A History of Multicultural America.* Boston: Little, Brown.

Torgovnick, Marianna. 1990. *Gone Primitive: Savage Intellects, Modern Lives.* Chicago: University of Chicago Press.

Turner, Patricia A. 1994. *Ceramic Uncles and Celluloid Mammies: Black Images and Their Influence on Culture.* New York: Anchor.

Wallace, Michele. 1990. *Invisibility Blues: From Pop to Theory.* New York: Verso.

Watkins, S. Craig. 1998. *Representing: Hip Hop Culture and the Production of Black Cinema.* Chicago: University of Chicago Press.

Wilson, William Julius. 1996. *When Work Disappears: The World of the New Urban Poor.* New York: Knopf.

Winant, Howard. 2001. *The World Is a Ghetto: Race and Democracy Since World War II.* New York: Basic Books.

Young, Robert J. C. 1995. *Colonial Desire: Hybridity in Theory, Culture and Race.* New York: Routledge.

Yuval-Davis, Nira. 1997. *Gender and Nation.* Thousand Oaks, Calif.: Sage.

Loving Women in the Modern World

What does it mean to be a "lesbian" in the modern world? In the 21st century it means loving women, desiring women, forming relationships with women, engaging in sexual behaviour with women, claiming an identity as a lesbian, and perhaps forming communities with other lesbians, although not all of these are necessary to the definition. But what do we make of women who loved, desired, formed relationships with and had sex with women before the concept and identity of "lesbian" were available? What do we make of such women in cultures that have different categories of gender and sexual behaviour? We might call them "lesbian-like" or talk of same-sex love, desire or sexual acts.[1] What is crucial is that we contemplate, as best we can, the ways in which women in the past and in different parts of the world negotiated and understood their desire, love and self-conceptions.

I explore here different patterns of loving women in various parts of the world, from around the beginning of the 19th century up to the present. It is impossible, of course, to be comprehensive, since research on many societies remains sketchy or is entirely lacking. Nor is there space to do justice to more than a few places. But my aim is to give a sense of women's lives with other women before, during and after the "discovery," naming and claiming of lesbian identity. Although lesbianism is often dismissed in societies subject to Western imperialism as an imported perversion (and in Western societies traditionally attributed to those of "other" races, classes or nations), women all around the world have found many ways of loving other women.

The story of loving women in the modern world is a tale of women who dressed and passed as men and who married women, of female husbands and manly women, of romantic friends who made lives together, of trysts in domestic spaces, of secretive and not-so-secretive communities, of sapphists and female inverts and marriage-resisters and bulldaggers and butches and fems and lesbians. Yet it is not simply a tale of women with same-sex desires freeing and naming themselves as the modern world came into being. What history teaches us is how differently sexuality has been conceived and practised in the past and in various societies, and how mistaken we are to think solely in terms of progress. As a way of disrupting a narrative of progress, I have approached the history of loving women thematically, looking first at marrying women, then desiring women, and finally at women claiming diverse identities.

MARRYING WOMEN

One of the most persistent patterns of what may or may not accurately be called female same-sex sexuality is the case of women crossing the gender line to live as men and to marry women. What we do not know in such cases is whether women became men solely for the economic and social freedom that male dress and employment provided, whether a sexual motivation figured in their decisions, or whether they conceived of themselves as something akin to transgendered, even if no such concept existed. We are particularly in the dark about the motives of their wives. What we do know is that such gender-crossing and marriage to women existed in a number of contexts.

Consider the story of Edward De Lacy Evans, born a woman, who lived as a man for twenty-three years in Victoria, Australia.[2] The case came to light in 1879 when he was forcibly stripped for a bath, having just arrived at Kew Asylum in Melbourne. Evans had emigrated to Australia from Ireland in 1856 as Ellen Tremaye, but after working for a short time as a domestic servant began dressing as a man and married one of his shipmates. He went to work as a miner and, when his first wife left him for another man, explaining that Evans was actually a woman, he married a young Irishwoman. When she died, he married a third young woman, who bore a child after being impregnated by her sister's husband. Although Evans claimed the child as his own, it was the birth, it seems, that sent Evans to the asylum.

What grabbed public interest was not the masquerade itself but the three marriages. Newspaper stories reported Evans's interest in women on board ship, and one journalist concluded that "the woman must have been mad on the subject of sex from the time she left Ireland."[3] The fact that Evans had been committed may have explained his sexual deviance, but how was one to account for his wives? It was difficult to ignore the fact that his third wife had borne a child, so therefore must have engaged in sexual intercourse with a man. Although she claimed not to know either that Evans was a woman or how she became pregnant, her speculation that Evans had one night substituted a real man for himself suggested that she and Evans did indeed regularly have sex. One newspaper story reported that his wives did not expose him because they were "nymphomaniacs," suggesting knowledge of the emerging medical literature that linked excessive heterosexual desire and prostitution with female same-sex sexuality. When Evans's wife eventually named her brother-in-law as the father of the child in a bid for support, Evans testified in court that he had witnessed the two in bed together, but that it was so painful he could barely speak of it.

Evans's story, like so many tales of women who became men and married women, leaves us uncertain what to think.[4] Clearly there was more here at stake than occupational mobility. That Evans loved and desired women seems evident, but did he think of himself as male? Did his wives? What was crucial to the public commentary was the insistence that gender transgression was a sign of mental illness, and in fact the doctors proclaimed Evans cured only when he donned female clothing.

In other cultures in other parts of the world, "manly women" might marry women without the need for deception. The crucial difference was societal acceptance of gender-crossing or the existence of a third (or more) category of gender. In some Native American cultures, what are called "two-spirit" manly females are conceptualized as a mixture of the masculine and feminine, a gender apart from either women, men or womanly men. The two-spirit role has to do with spirituality, occupation, personality and gender more than sexuality, so when sex does take place between a manly woman and another woman, it may technically be "same-sex sex"—because the bodies involved are physiologically alike—but in fact the sex is more accurately conceptualized as cross-gender.[5] Among the Mohaves, *hwames* are women who take on male roles and who are able to marry women and serve as fathers of children borne by their wives.

Oral tradition among the Kutenai of British Columbia tells of a female member who married a white fur trader in the early 19th century but returned a year later announcing that her husband had transformed her into a man. She took the name "Gone-To-The-Spirits" and began to dress and act like a man and to court women. She married a woman who had divorced her husband, and rumour spread that she had made a phallus out of leather with which to pleasure her wife. When her wife left because of Gone-To-The-Spirits' gambling, she pursued a series of women. With one of them she took up the role of guide for white traders, one of whom described them as "two strange Indians, in the character of man and wife," although he later noted that "they were in fact both women."[6] She became known as the "Manlike Woman" among the white traders.

Native American societies were not the only ones that conceptualized multiple genders and allowed same-sex but cross-gender relationships, nor were they the only social group in which two biological women might marry one another. In more than thirty African groups woman–woman marriage has been, and in some cases still is, a possibility. As among the Mohaves, a female husband could be the father of children born to her wife from a union with a biological male. In that sense, she is a "social male." In at least some cases, such a role involved male dress and occupations, as for third-gender Native Americans. In Nigeria in the 1990s, an elderly Ohagia Igbo *dike-nwami* ("brave-woman") by the name of Nne Uko told an ethnographer that she "was interested in manly activities" and felt that she was "meant to be a man."[7] Although she was divorced from a husband, she farmed and hunted, joined men's societies and married two women who gave birth to children biologically fathered by her brother. The fundamental reason for the existence of such marriages is economic and familial: if a woman cannot conceive, she can continue her family line by taking a wife who will bear children. Women might choose a female husband for a number of reasons, including the possibility of greater sexual freedom, more companionship, less quarrelling and physical violence, distaste for men, more input in household decisions or more bridewealth.[8] We know little or nothing about the emotional and sexual aspects of having a female husband, although scholars tend to insist that sex is not a part of such marriages. One ethnographer who spent two years studying the Bangwa of Cameroon in the 1970s suggested the presence of at least an emotional component when he described his best woman informant's relationship with one of her wives, commenting on "their obvious satisfaction in each other's company."[9]

A quite different kind of marriage from one in which a partner passed as a man or became a social male developed in the Euro-American world in the late 18th and early 19th centuries. As an ideology of sexual difference between women and men took hold among the urban middle classes, the phenomenon known as "romantic friendship" flourished. Women, assigned the domestic sphere of the home and assumed to be emotional and asexual, developed strong and passionate ties to other women that thrived in addition to or alongside marriage to men. When romantic friends in certain privileged circumstances chose not to marry as expected, they sometimes formed marriage-like relationships that became known in the United States, because of their prevalence in the northeast, as "Boston marriages."

No doubt the most famous marriage between romantic friends was that of Eleanor Butler and Sarah Ponsonby, who ran away together from their aristocratic Irish homes in 1778 when they were thirty-nine and twenty-three respectively. Although Butler, the elder of the pair, dressed and behaved in a masculine manner, they lived respectably, if eccentrically and not without occasional criticism, in a rural retreat in Wales for fifty-one years. As the "Ladies of Llangollen" they came to embody romantic friendship and the possibility of marriage, in practice if not in name, between two women. They called each other "my Better Half," "My Sweet Love" and "my Beloved."[10] Visitors flocked to their home, newspaper accounts described their house and garden, and other women who loved women viewed them as icons of female love. Anne Lister, a member of the Yorkshire gentry who was quite forthright about her love and lust for women, visited the Ladies in 1822 and felt a connection. She concluded that the long marriage between the two women must have been held together by "something more tender still than friendship."[11] When Butler died, leaving Ponsonby almost penniless, friends managed to arrange for Butler's pension to be paid to her—in effect a recognition that they had been married.

Anne Lister's particular interest in the relationship of the Ladies of Llangollen may be attributable to the fact that she longed to marry her own lover, Mariana Belcombe, who for economic reasons ended up married to a man. Before the wedding, Lister gave Mariana a ring to wear in place of the one she had been given by her husband-to-be, insisting that their marriage was the real one and wanting Mariana to acknowledge her as her "first husband."[12] Despite her belief in her marriage to Mariana, however, she agonized over whether they were in fact committing adultery.

In 1824, despite her continued love for Mariana, Lister visited Paris and fell in with a widow, Maria Barlow, who wanted to be Lister's wife but had to settle for the status of "mistress." Barlow thought that Lister, with her masculine appearance, could pass as a man and marry her publicly and openly. "It would have been better had you been brought up as your father's son," Barlow told Lister, but Lister was not keen on the idea of having no access to women's company, since she found so many lovers that way.[13] Instead, Lister recommitted herself to Mariana, exchanging pubic hair to wear in lockets, and Barlow sadly accepted her "divorce."[14]

At the end of her life, Lister obtained her wish to marry a woman when she courted Ann Walker, an heiress whose property adjoined hers. At first Walker described their relationship as "as good as a marriage"; later they exchanged rings, moved in together, rewrote their wills, and in every other way acted as husband and wife.[15] Although Lister was considered odd by her community, she also held economic and social power. Despite gossip and even incidents in which neighbours witnessed Lister and Walker kissing, the two women lived together without censure.

The Ladies of Llangollen and Anne Lister and her wives and mistress lived in societies that did not have a category for women who married women. Their relationships were nonetheless accepted, or at least tolerated, because of class privilege and because of ignorance, wilful or otherwise, that sexual relationships formed part of the arrangements. In 19th-century England and Wales, as throughout Europe and the United States, romantic friendships crossed the boundaries of respectability if there was too much gender transgression or suspicion of sexual activity beyond kissing and cuddling, as we shall see. But by the end of the 19th century, as the science of sexology began to describe and categorize masculine women and women with same-sex desires as "inverts" or "perverts," everything began to change.

Consider the case of Alice Mitchell and Freda Ward in late 19th-century Memphis, Tennessee. Mitchell, a middle-class white nineteen-year-old, fell in love with her seventeen-year-old friend Freda Ward (known as "Fred") and hatched a plot to dress as a man, run away with her and marry her. To this point their attachment seemed, to their families, to fit the familiar pattern of romantic friendship. Then Ward's family uncovered the plot and sent back Mitchell's engagement ring and other tokens of their love, forbidding them to see each other. Even worse from Mitchell's perspective, Ward began to be courted by a man. Early on in their plans to run away, Mitchell had said that she would kill Ward if she backed out of her promise to marry her, and she acted on this threat by slashing Ward's throat on the streets of Memphis in 1892. The case attracted attention from doctors and the popular press not only because of its drama, but also because it seemed to fit so perfectly the newly emerging theory of gender inversion and sexual deviance as inextricably linked. That is, Alice Mitchell became the embodiment of the "invert" or "lesbian" in American medical and popular discourse.[16] Her family's strategy for the defence was to have her declared insane, and she died in an asylum.

Across the Atlantic, at about the same time, the Hungarian count Sandor Vay was accused by his father-in-law not only of forgery, but also of fraud, since he "was only a woman, walking around in masculine clothes."[17] Unlike Mitchell, Vay was a "passing woman" who was raised as a boy, had affairs with women and worked as a journalist and writer. His father-in-law testified that one could see the shape of (rather large) male equipment between Vay's legs, and Vay's wife reported that she had given herself to him and had had no idea prior to his arrest that he was not biologically a man. Yet other witnesses testified that they knew the count to be a woman. The doctor who reported on the case to the court was himself confused, finding it difficult to deal with the masculine countess as a lady and much "easier, natural, and more correct" to think of Sandor as "a jovial, somewhat boyish student."[18] At this point the medical authorities proceeded from the story of a passing woman to a diagnosis of inversion and mental illness. As in the case of Alice Mitchell, the emerging ideas of the sexologists concerning gender inversion and same-sex sexual desire came to the fore. Sandor Vay was to Hungary, and to Europe more generally, what Alice Mitchell was to the United States: the embodiment of a sexual invert.

Once women who passed as men became defined in Euro-American cultures as sexual inverts and subsequently as mannish lesbians, marriages between women—whether passing women, manly women, social males, female husbands or romantic friends—had the potential to take on an air of sexual deviance. Nevertheless, some women continued to cross the gender line secretly, to live their lives as men and to marry women. Billy Tipton, a US jazz musician, originally invented himself as a man in order to earn a living during the Depression, but in 1989, when he died, his secret was revealed. He had been married several times and had adopted sons, and none of his immediate family—including his wives—knew that he had been born a woman.[19]

In the contemporary world, women in a few places can actually marry. In Belgium, Canada, Denmark, The Netherlands, Sweden and, in the United States, Massachusetts, lesbian marriages are taking place. Even in India, a society that does not condone same-sex relations, the fact that the Hindu Marriage Act allows diverse communities to define marriage means that some same-sex couples are able get married.[20] In the 1990s in a very poor rural region of India, Geeta, a woman from a *dalit* or "untouchable" family who was married to an abusive husband, met Manju, an older woman whose masculinity had won her a great deal of respect and power in her village. They came to know each other at a residential school run by a women's organization devoted to equality and empowerment, and they fell in love. As Geeta put it, "I do not know what happened to me when I met Manju but I forgot my man. I forgot that I had been married. We were so attracted to each other that we immediately felt like husband and wife."[21] Geeta accepted Manju as her husband at a Shiva temple, Manju's family accepted Geeta as a daughter-in-law, and Manju became both a second mother and a father to Geeta's daughter.

Marriage between women, then, has a long and complicated history. Many of the stories of women who married other women involve gender transgression, whether secret or open. Some take place in societies that recognize more than two genders or, for a variety of reasons, accept the idea of women as social males. There are many reasons why women might choose to cross the gender line or identify with a third or fourth gender, sexual desire for other women being only one. We know even less about why women might choose to marry female husbands. But what is clear is that women in various places in modern history have chosen to live their lives with other women.

DESIRING WOMEN

What do we know of women's sexual activities with one another, much less of their desires? This is a question not only of evidence, but also of interpretation. What counts as "sex"? Kissing, hugging, cuddling? And what about acts that seem clearly sexual from a contemporary Western perspective but might have little to do with erotic desire in other contexts? These are tricky questions. What we do know is that, despite all the obstacles, some record of women's same-sex desires has survived.

Let us begin with romantic friendship in the 18th- and 19th-century Western world, since one of the central debates in the history of sexuality hinges on the question of whether or not these passionate, intense, loving and physically affectionate relationships included sex, by which we presumably mean the involvement of genitals and/or sexual desire and/or sexual gratification. Certainly some of what romantic friends wrote to each other sounds like declarations of desire. There is Alice Baldy, a white woman from the US state of Georgia, writing in 1870 to her beloved, Josie Varner. "Do you know that if you only touch me, or speak to me there is not a nerve or fibre in my body that does not respond with a thrill of delight?"[22] Or 19th-century Czech writer Božena Němcová writing to Sofie Rottová, a fellow author: "Believe me, sometimes I dream that your eyes are right in front of me, I am drowning in them, and they have the same sweet expression as they did when they used to ask: 'Božena, what's wrong? Božena, I love you.'"[23] Or African-American poet Angelina Weld Grimké writing in 1896 to her school friend Mamie Burrell: "Oh Mamie if you only knew how my heart beats when I think of you and it yearns and pants to gaze, if only for one second upon your lovely face."[24] Are these expressions of physical desire? Formulaic expressions of friendship? Or sometimes the former, sometimes the latter and sometimes both?

One of the cases that most troubles our understanding of the relationship between romantic friendship and sexual desire is that of Scottish schoolteachers Jane Pirie and Marianne Woods. In the early 19th century, Pirie and Woods fulfilled a dream by establishing a school together in Edinburgh. Then their plans all came crashing down one day when one of their students, Jane Cumming, born of a liaison between an Indian woman and an aristocratic Scottish man serving the empire in the East, reported shocking behaviour to her grandmother. According to Jane Cumming, the two teachers visited each other in bed, lay one on top of the other, kissed and shook the bed. Furthermore, Cumming reported that Jane Pirie said one night, "You are in the wrong place," and Marianne Woods replied "I know," and asserted that she was doing it "for fun." Another night, said Cumming, Pirie had whispered, "Oh, do it, darling." And she described a noise she heard as similar to "putting one's finger into the neck of a wet bottle."[25]

One can only imagine the reactions of the judges in the case, forced to make an impossible choice between believing that respectable Scottish schoolteachers might engage in sexual behaviour or believing that decent schoolgirls could make up such tales. As one judge put it, making clear the acceptability of normal romantic friendship, "Are we to say that every woman who has formed an intimate friendship and has slept in the same bed with another is guilty? Where is the innocent woman in Scotland?"[26] Ultimately, they had to decide whether Pirie and Woods kissed, caressed and fondled "more than could have resulted from ordinary female friendship," suggesting a line between affectionate behaviour and sexuality that could be crossed.[27] The only way out of the dilemma was provided by Jane Cumming's heritage and childhood in India, where surely, many of the judges decided, she must have learned not only about sex, but also about sexual relations between women—something no respectable Scottish schoolgirl would be able to imagine.

That romantic friendship could indeed contain sexual desire and sexual activity is suggested by all-too-rare evidence from outside the walls of a courtroom. Anne Lister left us the most extensive record of her activities as a "female rake."[28] In her voluminous diary, some of it kept in code, Lister wrote of her lovemaking with Mariana Belcombe, using "kiss" to mean "orgasm": "From the kiss she gave me it seemed as if she loved me as fondly as ever. By & by, we seemed to drop asleep but, by & by, I perceived she would like another kiss & she whispered, 'Come again a bit, Freddy,' . . . But soon, I got up a second time, again took off, went to her a second time &, in spite of all, she really gave me pleasure, & I told her no one had ever given me kisses like hers."[29]

And Mariana was not the only lover to enjoy kisses with Lister. Maria Barlow, the widow Lister courted in Paris, came to her room one night and climbed into bed with her. "I was contented that my naked left thigh should rest upon her naked left thigh and thus she let me grubble her over her petticoats. All the while I was pressing her between my thighs. . . . Now and then I held my hand still and felt her pulsation, let her rise towards my hand two or three times and gradually open her thighs, and felt . . . that she was excited."[30]

If Lister is exceptional in both the extent of her conquests and her explicit depictions of them, she is not the only 19th-century woman to have left a record of sexual activities. As Brett Genny Beemyn relates in an earlier chapter, two African-American women across the Atlantic, freeborn domestic servant Addie Brown and schoolteacher Rebecca Primus, shared a passionate relationship in Hartford, Connecticut, in the 1860s. Some of their correspondence echoes the expressions of love and longing of other romantic friends: "Rebecca, when I bid you good by it's seem to me that my very heart broke. . . . My Darling Friend I shall never be happy again unless I am near you."[31] Yet Brown also refers to Primus's caressing of her breasts and compares Rebecca's kisses with those of her male employers, concluding "No *kisses* is like youres."[32]

The stories of Addie Brown and Rebecca Primus, Anne Lister, Mariana and Maria, and of Marianne Woods and Jane Pirie complicate the notion that intense and passionate relationships between women found acceptance in the Western world in the 19th century because no one imagined that women might indulge in sexual behaviour together. These tales do not mean that all romantic friendships involved the caressing of breasts or the exchange of "kisses." But they do open up the possibility that more romantic friends than we know of might have acted on their erotic desires, regardless of how they considered such activities.

Romantic friendship attracts so much attention because literate women often left a written record of their love for one another in letters and in diaries. But other kinds of sources allow us a glimpse into the lives of women whose voices do not reach us directly. In 19th-century northern India, for example, Urdu *Rekhti* poetry, written by men but in the personae and language of women, spoke of love between women. A poem might praise the beauty of a woman's female friend and lover: "Why should my heart not throb in my breast?/Your beauty is like that of gold."[33] Relationships between women needed to be kept secret, so poems refer to lovers sneaking into each other's rooms and hiding their love behind the screen of friendship. But the poems make clear—as does the vocabulary used to describe love and sex between women—that such relationships were not unknown. Poems describe sexual acts, including tribadism (the mutual rubbing

of vulvas), stroking with fingers, and the use of dildoes: "The way you rub me, ah! It drives my heart wild/Stroke me a little more, my sweet *Dogana* (woman friend)." Verses also compare female same-sex love-making favourably with heterosexual intercourse: "Let her go to men who want stakes hammered into her/Can she ever get these hours and hours of pleasure?" Says another, "There's no pleasure in the world like clinging to a woman."[34]

Although some scholars have dismissed *Rekhti* as pornographic, we should not assume so easily that representations of love and sexual activity between women, even if intended in whole or part to titillate men, bear no relationship to behaviour. The men who wrote *Rekhti* used the language of prostitutes, making it clear that they had contact with courtesans, some of whom at this time were educated and highly accomplished women. Women's quarters and courtesans' households provided the kind of female space in which love between women might be pursued in an otherwise restrictive society. An earlier commentary on the *Kamasutra* made this point: "Sometimes, in the secret of their inner rooms, with total trust in one another, they [women] lick each other's vulva, just like whores."[35] This comment suggests both the private spaces in which women's sexual activities took place, meaning that they left little trace in the public record, and a historical connection between female same-sex love and prostitution.

In fact, the assumption that prostitutes made love with each other, and not just for the pleasure of men, is one that crops up in other societies as well. In his 1836 study of prostitution in Paris, pioneering sexologist Alexandre-Jean-Baptiste Parent-Duchâtelet made the connection between commercial sex with men and sex with women.[36] For although, on the surface, women who had sex with men for money might seem to belong to the opposite end of a sexual spectrum from women who preferred to make love with women, both were deemed to suffer from hypersexuality. That the connection was not merely a fantasy of sexologists is suggested by such evidence as Parisian street songs from the late 19th century. One referred to a famous brothel: "The girls from la Farsy's place / Are lezzies (*gougnottes*), my girlfriends. / Happy the girl to whom God gives / A real tough dyke (*gousse*) from la Farsy's place." Another referred to women arrested for prostitution: "You've got to see this at night in the holding cell, / The little women kissing like mad / On the straw. / And when the sun goes down, / They go down too, / Without a fuss. / It's a helluvah lot more fun."[37] Such sources suggest that, even if sexologists like Parent-Duchâtelet were wrong when they claimed it was "repugnance for the most disgusting and perverse acts ... which men perform on prostitutes" that was responsible for "driving these unfortunate creatures to lesbian love," we can nevertheless learn something about sex between women from what went on in brothels.[38]

In describing and defining lesbianism, sexologists have left us some of the first detailed and reliable records of female same-sex sexual behaviour. Despite the filter of the doctors' own intentions and interpretations, women's voices do sometimes break through. In one famous US study of "sex variants" in New York in the 1930s, women described their sex lives and bragged about their ability to satisfy their lovers. Perhaps playing with both traditional notions about lesbians and the experts' belief in the hypersexuality of black women, a number of African-American subjects boasted of their sexual technique: "I insert my clitoris in the vagina just like the penis of a man. . . . Women enjoy it so much they leave their husbands."[39] Far more reliable are oral histories collected by historians sympathetic to their narrators. In the working-class lesbian bar culture of 1940s and 1950s Buffalo, New York, white, black and Native American butches saw their role as pleasuring their fems, primarily through tribadism or what they called "friction."[40] Oral sex became more acceptable in the 1950s at the same time that the idea of the "untouchable" or "stone butch"—the "doer" who did not let her lover make love to her—became more firmly entrenched. As one stone butch from the 1950s put it, "I wanted to satisfy them, and I wanted to make love—I love to make love. I still say that's the greatest thing in the world."[41]

These varied sources from different places provide evidence of kissing, the caressing of breasts, tribadism, manual stimulation, the use of dildoes, and oral sex. Sex practices change over time and vary in different cultures. But what all this evidence makes clear is that there is a long history of women desiring other women and acting on that desire. How women thought about what they did with each other, both before and after "lesbian" became a possible identity, we know less about. Yet women who loved women did, in different contexts, come to define identities that were based on their love and desire.

CLAIMING AN IDENTITY

The story of the emergence of lesbian identity has both geographical and chronological limitations, but the notion of love, sexual desire or sexual activity making

one a kind of person has more fluid boundaries. That is, the term "lesbian" has a relatively recent origin in Western culture, but there were other words or concepts that women applied to themselves to describe their desires and actions. Before the invention of the term "homosexuality" in 1869, Anne Lister saw her love and desire for women as a defining characteristic. She knew the term "Saffio," considered her attraction to women natural, and proclaimed proudly that "I love, & only love, the fairer sex & thus beloved by them in turn, my heart revolts from any other love than theirs."[42]

At the same time we need to remember that there have always been, and still are, women who love and desire other women but do not see that as defining their identities in any way. In Lesotho, for example, a small, poor country entirely enclosed by South Africa, women love other women and engage in activities that seem to a modern Western sensibility to be sexual; yet they neither identify as a particular category of "sexual being" nor even define what they do as "sex," which in Lesotho requires a penis.[43] As in much of the rest of the world, women must expect to marry and bear children. But boarding-school girls pair up as "Mummy" and "Baby" and kiss, rub each others' bodies, sometimes have genital contact, and jealously guard their relationships. Older women greet each other with long "French" kisses, fondle one another and engage in tribadism and cunnilingus, all of which they describe as "loving each other," "staying together nicely," "holding each other" or "having a nice time together," but not as sex.[44] And they are not lesbians.

In other cultures, women may engage in actions that provide an identity, but not one that corresponds to the concept "lesbian." At the end of the 19th century in Canton, a Chinese silk-producing area, women organized "sworn sisterhoods" (*zishu*) and identified as "marriage-resisters" (*dushen zhyyi nüzi*, literally "women believing in remaining single").[45] Although there were economic and cultural reasons behind their decision, commentators at the time attributed the phenomenon in part to the fact that women "acquired intimate friends with whom they practiced homosexual love."[46]

Once the sexologists had undertaken the process of naming and defining the kind of people who loved others of the same sex, what did such definitions mean to women who loved other women? For some, the medicalization of same-sex love brought unwanted attention and shame; for others, self-understanding and an identity. Jeannette Marks, a professor of English at Mount Holyoke College, Massachusetts, who lived in an intimate relationship with Mary Woolley, the college's president from 1901 to 1937, was one who worried that others might see her as a lesbian. In her writing she denounced "unwise college friendships," such as the one she had shared with Woolley, as "abnormal," and insisted that the only relationship that could "fulfill itself and be complete is that between a man and a woman."[47] Others were less vehement but worked to distinguish themselves from the pathologized subjects described by the sexologists. In a 1930 autobiography, the pseudonymous "Mary Casal" described her sexual relationship with another woman as "the very highest type of love" and "on a much higher plane than those of *the real inverts*."[48] In the same vein, US prison reformer Miriam Van Waters, in an intimate relationship with her benefactor Geraldine Thompson from the 1920s until Thompson's death in 1967, struggled to differentiate her own "normality" from the gender inversion and pathology of lesbianism as described in medical literature and attacked in the women's reformatory that she supervised.[49]

On the other hand, the concept of lesbianism as a defining characteristic allowed some women to embrace their own sexuality more fully. British feminist Frances Wilder expressed her gratitude to homosexual sexologist Edward Carpenter, whose work made her realize that she "was more closely related to the intermediate sex than I had hitherto imagined."[50] In *The Well of Loneliness,* Radclyffe Hall had her famous character Stephen discover her true nature when she finds a copy of Richard von Krafft-Ebing's monumental work *Psychopathia Sexualis.* Hall hoped that her novel would help young women like herself come to terms with their desires, as well as elicit sympathy from heterosexual readers.[51]

But it would be a mistake to assume that the experts defined lesbian identity independently, leaving women-loving women either to reject or embrace what was offered them. For the sexologists fashioned their analyses from what they saw around them, including the cases of women such as Alice Mitchell and Sandor Vay. And in the early 20th century a self-fashioning of the modern lesbian was taking place in communities where women with same-sex desires found others like themselves.

In Paris, the salon of the American Natalie Clifford Barney was the heart of one such lesbian community from the 1890s to the 1930s. A wealthy heiress, Barney wasted no time agonizing over the conclusions of the sexologists. Secure in her sexual desire for women, feminine in her self-presentation and protected by class privilege, Barney flourished in an environment in which homosexuality was celebrated among the elite. In her salon, she gathered around her a coterie of writers, artists and lovers whose works celebrated lesbianism. And she eschewed shame: "Albinos aren't reproached for having pink eyes and whitish hair, why should they [society] hold it against me for being a lesbian? It's a question of nature: my queerness isn't a vice, isn't 'deliberate,' and harms no one."[52] Flamboyant and self-confident, Barney had no qualms about flaunting her non-monogamous lesbianism.

Berlin, too, was home in the 1920s to a vibrant lesbian world. Until the Nazi rise to power, an astonishing number of lesbian clubs, bars, balls, groups, circles and publications catered to women who loved women, and cabaret acts openly represented lesbian love.[53] The periodical *Die Freundin* ("The Girlfriend"), published in Berlin from 1924 to 1933, directed its stories and articles to women described as "same-sex loving" (*gleichgeschlechtlichliebend*), "homosexual" (*homosexuell*), "homoerotic" (*homoerotisch*) or "lesbian" (*lesbisch*).[54] The transnational aspects of lesbian culture among elites is evident in the title of another periodical published in Berlin in the 1930s. *Garçonne* (the French for "boy" with an added feminine ending, meaning also an "emancipated woman") catered to a lesbian and male transvestite audience.[55] Both periodicals featured photographs and illustrations of a variety of lesbians: some cross-dressed, some in butch–fem couples, some entirely feminine.

New York was also home to commercial and private venues that catered to a crowd with same-sex desires, and not just to elite women. By the 1920s, two neighbourhoods—Greenwich Village and Harlem—had established reputations as welcoming places for lesbians as well as gay men. Like Paris and Berlin, both districts were also artistic and bohemian centres. The Harlem Renaissance in particular spread word of lesbian love through literature, art and the blues. Lucille Bogan, in "B.D. Women Blues," sang of "bulldagger" women, and in fact many of the great women blues singers were themselves lesbian or bisexual. Mabel Hampton, a black performer who in her teens lived in Harlem, described private parties where women who desired women might meet: "The bulldykers used to come and bring their women with them, you know."[56]

Such vibrant lesbian communities were the exception rather than the rule, however, for in much of the world the idea that women should live independently of men remained unthinkable. But even where the conditions for such lesbian communities were lacking, the language of same-sex love began to enter the vernacular. In Republican China, indigenous developments—such as the emergence of marriage resistance, the widespread existence of same-sex love relations in sex-segregated schools, and changes in gender roles accompanying urbanization—combined with the translation of the work of Western sexologists and drew attention to the new concept of "same-sex love" (*tongxing ai*) that had migrated from Japan.[57] A number of women writers from the progressive May Fourth movement wrote about love between women, often telling of relationships between women in school. One such author, Lu Yin, in *Lishi's Diary* (1923) tells the story of a woman who does not wish to marry and whose feelings for her school friend Yuanqing change from "ordinary friendship" to "same-sex romantic love." They make plans to live together, and Lishi that night dreams that they are rowing a boat in the moonlight. Then Yuanqing's mother forces her to move away and plans to marry her off to her cousin. Yuanqing writes to Lishi, "Ah, Lishi! Why didn't you plan ahead! Why didn't you dress up in men's clothes, put on a man's hat, act like a man, and visit my parents to ask for my hand?"[58] In the end, Yuanqing repudiates their dream and Lishi dies of melancholia. Lu Yin herself married twice, but her writings suggest that she struggled with lesbian desire. She described her urge to dress as a man and visit a brothel, although she feared that if anyone found out, they would have "dreadful suspicions" about her.[59]

In Japan, too, the work of Western sexologists made an impact, and in the early 20th century discussion of lesbians and cross-dressing women came to public attention. By the first years of the 20th century loanwords such as "homosexual" (*homosekushuaru* or *dōseiaisha*), "lesbian" (*rezubian*) and "garçon" (*garuson*), meaning a masculine woman, had become household words.[60] As Japan undertook a programme of modernization and urban men adopted Western dress, masculine or "new" women came to be identified with lesbianism and to represent the threat of social disorder. In this context, tales of butch–fem couples attempting suicide out of love captured the public imagination. Such was the case when Saijō Eriko, who played a woman's part in an all-female revue, and Masuda Yasumare, a masculine zealous fan who had taken on a male name, failed to carry out their love pact in 1935. Their story seemed symptomatic of what one account called the "recent, disturbing increase . . . in lesbian affairs between upper-class girls and women."[61]

The process of building a lesbian community and constructing a lesbian identity required some level of economic independence and the creation of social spaces, things not available to women in all cultures. In much of the world, marriage to men was and remains essential for women, so that even if a society is tolerant of same-sex female relations, they take place at the margins of heterosexual marriage. In most of Latin America, for example, until the 1970s women who loved women had few options besides marriage or the convent, and even women who worked to support themselves and could refrain from marriage had to conduct their relationships with women in a clandestine manner. The same is true in contemporary Egypt, where women with female lovers seem to lead normative heterosexual lives.[62]

In the 1960s and 1970s, in conjunction with movements for social justice that were appearing around the world, women who identified as lesbians began to speak out and organize public protests, even in places where that put them in a great deal of danger. When the United Nations–sponsored first International Women's Year Conference came to Mexico City in 1975, the press attacked the lesbian presence as imported and alien to Mexican culture, but four years later a group of lesbians promoted their cause publicly at the first World Sexology Congress.[63] In South Africa, groups such as Sunday's Women in Durban, the GLOW (Gay and Lesbian Organization of the Witwatersrand), Lesbian Forum in Soweto-Johannesburg, and Lesbians in Love and Compromising Situations (LILACS) in Cape Town emerged during the 1980s.[64] Today, lesbians with sufficient class or organizational privilege connect at international feminist and gay/lesbian conferences such as those sponsored by the International Lesbian and Gay Association. The Asian Lesbian Network brings together lesbians from ten Asian countries and Asian lesbians living outside Asia, and the Encuentros de Lesbianas Feministas are conferences for lesbians in Latin America and the Caribbean.[65]

Claiming an identity—as Saffic or lesbian; as a marriage-resister, a *garçonne* or a bulldagger; as *bombero* (literally "firefighter," for butch) or *mucama* ("housemaid," for fem) in Argentina, or as *chapatbaz* (women who engage in tribadism) in Urdu—requires one to have a concept of a particular kind of person with which one can relate, a notion that there are others like oneself with whom one might build a community. Although identity is important to the construction of the modern lesbian, we must remember that there are still women all around the globe who are crossing the gender line, loving women and engaging in sexual relations without thinking of themselves as lesbians.

LOVING WOMEN

What does it mean to love women in the modern world? As all of these manifestations of relationships between women make clear, there are many and various ways in which women love other women. Some cross the gender line to marry their lovers, as did Edward De Lacy Evans, Gone-To-The-Spirits, Sandor Vay and Billy Tipton. Others—with varying degrees of success—form marriage-like relationships, as did Elea-

nor Butler and Sarah Ponsonby, Anne Lister and Ann Walker, Geeta and Manju. Some, like the *hwame* of the Mohave people and the *garçonnes* of Berlin, embrace gender crossing or blurring, whereas others adopt feminine personae. Some, such as Alice Baldy, Sofie Rottová, Angelina Weld Grimké and the women of *Rekhti* poetry, express their love in passionate language. Some, such as Anne Lister, Addie Brown and Rebecca Primus, the jailed French prostitutes of street songs, the women of the New York sex study, 1950s butches and fems, and Natalie Clifford Barney, made love to each other with hands and tongues and vulvas. And others, in different ways, celebrated their love, claimed an identity and joined together to make the world a more hospitable place for loving women.

NOTES

1. Judith M. Bennett, "'Lesbian-Like' and the Social History of Lesbianisms," *Journal of the History of Sexuality*, vol. 9, no. 1–2 (2000), pp. 1–24; Leila J. Rupp, "Toward a Global History of Same-Sex Sexuality," *Journal of the History of Sexuality*, vol. 10, no. 2 (2001), pp. 287–302.
2. Lucy Chesser, "'A Woman Who Married Three Wives': Management of Disruptive Knowledge in the 1879 Australian Case of Edward De Lacy Evans," *Journal of Women's History*, vol. 9, no. 4 (1998), pp. 53–77.
3. Ibid., p. 60.
4. See Rudolf Dekker and Lott van de Pol, *The Tradition of Female Transvestism in Early Modern Europe* (London 1989), and Julie Wheelwright, *Amazons and Military Maids: Women Who Dressed as Men in Pursuit of Life, Liberty and Happiness* (London 1989).
5. See Sabine Lang, "Various Kinds of Two-Spirit People: Gender Variance and Homosexuality in Native American Communities," in Sue-Ellen Jacobs, Wesley Thomas and Sabine Lang (eds), *Two-Spirit People* (Urbana, IL 1997), pp. 100–118; and Walter L. Williams, *The Spirit and the Flesh: Sexual Diversity in American Indian Culture* (Boston, MA 1986).
6. Quoted in Williams, *The Spirit and the Flesh*, p. 237.
7. Quoted in Joseph M. Carrier and Stephen O. Murray, "Woman–Woman Marriage in Africa," in Stephen O. Murray and Will Roscoe (eds), *Boy-Wives and Female Husbands: Studies in African Homosexualities* (New York 1998), p. 259.
8. See Carrier and Murray, *Boy-Wives*.
9. Quoted in Carrier and Murray, *Boy-Wives*, p. 263.
10. Quoted in Martha Vicinus, *Intimate Friends: Women Who Loved Women, 1778–1928* (Chicago 2004), p. 9.
11. Ibid., p. 45.
12. Ibid., p. 20.
13. Ibid., p. 22.
14. Ibid., p. 23.
15. Ibid., p. 26.
16. See Lisa Duggan, *Sapphic Slashers: Sex, Violence, and American Modernity* (Durham, NC 2000).
17. Quoted in Geertje Mak, "Sandor/Sarolta Vay: From Passing Woman to Invert," *Journal of Women's History*, vol. 16, no. 1 (2004), p. 54.
18. Ibid., p. 61.
19. See Diane Wood Middlebrook, *Suits Me: The Double Life of Billy Tipton* (New York 1998).
20. Ruth Vanita, "CLAGS Reports," *Centre for Lesbian and Gay Studies News*, vol. 14, no. 2 (2004), p. 14.
21. Quoted in Amanda Lock Swarr and Richa Nagar, "Dismantling Assumptions: Interrogating 'Lesbian' Struggles for Identity and Survival in India and South Africa," *Signs: Journal of Women in Culture and Society*, vol. 29 (2004), p. 500.
22. Quoted in Elizabeth W. Knowlton, "'Only a Woman Like Yourself': Rebecca Alice Baldy, Dutiful Daughter, Stalwart Sister, and Lesbian Lover of Nineteenth-Century Georgia," in John Howard (ed), *Carryin'on in the Lesbian and Gay South* (New York 1997), p. 48.
23. Quoted in Dasa Francikova, "Female Friends in Nineteenth-Century Bohemia: Troubles with Affectionate Writing and 'Patriotic Relationships,'" *Journal of Women's History*, vol. 12, no. 3 (2000), pp. 23–28, quotation on p. 24.
24. Quoted in Gloria T. Hull, *Color, Sex, and Poetry: Three Women Writers of the Harlem Renaissance* (Bloomington, IN 1987), p. 139.
25. Quoted in Lillian Faderman, *Scotch Verdict* (New York 1983), p. 147.
26. Ibid., p. 281.
27. Ibid., p. 82.
28. "Female rake" is the term used by Vicinus in *Intimate Friends*. She provides an extensive analysis of Lister.
29. Anne Lister, *I Know My Own Heart: The Diaries of Anne Lister (1791–1840)*, ed. Helena Whitbread (London 1988), p. 104.

30. Anne Lister, *No Priest but Love: The Journals of Anne Lister from 1824–1826*, ed. Helena Whitbread (New York 1992), p. 65.

31. Quoted in Karen V. Hansen, "'No *Kisses* Is Like Youres': An Erotic Friendship Between Two African-American Women During the Mid-Nineteenth Century," *Gender and History*, vol. 7 (August), pp. 159, 160.

32. Ibid., p. 162.

33. Quoted in Ruth Vanita, "'Married Among Their Companions': Female Homoerotic Relations in Nineteenth-Century Urdu *Rekhti* Poetry in India," *Journal of Women's History*, vol. 16, no. 1 (2004), p. 22.

34. Ibid., p. 28.

35. Ibid., p. 34.

36. See Heather Lee Miller, "Sexologists Examine Lesbians and Prostitutes in the United States, 1840–1940," *NWSA Journal*, vol. 12, no. 3 (2000), pp. 67–91.

37. Quoted in Francesca Canadé Sautman, "Invisible Women: Lesbian Working-Class Culture in France, 1880–1930," in Jeffrey Merrick and Bryant T. Ragan, Jr. (eds), *Homosexuality in Modern France* (New York 1996), pp. 191–92.

38. Quoted in Miller, "Sexologists Examine Lesbians and Prostitutes," p. 70.

39. Quoted in Jennifer Terry, *An American Obsession: Science, Medicine, and Homosexuality in Modern Society* (Chicago 1999), p. 242.

40. See Elizabeth Lapovsky Kennedy and Madeline D. Davis, *Boots of Leather, Slippers of Gold: The History of a Lesbian Community* (New York 1993).

41. Ibid., p. 204.

42. Lister, *I Know My Own Heart*, p. 145.

43. Kendall, "'When a Woman Loves a Woman' in Lesotho: Love, Sex, and the (Western) Construction of Homophobia," in Stephen O. Murray and Will Roscoe (eds), *Boy-Wives and Female Husbands: Studies in African Homosexualities* (New York 1998), pp. 223–41.

44. Ibid., p. 233. On boarding-school relationships, Kendall cites Judith Gay, "Mummies and Babies and Friends and Lovers in Lesotho," *Journal of Homosexuality*, vol. 11, no. 3–4 (1985), pp. 97–116.

45. See Tze-lan D. Sang, *The Emerging Lesbian: Female Same-Sex Desire in Modern China* (Chicago 2003), pp. 52, 377.

46. Ibid., p. 52.

47. Quoted in Lillian Faderman, *Odd Girls and Twilight Lovers: A History of Lesbian Life in Twentieth-Century America* (New York 1991), p. 53.

48. Ibid., p. 54.

49. See Estelle B. Freedman, *Maternal Justice: Miriam Van Waters and the Female Reform Tradition* (Chicago 1996).

50. Quoted in Carroll Smith-Rosenberg, "Discourses of Sexuality and Subjectivity: The New Woman, 1870–1936," in Martin Bauml Duberman, Martha Vicinus and George Chauncey (eds), *Hidden from History: Reclaiming the Gay and Lesbian Past* (New York 1989), p. 275.

51. See Vicinus, *Intimate Friends*, p. 217.

52. Ibid., pp. 189–90.

53. See the articles in *Eldorado: Homosexuelle Frauen und Männer in Berlin 1850–1950*, exh. cat., Berlin, Schwules Museum (Berlin 1984).

54. Katharine Vogel, "Zum Selbstverständnis lesbischer Frauen in der Weimarer Republik," in *Eldorado*, pp. 162–68.

55. Quoted in Petra Schlierkamp, "Die Garçonne," in *Eldorado*, p. 173.

56. Joan Nestle, "Excerpts from the Oral History of Mabel Hampton," *Signs: Journal of Women in Culture and Society*, vol. 18 (1993), p. 933.

57. See Sang, *The Emerging Lesbian*.

58. Ibid., p. 139.

59. Ibid., p. 144.

60. See Jennifer Robertson, "Dying to Tell: Sexuality and Suicide in Imperial Japan," *Signs: Journal of Women in Culture and Society*, vol. 25 (1999), pp. 1–35.

61. Ibid., p. 16.

62. Didi Khayatt, "Egypt," in Bonnie Zimmerman (ed), *Lesbian Histories and Cultures* (New York 2000), pp. 257–58.

63. Claudia Hinojosa, "Mexico," in Zimmerman, *Lesbian Histories and Cultures*, pp. 494–96.

64. Ian Barnard, "South Africa," in Zimmerman, *Lesbian Histories and Cultures*, pp. 721–22.

65. Julie Dorf, "International Organizations," in Zimmerman, *Lesbian Histories and Cultures*, pp. 398–400.

36 **Michael A. Messner**

Becoming 100% Straight

In 1995, as part of my job as the President of the North American Society for the Sociology of Sport, I needed to prepare a one-hour long Presidential Address for the annual meeting of some 200 people. This presented a challenge to me: how might I say something to my colleagues that was challenging, at least somewhat original, and above all, not boring. Students may think that their professors are especially boring in the classroom, but believe me, we are usually much worse at professional meetings. For some reason, many of us who are able to speak to our students in the classroom in a relaxed manner, and using relatively jargon-free language, seem at these meetings to become robots, dryly reading our papers—packed with impressively unclear jargon—to our yawning colleagues.

Since I desperately wanted to avoid putting 200 sport studies scholars to sleep, I decided to deliver a talk which I entitled "studying up on sex." The title, which certainly did get my colleagues' attention, was intended as a play on words—a double entendre. "Studying up" has one, generally recognizable colloquial meaning, but in sociology, it has another. It refers to studying "up" in the power structure. Sociologists have perhaps most often studied "down"—studied the poor, the blue or pink-collar workers, the "nuts, sluts and perverts," the incarcerated. The idea of "studying up" rarely occurs to sociologists unless and until we are living in a time when those who are "down" have organized movements that challenge the institutional privileges of elites. So, for instance, in the wake of labor movements, some sociologists like C. Wright Mills studied up on corporate elites. And recently, in the wake of racial/ethnic civil rights movements, some scholars like Ruth Frankenberg have begun to study the social meanings of "whiteness." Much of my research, inspired by feminism, has involved a studying up on the social construction of masculinity in sport. Studying up, in these cases, has raised some fascinating new and important questions about the workings of power in society.

However, I realized, when it comes to understanding the social and interpersonal dynamics of sexual orientation in sport, we have barely begun to scratch the surface of a very complex issue. Although sport studies has benefited from the work of scholars like Helen Lenskyj, Brian Pronger, and others who have delineated the experiences of lesbians and gay men in sports, there has been very little extension of these scholars' insights into a consideration of the social construction of heterosexuality in sport. In sport, just as in the larger society, we seem obsessed with asking "how do people become gay?" Imbedded in this question is the assumption that people who identify as heterosexual, or "straight," require no explanation, since they are simply acting out the "natural" or "normal" sexual orientation. It's the "sexual deviants" who require explanation, we seem to be saying, while the experience of heterosexuals, because we are considered normal, seems to require no critical examination or explanation. But I knew that a closer look at the development of sexual orientation or sexual identity reveals an extremely complex process. I decided to challenge myself and my colleagues by arguing that although we have begun to "study up" on corporate elites in sport, on whiteness, on masculinity, it is now time to extend that by studying up on heterosexuality.

But in the absence of systematic research on this topic, where could I start? How could I explore, raise questions about, and begin to illuminate the social construction of heterosexuality for my colleagues? Fortunately, I had for the previous two years been working with a group of five men (three of whom identified as heterosexual, two as gay) who were mutually exploring our own biographies in terms of our earlier bodily experiences that helped to shape our gender and sexual identities. We modeled our project after that of a German group of feminist women, led by Frigga Haug, who created a research method which they call " memory work." In short, the women would mutually choose a body part, such as "hair," and each of them would then write a short story, based on a particularly salient childhood memory that related to their hair (for example, being forced by parents to cut your hair, deciding to straighten one's curly hair, in order to look more like other girls, etc.). Then, the group would read all of the stories, discuss them one-by-one, with the hope of gaining some more general understanding of, and raising new questions about, the social construction of "femininity." What resulted from this project was a fascinating book called *Female Sexualization*, which my men's group used as an inspiration for our project.

As a research method, memory work is anything but conventional. Many sociologists would argue that this is not really a "research method" at all, because the information that emerges from the project can't be used very confidently as a generalizable "truth," and especially because in this sort of project, the researcher is simultaneously part of what is being studied. How, my more scientifically oriented colleagues might ask, is the researcher to maintain his or her objectivity in this project? My answer is that in this kind of research, objectivity is not the point. In fact, the strength of this sort of research is the depth of understanding that might be gained through a systematic group analysis of one's experience, one's *subjective* orientation to social processes. A clear understanding of the subjective aspect of social life—one's bodily feelings, emotions, and reactions to others—is an invaluable window that allows us to see and ask new sociological questions about group interaction and social structure. In short, group memory work can provide an important, productive, and fascinating insight into aspects of social reality, though not a complete (or completely reliable) picture.

So, as I pondered the lack of existing research on the social construction of heterosexuality in sport, I decided to draw on one of my own stories from my memory work men's group. Some of my most salient memories of embodiment are sports memories. I grew up the son of a high school coach, and I eventually played point guard on my dad's team. In what follows, I juxtapose one of my stories with that of a gay former Olympic athlete, Tom Waddell, whom I had interviewed several years earlier for a book that I wrote on the lives of male athletes.

TWO SEXUAL STORIES

Many years ago I read some psychological studies that argued that even for self-identified heterosexuals, it is a natural part of their development to have gone through "bisexual" or even "homosexual" stages of life. When I read this, it seemed theoretically reasonable, but it did not ring true in my experience. I have always been, I told myself, 100% heterosexual! The group process of analyzing my own autobiographical stories challenged this conception I had developed of myself, and also shed light on the way that the institutional context of sport provided a context for the development of my definition of myself as "100% straight." Here is one of the stories.

When I was in the 9th grade, I played on a "D" basketball team, set up especially for the smallest of high school boys. Indeed, though I was pudgy with baby fat, I was a short 5'2", still pre-pubescent with no facial hair and a high voice that I artificially tried to lower. The first day of practice, I was immediately attracted to a boy I'll call Timmy, because he looked like the boy who played in the Lassie TV show. Timmy was short, with a high voice, like me. And like me, he had no facial hair yet. Unlike me, he was very skinny. I liked Timmy right away, and soon we were together a lot. I *noticed* things about him that I didn't notice about other boys: he said some words a certain way, and it gave me pleasure to try to talk like him. I remember liking the way the light hit his boyish, nearly hairless body. I thought about him when we weren't together. He was in the school band, and at the football games, I'd squint to see where he was in the mass of uniforms. In short, though I wasn't conscious of it at the time, I was infatuated with Timmy—I had a crush on him. Later that basketball season, I decided—for no reason that I could really articulate then—that I hated Timmy. I aggressively rejected him, began to make fun of him around other boys. He was, we all agreed, a geek. He was a faggot.

Three years later, Timmy and I were both on the varsity basketball team, but had hardly spoken a word to each other since we were freshmen. Both of us now had lower voices, had grown to around 6 feet tall, and we both shaved, at least a bit. But Timmy was a skinny, somewhat stigmatized reserve on the team, while I was the team captain and starting point guard. But I wasn't so happy or secure about this. I'd always dreamed of dominating games, of being the hero. Halfway through my senior season, however, it became clear that I was not a star, and I figured I knew why. I was not aggressive enough.

I had always liked the beauty of the fast break, the perfectly executed pick and roll play between two players, and especially the long twenty-foot shot that touched nothing but the bottom of the net. But I hated and feared the sometimes brutal contact under the basket. In fact, I stayed away from the rough fights for rebounds and was mostly a perimeter player, relying on my long shots or my passes to more aggressive teammates under the basket. But now it became apparent to me that time was running out in my quest for greatness: I needed to change my game, and fast. I decided one day before practice that I was gonna get aggressive. While practicing one of our standard plays, I passed the ball to a teammate, and then ran to the spot at which I was to set a pick on a defender. I knew that one could sometimes get away with setting a face-up screen on a player, and then as he makes contact with you, roll your back to him and plant your elbow hard in his stomach. The beauty of this move is that your own body "roll" makes the elbow look like an accident. So I decided to try this move. I approached the defensive player, Timmy, rolled, and planted my elbow deeply into his solar plexus. Air exploded audibly from Timmy's mouth, and he crumbled to the floor momentarily.

Play went on as though nothing had happened, but I felt bad about it. Rather than making me feel better, it made me feel guilty and weak. I had to admit to myself why I'd chosen Timmy as the target against whom to test out my new aggression. He was the skinniest and weakest player on the team.

At the time, I hardly thought about these incidents, other than to try to brush them off as incidents that made me feel extremely uncomfortable. Years later, I can now interrogate this as a *sexual* story, and as a *gender* story unfolding within the context of the heterosexualized and masculinized institution of sport. Examining my story in light of research conducted by Alfred Kinsey a half-century ago, I can recognize in myself what Kinsey saw as a very common **fluidity and changeability of sexual desire over the life-course.** Put simply, Kinsey found that large numbers of adult, "heterosexual" men had previously, as adolescents and young adults, experienced sexual desire for males. A surprisingly large number of these men had experienced sexual contact to the point of orgasm with other males during adolescence or early adulthood. Similarly, my story invited me to consider what is commonly called the **"Freudian theory of bisexuality."** Sigmund Freud shocked the post-Victorian world by suggesting that all people go through a stage, early in life, when they are attracted to people of the same sex. Adult experiences, Freud argued, eventually led most people to shift their sexual desire to what Freud called

an appropriate "love object"—a person of the opposite sex. I also considered my experience in light of what lesbian feminist author Adrienne Rich called **institution of compulsory heterosexuality.** Perhaps the extremely high levels of homophobia that are often endemic in boys' and men's organized sports led me to deny and repress my own homoerotic desire through a direct and overt rejection of Timmy, through homophobic banter with male peers, and through the resultant stigmatization of the feminized Timmy. And eventually, I considered my experience in light of what the radical theorist Herbert Marcuse called the **sublimation of homoerotic desire** into an aggressive, violent act as serving to construct a clear line of demarcation between self-and-other. Sublimation, according to Marcuse, involves the driving underground, into the unconscious, of sexual desires that might appear dangerous due to their socially stigmatized status. But sublimation involves more than simple repression into the unconscious—it involves a transformation of sexual desire into something else—often into aggressive and violent acting out toward others, acts that clarify boundaries between one's self and others and therefore lessen any anxieties that might be attached to the repressed homoerotic desire.

Importantly, in our analysis of my story, my memory group went beyond simply discussing the events in psychological terms. My story did suggest some deep psychological processes at work, perhaps, but it also revealed the importance of social context—in this case, the context of the athletic team. In short, my rejection of Timmy and the joining with teammates to stigmatize him in ninth grade stands as an example of what sociologist R. W. Connell calls a **moment of engagement with hegemonic masculinity,** where I actively took up the male group's task of constructing heterosexual/masculine identities in the context of sport. The elbow in Timmy's gut three years later can be seen as a punctuation mark that occurred precisely because of my fears that I might be failing at this goal.

It is helpful, I think, to compare my story with gay and lesbian "coming out" stories in sport. Though we have a few lesbian and bisexual coming out stories among women athletes, there are very few gay male coming out stories. Tom Waddell, who as a closeted gay man finished sixth in the decathlon in the 1968 Olympics, later came out and started the Gay Games, an athletic and cultural festival that draws tens of thousands of people every four years. When I interviewed Tom Waddell over a decade ago about his sexual identity and athletic career, he made it quite clear that for many years sports *was* his closet. Tom told me,

> When I was a kid, I was tall for my age, and was very thin and very strong. And I was usually faster than most other people. But I discovered rather early that I liked gymnastics and I liked dance. I was very interested in being a ballet dancer . . . [but] something became obvious to me right away—that male ballet dancers were effeminate, that they were what most people would call faggots. And I thought I just couldn't handle that . . . I was totally closeted and very concerned about being male. This was the fifties, a terrible time to live, and everything was stacked against me. Anyway, I realized that I had to do something to protect my image of myself as a male—because at that time homosexuals were thought of primarily as men who wanted to be women. And so I threw myself into atheletics—I played football, gymnastics, track and field . . . I was a *jock*—that's how I was viewed, and I was comfortable with that.

Tom Waddell was fully conscious of entering sports and constructing a masculine/heterosexual athletic identity precisely because he feared being revealed as gay. It was clear to him, in the context of the 1950s, that being revealed as gay would undercut his claims to the status of manhood. Thus, though he described the athletic closet as "hot and stifling," he remained in the closet until several years after his athletic retirement. He even knowingly played along with locker room discussions about sex and women, knowing that this was part of his "cover":

> I wanted to be viewed as male, otherwise I would be a dancer today. I wanted the male, macho image of an athlete. So I was protected by a very hard shell. I was clearly aware of what I was doing . . . I often felt compelled to go along with a lot of locker room garbage because I wanted that image—and I know a lot of others who did too.

Like my story, Waddell's story points to the importance of the athletic institution as a context in which peers mutually construct and re-construct narrow definitions of masculinity—and heterosexuality is considered to be a rock-solid foundation of this conception of masculinity. But unlike my story, Waddell's story may invoke what sociologist Erving Goffman called a "dramaturgical analysis": Waddell seemed to be consciously "acting" to control and regulate others' perceptions of him by constructing a public "front stage" persona that differed radically from what he believed to be his "true"

inner self. My story, in contrast, suggests a deeper, less consciously strategic repression of my homoerotic attraction. Most likely, I was aware on some level of the dangers of such feelings, and was escaping the dangers, disgrace, and rejection that would likely result from being different. For Waddell, the decision to construct his identity largely within sport was a decision to step into a fiercely heterosexual/masculine closet that would hide what he saw to be his "true" identity. In contrast, I was not so much stepping into a "closet" that would hide my identify—rather, I was stepping out into an entire world of heterosexual privilege. My story also suggests how a *threat* to the promised privileges of hegemonic masculinity—my failure as an athlete—might trigger a momentary sexual panic that could lay bare the constructedness, indeed, the *instability* of the heterosexual/masculine identity.

In either case—Waddell's or mine—we can see how, as young male athletes, heterosexuality and masculinity were not something we "were," but something we were *doing*. It is very significant, I think, that as each of us was "doing heterosexuality," neither of us was actually "having sex" with women (though one of us desperately wanted to!). This underscores a point made by some recent theorists, that heterosexuality should not be thought of simply as sexual acts between women and men; rather, **heterosexuality is a constructed identity, a performance, and an institution** that is not necessarily linked to sexual acts. Though for one of us it was more conscious than for the other, we were both "doing heterosexuality" as an ongoing practice through which we sought (a) to avoid stigma, embarrassment, ostracism, or perhaps worse if we were even suspected of being gay; and (b) to link ourselves into systems of power, status, and privilege that appear to be the birthright of "real men" (i.e., males who are able to successfully compete with other males in sport, work, and sexual relations with women). In other words, each of us actively scripted our own sexual/gender performances, but these scripts were constructed within the constraints of a socially organized (institutionalized) system of power and pleasure.

QUESTIONS FOR FUTURE RESEARCH

As I prepared to tell my above sexual story publicly to my colleagues at the sport studies conference, I felt extremely nervous. Part of the nervousness was due to the fact that I knew some of my colleagues would object to my claim that telling personal stories can be a source of sociological insights. But a larger part of the reason for my nervousness was due to the fact that I was revealing something very personal about my sexuality in such a public way. Most of us aren't used to doing this, especially in the context of a professional conference. But I had learned long ago, especially from feminist women scholars, and from gay and lesbian scholars, that biography is linked to history, and that part of "normal" academic discourse has been to hide "the personal" (including the fact that the researcher is himself or herself a person, with values, feelings, and, yes, biases) behind a carefully constructed facade of "objectivity." Rather than trying to hide—or be ashamed of—one's subjective experience of the world, I was challenging myself to draw on my experience of the world as a resource. Not that I should trust my experience as the final word on "reality"—white, heterosexual males like myself have made the mistake for centuries of calling their own experience "objectivity," and then punishing anyone who does not share their world view as "deviant." Instead, I hope to use my experience as an example of how those of us who are in dominant sexual/racial/gender/class categories can get a new perspective on the "constructedness" of our identities by juxtaposing our subjective experiences against the recently emerging world views of gay men and lesbians, women, and people of color.

Finally, I want to stress that, juxtaposed, my and Tom Waddell's stories do not shed much light on the question of why some individuals "become gay" while others "become" heterosexual or bisexual. Instead, I'd like to suggest that this is a dead-end question, and that there are far more important and interesting questions to be asked:

- How has heterosexuality, as an institution and as an enforced group practice, constrained and limited all of us—gay, straight, and bi?
- How has the institution of sport been an especially salient institution for the social construction of heterosexual masculinity?
- Why is it that when men play sports they are almost always automatically granted masculine status, and thus assumed to be heterosexual, while when women play sports, questions are raised about their "femininity" and their sexual orientation?

These kinds of questions aim us toward an analysis of the workings of power within institutions—including the ways that these workings of power shape and constrain our identities and relationships—and point us toward imagining alternative social arrangements that are less constraining for everyone.

REFERENCES

Haug, Frigga. 1987. *Female Sexualization: A Collective Work of Memory*. London: Verso.

Katz, Jonathan Ned. 1995. *The Invention of Heterosexuality*. New York: Dutton.

Messner, Michael A. 1992. *Power at Play: Sports and the Problem of Masculinity*. Boston: Beacon Press.

———. 1994. "Gay Athletes and the Gay Games: An Interview with Tom Waddell," in M. A. Messner & D. F. Sabo (Eds.), *Sex, Violence and Power in Sports: Rethinking Masculinity* (pp. 113–119). Freedom, CA: The Crossing Press.

Pronger, Brian. 1990. *The Arena of Masculinity: Sports, Homosexuality, and the Meaning of Sex*. New York: St. Martin's Press.

SECTION 8

Bodies

It might seem that women's bodies and physical health are biological rather than social matters. However, factors such as access to health care, working conditions, and nutrition are all socially determined and have a big impact on our physical selves. In addition, cultural ideologies about women's bodies affect how we perceive our own bodies, as well as how social institutions regulate women's bodies and health. As with the other aspects of women's lives that we have explored so far, class, race, ethnicity, nationality, sexuality, and ability intersect with gender in shaping the social and cultural forces that affect women's health and physical well-being.

Women's bodies are contested terrain, the subject of struggle over political rights, reproductive rights, health care, and medical research. The ability to control reproduction, to live and work in conditions not injurious to health, and to receive safe, effective, and affordable medical care are central to all women's welfare. In recent decades, feminists have devoted considerable energy to changing public health policy on women's behalf and to increasing research funding for women's health issues.

In the 1970s, a women's health movement developed in the United States as an outgrowth of the feminist and consumer health movements. Women's health advocates criticized and challenged the medical establishment's tendency to view women as abnormal and inherently diseased simply because the female reproductive cycle deviates from that of the male. Today, women across the world are asserting the right to control their own bodies by exposing and resisting the medical abuse of women in forms ranging from

forced sterilization and sex selection favoring male children to pharmaceutical experimentation. Women are also increasing their control over their own health care by enhancing access to information and specialized training that allows them more accurately to assess their health care needs and make informed decisions about medical treatment. These movements focused on improving women's health care have recently worked alongside other movements, such as those organizing against AIDS or working for improved nutrition and preventative health care for the poor in the United States as well as in Third World countries.

This section explores different aspects of the social construction of women's bodies and the experiences of diverse women with body issues. Suzanne Kessler's article in Section 2 ("The Medical Construction of Gender") showed that the medical system actively constructs sex categories. In "The Bare Bones of Sex: Part I—Sex and Gender," biologist Anne Fausto-Sterling uses the case of bone density and bone health to show how aspects of bodies that are generally considered purely biological are in fact affected in profound ways by cultural factors. Her analysis once again raises questions about the relationship of sex and gender, nature and nurture. Fausto-Sterling proposes a life course systems approach to thinking about bodies and culture. She argues that a consideration of biological and social factors at different stages of life, from the womb to old age, not only helps us to think in a more complex way about sex and gender but also has important consequences for public health policy. What are the factors that make women's bones different from men's? What are some of the examples that

Fausto-Sterling gives for how bones are affected by the way we live? What other conditions that we think of as physical might be shaped by culture?

Social contexts shape and create health problems as well. Becky Wangsgaard Thompson also explores the ways that social contexts shape and create health problems. In "'A Way Outa No Way': Eating Problems Among African-American, Latina, and White Women," she argues that compulsive eating, compulsive dieting, anorexia, and bulimia are all coping strategies that women employ in response to sexual abuse, poverty, heterosexism, racism, and "class injuries." Eating problems thus are not just about conforming to a norm of physical appearance but are also a "serious response to injustices." Thompson's article illustrates how examining women's multiple oppressions—race, class, and sex, as well as gender—can alter feminist analyses. What differences does she see between the different groups she examines? What kinds of social change would be necessary to eliminate eating problems?

In "Loose Lips Sink Ships," Simone Weil Davis looks at a different kind of bodily "problem" beginning to gain attention in the United States: droopy labia. She compares women's dissatisfaction with their genitals, leading them to embrace cosmetic surgery, to the motivations behind genital cutting in some African societies. At the same time that she argues against genital surgery of any kind, she challenges us to forego the assumption that U.S. women "choose" such surgeries while African women are helpless victims forced to undergo them. What are the forces that lead women in different contexts to alter their bodies? How does Davis's analysis compare to Debra Gimlin's article in Section 3 about other forms of cosmetic surgery? What do you think about the practice of labiaplasty? About other kinds of genital surgery?

Andrea Smith, in "Beyond Pro-Choice Versus Pro-Life," questions the approaches of both sides of the abortion debate from the perspective of women of color, poor women, and women with disabilities. Beginning with the complicated responses of Native American women to the question of whether they were "pro-choice" or "pro-life," Smith challenges the reliance of both groups on criminalization or choice as an approach to issues of reproductive rights. Arguing that neither side attends to the issues of marginalized women, she advocates a more complex response to the barriers to reproductive justice for women both in the United States and abroad. What kinds of approaches might make a difference? How might feminists go about fighting for what Smith calls "reproductive justice"?

The last article in this section takes an irreverent approach to the "cult of the survivor" of cancer—specifically, breast cancer. Barbara Ehrenreich tells the story of her cancer and chemotherapy, taking off from her own experience to analyze the politics and culture of cancer. Ehrenreich is critical of the pink-ribbon culture and its insistence that having cancer somehow ennobles one. Instead, she questions the role of environmental factors as a cause of cancer and critiques the role of drug companies in promoting the culture of cancer survivorship. How gendered is her experience of cancer? Do you agree with her criticism of the focus on the positive side of surviving cancer? How would you compare the treatment of women with breast cancer to that of women with other illnesses, such as cerebral palsy (see the boxed insert by Eli Clare)?

Together, these articles show the diverse ways in which bodies are socially constructed. What might a feminist agenda for the body include?

37 **Anne Fausto-Sterling**

The Bare Bones of Sex: Part 1—Sex and Gender

Here are some curious facts about bones. They can tell us about the kinds of physical labor an individual has performed over a lifetime and about sustained physical trauma. They get thinner or thicker (on average in a population) in different historical periods and in response to different colonial regimes (Molleson 1994; Larsen 1998). They can indicate class, race, and sex (or is it gender—wait and see). We can measure their mineral density and whether on average someone is likely to fracture a limb but not whether a particular individual with a particular density will do so. A bone may break more easily even when its mineral density remains constant (Peacock et al. 2002).[1]

Culture shapes bones. For example, urban ultraorthodox Jewish adolescents have lowered physical activity, less exposure to sunlight, and drink less milk than their more secular counterparts. They also have greatly decreased mineral density in the vertebrae of their lower backs, that is, the lumbar vertebrae (Taha et al. 2001). Chinese women who work daily in the fields have increased bone mineral content and density. The degree of increase correlates with the amount of time spent in physical activity (Hu et al. 1994); weightlessness in space flight leads to bone loss (Skerry 2000); gymnastics training in young women ages seventeen to twenty-seven correlates with increased bone density despite bone resorption caused by total lack of menstruation (Robinson et at. 1995). Consider also some recent demographic trends: in Europe during the past thirty years, the number of vertebral fractures has increased three- to fourfold for women and more than fourfold for men (Mosekilde 2000); in some groups the relative proportions of different parts of the skeleton have changed in recent generations.[2]

What are we to make of reports that African Americans have greater peak bone densities than Caucasian Americans (Aloia et al. 1996; Gilsanz et al. 1998),[3] although this difference may not hold when one compares Africans to British Caucasians (Dibba et al. 1999),

or that white women and white men break their hips more often than black women and black men (Kellie and Brody 1990)?[4] How do we interpret reports that Caucasian men have a lifetime fracture risk of 13–25 percent compared with Caucasian women's lifetime risk of 50 percent even though once peak bone mass is attained men and women lose bone at the same rate (Seeman 1997, 1998; NIH Consensus Statement Online 2000)?

Such curious facts raise perplexing questions. Why have bones become more breakable in certain populations? What does it mean to say that a lifestyle behavior such as exercise, diet, drinking, or smoking is a risk factor for osteoporosis? Why do we screen large numbers of women for bone density even though this information does not tell us whether an individual woman will break a bone?[5] Why was a major public policy statement on women's health unable to offer a coherent account of sex (or is it gender?) differences in bone health over the life cycle (Wizemann and Pardue 2001)? Why, if bone fragility is so often considered to be a sex-related trait, do so few studies examine the relationships among childbirth, lactation, and bone development (Sowers 1996; Glock, Shanahan, and McGowan 2000)?

Such curious facts and perplexing questions challenge both feminist and biomedical theory. If "facts" about biology and "facts" about culture are all in a muddle, perhaps the nature/nurture dualism, a mainstay of feminist theory, is not working as it should. Perhaps, too, parsing medical problems into biological (or genetic or hormonal) components in opposition to cultural or lifestyle factors has outlived its usefulness for biomedical theory. I propose that already well-developed dynamic systems theories can provide a better understanding of how social categories act on bone production. Such a framework, especially if it borrows from a second analytic trend called "life course analysis of chronic disease epidemiology" (Kuh and Ben-Shlomo 1997; Ben-Shlomo and Kuh 2002; Kuh and Hardy 2002), can improve our approaches to public health policy, prediction of individual health conditions, and the treatment of individuals with unhealthy bones.[6] To see why we should follow new roads, I consider gender, examining where we—feminist theorists and medical scientists—have recently been. . . .

SEX AND GENDER (AGAIN)

For centuries, scholars, physicians, and lay people in the United States and Western Europe used biological models to explain the different social, legal, and political statuses of men and women and people of different hues.[7] When the feminist second wave burst onto the political arena in the early 1970s, we made the theoretical claim that sex differs from gender and that social institutions produce observed social differences between men and women (Rubin 1975). Feminists assigned biological (especially reproductive) differences to the word *sex* and gave to *gender* all other differences.

"Sex," however, has become the Achilles' heel of 1970s feminism. We relegated it to the domain of biology and medicine, and biologists and medical scientists have spent the past thirty years expanding it into arenas we firmly believed to belong to our ally gender. Hormones, we learn (once more), cause naturally more assertive men to reach the top in the workplace (Dabbs and Dabbs 2001). Rape is a behavior that can be changed only with the greatest difficulty because it is wired somehow into men's brains (Thornhill and Palmer 2001). The relative size of eggs and sperm dictate that men are naturally polygamous and women naturally monogamous. And more. (See Zuk 2002; Travis 2003 for a critique of these claims.) Feminist scholars have two choices in response to this spreading oil spill of sex. Either we can contest each claim, one at a time, doing what Susan Oyama calls "hauling the theoretical body back and forth across the sex/gender border" (2000a, 190), or, as I choose to do here, we can reconsider the 1970s theoretical account of sex and gender.

In thinking about both gender and race, feminists must accept the body as simultaneously composed of genes, hormones, cells, and organs—all of which influence health and behavior—and of culture and history (Verbrugge 1997). As a biologist, I focus on what it might mean to claim that our bodies physically imbibe culture. How does experience shape the very bones that support us?[8] Can we find a way to talk about the body without ceding it to those who would fix it as a naturally determined object existing outside of politics, culture, and

social change? This is a project already well under way, not only in feminist theoretical circles but in epidemiology, medical sociology, and anthropology as well.

EMBODIMENT MERGES BIOLOGY AND CULTURE

During the 1990s, feminist reconsideration of the sex/gender problem moved into full swing.[9] Early in the decade Judith Butler argued compellingly for the importance of reclaiming the term *sex* for feminist inquiry but did not delve into the nuts and bolts of how sex and gender materialize in the body. Philosopher Elizabeth Grosz (1994) claimed that sex is neither fixed nor given. In drawing on philosophers such as Maurice Merleau-Ponty (1962) and Alfred North Whitehead ([1929] 1978), Grosz differentiates herself from Butler, holding that materiality is "primordial, not merely the effect of power" (Alcoff 2000, 858). Primordial materiality, however, does not mean that purely biological accounts of human development—no matter how intricate their stories of cellular function—can explain the emergence of lived and differently gendered realities. . . .[10]

Efforts to reincorporate the body into social theory also come from the field of disability studies. Here too an emphasis on the social construction of disability has been enormously productive. Yet several authors have broached the limitations of an exclusively constructivist approach. At least two different types of critique parallel and foreshadow possible feminist approaches to a reconsideration of the body. The first demands that we recognize the material constraints on the disabled body in its variable forms and that we integrate that recognition into theory (Williams and Busby 2000). The second, more radical move is to suggest that "the disabled body changes the process of representation itself" (Siebers 2001, 738). This latter approach offers a rich resource for feminist theories of representation and another possible entry point into the analysis of materiality in actual, lived-in bodies (see also Schriempf 2001).

SEX AND GENDER IN THE WORLD OF BIOLOGY AND MEDICINE

In contrast to these new feminist explorations of the body, in the field of medicine a more limited view of sex differences prevails. Consider a recent report on sex differences issued by the National Institute of Medicine and, more broadly, the professional movement called "gender-based medicine" promoted by the Society for Women's Health Research (SWHR). The SWHR describes itself as "the nation's only not-for-profit organization whose sole mission is to improve the health of women through research. . . . The Society . . . encourages the study of sex differences that may affect the prevention, diagnosis and treatment of disease and promotes the inclusion of women in medical research studies" (Schachter 2001, 29).[11] The society lobbies Congress, sponsors research conferences, and publishes a peer-reviewed academic journal, the *Journal of Women's Health and Gender-Based Medicine*.

A traditional biomedical model of health and disease provides the intellectual framework for the research conferences (Krieger and Zierler 1995). Although much of the research publicized through such conferences seems strictly to deal with *sex* in the 1970s feminist meaning of the word, sex sometimes strays into arenas that traditional feminists claim for gender. Consider a presentation that was said to provide evidence that prenatal testosterone exposure affects which toys little girls and boys prefer to play with (Berenbaum 2001). Working within a 1970s definition of the sex/gender dualism, the author of this study logically extends the term *sex* into the realm of human behavior.

For those familiar with contemporary feminist theory, it might seem that the large number of biological psychologists who follow similar research programs and the biomedical researchers interested in tracking down all of the medically interesting differences between men and women live in a time warp. But members of the feminist medical establishment, that is, those researchers and physicians for whom the activities and programs of the SWHR make eminent sense, see themselves perched on the forward edge of a nascent movement to bring gender equity to the health-care system. These feminists work outside of an intellectual milieu that would permit the more revolutionary task proposed by Grosz and Wilson, among others, that of contesting not only "the domination of the body by biological terms but also [contesting] the terms of biology itself" (Grosz 1994, 20). . . .

Helen Keane and Marsha Rosengarten (2002) have explored the body as a dynamic process out of which gender emerges. . . . I have chosen bone development—an area often accepted as an irrefutable site of sex difference—to examine Keane and Rosengarten's formulation. First, to what extent can we understand bone formation as an effect of culture rather than a passive unfolding of biology? Second, can we use dynamic (developmental) systems to ask better research questions and to formulate better public-health responses to bone disease?

WHY BONES?

Bones are eloquent. Archaeologists read old bone texts to find out how prehistoric peoples lived and worked. A hyperflexed and damaged big toe, a bony growth on the femur, the knee, or the vertebrae, for example, tell bioarchaeologist Theya Molleson that women in a Near Eastern agricultural community routinely ground grain on all fours, grasping a stone grinder with their hands and pushing back and forth on a saddle-shaped stone. The bones of these neolithic people bear evidence of a gendered division of labor, culture, and biology intertwined (Molleson 1994).[12]

. . . Osteoporosis is a condition that reveals all of the problems of defining sex apart from gender. A close reading of the osteoporosis literature further reveals the difficulties of adding the variable of race to the mix (a point I will develop in a forthcoming paper [Fausto-Sterling in preparation]) while also exemplifying the claim that disease states are socially produced, both by rhetoric and measurement (e.g., Petersen 1998) and by the manner in which cultural practice shapes the very bones in our bodies (Krieger and Zierler 1995).

OF BONES AND (WO)MEN

The accuracy of the claim that osteoporosis occurs four times more frequently in women than in men (Glock, Shanahan, and McGowan 2000) depends on how we define osteoporosis, in which human populations (and historical periods) we gather statistics, and what portions of the life cycle we compare. The NIH (2000) defines osteoporosis as a skeletal disorder in which weakened bones increase the risk of fracture. When osteoporosis first wandered onto the medical radar screen, the only signal that a person suffered from it was a bone fracture. Post hoc, a doctor could examine a person with a fracture either [by] using a biopsy to look at the structural competence of the bone or by assessing bone density.

If one looks at lifetime risks for fracture, contemporary Caucasian men range from 13 to 25 percent (Bilezikian, Kurkland, and Rosen 1999) while Caucasian women (who also live longer) have a 50 percent risk. But not all fractures result from osteoporosis. One study looked at fracture incidence in men and women at different ages and found that between the ages of five and forty-five men break more limbs than women.[13] The breaks, however, result from significant work- and sports-related trauma suffered by healthy bones. After the age of fifty, women break their bones more often than men, although after seventy years of age men do their best to catch up (Melton 1988).

The most commonly used medical standard for a diagnosis of osteoporosis no longer depends on broken bones. With the advent of machines called densitometers used to measure bone mineral density (of which more in a moment), the World Health Organization (WHO) developed a new "operational" definition: a woman has osteoporosis if her bone mineral density measures 2.5 times the standard deviation below a peak reference standard for young (white) women. The densitometer manufacturer usually provides the reference data to a screening facility (Seeman 1998), and thus rarely, if ever, do assessments of osteoporosis reflect what Margaret Lock calls "local biologies" (Lock 1998, 39).[14] With the WHO definition, the prevalence of osteoporosis for white women is 18 percent, although there is not necessarily associated pathology, since now, by definition, one can "get" or "have" osteoporosis without ever having a broken bone. The WHO definition is controversial, since bone mineral density (BMD, or grams/cm^2) accounts for approximately 70 percent of bone strength, while the other 30 percent derives from the internal structure of bone and overall bone size. And while women with lower bone density are 2.5 times more likely to experience a hip fracture than women with high bone densities, high risks of hip fracture emerge even in women with high bone densities when five or more other risk factors are present (Cummings et al. 1995).[15] Furthermore, it is hard to know how to apply the criterion, based on a baseline of young white women, to men, children, and members of other ethnic groups. To make matters worse, there is a lack of standardization between instruments and sites at which measurements are taken.[16] Thus it comes as no surprise that "controversy exists among experts regarding the continued use of this [WHO] diagnostic criterion" (NIH Consensus Statement Online 2000, 3).

There is a complicated mixture at play. First, osteoporosis—whether defined as fractures or bone density—is on the rise, even when the increased age of a population is taken into account (Mosekilde 2000). At the same time, it is hard to assess the danger of osteoporosis, in part due to drug company–sponsored "public awareness" campaigns. For example, in preparation for the sales campaign for its new drug, Fosamax,

Merck Pharmaceuticals gave a large osteoporosis education grant to the National Osteoporosis Foundation to educate older women about the dangers of osteoporosis (Tanouye 1995).[17] Merck also directly addressed consumers with television ads contrasting frail, pain-wracked older women with lively, attractive seniors, implying the urgent need for older women to use Fosamax (Fugh-Berman, Pearson, Allina, Zones, Worcester, and Whatley 2002).

Mass marketing a new drug, however, requires more than a public awareness campaign. There must also be an easy, relatively inexpensive method of diagnosis. Here the slippage between the new technological measure—bone density—and the old definition of actual fractures and direct assessment of bone structure looms large. Merck promoted affordable bone density testing even before it put Fosamax on the market. The company bought an equipment manufacturing company and ramped up its production of bone density machines while at the same time helping consumers find screening locations by giving a grant to the National Osteoporosis Foundation to push a toll-free number that consumers (presumably alarmed by the Merck TV ads) could call to find a bone density screener in a locale near them (Tanouye 1995; Fugh-Berman, Pearson, Allina, Zones, Worcester, and Whatley 2002).

The availability of a simple technological measure for osteoporosis also made scientific research easier and cheaper. The majority of the thousands upon thousands of research papers on osteoporosis published in the ten years from 1995 to 2005 use BMD as a proxy for osteoporosis. This is true despite a critical scientific literature that insists that the more expensive volumetric measure (grams/cm^3) more accurately measures bone strength and that knowledge of internal bone structure (bone histomorphometry) provides essential information for understanding the actual risk of fracture (Meunier 1988).[18] The explosion of knowledge about osteoporosis codifies a new disorder, still called osteoporosis but sporting a newly simplified account of bone health and disease.[19] . . .

Weaving together these threads—increasing lifetime risk, new disease definitions, and easier measurement—produces an epistemological transformation in our scientific accounts of bones and why they break. The transformation is driven by a combination of cultural forces (why are fracture rates increasing?) and new technologies generated by drug companies interested in creating new markets, disseminated with the help of market forces drummed up by the self-same drug companies, and aided by consumer health movements, including feminist health organizations such as the Society for Women's Research, which argue that gender-based differences in disease have been too long neglected.

Analyzing bone development within the framework of sex versus gender (nature vs. nurture) makes it difficult to understand bone health in men as well as women. Those trying to decide on a proper standard to measure fracture risk in men (should they use a separate male baseline or the only one available, which is for young, white women?) struggle with this problem of gender standardization (Melton et al. 1998). There are differences between men and women, although osteoporosis in men is vastly understudied. In a bibliography of 2,449 citations of papers from 1995 to 1999 (Glock, Shanahan, and McGowan 2000), only 47 (2 percent) addressed osteoporosis in men. But making sense of patterns of bone health for either or both sexes requires a dynamic systems approach. A basic starting place is to ask the development question.

For instance, we find no difference in bone mineral density in (Caucasian) boys and girls under age sixteen but a higher bone mineral density in males than in females thereafter (Zanchetta et al. 1995). This difference (combined with others that develop during middle adulthood) becomes important later in life, since men and women appear to lose bone at the same rate once they have reached a peak bone mass; those starting the loss phase of the life cycle with more bone in place will be less likely to develop highly breakable bones. Researchers offer different explanations for this divergence. Some note that boys continue to grow for an average of two years longer than girls (Seeman 1997). The extra growth period strengthens their bones by adding overall size. Others point additionally to hormones, diet, physical activity, and body weight as contributing to the emerging sex (or is it gender?) difference at puberty (Rizzoli and Bonjour 1999).

So differences in bone mineral density between boys and girls emerge during and after puberty, while for both men and women peak bone mass and strength is reached at twenty-five to thirty years of age (Seeman 1999). Vertebral height is the same in men and women, but vertebral width is greater in men. The volume of the inner latticework does not differ in men and women, but the outer layer of bone (periosteum) is thicker in men. Both width and outer thickness strengthen the bone. In general, sex/gender bone differences at peak are in size rather than density (Bilezikian, Kurkland, and Rosen 1999).

This life-cycle analysis reveals three major differences in the pattern of bone growth and loss in men compared with that in women. First, at peak, men have 20 to 30 percent more bone mass and strength than women. Second, following peak, men but not women compensate for bone loss with new increases in vertebral width that continue to strengthen the vertebrae. Over time both men and women lose 70 to 80 percent of bone strength (Mosekilde 2000), but the pattern of loss differs. In men the decline is gradual, barring secondary causes.[20] In women it is gradual until perimenopause, accelerates for several years during and after the menopause, and then resumes a gradual decline.[21] Lis Moskilde (2000) points out that the rush to link menopause to osteoporosis has led to the neglect of two of the three major differences in the pattern of bone growth between men and women. Yet these two factors are specifically linked to physical activity, and thus amenable to change earlier in life.

Indeed, many studies on children and adolescents address the contribution sociocultural components of bone development make to male-female differences that emerge just after puberty. But the overwhelming focus on menopause as the period of the life cycle in which women enter the danger zone steers us away from examining how earlier sociocultural events shape our bones (see Lock 1998). Once menopause enters the picture, the idea that hormones are at the heart of the problem overwhelms other modes of thought.[22] Nor is it clear how hormones affect bone development and loss. In childhood, growth hormone is essential for long bone growth, the gonadal steroids are important for the cessation of bone growth at puberty, and probably both estrogen and testosterone are important for bone health maintenance (Damien, Price, and Lanyon 1998). The details at the cellular level have yet to be understood (Gasperino 1995).[23] . . .

THINKING SYSTEMATICALLY ABOUT BONE

There are better ways to think about gender and the bare bones of sex. One cannot easily separate bone biology from the experiences of individuals growing, living, and dying in particular cultures and historical periods and under different regimens of social gender.[24] But how can we integrate the varied information presented in this essay in a manner that helps us ask better research and public policy questions and that, in posing better questions, allows us to find better answers? By *better*, I mean several things: in terms of the science I want to take more of the "curious facts" about bone into account when responding to public health problems. I favor emphasizing lifelong healthful habits that might prevent or lessen the severity of bone problems in late life, but I would also like us to have a better idea of how to help people whose bones are already thin. What dietary changes, what regimens of exercise and sun exposure, what body mass index work best with which medications? How do the medications we choose work? What unintended effects do they have? Finally, *better* includes an ability to predict outcomes for individuals, based on their particular life histories and genetic makeups, rather than merely making probability statements about large and diverse categories of people.

How can we get there from here? Below, I outline in fairly general form the possibilities of dynamic systems and developmental systems approaches. Such formulations allow us to work with the idea that we are always 100 percent nature and 100 percent nurture. I further point to important theoretical and empirical work currently under way by social scientists who study chronic diseases using a life-course approach. Before turning to the specifics of bone development, let me offer a general introduction to these complementary modes of thought.

. . . Ludwig von Bertalanffy is usually cited as the originator of "general systems theory," a program for studying complex systems such as organisms as whole entities rather than the traditional approach of reducing the whole to its component parts (Bertalanffy 1969), but the idea of studying developmental outcomes as a result of the combined action of genes and environment began in the early twentieth century before a clear theoretical statement was achieved in the 1940s.[25]

Systems theorists also write about the brain and behavior. D. O. Hebb (1949) linked psychology and physiology by thinking about how functional cellular groups develop in the brain, thus developing a form of systems theory called connectionism. As Esther Thelen and Linda Smith put it, "the connection weights between layers—the response of the network to a particular input—thus depend on the statistical regularities in the network's *history* of experiences" (Thelen and Smith 1998, 580). Thus an organism's current and future behaviors are shaped by past experiences via a direct effect on the strength of connections between cells in the brain.[26]

The varied systems approaches to understanding development share certain features in common. All

understand that cells, nervous systems, and whole organisms develop through a process of self-organization rather than according to a preformed set of instructions.[27] The varying relationships among system components lead to change, and new patterns are dynamically stable because the characteristics of the system confer stability. But if the system is sufficiently perturbed, instability ensues and significant fluctuations occur until a new pattern, again dynamically stable, emerges. Bone densities, for example, are often dynamically stable in midlife but destabilize during old age; most medical interventions aim to restabilize the dynamic system that maintains bone density. But we really do not understand how the transition from a stable to an unstable system of bone maintenance occurs.

To address the bare bones of sex, I highlight, in figure 1, seven systems that contribute to bone strength throughout the life cycle.[28] I also describe some of the known interrelationships between them.[29] Each of the seven—physical activity, diet, drugs, bone formation in fetal development, hormones, bone cell metabolism, and biomechanical effects on bone formation—can be analyzed as a complex system in its own right. Bone strength emerges from the interrelated actions of each (and all) of these systems as they act throughout the life cycle. As a first step toward envisioning bone from a systems viewpoint we can construct a theoretical diagram of their interactions. The diagram in systems approaches can be thought of as a theoretical model, to be tested in part or whole and modified as needed.[30] As ways to describe each component system using numerical proxies become available, the pictorial model can provide the framework for a mathematical model. Figure 1 represents one possible diagram of a life-course systems account of bone development.

This feminist systems account embeds the proposed subsystems within the dimensions of gender, socioeconomic position, and culture.[31] Consider the diet system. Generally, of course, diet is shaped by culture and subculture, including race and ethnicity (Bryant, Cadogan, and Weaver 1999). But gender further influences diet. For example, one study reports that 27 percent of U.S. teenage girls (compared with 10 percent of adolescent boys) who think they weigh the correct amount are nevertheless trying to lose weight (Walsh and Devlin 1998). It may also be true that there are sex/gender differences in basal metabolism rates that influence food intake.

Figure 1 also indicates the cumulative effects of diet on bone formation. Key events may be clustered at

FIGURE 1: A LIFE HISTORY–SYSTEMS OVERVIEW OF BONE DEVELOPMENT. (1) PHYSICAL ACTIVITY HAS DIRECT EFFECTS ON BONE CELL RECEPTORS AND INDIRECT EFFECTS BY BUILDING STRONGER MUSCLES, WHICH EXERT PHYSICAL STRAIN ON BONES, THUS STIMULATING BONE SYNTHESIS. (2) PHYSICAL ACTIVITY THAT TAKES PLACE OUTDOORS INVOLVES EXPOSURE TO SUNLIGHT, THUS STIMULATING VITAMIN D SYNTHESIS, PART OF THE HORMONAL SYSTEM REGULATING CALCIUM METABOLISM. (3) BIOMECHANICAL STRAIN AFFECTS BONE CELL METABOLISM BY ACTIVATING GENES CONCERNED WITH BONE CELL DIVISION AND BONE (RE)MODELING. (4) HORMONES AFFECT BONE CELL METABOLISM BY ACTIVATING GENES CONCERNED WITH BONE CELL DIVISION, CELL DEATH, BONE (RE)MODELING, AND NEW HORMONE SYNTHESIS.

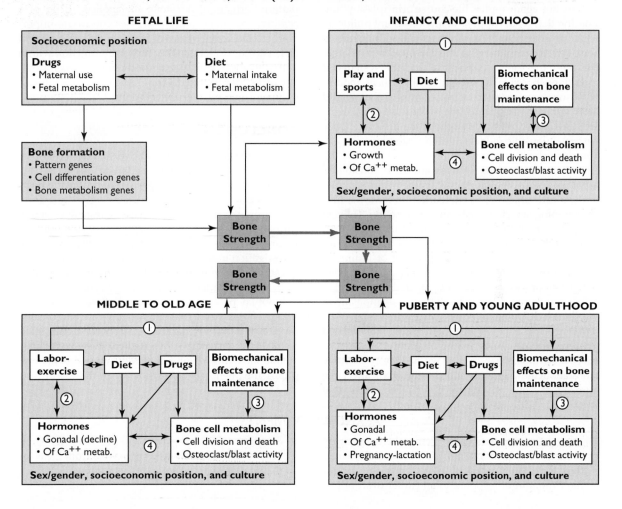

certain points in the life cycle.[32] For example, adolescent girls in the United States often diet more and exercise less than during earlier childhood. Diseases such as anorexia nervosa, which have devastating effects on bone development, may also emerge during adolescence. As Yoav Ben-Shlomo and Diana Kuh (2002) point out, such clustering of adverse events is common and may be thought of in terms of "chains of risk" (or benefit). In a life-course approach, prior events set the limits on later ones. If girls and women enter into adulthood with weakened bones, therefore, they can rebuild them, but their peak density may be less than if they had built stronger bones in adolescence.[33] Alternatively, achieving a safe peak bone density might require more sustained and intense work for a person of one history compared with a person of a different history.

Sex/gender, race, class, and culture also differentiate individuals by forms of play in childhood and beyond (Boot et al. 1997), by choices of formal exercise programs, and, in adulthood, by forms of labor, physical and otherwise. In analyzing the system of physical activity one again applies life-course principles by considering that what happens at any one point builds on what has gone before. Important events with regard to bone development may be clustered and interrelated. For both the diet and physical activity systems, it should be possible to design mathematical models based on some measure of bone strength that would incorporate the effects of each of these social systems on bone development throughout the life cycle; once we have plausible models of each system, we can ask questions about their interactions.

The remaining four systems are often considered within the realm of biology, as if biology were separate from culture, although recent work from some medical epidemiologists challenges this distinction (Ellison 1996; Hertzman 1999; Lamont et al. 2000). The system of biomechanical effects on bone synthesis, for example, requires further investigation of all of its inputs (physical strain, activation of genes that stimulate bone cell development or death, etc. [Harada and Rodan 2003]), but these must then be studied in relationship to the gender-differentiated physical activity system. The different body shapes of adult men and women (related to hormones at puberty among other things) may also effect bone biomechanics, and we need, too, to know more about how growth and development affect the number of bone mechanoreceptors—molecules that translate mechanical stress in biochemical activity (Boman et al. 1998; Pavalko et al. 2003).

The impact of hormones on bone development and maintenance requires research attention of a sort currently lacking in the bone literature. We need to know both about the molecular biology of hormones and bone cell hormone receptors and about life-course effects on hormone systems (Ellison 1996; Worthman 2002). Finally, genes involved in bone cell metabolism, pattern formation, hormone metabolism, drug processing, and many other processes contribute importantly to the development of bone strength (Zelzer and Olsen 2003). Understanding how they function within both the local and global (body and sociocultural) networks contributing to bone development requires a systems-level analysis not yet found in the literature.

CONCLUSION

This article is a call to arms. The sex-gender or nature-nurture accounts of difference fail to appreciate the degree to which culture is a partner in producing body systems commonly referred to as biology—something apart from the social. I introduce an alternative—a life-course systems approach to the analysis of sex/gender. Figure 1 is a research proposal for multiple programs of investigation in several disciplines. We need to ask old questions in new ways so that we can think systematically about the interweaving of bodies and culture. We will not lay bare the bones of sex, but we will come to understand, instead, that our skeletons are part of a life process. If process rather than stasis becomes our intellectual goal, we will improve medical practice and have a more satisfying account of gender and sex as, to paraphrase the phenomenologists, being-in-the-world.

ACKNOWLEDGMENTS

Thanks to the members of the Pembroke Seminar on Theories of Embodiment for a wonderful year of thinking about the process of body making and for their thoughtful response to an earlier draft of this essay. Credit for the title goes to Greg Downey. Thanks also to anonymous reviewers from *Signs* for making me sharpen some of the arguments.

NOTES

1. Munro Peacock et al. write: "The pathogenesis of a fragility fracture almost always involves trauma and is not necessarily associated with reduced bone mass. Thus, fragility fracture should neither be used synonymously nor interchangeably as a phenotype for osteoporosis" (2002, 303).

2. For example, sitting height reflects trunk length (vertebral height) vs. standing height, which reflects the length of the leg bones. These can change independently of one another. Thus height increases can result from changes in long bone length, vertebral height, or both. See Meredith 1978; Tanner et al. 1982; Malina, Brown, and

Zavaleta 1987; Balthazart, Tlemçani, and Ball 1996; Seeman 1997.

3. The use of racial terms such as *Caucasian* and others in this article is fraught. But for the duration of this article I will use the terms as they appear in the sources I cite, leaving an analysis of this problematic terminology to future publications, e.g., Fausto-Sterling 2004.

4. Since a number of studies show no sex difference in hip fracture incidence between African American men and women, the "well-known" gender difference in bone fragility may really only be about white women. As so often happens, the word *gender* excludes women of color (Farmer et al. 1984).

5. Peacock et al. write, "Key bone phenotypes involved in fracture risk relate not only to bone mass but also to bone structure, bone loss, and possibly bone turnover" (2002, 306).

6. I am grateful to Peter Taylor for insisting that I read the work in life-course analysis.

7. Stepan 1982; Kasten 1989; Hubbard 1990; Fausto-Sterling 1992.

8. I use the term *experience* rather than the term *environment* here to refer to functional activity. For more detail see Gottlieb, Whalen, and Lickliter 1998.

9. Butler 1990, 1993; Gatens 1996; Kirby 1997; Birke 1999.

10. The "rediscovery" of phenomenology and its application to gendered body image remains a fruitful arena of feminist body theory, e.g., Weiss 1999.

11. Since the society receives both foundation and pharmaceutical company funding, its claim to independence requires scrutiny. The Sex and Gene Expression conferences were funded by Aventis Pharmaceuticals as well as private foundations. Industry and mainstream medical care sponsorship does not unethically direct work, but it limits the permissible ontological and epistemological approaches to the study of women's health and sex differences.

12. Perhaps because the field of archaeology is still struggling to bring gender into the fold, its practitioners often insist on the centrality of the sex/gender distinction. Yet their own conclusions undermine this dualism, precisely because they use a biological product, bone, to draw conclusions about culture and behavior (Ehrenberg 1989; Gero and Conkey 1991; Wright 1996; Armelagos 1998).

13. This study (cited in Melton 1988) dates from 1979, and it seems likely that subsequent cultural changes have led to different patterns of breakage; fracture incidence is a moving target.

14. Local biologies reflect local differences in biology. For example, hot flashes are far less frequent in Japan than in the United States, possibly for reasons pertaining to diet. The normalization question here is: Is it best to compare a population to its own group or some group with similar environmental and genetic histories, or to some outgroup standard?

15. These factors include: a mother having broken her hip, especially before age eighty; height at age twenty-five (taller women are more likely to break hips); extreme thinness; sedentary lifestyle; poor vision; high pulse rate; the use of certain drugs; etc.

16. One researcher states: "I think what is also of note, is that the between-center differences are greater than between-sex differences within certain centers" (Lips 1997, 95).

17. Fosamax seems to be able to prevent further bone loss in people who are losing bone and to build back lost bone at least in the hip and spine. In discussing Merck's campaign, I do not argue that the drug is useless (in fact, I am taking it!), merely (!) that drug companies play an important role in the creation of new "disease" and profit as a result.

18. "An association between the change in areal bone density and the change in fracture rates has never been documented" (Seeman 1997, 517). According to the NIH Consensus Statement Online: "Currently there is no accurate measure of overall bone strength" (2000, 5). But BMD is often used as a proxy. The National Women's Health Network cites the pitfalls of using BMD to predict future fractures (Fugh-Berman, Pearson, Allina, Zones, Worcester, Whatley, Massion, et al. 2002), but others cite a strong association between BMD and fracture rate (e.g., Melton et al. 1998; Siri et al. 2001). One overview of studies that attempted to predict osteoporosis-linked fractures with bone mineral density concluded: "Measurements of bone mineral density can predict fracture risk but cannot identify individuals who will have a fracture. We do not recommend a programme of screening menopausal women for osteoporosis by measuring bone density" (Marshall, Johnell, and Wedell 1996, 1254). See also Nelson et al. 2002.

19. For a history of the concept of osteoporosis, see Klinge 1998.

20. A secondary cause might be bone loss due to an eating disorder or a metabolic disease, or the prolonged use of a bone-leaching drug such as cortisone.

21. When I use the words *men* and *women* I refer to particular populations on which these studies were done. These are mostly Caucasian and Northern European or North American. Most of the studies have been done since the 1980s, but bone size, shape, and growth patterns would have differed at the beginning of the twentieth century compared with their appearance at the beginning of the twenty-first. I will not make these points every time I use these words.

22. So powerful is the focus on old age that the long NIH bibliography on menopause completely ignores the possible importance of pregnancy and lactation on bone development. These two processes are profoundly implicated in calcium metabolism, and if there is *no* effect on later bone strength it would be important to find out why. What physiological mechanisms protect the bone of pregnant and lactating women? This is an example of a biological question that lies fallow because of the focus on supposed estrogen deficiency in old age.

23. For a discussion of bone biology, see the full article from which this reading as excerpted.

24. I found one eloquent but wordless example on the Web in an article on causes of vitamin D deficiency. The short segment titled "Insufficient Exposure to Sunlight" was

accompanied by a photograph of two women, standing in the blazing sun, covered from head to toe in burkas, clearly insufficiently exposed to sunlight but not for want of being outdoors in the sun.

25. Brief histories of these ideas as well as accounts of present-day embryology, genetics, and evolution based on systems theory may be found in Waddington 1957; Kauffman 1993; Webster and Goodwin 1996; Schlichting and Pigliucci 1998; van der Weele 1999; Oyama 2000a, 2000b.

26. The implications of these ideas for an integrative theory of the development of gender differences in behavior and psychological skills have not escaped me and are the subject of a work in progress. The explosion of knowledge about the plastic nature of brain development and an increasing understanding of neuroplasticity in adults suggest that far from being destiny, anatomy is dynamic history. A rich literature that joins mathematical models of nonlinear equations (Kelso 1995) has begun to join forces with experimental scientists who study animal behavior (Gottlieb 1997) and those who now use dynamic systems approaches to reconceptualize human behavioral development (Smith and Thelen 1993; Thelen and Smith 1994, 1998; Thelen 1995; Thelen et al. 2001).

27. Among biologists the idea that genes provide such instructions is giving way to a systems account of cell function. The metaphor of the genome (DNA) as a blueprint or set of direction for building cells and organisms is giving way to a new metaphor—genomes as parts list (Vukmirovic and Tilghmann 2000; Tyson, Csikasz-Nagy, and Novak 2002). If the genome lists only the component parts (codes for RNA and protein), the location of the assembly directions becomes uncertain: one needs to specify a cell or organism's past history and current conditions in order to predict a current developmental event accurately. Cell biologists have now turned in earnest to complexity and systems theory to help learn the rules by which organisms are assembled. (See entire December 2002 issue of *Bioessays*

devoted to "Modeling Complex Biological Systems.") In another example, authors extend and twist the book metaphor. "Just as words must be assembled into sentences, paragraphs, chapters and books to make sense, vital cellular functions are performed by structured ensembles of proteins . . . not by freely diffusing and occasionally colliding proteins" (Sali et al. 2003, 216).

28. I use Peter Taylor's definition of systems as "units that have clearly defined boundaries, coherent internal dynamics, and simply mediated relations with their external context" (personal communication 2003).

29. This choice of systems emerges from the data presented earlier in this article. Since this is a model, others might argue for dividing the pie in a different way. To keep the diagram readable and the discussion manageable, I have not emphasized that the entire grouping of systems is embedded in a larger system I call "general health." There are many disease states that secondarily affect bone (e.g., kidney disease or endocrine disorders) by affecting calcium metabolism or preventing exercise. The relationships among the systems affecting bone strength would be shifted in dramatic ways worthy of study in their own right under such circumstances.

30. Choice of model has profound implications. For a discussion of a lifestyle model of disease that emphasizes individual choice vs. a "social production model," see Krieger and Zierler 1995. For an update on current theories of social epidemiology, see Krieger 2001.

31. To the extent that race is a legitimate category separate from class and culture, I will incorporate it into the bone systems story in pt. 2 of this work. For a model of social pathways in childhood that lead to adult health, see Kuh and Ben-Shlomo 1997.

32. Bonjour et al. 1997; Boot et al. 1997; Perry 1997; Wang et al. 2003.

33. For the effects of dietary calcium later in life, see Heaney 2000.

REFERENCES

Alcoff, Linda Martín. 2000. "Philosophy Matters: A Review of Recent Work on Feminist Philosophy." *Signs: Journal of Women in Culture and Society* 25(3):841–42.

Aloia, J. F., A. N. Vaswani, J. K. Yeh, and E. Flaster. 1996. "Risk for Osteoporosis in Black Women." *Calcified Tissue International* 59(6):415–23.

Armelagos, George J. 1998. "Introduction: Sex, Gender and Health Status in Prehistoric and Contemporary Populations." In *Sex and Gender in Paleopathological Perspective*, ed. Anne L. Grauer and Patricia Stuart-Macadam, 1–10. Cambridge: Cambridge University Press.

Bachrach, Laura K. 2001. "Acquisition of Optimal Bone Mass in Childhood and Adolescence." *Trends in Endocrinology and Metabolism* 12(1):22–28.

Balthazart, Jacques, Omar Tlemçani, and Gregory F. Ball. 1996. "Do Sex Differences in the Brain Explain Sex Differences in Hormonal Induction of Reproductive Behavior? What 25 Years of Research on the Japanese Quail Tells Us." *Hormones and Behavior* 30(4):627–61.

Bassey, E. J., and S. J. Ramsdale. 1994. "Increase in Femoral Bone Density in Young Women Following High-Impact Exercise." *Osteoporosis International* 4:72–75.

Bassey, E. J., M. C. Rothwell, J. J. Littlewood, and D. W. Pye. 1998. "Pre- and Post-Menopausal Women Have Different Bone Mineral Density Responses to the Same High-Impact Exercise." *Journal of Bone and Mineral Research* 13(12):1805–13.

Ben-Shlomo, Yoav, and Diana Kuh. 2002. "A Life Course Approach to Chronic Disease Epidemiology: Conceptual

Models, Empirical Challenges, and Interdisciplinary Perspectives." *International Journal of Epidemiology* 31(2):285–93.

Berenbaum, Sheri. 2001. "Prenatal Androgen Effects on Cognitive and Social Development." Paper presented at the Second Annual Conference on Sex and Gene Expression, March 8–11, Winston-Salem, North Carolina.

Bertalanffy, Ludwig von. 1969. *General System Theory: Foundations, Development, Applications.* New York: Braziller.

Bilezikian, John P., Etah S. Kurland, and Clifford S. Rosen. 1999. "Male Skeletal Health and Osteoporosis." *Trends in Endocrinology and Metabolism* 10(6):244–50.

Birke, Lynda. 1999. *Feminism and the Biological Body.* Edinburgh: Edinburgh University Press.

Boman, U. Wide, A. Möller, and K. Albertsson-Wikland. 1998. "Psychological Aspects of Turner Syndrome." *Journal of Psychosomatic Obstetrics and Gynaecology* 19(1):1–18.

Bonjour, Jean-Phillippe, Anne-Lise Carrie, Serge Ferrari, Helen Clavien, Daniel Slosman, and Gerald Theintz. 1997. "Calcium-Enriched Foods and Bone Mass Growth in Prepubertal Girls: A Randomized, Double-Blind, Placebo-Controlled Trial." *Journal of Clinical Investigation* 99(6): 1287–94.

Boot, Annemieke M., Maria A. J. de Ridder, Huibert A. P. Pols, Eric P. Krenning, and Sabine M. P. F. de Muinck Keizer-Schrama. 1997. "Bone Mineral Density in Children and Adolescents: Relation to Puberty, Calcium Intake, and Physical Activity." *Journal of Clinical Endocrinology and Metabolism* 82(1):57–62.

Bryant, Rebecca J., Jo Cadogan, and Connie M. Weaver. 1999. "The New Dietary Reference Intakes for Calcium: Implications for Osteoporosis." *Journal of the American College of Nutrition* 18(5):S406–S412.

Butler, Judith. 1990. *Gender Trouble: Feminism and the Subversion of Identity.* New York: Routledge.

———. 1993. *Bodies That Matter: On the Discursive Limits of "Sex."* New York: Routledge.

Csordas, Thomas J. 1999. "Embodiment and Cultural Phenomenology." In *Perspectives on Embodiment: The Intersections of Nature and Culture,* ed. Gail Weiss and Honi Fern Haber, 143–62. New York: Routledge.

Cummings, Steven R., Michael C. Nevitt, Warren S. Browner, Katie Stone, Kathleen M. Fox, Kristine E. Ensrud, Jane Cauley, Dennis Black, and Thomas M. Vogt. 1995. "Risk Factors for Hip Fracture in White Women." *New England Journal of Medicine* 332(12):767–73.

Dabbs, James McBride, and Mary Godwin Dabbs. 2001. *Heroes, Rogues, and Lovers: Testosterone and Behavior,* New York: McGraw-Hill.

Daly, Robin M., Peter A. Rich, Rudi Klein, and Shona Bass. 1999. "Effects of High-Impact Exercise on Ultrasonic and Biochemical Indices of Skeletal Status: A Prospective Study in Young Male Gymnasts." *Journal of Bone and Mineral Research* 14(7):1222–30.

Damien, E., J. S. Price, and L. E. Lanyon. 1998. "The Estrogen Receptor's Involvement in Osteoblasts' Adaptive Response to Mechanical Strain." *Journal of Bone and Mineral Research* 13(8):1275–82.

Dawson-Hughes, Bess, Susan S. Harris, Elizabeth A. Krall, and Gerard E. Dallal. 1997. "Effect of Calcium and Vitamin D Supplementation on Bone Density in Men and Women 65 Years of Age or Older." *New England Journal of Medicine* 337 (September 4): 670–76.

Dibba, Bakary, Ann Prentice, Ann Laskey, Dot Stirling, and Tim Cole. 1999. "An Investigation of Ethnic Differences in Bone Mineral, Hip Axis Length, Calcium Metabolism and Bone Turnover Between West African and Caucasian Adults Living in the United Kingdom." *Annals of Human Biology* 26(3):229–42.

Ehrenberg, Margaret. 1989. *Women in Prehistory.* London: British Museum Press.

Ellison, Peter T. 1996. "Developmental Influences on Adult Ovarian Hormonal Function." *American Journal of Human Biology* 8(6):725–34.

Farmer, Mary E., Lon R. White, Jacob A. Brody, and Kent R. Bailey. 1984. "Race and Sex Differences in Hip Fracture Incidence." *American Journal of Public Health* 74(12): 1374–80.

Fausto-Sterling, Anne. 1992. *Myths of Gender: Biological Theories About Women and Men.* 2d ed. New York: Basic Books.

———. 2004. "Refashioning Race: DNA and the Politics of Health Care." *Differences: A Journal of Feminist Cultural Studies.* In Press.

———. In preparation. "The Bare Bones of Sex: Part II—Race."

Friedlander, Anne L., Harry K. Genant, Steven Sadowsky, Nancy Byl, and Claus C. Gluer. 1995. "A Two-Year Program of Aerobics and Weight Training Enhances Bone Mineral Density of Young Women." *Journal of Bone and Mineral Research* 10(4):574–85.

Frost, Harold M. 1992. "The Role of Changes in Mechanical Usage Set Points in the Pathogenesis of Osteoporosis." *Journal of Bone and Mineral Research* 7(3):253–61.

Fugh-Berman, Adriane, C. K. Pearson, Amy Allina, Jane Zones, Nancy Worcester, and Marianne Whatley. 2002. "Manufacturing Need, Manufacturing 'Knowledge.'" *Network News* (May/June):1, 4.

Fugh-Berman, Adriane, C. K. Pearson, Amy Allina, Jane Zones, Nancy Worcester, Mariamne Whatley, Charlea Massion, and Ellen Michaud. 2002. "Hormone Therapy and Osteoporosis: To Prevent Fractures and Falls, There Are Better Options Than Hormones." *Network News* (July/August): 4–5.

Fujita, Y., K. Katsumata, A. Unno, T. Tawa, and A. Tokita. 1999. "Factors Affecting Peak Bone Density in Japanese Women." *Calcified Tissue International* 64(2):107–11.

Gasperino, James. 1995. "Androgenic Regulation of Bone Mass in Women." *Clinical Orthopaedics and Related Research* 311:278–86.

Gatens, Moira. 1996. *Imaginary Bodies: Ethics, Power, and Corporeality.* London: Routledge.

Gero, Joan M., and Margaret W. Conkey, eds. 1991. *Engendering Archeology: Women in Prehistory.* Oxford: Blackwell.

Gilsanz, Vicente, David L. Skaggs, Arzu Kovanlikaya, James Sayre, M. Luiza Loro, Francine Kaufman, and Stanley G. Korenman. 1998. "Differential Effect of Race on the Axial and Appendicular Skeletons of Children." *Journal of Clinical Endocrinology and Metabolism* 83(5):1420–27.

Glock, Martha, Kathleen A. Shanahan, Joan A. McGowan, and compilers, eds. 2000. "Osteoporosis [Bibliography Online]: 2,449 Citations from January 1995 Through December 1999." Available online at http://www.nlm.nih.gov/pubs/cbm/osteoporosis.html. Last accessed May 5, 2004.

Goodman, Alan H. 1997. "Bred in the Bone?" *Sciences* 37(2):20–25.

Gottlieb, Gilbert. 1997. *Synthesizing Nature-Nurture: Prenatal Roots of Instinctive Behavior.* Mahwah, N.J.: Erlbaum.

Gottlieb, Gilbert, Richard E. Whalen, and Robert Lickliter. 1998. "The Significance of Biology for Human Development: A Developmental Psychobiological Systems View." In *Handbook of Child Psychology,* ed. Richard M. Lerner, 233–73. New York: Wiley.

Grosz, Elizabeth. 1994. *Volatile Bodies: Toward a Corporeal Feminism.* Bloomington: Indiana University Press.

Haapasalo, Heidi, Harri Sievanen, Pekka Kannus, Ari Heinonen, Pekka Oja, and Ilkka Vuori. 1996. "Dimensions and Estimated Mechanical Characteristics of the Humerus After Long-Term Tennis Loading." *Journal of Bone and Mineral Research* 11(6):864–72.

Harada, Shun-ichi, and Gideon A. Rodan. 2003. "Control of Osteoblast Function and Regulation of Bone Mass." *Nature* 423 (May 15):349–55.

Heaney, Robert P. 2000. "Calcium, Dairy Products, and Osteoporosis." *Journal of the American College of Nutrition* 19(2):S83–S99.

Hebb, D. O. 1949. *The Organization of Behavior: A Neuropsychological Theory.* New York: Wiley.

Hertzman, Clyde. 1999. "The Biological Embedding of Early Experience and Its Effects on Health in Adulthood." *Annals of the New York Academy of Science* 896:85–95.

Hu, J. F., X. H. Zhao, J. S. Chen, J. Fitzpatrick, B. Parpia, and T. C. Campbell. 1994. "Bone Density and Lifestyle Characteristics in Premenopausal and Postmenopausal Chinese Women." *Osteoporosis International* 4:288–97.

Hubbard, Ruth. 1990. *The Politics of Women's Biology.* New York: Routledge.

Jones, Henry H., James D. Priest, Wilson C. Hayes, Carol Chin Tichenor, and Donald A. Nagel. 1977. "Humeral Hypertrophy in Response to Exercise." *Journal of Bone and Joint Surgery* 59-A(2):204–8.

Kauffman, Stuart. 1993. *The Origins of Order: Self-Organization and Selection in Evolution.* New York: Oxford University Press.

Keane, Helen, and Marsha Rosengarten. 2002. "On the Biology of Sexed Subjects." *Australian Feminist Studies* 17(39):261–79.

Kellie, Shirley E., and Jacob A. Brody. 1990. "Sex-Specific and Race-Specific Hip Fracture Rates." *American Journal of Public Health* 80(3):326–28.

Kelso, J. A. Scott. 1995. *Dynamic Patterns: The Self-Organization of Brain and Behavior.* Cambridge, Mass.: MIT Press.

Kirby, Vicki. 1997. *Telling Flesh: The Substance of the Corporeal.* New York: Routledge.

Klinge, Ineke. 1998. "Gender and Bones: The Production of Osteoporosis, 1941–1996." Ph.D. dissertation, University of Utrecht.

Krieger, Nancy. 2001. "Theories for Social Epidemiology in the Twenty-First Century: An Ecosocial Perspective." *International Journal of Epidemiology* 30(4): 668–77.

Krieger, Nancy, and Sally Zierler. 1995. "Accounting for Health of Women." *Current Issues in Public Health* 1:251–56.

Kuh, Diana, and Yoav Ben-Shlomo, eds. 1997. *A Life Course Approach to Chronic Disease Epidemiology.* Oxford: Oxford University Press.

Kuh, Diana, and Rebecca Hardy, eds. 2002. *A Life Course Approach to Women's Health.* Oxford: Oxford University Press.

Lamont, Douglas, Louise Parker, Martin White, Nigel Unwin, Stuart M. A. Bennett, Melanie Cohen, David Richardson, Heather O. Dickinson, K. G. M. M. Alberti, and Alan W. Kraft. 2000. "Risk of Cardiovascular Disease Measured by Carotid Intima-Media Thickness at Age 49–51: A Lifecourse Study." *British Medical Journal* 320 (January 29): 273–78.

Larsen, Clark Spencer. 1998. "Gender, Health, and Activity in Foragers and Farmers in the American Southeast: Implications for Social Organization in the Georgia Bight." In *Sex and Gender in Paleopathological Perspective,* ed. Anne L. Grauer and Patricia Stuart-Macadam, 165–87. Cambridge: Cambridge University Press.

Lips, Paul. 1997. "Epidemiology and Predictors of Fractures Associated with Osteoporosis." *American Journal of Medicine* 103(2A): S3–S11.

Lock, Margaret. 1998. "Anomalous Ageing: Managing the Postmenopausal Body." *Body and Society* 4(1):35–61.

Malina, Robert M., Kathryn H. Brown, and Antonio N. Zavaleta. 1987. "Relative Lower Extremity Length in Mexican American and in American Black and White Youth." *American Journal of Physical Anthropology* 72:89–94.

Marshall, Deborah, Olof Johnell, and Hans Wedel. 1996. "Meta-Analysis of How Well Measures of Bone Mineral Density Predict Occurrence of Osteoporotic Fractures." *British Medical Journal* 312(7041):1254–59.

Mckay, H. A., M. A. Petit, K. M. Khan, and R. W. Schutz. 2000. "Lifestyle Determinants of Bone Mineral: A Comparison Between Prepubertal Asian- and Caucasian-Canadian Boys and Girls." *Calcified Tissue International* 66(5): 320–24.

Melton, L. Joseph, III. 1988. "Epidemiology of Fractures." In *Osteoporosis: Etiology, Diagnosis, and Management,* ed.

B. Lawrence Riggs and L. Joseph Melton, III, 133–54. New York: Raven.

Melton, L. Joseph, III, Elizabeth J. Atkinson, Michael K. O'Connor, W. Michael O'Fallon, and B. Lawrence Riggs. 1998. "Bone Density and Fracture Risk in Men." *Journal of Bone and Mineral Research* 13(12): 1915–23.

Meredith, Howard V. 1978. "Secular Change in Sitting Height and Lower Limb Height of Children, Youths, and Young Adults of Afro-Black, European, and Japanese Ancestry." *Growth* 42(1):37–41.

Merleau-Ponty, Maurice. 1962. *Phenomenology of Perception.* Trans. Colin Smith. New York: Humanities Press.

Messier, Stephen P., Todd D. Royer, Timothy E. Craven, Mary L. O'Toole, Robert Burns, and Walter H. Ettinger. 2000. "Long-Term Exercise and Its Effects on Balance in Older, Osteoarthritic Adults: Results from Fitness, Arthritis, and Seniors Trial (Fast)." *Journal of the American Geriatrics Society* 48(2):131–38.

Meunier, Pierre J. 1988. "Assessment of Bone Turnover by Histormorphometry." In *Osteoporosis: Etiology, Diagnosis, and Management,* ed. B. Lawrence Riggs and L. Joseph Melton III, 317–32. New York: Raven.

Moggs, Jonathan G., Damian G. Deavall, and George Orphanides. 2003. "Sex Steroids, Angels, and Osteoporosis." *BioEssays* 25(3):195–99.

Molleson, Theya. 1994. "The Eloquent Bones of Abu Hureyra." *Scientific American* 2:70–75.

Morel, J., B. Combe, J. Fracisco, and J. Bernard. 2001. "Bone Mineral Density of 704 Amateur Sportsmen Involved in Different Physical Activities." *Osteoporosis International* 12(2):152–57.

Mosekilde, Lis. 2000. "Age-Related Changes in Bone Mass, Structure, and Strength—Effects of Loading." *Zeitschrift für Rheumatologie* 59 (Supplement 1): I/1–I/9.

Muñoz, M. T., and J. Argente. 2002. "Anorexia Nervosa in Female Adolescents: Endocrine and Bone Mineral Density Disturbances." *European Journal of Endocrinology* 147(3):275–86.

Nelson, Heidi D., Mark Helfand, Steven H. Woolf, and Janet D. Allan. 2002. "Screening for Postmenopausal Osteoporosis: A Review of the Evidence for the U.S. Preventive Services Task Force." *Annals of Internal Medicine* 137(6):529–41.

NIH Consensus Statement Online. 2000. 17(1):1–36.

Nordstrom, P., K. Thorsen, E. Bergstrom, and R. Lorentzon. 1996. "High Bone Mass and Altered Relationship Between Bone Mass, Muscle Strength, and Body Constitution in Adolescent Boys on a High Level of Physical Activity." *Bone* 19(2):189–95.

Nordstrom, P., G. Nordstrom, and R. Lorentzon. 1997. "Correlation of Bone Density to Strength and Physical Activity in Young Men with a Low or Moderate Level of Physical Activity." *Calcified Tissue International* 60(4):332–37.

Oyama, Susan. 2000a. *Evolution's Eye: A System's View of the Biology-Culture Divide.* Durham, N.C.: Duke University Press.

———. 2000b. *The Ontogeny of Information: Developmental Systems and Evolution.* Durham, N.C.: Duke University Press.

Pavalko, Fred M., Suzanne M. Norvell, David B. Burr, Charles H. Turner, Randall L. Duncan, and Joseph P. Bidwell. 2003. "A Model for Mechanotransduction in Bone Cells: The Load-Bearing Mechanosomes." *Journal of Cellular Biochemistry* 88(1):104–12.

Peacock, Munro, Charles H. Turner, Michael J. Econs, and Tatiana Foroud. 2002. "Genetics of Osteoporosis." *Endocrine Reviews* 23(3):303–26.

Pead, Matthew J., Timothy M. Skerry, and Lance E. Lanyon. 1988. "Direct Transformation from Quiesence to Bone Formation in the Adult Periosteum Following a Single Brief Period of Bone Loading." *Journal of Bone and Mineral Research* 3(6):647–56.

Perry, Ivan J. 1997. "Fetal Growth and Development: The Role of Nutrition and Other Factors." In Kuh and Ben-Schlomo 1997, 145–68.

Petersen, Alan. 1998. "Sexing the Body: Representations of Sex Differences in *Gray's Anatomy,* 1858 to the Present." *Body and Society* 4(1):1–15.

Pettersson, U., H. Alfredson, P. Nordstrom, K. Henriksson-Larsen, and R. Lorentzon. 2000. "Bone Mass in Female Cross-Country Skiers: Relationship Between Muscle Strength and Different BMD Sites." *Calcified Tissue International* 67(3):199-206.

Rizzoli, R., and J.-P. Bonjour. 1999. "Determinants of Peak Bone Mass and Mechanisms of Bone Loss." *Osteoporosis International* 9 (Supplement 2): S17–S23.

Robinson, T. L., C. Snow-Harter, D. R. Taaffe, D. Gillis, J. Shaw, and R. Marcus. 1995. "Gymnasts Exhibits Higher Bone Mass Than Runners Despite Similar Prevalence of Amenorrhea and Oligomenorrhea." *Journal of Bone and Mineral Research* 10(1):26–35.

Rubin, Gayle. 1975. "The Traffic in Women: Notes on the 'Political Economy' of Sex." In *Toward an Anthropology of Women,* ed. Rayna R. Reiter, 157–210. New York: Monthly Review Press.

Russett, Cynthia Eagle. 1989. *Sexual Science: The Victorian Construction of Womanhood.* Cambridge, Mass.: Harvard University Press.

Sali, Andrej, Robert Glaeser, Thomas Earnest, and Wolfgang Baumeister. 2003. "From Words to Literature in Structural Proteins." *Nature* 422(6928):216–55.

Schacter, Beth. 2001. "About the Society for Women's Health Research." Proceedings from the Second Annual Conference on Sex and Gene Expression, March 8–11, Winston-Salem, North Carolina.

Schlichting, Carl D., and Massimo Pigliucci. 1998. *Phenotypic Evolution: A Reaction Norm Perspective.* Sunderland, Mass.: Sinauer Associates.

Schriempf, Alexa. 2001. "(Re)fusing the Amputated Body: An Interactionist Bridge for Feminism and Disability." *Hypatia* 16(4): 53–79.

Seeman, E. 1997. "Perspective: From: Density to Structure: Growing Up and Growing Old on the Surfaces of Bone." *Journal of Bone and Mineral Research* 12(4):509–21.

———. 1998. "Editorial: Growth in Bone Mass and Size—Are Racial and Gender Differences in Bone Mineral Density More Apparent Than Real?" *Journal of Clinical Endocrinology and Metabolism* 83(5): 1414–19.

———. 1999. "The Structural Basis of Bone Fragility in Men." *Bone* 25 (1):143–47.

Siebers, Tobin. 2001. "Disability in Theory: From Social Constructionism to the New Realism of the Body." *American Literary History* 13(4): 737–54.

Siris, Ethel S., Paul D Miller, Elizabeth Barrett-Connor, Kenneth G. Faulkner, Lois E. Wehren, Thomas A. Abbott, Marc L. Berger, Arthur C. Santora, and Louis M. Sherwood. 2001. "Identification and Fracture Outcomes of Undiagnosed Low Bone Mineral Density in Postmenopausal Women: Results from the National Osteoporosis Risk Assessment." *Journal of the American Medical Association* 286(22):2815–22.

Skerry, Tim. 2000. "Biomechanical Influences on Skeletal Growth and Development." In *Development, Growth, and Evolution: Implications for the Study of the Hominid Skeleton,* ed. Paul O' Higgins and Martin J. Cohn, 29–39. London: Academic Press.

Skerry, Tim, and Lance E. Lanyon. 1995. "Interruption of Disuse by Short Duration Walking Exercise Does Not Prevent Bone Loss in the Sheep Calcaneus." *Bone* 16(2): 269–74.

Smith, Linda B., and Esther Thelen, eds. 1993. *A Dynamic Systems Approach to Development: Applications.* Cambridge, Mass.: MIT Press.

Snow-Harter, Christine, Mary L. Bouxsein, Barbara Lewis, Dennis Carter, and Robert Marcus. 1992. "Effects of Resistance and Endurance Exercise on Bone Mineral Status of Young Women: A Randomized Exercise Intervention Trial." *Journal of Bone and Mineral Research* 7(7):761–69.

Soderman, K., E. Bergstrom, R. Lorentzon, and H. Alfredson,: 2000. "Bone Mass and Muscle Strength in Young Female Soccer Players." *Calcified Tissue International* 67(4):297–303.

Sowers, Maryfran. 1996. "Pregnancy and Lactation as Risk Factors for Subsequent Bone Loss and Osteoporosis." *Journal of Bone and Mineral Research* 11(8):1052–60.

Stepan, Nancy. 1982. *The Idea of Race in Science: Great Britain, 1800–1960.* London: Macmillan.

Taha, Wael, Daisy Chin, Arnold Silverberg, Larisa Lashiker, Naila Khateeb, and Henry Anhalt. 2001. "Reduced Spinal Bone Mineral Density in Adolescents of an Ultra-Orthodox. Jewish Community in Brooklyn." *Pediatrics* 107 (5): e79–e85.

Tanner, J. M., T. Hayashi, M. A. Preece, and N. Cameron. 1982. "Increase in Length of Leg Relative to Trunk in Japanese Children and Adults from 1957 to 1977: Comparison with British and Japanese Children." *Annals of Human Biology* 9(5): 411–23.

Tanouye, Elyse. 1995. "Merck's Osteoporosis Warnings Pave the Way for Its New Drug." *Wall Street Journal,* June 28, B1, B4.

Thelen, Esther. 1995. "Motor Development: A New Synthesis." *American Psychologist* 50(2): 79–95.

Thelen, Esther, Gregor Schoner, Christian Scheier, and Linda B. Smith. 2001. "The Dynamics of Embodiment: A Field Theory of Infant Perseverative Reachring" *Behavioral and Brain Sciences* 24(1): 1–86.

Thelen, Esther, and Linda B. Smith. 1994. *A Dynamic Systems Approach to the Development of Cognition and Action.* Cambridge, Mass: MIT Press.

———. 1998. "Dynamic Systems Theories," In *Handbook of Child Psychology: Theoretical Models of Human Development,* ed. Richard M. Lerner, 563–634. New York: Wiley.

Thornhill, Randy, and Craig T. Palmer. 2001. *A Natural History of Rape.* Cambridge, Mass.: MIT Press.

Travis, Cheryl Brown, ed. 2003. *Evolution, Gender, and Rape.* Cambridge, Mass.: MIT Press.

Tyson, John J., Attila Csikasz-Nagy, and Bela Novak. 2002. "The Dynamics of Cell Cycle Regulation." *BioEssays:* 24(12):1095–1109.

Van der Weele, Cor. 1999. *Images of Development: Environmental Causes of Ontogeny.* Albany: State University of New York Press.

Verbrugge, Marth H. 1997. "Recreating the Body. Women's Physical Education and the Science of Sex Differences in America, 1900–1940." *Bulletin of the History of Medicine* 71(2):273–304.

Vukmirovic, Ognenka Gog, and Shirley M. Tilghmann. 2000. "Exploring Genome Space." *Nature* 405(6793): 820–22.

Waddington, C. H. 1957. *The Strategy of the Genes: A Discussion of Some Aspects of Theoretical Biology.* London: Allen & Unwin.

Walsh, Timothy B., and Michael J. Devlin. 1998. "Eating Disorders: Progress and Problems." *Science* 280(5638):1387–90.

Wang, May-Choo, Patricia B. Crawford, Mark Hudes, Marta Van Loan, Kirstin Siemering, and Laura K. Bachrach. 2003. "Diet in Midpuberty and Sedentary Activity in Prepuberty Predict Peak Bone Mass." *American Journal of Clinical Nutrition* 77(2):495–503.

Webster, Gerry, and Brian Goodwin. 1996. *Form and Transformation: Generative and Relational Principles in Biology.* Cambridge: Cambridge University Press.

Weiss, Gail. 1999. *Body Images: Embodiments as Intercorporeality.* New York: Routledge.

Welton, D. C., H. C. G. Kemper, G. B. Post, W. Van Mechelen, J. Twisk, P. Lips, and G. J. Teule. 1994. "Weight-Bearing Activity During Youth Is a More Important Factor for Peak Bone Mass Than Calcium Intake." *Journal of Bone and Mineral Research* 9(7):1089–96.

Whitehead, Alfred North. (1929) 1978. *Process and Reality: An Essay in Cosmology.* New York: Macmillan.

Williams, Gareth, and Helen Busby. 2000. "The Politics of 'Disabled' Bodies." In *Health, Medicine and Society: Key Theories, Future Agendas,* ed. Simon J. Williams, Jonathan Gabe, and Michael Calnan, 169–85. London: Routledge.

Wizemann, Theresa M., and Mary-Lou Pardue, eds. 2001. *Exploring the Biological Contributions to Human Health: Does Sex Matter?* Washington, D.C.: National Academy Press.

Worthman, Carol M. 2002. "Endocrine Pathways in Differential Well-Being Across the Life Course." In Kuh and Hardy 2002, 197–216.

Wright, Rita P., ed. 1996. *Gender and Archeology.* Philadelphia: University of Pennsylvania Press.

Zanchetta, J. R., H. Plotkin, and M. L. Alvarez Filgueira. 1995. "Bone Mass in Children: Normative Values for the 2–20-Year-Old Population." *Bone* 16 (Supplement 4): S393–S399.

Zelzer, Elazar, and Bjorn R. Olsen. 2003. "The Genetic Basis for Skeletal Diseases." *Nature* 423(6937):343–48.

Zuk, Marlene. 2002. *Sexual Selections: What We Can and Can't Learn About Sex from Animals.* Berkeley: University of California Press.

R E A D I N G *38*   **Becky Wangsgaard Thompson**

"A Way Outa No Way": Eating Problems Among African-American, Latina, and White Women

Bulimia, anorexia, binging, and extensive dieting are among the many health issues women have been confronting in the last twenty years. Until recently, however, there has been almost no research about eating problems among African-American, Latina, Asian-American, or Native American women, working-class women, or lesbians.[1] In fact, according to the normative epidemiological portrait, eating problems are largely a white, middle-, and upper-class heterosexual phenomenon. Further, while feminist research has documented how eating problems are fueled by sexism, there has been almost no attention to how other systems of oppression may also be implicated in the development of eating problems.

In this article, I reevaluate the portrayal of eating problems as issues of appearance based in the "culture of thinness." I propose that eating problems begin as ways women cope with various traumas, including sexual abuse, racism, classism, sexism, heterosexism, and poverty. Showing the interface between these traumas and the onset of eating problems explains why women may use eating to numb pain and cope with violations to their bodies. This theoretical shift also permits an understanding of the economic, political, social, educational, and cultural resources that women need to change in correcting their relationship to food and their bodies.

EXISTING RESEARCH ON EATING PROBLEMS

There are three theoretical models used to explain the epidemiology, etiology, and treatment of eating problems. The biomedical model offers important scientific research about possible physiological causes of eating problems and the physiological dangers of purging and starvation (Copeland 1985; Spack 1985). However, this model adopts medical treatment strategies that may disempower and traumatize women (Garner 1985; Orbach 1985). In addition, this model ignores many social, historical, and cultural factors that influence women's eating patterns. The psychological model identifies eating problems as "multidimensional disorders" that are influenced by biological, psychological, and cultural factors (Garfinkel and Garner 1982). While useful in its exploration of effective therapeutic treatments, this model, like the biomedical one, tends to neglect women of color, lesbians, and working-class women.

The third model, offered by feminists, asserts that eating problems are gendered. This model explains why the vast majority of people with eating problems are women, how gender socialization and sexism may relate to eating problems, and how masculine models of psychological development have shaped theoretical interpretations. Feminists offer the culture-of-thinness model as a key reason why eating problems predominate among women. According to this model, thinness is a culturally, socially, and economically enforced requirement for female beauty. This imperative makes women vulnerable to cycles of dieting, weight loss, and subsequent weight gain, which may lead to anorexia and bulimia (Chernin 1981; Orbach 1978, 1985; Smead 1984).

Feminists have rescued eating problems from the realm of individual psychopathology by showing how the difficulties are rooted in systematic and pervasive attempts to control women's body sizes and appetites. However, researchers have yet to give significant attention to how race, class, and sexuality influence women's understanding of their bodies and appetites. The handful of epidemiological studies that include African-American women and Latinas casts doubt on the accuracy of the normative epidemiological portrait. The studies suggest that this portrait reflects which particular populations of women have been studied rather than actual prevalence (Andersen and Hay 1985; Gray, Ford, and Kelly 1987; Hsu 1987; Nevo 1985; Silber 1986).

More important, this research shows that bias in research has consequences for women of color. Tomas Silber (1986) asserts that many well-trained professionals have either misdiagnosed or delayed their diagnoses of eating problems among African-American and Latina women due to stereotypical thinking that these problems are restricted to white women. As a consequence, when African-American women or Latinas are diagnosed, their eating problems tend to be more severe due to extended processes of starvation prior to intervention. In her autobiographical account of her eating problems, Retha Powers (1989), an African-American woman, describes being told not to worry about her eating problems since "fat is more acceptable in the Black community" (p. 78). Stereotypical perceptions held by her peers and teachers of the "maternal Black woman" and the "persistent mammy-brickhouse Black woman image" (p. 134) made it difficult for Powers to find people who took her problems with food seriously.

Recent work by African-American women reveals that eating problems often relate to women's struggles against a "simultaneity of oppression" (Clarke 1982; Naylor 1985; White 1991). Byllye Avery (1990), the founder of the National Black Women's Health Project, links the origins of eating problems among African-American women to the daily stress of being undervalued and overburdened at home and at work. In Evelyn C. White's (1990) anthology, *The Black Woman's Health Book: Speaking for Ourselves*, Georgiana Arnold (1990) links her eating problems partly to racism and racial isolation during childhood.

Recent feminist research also identifies factors that are related to eating problems among lesbians (Brown 1987; Dworkin 1989; Iazzetto 1989; Schoenfielder and Wieser 1983). In her clinical work, Brown (1987) found that lesbians who have internalized a high degree of homophobia are more likely to accept negative attitudes about fat than are lesbians who have examined their internalized homophobia. Autobiographical accounts by lesbians have also indicated that secrecy about eating problems among lesbians partly reflects their fear of being associated with a stigmatized illness ("What's Important" 1988).

Attention to African-American women, Latinas, and lesbians paves the way for further research that explores the possible interface between facing multiple oppressions and the development of eating problems. In this way, this study is part of a larger feminist and sociological research agenda that seeks to understand how race, class, gender, nationality, and sexuality inform women's experiences and influence theory production.

METHODOLOGY

I conducted eighteen life history interviews and administered lengthy questionnaires to explore eating problems among African-American, Latina, and white women. I employed a snowball sample, a method in which potential respondents often first learn about the study from people who have already participated. This method was well suited for the study since it enabled women to get information about me and the interview process from people they already knew. Typically, I had much contact with the respondents prior to the interview. This was particularly important given the secrecy associated with this topic (Russell 1986; Silberstein, Striegel-Moore, and Rodin 1987), the necessity of women of color and lesbians to be discriminating about how their lives are studied, and the fact that I was conducting across-race research.

To create analytical notes and conceptual categories from the data, I adopted Glaser and Strauss's (1967) technique of theoretical sampling, which directs the researcher to collect, analyze, and test hypotheses during the sampling process (rather than imposing theoretical categories onto the data). After completing each interview transcription, I gave a copy to each woman who wanted one. After reading their interviews, some of the women clarified or made additions to the interview text.

Demographics of the Women in the Study

The eighteen women I interviewed included five African-American women, five Latinas, and eight white women. Of these women, twelve are lesbian and six are heterosexual. Five women are Jewish, eight are Catholic, and five are Protestant. Three women grew up outside of the United States. The women represented a range of class backgrounds (both in terms of origin and current class status) and ranged in age from nineteen to forty-six years old (with a median age of 33.5 years).

The majority of the women reported having had a combination of eating problems (at least two of the following: bulimia, compulsive eating, anorexia, and/or extensive dieting). In addition, the particular types of eating problems often changed during a woman's life span. (For example, a woman might have been bulimic during adolescence and anorexic as an adult.) Among the women, 28 percent had been bulimic, 17 percent had been bulimic and anorexic, and 5 percent had been anorexic. All of the women who had been anorexic or bulimic also had a history of compulsive eating and extensive dieting. Of the women, 50 percent were compulsive eaters and dieters (39 percent) or compulsive eaters (11 percent) but had not been bulimic or anorexic.

Two-thirds of the women have had eating problems for more than half of their lives, a finding that contradicts the stereotype of eating problems as transitory. The weight fluctuation among the women varied from 16 to 160 pounds, with an average fluctuation of 74 pounds. This drastic weight change illustrates the degree to which the women adjusted to major changes in body size at least once during their lives as they lost, gained, and lost weight again. The average age of onset was eleven years old, meaning that most of the women developed eating problems prior to puberty. Almost all

of the women (88 percent) consider themselves as still having a problem with eating, although the majority believe they are well on the way to recovery.

THE INTERFACE OF TRAUMA AND EATING PROBLEMS

One of the most striking findings in this study was the range of traumas the women associated with the origins of their eating problems, including racism, sexual abuse, poverty, sexism, emotional or physical abuse, heterosexism, class injuries, and acculturation.[2] The particular constellation of eating problems among the women did not vary with race, class, sexuality, or nationality. Women from various race and class backgrounds attributed the origins of their eating problems to sexual abuse, sexism, and emotional and/or physical abuse. Among some of the African-American and Latina women, eating problems were also associated with poverty, racism, and class injuries. Heterosexism was a key factor in the onset of bulimia, compulsive eating, and extensive dieting among some of the lesbians. These oppressions are not the same nor are the injuries caused by them. And certainly, there are a variety of potentially harmful ways that women respond to oppression (such as using drugs, becoming a workaholic, or committing suicide). However, for all these women, eating was a way of coping with trauma.

Sexual Abuse

Sexual abuse was the most common trauma that the women related to the origins of their eating problems. Until recently, there has been virtually no research exploring the possible relationship between these two phenomena. Since the mid-1980s, however, researchers have begun identifying connections between the two, a task that is part of a larger feminist critique of traditional psychoanalytic symptomatology (DeSalvo 1989; Herman 1981; Masson 1984). Results of a number of incidence studies indicate that between one-third and two-thirds of women who have eating problems have been abused (Oppenheimer et al. 1985; Root and Fallon 1988). In addition, a growing number of therapists and researchers have offered interpretations of the meaning and impact of eating problems for survivors of sexual abuse (Bass and Davis 1988; Goldfarb 1987; Iazzetto 1989; Swink and Leveille 1986).

Kearney-Cooke (1988) identifies dieting and binging as common ways in which women cope with frequent psychological consequences of sexual abuse (such as body image disturbances, distrust of people and one's own experiences, and confusion about one's feelings). Root and Fallon (1989) specify ways that victimized women cope with assaults by binging and purging: bulimia serves many functions, including anesthetizing the negative feelings associated with victimization. Iazzetto's innovative study (1989), based on in-depth interviews and art therapy sessions, examines how a woman's relationship to her body changes as a consequence of sexual abuse. Iazzetto discovered that the process of leaving the body (through progressive phases of numbing, dissociating, and denying) that often occurs during sexual abuse parallels the process of leaving the body made possible through binging.

Among the women I interviewed, 61 percent were survivors of sexual abuse (eleven of the eighteen women), most of whom made connections between sexual abuse and the beginning of their eating problems. Binging was the most common method of coping identified by the survivors. Binging helped women "numb out" or anesthetize their feelings. Eating sedated, alleviated anxiety, and combated loneliness. Food was something that they could trust and was accessible whenever they needed it. Antonia (a pseudonym) is an Italian-American woman who was first sexually abused by a male relative when she was four years old. Retrospectively, she knows that binging was a way she coped with the abuse. When the abuse began, and for many years subsequently, Antonia often woke up during the middle of the night with anxiety attacks or nightmares and would go straight to the kitchen cupboards to get food. Binging helped her block painful feelings because it put her back to sleep.

Like other women in the study who began binging when they were very young, Antonia was not always fully conscious as she binged. She described eating during the night as "sleep walking. It was mostly desperate—like I had to have it." Describing why she ate after waking up with nightmares, Antonia said, "What else do you do? If you don't have any coping mechanisms, you eat." She said that binging made her "disappear," which made her feel protected. Like Antonia, most of the women were sexually abused before puberty; four of them before they were five years old. Given their youth, food was the most accessible and socially acceptable drug available to them. Because all

of the women endured the psychological consequences alone, it is logical that they coped with tactics they could do alone as well.

One reason Antonia binged (rather than dieted) to cope with sexual abuse is that she saw little reason to try to be the small size girls were supposed to be. Growing up as one of the Italian Americans in what she described as a "very WASP town," Antonia felt that everything from her weight and size to having dark hair on her upper lip were physical characteristics she was supposed to hide. From a young age she knew she "never embodied the essence of the good girl. I don't like her. I have never acted like her. I can't be her. I sort of gave up." For Antonia, her body was the physical entity that signified her outsider status. When the sexual abuse occurred, Antonia felt she had lost her body. In her mind, the body she lived in after the abuse was not really hers. By the time Antonia was eleven, her mother put her on diet pills. Antonia began to eat behind closed doors as she continued to cope with the psychological consequences of sexual abuse and feeling like a cultural outsider.

Extensive dieting and bulimia were also ways in which women responded to sexual abuse. Some women thought that the men had abused them because of their weight. They believed that if they were smaller, they might not have been abused. For example when Elsa, an Argentine woman, was sexually abused at the age of eleven, she thought her chubby size was the reason the man was abusing her. Elsa said, "I had this notion that these old perverts liked these plump girls. You heard adults say this too. Sex and flesh being associated." Looking back on her childhood, Elsa believes she made fat the enemy partly due to the shame and guilt she felt about the incest. Her belief that fat was the source of her problems was also supported by her socialization. Raised by strict German governesses in an upper-class family, Elsa was taught that a woman's weight was a primary criterion for judging her worth. Her mother "was socially conscious of walking into places with a fat daughter and maybe people staring at her." Her father often referred to Elsa's body as "shot to hell." When asked to describe how she felt about her body when growing up, Elsa described being completely alienated from her body. She explained,

Remember in school when they talk about the difference between body and soul? I always felt like my soul was skinny. My soul was free. My soul sort of flew. I was tied down by this big bag of rocks that was my body. I had to drag it around. It did pretty much what it wanted and I had a lot of trouble controlling it. It kept me from doing all the things that I dreamed of.

As is true for many women who have been abused, the split that Elsa described between her body and soul was an attempt to protect herself from the pain she believed her body caused her. In her mind, her fat body was what had "bashed in her dreams." Dieting became her solution, but, as is true for many women in the study, this strategy soon led to cycles of binging and weight fluctuation.

Ruthie, a Puerto Rican woman who was sexually abused from twelve until sixteen years of age, described bulimia as a way she responded to sexual abuse. As a child, Ruthie liked her body. Like many Puerto Rican women of her mother's generation, Ruthie's mother did not want skinny children, interpreting that as a sign that they were sick or being fed improperly. Despite her mother's attempts to make her gain weight, Ruthie remained thin through puberty. When a male relative began sexually abusing her, Ruthie's sense of her body changed dramatically. Although she weighed only 100 pounds, she began to feel fat and thought her size was causing the abuse. She had seen a movie on television about Romans who made themselves throw up and so she began doing it, in hopes that she could look like the "little kid" she was before the abuse began. Her symbolic attempt to protect herself by purging stands in stark contrast to the psychoanalytic explanation of eating problems as an "abnormal" repudiation of sexuality. In fact, her actions and those of many other survivors indicate a girl's logical attempt to protect herself (including her sexuality) by being a size and shape that does not seem as vulnerable to sexual assault.

These women's experiences suggest many reasons why women develop eating problems as a consequence of sexual abuse. Most of the survivors "forgot" the sexual abuse after its onset and were unable to retrieve the abuse memories until many years later. With these gaps in memory, frequently they did not know why they felt ashamed, fearful, or depressed. When sexual abuse memories resurfaced in dreams, they often woke feeling upset but could not remember what they had dreamed. These free-floating, unexplained feelings left the women feeling out of control and confused. Binging or focusing on maintaining a new diet were ways women distracted or appeased themselves, in turn,

helping them regain a sense of control. As they grew older, they became more conscious of the consequences of these actions. Becoming angry at themselves for binging or promising themselves they would not purge again was a way to direct feelings of shame and self-hate that often accompanied the trauma.

Integral to this occurrence was a transference process in which the women displaced onto their bodies painful feelings and memories that actually derived from or were directed toward the persons who caused the abuse. Dieting became a method of trying to change the parts of their bodies they hated, a strategy that at least initially brought success as they lost weight. Purging was a way women tried to reject the body size they thought was responsible for the abuse. Throwing up in order to lose the weight they thought was making them vulnerable to the abuse was a way to try to find the body they had lost when the abuse began.

Poverty

Like sexual abuse, poverty is another injury that may make women vulnerable to eating problems. One woman I interviewed attributed her eating problems directly to the stress caused by poverty. Yolanda is a Black Cape Verdean mother who began eating compulsively when she was twenty-seven years old. After leaving an abusive husband in her early twenties, Yolanda was forced to go on welfare. As a single mother with small children and few financial resources, she tried to support herself and her children on $539 a month. Yolanda began binging in the evenings after putting her children to bed. Eating was something she could do alone. It would calm her, help her deal with loneliness, and make her feel safe. Food was an accessible commodity that was cheap. She ate three boxes of macaroni and cheese when nothing else was available. As a single mother with little money, Yolanda felt as if her body was the only thing she had left. As she described it,

> I am here, [in my body] 'cause there is no where else for me to go. Where am I going to go? This is all I got . . . that probably contributes to putting on so much weight cause staying in your body, in your home, in yourself, you don't go out. You aren't around other people. . . . You hide and as long as you hide you don't have to face . . . nobody can see you eat. You are safe.

When she was eating, Yolanda felt a momentary reprieve from her worries. Binging not only became a logical solution because it was cheap and easy but also because she had grown up amid positive messages about eating. In her family, eating was a celebrated and joyful act. However, in adulthood, eating became a double-edged sword. While comforting her, binging also led to weight gain. During the three years Yolanda was on welfare, she gained seventy pounds.

Yolanda's story captures how poverty can be a precipitating factor in eating problems and highlights the value of understanding how class inequalities may shape women's eating problems. As a single mother, her financial constraints mirrored those of most female heads of households. The dual hazards of a race- and sex-stratified labor market further limited her options (Higginbotham 1986). In an article about Black women's health, Byllye Avery (1990) quotes a Black woman's explanation about why she eats compulsively. The woman told Avery,

> I work for General Electric making batteries, and, I know it's killing me. My old man is an alcoholic. My kid's got babies. Things are not well with me. And one thing I know I can do when I come home is cook me a pot of food and sit down in front of the TV and eat it. And you can't take that away from me until you're ready to give me something in its place. (p. 7)

Like Yolanda, this woman identifies eating compulsively as a quick, accessible, and immediately satisfying way of coping with the daily stress caused by conditions she could not control. Connections between poverty and eating problems also show the limits of portraying eating problems as maladies of upper-class adolescent women.

The fact that many women use food to anesthetize themselves, rather than other drugs (even when they gained access to alcohol, marijuana, and other illegal drugs), is partly a function of gender socialization and the competing demands that women face. One of the physiological consequences of binge eating is a numbed state similar to that experienced by drinking. Troubles and tensions are covered over as a consequence of the body's defensive response to massive food intake. When food is eaten in that way, it effectively works like a drug with immediate and predictable effects. Yolanda said she binged late at night rather than getting drunk because she could still get up in the morning, get her children ready for school, and be clearheaded for the college classes she attended. By binging, she avoided the hangover or sickness that results from alcohol or illegal drugs.

In this way, food was her drug of choice since it was possible for her to eat while she continued to care for her children, drive, cook, and study. Binging is also less expensive than drinking, a factor that is especially significant for poor women. Another woman I interviewed said that when her compulsive eating was at its height, she ate breakfast after rising in the morning, stopped for a snack on her way to work, ate lunch at three different cafeterias, and snacked at her desk throughout the afternoon. Yet even when her eating had become constant, she was still able to remain employed. While her patterns of eating no doubt slowed her productivity, being drunk may have slowed her to a dead stop.

Heterosexism

The life history interviews also uncovered new connections between heterosexism and eating problems. One of the most important recent feminist contributions has been identifying compulsory heterosexuality as an institution which truncates opportunities for heterosexual and lesbian women (Rich 1986). All of the women interviewed for this study, both lesbian and heterosexual, were taught that heterosexuality was compulsory, although the versions of this enforcement were shaped by race and class. Expectations about heterosexuality were partly taught through messages that girls learned about eating and their bodies. In some homes, boys were given more food than girls, especially as teenagers, based on the rationale that girls need to be thin to attract boys. As the girls approached puberty, many were told to stop being athletic, begin wearing dresses, and watch their weight. For the women who weighed more than was considered acceptable, threats about their need to diet were laced with admonitions that being fat would ensure becoming an "old maid."

While compulsory heterosexuality influenced all of the women's emerging sense of their bodies and eating patterns, the women who linked heterosexism directly to the beginning of their eating problems were those who knew they were lesbians when very young and actively resisted heterosexual norms. One working-class Jewish woman, Martha, began compulsively eating when she was eleven years old, the same year she started getting clues of her lesbian identity. In junior high school, as many of her female peers began dating boys, Martha began fantasizing about girls, which made her feel utterly alone. Confused and ashamed about her fantasies, Martha came home every day from school and binged. Binging was a way she drugged herself so that being alone was tolerable. Describing binging, she said, "It was the only thing I knew. I was looking for a comfort." Like many women, Martha binged because it softened painful feelings. Binging sedated her, lessened her anxiety, and induced sleep.

Martha's story also reveals ways that trauma can influence women's experience of their bodies. Like many other women, Martha had no sense of herself as connected to her body. When I asked Martha whether she saw herself as fat when she was growing up she said, "I didn't see myself as fat. I didn't see myself. I wasn't there. I get so sad about that because I missed so much." In the literature on eating problems, *body image* is the term that is typically used to describe a woman's experience of her body. This term connotes the act of imagining one's physical appearance. Typically, women with eating problems are assumed to have difficulties with their body image. However, the term *body image* does not adequately capture the complexity and range of bodily responses to trauma experienced by the women. Exposure to trauma did much more than distort the women's visual image of themselves. These traumas often jeopardized their capacity to consider themselves as having bodies at all.

Given the limited connotations of the term *body image*, I use the term *body consciousness* as a more useful way to understand the range of bodily responses to trauma.[3] By body consciousness I mean the ability to reside comfortably in one's body (to see oneself as embodied) and to consider one's body as connected to oneself. The disruptions to their body consciousness that the women described included leaving their bodies, making a split between their body and mind, experiencing being "in" their bodies as painful, feeling unable to control what went in and out of their bodies, hiding in one part of their bodies, or simply not seeing themselves as having bodies. Binging, dieting, or purging were common ways women responded to disruptions to their body consciousness.

Racism and Class Injuries

For some of the Latinas and African-American women, racism coupled with the stress resulting from class mobility related to the onset of their eating problems. Joselyn, an African-American woman, remembered her white grandmother telling her she would never be as pretty as her cousins because they were lighter skinned. Her grandmother often humiliated Joselyn in front of others, as she made fun of Joselyn's body while she was naked and told her she was fat. As a young child, Joselyn began to think that although she could not change her skin color, she could at least try to be thin. When Joselyn was young, her grandmother was the only family member who objected to Joselyn's weight. However, her father also began encouraging his wife and daughter to be thin as the family's class standing began to change. When the family was working class, serving big meals, having chubby children, and keeping plenty of food in the house was a sign the family was doing well. But, as the family became mobile, Joselyn's father began insisting that Joselyn be thin. She remembered, "When my father's business began to bloom and my father was interacting more with white businessmen and seeing how they did business, suddenly thin became important. If you were a truly well-to-do family, then your family was slim and elegant."

As Joselyn's grandmother used Joselyn's body as territory for enforcing her own racism and prejudice about size, Joselyn's father used her body as the territory through which he channeled the demands he faced in the white-dominated business world. However, as Joselyn was pressured to diet, her father still served her large portions and bought treats for her and the neighborhood children. These contradictory messages made her feel confused about her body. As was true for many women in this study, Joselyn was told she was fat beginning when she was very young even though she was not overweight. And, like most of the women, Joselyn was put on diet pills and diets before even reaching puberty, beginning the cycles of dieting, compulsive eating, and bulimia.

The confusion about body size expectations that Joselyn associated with changes in class paralleled one Puerto Rican woman's association between her eating problems and the stress of assimilation as her family's class standing moved from poverty to working class. When Vera was very young, she was so thin that her mother took her to a doctor who prescribed appetite stimulants. However, by the time Vera was eight years old, her mother began trying to shame Vera into dieting. Looking back on it, Vera attributed her mother's change of heart to competition among extended family members that centered on "being white, being successful, being middle class, . . . and it was always, 'Ay Bendito. She is so fat. What happened?'"

The fact that some of the African-American and Latina women associated the ambivalent messages about food and eating to their family's class mobility and/or the demands of assimilation while none of the eight white women expressed this (including those whose class was stable and changing) suggests that the added dimension of racism was connected to the imperative to be thin. In fact, the class expectations that their parents experienced exacerbated standards about weight that they inflicted on their daughters.

EATING PROBLEMS AS SURVIVAL STRATEGIES

Feminist Theoretical Shifts

My research permits a reevaluation of many assumptions about eating problems. First, this work challenges the theoretical reliance on the culture-of-thinness model. Although all of the women I interviewed were manipulated and hurt by this imperative at some point in their lives, it is not the primary source of their problems. Even in the instances in which a culture of thinness was a precipitating factor in anorexia, bulimia, or binging, this influence occurred in concert with other oppressions.

Attributing the etiology of eating problems primarily to a woman's striving to attain a certain beauty ideal is also problematic because it labels a common way that women cope with pain as essentially appearance-based disorders. One blatant example of sexism is the notion that women's foremost worry is about their appearance. By focusing on the emphasis on slenderness, the eating-problems literature falls into the same trap of assuming that the problems reflect women's "obsession" with appearance. Some women were raised in families and communities in which thinness was not considered a criterion for beauty. Yet, they still developed eating problems. Other women were taught that women should be thin, but their eating problems were not primarily in reaction to this imperative. Their eating strategies began as logical solutions to problems rather than problems themselves as they tried to cope with a variety of traumas.

Establishing links between eating problems and a range of oppressions invites a rethinking of both the groups of women who have been excluded from research and those whose lives have been the basis of theory formation. The construction of bulimia and anorexia as appearance-based disorders is rooted in a notion of femininity in which white middle- and upper-class women are portrayed as frivolous, obsessed with their bodies, and overly accepting of narrow gender roles. This portrayal fuels women's tremendous shame and guilt about eating problems—as signs of self-centered vanity. This construction of white middle- and upper-class women is intimately linked to the portrayal of working-class white women and women of color as their opposite: as somehow exempt from accepting the dominant standards of beauty or as one step away from being hungry and therefore not susceptible to eating problems. Identifying that women may binge to cope with poverty contrasts the notion that eating problems are class bound. Attending to the intricacies of race, class, sexuality, and gender pushes us to rethink the demeaning construction of middle-class femininity and establishes bulimia and anorexia as serious responses to injustices.

Understanding the link between eating problems and trauma also suggests much about treatment and prevention. Ultimately, their prevention depends not simply on individual healing but also on changing the social conditions that underlie their etiology. As Bernice Johnson Reagon sings in Sweet Honey in the Rock's song "Oughta Be a Woman," "A way outa no way is too much to ask/too much of a task for any one woman" (Reagon 1980).[4] Making it possible for women to have healthy relationships with their bodies and eating is a comprehensive task. Beginning steps in this direction include insuring that (1) girls can grow up without being sexually abused, (2) parents have adequate resources to raise their children, (3) children of color grow up free of racism, and (4) young lesbians have the chance to see their reflection in their teachers and community leaders. Ultimately, the prevention of eating problems depends on women's access to economic, cultural, racial, political, social, and sexual justice.

NOTES

1. I use the term *eating problems* as an umbrella term for one or more of the following: anorexia, bulimia, extensive dieting, or binging. I avoid using the term *eating disorder* because it categorizes the problems as individual pathologies, which deflects attention away from the social inequalities underlying them (Brown 1985). However, by using the term *problem* I do not wish to imply blame. In fact, throughout, I argue that the eating strategies that women develop begin as logical solutions to problems, not problems themselves.

2. By trauma I mean a violating experience that has long-term emotional, physical, and/or spiritual consequences that may have immediate or delayed effects. One reason the term *trauma* is useful conceptually is its association

with the diagnostic label *post-traumatic stress disorder (PTSD)* (American Psychological Association 1987). PTSD is one of the few clinical diagnostic categories that recognize social problems (such as war or the Holocaust) as responsible for the symptoms identified (Trimble 1985). This concept adapts well to the feminist assertion that a woman's symptoms cannot be understood as solely individual, considered outside of her social context, or prevented without significant changes in social conditions.

3. One reason the term *consciousness* is applicable is its intellectual history as an entity that is shaped by social context and social structures (Delphy 1984; Marx 1964). This link aptly applies to how the women described their bodies because their perceptions of themselves as embodied (or not embodied) directly relate to their material conditions (living situations, financial resources, and access to social and political power).

4. Copyright © 1980. Used by permission of Songtalk Publishing.

REFERENCES

American Psychological Association. 1987. *Diagnostic and Statistical Manual of Mental Disorders.* 3rd ed. rev. Washington, DC: American Psychological Association.

Andersen, Arnold, and Andy Hay. 1985. Racial and socioeconomic influences in anorexia nervosa and bulimia. *International Journal of Eating Disorders* 4:479–87.

Arnold, Georgiana. 1990. Coming home: One Black woman's journey to health and fitness. In *The Black Women's Health Book: Speaking for Ourselves* , Evelyn C. White. Seattle, WA: Seal Press.

Avery, Byllye Y. 1990. Breathing life into ourselves: The evolution of the National Black Women's Health Project. In *The Black Women's Health Book: Speaking for Ourselves*, Evelyn C. White. Seattle, WA: Seal Press.

Bass, Ellen, and Laura Davis. 1988. *The Courage to Heal: A Guide for Women Survivors of Child Sexual Abuse.* New York: Harper & Row.

Brown, Laura S. 1985. Women, weight and power: Feminist theoretical and therapeutic issues. *Women and Therapy* 4:61–71.

———. 1987. Lesbians, weight and eating: New analyses and perspectives. In *Lesbian Psychologies*, the Boston Lesbian Psychologies Collective. Champaign: University of Illinois Press.

Chernin, Kim. 1981. *The Obsession: Reflections of the Tyranny of Slenderness.* New York: Harper & Row.

Clarke, Cheryl. 1982. *Narratives.* New Brunswick, NJ: Sister Books.

Copeland, Paul M. 1985. Neuroendocrine aspects of eating disorders. In *Theory and Treatment of Anorexia Nervosa and Bulimia: Biomedical, Sociocultural, and Psychological Perspectives*, Steven Wiley Emmett. New York: Brunner/Mazel.

Delphy, Christine. 1984. *Close to Home: A Materialist Analysis of Women's Oppression.* Amherst: University of Massachusetts Press.

DeSalvo, Louise. 1989. *Virginia Woolf: The Impact of Childhood Sexual Abuse on Her Life and Work.* Boston, MA: Beacon.

Dworkin, Sari H. 1989. Not in man's image: Lesbians and the cultural oppression of body image. In *Loving Boldly: Issues Facing Lesbians*, Ester D. Rothblum and Ellen Cole. New York: Harrington Park Press.

Garfinkel, Paul E., and David M. Garner. 1982. *Anorexia Nervosa: A Multidimensional Perspective.* New York: Brunner/Mazel.

Garner, David. 1985. Iatrogenesis in anorexia nervosa and bulimia nervosa. *International Journal of Eating Disorders* 4:701–26.

Glaser, Barney G., and Anselm L. Strauss. 1967. *The Discovery of Grounded Theory: Strategies for Qualitative Research.* New York: Aldine DeGruyter.

Goldfarb, Lori. 1987. Sexual abuse antecedent to anorexia nervosa, bulimia and compulsive overeating: Three case reports. *International Journal of Eating Disorders* 6:675–80.

Gray, James, Kathryn Ford, and Lily M. Kelly. 1987. The prevalence of bulimia in a Black college population. *International Journal of Eating Disorders* 6:733–40.

Herman, Judith. 1981. *Father-Daughter Incest.* Cambridge, MA: Harvard University Press.

Higginbotham, Elizabeth. 1986. We were never on a pedestal: Women of color continue to struggle with poverty, racism and sexism. In *For Crying Out Loud*, Rochelle Lefkowitz and Ann Withorn. Boston, MA: Pilgrim Press.

Hsu, George. 1987. Are eating disorders becoming more common in Blacks? *International Journal of Eating Disorders* 6:113–24.

Iazzetto, Demetria. 1989. When the body is not an easy place to be: Women's sexual abuse and eating problems. Ph.D. diss., Union for Experimenting Colleges and Universities, Cincinnati, Ohio.

Kearney-Cooke, Ann. 1988. Group treatment of sexual abuse among women with eating disorders. *Women and Therapy* 7:5–21.

Marx, Karl. 1964. *The Economic and Philosophic Manuscripts of 1844.* New York: International.

Masson, Jeffrey. 1984. *The Assault on the Truth: Freud's Suppression of the Seduction Theory.* New York: Farrar, Strauss & Giroux.

Naylor, Gloria. 1985. *Linden Hills.* New York: Ticknor & Fields.

Nevo, Shoshana. 1985. Bulimic symptoms: Prevalence and the ethnic differences among college women. *International Journal of Eating Disorders* 4:151–68.

Oppenheimer, R., K. Howells, R. L. Palmer, and D. A. Chaloner. 1985. Adverse sexual experience in childhood and clinical eating disorders: A preliminary description. *Journal of Psychiatric Research* 19:357–61.

Orbach, Susie. 1978. *Fat Is a Feminist Issue*. New York: Paddington.

———. 1985. Accepting the symptom: A feminist psycho-analytic treatment of anorexia nervosa. In *Handbook of Psychotherapy for Anorexia Nervosa and Bulimia*, David M. Garner and Paul E. Garfinkel. New York: Guilford.

Powers, Retha. 1989. Fat is a Black women's issue. *Essence*, Oct., 75, 78, 134, 136.

Reagon, Bernice Johnson. 1980. "Oughta be a woman." On Sweet Honey in the Rock's album *Good News*. Music by Bernice Johnson Reagon; lyrics by June Jordan. Washington, DC: Songtalk.

Rich, Adrienne. 1986. Compulsory heterosexuality and lesbian existence. In *Blood, Bread and Poetry*. New York: Norton.

Root, Maria P. P., and Patricia Fallon. 1988. The incidence of victimization experiences in a bulimic sample. *Journal of Interpersonal Violence* 3:161–73.

———. 1989. Treating the victimized bulimic: The functions of binge–purge behavior. *Journal of Interpersonal Violence* 4:90–100.

READING *39* **Simone Weil Davis**

Loose Lips Sink Ships

[They are] two excrescences of muscular flesh which hang, and in some women, fall outside the neck of the womb; lengthen and shorten as does the comb of a turkey, principally when they desire coitus. . . .

—Ambroise Paré (1579), quoted in Lisa Jean Moore and Adele E. Clarke, "Clitoral Conventions and Transgressions: Graphic Representations in Anatomy Texts, c1900–1991," Feminist Studies 21 (summer 1995)

DESIGNER VAGINAS

Perhaps you noticed some of the articles in women's magazines that came out in 1998; *Cosmopolitan, Marie Claire,* and *Harper's Bazaar* each carried one, as did *Salon* on-line, articles with titles like "Labia Envy," "Designer Vaginas," and "The New Sex Surgeries." More recently, *Jane* magazine covered the topic, and Dan Savage's nationally syndicated advice column, "Savage Love," stumbled explosively upon it as well. These pieces all discussed labiaplasty, a relatively recent plastic surgery procedure that involves trimming away labial tissue and sometimes injecting fat from another part of the body into labia that have been deemed excessively droopy. In contrast to the tightening operation known as "vaginal rejuvenation," labiaplasty is sheerly cosmetic in purpose and purports to have no impact on sensation (unless something were to go terribly awry).[1] Throughout coverage here and in Canada, the aptly named Doctors Alter, Stubbs, and Matlock shared much of the glory and the public relations. In the name of consumer choice, these articles provoke consumer anxiety. The *Los Angeles Times* quotes Dr. Matlock: "The woman is the designer . . . the doctor is just the instrument. . . . Honestly, if you look at *Playboy,* those women, on the outer vagina area, the vulva is very aesthetically appealing, the vulva is rounded. It's full, not flat. . . . Women are coming in saying, I want something different, I want to change things. They look at *Playboy,* the ideal woman per se, for the body and the shape and so on. You don't see women in there with excessively long labia minora."[2]

All the popular articles about the "new sex surgeries" that I've reviewed also include remarks from skeptical colleagues and from polled readers who feel okay about their labia. (In an unfortunate turn of phrase, one plastic surgeon describes Dr. Matlock as a bit too "cutting edge.") Despite this apparently balanced coverage, a brand-new worry is being planted, with the declaration in *Salon* that "many women had been troubled for years about the appearance of their labia minora," and with the use of words like "normal" and "abnormal" to describe nonpathological variations among genitalia. The November 1998 article in *Cosmopolitan* has an eye-catching blurb: "My labia were so long, they'd show through my clothes!" Having taken *that* in, the reader suddenly looks up at the accompanying photo with new eyes: the photograph is of a slim woman in fairly modest underwear; because of the picture's cropping, she is headless, but the posture is distinctive, awkward. She's somewhat hunched forward, her hands are both crotch-bound, and one finger slips beneath the edge of her panties. Having read the caption, you think, "My God, she's tucking in her labia!"[3]

Ellen Frankfort's 1972 book, the women's liberationist *Vaginal Politics,* begins with the following scene.[4] Carol from the Los Angeles Self-Help Clinic "slips out of her dungarees and underpants," hops onto a long table in an old church basement and inserts a speculum into her vagina. The 50 other women present file up and look with a flashlight, and learn, too, how to self-examine with a speculum and a dimestore mirror. This self-exploration of what has often been referred to as "the dark continent" or just "down there" seemed the perfect symbol for the early claim of women's liberation that "the personal is political." How could a woman call for sexual autonomy without self-awareness? To reverse the phrasing of one of Second Wave feminism's most famous byproducts, how could we know "our selves" without knowing "our bodies" first?[5] This image of women using a well-placed mirror to demystify and reclaim their own bodies is rooted dimly in my teen-years memory. I found it eerily resurrected when the *Salon* piece by Louisa Kamps came up on my computer screen. Kamps starts off like this: "'Ladies, get out your hand mirrors,' begins a curious press release I find at my desk one Monday morning. 'Yes, it is true . . . the newest trend in surgically enhanced body beautification: Female Genital Cosmetic Surgery.'" The hand mirror this time is used to alert the would-be vagina shopper to any deficiencies "down below" that she may have been blithely ignoring. From 1970s' consciousness-raising groups and Judy Chicago's dinner plates, through Annie Sprinkle's speculum parties of the 1980s, and on to Eve Ensler's collaborative *Vagina Monologues,*[6] we came at the end of the 1990s to Dr. Alter and Dr. Stubbs. What's the trajectory from Second Wave feminist "self-discovery and celebration" to the current almost-craze for labiaplasty? And does the fact of this trajectory provide us with a warning?

THE CLEAN SLIT

The vagina. According to Freud, its first sighting is the first scandal. It is *the* secret, invariably broken, that, once seen, changes you forever, especially if "you" are a little boy in turn-of-the-century Vienna, stumbling in upon your mother *en déshabillé.* You discover, all at once, in a rude shock, that she lacks a penis. You tremble at the threat that her missing phallus implies to *your* little member: if it happened to her, it could happen to you (especially because you've got the gall to compete with your father for your mother's affections). For Freud, his followers, and even many of his feminist revisionists, the "scandal" of a woman's genitals is supposed to be due to what *isn't* there, not what *is.* This article is not about lack, however. It is about excess. And it is not (exactly) about what Jacques Lacan and Hélène Cixous celebrated as *jouissance.* It's about labia.

So the vagina betokens the horror of castration, we're told. Many have remarked that perhaps this scandal is more accurately defined as one of interiority. In a society that revolves around the visual, an orgasm that doesn't include ejaculation can seem maddeningly uncontrollable: you can't prove it (outside of a laboratory), and thus it can be faked.[7] Discussing hard-core cinematic pornography, Linda Williams claims that "[t]he woman's ability to fake the orgasm that the man can never fake . . . seems to be at the root of all the genre's attempts to solicit what it can never be sure of: the out-of-control confession of pleasure, a hard-core 'frenzy of the visible.'"[8]

In the Amero-European world of the late-eighteenth and the early-nineteenth centuries, an earlier notion of women's natural lustiness was transformed into the myth of feminine modesty.[9] This purported lady-like decorum has always been depicted as simultaneously innate for the female *and* a massively big job. For the same social world that generated the mythos of the delicate, proper lady has also continually spawned and recycled dirty jokes about "vagina dentata," fatal odors, and other horror-story imagery about female genitalia.[10] The off-color disgust has always been tied in a complex way to a vast, off-color desire, and these both have been concomitant with the prescription to stay dainty—no matter what—for at least three hundred years. The paradoxical welding of abhorrence and adoration is often "resolved" socially through a stereotyped decoupling of the two, although mythologies of the lurid and the pure female are in fact too interdependent ever to be truly unbraided. Women have been branded good or bad, refined or fallen, on the basis of their race, their profession, their station in life, and so forth, with the judgments conveniently supporting the political, economic, and racial status quo (about which, more later). That being said, the paradox is also one that women negotiate individually, and this has been so for a remarkably long time. . . .

Although "feminine modesty" used to be the answer to this subtextual concern about vaginas, now the shameful zone needs to be brought into line for display, rather than hidden. The vulva is becoming a pioneer territory for cosmetic enhancement—surgical practitioners need above all to capitalize both on that preexisting shame and on the ever-greater need to provide a cyborgian spectacle of porno-gloss. The relative mainstreaming of the sex industry (think of Demi Moore in *Striptease,* for example) and the blurring of the lines between hard-core and advertising imagery (think Calvin Klein) have led to a perpetually increasing sense of pressure among many women, the pressure to develop and present a seamlessly sexualized, "airbrushed" body.[11] Drs. Alter, Stubbs, and Matlock want that sought-after body to include a specific labial look, one desirable enough to be worth "buying."

Before people will spend money on something as expensive and uncomfortable as cosmetic surgery, they need to be motivated not only by desire but by concern or self-doubt. Bringing the authoritative language of medical science to the aestheticization of the vagina is one key way to trigger such anxiety. Advertisers have frequently invoked and generated medicalized norms to sell products. Roland Marchand describes perhaps the classic example of this phenomenon: after the liquid known as Listerine proved a lackluster general antiseptic, it was decided to dramatize its function as a mouthwash. Foul tasting as it was, consumer incentive would be needed. The term "halitosis" was "exhumed from an old medical dictionary" by an advertising firm and became the driving force behind a subsequent, energetic scare campaign about the medical, social, and romantic risks of bad breath.[12] Advertisers have always been both matter-of-fact and explicit about delineating and then steadily working to create a sense of deficiency where once there was indifference or even, God forbid, enjoyment, working to incite new arenas of insecurity, new personal anxieties, so that more things can be marketed and sold.

Cosmetic surgery has worked with the same principles throughout its more than 100-year history, as detailed in histories of the profession by Kathy Davis, Elizabeth Haiken, and Sander Gilman.[13] For instance, in a particularly unnerving chapter on "micromastia" (the "disease" of flat-chestedness) and the surgeries developed to "correct" it, Haiken quotes a 1958 article by plastic surgeon Milton T. Edgerton and psychiatrist A. R. McClary, on "the psychiatry of breast augmentation": "Literally thousands of women in this country alone, are seriously disturbed by feelings of inadequacy in regard to concepts of the body image. Partly as a result of exposure to advertising propaganda and questionable publicity, many physically normal women develop an almost paralyzing self-consciousness focused on the feeling that they do not have the correct size bosom."[14] The rationale laid out here, which explains *but also helps create* "inferiority complexes," can be applied across the full topography of the human form, as borne out by the increasing prevalence of liposuction, face-lifts, buttock and tummy tucks. The latest realm to be scoured for "abnormalities" is the vagina, formerly spared from the scrutiny of the market because it was considered both too reviled and too quakingly desired to be addressed commercially.

These days, in part because of the video dissemination and the main-streaming of pornography, women, regardless of gender preference, can see the vaginas of a lot of different other women. They may desire those vaginas, they may simultaneously identify with them, but if they are rich enough or have great credit, they can definitely have them built.[15] A 1997 article in the Canadian magazine *See* interviews a patient of Dr. Stubbs in Toronto. Deborah "has had her eyes done and had breast implants and some liposuction. She says that she started thinking about her labia when her first husband brought home porn magazines and she started comparing herself. 'I saw some other ones that were cuter than mine' and I thought, 'Hey, I want that one,' she laughs."[16] Of course, the images we relish or bemoan in pornography are almost always tweaked technically. As Deborah did her "catalog shopping," the women she was admiring were perhaps themselves surgically "enhanced," but additionally, they were posed, muted with makeup and lighting, and the resultant photographic images were then edited with an airbrush or the digital modifications of Photoshop.

This is especially true of pornography that presents itself as "upscale," whether soft or hard core. As Laura Kipnis helps us realize, there's a crucial link between

Hustler's targeting of a working-class market and its being the first of the big three glossy "wank mags" to show what it called "the pink."[17] *Hustler's* aggressive celebration of vulgarity informed its initial rejection of soft-core decorum about genitals; thus, its representations of vaginas were matter-of-fact, and often enough contextualized with very explicit, poorly lit Polaroid shots sent in by readers. When the vagina finally came to the pages of *Penthouse*, by contrast, it was as flaw-free and glossy as the rest of the models' figures. In "The Pussy Shot: An Interview with Andrew Blake," sex writer Susie Bright discusses the classed aesthetics of this pornographer, whose trademarks are his lavish sets (straight out of *Architectural Digest*, Bright remarks) and high-end production values: in this posh setting, it comes as no surprise that the star's labia are small and her "pussy is perfectly composed, with every hair in place."[18]

The evolution of a new strict standard of "beauty," rigid enough to induce surgery, does not occur in a vacuum. Among other factors, economics are in play—not just in the eagerness of a few cosmetic surgeons to up their patient load but in a far more intricate web of drives and desires intersecting with technological shifts and cultural and financial power plays. I will only nod here to the complexity of this phenomenon. A first example: in *Venus Envy: A History of Cosmetic Surgery*, Haiken points out that research catalyzed by World War I and II led to technological innovations that furthered the cosmetic surgery industry. Wars, which maim and disfigure people, increase the demand for and respectability of plastic surgery, allowing surgeons the grim opportunity to improve their skills and their public relations. Additionally, war means the invention and/or increased availability of new materials, like silicone and polyurethane, both of which were used for breast augmentation in the wake of World War II.[19] Could this new material on hand have *led* (in part) to the 1950s' notorious obsession with large breasts?

Here is a more recent example of the subtle interplay of cultural and economic forces that can help shape changes in beauty standards: Perhaps Rudolph Giuliani's New York City should be thought of as undergoing an urban labiaplasty. In this zoned, regulated era, newly comfortable for tourists if not for New Yorkers, the sex industry has been radically curtailed. This change has meant, tellingly enough, that almost all the sex clubs "connected" enough to remain open after 1998 favor "clone" women—Caucasian bodies, tidy tan lines, big blonde hair, collagen lips, surgically removed ribs, liposucked bottoms, and implanted breasts. With time, their labia may also be ubiquitously trimmed. Many women with bodies that diverge from the approved stereotype—biker chicks, Latina and Black dancers, plump or small-breasted women, the pierced girl with the monster tattoo—women who used to be able to dance erotically for an income, have been "sheered away," forced into unemployment, prostitution, or departure. These days in New York, only the clones can dance, and it is clone bodies alone that New York City strip club patrons now ogle.[20] The ripple effects such a change works, no doubt, multiply, and the Bloomberg era will see them continue.

In part because of the prevalence of just such a mainstreamed *Penthouse* and *Playboy* aesthetic, labias in pornography are often literally tucked away (in the most low-tech variant of body modification).[21] If you review enough porn, however, especially lesbian porn or that which is unsqueamishly "déclassé" as in *Hustler*, you will see a wide variety in the female genitalia on display—wide enough to evoke the "snowflake uniqueness" analogy that is bandied around in popular coverage of the new cosmetic enhancement surgeries. And indeed the before-and-after shots available at some of the surgeons' web sites that I've found so far do reveal, unsurprisingly, that the single favored look for these "designer vaginas" is . . . the clean slit. Louisa Kamps of *Salon* magazine agrees: "What strikes me in the 'after' shots is the eerie similarity between the women . . . their genitalia are carbon copies of each other."

In a subtle but nontrivial way, this particular aesthetic and the surgery that manifests it cut back on women's experience of self-on-self contact, of tactility: Luce Irigaray celebrates the nonvisual, sensory experience women perpetually enjoy as their vaginal lips press and move against one another. She suggests that this physiological status makes women psychologically less invested in the myth of the monadic, self-reliant individual than are men. Irigaray's "two lips which are not one" would not touch each other much in a world of women "Altered."[22] What do the aesthetics of a streamlined vulva signify? The smooth groin of our favorite plastic android prototype, Barbie? A desire to approximate prepubescence? A fastidious minimization of marginal zones?[23]

Mary Russo writes of "the female grotesque" in terms that are relevant here: "The images of the grotesque body are precisely those which are abjected from the bodily canons of classical aesthetics. The classical body is transcendent and monumental, closed, static, self-contained, symmetrical, and sleek. . . . The grotesque body is open, protruding, secreting, multiple and changing. . . ."[24] Russo's contrasting of the grotesque with the classical is particularly resonant in this context, as plastic surgeons often invoke classical aesthetics and the metaphor of surgeon-as-sculptor; Stubbs even illustrates his site with photographs of classical statuary and presents his "before-and-after" shots in a "Surgical Art Gallery" captioned by Hippocrates: "'*Ars longa, vita brevis*'—Art is long and life is short."[25] Elizabeth Haiken discusses "the classical context in which [early plastic surgeons] wished to place themselves; the term *plastic surgery* derives from the Greek *plastikos,* to shape or mold."[26] The asymmetries, protrusions, and changeability of Russo's grotesque are what the labiaplasty is meant to "shape or mold" and *cut* away.

Bodies do change with the passage of time, of course. If the living body is to approximate sculpture, change itself must be managed, *fixed* . Reading the following quote from Dr. Alter's web site, one is reminded of the Renaissance theory of the wandering womb, whereby female hysteria and misbehavior were deemed the results of a uterus that had dislodged and begun to storm about internally, wreaking havoc. A woman's "womb was like a hungry animal; when not amply fed by sexual intercourse or reproduction, it was likely to wander about her body, overpowering her speech and senses."[27] In Dr. Alter's prose, the older woman, "in dialogue with gravity,"[28] may find her previously pleasing vagina dangerously "on the move": "The aging female may dislike the descent of her pubic hair and labia and desire re-elevation to its previous location," Dr. Alter warns. So, it is woman's work to make sure her genitalia are snug, not wayward.

We are talking about vaginal aesthetics, and aesthetic judgments almost always evidence socially relevant metaphors at work on the material and visual planes. Ideas about feminine beauty are ever-changing: the classic example is a comparison of Rubens's fleshy beauties and the wraithlike super-model Kate Moss (who succeeded Twiggy). But, in a world where many women have never thought about judging the looks of their genitals, even if they care about their appearance more generally, we should ask what criteria make for a good-looking vagina, and who is assigned as arbiter. These (mutating) criteria should tell us something about the value system that generates them. To tease out some answers to these questions, this article goes on to put the labiaplasty phenomenon in a contextual frame with other vaginal modifications.

MODIFYING/CLASSIFYING

What representations of vulvas circulate in our society? And who, beyond Dr. Tight, is modifying the female genitalia, how and why? For one, among alternative youth (and the not-so-alternative, not-so-youthful, too) piercings are being sought to modify and decorate the labia, sometimes to extend them, and, ideally, to add to clitoral stimulation. What sensibilities mark these changes? Among body modifiers on the Web, conversation about body image, self-mutilation, and, contrarily, healing, is common, with an accepted understanding that many turn to piercing as a means of overcoming perceived past abuse. "'Most folks use BodMod to get back in touch with the parts of themselves that were hurt or misused by others.' 'BodMod has helped me undemonize pain. . . . I was able to handle [childbirth] better, knowing that I'd survived . . . two ten-gauge labial piercings. . . .'" Changing one's relationship to one's genitalia by becoming their "modifier" leads here to an aesthetic reassessment: " 'You know, I never liked to look at my puss until I got my rings. I have well-developed inner labia that always show, and I was always envious of those women who seemed to have nice neat little pussies with everything tucked inside. My puss looked like an old whore's cunt to me! So one reason I *know* I wasn't mutilating myself when I got my privates pierced was how much I liked to look at myself after the work was done. You might actually say I'm *glad* my labia are the way they are now.'"[29]

"Glad" is what the cosmetic surgeons do *not* want you to be about prominent labia minora. If you look at the opening paragraph of Ensler's *Vagina Monologues,* you begin to wonder if the unruliness now coming under the governance of the cosmetic surgeon isn't at least as symbolic as it is aesthetic. This is Ensler, introducing her project (interviews with real women, transcribed, performed onstage, and then collected in a book):

I was worried about vaginas. I was worried about what we think about vaginas, and even more worried that we don't think about them. . . . So I decided to talk to women about their vaginas, to do vagina interviews, which became vagina monologues. I talked with over two hundred women. I talked to old women, young women, married women, single women, lesbians, college professors, actors, corporate professionals, sex workers, African American women, Hispanic women, Asian American women, Native American women, Caucasian women, Jewish women. At first women were reluctant to talk. They were a little shy. But once they got going, you couldn't stop them.[30]

Just as Ensler's own catalog of interviewees seems to burgeon and proliferate, so too the women with whom she spoke were "unstoppable." With a similar metaphoric expansion, in the cosmetic surgeons' promotional material, not only are women's *labia* depicted as in danger of distention, but one woman customer also described her *"hang-up"* about her preoperative labia as "just growing and growing," until the doctor cut it short, that is. Loose lips sink ships.

I received a "free consultation" from one doctor who performs labiaplasties, and this doctor explained to me that the ideal look for labia minora was not only minimal and unextended but also symmetrical, "homogeneously pink," and "not wavy."[31] To the dangers and allures of what's hidden about the vagina, now is added the "too muchness" of labial tissue. In their heterogeneous dappling and their moist curves, labia mark the lack of tidy differentiation between inside and outside and that's just *too much.* One effect of this procedure is to reduce this sense of a "marginal" site between exterior and interior corporeality. Labia can be seen as "gateway" tissue, in other words, tissue that is somewhat indeterminate in texture and hue, yielding slowly from outer to inner and blurring the boundary between the fetishized gloss of the outer dermis and the wet, mushy darkness of the inside. This indeterminacy, actually a function of the labia's protective role, may be part of their association with excess.[32] In *Public Privates: Performing Gynecology from Both Ends of the Speculum,* Terry Kapsalis "reads" the images in a widely used medical text, *Danforth's Obstetrics and Gynecology.* She is struck by the lack of representations of healthy vaginas in *Danforth's* and argues that ultimately the work's visual logic pathologizes female genitalia per se. Using language parallel to that which I have used here, she writes: "Perhaps it is not a lack that is threatening, but an excess. The fact is that even if no pathology exists, there *is* something there— namely, a vulva with labia, a clitoris, and so on, a marginal site occupying both the inside and the outside, an abject space (according to Julia Kristeva) that threatens to devour the penis (vagina dentata)."[33]

In the medical realm, much effort is expended to overcome the mysterious liminality of the vagina. Since the eras of the ancient anatomists Galen and Hippocrates and especially since the rise of gynecology in the nineteenth century, vaginas have been diagrammed and cataloged in medical textbooks. Running parallel, a variant of pornography has always picked up and parodied the objectifying eroticism of scientific conquest.[34] In this realm, large labia have often been associated with deviance—at least since the sixteenth century they have indicated to doctors the alleged presence of hypersexuality, onanism, and possible "tribadism" or lesbian tendencies. Jennifer Terry discusses a 1930s' study conducted in New York City, "under the auspices of the Committee for the Study of Sex Variants," in order "to identify, treat, and prevent homosexuality." A moderate-sized group of self-proclaimed lesbians were examined by a battery of experts, so that their "traits" could be characterized and profiled. These experts included gynecologists. The overseer of the project, one Dr. Dickinson, ultimately "identified ten characteristics which he argued set the sex variant [lesbian] apart from 'normal' women: (1) larger than average vulvas; (2) longer labia minora; (3) 'labia minora protrude between the labia majora and are wrinkled, thickened, or *brawny*'; (4) 'the prepuce is large or wrinkled or in folds'; (5) the clitoris is 'notably erectile' . . . , (6) 'eroticism is clearly in evidence on examination, as shown by dusky flush of the parts, with free flow of clear, glairy mucus, and with definite clitoris erection. . . .'" The study concludes that all "these findings can be the result of strong sex urge [presumably an innate or congenital condition], plus: (a) Vulvar and vulvovaginal self-friction; or (b) Homosexual digital or oral play; or (c) Heterosexual manual or coital techniques, singly or in any combination."[35] Terry rightly emphasizes the researchers' apparent fascination with the concept that homo/hypersexual desire (often conflated) could be strong enough that it could make the vulva a site of transformation. The prurience behind this possibility that perverted sex play could "rebuild" a vagina seems great enough that it is allowed to overshadow the theory of a congenital distinction between heterosexual and homosexual anatomy.

Many American and British clitoridectomies and female castrations (the removal of healthy ovaries) were performed in the nineteenth century and as recently as the 1970s, as a response to just such indicators.[36] Isaac Baker Brown began to perform clitoridectomies in Britain in 1858, in order to reduce "hysteria" and other nervous ailments, but particularly to combat "excessive" masturbation. He was, by the 1860s, soundly critiqued in his own country and indeed expelled from Britain's Obstetrical Society in 1867; but his procedure (and its milder variant, circumcision of the clitoral hood) became popular in the United States by the late 1860s and was performed in this country for decades. Although experimentation in the development phases of sexual surgeries generally was exacted on the bodies of poor and disenfranchised women (mostly African American), the lady of leisure became the expressed target for these operations. Upper-middle-class and upper-class women had disposable incomes and time on their hands (to masturbate . . . or to recover from genital surgery). Robert Battey developed the practice of removing healthy ovaries to address a whole slew of complaints, from kleptomania to epilepsy, and this procedure was surprisingly widespread, particularly between 1880 and 1910. One 1893 proponent of female castration claimed that "the moral sense of the patient is elevated. . . . She becomes tractable, orderly, industrious and cleanly." Although depleted misrule seems an unsurprising "benefit" of such operations, one would not expect *aesthetics* to spring up as a concern in this context, but Ben Barker-Benfield cites some clitoridectomy and castration patients who thought of the trend as a "fashionable fad" and found their scars "as pretty as the dimple on the cheek of sweet sixteen."[37]

In the 1970s and 1980s, James Burt, an Ohio gynecologist, gained notoriety—and eventually lost his license—performing what he called "the surgery of love" on more than 4,500 patients, apparently often without even garnering the pretense of informed consent, while they were anesthetized and "on the table" for another procedure. This procedure included a clitoral circumcision and a vaginal reconstruction that changed the angle of the vagina; he insisted before and after the malpractice suits that he had enhanced the sexual pleasure of 99 percent of the women upon whom he'd operated and that he was "correcting" the female anatomy, which he saw as God's mistake, by repositioning the genitalia. Women were left with loss of erotic sensation, enormous pain during intercourse, chronic bowel and urination problems requiring regular catheter use, and ongoing serious infections; the same set of medical sequelae have been reported among infibulated women.[38] In 1997, the Ohio Supreme Court ultimately awarded forty women compensation amounting to a total of $20 million. This award came after spectacular struggles in the courts over an eleven-year-period. The organization Patients-in-Arms, led by Carla Miller (who describes herself as "a victim of FGM" [female genital mutilation]), is devoted to helping women speak out about abuse and disfigurement at the hands of gynecologists. A review of the cases toward which Ms. Miller can direct one makes it excruciatingly clear both that this phenomenon is quite widespread and that it is made possible by the common and interlinked phenomenon of the "white wall of silence" that reduces the doctors' risk of being brought to task.[39]

In a related phenomenon that persists to this day, the erotic tissue of "intersexed" or ambiguously gendered babies and children is routinely, in fact just about ubiquitously, modified through surgery without the minor's consent, in what the medical profession calls a "psychosocial emergency." These modifications have been shown to leave behind serious psychological scarring; often enough, the surgeries profoundly compromise the sexual sensation of the people forced to undergo them. In a piece called "The Tyranny of the Aesthetic: Surgery's Most Intimate Violation," Martha Coventry explains that "girlhood is [almost always] the gender approximated through surgery in such circumstances." "It's easier to poke a hole than build a pole," as one surgeon remarks. Coventry quotes Suzanne Kessler, whose work represents an important contribution to the study of intersexed experience: "Genital ambiguity is corrected not because it is threatening to the infant's life, but because it is threatening to the infant's culture."[40]

The genitalia are cultural terrain that must conform to identificatory norms; this has been driven home by the historians of gynecological science. When mid-nineteenth-century physician Marion Sims developed the duck-billed speculum and an examination protocol that gave him a good view, he used the language of an imperial conquistador, beholding still uncharted territory: "I saw everything, as no man had seen before."[41] Much has been written, particularly by Irigaray, about the mythologization of female genitalia as "the dark continent," the "nothing to see," an Unknown supposedly waiting to be penetrated by pioneering masculine experts; Mary Ann Doane and Anne McClintock are among those who have etched out the linkage that such a metaphor immediately suggests between gender politics and racial imperialism.[42]

What if the "nothing," the furor about female absence, is in part a stand-in scandal for the *something* that is the vaginal bloom—just as the "vast wildernesses" of the Americas and Africa were an invader's myth that suppressed the inconvenient fact of inhabitation? It is exactly in the realms where gender and race intersect that we can see this being played out. Sander Gilman and Michele Wallace are among those who have discussed Saartjie (or Sara) Baartman, dubbed the

Hottentot Venus. She and other African women were taken from their homes and put on show in the early nineteenth century; in this display, their labial "aprons" were rumored about and peeked at with as much eroticized condemnation as were their "steoptygic" buttocks, although the latter were more plainly in view.[43] When George Cuvier, Geoffrey St. Hilaire, and Henri de Blainville, eminent naturalists all, attempted to force a scientific examination of Baartman, de Blainville reported that "she hid her apron carefully between her thighs—her movements were brusque and capricious like those of apes. . . . It was only with great sorrow that she let drop her handkerchief for a moment."[44] The outrage of invasion so evident here is aggravated by the dehumanization of Baartman that drove the tragic endeavor. In the same commentary, Cuvier describes elements of her appearance as being "like an orangutan," "like an animal," and "like a dog."[45] Eager to inspect her labia, particularly as they were seeking a classificatory wedge that would distinguish the Hottentot from the European on the level of species, the scientists spent three days trying to convince Baartman to submit to the physical, even offering her money, which she refused. Alas, her early death afforded them ready access to her private parts, however, and Cuvier made a plaster cast of her body and had her brain and genitals preserved in jars. Although the skeleton remains at Paris's Musée de l'Homme, her body is due to be returned to South Africa for burial . . . and her brain and genitals have disappeared.[46]

It is no coincidence that the aforementioned Marion Sims, early American gynecologist, developed his surgery techniques only by repeated, public operations on the bodies of African American slaves and poor, white "washerwomen."[47] Doing symbolic work, nonwhite women in the Euro-American context have endured the exposure of their bodies only to have them decried and desired, first as heathenish, then as "abnormal." Meanwhile, the nonprostitute white woman's vagina was hidden, protected—shamed, too, but out of the limelight.

OUR VULVAS, OUR SELVES

Perhaps this context needs to be kept in mind when we consider another role played contemporarily by images of female genitals: among activists opposed to the circumcision of African females, even among those who are extremely sensitive to the liabilities of cultural bias, the documenting photo has a special, and somewhat problematic, status. In "Desiring the 'Mutilated' African Woman," Wacuka Mungai points out that there is a heated and eerily prurient interest expressed over the Web in accessing documentary photos of girls and women who have undergone cliterodectomies, excisions, and infibulation.[48] Although photographs of excised and infibulated vaginas are available at "kinky" web sites alongside other images deemed freakish or gory, I agree with Mungai that, even beyond the overtly pornographic, their status as emblems of an "Othered" barbarity is also tinged with unacknowledged eroticism. As Mungai explains, these photos are typically taken with something like consent, but under circumstances when a girl would be hard pressed to withhold permission—in exchange for treatment, a foreign, light-skinned doctor who doesn't speak your language asks that you let her photograph you. You are not likely to refuse her, even though there may be trauma in the taking, and even though the photos then circulate the globe, representing only the wounded status of the African female. Like the gynecological diagram, like Baartman's genitals so long on formaldehyde display in Paris, like the "monster shot" in porn flicks, these images are partial, headless . . . vaginas emphatically disseevered from whole people, made creatures of their own—treated perhaps as the essence of the woman, the cut vagina the truest thing about her, a dangerous metonymy. Mungai points out that, by the same token, in media coverage of the debates over female circumcision among immigrants, the portraits of "cut" women's faces that accompany articles decrying the practice often serve to bring about the same delimiting reduction.

One North American woman with whom I spoke who had elected to have a labiaplasty laughed uproariously with me at the nerve of a European television news program that had approached her to ask if she'd like to do a segment on their show about her operation. The very *thought* of her face being linked to her imagined, modified vagina was preposterous to her, and she would certainly never have consented to being part of the show. Our laughter should continue to ring until it has turned livid, as we think about the many African girls and women who experience just this representational conflation. . . .

CONFOUNDING THE BOUNDARIES

The U.S. Congress passed a measure criminalizing the circumcision of a minor female in 1996, and nine or ten states have passed anti-FGO acts since 1996 as well. In

Illinois, Minnesota, Rhode Island, and Tennessee, this legislation felonizes operations performed on adults as well as on minors. But *which* operations? Anti-FGO laws that now exist in a number of U.S. states describe procedures that would definitely include those practiced by Drs. Alter and Matlock, but they use only language that addresses the "ritual" or custom and belief-based cutting of African immigrant bodies. Meanwhile, this legal language either elides or okays both the "corrective" cutting of the intersexed child and the surgery sought by the unsettled consumer who has been told by plastic surgeons that her labia are unappealing and aberrant. Thus American law marks out relations between the state and its citizen bodies that differ depending on birthplace, cultural context, and skin color.

In fact, however, it is a (prevalent) mistake to imagine a quantum distinction between Euro-American and African reshapings of women's bodies: far too often, they are measured with entirely different yardsticks, rather than on a continuum. Nahid Toubia, executive director of the advocacy group Rainbo, remarks that "[t]he thinking of an African woman who believes that 'FGM is the fashionable thing to do to become a real woman' is not so different from that of an American woman who has breast implants to appear more feminine."[49] In keeping with Toubia's remark, I propose here that a subtler and less culturally binaristic analysis of such phenomena will lead, not to political paralysis in the name of cultural relativism, but to deeper understanding of core issues like the nature of consent, of bodily aesthetics and social control, and of cross-cultural activist collaboration.[50]

Soraya Miré, Somali maker of the film *Fire Eyes,* remarks in Inga Muscio's (wo)manifesto, *Cunt: A Declaration of Independence:* "[Western women] come into conversations waving the American flag, forever projecting the idea that they are more intelligent than I am. I've learned that American women look at women like me to hide from their own pain. . . . In America, women pay *the money that is theirs and no one else's* to go to a doctor who cuts them up so they can create or sustain an image men want. Men are the mirror. Western women cut themselves up voluntarily."[51] Significantly, in Miré's construction, consent to genital surgery does *not* okay it so much as it marks the degrading depths of women's oppression. Although consent is at the heart of the issue of genital operations on children, a topic both urgent and not to be downplayed, we must also look at the social and cultural means whereby consent

is manufactured, regardless of age, in the West as well as in African and other countries engaging in FGOs. In the North American popular imagination, the public address of advertising is not understood as infringing upon our power of consent. Indeed, the freedom to "pay the money that is [one's] own" is too often inscribed as the quintessential exemplar of life in a democracy. Perhaps due to that presumption, beauty rituals hatched on Madison Avenue or in Beverly Hills do not bear the onus of "barbarism" here, despite the social compulsions, psychological drives, and magical thinking that impel them.

By the same token, American oversimplifications suppress the fact that African women's relations to female genital operations are complex and variable, as are the operations themselves, of course. The operations can be roughly grouped into four sorts: circumcision, the removal of the clitoral hood or "female prepuce"; clitoridectomy, "the partial or total removal of the clitoris"; excision, "the removal of the clitoris and all or part of the labia minora"; and infibulation, "the removal of all external genitalia followed by the stitching together of most of the vaginal opening."[52] As will be discussed, motivations for any of these practices are highly variable across time and between individuals as well as between cultures. Vicki Kirby points out the distortions that come with Western monolithizing: "What is 'other' for the West must thereby forfeit its own internal contradictions and diversities in this singular and homogenizing determination of alterity."[53]

Additionally, African vaginal aesthetics are not limited to such sheerings away of vulvular tissue. Although now it is predominantly the members of the royal family who still practice this technique (which is thus a sign of status), the Buganda people in Uganda have a tradition of stretching and massaging the labia and clitoris from childhood to extend them (for feminine beautification). As Londa Schiebinger describes, some say that the "Hottentot aprons," so fetishized by Europeans, were also the result of cosmetic manipulations, on the part of African women seeking beauty.[54]

If one considers all female circumcision practices in Africa to be analogous, as is too commonly the case in popular American analysis of the phenomenon, not only does one miss the dramatic differences between the different forms of FGO, but one also fails to understand the relevant differences between people who practice it as a part of their cultural life and those who experience it as a part of their religious life. Crucial issues of consent are blurred with such elisions.

Western critics of African genital surgeries can also miss completely the role that it often plays in the symbolism of resistance and political struggle, both colonial and tribal.[55] In *Facing Mt. Kenya: The Tribal Life of the Kikuyu* (1953), Jomo Kenyatta remarks that "the overwhelming majority of [the local people] believe that it is the secret aim of those who attack this country's old customs to disintegrate their social order and thereby hasten their Europeanization."[56] An additional point: although female circumcision is not explicitly directed by any religious text, it is practiced as an expression of Muslim, Christian, and Jewish religious observance among various African populations. Overall, it should not be imagined as concomitant with Islam (which it regularly is, often in an anti-Arab conflation), or even as a primarily religious practice.

In most regions, female circumcision practices are determined more by cultural factors, and by ethnic, national, tribal, and postcolonial politics, than by religion. They are by no means solely or exotically "ritualistic" in a way that entirely distinguishes them from nonimmigrant American operations on vaginas. Female genital operations are understood, variously, as hygiene, as beautification, as a curb to female sexuality, as a clarification of the difference between the sexes, as an enhancement of male sexual pleasure, as conducive to fertility and/or monogamy, as disease prevention, and as a means of conforming with social norms and ensuring that one's daughter will be marriageable, that she will be able to take her place among her age set, and that the solidarity and social strength of older women's organizations will be able to flourish.[57]

SURGERY, SISTERLINESS, AND THE "RIGHT TO CHOOSE"

Among the key motivating factors raised by African women who favor female genital surgeries are beautification, transcendence of shame, and the desire to conform; these clearly matter to American women seeking cosmetic surgery on their labia, as well. Thus, the motivations that impel African-rooted FGOs and American labiaplasties should not be envisioned as radically distinct. Not only does such oversimplification lead to a dangerous reanimation of the un/civilized binary, but it also leaves the feminist with dull tools for analysis of either phenomenon. There are aesthetic parallels between the Western and the African procedures. The enthusiasm for the clean slit voiced so vigorously by

the American plastic surgeon I consulted is echoed among a group of Egyptian mothers discussing female genital operations for their daughters in the 1990 documentary, *Hidden Faces*. Although several of the women laughingly nudge each other and say they wouldn't want the excisers to interfere much with "the front" (showing a clear zest for clitoral pleasure), one woman voices an aesthetic principle about which she feels strongly. Energetically, she decries the ugliness of dangling labia, and explains to the filmmaker, with appropriate hand gestures, "Do you want her to be like a boy, with this floppy thing hanging down? Now, it should be straight. Shhh. Smooth as silk." This aesthetic judgment is in keeping not only with the views of labiaplasters in the United States but also with the vocabulary of Mauritanian midwives: one such woman, who has argued to her colleagues for a milder version of circumcision in place of vigorous excision, "use[s] two words to refer to female circumcision, 'tizian,' which means to make more beautiful, and 'gaaad,' which means to cut off and make even."[58]

The group of women chatting on a rooftop in *Hidden Faces* invokes another continuum between African and American women's approaches to feminine beauty rituals and vaginal modifications. Simplistic depictions of a global patriarchy, wherein men curb, cow, cut, and dominate "their" women, may drive home the ubiquity of female subjugation, but they leave out an important factor at the same time: although both labiaplasties and African female circumcision should be (and are here) investigated through a feminist lens, that feminism should be informed by an awareness of women's agency. A knee-jerk celebration of that agency misleads, but its disavowal in the name of victimhood leads to dangerous blind spots. Across many different cultural contexts, female genital operations are contemplated and undergone by girls and women in a social and psychological framework shaped *in part* by other women.

The plastic surgeon whose office I visited provided me with two referrals, patients who had had the procedure done by him. As part of what seemed a well-worn sales pitch, he referred often to "self-help groups," a network of supportive, independent women helping each other find the professional care they wanted and deserved, in the face of an unfeeling, disbelieving medical profession. I was interested by what seemed an invocation of rather feminist sensibilities and wondered about this swelling, grassroots support group he seemed to be conjuring up for me. And, indeed, the image of the surgery consumer as a liberated woman and an independent self-fashioner did provide a crucial spin for the doctor, throughout his consultation. The consumer-feminist in support of other women he condoned; by contrast, he expressed an avowed disapproval of the women who came to him solely to please a domineering partner. He brought up this posited bad, weak, man-centric woman three times as we spoke, and each time his face clouded, he frowned, and his brow furrowed: he said that it was only this type of woman who complained of pain after the procedure, for instance, just to get the attention of her partner, whereas for most women, he insisted, the pain was minimal. He seemed to use these diverging models of female behavior to answer in advance any reservations the prospective client might have about a cosmetic operation on the genitalia (such as, "Should I really do something so drastic to my body just to please men?"). By insisting on his antipathy toward women who kowtowed to the male perspective, and celebrating the fearless vision of the pioneer consumer of "cutting edge" surgery, the doctor tried, I suspect, to ward off potential surges of feminist resistance to the procedure.

In the same spirit, one web site advertising the surgery fuels itself on a long-standing feminist call for a more responsive medical establishment by contrasting the surgeon being advertised with other doctors less sensitive to the needs of women. "Very few physicians are concerned with the appearance of the female external genitalia. A relative complacency exists that frustrates many women."[59] Rachel Bowlby has addressed the theoretical conflations between feminist freedom and the "freedom" to choose as a consumer.[60] The surgeon to whose sales pitch I listened and the creators of the web site noted here certainly understood that the feminist discourse of choice can be appropriated, funneled toward the managed choosing-under-duress of the consumer, becoming saturated along the way with commodity culture's directives.

One goal of this article is to raise the question of this ready appropriation. In *States of Injury: Power and Freedom in Late Modernity,* Wendy Brown examines some of the liabilities of the Left's reliance on the rhetoric of identity, injury, and redress, suggesting that it can result in a politics of state domination.[61] From Bakke on, we have certainly seen the language of affirmative action hauled into the arena of "reverse racism." Perhaps by the same token, the language of choice, as central to the feminist project in this country as we could

imagine, sprang up in a culture where the glories of consumer "choice" had already been mythologized. Revisiting and perhaps refiguring the conceptual framework behind "choice" in the face of manufactured consent, then, is to enable, not critique feminism. The hand mirror that allowed feminists of the 1960s and 1970s to get familiar with "our bodies, our selves" is positioned again so that we can see our vaginas. Only, it comes now with the injunction to look critically at what we see and to exert our selfhood through expenditure and remodeling of a body that is not "ourself" any longer but which is "ours," commodified and estranged, to rebuild.

Although the approach of the doctor I visited seemed agenda-driven and rather theatricalized, when I talked with the women to whom he referred me, I was struck by how very friendly and supportive they *did* seem. I had found the doctor likable but showy, like a much rehearsed salesman, but these women were engaged, candid, and genuinely warm. They were generous with their time (and with their permission to be cited anonymously in the present article), and they made it clear that they really did want to help other women with their "experience, strength, and hope." Perhaps these women were "incentivized" to speak well of the doctor (about whose care they raved): maybe they received discounted work in exchange for talking with prospective clients. Even with this possibility in mind they seemed sincerely ready to assume a common perspective, in fact an intimacy, between women discussing their bodies and body image. To overlook their candor, generosity, and *sisterliness* in order to critique the misogynist judgments that may have driven them to surgery would be to mischaracterize the phenomenon of gender display. We typically learn about and develop a gendered bodily performance, not in isolation, but as members of both real and imagined female "communities."[62] And in 2002, one senses the cultural shading that twentieth-century feminism has, ironically, brought to this community building: the rhetoric of choice making and of solidarity developed during the Second Wave ghosts through our conversations. It's a stereotypical joke that women *really* dress for each other—a deeper look at how this female-to-female hodgepodge of peer pressure and peer support really manifests itself is useful. And again, a look at the web of relations among women is helpful in understanding African female genital operations as well.

One on-line World Health Organization report discusses the impact of female circumcisions on girls' psychological health. Importantly, it mentions not only "experiences of suffering, devaluation and impotence" but also the "desirability of the ceremony for the child, with its social advantage of peer acceptance, personal pride and material gifts." Claire Robertson points out that among the functions of the circumcision ceremony in Central Kenya is the role female initiation plays in maintaining the social strength of organizations of older women.[63] The flip side of approving support, of course, is peer pressure. "When girls of my age were looking after the lambs, they would talk among themselves about their circumcision experiences and look at each other's genitals to see who had the smallest opening. If there was a girl in the group who was still uninfibulated, she would always feel ashamed since she had nothing to show the others."[64]

A reminiscent bodily shame lurks behind the support for labial modifications that my American patient contacts expressed. One (heterosexual) woman explained to me that although none of her boyfriends had ever remarked on her labia, "ever since I was fourteen, I felt like I had this abnormalcy; I felt uncomfortable changing in front of girl-friends." She went on to say that she felt she had to hide her vagina around other women and could never enjoy skinny-dipping because of her concerns about other women judging her appearance. Another labiaplasty patient reported a "120% shift" in her "mental attitude," and a "night-and-day" improvement in the looks of her genitalia, thanks to the surgery. "As sad as it is, it makes you feel inferior," she commented.[65] Her use of the second person (or the ethical dative, as it's known), so intimate in its extension of subjectivity, meant that her language included me. . . . I too felt sad, I too felt inferior. And for a fee, the kind doctor was there to correct me.

NEW RITES

It is probably obvious from this piece that, even in the age where both informational and medical technology have led to bodies being reshaped, extended, reconfigured, and reconceptualized like never before, I believe that erotic tissue is far better enjoyed than removed.[66] In approaching the politics of female genital operations, however, I would argue that it is imperative that both consent issues and vaginal modifications themselves be considered *on a continuum* that is not determined along hemispheric, national, or racial lines. Instead, we peer at female genital operations with a prurient, bifurcating tunnel vision and pretend a clean

break between the "primitive barbarism" of "ritual" cutting of African women, who are far too often represented as undifferentiated victims, and the aesthetic or medical "fixings" of those Amero-European women who are presented as either mildly deformed people in the wise hands of experts or consumer-designers of a cyborgian gender display.

In "Arrogant Perception, World-Traveling, and Multicultural Feminism: The Case of Female Genital Surgeries," Isabelle R. Gunning attempts to define and model a responsible approach to thinking about genital operations across cultures. She urges activists "to look at one's own culture anew and identify [. . .] practices that might prove 'culturally challenging' or negative to some other," and "to look in careful detail at the organic social environment of the 'other' which has produced the culturally challenging practice being explored."[67] I have tried, in this article, to meet her first criterion, and I hope that rendering American cosmetic surgery strange through a heedful look at this latest, not-yet-naturalized procedure can aid us in contextualizing and understanding genital surgeries born in other contexts as well.

Gunning examines some of the ramifications of legal "remedies" for African genital operations and concludes that criminalization of FGOs, whether on the grounds of violating human rights, women's rights, or children's rights, can seem to characterize African women and men as morally blighted, criminally bad parents, and blinded by a cultural tradition that would best be replaced with Western values. Stan Meuwese and Annemieke Wolthuis of Defense for Children International remark that a "legal approach to the phenomenon . . . especially the use of criminal law, shows very clearly the limitations of the juridical system to combat historically and socially deeply-rooted behavior." One Somali woman points out that "if Somali women change, it will be a change done by us, among us. When they order us to stop, tell us what we must do, it is offensive to the black person or Muslim person who believes in circumcision. To advise is good, but not to order."[68]

Gunning, Robertson, and writers at Rainbo's web site are among those who advise that the socioeconomic dependency of women upon men is perhaps the key context for understanding and ultimately abandoning female genital surgeries.[69] They call for a two-pronged strategy: (1) work to improve women's socioeconomic autonomy, both globally and locally and (2) facilitate autonomous, community-generated cultural evolution rather than imposing punitive restrictions. These do seem fruitful emphases, as applicable in the American as in the African context. That they are realizable can be seen with the following story.

In 1997, Malik Stan Reaves reported in the *African News Service* about an alternative ritual that was replacing female circumcision in some rural sections of Kenya. I quote from his article:

> A growing number of rural Kenyan families are turning to an alternative to the rite of female circumcision for their daughters. "Circumcision Through Words" grows out of collaborations between rural families and the Kenyan national women's group, Maendeleo ya Wanawake Organization (MYWO), which is committed to ending FGM in Kenya, . . . with the close cooperation of the Program for Appropriate Technology in Health (PATH), a nonprofit, nongovernmental, international organization which seeks to improve the health of women and children. . . .
>
> "People think of the traditions as themselves," said Leah Muuya of MYWO. "They see themselves in their traditions. They see they are being themselves because they have been able to fulfill some of the initiations." . . . Circumcision Through Words brings the young candidates together for a week of seclusion during which they learn traditional teachings about their coming roles as women, parents, and adults in the community, as well as more modern messages about personal health, reproductive issues, hygiene, communications skills, self-esteem, and dealing with peer pressure. The week is capped by a community celebration of song, dancing, and feasting which affirms the girls and their new place in the community.[70]

Willow Gerber, of PATH, confirms that as of December 2001, the Circumcision Through Words program is still ongoing and has been, over the last several years, expanded to other districts by a consortium of donors.[71] Considering this impressive endeavor, which has seen more than 1,900 girls grow to womanhood uncut, one is reminded of the words of Claire Robertson: "Central Kenyan women have been making increasingly successful efforts to stop FGM . . . [they show] strengths that U.S. women might well emulate in seeking to better their own status."[72]

How *might* we emulate "Circumcision Through Words"? Newly formed rituals in this country, at least those formally recognized as such, usually emerge in either New Age or evangelical settings and can grate

the sensibilities of people beyond those spheres. Initiation of our girls into womanhood is often enough left to the devices of Madison Avenue and magazines like *YM, Teen People,* and *CosmoGirl.* And yet, for all the unconsciousness with which so many of us muddle through our life transitions in this country, nonetheless we too "feel that we have been ourselves" when we fulfill what we see as society's expectations for people at our stage of life. This is not an emotion to be belittled. (One Arabic term for the genital scar is *nafsi* , "my own self.")[73] Without the "years of research and discussion" that helped MYWO develop Circumcision Through Words, we would be hard pressed to generate new ways of bringing "our bodies, ourselves" into a symbolic relation with the social world that would prove both intelligible and affirmative. Just as analogies between genital cuttings are both important and exceedingly difficult to draw, so too is the conscious development of new, performative practices both worth emulating and only circuitously "applicable." Even in rural Kenya, the approach to "circumcision through words" varies dramatically from district to district."[74]

So I will not conclude this article with a glib, faux ritual for American women trained to hate the specificities of their bodies in the interest of capital accumulation. I will see, however, if I can leave you in a performative mode, offering a coda that I hope can "act" upon and through the reader as a textual "rite of antidote," speaking back to the cited language of abnormality, pathology, and sexual distrust with which this article began.

CODA

Dan Savage, syndicated sex advice columnist, responded to one reader concerned about the aesthetic effect of her long labia minora, by suggesting the work of Dr. Stubbs. He received many letters of protest, providing paeans to the appeal of prominent labia and/or suggesting that he advise self-admiration, not surgery. The enthusiastic adjectives these letter writers employed ("lavish," "luscious," "extravagant"), coupled with their emphasis on erotic pleasure, can remind us that perhaps "beauty" results from a harmony between form and function, and one key genital function is *pleasure*. I offer excerpts from some of these letters here.[75]

- . . . You might have told Jagger Lips to toss her unappreciative lovers out of bed and find a boyfriend who sees the beauty of her as she exists. . . .

- . . . I have long inner labia and most of the women I've seen naked have inner labia that extend past the outer labia. . . . If someone wants to see what vulvas really look like, they should put down *Penthouse* and start sleeping with lots of women.
- . . . many men, myself included, don't find a thing wrong with longer labia minora. My girlfriend has one [*sic*] and I find it quite the enjoyable thing to suck on. . . .
- Does female sexual pleasure mean anything to you? Not only do the labia minora engorge during sexual stimulation and have lots of nerve endings, they also increase friction. . . .
- I am writing to Jagger Lips to discourage her from chopping off her labia minora. I prefer long labia. I find that they lend themselves more readily to being tugged, stretched, nibbled, etc. . . .
- . . . I remember a gorgeous actor, Savannah, who sadly committed suicide in the mid-1990s, who had a beautiful snatch with extravagant labia spilling (an inch and a half, easy) from her soft and salty cornucopia of love. She was rad, I hope she's resting in peace, and I'd recommend your reader try and rustle up a video. . . .
- Our society tends not to be so pussy-positive, and most commercial pussy pictures are airbrushed on Planet Barbie, and shouldn't be considered reality. Labia (inner and outer) have lots of nerves and feel really good when they get stroked.
- . . . Please tell the woman with the lavish labia not to have them removed. . . . You were much too hasty to recommend clipping her butterfly wings! . . .

ACKNOWLEDGMENTS

Thanks to former students Jenn Sanders and Wacuka Mungai for their help in developing this article.

NOTES

1. Things certainly can happen. See Louisa Kamps, "Labia Envy," 16 March 1998, <http://www.salon.com/mwt/feature/1998/03/16feature.html> (9 Dec. 2001).
2. *Los Angeles Times*, 5 Mar. 1998. See, too, the following Internet resources on labiaplasty: Dr. Alter: "Female Cosmetic and Reconstructive Genital Surgery," <http://www.altermd.com/female/index.html> (9 Dec. 2001); Julia Scheeres, "Vaginal Cosmetic Surgery," 16 Apr. 2001, <http://thriveonline.oxygen.com/sex/sexpressions/vaginal-cosmetic-surgery.html> (9 Dec. 2001); Dr. Stubbs, <http://psurg.com>; Laser Rejuvenation Center of LA, <http://www.drmatlock.com>; Dan Savage, "Long in the Labia," 16 Dec. 1999, <http://www.thestranger.com/1999-12-16/savage.html> (13 Dec. 2001); iVillage.com Archive Message Board, "Cosmetic Surgery," 7 Jan. 2000, <http://boards.allhealth.com/messages/get/bhcosmeticsx2.html> (13 Dec. 2001); Patients' chatboard, <http://boards.allhealth.com/messages/get/bhcosmeticsx2.html>
3. See Kamps. Also, see Carrie Havranek, "The New Sex Surgeries," *Cosmopolitan*, November 1998, 146.
4. Ellen Frankfort, *Vaginal Politics* (New York: Quadrangle, 1972). See, too, Julia Scheeres, "Vulva Goldmine: How Cosmetic Surgeons Snatch Your Money," *Bitch* 11 (January 2000): 70–84.
5. Boston Women's Health Collective, *Our Bodies, Ourselves* (New York: Simon & Schuster, 1973). Updated editions have continued to be released. See Boston Women's Health Collective, *Our Bodies, Ourselves for the New Century:*

A Book by and for Women (New York: Simon & Schuster, 1998).
6. See Amelia Jones, ed., *Sexual Politics: Judy Chicago's Dinner Party in Feminist Art History* (Berkeley: University of California Press, 1996); Shannon Bell, "Prostitute Performances: Sacred Carnival Theorists of the Female Body," from her *Reading, Writing, and Rewriting the Prostitute Body* (Bloomington: Indiana University Press, 1994), 137–84; and Eve Ensler, *The Vagina Monologues* (New York: Villard Press, 1998).
7. Although some women enjoy orgasmic ejaculation, it remains an exception to the rule.
8. Linda Williams's book is about pornographic films, especially those of the 1970s: *Hard Core: Power, Pleasure, and the "Frenzy of the Visible"* (Berkeley: University of California Press, 1989), 50.
9. See Michel Foucault, *The History of Sexuality*, vol. 1, *An Introduction* (New York: Random House, 1978).
10. See Gershon Legman, *Rationale of the Dirty Joke: An Analysis of Sexual Humor* (New York: Breaking Point Press, 1975), 547.
11. In a mode that both ridicules and familiarizes the body modifications of plastic surgery, tabloids regularly feature articles about the "work" being done on celebrities, with a special emphasis on implant disasters. See, for instance, "Hollywood's Plastic Surgery Nightmares: When Breast Implants Go Bad," *National Enquirer*, 4 May 1999, 28–33. Kathy Davis discusses popular coverage of celebrity

surgeries in *Reshaping the Female Body: The Dilemma of Cosmetic Surgery* (New York: Routledge, 1995), 18.

12. See the work of the late historian Roland Marchand, *Advertising the American Dream: Making Way for Modernity, 1920–1940* (Berkeley: University of California Press, 1985), 18–20.

13. Davis; Elizabeth Haiken, *Venus Envy: A History of Cosmetic Surgery* (Baltimore: Johns Hopkins University Press, 1997); Sander Gilman, *Making the Body Beautiful: A Cultural History of Aesthetic Surgery* (Princeton: Princeton University Press, 1999). Also, see Claudia Springer, *Electronic Eros: Bodies and Desire in the Postindustrial Age* (Austin: University of Texas Press, 1996).

14. Milton T. Edgerton and H.R. McClary, quoted in Haiken, 244.

15. On the thin line between identification and desire, between wanting to be like someone and wanting to bed down with them (so exploited in consumer culture), see Diana Fuss, "Fashion and the Homospectatorial Look," in *On Fashion*, ed. Shari Benstock and Suzanne Ferriss (New Brunswick, N.J.: Rutgers University Press, 1994), 211–32; and Judith Butler, *Gender Trouble: Feminism and the Subversion of Identity* (New York: Routledge, 1990), esp. 57–72.

16. Josey Vogels, "My Messy Bedroom," *See*, 10 July 1997, <http://www.greatwest.ca/SEE/Issues/1997/970710/josey.html> (13 Dec. 2001).

17. Laura Kipnis, *Bound and Gagged: Pornography and the Politics of Fantasy in America* (New York: Grove, 1996).

18. Susie Bright, "The Pussy Shot: An Interview with Andrew Blake," *Sexwise* (New York: Cleis Press, 1995), 82.

19. Haiken, 29–34, 136–45, 237, 246.

20. See Richard Goldstein, "Porn Free," *Village Voice*, 1 Sept. 1998, 28–34. My own research for a work-in-progress, "Choosing the Moves: Choreography in the Strip Club," also bears this out.

21. See Nedahl Stelio, "Do You Know What a Vagina Looks Like?" *Cosmopolitan*, August 2001, 126–28, on sex magazines' doctoring of vaginas and the increased prevalence of labiaplasty.

22. Luce Irigaray, *This Sex Which Is Not One*, trans. Catherine Porter (Ithaca: Cornell University Press, 1985), 209. Also see her *Speculum of the Other Woman* (Ithaca: Cornell University Press, 1986).

23. See Mary Douglas on a cross-cultural tendency to approach marginal zones, marginal people, and marginal periods with great apprehension, in *Purity and Danger: An Analysis of the Concepts of Pollution and Taboo* (1966; reprint, New York: Routledge, 1992).

24. Mary Russo, *The Female Grotesque: Risk, Excess, and Modernity* (New York: Routledge, 1994), 8.

25. See <http://www.psurg.com/gallery.html> (13 Dec. 2001).

26. Haiken, 5.

27. Natalie Zemon Davis, "Women on Top," in her *Society and Culture in Early Modern France* (Stanford: Stanford University Press, 1975), 124. See 124–31.

28. Denise Stoklos, remark made in Solo Performance Composition, her course offered by the Performance Studies Department, New York University, Spring 2000. "Our primary dialogue is with gravity," Stoklos says.

29. See Ambient, Inc., "Body Modification: Is It Self-Mutilation—Even if Someone Else Does It for You?" 2 Feb. 1998, <http://www.ambient.on.ca/bodmod/mutilate.htm> (13 Dec. 2001). Another web site dealing with body modification is <www.perforations.com> (13 Dec. 2001).

30. Ensler, 3–5.

31. This and all subsequent quotations from this plastic surgeon are from an office visit in a major American city—location to remain unspecified to ensure anonymity—in April 1999.

32. Elizabeth Grosz: "[W]omen's corporeality is inscribed as a mode of seepage." See her *Volatile Bodies: Toward a Corporeal Feminism* (Bloomington: Indiana University Press, 1994), 203.

33. Terri Kapsalis, *Public Privates: Performing Gynecology from Both Ends of the Speculum* (Durham: Duke University Press, 1997), 89. She references Julia Kristeva, *Powers of Horror: An Essay on Abjection* (New York: Columbia University Press, 1982). On the cultural and political implications of representations of genitalia in anatomical textbooks, see Lisa Jean Moore and Adele E. Clarke, "Clitoral Conventions and Transgressions: Graphic Representations in Anatomy Texts, c1900–1991," *Feminist Studies* 21 (summer 1995): 255–301; and Susan C. Lawrence and Kae Bendixen, "His and Hers: Male and Female Anatomy in Anatomical Texts for U.S. Medical Students, 1890–1989," *Social Science and Medicine* 35 (October 1992): 925–34. Also, see Katharine Young, "Perceptual Modalities: Gynecology," in her *Presence in the Flesh* (Cambridge: Harvard University Press, 1997), 46–79.

34. Thomas Laqueur, *Making Sex: Body and Gender from the Greeks to Freud* (Cambridge: Harvard University Press, 1990). And see Lynn Hunt, *The Invention of Pornography* (New York: Zone, 1993).

35. Jennifer Terry, "Lesbians under the Medical Gaze: Scientists Search for Remarkable Differences," *Journal of Sex Research* 27 (August 1990): 317–39, 332 (emphasis added), 333.

36. See Ben Barker-Benfield, "Sexual Surgery in Late-Nineteenth-Century America," *International Journal of Health Services* 5, no. 2 (1975): 279–98; Andrew Scull and Diane Favreau, "The Clitoridectomy Craze," *Social Research* 53 (summer 1986): 243; Barbara Ehrenreich and Deirdre English, *Complaints and Disorders: The Sexual Politics of Sickness* (New York: City University of New York Press, 1973); and Rachel P. Maines, *The Technology of Orgasm: "Hysteria," the Vibrator, and Women's Sexual Satisfaction* (Baltimore: Johns Hopkins University Press, 1999).

37. Barker-Benfield, 287, 298.

38. See Daniel Gordon, "Female Circumcision and Genital Operations in Egypt and the Sudan: A Dilemma for

Medical Anthropology," *Medical Anthropology Quarterly* 5 (March 1991): 7.

39. For more on this and similar cases, see Carla Miller's statement at <www.InMemoryoftheSufferingChild.com> . For coverage of the Burt case, see, for instance, Sandy Theis, "His Peers Waved Red Flags: Monitors' Concern Went Beyond Love Surgery," *Dayton Daily News*, 4 Aug. 1991, 1A; Rob Modic, "Painful Testimony: Woman Testifies of Trust for Gynecologist Burt," *Dayton Daily News*, 1 June 1991, 1A; Judith Adler Hennessee, "The Love Surgeon," *Mademoiselle,* August 1989, 206; Gerry Harness and Judy Kelman, "A Mother's True Story: 'My Gynecologist Butchered Me!'" *Redbook* , July 1989, 22. Also see <http://www.nocirc.org> (13 Dec. 2001); <http://www.SexuallyMutilatedChild.org/index.html> (13 Dec. 2001).

40. See Suzanne Kessler, *Gender: An Ethnomethodological Approach* (1978; reprint, Chicago: University of Chicago Press, 1985), quoted by Martha Coventry in "The Tyranny of the Aesthetic: Surgery's Most Intimate Violation," <http://www.fgm.org/coventryarticle.html> (20 Dec. 2001).

41. Deborah Kuhn McGregor, *From Midwives to Medicine: The Birth of American Gynecology* (New Brunswick, N. J.: Rutgers University Press, 1998), 49. She is quoting Sims's autobiography. See also Kapsalis, chap. 2.

42. Mary Ann Doane, "Dark Continents: Epistemologies of Racial and Sexual Difference in Psychoanalysis and the Cinema," in her *Femmes Fatales: Feminism, Film Theory, Psychoanalysis* (New York: Routledge, 1991), 209–48; and Anne McClintock, *Imperial Leather: Race Gender, and Sexuality in the Colonial Contest* (New York: Routledge, 1995), esp. 1–4, and 21–31.

43. See Zola Maseko, director, *The Life and Times of Sara Baartman, "The Hottentot Venus,"* videorecording, London: Dominant 7, Mail and Guardian Television, France 3, and SABC 2, 1998.

44. Henri de Blainville, quoted in Maseko.

45. See Londa Schiebinger, *Nature's Body: Gender in the Making of Modern Science* (Boston: Beacon, 1995), chap. 5.

46. Maseko.

47. McGregor, 46–51.

48. Wacuka Mungai, "Desiring the 'Mutilated' African Woman," paper, 1999. Mungai is a doctoral student at New York University and assistant program director at Rainbo, an organization devoted in large part to advocating for African women around the issue of female circumcision.

49. Nahid Toubia, *Female Genital Mutilation: A Call for Global Action*, 3d ed. (New York: Women, Ink, 1995), 35.

50. See Janice Boddy, "Body Politics: Continuing the Anti-circumcision Crusade"; and Faye Ginsburg, "What Do Women Want? Feminist Anthropology Confronts Clitoridectomy," both in *Medical Anthropology Quarterly* 5 (March 1991): 15–19.

51. Inga Muscio, *Cunt: A Declaration of Independence* (Toronto: Seal Press, 1998), 134–35.

52. "Female Genital Mutilation: A Human Rights Information Pack" (London: Amnesty International, 1997).

53. Vicki Kirby, "On the Cutting Edge: Feminism and Clitoridectomy," *Australian Feminist Studies* 5 (summer 1987): 35–56.

54. In New York City, March 1999, Wacuka Mungai shared one anecdote with me about a Buganda woman who took one trip to a gynecologist in North America: the doctor was flabbergasted and wanted to rush in a crowd of residents to stare at her. Of course, this reaction was not welcomed by the patient and she shied away from the entire profession afterward, rather than risk a reoccurrence of the circus atmosphere the doctor had created. See also, Lauran Neergard, "Doctors See More Female Circumcision," 17 Sept. 1999, posted at <http://www.worldafricannet.com/news/news7861.html>. And see this web site, that catalogs body modifications across cultures: <http://www.cadewalk.com/mods/modify.htm>. Also, see Schiebinger.

55. See Claire Robertson, "Grassroots in Kenya: Women, Genital Mutilation, and Collective Action, 1920–1990," *Signs* 21 (spring 1996): 615–42, on some of the history of circumcision's changing meaning in Kenya over the course of the twentieth century. Mungai suggested that the *tribal* politics, in addition to the politics of colonial resistance, were perhaps more complex than Robertson's article describes. See also, Isabelle R. Gunning, "Arrogant Perception, World Traveling, and Multicultural Feminism: The Case of Female Genital Surgeries," *Columbia Human Rights Law Review* 23 (Summer 1992): 189–248.

56. Jomo Kenyatta, quoted in Gunning, 228.

57. See, for instance, Nadia Kamal Khalifa, "Reasons Behind Practicing Re-circumcision among Educated Sudanese Women," *Ahfad Journal* 11, no. 2 (1994): 16–32; Anke van der Kwaake, "Female Circumcision and Gender Identity: A Questionable Alliance?" *Social Science and Medicine* 35, no. 6 (1992): 777–87.

58. Claire Hunt and Kim Longinotto, with Safaa Fathay, *Hidden Faces,* videorecording (New York: Twentieth Century Vixen Production/Women Make Movies, 1990). And see Elizabeth Oram, introduction to Zainaba's "Lecture on Clitoridectomy to the Midwives of Touil, Mauritania" (1987), in *Opening the Gates: A Century of Arab Feminist Writing* , ed. Margot Badran and Miriam Cooke (Bloomington: Indiana University Press, 1990), 63–71.

59. See <http://www.altermd.com/female/index.html> (13 Dec. 2001).

60. See Rachel Bowlby, in *Shopping with Freud: Items on Consumerism, Feminism, and Psychoanalysis* (New York: Routledge, 1993), on theoretical conflations between feminist freedom and the "freedom" to choose as a consumer.

61. Wendy Brown, *States of Injury: Power and Freedom in Late Modernity* (Princeton: Princeton University Press, 1995).

62. Anonymous telephone interviews with two West Coast labiaplasty patients, August 1999. For an on-line example of this, see the fascinating archived chat between women

about cosmetic surgery at iVillage, "Cosmetic Surgery Archive Board," 7 Jan. 2001, <http://boards.allhealth.com/messages/get/bhcosmeticsx2.html> (13 Dec. 2001).

63. See Robertson.

64. Anab's story, from "Social and Cultural Implications of Infibulation in Somalia," by Amina Wasame, in *Female Circumcision: Strategies to Bring about Change* (Somali Women's Democratic Organization), quoted in Toubia, 41.

65. Anonymous telephone interview with author, August 1999.

66. An important caveat: As the transgendered community has made clear, for some individuals, erotic enjoyment is enhanced via the genital modification that comes along with reassigning gender, even if that surgery has resulted in a reduction in nerve endings or sensation.

67. Gunning, 213.

68. See Frances A. Althaus, "Female Circumcision: Rite of Passage or Violation of Rites?" *International Family Planning Perspectives* 23 (September 1997), <http://www.agiusa.org/pubs/journals/2313097.html#21> (20 Dec. 2001).

69. Alan Worsley, "Infibulation and Female Circumcision," *Journal of Obstetrics and Gynecology of the British Empire* 45, no. 4 (1938): 687.

70. For more information, see the web site for the Gender Learning Network, a partnership between twenty-three women-run NGOs, including MYWO, "working to promote women's rights and status in Kenya," <http://arcc.or.ke/gln/glnl3sec.html> (13 Dec. 2001). And here are two relevant links to PATH's web site: (1) Anonymous, "Alternative rituals raise hope for eradication of Female Genital Mutilation," 20 Oct. 1997, <http://www.path.org/resources/press/19971020-FGM.html> (13 Dec. 2001), and (2) Anonymous, "Modern Rites of Passage," <http://www.path.org/resources/closerlooks/f_modern_rites_of_passage.htm> (13 Dec. 2001).

71. PATH's Michelle Folsom heads a ten-year office in Kenya, and oversees the organization's collaboration on this and other projects with MYWO, and their work receives the support of the Kenyan government. See "Program for Appropriate Technology in Health," *Promoting a Healthy Alternative to FGM: A Tool for Program Implementers* (Washington, D.C.: PATH, 2001). See also, Davan Maharaj, "Kenya to Ban Female Genital Excision," *Los Angeles Times*, 15 Dec. 2001.

72. Robertson, 615. See also, Carolyn Sargent, "Confronting Patriarchy: The Potential for Advocacy in Medical Anthropology," *Medical Anthropology Quarterly* 5 (March 1991): 24–25.

73. Alan Worsley, 687.

74. See "Modern Rites of Passage," <http://www.path.org/closerlooks/f_modern_rites_of_passage.html> (13 Dec. 2001).

75. All letters quoted in Dan Savage, "Savage Love," *Village Voice*, 18 Jan. 2000, 126.

READING *40* **Andrea Smith**

Beyond Pro-Choice Versus Pro-Life: Women of Color and Reproductive Justice

Once, while taking an informal survey of Native women in Chicago about their position on abortion—were they "pro-life" or "pro-choice"—I quickly found that their responses did not neatly match up with these media-mandated categories.

Example 1:

ME: Are you pro-choice or pro-life?

RESPONDENT 1:   Oh I am definitely pro-life.

ME: So you think abortion should be illegal?

RESPONDENT 1:   No, definitely not. People should be able to have an abortion if they want.

ME: Do you think then that there should not be federal funding for abortion services?

RESPONDENT 1:   No, there should be funding available so that anyone can afford to have one.

Example 2:

ME: Would you say you are pro-choice or pro-life?

RESPONDENT 2:   Well, I would say that I am pro-choice, but the most important thing to me is promoting life in Native communities.

These responses make it difficult to categorize the Native women queried neatly into "pro-life" or "pro-choice" camps. Is Respondent #1 pro-life because she says she is pro-life? Or is she pro-choice because she supports the decriminalization of and public funding for abortion? I would argue that, rather than attempt to situate these respondents in pro-life or pro-choice camps, it is more useful to recognize the limitations of the pro-life/pro-choice dichotomy for understanding the politics around reproductive justice. Unlike pro-life versus pro-choice advocates who make their overall political goal either the criminalization or decriminalization of abortion, the reproductive frameworks these Native women are implicitly articulating are based on fighting for life and self-determination of their communities. The criminalization of abortion may or may not be a strategy for pursuing that goal.

In previous works, I have focused more specifically on Native women and reproductive justice (Smith 2001). Here, I am using these Native women's responses to questions about abortion to argue that the pro-life versus pro-choice paradigm is a model that marginalizes women of color, poor women, and women with disabilities. The pro-life versus pro-choice paradigm reifies and masks the structures of white supremacy and capitalism that undergird the reproductive choices that women make, and it also narrows the focus of our political goals to the question of criminalization of abortion. Ironically, I will contend, while the pro-choice and pro-life camps on the abortion debate are often articulated as polar opposites, both depend on similar operating assumptions that do nothing to support either life or real choice for women of color. In developing this analysis, I seek to build on previous scholarship that centers women of color as well as reflect on my fifteen years as an activist in the reproductive justice movement through such organizations as Illinois National Abortion and Reproductive Rights Action League (NARAL), the Chicago Abortion Fund, Women of All Red Nations, Incite! Women of Color Against Violence, and Committee on Women, Population and the Environment. I begin by examining the limitations of the pro-life position. I then explore the problems with the pro-choice position. The paper concludes with suggestions for moving

beyond this binary stalemate between "pro-life" and "pro-choice."

PRO-LIFE POLITICS, CRIMINALIZATION OF ABORTION, AND THE PRISON INDUSTRIAL COMPLEX

The fetus is a life—but sometimes that life must be ended.

—Jeanette Bushnell, Seattle-based Native health activist (2004)

The pro-life position maintains that the fetus is a life; hence abortion should be criminalized. Consequently, the pro-life camp situates its position around moral claims regarding the sanctity of life. In a published debate on pro-life versus pro-choice positions on the issue of abortion, Gray Crum (former vice-president of South Carolina Citizens for Life) argues that the pro-life position is "ethically pure" (Crum and McCormack 1992, 54). Because of the moral weight he grants to the protection of the life of the fetus, Crum contends that abortion must be criminalized. Any immoral actions that impact others should be a "serious crime under the law" (1992, 28). The pro-choice position counters this argument by asserting that the fetus is not a life, and hence policy must be directed toward protecting a woman's ability to control her own body. To quote sociologist Thelma McCormack's response to Crum: "Life truly begins in the . . . hospital room, not in the womb" (Crum and McCormack 1992, 121). Gloria Feldt, president of Planned Parenthood, similarly asserts that if the fetus is established as a life, the principles of *Roe v. Wade* must necessarily be discarded (Feldt 2004, 90).

Jeanette Bushnell's statement that *"The fetus is a life—but sometimes that life must be ended"* suggests, however, a critical intervention in the pro-life argument. That is, the major flaw in the pro-life position is NOT the claim that the fetus is a life, but the conclusion it draws from this assertion: that because the fetus is a life, abortion should be criminalized. In this regard, reproductive rights activists and scholars could benefit from the analysis of the anti-prison movement which questions criminalization as an appropriate response to social issues. As I shall demonstrate, assuming a criminal justice regime fails to address social problems or to adjudicate reproductive issues and results in further marginalization of poor women and women of color. To make this connection, I must first provide a critical history of the failures of the prison system to deal effectively with social problems.

The anti-prison industrial complex movement has highlighted the complete failure of the prison system to address social concerns. In fact, not only do prisons not solve social problems, such as "crime," they are more likely to increase rather than decrease crime rates (Currie 1998; Donziger 1996; Walker 1998). Most people in prison are there for drug or poverty-related crimes. Prisons do not provide treatment for drug addiction, and it is often easier to access drugs in prison than on the outside. For people who are in prison because of poverty-related crimes, a prison record ensures that it will be much more difficult for them to secure employment once they are released. Consistently, study after study indicates that prisons do not have an impact on decreasing crime rates. . . . In fact, changes in crime rates often have more to do with fluctuations in employment rates than with increased police surveillance or increased incarceration rates (Box and Hale 1982; Jankovic 1977). In addition, as documented by prison activist groups such as the Prison Activist Resource Center, government monies are siphoned away from education and social services into prisons, thus destabilizing communities of color and increasing their vulnerability to incarceration (Prison Activist Resource Center 2004).

The failure of prisons is well known to policymakers. . . . Given that this failure is well known, it then becomes apparent that the purpose of prisons has never been to stop crime. Rather, as a variety of scholars and activists have argued, the purpose has been in large part to control the population of communities of color. . . . In 1994, for instance, one out of every three African American men between the ages of 20 and 29 was under some form of criminal justice supervision (Mauer 1999). Two-thirds of men of color in California between the ages of 18 and 30 have been arrested (Donziger 1996, 102–4). Six of every ten juveniles in federal custody are American Indian and two-thirds of women in prison are women of color (Prison Activist Resource Center 2004).

In a statement that also applies to the criminalization of abortion, Davis further argues that it is critical to disarticulate the equation between crime and punishment because the primary purpose is not to solve the problem of crime. . . . Prisons simply are not only ineffective institutions for addressing social concerns,

they drain resources from institutions that could be more effective. They also mark certain peoples, particularly people of color, as inherently "criminal," undeserving of civil and political rights—thus increasing their vulnerability to poverty and further criminalization.

Davis's principle of disarticulation is critical in reassessing the pro-life position. That is, whether or not one perceives abortion to be a crime, it does not therefore follow that punishment in the form of imprisonment is a necessary response. Criminalization individualizes solutions to problems that are the result of larger economic, social, and political conditions. Consequently, it is inherently incapable of solving social problems or addressing crime. . . . Thus, even if we hold that a top social priority is to reduce the number of abortions, there is no evidence to suggest that involving the criminal justice system will accomplish that goal, given that it has not been effective in reducing crime rates or addressing social problems. In addition, increased criminalization disproportionately affects people of color—and in the case of abortion, women of color and poor women. An interrogation of the assumptions behind the pro-life movement suggests that what distinguishes the pro-life position is not so much a commitment to life (since criminalization promotes death rather than life, particularly in communities of color and poor communities), but rather a commitment to criminal justice interventions in reproductive justice issues. . . .

. . . The pro-life position implicitly supports the prison industrial complex by unquestioningly supporting a criminal justice approach that legitimizes rather than challenges the prison system. As Davis (2003) argues, it is not sufficient to challenge the criminal justice system; we must build alternatives to it. Just as the women of color anti-violence movement is currently developing strategies for ending violence (Smith 2005/in press), a consistent pro-life position would require activists to develop responses to abortion that do not rely on the prison industrial complex. Otherwise, these pro-life activists will continue to support policies that are brutally oppressive, particularly to communities of color and poor communities.

Interestingly, this critique of the prison system is prevalent even within conservative evangelical circles. For example, Charles Colson, a prominent Christian Right activist, founder of Prison Fellowship, and former attorney with the Nixon administration, served time in prison for his role in the Watergate break-in. Following his imprisonment, Colson began to work on prison reform, organizing the Prison Fellowship and its associated lobbying arm, Justice Fellowship. . . . In fact, Colson argues that 50 percent of people in prison today should be released immediately (Fager 1982, 23). To quote Colson:

> The whole system of punishment today is geared toward taking away people's dignity, putting them in an institution, and locking them up in a cage. Prisons are overcrowded, understaffed, dirty places. Eighty percent of American prisons are barbaric—not just brutal, but barbaric. . . . Prison as a punishment is a failure. Mandatory sentences and longer sentences are counterproductive . . . the tougher the laws, I'm convinced, the more lawless and violent we will become. As for public safety, it can hardly be said that prisons contribute to public safety. . . . Prisons obviously are not deterring criminal conduct. The evidence is overwhelming that the more people we put in prison, the more crime we have. All prisons do is warehouse human beings and at exorbitant cost. (Colson 1983, 15; Fager 1982, 23; Forbes 1982, 34)[1]

Yet, despite his sustained critique of the failure of the prison system, Colson never critiques the wisdom of criminalization as the appropriate response to abortion. In the name of promoting life, the pro-life movement supports one of the biggest institutions of violence and death in this society. But given that this critique of criminalization is not inaccessible to large sectors of the pro-life movement, there should be opportunities to make anti-criminalization interventions into pro-life discourse. Thus, the major flaw in the pro-life position is not so much its claim that the fetus is a life, but its assumption that because the fetus is a life, abortion should be criminalized. A commitment to criminalization of social issues necessarily contributes to the growth of the prison system because it reinforces the notion that prisons are appropriate institutions for addressing social problems rather than causes of the problems. Given the disproportionate impact of criminalization on communities of color, support for criminalization as public policy also implicitly supports racism.

In addition, I am suggesting that those committed to pro-choice positions will be more effective and politically consistent if they contest the pro-life posi-tion from an anti-prison perspective. For instance, increasingly, poor women and women of color are finding their pregnancies criminalized. As Dorothy Roberts (1997) and others have noted, women of color are more likely to be arrested and imprisoned for drug use because, as a result of greater rates of poverty in communities of color, they are more likely to be in contact with government agencies where their drug use can be detected. While white pregnant women are slightly *more* likely to engage in substance abuse than black women, public health facilities and private doctors are more likely to report black women than white women to criminal justice authorities (Maher 1990; Roberts 1997, 175). Meanwhile, pregnant women who would like treatment for their addiction can seldom get it because treatment centers do not meet the needs of pregnant women. One study found that two-thirds of drug treatment centers would not treat pregnant women (Roberts 1997, 189). Furthermore, the criminalization approach is more likely to drive pregnant women who are substance abusers from seeking prenatal or other forms of health care for fear of being reported to the authorities (Roberts 1997, 190). Roberts critiques communities of color for often supporting the criminalization of women of color who have addictions and for failing to understand this criminalization as another strategy of white supremacy that blames women for the effects of poverty and racism. Lisa Maher (1990) and Rickie Solinger (2001, 148) note that a simple choice perspective is not effective for addressing this problem because certain women become marked as women who make "bad choices" and hence deserve imprisonment.

Similarly, Elizabeth Cook-Lynn (1998) argues in "The Big Pipe Case" that at the same time Native peoples were rallying around Leonard Peltier, no one stood beside Marie Big Pipe when she was incarcerated on a felony charge of "assault with intent to commit serious bodily harm" because she breast-fed her child while under the influence of alcohol. She was denied services to treat her substance abuse problem and access to abortion services when she became pregnant. But not only did her community not support her, it supported her incarceration. Cook-Lynn argues that in doing so, the community supported the encroachment of U.S. federal jurisdiction on tribal lands for an issue that would normally be under tribal jurisdiction (1998, 110–25). Cook-Lynn recounts how this demonization of Native women was assisted by the publication of

Michael Dorris's (1989) *The Broken Cord*, which narrates his adoption of a Native child who suffered from fetal alcohol syndrome. While this book has been crucial in sensitizing many communities to the realities of fetal alcohol syndrome, it also portrays the mother of the child unsympathetically and advocates repressive legislative solutions targeted against women substance abusers. Thus, within Native communities, the growing demonization of Native women substance abusers has prompted tribes to collude with the federal government in whittling away their own sovereignty.

In the larger society, Barbara Harris started an organization called CRACK (Children Requiring a Caring Kommunity) in Anaheim, California, which gives women $200 to have sterilizations. Their mission is to "'save our welfare system' and the world from the exorbitant cost to the taxpayer for each 'drug addicted birth' by offering 'effective preventive measures to reduce the tragedy of numerous drug-affected pregnancies'" (Kigvamasud'Vashi 2001). Some of CRACK's initial billboards read, "Don't let a pregnancy ruin your drug habit" (Kigvamasud'Vashi 2001). The organization has since opened chapters in several cities around the country, and has changed its name to Positive Prevention to present a less inflammatory image. Nonetheless, its basic message is the same—that poor women who are substance abusers are the cause of social ills and that the conditions that give rise to poor women becoming substance abusers do not need to be addressed.

Unfortunately, as both Roberts (1997) and Cook-Lynn (1998) point out, even communities of color, including those who identify as both pro-life and pro-choice, have supported the criminalization of women of color who have addiction issues. The reason they support this strategy is because they focus on what they perceive to be the moral culpability of women of color for not protecting the life of their children. If we adopt an anti-prison perspective, however, it becomes clear that even on the terms of moral culpability (which I am not defending) it does not follow that the criminal justice approach is the appropriate way to address this social concern.[2] In fact, criminal justice responses to unwanted pregnancies and/or pregnant women who have addiction issues demonstrate an inherent contradiction in the pro-life position. Many pro-life organizations have been ardent opponents of population control programs and policies—advocating against the promotion of dangerous contraceptives or the promotion of sterilization in third-world countries. Yet, their

position depends on the prison industrial complex that is an institution of population control for communities of color in the United States.

Meanwhile, many pro-choice organizations, such as Planned Parenthood, have supported financial incentives for poor and criminalized women to be sterilized or to take long-acting hormonal contraceptives (Saletan 2003).[3] As I will discuss later, part of this political inconsistency is inherent in the articulation of the pro-choice position. But another reason is that many in the pro-choice camp have also not questioned criminalization as the appropriate response for addressing reproductive health concerns. The pro-choice camp may differ from pro-life groups regarding which acts should be criminalized, but it does not necessarily question the criminalization regime itself.

THE PRO-CHOICE POSITION AND CAPITALISM

The pro-choice camp claims a position that offers more choices for women making decisions about their reproductive lives. A variety of scholars and activists have critiqued the choice paradigm because it rests on essentially individualist, consumerist notions of "free" choice that do not take into consideration all the social, economic, and political conditions that frame the so-called choices that women are forced to make (Patchesky 1990; Smith 1999; Solinger 2001). Solinger further contends that in the 1960s and 1970s, abortion rights advocates initially used the term "rights" rather than choice; rights are understood as those benefits owed to all those who are human regardless of access to special resources. By contrast, argues Solinger, the concept of choice is connected to possession of resources, thus creating a hierarchy among women based on who is capable of making legitimate choices (2001, 6). Consequently, since under a capitalist system, those with resources are granted more choices, it is not inconsistent to withdraw reproductive rights choices from poor women through legislation such as the Hyde Amendment (which restricts federal funding for abortion) or family caps for TANF (Temporary Assistance for Needy Families) recipients.[4] Solinger's argument can be demonstrated in the writings of Planned Parenthood. In 1960, Planned Parenthood commissioned a study which concluded that poor and working-class families lacked the rationality to do family planning, and that this lack of "rationality and early family planning as middle-class couples" was "embodied in the particular personalities, world views, and ways of life" of the poor themselves (Rainwater 1960, 5, 167). As Solinger states:

"Choice" also became a symbol of middle-class women's arrival as independent consumers. Middle-class women could afford to choose. They had earned the right to choose motherhood, if they liked. According to many Americans, however, when choice was associated with poor women, it became a symbol of illegitimacy. Poor women had not earned the right to choose. (2001, 199–200)

What Solinger's analysis suggests is that, ironically, while the pro-choice camp contends that the pro-life position diminishes the rights of women in favor of "fetal" rights; the pro-choice position actually does not ascribe inherent rights to women either. Rather, women are viewed as having reproductive choices if they can afford them or if they are deemed legitimate choice-makers.

William Saletan's (1998) history of the evolution of the pro-choice paradigm illustrates the extent to which this paradigm is a conservative one. Saletan contends that pro-choice strategists, generally affiliated with National Abortion and Reproductive Rights Action League (NARAL), intentionally rejected a rights-based framework in favor of one that focused on privacy from *big government*. That is, government should not intervene in the woman's right to decide if she wants to have children. This approach appealed to those with libertarian sensibilities who otherwise might have had no sympathy with feminist causes. The impact of this strategy was that it enabled the pro-choice side to keep *Roe v. Wade* intact—but only in the most narrow sense. This strategy undermined any attempt to achieve a broader pro-choice agenda because the strategy could be used against a broader agenda. For instance, the argument that government should not be involved in reproductive rights decisions could also be used by pro-life advocates against federal funding for abortions (Saletan 2003). Consequently, Saletan argues, "Liberals have not won the struggle for abortion rights. Conservatives have" (1998, 114).

Furthermore, this narrow approach has contributed to some pro-choice organizations, such as Planned Parenthood and NARAL, often developing strategies that marginalize women of color. Both supported the Freedom of Choice Act in the early 1990s that retained the Hyde Amendment (Saletan 2003). The

Hyde Amendment, besides discriminating against poor women by denying federal funding for abortion services, discriminates against American Indian women who largely obtain healthcare through Indian Health Services, a federal agency. One of NARAL's petitions stated: "The Freedom of Choice Act (FOCA) will secure the original vision of *Roe v. Wade*, giving *all* women reproductive freedom and securing that right for future generations [emphasis mine]."[5] Apparently, poor women and indigenous women do not qualify as "women."[6]

Building on this analysis, I would argue that while there is certainly a sustained critique of the choice paradigm, particularly among women of color reproductive rights groups, the choice paradigm continues to govern much of the policies of mainstream groups in a manner that sustains the marginalization of women of color, poor women, and women with disabilities. One example is the extent to which pro-choice advocates narrow their advocacy around legislation that affects the one choice of whether or not to have an abortion without addressing all the conditions that gave rise to a woman having to make this decision in the first place. Consequently, politicians, such as former President Bill Clinton, will be heralded as "pro-choice" as long as they do not support legislative restrictions on abortion regardless of their stance on other issues that may equally impact the reproductive choices women make. Clinton's approval of federal welfare reform that places poor women in the position of possibly being forced to have an abortion because of cuts in social services, while often critiqued, is not viewed as an "anti-choice" position. On Planned Parenthood's and NARAL's websites (www.plannedparenthood.org; www.naral.org) there is generally no mention of welfare policies in these organizations' pro-choice legislation alerts.

A consequence of the choice paradigm is that its advocates frequently take positions that are oppressive to women from marginalized communities. For instance, this paradigm often makes it difficult to develop nuanced positions on the use of abortion when the fetus is determined to have abnormalities. Focusing solely on the woman's choice to have or not have the child does not address the larger context of a society that sees children with disabilities as having worthless lives and that provides inadequate resources to women who may otherwise want to have them. As Martha Saxton notes: "Our society profoundly limits the 'choice' to love and care for a baby with a disability" (1998, 375). If our response to disability is to simply facilitate the process by which women can abort fetuses that may have disabilities, we never actually focus on changing economic policies that make raising children with disabilities difficult. Rashmi Luthra (1993) notes, by contrast, that reproductive advocates from other countries such as India, who do not operate from this same choice paradigm, are often able to develop more complicated political positions on issues such as this one.

Another example is the difficulty pro-choice groups have in maintaining a critical perspective on dangerous or potentially dangerous contraceptives, arguing that women should have the "choice" of contraceptives. Many scholars and activists have documented the dubious safety record of Norplant and Depo-Provera, two long-acting hormonal contraceptives (Krust and Assetoyer 1993; Masterson and Guthrie 1986; Roberts 1997; Smith 2001). In fact, lawsuits against Norplant have forced an end to its distribution (although Norplant that remains on the shelves can be sold to women). In 1978, the FDA denied approval for Depo-Provera on the grounds that: (1) dog studies confirmed an elevated rate of breast cancer; (2) there appeared to be an increased risk of birth defects in human fetuses exposed to the drug; and (3) there was no pressing need shown for use of the drug as a contraceptive (Masterson and Guthrie 1986). In 1987, the FDA changed its regulations and began to require cancer testing in rats and mice instead of dogs and monkeys; Depo-Provera did not cause cancer in these animals, but major concerns regarding its safety persist (Feminist Women's Health Centers 1997). Also problematic is the manner in which these contraceptives are frequently promoted in communities of color and often without informed consent (Krust and Assetoyer 1993; Masterson and Guthrie 1986; Smith 2001).[7] Yet none of the mainstream pro-choice organizations have ever seriously taken a position on the issue of informed consent as part of their agenda.[8] Indeed, Gloria Feldt, president of Planned Parenthood, equates opposition to Norplant and Depo-Provera as opposition to "choice" in her book *The War on Choice* (Feldt 2004, 34, 37). Planned Parenthood and NARAL opposed restrictions against sterilization abuse, despite the thousands of women of color who were being sterilized without their consent, because they saw such policies as interfering with a woman's "right to choose" (Nelson 2003, 144; Patchesky 1990, 8).

Particularly disturbing has been some of the support given by these organizations to the Center for Research on Population and Security, headed by Stephen Mumford and Elton Kessel, which distributes globally a form of sterilization, Quinacrine. Quinacrine is a drug that is used to treat malaria. It is inserted into the uterus where it dissolves, causing the fallopian tubes to scar, rendering the woman irreversibly sterile. Family Health International conducted four *in vitro* studies and found Quinacrine to be mutagenic in three of them (Controversy over Sterilization Pellet 1994; Norsigian 1996). It, as well as the World Health Organization, recommended against further trials for female sterilization, and no regulatory body supports Quinacrine. However, the North Carolina–based Center for Research on Population and Security has circumvented these bodies through private funding from such organizations as the Turner Foundation and Leland Fykes organization (which incidentally funds pro-choice *and* anti-immigrant groups). The Center for Research on Population and Security has been distributing Quinacrine for free to researchers and government health agencies. There are field trials in eleven countries, with more than 70,000 women sterilized. In Vietnam, a hundred female rubber plant workers were given routine pelvic exams during which the doctor inserted the Quinacrine without their consent. Thus far, the side effects linked to Quinacrine include ectopic pregnancy, puncturing of the uterus during insertion, pelvic inflammatory disease, and severe abdominal pains. Other possible concerns include heart and liver damage and exacerbation of pre-existing viral conditions. In one of the trials in Vietnam, a large number of cases that had serious side effects were excluded from the data (Controversy over Sterilization Pellet 1994; Norsigian 1996).

Despite the threat to reproductive justice that this group represents, Feminist Majority Foundation featured the Center for Research on Population and Security at its 1996 Feminist Expo because, I was informed by the organizers, they promoted choice for women. Then in 1999, Planned Parenthood almost agreed to sponsor a Quinacrine trial in the United States until outside pressure forced it to change its position (Committee on Women, Population and the Environment 1999). A prevalent ideology within the mainstream pro-choice movement is that women should have the choice to use whatever contraception they want. This position does not consider: (1) that a choice among dangerous contraceptives is not much of a choice; (2) the millions of dollars pharmaceutical companies and the medical industry have to promote certain contraceptives, compared to the few resources women's advocacy groups have to provide alternative information on these same contraceptives; and (3) the social, political, and economic conditions in which women may find themselves are such that using dangerous contraceptives may be the best of even worse options.

One reason that such groups have not taken a position on informed consent in the case of potentially dangerous contraceptives is due to their investment in population control. As Betsy Hartmann (1995) has argued, while contraceptives are often articulated as an issue of choice for white women in the first world, they are articulated as an instrument of population control for women of color and women in the third world (Hartmann 1995). The historical origins of Planned Parenthood are inextricably tied to the eugenics movement. Its founder, Margaret Sanger, increasingly collaborated with eugenics organizations during her career and framed the need for birth control in terms of the need to reduce the number of those in the "lower classes" (Roberts 1997, 73). In a study commissioned in 1960, Planned Parenthood concluded that poor people "have too many children" (Rainwater 1960, 2); yet something must be done to stop this trend in order to "disarm the population bomb" (Rainwater 1960, 178). Today, Planned Parenthood is particularly implicated in this movement as can be seen clearly by the groups it lists as allies on its website (www.plannedparenthood. org): Population Action International, the Population Institute, Zero Population Growth, and the Population Council. A central campaign of Planned Parenthood is to restore U.S. funding to the United Nations Population Fund. In addition it asserts its commitment to addressing *rapid population growth* on this same website. I will not repeat the problematic analysis, critiqued elsewhere, of this population paradigm that essentially blames third-world women for poverty, war, environmental damage, and social unrest, without looking at the root causes of all these phenomena (including population growth)—colonialism, corporate policies, militarism, and economic disparities between poor and rich countries (Bandarage 1997; Hartmann 1995; Silliman and King 1999).

As Hartmann (1995) documents, the United Nations Population Fund has long been involved in coercive contraceptive policies throughout the world. The Population Council produced Norplant and assisted in Norplant trials in Bangladesh and other countries without the informed consent of the trial participants (Hartmann 1995). In fact, trial administrators often refused to remove Norplant when requested (Cadbury 1995). All of these population organizations intersect to promote generally long-acting hormonal contraceptives of dubious safety around the world (Hartmann 1995). Of course, Planned Parenthood provides valuable family planning resources to women around the world as well, but it does so through a population framework that inevitably shifts the focus from family planning as a right in and of itself to family planning as an instrument of population control. While population control advocates, such as Planned Parenthood, are increasingly more sophisticated in their rhetoric and often talk about ensuring social, political, and economic opportunity, the *population* focus of this model still results in its advocates working to reduce population rather than to provide social, political, and economic opportunity.

Another unfortunate consequence of uncritically adopting the choice paradigm is the tendency of reproductive rights advocates to make simplistic analyses of who our political friends and enemies are in the area of reproductive rights. That is, all those who call themselves pro-choice are our political allies while all those who call themselves pro-life are our political enemies. An example of this rhetoric is Gloria Feldt's description of anyone who is pro-life as a "right-wing extremist" (Feldt 2004, 5). As I have argued elsewhere, this simplistic analysis of who is politically progressive versus conservative does not actually do justice to the complex political positions people inhabit (Smith 2002). As a result, we often engage uncritically in coalitions with groups that, as anti-violence activist Beth Richie states, "do not pay us back" (2000, 31). Meanwhile, we often lose opportunities to work with people with whom we may have sharp disagreements, but who may, with different political framings and organizing strategies, shift their positions.

To illustrate: Planned Parenthood is often championed as an organization that supports women's rights to choose with whom women of color should ally. Yet, as discussed previously, its roots are in the eugenics movement and today it is heavily invested in the population establishment. It continues to support population control policies in the third world, it almost supported the development of Quinacrine in the United States, and it opposed strengthening sterilization regulations that would protect women of color. Meanwhile, the North Baton Rouge Women's Help Center in Louisiana is a crisis pregnancy center that articulates its pro-life position from an anti-racist perspective. It argues that Planned Parenthood has advocated population control, particularly in communities of color. It critiques the Black Church Initiative for the Religious Coalition for Reproductive Choice for contending that charges of racism against Sanger are *scare tactics* (Blunt 2003, 22). It also attempts to provide its services from a holistic perspective—it provides educational and vocational training, GED classes, literacy programs, primary health care and pregnancy services, and child placement services. Its position: "We cannot encourage women to have babies and then continue their dependency on the system. We can't leave them without the resources to care for their children and then say, 'Praise the Lord, we saved a baby'" (Blunt 2003, 23).

It would seem that while the two organizations support some positions that are beneficial to women of color, they both equally support positions that are detrimental to them. If we are truly committed to reproductive justice, why should we presume that we should necessarily work with Planned Parenthood and reject the Women's Help Center? Why would we not instead position ourselves independently from both of these approaches and work to shift their positions to a stance that is truly liberatory for all women?

BEYOND PRO-LIFE VERSUS PRO-CHOICE

To develop an independent position, it is necessary to reject the pro-life versus pro-choice model for understanding reproductive justice. Many reproductive advocates have attempted to expand the definitions of either pro-life or pro-choice depending on which side of this divide they may rest. Unfortunately, they are trying to expand concepts that are inherently designed to exclude the experiences of most women, especially poor women, women of color, indigenous women, and women with disabilities.

If we critically assess the assumptions behind both positions, it is clear that these camps are more similar than they are different. As I have argued, they both assume a criminal justice regime for adjudicating reproductive issues (although they may differ as to which women should be subjected to this regime). Neither position endows women with inherent rights to their body—the pro-life position pits fetal rights against women's rights whereas the pro-choice position argues that women should have freedom to make choices rather than possess inherent rights to their bodies regardless of their class standing. They both support positions that reinforce racial and gender

hierarchies that marginalize women of color. The pro-life position supports a criminalization approach that depends on a racist political system that will necessarily impact poor women and women of color who are less likely to have alternative strategies for addressing unwanted pregnancies. Meanwhile, the pro-choice position often supports population control policies and the development of dangerous contraceptives that are generally targeted toward communities of color. And both positions do not question the capitalist system—they focus solely on the decision of whether or not a woman should have an abortion without addressing the economic, political, and social conditions that put women in this position in the first place.

Consequently, it is critical that reproductive advocates develop a framework that does not rest on the pro-choice versus pro-life framework. Such a strategy would enable us to fight for reproductive justice as a part of a larger social justice strategy. It would also free us to think more creatively about who we could work in coalition with while simultaneously allowing us to hold those who claim to be our allies more accountable for the positions they take. To be successful in this venture, however, it is not sufficient to simply articulate a women of color reproductive justice agenda—we must focus on developing a nationally coordinated women of color movement. While there are many women of color reproductive organizations, relatively few actually focus on bringing new women of color into the movement and training them to organize on their own behalf. And to the extent that these groups do exist, they are not generally coordinated as national mobilization efforts. Rather, national work is generally done on an advocacy level with heads of women of color organizations advocating for policy changes, but often working without a solid base to back their demands (Silliman et al. 2005/in press).

Consequently, women of color organizations are not always in a strong position to negotiate with power brokers and mainstream pro-choice organizations or to hold them accountable. As an example, many women of color groups mobilized to attend the 2004 March for Women's Lives in Washington, D.C., in order to expand the focus of the march from a narrow pro-choice abortion rights agenda to a broad-based reproductive rights agenda. While this broader agenda was reflected in the march, it became co-opted by the pro-choice paradigm in the media coverage of the event. My survey of the major newspaper coverage of the march indicates that virtually no newspaper described it as anything other than a pro-choice or abortion rights march.[9] To quote New Orleans health activist Barbara Major, "When you go to power without a base, your demand becomes a request" (2003). Base-building work, on which many women of color organizations are beginning to focus, is very slow work that may not show results for a long time. After all, the base-building of the Christian Right did not become publicly visible for 50 years (Diamond 1989). Perhaps one day, we will have a march for women's lives in which the main issues addressed and reported will include: (1) repealing the Hyde Amendment; (2) stopping the promotion of dangerous contraceptives; (3) decriminalizing women who are pregnant and who have addictions; and (4) ending welfare policies that punish women, in addition to other issues that speak to the intersections of gender, race, and class in reproductive rights policies.

At a meeting of the United Council of Tribes in Chicago, representatives from the Chicago Pro-Choice Alliance informed us that we should join the struggle to keep abortion legal or else we would lose our reproductive rights. A woman in the audience responded, "Who cares about reproductive rights; we don't have any rights, period." What her response suggests is that a reproductive justice agenda must make the dismantling of capitalism, white supremacy, and colonialism *central* to its agenda, and not just as principles added to organizations' promotional material designed to appeal to women of color, with no budget to support making these principles a reality. We must reject single-issue, pro-choice politics of the mainstream reproductive rights movement as an agenda that not only does not serve women of color, but actually promotes the structures of oppression which keep women of color from having real choices or healthy lives.

NOTES

1. This block quote is a compilation of Colson quotes from three different sources (Colson 1983, 15; Fager 1982, 23; Forbes 1982, 34).

2. As Roberts (1997) and Maher (1990) note, addiction is itself a result of social and political conditions, such as racism and poverty, which the U.S. government does not take steps to alleviate, and then blames women who are victimized by these conditions. Furthermore, the government provides no resources for pregnant women to end their addictions; it simply penalizes them for continuing a pregnancy. Thus assigning moral culpability primarily to pregnant women with addiction problems is a dubious prospect.

3. Additionally, several reproductive rights advocates at the historic *SisterSong* Conference on Women of Color and Reproductive Justice held in Atlanta, November 13–16, 2003, noted that some local Planned Parenthood agencies were currently offering financial incentives for women who are addicted to accept long-acting contraceptives or were distributing literature from CRACK. This policy was not uniform among Planned Parenthood chapters, however, and many Planned Parenthood chapters condemn this practice.

4. For further analysis of how welfare reform marks poor women and women of color as women who make "bad choices" and hence should have these choices restricted through marriage promotion, family caps (or cuts in payments if recipients have additional children), and incentives to use long-acting hormonal contraceptives, see Mink 1999.

5. The petition can be found on the Web at http://www .wanaral.org/s01takeaction/200307101.shtml

6. During this period, I served on the board of Illinois National Abortion and Reproductive Rights Action League (NARAL), which was constituted primarily of women of color. Illinois NARAL broke with National NARAL in opposing the Freedom of Choice Act (FOCA). Despite many heated discussions with NARAL president Kate Michelman, she refused to consider the perspective of women of color on this issue.

7. I was a co-organizer of a reproductive rights conference in Chicago in 1992. There, hotline workers from Chicago Planned Parenthood reported that they were told to tell women seeking contraception that Norplant had no side effects. In 2000, women from a class I was teaching at University of California, Santa Cruz, informed the class that when they asked Planned Parenthood workers what were the side effects of Depo-Provera, the workers said that they were not allowed to tell them the side effects because they were supposed to promote Depo-Provera. Similar problems in other Planned Parenthood offices were reported at the previously mentioned *SisterSong* conference. These problems around informed consent are not necessarily a national Planned Parenthood policy or uniform across all Planned Parenthood agencies.

8. In 1994 when NARAL changed its name from the National Association for the Repeal of Abortion Laws to the National Abortion and Reproductive Rights Action League, it held a strategy session for its state chapters which I attended. Michelman and her associates claimed that this name change was reflective of NARAL's interest in expanding its agenda to new communities, and informed consent around contraceptives would be included in this expanded agenda. I asked how much of NARAL's budget was going to be allocated to this new agenda. Their reply: none. They were going to release a report on these new issues, but they were going to work only on the issues NARAL had addressed traditionally.

9. Newspapers surveyed which focused solely on abortion rights include *The New York Times* (Toner 2004); *Connecticut Post* ("Abortion-Rights Marchers Crowd D.C." 2004); *New York Newsday* (Phelps 2004); *Syracuse Post Standard* (Gadoua 2004); *The Record* (Varoqua 2004); *The Baltimore Sun* (Gibson 2004); *The Commercial Appeal* (Wolfe 2004); *Richmond Times Dispatch* (Smith 2004); *Marin Independent Journal* ("Marchers Say Bush Policies Harm Women" 2004); *Salt Lake Tribune* (Stephenson 2004); *The Capital Times* (Segars 2004); *Dayton Daily News* (Dart 2004); *Milwaukee Journal Sentinel* (Madigan 2004); *Cleveland Plains Dealer* (Diemer 2004); *Minneapolis Star Tribune* (O'Rourke 2004); *Chicago Daily Herald* (Ryan 2004); *Chicago Sun-Times* (Sweeney 2004); *The Columbus Dispatch* (Riskind 2004); *San Francisco Chronicle* (Marinucci 2004); and *Dayton Daily News* (Wynn 2004). The coverage of "other" issues in a few papers was limited to "The concerns they voiced extended beyond the issues of abortion to health care access, AIDS prevention, birth control and civil rights" in *San Francisco Chronicle* (Marinucci 2004); "Another group flashed signs calling for the government to recognize same-sex marriage" in the *Houston Chronicle* (Black 2004); "Various trends and vendors on the Mall also promoted other political causes, including welfare, the Falun Gong movement in China, homosexual 'marriage,' the socialist movement, environmentalism, and striking Utah coal miners" in the *Atlanta Journal-Constitution* (Dart and Pickel 2004); "'This morning I was saying that I was mainly here for abortion,' said Gresh, reflecting on the march. 'But now, going through this, I realize that there are so many issues. Equal pay is a big issue. And globalization, and women's rights around the world'" in the *Pittsburgh Post-Gazette* (Belser 2004).

REFERENCES

"Abortion-Rights Marchers Crowd D.C." 2004. *Connecticut Post,* April 26.

Bandarage, Asoka. 1997. *Women, Population and Global Crisis.* London: Zed.

Belser, Ann. 2004. "Local Marchers Have Many Issues." *Pittsburgh Post-Gazette,* April 26, A4.

Black, Joe. 2004. "Marchers Rally for Abortion Rights." *Houston Chronicle,* April 26, A1.

Blunt, Sheryl. 2003. "Saving Black Babies." *Christianity Today* 47 (February):21–23.

Box, Steve, and Chris Hale. 1982. "Economic Crisis and the Rising Prisoner Population in England and Wales." *Crime and Social Justice* 17:20–35.

Bushnell, Jeanette. 2004. Interview with author, 21 May.

Committee on Women, Population and the Environment. 1999. Internal correspondence.

Controversy over Sterilization Pellet. 1994. *Political Environments* 1 (Spring):9.

Cook-Lynn, Elizabeth. 1998. *Why I Can't Read Wallace Stegner and Other Essays.* Madison: University of Wisconsin Press.

Crum, Gary, and Thelma McCormack. 1992. *Abortion: Pro-Choice or Pro-Life?* Washington, DC: American University Press.

Currie, Elliott. 1998. *Crime and Punishment in America.* New York: Metropolitan Books.

Dart, Bob. 2004. "Abortion-Rights Backers March." *Dayton Daily News,* April 26, A1.

Dart, Bob, and Mary Lou Pickel. 2004. "Abortion Rights Supporters March." *Atlanta Journal-Constitution,* April 26, 1A.

Davis, Angela. 2003. *Are Prisons Obsolete?* New York: Seven Stories Press.

Diamond, Sara. 1989. *Spiritual Warfare.* Boston: South End Press.

Diemer, Tom. 2004. "Thousands Rally for Choice: 500,000 to 800,000 March in D.C. in Support of Abortion Rights." *Cleveland Plains Dealer,* April 26, A1.

Donziger, Steven. 1996. *The Real War on Crime.* New York: HarperCollins.

Dorris, Michael. 1989. *The Broken Cord.* New York: Harper & Row.

Feldt, Gloria. 2004. *The War on Choice.* New York: Bantam Books.

Feminist Women's Health Centers. 1997. "Depo-Provera (The Shot)," http://www.fwhc.org/bcdepo.html.

Gadoua, Renee. 2004. "A Woman Should Decide." *Post-Standard,* April 26, B1.

Gibson, Gail. 2004. "Thousands Rally for Abortion Rights." *Baltimore Sun,* April 26, 1A.

Hartmann, Betsy. 1995. *Reproductive Rights and Wrongs: The Global Politics of Population Control.* Boston: South End Press.

Jankovic, Ivan. 1977. "Labour Market and Imprisonment." *Crime and Social Justice* 8:17–31.

Kigvamasud'Vashi, Theryn. 2001. "Fact Sheet on Positive Prevention/CRACK (Children Requiring a Caring Kommunity)." Seattle: Communities Against Rape and Abuse.

Krust, Lin, and Charon Assetoyer. 1993. "A Study of the Use of Depo-Provera and Norplant by the Indian Health Services." Lake Andes: South Dakota: Native American Women's Health Education Resource Center.

Luthra, Rashmi. 1993. "Toward a Reconceptualization of 'Choice': Challenges at the Margins." *Feminist Issues* 13 (Spring):41–54.

Madigan, Erin. 2004. "Hundreds of Thousands March for Abortion Rights." *Milwaukee Journal Sentinel,* April 26, 3A.

Maher, Lisa. 1990. "Criminalizing Pregnancy—The Downside of a Kinder, Gentler Nation?" *Social Justice* 17 (Fall): 111–35.

Major, Barbara. 2003. Keynote Address, National Women's Studies Association National Conference. New Orleans, June.

"Marchers Say Bush Policies Harm Women." 2004. *Marin Independent Journal,* April 26, Nation/World.

Marinucci, Carla. 2004. "Hundreds of Thousands in D.C. Pledge to Take Fight to Polls." *San Francisco Chronicle,* April 26, A1.

Masterson, Mike, and Patricia Guthrie. 1986. "Taking the Shot." *Arizona Republic,* n.p.

Mauer, Marc. 1999. *Race to Incarcerate.* New York: New Press/ W.W. Norton.

Mink, Gendolyn, ed. 1999. *Whose Welfare?* Ithaca: Cornell University Press.

Nelson, Jennifer. 2003. *Women of Color and the Reproductive Rights Movement.* New York: New York University Press.

Norsigian, Judy. 1996. "Quinacrine Update." *Political Environments* 3 (Spring):26–27.

O'Rourke, Lawrence. 2004. "Thousands Rally for Abortion Rights." *Star Tribune,* April 26, 1A.

Patchesky, Rosalind. 1990. *Abortion and Woman's Choice.* Boston: Northeastern University Press.

Phelps, Timothy. 2004. "Demonstration in D.C." *New York Newsday,* April 26, A05.

Prison Activist Resource Center. 2004. http://www .prisonactivist.org.

Rainwater, Lee. 1960. *And the Poor Get Children.* Chicago: Quadrangle Books.

Richie, Beth. 2000. "Plenary Presentation." In *The Color of Violence: Violence Against Women of Color,* ed. Incite! Women of Color Against Violence, 124. University of California, Santa Cruz: Incite! Women of Color Against Violence.

Riskind, Jonathan. 2004. "Supporters of Abortion Rights Seek Forefront." *The Columbus Dispatch,* April 25, 1A.

Roberts, Dorothy. 1997. *Killing the Black Body.* New York: Pantheon Books.

Ryan, Joseph. 2004. "Abortion Rights Supporters Jump in to Rejuvenate Cause." *Chicago Daily Herald,* April 26, 15.

Saletan, William. 2003. *Bearing Right.* Berkeley: University of California Press.

———. 1998. "Electoral Politics and Abortion." In *The Abortion Wars,* ed. Rickie Solinger, 111–23. Berkeley: University of California Press.

Saxton, Martha. 1998. "Disability Rights." In *The Abortion Wars,* ed. Rickie Solinger, 374–93. Berkeley: University of California Press.

Segars, Melissa. 2004. "Rally For Women's Rights." *The Capital Times,* April 26, 1A.

Silliman, Jael, Loretta Ross, Marlene Gerber Fried, and Elena Gutierrez. 2005/in press. *Undivided Rights.* Boston: South End Press.

Silliman, Jael, and Ynestra King, eds. 1999. *Dangerous Intersections: Feminist Perspectives on Population, Environment and Development.* Boston: South End Press.

Smith, Andrea. 2005/in press. "Domestic Violence, the State, and Social Change." In *Domestic Violence at the Margins: A Reader at the Intersections of Race, Class, and Gender,* ed. Natalie Sokoloff. New Brunswick: Rutgers University Press.

———. 2002. "Bible, Gender and Nationalism in American Indian and Christian Right Activism." Santa Cruz: University of California.

———. 2001. "'Better Dead Than Pregnant' The Colonization of Native Women's Health." In *Policing the National Body,* ed. Anannya Bhattacharjee and Jael Silliman, 123–46. Boston: South End Press.

Smith, Justine. 1999. "Native Sovereignty and Social Justice: Moving Toward an Inclusive Social Justice Framework." In *Dangerous Intersections: Feminist Perspectives on Population, Environment and Development,* ed. Jael Silliman and Ynestra King, 202–13. Boston: South End Press.

Smith, Tammie. 2004. "Marchers Call for 'A Choice' About Reproductive Rights." *Richmond Times Dispatch,* April 26, A1.

Solinger, Rickie. 2001. *Beggers and Choosers.* New York: Hill and Wang.

Stephenson, Kathy. 2004. "Utahns Take Part in D.C. and at Home." *Salt Lake Tribune,* April 26, A6.

Sweeney, Annie. 2004. "Chicagoans Head to D.C. for Pro-Choice March." *Chicago Sun-Times,* April 26, 18.

Toner, Robin. 2004. "Abortion Rights Marches Vow to Fight Another Bush Term." *The New York Times,* April 26, A1.

Varoqua, Eman. 2004. "N.J. Supporters Form Large Column for Rights." *The Record,* April 26, A01.

Walker, Samuel. 1998. *Sense and Nonsense About Crime.* Belmont: Wadsworth.

Wolfe, Elizabeth. 2004. "Rights March Packs Mall." *The Commercial Appeal,* April 26, A4.

Wynn, Kelli. 2004. "Hundreds Go to D.C. for March Today." *Dayton Daily News,* April 25, B1.

Welcome to Cancerland

A mammogram leads to a cult of pink kitsch.

I was thinking of it as one of those drive-by mammograms, one stop in a series of mundane missions including post office, supermarket, and gym, but I began to lose my nerve in the changing room, and not only because of the kinky necessity of baring my breasts and affixing tiny X-ray opaque stars to the tip of each nipple. I had been in this place only four months earlier, but that visit was just part of the routine cancer surveillance all good citizens of HMOs or health plans are expected to submit to once they reach the age of fifty, and I hadn't really been paying attention then. The results of that earlier session had aroused some "concern" on the part of the radiologist and her confederate, the gynecologist, so I am back now in the role of a suspect, eager to clear my name, alert to medical missteps and unfair allegations. But the changing room, really just a closet off the stark windowless space that houses the mammogram machine, contains something far worse, I notice for the first time now—an assumption about who I am, where I am going, and what I will need when I get there. Almost all of the eye-level space has been filled with photocopied bits of cuteness and sentimentality: pink ribbons, a cartoon about a woman with iatrogenically flattened breasts, an "Ode to a Mammogram," a list of the "Top Ten Things Only Women Understand" ("Fat Clothes" and "Eyelash Curlers" among them), and, inescapably, right next to the door, the poem "I Said a Prayer for You Today," illustrated with pink roses.

It goes on and on, this mother of all mammograms, cutting into gym time, dinnertime, and lifetime generally. Sometimes the machine doesn't work, and I get squished into position to no purpose at all. More often, the X ray is successful but apparently alarming to the invisible radiologist, off in some remote office, who calls the shots and never has the courtesy to show her face with an apology or an explanation. I try pleading with the technician: I have no known risk factors, no breast cancer in the family, had my babies relatively young and nursed them both. I eat right, drink sparingly, work out, and doesn't that count for something? But she just gets this tight little professional smile on her face, either out of guilt for the torture she's inflicting or because she already knows something that I am going to be sorry to find out for myself. For an hour and a half the procedure is repeated: the squishing, the snapshot, the technician bustling off to consult the radiologist and returning with a demand for new angles and more definitive images. In the intervals while she's off with the doctor I read the *New York Times* right down to the personally irrelevant sections like theater and real estate, eschewing the stack of women's magazines provided for me, much as I ordinarily enjoy a quick read about sweat-proof eyeliners and "fabulous sex tonight," because I have picked up this warning vibe in the changing room, which, in my increasingly anxious state, translates into: femininity is death. Finally there is nothing left to read but one of the free local weekly newspapers, where I find, buried deep in the classifieds, something even more unsettling than the growing prospect of major disease—a classified ad for a "breast cancer teddy bear" with a pink ribbon stitched to its chest.

Yes, atheists pray in their foxholes—in this case, with a yearning new to me and sharp as lust, for a clean and honorable death by shark bite, lightning strike, sniper fire, car crash. Let me be hacked to death by a madman, is my silent supplication—anything but suffocation by the pink sticky sentiment embodied in that bear and oozing from the walls of the changing room.

My official induction into breast cancer comes about ten days later with the biopsy, which, for reasons I cannot ferret out of the surgeon, has to be a surgical one, performed on an outpatient basis but under general anesthesia, from which I awake to find him standing perpendicular to me, at the far end of the gurney, down near my feet, stating gravely, "Unfortunately, there is a cancer." It takes me all the rest of that drug-addled day to decide that the most heinous thing about that sentence is not the presence of cancer but the absence of me—for I, Barbara, do not enter into it even as a location, a geographical reference point. Where I once was—not a commanding presence perhaps but nonetheless a standard assemblage of flesh and words and gesture—"there is a cancer." I have been replaced by it, is the surgeon's implication. This is what I am now, medically speaking. . . .

After a visit to my pathologist, my biological curiosity drops to a lifetime nadir. I know women who followed up their diagnoses with weeks or months of self-study, mastering their options, interviewing doctor after doctor, assessing the damage to be expected from the available treatments. But I can tell from a few hours of investigation that the career of a breast-cancer patient has been pretty well mapped out in advance for me: You may get to negotiate the choice between lumpectomy and mastectomy, but lumpectomy is commonly followed by weeks of radiation, and in either case if the lymph nodes turn out, upon dissection, to be invaded—or "involved," as it's less threateningly put—you're doomed to chemotherapy, meaning baldness, nausea, mouth sores, immunosuppression, and possible anemia. These interventions do not constitute a "cure" or anything close, which is why the death rate from breast cancer has changed very little since the 1930s, when mastectomy was the only treatment available. Chemotherapy, which became a routine part of breast-cancer treatment in the eighties, does not confer anywhere near as decisive an advantage as patients are often led to believe, especially in postmenopausal women like myself—a two or three percentage point difference in ten-year survival rates,[1] according to America's best known breast-cancer surgeon, Dr. Susan Love.

I know these bleak facts, or sort of know them, but in the fog of anesthesia that hangs over those first few weeks, I seem to lose my capacity for self-defense. The pressure is on, from doctors and loved ones, to do something right away—kill it, get it out now. The endless exams, the bone scan to check for metastases, the high-tech heart test to see if I'm strong enough to withstand chemotherapy—all these blur the line between selfhood and thing-hood anyway, organic and inorganic, me and it. As my cancer career unfolds, I will, the helpful pamphlets explain, become a composite of the living and the dead—an implant to replace the breast, a wig to replace the hair. And then what will I

mean when I use the word "I"? I fall into a state of unreasoning passive aggressivity: They diagnosed this, so it's their baby. They found it, let them fix it.

I could take my chances with "alternative" treatments, of course. . . . Or I could choose to do nothing at all beyond mentally exhorting my immune system to exterminate the traitorous cellular faction. But I have never admired the "natural" or believed in the "wisdom of the body." . . . I will put my faith in science, even if this means that the dumb old body is about to be transmogrified into an evil clown—puking, trembling, swelling, surrendering significant parts, and oozing post-surgical fluids. The surgeon—a more genial and forthcoming one this time—can fit me in; the oncologist will see me. Welcome to Cancerland.

Fortunately, no one has to go through this alone. Thirty years ago, before Betty Ford, Rose Kushner, Betty Rollin, and other pioneer patients spoke out, breast cancer was a dread secret, endured in silence and euphemized in obituaries as a "long illness." Something about the conjuncture of "breast," signifying sexuality and nurturance, and that other word, suggesting the claws of a devouring crustacean, spooked almost everyone. Today however, it's the biggest disease on the cultural map, bigger than AIDS, cystic fibrosis, or spinal injury, bigger even than those more prolific killers of women—heart disease, lung cancer, and stroke. There are roughly hundreds of websites devoted to it, not to mention newsletters, support groups, a whole genre of first-person breast-cancer books; even a glossy, upper-middle-brow, monthly magazine, *Mamm*. There are four major national breast-cancer organizations, of which the mightiest, in financial terms, is The Susan Komen Foundation, headed by breast-cancer veteran and Bush's nominee for ambassador to Hungary Nancy Brinker. G. Komen organizes the annual Race for the Cure, which attracts about a million people—mostly survivors, friends, and family members. Its website provides a microcosm of the new breast-cancer culture, offering news of the races, message boards for accounts of individuals' struggles with the disease, and a "marketplace" of breast-cancer-related products to buy.

More so than in the case of any other disease, breast-cancer organizations and events feed on a generous flow of corporate support. Nancy Brinker relates how her early attempts to attract corporate interest in promoting breast cancer "awareness" were met with rebuff. A bra manufacturer, importuned to affix a mammogram-reminder tag to his product, more or less wrinkled his nose. Now breast cancer has blossomed from wallflower to the most popular girl at the corporate charity prom. While AIDS goes begging and low-rent diseases like tuberculosis have no friends at all, breast cancer has been able to count on Revlon, Avon, Ford, Tiffany, Pier 1, Estee Lauder, Ralph Lauren, Lee Jeans, Saks Fifth Avenue, JC Penney, Boston Market, Wilson athletic gear—and I apologize to those I've omitted. You can "shop for the cure" during the week when Saks donates 2 percent of sales to a breast-cancer fund; "wear denim for the cure" during Lee National Denim Day, when for a $5 donation you get to wear blue jeans to work. You can even "invest for the cure," in the Kinetics Assets Management's new no-load Medical Fund, which specializes entirely in businesses involved in cancer research.

If you can't run, bike, or climb a mountain for the cure—all of which endeavors are routine beneficiaries of corporate sponsorship—you can always purchase one of the many products with a breast-cancer theme. There are 2.2 million American women in various stages of their breast-cancer careers, who, along with anxious relatives, make up a significant market for all things breast-cancer-related. Bears, for example: I have identified four distinct lines, or species, of these creatures, including "Carol," the Remembrance Bear; "Hope," the Breast Cancer Research Bear, which wears a pink turban as if to conceal chemotherapy-induced baldness; the "Susan Bear," named for Nancy Brinker's deceased sister, Susan; and the new Nick & Nora Wish Upon a Star Bear, available, along with the Susan Bear, at the Komen Foundation website's "marketplace."

And bears are only the tip, so to speak, of the cornucopia of pink-ribbon-themed breast-cancer products. You can dress in pink-beribboned sweatshirts, denim shirts, pajamas, lingerie, aprons, loungewear, shoelaces, and socks; accessorize with pink rhinestone brooches, angel pins, scarves, caps, earrings, and bracelets; brighten up your home with breast-cancer candles, stained-glass pink-ribbon candleholders, coffee mugs, pendants, wind chimes, and night-lights; pay your bills with special BreastChecks or a separate line of Checks for the Cure. "Awareness" beats secrecy and stigma of course, but I can't help noticing that the existential space in which a friend has earnestly advised me to "confront [my] mortality" bears a striking resemblance to the mall.

This is not, I should point out, a case of cynical merchants exploiting the sick. Some of the breast-cancer tchotchkes and accessories are made by breast-cancer survivors themselves, such as "Janice," creator of the "Daisy Awareness Necklace," among other things, and in most cases a portion of the sales goes to breast-cancer research. Virginia Davis of Aurora, Colorado, was inspired to create the "Remembrance Bear" by a friend's double mastectomy and sees her work as more of a "crusade" than a business. This year she expects to ship 10,000 of these teddies, which are manufactured in China, and send part of the money to the Race for the Cure. If the bears are infantilizing—as I try ever so tactfully to suggest is how they may, in rare cases, be perceived—so far no one has complained. "I just get love letters," she tells me, "from people who say, 'God bless you for thinking of us.'"

The ultrafeminine theme of the breast-cancer "marketplace"—the prominence, for example, of cosmetics and jewelry—could be understood as a response to the treatments' disastrous effects on one's looks. But the infantilizing trope is a little harder to account for, and teddy bears are not its only manifestation. A tote bag distributed to breast cancer patients by the Libby Ross Foundation (through places such as the Columbia Presbyterian Medical Center) contains, among other items, a tube of Estee Lauder Perfumed Body Creme, a hot-pink satin pillowcase, an audiotape "Meditation to Help You with Chemotherapy," a small tin of peppermint pastilles, a set of three small inexpensive rhinestone bracelets, a pink-striped "journal and sketch book," and—somewhat jarringly—a small box of crayons. Maria Willner, one of the founders of the Libby Ross Foundation, told me that the crayons "go with the journal for people to express different moods, different thoughts . . ." though she admitted she has never tried to write with crayons herself. Possibly the idea is that regression to a state of childlike dependency puts one in the best frame of mind with which to endure the prolonged and toxic treatments. Or it may be that, in some versions of the prevailing gender ideology, femininity is by its nature incompatible with full adulthood—a state of arrested development. Certainly men diagnosed with prostate cancer do not receive gifts of Matchbox cars.

But I, no less than the bear huggers, need whatever help I can get, and start wading out into the Web in search of practical tips on hair loss, lumpectomy versus mastectomy, how to select a chemotherapy regimen, what to wear after surgery and eat when the scent of food sucks. There is, I soon find, far more than I can usefully absorb, for thousands of the afflicted have posted their stories, beginning with the lump or bad mammogram, proceeding through the agony of the treatments; pausing to mention the sustaining forces of family, humor, and religion; and ending, in almost all cases, with warm words of encouragement for the neophyte. Some of these are no more than a paragraph long—brief waves from sister sufferers; others offer almost hour-by-hour logs of breast-deprived, chemotherapized lives:

> Tuesday, August 15, 2000: Well, I survived my 4th chemo. Very, very dizzy today. Very nauseated, but no barfing! It's a first. . . . I break out in a cold sweat and my heart pounds if I stay up longer than 5 minutes.
>
> Friday, August 18, 2000: . . . By dinner time, I was full out nauseated. I took some meds and ate a rice and vegetable bowl from Trader Joe's. It smelled and tasted awful to me, but I ate it anyway. . . . Rick brought home some Kern's nectars and I'm drinking that. Seems to have settled my stomach a little bit.

I can't seem to get enough of these tales, reading on with panicky fascination about everything that can go wrong—septicemia, ruptured implants, startling recurrences a few years after the completion of treatments, "mets" (metastases) to vital organs, and—what scares me most in the short term—"chemo-brain," or the cognitive deterioration that sometimes accompanies chemotherapy. I compare myself with everyone, selfishly impatient with those whose conditions are less menacing, shivering over those who have reached Stage IV ("There is no Stage V," as the main character in Wit, who has ovarian cancer, explains), constantly assessing my chances.

Feminism helped make the spreading breast-cancer sisterhood possible, and this realization gives me a faint feeling of belonging. Thirty years ago, when the disease went hidden behind euphemism and prostheses, medicine was a solid patriarchy, women's bodies its passive objects of labor. The Women's Health Movement, in which I was an activist in the seventies and eighties, legitimized self-help and mutual support and encouraged women to network directly, sharing their stories, questioning the doctors, banding together. It is hard now to recall how revolutionary these activities once seemed, and probably few participants in breast-cancer chat rooms and message boards realize that when post-mastectomy patients first proposed meeting in support groups in the mid-1970s, the American Cancer Society responded with a firm and fatherly

"no." Now no one leaves the hospital without a brochure directing her to local support groups and, at least in my case, a follow-up call from a social worker to see whether I am safely ensconced in one. This cheers me briefly, until I realize that if support groups have won the stamp of medical approval this may be because they are no longer perceived as seditious.

In fact, aside from the dilute sisterhood of the cyber (and actual) support groups, there is nothing very feminist—in an ideological or activist sense—about the mainstream of breast-cancer culture today. Let me pause to qualify: You can, if you look hard enough, find plenty of genuine, self-identified feminists within the vast pink sea of the breast-cancer crusade, women who are militantly determined to "beat the epidemic" and insistent on more user-friendly approaches to treatment. It was feminist health activists who led the campaign, in the seventies and eighties, against the most savage form of breast-cancer surgery—the Halsted radical mastectomy, which removed chest muscle and lymph nodes as well as breast tissue and left women permanently disabled. It was the Women's Health Movement that put a halt to the surgical practice, common in the seventies, of proceeding directly from biopsy to mastectomy without ever rousing the patient from anesthesia. More recently, feminist advocacy groups such as the San Francisco–based Breast Cancer Action and the Cambridge-based Women's Community Cancer Project helped blow the whistle on "high-dose chemotherapy," in which the bone marrow was removed prior to otherwise lethal doses of chemotherapy and later replaced—to no good effect, as it turned out.

Like everyone else in the breast-cancer world, the feminists want a cure, but they even more ardently demand to know the cause or causes of the disease without which we will never have any means of prevention. "Bad" genes of the inherited variety are thought to account for fewer than 10 percent of breast cancers, and only 30 percent of women diagnosed with breast cancer have any known risk factor (such as delaying childbearing or the late onset of menopause) at all. Bad lifestyle choices like a fatty diet have, after brief popularity with the medical profession, been largely ruled out. Hence suspicion should focus on environmental carcinogens, the feminists argue, such as plastics, pesticides (DDT and PCBs, for example, though banned in this country, are still used in many Third World sources of the produce we eat), and the industrial runoff in our ground water. No carcinogen has been linked definitely to human breast cancer yet, but many have been found to cause the disease in mice, and the inexorable increase of the disease in industrialized nations—about one percent a year between the 1950s and the 1990s—further hints at environmental factors, as does the fact that women migrants to industrialized countries quickly develop the same breast-cancer rates as those who are native born. Their emphasis on possible ecological factors, which is not shared by groups such as Komen and the American Cancer Society, puts the feminist breast-cancer activists in league with other, frequently rambunctious, social movements—environmental and anticorporate.

But today theirs are discordant voices in a general chorus of sentimentality and good cheer; after all, breast cancer would hardly be the darling of corporate America if its complexion changed from pink to green. It is the very blandness of breast cancer, at least in mainstream perceptions, that makes it an attractive object of corporate charity and a way for companies to brand themselves friends of the middle-aged female market. With breast cancer, "there was no concern that you might actually turn off your audience because of the life style or sexual connotations that AIDS has," Amy Langer, director of the National Alliance of Breast Cancer Organizations, told the *New York Times* in 1996. "That gives corporations a certain freedom and a certain relief in supporting the cause." Or as Cindy Pearson, director of the National Women's Health Network, the organizational progeny of the Women's Health Movement, puts it more caustically: "Breast cancer provides a way of doing something for women, without being feminist."

In the mainstream of breast-cancer culture, one finds very little anger, no mention of possible environmental causes, few complaints about the fact that, in all but the more advanced, metastasized cases, it is the "treatments," not the disease, that cause illness and pain. The stance toward existing treatments is occasionally critical—in *Mamm*, for example—but more commonly grateful; the overall tone, almost universally upbeat. The Breast Friends website, for example, features a series of inspirational quotes: "Don't Cry over Anything That Can't Cry over You," "I Can't Stop the Birds of Sorrow from Circling My Head, But I Can Stop Them from Building a Nest in My Hair," "When Life Hands Out Lemons, Squeeze Out a Smile," "Don't wait for your ship to come in . . . Swim out to meet it," and much more of that ilk. Even in the relatively sophisticated *Mamm*, a columnist bemoans not cancer or chemotherapy but the end of chemotherapy, and humorously proposes to deal with her separation anxi-

ety by pitching a tent outside her oncologist's office. So pervasive is the perkiness of the breast-cancer world that unhappiness requires a kind of apology, as when "Lucy," whose "long term prognosis is not good," starts her personal narrative on breastcancertalk.org by telling us that her story "is not the usual one, full of sweetness and hope, but true nevertheless."

There is, I discover, no single noun to describe a woman with breast cancer. As in the AIDS movement, upon which breast-cancer activism is partly modeled, the words "patient" and "victim," with their aura of self-pity and passivity, have been ruled un-P.C. Instead, we get verbs: Those who are in the midst of their treatments are described as "battling" or "fighting," sometimes intensified with "bravely" or "fiercely"— language suggestive of Katharine Hepburn with her face to the wind. Once the treatments are over, one achieves the status of "survivor," which is how the women in my local support group identify themselves, A.A.-style, as we convene to share war stories and rejoice in our "survivorhood": "Hi, I'm Kathy and I'm a three-year survivor." For those who cease to be survivors and join the more than 40,000 American women who succumb to breast cancer each year—again, no noun applies. They are said to have "lost their battle" and may be memorialized by photographs carried at races for the cure—our lost, brave sisters, our fallen soldiers. But in the overwhelmingly Darwinian culture that has grown up around breast cancer, martyrs count for little; it is the "survivors" who merit constant honor and acclaim. They, after all, offer living proof that expensive and painful treatments may in some cases actually work.

Scared and medically weakened women can hardly be expected to transform their support groups into bands of activists and rush out into the streets, but the equanimity of breast-cancer culture goes beyond mere absence of anger to what looks, all too often, like a positive embrace of the disease. As "Mary" reports, on the Bosom Buds message board:

> I really believe I am a much more sensitive and thought-ful person now. It might sound funny but I was a real worrier before. Now I don't want to waste my energy on worrying. I enjoy life so much more now and in a lot of aspects I am much happier now.

Or this from "Andee":

> This was the hardest year of my life but also in many ways the most rewarding. I got rid of the baggage,

made peace with my family, met many amazing people, learned to take very good care of my body so it will take care of me, and reprioritized my life.

Cindy Cherry, quoted in the *Washington Post*, goes further:

> If I had to do it over, would I want breast cancer? Absolutely. I'm not the same person I was, and I'm glad I'm not. Money doesn't matter anymore. I've met the most phenomenal people in my life through this. Your friends and family are what matter now.

The First Year of the Rest of Your Life, a collection of brief narratives with a foreword by Nancy Brinker and a share of the royalties going to the Komen Foundation, is filled with such testimonies to the redemptive powers of the disease: "I can honestly say I am happier now than I have ever been in my life—even before the breast cancer." "For me, breast cancer has provided a good kick in the rear to get me started rethinking my life. . . ." "I have come out stronger, with a new sense of priorities. . . ." Never a complaint about lost time, shattered sexual confidence, or the long-term weakening of the arms caused by lymph-node dissection and radiation. What does not destroy you, to paraphrase Nietzsche, makes you a spunkier, more evolved, sort of person.

The effect of this relentless brightsiding is to transform breast cancer into a rite of passage—not an injustice or a tragedy to rail against, but a normal marker in the life cycle, like menopause or graying hair. Everything in mainstream breast-cancer culture serves, no doubt inadvertently, to tame and normalize the disease: the diagnosis may be disastrous, but there are those cunning pink rhinestone angel pins to buy and races to train for. Even the heavy traffic in personal narratives and practical tips, which I found so useful, bears an implicit acceptance of the disease and the current barbarous approaches to its treatment: you can get so busy comparing attractive head scarves that you forget to question a form of treatment that temporarily renders you both bald and immunoincompetent. Understood as a rite of passage, breast cancer resembles the initiation rites so exhaustively studied by Mircea Eliade: First there is the selection of the initiates—by age in the tribal situation, by mammogram or palpation here. Then come the requisite ordeals—scarification or circumcision within traditional cultures, surgery and chemotherapy for the cancer patient. Finally, the initiate emerges into a new

and higher status—an adult and a warrior—or in the case of breast cancer, a "survivor."

And in our implacably optimistic breast-cancer culture, the disease offers more than the intangible benefits of spiritual upward mobility. You can defy the inevitable disfigurements and come out, on the survivor side, actually prettier, sexier, more femme. In the lore of the disease—shared with me by oncology nurses as well as by survivors—chemotherapy smoothes and tightens the skin, helps you lose weight; and, when your hair comes back, it will be fuller, softer, easier to control, and perhaps a surprising new color. These may be myths, but for those willing to get with the prevailing program, opportunities for self-improvement abound. The American Cancer Society offers the "Look Good . . . Feel Better" program, "dedicated to teaching women cancer patients beauty techniques to help restore their appearance and self-image during cancer treatment." Thirty thousand women participate a year, each copping a free makeover and bag of makeup donated by the Cosmetic, Toiletry, and Fragrance Association, the trade association of the cosmetics industry. As for that lost breast: after reconstruction, why not bring the other one up to speed? Of the more than 50,000 mastectomy patients who opt for reconstruction each year, 17 percent go on, often at the urging of their plastic surgeons, to get additional surgery so that the remaining breast will "match" the more erect and perhaps larger new structure on the other side.

Not everyone goes for cosmetic deceptions, and the question of wigs versus baldness, reconstruction versus undisguised scar, defines one of the few real disagreements in breast-cancer culture. On the more avant-garde, upper-middle-class side, *Mamm* magazine—which features literary critic Eve Kosofsky Sedgwick as a columnist—tends to favor the "natural" look.

Here, mastectomy scars can be "sexy" and baldness something to celebrate. The January 2001 cover story features women who "looked upon their baldness not just as a loss, but also as an opportunity: to indulge their playful sides . . . to come in contact, in new ways, with their truest selves." One decorates her scalp with temporary tattoos of peace signs, panthers, and frogs; another expresses herself with a shocking purple wig; a third reports that unadorned baldness makes her feel "sensual, powerful, able to recreate myself with every new day." But no hard feelings toward those who choose to hide their condition under wigs or scarves; it's just a matter, *Mamm* tells us, of "different aesthetics." Some go for pink ribbons; others will prefer the

Ralph Lauren Pink Pony breast-cancer motif. But everyone agrees that breast cancer is a chance for creative self-transformation—a makeover opportunity, in fact.

Now, cheerfulness, up to and including delusion and false hope, has a recognized place in medicine. There is plenty of evidence that depressed and socially isolated people are more prone to succumb to diseases, cancer included, and a diagnosis of cancer is probably capable of precipitating serious depression all by itself. To be told by authoritative figures that you have a deadly disease, for which no real cure exists, is to enter a liminal state fraught with perils that go well beyond the disease itself. Consider the phenomenon of "voodoo death"—described by ethnographers among, for example, Australian aborigines—in which a person who has been condemned by a suitably potent curse obligingly shuts down and dies within a day or two. Cancer diagnoses could, and in some cases probably do, have the same kind of fatally dispiriting effect. So, it could be argued, the collectively pumped-up optimism of breast-cancer culture may be just what the doctor ordered. Shop for the Cure, dress in pink-ribbon regalia, organize a run or hike—whatever gets you through the night. . . .

"Culture" is too weak a word to describe all this. What has grown up around breast cancer in just the last fifteen years more nearly resembles a cult—or, given that it numbers more than two million women, their families, and friends—perhaps we should say a full-fledged religion. The products—teddy bears, pink-ribbon brooches, and so forth—serve as amulets and talismans, comforting the sufferer and providing visible evidence of faith. The personal narratives serve as testimonials and follow the same general arc as the confessional autobiographies required of seventeenth-century Puritans: first there is a crisis, often involving a sudden apprehension of mortality (the diagnosis or, in the old Puritan case, a stern word from on high); then comes a prolonged ordeal (the treatment or, in the religious case, internal struggle with the Devil); and finally, the blessed certainty of salvation, or its breast-cancer equivalent, survivorhood. And like most recognized religions, breast cancer has its great epideictic events, its pilgrimages and mass gatherings where the faithful convene and draw strength from their numbers. These are the annual races for a cure, attracting a total of about a million people at more than eighty sites—70,000 of them at the largest event, in Washington, D.C., which in recent years has been attended by Dan and Marilyn Quayle and Al and Tipper Gore. Every-

thing comes together at the races: celebrities and corporate sponsors are showcased; products are hawked; talents, like those of the "Swinging, Singing Survivors" from Syracuse, New York, are displayed. It is at the races, too, that the elect confirm their special status. As one participant wrote in the *Washington Post:*

> I have taken my "battle scarred" breasts to the Mall, donned the pink shirt, visor, pink shoelaces, etc. and walked proudly among my fellow veterans of the breast cancer war. In 1995, at the age of 44, I was diagnosed and treated for Stage II breast cancer. The experience continues to redefine my life.

Feminist breast-cancer activists, who in the early nineties were organizing their own mass outdoor events—demonstrations, not races—to demand increased federal funding for research, tend to keep their distance from these huge, corporate-sponsored, pink gatherings. Ellen Leopold, for example—a member of the Women's Community Cancer Project in Cambridge and author of *A Darker Ribbon: Breast Cancer, Women, and Their Doctors in the Twentieth Century*—has criticized the races as an inefficient way of raising money. She points out that the Avon Breast Cancer Crusade, which sponsors three-day, sixty-mile walks, spends more than a third of the money raised on overhead and advertising, and Komen may similarly fritter away up to 25 percent of its gross. At least one corporate-charity insider agrees. "It would be much easier and more productive," says Rob Wilson, an organizer of charitable races for corporate clients, "if people, instead of running or riding, would write out a check to the charity."

To true believers, such criticisms miss the point, which is always, ultimately, "awareness." Whatever you do to publicize the disease—wear a pink ribbon, buy a teddy, attend a race—reminds other women to come forward for their mammograms. Hence, too, they would argue, the cult of the "survivor": If women neglect their annual screenings, it must be because they are afraid that a diagnosis amounts to a death sentence. Beaming survivors, proudly displaying their athletic prowess, are the best possible advertisement for routine screening mammograms, early detection, and the ensuing round of treatments. Yes, miscellaneous businesses—from tiny distributors of breast-cancer wind chimes and note cards to major corporations seeking a woman-friendly image—benefit in the process, not to mention the breast-cancer industry itself, the estimated $12–16-billion-a-year business in surgery, "breast health centers," chemotherapy "infusion suites," radiation treatment centers, mammograms, and drugs ranging from anti-emetics (to help you survive the nausea of chemotherapy) to tamoxifen (the hormonal treatment for women with estrogen-sensitive tumors). But what's to complain about? Seen through pink-tinted lenses, the entire breast-cancer enterprise—from grassroots support groups and websites to the corporate providers of therapies and sponsors of races—looks like a beautiful example of synergy at work: cult activities, paraphernalia, and testimonies encourage women to undergo the diagnostic procedures, and since a fraction of these diagnoses will be positive, this means more members for the cult as well as more customers for the corporations, both those that provide medical products and services and those that offer charitable sponsorships.

But this view of a life-giving synergy is only as sound as the science of current detection and treatment modalities, and, tragically, that science is fraught with doubt, dissension, and what sometimes looks very much like denial. Routine screening mammograms, for example, are the major goal of "awareness," as when Rosie O'Donnell exhorts us to go out and "get squished." But not all breast-cancer experts are as enthusiastic. At best the evidence for the salutary effects of routine mammograms—as opposed to breast self-examination—is equivocal, with many respectable large-scale studies showing a vanishingly small impact on overall breast-cancer mortality. For one thing, there are an estimated two to four false positives for every cancer detected, leading thousands of healthy women to go through unnecessary biopsies and anxiety. And even if mammograms were 100 percent accurate, the admirable goal of "early" detection is more elusive than the current breast-cancer dogma admits. A small tumor, detectable only by mammogram, is not necessarily young and innocuous; if it has not spread to the lymph nodes, which is the only form of spreading detected in the common surgical procedure of lymph-node dissection, it may have already moved on to colonize other organs via the bloodstream. David Plotkin, director of the Memorial Cancer Research Foundation of Southern California, concludes that the benefits of routine mammography "are not well established; if they do exist, they are not as great as many women hope." Alan Spievack, a surgeon recently retired from the Harvard Medical School, goes further, concluding from his analysis of dozens of studies that routine screening mammography is, in the words of famous British surgeon Dr. Michael Baum, "one of the greatest deceptions perpetrated on the women of the Western world."

Even if foolproof methods for early detection existed,[2] they would, at the present time, serve only as portals to treatments offering dubious protection and considerable collateral damage. Some women diagnosed with breast cancer will live long enough to die of something else, and some of these lucky ones will indeed owe their longevity to a combination of surgery, chemotherapy, radiation, and/or anti-estrogen drugs such as tamoxifen. Others, though, would have lived untreated or with surgical excision alone, either because their cancers were slow-growing or because their bodies' own defenses were successful. Still others will die of the disease no matter what heroic, cell-destroying therapies are applied. The trouble is, we do not have the means to distinguish between these three groups. So for many of the thousands of women who are diagnosed each year, Plotkin notes, "the sole effect of early detection has been to stretch out the time in which the woman bears the knowledge of her condition." These women do not live longer than they might have without any medical intervention, but more of the time they do live is overshadowed with the threat of death and wasted in debilitating treatments.

To the extent that current methods of detection and treatment fail or fall short, America's breast-cancer cult can be judged as an outbreak of mass delusion, celebrating survivorhood by downplaying mortality and promoting obedience to medical protocols known to have limited efficacy. And although we may imagine ourselves to be well past the era of patriarchal medicine, obedience is the message behind the infantilizing theme in breast-cancer culture, as represented by the teddy bears, the crayons, and the prevailing pinkness. You are encouraged to regress to a little-girl state, to suspend critical judgment, and to accept whatever measures the doctors, as parent surrogates, choose to impose.

Worse, by ignoring or underemphasizing the vexing issue of environmental causes, the breast-cancer cult turns women into dupes of what could be called the Cancer Industrial Complex: the multinational corporate enterprise that with the one hand doles out carcinogens and disease and, with the other, offers expensive, semi-toxic pharmaceutical treatments. Breast Cancer Awareness Month, for example, is sponsored by AstraZeneca (the manufacturer of tamoxifen), which, until a corporate reorganization in 2000, was a leading producer of pesticides, including acetochlor, classified by the EPA as a "probable human carcinogen."

This particularly nasty conjuncture of interests led the environmentally oriented Cancer Prevention Coalition (CPC) to condemn Breast Cancer Awareness Month as "a public relations invention by a major polluter which puts women in the position of being unwitting allies of the very people who make them sick." Although Astra-Zeneca no longer manufactures pesticides, CPC has continued to criticize the breast-cancer crusade—and the American Cancer Society for its unquestioning faith in screening mammograms and careful avoidance of environmental issues. In a June 12, 2001, press release, CPC chairman Samuel S. Epstein, M.D., and the well-known physician activist Quentin Young castigated the American Cancer Society for its "longstanding track record of indifference and even hostility to cancer prevention. . . . Recent examples include issuing a joint statement with the Chlorine Institute justifying the continued global use of persistent organochlorine pesticides, and also supporting the industry in trivializing dietary pesticide residues as avoidable risks of childhood cancer. ACS policies are further exemplified by allocating under 0.1 percent of its $700 million annual budget to environmental and occupational causes of cancer."

In the harshest judgment, the breast-cancer cult serves as an accomplice in global poisoning—normalizing cancer, prettying it up, even presenting it, perversely, as a positive and enviable experience.

When, my three months of chemotherapy completed, the oncology nurse calls to congratulate me on my "excellent blood work results," I modestly demur. I didn't do anything, I tell her, anything but endure—marking the days off on the calendar, living on Protein Revolution canned vanilla health shakes, escaping into novels and work. Courtesy restrains me from mentioning the fact that the tumor markers she's tested for have little prognostic value, that there's no way to know how many rebel cells survived chemotherapy and may be carving out new colonies right now. She insists I should be proud; I'm a survivor now and entitled to recognition at the Relay for Life being held that very evening in town.

So I show up at the middle-school track where the relay's going on just in time for the Survivors' March: about 100 people, including a few men, since the funds raised will go to cancer research in general, are marching around the track eight to twelve abreast while a loudspeaker announces their names and survival times and a thin line of observers, mostly people staffing the raffle and food booths, applauds. It could be almost any kind of festivity, except for the distinctive stacks of cellophane-wrapped pink Hope Bears for sale in some of the booths. I cannot help but like the funky small-town Gemutlichkeit of the event, especially when the audio system strikes up that universal anthem of solidarity, "We Are Family," and a few people of various ages start twisting to the music on the gerry-rigged stage. But the money raised is going far away, to the American Cancer Society, which will not be asking us for our advice on how to spend it.

I approach a woman I know from other settings, one of our local intellectuals, as it happens, decked out here in a pink-and-yellow survivor T-shirt and with an American Cancer Society "survivor medal" suspended on a purple ribbon around her neck. "When do you date your survivorship from?" I ask her, since the announced time, five and a half years, seems longer than I recall. "From diagnosis or the completion of your treatments?" The question seems to annoy or confuse her, so I do not press on to what I really want to ask: At what point, in a downwardly sloping breast-cancer career, does one put aside one's survivor regalia and admit to being in fact a die-er? For the dead are with us even here, though in much diminished form. A series of paper bags, each about the right size for a junior burger and fries, lines the track. On them are the names of the dead, and inside each is a candle that will be lit later, after dark, when the actual relay race begins.

My friend introduces me to a knot of other women in survivor gear, breast-cancer victims all, I learn, though of course I would not use the V-word here. "Does anyone else have trouble with the term 'survivor'?" I ask, and, surprisingly, two or three speak up. It could be "unlucky," one tells me; it "tempts fate," says another, shuddering slightly. After all, the cancer can recur at any time, either in the breast or in some more strategic site. No one brings up my own objection to the term, though: that the mindless triumphalism of "survivorhood" denigrates the dead and the dying. Did we who live "fight" harder than those who've died? Can we claim to be "braver," better, people than the dead? And why is there no room in this cult for some gracious acceptance of death, when the time comes, which it surely will, through cancer or some other misfortune?

No, this is not my sisterhood. For me at least, breast cancer will never be a source of identity or pride. As my dying correspondent Gerri wrote [on an Internet message board]: "IT IS NOT O.K.!" What it is, along with cancer generally or any slow and painful way of dying, is an abomination, and, to the extent that it's manmade, also a crime. This is the one great truth that I bring out of the breast-cancer experience, which did not, I can now report, make me prettier or stronger, more feminine or spiritual—only more deeply angry. What sustained me through the "treatments" is a purifying rage, a resolve, framed in the sleepless nights of chemotherapy, to see the last polluter, along with, say, the last smug health-insurance operative, strangled with the last pink ribbon. Cancer or no cancer, I will not live that long of course. But I know this much right now for sure: I will not go into that last good night with a teddy bear tucked under my arm.

NOTES

1. In the United States, one in eight women will be diagnosed with breast cancer at some point. The chances of her surviving for five years are 86.8 percent. For a black woman this falls to 72 percent; and for a woman of any race whose cancer has spread to the lymph nodes, to 77.7 percent.

2. Some improved prognostic tools, involving measuring a tumor's growth rate and the extent to which it is supplied with blood vessels, are being developed but are not yet in use.

STOLEN BODIES, RECLAIMED BODIES: DISABILITY AND QUEERNESS

Eli Clare

I want to write about the body, not as a metaphor, symbol, or representation, but simply as the body. To write about my body, our bodies, in all their messy, complicated realities. I want words shaped by my slurring tongue, shaky hands, almost steady breath; words shaped by the fact that I am a walkie—someone for whom a flight of stairs without an accompanying elevator poses no problem—and by the reality that many of the people I encounter in my daily life assume I am "mentally retarded." Words shaped by how my body—and I certainly mean to include the mind as part of the body—moves through the world.

Sometimes we who are activists and thinkers forget about our bodies, ignore our bodies, or reframe our bodies to fit our theories and political strategies. For several decades now, activists in a variety of social change movements, ranging from black civil rights to women's liberation, from disability rights to queer liberation, have said repeatedly that the problems faced by any marginalized group of people lie, not in their bodies, but in the oppression they face. But in defining the external, collective, material nature of social injustice as separate from the body, we have sometimes ended up sidelining the profound relationships that connect our bodies with who we are and how we experience oppression.

. . .

Disentangling the body from the problems of social injustice has served the disability rights movement well. The dominant paradigms of disability—the medical, charity, supercrip, and moral models—all turn disability into problems faced by individual people, locate those problems in our bodies, and define those bodies as wrong. The medical model insists on disability as a disease or condition that is curable and/or treatable. The charity model declares disability to be a tragedy, a misfortune, that must be tempered or erased by generous giving. The supercrip model frames disability as a challenge to overcome and disabled people as superheroes just for living our daily lives. The moral model transforms disability into a sign of moral weakness. . . .

In resistance to this, the disability rights movement has created a new model of disability, one that places emphasis on how the world treats disabled people: Disability, not defined by our bodies, but rather by the material and social conditions of ableism; not by the need to use a wheelchair, but rather by the stairs that have no accompanying ramp or

(Continued)

elevator. Disability activists fiercely declare that it's not our bodies that need curing. Rather, it is ableism—disability oppression, as reflected in high unemployment rates, lack of access, gawking, substandard education, being forced to live in nursing homes and back rooms, being seen as childlike and asexual—that needs changing. . . .

. . .

Irrevocable difference could be a cause for celebration, but in this world it isn't. The price we pay for variation from the norm that's defined and upheld by white supremacy, patriarchy, and capitalism is incredibly high. And in my life, that price has been body centered. I came to believe that my body was utterly wrong. Sometimes I wanted to cut off my right arm so it wouldn't shake. My shame was that plain, that bleak. Of course, this is one of the profound ways in which oppression works—to mire us in body hatred. Homophobia is all about defining queer bodies as wrong, perverse, immoral. Transphobia, about defining trans bodies as unnatural, monstrous, or the product of delusion. Ableism, about defining disabled bodies as broken and tragic. Class warfare, about defining the bodies of workers as expendable. Racism, about defining the bodies of people of color as primitive, exotic, or worthless. Sexism, about defining female bodies as pliable objects. These messages sink beneath our skin.

There are so many ways oppression and social injustice can mark a body, steal a body, feed lies and poison to a body. I think of the kid tracked into "special education" because of his speech impediment, which is actually a common sign of sexual abuse. I think of the autoimmune diseases, the cancers, the various kinds of chemical sensitivities that flag what it means to live in a world full of toxins. I think of the folks who live with work-related disabilities because of exploitative, dangerous work conditions. I think of the people who live downwind of nuclear fallout, the people who die for lack of access to health care, the rape survivors who struggle with post-traumatic stress disorder. The list goes on and on.

The stolen bodies, the bodies taken for good, rise up around me. Rebecca Wight, a lesbian, shot and killed as she hiked the Appalachian Trail with her lover. James Byrd Jr., an African American, dragged to death behind a pickup driven by white men. Tyra Hunter, a transgendered person living as a woman, left to bleed to death on the streets of D.C. because the EMT crew discovered she had a penis and stopped their work. Tracy Latimer, a twelve-year-old girl with severe cerebral palsy, killed by her father, who said he did it only to end her unbearable suffering. Bodies stolen for good. Other bodies live on—numb, abandoned, full of self-hate, trauma, grief, aftershock. The pernicious stereotypes, lies, and false images can haunt a body, stealing it away as surely as bullets do.

But just as the body can be stolen, it can also be reclaimed. The bodies irrevocably taken from us, we can memorialize in quilts, granite walls, and candlelight vigils. We can remember and mourn them, use their deaths to strengthen our will. And as for the lies and false images: we need to name them, transform them, create something entirely new in their place. Something that comes close and finally true to the bone, entering our bodies as liberation, as joy, as fury, as a will to refigure the world. . . .

. . .

In the end, I am asking that we pay attention to our bodies—our stolen bodies and our reclaimed bodies. To the wisdom that tells us the causes of the injustice we face lie outside our bodies, and also to the profound relationships our bodies have to that injustice, to the ways our identities are inextricably linked to our bodies. We need to do this because there are disability activists so busy defining disability as an external social condition that they neglect the daily realities of our bodies: the reality of living with chronic pain; the reality of needing personal attendants to help us pee and shit (and of being at once grateful for those PAs and deeply regretting our lack of privacy); the reality of disliking the very adaptive equipment that makes our day-to-day lives possible. We need to do this because there are disability thinkers who can talk all day about the body as metaphor and symbol but never mention flesh, and blood, bone and tendon—never even acknowledge their own bodies. We need to do this because without our bodies, without the lived bodily experience of identity and oppression, we won't truly be able to refigure the world. . . .

SECTION 9

Violence Against Women

Violence against women manifests itself in many forms. Verbal harassment, sexual imposition, sexual assault, rape, domestic battering, lesbian bashing, and child abuse all contribute to a social climate that encourages women to comply with men's desires or to restrict their activities in order to avoid assault. The threat of violence against women is pervasive across cultures. In addition to violence against women and girls, other forms of violence—against gay men (or those presumed to be gay), boys, people of color, and transgendered people—serve to reinforce the subordination of those groups and, often, to reinforce the notion that transgressing acceptable boundaries of gender is risky and dangerous. Feminist analyses of violence against women focus on the extent to which violence serves as a means for the institutionalized control of women, children, and sexual minorities by men. The articles in this section analyze various forms of violence against women and contrast beliefs and actualities about various kinds of male violence. Often, sexist ideologies encourage us to accept violence against women as either harmless or deserved. Feminist analyses take the position that this violence constitutes a system through which men frighten, and therefore control and dominate, women.

Patricia Yancey Martin and Robert A. Hummer also explore the implications of heterosexual male bonding in "Fraternities and Rape on Campus." Fraternity members' negative attitudes toward women, rigid ideas about masculinity, and pressures to demonstrate simultaneously their heterosexuality and their utter loyalty to the "brotherhood" create fraternity cultures in which men use women to prove their masculinity

and worth. What are some other social contexts in which similar pressures for men to be hypermasculine exist? How does this research fit with Laura Hamilton's on college women in Section 7?

Hate crimes are crimes motivated by prejudice against particular groups. Because violence against women is so widespread, we sometimes fail to recognize it as a crime of hate. In "Supremacy Crimes," Gloria Steinem argues that mass killings in schools such as Columbine, Colorado, and Jonesboro, Arkansas, serial killings by criminals such as Edmond Kemper and Son of Sam, and other multiple sadistic killings of strangers are linked to issues of male domination. According to Steinem, we should regard most such crimes not as individual and apolitical assaults by deranged men. Rather, they are crimes against women as a group, committed for the most part by white heterosexual males and motivated by their desire for power and superiority. Think about the coverage of the mass killings in schools and universities that occurred during the 1990s and 2000s. Did the media acknowledge the gender of the killers and most of the victims and the role that gender might have played in what happened?

Violence against women is shaped by the intersections between race, class, and gender. In "Mapping the Margins: Intersectionality, Identity Politics, and Violence Against Women of Color," Kimberlé Crenshaw examines the relationship between gender and race in domestic violence. Domestic violence, she shows, is shaped by race in several ways. First, there are proscriptions within communities of color against publicizing or politicizing domestic violence, out of the fear of reinforcing stereotypes of black men as violent. Controversy over feminism (often seen as a white movement) and reluctance to report violence to an often-racist police force further contribute to the problem. At the same time, efforts to address domestic violence by feminists and policy makers often either ignore women of color or include them in a tokenistic way. Services to help women who are battered, such as shelters, are often inaccessible to women of color because of language barriers or the lack of incorporation of women of color into leadership positions in shelters. What does Crenshaw suggest would be necessary to address domestic violence more effectively in all communities? To what extent do the other readings in this section use an intersectional approach to violence, taking into account how it is shaped by race as well as gender?

Violence against women, as all these articles point out, is not simply the act of individual men against individual women. Instead, it is created and perpetuated by social institutions. In the final article in this section, "Sex and War: Fighting Men, Comfort Women, and the Military-Sexual Complex," Joane Nagel discusses the many ways that violence against women is related to military organizations and ethnic conflict. These include Korean prostitution—around military bases in South Korea and within the United States—and similar sexual dynamics around other military bases. Reinforcing both the masculinity of U.S. soldiers and the exoticized sexual image of the women, prostitution serves many interests, Nagel argues. During wartime, Nagel asserts, rape is one weapon in ethnic conflicts, and it serves not only to attack the women who are raped but also to "terrorize and humiliate" the enemy as a whole. According to UN reports, Serbian soldiers raped and tortured Bosnian women as a systematic tool of war, and the hearings surrounding these horrific events have raised international awareness about sexual assault as a violation of human rights.

Despite the overt nature of sex crimes during war, Nagel contends that sex is militarized during peacetime as well, through the network of military bases, which she argues have institutionalized prostitution on a large scale around the world. In general, Nagel points out, these sexual relationships occur between military members and local residents who are seen as different, or Other, because of their race, ethnicity, and nationality. These "ethnosexual" industries also exist outside the military. Building from the prostitution and "entertainment" networks created during the Vietnam War, a large sex tourism industry has arisen in Thailand that now serves men from Japan, Europe, Australia, and the United States. For Nagel, the dynamics and industries she describes are not simply a manifestation of male dominance over women but represent a sexualization of ethnic dominance, a "sexual means to an ethnic end."

Can you identify other instances of the sexualization of ethnic difference and conflict? How prevalent is prostitution in your own community, and in what ways is it shaped by ethnic inequalities? Locate news accounts of recent developments in the UN-sponsored International Criminal Tribunals dealing with the former Yugoslavia or Rwanda. How are sexual assaults discussed in these hearings, and what are the attitudes exhibited toward these assaults? What evidence is there of the use of sexual violence in the Iraq War? What effects would you expect the Iraq War to have on what Nagel calls the "military-sexual complex"? How is rape in wartime similar to and different from rape in the contexts described in the other articles in this section?

42 **Patricia Yancey Martin**
Robert A. Hummer

Fraternities and Rape on Campus

Rapes are perpetrated on dates, at parties, in chance encounters, and in specially planned circumstances. That group structure and processes, rather than individual values or characteristics, are the impetus for many rape episodes was documented by Blanchard (1959) thirty years ago (also see Geis 1971), yet sociologists have failed to pursue this theme (for an exception, see Chancer 1987). A recent review of research (Muehlenhard and Linton 1987) on sexual violence, or rape, devotes only a few pages to the situational contexts of rape events, and these are conceptualized as potential risk factors for individuals rather than qualities of rape-prone social contexts.

Many rapes, far more than come to the public's attention, occur in fraternity houses on college and university campuses, yet little research has analyzed fraternities at American colleges and universities as rape-prone contexts (cf. Ehrhart and Sandler 1985). Most of the research on fraternities reports on samples of individual fraternity men. One group of studies compares the values, attitudes, perceptions, family socioeconomic status, psychological traits (aggressiveness, dependence), and so on, of fraternity and nonfraternity men (Bohrnstedt 1969; Fox, Hodge, and Ward 1987; Kanin 1967; Lemire 1979; Miller 1973). A second group attempts to identify the effects of fraternity membership over time on the values, attitudes, beliefs, or moral precepts of members (Hughes and Winston 1987; Marlowe and Auvenshine 1982; Miller 1973; Wilder, Hoyt, Doren, Hauck, and Zettle 1978; Wilder, Hoyt, Surbeck, Wilder, and Carney 1986). With minor exceptions, little research addresses the group and organizational context of fraternities or the social construction of fraternity life (for exceptions, see Letchworth 1969; Longino and Kart 1973; Smith 1964).

Gary Tash, writing as an alumnus and trial attorney in his fraternity's magazine, claims that over 90 percent of all gang rapes on college campuses involve fraternity men (1988, p. 2). Tash provides no evidence to substantiate this claim, but students of violence against women have been concerned with fraternity men's frequently reported involvement in rape episodes (Adams and Abarbanel 1988). Ehrhart and Sandler (1985) identify over fifty cases of gang rapes on campus perpetrated by fraternity men, and their analysis points to many of the conditions that we discuss here. Their analysis is unique in focusing on conditions in fraternities that make gang rapes of women by fraternity men both feasible and probable. They identify excessive alcohol use, isolation from external monitoring, treatment of women as prey, use of pornography, approval of violence, and excessive concern with competition as precipitating conditions to gang rape (also see Merton 1985; Roark 1987).

The study reported here confirmed and complemented these findings by focusing on both conditions and processes. We examined dynamics associated with the social construction of fraternity life, with a focus on processes that foster the use of coercion, including rape, in fraternity men's relations with women. Our examination of men's social fraternities on college and university campuses as groups and organizations led us to conclude that fraternities are a physical and sociocultural context that encourages the sexual coercion of women. We make no claims that all fraternities are "bad" or that all fraternity men are rapists. Our observations indicated, however, that rape is especially probable in fraternities because of the kinds of organizations they are, the kinds of members they have, the practices their members engage in, and a virtual absence of university or community oversight. Analyses that lay blame for rapes by fraternity men on "peer pressure" are, we feel, overly simplistic (cf. Burkhart 1989; Walsh 1989). We suggest, rather, that fraternities create a sociocultural context in which the use of coercion in sexual relations with women is normative and in which the mechanisms to keep this pattern of behavior in check are minimal at best and

471

absent at worst. We conclude that unless fraternities change in fundamental ways, little improvement can be expected.

METHODOLOGY

Our goal was to analyze the group and organizational practices and conditions that create in fraternities an abusive social context for women. We developed a conceptual framework from an initial case study of an alleged gang rape at Florida State University that involved four fraternity men and an eighteen-year-old coed. The group rape took place on the third floor of a fraternity house and ended with the "dumping" of the woman in the hallway of a neighboring fraternity house. According to newspaper accounts, the victim's blood-alcohol concentration, when she was discovered, was .349 percent, more than three times the legal limit for automobile driving and an almost lethal amount. One law enforcement officer reported that sexual intercourse occurred during the time the victim was unconscious: "She was in a life-threatening situation" (*Tallahassee Democrat* 1988b). When the victim was found, she was comatose and had suffered multiple scratches and abrasions. Crude words and a fraternity symbol had been written on her thighs (*Tampa Tribune* 1988). When law enforcement officials tried to investigate the case, fraternity members refused to cooperate. This led, eventually, to a five-year ban of the fraternity from campus by the university and by the fraternity's national organization.

In trying to understand how such an event could have occurred, and how a group of over 150 members (exact figures are unknown because the fraternity refused to provide a membership roster) could hold rank, deny knowledge of the event, and allegedly lie to a grand jury, we analyzed newspaper articles about the case and conducted open-ended interviews with a variety of respondents about the case and about fraternities, rapes, alcohol use, gender relations, and sexual activities on campus. Our data included over 100 newspaper articles on the initial gang rape case; open-ended interviews with Greek (social fraternity and sorority) and non-Greek (independent) students (*n* = 20); university administrators (*n* = 8, five men, three women); and alumni advisers to Greek organizations (*n* = 6). Open-ended interviews were held also with judges, public and private defense attorneys, victim advocates, and state prosecutors regarding the processing of sexual assault cases. Data were analyzed using the grounded theory method (Glaser 1978; Martin and Turner 1986). In the following analysis, concepts generated from the data analysis are integrated with the literature on men's social fraternities, sexual coercion, and related issues.

FRATERNITIES AND THE SOCIAL CONSTRUCTION OF MEN AND MASCULINITY

Our research indicated that fraternities are vitally concerned—more than with anything else—with masculinity (cf. Kanin 1967). They work hard to create a macho image and context and try to avoid any suggestion of "wimpishness," effeminacy, and homosexuality. Valued members display, or are willing to go along with, a narrow conception of masculinity that stresses competition, athleticism, dominance, winning, conflict, wealth, material possessions, willingness to drink alcohol, and sexual prowess vis-à-vis women.

Valued Qualities of Members

When fraternity members talked about the kind of pledges they prefer, a litany of stereotypical and narrowly masculine attributes and behaviors was recited and feminine or woman-associated qualities and behaviors were expressly denounced (cf. Merton 1985). Fraternities seek men who are "athletic," "big guys," good in intramural competition, "who can talk college sports." Males "who are willing to drink alcohol," "who drink socially," or "who can hold their liquor" are sought. Alcohol and activities associated with the recreational use of alcohol are cornerstones of fraternity social life. Nondrinkers are viewed with skepticism and rarely selected for membership.[1]

Fraternities try to avoid "geeks," nerds, and men said to give the fraternity a "wimpy" or "gay" reputation. Art, music, and humanities majors, majors in traditional women's fields (nursing, home economics, social work, education), men with long hair, and those whose appearance or dress violate current norms are rejected. Clean-cut, handsome men who dress well (are clean, neat, conforming, fashionable) are preferred. One sorority woman commented that "the top-ranking fraternities have the best looking guys."

One fraternity man, a senior, said his fraternity recruited "some big guys, very athletic" over a two-year period to help overcome its image of wimpiness. His fraternity had won the interfraternity competition for highest grade-point average several years running but was looked down on as "wimpy, dancy, even gay." With their bigger, more athletic recruits, "our reputation improved; we're a much more recognized fraternity now." Thus a fraternity's reputation and status depend on members' possession of stereotypically masculine qualities. Good grades, campus leadership, and community service are "nice" but masculinity dominance—for example, in athletic events, physical size of members, athleticism of members—counts most.

Certain social skills are valued. Men are sought who "have good personalities," are friendly, and "have the ability to relate to girls" (cf. Longino and Kart 1973). One fraternity man, a junior, said: "We watch a guy [a potential pledge] talk to women . . . we want guys who can relate to girls." Assessing a pledge's ability to talk to women is, in part, a preoccupation with homosexuality and a conscious avoidance of men who seem to have effeminate manners or qualities. If a member is suspected of being gay, he is ostracized and informally drummed out of the fraternity. A fraternity with a reputation as wimpy or tolerant of gays is ridiculed and shunned by other fraternities. Militant heterosexuality is frequently used by men as a strategy to keep each other in line (Kimmel 1987).

Financial affluence or wealth, a male-associated value in American culture, is highly valued by fraternities. In accounting for why the fraternity involved in the gang rape that precipitated our research project had been recognized recently as "the best fraternity chapter in the United States," a university official said: "They were good-looking, a big fraternity, had lots of BMWs [expensive, German-made automobiles]." After the rape, newspaper stories described the fraternity members' affluence, noting the high number of members who owned expensive cars (*St. Petersburg Times* 1988).

The Status and Norms of Pledgeship

A pledge (sometimes called an associate member) is a new recruit who occupies a trial membership status for a specific period of time. The pledge period (typically ranging from ten to fifteen weeks) gives fraternity brothers an opportunity to assess and socialize new recruits. Pledges evaluate the fraternity also and decide if they want to become brothers. The socialization experience is structured partly through assignment of a Big Brother to each pledge. Big Brothers are expected

to teach pledges how to become a brother and to support them as they progress through the trial membership period. Some pledges are repelled by the pledging experience, which can entail physical abuse; harsh discipline; and demands to be subordinate, follow orders, and engage in demeaning routines and activities, similar to those used by the military to "make men out of boys" during boot camp.

Characteristics of the pledge experience are rationalized by fraternity members as necessary to help pledges unite into a group, rely on each other, and join together against outsiders. The process is highly masculinist in execution as well as conception. A willingness to submit to authority, follow orders, and do as one is told is viewed as a sign of loyalty, togetherness, and unity. Fraternity pledges who find the pledge process offensive often drop out. Some do this by openly quitting, which can subject them to ridicule by brothers and other pledges, or they may deliberately fail to make the grades necessary for initiation or transfer schools and decline to reaffiliate with the fraternity on the new campus. One fraternity pledge who quit the fraternity he had pledged described an experience during pledgeship as follows:

> This one guy was always picking on me. No matter what I did, I was wrong. One night after dinner, he and two other guys called me and two other pledges into the chapter room. He said, "Here, X, hold this 25-pound bag of ice at arms' length 'til I tell you to stop." I did it even though my arms and hands were killing me. When I asked if I could stop, he grabbed me around the throat and lifted me off the floor. I thought he would choke me to death. He cussed me and called me all kinds of names. He took one of my fingers and twisted it until it nearly broke. . . . I stayed in the fraternity for a few more days, but then I decided to quit. I hated it. Those guys are sick. They like seeing you suffer.

Fraternities' emphasis on toughness, withstanding pain and humiliation, obedience to superiors, and using physical force to obtain compliance contributes to an interpersonal style that de-emphasizes caring and sensitivity but fosters intragroup trust and loyalty. If the least macho or most critical pledges drop out, those who remain may be more receptive to, and influenced by, masculinist values and practices that encourage the use of force in sexual relations with women and the covering up of such behavior (cf. Kanin 1967).

Norms and Dynamics of Brotherhood

Brother is the status occupied by fraternity men to indicate their relations to each other and their membership in a particular fraternity organization or group. Brother is a male-specific status; only males can become brothers, although women can become "Little Sisters," a form of pseudomembership. "Becoming a brother" is a rite of passage that follows the consistent and often lengthy display by pledges of appropriately masculine qualities and behaviors. Brothers have a quasifamilial relationship with each other, are normatively said to share bonds of closeness and support, and are sharply set off from nonmembers. Brotherhood is a loosely defined term used to represent the bonds that develop among fraternity members and the obligations and expectations incumbent upon them (cf. Marlowe and Auvenshine [1982] on fraternities' failure to encourage "moral development" in freshman pledges).

Some of our respondents talked about brotherhood in almost reverential terms, viewing it as the most valuable benefit of fraternity membership. One senior, a business-school major who had been affiliated with a fairly high-status fraternity throughout four years on campus, said:

> Brotherhood spurs friendship for life, which I consider its best aspect, although I didn't see it that way when I joined. Brotherhood bonds and unites. It instills values of caring about one another, caring about community, caring about ourselves. The values and bonds [of brotherhood] continually develop over the four years [in college] while normal friendships come and go.

Despite this idealization, most aspects of fraternity practice and conception are more mundane. Brotherhood often plays itself out as an overriding concern with masculinity and, by extension, femininity. As a consequence, fraternities comprise collectivities of highly masculinized men with attitudinal qualities and behavioral norms that predispose them to sexual coercion of women (cf. Kanin 1967; Merton 1985; Rapaport and Burkhart 1984). The norms of masculinity are complemented by conceptions of women and femininity that are equally distorted and stereotyped and that may enhance the probability of women's exploitation (cf. Ehrhart and Sandler 1985; Sanday 1981, 1986).

Practices of Brotherhood

Practices associated with fraternity brotherhood that contribute to the sexual coercion of women include a preoccupation with loyalty, group protection and secrecy, use of alcohol as a weapon, involvement in violence and physical force, and an emphasis on competition and superiority.

Loyalty, Group Protection, and Secrecy   Loyalty is a fraternity preoccupation. Members are reminded constantly to be loyal to the fraternity and to their brothers. Among other ways, loyalty is played out in the practices of group protection and secrecy. The fraternity must be shielded from criticism. Members are admonished to avoid getting the fraternity in trouble and to bring all problems "to the chapter" (local branch of a national social fraternity) rather than to outsiders. Fraternities try to protect themselves from close scrutiny and criticism by the Interfraternity Council (a quasigoverning body composed of representatives from all social fraternities on campus), their fraternity's national office, university officials, law enforcement, the media, and the public. Protection of the fraternity often takes precedence over what is procedurally, ethically, or legally correct. Numerous examples were related to us of fraternity brothers' lying to outsiders to "protect the fraternity."

Group protection was observed in the alleged gang rape case with which we began our study. Except for one brother, a rapist who turned state's evidence, the entire remaining fraternity membership was accused by university and criminal justice officials of lying to protect the fraternity. Members consistently failed to cooperate even though the alleged crimes were felonies, involved only four men (two of whom were not even members of the local chapter), and the victim of the crime nearly died. According to a grand jury's findings, fraternity officers repeatedly broke appointments with law enforcement officials, refused to provide police with a list of members, and refused to cooperate with police and prosecutors investigating the case (*Florida Flambeau* 1988).

Secrecy is a priority value and practice in fraternities, partly because full-fledged membership is premised on it (for confirmation, see Ehrhart and Sandler 1985; Longino and Kart 1973; Roark 1987). Secrecy is also a boundary-maintaining mechanism, demarcating in-group from out-group, us from them. Secret rituals, handshakes, and mottoes are revealed to pledge brothers as they are initiated into full brotherhood. Since only brothers are supposed to know a fraternity's secrets, such knowledge affirms membership in the fraternity and separates a brother from others. Extending secrecy tactics from protection of private knowledge to protection of the fraternity from criticism is a predictable development. Our interviews indicated that individual members knew the difference between right and wrong, but fraternity norms that emphasize loyalty, group protection, and secrecy often overrode standards of ethical correctness.

Alcohol as Weapon   Alcohol use by fraternity men is normative. They use it on weekdays to relax after class and on weekends to "get drunk," "get crazy," and "get laid." The use of alcohol to obtain sex from women is pervasive—in other words, it is used as a weapon against sexual reluctance. According to several fraternity men whom we interviewed, alcohol is the major tool used to gain sexual mastery over women (cf. Adams and Abarbanel 1988; Ehrhart and Sandler 1985). One fraternity man, a twenty-one-year-old senior, described alcohol use to gain sex as follows: "There are girls that you know will fuck, then some you have to put some effort into it. . . . You have to buy them drinks or find out if she's drunk enough."

A similar strategy is used collectively. A fraternity man said that at parties with Little Sisters: "We provide them with 'hunch punch' and things get wild. We get them drunk and most of the guys end up with one." "'Hunch punch,'" he said, "is a girls' drink made up of overproof alcohol and powdered Kool-Aid, no water or anything, just ice. It's very strong. Two cups will do a number on a female." He had plans in the next academic term to surreptitiously give hunch punch to women in a "prim and proper" sorority because "having sex with prim and proper sorority girls is definitely a goal." These women are a challenge because they "won't openly consume alcohol and won't get openly drunk as hell." Their sororities have "standards committees" that forbid heavy drinking and easy sex.

In the gang rape case, our sources said that many fraternity men on campus believed the victim had a drinking problem and was thus an "easy make." According to newspaper accounts, she had been drinking alcohol on the evening she was raped; the lead assailant is alleged to have given her a bottle of wine after she arrived at his fraternity house. Portions of the rape occurred in a shower, and the victim was reportedly so drunk that her assailants had difficulty holding her in a standing position (*Tallahassee Democrat* 1988a). While raping her, her assailants repeatedly told her they were members of another fraternity under the apparent belief that she was too drunk to know the

difference. Of course, if she w[...] who they were, she was too dr[...] Allgeier 1986; Tash 1988).

One respondent told us that gang [...] and can get one expelled, but he seemed to see no [...] wrong in sexual coercion one-on-one. He seemed unaware that the use of alcohol to obtain sex from a woman is grounds for a claim that a rape occurred (cf. Tash 1988). Few women on campus (who also may not know these grounds) report date rapes, however; so the odds of detection and punishment are slim for fraternity men who use alcohol for "seduction" purposes (cf. Byington and Keeter 1988; Merton 1985).

Violence and Physical Force   Fraternity men have a history of violence (Ehrhart and Sandler 1985; Roark 1987). Their record of hazing, fighting, property destruction, and rape has caused them problems with insurance companies (Bradford 1986; Pressley 1987). Two university officials told us that fraternities "are the third riskiest property to insure behind toxic waste dumps and amusement parks." Fraternities are increasingly defendants in legal actions brought by pledges subjected to hazing (Meyer 1986; Pressley 1987) and by women who were raped by one or more members. In a recent alleged gang rape incident at another Florida university, prosecutors failed to file charges but the victim filed a civil suit against the fraternity nevertheless (*Tallahassee Democrat* 1989).

Competition and Superiority   Interfraternity rivalry fosters in-group identification and out-group hostility. Fraternities stress pride of membership and superiority over other fraternities as major goals. Interfraternity rivalries take many forms, including competition for desirable pledges, size of pledge class, size of membership, size and appearance of fraternity house, superiority in intramural sports, highest grade-point averages, giving the best parties, gaining the best or most campus leadership roles, and, of great importance, attracting and displaying "good-looking women." Rivalry is particularly intense over members, intramural sports, and women (cf. Messner 1989).

FRATERNITIES' COMMODIFICATION OF WOMEN

In claiming that women are treated by fraternities as commodities, we mean that fraternities knowingly, and intentionally, *use* women for their benefit.

.ernities use women as bait for new members, as ervers of brothers' needs, and as sexual prey.

Women as Bait

Fashionably attractive women help a fraternity attract new members. As one fraternity man, a junior, said, "They are good bait." Beautiful, sociable women are believed to impress the right kind of pledges and give the impression that the fraternity can deliver this type of woman to its members. Photographs of shapely, attractive coeds are printed in fraternity brochures and videotapes that are distributed and shown to potential pledges. The women pictured are often dressed in bikinis, at the beach, and are pictured hugging the brothers of the fraternity. One university official says such recruitment materials give the message: "Hey, they're here for you, you can have whatever you want," and, "we have the best-looking women. Join us and you can have them too." Another commented: "Something's wrong when males join an all-male organization as the best place to meet women. It's so illogical."

Fraternities compete in promising access to beautiful women. One fraternity man, a senior, commented that "the attraction of girls [i.e., a fraternity's success in attracting women] is a big status symbol for fraternities." One university official commented that the use of women as a recruiting tool is so well entrenched that fraternities that might be willing to forgo it say they cannot afford to unless other fraternities do so as well. One fraternity man said, "Look, if we don't have Little Sisters, the fraternities that do will get all the good pledges." Another said, "We won't have as good a rush [the period during which new members are assessed and selected] if we don't have these women around."

In displaying good-looking, attractive, skimpily dressed, nubile women to potential members, fraternities implicitly, and sometimes explicitly, promise sexual access to women. One fraternity man commented that "part of what being in a fraternity is all about is the sex" and explained how his fraternity uses Little Sisters to recruit new members:

> We'll tell the sweetheart [the fraternity's term for Little Sister], "You're gorgeous; you can get him." We'll tell her to fake a scam and she'll go hang all over him during a rush party, kiss him, and he thinks he's done wonderful and wants to join. The girls think it's great too. It's flattering for them.

Women as Servers

The use of women as servers is exemplified in the Little Sister program. Little Sisters are undergraduate women who are rushed and selected in a manner parallel to the recruitment of fraternity men. They are affiliated with the fraternity in a formal but unofficial way and are able, indeed required, to wear the fraternity's Greek letters. Little Sisters are not full-fledged fraternity members, however; and fraternity national offices and most universities do not register or regulate them. Each fraternity has an officer called Little Sister Chairman who oversees their organization and activities. The Little Sisters elect officers among themselves, pay monthly dues to the fraternity, and have well-defined roles. Their dues are used to pay for the fraternity's social events, and Little Sisters are expected to attend and hostess fraternity parties and hang around the house to make it a "nice place to be." One fraternity man, a senior, described Little Sisters this way: "They are very social girls, willing to join in, be affiliated with the group, devoted to the fraternity." Another member, a sophomore, said: "Their sole purpose is social—attend parties, attract new members, and 'take care' of the guys."

Our observations and interviews suggested that women selected by fraternities as Little Sisters are physically attractive, possess good social skills, and are willing to devote time and energy to the fraternity and its members. One undergraduate woman gave the following job description for Little Sisters to a campus newspaper:

> It's not just making appearances at all the parties but entails many more responsibilities. You're going to be expected to go to all the intramural games to cheer the brothers on, support and encourage the pledges, and just be around to bring some extra life to the house. [As a Little Sister] you have to agree to take on a new responsibility other than studying to maintain your grades and managing to keep your checkbook from bouncing. You have to make time to be a part of the fraternity and support the brothers in all they do. (*The Tomahawk* 1988)

The title of Little Sister reflects women's subordinate status; fraternity men in a parallel role are called Big Brothers. Big Brothers assist a sorority primarily with the physical work of sorority rushes, which, compared to fraternity rushes, are more formal, structured, and intensive. Sorority rushes take place in the daytime and fraternity rushes at night so fraternity men are free to help. According to one fraternity member, Little Sister status is a benefit to women because it gives them a social outlet and "the protection of the brothers." The gender-stereotypic conceptions and obligations of these Little Sister and Big Brother statuses indicate that fraternities and sororities promote a gender hierarchy on campus that fosters subordination and dependence in women, thus encouraging sexual exploitation and the belief that it is acceptable.

Women as Sexual Prey

Little Sisters are a sexual utility. Many Little Sisters do not belong to sororities and lack peer support for refraining from unwanted sexual relations. One fraternity man (whose fraternity has sixty-five members and eighty-five Little Sisters) told us they had recruited "wholesale" in the prior year to "get lots of new women." The structural access to women that the Little Sister program provides and the absence of normative supports for refusing fraternity members' sexual advances may make women in this program particularly susceptible to coerced sexual encounters with fraternity men.

Access to women for sexual gratification is a presumed benefit of fraternity membership, promised in recruitment materials and strategies and through brothers' conversations with new recruits. One fraternity man said: "We always tell the guys that you get sex all the time, there's always new girls. . . . After I became a Greek, I found out I could be with females at will." A university official told us that, based on his observations, "no one [i.e., fraternity men] on this campus wants to have 'relationships.' They just want to have fun [i.e., sex]." Fraternity men plan and execute strategies aimed at obtaining sexual gratification, and this occurs at both individual and collective levels.

Individual strategies include getting a woman drunk and spending a great deal of money on her. As for collective strategies, most of our undergraduate interviewees agreed that fraternity parties often culminate in sex and that this outcome is planned. One fraternity man said fraternity parties often involve sex and nudity and can "turn into orgies." Orgies may be planned in advance, such as the Bowery Ball party held by one fraternity. A former fraternity member said of this party:

> The entire idea behind this is sex. Both men and women come to the party wearing little or nothing. There are pornographic pinups on the walls and usually porno

movies playing on the TV. The music carries sexual overtones. . . . They just get schnockered [drunk] and, in most cases, they also get laid.

When asked about the women who come to such a party, he said: "Some Little Sisters just won't go. . . . The girls who do are looking for a good time, girls who don't know what it is, things like that."

Other respondents denied that fraternity parties are orgies but said that sex is always talked about among the brothers and they all know "who each other is doing it with." One member said that most of the time, guys have sex with their girlfriends "but with socials, girlfriends aren't allowed to come and it's their [members'] big chance [to have sex with other women]." The use of alcohol to help them get women into bed is a routine strategy at fraternity parties.

CONCLUSIONS

In general, our research indicated that the organization and membership of fraternities contribute heavily to coercive and often violent sex. Fraternity houses are occupied by same-sex (all men) and same-age (late teens, early twenties) peers whose maturity and judgment is often less than ideal. Yet fraternity houses are private dwellings that are mostly off-limits to, and away from scrutiny of, university and community representatives, with the result that fraternity house events seldom come to the attention of outsiders. Practices associated with the social construction of fraternity brotherhood emphasize a macho conception of men and masculinity, a narrow, stereotyped conception of women and femininity, and the treatment of women as commodities. Other practices contributing to coercive sexual relations and the coverup of rapes include excessive alcohol use, competitiveness, and normative support for deviance and secrecy (cf. Bogal-Allbritten and Allbritten 1985; Kanin 1967).

Some fraternity practices exacerbate others. Brotherhood norms require "sticking together" regardless of right or wrong; thus rape episodes are unlikely to be stopped or reported to outsiders, even when witnesses disapprove. The ability to use alcohol without scrutiny by authorities and alcohol's frequent association with violence, including sexual coercion, facilitates rape in fraternity houses. Fraternity norms that emphasize the value of maleness and masculinity over femaleness and femininity and that elevate the status of men and lower the status of women in members' eyes undermine perceptions and treatment of women as persons who deserve consideration and care (cf. Ehrhart and Sandler 1985; Merton 1985).

Androgynous men and men with a broad range of interests and attributes are lost to fraternities through their recruitment practices. Masculinity of a narrow and stereotypical type helps create attitudes, norms, and practices that predispose fraternity men to coerce women sexually, both individually and collectively (Allgeier 1986; Hood 1989; Sanday 1981, 1986). Male athletes on campus may be similarly disposed for the same reasons (Kirshenbaum 1989; Telander and Sullivan 1989).

Research into the social contexts in which rape crimes occur and the social constructions associated with these contexts illumine rape dynamics on campus. Blanchard (1959) found that group rapes almost always have a leader who pushes others into the crime. He also found that the leader's latent homosexuality, desire to show off to his peers, or fear of failing to prove himself a man are frequently an impetus. Fraternity norms and practices contribute to the approval and use of sexual coercion as an accepted tactic in relations with women. Alcohol-induced compliance is normative, whereas, presumably, use of a knife, gun, or threat of bodily harm would not be because the woman who "drinks too much" is viewed as "causing her own rape" (cf. Ehrhart and Sandler 1985).

Our research led us to conclude that fraternity norms and practices influence members to view the sexual coercion of women, which is a felony crime, as sport, a contest, or a game (cf. Sato 1988). This sport is played not between men and women but between men and men. Women are the pawns or prey in the interfraternity rivalry game; they prove that a fraternity is successful or prestigious. The use of women in this way encourages fraternity men to see women as objects and sexual coercion as sport. Today's societal norms

support young women's right to engage in sex at their discretion, and coercion is unnecessary in a mutually desired encounter. However, nubile young women say they prefer to be "in a relationship" to have sex while young men say they prefer to "get laid" without a commitment (Muehlenhard and Linton 1987). These differences may reflect, in part, American puritanism and men's fears of sexual intimacy or perhaps intimacy of any kind. In a fraternity context, getting sex without giving emotionally demonstrates "cool" masculinity. More important, it poses no threat to the bonding and loyalty of the fraternity brotherhood (cf. Farr 1988). Drinking large quantities of alcohol before having sex suggests that "scoring" rather than intrinsic sexual pleasure is a primary concern of fraternity men.

Unless fraternities' composition, goals, structures, and practices change in fundamental ways, women on campus will continue to be sexual prey for fraternity men. As all-male enclaves dedicated to opposing faculty and administration and to cementing in-group ties, fraternity members eschew any hint of homosexuality. Their version of masculinity transforms women, and men with womanly characteristics, into the out-group. "Womanly men" are ostracized; feminine women are used to demonstrate members' masculinity. Encouraging renewed emphasis on their founding values (Longino and Kart 1973), service orientation and activities (Lemire 1979), or members' moral development (Marlowe and Auvenshine 1982) will have little effect on fraternities' treatment of women. A case for or against fraternities cannot be made by studying individual members. The fraternity qua group and organization is at issue. Located on campus along with many vulnerable women, embedded in a sexist society, and caught up in masculinist goals, practices, and values, fraternities' violation of women—including forcible rape—should come as no surprise.

ACKNOWLEDGMENTS

We gratefully thank Meena Harris and Diane Mennella for assisting with data collection. The senior author thanks the graduate students in her fall 1988 graduate research methods seminar for help with developing the initial conceptual framework. Judith Lorber and two anonymous *Gender & Society* referees made numerous suggestions for improving our article and we thank them also.

NOTE

1. Recent bans by some universities on open-keg parties at fraternity houses have resulted in heavy drinking before coming to a party and an increase in drunkenness among those who attend. This may aggravate, rather than improve, the treatment of women by fraternity men at parties.

REFERENCES

Adams, Aileen, and Gail Abarbanel. 1988. *Sexual Assault on Campus: What Colleges Can Do.* Santa Monica, CA: Rape Treatment Center.

Allgeier, Elizabeth. 1986. "Coercive Versus Consensual Sexual Interactions." G. Stanley Hall Lecture to American Psychological Association Annual Meeting, Washington, DC, August.

Blanchard, W. H. 1959. "The Group Process in Gang Rape." *Journal of Social Psychology* 49: 259–66.

Bogal-Allbritten, Rosemarie B., and William L. Allbritten. 1985. "The Hidden Victims: Courtship Violence Among College Students." *Journal of College Student Personnel* 43: 201–4.

Bohrnstedt, George W. 1969. "Conservatism, Authoritarianism and Religiosity of Fraternity Pledges." *Journal of College Student Personnel* 27: 36–43.

Bradford, Michael. 1986. "Tight Market Dries Up Nightlife at University." *Business Insurance* (March 2): 2, 6.

Burkhart, Barry. 1989. Comments in Seminar on Acquaintance/Date Rape Prevention: A National Video Teleconference, February 2.

Burkhart, Barry R., and Annette L. Stanton. 1985. "Sexual Aggression in Acquaintance Relationships." Pp. 43–65 in *Violence in Intimate Relationships*, ed. G. Russell. Englewood Cliffs, NJ: Spectrum.

Byington, Diane B., and Karen W. Keeter. 1988. "Assessing Needs of Sexual Assault Victims on a University Campus." Pp. 23–31 in *Student Services: Responding to Issues and Challenges*. Chapel Hill: University of North Carolina Press.

Chancer, Lynn S. 1987. "New Bedford, Massachusetts, March 6, 1983–March 22, 1984: The 'Before and After' of a Group Rape." *Gender & Society* 1: 239–60.

Ehrhart, Julie K., and Bernice R. Sandler. 1985. *Campus Gang Rape: Party Games?* Washington, DC: Association of American Colleges.

Farr, K. A. 1988. "Dominance Bonding Through the Good Old Boys Sociability Network." *Sex Roles* 18: 259–77.

Florida Flambeau. 1988. "Pike Members Indicted in Rape." (May 19): 1, 5.

Fox, Elaine, Charles Hodge, and Walter Ward. 1987. "A Comparison of Attitudes Held by Black and White Fraternity Members." *Journal of Negro Education* 56: 521–34.

Geis, Gilbert. 1971. "Group Sexual Assaults." *Medical Aspects of Human Sexuality* 5: 101–13.

Glaser, Barney G. 1978. *Theoretical Sensitivity: Advances in the Methodology of Grounded Theory.* Mill Valley, CA: Sociology Press.

Hood, Jane. 1989. "Why Our Society Is Rape-Prone." *New York Times*, May 16.

Hughes, Michael J., and Roger B. Winston, Jr. 1987. "Effects of Fraternity Membership on Interpersonal Values." *Journal of College Student Personnel* 45: 405–11.

Kanin, Eugene J. 1967. "Reference Groups and Sex Conduct Norm Violations." *The Sociological Quarterly* 8: 495–504.

Kimmel, Michael, ed. 1987. *Changing Men: New Directions in Research on Men and Masculinity.* Newbury Park, CA: Sage.

Kirshenbaum, Jerry. 1989. "Special Report, An American Disgrace: A Violent and Unprecedented Lawlessness Has Arisen Among College Athletes in all Parts of the Country." *Sports Illustrated* (February 27): 16–19.

Lemire, David. 1979. "One Investigation of the Stereotypes Associated with Fraternities and Sororities." *Journal of College Student Personnel* 37: 54–57.

Letchworth, G. E. 1969. "Fraternities Now and in the Future." *Journal of College Student Personnel* 10: 118–22.

Longino, Charles F., Jr., and Cary S. Kart. 1973. "The College Fraternity: An Assessment of Theory and Research." *Journal of College Student Personnel* 31: 118–25.

Marlowe, Anne F., and Dwight C. Auvenshine. 1982. "Greek Membership: Its Impact on the Moral Development of College Freshmen." *Journal of College Student Personnel* 40: 53–57.

Martin, Patricia Yancey, and Barry A. Turner. 1986. "Grounded Theory and Organizational Research." *Journal of Applied Behavioral Science* 22: 141–57.

Merton, Andrew. 1985. "On Competition and Class: Return to Brotherhood." *Ms.* (September): 60–65, 121–22.

Messner, Michael. 1989. "Masculinities and Athletic Careers." *Gender & Society* 3: 71–88.

Meyer, T. J. 1986. "Fight Against Hazing Rituals Rages on Campuses." *Chronicle of Higher Education* (March 12): 34–36.

Miller, Leonard D. 1973. "Distinctive Characteristics of Fraternity Members." *Journal of College Student Personnel* 31: 126–28.

Muehlenhard, Charlene L., and Melaney A. Linton. 1987. "Date Rape and Sexual Aggression in Dating Situations: Incidence and Risk Factors." *Journal of Counseling Psychology* 34: 186–96.

Pressley, Sue Anne. 1987. "Fraternity Hell Night Still Endures." *Washington Post* (August 11): B1.

Rapaport, Karen, and Barry R. Burkhart. 1984. "Personality and Attitudinal Characteristics of Sexually Coercive College Males." *Journal of Abnormal Psychology* 93: 216–21.

Roark, Mary L. 1987. "Preventing Violence on College Campuses." *Journal of Counseling and Development* 65: 367–70.

Sanday, Peggy Reeves. 1981. "The Socio-Cultural Context of Rape: A Cross-Cultural Study." *Journal of Social Issues* 37: 5–27.

———. 1986. "Rape and the Silencing of the Feminine." Pp. 84–101 in *Rape*, ed. S. Tomaselli and R. Porter. Oxford: Basil Blackwell.

St. Petersburg Times. 1988. "A Greek Tragedy." (May 29): 1F, 6F.

Sato, Ikuya. 1988. "Play Theory of Delinquency: Toward a General Theory of 'Action.'" *Symbolic Interaction* 11: 191–212.

Smith, T. 1964. "Emergence and Maintenance of Fraternal Solidarity." *Pacific Sociological Review* 7: 29–37.

Tallahassee Democrat. 1988a. "FSU Fraternity Brothers Charged" (April 27): 1A, 12A.

———. 1988b. "FSU Interviewing Students about Alleged Rape" (April 24): 1D.

———. 1989. "Woman Sues Stetson in Alleged Rape" (March 19): 3B.

Tampa Tribune. 1988. "Fraternity Brothers Charged in Sexual Assault of FSU Coed" (April 27): 6B.

Tash, Gary B. 1988. "Date Rape." *The Emerald of Sigma Pi Fraternity* 75(4): 1–2.

Telander, Rick, and Robert Sullivan. 1989. "Special Report, You Reap What You Sow." *Sports Illustrated* (February 27): 20–34.

The Tomahawk. 1988. "A Look Back at Rush, a Mixture of Hard Work and Fun" (April/May): 3D.

Walsh, Claire. 1989. Comments in Seminar on Acquaintance/Date Rape Prevention: A National Video Teleconference, February 2.

Wilder, David H., Arlyne E. Hoyt, Dennis M. Doren, William E. Hauck, and Robert D. Zettle. 1978. "The Impact of Fraternity and Sorority Membership on Values and Attitudes." *Journal of College Student Personnel* 36: 445–49.

Wilder, David H., Arlyne E. Hoyt, Beth Shuster Surbeck, Janet C. Wilder, and Patricia Imperatrice Carney. 1986. "Greek Affiliation and Attitude Change in College Students." *Journal of College Student Personnel* 44: 510–19.

READING *43*   **Gloria Steinem**

Supremacy Crimes

From domestic violence to sexual harassment, naming a crime has been the first step toward solving it. But another crime is hiding in plain sight. You've seen the ocean of television coverage, you've read the headlines: "How to Spot a Troubled Kid," "Twisted Teens," "When Teens Fall Apart."

After the slaughter in Colorado that inspired those phrases, dozens of copycat threats were reported in the same generalized way: "Junior high students charged with conspiracy to kill students and teachers" (in Texas); "Five honor students overheard planning a June graduation bombing" (in New York); "More than 100 minor threats reported statewide" (in Pennsylvania). In response, the White House held an emergency strategy session titled "Children, Violence, and Responsibility." Nonetheless, another attack was soon reported: "Youth with 2 Guns Shoots 6 at Georgia School."

I don't know about you, but I've been talking back to the television set, waiting for someone to tell us the obvious: it's not "youth," "our children," or "our teens." It's our sons—and "our" can usually be read as "white," "middle class," and "heterosexual." We know that hate crimes, violent and otherwise, are overwhelmingly committed by white men who are apparently straight. The same is true for an even higher percentage of impersonal, resentment-driven, mass killings like those in Colorado; the sort committed for no economic or rational gain except the need to say, "I'm superior because I can kill." Think of Charles Starkweather, who reported feeling powerful and serene after murdering ten women and men in the 1950s; or the shooter who climbed the University of Texas Tower in 1966, raining down death to gain celebrity. Think of the engineering student at the University of Montreal who resented females' ability to study that subject, and so shot to death fourteen women students in 1989, while saying, "I'm against feminism." Think of nearly all those who have killed impersonally in the workplace, the post office, McDonald's.

White males—usually intelligent, middle class, and heterosexual, or trying desperately to appear so—also account for virtually all the serial, sexually motivated, sadistic killings, those characterized by stalking, imprisoning, torturing, and "owning" victims in death. Think of Edmund Kemper, who began by killing animals, then murdered his grandparents, yet was released to sexually torture and dismember college students and other young women until he himself decided he "didn't want to kill *all* the coeds in the world." Or David Berkowitz, the Son of Sam, who murdered some women in order to feel in control of all women. Or consider Ted Bundy, the charming, snobbish young would-be lawyer who tortured and murdered as many as forty women, usually beautiful students who were symbols of the economic class he longed to join. As for John Wayne Gacy, he was obsessed with maintaining the public mask of masculinity, and so hid his homosexuality by killing and burying men and boys with whom he had had sex.

These "senseless" killings begin to seem less mysterious when you consider that they were committed disproportionately by white, nonpoor males, the group most likely to become hooked on the drug of superiority. It's a drug pushed by a male-dominant culture that presents dominance as a natural right; a racist hierarchy that falsely elevates whiteness; a materialist society that equates superiority with possessions, and a homophobic one that empowers only one form of sexuality.

As Elliott Leyton reports in *Hunting Humans: The Rise of the Modern Multiple Murderer*, these killers see their behavior as "an appropriate—even 'manly'—response to the frustrations and disappointments that are a normal part of life." In other words, it's not their life experiences that are the problem, it's the impossible expectation of dominance to which they've become addicted.

This is not about blame. This is about causation. If anything, ending the massive cultural cover-up of supremacy crimes should make heroes out of boys and men who reject violence, especially those who reject the notion of superiority altogether. Even if one believes in a biogenetic component of male aggression, the very existence of gentle men proves that socialization can override it.

Nor is this about attributing such crimes to a single cause. Addiction to the drug of supremacy is not their only root, just the deepest and most ignored one. Additional reasons why this country has such a high rate of violence include the plentiful guns that make killing seem as unreal as a video game; male violence in the media that desensitizes viewers in much the same way that combat killers are desensitized in training; affluence that allows maximum access to violence-as-entertainment; a national history of genocide and slavery; the romanticizing of frontier violence and organized crime; not to mention extremes of wealth and poverty and the illusion that both are deserved.

But it is truly remarkable, given the relative reasons for anger at injustice in this country, that white, nonpoor men have a near-monopoly on multiple killings of strangers, whether serial and sadistic or mass and random. How can we ignore this obvious fact? Others may kill to improve their own condition—in self-defense, or for money or drugs; to eliminate enemies; to declare turf in drive-by shootings; even for a jacket or a pair of sneakers—but white males addicted to supremacy kill even when it worsens their condition or ends in suicide.

Men of color and females are capable of serial and mass killing, and commit just enough to prove it. Think of Colin Ferguson, the crazed black man on the Long Island Railroad, or Wayne Williams, the young black man in Atlanta who kidnapped and killed black boys, apparently to conceal his homosexuality. Think of Aileen Carol Wuornos, the white prostitute in Florida who killed abusive johns "in self-defense," or Waneta Hoyt, the upstate New York woman who strangled her five infant children between 1965 and 1971, disguising their cause of death as sudden infant death syndrome. Such crimes are rare enough to leave a haunting refrain of disbelief, as evoked in Pat Parker's poem "jonestown": "Black folks do not/Black folks do not/Black folks do not commit suicide." And yet they did.

Nonetheless, the proportion of serial killings that are not committed by white males is about the same as the proportion of anorexics who are not female. Yet we discuss the gender, race, and class components of anorexia, but not the role of the same factors in producing epidemics among the powerful.

The reasons are buried deep in the culture, so invisible that only by reversing our assumptions can we reveal them.

Suppose, for instance, that young black males—or any other men of color—had carried out the slaughter in Colorado. Would the media reports be so willing to describe the murderers as "our children"? Would there be so little discussion about the boys' race? Would experts be calling the motive a mystery, or condemning the high school cliques for making those young men feel like "outsiders"? Would there be the same empathy for parents who gave the murderers luxurious homes, expensive cars, even rescued them from brushes with the law? Would there be as much attention to generalized causes, such as the dangers of violent video games and recipes for bombs on the Internet?

s, if racial identities had been rever- ⸺ emain so little discussed? In fact, the ⸺ said they were targeting blacks and athletes ⸺ a racial epithet, shot a black male student in the head, and then laughed over the fact that they could see his brain. What if *that* had been reversed?

What if these two young murderers, who were called "fags" by some of the jocks at Columbine High School, actually had been gay? Would they have got the same sympathy for being gay-baited? What if they had been lovers? Would we hear as little about their sexuality as we now do, even though only their own homophobia could have given the word "fag" such power to humiliate them?

Take one more leap of the imagination: suppose these killings had been planned and executed by young women—of any race, sexuality, or class. Would the media still be so uninterested in the role played by gender-conditioning? Would journalists assume that female murderers had suffered from being shut out of access to power in high school, so much so that they were pushed beyond their limits? What if dozens, even hundreds of young women around the country had made imitative threats—as young men have done— expressing admiration for a well-planned massacre and promising to do the same? Would we be discussing their youth more than their gender, as is the case so far with these male killers?

I think we begin to see that our national self-examination is ignoring something fundamental, precisely because it's like the air we breathe: the white male factor, the middle-class and heterosexual one, and the promise of superiority it carries. Yet this denial is self-defeating—to say the least. We will never reduce the number of violent Americans, from bullies to killers, without challenging the assumptions on which masculinity is based: that males are superior to females, that they must find a place in a male hierarchy, and that the ability to dominate *someone* is so important that even a mere insult can justify lethal revenge. There are plenty of studies to support this view. As Dr. James Gilligan concluded in *Violence: Reflections on a National Epidemic*, "If humanity is to evolve beyond the propensity toward violence . . . then it can only do so by recognizing the extent to which the patriarchal code of honor and shame generates and obligates male violence."

I think the way out can only be found through a deeper reversal: just as we as a society have begun to raise our daughters more like our sons—more like whole people—we must begin to raise our sons more like our daughters—that is, to value empathy as well as hierarchy; to measure success by other people's welfare as well as their own.

But first, we have to admit and name the truth about supremacy crimes.

UNDERSTANDING SEXUAL HARASSMENT: A PRIMER FOR DUDES

Silvana Naguib

I want to take a moment to clear some things up about sexual harassment. . . .

1. Men don't see street harassment, so they have very little first-hand understanding of 1) what it usually consists of, or 2) how often it happens. This is for two reasons.

   First, is a pretty obvious point, that no one harasses women when men are around. If I'm with any man, be it my boyfriend, friend, father, brother, or boss, no one says anything to me. An accompanied woman is automatically off-limits, apparently, in the world of street harassers. I assume this is mostly to avoid confrontation. That's part of the reason I want to confront people, so at least a few men are disabused of the notion that a woman alone will receive sexual comments about her body without imposing consequences on them.

   Second is a more subtle point. Even though men are out and about in the same streets where women are being harassed, they very rarely detect it, because most harassment is designed to be only barely detectable by the person it's directed at. It's almost always at a volume where you can hear it, but not as loud as the person would be talking if they were trying to get your attention, or addressing you normally. This is not loud enough for anyone standing nearby to hear. In fact, many people don't hear it when it's directed *at* them, because of a blinders-on-the-eyes-straight-ahead way they walk around in the world. This volume fact has two effects: no one can hear it except you, and you yourself aren't always even sure you heard it, or that it was directed at you.

This is problematic. It's different when someone yells "suck my dick, bitch!" than when someone mutters under their breath "damn, you got a sexy ass" as you walk by. In the second case, it seems disproportionate to call someone out; they only muttered something, after all. Furthermore, you often think, "was he saying that to me?" Like the time when I was walking by a group of guys sitting on a stoop and one guy muttered "damn, those are like watermelons." I flipped around and stared at him, but he looked off into space, as if there would be no reason for my staring. Since I wasn't even sure of what he'd said, and whether it was to me, I just walked on. This makes you feel like you're going fucking crazy, like the world is full of people muttering things about you under their breath (and it is, believe me), and you're always just a step behind being about to call them out on it.

It's designed to be just above detection for the person it's directed at, and just below detection for everyone else.

2. Sexual harassment is humiliating. [Elsewhere,] I explained it as follows: "You know those naked dreams, where you are naked in a public place, and everyone is looking at your naked body? That's what being a woman in your twenties (or teens, or thirties, or forties, or fifties) in a big city feels like. Everyone is looking at your body, all the time, and saying things about it."

And it's not just looking at your body [in a] normal, perception way, like "hey, there is a person over there." It's looking in a way that makes you feel *exposed,* because it is a sexualized gaze, it is analytical, it is evaluative, it is unwelcome. Of course, people who don't harass are engaging in this same looking, which is another issue, but a much more complex one that I won't get into. The problem is that street harassers are telling you that they are looking at you and evaluating your body in a sexual way, and they perceive your status as such that they can make you aware of your sexuality without consequence. It's humiliating, because it makes you feel small, powerless, and like an agglomeration of sexual parts for public consumption.

Great, Start 'Em Young

. . . So, last night, I was walking to the delightful Asian Grocery Store a half-mile or so from my apartment. My brain was filled with thoughts of the delicious Thai food I was going to cook for me and my dude, and also nervous twitchy thoughts about the upcoming bar exam results (I passed! Woot!). In a sort of dark spot on the sidewalk of a pretty major street (but not too dark; it was only an hour or so after sundown), I came across some kids on bikes. You know, riding around in circles, attempting to do tricks, etc.

The first kid I passed said, in that voice that isn't super loud but loud enough to hear, "big titties." To me. My age estimator isn't the greatest, but I'd put this kid at about 12, 13 at the most.

I've been trying for several months now not to let anyone get away with saying shit to me, even the smallest, barely heard thing. Not just to make myself feel more powerful, but also in the secret hopes that maybe, just maybe, it will have an effect on someone. Shake them, the way their comments shake me. Make them feel afraid, uncomfortable.

So I flip around, and say "Excuse me? What did you say?"

"I said big . . . (trails off)."

"What was that? I didn't hear you, punk."

He murmurs "Sorry."

(continued)

f riding away from me,
ids are behind him, and
g scared of this puny-ass
Come here." The kid turns

eak to women like that.
You're too fucking young for that and you know it.
Actually, don't do it when you're older, either."

I walk away, and I'm pretty sure I heard the kid
or one of his friends yell "big titties!" when I was at
sufficient distance.

It's even hard to write about this, because it's so
humiliating. I proceed because I think acting like
it's not humiliating will somehow reduce the humiliation. I mean, seriously, I'm 25, an attorney, and
totally brilliant, but I still have to deal with what
amounts to basically teasing from children?

It makes me angry. It makes my blood run hot
and makes me feel violent. What kind of society is
this, where pre-teens comment on adult women's
bodies in public to show off for their friends, as
part of the rite into "manhood"? These kids are
pre-pubescent or barely puberty-onset, and if they
are thinking about girls in a sexual way, I doubt
they're really getting it up for an old biddy like
me. This is so *obviously* not about sexual attraction.
It's about power, it's about getting away with
something, it's about giving yourself a little
satisfaction.

It was a good thing for my criminal record that
no adult tried to make any comments to me on the
rest of my journey, because I was resolved that if
someone did, I was going to put my grocery bags
down and hit them in the face.

READING *44*   **Kimberlé Crenshaw**

Mapping the Margins: Intersectionality, Identity Politics, and Violence Against Women of Color

. . . My objective [is to explore] the race and gender
dimensions of violence against women of color. . . . I
consider how the experiences of women of color are
frequently the product of intersecting patterns of racism and sexism. . . .

[Based on] a brief field study of battered women's
shelters located in minority communities in Los
Angeles,[1] [I found that in most cases], the physical
assault that leads women to these shelters is merely the
most immediate manifestation of the subordination
they experience. Many women who seek protection are
unemployed or under-employed, and a good number
of them are poor. Shelters serving these women cannot
afford to address only the violence inflicted by the bat-
terer; they must also confront the other multilayered
and routinized forms of domination that often converge

in these women's lives, hindering their ability to create
alternatives to the abusive relationships that brought
them to shelters in the first place. Many women of color,
for example, are burdened by poverty, child care
responsibilities, and the lack of job skills.[2] These burdens, largely the consequence of gender and class
oppression, are then compounded by the racially discriminatory employment and housing practices women
of color often face, as well as by the disproportionately
high unemployment among people of color that makes
battered women of color less able to depend on the support of friends and relatives for temporary shelter.[3]

Where systems of race, gender, and class domination converge, as they do in the experiences of battered
women of color, intervention strategies based solely on
the experiences of women who do not share the same

class or race backgrounds will be of limited help to women who because of race and class face different obstacles.[4] Such was the case in 1990 when Congress amended the marriage fraud provisions of the Immigration and Nationality Act to protect immigrant women who were battered or exposed to extreme cruelty by the United States citizens or permanent residents these women immigrated to the United States to marry. Under the marriage fraud provisions of the Act, a person who immigrated to the United States to marry a United States citizen or permanent resident had to remain "properly" married for two years before even applying for permanent resident status,[5] at which time applications for the immigrant's permanent status were required of both spouses. Predictably, under these circumstances, many immigrant women were reluctant to leave even the most abusive of partners for fear of being deported.[6] When faced with the choice between protection from their batterers and protection against deportation, many immigrant women chose the latter. Reports of the tragic consequences of this double subordination put pressure on Congress to include in the Immigration Act of 1990 a provision amending the marriage fraud rules to allow for an explicit waiver for hardship caused by domestic violence.[7] Yet many immigrant women, particularly immigrant women of color, have remained vulnerable to battering because they are unable to meet the conditions established for a waiver. The evidence required to support a waiver "can include but is not limited to, reports and affidavits from police, medical personnel, psychologists, school officials, and social service agencies."[8] For many immigrant women, limited access to these resources can make it difficult for them to obtain the evidence needed for a waiver. And cultural barriers often further discourage immigrant women from reporting or escaping battering situations. Tina Shum, a family counselor at a social service agency, points out that "[t]his law sounds so easy to apply, but there are cultural complications in the Asian community that make even these requirements difficult. . . . Just to find the opportunity and courage to call us is an accomplishment for many."[9] The typical immigrant spouse, she suggests, may live "[i]n an extended family where several generations live together, there may be no privacy on the telephone, no opportunity to leave the house and no understanding of public phones."[10] As a consequence, many immigrant women are wholly dependent on their husbands as their link to the world outside their homes.

Immigrant women are also vulnerable to spousal violence because so many of them depend on their husbands for information regarding their legal status.[11] Many women who are now permanent residents continue to suffer abuse under threats of deportation by their husbands. Even if the threats are unfounded, women who have no independent access to information will still be intimidated by such threats. And even though the domestic violence waiver focuses on immigrant women whose husbands are United States citizens or permanent residents, there are countless women married to undocumented workers (or who are themselves undocumented) who suffer in silence for fear that the security of their entire families will be jeopardized should they seek help or otherwise call attention to themselves.

Language barriers present another structural problem that often limits opportunities of non-English-speaking women to take advantage of existing support services. Such barriers not only limit access to information about shelters, but also limit access to the security shelters provide. Some shelters turn non-English-speaking women away for lack of bilingual personnel and resources.[12]

These examples illustrate how patterns of subordination intersect in women's experience of domestic violence. . . .

A. THE POLITICIZATION OF DOMESTIC VIOLENCE

[T]he political interests of women of color are obscured and sometimes jeopardized by political strategies that ignore or suppress intersectional issues, [as] is illustrated by my [research]. I attempted to review Los Angeles Police Department statistics reflecting the rate of domestic violence interventions by precinct because such statistics can provide a rough picture of arrests by racial group, given the degree of racial segregation in Los Angeles.[13] L.A.P.D., however, would not release the statistics. A representative explained that one reason the statistics were not released was that domestic violence activists both within and outside the Department feared that statistics reflecting the extent of domestic violence in minority communities might be selectively interpreted and publicized so as to undermine long-term efforts to force the Department to address domestic violence as a serious problem. I was told that activists were worried that the statistics might permit opponents to dismiss domestic violence as a minority problem and, therefore, not deserving of aggressive action.

The informant also claimed that representatives from various minority communities opposed the release of the statistics. They were concerned, apparently, that the data would unfairly represent Black and Brown communities as unusually violent, potentially reinforcing stereotypes that might be used in attempts to justify oppressive police tactics and other discriminatory practices. These misgivings are based on the familiar and not unfounded premise that certain minority groups—especially Black men—have already been stereotyped as uncontrollably violent. Some worry that attempts to make domestic violence an object of political action may only serve to confirm such stereotypes and undermine efforts to combat negative beliefs about the Black community.

This account sharply illustrates how women of color can be erased by the strategic silences of antiracism and feminism. The political priorities of both were defined in ways that suppressed information that could have facilitated attempts to confront the problem of domestic violence in communities of color.

1. Domestic Violence and Antiracist Politics

Within communities of color, efforts to stem the politicization of domestic violence are often grounded in attempts to maintain the integrity of the community. The articulation of this perspective takes different forms. Some critics allege that feminism has no place within communities of color, that the issues are internally divisive, and that they represent the migration of white women's concerns into a context in which they are not only irrelevant but also harmful. At its most extreme, this rhetoric denies that gender violence is a problem in the community and characterizes any effort to politicize gender subordination as itself a community problem. This is the position taken by Shahrazad Ali in her controversial book, *The Blackman's Guide to Understanding the Blackwoman.*[14] In this stridently antifeminist tract, Ali draws a positive correlation between domestic violence and the liberation of African Americans. Ali blames the deteriorating conditions within the Black community on the insubordination of Black women and on the failure of Black men to control them.[15] Ali goes so far as to advise Black men to physically chastise Black women when they are "disrespectful."[16] While she cautions that Black men must use moderation in disciplining "their" women, she argues that Black men must sometimes resort to physical force to reestablish the authority over Black women that racism has disrupted.[17]

Ali's premise is that patriarchy is beneficial for the Black community, and that it must be strengthened through coercive means if necessary. Yet the violence that accompanies this will to control is devastating, not only for the Black women who are victimized, but also for the entire Black community. The recourse to violence to resolve conflicts establishes a dangerous pattern for children raised in such environments and contributes to many other pressing problems. It has been estimated that nearly forty percent of all homeless women and children have fled violence in the home,[18] and an estimated sixty-three percent of young men between the ages of eleven and twenty who are imprisoned for homicide have killed their mothers' batterers.[19] And yet, while gang violence, homicide, and other forms of Black-on-Black crime have increasingly been discussed within African-American politics, patriarchal ideas about gender and power preclude the recognition of domestic violence as yet another compelling incidence of Black-on-Black crime.

Efforts such as Ali's to justify violence against women in the name of Black liberation are indeed extreme. The more common problem is that the political or cultural interests of the community are interpreted in a way that precludes full public recognition of the problem of domestic violence. While it would be misleading to suggest that white Americans have come to terms with the degree of violence in their own homes, it is nonetheless the case that race adds yet another dimension to why the problem of domestic violence is suppressed within nonwhite communities. People of color often must weigh their interests in avoiding issues that might reinforce distorted public perceptions against the need to acknowledge and address intracommunity problems. Yet the cost of suppression is seldom recognized in part because the failure to discuss the issue shapes perceptions of how serious the problem is in the first place.

The controversy over Alice Walker's novel *The Color Purple* can be understood as an intracommunity debate about the political costs of exposing gender violence within the Black community.[20] Some critics chastised Walker for portraying Black men as violent brutes.[21] One critic lambasted Walker's portrayal of Celie, the emotionally and physically abused protagonist who finally triumphs in the end. Walker, the critic contended, had created in Celie a Black woman whom she couldn't imagine existing in any Black community she knew or could conceive of.[22]

The claim that Celie was somehow an unauthentic character might be read as a consequence of silencing discussion of intracommunity violence. Celie may be unlike any Black woman we know because the real terror experienced daily by minority women is routinely concealed in a misguided (though perhaps understandable) attempt to forestall racial stereotyping. Of course, it is true that representations of Black violence—whether statistical or fictional—are often written into a larger script that consistently portrays Black and other minority communities as pathologically violent. The problem, however, is not so much the portrayal of violence itself as it is the absence of other narratives and images portraying a fuller range of Black experience. Suppression of some of these issues in the name of antiracism imposes real costs. Where information about violence in minority communities is not available, domestic violence is unlikely to be addressed as a serious issue.

The political imperatives of a narrowly focused antiracist strategy support other practices that isolate women of color. For example, activists who have attempted to provide support services to Asian- and African-American women report intense resistance from those communities.[23] At other times, cultural and social factors contribute to suppression. Nilda Rimonte, director of Everywoman's Shelter in Los Angeles, points out that in the Asian community, saving the honor of the family from shame is a priority.[24] Unfortunately, this priority tends to be interpreted as obliging women not to scream rather than obliging men not to hit.

Race and culture contribute to the suppression of domestic violence in other ways as well. Women of color are often reluctant to call the police, a hesitancy likely due to a general unwillingness among people of color to subject their private lives to the scrutiny and control of a police force that is frequently hostile. There is also a more generalized community ethic against public intervention, the product of a desire to create a private world free from the diverse assaults on the public lives of racially subordinated people. The home is not simply a man's castle in the patriarchal sense, but may also function as a safe haven from the indignities of life in a racist society. However, but for this "safe haven" in many cases, women of color victimized by violence might otherwise seek help.

There is also a general tendency within antiracist discourse to regard the problem of violence against women of color as just another manifestation of racism.

In this sense, the relevance of gender domination within the community is reconfigured as a consequence of discrimination against men. Of course, it is probably true that racism contributes to the cycle of violence, given the stress that men of color experience in dominant society. It is therefore more than reasonable to explore the links between racism and domestic violence. But the chain of violence is more complex and extends beyond this single link. Racism is linked to patriarchy to the extent that racism denies men of color the power and privilege that dominant men enjoy. When violence is understood as an acting-out of being denied male power in other spheres, it seems counterproductive to embrace constructs that implicitly link the solution to domestic violence to the acquisition of greater male power. The more promising political imperative is to challenge the legitimacy of such power expectations by exposing their dysfunctional and debilitating effect on families and communities of color. Moreover, while understanding links between racism and domestic violence is an important component of any effective intervention strategy, it is also clear that women of color need not await the ultimate triumph over racism before they can expect to live violence-free lives.

2. Race and the Domestic Violence Lobby

Not only do race-based priorities function to obscure the problem of violence suffered by women of color; feminist concerns often suppress minority experiences as well. Strategies for increasing awareness of domestic violence within the white community tend to begin by citing the commonly shared assumption that battering is a minority problem. The strategy then focuses on demolishing this strawman, stressing that spousal abuse also occurs in the white community. Countless first-person stories begin with a statement like, "I was not supposed to be a battered wife." That battering occurs in families of all races and all classes seems to be an ever-present theme of anti-abuse campaigns. First-person anecdotes and studies, for example, consistently assert that battering cuts across racial, ethnic, economic, educational, and religious lines.[25] Such disclaimers seem relevant only in the presence of an initial, widely held belief that domestic violence occurs primarily in minority or poor families. Indeed some authorities explicitly renounce the "stereotypical myths" about battered women.[26] A few commentators have even transformed the message that battering is not exclusively a problem of the poor or minority communities into a claim that it equally affects all races and classes.[27] Yet these comments seem less concerned with exploring domestic abuse within "stereotyped" communities than with removing the stereotype as an obstacle to exposing battering within white middle- and upper-class communities.

Efforts to politicize the issue of violence against women challenge beliefs that violence occurs only in homes of "others." While it is unlikely that advocates and others who adopt this rhetorical strategy intend to exclude or ignore the needs of poor and colored women, the underlying premise of this seemingly universalistic appeal is to keep the sensibilities of dominant social groups focused on the experiences of those groups. Indeed, as subtly suggested by the opening comments of Senator David Boren (D-Okla.) in support of the Violence Against Women Act of 1991, the displacement of the "other" as the presumed victim of domestic violence works primarily as a political appeal to rally white elites. Boren said:

> Violent crimes against women are not limited to the streets of the inner cities, but also occur in homes in the urban and rural areas across the country.
>
> Violence against women affects not only those who are actually beaten and brutalized, but indirectly affects all women. Today, our wives, mothers, daughters, sisters, and colleagues are held captive by fear generated from these violent crimes—held captive not for what they do or who they are, but solely because of gender.[28]

Rather than focusing on and illuminating how violence is disregarded when the home is "othered," the strategy implicit in Senator Boren's remarks functions instead to politicize the problem only in the dominant community. This strategy permits white women victims to come into focus, but does little to disrupt the patterns of neglect that permitted the problem to continue as long as it was imagined to be a minority problem. The experience of violence of minority women is ignored, except to the extent it gains white support for domestic violence programs in the white community.

Senator Boren and his colleagues no doubt believe that they have provided legislation and resources that will address the problems of all women victimized by domestic violence. Yet despite their universalizing rhetoric of "all" women, they were able to empathize with female victims of domestic violence only by looking past the plight of "other" women and by recognizing the familiar faces of their own. The strength of the appeal to "protect our women" must be its race and class specificity. After all, it has always been someone's wife, mother, sister, or daughter that has been abused, even when the violence was stereotypically Black or Brown, and poor. The point here is not that the Violence Against Women Act is particularistic on its own terms, but that unless the Senators and other policymakers ask why violence remained insignificant as long as it was understood as a minority problem, it is unlikely that women of color will share equally in the distribution of resources and concern. It is even more unlikely, however, that those in power will be forced to confront this issue. As long as attempts to politicize domestic violence focus on convincing whites that this is not a "minority" problem but their problem, any authentic and sensitive attention to the experiences of Black and other minority women probably will continue to be regarded as jeopardizing the movement.

While Senator Boren's statement reflects a self-consciously political presentation of domestic violence, an episode of the CBS news program *48 Hours*[29] shows how similar patterns of "othering" nonwhite women are apparent in journalistic accounts of domestic violence as well. The program presented seven women who were victims of abuse. Six were interviewed at some length along with their family members, friends, supporters, and even detractors. The viewer got to know something about each of these women. These victims were humanized. Yet the seventh woman, the only nonwhite one, never came into focus. She was literally unrecognizable throughout the segment, first introduced by photographs showing her face badly beaten and later shown with her face electronically altered in the videotape of a hearing at which she was forced to testify. Other images associated with this woman included shots of a bloodstained room and blood-soaked pillows. Her boyfriend was pictured handcuffed while the camera zoomed in for a close-up of his bloodied sneakers. Of all the presentations in the episode, hers was the most graphic and impersonal. The overall point of the segment "featuring" this woman was that battering might not escalate into homicide if battered women would only cooperate with prosecutors. In focusing on its own agenda and failing to explore why this woman refused to cooperate, the program diminished this woman, communicating, however subtly, that she was responsible for her own victimization.

Unlike the other women, all of whom, again, were white, this Black woman had no name, no family, no context. The viewer sees her only as victimized and uncooperative. She cries when shown pictures. She pleads not to be forced to view the bloodstained room and her disfigured face. The program does not help the viewer to understand her predicament. The possible reasons she did not want to testify—fear, love, or possibly both—are never suggested. Most unfortunately, she, unlike the other six, is given no epilogue. While the fates of the other women are revealed at the end of the episode, we discover nothing about the Black woman. She, like the "others" she represents, is simply left to herself and soon forgotten.

I offer this description to suggest that "other" women are silenced as much by being relegated to the margin of experience as by total exclusion. Tokenistic, objectifying, voyeuristic inclusion is at least as disempowering as complete exclusion. The effort to politicize violence against women will do little to address Black and other minority women if their images are retained simply to magnify the problem rather than to humanize their experiences. Similarly, the antiracist agenda will not be advanced significantly by forcibly suppressing the reality of battering in minority communities. As the *48 Hours* episode makes clear, the images and stereotypes we fear are readily available and are frequently deployed in ways that do not generate sensitive understanding of the nature of domestic violence in minority communities.

3. Race and Domestic Violence Support Services

Women working in the field of domestic violence have sometimes reproduced the subordination and marginalization of women of color by adopting policies, priorities, or strategies of empowerment that either elide or wholly disregard the particular intersectional needs of women of color. While gender, race, and class intersect to create the particular context in which women of color experience violence, certain choices made by "allies" can reproduce intersectional subordination within the very resistance strategies designed to respond to the problem.

This problem is starkly illustrated by the inaccessibility of domestic violence support services to many non-English-speaking women. In a letter written to the deputy commissioner of the New York State Department of Social Services, Diana Campos, Director of

Human Services for Programas de Ocupaciones y Desarrollo Economico Real, Inc. (PODER), detailed the case of a Latina in crisis who was repeatedly denied accommodation at a shelter because she could not prove that she was English-proficient. The woman had fled her home with her teenaged son, believing her husband's threats to kill them both. She called the domestic violence hotline administered by PODER seeking shelter for herself and her son. Because most shelters would not accommodate the woman with her son, they were forced to live on the streets for two days. The hotline counselor was finally able to find an agency that would take both the mother and the son, but when the counselor told the intake coordinator at the shelter that the woman spoke limited English, the coordinator told her that they could not take anyone who was not English-proficient. When the women in crisis called back and was told of the shelter's "rule," she replied that she could understand English if spoken to her slowly. As Campos explains, Mildred, the hotline counselor, told Wendy, the intake coordinator

> that the woman said that she could communicate a little in English. Wendy told Mildred that they could not provide services to this woman because they have house rules that the woman must agree to follow. Mildred asked her, "What if the woman agrees to follow your rules? Will you still not take her?" Wendy responded that all of the women at the shelter are required to attend [a] support group and they would not be able to have her in the group if she could not communicate. Mildred mentioned the severity of this woman's case. She told Wendy that the woman had been wandering the streets at night while her husband is home, and she had been mugged twice. She also reiterated the fact that this woman was in danger of being killed by either her husband or a mugger. Mildred expressed that the woman's safety was a priority at this point, and that once in a safe place, receiving counseling in a support group could be dealt with.[30]

The intake coordinator restated the shelter's policy of taking only English-speaking women, and stated further that the woman would have to call the shelter herself for screening. If the woman could communicate with them in English, she might be accepted. When the woman called the PODER hotline later that day, she was in such a state of fear that the hotline counselor who had been working with her had difficulty understanding her in Spanish.[31] Campos directly intervened at this point, calling the executive director of the shelter. A counselor called back from the shelter. As Campos reports,

> Marie [the counselor] told me that they did not want to take the woman in the shelter because they felt that the woman would feel isolated. I explained that the son agreed to translate for his mother during the intake process. Furthermore, that we would assist them in locating a Spanish-speaking battered women's advocate to assist in counseling her. Marie stated that utilizing the son was not an acceptable means in communication for them, since it further victimized the victim. In addition, she stated that they had similar experiences with women who were non-English-speaking, and that the women eventually just left because they were not able to communicate with anyone. I expressed my extreme concern for her safety and reiterated that we would assist them in providing her with the necessary services until we could get her placed someplace where they had bilingual staff.[32]

After several more calls, the shelter finally agreed to take the woman. The woman called once more during the negotiation; however, after a plan was in place, the woman never called back. Said Campos, "After so many calls, we are now left to wonder if she is alive and well, and if she will ever have enough faith in our ability to help her to call us again the next time she is in crisis."[33]

Despite this woman's desperate need, she was unable to receive the protection afforded English-speaking women, due to the shelter's rigid commitment to exclusionary policies. Perhaps even more troubling than the shelter's lack of bilingual resources was its refusal to allow a friend or relative to translate for the woman. This story illustrates the absurdity of a feminist approach that would make the ability to attend a support group without a translator a more significant consideration in the distribution of resources than the risk of physical harm on the street. The point is not that the shelter's image of empowerment is empty, but rather that it was imposed without regard to the disempowering consequences for women who didn't match the kind of client the shelter's administrators imagined. And thus they failed to accomplish the basic priority of the shelter movement—to get the woman out of danger.

Here the woman in crisis was made to bear the burden of the shelter's refusal to anticipate and provide for the needs of non-English-speaking women. Said Campos, "It is unfair to impose more stress on victims by placing them in the position of having to demonstrate their proficiency in English in order to receive services that are readily available to other battered women."[34] The problem is not easily dismissed as one of well-intentioned ignorance. The specific issue of monolingualism and the monistic view of women's experience that set the stage for this tragedy were not new issues in New York. Indeed, several women of color reported that they had repeatedly struggled with the New York State Coalition Against Domestic Violence over language exclusion and other practices that marginalized the interests of women of color.[35] Yet despite repeated lobbying, the Coalition did not act to incorporate the specific needs of nonwhite women into its central organizing vision.

Some critics have linked the Coalition's failure to address these issues to the narrow vision of coalition that animated its interaction with women of color in the first place. The very location of the Coalition's headquarters in Woodstock, New York—an area where few people of color live—seemed to guarantee that women of color would play a limited role in formulating policy. Moreover, efforts to include women of color came, it seems, as something of an afterthought. Many were invited to participate only after the Coalition was awarded a grant by the state to recruit women of color. However, as one "recruit" said, "they were not really prepared to deal with us or our issues. They thought that they could simply incorporate us into their organization without rethinking any of their beliefs or priorities and that we would be happy."[36] Even the most formal gestures of inclusion were not to be taken for granted. On one occasion when several women of color attended a meeting to discuss a special task force on women of color, the group debated all day over including the issue on the agenda.[37]

The relationship between the white women and the women of color on the Board was a rocky one from beginning to end. Other conflicts developed over differing definitions of feminism. For example, the Board decided to hire a Latina staffperson to manage outreach programs to the Latino community, but the white members of the hiring committee rejected candidates favored by Latina committee members who did not have recognized feminist credentials. As Campos pointed out, by measuring Latinas against their own biographies, the white members of the Board failed to recognize the different circumstances under which feminist consciousness develops and manifests itself within minority communities. Many of the women who interviewed for the position were established activists and leaders within their own community, a fact in itself suggesting that these women were probably familiar with the specific gender dynamics in their communities and were accordingly better qualified to handle outreach than other candidates with more conventional feminist credentials.[38]

The Coalition ended a few months later when the women of color walked out.[39] Many of these women returned to community-based organizations, preferring to struggle over women's issues within their communities rather than struggle over race and class issues with white middle-class women. Yet as illustrated by the case of the Latina who could find no shelter, the dominance of a particular perspective and set of priorities within the shelter community continues to marginalize the needs of women of color.

The struggle over which differences matter and which do not is neither an abstract nor an insignificant debate among women. Indeed, these conflicts are about more than difference as such; they raise critical issues of power. The problem is not simply that women who dominate the antiviolence movement are different from women of color but that they frequently have power to determine, either through material or rhetorical resources, whether the intersectional differences of women of color will be incorporated at all into the basic formulation of policy. Thus, the struggle over incorporating these differences is not a petty or superficial conflict about who gets to sit at the head of the table. In the context of violence, it is sometimes a deadly serious matter of who will survive—and who will not. . . .

NOTES

1. During my research in Los Angeles, California, I visited Jenessee Battered Women's Shelter, the only shelter in the Western states primarily serving Black women, and Everywoman's Shelter, which primarily serves Asian women. I also visited Estelle Chueng at the Asian Pacific Law Foundation, and I spoke with a representative of La Casa, a shelter in the predominantly Latino community of East L.A.

2. One researcher has noted, in reference to a survey taken of battered women's shelters, that "many Caucasian women were probably excluded from the sample, since they are more likely to have available resources that enable them to avoid going to a shelter. Many shelters admit only women with few or no resources or alternatives." Mildred Daley Pagelow, *Woman-Battering: Victims and Their Experiences*, 97 (1981). On the other hand, many middle- and upper-class women are financially dependent upon their husbands and thus experience a diminution in their standard of living when they leave their husbands.

3. More specifically, African Americans suffer from high unemployment rates, low incomes, and high poverty rates. According to Dr. David Swinton, Dean of the School of Business at Jackson State University in Mississippi, African Americans "receive three-fifths as much income per person as whites and are three times as likely to have annual incomes below the federally defined poverty level of $12, 675 for a family of four." Urban League Urges Action, *N.Y. Times*, Jan 9, 1991, at A14. In fact, recent statistics indicate that racial economic inequality is "higher as we begin the 1990s than at any other time in the last 20 years." David Swinton, The Economic Status of African Americans: "Permanent" Poverty and Inequality, in *The State of Black America* 1991, 25 (1991).

The economic situation of minority women is, expectedly, worse than that of their male counterparts. Black

women, who earn a median of $7,875 a year, make considerably less than Black men, who earn a median income of $12,609 a year, and white women, who earn a median income of $9,812 a year. *Id.* at 32 (Table 3). Additionally, the percentage of Black female-headed families living in poverty (46.5%) is almost twice that of white female-headed families (25.4%). *Id.* at 43 (Table 8). Latino households also earn considerably less than white households. In 1988, the median income of Latino households was $20,359 and for white households, $28,840—a difference of almost $8,000. *Hispanic Americans: A Statistical Sourcebook* 149 (1991), Analyzing by origin, in 1988, Puerto Rican households were the worst off, with 34.1% earning below $10,000 a year and a median income for all Puerto Rican households of $15,447 per year. *Id.* at 155. 1989 statistics for Latino men and women show that women earned an average of $7,000 less than men. *Id.* at 169.

4. . . . Racial differences marked an interesting contrast between Jenessee's policies and those of other shelters situated outside the Black community. Unlike some other shelters in Los Angeles, Jenessee welcomed the assistance of men. According to the Director, the shelter's policy was premised on a belief that given African Americans' need to maintain healthy relations to pursue a common struggle against racism, anti-violence programs within the African American community cannot afford to be antagonistic to men. For a discussion of the different needs of Black women who are battered, see Beth Richie, Battered Black Women: A Challenge for the Black Community, *Black Scholar* 40 (Mar./Apr. 1985).

5. §U.S.C. §1186a (1988), . . .

6. Immigration activists have pointed out that "[t]he 1986 Immigration Reform Act and the Immigration Marriage Fraud Amendment have combined to give the spouse

applying for permanent residence a powerful tool to control his partner." Jorge Banales, Abuse Among Immigrants: As Their Numbers Grow So Does the Need for Services, *Washington Post*, Oct. 16, 1990, at E5. . . . In one egregious instance described by Beckie Masaki, executive director of the Asian Women's Shelter in San Francisco, the closer the Chinese bride came to getting her permanent residency in the United States, the more harshly her Asian-American husband beat her. Her husband, kicking her in the neck and face, warned her that she needed him, and if she did not do as he told her, he would call immigration officials. Deanna Hodgin, "Mail-Order" Brides Marry Pain to Get Green Cards, *Washington Times*, Apr. 16, 1991, at El.

7. Immigration Act of 1990, Pub. L. No. 101–649, 104 Stat. 4978. . . .

8. H.R.Rep. No. 723(1). 101st Cong., 2d Sess. 79 (1990), *reprinted in* 1990 U.S.C.C.A.N. 6710, 6759.

9. Hodgin, *supra* note 6.

10. *Id.*

11. A citizen or permanent resident spouse can exercise power over an alien spouse by threatening not to file a petition for permanent residency. If he fails to file a petition for permanent residency, the alien spouse continues to be undocumented and is considered to be in the country illegally. These constraints often restrict an alien spouse from leaving. Dean Ito Taylor tells the story of "one client who has been hospitalized—she's had him arrested for beating her—but she keeps coming back to him because he promises he will file for her. . . . He holds that green card over her head." Hodgin, *supra* note 6. . . .

12. . . . To combat this lack of appropriate services for women of color at many shelters, special programs have been created specifically for women from particular communities. A few examples of such programs include the Victim Intervention Project in East Harlem for Latina women, Jenessee Shelter for African American women in Los Angeles, Apna Gar in Chicago for South Asian women, and, for Asian women generally, the Asian Women's Shelter in San Francisco, the New York Asian Women's Center, and the Center for the Pacific Asian Family in Los Angeles. Programs with hotlines include Sakhi for South Asian Women in New York, and Manavi in Jersey City, also for South Asian women, as well as programs for Korean women in Philadelphia and Chicago.

13. Most crime statistics are classified by sex or race but none are classified by sex and race. Because we know that most rape victims are women, the racial breakdown reveals, at best, rape rates for Black women. Yet, even given this head start, rates for other non-white women are difficult to collect. While there are some statistics for Latinas, statistics for Asian and Native American women are virtually nonexistent. Cf. G. Chezia Carraway, Violence Against Women of Color, *Stan. L. Rev.* 43 (1993); 1301.

14. Shahrazad Ali, *The Blackman's Guide to Understanding the Blackwoman* (1989). Ali's book sold quite well for an independently published title, an accomplishment no doubt due in part to her appearances on the Phil Donahue, Oprah Winfrey, and Sally Jesse Raphael television talk shows. For public and press reaction, see Dorothy Gilliam, Sick, Distorted Thinking, *Washington Post*, Oct. 11, 1990, at D3; Lena Williams, Black Woman's Book Starts a Predictable Storm, *New York Times*, Oct 2, 1990, at C11; see also Pearl Cleague, *Mad at Miles: A Black Women's Guide to Truth* (1990). The title clearly styled after Ali's, *Mad at Miles* responds not only to issues raised by Ali's book, but also to Miles Davis's admission in his autobiography, *Miles: The Autobiography* (1989), that he had physically abused, among other women, his former wife, actress Cicely Tyson.

15. Shahrazad Ali suggests that the "[Blackwoman] certainly does not believe that her disrespect for the Blackman is destructive, nor that her opposition to him has deteriorated the Black nation." S. Ali, *supra* note 14, at viii. Blaming the problems of the community on the failure of the Black woman to accept her "real definition," Ali explains that "[n]o nation can rise when the natural order of the behavior of the male and the female have been altered against their wishes by force. No species can survive if the female of the genus disturbs the balance of her nature by acting other than herself." *Id.* at 76.

16. Ali advises the Blackman to hit the Blackwoman in the mouth, "[b]ecause it is from that hole, in the lower part of her face, that all her rebellion culminates into words. Her unbridled tongue is a main reason she cannot get along with the Blackman. She often needs a reminder." *Id.* at 169. Ali warns that "if [the Blackwoman] ignores the authority and superiority of the Blackman, there is a penalty. When she crosses this line and becomes viciously insulting, it is time for the Blackman to soundly slap her in the mouth." *Id.*

17. Ali explains that, "[r]egretfully some Blackwomen want to be physically controlled by the Blackman." *Id.* at 174. "The Blackwoman, deep inside her heart" Ali reveals, "wants to surrender but she wants to be coerced." *Id.* at 72. "[The Blackwoman] wants [the Blackman] to stand up and defend himself even if it means he has to knock her out of the way to do so. This is necessary whenever the Blackwoman steps out of the protection of womanly behavior and enters the dangerous domain of masculine challenge." *Id.* at 174.

18. [Women and Violence: Hearings Before the Senate Comm. on the Judiciary on Legislation to Reduce the Growing Problem of Violent Crime Against Women, 101st Cong., 2d Sess., pt. 2, at 142] (statement of Susan Kelly-Dreiss) (discussing several studies in Pennsylvania linking homelessness to domestic violence).

19. *Id.* at 143 (statement of Susan Kelly-Dreiss).

20. Alice Walker, *The Color Purple* (1982). The most severe criticism of Walker developed after the book was filmed as a movie. Donald Bogle, a film historian, argued that part of

the criticism of the movie stemmed from the one-dimensional portrayal of Mister, the abusive man. See Jacqueline Trescott, Passions over Purple; Anger and Unease over Film's Depiction of Black Men, *Washington Post*, Feb. 5, 1986, at C1. Bogle argues that in the novel, Walker linked Mister's abusive conduct to his oppression in the white world—since Mister "can't be himself, he has to assert himself with the black woman." The movie failed to make any connection between Mister's abusive treatment of Black women and racism, and thereby presented Mister only as an "insensitive, callous man." *Id.*

21. See, e.g., Gerald Early, Her Picture in the Papers: Remembering Some Black Women, *Antaeus*, Spring 1988, at 9; Daryl Pickney, Black Victims, Black Villains, *New York Review of Books*, Jan. 29, 1987, at 17; Trescott, *supra* note 20.

22. Trudler Harris, On the Color Purple, Stereotypes, and Silence, *Black Am. Lit. F.* 18 (1984), 155.

23. The source of the resistance reveals an interesting difference between the Asian-American and African-American communities. In the African-American community, the resistance is usually grounded in efforts to avoid confirming negative stereotypes of African-Americans as violent; the concern of members in some Asian-American communities as to avoid tarnishing the model minority myth. Interview with Nilda Rimonte, Director of the Everywoman Shelter, in Los Angeles, California (April 19, 1991).

24. Nilda Rimonte, A Question of Culture: Cultural Approval of Violence Against Women in the Pacific-Asian Community and the Cultural Defense, *Stan. L. Rev.* 43 (1991), 1311; see also Nilda Rimonte, Domestic Violence Against Pacific Asians, in Asian Women United of California ed., *Making Waves: An Anthology of Writings by and About Asian American Women*; 327, 328 (1989). . . .

When—or, more importantly, how—to take culture into account when addressing the needs of women of color is a complicated issue. Testimony as to the particularities of Asian "culture" has increasingly been used in trials to determine the culpability of both Asian immigrant women and men who are charged with crimes of interpersonal violence. A position on the use of the "cultural defense" in these instances depends on how "culture" is being defined as well as on whether and to what extent the "cultural defense" has been used differently for Asian men and Asian women. See Leti Volpp, (Mis) Identifying Culture: Asian Women and the "Cultural Defense," (unpublished manuscript).

25. See, e.g., Lenore F. Walker, *Terrifying Love: Why Battered Women Kill and How Society Responds*, 101–102 (1989). ("Battered women come from all types of economic, cultural, religious, and racial backgrounds. . . . They are women like you. Like me. Like those whom you know and love."); Murray A. Straus, Richard J. Gelles & Suzanne K. Steinmetz, *Behind Closed Doors: Violence in the American Family*, 31 (1980) ("Wife-beating is found in every class, at every income level."). . . .

26. For example, Susan Kelly-Dreiss states: "T[h] many myths about battered women—they are [ ] are women of color, they are uneducated, they [ ] welfare, they deserve to be beaten and they even li[ ] However, contrary to common misperceptions, domesti[ ] violence is not confined to any one socioeconomic, ethnic, religious, racial or age group." Hearings on Violent Crime Against Women, *supra* note 18, pt. 2, at 139 (testimony of Susan Kelly-Dreiss, Executive Director, Pennsylvania Coalition Against Domestic Violence). Kathleen Waits offers a possible explanation for this misperception: "It is true that battered women who are also poor are more likely to come to the attention of governmental officials than are their middle- and upper-class counterparts. However, this phenomenon is caused more by the lack of alternative resources and the intrusiveness of the welfare state than by any significantly higher incidence of violence among lower-class families." Kathleen Waits, The Criminal Justice System's Response to Battering: Understanding the Problem, Forging the Solutions, *Washington U.L. Rev.* 60 (1985), 267, 276–277.

27. However, no reliable statistics support such a claim. In fact, some statistics suggest that there is a greater frequency of violence among the working classes and the poor. See M. Straus, R. Gelles & S. Steinmetz, *supra* note 25, at 31. Yet these statistics are also unreliable because, to follow Waits's observation, violence in middle- and upper-class homes remains hidden from the view of statisticians and governmental officials alike. I would suggest that assertions that the problem is the same across race and class are driven less by actual knowledge about the prevalence of domestic violence in different communities than by advocates' recognition that the image of domestic violence as an issue involving primarily the poor and minorities complicates efforts to mobilize against it.

28. 137 Cong. Rec. S611 (daily ed. Jan. 14, 1991) (statement of Sen. Boren). Senator William Cohen (D-Me.) followed with a similar statement. . . . *Id.* (statement of Sen. Cohen).

29. *48 Hours: Till Death Do Us Part* (CBS television broadcast, Feb. 6, 1991).

30. Letter of Diana M. Campos, Director of Human Services, PODER, to Joseph Semidei, Deputy Commissioner, New York State Department of Social Services (Mar. 26, 1992).

31. The woman had been slipping back into her home during the day when her husband was at work. She remained in a heightened state of anxiety because he was returning shortly and she would be forced to go back out into the streets for yet another night.

32. PODER Letter, *supra* note 30.

33. *Id.*

34. *Id.*

35. Roundtable Discussion on Racism and the Domestic Violence Movement (April 2, 1992). The participants in the discussion—Diana Campos, Director, Bilingual Outreach

ɔalition Against Domestic
Director, Victim Intervened project in East Harlem,
men); and Haydee Rosario,
Harlem Council for Human
vention Project volunteer—
to race and culture during
New York State Coalition
Against Dom... , a state oversight group that
distributed resources to battered women's shelters
throughout the state and generally set policy priorities for
the shelters that were part of the Coalition.

36. *Id.*
37. *Id.*
38. *Id.*
39. Ironically, the specific dispute that led to the walk-out concerned the housing of the Spanish-language domestic violence hotline. The hotline was initially housed at the Coalition's headquarters, but languished after a succession of coordinators left the organization. Latinas on the Coalition board argued that the hotline should be housed at one of the community service agencies, while the board insisted on maintaining control of it. The hotline is now housed at PODER. *Id.*

R E A D I N G *45* **Joane Nagel**

Sex and War: Fighting Men, Comfort Women, and the Military-Sexual Complex

Several years ago a student came to see me during office hours to discuss a research project he was planning for that semester. He said he wanted to write a paper on Korean prostitution in Junction City, Kansas. I looked at him blankly, thinking there was some kind of miscommunication between us. He was an international student, and perhaps we were having a language problem. Either I did not understand his description of the project or he did not understand the assignment. What would Koreans (especially Korean prostitutes) be doing in a small town 150 miles west of Kansas City? As we discussed his project further, I began to understand what this Korean student already knew—that both South Korea and Kansas are ethnosexual destinations where the global meets the local in the pursuit of racialized sex and romance.

. . . This [reading] will focus on the geopolitics of ethnicity and sexuality mainly in the twentieth century, and will examine the ethnosexual dimensions of international conflicts, civil wars, the Cold War, and the post-Soviet "new world order." We will survey the ways that sexuality is deployed in military missions and the uses of sexual technologies in making war and keeping the peace.

SEX AND THE MILITARY MAN

Since the Korean War of 1950–1953 hundreds of thousands of U.S. armed services personnel have been stationed on dozens of military bases and installations in South Korea. For instance, in 2001 U.S. Forces in Korea officials reported that there were ninety-five military bases and installations of various sorts in South Korea, forty-one of which were "major sized bases/installations" staffed by approximately thirty-seven thousand troops and service personnel.[1] Some of these troops are based stateside in Junction City, Kansas, home of the U.S. Army's First Infantry Division—"The Big Red One." While they are stationed in South Korea many American servicemen frequent hundreds of bars and brothels surrounding military bases, some of which were set up and are inspected by U.S. and Korean authorities. These Americans sate their sexual desire and spread their sexual seed among thousands of Korean and other mainly Asian prostitutes servicing these servicemen. For instance, Katharine Moon estimates that

[s]ince the war, over one million Korean women have served as sex providers for the U.S. military. And

millions of Koreans and Americans have shared a sense of special bonding, for they have together shed blood in battle and mixed blood through sex and Amerasian offspring.[2]

GIs in Korea do not simply have sex with local women, some marry Korean women who return with them to the United States when the men complete their tours of duty. Moon reports that "from the early 1950s to the early 1990s, over 100,000 Korean women have immigrated to the United States as wives of servicemen."[3] Some of these marriages are, no doubt, affairs of convenience arranged for profit or immigration purposes, and some are matches made for love or romance. Some marriages last, some do not.

In the United States, Korean women from dissolved unions often find themselves strangers in a new land, attempting to establish an independent life, possessing only a limited knowledge of English and few job skills, competing for employment in local labor markets primarily oriented to providing services to the military base. These women have easy access linguistically and culturally to already established Korean businesses catering to soldiers, and many find work as waitresses, bargirls, dancers, masseuses, and prostitutes. This combination of military, marriage, and migration accounted for what initially seemed to me to be the unlikely presence of Korean prostitutes in Junction City, Kansas.

The number of Korean prostitutes in Junction City is no doubt small and represents a tiny proportion of the number of American prostitutes working near U.S. military bases across the United States. Korean prostitutes in Junction City are, of course, only a tiny fraction of the number of Korean and other Asian prostitutes working near U.S. military bases in Korea, and still a smaller fraction of German and other European prostitutes working near U.S. military bases in Germany, or the number of Japanese, Okinawan, and other Asian prostitutes working near U.S. military bases in Japan,[4] or Filipino prostitutes who worked near U.S. military bases in the Philippines until those bases were closed in 1992,[5] or Panamanian and Latin American prostitutes who worked near bases in the former U.S. Canal Zone before the canal was turned over to Panama in 1999. These are to name but a few of the ethnosexual work zones surrounding U.S. and other countries' military bases around the world. These militarized ethnosexual frontiers are collateral creations of the global defense and warfare system.

An important aspect of Korean prostitution in Korea and Kansas involves the place of Asian women in Western erotic meaning systems. Lynn Thiesmeyer argues that the imaginary construction of Asian women's sexuality is accomplished by "discourses of seduction" in which the Asian female body is characterized by servile sexual availability. She argues that this long-standing, performative Western sexual stereotype of Asian women works to silence dissident discourses and mask inconvenient realities of Asian women's physical abuse, forced servitude, and sexual exploitation by both Western and non-Western men.

> The western image of the Asian female, the Asian body, and Asian sexuality has been reproduced, yet scarcely updated for centuries. As a late twentieth-century representative body of cultural feudalism and exoticism, the Asian/Asian-American woman has no parallel in the fantasies of the West. Wendy Chapkis points out that "advertisements using Asian women, for example, are evocative not only of the sexual mystery but also the docility and subservience supposedly 'natural to the oriental female.' . . . These women thus become metaphors for adventure, cultural difference, and sexual sub-servience."[6]

Thus, for American servicemen the sexual recreation areas that surround U.S. military bases, especially in Asia, are ethnosexual sites where Western fantasies of Asian female sexuality meet material manifestations of Asian women, and where the marriage of geopolitics and racial cosmologies is consummated nightly.

Although the presence of U.S. bases provides the customer base for the local and immigrant prostitutes, the bars and brothels that ring military installations are owned and regulated by a variety of economic players. Aida Santos argues that there are many local groups and actors directly or indirectly involved in the sex industry: local club owners, organized crime rings, politicians and party officials, law enforcement; she also cites local patriarchal cultural patterns, especially "male political privilege that underlies the institutionalized use of women's bodies."[7] Saundra Sturdevant and Brenda Stoltzfus's discussion of the bar system in Olongapo that was situated near the Subic Bay U.S. military base in the Philippines described a similar local/foreign partnership:

> The bar owners are Filipinos, Chinese, and American ex-Navy men who either have married a Filipina or

have a front in order to own a bar. They are community members active in the Lion's and Rotary Clubs. The mayor also owns several clubs. The club owners have an association, which enables them to control what happens in the bar system.[8]

There are many interests served by the sexual service industry. There is money to be made, troops to be entertained, tensions to be released, strategic interests to be protected, and masculinity to be militarized. Cynthia Enloe argues that militaries and military operations depend on

particular presumptions about masculinity in order to sustain soldiers' morale and discipline. Without a sexualized "rest and recreation" (R&R) period, would the U.S. military command be able to send young men off on long, often tedious sea voyages and ground maneuvers? Without myths of Asian women's compliant sexuality would many American men be able to sustain their own identities of themselves as manly enough to act as soldiers. Women who . . . work as prostitutes around American bases in Asia tell us how a militarized masculinity is constructed and reconstructed in smoky bars and in sparsely furnished boardinghouses. If we only look at boot camps and the battlefield—the focus of most investigations into the formation of militarized masculinity—we will not be able adequately to explain just how masculinity is created and sustained in the peculiar ways necessary to sustain a military organization.[9]

Enloe is joined by a number of critics of the U.S. global military presence who argue that the military mobilization of masculinity to serve national interests—economic and geopolitical, foreign and domestic—is not without its costs—to the men themselves and to the country as a whole. The presence of the U.S. military is deeply resented in many countries, not the least because of the local presence of American culture and consumers, especially sexual consumers. Chalmers Johnson argues that

[f]ew Americans who have never served in the armed forces overseas have any conception of the nature or impact of an American base complex, with its massive military facilities, post exchanges, dependents' housing estates, swimming pools, and golf courses, and the associated bars, strip clubs, whore-houses, and venereal disease clinics that they attract. . . . They can extend

for miles, dominating localities and in some cases whole nations.[10]

In such cases, the American presence can be experienced by locals as an occupation by foreign men, women, equipment, vehicles, buildings, war machinery and materiel, as an invasion of Western culture, ideas, and desires, and as a source of pollution and corruption. Johnson links anti-American sentiment and actions, such as attacks on U.S. military and civilian targets, to the "blowback" from America's international presence and foreign policy that, he argues, are hidden from average Americans or conveniently denied by informed Americans and their government.[11]

FIGHTING MEN AND COMFORT WOMEN

As Enloe notes, sexuality has always been an important, though often disregarded, aspect of all militaries and military operations. Throughout history women have been among "camp followers" providing services such as laundry, nursing, companionship, and sex to soldiers on military missions during peace and war.[12] Sometimes these women have been wives, relatives, or girlfriends, but always among their ranks have been prostitutes as well. Women who have had sex with servicemen around the world, however, have not always been volunteers. Throughout history local women have been involuntarily "drafted" in the sexual service of militaries as rape victims and sexual slaves.[13]

Rape in war is at its core an ethnosexual phenomenon. Whether a war is fought across national borders or inside state boundaries, the military front is typically an ethnosexual frontier. Differences in nationality, race, or ethnicity separate the combatants and identify the targets of aggression in military operations. Whether violence in war is from combat or sexual attack, and whether it is guns or bodies that are used as weapons, those who are physically or sexually assaulted almost always are different in some ethnic way. Men at war do not, as a rule, rape their "own" women unless, of course, those women are suspected of disloyalty, especially sexual disloyalty or "collaboration."

Sexual exploitation and abuse are important weapons of war, and rape is perhaps the most common component of war's sexual arsenal. Susan Brownmiller documents the routine practice of rape, especially gang rape, in war.[14] Moving or occupying armies use the rape of "enemy" women and girls as both a carrot and a stick: raping local women is a spoil of war for the troops to enjoy, and rape is also a technique of terror and warfare designed to dominate and humiliate enemy men by sexually conquering their women. Rape in war, as in many other ethnosexual settings, is best understood as a transaction between men, where women are the currency used in the exchange. Sexually taking an enemy's women amounts to gaining territory and psychological advantage. In countries around the world, rape often is defined as a polluting action, a way to soil the victim, her kin, and her nation physically and symbolically. Sexual warfare can extend beyond the moment of violation in situations where victims are reputationally smeared, physically mutilated, or when pregnancies or births result from sexual assaults. For instance, the widespread rape of mainly Muslim and some Croatian women by Serbian men in Bosnia in the early 1990s was partly intended to impregnate the women so that they would bear Serbian babies, "little Chetniks."[15] In order to guarantee that these rape victims could not obtain abortions, the Serbs set up concentration camps where pregnant women were imprisoned until they gave birth.[16]

Probably the best-known instance of rape in war is the so-called Rape of Nanking that occurred during the Japanese invasion of China in the winter and spring of 1938–1939, when Japanese soldiers raped an estimated eighty thousand Chinese women and girls.[17] A less well-known instance of Japanese wartime sexual exploits was the sexual enslavement of thousands of mainly Asian women by the Japanese Imperial Army during World War II. Sexual slavery in war is a variation on the theme of wartime rape. Slavery extends the tactic of rape as a short-term strategy of a military mission into a permanent feature of military operations. The Japanese military established camps of so-called military comfort women (*Jugun Ianfu*) in Japan and other countries where Japanese troops were stationed. While there were some mainly lower-class Japanese women forced into sexual slavery, most of the estimated 200,000 women enslaved by the Japanese army were ethnic or national Others brought from Korea, China, Taiwan, Indonesia, Malaysia, and the Philippines to sexually service the troops.[18] Kazuko Watanabe reports that in such settings a woman's worth as a sexual commodity was based on her class and her ethnicity.[19] . . .

Soldiers' rankings of and preferences for women of particular races and nationalities enslaved in rape camps were not unique to the Japanese military.[20] Japan was not the only country that established large-scale organized operations of forced sexual servitude during World War II. The Nazis used concentration camps in Germany and other occupied countries for more than industrial and war-related labor, their program of genocide against the Jews, and the mass deportation and killing of Roma (gypsies) and other "non-Aryan" peoples. Sexual labor was also demanded of women internees, and both men and women prisoners were used for sexual experimentation by Nazi scientists and physicians. German concentration camps were sites of forced prostitution and sexual assault, and as was the case with Japan, not all women in the German camps were treated as "equal" when it came to sexual abuse. A woman's age, youth, and physical appearance made her more or less likely to be the target of Nazi sexual aggression.[21] And, as in so many areas of social life, even (especially) in wartime concentration camps, ethnicity mattered. There were official prohibitions against German soldiers having sex with Jewish women, though these rules often were not enforced. Many Jewish women survivors reported extensive sadistic sexual torture, as well as rape, and these assaults often were accompanied by a barrage of racial and anti-Semitic verbal abuse.[22]

The Allies also were involved in sexual violence and exploitation during World War II. Some was in the form of mass rapes, such as those committed against German women by the Soviet army.[23] In other cases, sexual abuse and exploitation resulted when military personnel capitalized on the vulnerability of women who faced economic hardship, malnourishment, or starvation because of the war's disruption of local economies and food production. Many women in occupied or liberated countries found sexual liaisons or prostitution preferable to the grim alternatives available for themselves and their dependent families. U.S. troops also committed rapes during the war and the occupation that followed. In her examination of U.S. Army records, Brownmiller found 947 rape *convictions*, not simply charges or trials of American soldiers in Army general courts-martial during the period from January 1942 to July 1947.[24]

Wartime rape did not stop at the end of World War II, nor did its ethnosexual character change after 1945. The practice of rape in war extended into major and minor conflicts during the second half of the twentieth century—in civil wars, wars of independence, and military invasions, interventions, and operations in countries and regions around the world including Bangladesh, Vietnam, Iraq, Kuwait, Bosnia, Croatia, Serbia, Rwanda, Liberia, Kashmir, and Sierra Leone.[25] The logic of rape in war is always the same: rapes are committed across ethnosexual boundaries, and rape is used by both sides for the familiar time-honored reasons—to reward the troops, to terrorize and humiliate the enemy, and as a means of creating solidarity and protection through mutual guilt among small groups of soldiers. Ethnic loyalty and ethnic loathing join hands in rape in war.

In the post–Soviet era East European nationalist conflicts the use of rape as a weapon of war has begun to move from the shadows more fully into view. For instance, during the 1990s warfare occurred along a number of ethnic and national borders in the former Yugoslavia—between Croats and Serbs, Christians and Muslims, and against Roma, among others. The most notorious of these ethnic conflicts was in Bosnia; the conflict's notoriety stemmed in part from its sexual character, especially the mass rape of Bosnian Muslim women by Orthodox Christian Serbian men. Many of these men and women were former neighbors. Muslims and Christians had lived side by side in the city of Sarajevo and elsewhere in Bosnia for decades and many had intermarried. That peace was shattered in 1992 when "ethnic cleansing" began.

Ethnic cleansing, or the removal of one ethnic group from a territory claimed by another, followed a common pattern across the region. Groups of armed Serbian men (sometimes uniformed troops and sometimes "irregulars" who were not officially in the military and not in uniform) roamed Bosnian towns and villages in groups, opportunistically looting and pillaging houses and businesses, raping and killing mainly unarmed Muslims they encountered along the way. Survivors reported that the Serbs came through the same towns several times in waves. During the first wave, typically, some of the Muslim men were killed and the rest were rounded up to be killed later or to be interned in concentration camps. Muslim women, children, and the elderly were left behind. It was during the next waves of Serbs passing through the towns that they raped local non-Serbian girls and women.

Munevra was a forty-eight-year-old widow with three sons ranging in age from fourteen to twenty-four, ages that made them targets for the Serbs to kill or deport to concentration camps. She kept the young men hidden in the cellar as small groups of armed Serbian men repeatedly came through the town. In the spring of 1992, two men came to her house and sexually assaulted her. Please note, Munevra's account of her abuse and the testimony of other rape victims below may be very disturbing to some readers.

I was afraid my sons would hear me. I was dying of fear 'cause of my sons. They're decent people. . . . Then this man touched my breasts. He pulled up my blouse and took out my breasts. . . . He said, "For a woman your age your breasts aren't bad." Then they brought me to the other room. . . . I begged him and cried, and I crossed my legs. Then he took out his thing, you know, and he did it and sprayed it on me. When he was done the other one came and did the same thing. . . . When they left, my sons came out and . . . they asked me what happened: "What'd they do to you?" I said, "Nothing." I couldn't tell them about it. . . . I'd rather die than have them find out about it.[26]

Women's and families' shame about such incidents were part of the process of victimization and violation.[27] Munevra's experience occurred relatively early in the nationalist conflict; far worse sexual violations were in store for women as the war escalated.

The scene in Serbian so-called rape camps was a longer, more brutal nightmare for Muslim and other non-Serbian women and girls. Twenty-six-year-old Ifeta was arrested by Serbian soldiers, most of whom she knew, and taken to a women's camp in Doboj:

Three drunken [Serbian army] soldiers . . . dragged her into a classroom . . . here she was raped by all three men "at the same time," says Ifeta, pointing to her mouth and backside. "And while they were doing it they said I was going to have a baby by them.". . . After that the rapes were a part of Ifeta's daily life. . . . It was always a gang rape, they always cursed and humiliated her during it, and the rapists very frequently forced her to have oral sex with them.[28]

Another camp internee, Kadira, described the weeks she spent at Doboj:

"They pushed bottle necks into our sex, they even stuck shattered, broken bottles into some women. . . . Guns too. And then you don't know if he's going to fire, you're scared to death." . . . Once she was forced to urinate on the Koran. Another time she and a group of women had to dance naked for the Serbian guards and sing Serbian songs. . . . She has forgotten how many times she was raped.[29]

The same pattern of sexual terror, torture, and rape used by the Serbs in their campaigns of ethnic cleansing and warfare in Bosnia was repeated in Kosovo,

Yugoslavia, in 1998–1999. Once again groups of Serbian men—police, soldiers, irregulars—swept through villages invading homes and raping Kosovar Albanian (mainly Muslim) female occupants, sexually attacking Kosovar Albanian women refugees fleeing combat zones, and sexually assaulting Kosovar Albanian women who were being held hostage or detained. The Kosovo conflict ended when NATO troops entered Kosovo in June 1999.[30]

In spring 2000, the UN convened the *International Criminal Tribunal for the Former Yugoslavia* in The Hague, Netherlands, to investigate and prosecute those ordering mass killing and mass rape in the various ethnic conflicts in the former Yugoslavia.[31] This investigation raised the issue of whether rape and sexual slavery are "crimes against humanity." Enloe argues that this question reflects a new awareness and public airing of what has been a long hidden history of sexual assault, torture, and exploitation of women during war:

> [T]he rapes in Bosnia have been documented by women's organizations . . . [that] have helped create an international political network of feminists who are making news of the Bosnian women's victimization not to institutionalize women as victims, not to incite men to more carnage, but to explain anew how war makers rely on peculiar ideas about masculinity. . . . [F]eminist reporters are using news of wartime sexual assaults by male soldiers to rethink the very meanings of both sovereignty and national identity. . . . If they succeed, the construction of the entire international political arena will be significantly less vulnerable to patriarchy.[32]

As the reports of human rights hearings and organizations document every year, it is not only enemy women who are the targets of sexual abuse and torture in war. I have not seen reported the establishment of rape camps with men as sexual slaves; however, men often are assaulted sexually as part of intimidation, torture, and combat in international conflicts and wars, as well as in military or paramilitary operations against internal political or ethnic insurgents. For instance, in Bosnia, there were numerous reports of cases in which Muslim and Croatian men were castrated or forced to castrate one another:

> In villages, towns, cities, the countryside, and concentration camps, male and female adults and children are raped as part of more extensive torture. Many of the atrocities committed are centered on the genitalia. . . .

[T]estimonies of castrations enforced on Bosnian-Herzegovinian and Croatian prisoners, and in particular of orders under threat of death that they castrate each other with various instruments and at times with their teeth, are widely available, as the [United Nations] Bassiouni Report makes clear.[33]

Men also can be vulnerable to sexualized warfare in more indirect ways. In her critique of Japan's patriarchal Confucianist view of all women and racist treatment of non-Japanese men and women, Kazuko Watanabe also identifies a danger for men. She argues that in many countries men are trapped in masculinist roles, and forced to act out patriarchal and sexual scripts that commodify and endanger them as well as the women they victimize. . . .[34]

Watanabe's analysis suggests that although they are perpetrators of the rape and sexual abuse of both women and other men in times of war, men pay a psychological, social, and physical price for their complicity in patriarchal masculinist systems of sexual and ethnosexual violence. For instance, many soldiers display varying degrees of post-traumatic stress or "shell shock" following combat. Michael Kimmel reports that during World War I officers and doctors tended to view such disorders as "failures to conform to gender demands":

> Most psychiatric treatments for shell shock involved treating the disease as the result of insufficient manliness. T. J. Calhoun, assistant surgeon with the Army of the Potomac, argued that if the soldier could not be "laughed out of it by his comrades" or by "appeals to his manhood," then a good dose of battle was the best "curative."[35]

Although modern-day soldiers suffering from post-traumatic stress are viewed with more sympathy than their historical counterparts, many, including those working in the health care industry, still view soldiers exhibiting symptoms arising from combat and military operations with some suspicion, as malingerers, frauds, or weaklings.[36]

SEX AND PEACE

A state of war is not a necessary condition for the militarization of sex. Even in peacetime or as part of a "defense" strategy, the presence of military troops, operations, or bases creates a convenient and lucrative market for the sex industry, and occupying or peace-keeping troops find ample opportunity for sexual associations with and sexual attacks against local women and girls. It is the scale of military operations, not the occurrence of actual combat, that determines the amount and intensity of sexual action—commercial, congenial, and coercive—on the ethnosexual frontiers surrounding military installations and troops. For instance, the Cold War changed the character of military-related prostitution, which was already operating on a large scale at the end of World War II. After the war, the Allied powers established permanent military bases in former hostile states (e.g., Germany, Japan, Italy) and in many friendly countries as part of the North Atlantic Treaty Organization (NATO) and various mutual defense agreements and treaties (e.g., with the Philippines, Panama, Guam).

During the Cold War, the creation of a global network of military bases and pacts by the U.S. and its allies and by the Soviet Union and its allies greatly expanded the number of armed forces and military installations around the world. These new military consumers generated unprecedented demand for many products and services for military operations and personnel, including sexual services. Military bases became permanent features of the geopolitical landscape in the second half of the twentieth century, and expanded in size and personnel during various Cold War proxy combat engagements such as those in Korea, Vietnam, Central America, and Southern Africa. Prostitution became a large-scale, stable industry around military bases in many parts of the world. Not just U.S. bases were involved. Soldiers are a diverse set of global ethnosexual adventurers. For instance, Enloe reported during the 1980s there were

> British bases in West Germany, Cyprus, the Falklands and Belize . . . [and] Northern Ireland. . . . The Indian government stationed 45,000 of its soldiers on counter-insurgency duty in Sri Lanka. There have been 50,000 Cuban soldiers stationed in Angola. The Soviet Union maintains bases in Vietnam and Eastern Europe. Vietnamese troops only now are withdrawing from Kampuchea. The French military bases 8,000 of its soldiers in Chad, the Central African Republic, Gabon, Senegal, the Ivory Coast and Djibouti, as well as others in its remaining Pacific and Caribbean colonies. Canada sends troops to its bases in West Germany. Finnish, Fijian, Irish and other men serve overseas as part of United Nations peace-keeping forces.[37]

The sex workers who provided services to these troops typically were ethnically distinct from their clients since soldiers often are stationed in regions of a country with ethnically different populations or in countries where local or immigrant sex workers are of different nationalities from occupying forces. It is important to note in this thus far almost exclusively heterosexual discussion that the sex workers visited by military men are not always women. For instance, U.S. servicemen stationed abroad also seek exotic sexual encounters with Other men. During his tour in the U.S. Marine Corps in the 1980s, former Chief Scout/Sniper David Anthony Tyeeme Clark reported much gossip and bragging by Marines about their sexual exploits with "benny boys"—male sex workers who provided presumably straight Marines with something new and different during their shore "liberty."

> My enlistment was for six years beginning in 1982 . . . [those] years corresponded with the Reagan/Gipper/John Wayne administration . . . when men were men and benny boys provided the best shore leave memories. . . . In my memory of those conversations, guys would insist that benny boys were even better than women (the logic was something like benny boys had insider [sexual] knowledge, something women had to depend on men for learning).[38]

Clark argues that by othering these often gay, ethnically different male sex workers, Marines managed to create the distance they needed to maintain a hyper-masculine, hyperheterosexual image of themselves and the Marine Corps. The exotic strangeness they attributed to the benny boys seemed to allow the Marines to camouflage the fact that they were having sex with other men.[39]

The last five decades of postwar global militarization has institutionalized female and male prostitution on an unparalleled scale in the many countries around the world that served NATO and Eastern bloc military operations. The disintegration of the Soviet Union in the early 1990s and the subsequent end of the Cold War changed the logic of many of these military base and personnel placements from superpower competition to international peacekeeping. UN and NATO peacekeeping operations have expanded as has the U.S. military's involvement in peacekeeping. As a result, the international circulation of soldiers remains an important feature of the global system. These new peacekeeping troops are no more celibate than their

Cold War predecessors, and the new military missions have generated continuing demand for sexual services. For instance, Judith Stiehm reports that during the United Nations' peacekeeping mission in Namibia in 1989–1990

> some male peacekeepers moved local women into their quarters, UN vehicles were parked in front of brothels, and even high-ranking officials were believed to exploit local women hired by the UN. . . . [In Cambodia in the early 1990s] the abuse of local women and children by UN troops and civilian police was brought to public attention. . . . Apparently the fear of AIDS made "virgins" highly desirable, and younger and younger girls were being recruited for prostitution.[40]

In contrast to the historically casual, even approved links between national armies and sexual service suppliers, Stiehm found that international peacekeeping troops and officials' sexual excursions into local towns and countrysides became controversial as the 1990s progressed. For the first time serious questions were being raised about the taken-for-granted, "boys will be boys" attitude of UN senior officials. Stiehm attributes this change of heart and mind to the presence of women UN workers and peacekeepers and to the involvement of religious NGOs (nongovernmental organizations, such as charitable or relief organizations), both of whom challenged longstanding military men's sexual perquisites.[41] Exposure and criticism of UN troops' ethnosexual appetites and indulgences pressured United Nations officials to design new policies to restrict such behavior. Established ethnosexual practices die hard, however, especially where there is money to be made. . . .

An important aspect of military-related prostitution, even in peacekeeping settings, is that it illustrates very clearly the links among geopolitics, ethnicity, and sexuality. Even away from war fronts with their direct ethnic and national confrontations, sexual encounters involving foreign military personnel and local people are almost without exception ethnosexual encounters. The women and men providing sexual services to peace-time military and police personnel are invariably racial, ethnic, and national Others. Such sexual encounters often are the only real interactions that occur between locals and foreign soldiers. As a result of this limited, distorted relationship, the commercial sexualized image each has of the other magnifies the stereotypes and prejudices that so often are associated with racial, ethnic, or national differences. The hypersexualization of local women, the commercialization of sexual culture, and the presence of an entrenched sex industry, all of which stem from the militarization of sexuality, often persist long after the wars are over. . . .

THE MILITARY-SEXUAL COMPLEX

Despite the end of the Korean War, Vietnam War, and Cold War, the sex industries they helped to generate and expand have remained permanent niches in many national economies. Besides continuing to service ongoing military operations around the world, a central legacy of the militarized global sex trade is sex tourism.[42] Sex tourism is part of a large sex-for-profit industry which includes, for example, prostitution, pornography, sexual media, materials, and equipment, and nude and exotic dancing. Sex tourism destinations are concentrated commercial sex spaces that provide a wide array of establishments and services to which consumers travel for sex. Sex tourist destinations can draw customers from local populations or from more distant national and international venues. Sex tours often are advertised and arranged by agencies and organizations specializing in sex tourism. Both sex tourism and the broader sex industry of which it is a part are organized commercial operations with legal and illegal components and with some well-paid and some exploited workers.

Sex tourism represents another chapter in the history of sex and war. Sex tourism developed as the international industry it is today with the help of the U.S. military. The strategy of delivering large groups of consumers to commercial sex service destinations began, in part, as a strategy for entertaining the troops during the Vietnam War. Ryan Bishop and Lillian Robinson argue that there is a historical connection between sex-for-sale operations catering to soldiers and sex for sale to tourists: "sex tourism builds on an infrastructure established for military R&R and extended through corporate recreational contracts. . . .[43] They detail a fascinating link between the U.S. military and the World Bank in the development of the notorious Thai sex industry:

> In 1967, Thailand contracted with the U.S. government to provide "Rest and Recreation" . . . services to the troops during the Vietnam War. Today's customers at the go-go bars spawned by those contracts are not only white Americans but also European and Australian—all

farangs to the Thais. . . . It was in 1971, while the war in Southeast Asia still raged, that World Bank President Robert McNamara, who had been U.S. Secretary of Defense when the R&R contracts with Thailand were signed, went to Bangkok to arrange for the bank's experts to produce a study of Thailand's postwar tourism prospects.[44]

Because of the presence and profitability of the wartime sex industry, the World Bank's advice, which Thailand followed, to specialize in tourism resulted in a large-scale sexualization of the tourist trade. The U.S. military and the World Bank thus became partners in developing what is perhaps the most famous, or infamous depending on one's point of view, sex industry in the world. Phil Williams concurs with Bishop and Robinson's summary of this connection:

The importance of Thailand in the global sex industry, for example, is generally traced back to the late 1960s and the use of Thailand as a place for "rest and recreation" for American G.I.s in Vietnam. The recommendation by the World Bank in [the 1970s] that Thailand develop "mass tourism" as a means to pay off its debts, encouraged what became, in effect, the peace-time institutionalization of the sex industry in Thailand.[45]

Some scholars argue that historical and cultural aspects of Thai society made it especially suitable for the development of a large-scale sex sector. For instance, although David Leheny agrees with other researchers about the link between Thailand's agreement to provide R&R for U.S. soldiers during the Vietnam war and the burgeoning of its sex industry, he also cites earlier agreements and legislation that set the stage for the present, in particular

the Bowring Treaty of 1855 which opened Thailand to foreign laborers. Most immigrants were young men from rural South China, planning to earn money for their families by mining tin in Phuket. A large number of Chinese prostitutes accompanied the men, establishing the largest sex centers Thailand had experienced at that time. . . . A 1909 law to prevent the spread of venereal disease effectively legalized prostitution.[46]

Ryan Bishop also supports analyses that identify historical antecedents to contemporary patterns of ethnosexual commerce. He is suspicious of other claims, however, especially those made by sex tourists, that Thai Buddhism and traditions of concubinage provide religious and cultural support for the commercial sex industry:

It is a bit too neat that "going native" just happens to mesh with one's deepest, darkest desires. . . . [Thailand's] Theravada Buddhism is just as proscriptive about premarital sex, if not more so, than any monotheistic system. In fact, virginity is such an important part of a woman's status as a desirable bride that procurers for the sex trade regularly rape young women, rendering them "damaged goods" and unavailable for marriage.[47]

Kazuko Watanabe sees reflections more of history than of any specific religious or cultural traditions in the present-day sex trade throughout Asia. She argues, for instance, that there are many social, political, and economic parallels between Japan's wartime policy of forcing mainly foreign women into prostitution and its current role as a consumer market for the sex industry, in particular sex tourism, which also involves mainly foreign women as sexual service provider. . . .[48]

CONCLUSION

Ethnicity and sexuality are unlikely but constant companions on war fronts around the world. Ethnosexual exploitation is a common weapon of war and a routine price of peace. In conflicts across and within national borders, differences in language, religion, culture, and color often become justifications for sexual assault; alien ethnic homelands are sighted for sexual strikes and sexual warfare is waged against ethnically defined enemies. Casualties of ethnosexual assaults are not collateral damage associated with military campaigns; they are designated targets of sexual attack; they are victims who are guilty of ethnic Otherness; they are in the wrong skin in the wrong place at the wrong time; they are the sexual means to an ethnic end, a sexual stopover on the path toward a final solution.

The drama of sex and war is not restricted to combat theatres. The post–World War II period with its economic competition and superpower geopolitical rivalry produced a massive military-sexual complex to feed its large-scale manpower's equally large-scale sexual appetites. The militarization of sexuality has outlived the Cold War in the form of an international sex industry that serves military personnel around the world in conflicts and peacekeeping operations and satisfies the growing civilian market for ethnosex.

NOTES

1. Major William H. MacDonald, EUSA/USFK Public Affairs Office, personal communication, July 11, 2001; for a critical view of the U.S. military presence in South Korea, see http://www.apcjp.org/women's_network/skorea.htm.

2. Katharine H. S. Moon, *Sex Among Allies: Military Prostitution in U.S.-Korea Relations* (New York: Columbia University Press, 1997), 1.

3. Ibid., 175, fn. 42.

4. U.S. military bases were established in Japan during the Allied occupation of the country following the end of World War II; 75 percent of U.S. military bases in Japan are on Okinawa Island; Kazuko Watanabe reports that controversies and demands that the U.S. close its military bases in Japan are the result not only of public opposition to the large sex industry on the island, but also because of the history of sexual assaults against Okinawan women by U.S. soldiers; see Kazuko Watanabe, "Trafficking in Women's Bodies, Then and Now: The Issue of Military Comfort Women," *Peace & Change* 20 (1995): 501–14. For a discussion of sexual collaboration between U.S. and Japanese authorities during the allied occupation of Japan, see Yuki Tanaka. *Japan's Comfort Women: Sexual Slavery and Prostitution During World War II and the U.S. Occupation* (New York: Routledge, 2002): my thanks to Ayako Mizumura for bringing this book to my attention.

5. Jean Enriquez reports that in recent years since the closing of U.S. bases in the Philippines and the beginning of the Asian economic crisis, "Filipino women have been migrating in flocks to neighboring countries"; many of these women go to South Korea which now "ranks 7th in terms of destination of deployed overseas Filipino workers"; some of these women are willingly recruited and others are unwillingly required to work in the Korean sex industry; see Jean Enriquez, "Filipinas in Prostitution Around U.S. Military Bases in Korea: A Recurring Nightmare," *Coalition Against Trafficking in Women-Asia-Pacific*, July 11, 2001, http://www.uri.edu/artsci/wms/hughes/catw/filkorea.htm.

6. Lynn Thiesmeyer, "The West's 'Comfort Women' and the Discourses of Seduction," in *Transnational Asia Pacific: Gender, Culture, and the Public Sphere*, ed. Shirley G. Lim, Larry E. Smith, and Wimal Dissanayake (Urbana: University of Illinois Press, 1999), 81; see also, Wendy Chapkis, *Beauty Secrets: Women and the Politics of Appearance* (Boston: South End Press, 1986), 53–54; Lisa Lowe argues that there is not a unified Euro-American historical imagining of Asian women, rather there are similarities between regional and historical different "orientalisms"; Lowe, *Immigrant Acts*, 178, n. 7.

7. Aida F. Santos, "Gathering the Dust: The Base Issue in the Philippines," in *Let the Good Times Roll: Prostitution and the U.S. Military in Asia*, ed. Saundra Pollock Sturdevant and Brenda Stoltzfus (New York: The New Press, 1992), 39;

Cynthia Enloe provides an even more extensive list of men she argues "contribute to the construction and maintenance of prostitution around any government's military base: husbands and lovers, bar owners, local and foreign, local public-health officials, local government zoning-board members, local police officials, local mayors, national treasury or finance-ministry officials, national-defense officials, male soldiers in the national forces, local male prostitution customers, foreign male soldier-customers, foreign male soldiers' buddies, foreign base commanders, foreign military medical officers, foreign national-defense planners, foreign national legislators" (Cynthia Enloe, "It Takes Two," in *Let the Good Times Roll*, 24–25); see also Cynthia Enloe, *The Morning After: Sexual Politics and the End of the Cold War* (Berkeley: University of California Press, 1993).

8. Saundra Pollock Sturdevant and Brenda Stoltzfus, "Olongapo: The Bar System," in *Let the Good Times Roll*, 46–47.

9. Enloe, "It Takes Two," 23–24.

10. Chalmers Johnson, *Blowback: The Costs and Consequences of American Empire* (New York: Metropolitan Books, 2000), 35; see also Cynthia Enloe, *Maneuvers: The International Politics of Militarizing Women's Lives* (Berkeley: University of California Press, 2000).

11. Ibid., as its 2000 publication date indicates, Johnson's book was written before the September 11, 2001, attacks on New York and Washington, but he does link the 1996 bombing of the Khobar Towers apartments in Saudi Arabia, an attack that has been attributed to the same suspected perpetrators of the 2001 attacks, to the presence of U.S. military in Saudi Arabia, a presence that was invited by the Saudi government in the early 1990s following Iraq's invasion of Kuwait, but which is resented by "devoutly Muslim citizens of that kingdom [who] see [U.S.] presence as a humiliation to the country and an affront to their religion" (92); my thanks to Norm Yetman, American Studies, University of Kansas, for bringing this book to my attention.

12. See for instance, Butler, *Daughters of Joy, Sisters of Misery*.

13. For a recent overview see Barstow, *War's Dirty Secret*.

14. Brownmiller, *Against Our Will*.

15. Allen, *Rape Warfare*, 96.

16. Ibid., 96.

17. See Iris Chang, *The Rape of Nanking: The Forgotten Holocaust of World War II* (New York: Basic Books, 1997); James Yin and Shi Young, *The Rape of Nanking: An Undeniable History in Photographs* (Chicago: Innovative Publishing Group, 1997).

18. Japan has yet to make satisfactory restitution to Korean and Filipina "comfort women" who were sexually enslaved during World War II, and some former victims have come forward to demand a public apology and accounting for their treatment; see Seth Mydans, "Inside a Wartime Brothel: The Avenger's Story," *New York Times*, November 12, 1996:A3; Maria Rosa Henson, *Comfort*

Woman: A Filipina's Story of Prostitution and Slavery Under the Japanese Military (Lanham, MD: Rowman & Littlefield Publishers, 1999); Sangmie Choi Schellstede, *Comfort Women Speak: Testimony by Sex Slaves of the Japanese Military* (New York: Holmes and Meier, 2000); for discussions of Japan's system of brothels, see George L. Hicks, *The Comfort Women: Japan's Brutal Regime of Enforced Prostitution in the Second World War* (New York: W.W. Norton, 1995); Keith Howard, *True Stories of the Korean Comfort Women* (London: Cassell, 1995); Sayoko Yoneda, "Sexual and Racial Discrimination: A Historical Inquiry into the Japanese Military's 'Comfort' Women System of Enforced Prostitution," in *Nation, Empire, Colony: Historicizing Gender and Race*, ed. Ruth Roach Pierson and Nupur Chaudhuri (Bloomington: Indiana University Press, 1989), 237–50; for a discussion of restitution in general and specifically as it relates to the women enslaved by Japan during World War II, see Elazar Barkan, *The Guilt of Nations: Restitution and Negotiating Historical Injustices* (New York: W.W. Norton, 2000), especially chapter 3.

19. Watanabe, "Trafficking in Women's Bodies," 503–504.

20. Both sexual and nonsexual labor were also demanded of women enslaved by the Japanese (ibid., 503); the Japanese also used rape as an instrument of terror and domination, most infamous is the "rape of Nanking" in which thousands of women were raped and killed; see Brownmiller, *Against Our Will*, 53–60.

21. Brownmiller, *Against Our Will*, 61–62.

22. For firsthand accounts of women's treatment in the camps, see Sarah Nomberg-Przytyk, *Tales from a Grotesque Land* (Chapel Hill: University of North Carolina Press, 1985), 14–20; Livia E. Bitton Jackson, *Elli: Coming of Age in the Holocaust* (New York: Times Books, 1980) 59–61; Cecile Klein, *Sentenced to Live* (New York: Holocaust Library, 1988), 73–77; Lore Shelley, *Auschwitz: The Nazi Civilization* (Lanham, MD: University Press of America, 1992).

23. See Cornelius Ryan, *The Last Battle* (New York: Simon & Schuster, 1966); Barstow, *War's Dirty Secret*.

24. Brownmiller, *Against Our Will*, 76–77; these 947 convictions are only part of a much greater universe of sexual assault by U.S. troops for several reasons: most rape is not reported and when it is, convictions are relatively rare even today, much less back in the 1940s during a state of war and/or military occupation; further, these were *convictions* where the soldier was found guilty, and did not include what could only have been a much larger number of charges filed and trials conducted; further still, these records were only for convictions of Army and Air Force personnel, and did not include data on the U.S. Navy or Marine Corps; finally, these records did not include information on charges, trials, or convictions for lesser sexual crimes than rape, such as sodomy or assault with the intent to commit rape or sodomy.

25. See Americas Watch and the Women's Rights Project, *Untold Terror: Violence Against Women in Peru's Armed Conflict* (New York: Americas Watch, 1992); Asia Watch and Physicians for Human Rights, *Rape in Kashmir: A Crime of War* (New York: Asia Watch, 1993); Ximena Bunster, "Surviving Beyond Fear: Women and Torture in Latin America," in *Women and Change in Latin America*, ed. June Nash and Helen Safa (South Hadley, MA: Bergin & Garvey, 1986), 297–325; Samir al-Khalil, *Republic of Fear: The Politics of Modern Iraq* (Berkeley: University of California Press, 1989).

26. Stiglmayer, "The Rapes in Bosnia-Herzegovina," 101.

27. See Elizabeth Bumiller, "Deny Rape or Be Hated: Kosovo Victims' Choice," *New York Times*, June 22, 1999:1; Peter Finn, "Signs of Rape Sear Kosovo; Families' Shame Could Hinder Investigation," *Washington Post*, June 27, 1999:1.

28. Stiglmayer, "The Rapes in Bosnia-Herzegovina," 117–18.

29. Ibid., 118–19.

30. Human Rights Watch reports that although both sides committed sexual assault during the conflict, rates of rape by Serbian men far outnumbered instances of sexual abuse by Kosovar Albanian men during the conflict; see Human Rights Watch Report, "Kosovo: Rape as a Weapon of 'Ethnic Cleansing'" (March 21, 2000); my thanks to Hsui-hua Shen, Department of Sociology, University of Kansas, for bringing this report to my attention.

31. For early reports on the hearings and judgments of that tribunal, see Marlise Simons, "Bosnian Serb Trial Opens: First on Wartime Sex Crimes," *New York Times*, March 21, 2000:3; John-Thor Dahlburg, "Bosnian Witness Says She Endured Series of Rapes; Courts: Victim No. 50 Testifies in The Hague," *Los Angeles Times*, March 30, 2000:1; Chris Bird, "UN Tribunal Told of Bosnian Rape Camp Horrors," *Guardian*, April 21, 2000:1; Roger Thurow, "A Bosnian Rape Victim Suffers from Scars That Do Not Fade," *Wall Street Journal*, July 17, 2000:18.

32. Cynthia Enloe, "Afterword: Have the Bosnian Rapes Opened a New Era of Feminist Consciousness?" in *Mass Rape*, 219–30; progress continues to be made, slowly, in the shift toward defining rape as a human rights violation and in the prosecution of those responsible for the sexual assaults in the former Yugoslavia: on June 29, 2001, the Serbian government turned over former Yugoslavian president Slobodan Milosevic to the United Nations war crimes tribunal in The Hague, Netherlands; Marlise Simons with Carlotta Gall, "Milosevic Is Given to U.N. for Trial in War-Crime Case," *New York Times*, June 29, 2001:1; it is important to note that at about the same time the rapes and killings were happening in Yugoslavia and Bosnia, millions of men, women, and children were being raped, mutilated, and murdered in Rwanda; while Western governments dithered and delayed responding to both the Yugoslavian and Rwandan massacres and atrocities, and while an international tribunal was established in 1994 to prosecute Rwandans for their war crimes, the issue of rape as a war crime came to the fore in Yugoslavia, but not in the much larger-scale Rwandan case; perhaps it required reports of the mass rapes and sexual enslavement of white women, albeit Muslim white women, for the "civilized" world to take notice of ethnosexual violence in war.

33. Allen, *Rape Warfare,* 78; the "Bassiouni Report" is the result of an October 1992 decision by the Secretary-General of the United Nations to appoint a commission of experts "to examine and analyze information gathered with a view to providing the Secretary-General with its conclusions on the evidence of grave breaches of the Geneva Conventions and other violations of international humanitarian law committed in the territory of the former Yugoslavia" (ibid., 43).

34. Watanabe, "Trafficking in Women's Bodies," 506–507.

35. Kimmel, *Manhood in America,* 133–34.

36. See, for instance, Tracy X. Karner, *Masculinity, Trauma, and Identity: Life Narratives of Vietnam Veterans with Post Traumatic Stress Disorder* (Ph.D. diss., University of Kansas, 1994).

37. Enloe, *Bananas, Beaches, and Bases,* 66.

38. Personal communication, July 22, 2001; Clark was a Corporal in the First Battalion, Seventh Marines, Strategic and Target Acquisition (STA) Platoon.

39. Ibid.; Clark goes on to say:

> It is funny that during a period in U.S. military history when a "good" president restored military "honor," guys were in the Philippines and Thailand receiving oral sex (and who knows what else) from guys—and then talking about it later, giving no indication at all that they might just have participated in sex acts that challenged their masculinity. At the same time, new recruits were being instructed in the "manly" arts of beating up "fags," Naval Intelligence was hunting down "evidence" that guys with HIV and AIDS actually were gay, and Marines having sex with Marines (men) and caught in the "act" were being "punished" with hysterical physical violence in response. (ibid.)

> See also Steven Zeeland, *The Masculine Marine: Homoeroticism in the U.S. Marine Corps* (New York: Harrington Park Press, 1996); Tim Bergling, "A Few Good Men," *Genre* (November/ December 1997) (http://www.davidclemens.com/gaymilitary/fgm.htm) and Anonymous, "Standby Warning" (http://www.subicbaymarines.com/Standby.htm).

40. Judith Hicks Stiehm, "United Nations Peacekeeping: Men's and Women's Work," in *Gender Politics in Global Governance,* ed. Mary K. Meyer and Elisabeth Prugl (Lanham, MD: Rowman & Littlefield, 1999), 50–54.

41. Stiehm attributes the "boys will be boys" comment to Yasushi Akashi of Japan, the head of the UN peacekeeping mission in Cambodia; the comment was in response to "a letter signed by more than 180 women [that] was sent to Akashi charging sexual harassment of staff by UNTAC personnel and harassment of women on the street and asserting that there was no channel for redressing this behavior" (ibid., 54).

42. Sex tourism is distinct from the general sex industry in that it is the sector of the sex trade that actually provides organized travel and tours to bring sex consumers to concentrated sex service destinations.

43. Ryan Bishop and Lillian S. Robinson, *Night Market: Sexual Cultures and the Thai Economic Miracle* (New York: Routledge, 1998), 248.

44. Ibid., 8–9.

45. Phil Williams, "Trafficking in Women and Children: A Market Perspective," in *Illegal Immigration and Commercial Sex: The New Slave Trade,* ed. Phil Williams (London: Frank Cass, 1999), 154; see also Lisa Law, "A Matter of 'Choice': Discourses on Prostitution in the Philippines," in *Sites of Desire, Economies of Pleasure: Sexualities in Asia and the Pacific,* ed. Lenore Manderson and Margaret Jolly (Chicago: University of Chicago Press, 1997), 233–61.

46. David Leheny, "A Political Economy of Asian Sex Tourism," *Annals of Tourism Research* 22 (1995): 367–84, 373; Annette Hamilton also finds images of a sexualized Thailand in 1950s fiction, images that lead her to argue that Thailand was already a "privileged site" in the "Western masculinist imagination" before the Vietnam War era; she does not conclude, however, that the large-scale commercialization of sex that occurred as a result of the war was irrelevant to contemporary images of a sexualized Thailand; see Annette Hamilton, "Primal Dream: Masculinism, Sin, and Salvation in Thailand's Sex Trade," in *Sites of Desire, Economies of Pleasure,* 157.

47. Ryan Bishop, personal communication, March 16, 2001; see also Bishop and Robinson, *Night Market,* 160–61; see also Thanh-Dam Truong, *Sex, Money, and Morality: Prostitution and Tourism in South-East Asia* (London: Zed Books, 1990); Lenore Manderson, "Public Sex Performances in Patpong and Explorations of the Edges of Imagination," *The Journal of Sex Research* 29 (1992): 451–75.

48. Watanabe, "Trafficking in Women's Bodies," 506. Sex tourism has become a controversial business in many destination and consumer countries. In Thailand, a number of organizations, including "Empower" and "Friends of Women," work directly with women in the sex tourism industry to teach them about AIDS prevention, and "Daughters Education Programme" provides education for village girls to increase their employability outside of sex tourism and to enhance their local status; Enloe, *Bananas, Beaches and Bases,* 38; June Kane, *Sold for Sex* (Brookfield, VT: Arena, 1998), 122–23. Other international anti–sex trade/sex tourism organizations include the Asian Women's Human Rights Council, ECPAT (End Child Prostitution in Asian Tourism), the Global Alliance Against Traffic in Women, and the Coalition Against Trafficking in Women; see Skrobanek et al., *The Traffic in Women,* 81, 110–16; Kane, *Sold for Sex,* 4; the website for the Coalition Against Trafficking in Women is http://www.uri.edu/artsci/wms/hughes/catw/catw.htm; Julia Davidson reports several demonstrative methods of protesting sex tourism:

> There have been instances of direct action against clients—for example, that organized by Japanese feminist groups at airports, which involved ridiculing and insulting men arriving home from sex tours, and that proposed by the Filipino guerrilla group that adopted the slogan, "Kill a sex tourist a day." Public humiliation has also been used as an instrument to control Taiwanese businessmen caught using prostitutes

while in mainland China. (Davidson, *Prostitution, Power, and Freedom,* 198)

Davidson quotes Ren's description of Chinese humiliation techniques:

> Chinese authorities not only sent them to a poultry farm in the outskirts of Bejing for a short period of labor reform, but also sent letters to their employers in Taiwan to inform them of the "repulsive deeds" committed by their employees in China. Hoping that public exposure will deter such behavior, Chinese authorities have also stamped the words "patron of prostitution" on the travel documents of those men who have been found guilty of committing "repulsive deeds." (Ren, "China," in *Prostitution: An International Handbook on Trends, Problems, and Policies,* ed. Nanette Davis [Westport, CT: Greenwood Press, 1993], 102–103)

PART FOUR

SOCIAL CHANGE

Thus far we have emphasized the stability of gender inequality. We have examined how socialization, social definitions of gender, and the structure and content of all the major institutional arenas of social life converge to produce a world in which males and females are understood as essentially different and are differentially valued and rewarded. The forces that perpetuate gender inequality are so intricately interwoven into the social fabric and so deeply embedded in the identities of individuals that changing them is beyond the power of any one individual, no matter how well intentioned.

Yet societies can and do change. Anyone who has lived through the past three decades in the United States cannot help but notice that there has been substantial change in the position, behaviors, and consciousness of women and men. In earlier readings, we discussed some of the dynamic forces that have unintentionally recast gender consciousness and inequality, including new cultural meanings, technological innovations, demographic processes, and economic factors. To understand fully how systems of gender inequality change, we must also examine the ways that women have sought collectively and intentionally to reduce their disadvantage. Certainly, every society or group contains individuals who are nonconformists, but significant and lasting social change is ultimately the result of collective rather than individual action.

In Part Four, we turn our attention to struggles to transform culture and social institutions in two arenas. Section 10 focuses on the politicization of gender in the state and in global politics. Section 11 documents the rich history and diversity of women's movements and examines continuity and change in the history of American feminism. To understand the part that women themselves have played in improving their status, we focus, on the one hand, on women's actions "within the system" by conventional and orderly means and, on the other, on women's collective actions "outside the system" by unconventional and disorderly means.

Politics is generally thought to refer to the institutionalized or authoritative system by which a society makes decisions, allocates power, and distributes resources. According to the traditional view, voting, campaigning, lobbying, conducting organizational activities, holding office, and working in political parties are classified as politics because they take place in the context of formal governmental structure.

Feminist scholars have pointed out that the standard definition of politics is too narrow, however, for understanding women's political participation. It not only assumes a particular type of state and political system but ignores the fact that, until fairly recently in most industrialized societies, women have been denied access to the formal political process.

In the United States, women were not allowed to vote, hold office, or sit on juries until the twentieth century. Even after women received the vote with the passage of the Nineteenth Amendment to the U.S. Constitution in 1920, their participation in electoral politics, involvement in major political parties, and election to public offices lagged significantly behind men's. African-American women, moreover, like African-American men, remained effectively disenfranchised in southern states by racist voter registration rules until the late 1960s.

It was not until a half century after women got the vote that the gap between men's and women's political party involvement and office holding began to shrink, and even today women fare better in local and state politics than in the national arena. Voting turnout differences between women and men finally disappeared in 1976. But it took until 1980 for women to use the electoral process to express their collective dissatisfaction by voting in line with their interests in women's equality, creating for the first time what has come to be known as the "gender gap." It is striking, however, that women have ascended to the leadership of their countries in other parts of the world earlier than in the United States.

Holding elections, participating in party politics, running for office, and lobbying are not, however, the only ways to express grievances, influence public policy, and achieve social change. Politics also include social movements, protests, and other group actions intended to change cultural beliefs and influence the distribution of power and resources in a state or community. This definition is broad enough to encompass women's long history of participation in collective action on their own behalf through the feminist movement, as well as in pursuit of other human rights causes through female reform societies, women's church groups, alternative religious societies, women's clubs, and other social groups and movements.

Social movements are collective attempts to bring about change. They originate outside of the established political system, forge links between individuals and groups who share common concerns, and mobilize the people and resources necessary to pursue the goal of social change. In democratic societies, social movements and the tactics they employ—marches, boycotts, strikes, demonstrations, and protests—are a regular part of the democratic process. Movements act as pressure groups on behalf of people excluded from routine decision-making processes and the dominant power structure; they are a major source of new social patterns and cultural understandings.

Because participants in social movements typically challenge conventional ideas and behaviors, they are often stereotyped by the larger society as deviant and irrational and accused of exaggerating their claims. If we take a historical perspective on social movements, however, we will often find that today's social institution is likely to have been yesterday's social movement. In other words, social movement participants are not qualitatively different from other kinds of social actors, and their actions are governed by the same norms that underlie other groups.

Although popular opinion often presents the women's movement as a relatively recent phenomenon, its roots are well grounded historically. Indeed, the similarities between the views of contemporary feminists and earlier feminists can be remarkable. More than 200 years ago, for example, Abigail Adams gave this warning to her husband, John, when he was helping to fashion the Constitution of the United States:

In the new code of laws which I suppose will be necessary for you to make, I desire you would remember the ladies and be more generous and favorable to them than your ancestors. Do not put such unlimited power in the hands of husbands. Remember, all men would be tyrants if they could. If particular care and attention is not paid to the ladies, we are determined to foment a rebellion, and will not hold ourselves bound by any laws in which we have no voice or representation.

Unfortunately, John Adams failed to take his wife's warning seriously. He urged her to be patient and said that there were more important issues than the rights of "ladies."

As this example illustrates, in the United States, as in much of the industrialized world, the history of feminist activism is long and rich. Until the past three decades, however, knowledge of the women's movement remained mostly buried. Initially, most scholars studying the women's movement held that feminism in the United States has come in waves. The first wave began in the nineteenth century as a broad attack on male domination, continued for almost a century, and then died precipitously in 1920 with the passage of the suffrage amendment granting women the right to vote, which by then had become the movement's major goal. Supposedly, a forty-year lull followed before the second wave, or new feminist movement, erupted in the mid-1960s.

As a result of new research, a different interpretation of the history of the U.S. women's movement has recently emerged that emphasizes the continuity and persistence of women's resistance. The newer work recognizes the great waves of mass feminist activism but also points to the survival of feminism in less highly mobilized periods. It focuses not only on the continuity of the movement but on changes in feminist ideology, goals, constituency, tactics, and organizational style. In addition to self-proclaimed feminists, working-class women and women of color also have a long history of struggle on their own behalf, in labor unions, socialist and communist groups, and women's clubs and within churches and communities. Any analysis of contemporary feminism and the backlash against it must consider the multiple forms of the enduring struggle against gender inequality.

The readings thus far suggest the depth, pervasiveness, and persistence of gender inequality and the intersection of gender with inequalities of race, class, and sexuality. It is not surprising, then, that contemporary feminism encompasses a wide range of struggles, from local efforts to improve women's daily lives to broad visions of fundamentally restructuring all institutions that perpetuate and sustain male dominance. The media have repeatedly proclaimed the present period the "postfeminist era," and many women disavow the feminist label—yet, as we shall see, women's movements remain very much alive. Feminist groups can be found within every major institution: in the professions, academia, labor, religion, politics, the arts, music, and literature. Feminist groups have mobilized around practically every issue imaginable, including employment and equal pay issues, reproductive rights, health, depression, substance abuse, pornography, prostitution, disability rights, spirituality, child care, nuclear weaponry, lesbianism, incest, battering, racism, and older women's rights. Feminists organize around sexual, racial, ethnic, and class identities.

The flourishing of women's organizing in these multiple forms has been considered a "third wave" of feminism that builds on the successes and lessons of earlier activism. Third-wave feminism is characterized by the view that gender is multiple and variable because it is also shaped by race, class, sexuality, nationality, and other factors. But the differences and conflicts between second- and third-wave feminism have also been exaggerated. What is important is that, because feminism addresses every facet of social life, it has had a major and lasting impact not only on economic, political, and cultural institutions but also on the consciousness and lives of individual women and men.

In Part Four, we examine the diversity of women's participation in contemporary women's movements, emphasizing the continuity and global nature of feminist challenges as well as changes and differences in feminist goals, constituencies, and tactics. The readings document the multiple forms that feminist resistance can take. They recognize that protest can be directed at the structural, cultural, or individual level and that resistance varies across cultural and national contexts. We begin with an overview of the U.S. women's movement and a look to the future. As you read these selections, think about the ways in which the efforts of women to transform gender have succeeded.

Global Politics and the State

National governments, international relations, and transnational economies and cultures exert wide-ranging influence on gender systems. Government-controlled economies shape differences in women's and men's wages and the prices of goods that women and men produce and consume. National and international policies on education, welfare, health, and various forms of violence against women affect women's daily lives in profound ways.

Because governmental policies frequently reflect dominant antiwoman ideologies, they often serve to reinforce the disadvantaged position of women in most countries. The state, in fact, plays a central part in maintaining a social structure of inequalities between women and men and between people of different social groups. That is, the state plays a crucial role in perpetuating inequalities of class (through regulation of the labor market or of minimum wages, for example) and of race and ethnicity and nationality (for example, through legislative policies regarding affirmative action or immigration).

Feminist scholars focus on the ways that state actions and policies create and perpetuate gender categories, ideologies of women's inferiority, and differential access of women and men to valued resources and power. The state's role in upholding gender stratification, of course, is inextricably linked to its role in reinforcing race and class stratification, as the articles in this section point out.

The increasing forces of globalization mean that women's lives are shaped not only by the governmental policies of their own countries but also by transnational politics and economics as well, as we have already seen in the case of Latina domestic workers in Los Angeles. A complex web of interrelationships among transnational corporations, states, transnational social movements, technology, and ideologies of gender, race, ethnicity, and religion shapes relations among women, states, and global politics. In this section, contributors examine the relationships among constructions of gender, the forces of globalization, women's lives and activism, and the state, both in the United States and transnationally.

We begin with Cynthia Enloe's discussion of the transnational economics and politics of women's labor in her classic article "The Globe Trotting Sneaker." Enloe makes clear that women workers' interests have been left behind as outsourcing and globalization have increased. Taking sneaker manufacturing as an example, she shows how multinational corporations profit from the labor of underpaid and exploited women workers on the global assembly line. Documenting the activism of women workers in South Korea, Enloe shows why Nike moved its manufacturing from South Korea to countries such as China and Indonesia, where women were less organized. Yet, she suggests, increasing transnational organizing by women workers holds the potential for social change, particularly if women in the United States and other countries of the global North join them. Where are your running shoes and clothing produced? How does your standard of living depend on the work of the women workers Enloe discusses? What would be the consequences if workers earned a living wage all around the globe? What might you and other Americans do to improve the living situation of women workers abroad?

Women work in the global economy not only on the assembly line but also as sex workers. Feminist scholarship on prostitution and sex work has tended to fall into two polarized camps, focusing either on sex trafficking and sexual slavery or on sex as work that women might choose. Jo Doezema, in "Forced to Choose: Beyond the Voluntary v. Forced Prostitution Dichotomy," takes the latter position. She sees the distinction between forced and voluntary prostitution as increasingly replacing the notion that all prostitution is wrong and should be abolished in international agreements. While the distinction does recognize that some women might choose sex work, it continues the division between innocent victims and guilty and sexually transgressive women, and it focuses attention on saving the innocent rather than protecting the rights of sex workers. Further, this new model tends to assume that poor Third World women are forced into prostitution while those who choose sex work come from more privileged positions in the West. Are you convinced by Doezema's arguments? What assumptions underlie the forced versus voluntary prostitution dichotomy? What measures might both protect women from exploitation and protect the rights of sex workers?

When the United States went to war in Afghanistan after the attacks of September 11, one of the rationales was the need to liberate Afghan women. Lila Abu-Lughod addresses the question "Do Muslim Women Really Need Saving?" reminding us that Afghan women, like Filipinas and Latinas in North America, have their own history of activism. Critiquing the "missionary" notion of saving other women, Abu-Lughod calls for a serious appreciation of differences among women around the globe. Why do you think there is so much focus in the United States on the "oppression" of Muslim women? How does Abu-Lughod suggest that we deal with differences?

The final articles in this section return to the United States, where the welfare reform of 1996 parallels the cutting of social services in countries undergoing structural adjustment, a topic addressed in the next section by Grace Chang. In this section, Gwendolyn Mink, a feminist scholar and activist, argues that income support for caregivers is essential for women's equality—meaning that welfare should be an inalienable right of poor single mothers. Do you agree? Why was the women's movement so uninvolved in the fight against welfare reform?

Melanie Heath, in "The Marriage Promotion Movement," also takes up the question of government policy and its impact on women of different classes. Her study of the marriage promotion movement in Oklahoma, the state in the forefront of the attempt to shore up heterosexual marriage, shows how state policy is motivated by the desire to reinforce conservative gender norms. Ostensibly designed to combat poverty by encouraging two-parent families, the marriage promotion movement in fact shifts resources to white, middle-class women, promoting not so much marriage as heteronormativity and gender conformity. How does the marriage promotion movement echo the agenda of doctors in the 1950s, according to Carolyn Herbst Lewis in Section 6? What assumptions underlie the marriage promotion movement? Why does the government promote heterosexual marriage but ban gay marriage? Why is marriage a political issue?

As the forces of globalization increase, the economic, political, and cultural power of the global North affects women everywhere. Yet we need to be respectful of difference, as Lila Abu-Lughod argues. Once again, this section returns to the question of the commonalities and differences among women. Given the disparities of wealth and power among women around the world, especially between the global North and South, do you think diverse women have anything in common by virtue of their gender?

The Globe Trotting Sneaker

Four years after the fall of the Berlin Wall marked the end of the Cold War, Reebok, one of the fastest- growing companies in United States history, decided that the time had come to make its mark in Russia. Thus it was with considerable fanfare that Reebok's executives opened their first store in downtown Moscow in July 1993. A week after the grand opening, store managers described sales as well above expectations.

Reebok's opening in Moscow was the perfect post–Cold War scenario: commercial rivalry replacing military posturing; consumerist tastes homogenizing heretofore hostile peoples; capital and managerial expertise flowing freely across newly porous state borders. Russians suddenly had the "freedom" to spend money on US cultural icons like athletic footwear, items priced above and beyond daily subsistence: at the end of 1993, the average Russian earned the equivalent of $40 a month. Shoes on display were in the $100 range. Almost 60 percent of single parents, most of whom were women, were living in poverty. Yet in Moscow and Kiev, shoe promoters had begun targeting children, persuading them to pressure their mothers to spend money on stylish, western sneakers. And as far as strategy goes, athletic shoe giants have, you might say, a good track record. In the United States many inner-city boys who see basketball as a "ticket out of the ghetto" have become convinced that certain brand-name shoes will give them an edge.

But no matter where sneakers are bought or sold, the potency of their advertising imagery has made it easy to ignore this mundane fact: Shaquille O'Neal's Reeboks are stitched by someone; Michael Jordan's Nikes are stitched by someone; so are your roommate's, so are your grandmother's. Those someones are women, mostly Asian women who are supposed to believe that their "opportunity" to make sneakers for US companies is a sign of their country's progress— just as a Russian woman's chance to spend two months'

salary on a pair of shoes for her child allegedly symbolizes the new Russia.

As the global economy expands, sneaker executives are looking to pay women workers less and less, even though the shoes that they produce are capturing an ever-growing share of the footwear market. By the end of 1993, sales in the United States alone had reached $11.6 billion. Nike, the largest supplier of athletic footwear in the world, posted a record $298 million profit for 1993—earnings that had nearly tripled in five years. And sneaker companies continue to refine their strategies for "global competitiveness"—hiring supposedly docile women to make their shoes, changing designs as quickly as we fickle customers change our tastes, and shifting factories from country to country as trade barriers rise and fall.

The logic of it all is really quite simple; yet trade agreements such as the North American Free Trade Agreement (NAFTA) and the General Agreement of Tariffs and Trade (GATT) are, of course, talked about in a jargon that alienates us, as if they were technical matters fit only for economists and diplomats. The bottom line is that all companies operating overseas depend on trade agreements made between their own governments and the regimes ruling the countries in which they want to make or sell their products. Korean, Indonesian, and other women workers around the world know this better than anyone. They are tackling trade politics because they have learned from hard experience that the trade deals their governments sign do little to improve the lives of workers. Guarantees of fair, healthy labor practices, of the rights to speak freely and to organize independently, will usually be left out of trade pacts—and women will suffer. The recent passage of both NAFTA and GATT ensures that a growing number of private companies will now be competing across borders without restriction. The result? Big business will step up efforts to pit working women in industrialized countries against much lower-paid

FIGURE I   HOURLY WAGES IN ATHLETIC FOOTWEAR FACTORIES

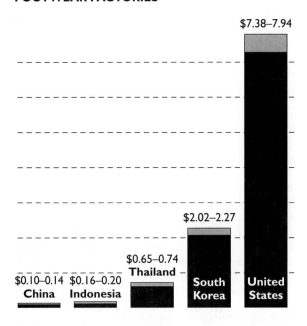

$7.38–7.94

$2.02–2.27

$0.65–0.74
Thailand

$0.10–0.14 $0.16–0.20
China   Indonesia

South Korea   United States

working women in "developing" countries, perpetuating the misleading notion that they are inevitable rivals in the global job market. (See Figure 1.)

All the "New World Order" really means to corporate giants like athletic shoemakers is that they now have the green light to accelerate long-standing industry practices. In the early 1980s, the field marshals commanding Reebok and Nike, which are both US-based, decided to manufacture most of their sneakers in South Korea and Taiwan, hiring local women. L.A. Gear, Adidas, Fila, and Asics quickly followed their lead. In short time, the coastal city of Pusan, South Korea, became the "sneaker capital of the world." Between 1982 and 1989 the United States lost 58,500 footwear jobs to cities like Pusan, which attracted sneaker executives because its location facilitated international transport. More to the point, South Korea's military government had an interest in suppressing labor organizing, and it had a comfortable military alliance with the United States. Korean women also seemed accepting of Confucian philosophy, which measured a woman's morality by her willingness to work hard for her family's well-being and to acquiesce to her father's and husband's dictates. With their sense of patriotic duty, Korean women

seemed the ideal labor force for export-oriented factories.

US and European sneaker company executives were also attracted by the ready supply of eager Korean male entrepreneurs with whom they could make profitable arrangements. This fact was central to Nike's strategy in particular. When they moved their production sites to Asia to lower labor costs, the executives of the Oregon-based company decided to reduce their corporate responsibilities further. Instead of owning factories outright, a more efficient strategy would be to subcontract the manufacturing to wholly foreign-owned—in this case, South Korean—companies. Let them be responsible for workers' health and safety. Let them negotiate with newly emergent unions. Nike would retain control over those parts of sneaker production that gave its officials the greatest professional satisfaction and the ultimate word on the product: design and marketing. Although Nike was following in the footsteps of garment and textile manufacturers, it set the trend for the rest of the athletic footwear industry.

But at the same time, women workers were developing their own strategies. As the South Korean pro-democracy movement grew throughout the 1980s, increasing numbers of women rejected traditional notions of feminine duty. Women began organizing in response to the dangerous working conditions, daily humiliations, and low pay built into their work. Such resistance was profoundly threatening to the government, given the fact that South Korea's emergence as an industrialized "tiger" had depended on women accepting their "role" in growing industries like sneaker manufacture. If women reimagined their lives as daughters, as wives, as workers, as citizens, it wouldn't just rattle their employers; it would shake the very foundations of the whole political system.

At the first sign of trouble, factory managers called in government riot police to break up employees' meetings. Troops sexually assaulted women workers, stripping, fondling, and raping them "as a control mechanism for suppressing women's engagement in the labor movement," reported Jeong-Lim Nam of Hyosung Women's University in Taegu. It didn't work. It didn't work because the feminist activists in groups like the Korean Women Workers Association (KWWA) helped women understand and deal with the assaults. The KWWA held consciousness-raising sessions in which notions of feminine duty and respectability were tackled along with wages and benefits. They organized independently of the male-led labor unions to ensure that their issues would be taken seriously, in labor negotiations and in the prodemocracy movement as a whole.

The result was that women were at meetings with management, making sure that in addition to issues like long hours and low pay, sexual assault at the hands of managers and health care were on the table. Their activism paid off: in addition to winning the right to organize women's unions, their earnings grew. In 1980, South Korean women in manufacturing jobs earned 45 percent of the wages of their male counterparts; by 1990, they were earning more than 50 percent. Modest though it was, the pay increase was concrete progress, given that the gap between women's and men's manufacturing wages in Japan, Singapore, and Sri Lanka actually *widened* during the 1980s. Last but certainly not least, women's organizing was credited with playing a major role in toppling the country's military regime and forcing open elections in 1987.

Without that special kind of workplace control that only an authoritarian government could offer, sneaker executives knew that it was time to move. In Nike's case, its famous advertising slogan—"Just Do It"—proved truer to its corporate philosophy than its women's "empowerment" ad campaign, designed to rally women's athletic (and consumer) spirit. In response to South Korean women workers' newfound activist self-confidence, the sneaker company and its subcontractors began shutting down a number of their South Korean factories in the late 1980s and early 1990s. After bargaining with government officials in nearby China and Indonesia, many Nike subcontractors set up shop in those countries, while some went to Thailand. China's government remains nominally Communist; Indonesia's ruling generals are staunchly anti-Communist. But both are governed by authoritarian regimes who share the belief that if women can be kept hard at work, low paid, and unorganized, they can serve as a magnet for foreign investors.

Where does all this leave South Korean women—or any woman who is threatened with a factory closure if she demands decent working conditions and a fair wage? They face the dilemma confronted by thousands of women from dozens of countries. The risk of job loss is especially acute in relatively mobile industries; it's easier for a sneaker, garment, or electronics manufacturer to pick up and move than it is for an automaker or a steel producer. In the case of South Korea, poor

women had moved from rural villages into the cities searching for jobs to support not only themselves but parents and siblings. The exodus of manufacturing jobs has forced more women into the growing "entertainment" industry. The kinds of bars and massage parlors offering sexual services that had mushroomed around US military bases during the Cold War have been opening up across the country.

But the reality is that women throughout Asia are organizing, knowing full well the risks involved. Theirs is a long-term view; they are taking direct aim at companies' nomadic advantage, by building links among workers in countries targeted for "development" by multinational corporations. Through sustained grassroots efforts, women are developing the skills and confidence that will make it increasingly difficult to keep their labor cheap. Many are looking to the United Nations conference on women in Beijing, China [1996], as a rare opportunity to expand their cross-border strategizing.

The Beijing conference will also provide an important opportunity to call world attention to the hypocrisy of the governments and corporations doing business in China. Numerous athletic shoe companies followed Nike in setting up manufacturing sites throughout the country. This included Reebok—a company claiming its share of responsibility for ridding the world of "injustice, poverty, and other ills that gnaw away at the social fabric," according to a statement of corporate principles.

Since 1988, Reebok has been giving out annual human rights awards to dissidents from around the world. But it wasn't until 1992 that the company adopted its own "human rights production standards"—after labor advocates made it known that the quality of life in factories run by its subcontractors was just as dismal as that at most other athletic shoe suppliers in Asia. Reebok's code of conduct, for example, includes a pledge to "seek" those subcontractors who respect workers' rights to organize. The only problem is that independent trade unions are banned in China. Reebok has chosen to ignore that fact, even though Chinese dissidents have been the recipients of the company's own human rights award. As for working conditions, Reebok now says it sends its own inspectors to production sites a couple of times a year. But they have easily "missed" what subcontractors are trying to hide—like 400 young women workers locked at night into an overcrowded dormitory near a Reebok-contracted factory in the town of Zhuhai, as reported last August in the *Asian Wall Street Journal Weekly*.

Nike's cofounder and CEO, Philip Knight, has said that he would like the world to think of Nike as "a company with a soul that recognizes the value of human beings." Nike, like Reebok, says it sends in inspectors from time to time to check up on work conditions at its factories; in Indonesia, those factories are run largely by South Korean subcontractors. But according to Donald Katz in a recent book on the company, Nike spokesman Dave Taylor told an in-house newsletter that the factories are "[the subcontractors'] business to run." For the most part, the company relies on regular reports from subcontractors regarding its "Memorandum of Understanding," which managers must sign, promising to impose "local government standards" for wages, working conditions, treatment of workers, and benefits.

In April, the minimum wage in the Indonesian capital of Jakarta will be $1.89 *a day*—among the highest in a country where the minimum wage varies by region. And managers are required to pay only 75 percent of the wage directly; the remainder can be withheld for "benefits." By now, Nike has a well-honed response to growing criticisms of its low-cost labor strategy. Such wages should not be seen as exploitative, says Nike, but rather as the first rung on the ladder of economic opportunity that Nike has extended to workers with few options. Otherwise, they'd be out "harvesting coconut meat in the tropical sun," wrote Nike spokesman Dusty Kidd, in a letter to the *Utne Reader*. The all-is-relative response craftily shifts attention away from reality: Nike didn't move to Indonesia to help Indonesians; it moved to ensure that its profit margin continues to grow. And that is pretty much guaranteed in a country where "local standards" for wages rarely take a worker over the poverty line. A 1991 survey by the International Labor Organization (ILO) found that 88 percent of women working at the Jakarta minimum wage at the time—slightly less than a dollar a day— were malnourished.

A woman named Riyanti might have been among the workers surveyed by the ILO. Interviewed by the *Boston Globe* in 1991, she told the reporter who had asked about her long hours and low pay: "I'm happy working here. . . . I can make money and I can make friends." But in fact, the reporter discovered that Riyanti had already joined her co-workers in two strikes, the first to force one of Nike's Korean subcon-

tractors to accept a new women's union and the second to compel managers to pay at least the minimum wage. That Riyanti appeared less than forthcoming about her activities isn't surprising. Many Indonesian factories have military men posted in their front offices who find no fault with managers who tape women's mouths shut to keep them from talking among themselves. They and their superiors have a political reach that extends far beyond the barracks. Indonesia has all the makings for a political explosion, especially since the gap between rich and poor is widening into a chasm. It is in this setting that the government has tried to crack down on any independent labor organizing—a policy that Nike has helped to implement. Referring to a recent strike in a Nike-contracted factory, Tony Nava, Nike representative in Indonesia, told the *Chicago Tribune* in November 1994 that the "troublemakers" had been fired. When asked about Nike policy on the issue, spokesman Keith Peters struck a conciliatory note: "If the government were to allow and encourage independent labor organizing, we would be happy to support it."

Indonesian workers' efforts to create unions independent of governmental control were a surprise to shoe companies. Although their moves from South Korea have been immensely profitable (see Figure 2), they do not have the sort of immunity from activism that they had expected. In May 1993, the murder of a female labor activist outside Surabaya set off a storm of local and international protest. Even the US State Department was forced to take note in its 1993 worldwide human rights report, describing a system similar to that which generated South Korea's boom twenty years earlier: severely restricted union organizing, security forces used to break up strikes, low wage for men, lower wages for women—complete with government rhetoric celebrating women's contribution to national development.

Yet when President Clinton visited Indonesia last November, he made only a token effort to address the country's human rights problem. Instead, he touted the benefits of free trade, sounding indeed more enlightened, more in tune with the spirit of the post–Cold War era than do those defenders of protectionist trading policies who coat their rhetoric with "America first" chauvinism. But "free trade" as actually being practiced today is hardly *free* for any workers—in the United States or abroad—who have to accept the Indonesian, Chinese, or Korean workplace model as the price of keeping their jobs.

FIGURE 2   A $70 PAIR OF NIKE PEGASUS: WHERE THE MONEY GOES

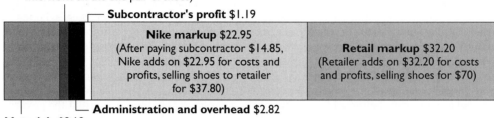

The not-so-new plot of the international trade story has been "divide and rule." If women workers and their government in one country can see that a sneaker company will pick up and leave if their labor demands prove more costly than those in a neighbor country, then women workers will tend to see their neighbors not as regional sisters, but as competitors who can steal their precarious livelihoods. Playing women off against each other is, of course, old hat. Yet it is as essential to international trade politics as is the fine print in GATT.

But women workers allied through networks like the Hong Kong-based Committee for Asian Women are developing their own post–Cold War foreign policy, which means addressing women's needs: how to convince fathers and husbands that a woman going out to organizing meetings at night is not sexually pro-miscuous; how to develop workplace agendas that respond to family needs; how to work with male unionists who push women's demands to the bottom of their lists; how to build a global movement.

These women refuse to stand in awe of the corporate power of the Nike or Reebok or Adidas executive. Growing numbers of Asian women today have concluded that trade politics have to be understood by women on their own terms. They will be coming to Beijing this September [1996] ready to engage with women from other regions to link the politics of consumerism with the politics of manufacturing. If women in Russia and Eastern Europe can challenge Americanized consumerism, if Asian activists can solidify their alliances, and if US women can join with them by taking on trade politics—the post–Cold War sneaker may be a less comfortable fit in the 1990s.

ACKNOWLEDGMENTS

This article draws from the work of South Korean scholars Hyun Sook Kim, Seung-kyung Kim, Katherine Moon, Seungsook Moon, and Jeong-Lim Nam.

Forced to Choose: Beyond the Voluntary v. Forced Prostitution Dichotomy

INTRODUCTION

At the 1995 United Nations Fourth World Conference on Women in Beijing, I and other delegates from the Network of Sex Work Projects (NSWP) and the Global Alliance Against Trafficking in Women (GAATW) lobbied to ensure that every mention of prostitution as a form of violence against women in the final conference document would be prefaced by the word "forced."[1] Because sex workers' human rights were not mentioned in the draft document, it was impossible to introduce this concept at the Conference. The best we could do was "damage limitation," keeping abolitionist language out of the final document. Ironically, I found myself lobbying for a recognition of the distinction between voluntary prostitution and forced prostitution, a distinction I and other sex worker activists had come to realize had been subverted in such a way that it had become a new justification for denying sex workers their human rights.

Does this mean that I deny that some women in the sex industry work in slavery-like conditions or that I deny that it is possible to choose prostitution as a profession? It does not. It means that I argue that the voluntary/forced dichotomy is the wrong theoretical framework with which to analyze the experience of sex workers. The necessity to critically examine the form this theory is taking is all the more pressing now that it is replacing abolitionism as the dominant model of prostitution at the international level.

In this [article] I examine the rise to prominence of the "voluntary" versus "forced" model of sex worker experience, and the implications and consequences of this rise for sex workers' rights. In the first section, I give a short history of feminist attempts to get prostitution on the international political agenda. Second, an examination of relevant international instruments demonstrates that the voluntary/forced dichotomy is replacing the abolitionist model of prostitution. Finally, I seek to show that this dichotomy has become another way of denying sex workers their human rights.

PROSTITUTION AND INTERNATIONAL POLITICS

A Brief History

Early attempts to deal with prostitution internationally were heavily influenced by nineteenth-century feminist activism. It was women like Josephine Butler who first brought the issue of the "white slave trade" to international attention, via a campaign to protect morals of both men and women. The feminist campaign, founded by Butler, began with attempts to repeal the Contagious Diseases Acts in Britain.[2] Under the acts, any woman identified as a "common prostitute" was forced to undergo a fortnightly internal examination. Infected women were interned in specially designated hospital wards, "pseudomedical prisons for whores."[3]

Feminists in the repeal movement were ambivalent in their attitudes to prostitutes. They recognized a commonality of interests with prostitutes, realizing that the Acts were a threat to the civil liberties of all women. Because any woman could be identified on the word of a police officer as a "common prostitute," any woman, especially a working-class woman, on her own in a certain area at a certain time could be detained and forced to submit to an internal examination. On the other hand, prostitution was seen as "the great social evil," and prostitutes as victims of male vice, who needed to be rescued. Thus, controlling male vice was seen as the key to ending prostitution. Regulation of prostitution was condemned as an official licensing of male vice.

After the repeal of the Acts in 1883, the focus of the campaign shifted from the rejection of government attempts to monitor sexuality to the promotion of repressive measures designed to end vice. The agenda of the social purity movement was dominated by the mirages of white slave trade and child prostitution. This campaign was helped enormously by sensationalist journalists who seized on the titillating tales of deflowered innocence. . . . Research indicates that most of the "trafficking victims" were actually prostitutes migrating, like thousands of others, in hope of finding a better life. . . . Although the Contagious Disease Acts were finally repealed in 1886, in many places their regime was continued under a different name, with purity activists now patrolling the streets instead of the police.[4]

The movement for social purity had success in the US and the continent as well as in Britain. By the turn of the century, most of the existing regulatory systems in Europe and the United States had ended, and international efforts had begun to target the "white slave trade." In the five years before the end of the nineteenth century, three international conferences on the prevention of trafficking in women were held.[5] In the early years of the century, two international instruments concerning the trade were created.[6] The League of Nations adopted two conventions dealing with the traffic in women and children.[7] In 1949, the UN adopted the Convention for the Suppression of the Traffic in Persons and the Exploitation of the Prostitution of Others, which combined and superseded the earlier agreements.

Current Approaches

After the 1949 Convention was adopted, both feminist and international concern for prostitution and the traffic in women abated for a time. But since the middle of the 1980s, there has been a new wave of feminist-backed campaigning against trafficking in women, child prostitution and sex tourism. Campaign efforts have succeeded in putting prostitution back at the top of the international agenda. . . .

The modern anti-trafficking campaign is split along ideological lines on views of prostitution. The fundamental difference of opinion concerns the question of whether or not a person can choose prostitution as a profession. Some feminists argue that all prostitution constitutes a human rights violation. The strongest advocate of this "neo-abolitionist" view internationally is the Coalition Against Trafficking in Women (CATW), founded by Kathleen Barry. Their "Convention on the Elimination of All Forms of Sexual Exploitation of Women" defines prostitution as a form of sexual exploitation just like rape, genital mutilation, incest and battering.[8] Sexual exploitation is defined as "a practice by which women are sexually subjugated through abuse of women's sexuality and/or violation of physical integrity as a means of achieving power and domination including gratification, financial gain, advancement."[9] Prostitution is explicitly named as a violation of women's human rights, and is also held responsible for "subordinating women as a group."[10]

The distinction between free and forced prostitution was developed by the prostitutes' rights movement in response to feminists (and others) who saw all prostitution as abusive.[11] The World Charter for Prostitutes Rights (1985) states "Decriminalize all aspects of adult prostitution resulting from individual decision."[12] This distinction was included in the analysis of some anti-trafficking organizations, such as the Global Alliance Against Trafficking in Women (GAATW) based in Thailand. The GAATW objects to international instruments for "disregarding the will of adult persons engaged in prostitution" and demand that instruments to combat trafficking be "based on respect for human rights, specifically the right of all persons to self determination."[13] Traffic in persons and forced prostitution are "manifestations of violence against women and the rejection of these practices, which are a violation of the right to self determination, must hold within itself the respect for the self determination of adult persons who are voluntarily engaged in prostitution."[14]

CHANGING THE DOMINANT DISCOURSE

The abolitionist viewpoint has defined the terms of the international discourse on prostitution for almost 100 years. This discourse is being challenged by those who see sex work as a legitimate occupation. An examination of relevant UN instruments shows that there has been a shift away from mechanisms based on abolitionist ideology and toward an approach that respects the right to self-determination. This trend is most evident in those UN instruments dealing specifically with women's human rights and violence against women.

The watershed for the shift can be located in the mid-1980s.[15] Before then, UN instruments were abolitionist in character. Since that time, the majority make a distinction between voluntary and forced prostitution. Prostitution is dealt with in many different UN bodies; it is beyond the scope of this [article] to examine them all. Rather, I will focus on key documents and the work of the main bodies to illustrate the shift towards a new discourse.

Abolitionist Instruments

The Preamble to the 1949 Convention for the Suppression of Traffic in Persons and of the Exploitation of the Prostitution of Others states that "prostitution and . . . traffic in persons for the purposes of prostitution are incompatible with the dignity and worth of the human person. . . ." The convention has come under attack from both "sides" in the anti-trafficking debate. There is fundamental disagreement about the ideological approach of the convention. An examination of this disagreement is useful for the light it sheds on the issue of "voluntary" and "forced" prostitution.

Modern abolitionists, ironically, criticize the Trafficking Convention for making a distinction between "voluntary" and "forced" prostitution.[16] . . .

. . . The distinction between "voluntary" and "forced" prostitution, as it is currently understood, had no relevance at the time the international instruments to combat trafficking in women were drafted. For the regulationists, the prostitute was a fallen woman, whose personal pathology or inclination to vice, weakness, stupidity, and/or vanity led inevitably to life as a prostitute. Abolitionist ideology firmly fixed the prostitute as a victim. The image of the prostitute as agent, who willingly chooses her occupation, was unimaginable in either of these models. *Prostitution as a matter of personal choice and a form of work* is a concept developed by sex workers that radically contradicts both the regulationist and abolitionist versions of prostitute reality. To equate or collapse the very different analysis of the regulationists and prostitutes' rights supporters denies the radical implications of sex workers' politics. . . .

The Convention on the Elimination of All Forms of Discrimination Against Women (CEDAW) was adopted in 1979. Article 6 deals with prostitution and trafficking in women. It uses the same wording as the 1949 convention, calling upon state parties to "take all appropriate measures . . . to suppress all forms traffic in women and the exploitation of prostitution of women." This would seem to imply that the drafters' intent was abolitionist. However, when the text was being drafted, Morocco introduced an amendment to Article 6 which called for the suppression of prostitution in addition to the suppression of the exploitation of prostitution. This amendment was found unacceptable by the Netherlands and Italy, because they considered that the new element of suppression of prostitution unacceptable.[17] The amendment was rejected; thus it can be argued that Article 6 does not consider all prostitution inherently coercive.[18] The Mexico Declaration on the Equality of Women, adopted at the Second UN Conference on Women in 1975, makes no distinction between forced and voluntary prostitution: "Women all over the world should unite to eliminate violations of human rights committed against women and girls such as rape, prostitution. . . ."[19]

Toward a New Perspective

General Recommendation 19 of CEDAW (1992) on violence against women includes specific paragraphs relating to Article 6 (see above) of the Convention. It reaffirms the requirements of Article 6 for states to "suppress all forms of traffic in women and exploitation of the prostitution of others," but also states that "Poverty and unemployment force many women . . . into prostitution. Prostitutes are especially vulnerable to violence because their status, which may be unlawful, tends to marginalize them. They need the equal protection of laws against rape and other forms of violence." Though this text does not specifically distinguish between forced and voluntary prostitution, an important shift in emphasis is apparent. Rather than focusing on repressive measures to eliminate the practice of prostitution, the Committee instead focuses on the prostitute as a subject whose rights can be violated.

The first document to make a clear departure from an abolitionist view of prostitution is the Declaration on the Elimination of Violence Against Women (1993). "Violence against women shall be understood to encompass, but not be limited to, the following: Physical, sexual and psychological violence occurring within the general community, including rape, sexual abuse, sexual harassment and intimidation at work, in educational institutions and elsewhere, trafficking in women and forced prostitution."[20] . . .

The Declaration on Violence Against Women is the standard against which the activities of the international community must be measured.[21] The implicit distinction between forced and non-forced prostitution recognized by the Declaration signalled that the international community's view of prostitution had changed. Since the adoption of the Declaration, the majority of international agreements denote forced prostitution and trafficking, rather than prostitution itself, as violence against women. The Vienna Declaration and Program of Action of the 1993 World Conference on Human Rights, recognized women's rights as human rights, and urged state parties to adopt the Declaration on Violence Against Women.[22] At the Fourth World Conference on Women, Beijing 1995, the draft of the Platform for Action included abolitionist language in a number of paragraphs, but this language was not retained in the final document. The final document condemns only forced prostitution, not prostitution as such.[23]

Radhika Coomaraswamy, the UN Special Rapporteur on Violence Against Women, also distinguishes between voluntary and forced prostitution: "Some women become prostitutes through 'rational choice,' others become prostitutes as a result of coercion, deception or economic enslavement."[24] . . .

This shift toward a new perspective on prostitution, while clearly evident, is not occurring at the same speed in all areas of the United Nations dealing with prostitution and trafficking. There is no commitment in the United Nations to an integrated and coordinated prostitution policy.[25] As a result, UN approaches are highly fragmented, with different UN instruments and bodies taking different ideological stances, and even with contradictory positions within the same body or agreement.[26] Some UN organizations, such as UNESCO and the Working Group on Contemporary Forms of Slavery, continue to argue that prostitution itself is a human rights violation.

BEYOND VOLUNTARY/FORCED

So should sex worker organizations be jumping for joy that the right to self-determination is being recognized, at least implicitly, at [the] international level? Does this mean that the United Nations and other international organizations are now going to start taking sex workers' human rights seriously, instead of cloaking moral condemnation of sex work under paternalistic "save us for our own good" rhetoric? Before we break out the party hats, we should look at how the concept of self-determination and the distinction between free and forced prostitution are interpreted and being translated into policy by NGOs, governments and intergovernmental agencies. Are the same old stereotypes and moral judgments now being expressed as loathing of forced prostitution?

Criticisms of the Campaigns

The distinction between free and forced prostitution has implicitly been recognized by the international community. But international actors and agreements are rarely as vocal about promoting prostitutes rights as they are in condemning forced prostitution. No international agreement condemns the abuse of human rights of sex workers who were not "forced."

I believe that this is the result of two factors. Firstly, though the international community may be agreeing on condemning only forced prostitution as a human rights violation, this does not imply agreement on how to deal with voluntary prostitution; how it is to be defined, if it should be regulated by the state or left to the workers to organize, or even if it exists at all. In fact, it is because there is no agreement about "voluntary" prostitution in the first place that the consensus on "forced" prostitution has come into being. It can be seen as a compromise: those who, for whatever reason, wish to eliminate all prostitution can at least be satisfied that the "worst" abuses are being dealt with and those who support self-determination are relieved that this right is not threatened.

Secondly, most organizations that acknowledge and support the right to self-determination place much more emphasis on stopping forced prostitution than on sex workers' rights. Partly this is because it is felt that this is more properly the domain of sex worker organizations. Given the fact that sex workers have long demanded the right to speak for themselves, this hesitance is somewhat justified. However, this reluctance to address sex workers' rights can also be attributed to the fact that it is easier to gain support for victims of evil traffickers than for challenging structures that violate sex workers' human rights.

The campaigning efforts of anti-trafficking groups have been instrumental in creating a climate wherein the great majority of sex work, and practically all sex work involving young men and women and women in developing countries, is seen as abuse. Forced prostitution, child prostitution and sex tourism are linked together and made indistinguishable. In the race to produce yet more horrifying stories, and higher numbers, concern for rights loses out to hysteria over victims.

Though most of the criticism of the prostitutes rights' movement has focused on the abolitionist view of sex work, sex workers are now increasingly critical of anti-trafficking campaigners and human rights activists who distinguish between voluntary and forced prostitution, yet who place all their campaigning energy into stopping forced prostitution. They have been criticized for initiating their campaigns without consultation with sex workers and for using the same emotive language as abolitionists, thus perpetuating "the stereotype of Asian sex workers as passive and exploited victims."[27] Such victimization "has grave consequences for all sex workers as it perpetuates the old stereotype that prostitution is bad and should be abolished."[28]. . . The "voluntary" prostitute is a Western sex worker, seen as capable of making independent decisions about whether or not to sell sexual services, while the sex worker from a developing country is deemed unable to make this same choice: she is passive, naive, and ready prey for traffickers.[29] Potentially the most frightening division, however, created by the voluntary/forced dichotomy is that of sex workers into guilty/"voluntary" and innocent/"forced" prostitutes, which reinforces the belief that women who transgress sexual norms deserve to be punished. This division is thus a threat to the entire concept of women's human rights.

Innocent Victims

"In any given year, many thousands of young women and girls . . . are lured . . . into forced prostitution."[30] For the general public and bodies concerned with this issue, forced prostitution is very much a matter of coerced innocence. The picture of the "duped innocent" is a pervasive and tenacious cultural myth.[31] High profile campaigns by NGOs and in the media, with their continued focus on the victim, adds yet more potency to the myths. The public is convinced that huge numbers of innocent (read, sexually pure) women and children are being subjected to the perverse whims of degenerate Western men.

In the new discourse of voluntary/forced prostitution, the innocence of the victim determines which side of the dichotomy she will fall under. One of the consequences of thinking about prostitution in terms of choice and force is that it becomes necessary to show that instances of abuse are in fact "forced prostitution." In reports on trafficking, it is often stressed that the women did not "choose" to be prostitutes. Emotive words like "duped," "tricked" or "lured" are used time and time again to show that the women involved did not know what they were letting themselves in for. A good example of the standard scenario runs as follows: "Many women from Russia, Hungary, Poland and other countries in the region are tricked into prostitution in the West, where they had been promised jobs in offices, in restaurants, or as domestic servants. Instead,

they find themselves locked up in a brothel, their papers are taken away and their earnings are kept back to repay their 'debt.'"[32]

Human Rights Watch, who did a study of Burmese women and girls trafficked into Thailand, conclude that the "combination of debt-bondage and illegal confinement renders the employment of the Burmese women and girls tantamount to forced labor, which is prohibited under international law."[33] However, the researchers found it necessary to state that only four of the twenty-nine women they interviewed knew they were going to be prostitutes.[34] It is hard to see what relevance this has: surely debt bondage and illegal confinement amount to slavery, whether or not there was initial agreement to work as a prostitute. Still, the innocence of the victim is seen to be of primary importance.

Other reports of "forced prostitution" focus on the aspect of poverty. "Susie is the face of contemporary poverty. That her job as a debt-bonded sex worker is the best economic option available to her is a metaphor for most of the world's women, whose grinding impoverishment in the Third World is accelerating."[35] This "poverty as force" approach has been criticized for its underlying racist and classist implications; even those who would accept "voluntary" prostitution, on the part of well-off Western women, refuse to respect the choice of a woman from a developing country.[36] On the one hand, this shows an underlying rejection of prostitution as a profession—no "normal" woman would choose the work unless "forced" by poverty. On the other, equating poverty with "force" is, like the focus on deceit, a way of establishing the innocence of "trafficked victims" and thus their eligibility for human rights protection.

A third way "innocence" is established is by focusing on the youth of the "victim" as children are assumed to be sexless and thus beyond "guilt."[37] Campaign pamphlet titles like "The Rape of the Innocents" and sickening stories of child abuse galvanize public opinion and get donations.[38] Tellingly, the distinctions between child and adult are blurred so as to include as many as possible in the category of unquestionable innocents. According to a United Nations report on trafficking in Burma, "With the growth of sex tourism and the commercial sex trade in neighboring countries of the region, child abuse and exploitation has assumed a new form: sexual trafficking of children across international borders . . . the number of Myanmar [Burma] girls working in Thai brothels has been conservatively estimated at between 20,000 to 30,000, with approximately 10,000 new recruits brought in yearly. *The majority are between 12 and 25 years old.*"[39]

Reality: So What's Going On?

When subjected to scrutiny, the image of the "trafficking" victim turns out to be a figment of neo-Victorian imaginations. Just as the turn of the century obsession with the "white slave trade" turned out to be based on actual prostitute migration, the Dutch Foundation Against Trafficking in Women (STV) and the GAATW, in their report on trafficking to the UN Special Rapporteur on Violence against Women, conclude that slavery-like conditions in sex work are primarily problems for those already working in the sex trade: thus for prostitutes who migrate.[40] But the campaign juggernaut remains unaffected by fact. From the Arab sheikh's harem slave to the village girl chained to her bed in the brothels of Bangkok, the image of the defiled innocent has a particular fascination.[41] It is reminiscent of sentiment expressed during a meeting of anti–white slave trade activists at the turn of the century. The women present were exhorted by the speaker to "Remember, ladies . . . 'it is more important to be aroused than to be accurate. Apathy is more of a crime than exaggeration in dealing with this subject.'"[42]

Parallels between the two movements are easily drawn. As a symbol, the "white slave" personified conservative moral fears of women's sexuality and economic independence, and of the growing power of the working class, and reflected racist stereotypes. The nineteenth-century sex slave was a white woman, victim of the animal lusts of the dark races. In the modern myth, the racism has changed focus: "passive," unemancipated women from the developing world are the new sex slaves.

A number of today's campaigns have become a platform for reactionary and paternalistic voices, advocating a rigid sexual morality under the guise of protecting women, and incorporating racist and classist perceptions in their analysis of the sex industry in developing countries. This is particularly the case when campaigners actually succeed in getting governments to do something about "trafficking," for then the focus shifts from women's rights to a hysterical and paranoid reaction to women's increasing sexual autonomy, the "breakdown of the family" and migration. Often, "trafficking" is used by states to initiate and justify restrictive policies.[43] There are still many governments with moral objections to prostitution. At the

international level, however, most are politically savvy enough to cloak moral indignation in terms of "victimization of women."

If it is recognized that the majority of those in the sex industry who end up in debt-bondage or slavery-like conditions were *already* working as sex workers, it is impossible to avoid the conclusion that it is prostitutes whose human rights are being violated on a massive scale. Of course this is unpalatable to the international community: it is one thing to save innocent victims of forced prostitution, quite another to argue that prostitutes deserve rights. It is not only governments who prefer saving innocent women to giving rights to guilty ones. Most feminist discourse on trafficking limits itself to the fight against "forced prostitution," the "voluntary" prostitute is not condemned—she is ignored.

Many governments place the distinction between "guilty" and "innocent" women at the heart of their legislation on prostitution and trafficking. In Germany, the penalty for trafficking is reduced in cases where the victim knew she was going to be a prostitute or when deceit was used on a person who is "not far from being a prostitute."[44] In Colombia, the use of violence to force a person into prostitution is only prohibited in cases where the woman concerned is "of undisputed virtue."[45] Other countries, including Uganda, Canada, Japan, Brazil and El Salvador, have similar provisions.[46] But even in those countries where "the virtue of the woman is not mentioned as an explicit criterion in law," it still "implicitly or explicitly plays a crucial role in the interpretation and enforcement of the law."[47] In the Netherlands, for example, police will refuse to investigate complaints of trafficking by women who continue working as prostitutes. "Supposedly there is no victim: she wanted it all the time, at least, that is what they can conclude from the fact that the woman is willing to work again in prostitution after having filed charges."[48]

Because feminists are undecided about whether or not "voluntary" prostitution exists or how it should be dealt with, their analysis of forced prostitution reinforces rather than challenges stereotypical views of female sexuality. For example, Human Rights Watch Women's Rights Project, in their report on global human rights abuses of women, states that it "takes no position on prostitution per se. However, we strongly condemn laws and official policies and practices that fail to distinguish between prostitutes and victims of forced trafficking."[49]

Focusing on forced prostitution provides a way out for those who are unwilling to admit that the issues raised by the prostitutes' rights movement have to be faced. Governments do not have to be challenged about their treatment of voluntary prostitutes; i.e., "While we recognize the right of governments to make and enforce laws that regulate national borders, they must distinguish between those who purposefully violate immigration laws and others who are victims of forced prostitution."[50] The report is not clear about how a prostitute is to be distinguished from a victim of trafficking. In order for a "victim" to be eligible for the protection recommended by Human Rights Watch, she would have to prove her innocence, i.e., that she didn't know she was going to be a prostitute. This bears a frightening resemblance to rape trials, in which a victim's chastity status will determine the severity of the crime.

The peculiarities of viewing sex work through the distorting lens of the voluntary/forced dichotomy cause what are clearly abuses of sex workers' rights to be condemned as examples of forced prostitution. Human Rights Watch reports that women in India who are arrested for prostitution are sent to "protective homes" where "inmates complained of grave mistreatment, including branding with hot irons, rapes, and sexual assaults. Almost all inmates were suffering from malnutrition. Many also had skin diseases and tuberculosis."[51] Yet, in the face of this horrific abuse of sex workers' human rights, the best Human Rights Watch can do is reiterate that "victims of trafficking" should be treated differently from prostitutes. Sex workers who are imprisoned and detained, subjected to cruel and degrading mistreatment, who suffer violence at the hands of the state or by private individuals with the state's support, are disqualified from human rights considerations if their status is "voluntary." This is the voluntary/forced dichotomy taken to its extreme and logical conclusion. Human rights organizations and bodies in the United Nations seem content to let governments trample on the rights of sex workers, as long as the morals of "innocent" women are protected.

CONCLUSION

The distinction between "voluntary" and "forced" prostitution has largely replaced the abolitionist model of prostitution in international discourse. This would seem to imply a recognition of the right to self-determination. However, this dichotomy creates divisions between sex workers. The most frightening division created by the voluntary/forced dichotomy is that it reproduces the whore/madonna division within the category "prostitute." Thus, the madonna is the "forced prostitute"—the child, the victim of trafficking; she who, by virtue of her victim status, is exonerated from sexual wrong-doing. The "whore" is the voluntary prostitute: because of her transgression, she deserves whatever she gets. The distinction between voluntary and forced prostitution, a radical and resistive attack on previous discourses that constructed all prostitutes as victims and/or deviants, has been co-opted and inverted, and incorporated to reinforce systems that abuse sex workers' rights.

The campaign for sex workers' rights began with challenging the myths surrounding prostitution and women's sexuality. Claiming that prostitution could be a choice was a major step. Yet now, as old myths are being given new impetus under the guise of accepting choice; it is time to reconsider the usefulness of "choice" versus "force" as the model of sex workers' experience.

NOTES

1. The Beijing Declaration and Platform for Action, 1995.
2. These acts, passed in 1864, 1866, and 1869, targeted prostitutes in an attempt to control the spread of venereal disease. See Judith Walkowitz, *Prostitution and Victorian Society: Women. Class and the State* (Cambridge: Cambridge University Press, 1982).
3. Nicky Roberts, *Whores in History: Prostitution in Western Society* (London: HarperCollins, 1992) 248.
4. Ibid., p. 258.
5. See Lenke Fereh, "Forced Prostitution and Traffic in Persons," in Marieke Klap, Yvonne Klerk and Jaqueline Smith, eds., *Combating Traffic in Persons: Proceedings of the Conference on Traffic in Persons* (Utrecht: IMS, Netherlands Institute of Human Rights, 1995) 68.
6. The International Agreement for the Suppression of the White Slave Traffic, Paris (1904), and the International Convention for the Suppression of the White Slave Traffic (1910).
7. The International Convention to Combat the Traffic in Women and Children (1921) and the International Convention for the Suppression of the Traffic in Women of Full Age (1933). Nicky Roberts links the League's concern with the traffic in women with the re-opening, after World War I, of actual international migration networks and routes used by prostitutes (279).
8. Developed as a replacement for the United Nations 1949 Convention for the Suppression of the Traffic in Persons and of the Exploitation of the Prostitution of Others by the

Coalition Against Trafficking in Women (CATW). (Draft) Convention on the Elimination of All Forms of Sexual Exploitation of Women, 1993 Art. 2(b).

9. CATW: (Draft) Convention on the Elimination of All Forms of Sexual Exploitation of Women, 1993 Art. I.

10. Ibid.

11. For a history of the development of sex worker politics to 1986, see Gail Pheterson, ed., *A Vindication of the Rights of Whores* (Washington: Seal Press, 1989) 3–30.

12. International Committee for Prostitutes Rights, printed in Pheterson, 1989, pp. 40–42.

13. GAATW/STV, "A Proposal to Replace the Convention for the Suppression of the Traffic in Persons and of the Exploitation of the Prostitution of Others," Utrecht, 1994, par. II.2 and par. III.1, emphasis added.

14. Ibid., par. III.1.

15. This was also the time when the international movement for sex workers' rights reached its peak of organization, with two international conferences held in 1985 and 1986. For documentation of these conferences, see Gail Pheterson, ed., *A Vindication of the Rights of Whores* (Washington: Seal Press, 1989).

16. See Laura Reanda, "Prostitution as a Human Rights Question, Problems and Prospects of United Nations Action," *Human Rights Quarterly* 13 (1991) 209–211, and UNESCO/CATW, "The Penn State Report," 1–2. Pennsylvania, 1992.

17. See Lars Adam Rehof, *Guide to the Travaux Preparatoire of the United Nations Convention on the Elimination of All Forms of Discrimination Against Women* (Dordrecht: Martinus Nijhoff/Kluwer, 1993) 91.

18. This conclusion is supported by R. Haverman and J. C. Hes in "Vrouwenhandel en Exploitatie van Prostitutie," A. W. Heringa et al., eds., *Het Vrouwenverdrag: Een beeld van een Verdrag* (Antwerpen and Amersfoort: MAKLU, 1994).

19. Declaration of Mexico on the Equality of Women, UN 1975, par. 28, 34.

20. Declaration of Mexico on the Equality of Women, UN 1975, Art. 2.

21. Maria Hartle, "Traffic in Women as a Form of Violence Against Women," in Klap et al., eds., *Combating Traffic in Persons: Proceedings of the Conference on Traffic in Persons* (Utrecht: IMS, Netherlands Institute of Human Rights, 1995).

22. The Vienna Declaration and Program of Action, par. 38.

23. Draft Platform for Action (A/CONF.177.1, 24 May 1995) notably par. 122, 131d, 225; and the Beijing Declaration and Platform for Action, par. 123, 131d, 224.

24. UN EICN 411995142.

25. Miller, 1991, p. 1.

26. The above instruments are not all inherently consistent in that several call upon states to ratify the abolitionist Trafficking Convention. However, in calling for the elimination of only "forced prostitution and trafficking" rather than prostitution itself, an implicit recognition of the right to self-determination is evident.

27. See "A Joint Statement of Policy," by the Prostitutes' Rights Organization for Sex Workers; the Sex Workers Outreach Project; Workers in Sex Employment in the ACT; Self-Help for Queensland Workers in the Sex Industry; The Support, Information, Education, Referral Association of Western Australia; The South Australian Sex Industry Network; The Prostitutes Association of South Australia; The Prostitute Association Northern Territory for Health, Education, Referrals; Cybelle, Sex Worker Organization Tasmania; Sydney Sexual Health Center, Sydney Hospital; The Queer and Esoteric Workers Union and representatives of Asian sex working communities in New South Wales (1996) 3.

28. Ibid., 3.

29. See also Jo Doezema, "Choice in Prostitution," in *Changing Faces of Prostitution* (Helsinki: Unioni, The League of Finnish Feminists, 1995).

30. *The Human Rights Watch Global Report on Women's Human Rights* (New York: Human Rights Watch, 1995) 196.

31. Roberts, p. 253.

32. Tasha David, *Worlds Apart, Women and the Global Economy* (Brussels: International Confederation of Free Trade Unions, 1996) 43.

33. *Human Rights Watch*, 1995, p. 213.

34. Ibid., p. 210.

35. Angela Matheson, "Trafficking in Asian Sex Workers," *Green Left Weekly* (26 October 1994) 1.

36. See J. Doezema, "Sex Worker Delegation to the Beijing Conference," in Network of Sex Works Projects internal communication, Amsterdam, March 1995, and Alison Murray's contribution to this book. Abject poverty is not usually the primary reason for women to choose sex work or to migrate as a sex worker. Apart from the obvious fact that not all poor women choose to become prostitutes, research shows that there are other important considerations motivating someone's choice to do sex work. . . .

37. . . . Heather Montgomery challenges some of the myths surrounding "child prostitution." See also Maggie Black, "Home Truths," *New Internationalist* (February 1994), 11–13, and Alison Murray, forthcoming, "On Bondage, Peers and Queers: Sexual Subcultures, Sex Workers and AIDS Discourses in the Asia-Pacific."

38. For example, see Ron O'Grady, *The Rape of the Innocent, End Child Prostitution in Asian Tourism* (Bangkok: ECPAT, 1994).

39. *Children and Women in Myanmar: A Situation Analysis* (UNICEF 1995) 38, emphasis added.

40. Marjan Wijers and Lin Lap-Chew, *Trafficking in Women: Forced Labor and Slavery-like Practices in Marriage, Domestic Labor and Prostitution* (Utrecht: The Foundation Against Trafficking in Women and the Global Alliance Against Trafficking in Women, 1996) 198.

41. This fascination has an erotic element: at an 1885 demonstration in London in the wake of a sensational articles

about the white slave trade "street vendors shifted record numbers of the pornographic magazine *The Devil*." See Roberts, 1992.

42. Roberts, 1992, p. 264.
43. Wijers and Lap-Chew, pp. 111–152.
44. Ibid., p. 126.
45. Ibid., p. 128.

46. Ibid., pp. 126–130.
47. Ibid., p. 153.
48. Marga de Boer, *Traffic in Women: Policy* Willem Pompe Institute for Criminal Law 29.
49. *Human Rights Watch*, 1995, p. 198.
50. Ibid., p. 200.
51. Ibid., p. 253.

FEMICIDE IN JUÁREZ

Pheona Donohoe

Pink and black crosses mark the street poles in downtown Ciudad Juárez. They are a constant reminder of how easy it is for a woman to disappear. Symbolizing the victims of femicide, each pole is hand-painted by a family member of the murdered and missing women from Juárez. Earlier this year Amnesty International estimated that 373 women had been murdered in Juárez since 1993. Many were killed as the result of domestic violence, gang or drug related, or from the horrifying kidnap, rape and torture by alleged serial killers. Despite the Juárez femicide becoming a mass-media commodity, these crimes have not ceased with two more murders in the past several months. This gross abuse of human rights is happening within kilometers of El Paso, Texas. On one side of the border is poverty and corruption. On the other is democracy, justice and freedom. America's international dominance has come at cost however, and is partially to blame for the moral chaos in Juárez.

Logos for American corporations are plastered on the exterior walls of 80% of the factories in Juárez. Some of these factories assemble parts for General Motors, Sony, Ford, Phillips and RCA. Since the North American Free Trade Agreement (NAFTA) took effect, Juárez [has become] the largest industrial zone in Mexico, housing almost 300 maquiladoras (foreign-owned sweatshops). A majority of the factory workers are female and many have relocated to Juárez from remote villages and towns from the south of Mexico. Over the past 10 years, many of the women employed at maquiladoras

have disappeared. Some bodies have been found in the Chihuahua desert, some remain missing.

The last victim in the Juárez femicide is Alma Brisa Molina Baca, a maquiladora worker who never made it home on Saturday July 24. Her body was found on waste ground several days later. Autopsies revealed she had been raped and strangled. This follows the death of Guadalupe Santos Gomez, a 24-year-old bar waitress originally from southern Mexico. Her strangled body was found in an empty lot in a south Juárez suburb on Monday May 28. Santos shared physical traits consistent with two thirds of the victims; dark skinned, tall and thin, with long, dark hair, aged between 11 and 25. Over one third of the victims have never been identified.

To date, the handling of the Juárez murders by local authorities has been a farce. State authorities have lost, contaminated and even washed evidence, wrongly identified bodies, announced victims' names to the media before their families, forced suspects into confessing after torturing them with electric prods, threatened and harassed family members of the victims, and allegedly have a direct involvement in the murders. In early July the Mexican government bowed to pressure and released its first report on the murders in Juárez. Compiled by Maria Lopez Urbina, the federal prosecutor in charge of investigating the femicide, this was the first real analysis of the situation despite its eleven-year history. This report was not why or how the women were killed,

(continued)

but rather how the investigation of their murders was handled by officials. Not surprisingly, 81 Chihuahua officials were harshly criticized for their incompetent handing of the cases; 24 police officers, 17 forensic experts, 30 state investigators and 3 investigative supervisors. Most alarmingly, the report only contained information on 50 of the murders.

In addition to victims' families receiving little to no help from authorities to solve the murders, they are currently being exploited by media outlets capitalizing on their loss and turning the femicide into pop culture. Dozens of movies, TV shows, songs, theatre performances, artwork and books are in production with storylines inspired by the femicide in Juárez, many sensationalizing and glorifying the murders. Most recently, Mexico's second largest television network, TV Azteca, began airing a five-part, soap-opera style drama called *Tan Infinito Como El Desierto (As Infinite as the Desert)*. Shot on location in Juárez, the series dramatizes a different type of murder [with] each episode suggesting women fell victim to snuff movies, satanic rituals and copycat murders inspired by serial killers. The executive producer, Genoveva Martinez, claims that the episodes are based on police investigations. Family members in Juárez are infuriated by the series and many have threatened legal action against the broadcast company for unauthorized use of their daughters' names and images.

In addition to the Mexican television show there is a film by Kevin James Dobson, *The Virgin of Juárez*, currently in production; a book by Diana Washington Valdez, *Harvest of Women*, due to be released later this year; a text/illustration book compiled by actress Mia Kirshner due in 2006; a song "Mujeres de Juárez" on the new los Tigres del Norte album; and other documentaries in the making. Chihuahua state has responded quickly and on April 21 the president of the state assembly, Victor Valencia, banned the los Tigres del Norte song claiming it was immoral for the band to be making money from singing about the murders. A respectful insight into the Juárez murders is the 2001 documentary *Senorita Extraviada (Young Missing Women)* by Mexican-American filmmaker Lourdes Portillo. Containing interviews with victims' families and a survivor of police brutality, the documentary helped to raise international awareness including a recent screening in Melbourne, Australia. The Melbourne documentary screening drew a sell-out crowd to the Australian Centre for the Moving Image and launched a fundraising campaign which also included a concert and series of t-shirts. AUD$5,500 [Australian dollars] was raised and forwarded to Amigos de las Mujeres de Juárez in New Mexico.

Despite the international attention, Mexican federal government reports and constant media coverage, the pink and black crosses continue to fill the streets of Juárez where men kill with impunity. Twenty-four years ago the Pop Group released an album *How Much Longer Do We Tolerate Mass Murder?* We've learned little in the quarter century since that album's release and in Juárez the authorities don't just tolerate it, they cover it up.

Do Muslim Women Really Need Saving? Anthropological Reflections on Cultural Relativism and Its Others

What are the ethics of the current "War on Terrorism," a war that justifies itself by purporting to liberate, or save, Afghan women? Does anthropology have anything to offer in our search for a viable position to take regarding this rationale for war?

I was led to pose the question of my title in part because of the way I personally experienced the response to the U.S. war in Afghanistan. Like many colleagues whose work has focused on women and gender in the Middle East, I was deluged with invitations to speak—not just on news programs but also to various departments at colleges and universities, especially women's studies programs. Why did this not please me, a scholar who has devoted more than 20 years of her life to this subject and who has some complicated personal connection to this identity? Here was an opportunity to spread the word, disseminate my knowledge, and correct misunderstandings. The urgent search for knowledge about our sister "women of cover" (as President George Bush so marvelously called them) is laudable and when it comes from women's studies programs where "transnational feminism" is now being taken seriously, it has a certain integrity (see Safire 2001).

My discomfort led me to reflect on why, as feminists in or from the West, or simply as people who have concerns about women's lives, we need to be wary of this response to the events and aftermath of September 11, 2001. I want to point out the minefields—a metaphor that is sadly too apt for a country like Afghanistan, with the world's highest number of mines per capita— of this obsession with the plight of Muslim women. I hope to show some way through them using insights from anthropology, the discipline whose charge has been to understand and manage cultural difference. At

the same time, I want to remain critical of anthropology's complicity in the reification of cultural difference.

CULTURAL EXPLANATIONS AND THE MOBILIZATION OF WOMEN

It is easier to see why one should be skeptical about the focus on the "Muslim woman" if one begins with the U.S. public response. I will analyze two manifestations of this response: some conversations I had with a reporter from the PBS *NewsHour with Jim Lehrer* and First Lady Laura Bush's radio address to the nation on November 17, 2001. The presenter from the *NewsHour* show first contacted me in October to see if I was willing to give some background for a segment on Women and Islam. I mischievously asked whether she had done segments on the women of Guatemala, Ireland, Palestine, or Bosnia when the show covered wars in those regions; but I finally agreed to look at the questions she was going to pose to panelists. The questions were hopelessly general. Do Muslim women believe "x"? Are Muslim women "y"? Does Islam allow "z" for women? I asked her: If you were to substitute Christian or Jewish wherever you have Muslim, would these questions make sense? I did not imagine she would call me back. But she did, twice, once with an idea for a segment on the meaning of Ramadan and another time on Muslim women in politics. One was in response to the bombing and the other to the speeches by Laura Bush and Cherie Blair, wife of the British Prime Minister.

What is striking about these three ideas for news programs is that there was a consistent resort to the cultural, as if knowing something about women and Islam or the meaning of a religious ritual would help one understand the tragic attack on New York's World Trade Center and the U.S. Pentagon, or how Afghanistan had come to be ruled by the Taliban, or what interests might have fueled U.S. and other interventions in the region over the past 25 years, or what the history of American support for conservative groups funded to undermine the Soviets might have been, or why the caves and bunkers out of which Bin Laden was to be smoked "dead or alive," as President Bush announced on television, were paid for and built by the CIA.

In other words, the question is why knowing about the "culture" of the region, and particularly its religious beliefs and treatment of women, was more urgent than exploring the history of the development of repressive regimes in the region and the U.S. role in this history. Such cultural framing, it seemed to me, prevented the serious exploration of the roots and nature of human suffering in this part of the world. Instead of political and historical explanations, experts were being asked to give religio-cultural ones. Instead of questions that might lead to the exploration of global interconnections, we were offered ones that worked to artificially divide the world into separate spheres— recreating an imaginative geography of West versus East, us versus Muslims, cultures in which First Ladies give speeches versus others where women shuffle around silently in burqas.

Most pressing for me was why the Muslim woman in general, and the Afghan woman in particular, were so crucial to this cultural mode of explanation, which ignored the complex entanglements in which we are all implicated, in sometimes surprising alignments. Why were these female symbols being mobilized in this "War against Terrorism" in a way they were not in other conflicts? Laura Bush's radio address on November 17 reveals the political work such mobilization accomplishes. On the one hand, her address collapsed important distinctions that should have been maintained. There was a constant slippage between the Taliban and the terrorists, so that they became almost one word—a kind of hyphenated monster identity: the Taliban-and-the-terrorists. Then there was the blurring of the very separate causes in Afghanistan of women's continuing malnutrition, poverty, and ill health, and their more recent exclusion under the Taliban from employment, schooling, and the joys of wearing nail polish. On the other hand, her speech reinforced chasmic divides, primarily between the "civilized people throughout the world" whose hearts break for the women and children of Afghanistan and the Taliban-and-the-terrorists,

the cultural monsters who want to, as she put it, "impose their world on the rest of us."

Most revealingly, the speech enlisted women to justify American bombing and intervention in Afghanistan and to make a case for the "War on Terrorism" of which it was allegedly a part. As Laura Bush said, "Because of our recent military gains in much of Afghanistan, women are no longer imprisoned in their homes. They can listen to music and teach their daughters without fear of punishment. . . . The fight against terrorism is also a fight for the rights and dignity of women" (U.S. Government 2002).

These words have haunting resonances for anyone who has studied colonial history. Many who have worked on British colonialism in South Asia have noted the use of the woman question in colonial policies where intervention into sati (the practice of widows immolating themselves on their husbands' funeral pyres), child marriage, and other practices was used to justify rule. As Gayatri Chakravorty Spivak (1988) has cynically put it: white men saving brown women from brown men. The historical record is full of similar cases, including in the Middle East. In Turn of the Century Egypt, what Leila Ahmed (1992) has called "colonial feminism" was hard at work. This was a selective concern about the plight of Egyptian women that focused on the veil as a sign of oppression but gave no support to women's education and was professed loudly by the same Englishman, Lord Cromer, who opposed women's suffrage back home.

Sociologist Marnia Lazreg (1994) has offered some vivid examples of how French colonialism enlisted women to its cause in Algeria. She writes:

> Perhaps the most spectacular example of the colonial appropriation of women's voices, and the silencing of those among them who had begun to take women revolutionaries . . . as role models by not donning the veil, was the event of May 16, 1958 [just four years before Algeria finally gained its independence from France after a long bloody struggle and 130 years of French control—L.A.]. On that day a demonstration was organized by rebellious French generals in Algiers to show their determination to keep Algeria French. To give the government of France evidence that Algerians were in agreement with them, the generals had a few thousand native men bused in from nearby villages, along with a few women who were solemnly unveiled by French women. . . . Rounding up Algerians and bringing them to demonstrations of loyalty to France was not in itself

an unusual act during the colonial era. But to unveil women at a well-choreographed ceremony added to the event a symbolic dimension that dramatized the one constant feature of the Algerian occupation by France: its obsession with women. (Lazreg 1994:135)

Lazreg (1994) also gives memorable examples of the way in which the French had earlier sought to transform Arab women and girls. She describes skits at awards ceremonies at the Muslim Girls' School in Algiers in 1851 and 1852. In the first skit, written by "a French lady from Algiers," two Algerian Arab girls reminisced about their trip to France with words including the following:

> Oh! Protective France: Oh! Hospitable France! . . .
> Noble land, where I felt free
> Under Christian skies to pray to our God: . . .
> God bless you for the happiness you bring us!
> And you, adoptive mother, who taught us
> That we have a share of this world,
> We will cherish you forever! (Lazreg 1994:68–69)

These girls are made to invoke the gift of a share of this world, a world where freedom reigns under Christian skies. This is not the world the Taliban-and-the-terrorists would "like to impose on the rest of us."

Just as I argued above that we need to be suspicious when neat cultural icons are plastered over messier historical and political narratives, so we need to be wary when Lord Cromer in British-ruled Egypt, French ladies in Algeria, and Laura Bush, all with military troops behind them, claim to be saving or liberating Muslim women.

POLITICS OF THE VEIL

I want now to look more closely at those Afghan women Laura Bush claimed were "rejoicing" at their liberation by the Americans. This necessitates a discussion of the veil, or the burqa, because it is so central to contemporary concerns about Muslim women. This will set the stage for a discussion of how anthropologists, feminist anthropologists in particular, contend with the problem of difference in a global world. In the conclusion, I will return to the rhetoric of saving Muslim women and offer an alternative.

It is common popular knowledge that the ultimate sign of the oppression of Afghan women under the Taliban-and-the-terrorists is that they were forced to

wear the burqa. Liberals sometimes confess their surprise that even though Afghanistan has been liberated from the Taliban, women do not seem to be throwing off their burqas. Someone who has worked in Muslim regions must ask why this is so surprising. Did we expect that once "free" from the Taliban they would go "back" to belly shirts and blue jeans, or dust off their Chanel suits? We need to be more sensible about the clothing of "women of cover," and so there is perhaps a need to make some basic points about veiling.

First, it should be recalled that the Taliban did not invent the burqa. It was the local form of covering that Pashtun women in one region wore when they went out. The Pashtun are one of several ethnic groups in Afghanistan and the burqa was one of many forms of covering in the subcontinent and Southwest Asia that has developed as a convention for symbolizing women's modesty or respectability. The burqa, like some other forms of "cover" has, in many settings, marked the symbolic separation of men's and women's spheres, as part of the general association of women with family and home, not with public space where strangers mingled.

Twenty years ago the anthropologist Hanna Papanek (1982), who worked in Pakistan, described the burqa as "portable seclusion." She noted that many saw it as a liberating invention because it enabled women to move out of segregated living spaces while still observing the basic moral requirements of separating and protecting women from unrelated men. Ever since I came across her phrase "portable seclusion," I have thought of these enveloping robes as "mobile homes." Everywhere, such veiling signifies belonging to a particular community and participating in a moral way of life in which families are paramount in the organization of communities and the home is associated with the sanctity of women.

The obvious question that follows is this: If this were the case, why would women suddenly become immodest? Why would they suddenly throw off the markers of their respectability, markers, whether burqas or other forms of cover, which were supposed to assure their protection in the public sphere from the harassment of strange men by symbolically signaling to all that they were still in the inviolable space of their homes, even though moving in the public realm? Especially when these are forms of dress that had become so conventional that most women gave little thought to their meaning.

To draw some analogies, none of them perfect, why are we surprised that Afghan women do not throw off their burqas when we know perfectly well that it would not be appropriate to wear shorts to the opera? At the time these discussions of Afghan women's burqas were raging, a friend of mine was chided by her husband for suggesting she wanted to wear a pantsuit to a fancy wedding: "You know you don't wear pants to a WASP wedding," he reminded her. New Yorkers know that the beautifully coiffed Hasidic women, who look so fashionable next to their dour husbands in black coats and hats, are wearing wigs. This is because religious belief and community standards of propriety require the covering of the hair. They also alter boutique fashions to include high necks and long sleeves. As anthropologists know perfectly well, people wear the appropriate form of dress for their social communities and are guided by socially shared standards, religious beliefs, and moral ideals, unless they deliberately transgress to make a point or are unable to afford proper cover. If we think that U.S. women live in a world of choice regarding clothing, all we need to do is remind ourselves of the expression, "the tyranny of fashion."

What had happened in Afghanistan under the Taliban is that one regional style of covering or veiling, associated with a certain respectable but not elite class, was imposed on everyone as "religiously" appropriate, even though previously there had been many different styles, popular or traditional with different groups and classes—different ways to mark women's propriety, or, in more recent times, religious piety. Although I am not an expert on Afghanistan, I imagine that the majority of women left in Afghanistan by the time the Taliban took control were the rural or less educated, from nonelite families, since they were the only ones who could not emigrate to escape the hardship and violence that has marked Afghanistan's recent history. If liberated from the enforced wearing of burqas, most of these women would choose some other form of modest headcovering, like all those living nearby who were not under the Taliban—their rural Hindu counterparts in the North of India (who cover their heads and veil their faces from affines [in-laws]) or their Muslim sisters in Pakistan.

Even *The New York Times* carried an article about Afghan women refugees in Pakistan that attempted to educate readers about this local variety (Fremson 2001). The article describes and pictures everything from the now-iconic burqa with the embroidered eyeholes, which a Pashtun woman explains is the proper dress for her community, to large scarves they call chadors, to the new Islamic modest dress that wearers refer to as *hijab*. Those in the new Islamic dress are characteristically students heading for professional careers, especially in medicine, just like their counterparts from Egypt to Malaysia. One wearing the large scarf was a school principal; the other was a poor street vendor. The telling quote from the young street vendor is, "If I did [wear the burqa] the refugees would tease me because the burqa is for 'good women' who stay inside the home" (Fremson 2001:14). Here you can see the local status associated with the burqa—it is for good respectable women from strong families who are not forced to make a living selling on the street.

The British newspaper *The Guardian* published an interview in January 2002 with Dr. Suheila Siddiqi, a respected surgeon in Afghanistan who holds the rank of lieutenant general in the Afghan medical corps (Goldenberg 2002). A woman in her sixties, she comes from an elite family and, like her sisters, was educated. Unlike most women of her class, she chose not to go into exile. She is presented in the article as "the woman who stood up to the Taliban" because she refused to wear the burqa. She had made it a condition of returning to her post as head of a major hospital when the Taliban came begging in 1996, just eight months after firing her along with other women. Siddiqi is described as thin, glamorous, and confident. But further into the article it is noted that her graying bouffant hair is covered in a gauzy veil. This is a reminder that though she refused the burqa, she had no question about wearing the chador or scarf.

Finally, I need to make a crucial point about veiling. Not only are there many forms of covering, which themselves have different meanings in the communities in which they are used, but also veiling itself must not be confused with, or made to stand for, lack of agency. As I have argued in my ethnography of a Bedouin community in Egypt in the late 1970s and 1980s (1986), pulling the black head cloth over the face in front of older respected men is considered a voluntary act by women who are deeply committed to being moral and have a sense of honor tied to family. One of the ways they show their standing is by covering their faces in certain contexts. They decide for whom they feel it is appropriate to veil.

To take a very different case, the modern Islamic modest dress that many educated women across the Muslim world have taken on since the mid-1970s now both publicly marks piety and can be read as a sign of educated urban sophistication, a sort of modernity (e.g., Abu-Lughod 1995, 1998; Brenner 1996; El Guindi 1999; MacLeod 1991; Ong 1990). As Saba Mahmood (2001) has so brilliantly shown in her ethnography of women in the mosque movement in Egypt, this new form of dress is also perceived by many of the women who adopt it as part of a bodily means to cultivate virtue, the outcome of their professed desire to be close to God.

Two points emerge from this fairly basic discussion of the meanings of veiling in the contemporary Muslim world. First, we need to work against the reductive interpretation of veiling as the quintessential sign of women's unfreedom, even if we object to state imposition of this form, as in Iran or with the Taliban. (It must be recalled that the modernizing states of Turkey and Iran had earlier in the century banned veiling and required men, except religious clerics, to adopt Western dress.) What does freedom mean if we accept the fundamental premise that humans are social beings, always raised in certain social and historical contexts and belonging to particular communities that shape their desires and understandings of the world? Is it not a gross violation of women's own understandings of what they are doing to simply denounce the burqa as a medieval imposition? Second, we must take care not to reduce the diverse situations and attitudes of millions of Muslim women to a single item of clothing. Perhaps it is time to give up the Western obsession with the veil and focus on some serious issues with which feminists and others should indeed be concerned.

Ultimately, the significant political-ethical problem the burqa raises is how to deal with cultural "others." How are we to deal with difference without accepting the passivity implied by the cultural relativism for which anthropologists are justly famous—a relativism that says it's their culture and it's not my business to judge or interfere, only to try to understand. Cultural relativism is certainly an improvement on ethnocentrism and the racism, cultural imperialism, and imperiousness that underlie it; the problem is that it is too late not to interfere. The forms of lives we find around the world are already products of long histories of interactions.

I want to explore the issues of women, cultural relativism, and the problems of "difference" from three angles. First, I want to consider what feminist anthropologists (those stuck in that awkward relationship, as Strathern [1987] has claimed) are to do with strange political bedfellows. I used to feel torn when I received the e-mail petitions circulating for the last few years

in defense of Afghan women under the Taliban. I was not sympathetic to the dogmatism of the Taliban; I do not support the oppression of women. But the provenance of the campaign worried me. I do not usually find myself in political company with the likes of Hollywood celebrities (see Hirschkind and Mahmood 2002). I had never received a petition from such women defending the right of Palestinian women to safety from Israeli bombing or daily harassment at checkpoints, asking the United States to reconsider its support for a government that had dispossessed them, closed them out from work and citizenship rights, refused them the most basic freedoms. Maybe some of these same people might be signing petitions to save African women from genital cutting, or Indian women from dowry deaths. However, I do not think that it would be as easy to mobilize so many of these American and European women if it were not a case of Muslim men oppressing Muslim women—women of cover for whom they can feel sorry and in relation to whom they can feel smugly superior. Would television diva Oprah Winfrey host the Women in Black, the women's peace group from Israel, as she did RAWA, the Revolutionary Association of Women of Afghanistan, who were also granted the *Glamour Magazine* Women of the Year Award? What are we to make of post-Taliban "Reality Tours" such as the one advertised on the internet by Global Exchange for March 2002 under the title "Courage and Tenacity: A Women's Delegation to Afghanistan"? The rationale for the $1,400 tour is that "with the removal of the Taliban government, Afghan women, for the first time in the past decade, have the opportunity to reclaim their basic human rights and establish their role as equal citizens by participating in the rebuilding of their nation." The tour's objective, to celebrate International Women's Week, is "to develop awareness of the concerns and issues the Afghan women are facing as well as to witness the changing political, economic, and social conditions which have created new opportunities for the women of Afghanistan" (Global Exchange 2002).

To be critical of this celebration of women's rights in Afghanistan is not to pass judgment on any local women's organizations, such as RAWA, whose members have courageously worked since 1977 for a democratic secular Afghanistan in which women's human rights are respected, against Soviet-backed regimes or U.S.-, Saudi-, and Pakistani-supported conservatives. Their documentation of abuse and their work through clinics and schools have been enormously important.

It is also not to fault the campaigns that exposed the dreadful conditions under which the Taliban placed women. The Feminist Majority campaign helped put a stop to a secret oil pipeline deal between the Taliban and the U.S. multinational Unocal that was going forward with U.S. administration support. Western feminist campaigns must not be confused with the hypocrisies of the new colonial feminism of a Republican president who was not elected for his progressive stance on feminist issues or of administrations that played down the terrible record of violations of women by the United States' allies in the Northern Alliance, as documented by Human Rights Watch and Amnesty International, among others. Rapes and assaults were widespread in the period of infighting that devastated Afghanistan before the Taliban came in to restore order.

It is, however, to suggest that we need to look closely at what we are supporting (and what we are not) and to think carefully about why. How should we manage the complicated politics and ethics of finding ourselves in agreement with those with whom we normally disagree? I do not know how many feminists who felt good about saving Afghan women from the Taliban are also asking for a global redistribution of wealth or contemplating sacrificing their own consumption radically so that African or Afghan women could have some chance of having what I do believe should be a universal human right—the right to freedom from the structural violence of global inequality and from the ravages of war, the everyday rights of having enough to eat, having homes for their families in which to live and thrive, having ways to make decent livings so their children can grow, and having the strength and security to work out, within their communities and with whatever alliances they want, how to live a good life, which might very well include changing the ways those communities are organized.

Suspicion about bedfellows is only a first step; it will not give us a way to think more positively about what to do or where to stand. For that, we need to confront two more big issues. First is the acceptance of the possibility of difference. Can we only free Afghan women to be like us or might we have to recognize that even after "liberation" from the Taliban, they might want different things than we would want for them? What do we do about that? Second, we need to be vigilant about the rhetoric of saving people because of what it implies about our attitudes.

Again, when I talk about accepting difference, I am not implying that we should resign ourselves to being cultural relativists who respect whatever goes on elsewhere as "just their culture." I have already discussed the dangers of "cultural" explanations; "their" cultures are just as much part of history and an interconnected world as ours are. What I am advocating is the hard work involved in recognizing and respecting differences—precisely as products of different histories, as expressions of different circumstances, and as manifestations of differently structured desires. We may want justice for women, but can we accept that there might be different ideas about justice and that different women might want, or choose, different futures from what we envision as best (see Ong 1988)? We must consider that they might be called to personhood, so to speak, in a different language.

Reports from the Bonn peace conference held in late November to discuss the rebuilding of Afghanistan revealed significant differences among the few Afghan women feminists and activists present. RAWA's position was to reject any conciliatory approach to Islamic governance. According to one report I read, most women activists, especially those based in Afghanistan who are aware of the realities on the ground, agreed that Islam had to be the starting point for reform. Fatima Gailani, a U.S.-based advisor to one of the delegations, is quoted as saying, "If I go to Afghanistan today and ask women for votes on the promise to bring them secularism, they are going to tell me to go to hell." Instead, according to one report, most of these women looked for inspiration on how to fight for equality to a place that might seem surprising. They looked to Iran as a country in which they saw women making significant gains within an Islamic framework—in part through an Islamically oriented feminist movement that is challenging injustices and reinterpreting the religious tradition.

The situation in Iran is itself the subject of heated debate within feminist circles, especially among Iranian feminists in the West (e.g., Mir-Hosseini 1999; Moghissi 1999; Najmabadi 1998, 2000). It is not clear whether and in what ways women have made gains and whether the great increases in literacy, decreases in birthrates, presence of women in the professions and government, and a feminist flourishing in cultural fields like writing and film-making are because of or despite the establishment of a so-called Islamic Republic. The concept of an Islamic feminism itself is also controversial. Is it an oxymoron or does it refer to a viable movement forged by brave women who want a third way?

One of the things we have to be most careful about in thinking about Third World feminisms, and feminism in different parts of the Muslim world, is how not to fall into polarizations that place feminism on the side of the West. I have written about the dilemmas faced by Arab feminists when Western feminists initiate campaigns that make them vulnerable to local denunciations by conservatives of various sorts, whether Islamist or nationalist, of being traitors (Abu-Lughod 2001). As some like Afsaneh Najmabadi are now arguing, not only is it wrong to see history simplistically in terms of a putative opposition between Islam and the West (as is happening in the United States now and has happened in parallel in the Muslim world), but it is also strategically dangerous to accept this cultural opposition between Islam and the West, between fundamentalism and feminism, because those many people within Muslim countries who are trying to find alternatives to present injustices, those who might want to refuse the divide and take from different histories and cultures, who do not accept that being feminist means being Western, will be under pressure to choose, just as we are: Are you with us or against us?

My point is to remind us to be aware of differences, respectful of other paths toward social change that might give women better lives. Can there be a liberation that is Islamic? And, beyond this, is liberation even a goal for which all women or people strive? Are emancipation, equality, and rights part of a universal language we must use? To quote Saba Mahmood, writing about the women in Egypt who are seeking to become pious Muslims, "The desire for freedom and liberation is a historically situated desire whose motivational force cannot be assumed a priori, but needs to be reconsidered in light of other desires aspirations, and capacities that inhere in a culturally and historically located subject" (2001:223). In other words, might other desires be more meaningful for different groups of people? Living in close families? Living in a godly way? Living without war? I have done fieldwork in Egypt over more than 20 years and I cannot think of a single woman I know, from the poorest rural to the most educated cosmopolitan, who has ever expressed envy of U.S. women, women they tend to perceive as bereft of community, vulnerable to sexual violence and social anomie, driven by individual success rather than morality, or strangely disrespectful of God.

Mahmood (2001) has pointed out a disturbing thing that happens when one argues for a respect for other traditions. She notes that there seems to be a difference in the political demands made on those who work on or are trying to understand Muslims and Islamists and those who work on secular-humanist projects. She, who studies the piety movement in Egypt, is consistently pressed to denounce all the harm done by Islamic movements around the world—otherwise she is accused of being an apologist. But there never seems to be a parallel demand for those who study secular humanism and its projects, despite the terrible violences that have been associated with it over the last couple of centuries, from world wars to colonialism, from genocides to slavery. We need to have as little dogmatic faith in secular humanism as in Islamism, and as open a mind to the complex possibilities of human projects undertaken in one tradition as the other.

BEYOND THE RHETORIC OF SALVATION

Let us return, finally, to my title, "Do Muslim Women Really Need Saving?" The discussion of culture, veiling, and how one can navigate the shoals of cultural difference should put Laura Bush's self-congratulation about the rejoicing of Afghan women liberated by American troops in a different light. It is deeply problematic to construct the Afghan woman as someone in need of saving. When you save someone, you imply that you are saving her from something. You are also saving her *to* something. What violences are entailed in this transformation, and what presumptions are being made about the superiority of that to which you are saving her? Projects of saving other women depend on and reinforce a sense of superiority by Westerners, a form of arrogance that deserves to be challenged. All one needs to do to appreciate the patronizing quality of the rhetoric of saving women is to imagine using it today in the United States about disadvantaged groups such as African American women or working-class women. We now understand them as suffering from structural violence. We have become politicized about race and class, but not culture.

As anthropologists, feminists, or concerned citizens, we should be wary of taking on the mantles of those 19th-century Christian missionary women who devoted their lives to saving their Muslim sisters. One of my favorite documents from that period is a collection called *Our Moslem Sisters,* the proceedings of a conference of women missionaries held in Cairo in 1906 (Van Sommer and Zwemmer 1907). The subtitle of the book is *A Cry of Need from the Lands of Darkness*

Interpreted by Those Who Heard It. Speaking of the ignorance, seclusion, polygamy, and veiling that blighted women's lives across the Muslim world, the missionary women spoke of their responsibility to make these women's voices heard. As the introduction states, "They will never cry for themselves, for they are down under the yoke of centuries of oppression" (Van Sommer and Zwemer 1907:15). "This book," it begins, "with its sad, reiterated story of wrong and oppression is an indictment and an appeal. . . . It is an appeal to Christian womanhood to right these wrongs and enlighten this darkness by sacrifice and service" (Van Sommer and Zwemer 1907:5).

One can hear uncanny echoes of their virtuous goals today, even though the language is secular, the appeals not to Jesus but to human rights or the liberal West. The continuing currency of such imagery and sentiments can be seen in their deployment for perfectly good humanitarian causes. In February 2002, I received an invitation to a reception honoring an international medical humanitarian network called Médecins du Monde/Doctors of the World (MdM). Under the sponsorship of the French Ambassador to the United States, the Head of the delegation of the European Commission to the United Nations, and a member of the European Parliament, the cocktail reception was to feature an exhibition of photographs under the clichéd title "Afghan Women: Behind the Veil."

The invitation was remarkable not just for the colorful photograph of women in flowing burqas walking across the barren mountains of Afghanistan but also for the text, a portion of which I quote:

> For 20 years MdM has been ceaselessly struggling to help those who are most vulnerable. But increasingly, thick veils cover the victims of the war. When the Taliban came to power in 1996, Afghan Women became faceless. To unveil one's face while receiving medical care was to achieve a sort of intimacy, find a brief space for secret freedom and recover a little of one's dignity. In a country where women had no access to basic medical care because they did not have the right to appear in public, where women had no right to practice medicine, MdM's program stood as a stubborn reminder of human rights. . . . Please join us in helping to lift the veil.

Although I cannot take up here the fantasies of intimacy associated with unveiling, fantasies reminiscent of the French colonial obsessions so brilliantly unmasked by Alloula in *The Colonial Harem* (1986), I can ask why

humanitarian projects and human rights discourse in the 21st century need rely on such constructions of Muslim women.

Could we not leave veils and vocations of saving others behind and instead train our sights on ways to make the world a more just place? The reason respect for difference should not be confused with cultural relativism is that it does not preclude asking how we, living in this privileged and powerful part of the world, might examine our own responsibilities for the situations in which others in distant places have found themselves. We do not stand outside the world, looking out over this sea of poor benighted people, living under the shadow—or veil—of oppressive cultures; we are part of that world. Islamic movements themselves have arisen in a world shaped by the intense engagements of Western powers in Middle Eastern lives.

A more productive approach, it seems to me, is to ask how we might contribute to making the world a more just place. A world not organized around strategic military and economic demands; a place where certain kinds of forces and values that we may still consider important could have an appeal and where there is the peace necessary for discussions, debates, and transformations to occur within communities. We need to ask ourselves what kinds of world conditions we could contribute to making such that popular desires will not be overdetermined by an overwhelming sense of helplessness in the face of forms of global injustice. Where we seek to be active in the affairs of distant places, can we do so in the spirit of support for those within those communities whose goals are to make women's (and men's) lives better (as Walley has argued in relation to practices of genital cutting in Africa [1997])? Can we use a more egalitarian language of alliances, coalitions, and solidarity, instead of salvation?

Even RAWA, the now celebrated Revolutionary Association of the Women of Afghanistan, which was so instrumental in bringing to U.S. women's attention the excesses of the Taliban, has opposed the U.S. bombing from the beginning. They do not see in it Afghan women's salvation but increased hardship and loss. They have long called for disarmament and for peacekeeping forces. Spokespersons point out the dangers of confusing governments with people, the Taliban with innocent Afghans who will be most harmed. They consistently remind audiences to take a close look at the ways policies are being organized around oil interests, the arms industry, and the international drug trade. They are not obsessed with the veil, even though they are the most radical feminists working for a secular democratic Afghanistan. Unfortunately, only their messages about the excesses of the Taliban have been heard, even though their criticisms of those in power in Afghanistan have included previous regimes. A first step in hearing their wider message is to break with the language of alien cultures, whether to understand or eliminate them. Missionary work and colonial feminism belong in the past. Our task is to critically explore what we might do to help create a world in which those poor Afghan women, for whom "the hearts of those in the civilized world break," can have safety and decent lives.

ACKNOWLEDGMENTS

I want to thank Page Jackson, Fran Mascia-Lees, Tim Mitchell, Rosalind Morris, Anupama Rao, and members of the audience at the symposium "Responding to War," sponsored by Columbia University's Institute for Research on Women and Gender (where I presented an earlier version), for helpful comments, references, clippings, and encouragement.

REFERENCES

Abu-Lughod, Lila. 1986. *Veiled Sentiments: Honor and Poetry in a Bedouin Society.* Berkeley: University of California Press.

———. 1995. Movie Stars and Islamic Moralism in Egypt. *Social Text* 42:53–67.

———. 1998. *Remaking Women: Feminism and Modernity in the Middle East.* Princeton: Princeton University Press.

———. 2001. Orientalism and Middle East Feminist Studies. *Feminist Studies* 27(1):101–113.

Ahmed, Leila. 1992. *Women and Gender in Islam.* New Haven, CT: Yale University Press.

Alloula, Malek. 1986. *The Colonial Harem.* Minneapolis: University of Minnesota Press.

Brenner, Suzanne. 1996. Reconstructing Self and Society: Javanese Muslim Women and "the Veil." *American Ethnologist* 23(4):673–697.

El Guindi, Fadwa. 1999. *Veil: Modesty, Privacy and Resistance.* Oxford: Berg.

Fremson, Ruth. 2001. Allure Must Be Covered. Individuality Peeks Through. *New York Times*, November 4: 14.

Global Exchange. 2002. Courage and Tenacity: A Women's Delegation to Afghanistan. Electronic document, http://www.globalexchange.org/tours/auto/2002-03-05_CourageandTenacityAWomensDele.html. Accessed February 11.

Goldenberg, Suzanne. 2002. The Woman Who Stood Up to the Taliban. *The Guardian*, January 24. Electronic document, http://222.guardian.co.ur/afghanistan/story/0,1284,63840.

Hirschkind, Charles, and Saba Mahmood. 2002. Feminism, the Taliban, and the Politics of Counter-Insurgency. *Anthropological Quarterly* 75(2):107–122.

Lazreg, Marnia. 1994. *The Eloquence of Silence: Algerian Women in Question.* New York: Routledge.

MacLeod, Arlene. 1991. *Accommodating Protest.* New York: Columbia University Press.

Mahmood, Saba. 2001. Feminist Theory, Embodiment, and the Docile Agent: Some Reflections on the Egyptian Islamic Revival. *Cultural Anthropology* 16(2):202–235.

Mir-Hosseini, Ziba. 1999. *Islam and Gender: The Religious Debate in Contemporary Iran.* Princeton: Princeton University Press.

Moghissi, Haideh. 1999. *Feminism and Islamic Fundamentalism.* London: Zed Books.

Najmabadi, Afsaneh. 1998. Feminism in an Islamic Republic. In *Islam, Gender and Social Change.* Yvonne Haddad and John Esposito, eds. Pp. 59–84. New York: Oxford University Press.

———. 2000. (Un)Veiling Feminism. *Social Text* 64:29–45.

Ong, Aihwa. 1988. Colonialism and Modernity: Feminist RePresentations of Women in Non-Western Societies. *Inscriptions* 3–4:79–93.

———. 1990. State Versus Islam: Malay Families, Women's Bodies, and the Body Politic in Malaysia. *American Ethnologist* 17(2):258–276.

Papanek, Hanna. 1982. Purdah in Pakistan: Seclusion and Modern Occupations for Women. In *Separate Worlds.* Hanna Papanek and Gail Minault, eds. Pp. 190–216. Columbia, MO: South Asia Books.

Safire, William. 2001. "On Language." *New York Times Magazine*, October 28: 22.

Spivak, Gayatri Chakravorty. 1988. Can the Subaltern Speak? In *Marxism and the Interpretation of Culture.* Cary Nelson and Lawrence Grossberg, eds. Pp. 271–313. Urbana: University of Illinois Press.

Strathern, Marilyn. 1987. An Awkward Relationship: The Case of Feminism and Anthropology. *Signs* 12: 276–292.

U.S. Government. 1907. *Our Moslem Sisters: A Cry of Need from Lands of Darkness Interpreted by Those Who Heard It.* New York: Fleming H. Revell.

———. 2002. Electronic document, http://www.whitehouse.gov/news/releases/2001/11/20011117. Accessed January 10.

Walley, Christine. 1997. Searching for "Voices": Feminism, Anthropology, and the Global Debate over Female Genital Operations. *Cultural Anthropology* 12(3):405–438.

BAGHDAD BURNING: GIRL BLOG FROM IRAQ

Riverbend

Saturday, August 23, 2003: We've Only Just Begun . . .

Females can no longer leave their homes alone. Each time I go out, E. and either a father, uncle, or cousin has to accompany me. It feels like we've gone back 50 years ever since the beginning of the occupation. A woman, or girl, out alone, risks anything from insults to abduction. An outing has to be arranged at least an hour beforehand. I state that I need to buy something or have to visit someone. Two males have to be procured (preferably large) and "safety arrangements" must be made in this total state of lawlessness. And always the question: "But do you have go out and buy it? Can't I get it for you?" No you can't, because the kilo of eggplant I absolutely have to select with my own hands is just an excuse to see the light of day and walk down a street. The situation is incredibly frustrating to females who work or go to college.

Before the war, around 50% of the college students were females, and over 50% of the working force was composed of women. Not so anymore. We are seeing an increase of fundamentalism in Iraq which is terrifying.

For example, before the war, I would estimate (roughly) that about 55% of females in Baghdad wore a hijab—or headscarf. Hijabs do not signify fundamentalism. That is far from the case—although I, myself, don't wear one, I have family and friends who do. The point is that, before, it didn't really matter. It was *my* business whether I wore one or not—not the business of some fundamentalist on the street.

For those who don't know (and I have discovered they are many more than I thought), a hijab only covers the hair and neck. The whole face shows and some women even wear it Grace Kelly style with a few locks of hair coming out of the front. A "burqa" on the other hand, like the ones worn in Afghanistan, covers the whole head—hair, face, and all.

I am female and Muslim. Before the occupation, I more or less dressed the way I wanted to. I lived in jeans and cotton pants and comfortable shirts. Now, I don't dare leave the house in pants. A long skirt and loose shirt (preferably with long sleeves) has become necessary. A girl wearing jeans risks being attacked, abducted, or insulted by fundamentalists who have been . . . liberated!

Fathers and mothers are keeping their daughters stashed safe at home. That's why you see so few females in the streets (especially after 4 pm). Others are making their daughters, wives, and sisters wear a hijab. Not to oppress them, but to protect them.

I lost my job for a similar reason. Girls are being made to quit college and school. My 14-year-old cousin (a straight-A student) is going to have to repeat the year because her parents decided to keep her home ever since the occupation. Why? Because the Supreme Council of the Islamic Revolution in Iraq overtook an office next to her school and opened up a special "bureau."

Men in black turbans (M.I.B.T.s as opposed to M.I.B.s) and dubious, shady figures dressed in black, head to foot, stand around the gates of the bureau in clusters, scanning the girls and teachers entering, the secondary school. The dark, frowning figures stand ogling, leering and sometimes jeering at the ones not wearing a hijab or whose skirts aren't long enough. In some areas, girls risk being attacked with acid if their clothes aren't "proper."

The Supreme Council for the Islamic Revolution in Iraq (SCIRI—but I prefer "SCAREY") was established in 1982 in Tehran. Its main goal is to import the concept of the "Islamic Revolution" from Iran to Iraq. In other words, they believe that Iraq should be a theocracy led by Shi'a Mullahs. Abdul Aziz Al-Hakim, the deputy leader of SCIRI, is a part of the nine-member rotating presidency and will soon have a go at ruling Iraq.

The SCIRI would like to give the impression that they have the full support of all Shi'a Muslims in Iraq. The truth is that many Shi'a Muslims are terrified of them and of the consequences of having them as a ruling power. Al-Hakim was responsible for torturing and executing Iraqi POWs in Iran all through the Iran-Iraq war and after. Should SCIRI govern Iraq, I imagine the first step would be to open the borders with Iran and unite the two countries. Bush can then stop referring to the two countries as a part of his infamous "Axis of Evil" and can just begin calling us the "Big Lump of Evil and Bad North Korea" (which seems more in accord with his limited linguistic abilities).

Ever since entering Iraq, Al-Hakim has been blackmailing the CPA in Baghdad with his "major Shi'a following." He entered Iraq escorted by "Jaysh Badir" or "Badir's Army." This "army" is composed of thousands of Iraqi extremists led by Iranian extremists and trained in Iran. All through the war, they were lurking on the border, waiting for a chance to slip inside. In Baghdad, and the south, they have been a source of terror and anxiety to Sunnis, Shi'a, and Christians alike. They, and some of their followers, were responsible for a large portion of the looting and the burning (you'd think they were going to get reconstruction contracts . . .). They were also responsible for hundreds of religious and political abductions and assassinations.

The whole situation is alarming beyond any description I can give. Christians have become the victims of extremism also. Some of them are being threatened, others are being attacked. A few wannabe Mullahs came out with a "fatwa," or decree, in June that declared all females should wear the hijab and if they didn't, they could be subject to "punishment." Another group claiming to be a part of the "Hawza Al Ilmia" decreed that not a single girl over the age of 14 could remain unmarried—even if it meant that some members of the Hawza would have to have two, three, or four wives. This decree included females of other religions. In the south, female UN and Red Cross aides received death threats if they didn't wear the hijab. This isn't done in the name of God—it's done in the name of power. It tells people—the world—that "Look—we have power, we have influence."

Liquor stores are being attacked and bombed. The owner usually gets a "threat" in the form of a fatwa claiming that if they didn't shut down the store permanently, there would be consequences.

The consequences are usually either a fire or a bomb. Similar threats have been made to hairdressers in some areas in Baghdad. It's frightening and appalling, but true.

Don't blame it on Islam. Every religion has its extremists. In times of chaos and disorder, those extremists flourish. Iraq is full of moderate Muslims who simply believe in "live and let live." We get along with each other—Sunnis and Shi'a, Muslims and Christians, and Jews and Sabi'a. We intermarry, we mix and mingle, we live. We build our churches and mosques in the same areas, our children go to the same schools . . . it was never an issue.

Someone asked me if, through elections, the Iraqi people might vote for an Islamic state. Six months ago, I would have firmly said, "No." Now, I'm not so sure. There's been an overwhelming return to fundamentalism. People are turning to religion for several reasons.

The first and most prominent reason is fear. Fear of war, fear of death, and fear of a fate worse than death (and yes, there are fates worse than death). If I didn't have something to believe in during this past war, I know I would have lost my mind. If there hadn't been a God to pray to, to make promises to, to bargain with, to thank—I wouldn't have made it through.

Encroaching Western values and beliefs have also played a prominent role in pushing Iraqis to embrace Islam. Just as there are ignorant people in the Western world (and there are plenty—I have the emails to prove it . . . don't make me embarrass you), there are ignorant people in the Middle East. In Muslims and Arabs, Westerners see suicide bombers, terrorists, ignorance, and camels. In Americans, Brits, etc. some Iraqis see depravity, prostitution, ignorance, domination, junkies, and ruthlessness. The best way people can find to protect themselves, and their loved ones, against this assumed threat is religion.

Finally, you have more direct reasons. 65% of all Iraqis are currently unemployed for one reason or another. There are people who have families to feed. When I say "families" I don't mean a wife and 2 kids . . . I mean around 16 or 17 people. Islamic parties supported by Iran, like Al-Daawa and SCIRI, are

(continued)

currently recruiting followers by offering "wages" to jobless men (an ex-soldier in the army, for example) in trade of "support." This support could mean anything—vote when the elections come around, bomb a specific shop, "confiscate," abduct, hijack cars (only if you work for Al-Chalabi . . .).

So concerning the anxiety over terror and fundamentalism—I would like to quote the Carpenters—worry? "We've only just begun . . . we've only just begun . . ."

Sunday, August 24, 2003: About Riverbend

A lot of you have been asking about my background and the reason why my English is good. I am Iraqi—born in Iraq to Iraqi parents, but was raised abroad for several years as a child. I came back in my early teens and continued studying in English in Baghdad—reading any book I could get my hands

on. Most of my friends are of different ethnicities, religions, and nationalities. I am bilingual. There are thousands in Iraq like me—kids of diplomats, students, expatriates, etc.

As to my connection with Western culture . . . you wouldn't believe how many young Iraqi people know so much about American/British/French pop culture. They know all about Arnold Schwarzenegger, Brad Pitt, Whitney Houston, McDonalds, and M.I.B.s . . . Iraqi tv stations were constantly showing bad copies of the latest Hollywood movies. (If it's any consolation, the Marines lived up to the Rambo/Terminator reputation which preceded them.)

But no matter what—I shall remain anonymous. I wouldn't feel free to write otherwise. I think Salam and Gee are incredibly brave . . . who knows, maybe one day I will be too. You know me as Riverbend, you share a very small part of my daily reality—I hope that will suffice.

R E A D I N G *49*   **Gwendolyn Mink**

The Lady and the Tramp (II): Feminist Welfare Politics, Poor Single Mothers, and the Challenge of Welfare Justice

I have worked in various political venues on welfare issues for ten years—for about as long as I have been researching and writing about women and U.S. social policy.[1] Most recently, I worked as a Steering Committee member and cochair of the Women's Committee of 100, a feminist mobilization against punitive welfare reform. I signed up with the Women's Committee of 100 in March or April of 1995—roughly a year after completing a book on welfare policy history and around the same time as the book's publication.[2]

I have always done both politics and scholarship, so directing my activism toward my field of professional

expertise at first did not seem especially odd or problematic. However, I had just published a book critical of experts like me—a book which, among other things, faulted solipsistic women welfare innovators of the early twentieth century for building a welfare state harmful to women and to gender equality. The book was barely between covers, and I had already embarked on a path of policy advocacy that veered disturbingly close to the reformers I had criticized. There I was, consorting with a group of supereducated, do-good feminists, most of whom would never need a welfare check. And there we were, using our social and professional positions to gain entry into congressional offices, where we spoke against reforms that would affect not us but poor women. It seemed to me that maybe I hadn't really internalized the lessons I had drawn from early-twentieth-century welfare history.

I struggled a bit with my own contradictions—between what I felt compelled to do as a feminist activist confronted by the political crisis of welfare reform and what I had cautioned against as a student of elite women reformers. But I didn't have to struggle long. It quickly became apparent that any historical analogies I feared were the product of academic overinterpretation. An awesome collection of women makes up the Committee of 100—none of whom, to my knowledge, has any interest in mothering the poor as our forebears did earlier in the century and all of whom reject the morally and culturally prescriptive politics of early-twentieth-century welfare innovation and of late-twentieth-century welfare reform.

We mobilized not to speak for poor mothers but with them—to speak for ourselves as feminists frustrated by the absence of women's voices and by the lack of gender equality concerns in the welfare debate. Although members of Congress paid scant attention, in our lobbying, letter writing, and media efforts, we repeatedly explained how welfare reform risks many of the rights and protections upon which women's security and equality depends. Often speaking of "welfare as a women's issue," we argued that "a war against poor women is a war against all women."

This was a strategically clever rallying cry, but it failed to rally many women—even feminists. In fact, the war against poor women was just that: a war against poor women. And it was a war in which many middle-class women participated on the anti-welfare side. All but one woman in the U.S. Senate supported the Personal Responsibility Act when it first was taken up in the summer of 1995.[3] In 1996, twenty-six of thirty-one Democratic women in the House of Representatives voted for their party's substitute bill, which, like the Personal Responsibility Act, stripped poor single mothers of their entitlement to welfare.[4] Meanwhile, across the country, a National Organization for Women Legal Defense and Education Fund appeal for contributions to support an economic justice litigator aroused so much hate mail that NOW LDEF stopped doing direct mail on the welfare issue.[5]

Although the feminist Women's Committee of 100 campaigned ardently against the welfare bill, Republicans won their war against poor single mothers with

the complicity of millions of other feminists. Feminist members of Congress did not write the Personal Responsibility Act, of course. Nor did NOW members or contributors to Emily's List comprise the driving force behind the most brutal provisions of the new welfare law. My point is not that feminists were uniquely responsible for how Congress reformed welfare. It is that they were uniquely positioned to make a difference. We have made a difference in many arenas across the years, even during inauspicious Republican presidencies—reforming rape laws, winning recognition of sexual harassment as a form of sex discrimination, and securing passage of a federal law against domestic violence. Feminists certainly could have made a difference when a friendly Democratic president began casting about for ways to reform welfare in 1993; and although we could not have changed Republican intentions in the 104th Congress, we surely could have pressured the Democrat we helped elect to the White House to veto the Republican bill.

In the absence of widespread feminist opposition to the welfare reform principles of the Personal Responsibility Act, the legislative record is devoid of a counternarrative that might temper administrative and judicial enforcement of the new law. Moreover, it is devoid of any discursive precedent for women-friendly, equality-enhancing amendments to the new law. Because most feminists did not contest or disturb the Republican welfare paradigm, about all they can do now to fix the new welfare mess is urge that more money be spent on job training and childcare and that broader exceptions for battered women be adopted. These are important goals, but they do not repair the damage wrought by the new welfare law on the lives and rights of poor single mothers.

Why were so many feminists unconcerned that welfare reform not only repealed poor single mothers' entitlement to cash assistance but encroached on their basic civil rights as well? Given the degree of harm inflicted on poor single mothers by the new welfare law, why were there no candlelight vigils like there were against O. J. Simpson? Why were there no marches like there have been to defend *Roe v. Wade?* Why were no boycotts waged like there were against the film *The People vs. Larry Flynt?*

These questions are the fruit of my frustration as a welfare activist. They have renewed my scholarly attention to the relationship between welfare and equality, on the one hand, and between welfare and feminism, on the other. Out of these concerns has emerged a new scholarly project . . . a new book.[6] The book is a broadside against the Personal Responsibility Act, culminating in defense of welfare. It is also a call to middle-class feminists to practice true "sisterhood": by upholding poor mothers' rights as we do our own.

Although the Personal Responsibility Act deserves boundless criticism for its seismic practical consequences—for driving a million more children into poverty, for example—my book is concerned less with the economic than with the political impact of welfare reform. The new welfare law distinguishes poor single mothers as a separate caste, subject to a separate system of law. Poor single mothers are the only people in America forced by law to work outside the home. They are the only people in America whose decisions to bear children are punished by government. They are the only people in America of whom government may demand the details of intimate relationships. And they are the only mothers in America compelled by law to make room for biological fathers in their families.

Based on lessons drawn from eighteen months of struggle against the Personal Responsibility Act, one of my goals in the book is to defend welfare as an affirmative right of poor single mothers, a right backed up by the reproductive, associational, family, and vocational rights assured to all persons under the Constitution. Toward this end, I argue that welfare (by which I mean income support for caregivers) is a condition of women's equality (by which I mean full and independent citizenship).

Without welfare, mothers who work inside the home are deprived of equal citizenship, for they alone are not paid for their labor. Moreover, lacking earnings for their economic and social contributions, women who work full- or part-time as caregivers for their children are ideologically unequal in a political culture that prizes income-producing work as the currency of virtue. Further, unwaged mothers do not have marital freedom: lacking the financial means to exit marriages, they lack the freedom to choose to stay in them. When they do dare to exit or avoid marriage, mothers do not enjoy vocational liberty: unpaid for their work in the home, they are forced either by law or by economic circumstance to choose wages over children.

We should not think of welfare as a subsidy for dependence but as insurance for the rights that comprise independence. Nor should we think of welfare as an income substitute for the wage earned by breadwinners—fathers—in the labor market. Rather, we should reconceive welfare as the income owed to persons who work inside the home caring for, nurturing, and protecting children—mothering.

The idea that welfare should support mothers in their caregiving roles should not be terribly controversial. This was a core premise of mothers' pension programs early in the century and a justification for including Aid to Dependent Children in the New Deal's Social Security Act.[7] The problem is that the caregiving work performed by poor mothers has lost its luster over the past thirty years; who welfare mothers are explains why.

In the popular imagination, welfare participants are reckless breeders who bear children to avoid work. Such vintage stereotypes have bipartisan roots and were popularized beginning in the 1960s by Republican Richard Nixon, southern Democrat Russell Long, and sometime Democrat George Wallace. Even Lyndon Johnson, often credited for expanding welfare as part of his War on Poverty, shared these views: he called for limits on payments to non-marital children and complained that their mothers "sit around and breed instead of going out to work."[8] Into the 1990s, the racial mythology of welfare cast the welfare mother as Black, pinned the need for reform on her character, and at least implicitly defined Black women as other people's workers rather than their own families' mothers.[9] Racially charged images of lazy, promiscuous, and matriarchal women have dominated welfare discourse for quite some time, inflaming demands that mothers who need welfare—although perhaps not their children—must pay for their improvident behavior through work, marriage, or destitution.[10]

If racism has permitted policymakers to negate poor single mothers as mothers, middle-class feminism has provided them an excuse. New attitudes about wage earning by mothers amplified by successful feminist challenges to employment discrimination have turned work outside the home into a rhetorical resource for critics of welfare. Middle-class feminists' emphasis on women's right to work outside the home also has inflected welfare politics among women, diminishing the scale of coalitions for welfare justice—especially by comparison to coalitions for abortion rights or against rape or domestic violence. This created something of a vacuum in the defense of poor mothers' political and economic rights.

Part of the problem, I think, is that white and middle-class feminists—who are the mainstream of the women's movement—view mothers who need welfare as mothers who need feminism. They see welfare mothers as victims—of patriarchy, maybe of racism, possibly of false consciousness. They don't see welfare mothers as feminist agents of their own lives—as women who are entitled to and capable of making independent and honorable choices about what kind of work they will do and how many children they will have and whether they will marry. As a result, when many white, middle-class feminists weighed into the welfare debate, it was to prescribe reforms to assimilate welfare mothers to white feminists' own goals—principally, independence through paid employment.

Most of the policy claims made by Second-Wave feminists have emphasized women's right to participate in men's world and have made work outside the home a defining element for women's full and equal citizenship. Middle-class feminists responded to their particular historical experiences, experiences drawn by an ethos of domesticity which confined middle-class women to the home. From this perspective, the home is the site of oppression for women, while the labor market is potentially liberating. But when middle-class women moved into the labor market, they did not trade in their caregiving obligations. Now doubly taxed by the dual responsibilities of earning and caring, many feminists have demanded labor market policies to address the family needs that fall disproportionately on women—parental leave and childcare, for example.[11] However, they have been less interested in winning social policies to support women where we meet our family responsibilities: in the home. In the absence of widespread feminist attention to the social value of the childraising and home management work mothers do, poor mothers' right to do motherwork has been only faintly defended.

The popular feminist claim that women earn independence, autonomy, and equality through wages historically has divided feminists along class and race lines, as women of color and poor white women have not usually earned equality from sweated labor. To the contrary. Especially for women of color, wage work has been a mark of inequality: expected by the white society for whom they work; necessary because their male kin cannot find jobs or cannot earn family-supporting wages; and exploitative because their earnings keep them poor. Thus, the right to care for their own children—to work inside the home—has been a touch-stone goal of their struggles for equality. The fact that women are positioned divergently in the nexus among caregiving, wage earning, and inequality separated feminists one from another on the welfare issue

and separated employed middle-class feminists from mothers who need welfare.

Out of the middle-class feminist emphasis on winning rights in the workplace has emerged, sotto voce, an expectation that women ought to work outside the home and an assumption that any job outside the home—including caring for other people's children—is more socially productive than caring for one's own. Feminists in Congress betrayed this bias, voting unfazed to require poor single mothers to work outside the home both as a condition of welfare and as a consequence of time limits.

Although feminism is fundamentally about winning women choices, our labor market bias has put much of feminism not on the side of vocational choice—the choice to work inside or outside the home—but on the side of wage earning for all women. Thus, most congressional feminists, along with many feminists across the country, have conflated their right to work outside the home with poor single mothers' obligation to do so. This is an obligation of no small significance for poor single mothers, who are conscripted into wagework under the new welfare law.

Most single mothers work outside the home, and most single mothers who receive welfare want to. The question is whether social policy should dictate that they must. Poor single mothers already shoulder a double burden in parenting: should social policy require them to perform yet another job?

Except for a few young men in my classes who insist that mothering is love, not work, I think most people understand that the caregiving mostly provided by mothers is work. Disagreements arise over whether that work is worth anything if it is performed for one's own family. Or, more accurately, disagreements arise over when that work is worth something and in what kinds of families.

When Republicans and Democrats have wanted to, they have acknowledged mothers' caregiving work in public policy: they've even remunerated it. The very week it negated the motherwork of poor single women by giving final approval to the Personal Responsibility Act, Congress affirmed the mother-work of middle-class homemakers by granting them rights to their own IRAs.[12] Representative Nancy Johnson hailed the measure as forwarding equality for homemakers. Others hailed it for honoring them. Viewed alongside welfare reform, IRAs for homemakers deepened existing differentiations in law between married and unmarried mothers, between white women and women of color, and between rich women and poor. It also created a distinction between poor single mothers' activities in the home and married, middle-class mothers' work there. IRAs, after all, are an untaxed portion of earned income.

Clearly, legislators do understand that what (some) domestic mothers do is not pass the time but work. The challenge, then, is to lead policymakers to give poor mothers' caregiving work the dignity it is due by providing it an income. Payments for mothers' caregiving work ought not to be too difficult to calculate, for much of the work done by caregiving mothers already has a market price if performed for someone else's family. We pay teachers, for example, as well as psychologists, nurses, accountants, chauffeurs, launderers, housecleaners, cooks, waitresses, even personal shoppers.[13]

To some extent we can derive a right to a caregiver's income through constitutional reasoning: a socially provided income guarantee ought to be a condition of reproductive, marital, family, and vocational freedoms—as well as a matter of equal protection. Although the Constitution does not oblige us to provide for one another's economic security, it does permit us to imagine different ways to enforce its meaning legislatively: the Fourteenth Amendment gives Congress the responsibility to enact laws that enforce its provisions, including its clause promising "equal protection of the law." Moreover, the Constitution permits us to defend rights with remedies, including remedial social supports—legal assistance for poor criminal defendants, for example—without which the rights of some citizens would disappear.

Welfare remedies poor single mothers' inequality, specifically the inequality of economic disfranchisement. Mothers' economic disfranchisement comes from our failure to impute economic value to the work that they do. In marriages, mothers who work inside the home surrender their economic personhood to husbands and occupy the legal status of dependent. Such married mothers' lack of their own economic resources—earnings—skew power relations in the family; some mothers may feel tethered to husbands because they could not survive the economic consequences of leaving them. Single mothers, meanwhile, must accept destitution as a condition of caring for their children. Unpaid and disdained, they are expected to forswear childraising for full-time wage earning. Full-time caregiving mothers, then, are disproportionately dependent on men if married and disproportionately poor, if not. These private inequalities have public effects, foreclosing mother-workers' independent citizenship.

We would begin to redress these inequalities by providing caregivers who are parenting alone an income in recognition of their family work. A socially provided income for solo parents who bear the dual responsibilities of providing care for their children and financing it, welfare is a condition of equality in the family, in the labor market, and in the state. As such, welfare should be a right, not an entitlement—a claim backed by law and courts that should be irresistible, or at least impossible for a rogue Congress to deny. Unless we can establish a right to welfare, we cannot cure inequality where it is most gendered—in sexual, reproductive, and family relations.

A right to income support in return for poor single mothers' caregiving work tackles the neglected side of the gender divide, the side that has defined women as the legal and economic dependents of men. But although a caregiver's income would address the gender divide, it need not reproduce that divide. Rights that accommodate mothers' caregiving work need not ascribe mother-work to all women, nor only to women: men can mother, too. Nor need rights that accommodate mothers' caregiving work disparage women's choices and equality claims in the labor market. Such rights should widen options for solo caregivers of either gender by backing up the choice to work outside the home with the means not to. Ending welfare by redefining it in this way will enable equality—in the safety net, between the genders, among women, and under the Constitution.

NOTES

1. "Lady and the tramp" refers to my essay, "The Lady and the Tramp: Gender, Race, and the Origins of the American Welfare State," in *Women, the State, and Welfare*, ed. Linda Gordon (Madison: University of Wisconsin Press, 1990), 92–122.

2. Gwendolyn Mink, *The Wages of Motherhood: Inequality in the Welfare State, 1917–1942* (Ithaca: Cornell University Press, 1995).

3. The Republican initiative (H.R. 4) was first introduced in January 1995. Passed by the House in March and by the Senate in the late summer, the bill died with the 1995 budget impasse. In 1996, the Congress passed and the president signed a new bill, H.R. 3734, or P.L. 104–193. The new law repealed the Aid to Families with Dependent Children program.

4. This was the Castle-Tanner substitute amendment to H.R. 3734. See *Congressional Record*, 18 July 1996, H7907–7974.

5. Felicia Kornbluh, "Feminists and the Welfare Debate: Too Little? Too Late?" *Dollars and Sense*, November/December 1996, 25.

6. Mink, *Welfare's End* (Ithaca: Cornell University Press, 1998). Some material in this article is taken from this book with the permission of the publisher.

7. Mink, *Wages of Motherhood* , chap. 6.

8. President Lyndon Johnson to his budget director, LBJ White House telephone tapes, CNN Morning News, 18 Oct. 1996.

9. Dorothy Roberts, "The Value of Black Mothers' Work," *Connecticut Law Review* 26 (spring 1994): 871–73; Lucy A. Williams, "Race, Rat Bites, and Unfit Mothers: How Media Discourse Informs Welfare Legislation Debate," *Fordham Urban Law Journal* 22 (summer 1995): 1159–96.

10. See, e.g., Charles Murray, *Losing Ground: American Social Policy, 1950–1980* (New York: Basic Books, 1984).

11. See, for example, Barbara Bergman and Heidi Hartmann, "A Welfare Reform Based on Help for Working Parents," *Feminist Economics* 1 (summer 1995): 85–91.

12. The IRAs for homemakers provision was part of the Small Business Job Protection and Minimum Wage Increase Act, H.R. 3448 (104th Congress, 2d session).

13. In 1972, Chase Manhattan Bank economists concluded that the weekly value of a family caregiver's work was at least $257.53, or $13,391.56 a year (1972 dollars). See Ann Crittenden Scott, "The Value of Housework: For Love or Money?" *Ms.*, July 1972, 56–59.

READING *50*   *Melanie Heath*

The Marriage Promotion Movement

We don't know as much as we'd like about how to help at-risk couples create healthy marriages, but that must not stop us from taking action. The need is there, and it's time to close the marriage gap between rich and poor. People who care about the future of this society—about social equality, about fighting poverty, about the welfare of our children—cannot sit idly by as the marriage gap grows wider. . . .

The poor want and deserve good, healthy marriages as much as the wealthy. A truly just society cannot let the powerful social and economic advantages of a good marriage become just another middle-class entitlement.

—*Wade Horn*, Closing the Marriage Gap

"What Is America's Most Serious Social Problem?" read the headline of the February 2006 Fact Sheet from the Institute for American Values. It continues, "America faces many urgent challenges. Crime. Poverty. Education. And many others. Each is important. But many leading scholars now conclude that our nation's single most important problem is the weakening of marriage." The fact sheet delivers a concise synopsis of why the decline of marriage is so serious. First, the weakening of marriage "drives" many other social problems:

Children raised outside of intact marriages are significantly more likely than other children to use drugs . . . to drop out of school . . . to commit crimes . . . to suffer from depression and emotional distress . . . to be neglected or abused . . . to be sexually active early . . . to commit or consider suicide . . . and later in life to get divorced themselves and to bear children outside of marriage.

It explains that the decline in marriage costs taxpayers billions of dollars by requiring an increase in jails, welfare payments, medical costs, remedial education, and juvenile justice systems. Second, marriage is linked to many social goods, including higher levels of health and happiness, as well as lower levels of substance abuse for adults and teenagers. Most significantly, the fact sheet claims marriage is "a wealth-creating institution." People who marry earn, save, and build more wealth in comparison to those who are single or living together.

Scholars, policymakers, and others who subscribe to this view generally identify with the "marriage movement," a diverse coalition of clergy and religious leaders, family practitioners (therapists, counselors, and educators), welfare officials and employees, politicians, think tank personnel, and other community activists. These individuals seek a "renaissance" for heterosexual marriage to turn the tide on the problem of marital decline in U.S. culture and end the upsurge of divorce, cohabitation, and unwed childbearing (Institute for American Values 2004). Officially set in motion in 2000 with the declaration of "The Marriage Movement: A Statement of Principles," its 113 signatories include a number of prominent family scholars and researchers, including David Blankenhorn, William Galston, Maggie Gallagher, Judith Wallerstein, Amitai Etzioni, James Q. Wilson, David Popenoe, Jean Bethke Elshtain, and Barbara Dafoe Whitehead. The marriage movement grew out of the responsible fatherhood movement in the 1990s, and the two share a number of key leaders. Wade Horn, former president of the National Fatherhood Initiative, a nonprofit organization that seeks to increase the number of children growing up with an involved father, has championed marriage promotion efforts in his current position as assistant secretary for Children and Families in U.S. Department of Health and Human Services (HHS).

The strategies of the marriage movement combine grassroots efforts with broader goals to influence public policy and law at the state and national level (Hull 2006). Diane Sollee, a family therapist, founded the Coalition for Marriage, Family, and Couples Education in 1996, a clearinghouse for the movement that sponsors the annual Smart Marriages conference to bring together those interested in building a marriage culture to spread the word that "married love is a possible, reasonable, normal, achievable goal" (Coalition for Marriage, Family, and Couples Education et al. 2000:7). The movement's growth has also been closely tied to federal policies that provide funding for marriage promotion and education. The Personal Responsibility and Work Opportunity Reconciliation Act of 1996, the law that ended over sixty years of federal welfare benefits to poor families, specifically designated marriage promotion in addition to job preparation and work as a sanctioned use of Temporary Assistance to Needy Families (TANF) state block grants to end the "dependence" of needy parents on government benefits. The focus on marriage marks an ideological shift in welfare legislation that is at heart of the controversy of who should marry and why.

In 2002, the Bush Administration launched its Healthy Marriage Initiative within HHS, funding demonstration projects nationwide to offer marriage education classes and disseminate a public message of the value of marriage. Most recently, Bush signed into law the Deficit Reduction Act, which reauthorizes welfare reform and sanctions an appropriation of up to $150 million per year from 2006 to 2010 to promote healthy marriages and responsible fatherhood (Roberts 2006). This is in addition to $100 million within existing programs that have already been diverted into marriage promotion (Olson 2005). A 2004 report from the Center for Law and Social Policy found that every state has undertaken at least one activity or made at least one policy or legal change designed to strengthen marriage and/or two-parent families in the last ten years (Ooms, Bouchet, and Park 2004). The report conveys that governors in 9 states have declared strengthening marriage a public objective, 40 states have government-funded programs to offer marriage-related services, and 36 states have revised their TANF eligibility rules to treat one-parent and two-parent households the same.

A main focus of marriage promotion has been the negative consequences of divorce and nonmarital childbearing on the economic and emotional well-being of children and adults. Census data reveal that children living with married parents have on average a higher family income than children living outside a married family. In 2000, 6 percent of married two-parent families lived in poverty compared to 33 percent of single-mother families (Coontz and Folbre 2002; U.S. Census 2000). Mothers who never marry face conditions of poverty more than any other group, including those who divorce (Alan Guttmacher Institute 1999; Coontz and Folbre 2002; Halpern 1999). Marriage promotion advocates have pointed to the relationship between single motherhood and poverty as an important reason for public policies to promote marriage. James Q. Wilson (2002) in *The Marriage Problem* refers the reader to the emergence of two nations in America, dividing the rich and the poor, a phenomenon first described a century ago by Benjamin Disraeli. Wilson explains how the more uneven distribution of wealth in past years has transformed the principle on which the nation is divided. Today, some children are raised in a "second world—the world without fathers, without safety, without a decent life or reasonable prospects for the future" (p. 2). The two worlds, he suggests, can only be joined by rebuilding a marriage culture.

The project to restore heterosexual marriage points to an important set of sociological questions for thinking about social change. What is driving these efforts to restore the significance of marriage in law and public policy? Ostensibly, marriage promotion advocates justify the necessity to promote marriage to secure the well-being of children and to fight poverty. However, marriage promotion seems a simplistic solution in the face of an increasingly global capitalist economy and seismic transformations in gender relations within and outside marriage that fuel high rates of divorce and nonmarital childbearing. Marriage no longer prevails as the primary setting for childbearing/rearing, and increases in divorce, cohabitation, and female labor force participation, along with the increasing visibility of lesbian and gay families, have precipitated a "deinstitutionalization" of marriage that challenges any dominant conception of "normal" family life (Cherlin 2004; Stacey 1996). In this context, what does it mean to promote marriage, and what is the impact on social change of this cultural project that offers a "marriage cure" to poverty?

With these questions in mind I set out to study the cultural politics of marriage in a state that possesses the most substantial and enduring marriage initiative in the nation. In 1999, the governor of Oklahoma launched a statewide marriage promotion program, the Oklahoma Marriage Initiative (OMI), which was financed with $10 million in undedicated TANF funds. By 2004, the year I spent in Oklahoma, the program had worked through many of its growing pains. It was often in the media limelight for its antipoverty efforts (Boo 2003). I traveled there to study the parameters of promoting heterosexual marriage, not only from the leadership's perspective but at the ground level. I wanted to find out what was actually involved in these politics, both ideologically and its effects on those it served. Who benefited and why?

In broad terms, I sought to understand the spoken and unspoken consequences on social inequality of state policy and local efforts to transform culture through marriage promotion. Sociologists of culture have mapped the ways social groups differentiate themselves through beliefs, practices, and institutions to produce inequality (Lamont and Fournier 1992). One level involves the interactional and symbolic. Language and culture shape material reality through symbolic boundaries to produce stigma and create the "other" (Goffman 1963). Another level is the macrosociological, which locates individuals within institutions and organizations. In this realm, culture serves as an ideology and means of domination (Lamont and Fournier 1992). Marriage promotion advocates point to the construction of symbolic boundaries that create a "marriage gap" between the middle class, who tend to delay marriage and bear children after marrying, and the poor, who bear children outside marriage at a younger age. For them, restoring marriage can bridge this gap. In this paper, I argue that state policy and local efforts to promote marriage, rather than bridging the gap between the more privileged and the poor, instead reproduce a symbolic and material divide motivated by fundamental anxieties over shifting gender relations of the past half century. Marriage promotion advocates reinforce a symbolic boundary of marriage that has focused resources away from poor women and toward the middle class.

The cultural politics of marriage includes two ideological frames—one of antipoverty and one of morality. A frame involves a set of ideas or images that shape the way individuals "locate, perceive, identify, and label" the social world (Goffman 1974:21). While frames enable individuals to make sense of their experiences, they do not transmit meaning in a neutral manner. Rather they contain discursive ambiguities that are "an explicit battleground of ideological wars" (Steinberg 1998:853). For example, the frame "welfare reform" suggests that welfare is something aberrant in need of remedy, setting the ground of a conservative political agenda (Grindstaff 2006). The two frames of the cultural politics of marriage emphasize on the one hand cultural concerns over poverty and inequality, and on the other morality and family values.

The antipoverty frame derives from the belief that heterosexual marriage between two biological parents provides the best outcomes for the well-being of children. It seeks to provide skills to impoverished, unwed parents to help them realize their dreams of marriage, to sustain these unions, and to help keep already married couples from divorcing. Its appeal is predominantly one of social health (McClain 2006; Waite and Gallagher 2000). The moral frame shares the belief that heterosexual marriage provides the best environment for rearing children, but it is more concerned with the moral and cultural values that families inculcate than with the social health of its members. Both agendas share a cultural emphasis on promoting heterosexual marriage as the superior family form, but with different strategies and emphases. In the following, I demonstrate how the moral frame of marriage promotion policy reinforces rather than rectifies the marriage gap. I argue that the underlying motivation behind marriage promotion is anxiety over gender and a push to reinforce conservative gender norms.

DATA AND METHODS

I chose to study marriage promotion in Oklahoma as it has been in the vanguard of efforts across the nation to promote and strengthen heterosexual marriage. Oklahoma is the 7th poorest state in the nation, with one out of every five children living below the poverty line. In 1998, the former Republican governor Frank Keating asked economists to conduct a study on the reasons for Oklahoma's poor economic performance. Two of the social indicators related to Oklahoma's high divorce rate. Thus began the governor's project to lift the state out of poverty by promoting marriage and lowering the divorce rate.

I met with two OMI employees at the Smart Marriages conference in 2003 and presented my idea of doing ethnographic research on the cultural impact of the marriage initiative on individual lives. They were enthusiastic, and when I arrived, I contacted them about attending workshops. Drawing on grounded theory (Glaser and Strauss 1967), I began attending classes listed on OMI's website for the general public, building theory as I went. After a couple months, I began attending more specialized classes, like the ones targeted for TANF recipients, for high school students, for adoptive couples, and for employees of the Chickasaw Nation. After each workshop, I returned home to type up and expand my handwritten field notes. Altogether, I attended 30 workshops for the general population.

As I attended workshops, I formulated interview questions for participants and staff. Over time, I conducted 45 semi-structured, in-depth interviews with OKDHS staff, with high school teachers, and with directors of programs involved in OMI that lasted between one and two hours. These included questions about their involvement with the Oklahoma Marriage Initiative and their perceptions of marriage and of the political project of the marriage initiative. My formal interviews with five OMI employees (who work for Public Strategies) came at the very end of my ethnographic research in November and December. These interviews confirmed much of what I already knew,

since I'd been working closely with OMI staff from the beginning of my fieldwork. I transcribed all the interviews, which with my field notes amounted to over 2,000 pages. I coded all of these using a qualitative software program, Atlas.ti.

I provided pseudonyms for all the participants with the exception of three high-profile leaders of the Oklahoma Marriage Initiative. All of these have been quoted in the media and have written about the marriage initiative in various capacities. I discussed with them the difficulty of protecting their identities given their high-profile position, and each agreed to let me use their real names. All agreed that the information they had provided to me was consistent with statements and interviews they had made in other public venues. My fieldwork and interviews held many surprises. Foremost was the unexpected finding that a small percentage of the classes were actually targeting a low-income population.

THE [PROTESTANT] OKLAHOMA MARRIAGE INITIATIVE

The Oklahoma Marriage Initiative had already received national news coverage when Katherine Boo's award-winning 2003 *New Yorker* story, "The Marriage Cure," was published. Yet, it was her highly ethnographic narrative that propelled Oklahoma's notoriety as a leader of marriage promotion and strengthening efforts. Boo's article chronicles the impact of marriage classes on the lives of two impoverished African American women living in an Oklahoma housing project. She followed them to a state-sponsored, three-day marriage education seminar taught by Pastor George Young, the African American pastor of Holy Temple Baptist Church. The article portrays Oklahoma to be at the forefront of antipoverty thinking that views marriage as a possible means to lift women out of poverty, the idea being "Two parents means two paychecks" (Boo 2003:109). It paints a picture of the OMI's efforts to offer marriage workshops to this population: door-to-door solicitations at a housing project and announcements at neighborhood churches and social service agencies. Boo also identifies obstacles and complications. Despite OMI's recruitment efforts, only five attended the workshop. Moreover, the only tangible outcome for the five was the breakup of the longest-term relationship among them.

Overall, the article leaves a strong message about antipoverty and marriage. Significant structural and economic barriers confront the cultural project to close the marriage gap among America's neediest women, a segment of the population who face daily employment and other forms of discrimination based on gender, race, and class. Boo concluded that the Oklahoma Marriage Initiative had its work cut out for it. When I arrived in Oklahoma, I assumed that a substantial amount of my time would be spent attending marriage classes with participants from impoverished neighborhoods such as the one covered in Boo's article. I learned, however, that marriage promotion in Oklahoma had a very different organization and focus from what the article had led me to expect. While OMI was pushing to get services to a low-income population, an effort that would seem to require substantial resources and time, I found that a large number of the free classes were attended by individuals who could afford to pay.

During the ten months I spent in Oklahoma, I realized that most workshops were largely populated by white, middle-class couples. Many of the OMI leaders and volunteers I interviewed sincerely viewed OMI's efforts through an antipoverty frame: they believed that providing low-income families with relationship skills could help families get or stay out poverty. A DHS employee who oversees the OMI contract told me: "We focus on low-income families. That is a target population because we want to build healthy and stronger families in relationships to reduce teen pregnancies." OMI was in the process of offering marriage education workshops to families of first-offender children, to families in federal prison, to high school students, and even to middle school students.

Given this goal, I was surprised to find that OMI's efforts were not concentrated on the targeted population. A DHS employee in charge of OMI's contract explained:

Well, the initial directive from the standpoint we made in Oklahoma was we wanted all Oklahomans to be able to access this information period, regardless. To some extent, many of us breathed a sigh of relief, because otherwise we are talking about income standards, and we'd have to be looking at things to determine who is eligible and who is not.

Although this employee was not part of the initial planning, she related what may have been a conscious decision to target the middle class:

I think there may have been some early discussions before I came into the picture that, if this was going to

be successful, we've got to get the middle class to buy into it. That's how Social Security in 1935 became successful because of the middle class. They were the bigger users of it right off the bat. To some extent, I see that is how this is too.

The DHS employee asserted that the goal of OMI is community building and confirmed that much of this effort, especially in the early stages, involved the middle class.

Several people who worked in organizations that contracted with OMI expressed concern over who actually benefits from its services. The director of an agency working directly with OMI raised a concern about taking money away from poor women:

I tell you that the amount of money that is spent on [OMI] really, really bothers me. I think it was $2 million this year![1] So, it was money that was taken away from poor women, and it hasn't been targeting poor women. In February on Valentine's weekend, there's a Sweetheart Getaway, and all these people come, and then you have the PREP spin-off for adopted couples and high school kids. Not that those things are not important, but they are being paid for with funds that were set aside for poor families.

Sweetheart Weekends are OMI's "big PR events," as one employee explained. These weekends take place across the state, are more highly publicized by local press, and draw a much larger crowd. Further critiquing the diversion of funds from poor women, she offered Nancy, a single mother who couldn't make ends meet:

This is somebody who wants to make it. She doesn't want to be on welfare, and I think about the Nancys of this world, and I love Mary Myrick [president of the company contracting with OMI], okay, I am very fond of Mary, but she will probably end up a millionaire off the Oklahoma Marriage Initiative, and Nancy doesn't have enough support that she can keep a job long enough to earn medical leave. There's just something wrong with this picture. . . . It's just so much money that so far has been spent on so many middle-class people. That's my rub with it.

During my fieldwork, I discovered that the logic behind the planning and implementation of OMI involved a moral frame that, at times, emphasized a

Christian doctrine of marriage. This frame has a nonreligious argument based on the vital connection of marriage to the social and moral order (see Wilson 2002), as well as a religious line of reasoning that traces marriage to God's divine plan (see Dobson 2004; Stanton 1997). OMI leaders created what they called a religious and secular track for marriage promotion. Significant effort in the initial planning was focused on the religious track, and conservative Christian leaders played a crucial role in developing the blueprint. The executive director of the Oklahoma Family Policy Council, a branch of James Dobson's Focus on the Family, was a representative of "family and faith" on OMI's original steering committee of six people. Three of the six people he named on that committee were from conservative Christian organizations, including the executive director of the Baptist General Convention of Oklahoma.

The weight given to building the initiative through the support of conservative religious leaders and churches meant a larger focus on white, middle-class families. When an OMI employee told me about a new OMI program to target poor, unwed couples having a baby, Transition to Parenthood, I responded enthusiastically that this seemed a positive direction, since it appeared to me that many of the services were going to . . . and she finished my sentence "the middle-class." I discussed this with a high-level DHS employee who worked directly with OMI. She said,

> It really took our team quite a while to really get to the low-income families. What we were trying to do was get it out there. Put some feet under it. A lot of people at first who were getting the services were in the middle-class. The church groups, you know, the building of it was through the churches, and frankly mostly Protestant churches. The Catholics and Jews have already got it figured out about counseling and marriage educations. . . . I kept thinking, well, this is more of a Protestant Oklahoma Marriage Initiative, but no one wanted to deal with that.

Many of the marriage education classes that were announced on the OMI website were held in churches and, even among those that were not, the leaders were often pastors or individuals very active in their church. Like the rest of the country, churches in Oklahoma are segregated by race and class, and most of OMI's efforts to reach out to religious leaders and churches have accessed white, middle-class Protestants.

The moral frame shaped an overall policy to emphasize the superiority of heterosexual marriage. I asked Mary Myrick whether the goal of OMI was to strengthen marriage or more generally to support relationships, whether married or unmarried. She replied,

> The goal of the initiative is to strengthen marriage, and we're really not unwavering about that goal. We believe that marriage is a different kind of relationship with different kinds of outcomes, and so we are not in any way, shape, or form going to do anything that sells that goal short.

Mary Myrick's words attest to the importance marriage promotion advocates place on sustaining a symbolic boundary of marriage. Family sociologist Andrew Cherlin (2003) argues that the marriage promotion language in the welfare reauthorization bill may be as or even more influential in spelling out the federal government's position on family life than on the actual money being spent on marriage programs. OMI's efforts to promulgate the symbolic importance of marriage reflect a moral agenda to reposition marriage as the morally superior family form for raising children, and most of its employees embrace this vision as a way to help people better their relationships as well as their lives.

A paradox was evident between the antipoverty frame that would entail targeting the population in which poverty is the most severe and the moral frame that sought to sustain the symbolic boundary of marriage. The logic of the antipoverty frame suggests that TANF monies would most desirably target exclusively TANF recipients who have historically low rates of marriage. Yet, many of the services have gone to more privileged families. The moral frame of marriage promotion seeks to strengthen marriage throughout the culture to change the moral climate that has influenced the unparalleled transformations in marriage and family on a local and global scale. The rationale implies that strengthening marriage within the culture to lower divorce rates and nonmarital births would mean fewer single mothers at risk of poverty. Rather than seeing these two at odds, marriage promotion figureheads argue that both are needed to better the welfare of children. But an imperative question persists: what are the consequences of redistributing TANF monies meant for needy families to those with more wealth? If the goal is to close the marriage gap between the more privileged classes and the poor, funneling money designated for poor families to strengthen the marriages of middle- and upper-middle-class families would seem to defeat the purpose.

This paradox is, in fact, written into the 1996 Personal Responsibility Act that links poverty to the problems of teenage pregnancy, out-of-wedlock births, single-parent families, and deadbeat dads (Hays 2003). Whereas the first goal offered in welfare reform specifies providing "assistance to *needy families* so that children may be cared for in their own homes" (U.S. Congress 1996, my emphasis), the last goal seeks to "encourage the formation and maintenance of two-parent families," a provision that might apply to the general population. With this wording, the welfare reform law sanctions the possible redistribution of resources from poor families to the middle and upper classes. This might even be a way of punishing poor single mothers for their "dependency" on welfare by signaling the greater importance of nurturing middle-class marriages, though no one in the Bush Administration or OMI would spell it out this way. Plausibly, the most direct way to accomplish the goal of promoting two-parent families involves focusing resources on the population with the lowest rates of marriage. But Oklahoma's statewide initiative has not done this. One high-level OMI employee gave me an estimate that not more than 5 percent of the services were going to TANF recipients. This finding demonstrates the dominance of the moral over the antipoverty frame in seeking to strengthen the symbolic boundary of marriage.

TEACHING THE IMPORTANCE OF GENDER AND HETEROSEXUALITY

During my participation in OMI workshops and the training for workshop leaders, I discovered an underlying anxiety over shifting gender relations that anchored the efforts to reinforce the symbolic boundary of marriage. In the past fifty years, the large number of married women entering the workforce has transformed the male breadwinner and female homemaker model of marriage, calling into question conservative gender norms. Drawing on West and Zimmerman's (1987) conceptualization of "doing gender," Berk (1985) demonstrates the connection between the household division of labor and the production of gender. For many marriage promotion advocates, the anxiety over poor women having babies outside marriage is eclipsed by challenges that shifting gender relations have wrought on marriage. The script for doing gender in marriage can no longer be taken for granted and is challenged by

a growing cultural assumption of gender egalitarianism, especially among couples who choose to cohabitate (Shelton and John 1993). In response to these challenges, the workshops and curriculum taught about the differences between men and women as a central component of married life, with men portrayed as the stronger, more rational spouse.

While the moral frame of marriage promotion contributes to social inequality by distributing economic and social resources to the more privileged, it also impacts gender inequality by instructing on the gendered dynamics in marriage. Many marriage promotion advocates do support gender egalitarianism. Moreover, the curriculum chosen by OMI, the Prevention and Relationship Enhancement Program (PREP), focuses on relationship skills that might promote egalitarian relationships, i.e., providing skills that would give each partner an equal footing for better communication. The creators of PREP argue that the curriculum helps partners "say what they need to say, get to the heart of problems, avoid standoffs and connect with each other instead of pushing each other away" (Oklahoma Marriage Initiative n.d.b.).

However, a more explicitly moral frame is offered in PREP's Christian version. The Oklahoma Marriage Initiative adopted Christian PREP (CPREP), which combines moral principles with the therapeutic language of PREP. As the curriculum unfolds, each new skill is followed by a Bible verse, and there is an emphasis throughout on God's design for marriage. CPREP provides ideas about God's design for a union of the "opposite sexes." The central theme is "Oneness" in marriage, which derives from a key biblical passage in Genesis that conservative Christians regularly cite as theological proof of marriage's original heterosexual union of one man, one woman: "For this reason a man will leave his father and mother and be united to his wife, and they will become one flesh" (Genesis 2:24 NIV). Oneness involves mystery that is hard to define. It is about "blood kinship as well as spiritual, emotional, psychological, and sexual union between husband and wife" (Stanley et al. 1996:21). The curriculum explains that in the "first marriage," things started out well but deteriorated because of sin. The first thing they did after their sin was cover up: "They hid from each other and they hid from God. What had been great intimacy between man and woman, and with God, was shattered" (p. 8). Marriage is not only designed by God but marital problems can be traced to original sin.

In the three-day PREP/CPREP training I attended, I found that the moral vision of the curriculum was largely based on defining and managing gender differences in marriage. Howard Markman and Scott Stanley, the creators of PREP, and Natalie Jenkins, vice president, instructed the training at Southern Nazarene University outside Oklahoma City. Overall, the crowd was largely white, and many present were counselors and educators who were receiving Continuing Education Units for their participation. The three presenters were lively and upbeat, offering the material with lots of banter and jokes. During my three days of observation, I discerned an underlying moral anxiety over changes in gender relations and what this means for an unspoken heterosexuality.

The first day, the presenters offered an overview of the state of marriage in the U.S. and in Oklahoma, providing many of the familiar statistics about divorce's negative effects on children. A good portion of the presentation focused on what men do versus women. Scott Stanley told the audience that he wanted to talk about gender differences and explained how researchers have found a pattern that involves females pursuing an issue and males withdrawing. He attributed this to biological factors that show males to be more physiologically reactive and females to be more aroused. Stanley admitted that these patterns of behavior are complex and that researchers have had difficulty deciding what is physiological and what is not. Yet, the pattern seems to reflect a greater need for men *not* to argue with their mate. The presenters threaded a biological explanation of gender difference throughout the training, offering examples and jokes that drew on biological and cultural differences between men and women. The clear message of the training was about how to manage gender differences that are essential to heterosexual relationships.

The curriculum includes a number of videos of real couples fighting. One shows a young African American couple who argue over the amount of time the guy spends watching sports. During the young man's explanation for why his time spent watching sports is not excessive, Howard Markman stopped the video to point out the way the he lifted his hands up and "gazes towards heaven." Markman called this the "beam me up Scotty response." He says, "This really is an appeal to God. We have a special message to the women in the room. If your partner, husband, son has this response, you might mistakenly think that he is withdrawing, but he is having a spiritual moment." I

laughed along with the audience, but what makes this statement funny is its connection to the cultural assumption that boys will be boys. Howard Markman implied that women can't really understand the nature of men, which leads to the kind of exasperation shown in the video.

Throughout the presentation, Scott, Howard, and Natalie performed gender in a way that is just as important as the message they offered about gender difference and its relationship to heterosexual marriage (Butler 1999; West and Zimmerman 1987). Their bantering constantly focused on gender differences. For example, Howard told a joke about how many men it takes to change the toilet paper with the punchline of there being no scientific answer because it hasn't happened yet. A little later, Howard flipped the remote as if he were surfing television channels, distracting Natalie's presentation. She told him to "sit" and informed us that she forgot to take the batteries out of the men's toy. Next, she conveyed that the reason she needs these guys is because she's not the most technologically advanced. As we watched a video of a couple fighting over the way the husband puts the laundry soap in the washer, Natalie asserted that the woman is "missing the miracle. He's doing the laundry!" Later on, Natalie discussed expectations and how, when she was first married, she wanted flowers because all her friends were getting flowers. She and her husband were having financial difficulties, so she found a 99 cent coupon for a dozen carnations and put four quarters and the coupon on the fridge with a note saying, "Honey, if this coupon expires, so will you."

All of this gender work solidifies for the audience the importance of the differences between men and women. Men play with their toys; women want flowers. To make a marriage work requires recognizing (and performing) these differences. As the presenters performed and instructed the normative expectations of gender, the program took on a "he said, she said" character that seemed to epitomize the nature of marriage. The three instructors taught about how gender motivates much of the friction in marital relationships, but they also just taught about gender. At heart, the lesson taught that gender difference is the glue that brings and keeps two people of the "opposite" sex together. These differences are tied to understandings of bodies to establish a moral vision of marriage. At one point in the PREP program, Scott Stanley held up a picture of his two sons and told the audience that his younger boy asked him, "How do two bodies know when they are married? How does the woman's body know when to have the baby?" He observed that his son asked these questions in the context of marriage, but he will soon learn that this is not the way its goes in this culture.

Providing a moral vision of marriage through gender difference and its connection to bodies and heterosexuality was even more pronounced in the CPREP training. Scott Stanley told the group of about 75 people how gender difference originates back in the Genesis passage that tells a man to leave his mother and father and unite with this wife. Stanley says of this foundational passage,

> I think it is interesting that it says man [will leave his mother and father] and not man and woman. I have come to believe from science (and this is going to sound sexist) why males are called to a higher level of commitment and sacrifice, biologically and scripturally. Women are inherently made more vulnerable than men because they have babies. Males need to protect. Unfortunately, in our culture, we have gutted that, and women bear the most burden by the lack of a sacrificial ethic.

Stanley recognized that many would label his comments that tie gender to women's biological capacity to have babies as sexist. His statement, however, offers an inherent message on gender difference throughout the training—men are naturally less emotional and better equipped for certain responsibilities in marriage— namely the need to protect their families. Relational skills are the strength of women, but in the face of her emotions, the man tends to withdraw. So, communication appears to become part of the sacrificial ethic for men.

Scott Stanley discussed how God recognized that leaving man alone was not good and how Adam's reaction to Eve was "pretty strong." He asked the audience what nakedness without shame means. Several people answered safe, proper, and then jokingly, proper temperature. When Adam and Eve recognized they were naked after eating from the forbidden tree, Stanley pointed out they tried to cover their genitals with their hands. He said,

> God meant something when he specified that there should be male and female and what to do with bodies. I don't just mean sex and physical union, but I mean oneness. They covered up where they are most obviously different. We don't cover up where we are similar. We fear rejection in relationships because of

the possibility of difference. Difference symbolizes physical union, which is now apparent to them.

Stanley sums up with the idea that CPREP speaks to deeper longings. There are some things that make it unsafe to be naked and unafraid, "to drop the fig leaf." The story of Genesis shows that there are many barriers to intimacy and oneness.

CPREP offers a substantive moral vision of marriage based on woman's vulnerability and essential physical and spiritual difference from man. Heterosexuality is an essential component of marriage not only in terms of sex but as an institution created by God to merge difference. Thus, to promote marriage is to promote the oneness of gender difference. The concept of oneness motivates a strong moral vision by means of the Genesis story to demonstrate the meaning of marriage through the sexual and spiritual union of "oppositely" sexed bodies. The emphasis on gender difference is much more subtle in the general PREP training but is likewise tied to heterosexual union. The message of the two curricula is not only one of managing difference but of creating a superior relationship— marriage—that unites gender difference through legitimate heterosexuality.

CONCLUSION

In this paper, I argued that marriage promotion, with its emphasis on child well-being and fighting poverty, upholds a moral frame to reinforce the symbolic boundary of marriage. The main material consequence has been the funneling of scarce resources earmarked for needy families—hence the appellation Temporary Assistance to *Needy Families*—to provide services to the general population, an outcome written into the welfare reform law of 1996, and that made its way into the 2005 Deficit Reduction Act that reauthorizes welfare. Many marriage-related programs financed with government money do focus on low-income families. Yet, of the seven states—Arizona, Louisiana, Michigan, New Mexico, Oklahoma, Utah, and Virginia— that have dedicated significant TANF funds to marriage-related activities, all offer marriage services to the general population and not just TANF recipients (Ooms, Bouchet, and Parke 2004). The Oklahoma Marriage Initiative's decision early on to target religious leaders and churches as a way to publicize the initiative has meant a strong concentration of the initiative being used by white, middle-class couples, which reinforces the idea that these couples are more marriage-oriented. Marriage promotion in this context may actually widen the marriage gap both economically and ideologically.

Underlying the dominance of the moral frame was a fundamental unease about gender and heterosexuality, and how the decline of marriage might impact their production. Gender and sexuality provide norms to regulate bodily practices and behavior (Butler 2004). Heterosexual marriage has been important to normalizing gendered behavior and to producing expectations about men's and women's "nature" that make gender and (hetero)sexuality appear instinctive and effortless. The decline of marriage and women's increased workforce participation over the last forty years has challenged these norms. As women now occupy a significant segment of the workforce, the "time bind" has heavily impacted the quality of family life in the United States, and most working mothers feel especially pinched for time struggling to juggle work and most of the household and childcare responsibilities (Hochschild 2001; Jacobs and Gerson 2005).

A majority of the workshops I attended for the general population emphasized conservative gender norms as the nuts and bolts of a harmonious marriage. Workshop leaders and trainers provided examples and offered gendered performances to focus on unequivocal differences between men and women that catered to cultural ideas of men as rational (strong) and women as emotional (weak). These performances provided simple answers to complex negotiations that many families face as they juggle tight work schedules along with raising children and try to manage their multifaceted households that often bring children from previous marriages or relationships. In sum, the public policy of marriage promotion, with its goal of reinforcing the symbolic boundary of marriage, rather than alleviating social inequality, actually appears to contribute to it, by funneling resources away from poor women and their children and teaching about gender in a manner that may reinforce gender inequality within marriage. At root, anxieties over gender have inspired a public policy agenda, as well as the welfare reform law, that does little to enhance the lives of those it claims to want to help.

NOTE

1. Governor Frank Keating designated $10 million in 1999 for four years. OMI spends between $2 and 3 million a year, and it renewed its contract in 2004.

REFERENCES

Alan Guttmacher Institute. 1999. "Married Mothers Fare the Best Economically, Even If They Were Unwed at the Time They Gave Birth." *Family Planning Perspectives* 31:258–260.

Berk, S. P. 1985. *The Gender Factory: The Apportionment of Work in American Households.* New York: Plenum.

Boo, Katherine 2003. "The Marriage Cure: Is Wedlock Really a Way Out of Poverty?" *The New Yorker,* August 18.

Butler, Judith. 1999. *Gender Trouble.* New York: Routledge.

Cherlin, Andrew. 2003. "Should the Government Promote Marriage?" *Contexts* 2:22–29.

———. 2004. "The Deinstitutionalization of American Marriage." *Journal of Marriage and Family* 66:848–861.

Coalition for Marriage, Family and Couples Education (CMFCE), Institute for American Values (IAV), and Religion, Culture, and Family Project (RCFP). 2000. *The Marriage Movement: A Statement of Principles.* New York: Institute for American Values.

Coontz, Stephanie and Nancy Folbre. 2002. "Marriage, Poverty, and Public Policy." *Discussion Paper from the Council on Contemporary Families.* www.contemporaryfamilies.org.

Dobson, James. 2004. *Marriage Under Fire: Why We Must Win This Battle.* Sisters: Multnomah Publishers.

Glaser, Barny and Anselm Strauss. 1967. *Discovery of Grounded Theory. Strategies for Qualitative Research.* Mill Valley: Sociology Press.

Goffman, Erving. 1963. *Stigma: Notes on the Management of Spoiled Identity.* Englewood Cliffs: Prentice-Hall.

Grindstaff, Laura. 2006. "The Facts Unframed Will Not Set You Free." *Contemporary Sociology* 35:341–346.

Halpern, Ariel. 1999. *Poverty Among Children Born Outside of Marriage: Preliminary Findings from the National Survey of America's Families.* Washington, DC: The Urban Institute.

Horn, Wade F. 2003. "Closing the Marriage Gap." *Crisis: Politics, Culture and the Church* 21:33–37.

Hays, Sharon. 2003. *Flat Broke with Children: Women in the Age of Welfare Reform.* Oxford: Oxford University Press.

Hull, Kathleen E. 2006. *Same-Sex Marriage: The Cultural Politics of Love and Law.* Cambridge: Cambridge University Press.

Institute for American Values. 2004. *What Next for the Marriage Movement?* New York: Institute for American Values.

Lamont, Michele and Michael Fournier. 1992. "Introduction." Pp. 1–20 in *Cultivating Differences: Symbolic Boundaries and the Making of Inequality,* edited by M. Lamont and M. Fournier. Chicago: University of Chicago Press.

McClain, Linda C. 2006. *The Place of Families: Fostering Capacity, Equality, and Responsibility.* Cambridge: Harvard University Press.

Olson, Sarah. 2005. "Marriage Promotion, Reproductive Injustice, and the War Against Poor Women of Color." *Dollars & Sense,* January/February.

Ooms, Theodora, Stacey Bouchet, and Mary Parke. 2004. *Beyond Marriage Licenses: Efforts in States to Strengthen Marriages and Two-Parent Families.* Washington, DC: Center for Law and Social Policy.

Roberts, Paula. 2006. "Update on the Marriage and Fatherhood Provisions of the 2006 Federal Budget and the 2007 Budget Proposal." *Center for Law and Social Policy,* February 10. http://www.clasp.org/publications/marriage_fatherhood_budget2006.pdf.

Shelton, B. A. and D. John. 1993. "Does Marital Status Make a Difference? Housework Among Married and Cohabiting Men and Women." *Journal of Family Issues* 14:401–420.

Stacey, Judith. 1996. *In the Name of the Family: Rethinking Family Values in the Postmodern Age.* Boston: Beacon Press.

Stanton, Glenn T. 1997. *Why Marriage Matters: Reasons to Believe in Marriage in Postmodern Society.* Navpress Publishing Group.

Steinberg, Marc W. 1998. "Tilting the Frame: Considerations on Collective Action Framing from a Discursive Turn." *Theory and Society* 27:845–872.

U.S. Bureau of the Census. 2000. "Historical Poverty Statistics—Table 4. Poverty Status of Families, by Type of Family, Presence of Related Children, Race, and Hispanic Origin: 1959–2000." Available at http://www.census.gov.

U.S. Congress. 1996. "Personal Responsibility and Work Opportunity Reconciliation Act of 1996." Public Law 104–93, H.R. 3734.

Waite, Linda J. and Maggie Gallagher. 2000. *The Case for Marriage: Why Married People Are Happier, Healthier, and Better Off Financially.* New York: Broadway Books.

West, Candace and Don Zimmerman. 1987. "Doing Gender." *Gender & Society* 1:125–151.

Wilson, James Q. 2002. *The Marriage Problem: How Our Culture Has Weakened Families.* New York: Harper Paperbacks.

SECTION *11*

Social Protest
and the Feminist Movement

Throughout *Feminist Frontiers,* we have examined the breadth and magnitude of the social forces working to differentiate women and men and to disadvantage women. Socialization, the organization of social institutions, and social and economic policies all come together to hinder women's full political participation, self-determination, economic security, and even health and safety.

Despite the ubiquitous forms of inequality embedded in our social institutions, women resist. As we have seen, women often struggle against oppression in individual ways. Women also come together to take collective action to pursue social change. This section explores contemporary forms of social protest, noting how feminist movements attract different constituencies, develop different ideas, articulate different goals, and utilize different tactics and strategies across time and place.

In the first article, Verta Taylor, Nancy Whittier, and Cynthia Fabrizio Pelak present an overview of the multiple ideologies and forms of the feminist movement in the United States from its emergence in the 1960s to the present. "The Women's Movement: Persistence Through Transformation" considers the larger social and economic conditions responsible for the rise of women's movements in the Western world and describes the transnational context of feminism. Taylor, Whittier, and Pelak focus on the way feminist movements have changed over time as a result of activists' own ideas and goals and

the larger social and political context, including antifeminist countermovements that have arisen to oppose the aims of the women's movement. Based on their analysis, what do you think might be the future of feminism?

Feminism, as this article demonstrates, has a long and vibrant history and strong prospects for the future. A great deal of attention has been devoted to the generational divisions in feminism. Some see a "third wave" of feminism; others see the death of feminism in the "postfeminist" generation. Pamela Aronson, in "Feminists or 'Postfeminists'? Young Women's Attitudes Toward Feminism and Gender Relations," explores attitudes toward feminism through interviews with a diverse sample of young women. She shows that the majority of her sample is aware that the women's movement increased opportunity and that inequality remains, but that young women embrace a range of positions on the question of whether they identify as feminists. What difference do class, race, and life experience make in shaping young women's perspectives? Where would you fit on a spectrum of attitudes toward feminism?

Grace Chang, in "From the Third World to the 'Third World Within': Asian Women Workers Fighting Globalization," like Cynthia Enloe in the previous section, attends to the ways that women workers are fighting the forces of globalization. In the context of the globalization of poverty and its consequences, including the migration of millions of women from the Third World to the First, Chang focuses on the activism of Filipina migrant workers in the United States and Canada. Chang links the impact on women of Structural Adjustment Programs forced on countries of the global South—from the slashing of social services to economic changes that leave no option for survival other than migration—to welfare reform in the United States. Her stories of Filipina workers echo those of the Latin American nannies recounted by Pierrette Hondagneu-Sotelo in Section 5. What strategies are women employing to resist the consequences of globalization? How might the feminist movement support the struggles of immigrant women workers?

In "Punks, Bulldaggers, and Welfare Queens: The Radical Potential of Queer Politics?" Cathy Cohen calls for a new form of progressive and transformative coalition building. She embraces queer activists' in-your-face strategies intended to challenge the invisibility of gay, lesbian, bisexual, and transgendered people and to embrace sexual difference. But she criticizes the narrowness of queer politics for its overemphasis on deconstructing the historically and culturally recognized categories of homosexual and heterosexual. Such a strategy, she argues, exaggerates the similarities among individuals categorized under the label of "heterosexual" and ignores the way other systems of oppression regulate the lives of women and men of all races, classes, and sexualities. A truly queer politics, she suggests, would bring together those, like punks, bulldaggers, and welfare queens, who live outside not heterosexuality, but heteronormativity. What might the kinds of coalitions Cohen envisages look like?

Women's movements in the twenty-first century are becoming more diverse than ever and hold great promise for transforming for the better the lives of both women and men. As you finish reading *Feminist Frontiers*, think about what changes you would like to see in your world. How do you propose to work for these changes?

Verta Taylor
Nancy Whittier
Cynthia Fabrizio Pelak

The Women's Movement: Persistence Through Transformation

INTRODUCTION

Popular authors and scholars alike described the 1980s and 1990s as a "postfeminist" era of political apathy during which former feminists traded their political ideals for career mobility and cell phones and younger women single-mindedly pursued career goals and viewed feminism as an anachronism. Yet this was not the first time that commentators proclaimed the death of feminism. In the 1920s, after women won the right to vote, images of young women abandoning the struggle for rights in favor of jobs and good times filled the media. Then as now, feminism changed form, but neither the movement nor the injustices that produced it have vanished. Of all the manifestations of social activism in the 1960s, feminism is one of the few that persist. We explore here continuity and change in the American women's movement from the 1960s to the present. First we consider the structural preconditions of women's movements in the Western world and the international context for activism. Then we focus on the changing ideologies, structures, political contexts, and strategies of the women's movement in the United States. We conclude our discussion by considering historically specific antifeminist countermovements that have emerged in response to challenges of the women's movement.

STRUCTURAL PRECONDITIONS OF WESTERN FEMINIST MOVEMENTS

From a social movement perspective, women have always had sufficient grievances to create the context for feminist activity. Indeed, instances of collective action on the part of women abound in history, especially if one includes female reform societies, women's church groups, alternative religious societies, and women's clubs. However, collective activity on the part of women directed specifically toward improving their own status has flourished primarily in periods of generalized social upheaval, when sensitivity to moral injustice, discrimination, and social inequality has been widespread in the society as a whole (Chafe 1977; Staggenborg 1998a). The first wave of feminism in the United States grew out of the abolitionist struggle of the 1830s and peaked during an era of social reform in the 1890s, and the contemporary movement emerged out of the general social discontent of the 1960s. Although the women's movement did not die between these periods of heightened activism, it declined sharply in the 1930s, 1940s, and 1950s after the passage of the Nineteenth Amendment to the Constitution guaranteeing women the right to vote as a response to the changing social, political, and economic context (Rupp and Taylor 1987). During this period, women who had played important roles in obtaining women's suffrage managed to keep the flames of feminism alive by launching a campaign to pass an Equal Rights Amendment (ERA) to the Constitution.

Despite national differences in feminist movements, scholars identify certain basic structural conditions that have contributed to the emergence of feminist protest in most parts of the Western world (Oppenheimer 1973; Huber and Spitze 1983; Chafetz and Dworkin 1986). Broad societal changes in the patterns of women's participation in the paid labor force, increases in women's formal educational attainment, and shifts in women's fertility rates and reproductive roles disrupt traditional social arrangements and set the stage for women's movements. As industrialization and urbanization bring greater education for women, expanding public roles create role and status conflicts for middle-class women, who then develop the discontent and gender consciousness necessary for political action (Chafetz and Dworkin 1986). Specifically, when women, especially married middle-class women, enter the paid labor force, their gender consciousness increases because they are more likely to use men as a reference group when assessing their access to societal rewards. Similarly, women often experience strains and discrepancies in their lives as their gender consciousness is raised through formal education (Klein 1984).

Other important structural factors that serve as preconditions for feminist mobilization include changes in family relationships, marriage, fertility, and sexual mores (Ferree and Hess 1994). Declines in women's childbearing and increases in their age at first marriage can improve women's educational attainment and participation in the paid labor force—which, in turn, raise their gender consciousness (Klein 1984). Moreover, changes in the traditional relationships between women and men in marriage and in sexual mores, such as the shift from authoritarian marriages to romantic or companionate marriages at the turn of the last century in the United States and the "sexual revolution" of the 1960s, can politicize gender relations and create the motivations for feminist mobilization.

Certainly, the specific configuration of structural preconditions underlying the genesis of feminist collective mobilizations varies with historical and geographic context. Not only the political context but also the demographic, economic, and cultural processes that have given rise to feminist movements in the United States are different from those in Third World countries. Such political and cultural variations are reflected in national and regional variations in the way women define their collective interests, in the distinct ideologies, organizational forms, and strategies adopted by feminist movements in different times and places, and ultimately in the possibilities for feminist mobilization. Nonetheless, scholars recognize some important commonalties among women's movements around the world.

FEMINIST MOVEMENTS IN AN INTERNATIONAL CONTEXT

We focus here on the women's movement in the United States. It is nonetheless important to acknowledge the multiple forms of feminist resistance around the world

and to underscore the importance of the historical and geographic specificity of feminist activism. Throughout modern history, women in all regions of the world have organized collectively against the injustice and oppression in their lives and communities (Basu 1995). Such mobilizations in diverse political, cultural, and historical contexts have varied widely in their organizations, strategies, ideologies, and structures. Gender oppression for some Third World feminists cannot be divorced from issues and histories of colonization, immigration, racism, or imperialism, and thus feminist activism in some Third World contexts may be organized around a constellation of oppressions rather than specifically around gender oppression (Jayawardena 1986; Mohanty, Russo, and Torres 1991).

In some instances, ideological, organizational, and strategic differences in women's movements lie in fundamental differences in the political culture of a region (Ray 1999). In Calcutta, India, for example, which is dominated by the Communist Party and a strong and traditional left culture, the women's movement functions more as a political party and uses the party structure to address issues such as employment, poverty, and literacy that do not directly threaten the gender status quo. The women's movement in Bombay, on the other hand, which exists in a more open, contested political field and culture, is more explicitly feminist and uses more autonomous forms of organizing to spotlight issues that are more threatening to men, such as violence against women, religious fundamentalism, and women's restricted roles in the family. Although national and regional differences exist, there are important commonalties that link women's movements over time and place (Chafetz and Dworkin 1986; Katzenstein and Mueller 1987; Giele 1995; Miles 1996).

Women's movements, particularly those in industrialized countries, generally have emerged in two waves of heightened activism. In their cross-cultural, historical analysis of forty-eight countries, Chafetz and Dworkin (1986) found that the mass-scale, independent women's movements of the first wave, such as those in European societies and the United States, occurred in the closing decades of the nineteenth century and the first decades of the twentieth century, while the second-wave women's movements have emerged since the 1960s. Major goals of the first wave of activism included women's suffrage, educational opportunities for women, basic legal reforms, inheritance and property rights, and employment opportunities for women. Women's demands during this first wave often were framed around middle-class women's roles as wives and mothers and reinforced gender difference by valorizing women's special virtues and moral superiority over men. Smaller-scale movements during the first wave were more likely to challenge basic role differentiation between women and men and to resist doctrines and images of femininity in the culture.

To the extent that the large-scale changes brought on by urbanization and industrialization in Western countries created dramatic changes in the workplace, the family, and the lives of women and men, it is not surprising there was considerable ideological debate and diversity among first-wave feminists. In the United States, for example, some factions of the nineteenth-century women's movement were grounded in essentialist views of sex differences and were more interested in nonfeminist social reforms, for which the vote was only a prerequisite (Buechler 1990; Giele 1995). Other branches of the nineteenth-century women's movement rejected essentialist notions of gender and, by pursuing more radical changes such as sexual freedom and the expansion of women's roles in the workplace and politics, sought to transform the gender order in more fundamental ways (Cott 1987).

Women's movements of the second wave in Western countries, blossoming since the 1960s, have mobilized around an even broader range of issues, such as reproductive rights, sexual and economic exploitation, and violence against women (Chafetz and Dworkin 1986; Ferree and Hess 1994). Modern feminist movements often have developed around women's commonalities, but differences of race, class, ethnicity, and nationality are also expressed in the collective identities deployed by feminists (Moraga and Anzaldúa 1981; Mohanty, Russo, and Torres 1991). African-American women have organized around interlocking structures of oppression that affect women differently depending on their ethnicity, class, or sexual identities (Collins 1990). For example, African-American and Latina women from low-income urban neighborhoods have struggled for quality education, affordable and safe housing, and expanded child care services for their families and communities (Naples 1992).

Since the 1970s, there has been a phenomenal growth in regional, interregional, and international networking among feminist groups (Miles 1996), although the origins of international women's organizations date back to the closing decades of the nineteenth century (Rupp 1997). The United Nations' International Women's Year (1975) and Decade for Women (1975–1985) helped foster global feminist dialogues and stimulated independent, locally based feminist activities in all parts of the world. Since the beginning of the UN Decade for Women, there have been four official UN world conferences of government representatives devoted to women's issues, with four unofficial forums of women's groups running alongside each of these conferences. Since the first forum in Mexico City in 1975, participation by women in the unofficial forums has increased sharply, challenging the notion that feminism has died in recent years.

Although these conferences and forums have been sites of considerable debate and conflict over the meaning of "women's issues" and the definition of feminism, the events have sparked multiple forms and foci of feminist resistance and a global awareness of women's oppression that reaches beyond women's groups. Feminists are forging global relations around a diverse set of issues including "health, housing, education, law reform, population, human rights, reproductive and genetic engineering, female sexual slavery and trafficking in women, violence against women, spirituality, peace and militarism, external debt, fundamentalism, environment, development, media, alternative technology, film, art and literature, publishing, and women's studies" (Miles 1996:142). The trajectory of the US women's movement can be fully understood only in this global context.

THE CONTEMPORARY FEMINIST MOVEMENT: CONTINUITY AND CHANGE

Most scholarly analyses of the women's movement of the late 1960s—what scholars call the "second-wave feminist movement"—divide it into two wings, with origins in the grievances and preexisting organizations of two groups of women: older professional women, who formed bureaucratic organizations with a liberal ideology and adopted legal reform strategies, and younger women from the civil rights and New Left movements, who formed small collective organizations with radical ideology and employed "personal as political" strategies such as consciousness-raising groups (Freeman 1975; Cassell 1977; Ferree and Hess 1994; Buechler 1990). During a period of resurgence dating to the founding of the National Organization for Women (NOW) in 1966, the movement established itself, forming organizations and ideologies and moving into the public eye (Buechler 1990; Ryan 1992). By 1971, major segments of feminism had crystallized: liberal feminism, embodied in the formation of groups such as NOW, the Women's Equity Action League (WEAL) in 1967, and the National Women's Political Caucus (NWPC) in 1971; radical feminism and socialist feminism, emerging from consciousness-raising groups, theory groups, and small action groups such as Redstockings and the Feminists in 1969; and lesbian feminism, organized in such groups as Radicalesbians in 1970 and the Furies (initially called "Those Women") in 1971 (Echols 1989).

The year 1972 was pivotal both for the movement's success and for its opposition. The Equal Rights Amendment (ERA) passed the Congress, and Phyllis Schlafly launched her first antifeminist attacks. This can be considered the movement's heyday because the feminist revolution seemed to be on the move. The campaign to ratify the ERA in the states brought mass mobilization, fostering female solidarity and enlisting women into feminism; women's studies programs proliferated on college campuses; the number and variety of feminist organizations increased phenomenally; and the movement entered the political arena and encountered active opposition (Matthews and DeHart 1990; Ryan 1992). Not only did feminism flourish in the ERA ratification campaign but it spread into the political mainstream, while radical and lesbian feminist organizing heightened outside it.

Following the ERA's defeat in 1982, the women's movement entered a period of the doldrums, in which it developed new structural forms to survive a declining membership and an increasingly nonreceptive environment. The 1980s saw a turning away from the values of equality, human rights, and social justice and even a deliberate backlash against the feminist momentum of the 1970s. Rights won by feminists in the 1960s and 1970s—from affirmative action to legal abortion—were under siege throughout the 1980s and 1990s. Yet the so-called postfeminist era of the 1980s and 1990s no more marks the death of the women's movement than did the earlier premature announcements of feminism's demise. In fact, although the women's movement of the turn of the twenty-first century takes a different form than it did twenty years earlier, it remains vital and influential.

Feminist Ideology

While ideas do not necessarily cause social movements, ideology is a central component in the life of any social movement (Morris and Mueller 1992). The modern feminist movement, like most social movements, is not ideologically monolithic. Feminist ideology encompasses numerous ideological strands that differ in the scope of change sought, the extent to which gender inequality is linked to other systems of domination—especially class, race, ethnicity, and sexuality—and the significance attributed to gender differences. We focus here on the evolution of the dominant ideologies that have motivated participants in the two major branches of the feminist movement from its inception, liberal feminism and radical feminism.

The first wave of the women's movement in the nineteenth century was, by and large, a liberal feminist reform movement. It sought equality within the existing social structure and, indeed, in many ways functioned like other reform movements to reaffirm existing values within the society (Ferree and Hess 1994). Nineteenth-century feminists believed that if they obtained the right to an education, the right to own property, the right to vote, employment rights—in other words, equal civil rights under the law—they would attain equality with men. Scholars have labeled this thinking "individualist" or "equity" feminism, linking the goal of equal rights to gender assumptions about women's basic sameness with men (Offen 1988; Black 1989).

The basic ideas identified with contemporary liberal or "mainstream" feminism have changed little since their formulation in the nineteenth century, when they seemed progressive, even radical (Eisenstein 1981). Contemporary liberal feminist ideology holds that women lack power simply because we are not, as women, allowed equal opportunity to compete and succeed in the male-dominated economic and political arenas but, instead, are relegated to the subordinate world of home, domestic labor, motherhood, and family. The major strategy for change is to gain legal and economic equalities and to obtain access to elite positions in the workplace and in politics. Thus, liberal feminists tend to place as much emphasis on changing individual women as they do on changing society. For instance, teaching women managerial skills or instructing rape victims in "survival" strategies strikes a blow at social definitions that channel women into traditionally feminine occupations or passive behaviors that make them easy targets of aggression from men.

Liberal feminists ironically provided ideological support through the 1970s and 1980s for the massive transformation in work and family life that was occurring as the United States underwent the transition to a postindustrial order (Mitchell 1986; Stacey 1987). Some writers even contend that by urging women to enter the workplace and adopt a male orientation, the equal opportunity approach to feminism unwittingly contributed to a host of problems that further disadvantaged women (especially working-class women and women of color), including the rise in divorce rates, the "feminization" of working-class occupations, and the devaluation of motherhood and traditionally female characteristics (Gordon 1991).

Radical feminist ideology dates to Simone de Beauvoir's early 1950s theory of "sex class," which was developed further in the late 1960s among small groups of radical women who fought the subordination of women's liberation within the New Left (Beauvoir 1952; Firestone 1970; Millett 1971; Atkinson 1974; Rubin 1975; Rich 1976, 1980; Griffin 1978; Daly 1978; Eisenstein 1981; Hartmann 1981; Frye 1983; Hartsock 1983; MacKinnon 1983). The radical approach recognizes women's identity and subordination as a "sex class," emphasizes women's fundamental difference from men, views gender as the primary contradiction and foundation for the unequal distribution of a society's rewards and privileges, and recasts relations between women and men in political terms (Echols 1989). Defining women as a "sex class" means no longer treating patriarchy in individual terms but acknowledging the social and structural nature of women's subordination. Radical feminists hold that in all societies, institutions and social patterns are structured to maintain and perpetuate gender inequality and female disadvantage permeates virtually all aspects of sociocultural and personal life. Further, through the gender division of labor, social institutions are linked so that male superiority depends upon female subordination (Hartmann 1981). In the United States, as in most industrialized societies, power, prestige, and wealth accrue to those who control the distribution of resources outside the home, in the economic and political spheres. The sexual division of labor that assigns child care and domestic responsibilities to women not only ensures gender inequality in the family system but perpetuates male advantage in political and economic institutions as well.

To unravel the complex structure on which gender inequality rests requires, from a radical feminist perspective, a fundamental transformation of all institutions in society. To meet this challenge, radical feminists formulated influential critiques of the family, marriage,

love, motherhood, heterosexuality, sexual violence, capitalism, reproductive policies, the media, science, language and culture, the beauty industry, sports, politics, the law, technology, and more. Radical feminism's ultimate vision is revolutionary in scope: a fundamentally new social order that eliminates the sex-class system and replaces it with new ways—based on women's difference—of defining and structuring experience. Central to the development of radical feminist ideology was the strategy of forming small groups for the purpose of "consciousness-raising." Pioneered initially among New Left women, consciousness-raising can be understood as a kind of conversion in which women come to view experiences previously thought of as personal and individual, such as sexual exploitation or employment discrimination, as social problems that are the result of gender inequality.

By the late 1970s, the distinction between liberal and radical feminism was becoming less clear (Carden 1978; Whittier 1995). Ideological shifts took place at both the individual and organizational levels. Participation in liberal feminist reform and service organizations working on such issues as rape, battering, abortion, legal and employment discrimination, and women's health problems raised women's consciousness, increased their feminist activism, and contributed to their radicalization as they came to see connections between these issues and the larger system of gender inequality (Schlesinger and Bart 1983; Whittier 1995). Women were also radicalized by working through their own personal experiences of sexual harassment, divorce, rape, abortion, and incest (Huber 1973; Klein 1984).

Radicalization has occurred at the group level as well. By the end of the 1970s, liberal feminist organizations such as NOW, the Women's Legal Defense Fund, and the National Abortion Rights Action League (NARAL), which had been pursuing equality within the law, began to adopt strategies and goals consistent with a more radical stance. NOW included in its 1979 objectives not only such legal strategies as the ERA and reproductive choice, but broader issues such as the threat of nuclear energy to the survival of the species, lesbian and gay rights, homemakers' rights, the exploitation of women in the home, and sex segregation in the workplace (Eisenstein 1981). Even the ERA, which sought equality for women within the existing legal and economic structure, was based on the fact that women are discriminated against as a "sex class" (Mansbridge 1986).

Beginning in the mid-1980s, with the defeat of the unifying issue of the ERA and the growing diversification of the movement, feminist ideology deemphasized the question of women's similarity to or difference from men in favor of "deconstructing" the term *woman*. Women of color, Jewish women, lesbians, and working-class women challenged radical feminists' idea of a "sex class" that implied a distinctive and essential female condition. Since women are distributed throughout all social classes, racial and ethnic groupings, sexual communities, cultures, and religions, disadvantage for women varies and is multidimensional (Spelman 1988). The recognition that the circumstances of women's oppression differ has given way to a new feminist paradigm that views race, class, gender, ethnicity, and sexuality as interlocking systems of oppression, forming what Patricia Hill Collins (1990) refers to as a "matrix of domination."

Some scholars have charged that focusing on women's differences from one another has resulted in a retreat to "identity politics" and the demise of the women's movement. Alice Echols (1989) links disputes over difference and a focus on identity to a concentration on building an alternative women's culture rather than confronting and changing social institutions. In a similar vein, Barbara Ryan (1989) argues that internal debates over the correctness of competing feminist theories and the political implications of personal choices—what she terms "ideological purity"—tore the women's movement apart. But other scholars see the sometimes vehement arguments over women's differences from one another as a sign of life (Taylor and Rupp 1993). Feminists organizing around diverse identities sometimes seek out new arenas of challenge that differ from traditional definitions of political activism and thus extend the reach of feminism. Self-help movements focused on the self and the body, for example—drug and alcohol abuse, incest, postpartum depression, battering, breast cancer—offer a complex challenge to traditional notions of femininity, motherhood, and sexuality and carry the potential to mobilize new constituencies (Taylor and Van Willigen 1996; Gagné 1998).

In any case, ideas alone are an incomplete explanation of either the direction or the consequences of a social movement (Marx and Wood 1975; McCarthy and Zald 1977). Much depends on a movement's structures and strategies, as well as on the larger political context.

Feminist Organizational Structures

Social movements do not generally have a single central organization or unified direction. Rather, the structure of any general, broad-based social movement is more diffuse—composed of a number of relatively independent organizations that differ in ideology, structure, goals, and tactics. A social movement is characterized by decentralized leadership; it is loosely connected by multiple and overlapping memberships and by friendship networks that work toward common goals (Gerlach and Hine 1970). The organizational structure of the modern feminist movement has conformed to this model from its beginnings (Freeman 1975; Cassell 1977; Ferree and Martin 1995). While the movement as a whole is characterized by a decentralized structure, the various organizations that comprise it vary widely in structure. The diversity of feminist organizational forms reflects both ideological differences and the movement's diverse membership base (Freeman 1979).

There have been two main types of organizational structure in the modern feminist movement since its resurgence, reflecting the two sources of feminist organizing in the late 1960s: bureaucratically structured movement organizations with hierarchical leadership and democratic decision-making procedures, such as the National Organization for Women; and smaller, collectively structured groups that formed a more diffuse social movement community held together by a feminist political culture. Collectively organized groups, at least in theory, strove to exemplify a better way of structuring society by constructing a distinctive women's culture that valorized egalitarianism, the expression of emotion, and the sharing of personal experience. It is important to recognize, however, that while the two strands of the women's movement emerged separately, they have not remained distinct and opposed to each other. Most women's movement organizations are mixed in form from the outset. The two structures have increasingly converged as bureaucratic organizations adopted some of the innovations of collectivism and feminist collectives became more formally structured (Staggenborg 1988, 1989; Martin 1990; Ryan 1992; Ferree and Martin 1995; Whittier 1995). In addition, many individual activists are involved in a variety of organizations with differing structures.

The bureaucratically structured and professionalized movement organizations initially adopted by liberal groups such as NOW were well suited to work within the similarly structured political arena and to members' previous experience in professional organizations. The structures that radical feminist groups initially adopted, on the other hand, built on their prior involvement in the New Left (Evans 1979). Collectivist organizations grew from radical feminists' attempts to structure relations among members, processes of decision making, and group leadership in a way that reflected or prefigured the values and goals of the movement (Rothschild-Whitt 1979; Breines 1982). Feminist collectivist organizations made decisions by consensus, rotated leadership and other tasks among members, and shared skills to avoid hierarchy and specialization. Such groups often failed to meet their ideals and did, in fact, spawn unacknowledged hierarchies (Freeman 1972/3). Nevertheless, the conscious effort to build a feminist collective structure has had a lasting impact on the women's movement and has led to the growth of a social movement community (Buechler 1990). That is, the movement consists of not only formal organizations but also more informally organized communities, made up of networks of people who share the movement's political goals and outlook and work toward common aims. The collectivist branch of the women's movement initially sparked the growth of a feminist social movement community in which alternative structures guided by a distinctively feminist women's culture flourished—including bookstores, theater groups, music collectives, poetry groups, art collectives, publishing and recording companies, spirituality groups, vacation resorts, self-help groups, and a variety of feminist-run businesses. This "women's culture," though it includes feminists of diverse political persuasions, has been largely maintained by lesbian feminists. It nurtures a feminist collective identity that is important to the survival of the women's movement as a whole (Taylor and Whittier 1992; Taylor and Rupp 1993).

Both bureaucratic organizations working within mainstream politics and the alternative feminist culture have expanded and converged since the movement's emergence in the 1960s. Organizations such as NOW and NARAL incorporated some of the innovations of collectivism, including consciousness-raising groups, modified consensus decision making, and the use of direct-action tactics and civil disobedience. A host of structural variations emerged, including formally structured groups that use consensus decision making, organizations with deliberately democratic

structures, and groups that officially operate by majority-rule democracy but in practice make most decisions by consensus (Staggenborg 1988, 1989; Martin 1990; Ryan 1992; Taylor 1996). At the same time, feminist collectives shifted their focus from consciousness-raising and radical feminist critique to the development of feminist self-help and service organizations such as rape crisis centers, shelters for battered women, job training programs for displaced homemakers, and lesbian peer counseling groups. Moreover, many feminist collectives revised their structure to depend less on consensus decision making and to permit specialization of skills. The widespread acceptance of the feminist analysis of rape as an act of violence and power rather than a strictly sexual act further attested to the impact of the feminist antirape movement. Feminist antirape groups received financial support from government agencies and private foundations to provide rape-prevention and treatment services in public schools and universities (Matthews 1994). The distinction between "working outside the system" and "working within the system," so important in the late 1960s, no longer had the same significance.

In conjunction with the ideological shift from a universal to a differentiated category of "woman," the structures of the women's movement diversified as well. Although individual women of color and working-class women had participated in the founding of NOW and in the early protests against sexism in the civil rights movement, the women's movement attracted primarily white middle-class women. Not that women of color and working-class or poor women experienced no oppression as women or opposed feminist goals. A 1989 New York Times/CBS News poll revealed that, while only 64 percent of white women saw a need for a women's movement, 85 percent of African-American women and 76 percent of Hispanic women thought the women's movement was needed (Sapiro 1991). Yet the feminist movement remained predominantly white both because it continued to define its goals based on the concerns of white middle-class women and because many Black women and other women of color placed a priority on working in their own racial communities to advance their collective interests, despite the recognition of sexism within such organizations (Barnett 1993; Robnett 1996).

Independent organizing by women of color did grow during the 1970s, and when African-American activists in the women's movement formed the National

Black Feminist Organization in 1973 it grew to a membership of 1,000 within its first year (Deckard 1983). In the 1980s and 1990s, independent feminist organizations and networks of women of color such as the National Black Women's Health Project and the National Coalition of 100 Black Women emerged. Women of color also formed active caucuses within predominantly white feminist organizations, such as the National Women's Studies Association, to work against racism within the women's movement (Leidner 1993). Likewise, Jewish women, who had historically played important roles within the women's movement, organized their own groups in the 1980s and spoke out against antisemitism within the movement (Beck 1980; Bulkin, Pratt, and Smith 1984). Some scholars have argued that the Black feminist movement generally does not mobilize through institutionalized formal organizations but operates through informal networks in local communities. Such informal networks include self-help groups, book clubs, "girlfriend" (women-only) parties and gatherings, and explicitly political groups. For example, in the 1990s, after the much publicized appeal of convicted rapist and professional boxer Mike Tyson, one such informal network served as a springboard to launch an antirape education program geared to the Black community (White 1999).

Union women played a significant role in the formation of NOW in 1966 by providing office space and clerical services until NOW's endorsement of the ERA in 1967 forced the women of the United Auto Workers, an organization that at the time opposed the ERA, to withdraw such support. Women committed to both feminism and the union movement, like women of color, formed their own organization, the Coalition of Labor Union Women (CLUW) in 1974 (Balser 1987). CLUW claimed 16,000 members by 1982 and had made progress in its fight to win AFL-CIO support for feminist issues. Union women also participated in deeply gendered ways in labor movement activity such as the 1985 Wheeling-Pittsburgh Steel strike, both affirming and challenging gender (Fonow 1998). The basic class and race composition of the movement may have changed little throughout the 1970s and 1980s, but by the beginning of the twenty-first century "a movement that began as unconsciously class-bound and race-bound has now become consciously class-bound and race-bound" (Buechler 1990:158).

Collective action by the women's movement has created new institutions and moved into almost every major institution of our society. However, in direct proportion to the successes of the women's movement, a countermovement successfully reversed some feminist gains, stalled progress on others, and changed the face of the women's movement.

The Antifeminist Political Context

The early 1980s saw a rapid decrease in the number of feminist organizations and a transformation in the form and activities of the women's movement. In part, this was a response to the successes of the New Right: so powerful were antifeminist sentiments and forces that members of the Republican party were elected in 1980 on a platform developed explicitly to "put women back in their place." After forty years of faithful support of the ERA, the Republican party dropped it from its platform, called for a constitutional amendment to ban abortion, and aligned itself with the economic and social policies of the New Right. After the election of the conservative Reagan administration in 1980, federal funds and grants were rarely available to feminist service organizations, and because other social service organizations were also hard hit by budget cuts, competition increased for relatively scarce money from private foundations. As a result, many feminist programs such as rape crisis centers, shelters for battered women, abortion clinics, and job training programs were forced to close or limit their services.

The failure of the ERA in 1982 seemed to reflect the changed political climate and set the stage for other setbacks throughout the 1980s. Abortion rights, won in 1973 with the Supreme Court's decision in *Roe v. Wade*, were curtailed in 1989 by the Supreme Court's decision in *Webster v. Reproductive Services* permitting states to enact restrictions on abortion (Staggenborg 1991: 137–38). Following the *Webster* decision, state governments set increasingly tight restrictions on abortion, ranging from "informed consent" laws that required a waiting period before women could obtain abortion surgery, to parental consent laws for underage women, to outright bans on abortion unless the woman's life was in danger. In 1991, the Supreme Court further limited abortion rights by ruling that federally funded family planning clinics could be barred from providing information on abortion. The antiabortion movement also escalated and hardened its tactics in the late 1980s and 1990s: it bombed abortion clinics, picketed doctors who performed abortions, and attempted to dissuade women entering clinics from having abortions (Staggenborg 1991; Simonds 1996).

[handwritten margin note: Gender Resistance can occur at 3 levels! (1) individual (2) social structural (3) cultural]

Further, women's studies programs in colleges and universities, which had been established in the 1970s in response to feminist agitation, came under attack by conservatives in the late 1980s and early 1990s. A backlash against "multiculturalism" and "political correctness" in academia sought to restore the traditional academic focus on the "great thinkers" of Western European history and thus to maintain the primacy of white male perspectives and experiences. Joining the attack, feminists such as Camille Paglia, Katie Roiphe, and Elizabeth Fox-Genovese drew media attention by holding radical and lesbian feminists responsible for alienating mainstream women and men from the women's movement.

The women's movement suffered not only from such attacks but also from its apparent success. Overt opposition to the feminist movement had been muted in the mid- to late 1970s. Elites in politics, education, and industry gave the appearance of supporting feminist aims through affirmative action programs and the appointment of a few token women to high positions in their respective areas. Meanwhile, the popular image of feminism advanced by the mass media suggested that the women's movement had won its goals. Despite the real-life difficulties women encountered trying to balance paid employment and a "second shift" of housework and child care (Hochschild 1989), the image of the working woman became the feminine ideal. The public discourse implied that since women had already achieved equality with men, they no longer needed a protest movement. Women who continued to press for gender equality were described increasingly in negative terms, as lesbians, man-haters, and, in the words of right-wing talk show host Rush Limbaugh, "feminazis."

But the women's movement did not die. Rather, it went into abeyance in order to survive in a hostile political climate. Movements in abeyance are in a holding pattern, during which activists from an earlier period maintain the ideology and structural base of the movement but few new recruits join (Taylor 1989). A movement in abeyance is primarily oriented toward maintaining itself rather than confronting the established order directly. Focusing on building an alternative culture, for example, is a means of surviving when external resources are not available and the political structure is not amenable to challenge. The structure and strategies of the women's movement have changed, then, as mass mobilization has declined and opposition to feminism has swelled. Nevertheless, feminist resistance continues—just in different forms.

Multiple Strategies and the Challenge to Gender

Gender resistance, challenge, and change can occur at three levels: the individual level of consciousness and interactions, the social structural level, and the cultural level (Collins 1990). This conceptualization of feminist activism allows us to recognize that movements adopt many strategies and to acknowledge the important role of women's movements in the reconstruction of gender.

Resisting Gender Practices   At the level of consciousness and social interactions, individual women can and do resist norms and expectations of the dominant gender system (Thorne 1994, 1995). It is, however, social movements or collectives, rather than isolated individuals, who perform the critical role of refashioning the gender code and calling institutions to account for gender inequality (Huber 1976; Chafetz 1990; Connell 1987). One of the primary goals of the modern feminist movement has been to change the unequal power relations between women and men. A general strategy used by feminists to achieve this goal has been to resist and challenge sexist practices within a diverse set of social contexts, ranging from heterosexual marriage to the gender division of labor in rearing and nurturing children to the gendered workplace and male-dominated medical establishment.

The formation of consciousness-raising groups facilitated the process of resisting and challenging gender practices and politicizing everyday life. Because consciousness-raising enables women to view the "personal as political," for most women it is an identity-altering experience. Becoming a feminist can transform a woman's entire self-concept and way of life: her biography, appearance, beliefs, behavior, and relationships (Cassell 1977; Esterberg 1997). As women's consciousness changes through personalized political strategies, women individually and collectively defy traditionally feminine role expectations for women and, in so doing, reconstruct the meanings of women, femininity, and interpersonal relationships between women and men. For example, some breast cancer activists have chosen to resist societal conceptions of femininity that link women's sexuality to breast beauty by refusing to wear prostheses or displaying mastectomy scars following breast surgery.

Women active in the feminist movement of the 1960s and 1970s continued to shape their lives in the

1980s and 1990s around their feminist beliefs, even when they were not involved in organized feminist activity. They continued to choose leisure activities, significant relationships, dress, and presentation of self consistent with feminist ideology (Whittier 1995). Many held jobs in government, social service organizations, or women's studies departments and other academic programs that allowed them to incorporate their political goals into their work. Even the consciousness and lives of women who did not identify as feminist have been altered by the women's movement. In a study of gender and family life in the Silicon Valley of California, Judith Stacey (1987) found that in the 1980s some women incorporated portions of feminism into traditional family and work structures by combining a feminist emphasis on developing satisfying careers, sharing household work with husbands, and increasing men's emotional expressiveness with fundamentalist Christianity and its focus on the importance of the family. Such women critiqued men's absence from families and lack of emotional expression, reflecting both feminism and traditional religion. The effects of the women's movement stretch far beyond policies and practices that are explicitly labeled feminist.

Another example of women resisting gender practices at the interactional level is found among young African-American women involved in little sister fraternity programs on college campuses in the 1990s. Such women embrace a collective identity built on notions of sisterhood and womanly strength to challenge the sexist practices of fraternities (Stombler and Padavic 1997). Further, these women use the fraternity little sister program to satisfy their own agendas of community service and self-enhancement. Even within the most traditional male-dominated organizations, then, gender relations are not immutable and women are employing diverse strategies to resist gender inequality.

Challenging the Structure of Gender Inequality   The challenge to gender inequality and the dominant gender order is also waged at the social structural level. As we have seen, the liberal bureaucratic strand of the modern feminist movement has employed legal reform strategies and engaged in street protests to counter sex discrimination in the economic, education, political, and domestic spheres. The legislative campaigns for equal pay for work of comparable worth and for maternity leave policies in the workplace challenge institutions that essentialize differences between women and men and rank "masculine" values and attributes above

those identified as "feminine" (Vogel 1993). The women's movement has created a feminist policy network of elected officials, lobbying organizations, social movement organizations, and individuals who have mobilized to address issues ranging from abortion rights, domestic violence, and pregnancy discrimination to day care, sexual harassment, and welfare rights (Ferree and Hess 1994; Staggenborg 1996; Gagné 1998).

As part of its legislative or legal strategies, the modern feminist movement has engaged in street protests such as picketing, mass demonstrations, and civil disobedience. Even within the conservative political climate of the 1980s, the feminist movement sparked some of the largest feminist demonstrations and actions in years. In April 1989, the National Organization for Women and abortion rights groups organized a national demonstration in Washington, DC, that drew between 300,000 and 600,000 women and men to protest restrictions on abortion. Additional national and local demonstrations followed. Prochoice activists organized electoral lobbying, defended abortion clinics, held conferences, and attempted to form coalitions across racial and ethnic lines and among women of different ages (Staggenborg 1991; Ryan 1992). The National Abortion Rights Action League experienced a growth in membership from 200,000 in 1989 to 400,000 in 1990 (Staggenborg 1991:138). NOW also continued to grow in the late 1980s and 1990s. After a decline in the early 1980s, it reached a membership of 250,000 in 1989 and maintained that membership level throughout the 1990s.

A wide variety of feminist organizations continued to pursue social change at state and local levels in the late 1990s (Ferree and Martin 1995). The Lesbian Avengers, a direct-action group founded in the 1990s with affiliates in several large cities, uses dramatic street theater to focus on issues of sexism and homophobia. For example, outside a police station in Delaware, Lesbian Avengers protested the police department's lack of action to catch a serial rapist by drawing chalk outlines of bodies on the sidewalk to represent women who had been raped during the past year. Veteran feminist organizations, such as NOW, continued to hold public protests in the late 1990s. For instance, in 1999, NOW chapters across the country staged pickets outside Wal-Mart retail stores to protest the corporation's refusal to sell the emergency contraception kit PREVEN to those who wish to prevent unintended pregnancies.

Beyond street politics, feminist activism in the 1980s and 1990s moved into diverse institutional settings. As an indication of the success and influence of feminist mobilization in earlier years, women found niches from which to challenge and transform institutional policies and structures, from pay equity to sexual harassment to occupational sex segregation (Blum 1991). Women in the military, for example, have formed pressure groups such as Women Military Aviators, who fought for the opening up of combat aviation positions for women. In the Catholic Church, radical religious orders have become protected spaces for women who challenge hierarchy within the institutional church (Katzenstein 1998). In major corporations, feminists have joined with gay activists to campaign successfully for domestic partnership benefits for lesbian and gay employees. Such unobtrusive mobilization within institutional boundaries refutes the notion of the death of feminism (Katzenstein 1997). Although the form and location of feminist protest have changed, this does not mean the women's movement has been deradicalized. The transformative potential of feminist activism within institutional settings may in some contexts be greater than that of pressure from outside.

Reconstructing the Culture of Gender　At the cultural level, the feminist social movement community has challenged cultural values, beliefs, and norms around gender and the gender order through building alternative social and cultural institutions for women outside mainstream institutions. The strategy of creating autonomous institutions is rooted in radical feminist ideology, which emphasizes that women need to have places and events away from patriarchal society where they can develop strength and pride as women. Since the early years of the women's movement, an extensive network of institutions has emerged within which a feminist culture flourishes (Taylor and Whittier 1992). Feminist communities contribute to the reconstruction of the culture of gender by challenging the devaluation of the feminine and undermining androcentric values and beliefs at the same time that they rearticulate alternative femininities and woman-centered values and beliefs (Taylor and Rupp 1993).

Into the new century, the feminist cultural community has continued to thrive with events such as an "annual multicultural multiracial conference on aging" for lesbians (*Off Our Backs* 1991:12), feminist cruises, annual women's music festivals, and women's comedy festivals in different parts of the country (Staggenborg 1998b). Gatherings and conferences include

groups such as Jewish lesbian daughters of holocaust survivors, women motorcyclists, fat dykes, pagans, Asian lesbians, practitioners of herbal medicine, and survivors of incest. Newsletters and publications exist for a multitude of groups, among them women recovering from addictions, women's music professionals and fans, lesbian separatists, disabled lesbians, lesbian mothers, feminists interested in sadomasochism, and feminists opposed to pornography.

The growth of the feminist community underscores the flowering of lesbian feminism in the late 1980s and 1990s (Esterberg 1997; Stein 1997). A wide variety of lesbian and lesbian feminist books and anthologies have been published on topics ranging from lesbian feminist ethics to separatism to sexuality to lesbian parenthood to commitment ceremonies for lesbian couples (see, for example, Hoagland 1988; Hoagland and Penelope 1988; Loulan 1990; Butler 1991), reflecting diverse perspectives that have been hotly debated in the pages of lesbian publications and at conferences and festivals. For example, a series of letters to the editor in a national lesbian newsletter during 1991 argued about the correct lesbian feminist response to lesbians serving in the armed forces in the Persian Gulf War: some readers held that the war was a manifestation of patriarchy and that lesbians in the military should be criticized; others argued that lesbian soldiers should be supported because they are lesbians in a homophobic institution, regardless of one's support of or opposition to the war; still others argued that the Gulf War was justified and that lesbian servicewomen should be celebrated for their patriotic service (*Lesbian Connection* 1991). Clearly, the task of building a community based on the identity "lesbian" has proven complex, if not impossible. Nevertheless, the institutional structure of the social movement community has continued to expand, and within the community feminists construct and reinforce a collective identity based on opposition to dominant conceptions of women and lesbians (Taylor and Whittier 1992).

Another example of resistance on the cultural level is the emergence of women's self-help groups, which sprang directly out of the early women's health movement and continue to model support groups on feminist consciousness-raising (Rapping 1996; Simonds 1996). Some feminist writers contend that women's self-help diverts the feminist agenda away from social and political change and directs women, instead, to change themselves (Kaminer 1992). Others argue that explicitly feminist self-help movements, such as strands of the postpartum depression and breast cancer movements, are contributing to the reconstruction of gender through the collective redefinition of womanhood and the cultural articulation of alternative femininities (Taylor 1996; Taylor and Van Willigen 1996; Klawiter 1999). These self-help movements are not depoliticized and purely individually focused; they perform a critical role of challenging institutional gender biases and refashioning the dominant gender code (Taylor 1996, 1999).

All of these diverse strategies, operating at different levels, challenge traditional societal definitions of femininity and masculinity and the dominant gender order. From the individual to the social structural to the cultural plane, we can see the continuous impact of the women's movement.

Movement Continuity and Change into the Twenty-first Century

Social movement scholars understand that social movements affect one another. The abolitionist movement in the mid-nineteenth century influenced the first wave of the women's movement in the United States, and the civil rights and New Left movements of the 1960s shaped the course of the second wave (Buechler 1990). In turn, the women's movement has had a substantial impact on other social movements. Meyer and Whittier (1994) argue that "the ideas, tactics, style, participants, and organizations of one movement often *spill over* its boundaries to affect other social movements" (277, emphasis in the original). The gay and lesbian, transgender, AIDS, recovery from addictions, New Age, and animal-rights movements have been profoundly influenced by feminist values and ideology, including the emphasis on collective structure and consensus, the notion of the personal as political, and the critique of patriarchy extended to the mistreatment of animals and ecological resources (Jasper and Poulsen 1995; Einwohner 1999).

The women's movement also trained a large number of feminist activists in the 1970s (particularly lesbians), who have participated in new social movements and integrated feminism into them (Cavin 1990; Whittier 1995). The gay and lesbian movement, for example, has expanded its health concerns to include breast cancer as well as AIDS and has used strategies of the feminist antirape movement to confront violence against gays and lesbians. In addition, feminists have renewed coalitions with the peace, environmental,

socialist, anti-US intervention in Latin America, and antiapartheid movements, transforming these movements both by creating separate feminist organizations that address these issues and by moving into mixed-sex organizations (Whittier 1995). In a sense the women's movement has come full circle, rejoining the 1990s versions of the movements that composed the New Left in the 1960s, when many feminists split off to form a separate autonomous women's movement.

Although the women's movement has changed form and location, the level of mass mobilization and confrontation of the social structural system has clearly declined since the 1980s. Because feminism came to focus more on consciousness and culture and established roots in other social movements of the period, feminist protest is less visible than it was during the heyday of the women's movement. According to some studies (Schneider 1988; Dill unpublished), despite support for feminist goals, many young women do not identify themselves as feminists, apparently because the term is stigmatized. A feminist is seen as someone who deviates from gender norms by being unattractive, aggressive, hostile to men, unfeminine, opposed to marriage and motherhood, and lesbian. Despite the gain made by women in some areas, gender norms are still so rigid and deeply internalized that they successfully deter many women who support the feminist agenda from participating in the movement.

Yet some younger women have joined the women's movement despite the risks entailed in identifying with a stigmatized and unpopular cause. A new generation of women has been recruited to feminism primarily through women's studies courses and through the transmission of feminism from mothers to daughters. The institutionalized gains of the heyday of feminist activism in the 1970s are enabling the women's movement to survive and to disseminate its ideas to new recruits. What direction the self-proclaimed "third-wave" feminists (Kamen 1991; Walker 1992, 1995) will take is not at all clear, but the history of the women's movement suggests that a new constituency will revise feminist ideology, renovate existing structures, respond to a changing political climate, and further develop feminist strategies.

ANTIFEMINIST COUNTERMOVEMENTS

The emergence of organized opposition is one indication of the successes of feminist movements. In general, it is when social movements pose a serious threat to the status quo that countermovements appear (Chafetz and Dworkin 1987). Antifeminist resistance movements mobilized in response to first- and second-wave feminist movements in the United States when feminists began to gain political legitimacy and influence. For example, as the first wave of the women's movement was building support for suffrage in the late nineteenth century, an organized antisuffrage movement began to coalesce (Marshall 1997). Likewise, when the feminist movement of the 1970s was gaining political ground on the ratification of the Equal Rights Amendment, an anti-ERA movement blossomed (Marshall 1984).

Antifeminist countermovements, like feminist movements, are not monolithic. They vary over time and place by ideology, strategy, and organization (Marshall 1985; Buechler 1990; Blee 1991). Chafetz and Dworkin (1987) contend that antifeminist countermovements are composed of two constituencies: vested-interest groups, which are typically male-dominated and oppose feminist change movements on the basis of class interests; and voluntary grassroots associations made up of women who are reacting to the threat to their status as privileged traditional women.

Compared to the scholarship on movements, countermovements have been understudied and undertheorized (Meyer and Staggenborg 1996). Research on organized opposition to feminism by women is also limited (Klatch 1990; Marshall 1997). Women's participation in antifeminist countermovements challenges the radical feminist notion that women are a "sex class" with clearly defined gender interests (Luker 1984; Blee 1991). Scholars often characterize antifeminist women as victims of false consciousness or as women who are passively expressing their husbands' interests. Marshall (1997) argues that these are overly simplistic interpretations and that an appreciation for the ways in which antisuffragist leaders used their wealth, social networks, and political power to build an oppositional identity in the antisuffrage movement suggests "a conceptual shift of the locus of conflict over suffrage from culture to politics" (p. 13). In this light, antifeminist women should be viewed as political actors who take up gendered class interests independently of their husbands (Marshall 1997).

The interaction between opposing movements is a prominent feature of contemporary US society. Any social movement analysis is incomplete without a consideration of the interdependence of movements and countermovements. For example, we cannot fully understand the tactics, strategies, organizational forms, and feminist identities characteristic of the feminist movement during the 1980s and 1990s without considering the effects of the antiabortion mobilization and the rise of the New Right.

The modern women's movement in the United States has been opposed by a variety of conservative antifeminist groups. In the early 1970s, the Stop ERA campaign initiated by Phyllis Schlafly fought to block passage of the ERA by state legislatures. Through the 1970s, the New Right grew larger and more influential, linking conservative issues like opposition to busing, abortion, gay rights, the ERA, and governmental regulation of business through affirmative action and health and safety programs (Klatch 1990). With the election of Ronald Reagan to the presidency in 1980, the New Right gained state support for its agenda.

The antifeminist movement in the late 1980s and 1990s spent considerable energy opposing abortion, and its successes in that area have been impressive in terms of judicial and legislative gains and disruptive demonstrations at abortion clinics (Staggenborg 1991; Simonds 1996). Over the years a number of aggressive splinter groups, such as Operation Rescue, developed out of the mainstream National Right to Life Committee, which originated within the Catholic Church. The murders of Drs. David Gunn in Pensacola, Florida, and Barnett Slepian in Buffalo, New York, are potent examples of the radical tactics advocated by some antiabortion rights groups.

The prevalence of antifeminist resistance throughout history highlights the significance of the family, sexuality, and reproduction for the maintenance of the dominant social order. The growth of antifeminism, however, does not imply that the women's movement has failed or run its course. On the contrary, it attests to feminism's successful challenge to the status quo.

CONCLUSION

The history of the women's movement and its present survival, despite the challenges it has confronted from within its own ranks and from a conservative political climate, suggest that because feminism is a response to the fundamental social cleavage of gender it will continue to exist (Taylor and Rupp 1993). As one generation of feminists fades from the scene with its ultimate goals unrealized, another takes up the challenge (Rossi 1982).

But each new generation of feminists does not simply carry on where the previous generation left off. Rather, it speaks for itself and defines its own objectives and strategies, often to the dismay and disapproval of feminists from earlier generations. A new generation of feminists may organize a "warm line" for women suffering postpartum depression (Taylor 1996), or construct a public clothesline of T-shirts representing the victims of domestic violence to raise awareness of violence against women, or march together in a Take Back the Night event to empower survivors of sexual violence and reclaim the streets for women. They may put on "drag king" performances to challenge the restrictions placed on expressions of women's sexuality, or distribute condoms and dental dams to women for AIDS prevention, or organize "kiss-ins" with Queer Nation. While earlier generations of activists may not view such endeavors as feminist, as Myra Ferree and Beth Hess (1985:182) point out, "feminism is not simply a form of received wisdom" but something that evolves with each new cycle of feminist activism. Just as the women's movement of the twentieth century has endured and persisted through transformation, feminism of the twenty-first century will be characterized by continuity and change.

REFERENCES

Atkinson, T. G. (1974). *Amazon Odyssey*. New York: Links.

Balser, Diane. (1987). *Sisterhood and Solidarity: Feminism and Labor in Modern Times*. Boston: South End Press.

Barnett, Bernice McNair. (1993). Invisible southern black women leaders in the civil rights movement: The triple constraints of gender, race, and class. *Gender & Society*, 7, 162–182.

Basu, Amrita, ed. (1995). *The Challenge of Local Feminisms: Women's Movements in Global Perspective*. Boulder, CO: Westview Press.

Beauvoir, S. de. (1952). *The Second Sex*. New York: Bantam.

Beck, E. T. (1980). *Nice Jewish Girls: A Lesbian Anthology*. Watertown, MA: Persephone.

Black, Naomi. (1989). *Social Feminism*. Ithaca, NY: Cornell University Press.

Blee, Kathleen M. (1991). *Women of the Klan: Racism and Gender in the 1920s*. Berkeley: University of California Press.

Blum, Linda M. (1991). *Between Feminism and Labor: The Significance of the Comparable Worth Movement*. Berkeley: University of California Press.

Breines, W. (1982). *Community and Organization in the New Left, 1962–68*. New York: Praeger.

Buechler, Steven M. (1990). *Women's Movements in the United States*. New Brunswick, NJ: Rutgers.

Bulkin, Elly, Minnie Bruce Pratt, & Barbara Smith. (1984). *Yours in Struggle: Three Feminist Perspectives on Anti-Semitism and Racism*. New York: Long Haul Press.

Butler, Becky. (1991). *Ceremonies of the Heart: Celebrating Lesbian Unions*. Seattle, WA: The Seal Press.

Carden, Maren. (1978). The proliferation of a social movement. In Louis Kriesberg, ed., *Research in Social Movements, Conflict, and Change*, vol. 1 (pp. 179–196). Greenwich, CT: JAI Press.

Cassell, J. (1977). *A Group Called Women: Sisterhood and Symbolism in the Feminist Movement*. New York: David McKay.

Cavin, Susan. (1990). The invisible army of women: Lesbian social protests, 1969–88. In Guida West & Rhoda Blumberg, eds. *Women and Social Protest* (pp. 321–332). New York: Oxford University Press.

Chafe, W. H. (1977). *Women and Equality: Changing Patterns in American Culture*. New York: Oxford University Press.

Chafetz, Janet. (1990). *Gender Equity: An Integrated Theory of Stability and Change*. Newbury Park, CA: Sage.

Chafetz, Janet, & Gary Dworkin. (1986). *Female Revolt*. Totowa, NJ: Rowman Allanheld.

———. (1987). In the face of threat: Organized antifeminism in comparative perspective. *Gender & Society*, 1, 33–60.

Collins, Patricia Hill. (1990). *Black Feminist Thought*. New York: Routledge.

Cornell, R. W. (1987). *Gender and Power*. Stanford, CA: Stanford University Press.

Cott, Nancy. (1987). *The Grounding of Modern Feminism*. New Haven, CT: Yale University Press.

Daly, Mary. (1978). *Gyn/ecology*. Boston: Beacon.

Deckard, Barbara Sinclair. (1983). *The Women's Movement*. New York: Harper & Row.

Dill, Kim. Unpublished. "Feminism in the nineties: The influence of collective identity and community on young feminist activists." Master's thesis, The Ohio State University, 1991.

Echols, Alice. (1989). *Daring to Be Bad: Radical Feminism in America 1967–1975*. Minneapolis: University of Minnesota Press.

Einwohner, Rachel L. (1999). Gender, class, and social movement outcomes: Identity and effectiveness in two animal rights campaigns. *Gender & Society*, 13, 56–76.

Eisenstein, Z. (1981). *The Radical Future of Liberal Feminism*. New York: Longman.

Esterberg, Kristin G. (1997). *Lesbian and Bisexual Identities: Constructing Communities, Constructing Selves*. Philadelphia: Temple University Press.

Evans, Sarah. (1979). *Personal Politics*. New York: Knopf.

Ferree, Myra Marx, & Beth B. Hess. [1985] (1994). *Controversy and Coalition: The New Feminist Movement*. Boston: Twayne.

Ferree, Myra Marx, & Patricia Yancey Martin. (1995). *Feminist Organizations: Harvest of the New Women's Movement*. Philadelphia: Temple University Press.

Firestone, S. (1970). *The Dialectic of Sex.* New York: William Morrow.

Fonow, Mary Margaret. (1998). Protest engendered: The participation of women steelworkers in the Wheeling-Pittsburgh steel strike of 1985. *Gender & Society,* 12, 710–728.

Freeman, Jo. (1972/3). The tyranny of structurelessness. *Berkeley Journal of Sociology,* 17, 151–164.

———. (1975). *The Politics of Women's Liberation.* New York: David McKay.

———. (1979). Resource mobilization and strategy: A model for analyzing social movement organization actions. In M. N. Zald & J. D. McCarthy, eds. *The Dynamics of Social Movements* (pp. 167–89). Cambridge, MA: Winthrop.

Frye, Marilyn. (1983). *The Politics of Reality: Essays in Feminist Theory.* Trumansburg, NY: Crossing Press.

Gagné, Patricia. (1998). *Battered Women's Justice: The Movement for Democracy and the Politics of Self-defense.* New York: Twayne Publishers.

Gerlach, L. P., & V. H. Hine. (1970). *People, Power, Change: Movements of Social Transformation.* Indianapolis: Bobbs-Merrill.

Giele, Janet Zollinger. (1995). *Two Paths to Women's Equality: Temperance, Suffrage, and the Origins of Modern Feminism.* New York: Twayne Publishers.

Gordon, Suzanne. (1991). *Prisoners of Men's Dreams.* New York: Little, Brown.

Griffin, S. (1978). *Women and Nature.* New York: Harper & Row.

Hartmann, Heidi. (1981). The family as the locus of gender, class, and political struggle: The example of housework. *Signs,* 6, 366–394.

Hartsock, Nancy. (1983). *Money, Sex, and Power: Toward a Feminist Historical Materialism.* New York: Longman.

Hoagland, Sarah Lucia. (1988). *Lesbian Ethics: Toward New Value.* Palo Alto, CA: Institute of Lesbian Studies.

Hoagland, Sarah Lucia, & Julia Penelope, eds. (1988). *For Lesbians Only.* London: Onlywomen Press.

Hochschild, Arlie. (1989). *The Second Shift.* New York: Avon.

Huber, Joan. (1973). From sugar and spice to professor. In A. S. Rossi & A. Calderwood, *Academic Women on the Move.* New York: Russell Sage Foundation.

———. (1976). Toward a sociotechnological theory of the women's movement. *Social Problems,* 23, 371–388.

Huber, Joan, & Glenna Spike. (1983). *Sex Stratification: Children, Housework, and Jobs.* New York: Academic.

Jasper, James M., & Jane D. Poulsen. (1995). Recruiting strangers and friends: Moral shocks and social networks in animal rights and anti-nuclear protests. *Social Problems,* 42, 493–512.

Jayawardena, Kumari. (1986). *Feminism and Nationalism in the Third World.* London: Zed Books.

Kamen, Paula. (1991). *Feminist Fatale: Voices from the "Twenty-something" Generation Explore the Future of the Women's Movement.* New York: Donald I. Fine.

Kaminer, Wendy. (1992). *I'm Dysfunctional, You're Dysfunctional: The Recovery Movement and Other Self-help Fashions.* Reading, MA: Addison-Wesley.

Katzenstein, Mary Fainsod. (1997). Stepsisters: Feminist movement activism in different institutional spaces. In David Meyer & Sidney Tarrow, eds., *A Movement Society? Contentious Politics for a New Century.* Boulder, CO. Rowman & Littlefield.

———. (1998). *Faithful and Fearless: Moving Feminist Protest Inside the Church and Military.* Princeton, NJ: Princeton University Press.

Katzenstein, Mary Fainsod, & Carol McClurg Mueller. (1987). *The Women's Movements of the United States and Western Europe.* Philadelphia: Temple University Press.

Klatch, Rebecca. (1990). The two worlds of women of the new right. In Louise A. Tilly & Patricia Gurin, eds., *Women, Politics and Change.* New York: Russell Sage Foundation.

Klawiter, Maren. (1999). Racing for the Cure, walking women, and toxic touring: Mapping cultures of action within the Bay Area terrain of breast cancer. *Social Problems,* 46, 104–126.

Klein, Ethel. (1984). *Gender Politics.* Cambridge, MA: Harvard University Press.

Leidner, Robin. (1993). Constituency, accountability, and deliberation: Reshaping democracy in the National Women's Studies Association. *NWSA Journal,* 5, 4–27.

Lesbian Connection. (1991). Vols. 13 & 14. Lansing, MI: Ambitious Amazons.

Loulan, JoAnn. (1990). *The Lesbian Erotic Dance.* San Francisco: Spinsters Book Company.

Luker, Kristin. (1984). *Abortion and the Politics of Motherhood.* Berkeley: University of California Press.

MacKinnon, C. A. (1983). Feminism, Marxism, method, and the state: Toward feminist jurisprudence. *Signs,* 8, 635–668.

Mansbridge, Jane. (1986). *Why We Lost the ERA.* Chicago: University of Chicago Press.

Marshall, Susan E. (1984). Keep us on the pedestal: Women against feminism in twentieth-century America. In Jo Freeman, ed., *Women: A Feminist Perspective* (pp. 568–581). Palo Alto: Mayfield.

———. (1985). Ladies against women: Mobilization dilemmas of antifeminist movements. *Social Problems,* 32, 348–362.

———. (1997). *Splintered Sisterhood: Gender and Class in the Campaign Against Woman Suffrage.* Madison: University of Wisconsin Press.

Martin, Patricia Yancey. (1990). Rethinking feminist organizations. *Gender & Society,* 4, 182–206.

Marx, G. T., & J. L. Wood. (1975). Strands of theory and research in collective behavior. *Annual Review of Sociology,* 1, 363–428.

Matthews, Nancy. (1994). *Confronting Rape: The Feminist Anti-rape Movement and the State.* London: Routledge.

Matthews, Donald G., & Jane Sheffon DeHart. (1990). *Sex, Gender and the Politics of ERA: A State and the Nation.* New York: Oxford.

McCarthy, J. D., & M. N. Zald. (1977). Resource mobilization and social movements: A partial theory. *American Journal of Sociology, 82,* 1212–1239.

Meyer, David S., & Nancy Whittier. (1994). Social movement spillover. *Social Problems, 41,* 277–298.

Meyer, David S., & Suzanne Staggenborg. (1996). Movements, countermovements, and the structure of political opportunity. *American Journal of Sociology, 101,* 1628–1660.

Miles, Angela. (1996). *Integrative Feminisms: Building Global Visions, 1960s–1990s.* New York: Routledge.

Millett, K. (1971). *Sexual Politics.* New York: Avon.

Mitchell, Juliet. (1986). Reflections on twenty years of feminism. In Juliet Mitchell & Ann Oakley, eds., *What Is Feminism?* (pp. 34–48). Oxford: Basil Blackwell.

Mohanty, Chandra Talpade, Ann Russo, & Lordes Torres, eds. (1991). *Third World Women and the Politics of Feminism.* Bloomington: Indiana University Press.

Moraga, Cherríe & Gloria Anzaldúa. (1981). *This Bridge Called My Back: Writings by Radical Women of Color.* Watertown, MA: Persephone.

Morris, Aldon D., & Carol McClurg Mueller, eds. (1992). *Frontiers in Social Movement Theory.* New Haven, CT: Yale University Press.

Naples, Nancy A. (1992). Activist mothering: Cross-generational continuity in the community work of women from low-income neighborhoods. *Gender & Society, 6,* 441–463.

Off Our Backs (1991). Passages 7—Beyond the barriers. Vol. 21 (6), 12.

Offen, Karen. (1988). Defining feminism: A comparative historical approach. *Signs, 14,* 119–157.

Oppenheimer, Valerie Kincade. (1973). Demographic influence on female employment and the status of women. In Joan Huber, ed., *Changing Women in a Changing Society* (pp. 184–199). Chicago: University of Chicago Press.

Rapping Elayne. (1996). *The Culture of Recovery: Making Sense of the Recovery Movement in Women's Lives.* Boston: Beacon Press.

Ray, Raka. (1999). *Fields of Protest: Women's Movements in India.* Minneapolis: University of Minnesota Press.

Rich, Adrienne. (1976). *Of Woman Born.* New York: Norton.

———. (1980). Compulsory heterosexuality and lesbian existence. *Signs, 5,* 631–660.

Robnett, Belinda. (1996). African-American women in the civil rights movement, 1954–1965: Gender, leadership, and micromobilization. *American Journal of Sociology, 101,* 1661–1693.

Rossi, Alice S. (1982). *Feminist in Politics: A Panel Analysis of the First National Women's Conference.* New York: Academic Press.

Rothschild-Whitt, Joyce. (1979). The collectivist organization: An alternative to rational-bureaucratic models. *American Sociological Review, 44,* 509–527.

Rubin, G. (1975). Traffic in women: Notes on the "political economy" of sex. In Rayne Reiter, ed., *Toward an Anthropology of Women,* New York: Monthly Review Press.

Rupp, Leila J. (1997). *Worlds of Women: The Making of an International Women's Movement.* Princeton, NJ: Princeton University Press.

Rupp, Leila J., & Verta Taylor. (1987). *Survival in the Doldrums: The American Women's Rights Movement, 1945 to 1960s.* New York: Oxford University Press.

Ryan, Barbara. (1989). Ideological purity and feminism: The U.S. women's movement from 1966 to 1975. *Gender & Society, 3,* 239–257.

———. (1992). *Feminism and the Women's Movement.* New York: Routledge.

Sapiro, V. (1991). In Janet Boles, ed., *The Annals of the American Academy of Political and Social Science,* May, 515.

Schlesinger, M. B., & P. Bart. (1983). Collective work and self-identity: The effect of working in a feminist illegal abortion collective. In L. Richardson & V. Taylor, eds., *Feminist Frontiers.* Reading, MA: Addison-Wesley.

Schneider, Beth. (1988). Political generations in the contemporary women's movement. *Sociological Inquiry, 58,* 4–21.

Simonds, Wendy. (1996). *Abortion at Work: Ideology and Practice in a Feminist Clinic.* New Brunswick, NJ: Rutgers University Press.

Spelman, Elizabeth. (1988). *Inessential Woman: Problems of Exclusion in Feminist Thought.* Boston: Beacon Press.

Stacey, Judith. (1987). Sexism by a subtler name? Postindustrial conditions and postfeminist consciousness. *Socialist Review, 17,* 7–28.

Staggenborg, Suzanne. (1988). The consequences of professionalization and formalization in the pro-choice movement. *American Sociological Review, 53,* 585–606.

———. (1989). Stability and innovation in the women's movement: A comparison of two movement organizations. *Social Problems, 36,* 75–92.

———. (1991). *The Pro-choice Movement.* New York: Oxford University Press.

———. (1996). The survival of the women's movement: Turnover and continuity in Bloomington, Indiana. *Mobilization, 1,* 143–158.

———. (1998a). *Gender, Family, and Social Movements.* Thousand Oaks, CA: Pine Forge Press.

———. (1998b). Social movement communities and cycles of protest: The emergence and maintenance of a local women's movement. *Social Problems, 45,* 180–204.

Stein, Arlene. (1997). *Sex and Sensibility: Stories of a Lesbian Generation.* Berkeley: University of California Press.

Stombler, Mindy, & Irene Padavic. (1997). Sister acts: Resisting men's domination in black and white fraternity little sister programs. *Social Problems, 44,* 257–275.

Taylor, Verta. (1989). Social movement continuity: The women's movement in abeyance. *American Sociological Review, 54,* 761–775.

————. (1996). *Rock-a-by Baby: Feminism, Self-help, and Postpartum Depression.* New York: Routledge.

————. (1999). Gender and social movements: Gender processes and women's self-help movements. *Gender & Society,* 13, 8–33.

Taylor, Verta, & Leila Rupp. (1993). Women's culture and lesbian feminist activism: A reconsideration of cultural feminism. *Signs,* 19, 32–61.

Taylor, Verta, & Marieke Van Willigen. (1996). Women's self-help and the reconstruction of gender: The postpartum support and breast cancer movements. *Mobilization: An International Journal,* 2, 123–142.

Taylor, Verta, & Nancy Whittier. (1992). Collective identity in social movement communities: Lesbian feminist mobilization. In Aldon Morris & Carol Mueller, eds., *Frontiers of Social Movement Theory.* New Haven, CT: Yale University Press.

Thorne, Barrie. (1994). *Gender Play: Girls and Boys in School.* New Brunswick, NJ: Rutgers University Press.

————. (1995). Symposium on West and Fenstermaker's "Doing Difference." *Gender & Society,* 9, 498–499.

Vogel, Lise. (1993). *Mothers on the Job: Maternity Policy in the U.S. Workplace.* New Brunswick, NJ: Rutgers University Press.

Walker, Rebecca. (1992). Becoming the third wave. *Ms.,* 2 (January/February), 39–41.

————. (1995). *To Be Real: Telling the Truth and Changing the Face of Feminism.* New York: Anchor.

White, Aaronette M. (1999). Talking feminist, talking back: Micromobilization processes in a collective protest against rape. *Gender & Society,* 13, 77–100.

Whittier, Nancy E. (1995). *Feminist Generations: The Persistence of the Radical Women's Movement.* Philadelphia: Temple University Press.

R E A D I N G *52*   **Pamela Aronson**

Feminists or "Postfeminists"? Young Women's Attitudes Toward Feminism and Gender Relations

A late 1990s cover of *Time* magazine with the caption "Is feminism dead?" featured photos of prominent feminist activists, including one of the flighty television lawyer character, Ally McBeal (Bellafante 1998). Such media pronouncements of the "death" of feminism rest on widespread presumptions that young women do not appreciate gains made by the women's movement, are not concerned about discrimination, and do not support feminism. These suppositions have rarely been tested.

How do young women view their own opportunities and obstacles, particularly when compared to those faced by women of their mothers' generation? How do they perceive and experience gender discrimination? How do they identify themselves with respect to feminism, and how can we make sense of their seemingly contradictory perspectives? Finally, what are the impacts of racial and class background and life experience on attitudes toward feminism? Although

prior studies have considered aspects of these questions, my research examines them through interviews with a diverse sample. This diversity reveals the importance not only of race and class, but also life experience, in the development of attitudes toward feminism. Furthermore, by not imposing a set definition of feminism but letting it emerge from the interviewees themselves, my study reveals great ambiguity in the meanings of feminism today and suggests that we need to rethink some of the assumptions about young women's identities.

GROWING UP IN THE SHADOW OF THE WOMEN'S MOVEMENT[1]

Since the mid-1980s, 30 to 40 percent of women have called themselves feminists, and by 1990, nearly 80 percent favored efforts to "strengthen and change women's status in society" (Marx Ferree and Hess 1995, 88).

Although the media often question why so few women call themselves feminists, Marx Ferree and Hess (1995) pointed out that the number of women who do so represents the same percentage of people who label themselves as Republicans or Democrats. Addressing the same concerns, Gurin (1985, 1987) distinguished between four components of gender consciousness: identification (recognizing women's shared interests), discontent (recognizing women's lack of power), assessment of legitimacy (seeing gender disparities as illegitimate), and collective orientation (believing in collective action). Although women historically have become more critical of men's claims to power, women's gender consciousness has been weaker than the group consciousness of African Americans, the working class, and the elderly. At the same time, women, especially employed women, are often conscious of women's structural disadvantage in the labor market (Gurin 1985). However, an average woman may have somewhat vague understandings of political labels such as "feminism," as activists and political elites are generally more consistent and coherent in their positions (Converse 1964; Unger 1989).

In the early 1980s, the media began to label women in their teens and twenties as the "postfeminist" generation[2] (Bellafante 1998; Bolotin 1982; Whittier 1995). Twenty years later, the term continues to be applied to young women, who are thought to benefit from the women's movement through expanded access to employment and education and new family arrangements but at the same time do not push for further political change. Postfeminism has been the subject of considerable debate, since its usage connotes the "death" of feminism and because the equality it assumes is largely a myth (Coppock, Haydon, and Richter 1995; Overholser 1986; Rosenfelt and Stacey 1987; Whittier 1995). The term has been used by researchers to reflect the current cycle and stage of the women's movement (Taylor 1989; Taylor and Rupp 1993; Whittier 1995). Indeed, Rossi (1982) has written of a cyclical generational pattern in the women's movement, with each feminist wave separated by roughly fifty years, or two generations. "Quiet periods" (Rossi 1982, 9) see diminished political action, but continued progress in private arenas, such as education and employment. Because movement stages greatly influence how women identify with the movement (Taylor 1989; Taylor and Rupp 1993; Whittier 1995), women's individual attitudes toward feminism are likely to vary.

The second-wave women's movement has simultaneously experienced great successes and backlash. Successes include the maintenance of movement organizations (Marx Ferree and Yancey Martin 1995; Whittier 1995), as well as a "broadly institutionalized and effective interest group," with an institutional base in academia, particularly women's studies programs (Brenner 1996, 24). Backlash is evident in a decline in grassroots mobilization and negative public discourse by antifeminist organizations and media figures (Faludi 1991; Marx Ferree and Hess 1995; Schneider 1988).

Scholars have found that young women tend to be depoliticized and individualistic and that few identify as feminists (Rupp 1988; Stacey 1987)—they typically focus on individual solutions (Budgeon and Currie 1995) and express feminist ideas without labeling them as such (Henderson-King and Stewart 1994; Morgan 1995; Percy and Kremer 1995; Renzetti 1987; Rupp 1988; Stacey 1987; Weis 1990). Many of these apolitical women assume that discrimination will not happen to them (Sigel 1996). The lack of grassroots mobilization results in no framework for understanding individual experiences in politicized terms (Aronson 2000; Taylor 1996) and limits "postfeminists" to viewing gender disparities as illegitimate, rather than in collective terms or in terms of women's shared interests (Gurin 1985, 1987). Their attitudes are also influenced by the media, which have supported the antifeminist backlash (Faludi 1991; Marx Ferree and Hess 1995) and have implied that "no further feminist action is needed" (Schneider 1988, 11).

This generally negative picture of contemporary feminist consciousness is occasionally countered by researchers who have been discovering a "third wave." They point to more than one micro cohort within the postfeminist generation, noting that women who came of age in the 1990s more frequently support feminist goals and are more politically active to achieve these goals (e.g., abortion rights activism) than women who came of age in the 1980s (Whittier 1995). From activists who seek to represent a diversity of young women's experiences (Walker 1995), to the Riot Grrrl movement in music (Rosenberg and Garofalo 1998; Wald 1998), third-wave feminism is said to explicitly embrace hybridity, contradiction, and multiple identities (particularly "connections between racial, sexual and gender identities," Heywood and Drake 1997, 7, 8, 15). However, this new emphasis is questioned by scholars arguing that African American and Chicana feminists have focused historically, and continue to focus, on organizing not only in terms of gender but also along racial lines (Hurtado 1998; Springer 2002). In addition, the third wave is sometimes perceived as nonactivist in nature (Heywood and Drake 1997).

Although not explicitly defining themselves as feminists, other women are said to have the "potential for feminist critique" (Weis 1990, 179). Stacey (1991, 262) argued that young women have "semiconsciously incorporated feminist principles into their gender and kinship expectations and practices." This approach includes "taking for granted" many recent gains: women's work opportunities, combining work with family, sexual autonomy and freedom, and male participation in domestic work and child rearing (Stacey 1991, 1987). This "simultaneous incorporation, revision and depoliticization" (Stacey 1987, 8) of feminism indicates that worldviews include more feminist principles while being less explicitly feminist.

The negative as well as the positive prognosis of these studies should be taken with a grain of salt. They tend to operate with uniform definitions of feminism, ignore generational differences, and/or study groups that are too homogeneous to provide conclusions about the full diversity of today's young women. My study seeks to correct each of these limitations and hopes to provide insights that are more nuanced, complex, and attentive to diversity. . . .

This [reading] explores young women's attitudes toward feminism in relation to differences in background and life experience. In contrast to prior research, I recognize the ambivalent and sometimes contradictory orientations of the women who have grown up in the shadow of the women's movement. While prior research has given some attention to the contexts within which feminist attitudes develop (Sigel 1996; Stacey 1987; Taylor 1996; Whittier 1995), many studies have not directly considered women's perceptions of some key goals of feminist organizing, such as advancing women's opportunities, and the obstacles and discrimination that feminism addresses. To discern the context of young women's attitudes toward gender relations, I begin my analysis with an examination of perceptions of women's opportunities, obstacles, and discrimination. I continue the analysis by considering young women's attitudes toward feminism and the impact of race, class, and life experience on these attitudes. Taken together, this article reveals support for feminist goals and complexity in attitudes toward the term *feminism*.

METHOD[3]

This study is based on in-depth interviews with members of a panel study of young people, the Youth Development Study, an ongoing longitudinal study of adolescent development and the transition to adulthood (Jeylan Mortimer is the principal investigator). The larger survey sample ($N = 1,000$) was randomly chosen from a list of enrolled ninth-grade students in St. Paul, Minnesota. Respondents completed surveys annually, with the first year (ninth grade) in 1988. Of the original 1,000 panel members who took part in the first year of data collection, the Youth Development Study retained 77.5 percent through 1995, the last year of the survey before my interview study.

For my in-depth interviews, I followed Glaser and Strauss's (1967) suggestions for theoretical sampling and interviewed women with varying trajectories of life experience and background, as reported in surveys during the four years following high school (1991 to 1995). I focused on differences in education, parenthood, and careers and interviewed nearly equal proportions of women in each group. . . . A "school" group had attended a four-year college or university for at least eight months annually in three of the four years following high school. A "parent" group had become mothers by the eighth year of the study and could also be engaged in school and/or work. A "labor force" group did not have an extensive school trajectory, nor had they become mothers. Instead, they typically worked full-time or moved between postsecondary school and work after high school. . . .

. . . The women were aged twenty-three or twenty-four at the time of my interviews. Among them, 33 percent were women of color (11.9 percent African American, 9.5 percent Asian American, 9.5 percent biracial and multiracial, and 2.4 percent Latina). Their socioeconomic backgrounds included 31 percent from working-class families, 48 percent from the middle class, and 21 percent from upper-middle-class backgrounds.[4] At the time of the interviews, two-thirds of the women were working full-time (28), 3 were working part-time, 7 were in school full-time (and not working), and 4 were out of the labor force for other reasons (2 were caring for their young children, 1 was not working as a result of a severe disability, and 1 was in prison). Slightly more than one-third had completed a bachelor's degree.

Half of the interviewees were involved in committed relationships: 10 were married, 3 were engaged,

8 were in exclusive relationships, and 1 was divorced and involved in a new relationship. Although none of the women directly labeled themselves as lesbians, 2 suggested this possibility.... Although it would be interesting to examine whether young lesbian and bisexual women would report different perceptions of feminism than heterosexual young women, this issue cannot be adequately addressed with my sample.

One-third (14) of the interviewees had become mothers by the time of the interviews. Ten of these women were single parents, while 4 of them were married. However, nearly all had previously been single parents; only 1 woman was married prior to becoming a parent.

... In the analysis that follows, using pseudonyms for my respondents, I examine several key issues that emerged during the interviews. First, to provide a context for attitudes toward feminism, I consider two themes about women's treatment by society: perceptions of opportunities and obstacles, and experiences with gender discrimination. I then explicate the five approaches to feminist identification that came out of my analysis of the interviews.

PERCEPTIONS OF OPPORTUNITIES AND OBSTACLES

My interviews revealed a general optimism about women's expanded opportunities, coupled with a realization that older women have struggled to create these new opportunities. At the same time, most (35 out of 42) of the interviewees were quite aware that gender-based obstacles still remained. These perspectives were shared by women of all racial and class backgrounds and life experiences.

A majority (36) of the interviewees discussed women's current opportunities in terms of expanded educational and career choices, which have in turn led to women's independence from men and new family arrangements. For example, Hoa, a middle-class Vietnamese American woman who was in law school at the time of the interview, said that women used to think "'I will *marry* a doctor. I will *marry* a lawyer.' It was never: 'I will *become* one.'" Nora, a working-class Hispanic woman, saw this issue in generational terms:

When my mom was growing up, *men* pretty much *ruled* it.... [Men] decided what would happen *when* and where you were going to go and where you're

going to live. Nowadays men have an opinion, but that's all it is.... Women have their opinions and can go with what they want to do.... They can make their own decisions without men.

There was widespread awareness that changes resulted from the struggles of older women, who helped to create new opportunities. Although most of the interviewees attributed these changes to an aggregate of individuals who became "fed up" or "got sick and tired" of gender inequalities, a number credited the women's movement directly.

At the same time, 35 of the interviewees also observed that women continue to face many obstacles, including sexism, difficulty balancing conflicting work and family demands, greater responsibility than men for child rearing and domestic work, and violence against women. For example, Esther, a working-class white woman, said, "Although it's changing, I think that there's a lot of things that are still real male dominated." Nine of the interviewees mentioned that new opportunities have produced new strains, particularly balancing work and family. As Linda, a middle-class white woman working in a traditionally male field, put it, "Companies aren't supportive yet of working mothers."

This recognition of the need for further social change diverges from prior research on the postfeminist generation in two ways. While the micro cohort of women I interviewed here may be more aware of obstacles than prior postfeminist micro cohorts (Whittier 1995), my respondents were more diverse in background than prior studies and thus may have been more apt to perceive obstacles. At the same time that this recognition of inequalities and their illegitimacy suggests significant gender consciousness, my interviewees stopped short of a collective orientation focused on women's movement activism (Gurin 1985, 1987).

EXPERIENCES WITH GENDER DISCRIMINATION

Have these young women experienced discrimination? Although only 6 (14 percent) of the 42 interviewees felt they had experienced blatant instances of gender discrimination, nearly all had experienced what they considered to be minor instances of discrimination or were aware of its possibility in the future. Specifically, a third (14) were concerned about workplace inequality and discrimination. Nearly a quarter (10) approached discrimination somewhat paradoxically: They did not expect that gender discrimination would have an impact on their lives, despite the subtle instances of discrimination that they had experienced. The final quarter (12 out of 42) of interviewees focused on individual solutions to discrimination, such as confronting their perpetrator. In all, these findings reveal a substantial awareness of gender discrimination.

Of the six women who recounted instances of blatant gender discrimination, the main problem was workplace discrimination and sexual harassment. For example, Shonda, a working-class African American woman, experienced both gender and racial discrimination on the job. Although she was aware that she could have filed a lawsuit, her more immediate concern of financially supporting her two children took precedence.

One-third of the women were concerned about future discrimination, including pay equity, hitting a "glass ceiling," and career advancement. Reflecting the career trajectories that these women anticipated, most of those with this approach were middle-class white women with college educations. For example, Linda, a middle-class white woman who worked in the field of accounting, said, "I can see being a woman coming in the way. I work for a company that does still have a little bit of the old boy's club at the upper management."

Nearly a quarter of the interviewees did not originally label their own experiences "discrimination" but realized through telling their stories that gender inequalities were, in fact, part of their life experience. For example, when I asked Sherri, an upper-middle-class white woman who worked in a hospital, whether she had experienced discrimination, she said, "I never thought about it. Probably because in my field it's mostly women." She went on to say the following:

> The highest paid people around here are *men*. I *do* think that's a big obstacle for women—that it's a male, white, male-dominated world, and they're the ones who make the rules. . . . It's not something that I worry about, but I think that's a big obstacle for women.

Similarly, Hillary, a working-class Korean American woman, never felt less "capable" as a result of being a woman, yet she described women's second shift with regard to household responsibilities and her anger at feeling afraid to walk alone at night. Illustrating both an awareness, and the minimizing, of gender

discrimination, she said, "Other than the constraints that I felt being a woman, I really don't think that I've . . . missed out on opportunities . . . because I'm a woman, luckily." This paradoxical approach indicates that some women are reluctant to label their experiences with inequality as "discrimination" because they define discrimination narrowly in terms of blatant workplace harassment.

The remaining quarter of the women in this study focused on individual solutions to the problem of discrimination, such as confronting the perpetrator. For example, Felicia, a middle-class white woman, said she wouldn't "tolerate" discrimination: "I feel . . . like I can take care of myself. Some man might want to put me back in my place, but I think I'm a tough little bitch . . . ! Take some karate classes!" Here, individual resistance to discrimination resulted in feelings of personal strength, yet it is important to note that this approach is based on an assumption that individuals must be strong enough to defend themselves against discriminatory actions. Other women focused on the impact of their own choices, particularly choosing female-dominated careers. For example, Kelly, a middle-class white woman who worked in female-dominated retail, said that discrimination "*definitely* hasn't affected me. . . . I haven't been in a situation where it's been more of a man's field. . . . I've never, *ever* felt discriminated [against]."[5]

In sum, although only a small proportion of the interviewees felt that they had experienced blatant gender discrimination, most of the women had known it in minor ways and expressed some concern about it in the future. These findings run contrary to past studies, which imply that young women are unrealistic about the forces that have the potential to hold them back (Coppock, Haydon, and Richter 1995; Sigel 1996; Stacey 1987).[6] At the same time, the term *discrimination* was itself often defined in a narrow way, to include only blatant instances of workplace inequality. This low level of awareness may result from the successes of the women's movement, which have made discrimination less pronounced than in the past. It may also reflect arguments made by other scholars: Women partially accept discrimination as a given because they try to protect themselves from its negative effects (Sigel 1996), or they may feel helpless when thinking of themselves as victims (Gurin 1987). The extent of gender consciousness observed here does not include a collective orientation (Gurin 1985, 1987) since the emphasis was on individual responsibility rather than a broader framework of inequality. It may be that such a political vision, based on social movement involvement, is not available to these women.

ATTITUDES TOWARD FEMINISM

When asked about their attitudes toward feminism, nearly half of these women's responses could be categorized on the continuums developed in previous studies (e.g., Kamen 1991; Taylor 1996) including those who identified as feminists, those who called themselves feminists but qualified their support, and those who said they were not feminists but supported a range of feminist issues. However, suggesting ambiguity in the term *feminism* and its negative connotations, more than half of these women did not want to explicitly define themselves in relation to feminism at all. Most of these interviewees were, in the words of one woman, "fence-sitters": They embraced a number of feminist principles yet rejected others and failed to classify themselves as either feminists or nonfeminists. In addition, nearly a quarter had never thought about feminism as a concept and were unable to articulate an opinion altogether. Despite this ambiguity, nearly all of the interviewees were supportive of feminist issues.

Racial and Class Background and Life Experience

Attitudes toward feminism were differentiated by racial and class background and life experience. . . . In the interviews, nearly a quarter of the women (10 out of 42) identified themselves as feminists. Among this group, 6 defined themselves as feminists without qualifying what they meant by the term *feminist,* while 4 qualified their support by outlining the specific aspects of feminism with which they agreed and disagreed. Those who did not qualify their support were nearly all white or middle class; all were college educated and came to feminism as a result of their experiences with women's studies courses. The women who qualified their feminist identities were women of color or white working-class women who had nearly all attended college but had no experience with women's studies courses.

As young women are most commonly characterized in other research, eight of the interviewees (19 percent) defined themselves as not being feminists but

agreed with many of the principles of feminist ideology. Nearly all of these interviewees were from quite privileged backgrounds—close to 90 percent were white and middle to upper-middle class. However, unlike the nearly all-white and middle-class group who called themselves feminists, only two of these women had attended college and neither had taken women's studies courses.

One-third of the interview sample (13 out of 42 interviewees) were what one woman called "fence-sitters" since they would not position themselves in relation to feminism as an identity. These women were evenly divided in their life experiences and proportionally divided along racial lines, although a greater proportion were from working-class backgrounds.

One-quarter of the interviewees (11 out of 42) were uncertain about their attitudes toward feminism yet endorsed an ideology of equality. Among these women who never thought about feminism, the majority (7 out of 11) were young parents—typically single parents—while the others were focused on the full-time labor force; none had completed a four-year college degree. In addition, a disproportionate number of these interviewees were women of color. A number of these women experienced great stress in daily living, leaving little time for reflection about such issues. This suggests that not only racial and class background but also life paths and life experience in early adulthood may be linked to attitudes toward feminism. I will now consider each of these approaches in turn.

"I'm a Feminist"

Among those who identified as feminists without qualifying their support, feminism was viewed primarily as an ideology of equality. The women in this group were supportive of equal opportunity, abortion rights, equality in childhood socialization, and "social justice" and were concerned about issues such as sexual assault. These interviewees largely came to see themselves as feminists as a result of taking women's studies courses. Tina, a working-class white woman, said that a woman's studies course "started the whole movement for *me.* . . . If I hadn't taken that class . . . I could be married with 6 children right now!" Involvement in women's studies courses reveals that young feminists are not only highly educated but also exposed to feminist ideologies through an institutional location that supports and legitimates feminist perspectives.

"I'm a Feminist, but . . ."

Those who defined themselves as feminists but quali-fied their support came to their views not through women's studies courses but through assumptions of equality inherent in the attitudes of their families when they were growing up. Although they called them-selves feminists, they also distanced themselves from certain negative associations of feminism. For example, Esther, a working-class white woman, said, "Feminism has gotten a bad rap . . . that it's sort of this *angry, radi-cal* [view-point]. . . . I consider myself a feminist, defi-nitely. I consider myself a *strong* feminist, but I'm not someone who is always needing to assert it." Although she endorsed an ideology of equality and supported diversity in men's and women's work and family arrangements, Esther distanced herself from two nega-tive associations with feminism: those who "always assert" their viewpoints and those who "want to alien-ate men."

These women grew up with an assumption of equality in their families, yet this may itself explain why they qualify their feminist identities. As Esther put it,

> Feminism isn't something that I've had to *discover* on my own. . . . People who *just* discover . . . *activism* or *feminism* . . . are . . . more vocal about it and . . . *cham-pion* it because it's new and different. And I feel like it's just a *given* that everyone should be treated equally. It's just a *given* that . . . because I'm a woman, that doesn't stop me from doing whatever I want to do.

"I'm Not a Feminist, but . . ."

Nineteen percent of the interviewees distanced them-selves from feminism while endorsing many of the principles of feminist ideology. One example of this perspective comes from Betsy, a middle-class white woman, who said, "I'm *not* a feminist, I would say. Probably a lot of feminists wouldn't like me. But, well, I mean I guess it depends on what feminism. . . . I think everybody should be treated equally at the base." These women gave several reasons for dis-tancing themselves from the identity of "feminist." A number of interviewees felt that feminism goes "too far." Whitney, a middle-class Korean American woman, said that "a lot of feminism goes overboard," yet she suspected that she had this view because she herself had never faced discrimination: "Maybe

people who are a little bit older or have been discrimi-nated against [call themselves feminists] and I haven't really experienced that. So, I mean if I had, maybe I would become a feminist, but I either don't *see* it [or] haven't *been*" discriminated against. Here, feminism is seen as a place where grievances against discrimi-nation can be voiced, rather than a perspective that sees power inequalities influencing every domain of gender relations.

Other interviewees distanced themselves from activism and political engagement. Dawn, an upper-middle-class white woman, appreciated the benefits of the women's movement, particularly educational and occupational opportunities, and was supportive of equality more generally. At the same time, she said, "I *don't* believe that I would consider *myself* a feminist." Implying that it was activism from which she distanced herself, she said, "I don't go out every day and say 'wom-en's rights and more opportunities for women. . . . I don't think about it on a day-to-day basis." Similarly, Linda, a middle-class white woman, said of feminism: "Folks should just live their lives and not get so caught up in everything." Clearly, these women's gender con-sciousness does not include a collective orientation (Gurin 1985, 1987).

These women also distanced themselves from femi-nism as a result of negative perceptions of feminists, particularly lesbianism and separatism from men. For example, although Alice, a middle-class white woman, said, "I just think that everybody is *equal*," she did not want to distance herself from men: "I don't go around bashing men. . . . I *like* men." Linda thought that being a feminist meant that she could not live the type of life she wanted to lead:

> I have a couple of feminist friends that have *very* differ-ent views than I do. . . . My boyfriend's sister is a femi-nist, and she will *never* have children. She will probably *never* get married. And that's fine, but that's not what I want to do. That's not the life that I want to lead. I want to raise a family.

This perspective reflects the antifeminist movement and the media's construction of feminists as lesbians and militants (Faludi 1991; Marx Ferree and Hess 1995). As was also the case in previous eras (e.g., Marshall 1997), the media have perpetuated "the social climate of antifeminism and thwart[ed] the possibility of mobilizing discontented women" (Rupp and Taylor 1987).

"I'm a Fence-Sitter"

The fence-sitting approach (taken by one-third of the women) reveals a paradox: support for feminist issues, as well as the ambiguous connotations of "feminism" today. Rather than identifying themselves in relation to feminist identity, these women focused on evaluating the ideologies and stereotypes associated with feminism. This group is distinct from the others because they would not classify themselves as either feminists or nonfeminists. In embracing ambiguity, they truly remained "on the fence." In some respects, they evaded the interview questions and chose instead to support and critique aspects of the term *feminism*.

One woman who took this approach was Ann, who is working class and white. When I asked her thoughts about feminism, she said, "I'd be supportive," yet she stopped short of calling herself a feminist. She went on to call herself a fence-sitter and said, "I would still be reserved about some things." When asked to elaborate, she discussed only her support of feminist issues: eradicating the "perpetuation" of stereotypes about women, violence against women, governmental cuts in welfare, and sexual harassment and favoring comparable worth and gay rights. Likewise, Susan, a middle-class white woman, said that "a lot of feminism is lesbianism" and she did not want to "go hate men." She also recognized this stereotype as a "big generalization" about feminists. In fact, she had enjoyed taking women's studies courses in college: "As far as identifying similar experiences and . . . feeling like you're not alone, that's what I *like* about feminism."

Other studies have also found that some women reject feminism because they are worried about creating "male antagonism" (Sigel 1996, 114). These views may reflect a general reluctance to express anger over discrimination because some women accept unfairness, see discrimination as realistic, or want to protect themselves from recognizing inequality (Sigel 1996). Stereotypes against feminists have been powerfully advanced by the antifeminist movement and the media, which may have influenced these women's views.

"I Never Thought About Feminism"

The remaining quarter (11 out of 42) of the interviewees expressed a great deal of uncertainty about their attitudes toward feminism, had no opinion on the topic, or had substantial difficulty defining the term itself. Of these women, most felt that they were unable to comment because they did not know enough about feminism or had never thought about it in enough depth to express an opinion. One interviewee who was unable to articulate an opinion was Kelly, a middle-class white woman. Although she felt that "women should have the same rights as a man does," she said that she had "never been a real *strong* activist." Kelly went on to explain her view as follows: "I don't really have a lot of feelings on that because I kind of take it as it is. . . . I don't really think about that kind of stuff." Kim, a middle-class white woman, said, "I don't even really know what [feminism] *is*."

Why were these women unable or unwilling to articulate an opinion of feminism? Some of the interviewees were simply confused over the definition of feminism. For others, feminism was implicitly defined as an activist approach that addressed discrimination and thus did not have personal relevance. For example, when I asked Caroline, an upper-middle-class white woman, about her view of feminism, she said that "nothing has *happened* to me that I would have to be that way." Here, being "that way" connotes that feminist perspectives go along with discrimination: without it, there was no need to think about feminism. Other women also saw feminism as irrelevant to their everyday lives. Jill, a middle-class, white, single parent of two children, was explicit that she had more pressing daily issues to worry about than feminism:

> I don't care. No big thing. I've never been treated unfairly by a man. I don't think I have. . . . I blow off things, because I'm an easy come, easy go [person]. I'm already stressed out with kids and a job. . . . I don't need to be stressed out about things like that. So [in terms of] *feminism*, I don't *care*. Who *cares*?

To Jill, feminism is irrelevant, perhaps even frivolous, when compared with the struggles of combining work and single motherhood. Feminism is primarily a way to redress workplace discrimination, in contrast to confronting issues that are central to basic survival as a woman. Ironically, both Caroline and Jill (in another part of the interview) also recounted their own experiences with domestic violence, suggesting that some of the women who would benefit the most from a feminist political perspective or agenda see it as the least relevant to their own lives.

At the same time, these women were supportive of equality between men and women. For example, Yolanda, a working-class biracial (African American and white) single parent said,

> I can change a tire. I can change oil . . . and I don't have a problem with it. And I can move my *own* furniture, *pregnant* or *not,* you know?! . . . When a guy tells me I can't do something, I'll tell him to *prove* it. . . . I'll tell a guy off real quick if he tells *me* that [I can't do something] because of my gender.

As I explore elsewhere (Aronson 1999, 2001), the young women in this study (even the engaged and married women) emphasized the importance of their own independence from men in many areas of their lives—career, finances, childbearing and child rearing, and self-development. In fact, marital status does not seem to make any difference in attitudes toward feminism, as women with different relationships to men were evenly dispersed among the groups examined here.

CONCLUSIONS

My findings about the widespread awareness of the extent of gender inequality run contrary to prior studies of the postfeminist generation (Renzetti 1987; Rupp 1988; Sigel 1996; Stacey 1987, 1991). And while many of the interviewees fit on a continuum of feminist identification previously defined by other researchers (Kamen 1991; Sigel 1996; Taylor 1989), more than half of the young women in this study approached feminism even more ambiguously than previously reported, especially the fence-sitters who embrace some aspects of feminism while rejecting others and avoid defining themselves in relation to the identity of feminist.

My findings also extend prior research by illustrating that attitudes toward feminism are shaped by racial and class background, and also by life experience. No prior studies have examined the role of diverse types of life experience in developing particular attitudes toward feminism. I have shown that the feminist identification without qualification and the "I'm not a feminist, but . . ." approach are associated with more privileged racial and class backgrounds. The feminists were more likely to be college educated, and most had taken women's studies courses. Those who qualified their feminist identities and those who had never

thought about feminism were disproportionately from less privileged racial and class backgrounds, but their life experience differentiates them from the other groups as well. The "qualified" feminists were college-educated, working-class women and/or women of color who came to feminism as a result of assumptions of equality when growing up. Among the women who had never thought about feminism, two-thirds had become parents early in life, and none had pursued a college degree.

My findings also indicate that young women's development of a feminist perspective and identity is tied closely with institutions that support and nurture such a perspective—particularly women's studies programs. This institutionalization of feminism has occurred at the same time as antifeminist organizations and media figures have advanced negative stereotypes that have become incorporated in some young women's conceptions of feminism. In addition, although the women of color that I interviewed were supportive of equality, most distanced themselves from the identity of feminist, suggesting that the institutional supports for feminism may be more appealing or available to white women.

This study also suggests that having the space to think about political issues such as feminism may be a luxury that some young women, especially single mothers, cannot afford. For these women, feminism was seen as lacking personal relevance and viewed primarily as a place to redress workplace discrimination. Many of these women had never thought about their positions on feminism or saw it as frivolous when compared with the struggles of supporting and raising their children. Obviously, this is a broader problem than simply creating better public relations within feminist organizations, as it involves developing new initiatives and expanding institutional power. A new wave of political organizing might in turn lead to new personal understandings of feminism at later points in the life course (Aronson 2000).

Most important, whether or not young women call themselves feminists, they support feminist goals. In fact, the young women I interviewed were more supportive of feminism than had been found in past research, and none expressed antifeminist sentiments. The fence-sitting stance, while not as politicized as in previous generations, is not entirely individualized and apolitical either. Although most researchers and the media have painted a pessimistic view of young women's ambivalence, I believe that my results offer some promise for feminism. Many of these young women may be passive supporters rather than agents of change, but they are supporters nonetheless. Their endorsement may represent the seeds of change, which, under the right historical conditions, and in interaction with the growth of grassroots feminist organizing, could blossom into the next wave of the women's movement.

ACKNOWLEDGMENTS

This research was supported by a National Research Service Award from the National Institute of Mental Health (Training Program in Identity, Self, Role, and Mental Health—PHST 32 MH 14588), the National Institute of Mental Health (MH 42843, Jeylan T. Mortimer, principal investigator), the Personal Narratives Award from the Center for Advanced Feminist Studies, University of Minnesota, and a Graduate School Block Grant Stipend Award from the Department of Sociology, University of Minnesota. The author would like to thank a number of people who provided comments and suggestions on earlier versions of this article: Ronald Aronson, Christine Bose, Donna Eder, Debbie Engelen-Eigles, Amy Kaler, Barbara Laslett, Jane McLeod, Jeylan T. Mortimer, Irene Padavic, Katie See, Beth Schneider, and Kim Simmons, as well as the social psychology seminar members at Indiana University and several anonymous reviewers.

NOTES

1. I would like to thank Karen Lutfey for the origination of this phrase.
2. This term had also been used after the first-wave women's movement (Taylor 1996).
3. For details about methodology, see the original article from which this selection is excerpted.
4. Social class background was based on parents' income and education as reported in the parent surveys in the first year of the study (1988). "Working class" includes those whose parents had less than a bachelor's degree and earned less than $30,000 per year in 1988. "Middle class" includes four subgroups: parents who had high educational attainment (at least a bachelor's degree) and low income (less than $30,000 per year in 1988), low educational attainment (less than a bachelor's degree) but high income (at least $50,000 per year in 1988), high education (at least a bachelor's degree) and middle income (between $30,000 and $50,000 per year in 1988), and low education (less than a bachelor's degree) and middle income. "Upper-middle class" includes those parents who had high educational attainment (at least a bachelor's degree) and earned a middle to high income (more than $50,000 per year in 1988).
5. This lack of salience of gender discrimination within female-dominated occupations is supported by Slevin and Wingrove's (1998) findings that African American women do not find race to be extremely salient when working in African American organizations.
6. It is possible that the differences between my study and prior findings result from historical shifts—that this micro cohort of young women is more aware of inequalities than prior micro cohorts of the postfeminist generation (Whittier 1995).

REFERENCES

Aronson, Pamela. 1999. The balancing act: Young women's expectations and experiences of work and family. In *Research in the sociology of work*, vol. 7, edited by Toby Parcel. Stamford, CT: JAI.

———. 2000. The development and transformation of feminist identities under changing historical conditions. In *Advances in life course research: Identity across the life course in cross-cultural perspective*, vol. 5, edited by Timothy J. Owens. Stamford, CT: JAI.

———. 2001. The markers and meanings of growing up: Contemporary young women's transition to adulthood. Paper presented at the annual meeting of the American Sociological Association, Anaheim, CA.

Bellafante, Ginia. 1998. Is feminism dead? *Time Magazine*, 29 June, 25.

Bolotin, Susan. 1982. Views from the post-feminist generation. *New York Times Magazine*, 17 October, 29–31, 103–16.

Brenner, Johanna. 1996. The best of times, the worst of times: Feminism in the United States. In *Mapping the women's movement: Feminist politics and social transformation in the North*, edited by Monica Threlfall. London: Verso.

Budgeon, Shelley, and Dawn Currie. 1995. From feminism to postfeminism: Women's liberation in fashion magazines. *Women's Studies International Forum* 18 (2): 173–86.

Coppock, Vicki, Deena Haydon, and Ingrid Richter. 1995. *The illusions of "post-feminism": New women, old myths*. London: Taylor and Francis.

Faludi, Susan. 1991. *Backlash: The undeclared war against American women*. New York: Crown.

Gurin, Patricia. 1985. Women's gender consciousness. *Public Opinion Quarterly* 49 (2): 143–63.

———. 1987. The political implications of women's statuses. In *Spouse, parent, worker: On gender and multiple roles*, edited by Faye J. Crosby. New Haven, CT: Yale University Press.

Henderson-King, Donna, and Abigail Stewart. 1994. Women or feminists? Assessing women's group consciousness. *Sex Roles* 31 (9–10): 505–16.

Heywood, Leslie, and Jennifer Drake. 1997. Introduction. *Third wave agenda: Being feminist, doing feminism*, edited by Leslie Heywood and Jennifer Drake. Minneapolis: University of Minnesota Press.

Hurtado, Aida. 1998. Sitios y lenguas: Chicanas theorize feminisms. *Hypatia* 13 (2): 134–61.

Kamen, Paula. 1991. *Feminist fatale: Voices from the "twenty-something" generation explore the future of the "women's movement."* New York: Donald I. Fine.

Marshall, Susan. 1997. *Splintered sisterhood: Gender and class in the campaign against woman suffrage.* Madison: University of Wisconsin Press.

Marx Ferree, Myra, and Beth B. Hess. 1995. *Controversy and coalition: The new feminist movement across four decades of change.* 3d ed. New York: Routledge.

Marx Ferree, Myra, and Patricia Yancey Martin. 1995. *Feminist organizations: Harvest of the new women's movement.* Philadelphia: Temple University Press.

Morgan, Debi. 1995. Invisible women: Young women and feminism. In *Feminist activism in the 1990s,* edited by Gabriele Griffin. London: Taylor and Francis.

Overholser, Geneva. 1986. What "post-feminism" really means. *New York Times,* 19 September, 30.

Percy, Carol, and John Kremer. 1995. Feminist identifications in a troubled society. *Feminism and Psychology* 5 (2): 201–22.

Renzetti, Claire. 1987. New wave or second stage? Attitudes of college women toward feminism. *Sex Roles* 16 (5/6): 265–77.

Rosenberg, Jessica, and Gitana Garofalo. 1998. Riot grrrl: Revolutions from within. *Signs: Journal of Women in Culture and Society* 23 (3): 809–41.

Rosenfelt, Deborah, and Judith Stacey. 1987. Second thoughts on the second wave. *Feminist Studies* 13 (2): 341–61.

Rossi, Alice. 1982. *Feminists in politics.* New York: Academic.

Rupp, Lelia, and Verta Taylor. 1987. *Survival in the doldrums: The American women's rights movement, 1945 to the 1960s.* New York: Oxford University Press.

Rupp, Rayna. 1988. Is the legacy of second-wave feminism postfeminism? *Socialist Review* (January–March): 52–57.

Schneider, Beth. 1988. Political generations and the contemporary women's movement. *Sociological Inquiry* 58: 4–21.

Sigel, Roberta. 1996. *Ambition and accommodation: How women view gender relations.* Chicago: University of Chicago Press.

Slevin, Kathleen F., and C. Ray Wingrove. 1998. *From stumbling blocks to stepping stones: The life experiences of fifty professional African American women.* New York: New York University Press.

Springer, Kimberly. 2002. Third wave Black feminism? *Signs: Journal of Women in Culture and Society* 27 (4): 1059–82.

Stacey, Judith. 1987. Sexism by a subtler name? Postindustrial conditions and postfeminist consciousness in the Silicon Valley. *Socialist Review* 17 (6): 7–28.

———. 1991. *Brave new families: Stories of domestic upheaval in late twentieth century America.* New York Basic Books.

Taylor, Verta. 1996. *Rock-a-by baby: Feminism, self-help, and postpartum depression.* New York: Routledge.

———. 1989. Social movement continuity: The women's movement in abeyance. *American Sociological Review* 54:761–75.

Taylor, Verta, and Lelia Rupp. 1993. Women's culture and lesbian feminist activism: A reconsideration of cultural feminism. *Signs: Journal of Women in Culture and Society* 19 (1): 32–61.

Unger, Rhoda. 1989. Explorations in feminist ideology: Surprising consistencies and unexamined conflicts. In *Representations: Social constructions of gender,* edited by Rhoda Unger. Amityville, NY: Baywood.

Wald, Gayle. 1998. Just a girl? Rock music, feminism, and the cultural construction of female youth. *Signs: Journal of Women in Culture and Society* 23 (3): 585–610.

Walker, Rebecca. 1995. *To be real: Telling the truth and changing the face of feminism.* New York: Anchor.

Weis, Lois. 1990. *Working class without work: High school students in a de-industrializing economy.* New York: Routledge.

Whittier, Nancy. 1995. *Feminist generations: The persistence of the radical women's movement.* Philadelphia: Temple University Press.

TRANSFORM THE WORLD:
WHAT YOU CAN DO WITH A DEGREE IN WOMEN'S STUDIES

Nikki Ayanna Stewart

A. Become the first woman president of Harvard University
B. Win a Rhodes Scholarship to study sexual civil rights
C. Advocate for domestic-violence survivors while starring on TV's *Survivor*
D. Teach the next generation
E. All of the above, and more

It's a typical question from parents, fellow students and even faculty: What can you do with your college degree? In an era of conservative impediments to progressive liberal arts education, a field such as women's studies seems a particularly common target for that query.

Recently, we have had at least one excellent role model to point to: Drew Gilpin Faust, the first woman president of Harvard. She may have earned her Ph.D. in American civilization, but she was formerly chair of the women's studies program at the University of Pennsylvania and founding dean of the Radcliffe Institute for Advanced Study. Under her leadership, Radcliffe—Harvard's former women's college—has become an interdisciplinary research center supporting "transformative works," with a special commitment to studying women, gender and society. In a similar fashion, many women's studies majors tend to intermix their fields of concentration in order to craft distinctive careers aimed at transforming our world.

How many women's studies grads are we talking about? According to the National Center for Education Statistics, in the 2003–2004 academic year U.S. institutions of higher education granted 1,024 bachelor's degrees, 135 master's degrees and five doctoral degrees in women's studies. These statistics, however, are suspect, given that the National Women's Studies Association (NWSA) has documented 750 active undergraduate and graduate women's studies programs in U.S. colleges and universities.

"It is very difficult to get a picture of women's studies as a field," says Allison Kimmich, executive director of the NWSA and a Ph.D. in women's studies from Emory University, "particularly the number of graduates now out in the workforce and the kinds of career paths those graduates have taken. Women's studies has not historically collected that data on itself." A clearer picture of women's studies programs should begin to emerge, however, as NWSA has embarked on a Ford Foundation–funded project to map women's and gender studies in the U.S. In the future, the association hopes to collect data on graduates' career paths.

Earlier studies of women's studies graduates, such as that by Barbara F. Luebke and Mary Ellen Reilly in their 1995 book *Women's Studies Graduates: The First Generation* (Teachers College Press), were similarly concerned with documenting the value of such degrees. They found that the fact that women's studies majors and graduates were persistently asked what could be done with their degrees reflected a continuing ignorance about women's studies as an academic discipline. In their study, Luebke and Reilly were also able to document a unique set of skills learned through women's studies programs: empowerment, self-confidence, critical thinking, building community, and understanding differences and intersections among racism, homophobia, sexism, classism, ableism, anti-Semitism and other types of oppression.

Moya Bailey, a B.A. in comparative women's studies at Spelman College (the first historically black U.S. college to offer a women's studies major) and now a Ph.D. student in women's studies at Emory University, has already been able to use some of her women's studies skills in community action. While at Spelman, Bailey participated in "The Nelly Protest," a nationally publicized demonstration against misogyny in hip-hop music and videos.

That and other protest actions were so meaningful to her that, as a doctoral student at Emory, she

(continued)

has studied how "intentional communities"—like the nurturing spaces often created by women's studies programs—assist marginalized groups to develop much-needed critical and political perspectives. Within 10 years, she hopes to be teaching women's studies at a historically black college or university, "adding gender, class and sexuality as important pieces of the conversation within an African American community context."

Similarly, Harvard undergraduate Ryan Thoreson hopes to develop a career focused on the intersection of multiple concerns. As a dual major in government and women/gender/sexuality studies, Thoreson believes that women's studies will enrich his planned practice of international sexual civil-rights law. "In my government courses I learned about political theory, but I found the political theory I learned in my women's studies curriculum to be much more broadly applicable," says Thoreson, a Rhodes Scholarship winner. "If I had only majored in government, I would not come to legal and policy questions as thoughtfully, wanting to understand the social and cultural context of groups affected by the law."

Maria Bevacqua, associate professor and chair of the Department of Women's Studies at Minnesota State University, Mankato, believes that women's studies has carved out a niche in the area of applied theory and practice. Like many programs, Mankato's women's studies curriculum includes internships in feminist organizations and collective action projects for course credit. Bevacqua—who has her own women's studies Ph.D. from Emory—has seen her program's graduates do everything from working in human service agencies to opening feminist businesses. Moreover, women's studies graduates act as "ambassadors of feminism, bringing the women's studies perspective into the rest of the world."

Beverly Guy-Sheftall, founding director of the Women's Research and Resource Center and professor of women's studies at Spelman, has increasingly seen students' take women's studies into the public sphere. "In the early years, women's studies graduates tended to work on gender-specific issues,

getting jobs in battered-women's shelters and rape crisis centers," she says. "But more and more we have students going into public health, international policy, journalism, electoral politics, filmmaking, K–12 education and other careers that allow them to effect large-scale change."

Guy-Sheftall has also seen students increasingly desire to be public intellectuals and media producers, so much so that Spelman has incorporated digital media production into its women's studies curriculum. "I think we are going to see many more women's studies graduates going into film and television, and many of our students already produce documentaries—even if they choose to do something else as a career."

Deborah Siegel, author of the forthcoming book *Sisterhood, Interrupted: From Radical Women to Grrls Gone Wild,* has noticed the same thing. She observes that in the 1970s, "women's studies was about bridging the divide between scholarship and activism. This current generation is bridging scholarship, activism and *media*."

Becky Lee is representative of this new generation. After acquiring a B.A. in women's studies from the University of Michigan in 2000, Lee went on to law school and then worked as an advocate for domestic-violence survivors. While doing this work, she was approached to audition for the popular reality TV show *Survivor*. Thinking it could serve as a good platform for her cause, she joined the cast, and while she found that most of her statements on domestic violence got left on the editing floor, she has used the *Survivor* experience to expand her advocacy.

"I came in third and used my $75,000 prize to found a fund for domestic-violence prevention with a special focus on immigrant women from marginalized communities," she says. "Now when I make public appearances for the show, I talk about the fund as a way to raise the issue of domestic violence for mainstream audiences."

So what can *you* do with a degree in women's studies? Perhaps transform enough minds through feminist education that this question is no longer asked.

Grace Chang

From the Third World to the "Third World Within": Asian Women Workers Fighting Globalization

The present form of globalization has not produced enough jobs for all those who seek them or in the places where they are most needed. This is probably its biggest failure.

—Juan Somavia, Director-General,
International Labor Organization[1]

I want to begin to dispel the myths. It's not about mail-order brides. Hello, this is a global world. . . . We are a global population.

—Mike Krosky, Owner, Cherry Blossoms[2]

INTRODUCTION

These observations on globalization probably could not have come from more distant corners. Juan Somavia's comment, addressed to representatives from 175 International Labor Organization member countries was intended to be sobering. He warned that the failure of globalization to create new jobs in developing countries has fueled and will continue to fuel massive migration worldwide. He estimated that about 500 million jobs will have to be created over the next decade just to accommodate the young people and women now entering the labor market.

In contrast, Mike Krosky's comment from an interview about his Cherry Blossoms business is positively celebratory. Krosky's business lists over 6000 women available for order through print catalogs and a web site, half of whom are Filipina. The next largest group is Indonesian, and the group showing the greatest increase comes from Eastern European countries. Krosky celebrates globalization not only because of huge business profits, but also for his personal satisfaction as the happy husband of a Filipina more than 18 years his junior, whom he met through his own service.

Both these comments speak directly or otherwise to an important but often neglected aspect of globalization: migrations of Third World people from their homes as a result of the destruction wrought by globalization on their abilities to survive at home.

I want to address this dimension of globalization, particularly Third World women's migrations, and, like Mike Krosky, I want to begin to dispel the myths. I also want to address the reality that in today's globalized context, virtually all migration can be seen as coerced through economic means, through the institutionalized underdevelopment and impoverishment of Third World nations and people.

A few years ago I had the privilege of speaking on an International Women's Day radio program with Ethel Long Scott of the Women's Economic Agenda Project. Scott remarked that we must talk about globalization in its proper terms, as the *globalization of poverty*—that is, the creation, perpetuation, and exacerbation of poverty worldwide. Scott also cautioned listeners not to think that the ravages of globalization are confined "over there" in the Third World but to examine its impacts in our own communities of color.[3] Scott raised an important point missing from many debates surrounding globalization—that those in the Third World and those in the "Third World within" First World countries share these conditions and thus are central to the struggles against this globalization of poverty.[4]

I will examine how women of color and migrant women in First World host nations experience the impact of globalization on their lives and livelihoods daily and forge resistance to these impact daily. Specifically, I look at the struggles of Filipina migrant workers in the U.S. and Canada—women who suffer these impacts on both ends of the global "trade route." I interviewed members of two migrant domestic worker organizations, one in

Vancouver, Canada, and the other in Bronx, New York, who provide important models for critical gender analyses of globalization and organized resistance against it.

Many of us who attended the 1995 Non-Governmental Organizations (NGO) Forum on Women as members of the U.S. women of color delegation were humbled by our Third World sisters who danced circles around us in their analyses and first-hand knowledge of global economic restructuring and its impact. Poor women of color throughout the world suffer first and worst under globalization. They experience so-called "development" and "free trade" as losses in status, freedom, safety, education, access to basic needs of food, water, housing, and health care—indeed, as assaults on their very survival. As the first victims of globalization, poor women of color are also the primary leaders in fighting back, in resisting the so-called "New World Order" that they know is not new at all but a continuation of neo-imperialist activities into the 21st century.

GLOBAL ECONOMIC RESTRUCTURING

At the Fourth World NGO Forum on Women held in China in 1995, women from Africa, Latin America, the Middle East, and Asia echoed the same truth in their testimonies: Global economic restructuring embodied in Structural Adjustment Programs (SAPs) strikes poor women of color around the world the hardest, rendering them most vulnerable to exploitation both at home and in the global labor market. Since the 1980s, the World Bank, International Monetary Fund (IMF), and other international financial institutions based in the First World have routinely prescribed structural adjustment policies to the governments of indebted countries as preconditions for loans. These prescriptions included cutting government expenditures on social programs, slashing wages, liberalizing imports, opening markets to foreign investment, expanding exports, devaluing local currency, and privatizing state enterprises.

Women have consistently reported increasing poverty and rapidly deteriorating nutrition, health, and work conditions as a direct result of SAPs. When wages and food subsidies are cut, wives and mothers adjust household budgets often at the expense of their own and their children's nutrition. As public health care and education vanish, women suffer from lack of prenatal care and become nurses to ill family members at

home; girls are the first family members to leave school to help at home or go to work. When export-oriented agriculture is encouraged—indeed, coerced—peasant families are evicted from their lands to make room for corporate farms, and women become seasonal workers in the fields or in processing areas instead of land-owning farmers.

Lands once used to raise staples like rice are used instead for raising shrimp, oranges, and orchids—all for export, not for local consumption—or for golf courses and luxury hotels for tourists. Essentially, SAPs lead to destruction of both subsistence and social service systems in Third World nations so that women have no viable options to sustain their families and leave them behind to migrate in search of work. Usually women go from villages to cities within their home countries first and then migrate to the First World to pursue service work, sex work, and manufacturing jobs.[5]

Since the 1995 NGO Forum, women of color around the world have spoken in no uncertain terms to these continuing trends that globalization imposes on their lives.[6] They report the persistence of the most devastating impact of globalization on their abilities to support their children and families in the form of increased assaults on their reproductive rights. In short, globalization threatens the very survival of people of color by hindering the ability of their women to reproduce and maintain their families and communities.

In 1999, before the Seattle protests against the World Trade Organization (WTO), the Northwest Labor and Employment Law Office (LELO), a multiracial community and labor organization, recognized the need for education to build awareness of these issues and the linkages between workers' struggles in the U.S. and abroad. LELO brought together several grassroots groups, including the Seattle Young People's Project, Committee Against Repression in Mexico, Community Coalition for Environmental Justice, and the Washington Alliance for Immigrant and Refugee Justice to form the Workers' Voices Coalition. The coalition sponsored the participation of eight women labor-rights organizers from Third World countries in the WTO protest activities and a post-WTO conference.

Cenen Bagon, a participant, responded to comments by Michael Moore, then WTO director-general, when he addressed the International Confederation of Free Trade Unions. Moore said, "There is also a darker side to the backlash against globalization. For some, the attacks on economic openness are part of a broader assault on internationalism, on foreigners, immigration, a more pluralistic and integrated world. . . ." Bagon, who works with Filipina and other immigrant women workers in Canada through the Vancouver Committee for Domestic Workers and Caregivers Rights, countered sharply:

> Moore and others like him, in his ideological dogma, forget to add, and I'm sure it's quite intentional, that what we are against are the realities brought about by trade authored by the backers of capitalist globalization. . . . And if these so-called leaders are really looking for indicators of whether their programs are truly creating economic improvements, they should look beyond the country's balance of payment and budget deficits and analyze how women are affected by these programs. . . . Supporters of structural adjustment programs should visit the night life in Japan, Hong Kong, and certain places in Canada and listen to the stories of Filipino and other women who unknowingly left their countries as entertainers and ended up being prostituted by their recruiters. They should also listen to the stories of domestic workers who left not only their countries . . . but their families and their own children, as well, to care for other women's children and households. . . . [7]

Bagon calls for world leaders to view the migration of women forced to leave their homelands and families because of the ravages of SAPs as true indicators of the impacts of global economic restructuring. Extending on this, the experiences of immigrant women workers can serve not only as measures of the effects, but as true indicators of the *intentions* of SAPs and other neo-liberal economic policies. The sheer magnitude of women's migration urges us to examine this phenomenon and view it as both an effect of globalization and as a calculated feature of global economic restructuring.

In other words, it is important to understand the economic interventions in Third World nations embodied in SAPs and free-trade policies as deliberate. They facilitate the extraction of resources, especially labor and people, from the Third World and their importation into the First World. In effect, they support trade in and traffic of migrant women workers and their exploitation at both ends of the so-called trade route. This trade or forced migration is orchestrated through economic interventions compelling migration from the Third World coupled with welfare, labor, and immigration policies in the First World that channel these women into service work at poverty wages in host or receiving countries.

I have argued elsewhere that structural adjustment in the Third World and welfare reform in the First World are inextricably linked; indeed, they are two sides of the same coin. For example, in the U.S., domestic forms of structural adjustment, including privatization and cutbacks in health care and the continued lack of subsidized child care, contribute to expanded demand among dual-career middle-class households for child care, elder care, home health care, and housekeeping workers. The slashing of benefits and social services under "welfare reform" helps guarantee that this demand is met by a pool of migrant women readily available to serve as cheap labor. The dismantling of public support in the U.S. in general and the denial of benefits and services to immigrants in particular act in tandem with structural adjustment in the Third World to force migrant women into low-wage service work in the U.S.[8]

Migrant women workers from indebted nations are kept pliable by both the dependence of their families on remittances sent home and by the severe restrictions on immigrant access to almost all forms of assistance in the U.S. Their vulnerability is further reinforced by First World immigration policies explicitly designed to recruit migrant women as contract or temporary workers yet deny them the protections and rights afforded citizens. This phenomenon is readily apparent in the cases of both U.S. and Canadian immigration policies structured to ensure a ready supply of women workers available for nursing aide, home care, domestic care, child care, and elder care work at low wages and under conditions most citizens would not accept.

"FILIPINOS FOR THE WORLD"

The massive migration of women from the Philippines to all corners of the First World illustrates clearly how structural adjustments imposed on the Philippines and welfare and immigration policies in First World receiving countries combine to make the global traffic in Filipinas an explicit government practice and highly profitable industry on both ends of the trade route. Every day, an average of 2700 people are estimated to leave the Philippines in search of work. Currently, more than 8 million Filipino migrant workers live in over 186 countries, and an estimated 65% are women.[9]

Although the Philippine government denies that it has an official export policy now, an agency called the Philippine Overseas Employment Administration (POEA) was established in the 1970s to promote migrant labor with the stated goals of (1) earning foreign currency and (2) easing the Philippines' unemployment rate.[10]

Confining the analysis for the moment only to the benefits of this trade to the Philippine government and capital, the numbers are staggering. One woman migrating to Canada reported paying 1900 pesos at the embassy in the Philippines, 1500 pesos for a medical examination, and 5000 pesos to the POEA according to the research by the Philippine Women's Centre.[11] If we multiply this total 8400 pesos ($181 US) for typical bureaucratic expenses paid by one individual migrating from the Philippines by the average daily exodus of 2700 people leaving the country, the Philippine government receives the equivalent of almost half a million U.S. dollars in revenue daily for processing exports of people. Moreover, the remittances sent home to families by Filipino workers overseas infuse into the economy what amounts to the Philippines' largest source of foreign currency—far more than income from sugar and mineral exports.

Although the absolute numbers are remarkable, taken in context they are particularly telling. For example, in the year 2000, remittances from overseas workers were estimated at $6.23 billion officially, reported as channeled through the Central Bank of the Philippines. This does not include funds received through informal channels. The $6.23 billion represented 5.2% of the gross domestic product and exceeded the entire interest payment on the country's foreign debt that hovers around $5 billion a year.[12]

Philippine President Gloria Macapagal-Arroyo launched a program known as "Filipinos for the World" to celebrate and further institutionalize this exportation of workers for profit. Arroyo (unaffectionately referred to as GMA) persists in glorifying these migrant workers, following a long line of Philippines officials who once called women in particular the country's "modern heroes." In even more crass economic terms, GMA now calls them "overseas Philippines investors" and "internationally shared resources."[13] She is promoting her new labor export plan announced in June of 2002 as a push to have 100 million overseas Filipinos serving others across the globe. Arroyo's program will certainly serve her interests well. As one observer remarked, "Arroyo seeks not only the remittances from the migrant workers, but their absentee ballots to keep her

in office and bolster her unstable position. She wants not only the dollars but the 8 million Filipinos abroad in her pocket at election time."[14]

It is particularly useful to examine the experiences of Filipinas trained as nurses who migrate to work in the U.S. and Canada. They provide cheap and highly skilled labor and also serve to further the neo-liberal agenda of privatizing health care. In both countries, immigration policy is structured to keep these trained workers underemployed and deskilled in exploitative situations closely resembling indentured servitude and debt bondage. Nursing schools graduating hundreds of thousands of registered nurses abound in the Philippines, but few graduates reside in their own country.

The Philippine Women Centre (PWC) of British Columbia, a group of Filipino–Canadian women working to educate, organize, and mobilize Filipina migrant workers in Canada, identifies this phenomenon as the "commodification of the nursing profession in the Philippines." The group observes that nursing training is promoted as "a quick route to work abroad," rather than as a means to serve the needs of Filipinos. As a result Filipina nurses are seen as exportable commodities.[15] A survey of members of the group revealed that 77% of participants studied nursing with the specific intention of going abroad, and 62% took entrance exams allowing foreigners to practice nursing in the U.S.[16]

Clearly, exclusion from both welfare benefits and workers' rights through immigration policy makes immigrant women workers available for—indeed, unable to refuse—low-wage service work in the U.S. In Canada, the connection between labor control and immigration policy is even more explicit because of the use of both immigration and nursing accreditation issues to prevent foreign-trained nurses from being able to practice nursing for several years after arrival in Canada. In tandem, the policies serve to exclude immigrant nurses from their professions and channel them into low-paid care work as nannies, domestics, and home support workers.

The Live-in Caregiver Program (LCP) is the immigration policy through which the vast majority of Filipina migrants enter Canada and become trapped in low-wage care work. Established in 1992 to facilitate the importation of primarily Filipino women, the program provides that a Canadian employer (individual or employment agency) may apply through the Canadian Employment Office for a prospective employee after showing that an attempt was made to find a Canadian to do the job. A job applicant must have 2 years of postsecondary education, 6 months of formal training or 12 months of experience in caregiving work, and be in good health. Once matched with an employer, she must notify the Ministry of Citizenship and Immigration if she wishes to change employers. After 2 years of live-in work, a nanny can apply for landed-immigrant status, but during those 2 years she is considered a temporary migrant. Three years after applying for landed-immigrant status, she can become a Canadian citizen.[17]

The PWC undertook a community-based participatory action research project, interviewing 30 Filipina nurses who entered Canada via the LCP and performed domestic work. According to Cecilia Diocson, founding chairperson of the PWC, the interviews revealed that women with up to 15 years of nursing experience in operating rooms, cancer units, and other facilities were becoming deskilled while working as nannies and home support workers.[18] Others were indeed using their skills, working around the clock and performing nursing tasks, but they were not recognized or compensated as such. Many of their tasks included heavy lifting; transferring; personal care duties; administering medications; and tube feeding for elderly, ill, and disabled clients. One nurse, Mary Jane reported:

Because of the LCP requirements, we become responsible for our employers 24 hours a day, but we are only paid for 8 hours, with no overtime pay. For some of us, we accompany our employers to the hospital and even sleep at our employer's bedside at the hospital.[19]

Many of those interviewed did not realize when they migrated that they would not be doing nursing work after they entered Canada through the LCP. Many believed that they would perform nursing in private homes or care for disabled children. Moreover, many did not know that working as a nanny would mean so much labor demanded of them beyond caring for children. For example, Pamela, a registered nurse in the Philippines who left three children behind to seek work in Vancouver, said:

I thought being a nanny, as the dictionary says, is child's nurse. In the Philippines, a yaya [Tagalog for nanny] works for the kids only, right? They don't do other jobs in the house. They just change the kids, feed them and put them to bed. . . . When I came here, I was shocked. I said, why is it a package? Three children in

a big house, 5 bedrooms, 1½ baths, and 3 living rooms. . . . I feel like I'm going to die. My female employer didn't work. She stays at home. Then, she said that I'm not clean enough. I told her that I have to prioritize the work and I asked her, what's more important, the kids or cleaning? . . . It was so hard I quit.[20]

After Pamela quit, her former employer refused to give her a reference, nanny agencies would not accept her, and she decided to advertise for a job caring for the elderly. Several prospective employers who answered her ad sought caregivers willing to provide sexual services. After several such experiences and trying to work as a nanny for one more family, she found a job caring for a single woman.

Pamela supports her husband, who is a student, and her three children in the Philippines by sending a quarter of her wages home each month. She spoke of the hardships of separation from her family and her doubts and fears about reuniting:

I'm confused whether I should get my family or not. The separation is really hard for me, but I also think if my family is here, my husband and I have to chip in. I fear that communication will be through messages on the refrigerator. We don't see each other any more. That's why sometimes I feel that maybe it's better for them to stay in the Philippines because they write to me and there's an attachment still. Here, it seems that you're not really intact.[21]

Mary Jane, another Filipina nurse working as a nanny, reflected on the pain of separation from her children and the great financial hardship of maintaining contact:

My children are now 5 and 8. I spent so much money on the long distance because sometimes when I call, my child will say, "Mommy I still want to sing." You know, you didn't see your child for 4 years and she will tell you she wants to sing, you cannot say no. . . . I said I will call everyday so that [her youngest child] will not forget my voice. I only stopped calling because my phone bill is over $500.

For these women, the agony of separation from their own children is surely not diminished by caring for their employers' children. For many of the women interviewed, the hope of eventually being able to bring their families to join them in Canada influenced them to stay in unhappy and often abusive working situations in order to fulfill the 2-year live-in work requirement of the LCP as quickly as possible. The policy prohibits them from earning any extra income to supplement their low wages as caregivers and explicitly stipulates that working for anyone other than the employer named on the employment authorization is illegal, and unauthorized employment will not count toward satisfying the 2-year employment requirement to apply for permanent residence.[22] Thus, women are effectively kept bonded to the employers named on their original LCP employment authorizations at whatever wages and conditions the employer chooses to provide. As Pamela reports:

> Filipinos are abused because they are pressured to stay with the 24-month requirement. . . . You stay because it's not that easy to find an employer. And you get exploited and we are highly educated. . . . That's really racism.

In addition to these barriers that essentially lock trained nurses into nanny and home support work for at least 2 years, migrant Filipinas face more hurdles in trying to gain accreditation to practice nursing even after serving the 2-year live-in requirement. Applicants must take English tests that are irrelevant and extremely costly, about US $410. According to Leah Diana, a registered nurse and volunteer with the Filipino Nurses Support Group (FNSG) in Vancouver, Filipino nurses are usually educated in English, used English while employed in the Philippines and elsewhere, and passed mandatory English interviews before arrival in Canada. Diana says, "The English tests required are only based on the racist assumption that people of color can't speak English." These barriers are particularly outrageous when viewed in the context of Canada's recognized nursing shortage. A Canadian Nurses' Association study showed an expected shortage of 59,000 to 113,000 registered nurses in Canada by the year 2011.[23]

Cecilia Diocson reports that the mainstream, predominantly white nursing unions in Canada have not been good allies. They have not supported allowing Filipina nurses to practice despite shortages. Diocson expressed outrage that the president of a nursing union tried to pass this off as concern that "the Philippines needs them." She said:

> We responded, "Don't give us that kind of rationalization. The nurses are already here, and in crisis, and we are seeking solidarity. Is the real issue that we are non-

white, from the Third World, and foreign-trained? Are you threatened by our presence?" It's so clear that this is just racism. Otherwise, they would support and struggle with us.

Beyond the presence of women of color born and trained in the Third World, the existence of a surplus of low-wage workers and ostensible competitors is perhaps most threatening. Migrant women workers are well aware that the Canadian government can and does use their presence in the country and their exclusion through the LCP from the nursing profession to render them available to do other low-wage care and service work while keeping Canadian citizen nurses wary of competition. As Gemma Gambito, a member of FNSG who graduated from nursing school in the Philippines in 1993 and went to Canada in 1997 under the LCP, says:

> Our presence in Canada is used to drive down the wages of Canadian nurses and health care workers. Once completing our temporary work contract and becoming landed immigrants, many become home support workers, nursing aides, or continue to do domestic work for low wages. A pool of highly skilled yet low paid health workers has been created by the Canadian government's LCP.[24]

The LCP and its attendant racism facilitate the privatization of health care and help ensure the lack of movement or alliance building for subsidized child care, health care, and other staples of feminist and worker agendas. Dr. Lynn Farrales, a co-chair of the PWC, observes that the LCP functions simply to bring in women who are educated and trained nurses to do domestic work and provide live-in child care and private home care for the disabled and elderly for less than minimum wage. Farrales says:

> Canada, a country without a national day care program and a health care system moving towards increased privatization, has established in the LCP a means of importing highly educated and skilled workers to fulfill the need for flexible and cheap labor in the spheres of child care and health care. The economic and social consequences of the LCP have been devastating for Filipino women. They are highly exploited, oppressed, and de-skilled. Despite being highly educated, many are trapped in minimum wage jobs after completion of the LCP, and are effectively legislated into poverty.[25]

Moreover, Farrales notes that these negative consequences extend to the next generation of Filipino youth as well, including the effects of years of separation of mothers and children and the systemic racism in Canadian institutions that Filipino–Canadian youths encounter. Because Filipino youths drop out of high school at high rates, they join their mothers working for low wages in the service sector. Thus, the Canadian government achieves what Farrales calls the "commodification of the migration of the entire family as a package deal of cheap labor."[26] Meanwhile, ironically, with rapidly privatizing health care and the continuing nursing shortage in the public sector, health care becomes inaccessible for working-class Canadians, including Filipina nurses and their families. Thus, the Canadian government provides middle- and upper-class Canadian citizens with quality, low-cost, in-home child care and health care, literally at the expense of Filipina women workers and their families, who cannot afford these services for themselves.

Filipina migrant workers understand all too well how the Philippine government benefits and profits from this trade in women and thus plays a calculated role in ensuring its smooth functioning. The following statement of the PWC reflects this analysis of the past and current complicity of the Philippine government in this trade:

> The migration and commodification of Filipinos is sanctioned by official Philippine government policy. Known as the Labour Export Policy (LEP), this scheme of systematically exporting labour is part of the Structural Adjustment Programs (SAPs) imposed by the IMF and World Bank as conditionalities for borrowing. Ultimately, the LEP and SAPs are part of the neoliberal policies of the globalization agenda. The LEP seeks to alleviate the continuing problems of massive unemployment, trade deficits, foreign debt and social unrest. . . . The government relies upon the remittances of these migrants to prop up the economy and pay off the massive foreign debt owed to the IMF and the World Bank. Instead of selling coconuts and sugar, the Philippine government is now engaged in the sophisticated practice of selling its own people to industrialized countries.[27]

This statement reflects these women's clear recognition that the official Philippine government labor export policy is part and parcel of structural adjustment programs that wreak havoc on their lives and

force them to migrate in the first place. The LEP institutionalizes the exportation of Filipina women to other countries for cheap labor and effectively guarantees that remittances from these migrant women workers are used to pay off foreign debt.

TURNING THE "NEW WORLD ORDER" UPSIDE DOWN

Carol de Leon is now program director for the Women Workers Project at CAAAV (formerly Committee Against Anti-Asian Violence): Organizing Asian Communities in the Bronx, New York. She grew up in the Philippines, where she was a youth activist until she left in 1987 to work abroad as a nanny. She recalls that when she was in Hong Kong she applied to go to Canada, but it did not materialize, and this was probably fortunate. In the mid-1980s, the Canadian government was "very lenient, inviting people to come into the country, so at the time it was so easy to find an employer and go to Canada." In the 1990s, the Canadian government instituted requirements such as educational background checks for 2 to 3 years of college education. She comments:

> It seems very appealing to go to Canada when you are in other countries . . . for a Third World woman to go there—but in reality that structure is not well-implemented. When you go there, you'll end up working for a family for 2 or 3 years, and if you are being exploited, you can't leave while applying for a change in status. So the employer has all of the control, because the worker will end up staying anyway.[28]

De Leon knows that she is lucky not to be speaking from the experience of being trapped as a live-in caregiver in Canada. Although some aspects of her initial experiences in the U.S. were very similar, she not only was able to escape these exploitative situations, but is now organizing women like her to mobilize against the common abuses they face.

De Leon says that although the U.S. has no program like the Canadian LCP, it has a formal legal structure for au pairs who are usually young students from Europe. She says employers can hire them through agencies and arrange for them to have connections to church and school here. She also emphasizes that these "young students are treated very well and respected for what they do, compared to immigrant women who work as professional nannies." Third World women working for corporate executives do not get working permits. De Leon says, "You just get a visa that is tied to an employer." She had a contract to work as a live-in nanny for a family; her working papers described her as a "personal servant to American family." She added, "I really hated that because it sounded like back in the days when women and men are being brought here from Africa against their will and became enslaved. To me, *servant* means *slave*, and I'm certainly not one." She started working a few months after arrival in the New York City suburb of Ardsley. The people and weather appeared strange. Her job conditions were "a nightmare—I did everything from waking up the children, giving them breakfast, walking the dog, shoveling the snow, and cleaning the house." She worked from 6:30 A.M. to 9 P.M. 6 days a week. After a year, she asked for another day off after noting that others had 2 days off. Her employer, who worked for Philip Morris Corporation, said that he had seen that the common practice in Hong Kong was only one day off and refused her request on that basis.

She took the initiative to call the labor department to find out about the minimum wage and overtime pay and asked her employer to adjust her salary. Again, her employer said that the contract they signed was based on earnings in Hong Kong. De Leon pointed out that she could not support herself on those wages. When she asked for overtime, saying she understood the law limited the workday to 8 hours, her employers demanded to know where she got the information. After telling them that her source was the labor department, they still refused, then gave her a $25 raise. De Leon calculated that her earnings after the raise amounted to $2 an hour when the minimum wage was $4. After that, she decided that she wanted to leave, but met the typical tactics of exploitative household employers:

> When I told them that I'd rather leave, they said I couldn't break the contract. I said that in a contract, either party can break the contract if you are not happy, so I'm giving you 2 weeks' notice. They insisted that I couldn't do it, and tried to manipulate me, asking where I was going, if I was going back to my country. To me, that's an implication that I was going to starve! I told her that it's none of her business.

Ultimately de Leon decided to stay because she signed a contract to work for 2 years—"the reality is that I felt I was legally trafficked." She remarks that women who are brought here by executives or diplo-

mats have no way to network with others and no assistance from employers to find a community. Instead, she observes, workers are discouraged from meeting others and deliberately isolated in the suburbs, where they had no contact with other nannies, not even in the park. She adds that, "Without other people giving me support, I decided to stay and finish my contract and just survive," recalling that this also happened to her in Hong Kong. She was finally able to leave and find a live-out job from 11 A.M. to 7 P.M. that allowed her to start going to the park:

> That's when I realized that in this industry the majority of workers are women from the Third World. I met other domestic workers from all over the Third World. I realized that these conditions were widespread, whether you were from Indonesia, Malaysia, Philippines, Barbados, Guyana, Trinidad, most domestic workers face long hours, low wages, and isolation, and lack of control of our living and working conditions. Labor laws are not enforced in this industry. And labor laws simply do not protect our basic human rights to decent housing, food, shelter, and livable wages. And many laws, like those protecting workers against discrimination in the workplace, including sexual harassment and racism, specifically exclude domestic workers.

De Leon recalls many accounts of women who were subject to abuse and exploitation, worked long hours even when they were sick, and were forced to terminate pregnancies. After 7 years, she met people from CAAAV when they were handing out fliers in the park. De Leon approached them, "they took my number, and the next week I met with them and ended up going to weekly meetings."

Now, de Leon leads the Women Workers Project, which holds monthly meetings to improve working and living conditions among women in the domestic work industry. The project members began drafting standard guidelines and a pay scale to make recommendations for how much should be paid per child, for housekeeping tasks, etc.:

> We started looking at the industry, and realized that we had to be strategic about it, doing outreach with women from other ethnicities, and women really embraced it. We did a survey in 2000 in parks, indoor playgrounds, train stations, to see the conditions of women—who gets minimum wage, overtime pay, sick days, holidays. One woman who was being sponsored

was forced to work 6 days a week, over 65 hours. She wanted to have one day to go to church. She started asking and showing papers from the labor department, and her employers were furious. Employers will try all their ways to not follow the regulations.

De Leon remarks on the lack of regulation of the industry: "We're not even protected from sexual harassment or any other abuses." Moreover, she notes that employers try many different tactics, including using race to divide household workers. For example, they make comparisons and say women from the Philippines are "better than from other countries, to create tensions between workers." They also "discriminate against us because of race, language, and immigration status."

Domestic Workers United, a project sponsored by CAAAV and Andolan, a South Asian workers' group, is pushing now for legislation that de Leon's group drafted. Led by a steering committee composed mostly of women from the Caribbean, the group used their research to design a standard contract and approached the New York City Council to pass a new law regulating the industry. Essentially, the law will regulate the Department of Consumer Affairs, the agency that licenses employment agencies recruiting and placing domestic workers. Seventy-five percent of domestic workers get their jobs through such agencies. The agencies should serve to protect these workers' rights, yet, de Leon says, when a worker has an abusive employer and calls her agency, "they advise you to stay for at least 3 or 4 months because they want to receive their fees from the employers." Otherwise, the agency will have to give the money back to the employer or provide another employee without a fee. De Leon explains, "What we are asking for is a code of conduct, so that the agency provides a contract with your work conditions, including minimum wage, 2 weeks' paid vacation, etc. and the agency should enforce it."[29]

The group introduced the bill in March 2002 and provided supporting testimony at a hearing in May with the chair of the committee on labor. Supporters like Councilwoman Gail Brewer said the bill should have been easy to pass because it involved no cost to the city. The group staged a city-wide action on October 5, 2002, starting with a rally at Washington Square Park, followed by a march to City Hall. Participants wore yellow rubber gloves and aprons, just as they did when they introduced the bill. Media coverage surpassed their expectations: although the turnout for the action was strong at 500, the press coverage put the numbers above 1000.[30]

De Leon reflects on the Women Workers' Project and the demands of the bill. She also describes the nature of her organization's work and, more broadly, the movement she is helping build. The measure is in some ways modest and yet revolutionary:

> The bill is very basic—how we should be treated, working conditions, minimum wage, overtime pay, legal holidays and sick days—but really, we want to turn the industry upside down and change the notions that immigrant workers are lazy and uneducated. Because it relates to history, because this country inherited this industry through American slavery and ideas that this is women's work, etc. We're calling for respect and recognition for women in this industry.

De Leon says the group continues to wait patiently for a meeting on the bill with the Department of Consumer Affairs but will stage another action if necessary. In the meantime, her project offers an immigrant rights law clinic through New York University students working with CAAAV to provide advice on negotiating with employers and maneuvering the health care system. The project also provides courses for nannies on child care, psychology, and cardiopulmonary resuscitation training leading to Red Cross certification.[31]

Similarly, while the PWC in Vancouver pursues its long-term campaign to dismantle the LCP, its members work to build the movement for immigrant workers' rights in Canada every day in myriad ways. For example, the PWC has rented a house for use as a drop-in center for members who yearn for camaraderie and some comforting elements of Philippine culture. Cecilia Diocson, founding chairperson and director, describes how the center serves as a place for women to congregate, eat, and talk with women in similar situations:

> The women started to educate each other, bringing their stories to discuss at the center. We have had a lot of successes in making these women more assertive in their employers' homes after gathering these stories over food. They report having to pay for their own room and board, sleeping in the garage without heat, and being "shared" by two employers. They say, "It's like being in prison from Monday through Friday." The majority work 14 to 16 hours and are underpaid. We found out that they are getting underfed too. They want rice at least twice a day, but lots of white employers

don't eat rice, just pasta and potatoes. The regulars on Friday afternoon would be rushing to the kitchen, saying "I'm so hungry. I haven't had rice all week." They could hardly work because they were so hungry.

Clearly, the drop-in center provides more than a refuge for hungry workers. It serves as a space for these women to build a community base from which to organize. The effectiveness of the other work of the PWC is closely tied to this base, as much of it evolves from participatory research and is advanced through popular education including cultural events and political theater. The center has been able to conduct longitudinal studies, following women through 8- to 10-year time spans, to document the segregation and lack of mobility Filipinas face in the labor market in Canada.

The most recent research relates to the way the increasing number of Filipinas who enter Canada via the LCP led to growth over the past 20 years of the mail-order bride industry—"another category of slave," as Diocson says. The PWC also plans to launch a women's studies program with guest lecturers at the center for women who cannot afford to attend universities.[32]

At a recent international women's conference, Diocson presented an analysis of global migration and particularly the cases of Filipina women forced to migrate to Canada in the context of global capitalism. Her cogent analysis, both as a trained nurse who migrated from the Philippines and as a radical political organizer, is one of the most well-articulated analyses I have encountered in a variety of contexts. She commented about the LCP:

Instead of instituting a universal day care system to address the needs of women who are leaving the home to join the workplace, the Canadian state's response to this economic restructuring is to import cheap but highly educated and relatively skilled foreign domestic workers. This confers several advantages both to the Canadian state and Canadians who can afford a foreign domestic worker. . . . [T]he Canadian state earns revenue through the processing of migration documents and taxation of these foreign domestic workers. . . . [F]oreign domestic workers help provide a stable base of cheap "reserve army of labor" that keeps wages down and ensures continuous accumulation of capital. . . . Thus, the foreign domestic worker is functional to the maintenance of the existing capitalist system in Canada. On the other side of the ledger, the sending country also benefits much from its export of foreign domestic workers.[33]

In my experience, Third World women migrant workers have always been many steps ahead of us in formulating and articulating these analyses of globalization, perhaps because of its direct and dire impacts on the conditions of these women's lives. They have much at stake to develop strategies to resist these conditions effectively, and it is only fitting that those who have suffered first and worst under globalization will lead the way out from under its oppressive forces. The women of the Workers' Voices Coalition, the PWC, Domestic Workers United, and many other grassroots organizations are doing revolutionary work in the face of what they all know is surely not new under globalization. They remind us through their fierce struggles and sharp analyses that they will revolutionize not only their work force and their adopted societies, but the antiglobalization movement itself.

ACKNOWLEDGMENTS

Portions of this [reading] are reprinted from Chang, G., "The Global Trade in Filipina Workers," in *Dragon Ladies: Asian American Feminists Breathe Fire*, South End Press, Boston, 1997, p. 132; Chang, G., *Disposable Domestics: Immigrant Women Workers in the Global Economy*, South End Press, Boston, 2000, p. 123.

NOTES

1. "Globalization's Inability to Create Jobs Fuels Mass Migration: ILO Chief," *Tehran Times*, June 13, 2002.
2. Nishioka, J., "Marriage by Mail: The Internet Makes It Easier for Potential Mates to Connect Across Seas," *Asian-Week*, July 29, 1999. [Cherry Blossoms is identified by all but Krosky as an international mail-order bride business.]
3. KPFA Radio, Morning Show with host Andrea Lewis, International Women's Day Program, 2001, guests: Grace Chang and Ethel Long Scott.
4. See "Third World Within" cited in *CAAAV Voice*, Special Issue on Women, Race and Work, Vol. 10, Fall 2000, p. 17. Cindy Domingo, founder of the Workers' Voices Coalition, in her call for seizing the moment after the Battle at Seattle, 1999, said: "We saw the profound deterioration in the conditions of immigrant and women workers worldwide as a direct result of free trade policies, globalization and privatization. In the United States, immigrant workers have become scapegoats for the failures of the global economy

because U.S. workers don't see their interests as one and the same with workers in Latin America, Asia or Africa. The WTO coming to our city gave us a once-in-a-lifetime opportunity to draw links between conditions faced by working people in developing countries and those faced by immigrants and people of color in the United States," cited by Joy, K., in "Gender, Immigration and the WTO," *Network News,* Winter 2000, p. 12.

5. Testimony of representative of the International Organization of Prostitutes, Gabriela Workshop, September 3, 1995.

6. See Sandrasagra, M. J., "Globalisation Heightening Gender Inequalities," IPS, October 10, 2000; Tauli-Corpuz, V., "Asia-Pacific Women Grapple with Financial Crisis and Globalisation," Roundtable Discussion on the Economic, Social, and Political Impacts of the Southeast Asian Financial Crisis, Manila, April 12–14, 1998, and Rural and Indigenous Women Speak Out on the Impact of Globalisation, Chiangmai, Thailand, May 22–25, 1998.

7. Testimony of Cenen Bagon, "Voices of Working Women," Proceedings of "Beyond the WTO: Conference on Women and Immigration the Global Economy" organized by North-west Labor and Employment Law Office (LELO) and Workers' Voice Coalition, Seattle, Washington, December 4, 1999, p. 16.

8. See Chang, G., "The Global Trade in Filipina Workers," in *Dragon Ladies: Asian American Feminists Breathe Fire*, South End Press, Boston, 1997, p. 132; Chang, G., *Disposable Domestics: Immigrant Women Workers in the Global Economy*, South End Press, Boston, 2000, p. 123.

9. Filipino Nurses Support Group, "Contextualizing the Presence of Filipino Nurses in BC," in *Advancing the Rights and Welfare of Non-Practicing Filipino and Other Foreign-Trained Nurses,*" proceedings of national consultation for Filipino and other foreign-trained nurses, December 7–9, 2001. The Philippines Department of Labor and Employment estimates that about 2748 Filipinos leave the country daily.

10. This number does not include women who are trafficked, illegally recruited, or migrate for marriage or students and tourists who eventually become undocumented workers. Data compiled by Kanlungan Center Foundation from Philippine Overseas Employment Administration and Department of Labor and Employment statistics, 1995; Vincent, I., "Canada Beckons Cream of Nannies: Much-Sought Filipinas Prefer Work Conditions," *Globe and Mail*, January 20, 1996, p. A1. Other authors more extensively address trafficking in women for the sex, entertainment, and mail-order bride industries. See Rosca, N., "The Philippines' Shameful Export," *Nation*, April 17, 1995, p. 523; Kim, E., "Sex Tourism in Asia: A Reflection of Political and Economic Equality," *Critical Perspectives of Third World America*, 2, Fall 1984, p. 215; Blitt, C., producer, "Sisters and Daughters Betrayed: The Trafficking of Women and Girls and the Fight to End It," Video, Global Fund for Women.

11. Testimony of Pamela, "Filipino Nurses Doing Domestic Work in Canada: A Stalled Development," Philippine Women Centre of British Columbia, March 2000, p. 20.

12. Philippine Overseas Employment Administration, 2000, bulatlat.com.

13. Presentation by Ethel Farrales, Filipino–Canadian Youth Alliance, Vancouver, "Link Arms, Raise Fists: U.S. Out of the Philippines Now!" North American Conference, July 6–7, 2002.

14. Comments of youth member of Overseas Filipino Workers' Organization, Vancouver, "Link Arms, Raise Fists: U.S. Out of the Philippines Now!" North American Conference, San Francisco, July 6–7, 2002.

15. Philippine Women Centre of British Columbia, "Filipino Nurses Doing Domestic Work in Canada: A Stalled Development," Vancouver, March 2000, p. 10.

16. Ibid., p. 16.

17. Ibid., p. 11.

18. Diocson, C., Philippine Women Centre of British Columbia, Vancouver, phone interview, August 2002.

19. Statement of Sheila Farrales, "The Use of Filipino Nurses in the Scheme to Privatize Health Care," Conference Proceedings: Advancing the Rights and Welfare of Non-Practicing Filipino and Other Foreign-Trained Nurses, Filipino Nurses' Support Group, Burnaby, British Columbia, December 7–9, 2001, p. 51.

20. Testimony of Pamela, "Filipino Nurses Doing Domestic Work in Canada: A Stalled Development," Philippine Women Centre of British Columbia, March 2000, p. 19.

21. Ibid., p. 20.

22. Ibid., p. 29.

23. Statement of Sheila Farrales, ibid.

24. Statement of Gemma Gambito, ibid., p. 61.

25. Statement of Lynn Farrales, ibid., p. 42.

26. Ibid.

27. Philippine Women Centre of British Columbia, "Filipino Nurses Doing Domestic Work in Canada: A Stalled Development," March 2000, p. 7.

28. De Leon, C., Women Workers Project, CAAAV, Bronx, NY, phone interview, September 2002.

29. De Leon, C., Women Workers Project, CAAAV, Bronx, NY, phone interviews, September 2002 and February 2003.

30. Alapo, L., "Bill to Protect Domestic Workers," *Newsday*, March 25, 2002; Greenhouse, S., "Wage Bill Would Protect Housekeepers and Nannies," *New York Times*, March 25, 2002; Richardson, L., "A Union Maid? Actually a Nanny, Organizing," *New York Times*, April 4, 2002; Ginsberg, A., "Nannies March for Fair Pay, OT," *Daily News*, October 6, 2002; Ramirez, M., "Domestic Workers Seek Wage, Personal Protection," *Newsday*, October 6, 2002; Geron, T., "All in a Day's Work," *AsianWeek*, July 11, 2002; Lee, C., "Revolt of the Nannies," *Village Voice*, March 9, 2002.

31. De Leon, C., Women Workers Project, CAAAV, Bronx, NY, phone interview, September 2002.

32. Diocson, C., Philippine Women Centre of British Columbia, phone interview, August 2002.

33. Diocson, C., "Forced Migration: Perpetuation of Underdevelopment," paper presented at Ninth International Forum, Association for Women's Rights in Development, Guadalajara, Mexico, October 3–6, 2002.

54   ***Cathy J. Cohen***

Punks, Bulldaggers, and Welfare Queens: The Radical Potential of Queer Politics?

On the eve of finishing this essay my attention is focused not on how to rework the conclusion (as it should be) but instead on news stories of alleged racism at Gay Men's Health Crisis (GMHC). It seems that three black board members of this largest and oldest AIDS organization in the world have resigned over their perceived subservient position on the GMHC board. Billy E. Jones, former head of the New York City Health and Hospitals Corporation and one of the board members to quit, was quoted in the *New York Times* as saying, "Much work needs to be done at GMHC to make it truly inclusive and welcoming of diversity. . . . It is also clear that such work will be a great struggle. I am resigning because I do not choose to engage in such struggle at GMHC, but rather prefer to fight for the needs of those ravaged by HIV" (Dunlap).

This incident raises mixed emotions for me, for it points to the continuing practice of racism many of us experience on a daily basis in lesbian and gay communities. But just as disturbingly it also highlights the limits of a lesbian and gay political agenda based on a civil rights strategy, where assimilation into, and replication of, dominant institutions are the goals. Many of us continue to search for a new political direction and agenda, one that does not focus on integration into dominant structures but instead seeks to transform the basic fabric and hierarchies that allow systems of oppression to persist and operate efficiently. For some of us, such a challenge to traditional gay and lesbian politics was offered by the idea of queer politics. Here we had a potential movement of young antiassimilationist activists committed to challenging the very way people understand and respond to sexuality. These activists promised to engage in struggles that would disrupt dominant norms of sexuality, radically transforming politics in lesbian, gay, bisexual, and transgendered communities.

Despite the possibility invested in the idea of queerness and the practice of queer politics, I argue that a truly radical or transformative politics has not resulted from queer activism. In many instances, instead of destabilizing the assumed categories and binaries of sexual identity, queer politics has served to reinforce simple dichotomies between heterosexual and everything "queer." An understanding of the ways in which power informs and constitutes privileged and marginalized subjects on both sides of this dichotomy has been left unexamined.

I query in this essay whether there are lessons to be learned from queer activism that can help us construct a new politics. I envision a politics where one's relation to power, and not some homogenized identity, is privileged in determining one's political comrades. I'm talking about a politics where the *nonnormative* and *marginal* position of punks, bulldaggers, and welfare queens, for example, is the basis for progressive transformative coalition work. Thus, if there is any truly radical potential to be found in the idea of queerness and the practice of queer politics, it would seem to be located in its ability to create a space in opposition to dominant norms, a space where transformational political work can begin.

EMERGENCE OF QUEER POLITICS AND A NEW POLITICS OF TRANSFORMATION

Theorists and activists alike generally agree that it was in the early 1990s that we began to see, with any regularity, the use of the term "queer."[1] This term would come to denote not only an emerging politics, but also a new cohort of academics working in programs primarily in the humanities centered around social and cultural criticism (Morton 121). Individuals such as Judith Butler, Eve Sedgwick, Teresa de Lauretis, Diana

Fuss, and Michael Warner produced what are now thought of as the first canonical works of "queer theory." Working from a variety of postmodernist and poststructuralist theoretical perspectives, these scholars focused on identifying and contesting the discursive and cultural markers found within both dominant and marginal identities and institutions which prescribe and reify "heterogendered" understandings and behavior.[2] These theorists presented a different conceptualization of sexuality, one which sought to replace socially named and presumably stable categories of sexual expression with a new fluid movement among and between forms of sexual behavior (Stein and Plummer 182).

Through its conception of a wide continuum of sexual possibilities, queer theory stands in direct contrast to the normalizing tendencies of hegemonic sexuality rooted in ideas of static, stable sexual identities and behaviors. In queer theorizing the sexual subject is understood to be constructed and contained by multiple practices of categorization and regulation that systematically marginalize and oppress those subjects thereby defined as deviant and "other." And, at its best, queer theory focuses on and makes central not only the socially constructed nature of sexuality and sexual categories, but also the varying degrees and multiple sites of power distributed within all categories of sexuality, including the normative category of heterosexuality.

It was in the early 1990s, however, that the postmodern theory being produced in the academy (later to be recategorized as queer theory) found its most direct interaction with the real-life politics of lesbian, gay, bisexual, and transgendered activists. Frustrated with what was perceived to be the scientific "degaying" and assimilationist tendencies of AIDS activism, with their invisibility in the more traditional civil rights politics of lesbian and gay organizations, and with increasing legal and physical attacks against lesbian and gay community members, a new generation of activists began the process of building a more confrontational political formation—labeling it queer politics (Bérubé and Escoffier 12). Queer politics, represented most notoriously in the actions of Queer Nation, is understood as an "in your face" politics of a younger generation. Through action and analysis these individuals seek to make "queer" function as more than just an abbreviation for lesbian, gay, bisexual, and transgendered. Similar to queer theory, the queer politics articulated and pursued by these activists first and foremost recognizes and encourages the fluidity and movement of people's sexual lives. In queer politics sexual expression is something that always entails the possibility of change, movement, redefinition, and subversive performance—from year to year, from partner to partner, from day to day, even from act to act. In addition to highlighting the instability of sexual categories and sexual subjects, queer activists also directly challenge the multiple practices and vehicles of power which render them invisible and at risk. However, what seems to make queer activists unique, at this particular moment, is their willingness to confront normalizing power by emphasizing and exaggerating their own antinormative characteristics and nonstable behavior. Joshua Gamson, in "Must Identity Movements Self-Destruct? A Queer Dilemma," writes that

> queer activism and theory pose the challenge of a form of organizing in which, far from inhibiting accomplishments, the *destabilization* of collective identity is itself a goal and accomplishment of collective action.
>
> The assumption that stable collective identities are necessary for collective action is turned on its head by queerness, and the question becomes: *When and how are stable collective identities necessary for social action and social change?* Secure boundaries and stabilized identities are necessary not in general, but in the specific, a point social movement theory seems currently to miss. (403, original emphasis)

Thus queer politics, much like queer theory, is often perceived as standing in opposition, or in contrast, to the category-based identity politics of traditional lesbian and gay activism. And for those of us who find ourselves on the margins, operating through multiple identities and thus not fully served or recognized through traditional single-identity-based politics, *theoretical conceptualizations* of queerness hold great political promise. For many of us, the label "queer" symbolizes an acknowledgment that through our existence and everyday survival we embody sustained and multisited resistance to systems (based on dominant constructions of race and gender) that seek to normalize our sexuality, exploit our labor, and constrain our visibility. At the intersection of oppression and resistance lies the radical potential of queerness to challenge and bring together all those deemed marginal and all those committed to liberatory politics.

The problem, however, with such a conceptualization and expectation of queer identity and politics is that in its present form queer politics has not emerged as an encompassing challenge to systems of domination and oppression, especially those normalizing processes embedded in heteronormativity. By "heteronormativity" I mean both those localized practices and those centralized institutions which legitimize and privilege heterosexuality and heterosexual relationships as fundamental and "natural" within society. I raise the subject of heteronormativity because it is this normalizing practice/power that has most often been the focus of queer politics (Blasius 19–20; Warner xxi–xxv).

The inability of queer politics to effectively challenge heteronormativity rests, in part, on the fact that despite a surrounding discourse which highlights the destabilization and even deconstruction of sexual categories, queer politics has often been built around a simple dichotomy between those deemed queer and those deemed heterosexual. Whether in the infamous "I Hate Straights" publication or queer kiss-ins at malls and straight dance clubs, very near the surface in queer political action is an uncomplicated understanding of power as it is encoded in sexual categories: all heterosexuals are represented as dominant and controlling and all queers are understood as marginalized and invisible. Thus, even in the name of destabilization, some queer activists have begun to prioritize sexuality as the primary frame through which they pursue their politics.[3] Undoubtedly, within different contexts various characteristics of our total being—for example, race, gender, class, sexuality—are highlighted or called upon to make sense of a particular situation. However, my concern is centered on those individuals who consistently activate only one characteristic of their identity, or a single perspective of consciousness, to organize their politics, rejecting any recognition of the multiple and intersecting systems of power that largely dictate our life chances.

It is the disjuncture, evident in queer politics, between an articulated commitment to promoting an understanding of sexuality that rejects the idea of static, monolithic, bounded categories, on the one hand, and political practices structured around binary conceptions of sexuality and power, on the other hand, that is the focus of this article. Specifically, I am concerned with those manifestations of queer politics in which the capital and advantage invested in a range of sexual categories are disregarded and, as a result, narrow and homogenized political identities are reproduced that inhibit the radical potential of queer politics. It is my contention that queer activists who evoke a

single-oppression framework misrepresent the distribution of power within and outside of gay, lesbian, bisexual, and transgendered communities, and therefore limit the comprehensive and transformational character of queer politics.

Recognizing the limits of current conceptions of queer identities and queer politics, I am interested in examining the concept of "queer" in order to think about how we might construct a new political identity that is truly liberating, transformative, and inclusive of all those who stand on the outside of the dominant constructed norm of state-sanctioned white middle- and upper-class heterosexuality.[4] Such a broadened understanding of queerness must be based on an intersectional analysis that recognizes how numerous systems of oppression interact to regulate and police the lives of most people. Black lesbian, bisexual, and heterosexual feminist authors such as Kimberle Crenshaw, Barbara Ransby, Angela Davis, Cheryl Clarke, and Audre Lorde have repeatedly emphasized in their writing the intersectional workings of oppression. And it is just such an understanding of the interlocking systems of domination that is noted in the opening paragraph of the now famous black feminist statement by the Combahee River Collective:

> The most general statement of our politics at the present time would be that we are actively committed to struggling against racial, sexual, heterosexual, and class oppression and see as our particular task the development of *integrated* analysis and practice based upon the fact that the major systems of oppression are interlocking. The synthesis of these oppressions creates the conditions of our lives. As Black women we see Black feminism as the logical political movement to combat the manifold and simultaneous oppressions that all women of color face. (272)

This analysis of one's place in the world which focuses on the intersection of systems of oppression is informed by a consciousness that undoubtedly grows from the lived experience of existing within and resisting multiple and connected practices of domination and normalization. Just such a lived experience and analysis have determined much of the progressive and expansive nature of the politics emanating from people of color, people who are both inside and outside of lesbian and gay communities.

However, beyond a mere recognition of the intersection of oppressions, there must also be an understanding of the ways our multiple identities work to limit the entitlement and status some receive from obeying a heterosexual imperative. For instance, how would queer activists understand politically the lives of women—in particular women of color—on welfare, who may fit into the category of heterosexual, but whose sexual choices are not perceived as normal, moral, or worthy of state support? Further, how do queer activists understand and relate politically to those whose same-sex sexual identities position them within the category of queer, but who hold other identities based on class, race and/or gender categories which provide them with membership in and the resources of dominant institutions and groups?

Thus, inherent in our new politics must be a commitment to left analysis and left politics. Black feminists as well as other marginalized and progressive scholars and activists have long argued that any political response to the multilayered oppression that most of us experience must be rooted in a left understanding of our political, economic, social, and cultural institutions. Fundamentally, a left framework makes central the interdependency among multiple systems of domination. Such a perspective also ensures that while activists should rightly be concerned with forms of discursive and cultural coercion, we also recognize and confront the more direct and concrete forms of exploitation and violence rooted in state-regulated institutions and economic systems. The Statement of Purpose from the first Dialogue on the Lesbian and Gay Left comments specifically on the role of interlocking systems of oppression in the lives of gays and lesbians. "By leftist we mean people who understand the struggle for lesbian and gay liberation to be integrally tied to struggles against class oppression, racism, and sexism. While we might use different political labels, we share a commitment to a fundamental transformation of the economic, political and social structures of society."

A left framework of politics, unlike civil rights or liberal frameworks, brings into focus the systematic relationship among forms of domination, where the creation and maintenance of exploited, subservient, marginalized classes is a necessary part of, at the very least, the economic configuration. Urvashi Vaid, in *Virtual Equality,* for example, writes of the limits of civil rights strategies in confronting systemic homophobia:

Civil rights do not change the social order in dramatic ways; they change only the privileges of the group asserting those rights. Civil rights strategies do not challenge the moral and antisexual underpinnings of homophobia, because homophobia does not originate in our lack of full civil equality. Rather, homophobia arises from the nature and construction of the political, legal, economic, sexual, racial and family systems within which we live. (183)

Proceeding from the starting point of a system-based left analysis, strategies built upon the possibility of incorporation and assimilation are exposed as simply expanding and making accessible the status quo for more privileged members of marginal groups, while the most vulnerable in our communities continue to be stigmatized and oppressed.

It is important to note, however, that while left theorists tend to provide a more structural analysis of oppression and exploitation, many of these theorists and activists have also been homophobic and heterosexist in their approach to or avoidance of the topics of sexuality and heteronormativity. For example, Robin Podolsky, in "Sacrificing Queers and other 'Proletarian' Artifacts," writes that quite often on the left lesbian and gay sexuality and desire have been characterized as "more to do with personal happiness and sexual pleasure than with the 'material basis' of procreation—we were considered self-indulgent distractions from struggle . . . [an example of] 'bourgeois decadence'" (54).

This contradiction between a stated left analysis and an adherence to heteronormativity has probably been most dramatically identified in the writing of some feminist authors. I need only refer to Adrienne Rich's well-known article, "Compulsory Heterosexuality and Lesbian Existence," as a poignant critique of the white, middle-class heterosexual standard running through significant parts of feminist analysis and actions. The same adherence to a heterosexual norm can be found in the writing of self-identified black left intellectuals such as Cornel West and Michael Eric Dyson. Thus, while these writers have learned to make reference to lesbian, gay, bisexual, and transgendered segments of black communities—sparingly—they continue to foreground black heterosexuality and masculinity as the central unit of analysis in their writing—and most recently in their politics, witness their participation in the Million Man March.

This history of left organizing and the left's visible absence from any serious and sustained response to the AIDS epidemic have provoked many lesbian, gay, bisexual and transgendered people to question the relevance of this political configuration to the needs of our communities. Recognizing that reservations of this type are real and should be noted, I still hold that a left-rooted analysis which emphasizes economic exploitation and class structure, culture, and the systemic nature of power provides a framework of politics that is especially effective in representing and challenging the numerous sites and systems of oppression. Further, the left-centered approach that I embrace is one that designates sexuality and struggles against sexual normalization as central to the politics of all marginal communities.

THE ROOT OF QUEER POLITICS: CHALLENGING HETERONORMATIVITY?

In the introduction to the edited volume *Fear of a Queer Planet: Queer Politics and Social Theory*, Michael Warner asks the question: "What do queers want?" (vii). He suggests that the goals of queers and their politics extend beyond the sexual arena. Warner contends that what queers want is acknowledgment of their lives, struggles, and complete existence; queers want to be represented and included fully in left political analysis and American culture. Thus what queers want is to be a part of the social, economic, and political restructuring of this society; as Warner writes, queers want to have queer experience and politics "taken as starting points rather than as footnotes" in the social theories and political agendas of the left (vii). He contends that it has been the absence or invisibility of lived queer experience that has marked or constrained much of left social and political theories and "has posited and naturalized a heterosexual society" in such theories (vii).

The concerns and emerging politics of queer activists, as formulated by Warner and others interested in understanding the implications of the idea of queerness, are focused on highlighting queer presence and destroying heteronormativity not only in the larger dominant society but also in extant spaces, theories, and sites of resistance, presumably on the left. He suggests that those embracing the label of "queer" understand the need to challenge the assumption of heteronormativity in every aspect of their existence:

> Every person who comes to a queer self-understanding knows in one way or another that her stigmatization is connected with gender, the family, notions of individual freedom, the state, public speech, consumption

and desire, nature and culture, maturation, reproductive politics, racial and national fantasy, class identity, truth and trust, censorship, intimate life and social display, terror and violence, health care, and deep cultural norms about the bearing of the body. Being queer means fighting about these issues all the time, locally and piecemeal but always with consequences. (xiii)

Now, independent of the fact that few of us could find ourselves in such a grandiose description of queer consciousness, I believe that Warner's description points to the fact that in the roots of a lived "queer" existence are experiences with domination and in particular heteronormativity that form the basis for genuine transformational politics. By transformational, again, I mean a politics that does not search for opportunities to integrate into dominant institutions and normative social relationships, but instead pursues a political agenda that seeks to change values, definitions, and laws which make these institutions and relationships oppressive.

Queer activists experiencing displacement both within and outside of lesbian and gay communities rebuff what they deem the assimilationist practices and policies of more established lesbian and gay organizations. These organizers and activists reject cultural norms of acceptable sexual behavior and identification and instead embrace political strategies which promote self-definition and full expression. Members of the Chicago-based group Queers United Against Straight-acting Homosexuals (QUASH) state just such a position in the article "Assimilation Is Killing Us: Fight for a Queer United Front" published in their newsletter, WHY I HATED THE MARCH ON WASHINGTON:

> Assimilation is killing us. We are falling into a trap. Some of us adopt an apologetic stance, stating "that's just the way I am" (read: "I'd be straight if I could."). Others pattern their behavior in such a way as to mimic heterosexual society so as to minimize the glaring differences between us and them. No matter how much [money] you make, fucking your lover is still illegal in nearly half of the states. Getting a corporate job, a fierce car and a condo does not protect you from dying of AIDS or getting your head bashed in by neo-Nazis. The myth of assimilation must be shattered.
> . . . Fuck the heterosexual, nuclear family. Let's make families which promote sexual choices and liberation rather than sexual oppression. We must learn from the

legacy of resistance that is ours: a legacy which shows that empowerment comes through grassroots activism, not mainstream politics, a legacy which shows that real change occurs when we are inclusive, not exclusive. (4)

At the very heart of queer politics, at least as it is formulated by QUASH, is a fundamental challenge to the heteronormativity—the privilege, power, and normative status invested in heterosexuality—of the dominant society.

It is in their fundamental challenge to a systemic process of domination and exclusion, with a specific focus on heteronormativity, that queer activists and queer theorists are tied to and rooted in a tradition of political struggle most often identified with people of color and other marginal groups. For example, activists of color have, through many historical periods, questioned their formal and informal inclusion and power in prevailing social categories. Through just such a process of challenging their centrality to lesbian and gay politics in particular, and lesbian and gay communities more generally, lesbian, gay, bisexual, and transgendered people of color advanced debates over who and what would be represented as "truly gay." As Steven Seidman reminds us in "Identity and Politics in a 'Postmodern' Gay Culture: Some Historical and Conceptual Notes," beyond the general framing provided by postmodern queer theory, gay and lesbian—and now queer—politics owes much of its impetus to the politics of people of color and other marginalized members of lesbian and gay communities.

> Specifically, I make the case that postmodern strains in gay thinking and politics have their immediate social origin in recent developments in the gay culture. In the reaction by people of color, third-world-identified gays, poor and working-class gays, and sex rebels to the ethnic/essentialist model of identity and community that achieved dominance in the lesbian and gay cultures of the 1970s, I locate the social basis for a rethinking of identity and politics. (106)

Through the demands of lesbian, gay, bisexual, and transgendered people of color as well as others who did not see themselves or their numerous communities in the more narrowly constructed politics of white gays and lesbians, the contestation took shape over who and what type of issues would be represented in lesbian and gay politics and in larger community discourse.

While similarities and connections between the politics of lesbians, gay men, bisexuals, and transgendered people of color during the 1970s and 1980s and queer activists of today clearly exist, the present-day rendition of this politics has deviated significantly from its legacy. Specifically, while both political efforts include as a focus of their work the radicalization and/or expansion of traditional lesbian and gay politics, the politics of lesbian, gay, bisexual, and transgendered people of color have been and continue to be much broader in its understanding of transformational politics.

The politics of lesbian, gay, bisexual, and transgendered people of color has often been guided by the type of radical intersectional left analysis I detailed earlier. Thus, while the politics of lesbian, gay, bisexual, and transgendered activists of color might recognize heteronormativity as a primary system of power structuring our lives, it understands that heteronormativity interacts with institutional racism, patriarchy, and class exploitation to define us in numerous ways as marginal and oppressed subjects.[5] And it is this constructed subservient position that allows our sisters and brothers to be used either as surplus labor in an advanced capitalist structure and/or seen as expendable, denied resources, and thus locked into correctional institutions across the country. While heterosexual privilege negatively impacts and constrains the lived experience of "queers" of color, so too do racism, classism, and sexism.

In contrast to the left intersectional analysis that has structured much of the politics of "queers" of color, the basis of the politics of some white queer activists and organizations has come dangerously close to a single-oppression model. Experiencing "deviant" sexuality as the prominent characteristic of their marginalization, these activists begin to envision the world in terms of a "hetero/queer" divide. Using the framework of queer theory in which heteronormativity is identified as a system of regulation and normalization, some queer activists map the power and entitlement of normative heterosexuality onto the bodies of all heterosexuals. Further, these activists naively characterize all those who exist under the category of "queer" as powerless. Thus, in the process of conceptualizing a decentered identity of queerness, meant to embrace all those who stand on the outside of heteronormativity, a monolithic understanding of heterosexuality and queerness has come to dominate the political imagination and actions of many queer activists.

This reconstruction of a binary divide between heterosexuals and queers, while discernible in many of the actions of Queer Nation, is probably most evident in the manifesto "I Hate Straights." Distributed at gay pride parades in New York and Chicago in 1990, the declaration written by an anonymous group of queers begins,

I have friends. Some of them are straight.

Year after year, I see my straight friends. I want to see how they are doing, to add newness to our long and complicated histories, to experience some continuity.

Year after year I continue to realize that the facts of my life are irrelevant to them and that I am only half listened to, that I am an appendage to the doings of a greater world, a world of power and privilege, of the laws of installation, a world of exclusion. "That's not true," argue my straight friends. There is the one certainty in the politics of power; those left out of it beg for inclusion, while the insiders claim that they already are. Men do it to women, whites do it to blacks, *and everyone does it to queers.*

. . . *The main dividing line, both conscious and unconscious, is procreation . . . and that magic word—Family.* (emphasis added)

Screaming out from this manifesto is an analysis which places not heteronormativity, but heterosexuality, as the central "dividing line" between those who would be dominant and those who are oppressed. Nowhere in this essay is there recognition that "non-normative" procreation patterns and family structures of people who are labeled heterosexual have also been used to regulate and exclude *them.* Instead, the authors declare. "Go tell them [straights] to go away until they have spent a month walking hand in hand in public with someone of the same sex. After they survive that, then you'll hear what they have to say about queer anger. Otherwise, tell them to shut up and listen." For these activists, the power of heterosexuality is the focus, and queer anger the means of queer politics. Missing from this equation is any attention to, or acknowledgment of, the ways in which identities of race, class, and/or gender either enhance or mute the marginalization of queers, on the one hand, and the power of heterosexuals, on the other.

The fact that this essay is written about and out of queer anger is undoubtedly part of the rationale for its defense (Berlant and Freeman 200). But I question the degree to which we should read this piece as just an aberrational diatribe against straights motivated by intense queer anger. While anger is clearly a motivating factor for such writing, we should also understand this action to represent an analysis and politics structured around the simple dichotomy of straight and queer. We know, for instance, that similar positions have been put forth in other anonymously published, publicly distributed manifestos. For example, in the document *Queers Read This,* the authors write, "Don't be fooled, straight people own the world and the only reason you have been spared is you're smart, lucky or a fighter. Straight people have a privilege that allows them to do whatever they please and fuck without fear." They continue by stating: "Straight people are your enemy."

Even within this document, which seems to exemplify the narrowness of queer conceptions, there is a surprising glimpse at a more enlightened left intersectional understanding of what queerness might mean. For instance, the authors continue, "being queer is not about a right to privacy; it is about the freedom to be public, to just be who we are. It means everyday fighting oppression; homophobia, racism, misogyny, the bigotry of religious hypocrites and our own self-hatred." Evident in this one document are the inherent tensions and dilemmas many queer activists currently encounter: how does one implement in real political struggle a decentered political identity that is not constituted by a process of seemingly reductive "othering"?

The process of ignoring or at least downplaying queers' varying relationships to power is evident not only in the writing of queer activists, but also in the political actions pursued by queer organizations. I question the ability of political actions such as mall invasions (pursued by groups such as the Queer Shopping Network in New York and the Suburban Homosexual Outreach Program [SHOP] in San Francisco), to address the fact that queers exist in different social locations. Lauren Berlant and Elizabeth Freeman describe mall invasion projects as

[an attempt to take] the relatively bounded spectacle of the urban pride parade to the ambient pleasures of the shopping mall. "Mall visibility actions" thus conjoin the spectacular lure of the parade with Hare Krishna-style conversion and proselytizing techniques. Stepping into malls in hair-gelled splendor, holding hands and handing out fliers, the queer auxiliaries produce an "invasion" that conveys a different message. "We're here, we're queer, *you're* going shopping." (210)

The activity of entering or "invading" the shopping mall on the part of queer nationals is clearly one of attempted subversion. Intended by their visible presence in this clearly coded heterosexual family economic mecca is a disruption of the agreed-upon segregation between the allowable spaces for queer "deviant" culture and the rest of the "naturalized" world. Left unchallenged in such an action, however, are the myriad ways, besides the enforcement of normative sexuality, in which some queers feel alienated and excluded from the space of the mall. Where does the mall as an institution of consumer culture and relative economic privilege play into this analysis? How does this action account for the varying economic relationships queers have to consumer culture? If you are a poor or working-class queer the exclusion and alienation you experience when entering the mall may not be limited to the normative sexual codes associated with the mall, but may also be centered on the assumed economic status of those shopping in suburban malls. If you are a queer of color your exclusion from the mall may, in part, be rooted in racial norms and stereotypes which construct you as a threatening subject every time you enter this economic institution. Queer activists must confront a question that haunts most political organizing: How do we put into politics a broad and inclusive left analysis that can actually engage and mobilize individuals with intersecting identities?

Clearly, there will be those critics who will claim that I am asking too much from any political organization. Demands that every aspect of oppression and regulation be addressed in each political act seem, and are indeed, unreasonable. However, I make the critique of queer mall invasions neither to stop such events nor to suggest that every oppression be dealt with by this one political action. Instead, I raise these concerns to emphasize the ways in which varying relation to power exist not only among heterosexuals, but also among those who label themselves queer.

In its current rendition, queer politics is coded with class, gender, and race privilege, and may have lost its potential to be a politically expedient organizing tool for addressing the needs—and mobilizing the bodies—of people of color. As some queer theorists and activists call for the destruction of stable sexual categories, for example, moving instead toward a more

fluid understanding of sexual behavior, left unspoken is the class privilege which allows for such fluidity. Class or material privilege is a cornerstone of much of queer politics and theory as they exist today. Queer theorizing which calls for the elimination of fixed categories of sexual identity seems to ignore the ways in which some traditional social identities and communal ties can, in fact, be important to one's survival. Further, a queer politics which demonizes all heterosexuals discounts the relationships—especially those based on shared experiences of marginalization—that exist between gays and straights, particularly in communities of color.

Queers who operate out of a political culture of individualism assume a material independence that allows them to disregard historically or culturally recognized categories and communities or at the very least to move fluidly among them without ever establishing permanent relationships or identities within them. However, I and many other lesbian and gay people of color, as well as poor and working-class lesbians and gay men, do not have such material independence. Because of my multiple identities, which locate me and other "queer" people of color at the margins in this country, my material advancement, my physical protection and my emotional well-being are constantly threatened. In those stable categories and named communities whose histories have been structured by shared resistance to oppression, I find relative degrees of safety and security.

Let me emphasize again that the safety I feel is relative to other threats and is clearly not static or constant. For in those named communities I also find versions of domination and normalization being replicated and employed as more privileged/assimilated marshal group members use their associations with dominant institutions and resources to regulate and police the activities of other marginal group members. Any lesbian, gay, bisexual, or transgendered person of color who has experienced exclusion from indigenous institutions, such as the exclusion many out black gay men have encountered from some black churches responding to AIDS, recognizes that even within marginal groups there are normative rules determining community membership and power (Cohen). However, in spite of the unequal power relationships located in marginal communities, I am still not interested in disassociating politically from those communities, for queerness, as it is currently constructed, offers no viable political alternative, since it invites us to put forth a political agenda that makes invisible the prominence of race, class, and to varying degrees gender in determining the life chances of those on both sides of the hetero/queer divide.

So despite the roots of queer politics in the struggles of "queer" people of color, despite the calls for highlighting categories which have sought to regulate and control black bodies like my own, and despite the attempts at decentralized grassroots activism in some queer political organizations, there still exist—for some, like myself—great misgivings about current constructions of the term "queer." Personally speaking, I do not consider myself a "queer" activist or, for that matter, a "queer" anything. This is not because I do not consider myself an activist; in fact I hold my political work to be one of my most important contributions to all of my communities. But like other lesbian, gay, bisexual, and transgendered activists of color, I find the label "queer" fraught with unspoken assumptions which inhibit the radical political potential of this category.

The alienation, or at least discomfort, many activists and theorists of color have with current conceptions of queerness is evidenced, in part, by the minimal numbers of theorists of color who engage in the process of theorizing about the concept. Further, the sparse numbers of people of color who participate in "queer" political organizations might also be read as a sign of discomfort with the term. Most important, my confidence in making such a claim of distance and uneasiness with the term "queer" on the part of many people of color comes from my interactions with other lesbian, gay, bisexual, and transgendered people of color who repeatedly express their interpretation of "queer" as a term rooted in class, race, and gender privilege. For us, "queer" is a politics based on narrow sexual dichotomies which make no room either for the analysis of oppression of those we might categorize as heterosexual, or for the privilege of those who operate as "queer." As black lesbian activist and writer Barbara Smith argues in "Queer Politics: Where's the Revolution?":

> Unlike the early lesbian and gay movement, which had both ideological and practical links to the left, black activism and feminism, today's "queer" politicos seem to operate in a historical and ideological vacuum. "Queer" activists focus on "queer" issues, and racism, sexual oppression and economic exploitation do not qualify, despite the fact that the majority of "queers"

are people of color, female or working class. . . . Building unified, ongoing coalitions that challenge the system and ultimately prepare a way for revolutionary change simply isn't what "queer" activists have in mind. (13–14)

It is this narrow understanding of the idea of queer that negates its use in fundamentally reorienting the politics and privilege of lesbian and gay politics as well as more generally moving or transforming the politics of the left. Despite its liberatory claim to stand in opposition to static categories of oppression, queer politics and much of queer theory seem in fact to be static in the understanding of race, class, and gender and their roles in how heteronormativity regulates sexual behavior and identities. Distinctions between the status and the acceptance of different individuals categorized under the label of "heterosexual" go unexplored.

I emphasize the marginalized position of some who embrace heterosexual identities not because I want to lead any great crusade to understand more fully the plight of "the heterosexual." Rather, I recognize the potential for shared resistance with such individuals. This potential not only for coalitional work but for a shared analysis is especially relevant, from my vantage point, to "queer" people of color. Again, in my call for coalition work across sexual categories, I do not want to suggest that same-sex political struggles have not, independently, played an essential and distinct role in the liberatory politics and social movements of marginal people. My concern, instead, is with any political analysis or theory which collapses our understanding of power into a single continuum of evaluation.

Through a brief review of some of the ways in which nonnormative heterosexuality has been controlled and regulated through the state and systems of marginalization we may be reminded that differentials in power exist within all socially named categories. And through such recognition we may begin to envision a new political formation in which one's relation to dominant power serves as the basis of unity for radical coalition work in the twenty-first century.

HETEROSEXUALS ON THE (OUT)SIDE OF HETERONORMATIVITY

In this section I want to return to the question of a monolithic understanding of heterosexuality. I believe that through this issue we can begin to think critically about the components of a radical politics built not exclusively on identities, but on identities as they are invested with varying degrees of normative power. Thus, fundamental to my concern about the current structure and future agenda of queer politics is the unchallenged assumption of a uniform heteronormativity from which all heterosexuals benefit. I want again to be clear that there are, in fact, some who identify themselves as queer activists who do acknowledge relative degrees of power, and heterosexual access to that power, even evoking the term "straight queers." "Queer means to fuck with gender. There are straight queers, bi queers, tranny queers, lez queers, fag queers, SM queers, fisting queers in every single street in this apathetic country of ours" (anonymous, qtd. McIntosh 31).

Despite such sporadic insight, much of the politics of queer activists has been structured around the dichotomy of straight versus everything else, assuming a monolithic experience of heterosexual privilege for all those identified publicly with heterosexuality. A similar reductive dichotomy between men and women has consistently reemerged in the writing and actions of some feminists. And only through the demands, the actions, and the writing of many "feminists" and/or lesbians of color have those women who stand outside the norm of white, middle-class, legalized heterosexuality begun to see their lives, needs, and bodies represented in feminist theory (Carby; Collins; hooks). In a similar manner lesbian, gay, bisexual, and transgendered people of color have increasingly taken on the responsibility for at the very least complicating and most often challenging reductive notions of heteronormativity articulated by queer activists and scholars (Alexander; Farajaje-Jones; Lorde; Moraga and Anzaldúa; B. Smith).

If we follow such examples, complicating our understanding of both heteronormativity and queerness, we move one step closer to building the progressive coalition politics many of us desire. Specifically, if we pay attention to both historical and current examples of heterosexual relationships which have been prohibited, stigmatized, and generally repressed, we may begin to identify those spaces of shared or similar oppression and resistance that provide a basis for radical coalition work. Further, we may begin to answer certain questions: In narrowly positing a dichotomy of heterosexual privilege and queer oppression under which we all exist, are we negating a basis of political unity that could serve to strengthen many communities and movements seeking justice and societal

transformation? How do we use the relative degrees of ostracization all sexual/cultural "deviants" experience to build a basis of unity for broader coalition and movement work?

A little history (as a political scientist a little history is all I can offer) might be helpful in trying to sort out the various ways heterosexuality, especially as it has intersected with race, has been defined and experienced by different groups of people. It should also help to underscore the fact that many of the roots of heteronormativity are in white supremacist ideologies which sought (and continue) to use the state and its regulation of sexuality, in particular through the institution of heterosexual marriage, to designate which individuals were truly "fit" for full rights and privileges of citizenship. For example, the prohibition of marriages between black women and men imprisoned in the slave system was a component of many slave codes enacted during the seventeenth and eighteenth centuries. M. G. Smith, in his article on the structure of slave economic systems, succinctly states, "As property slaves were prohibited from forming legal relationships or marriages which would interfere with and restrict their owner's property rights" (71–72). Herbert G. Gutman, in *The Black Family in Slavery and Freedom, 1750–1925*, elaborates on the ideology of slave societies which denied the legal sanctioning of marriages between slaves and further reasoned that Blacks had no conception of family.

> The *Nation* identified sexual restraint, civil marriage, and family "stability" with "civilization" itself.
>   Such mid-nineteenth-century class and sexual beliefs reinforced racial beliefs about Afro-Americans. As slaves, after all, their marriages had not been sanctioned by the civil laws and therefore "the sexual passion" went unrestrained. . . . Many white abolitionists denied the slaves a family life or even, often, a family consciousness because for them [whites] the family had its origins in and had to be upheld by the civil law. (295)

Thus it was not the promotion of marriage or heterosexuality per se that served as the standard or motivation of most slave societies. Instead, marriage and heterosexuality, as viewed through the lenses of profit and domination, and the ideology of white supremacy, were reconfigured to justify the exploitation and regulation of black bodies, even those presumably engaged in heterosexual behavior. It was this system of state-sanctioned, white male, upper-class, heterosexual domination that forced these presumably black *heterosexual* men and women to endure a history of rape, lynching, and other forms of physical and mental terrorism. In this way, marginal group members, lacking power and privilege although engaged in heterosexual behavior, have often found themselves defined as outside the norms and values of dominant society. This position has most often resulted in the suppression or negation of their legal, social, and physical relationships and rights.

In addition to the prohibition of marriage between slaves, A. Leon Higginbotham, Jr., in *The Matter of Color—Race and the American Legal Process: The Colonial Period*, writes of the legal restrictions barring interracial marriages. He reminds us that the essential core of the American legal tradition was the preservation of the white race. The "mixing" of the races was to be strictly prohibited in early colonial laws. The regulation of interracial heterosexual relationships, however, should not be understood as exclusively relegated to the seventeenth, eighteenth and nineteenth centuries. In fact, Higginbotham informs us that the final law prohibiting miscegenation (the "interbreeding" or marrying of individuals from different "races"—actually meant to inhibit the "tainting" of the white race) was not repealed until 1967:

> Colonial anxiety about interracial sexual activity cannot be attributed solely to seventeenth-century values, for it was not until 1967 that the United States Supreme Court finally declared unconstitutional those statutes prohibiting interracial marriages. The Supreme Court waited thirteen years after its *Brown* decision dealing with desegregation of schools before, in *Loving v. Virginia*, it agreed to consider the issue of interracial marriages. (41)

It is this pattern of regulating the behavior and denigrating the identities of those heterosexuals on the outside of heteronormative privilege, in particular those perceived as threatening systems of white supremacy, male domination, and capitalist advancement, that I want to highlight. An understanding of the ways in which heteronormativity works to support and reinforce institutional racism, patriarchy, and class exploitation must therefore be a part of how we problematize current constructions of heterosexuality. As I stated previously, I am not suggesting that those involved in publicly identifiable heterosexual behavior do not

receive political, economic, and social advantage, especially in comparison to the experiences of some lesbian, transgendered, gay, and bisexual individuals. But the equation linking identity and behavior to power is not as linear and clear as some queer theorists and activists would have us believe.

A more recent example of regulated nonnormative heterosexuality is located in current debates and rhetoric regarding the "underclass" and the destruction of the welfare system. The stigmatization and demonization of single mothers, teen mothers, and, primarily, poor women of color dependent on state assistance has had a long and suspicious presence in American "intellectual" and political history. It was in 1965 that Daniel Patrick Moynihan released his "study" entitled *The Negro Family: The Case for National Action*. In this report, which would eventually come to be known as the Moynihan Report, the author points to the "pathologies" increasingly evident in so-called Negro families. In this document were allegations of the destructive nature of Negro family formations. The document's introduction argues that

> the fundamental problem, in which this is most clearly the case, is that of family structure. The evidence—not final, but powerfully persuasive—is that the Negro family in urban ghettos is crumbling. A middle-class group has managed to save itself, but for vast numbers of the unskilled, poorly educated city working class the fabric of conventional social relationships has all but disintegrated.

Moynihan, later in the document, goes on to describe the crisis and pathologies facing Negro family structure as being generated by the increasing number of single-female-headed households, the increasing number of "illegitimate" births and, of course, increasing welfare dependency:

> In essence, the Negro community has been forced into a matriarchal structure which, because it is so out of line with the rest of the American society, seriously retards the progress of the group as a whole, and imposes a crushing burden on the Negro male and, in consequence, on a great many Negro women as well. . . . In a word, most Negro youth are in danger of being caught up in the tangle of pathology that affects their world, and probably a majority are so entrapped. . . . Obviously, not every instance of social pathology afflicting the Negro community can be

traced to the weakness of family structure. . . . Nonetheless, at the center of the tangle of pathology is the weakness of the family structure. (29–30)

It is not the nonheterosexist behavior of these black men and women that is under fire, but rather the perceived nonnormative sexual behavior and family structures of these individuals, whom many queer activists—without regard to the impact of race, class, or gender—would designate as part of the heterosexist establishment or those mighty "straights they hate."

Over the last thirty years the demonization of poor women, engaged in nonnormative heterosexual relationships, has continued under the auspices of scholarship on the "underclass." Adolph L. Reed, in "The 'Underclass' as Myth and Symbol: The Poverty of Discourse About Poverty," discusses the gendered and racist nature of much of this literature, in which poor, often black and Latina women are portrayed as unable to control their sexual impulses and eventual reproductive decisions, unable to raise their children with the right moral fiber, unable to find "gainful" employment to support themselves and their "illegitimate children," and of course unable to manage "effectively" the minimal assistance provided by the state. Reed writes:

> The underclass notion may receive the greatest ideological boost from its gendered imagery and relation to gender politics. As I noted in a critique of Wilson's *The Truly Disadvantaged,* "family" is an intrinsically ideological category. The rhetoric of "disorganization," "disintegration," "deterioration" reifies one type of living arrangement—the ideal type of the bourgeois nuclear family—as outside history, nearly as though it were decreed by natural law. But—as I asked earlier—why exactly is out-of-wedlock birth pathological? Why is the female-headed household an indicator of disorganization and pathology? Does that stigma attach to *all* such households—even, say, a divorced executive who is a custodial mother? If not, what are the criteria for assigning it? The short answer is race and class bias inflected through a distinctively gendered view of the world. (33–34)

In this same discourse of the "underclass," young black men engaged in "reckless" heterosexual behavior are represented as irresponsible baby factories, unable to control or restrain their "sexual passion" (to borrow a term from the seventeenth century). And unfortunately, often it has been the work of professed liberals like William Julius Wilson, in his book *The Truly Disadvantaged,* that, while not using the word "pathologies," has substantiated in its own tentative way the conservative dichotomy between the deserving working poor and the lazy, Cadillac-driving, steak-eating welfare queens of Ronald Reagan's imagination. Again, I raise this point to remind us of the numerous ways that sexuality and sexual deviance from a prescribed norm have been used to demonize and to oppress various segments of the population, even some classified under the label "heterosexual."

The policies of politicians and the actions of law enforcement officials have reinforced, in much more devastating ways, the distinctions between acceptable forms of heterosexual expression and those to be regulated—increasingly through incarceration. This move toward the disallowance of some forms of heterosexual expression and reproductive choice can be seen in the practice of prosecuting pregnant women suspected of using drugs—nearly 80 percent of all women prosecuted are women of color; through the forced sterilization of Puerto Rican and Native American women; and through the state-dictated use of Norplant by women answering to the criminal justice system and by women receiving state assistance.[6] Further, it is the "nonnormative" children of many of these nonnormative women that Newt Gingrich would place in orphanages. This is the same Newt Gingrich who, despite his clear disdain for gay and lesbian "lifestyles," has invited lesbians and gay men into the Republican party. I need not remind you that he made no such offer to the women on welfare discussed above. Who, we might ask, is truly on the outside of heteronormative power—maybe *most* of us?

CONCLUSION: DESTABILIZATION AND RADICAL COALITION WORK

While all this may, in fact, seem interesting or troubling or both, you may be wondering: What does it have to do with the question of the future of queer politics? It is my argument, as I stated earlier, that one of the great failings of queer theory and especially queer politics has been their inability to incorporate into analysis of the world and strategies for political mobilization the roles that race, class, and gender play in defining people's differing relations to dominant and normalizing power. I present this essay as the beginning of a much longer and protracted struggle to acknowledge and delineate the distribution of power within and outside of queer communities. This is a discussion of how to build a politics organized not merely by reductive categories of straight and queer, but organized instead around a more intersectional analysis of who and what the enemy is and where our potential allies can be found. This analysis seeks to make clear the privilege and power embedded in the categorizations of, on the one hand, an upstanding, "morally correct," white, state-authorized, middle-class, male *heterosexual,* and on the other, a culturally deficient, materially bankrupt, state-dependent, *heterosexual* woman of color, the latter found most often in our urban centers (those that haven't been gentrified), on magazine covers, and on the evening news.

I contend, therefore, that the radical potential of queer politics, or any liberatory movement, rests on its ability to advance strategically oriented political identities arising from a more nuanced understanding of power. One of the most difficult tasks in such an endeavor (and there are many) is not to forsake the complexities of both how power is structured and how we might think about the coalitions we create. Far too often movements revert to a position in which membership and joint political work are based upon a necessarily similar history of oppression—but this is too much like identity politics (Phelan). Instead, I am suggesting that the process of movement building be rooted not in our shared history or identity, but in our shared marginal relationship to dominant power which normalizes, legitimizes, and privileges.

We must, therefore, start our political work from the recognition that multiple systems of oppression are in operation and that these systems use institutionalized categories and identities to regulate and socialize. We must also understand that power and access to dominant resources are distributed across the boundaries of "het" and "queer" that we construct. A model of queer politics that simply pits the grand "heterosexuals" against all those oppressed "queers" is ineffectual as the basis for action in a political environment dominated by Newt Gingrich, the Christian Right, and the recurring ideology of white supremacy. As we stand on the verge of watching those in power dismantle the welfare system through a process of demonizing poor and young, primarily poor and young women of color—many of whom have existed for their entire lives outside the white, middle-class, heterosexual norm—we have to ask if these women do not fit into society's categories of marginal, deviant, and "queer."

As we watch the explosion of prison construction and the disproportionate incarceration rates of young men and women of color, often as part of the economic development of poor white rural communities, we have to ask if these individuals do not fit society's definition of "queer" and expendable.

I am not proposing a political strategy that homogenizes and glorifies the experience of poor heterosexual people of color. In fact, in calling for a more expansive left political identity and formation I do not seek to erase the specific historical relation between the stigma of "queer" and the sexual activity of gay men, lesbians, bisexual, and transgendered individuals. And in no way do I mean to, or want to, equate the experiences of marginal heterosexual women and men to the lived experiences of queers. There is no doubt that heterosexuality, even for those heterosexuals who stand outside the norms of heteronormativity, results in some form of privilege and feelings of supremacy. I need only recount the times when other women of color, more economically vulnerable than myself, expressed superiority and some feelings of disgust when they realized that the nice young professor (me) was "that way."

However, in recognizing the distinct history of oppression lesbian, gay, bisexual, and transgendered people have confronted and challenged, I am not willing to embrace every queer as my marginalized political ally. In the same way, I do not assume that shared racial, gender, and/or class position or identity guarantees or produces similar political commitments. Thus, identities and communities, while important to this strategy, must be complicated and destabilized through a recognition of the multiple social positions and relations to dominant power found *within* any one category or identity. Kimberlé Crenshaw, in "Mapping the Margins: Intersectionality, Identity Politics, and Violence Against Women of Color," suggests that such a project use the idea of intersectionality to reconceptualize or problematize the identities and communities that are "home" to us. She demands that we challenge those identities that seem like home by acknowledging the other parts of our identities that are excluded:

With identity thus reconceptualized [through a recognition of intersectionality], it may be easier to understand the need to summon up the courage to challenge groups that are after all, in one sense, "home" to us, in the name of the parts of us that are not made at home. . . . The most one could expect is that we will dare to speak against internal exclusions and marginalizations, that we might call attention to how the identity of "the group" has been centered on the intersectional identities of a few. . . . Through an awareness of intersectionality, we can better acknowledge and ground the differences among us and negotiate the means by which these differences will find expression in constructing group politics. (1299)

In the same ways that we account for the varying privilege to be gained by a heterosexual identity, we must also pay attention to the privilege some queers receive from being white, male, and upper class. Only through recognizing the many manifestations of power, across and within categories, can we truly begin to build a movement based on one's politics and not exclusively on one's identity.

I want to be clear that what I and others are calling for is the destabilization, and not the destruction or abandonment, of identity categories.[7] We must reject a queer politics which seems to ignore, in its analysis of the usefulness of traditionally named categories, the roles of identity and community as paths to survival, using shared experiences of oppression and resistance to build indigenous resources, shape consciousness, and act collectively. Instead, I would suggest that it is the multiplicity and interconnectedness of our identities which provide the most promising avenue for the *destabilization and radical politicalization* of these same categories.

This is not an easy path to pursue because most often this will mean building a political analysis and political strategies around the most marginal in our society, some of whom look like us, many of whom do not. Most often, this will mean rooting our struggle in, and addressing the needs of, communities of color. Most often this will mean highlighting the intersectionality of one's race, class, gender, and sexuality and the relative power and privilege that one receives from being a man and/or being white and/or being middle class and/or being heterosexual. This, in particular, is a daunting challenge because so much of our political consciousness has been built around simple dichotomies such as powerful/powerless; oppressor/victim; enemy/comrade. It is difficult to feel safe and secure in those spaces where both your relative privilege and your experiences with marginalization are understood to shape your commitment to radical politics. However,

as Bernice Johnson Reagon so aptly put it in her essay, "Coalition Politics: Turning the Century," "if you feel the strain, you may be doing some good work" (362).

And while this is a daunting challenge and uncomfortable position, those who have taken it up have not only survived, but succeeded in their efforts. For example, both the needle exchange and prison projects pursued through the auspices of ACT UP New York point to the possibilities and difficulties involved in principled transformative coalition work. In each project individuals from numerous identities—heterosexual, gay, poor, wealthy, white, black, Latino—came together to challenge dominant constructions of who should be allowed and who deserved care. No particular identity exclusively determined the shared political commitments of these activists; instead their similar positions, as marginalized subjects relative to the state—made clear through the government's lack of response to AIDS—formed the basis of this political unity.

In the prison project, it was the contention of activists that the government which denied even wealthy gay men access to drugs to combat this disease must be regarded as the same source of power that denied incarcerated men and women access to basic health care, including those drugs and conditions needed to combat HIV and AIDS. The coalition work this group engaged in involved a range of people, from formerly incarcerated individuals, to heterosexual men and women of color, to those we might deem privileged white lesbians and gay men. And this same group of people who came together to protest the conditions of incarcerated people with AIDS also showed up to public events challenging the homophobia that guided the government's and biomedical industries' response to this epidemic. The political work of this group of individuals was undoubtedly informed by the public identities they embraced, but these were identities that they further acknowledged as complicated by intersectionality and placed within a political framework where their shared experience as marginal, nonnormative subjects could be foregrounded. Douglas Crimp, in his article "Right On, Girlfriend!" suggests that through political work our identities become remade and must therefore be understood as *relational*. Describing such a transformation in the identities of queer activists engaged in, and prosecuted for, needle exchange work, Crimp writes:

But once engaged in the struggle to end the crisis, these queers' identities were no longer the same. It's not that "queer" doesn't any longer encompass their sexual practices; it does, but it also entails a *relation* between those practices and other circumstances that make very different people vulnerable both to HIV infection and to the stigma, discrimination, and neglect that have characterized the societal and governmental response to the constituencies most affected by the AIDS epidemic. (317–18)

The radical potential of those of us on the outside of heteronormativity rests in our understanding that we need not base our politics in the dissolution of all categories and communities, but we need instead to work toward the destabilization and remaking of our identities. Difference, in and of itself—even that difference designated through named categories—is not the problem. Instead it is the power invested in certain identity categories and the idea that bounded categories are not to be transgressed that serve as the basis of domination and control. The reconceptualization not only of the content of identity categories, but the intersectional nature of identities themselves, must become part of our political practice.

We must thus begin to link our intersectional analysis of power with concrete coalitional work. In real terms this means identifying political struggles such as the needle exchange and prison projects of ACT UP that transgress the boundaries of identity to highlight, in this case, both the repressive power of the state and the normalizing power evident within both dominant and marginal communities. This type of principled coalition work is also being pursued in a more modest fashion by the Policy Institute of the National Gay and Lesbian Task Force. Recently, the staff at the Task Force distributed position papers not only on the topics of gay marriages and gays in the military, but also on right-wing attacks against welfare and affirmative action. Here we have political work based in the knowledge that the rhetoric and accusations of nonnormativity that Newt Gingrich and other right-wingers launch against women on welfare closely resemble the attacks of nonnormativity mounted against gays, lesbians, bisexuals, and transgendered individuals. Again it is the marginalized relation to power, experienced by both of these groups—and I do not mean to suggest that the groups are mutually exclusive—that frames the possibility for transformative coalition work. This prospect diminishes when we do not recognize and deal with the reality that the intersecting identities that gay people embody—in terms of race, class, and gender privilege—put some of us on Gingrich's side of the welfare struggle (e.g., Log Cabin Republicans). And in a similar manner a woman's dependence on state financial assistance in no way secures her position as one supportive of gay rights and/or liberation. While a marginal identity undoubtedly increases the prospects of shared consciousness, only an articulation and commitment to mutual support can truly be the test of unity when pursuing transformational politics.

Finally, I realize that I have been short on specifics when trying to describe how we move concretely toward a transformational coalition politics among marginalized subjects. The best I can do is offer this discussion as a starting point for reassessing the shape of queer/lesbian/gay/bisexual/transgendered politics as we approach the twenty-first century. A reconceptualization of the politics of marginal groups allows us not only to privilege the specific lived experience of distinct communities, but also to search for those interconnected sites of resistance from which we can wage broader political struggles. Only by recognizing the link *between* the ideological, social, political, and economic marginalization of punks, bulldaggers, and welfare queens can we begin to develop political analyses and political strategies effective in confronting the linked yet varied sites of power in this country. Such a project is important because it provides a framework from which the difficult work of coalition politics can begin. And it is in these complicated and contradictory spaces that the liberatory and left politics that so many of us work for is located.

ACKNOWLEDGMENTS

The author would like to thank Mark Blasius, Nan Boyd, Ed Cohen, Carolyn Dinshaw, Jeff Edwards, Licia Fiol-Matta, Joshua Gamson, Lynne Huffer, Tamara Jones, Carla Kaplan, Ntanya Lee, Ira Livingston, and Barbara Ransby for their comments on various versions of this paper. All shortcomings are of course the fault of the author.

NOTES

1. The very general chronology of queer theory and queer politics referred to throughout this article is not meant to write the definitive historical development of each phenomenon. Instead, the dates are used to provide the reader with a general frame of reference. See Epstein for a similar genealogy of queer theory and queer politics.

2. See Ingraham for a discussion of the heterogendered imaginary.

3. I want to be clear that in this essay I am including the destruction of sexual categories as part of the agenda of queer politics. While a substantial segment of queer activists and theorists call for the *destabilization* of sexual categories, there are also those self-avowed queers who embrace a politics built around the *deconstruction* and/or elimination of sexual categories. For example, a number of my self-identified queer students engage in sexual behavior that most people would interpret as *transgressive* of sexual identities and categories. However, these students have repeatedly articulated a different interpretation of their sexual behavior. They put forth an understanding that does not highlight their transgression of categories, but one which instead represents them as individuals who operate outside of categories and sexual identities altogether. They are sexual beings, given purely to desire, truly living sexual fluidity, and not constrained by any form of sexual categorization or identification. This interpretation seems at least one step removed from that held by people who embrace the fluidity of sexuality while still recognizing the political usefulness of categories or labels for certain sexual behavior and communities. One example of such people might be those women who identify as lesbians and who also acknowledge that sometimes they choose to sleep with men. These individuals exemplify the process of destabilization that I try to articulate within this essay. Even further removed from the queers who would do away with all sexual categories are those who also transgress what many consider to be categories of sexual behaviors while they publicly embrace one stable sexual identity (for example, those self-identified heterosexual men who sleep with other men sporadically and secretly).

4. I want to thank Mark Blasius for raising the argument that standing on the outside of heteronormativity is a bit of a misnomer, since as a dominant normalizing process it is a practice of regulation in which we are all implicated. However, despite this insight I will on occasion continue to use this phrasing, understanding the limits of its meaning.

5. See Hennessy for a discussion of left analysis and the limits of queer theory.

6. For an insightful discussion of the numerous methods used to regulate and control the sexual and reproductive choices of women, see Shende.

7. See Jones for an articulation of differences between the destabilization and the destruction of identity categories.

REFERENCES

Alexander, Jacqui. "Redrafting Morality: The Postcolonial State and the Sexual Offences Bill of Trinidad and Tobago." *Third World Women and the Politics of Feminism,* ed. C. T. Mohanty, A. Russo, and L. Torres. Bloomington: Indiana UP, 1991. 133–52.

Berlant, Lauren, and Elizabeth Freeman. "Queer Nationality." Warner 193–229.

Bérubé, Allan, and Jeffrey Escoffier. "Queer/Nation." *Out/Look: National Lesbian and Gay Quarterly* II (Winter 1991): 12–14.

Blasius, Mark. *Gay and Lesbian Politics: Sexuality and the Emergence of a New Ethic.* Philadelphia: Temple UP, 1994.

Butler, Judith. *Gender Trouble.* New York Routledge, 1990.

Carby, Hazel. *Reconstructing Womanhood: The Emergence of the Afro-American Woman Novelist.* New York: Oxford UP, 1987.

Clarke, Cheryl. "The Failure to Transform: Homophobia in the Black Community." Smith, *Home Girls* 197–208.

Cohen, Cathy J. "Contested Membership: Black Gay Identities and the Politics of AIDS." *Queer Theory/Sociology,* ed. S. Seidman. Oxford: Blackwell, 1996. 362–94.

Collins, Patricia Hill. *Black Feminist Thought: Knowledge, Consciousness, and the Politics of Sociology Empowerment.* New York: Harper, 1990.

Combahee River Collective. "The Combahee River Collective Statement." Smith, *Home Girls* 272–82.

Crenshaw, Kimberle. "Mapping the Margins: Intersectionality, Identity Politics, and Violence Against Women of Color." *Stanford Law Review* 43 (1991): 1241–99.

Crimp, Douglas. "Right On, Girlfriend!" Warner 300–20.

Davis, Angela Y. *Women, Race and Class.* New York Vintage, 1983.

De Lauretis, Teresa. "Queer Theory: Lesbian and Gay Sexualities." *Differences* 3.2 (Summer 1991): iii–xviii.

Dunlap, David W. "Three Black Members Quit AIDS Organization Board." *New York Times* 11 Jan. 1996: B2.

Dyson, Michael Eric. *Between God and Gangsta Rap.* New York: Oxford UP, 1996.

Epstein, Steven. "A Queer Encounter: Sociology and the Study of Sexuality." *Sociological Theory* 12 (1994): 188–202.

Farajaje-Jones, Elias. "Ain't I a Queer." Creating Change Conference, National Gay and Lesbian Task Force, Detroit, Michigan, 8–12 Nov. 1995.

Fuss, Diana, ed. *Inside/Outside.* New York: Routledge, 1991.

Gamson, Joshua. "Must Identity Movements Self-Destruct? A Queer Dilemma." *Social Problems* 42 (1995): 390–407.

Gutman, Herbert G. *The Black Family in Slavery and Freedom, 1750–1925.* New York: Vintage, 1976.

Hennessy, Rosemary. "Queer Theory, Left Politics," *Rethinking MARXISM* 7.3 (1994): 85–111.

Higginbotham, A. Leon, Jr. *In the Matter of Color—Race and the American Legal Process: The Colonial Period.* New York: Oxford UP, 1978.

hooks, bell. *Feminist Theory: From Margin to Center.* Boston: South End, 1984.

Ingraham, Chrys. "The Heterosexual Imaginary: Feminist Sociology and Theories of Gender." *Sociological Theory* 12 (1994): 203–19.

Jones, Tamara. "Inside the Kaleidoscope: How the Construction of Black Gay and Lesbian Identities Inform Political Strategies." Unpublished. Yale University, 1995.

Lorde, Audre. *Sister Outsider: Essays and Speeches by Audre Lorde.* New York: The Crossing P. 1984.

McIntosh, Mary. "Queer Theory and the War of the Sexes." *Activating Theory: Lesbian, Gay, Bisexual Politics,* ed. J. Bristow and A. R. Wilson. London: Lawrence and Wishart, 1993. 33–52.

Moraga, Cherríe, and Gloria Anzaldúa, eds. *This Bridge Called My Back: Writings by Radical Women of Color.* New York: Kitchen Table/Women of Color, 1981.

Morton, Donald. "The Politics of Queer Theory in the (Post) Modern Moment," *Genders* 17 (Fall 1993): 121–15.

Moynihan, Daniel Patrick. *The Negro Family: The Case for National Action.* Washington D.C.: Office of Policy Planning and Research, U.S. Department of Labor, 1965.

Phelan, Shane. *Identity Politics: Lesbian Feminism and the Limits of Community.* Philadelphia: Temple UP, 1989.

Podolsky, Robin. "Sacrificing Queer and other 'Proletarian' Artifacts." *Radical America* 25.1 (January 1991): 53–60.

Queer Nation. "I Hate Straights" manifesto. New York, 1990.

Queers United Against Straight-Acting Homosexuals. "Assimilation Is Killing Us: Fight for a Queer United Front." WHY I HATED THE MARCH ON WASHINGTON (1993): 4.

Ransby, Barbara, and Tracye Matthews. "Black Popular Culture and the Transcendence of Patriarchical Illusions." *Race & Class* 35.1 (July–September 1993): 57–70.

Reagon, Bernice Johnson. "Coalition Politics: Turning the Century." Smith, *Home Girls* 356–68.

Reed, Adolph L., Jr. "The 'Underclass' as Myth and Symbol: The Poverty of Discourse About Poverty." *Radical America* 24.1 (January 1990): 21–40.

Rich, Adrienne. "Compulsory Heterosexuality and Lesbian Existence." *Powers of Desire: The Politics of Sexuality,* ed. A. Snitow, C. Stansell and S. Thompson. New York: Monthly Review, 1983. 177–206.

Sedgwick, Eve. *The Epistemology of the Closet.* Berkeley: U of California P, 1990.

Seidman, Steven. "Identity and Politics in a 'Postmodern' Gay Culture." Warner 105–42.

Shende, Suzanne. "Fighting the Violence Against Our Sisters: Prosecution of Pregnant Women and the Coercive Use of Norplant." *Women Transforming Politics: An Alternative Reader,* ed. C. Cohen, K. Jones, and J. Tronto, New York: New York UP, 1997.

Smith, Barbara. "Queer Politics: Where's the Revolution?" *The Nation* 257.1 (July 5, 1993): 12–16.

——, ed. *Home Girls: A Black Feminist Anthology.* New York: Kitchen Table/Women of Color, 1983.

Smith, M. G. "Social Structure in the British Caribbean About 1820." *Social and Economic Studies* 1.4 (August 1953): 55–79.

"Statement of Purpose." Dialogue on the Lesbian and Gay Left. Duncan Conference Center in Del Ray Beach, Florida. 1–4 April 1993.

Stein, Arlene, and Ken Plummer. "'I Can't Even Think Straight': 'Queer' Theory and the Missing Sexual Revolution in Sociology." *Sociological Theory* 12 (1994): 178–87.

Vaid, Urvashi. *Virtual Equality: The Mainstreaming of Gay & Lesbian Liberation.* New York: Anchor, 1995.

Warner, Michael, ed. *Fear of a Queer Planet: Queer Politics and Social Theory.* Minneapolis: U of Minnesota P, 1993.

West, Cornel. *Race Matters.* Boston: Beacon, 1993.

Wilson, William Julius. *The Truly Disadvantaged: The Inner City, the Underclass, and Public Policy.* Chicago: U of Chicago P, 1987.

UN COMMISSION APPROVES DECLARATION REAFFIRMING GOALS OF 1995 WOMEN'S CONFERENCE AFTER U.S. DROPS ANTIABORTION AMENDMENT

08 Mar 2005

The 45-member . . . UN Commission on the Status of Women on Friday unanimously approved a one-page declaration supporting the Platform for Action adopted at the 1995 Fourth World Conference on Women in Beijing after the United States dropped an amendment that would have clarified that the platform does not include a right to abortion or create any new international human rights, the *AP/San Francisco Chronicle* reports (Lederer, *AP/San Francisco Chronicle*, 3/5). The UN commission at the end of last month—ahead of a two-week review of the conference, which began last week—proposed a declaration asking the participating countries to reaffirm progress toward the Beijing platform, which stated that abortion should be safe in places where it is legal and that criminal charges should not be filed against any woman who undergoes an illegal abortion. The platform also stated that women have the right to "decide freely and responsibly on matters related to their sexuality . . . free of coercion, discrimination and violence." Bush administration representatives at first said the United States would not sign the declaration because of concerns that the platform classified legal abortion as a human right and proposed an amendment that would reaffirm U.S. commitment to the platform and declaration "while reaffirming that they do not create any new international human rights and that they do not include the right to abortion." However, most member nations rejected even a "watered down" version of the U.S. amendment, with delegates from the European Union, African Union and Mercosur trading bloc in South America all insisting that the declaration remain in its original form (*Kaiser Daily Reproductive Health Report*, 3/4).

U.S. Drops Amendment, Declares Victory

U.S. Ambassador to the United Nations Ellen Sauerbrey on Friday said the U.S. delegation would drop its amendment after "receiving assurances" that the platform approved at the 1995 conference does not create "a new global right to abortion," the *AP/Chronicle* reports (*AP/San Francisco Chronicle*, 3/5). "We have heard from countries that our interpretation is their interpretation," Sauerbrey said at a news conference, adding, "so the amendment, we recognize, is really redundant, but it has accomplished its goals" (Lynch, *Washington Post*, 3/5). Charlotte Bunch, executive director of the Center for Women's Global Leadership, said the amendment was "an effort to inject U.S. politics into a broad international consensus," adding, "The reality is that [the United States] heard loud and clear the voices of 6,000 women here [at the conference] saying 'No,' echoing millions of other women worldwide" (*AP/San Francisco Chronicle*, 3/5).

FOURTH WORLD CONFERENCE ON WOMEN BEIJING DECLARATION

Declaration

1. We, the Governments participating in the Fourth World Conference on Women,

2. Gathered here in Beijing in September 1995, the year of the fiftieth anniversary of the founding of the United Nations,

3. Determined to advance the goals of equality, development and peace for all women everywhere in the interest of all humanity,

4. Acknowledging the voices of all women everywhere and taking note of the diversity of women and their roles and circumstances, honoring the women who paved the way and inspired by the hope present in the world's youth,

5. Recognize that the status of women has advanced in some important respects in the past decade but that progress has been uneven, inequalities between women and men have persisted and major obstacles remain, with serious consequences for the well-being of all people,

6. Also recognize that this situation is exacerbated by the increasing poverty that is affecting the lives of the majority of the world's people, in particular women and children, with origins in both the national and international domains,

7. Dedicate ourselves unreservedly to addressing these constraints and obstacles and thus enhancing further the advancement and empowerment of women all over the world, and agree that this requires urgent action in the spirit of determination, hope, cooperation and solidarity, now and to carry us forward into the next century.

We Reaffirm Our Commitment to:

8. The equal rights and inherent human dignity of women and men and other purposes and principles enshrined in the Charter of the United Nations, to the Universal Declaration of Human Rights and other international human rights instruments, in particular the Convention on the Elimination of All Forms of Discrimination against Women and the Convention on the Rights of the Child, as well as the Declaration on the Elimination of Violence against Women and the Declaration on the Right to Development;

9. Ensure the full implementation of the human rights of women and of the girl child as an inalienable, integral and indivisible part of all human rights and fundamental freedoms;

10. Build on consensus and progress made at previous United Nations conferences and summits— on women in Nairobi in 1985, on children in New York in 1990, on environment and development in Rio de Janeiro in 1992, on human rights in Vienna in 1993, on population and development in Cairo in 1994 and on social development in Copenhagen in 1995 with the objective of achieving equality, development and peace;

11. Achieve the full and effective implementation of the Nairobi Forward-Looking Strategies for the Advancement of Women;

12. The empowerment and advancement of women, including the right to freedom of thought, conscience, religion and belief, thus contributing to the moral, ethical, spiritual and intellectual needs of women and men, individually or in community with others and thereby guaranteeing them the possibility of realizing their full potential in society and shaping their lives in accordance with their own aspirations.

We Are Convinced That:

13. Women's empowerment and their full participation on the basis of equality in all spheres of society, including participation in the decision-making process and access to power, are fundamental for the achievement of equality, development and peace;

14. Women's rights are human rights;

15. Equal rights, opportunities and access to resources, equal sharing of responsibilities for the family by men and women, and a harmonious partnership between them are critical to their well-being and that of their families as well as to the consolidation of democracy;

16. Eradication of poverty based on sustained economic growth, social development, environmental protection and social justice requires the involvement of women in economic and social development, equal opportunities and the full and equal participation of women and men as agents and beneficiaries of people-centered sustainable development;

17. The explicit recognition and reaffirmation of the right of all women to control all aspects of their health, in particular their own fertility, is basic to their empowerment;

18. Local, national, regional and global peace is attainable and is inextricably linked with the advancement of women, who are a fundamental force for leadership, conflict resolution and the promotion of lasting peace at all levels;

19. It is essential to design, implement and monitor, with the full participation of women, effective, efficient and mutually reinforcing gender-sensitive policies and programmes, including development policies and programmes, at all levels that will foster the empowerment and advancement of women;

20. The participation and contribution of all actors of civil society, particularly women's groups and networks and other non-governmental organizations and community-based organizations, with full respect for their autonomy, in cooperation with Governments, are important to the effective implementation and follow-up of the Platform for Action;

21. The implementation of the Platform for Action requires commitment from Governments and the international community. By making national and international commitments for action, including those made at the Conference, Governments and the international community recognize the need to take priority action for the empowerment and advancement of women.

We Are Determined to:

22. Intensify efforts and actions to achieve the goals of the Nairobi Forward-Looking Strategies for the Advancement of Women by the end of this century;

23. Ensure the full enjoyment by women and the girl child of all human rights and fundamental freedoms and take effective action against violations of these rights and freedoms;

24. Take all necessary measures to eliminate all forms of discrimination against women and the girl child and remove all obstacles to gender equality and the advancement and empowerment of women;

25. Encourage men to participate fully in all actions towards equality;

26. Promote women's economic independence, including employment, and eradicate the persistent and increasing burden of poverty on women by addressing the structural causes of poverty through changes uneconomic, ensuring equal access for all women, including those in rural areas, as vital development agents, to productive resources, opportunities and public services;

27. Promote people-centered sustainable development, including sustained economic growth, through the provision of basic education, life-long education, literacy and training, and primary health care for girls and women;

28. Take positive steps to ensure peace for the advancement of women and, recognizing the leading role that women have played in the peace movement, work actively towards general and complete disarmament under strict and effective international control, and support negotiations on the conclusion, without delay, of a universal and multilaterally and effectively verifiable comprehensive nuclear-test-ban treaty which contributes to nuclear disarmament and the prevention of the proliferation of nuclear weapons in all its aspects;

29. Prevent and eliminate all forms of violence against women and girls;

30. Ensure equal access to and equal treatment of women and men in education and health care

(continued)

and enhance women's sexual and reproductive health as well as education;

31. Promote and protect all human rights of women and girls;

32. Intensify efforts to ensure equal enjoyment of all human rights and fundamental freedoms for all women and girls who face multiple barriers to their empowerment and advancement because of such factors as their race, age, language, ethnicity, culture, religion, or disability, or because they are indigenous people;

33. Ensure respect for international law, including humanitarian law, in order to protect women and girls in particular;

34. Develop the fullest potential of girls and women of all ages, ensure their full and equal participation in building a better world for all and enhance their role in the development process.

We Are Determined to:

35. Ensure women's equal access to economic resources, including land, credit, science and technology, vocational training, information, communication and markets, as a means to further the advancement and empowerment of women and girls, including through the enhancement of their capacities to enjoy the benefits of equal access to these resources, inter alia, by means of international cooperation;

36. Ensure the success of the Platform for Action, which will require a strong commitment on the part of Governments, international organizations and institutions at all levels. We are deeply convinced that economic development, social development and environmental protection are interdependent and mutually reinforcing components of sustainable development, which is the framework for our efforts to achieve a higher quality of life for all people. Equitable social development that recognizes empowering the poor, particularly women living in poverty, to utilize environmental resources sustainably is a necessary foundation for sustainable development. We also recognize that broad-based and sustained economic growth in the context of sustainable development is necessary to sustain social development and social justice. The success of the Platform for Action will also require adequate mobilization of resources at the national and international levels as well as new and additional resources to the developing countries from all available funding mechanisms, including multilateral, bilateral and private sources for the advancement of women; financial resources to strengthen the capacity of national, subregional, regional and international institutions; a commitment to equal rights, equal responsibilities and equal opportunities and to the equal participation of women and men in all national, regional and international bodies and policy-making processes; and the establishment or strengthening of mechanisms at all levels for accountability to the world's women;

37. Ensure also the success of the Platform for Action in countries with economies in transition, which will require continued international cooperation and assistance;

38. We hereby adopt and commit ourselves as Governments to implement the following Platform for Action, ensuring that a gender perspectives reflected in all our policies and programmes. We urge the United Nations system, regional and international financial institutions, other relevant regional and international institutions and all women and men, as well as non-governmental organizations, with full respect for their autonomy, and all sectors of civil society, in cooperation with Governments, to fully commit themselves and contribute to the implementation of this Platform for Action.

ACKNOWLEDGMENTS

Lila Abu-Lughod, "Do Muslim Women Really Need?" from *American Anthropologist* 104, no. 3 (2002). Copyright © 2002 by the American Anthropological Association. Reprinted with permission.

Paula Gunn Allen, "Where I Come From is Like This" from *The Sacred Hoop: Recovering the Feminine Side in American Indian Traditions*. Copyright © 1986 by Paula Gunn Allen. Reprinted with the permission of Beacon Press, Boston.

Pamela Aronson, "Feminists or Postfeminists?" from *Gender & Society* 17, no. 6 (December 2003). Copyright © 2003 by Sociologists for Women in Society. Reprinted with the permission of Sage Publications, Inc.

Ingrid Banks, "Hair Still Matters." Reprinted with the permission of the author.

Eileen Boris, "Desirable Dress: Rosies, Sky Girls, and the Politics of Appearance" from *International Labor and Working-Class History* 69 (Spring 2006): 123–142. Copyright © 2006 by International Labor and Working-Class History, Inc. Reprinted with the permission of the author and Cambridge University Press.

Eileen Boris, "The Living Wage as a Women's Issue" from *Living Wage Now! The Newsletter of the Coalition for a Living Wage* (February 2001). Reprinted with the permission of the Coalition for a Living Wage.

Christine E. Bose and Rachel Bridges Whaley, "Sex Segregation in the U.S. Labor Force" from *Gender Mosaics: Social Perspectives*, edited by Dana Vannoy. Copyright © 2001 by Roxbury Publishing Company. Reprinted with the permission of the publisher.

Grace Chang, "From the Third World to the 'Third World Within'" from *Labor Versus Empire: Race, Gender, and Migration*, edited by Gilbert G. Gonzalez, Raul Fernandez, Vivian Price, David Smith, and Linda Trinh Vo. Copyright © 2004 by Taylor & Francis Books, Inc. Reprinted with the permission of Routledge/Taylor & Francis Group, LLC.

Eli Clare, "Stolen Bodies" excerpt from "Stolen Bodies, Reclaimed Bodies: Disability and Queerness" from *Public Culture* 13(3): 359–365. Copyright © 2001 by Duke University Press. All rights reserved. Used by permission of the publisher.

Cathy Cohen, "Punks, Bulldaggers, and Welfare Queens: The Radical Potential of Queer Politics?" from *GLQ: A Journal of Lesbian and Gay Studies* 3, no. 4 (1997): 437–65. Copyright © 1997 by Duke University Press. All rights reserved. Used by permission of the publisher.

Patricia Hill Collins, from *Black Sexual Politics: African Americans, Gender, and the New Racism*. Copyright © 2004 by Routledge. Reprinted with the permission of Routledge/Taylor & Francis Group, LLC.

R. W. Connell, "Masculinities and Globalization" from *Men and Masculinities* 1 (1999). Copyright © 1999 by Sage Publications, Inc. Reprinted with the permission of Sage Publications, Inc.

Kimberlé Crenshaw, "Mapping the Margins: Intersectionality, Identity Politics, and Violence Against Women of Color" from *Stanford Law Review* 1241 (1991). Reprinted with the permission of the author and the *Stanford Law Review*, Stanford University School of Law.

Simone Weil Davis, "Loose Lips Sink Ships" from *Feminist Studies* 28, no. 1 (Spring 2002). Reprinted with the permission of the publisher, *Feminist Studies*, Inc.

Jo Doezema, "Forced to Choose: Beyond the Voluntary v. Forced Prostitution" from *Global Sex Workers: Rights, Resistance, and Redefinition*, edited by Kamala Kempadoo and Jo Doezema. Copyright © 1998 by Routledge. Reprinted with the permission of the author and Routledge/Taylor & Francis Books, Inc.

Pheona Donohoe, "Femicide in Juárez." Reprinted with the permission of the author.

Barbara Ehrenreich, "Welcome to Cancerland" from *Harper's* (November 2001). Copyright © 2001 by Barbara Ehrenreich. Reprinted with the permission of International Creative Management, Inc.

Cynthia Enloe, "The Globe Trotting Sneaker" from *Ms.* (March/April 1995). Copyright © 1995. Reprinted with the permission of the author.

Yen Le Espiritu, "We Don't Sleep Around Like White Girls Do" from *Signs: Journal of Women in Culture and Society* 26, no. 2 (Winter 2001). Copyright © 2001 by The University of Chicago. Reprinted with permission.

Rosemarie Garland-Thomson, "Feminism and Disability Studies" from *Emory Report* (July 6, 2004). Reprinted with the permission of the author.

Kathleen Gerson, "Moral Dilemmas, Moral Strategies, and the Transformation of Gender" from *Gender & Society* 16, No. 1 (February 2002): 8–28. Copyright © 2002 by Sociologists for Women in Society. Reprinted with the permission of the author and Sage Publications, Inc.

Debra Gimlin, "Cosmetic Surgery: Paying for Your Beauty" from *Body Work: Beauty and Self-Image in American Culture*. Copyright © 2002 by the Regents of the University of California. Reprinted with the permission of the University of California Press.

Robin Givhan, "Hilary Clinton's Tentative Dip into New Neckline Territory" from *The Washington Post* (July 20, 2007): C01. Copyright © 2007 by The Washington Post Company. Reprinted with permission.

Laura Hamilton, "Trading on Heterosexuality: College Women's Gender Strategies and Homophobia" from *Gender & Society* 21, No. 2 (April 2007): 145–172. Copyright © 2007 by Sociologists for Women in Society. Reprinted with the permission of the author and Sage Publications, Inc.

Melanie Heath, "The Marriage Promotion Movement" [editors' title. Originally titled "Making Marriage Count in Law and Public Policy: Symbolic Boundaries and Gendered Anxieties"]. Copyright © 2007 by Melanie Heath. Reprinted with the permission of the author.

Pierrette Hondagneu-Sotelo, "Maid in L.A." from *Doméstica: Immigrant Workers Cleaning and Caring in the Shadows of Affluence*. Copyright © 2001 by the Regents of the University of California. Reprinted with the permission of the University of California Press.

Hung Cam Thai, "For Better or Worse: Gender Allures in the Vietnamese Global Marriage Market." Revised by Verta Taylor and Nancy Whittier from Hung Cam Thai, "Clashing Dreams: Highly-Educated Vietnamese Brides and Their Low-Wage Overseas Husbands" in *Global Woman*, edited by Arlie Russell Hochschild and Barbara Ehrenreich (New York: Metropolitan Books, 2003). Reprinted with the permission of the author.

Miliann Kang, "The Managed Hand: The Commercialization of Bodies and Emotions in Korean Immigrant-Owned Nail Salons" from *Gender & Society* 17, no. 6 (December 2003): 820–839. Copyright © 2003 by Sociologists for Women in Society. Reprinted with the permission of the author and Sage Publications, Inc.

Suzanne J. Kessler, "The Medical Construction of Gender" from *Lessons from the Intersexed*. Copyright © 1990 by The University of Chicago. Copyright © 1998 by Suzanne J. Kessler. Reprinted with the permission of the author and The University of Chicago Press.

Michael Kimmel, "What Are Little Boys Made Of?" from *Ms.* (October/November 1999). Copyright © 1999. Reprinted with the permission of the author.

Catherine Kudlick, "The Blind Man's Harley: White Canes and Gender Identity in America" from *Signs: Journal of Women in Culture and Society* 30, no. 2 (2005). Copyright © 2005 by The University of Chicago. Reprinted with permission.

Silvana Naguib, "Understanding Sexual Harassment: A Primer for Dudes" from Rock, Paper, Swords (October 2, 2007), ***http://rockpaperswords.blogspot.com***. Copyright © 2007 by Silvana Naguib. Reprinted with the permission of the author.

Carolyn Herbst Lewis, "Waking Sleeping Beauty: The Premarital Pelvic Exam and Heterosexuality during the Cold War" from *Journal of Women's History* 17, No. 4 (Winter 2005): 86–110. Copyright © 2005 by the Journal of Women's History. Reprinted with permission.

Laura M. Lopez and Frances S. Hasso, "Frontlines and Borders: Identity Thresholds for Latinas and Arab-American Women" from *Everyday Inequalities: Critical Inquiries*, edited by Jodi O'Brien and Judith A. Howard. Copyright © 1998 by Blackwell Publishers, Ltd. Reprinted with the permission of the publisher.

Judith Lorber, "'Night to His Day': The Social Construction of Gender" from *Paradoxes of Gender*. Copyright © 1993 by Yale University. Reprinted with the permission of Yale University Press.

Audre Lorde, "The Master's Tools Will Never Dismantle the Master's House" from *Sister Outsider: Essays and Speeches*. Copyright © 1984 by Audre Lorde. Reprinted with the permission of The Crossing Press, Freedom, California.

Patricia Yancy Martin and Robert A. Hummer, "Fraternities and Rape on Campus" from *Gender & Society* 3, no. 4 (December 1989). Copyright © 1989 by Sociologists for Women in Society. Reprinted with the permission of the authors and Sage Publications, Inc.

Peggy McIntosh, "White Privilege: Unpacking the Invisible Knapsack." Copyright © 1988 by Peggy McIntosh. Permission to reprint must be obtained from the author, Wellesley College Center for Research on Women, Wellesley, MA 02481, (781) 283–2520, mmcintosh@wellesley.edu.

Michael A. Messner, "Becoming 100% Straight" from *Inside Sports*, edited by Jay Coakley and Peter Donnelly. Copyright © 1999 by Michael A. Messner. Reprinted with the permission of Taylor & Francis Books UK.

Gwendolyn Mink, "The Lady and the Tramp (II)" from *Feminist Studies* 24, no. 1 (Spring 1998): 55–64. Reprinted with the permission of the publisher, *Feminist Studies*, Inc.

Chandra Talpade Mohanty, from *Feminism Without Borders: Decolonizing Theory, Practicing Solidarity*. Copyright © 2002 by Duke University Press. All rights reserved. Used by permission of the publisher.

Melissa Morrison, "Bridal Wave" from *Bitch: Feminist Response to Pop Culture* (Summer 2004). Reprinted with the permission of the author.

Joane Nagel, "Sex and War" from *Race, Ethnicity, and Sexuality: Intimate Intersections, Forbidden Frontiers*. Copyright © 2003 by Oxford University Press, Inc. Reprinted with the permission of Oxford University Press, Ltd.

Nancy Naples, "Queer Parenting in the New Millennium" from *Gender & Society* 18, No. 6 (December 2004): 679-684. Copyright © 2004 by Sociologists for Women in Society. Reprinted with the permission of Sage Publications, Inc.

Kristen Nelson, "The Making of a Soldier: Gender in Military Recruitment." Copyright © 2007 by Kristen Nelson. Reprinted with the permission of the author.

Tara Parker-Pope, "Rewriting Rap to Empower Teens" from *The New York Times* (November 6, 2007). Copyright © 2007 by The New York Times Company. Reprinted with permission.

Barbara Reskin, excerpt from "The Realities of Affirmative Action in Employment" from *The Realities of Affirmative Action in Employment*. Copyright © 1998 by the American Sociological Association. Reprinted with the permission of the author and the American Sociological Association.

Laurel Richardson, "Gender Stereotyping in the English Language" adapted from *The Dynamics of Sex and Gender: A Sociological Perspective, Third Edition* (New York: Harper & Row, 1987). Copyright © 1981 by Houghton Mifflin Company. Copyright © 1987 by Harper & Row, Publishers, Inc. Reprinted with the permission of the author.

Riverbend, "We've Only Just Begun" and "About Riverbend" from *Baghdad Burning: Girl Blog from Iraq*. Copyright © 2005 by Riverbend. Reprinted with the permission of The Feminist Press at the City University of New York, www.feministpress.org. All rights reserved.

Judy Rohrer, "Haole Girl: Identity and White Privilege in Hawai'i" in *Social Process in Hawai'i* (Honolulu: University of Hawai'i Press, 1997). Copyright © 1997 by the University of Hawai'i. Reprinted with the permission of the Dr. Kiyoshi Ikeda, Department of Sociology, University of Hawai'i.

Leila J. Rupp, "Loving Women in the Modern World" from *Gay Life and Culture: A World History*, edited by Robert Aldrich. Copyright © 2006. Reprinted with the permission of Rizzoli International Publications, Inc.

Leila J. Rupp and Verta Taylor, "Learning from Drag Queens" from *Contexts* 5, # 3 (2006): 12–17. Copyright © 2006 by the American Sociological Association. All rights reserved. Reprinted with the permission of the University of California Press.

Denise A. Segura, "Working at Motherhood: Chicana and Mexican Immigrant Mothers and Employment" from *Mothering: Ideology, Experience, and Agency*, edited by Evelyn Nakano Glenn, Grace Chang, and Linda Rennie Forcey. Copyright © 1994 by Routledge. Reprinted with the permission of the author and Routledge/Taylor & Francis Books, Inc.

T. Denean Sharpley-Whiting, "I See the Same Ho': Video, Vixens, Beauty Culture, and Diasporic Sex Tourism" from *Pimps Up, Ho's Down: Hip Hop's Hold on Young Black Women*. Copyright © 2007 by New York University. Reprinted with the permission of New York University Press.

Andrea Smith, "Beyond Pro-Choice versus Pro-Life" from *NWSA Journal* 17.1 (2005): 119–140. Copyright © 2005. Reprinted with the permission of The Johns Hopkins University Press.

Kimberly Springer, "Being the Bridge: A Solitary Black Woman's Position in the Women's Studies Classroom as a Feminist Student and Professor" from *This Bridge We Call Home: Radical Visions for Transformation*, edited by Gloria Anzaldua and AnaLouise Keating. Copyright © 2002 by Gloria Anzaldua and AnaLouise Keating. Reprinted with the permission of Routledge/Taylor & Francis, Inc.

Gloria Steinem, "Supremacy Crimes" from *Ms.* (August—September 1999). Copyright © 1999 by Gloria Steinem. Reprinted with the permission of the author.

Anne Fausto Sterling, "The Bare Bones of Sex" from *Signs: Journal of Women in Culture and Society* 30, No. 2 (2005). Copyright © 2005 by The University of Chicago. All rights reserved. Reprinted with permission.

Nikki Ayanna Stewart, "Transform the World: What You Can Do with a Degree in Women's Studies" from *Ms.* (Spring 2007). Copyright © 2007. Reprinted with the permission of *Ms. Magazine*

Susan Stryker, "Transgender Feminism: Queering the Woman Question" from *Third Wave Feminism and Post-Feminism: A Critical Explanation*, Second Revised Edition, edited by Stacy Gillis, Gillian Howe, and Rebecca Munford. Reprinted with the permission of Palgrave.

Judith Taylor, "Feminist Consumerism and Fat Activists: A Comparative Study of Grassroots Activism and the Dove 'Real Beauty' Campaign" from *Signs: Journal of Women in Culture and Society* (Summer 2008). Copyright © 2008 by The University of Chicago. Reprinted with permission.

Verta Taylor, Nancy Whittier, Cynthia Fabrizio Pelak, "The New Feminist Movement: Persistence Through Transformation." Reprinted with the permission of the authors.

Becky Wangsgaard Thompson, "'A Way Outa No Way': Eating Problems among African American, Latina, and White Women" from *Gender & Society* 6, no. 4 (December 1992). Copyright © 1994 by Sociologists for Women in Society. Reprinted with the permission of the author.

Barrie Thorne, "Girls and Boys Together . . . But Mostly Apart: Gender Arrangements in Elementary Schools" from *Relationships and Development*, edited by Willard W. Hartup and Zick Rubin (Hillsdale, New Jersey: Lawrence Erlbaum Associates, 1986). Volume sponsored by the Social Science Research Council. Copyright © 1986 by Lawrence Erlbaum Associates. Reprinted with the permission of the author and publisher.

Deborah L. Tolman, "Doing Desire: Adolescent Girls' Struggles for/with Sexuality" from *Gender & Society* 8, no. 3 (September 1994). Copyright © 1994 by Sociologists for Women in Society. Reprinted with the permission of Sage Publications, Inc.

"UN Commission Approves Declaration Reaffirming Goals of 1995 Women's Conference" from Kaiser Daily Reproductive Health Report, March 4, 2005. Reprinted with the permission of the Kaiser Family Foundation, www.kaisernetwork.org.

France Winndance Twine, "Bearing Blackness in Britain: The Meaning of Racial Difference for White Birth Mothers of African-Descent Children" from *Social Identities* 5, no. 2 (June 1999). Copyright © 1999 by Taylor & Francis Ltd. Reprinted with permission.

Alice Walker, "Womanist" from *In Search of Our Mothers' Gardens: Womanist Prose*. Copyright © 1983 by Alice Walker. Reprinted by permission of Harcourt, Inc.

Gust Yep and Ariana ochoa Camacho, "The Normalization of Heterogendered Relations in *The Bachelor*" from *Feminist Media Studies* 4, No. 3 (November 2004). Copyright © 2004 by Taylor & Francis Ltd. Reprinted with permission.

Maxine Baca Zinn and Bonnie Thornton Dill, "Theorizing Difference from Multiracial Feminism" from *Feminist Studies* 22, no. 2 (Summer 1996). Reprinted with the permission of the publisher, *Feminist Studies*, Inc.